58th Annual Edition

Gun Digest®

2004

Edited by
Ken Ramage

—GUN DIGEST STAFF—

EDITOR
Ken Ramage

CONTRIBUTING EDITORS

Holt Bodinson – *Ammunition, Ballistics & Components; Web Directory*

Raymond Caranta – *The Guns of Europe*

J. W. "Doc" Carlson – *Blackpowder Review*

John Haviland – *Shotgun Review*

John Malloy – *Handguns Today: Autoloaders*

Charles E. Petty – *Handloading Update*

Layne Simpson – *Rifle Review*

John Taffin – *Handguns Today: Sixguns & Others*

Wayne van Zwoll – *Scopes & Mounts*

Editorial Comments and Suggestions

We're always looking for feedback on our books. Please let us know what you like about this edition. If you have suggestions for articles you'd like to see in future editions, please contact.

Ken Ramage/Gun Digest
700 East State St.
Iola, WI 54990
email: ramagek@krause.com

Manuscripts, contributions and inquiries, including first class return postage, should be sent to the GUN DIGEST Editorial Offices, Krause Publications, 700 E. State Street, Iola, WI 54990-0001. All materials received will receive reasonable care, but we will not be responsible for their safe return. Material accepted is subject to our requirements for editing and revisions. Author payment covers all rights and title to the accepted material, including photos, drawings and other illustrations. Payment is at our current rates.

CAUTION: Technical data presented here, particularly technical data on the handloading and on firearms adjustment and alteration, inevitably reflects individual experience with particular equipment and components under specific circumstances the reader cannot duplicate exactly. Such data presentations therefore should be used for guidance only and with caution. Krause Publications, Inc., accepts no responsibility for results obtained using this data.

Published by

krause publications
An F&W Publications Company

700 East State Street • Iola, WI 54990-0001
715-445-2214 • 888-457-2873
www.krause.com

Please call or write for our free catalog of publications. Our toll-free number to place an order or obtain a free catalog is 800-258-0929 or please use our regular business telephone, 715-445-2214.

Library of Congress Catalog Number: 44-32588
ISBN: 0-87349-589-6

Edited by Ken Ramage
Designed by Ethel Thulien, Patsy Howell, and Tom Nelsen

JOHN T. AMBER LITERARY AWARD

John L. Marshall

John Marshall has won the prestigious John T. Amber Award for his article *"Service 45s of the Twentieth Century,"* a work meticulously researched and published in the GUN DIGEST 2003, 57TH EDITION. He is a native of the Phoenix, Arizona area who has had a life-long interest in firearms that began at age 11 when he and his dad split the cost of a Model 69A Winchester bolt-action 22 rifle.

Active in both high school and college ROTC, Marshall received his bachelor's in business administration from Arizona State University, and later did some post-graduate work. He was commissioned in the U.S. Army and served two years on active duty, followed by service with the Arizona National Guard, in the 158th Infantry (Bushmasters). He participated actively in both rifle and pistol competition while in the service.

Following a long career in human resources administration and executive recruiting, Marshall went into semi-retirement to pursue a career "that would be more fun" in the firearms field. He is presently a technical sales representative for Dillon Precision Products, makers of reloading equipment and firearms accessories. He has become an active gun writer and

has had feature articles published in *American Gunsmith, Handguns* magazine, and Dillon's *Blue Press* catalog/magazine. Marshall's particular expertise is in U.S. military firearms, and he is currently writing a definitive collector's book on the Remington Nylon series of 22 rifles.

The only juried literary award in the firearms field, the John T. Amber Award replaced the Townsend Whelen Award, originated by the late John T. Amber and later re-named in his honor. Now, a $1,000 prize goes to the winner of this annual award.

Nominations for the competition are made by GUN DIGEST editor Ken Ramage and are judged by a distinguished panel of editors experienced in the firearms field. Entries are evaluated for felicity of expression and illustration, originality and scholarship, and subject importance to the firearms field.

This year's Amber Award nominees, in addition to Marshall, were:

Christopher R. Bartocci, *"AK47: The Path of A Legend"*

Hollis M. Flint, *"Smith & Wesson K-Frame 38 Special Target Revolvers"*

Jim Foral, *"Selling the American 303"*

Jim Foral, *"Wanted: A 22 Automatic Pistol"*

George J. Layman, *"The Brown-Merrill Bolt Action"*

Harvey T. Pennington, *"Thanks, Jack McPhee!"*

William R. Marshall, *"The 32-20 Revolver"*

Tom Schiffer, *"Long-Range Muzzleloading Rifles"*

Serving as judges for this year's competition were John D. Acquilino, editor of *Inside Gun News*; Bob Bell, former editor-in-chief of *Pennsylvania Game News*; James W. Bequette, editorial director of Primedia's outdoor group; David Brennan, editor of *Precision Shooting*; Sharon Cunningham, director of Pioneer Press; Pete Dickey, former technical editor of *American Rifleman*; Jack Lewis, former editor and publisher of *Gun World*; Bill Parkerson, former editor of *American Rifleman*, now director of research and information for the National Rifle Association, and Dave Petzal, executive editor of *Field & Stream*.

Introduction

IN THE YEAR past we lost two individuals who literally helped shape the shooting sports as we know them today, and who brought us firearms that have stirred our souls: Bill Ruger, Sr., and Val Forgett.

As I considered the preparation of this introduction, my thoughts turned to the Ruger arms in my gun rack. There are maybe a dozen, and each of the company's major product categories is represented. At the great risk of oversimplifying matters, Bill Ruger stands out because he did not overlook the subtleties when designing a new arm. His knowledge and appreciation of classic arms designs melded with his skill at designing product capable of being mass-produced. For example, his single-action revolvers were powered by coil springs, not traditional leaf springs. When it came time to stock the Model 77 bolt-action rifle, Ruger turned to a noted stock designer for the classic pattern that the rifle has carried ever since. There are other examples, of course.

Much has been written about Bill Ruger, the firearms he designed and the company he (and his associates) built. What many might not know about Ruger is that he had wide-ranging interests, and endeavors beyond his successful firearms business. The article "William Batterman Ruger" found within these pages is good reading, and some of the photos have never before been published.

Over the years I became acquainted with Bill Sr., beginning I believe in the mid-'70s when I first contacted him regarding a business matter, the Lyman Centennial Rifle project.

Val Forgett took a somewhat different approach, and was truly instrumental in creating the industry that supplies the replica firearms so many of us enjoy. His initiative and insight created a market for muzzleloaders (later, cartridge arms as well) produced by the craftsmen in the centuries-old arms-making region of northern Italy known as the Gardone Valley. The economic impact of this new arms manufacturing business was so dramatic that a grateful Italian government bestowed a knighthood on Forgett.

My acquaintanceship with Forgett dates to late '72. At the time I was in Connecticut, interviewing for a position with Lyman Products Co., of Middlefield. Lyman was in the early days of establishing a line of blackpowder rifles and revolvers, and Forgett's Navy Arms Company was involved in the process.

Although not yet signed aboard with Lyman, I was invited to an evening meeting. During the course of conversation, I mentioned that I had one of his 1851 Navy revolvers purchased in '61 from a small gun shop in Aberdeen, Maryland and rattled off the low serial number. Without a moment's hesitation, Val named the shop and its owner – Ellis Friedlander. I did get the job with Lyman, and I still have Navy #319…….

Generally, it has been a satisfactory year for the shooting sports industry. The legislative threat to arms ownership appears to diminish, and business – while not exceptional – has been reasonably good.

Once again, you'll notice changes to the Contributing Editors' masthead. After several years of debating the matter, Bob Bell has relinquished the annual optics report. Stepping into that assignment is Wayne van Zwoll, a well-known writer and author of the recently published book *Sporting Optics* (Krause Publications).

Bell is the senior contributor to GUN DIGEST and, according to our author/article index, his first article, "Hunting Scopes –A Critical Evaluation", was published in the GUN DIGEST, 15th Edition. Many others followed over the years, and books as well. Bell's article "Buhmiller's Big Boomers" that ran in GUN DIGEST, 54th Edition, received the 19th annual John T. Amber Award. We'll miss his annual report, but look forward to his articles.

Handloading editor Larry Sterett has also stepped down and will be missed, but his annual handloading column is in capable hands. Long-time author and handloader Charles Petty now reports on this interesting branch of the shooting sports family tree.

Within this edition of GUN DIGEST, we have a variety of articles for your reading pleasure. Be sure to read up on the new products, then look over the articles. I have my favorites among them, and have once again been tempted to add to my firearms inventory. Among our contributors, you'll find past winners of the John T. Amber Award as well as one or two authors that are new to you.

Among the latter is Michael Kluever, author of "The Lost Sport of Dump Rat Shooting," a short work that will likely strike a chord with over-30 readers from America's smaller communities. In corresponding with the author, I remarked that while he was after the dump rats outside Wausau, Wisconsin I was doing the same thing at the town dump in Leavenworth, Kansas. The challenge with this work was providing appropriate illustration. Fortunately, the well-known Western humorist Boots Reynolds agreed to do a few drawings—and perfectly captured the essence of the Wisconsin dump rat.

We hope you enjoy this 58th edition of GUN DIGEST. Comment is always welcome.

WHILE IN RENO last January attending both the Safari Club International show and the Firearms Engravers & Gunmakers Exhibition I enjoyed a close examination of the Guild raffle project #19. This rifle, chambered for the 22 LR cartridge, is a real beauty and is destined to be won by a lucky raffle ticket holder during the next Exhibition in Reno, scheduled for late January, 2004.

Joe Peitz did the metal work, and plenty of it. He started with a Model '98 Mauser action, and shortened it to accommodate the diminutive rimfire round. In the process, he also made the bolt shroud, cocking piece, magazines, bottom metal, the octagonal bolt handle, etc. He then barreled the shortened action with a half-octagon/half-round tube, machined with an integral quarter-rib. Among the remaining parts crafted by Peitz is the remarkable one-piece forend cap & sight ramp.

With the metal work and stocking completed, engraver Gil Rudolph went to work. His very extensive contribution consists of overlapping English scroll with raised 24-kt gold acorns and flush gold lines—all gold lines and borders are either decorated with line, or outlined with a border cut. Animals portrayed are small prairie or desert game, and all have their Latin names engraved around them. The receiver, and other parts of the rifle, have gold scroll, completed in 24-kt gold. Ultimately, various areas of the completed work were blued, French-greyed, or coin-finished.

Tickets at $20 each are available from Jan Billeb, ACGG, 22 Vista View Drive, Cody, WY 82414 (307) 587-4297 or through the ACGG website www.acgg.com. Ticket sales are limited to 4,000 and the winner does not have to be present at the drawing to be held in Reno, late January, 2004.

Ken Ramage, Editor

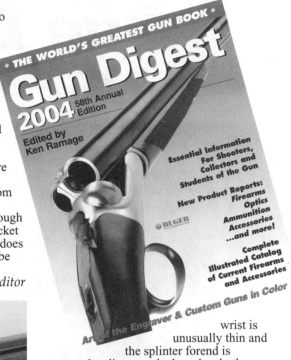

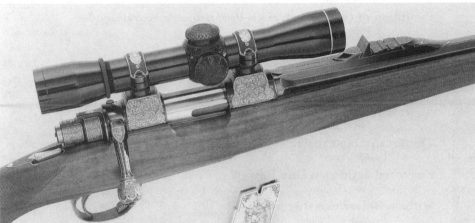

Perfectly proportioned, the 22 looks for all the world like a full-size custom rifle. Only the short action opening and magazine hint at the rimfire chambering. *Courtesy Tom Alexander Photography*

The rifle was stocked with French walnut in Mannlicher style *(including a pancake cheekpiece)* by Larry Amrine. He then fitted a specially shortened Biesen steel buttplate, finished the wood with Permalin and checkered the wrist and forearm in a fine 24 lpi point pattern.

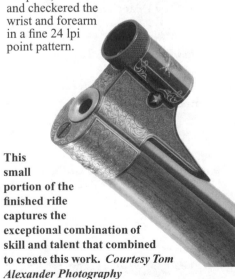

This small portion of the finished rifle captures the exceptional combination of skill and talent that combined to create this work. *Courtesy Tom Alexander Photography*

About Our Covers...

It is the custom of GUN DIGEST *to comment on the firearms that illustrate the covers of each edition. This year, a new side-by-side shotgun – the first offered by Sturm, Ruger & Co. – appears on both the front and back covers.*

The Gold Label Side-by-Side Shotgun

A world-class shotgun, traditionally produced by British and other European manufacturers employing skilled hand labor, must integrate several indispensable traits: durability, aesthetics and remarkable handling characteristics. Not easy to do, and certainly not in a modern production arm.

Ruger's objective was to create such a shotgun to be made by modern manufacturing techniques and materials and, after a design and development period of several years, the result is before you — the Gold Label Side-by-Side.

Weighing less than 6-1/2 pounds, the new gun can be comfortably carried for hours. Perhaps the first thing a person notices upon handling the gun is that the

wrist is unusually thin and the splinter forend is subordinate to the barrels—both classic characteristics of "best" European guns. The net result is that the gun rests deep in the shooter's hands and comes naturally to shoulder.

The Gold Label is a new design, from stem to stern.

Note the clean, rounded action lines that flow into the barrels—no accident thanks to the internal hammer interrupters, spring-assisted opening system, convenient safety/barrel selector, and absence of exposed pins or screws in the smooth, low profile stainless steel receiver. There are no protrusions from the rear of the barrels when the action is opened. The 3-inch chambers and positive extractors present themselves unobtrusively for fast and easy loading or unloading, and the Dickson-style selective ejectors reliably kick out empties. The selective single trigger allows a quick choice of either barrel, giving versatility for any field situation.

The 12-gauge hammer-forged barrels, with forcing cones relieved to lessen felt recoil and shot deformation, include a complete set of (5) steel shot-compatible, thin wall screw-in choke tubes: All contribute to uniform patterns, pattern flexibility, and superb handling dynamics. A matte steel rib with a gold bead sight draws the eye naturally to the muzzles of the 28-inch barrels just as surely as the graceful stock and splinter forend guide the hands toward the target.

The Gold Label balances gracefully, just 3/8-inch ahead of the barrel pivot point at the hinge pin, thus keeping its weight distributed between the shooter's hands for the lively response demanded by the upland game hunter. The gun is stocked with premium grade walnut, in either straight-grip or pistol-grip versions; the wrist and splinter forend carry crisp 22 lpi checkering.

Gun Digest 2004

The World's Greatest Gun Book

CONTENTS

Page 39

Page 49

Page 83

REPORTS FROM THE FIELD:

Page 113

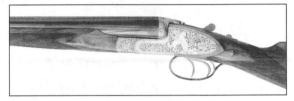

Page 212

CATALOG OF ARMS AND ACCESSORIES

The Winchester Model 12 Heavy Duck Gun

by Hollis M. Flint

"A new duck gun has appeared and it is one designed to interest gunners who frequent waterfowl passes, fox trails or the habitat of the wary gobbler. Oddly enough, it is a hammerless slide-action repeater, but then we have long ceased becoming surprised at anything that enterprising W.R.A. Co. may do."

American Rifleman, January 1936

Prologue

THE HISTORY OF Oliver F. Winchester (1810-1880) and his endeavors in the manufacturing of firearms at Bridgeport and New Haven, Connecticut, is filled with circumstances that could have led to corporate failure. However, Winchester and his succeeding family members successfully managed Winchester Repeating Arms Company from 1866 to 1919. During that time they largely made the right business decisions, hired the right people, and enjoyed a fair share of luck. That luck ran out following World War I when the arms industry declined and the management of Winchester was relinquished to outsiders.

Harold Williamson, in his book *Winchester, The Gun That Won the West*, relates that the new management of Winchester embarked "...*on a program that involved an extraordinary departure from the company's previous operations and the investment of borrowed capital in large amounts.*" Winchester struggled through a decade of inept product diversification that was terminated by the Great Depression. Winchester was bankrupt and went into receivership in January 1931. The committee appointed to study the requirements for continuing business reported "...*a successful reorganization would require the raising of a substantial amount of new capital.*" That capital was supplied by the Olin family of Olin Industries, owners of Western Cartridge Company.

Franklin W. Olin founded Western Cartridge Company in 1898. Western rapidly achieved a leading position in the ammunition industry through innovation

and skillful management. Franklin and his two sons John M. Olin and Spencer T. Olin were the managers of Olin Industries and Western Cartridge Company in 1931. The Olins bought Winchester for $8.1 million through a combination of $3.3 million cash and the balance in an issue of preferred stock. The Olins used the Western ammunition plant at East Alton, Illinois, as collateral for borrowing about four million in cash, no small feat in the fall of 1931. The survival of both Western and Winchester now depended on Olin management.

Edwin Pugsley, in charge of Winchester at the time of receivership, is quoted in Williamson's book: "*The purchase of the company by the Olin interests brought a breath of life to the institution and brought to Winchester many things. First of all was the end of management by people who were not familiar or sympathetic with the gun and ammunition business.*" The Olins were avid duck hunters.

It was John Olin who inspired Western's revolutionary "*Super-X*" shotshell in 1921. The short shot string put more shot into a duck whistling by at 50 yards. Western's 3-inch 12-gauge magnum with 1 3/8-ounces of shot was introduced the same year. The magnum led to new class of long-range double-barrel shotguns for waterfowl. Western's copper-plated shot, introduced about 1925, extended shotgun range even further. It was Western that produced the 3 1/2-inch 10-gauge magnum with 2 ounces of shot in 1932. Ithaca brought out their "*Magnum 10*" double to use the new shell. John Olin wanted a new 3-inch .410 shotshell with 3/4-ounce of shot for Winchester's new Model 42. Winchester designed the Model 42 to use the new shell and the combo went to market in 1932. The duck gun version of the Model 12, introduced in 1935, was a natural consequence of duck hunters in charge of Winchester. The Model 12, already 23 years old, was one of many successful designs by Thomas C. Johnson.

Thomas C. Johnson came to Winchester in 1885 and remained a dedicated employee until his death in 1934. Johnson, at once one of the great gun designers and one of the least known, produced a steady flow of new firearm designs for Winchester. Initially came a series of autoloading rifles, including the rimfire Model 1903 and centerfire rifles, culminating with the Model 1910, chambered for the 401 WSL cartridge. Johnson designed the Models 52 and 61 rimfire rifles and the Model 54 centerfire rifle. He was the chief designer of the Model 21 double, John Olin's favorite. However, the gun for which Johnson is best remembered is his Model 12 pump-action shotgun, *"The Perfect Repeater."*

The Model 12 shotgun, initially the Model 1912, hit the market in August 1912. It was an immediate success. Sales of 100,000 were recorded in the first two years of production. Thereafter, a staggering number of variations were produced during the 1912-1980 period. Total production reached two million. Dave Riffle in his book, *The Greatest Hammerless Repeating Shotgun Ever Built: The Model 12 1912-1964,* states *"The Winchester Model 12 was, and still remains, the only gun that was offered in over 100 different variations or configura-*

The Model 12 Duck Gun is a highly specialized tool for hunters who need to put a lot of shot on target at 60 yards or more. The duck gun's reputation was made with the one and five-eighths ounce load, the heaviest 12 magnum load from about 1935 to the mid-1950s.

tions during its lifetime." It is fair to say that Winchester produced Model 12 shotguns for every conceivable shotgunning special interest group, including duck hunters.

The Gun and the Times

The Model 12 duck gun examined by the staff of the *American Rifleman* in 1936 was the earliest version. The stock*"...has a hard-rubber plate and a real, full pistol grip carved close to the guard. It is the skeet style of stock with a comb drop of 1 1/2 X 2 1/2 inches, and a 14-inch length, butt to trigger."*

The gun weighed 8 1/2 pounds with its 32-inch Full choke barrel. *"The receiver is heavier and so is the barrel. The balance point is the takedown joint. It is not as slow or pokey as one might expect."* The staff shot skeet with the gun and concluded *"It is not as fast as the standard Model-12, but nearly so."* In further shooting tests the staff found *"We could not discern any practical difference in recoil effect when shooting standard three inch heavy duck loads."* Winchester supplied two boxes of 3-inch shells loaded with 1 3/8-ounces of #5

chilled shot pushed by four drams equivalent of powder. The load averaged 67.5% (range 62-72.5%), in a 30-inch circle at 40 yards. This percentage was disappointing compared to the 80% or better patterns obtained with other duck guns tested by the staff. An 80% pattern they felt *"...should make it a real 60-yard outfit with 1 ? ounces of No. 4 chilled shot."*

The new Model 12 duck gun was introduced to long-range waterfowl hunters habituated to heavy double shotguns chambered for 3-inch shells. The 3-inch shell was chambered originally in the famous Super Fox long-range double. Jack O'Connor was there and sets the scene nicely in the *Complete Book of Shooting.* *"Along in the 1920's a few bold souls had long-chambered [3-inch], overbored, long-barreled, and heavy, long range 12-gauge Magnum double guns built. These were turned out by the Hunter Arms Company of Fulton, N.Y. in L.C. Smith brand, by the A.H. Fox Company of Philadelphia, by Parker, and by Ithaca. These were called long-range waterfowl guns."* The Model 21 double seemed the reasonable choice for Winchester's duck gun. Thus it was that the *American Rifleman* staff thought it odd that Winchester brought out the 3-inch chamber in their Model 12 pump gun. Charles Askins may have influenced the decision.

Charles Askins was the leading expert on shotguns in the first half of the last century. He spent many

Some duck loads from the first half of the last century (drams equivalent/ounces shot x length). Twelve gauge: 3 3/4 / 1 1/4 x 2 3/4, 4 / 1? x 3, 4 1/4 / 1? x 3. Ten gauge: 4 / 1 1/4 x 2?, 4 3/4 / 1? x 2?, 5 / 2 x 3 1/2. Eight gauge: 5 1/4/ 1 3/4 x 3 1/4.

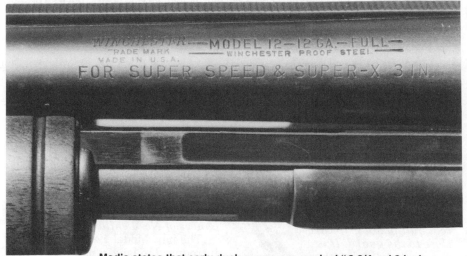

Madis states that early duck guns were marked "*2 3/4 and 3 inch chamber*". The later inscription, shown, prescribes Winchester / Western ammunition. All 3-inch and shorter shells work fine.

years as firearms editor for *Outdoor Life* and later *Field and Stream*, as well as shotgun editor for the *American Rifleman*. Askins wrote in his 1929 book *Modern Shotguns and Loads*: "*Perhaps half the game that is killed in America today is shot with repeating shotguns, pump or automatic. In duck shooting the proportion of magazine guns in use is much higher, probably four men in five using the repeater.*" Askins added, "*Fact is, personally, I have always thought that I was surer on the second bird with a repeater than I was with a double gun.*" On gauges for duck hunting: "*No fault is to be found with the twelve [gauge] as a duck gun, whether in double barrel with 3 inch cases or in repeaters with 2 3/4 inch*". Since "*Every shotgun manufacturer is a friend of mine*", Askins' views were well known in the industry. The Olins were businessmen first and duck hunters second. In their view, the Model 12 pump with 3-inch chamber was likely to sell better than a similarly chambered Model 21 double. The Model 21 received duck gun status in 1940, although 3-inch chambers could be ordered earlier. The Model 12 was the first magazine repeater chambered for 3-inch magnum shells.

Charles Askins commented on the new Model 12 duck gun in the March 1936 issue of *Outdoor Life*: "*This should be the best long-range repeating shotgun now made or that has been made.*" No faint praise, but hardly a surprise.

The Olins soon added to the attractiveness of the Model 12 duck gun by bringing out a new 1 5/8-ounce load for the 3-inch shell. Heretofore, you could only shoot this weight of shot in a 10-gauge double gun with 2 7/8-inch chambers, or the new Ithaca Magnum 10. Fanciers of long-range shotguns now had a 12-gauge repeater shooting a 10-gauge shot load. The $48 price tag was right. Enthusiastic hunters bought the new repeater.

George Madis indicates in his book *The Winchester Model Twelve* that about 18,000 Model 12 duck guns were sold during the 1935-1941 period. The magnitude of this sale is appreciated when you realize how few of the special 10- and 12-gauge magnum double guns were sold. A study of Michael McIntosh's book *Best Guns* indicates that a few thousand of the specialized waterfowl doubles of all brands were sold between 1921 and 1941. For example, only about 300 Super Fox and 800 of the Ithaca Magnum 10 doubles went into hunter's hands during the period. The era of the double gun was ending as World War II approached.

The era of plentiful ducks and liberal bag limits was also ending. The Model 12 duck gun came to market at the all-time low point of duck populations in the United States. Severe drought conditions gripped the United States and Canada during the 1930s. Reduced bag limits and shell capacities for repeating shotguns were introduced. The Duck Stamp Law of 1934 was enacted to provide funds for waterfowl propagation. The Pittman-Robertson Act of 1937 began an 11 percent excise tax on sporting arms and ammunition. The funds are returned to the states for wildlife restoration projects. Ducks Unlimited was born in 1937 to aid in restoration of wetland breeding areas, primarily in Canada. Winchester recognized the scarcity of ducks in their promotional advertisement of the new duck gun "*To Meet the New Wildfowling Conditions.*" I suspect most Model 12 duck guns bought before World War II were put to work on other game.

Winchester made changes to the stock of the Model 12 duck gun after its introduction. A red rubber Winchester recoil pad was added the first year of production. Length of pull was reduced from 14 to 13? inches in January 1936 to reflect the extra clothing worn by duck hunters. The drop at heel was reduced from 2-1/2 to 2-3/8 inches in December 1938. The straighter stock reduced perceived recoil. Downpitch remained 2-1/2 inches with the 30-inch barrel throughout production. The less pronounced pistol grip-style buttstock of the original Model 12 was discontinued in late 1934 and is not found on duck guns. The new 1935-style buttstock featured a closer and fuller pistol grip. The buttstock was reshaped on Model 12 shotguns again in the mid-1950s. The late style stock featured a flared pistol grip moved back a bit from the trigger. In 1960, length of pull was increased from 13? to 13-3/4 inches on duck guns. The straight grip stock, optional from 1935, was discontinued in the late 1950s.

The Winchester proof mark offset to the left of the rib indicates the rib was factory installed. Winchester used this proof mark on its shotguns beginning in 1905.

Buttstocks of duck guns had lead slugs inserted into the wood beneath the recoil pad. The lead slug added weight but more importantly maintained the balance point at the takedown joint. Madis comments *"Fancy walnut was considered too fancy for the rough treatment often given a duck gun."* Fancy walnut could be ordered and the few pidgeon-grade duck guns had fancy walnut. Some late duck guns came with special order Hydro-Coil stocks, according to Madis.

The slide handle of early duck guns was round with 18 circular grooves. The slide handle was given a larger diameter, flat bottom and 14 grooves on each side of the handle about 1947. The slide handle was enlarged in about 1956 to a slightly extended beavertail shape with 14 circular grooves. Keep in mind that all of these changes in stock design were *"running changes"* and thus some overlapping of designs occurred in production.

The barrels and receivers of Model 12 duck guns are made from *"Winchester Proof Steel."* This steel was first used in the Model 21 double introduced in 1931. Winchester proof steel replaced nickel steel in the manufacture of all Winchester firearms in the early 1930s. Winchester proof steel is chrome-molybdenum steel. In an ad in the October 1952 *American Rifleman*, Winchester proclaimed. *"Metal parts of the Model 12 are machined from chrome-molybdenum, the toughest, longest wearing and finest gun steel known."*

Barrel lengths were 30 or 32 inches, but 32-inch barrels were discontinued in 1948. Full choke was the only standard boring available. Winchester cautiously claimed *"70 to 75% pattern in a 30 inch circle at 40 yards."* Madis states *"Ventilated ribs were rarely offered on* [duck] *guns."* However, *"The fact is a few duck guns were provided with these ribs."* Dave Riffle's book and the various catalogs I have indicate that the Winchester new ventilated rib was an option from about 1954 to 1959. Only rib extensions of the same width as the factory ventilated rib are found on receivers of duck guns. Ronald Stadt states in *Winchester Shotguns and Shotshells*: *"All Winchester special ventilated rib magnum guns examined have sand-blasted receiver tops."* Solid ribs were offered until the mid-1950s, except as noted by Stadt: *"The 1960 wholesale-retail catalog listed 30-inch solid rib pidgeon magnums. This likely was the*

last mention of solid ribs in Winchester literature."* The duck gun was discontinued in 1963.

Model 12 duck guns had the same six-shot capacity as the standard Model 12: one in the chamber, five in the magazine. President Roosevelt signed the law limiting magazine repeaters to three shells for migratory game bird hunting in 1935. Winchester dutifully shipped its duck guns with a wooden plug installed to limit magazine capacity to two shells.

Winchester stated both *"2? and 2 3/4" shells perform satisfactorily in this* [duck] *gun."* The ejection port of the duck gun is about 1/8-inch longer than the standard port. Recent 3 1/2-inch 12-gauge shells

will create dangerous pressure in the 3-inch duck gun chamber. Winchester advises *"Do not use steel shot in any Winchester shotgun with a fixed choke."* Use tungsten polymer, tungsten matrix or bismuth shot for waterfowl hunting with your Model 12 duck gun.

Mechanically, the Model 12 duck gun differs little in design from the standard Model 12. In fact, Madis states *"Any twelve gauge Model Twelve could be rechambered and reworked to shoot three inch shells for a small additional charge* [by Winchester], *yet few guns were reworked in this way."* I can find no external differences in receiver dimensions, other than the ejection port, between standard and magnum versions.

The senior of the two crafty hunters in this ad is holding the "Magnum Duck Gun." This ad appeared on the back cover of the September 1953 issue of the *American Rifleman*. It is the only ad I could find showing the duck gun in the field.

All Model 12 shotguns have an action slide lock that keeps the action closed and locked in the event of a misfire or hangfire. If you pull the trigger and the shell does not fire you must push the slide handle forward to unlock the action. Consider the possibility of a hangfire, an occasional event in 1912, in a gun without the slide lock feature. You jack the shell out and it goes off under your nose. The slide lock is automatically released by the forward nudge of recoil in the Model 12. Later pump guns, such as the Remington Model 870 and Mossberg Model 500, do not have the slide lock feature. It is possible for the slide lock to fail to unlock the action during recoil. The duck gun sent to the *American Rifleman* staff in 1935 would not unlock during recoil. *"Most annoying was the failure of the action-slide lock to function properly. Its failure to release on discharge made it impossible to shoot doubles* [at skeet] *with this particular sample."* The staff concluded, *"Mechanically, the sample was not as good as other guns of the same model."* Noted were machine marks on the breech bolt, wood not closely fitted, primers struck off center and sharp edges at the chamber. Could it be that the intended rough usage led to lack of care in the fitting of parts of early duck guns?

Winchester undertook preparations for improvements in its firearms line following World War II. John Olin initiated an analysis of Winchester's commercial line in 1942. George Watrous, a longtime Winchester employee with many talents, was commissioned to investigate the good and bad points of Winchester's pre-war line and make suggestions for postwar improvement. Herbert Houze summarizes the Watrous report in his book *"Winchester Repeating Arms Company, It's History & Development from 1865 to 1981"*. Houze relates that for the Model 12 the Watrous report suggested *"…improve the smoothness of the action as it is criticized for being rough."* How this was to be accomplished is not related but closer hand-fitting and gauging of parts was likely.

Model 12 duck guns could be ordered in pidgeon grade, featuring fancy wood and meticulous fitting and finish of parts. Also available initially were standard trap and special trap grades. Checkered stocks and extension slide handles were available as options on the standard grade throughout most of the duck gun's production. Interchangeable barrels (forend assembly) for 2 3/4-inch shells and choke

A lead slug is permanently installed in the buttstock of Model 12 duck guns. The lead slug balances the weight of the heavier barrel, and reduces recoil.

of choice were special order. Optional dimensions for straight or pistol grip stocks, grip caps, front sights and recoil pads were also among early options.

Options for the Model 12 duck gun were reduced over the years, particularly following World War II. This was a result of the Watrous report, which recommended that many of the slow-selling options be discontinued following the war. By 1955, the options were matted rib, ventilated rib, straight or pistol grip stock and buttstock and extension slide handle checkered. The pidgeon-grade duck gun was discontinued in 1961. In 1963, when production ended, Riffle's book shows no options available. The price in 1963 was $122 compared to $109.50 for the standard Model 12. Duck guns always sold for a slight premium over the standard model.

The 3-inch "Super Twelve" Shotshell

My copy of Winchester's Catalog No. 80 of 1916 indicates seven empty 12-gauge paper shell lengths (2-1/2 to 3-1/4 inches). The *"standard length"* was 2-5/8 inches. There are 16 pages of loads for various shell lengths, shot sizes (dust through buck, soft or chilled), five powders, five shell grades and 11

gauges. There was only one way to go after World War I: standardize shell lengths, discontinue bastard gauges and reduce the load options. The standard 12-gauge duck load in 1921 was a 2 3/4-inch shell holding 3 3/4-drams equivalent powder and 1 1/4-ounces of shot.

Western brought out their Super-X 2-3/4 and 3-inch shotshells in 1921. McIntosh notes that the Super-X shotshell "…*was a breakthrough to the modern age of shotgun ammunition."* In a full-page ad in the September 1926 issue of the *American Rifleman*, Western claimed *"Killing power 15 to 20 yards beyond the effective range of ordinary loads."* This was based on a documented reduction in stringing of the shot charge, from about 20 feet to about 4 feet, at 42 yards. My 1951 Winchester *Ammunition Handbook* gives a comparison of 17 to 11 feet at 60 yards. Western's innovation was progressive-burning powder that deformed fewer shot during acceleration. Charles Askins confirmed the tighter patterns and greater effective range in the field. Duck hunters bought 12-gauge doubles with 3-inch chambers to use the new Super-X magnum load, the *Super Twelve as it was soon called.*

The takedown joint of the Model 12 is adjustable to compensate for wear. The machining and fitting required for the takedown joint is one of the reasons the Model 12 became too expensive to manufacture by 1963. The adjustment setting shown is the way it left the factory.

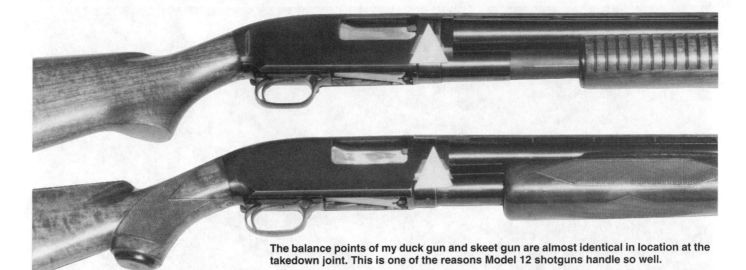

The balance points of my duck gun and skeet gun are almost identical in location at the takedown joint. This is one of the reasons Model 12 shotguns handle so well.

Nash Buckingham was one of the great duck-hunting writers of the period. H. Lea Lawrence relates in his 2001 GUN DIGEST article, The *Saga of Bo Whoop*, that in 1921 John Olin sent Buckingham his personal heavy double, a custom-choked Super Fox, for testing. Olin included his new Super-X magnum 3-inch shells loaded with 1 3/8-ounces of shot. Buckingham's tests led him to buy his own custom Super Fox, "*Bo Whoop*." Bo Whoop patterned about 90% at 40 yards with specially bored barrels. Buckingham had a solid 60-yard duck gun and was on his way to becoming a legend. Buckingham recorded his adventures in some of the best hunting stories ever written. I offer the following example from *What Rarer Day* in Buckingham's book *De Shootinest Gent'man and Other Tales* published in 1934.

We join Buckingham in his "*ducking skiff*" as he is poled through the bayou by Ab, his black guide. Buckingham is jump-shooting with his "*big double gun*". It is first shooting light. "*A smothered roar from around the corner! Ab steadies the boat. I pick them up through the*

TABLE 1

Model 12 Duck Guns Were Produced During the Years Shown Below. Serial Numbers are for the Beginning of the Indicated Year.

Year	Serial no.	Year	Serial no.	Year	Serial no.
1935	673995	1945	1043616	1955	1603588
36	686979	46	1055711	56	1673987
37	720137	47	1070801	57	1714231
38	754251	48	1102375	58	1770398
39	779456	49	1184056	59	1800014
40	814122	50	1234053	60	1857953
41	856500	51	1318795	61	1910910
42	945107	52	1398790	62	1928333
43	1000251	53`	1459676	63	1941576
44	1034750	54	1543941		

From Madis *The Winchester Model Twelve*

interlacing covert, a bunch of suspicious mallards driving for safety. But they must pass our way to clear! I hunker down and blaze away. Two birds tumble all awry from among the leaders. My second blast bites off a dismayed climber. Pandemonium! The marsh is in riot! Alarm calls! The surge of zooming pinions [wings]! Teal, mallard, widgeon and sprig [pintail] hover singly and in bunches overhead. It is, somehow,

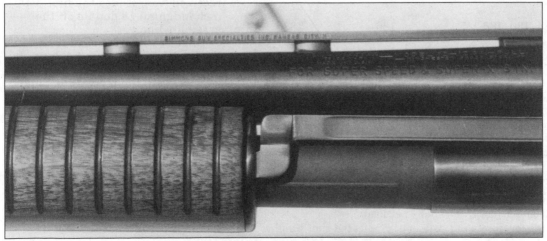

My 1952 duck gun has the infamous stamped "dog-leg" action slide rod. This rod could override the action slide spring during recoil and lock the action. Madis indicates about 12,000 of these action slide rods left the factory in the early 1950s. Winchester offered to replace them with straight style rods. I had no problems with this rod.

Results of an early morning duck hunt near Gwinner, North Dakota, about 1965. My wife Del is holding my Model 12 while I hold the photographer's double. Friend Dennis Nelson also has a Model 12. *Andy Terranova photo.*

TABLE 2

Specifications of Model 12 Duck Guns Tested

Serial number	Year produced	Trigger pull pounds[a]	Bore diameter[b]	Choke constriction[c]	Weight empty pounds
1418XXX	1952	6.5	.730	.033	8.82
1512XXX	1953	7.5	.729	.035	8.75

a Factory specified trigger pull is four and a half pounds.
b Winchester listed .730 as their 12-gauge bore diameter in the 1951 *Winchester Ammunition Handbook*.
c O'Connor in **The Shotgun Book** cites data showing an average of .031 constriction for Winchester 12-gauge Full choke barrels.

TABLE 3

Specifications of Shotshells Tested in Model 12 Duck Guns

Shell[a]	Shot counts/avg.[b]	Expected average[c]	Listed velocity,fps
Win. AA 2-1?-8	499, 503, 502/501	461	1145
Fed. TP Max-1?-4	184, 189, 188/187	186	1330
Win. XX 4-1?-4	223, 220, 222/222	219	1290
Win. XX 4-1?-4	260, 265, 264/263	252	1210
Fed. Prem. 4-2-2	166, 169, 168/168	180	1175

a Winchester AA = lead shot, Federal TP = Tungsten polymer shot, Winchester XX and Federal Premium = copper-plated lead shot. All but the AA trap load are buffered 3-inch magnum loads.
b Pellets were counted from each of three shells per load.
c From industry standards for number of pellets per indicated shot weight.

not easy to avoid shoving shells wrong end first into one's gun. But I manage to concentrate, find the combination, and center a pair of easy sprigs. I am tempted to stop off awhile and call. But the charm of idle jump-shooting is far too potent."

Charles Askins, in an article entitled *Long Range Shotguns* in the January 1930 issue of the *American Rifleman*, concludes that a 12-gauge magnum with 1 3/8-ounces of shot, patterning 80% or better "...*is pretty reliable* [on ducks] *at 65 yards.*" However, Askins goes on to say "*I have never, personally, had a shotgun which would reach far enough.*" Before the eight gauge was banned in 1918, Askins had a Greener eight-gauge double with 36-inch barrels weighing 13 pounds. His handload was a "...*heavy load of Herco powder and 2 ounces of shot, either 2's or 4's. It would stop ducks consistently at 80 yards.*" Two years after Askins wrote the above, he received from Ithaca the first 3 1/2-inch Magnum 10 double off the assembly line.

Charles Askins is the father of the late Colonel Charles Askins, Jr., of course.

Such were the men of the long-range duck-hunting cult. Their attitude is summed up by Elmer Keith in *Shotguns by Keith*: "...*the satisfaction of seeing big ducks crumple at long range and come down and bounce on the ground or splash high in the water is the cream of shotgun shooting.*"

It is my view that the long-range duck-hunting cult was a legacy from the days of market hunting. Bob

Hinman, in his 1972 GUN DIGEST article *Ten Cents a Duck*, notes that "*Shooting for the market was at one time a way of life for thousands of America's skilled shotgunners.*" Market hunting was legislated out of existence in the late teens. However, killing ducks at long range remained the objective of many duck hunters. The 12-gauge 3-inch magnum shotshell was developed to achieve this objective.

The 1 5/8-ounce load of the mid-'30s bought the 12 magnum a few more yards of range. Elmer Keith instructs: "*For the man who wants greater range and a bigger shot load for duck or goose shooting, the Model 12 Winchester is in a class by itself* [with] *the long 3" 1? ounce load.*" Nevertheless, the 1 7/8-ounce load appeared in the mid-'50s and now a full two ounces of shot can be had in the 12 magnum. Askins and Buckingham would sure be surprised at how far the 12 magnum has come.

Shooting the Model 12 Duck Gun

I own two Model 12 duck guns. Although acquired many years apart, the two duck guns are of nearly the same vintages, 1952 and 1953. The first thing you notice when you pick up a duck gun is its weight and solid feel. No other pump shotgun feels like the duck gun. The extra weight is meant to soak up the recoil of what once was thought to be a very hard-kicking load. It still is. Twelve magnum guns grew lighter over the years and consequently kick harder. The near nine-pound Model 12 duck gun is an anachronism among today's waterfowl hunting shotguns. However, the Model 12 duck gun should still be an excellent long-range waterfowl shotgun with the right ammunition. I have often wondered how well my guns would pattern with modern ammunition.

The duck gun made in 1952 has a Simmons ventilated rib. Winchester installed Simmons ribs and Simmons-designed ventilated ribs for several years. However, Winchester's ribs were not marked with the Simmons

This 48% pattern (pellet holes marked) was fired from 60 yards by Model 12 1418XXX and Winchester's 1 5/8-ounce load of #4 shot. Other percentages fired by this combination were 40, 45, 42 and 46% for an average of 44%. Putting one of these patterns on a flying duck at 60 yards is not easy.

name *and* Kansas City address as mine is. Also, the rib and its receiver extension cover the Winchester proof marks, a sure sign that it is not factory installed. My 1953 duck gun has the factory solid rib. Both guns have 30-inch Full choke barrels inscribed "*FOR SUPER SPEED & SUPER-X 3 IN.*" The bores are bright with no pitting. The takedown joints are tight (*See the instructions in Madis' book if your Model 12 has a loose takedown joint*). The locked breech bolts of both guns have little perceptible play when the rear of the bolt is pressed from the side. This test determines if excessive peening of the bolt locking cut in the receiver has occurred. Loose bolts and excess headspace occur only after long service. This test, along with a check of adjustment remaining in the takedown joint and functioning of the slide lock disconnector, are my standard mechani-

cal checks for a Model 12. The solid rib gun shows carrying wear while the ventilated rib gun was refinished when the rib was installed. Both guns were disassembled, cleaned and lightly oiled before testing.

I decided to test the patterning of the five loads detailed in the accompanying table. Emphasis was placed on loads of #4 shot because of its historical significance in waterfowl hunting and association with the long-range objectives of the Model 12 duck gun. I included tungsten polymer shot because it is non-toxic to waterfowl and has the same density as lead. Also, it was the only 1 3/8-ounce magnum load available. I included #2 shot because this size shot has always been my goose and turkey load in 3-inch shells. The trap load was included because trap shooting is suited to the duck gun.

It is general consensus that 10 patterns are required for an accurate appraisal of a given load and barrel combination. I fired 10 patterns for each of the five test loads in each of the two duck guns, for a total of 100 patterns. Range was 40 yards from gun muzzle to target frame. Patterns were fired from a benchrest, using American Target Company B21 silhouette targets measuring 35 by 45 inches. The silhouette provides a precise aiming point. Each fired target was turned over and a 30-inch cardboard disc

TABLE 4

Patterns Produced by Model 12 Duck Guns at 40 Yards

Pellets in 30-inch circle / percent of total pellets[a]					
Model 12	Win. 1?-8	Fed. 1?-4	Win. 1?-4	Win. 1?-4	Fed. 2-2
1418XXX	352/70±2	153/82±3	186/84±3	226/86±3	122/73±4
1512XXX	372/74±3	155/83±4	179/81±3	223/85±2	116/69±4

a Averages of 10 patterns per load ± standard deviation.

placed to cover the maximum number for pellet holes. The perimeter of the disc was then marked and the enclosed pellet holes counted. The number of pellet holes was divided by the average number of pellets in the load to produce the pattern percentage. Both shotguns shot to point of aim and all patterns were contained on the target paper due to precise aiming, facilitated by placing a 25-pound sack of lead shot between me and the gun butt.

Results and Discussion

The paired pattern percentages fired by the two duck guns with each of the five loads were not significantly different, judging by the overlapping standard deviations. Both guns averaged 80% or better patterns with all loads of #4 shot. Not shown in the table of results are the dense centers of patterns obtained with #4 shot compared to #8 and #2 shot. Some patterns of #4 shot might let a duck escape if it were caught just inside the margin of the 30-inch circle. On the other hand, a duck caught in the middle of one of these dense-centered patterns at 40 yards would receive a dozen or more pellets. Number 8 and 2 shot provided wider and more even patterns with no center thickening. Pattern percentages were around 70% with these latter loads.

Askins stated in *Modern Shotguns and Loads: "All shotguns which are intended for long range work…should be patterned at 60 yards."* Continuing, *"…loads which pattern around 85% [at 40 yards] have that quality which will permit them to continue a pattern on down the range."* Askins found that each yard of range beyond 40 yards reduced pattern density by an average of two percent. Curious, I fired five additional patterns at 60 yards with Model 12 number 1418XXX and

the Winchester load of 1 5/8-ounces of #4 shot. This combination, which averaged 83.6% at 40 yards, averaged 44.2% at 60 yards! Askins' rule of thumb of 70 years ago still pertains with modern lead-shot ammunition.

Madis states *"Winchester spent a great deal of time and effort to develop better chokes."* Furthermore, *"Winchester constantly experimented, searching for improvements in all chokes, even the old standby full choke."* Winchester almost certainly would have perfected their Full-choke Model 12 duck gun to maximize patterns with #4 lead shot, the size most mentioned for long-range duck shooting in publications prior to the advent of non-toxic shot. Winchester suggests their 3-inch 12-gauge shotshells with 1 3/8-ounces or 1 5/8-ounces of #4 shot for wildfowl hunting in their 1951 *Ammunition Handbook: "These shells were developed especially for extremes in long range shooting with 12-gauge Winchester Model 12 and Model 21 Heavy Duck Guns."*

Charles Askins provides data for the patterning of several of his personal shotguns with Western's Super-X shells loaded with their new #4 copper-plated shot. Writing in the March 1927 issue of the *American Riflemen*, Askins reports that his Remington Model 10 12-gauge pump averaged 89% of 1 1/4-ounces of shot in a 30-inch circle at 40 yards. His Super Fox 12 gauge magnum double averaged 83.7% (two-barrel average) of 1 3/8-ounces of shot under the same conditions. Askins' Ithaca 10-gauge double with 2 7/8-inch chambers averaged 86.9% with 1 5/8-ounces of shot. His shotguns were undoubtedly the best long-range duck guns he found in extensive testing. Askins concludes *"How far are we going to be able to kill ducks? Probably a lot farther than we can hit 'em. A lot of us will have to begin learning to hit long-range*

ducks." Sounds like an invitation to join the long-range duck hunting cult!

Keith stated in 1967: *"The old 70% standard is now obsolete and most any full choke gun will go 75% or better. Some will even go 85% to 90%, but rarely."* Keith, who obtained Askins' Ithaca 10 magnum double upon Askins' death, achieved 93% patterns with two ounces of copper-plated #3 shot in the big double. This was after extensive reworking of the chokes by Ithaca.

Model 12 duck guns are highly specialized tools for a very limited number of duck hunters who can regularly center a duck at 40-60 yards, *and need to.* That is why I have never used one of my duck guns for duck hunting. The ducks shot by me in the accompanying photograph were taken with Skeet boring and trap loads of #7 1/2-shot. My wife shot her share of ducks with a 20-gauge autoloader bored Improved Cylinder shooting one ounce of #7 1/2-shot. We limited our shooting to 25 yards or less and seldom missed. In those good old days of the 1960s the ducks flew just above the cattails and shots were plentiful. There was no need to shoot ducks at 60 yards.

Will Winchester ever build the Model 12 again? *"No."* says Madis. *"The nearest thing to a Model Twelve that could appear, whether domestic or foreign, would be a shotgun with the same model designation, but it would not and could not be a Model Twelve."* Browning, in fact, did import foreign-made copies of the Model 12 after Madis wrote the above. As good as the Brownings are, I'll just keep my Model 12s from New Haven. The Model 12 duck guns are still as suitable for *"…waterfowl passes, fox trails or the habitat of the wary gobbler"* as they were when the duck hunters at Winchester surprised the market in 1935. ●

Bibliography

Askins, Charles. Copper-Coated Shot. *American Rifleman*. March 1927.

Askins, Charles. Long Range Shotguns. *American Rifleman*. January 1930.

Askins, Charles. *Modern Shotguns and Loads*. Small Arms Technical Publishing Company. Marshalltown, Delaware. 1929.

Buckingham, Nash. *De Shootinest Gent'man and Other Tales*. G. P. Putnam's Sons. New York, New York. 1934.

Hinman, Bob. Ten Cents a Duck. GUN DIGEST. Krause Publications. Iola, Wisconsin. 1972.

Houze, Herbert G. *Winchester Repeating Arms Company*. Its History and Development. From 1865-1981. Krause Publications. Iola, Wisconsin. 1994.

Keith, Elmer. *Shotguns by Keith*. Bonanza Books. New York, Neew York. 1967.

Lawrence, H. Lea. The Saga of Bo Whoop. GUN DIGEST. Krause Publications. Iola, Wisconsin. 2001.

McIntosh, Michael. *Best Shotguns*. First Revised Edition. Countrysport Press. Selma, Alabama. 1999.

O'Connor, Jack. *The Shotgun Book*. Alfred A. Knopt. New York, New York. 1965.

O'Connor, Jack. Wildfowl Shooting in *Complete Book of Shooting*. Harper & Row. New York, New York. 1965.

Riffle, Dave. *The Greatest Hammerless Repeating Shotgun Ever Built. The Model 12 1912-1964*. Publishing Professiionals. Fort Myers, Florida.

Stadt, Ronald W. *Winchester Shotguns and Shotshells*. Second Edition. Krause Publications Inc., Iola, Wisconsin. 1995.

Staff Report. The Winchester Model-12 Heavy Duck Gun. *American Rifleman*. January 1936.

Watrous, George R. T*he History of Winchester Firearms 1866-1966*. Third Edition Winchester-Western Press. 1966.

Williamson, Harold F. *Winchester the Gun That Won the West*. Second Edition. H. S. Barnes and Company, Inc. New York, New York. 1961.

Winchester Arms and Accessories. Price list. *Winchester Repeating Arms Company*. New Haven, Connecticut. March 1939.

Winchester Arms and Accessories. Price list. Winchester Repeating Arms Company. New Haven, Connecticut. October 1946.

Winchester Catalog No. 80. 1916. Reprint. Springfield Printing and Binding Company. Springfield, Massachusetts. Undated.

Winchester Sales Manual 1938. Reprint. Lear Publications. Easton, Pennsylvania. 1970.

"Bootleg" Pistols

A.D. Hilliard pistol, #160.

by Ken Aiken

SAMUEL COLT WAS a promoter of laughing gas.[1] Oliver Winchester a successful manufacturer of shirts.[2] The guns we associate with the "Winning of the West" — the Colt "Peacemaker" of 1873[3] and the Winchester Model 1873 rifle[4] — were touted in that image by company advertising in the latter part of the 19th century and indelibly imprinted in our minds by Hollywood's dramatization in the 20th. But few of the pioneers who ventured West in the 1840s[5] and in the years following the discovery of gold in California carried the expensive percussion Colt revolvers; and the lever-action Henry, Spencer, and Ball cartridge rifles were guns of the future.[6] Most of the pioneers, farmers, and fortune-seekers who headed West in these early years were armed with single-shot, muzzle-loading rifles and "boot" pistols.

In the 18th and first half of the 19th century men wore high boots, and small pistols were often carried tucked into the top of these boots for easy access — holsters for pistols were generally limited to saddle-mounted scabbards for dragoon pistols until the Civil War — but the bulkiness of flintlock pistols, and the tendency of sidelock hammers to catch on boot tops when being withdrawn, limited their appeal. Around 1829 the availability of copper percussion caps[7] enabled a new class of firearm to be developed: the underhammer.

The under-hammer lock, with the hammer in front of the trigger on the underside of the barrel, was not a new concept. Flintlock under-hammer pistols and one rifle[8] are known, but the complications of striking the priming powder made these firearms a rarity. It was the availability of Joshua Shaw's percussion caps that made the under-hammer lock a practical mechanism and enabled the creation of a handgun suitable for being worn tucked into the top of a mans' boot, hence the name "boot" or "bootleg" pistol.

The story of the invention of the under-hammer lock by one of its most prolific makers, long accepted as historical fact *(but becoming more and more anecdotal as my research continues)*, was written by Guy Hubbard, in his 1922 *"Windsor Industrial History: Part I"*[9] as follows:

"During the latter part of the time when Asahel Hubbard was operating his shop between Windsor and the West Parish, Nicanor Kendall became, for certain reasons, a frequent visitor there. One day when this young gunsmith and the daughter of the house were riding in a sleigh along one of the country roads, he noticed a gray squirrel in a tree nearby, and having one of Story's side-hammer percussion rifles with him, he started to draw it from beneath the buffalo robe. As he did so, the hammer caught, and falling, exploded the rifle when the muzzle was pointed at the young lady's head. Believing his right hand to be blown to pieces, Kendall thrust it under the robe and horror-stricken turned to see what the fate of his companion has been. To his intense relief he found that at the moment of the explosion she had chanced to lean out of the sleigh to look back, so, aside from being badly frightened,

was uninjured. Without mentioning his own crippled condition, Kendall drove hurriedly to the house of the village doctor, where he was further gratified to find that his hand, instead of being shattered, was only burned, the ball having passed between his fingers.

This painful and alarming accident inspired Mr. Kendall to invent a type of gun lock in which the trigger and hammer might be protected by the same guard."

Nicanor Kendall, the son of the local blacksmith, was born in West Windsor, Vermont on December 20, 1807. Not much else is known, except that he worked for Asa Story, probably as an assistant rather than an apprentice, and that Asa Story is generally believed to have opened his gun shop in West Windsor in 1830. Located on the Connecticut River and the major stage roads, Windsor was at that time the wealthiest town in the state and a crossroad of commerce. Asahel Hubbard had invented a rotary water pump in 1828 and created the National Hydraulic Company in Proctorsville in 1829.[10] The "engine" company, as it was called, developed a nationwide network of independent agents and the machine shop on the Black River probably became a place where the latest inventions were discussed by the "mechanics" and traveling salesmen. Nicanor Kendall would have had plenty of opportunity to learn about any new development in firearms either at the "engine" works or in Asa Story's shop.[11] Kendall's first under-hammer guns were allegedly made in Asa Story's shop, but sometime early in 1835 N. Kendall organized financial back-

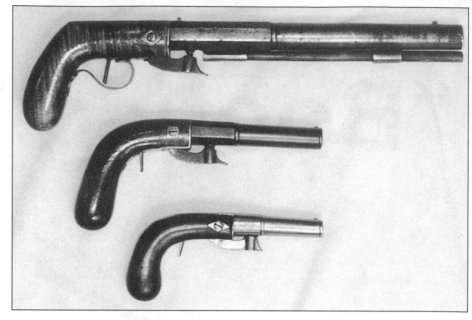

Boot pistols by N. Kendall & Co.

ing, formed N. Kendall & Company,[12] and contracted with the superintendent of the Vermont State Prison at Windsor to operate a shop within the prison walls for the employ of a number of convicts.[13] The company had already been producing firearms when they received an order for several hundred guns from the Republic of Texas in November of 1835; this order was completed sometime in 1836. Their success did not go unnoticed by other gunsmiths.

An under-hammer pistol made by Asa Story after 1838. The work is cruder than what was produced in the prison shops, so it probably dates after 1841. *Terry Tyler collection*

Exactly when the first percussion underhammers were made and by whom is open to conjecture. It wasn't Nicanor Kendall, although he appears to have been the first to apply an under-hammer percussion lock to a rifle, but probably Jedediah Caswell of Manlius, New York.[14] A boot pistol, made around 1830 and engraved LELAND, is believed to have been made by one of the Leland family of Sherborn, Massachusetts.[15] Two Kentucky-style under-hammer pistols are known, but there is nothing to indicate when they were made and they probably represent the work of individual gunsmiths after the boot pistol became popularized. Although

most famous gunsmiths developed their own versions of the under-hammer lock, the simplicity of this mechanism *(American and European pistols having only two moving parts are known)* made it possible for independent gunsmiths, many blacksmiths, and more than a few tinkers to

create firearms of their own design. The vast majority of these guns bear no trace of the maker's identity and often represent one-of-a-kind efforts, making it difficult to document the history of this popular firearm. Even when some limited documentation is available, questions remain.

Michael Carleton of Haverhill, NH *(located just south of the northernmost port on the Connecticut River and about 45 miles upstream from Windsor, Vermont)* developed a unique under-hammer lock in which the hammer was driven forward *(horizontally and in parallel with the barrel)* by the spring action of the trigger guard.[16] Although a patent was issued to M. Carleton for a "Percussion Lock" on December 23, 1830, it is unknown whether it was for this design. Also unknown is exactly when these unique pistols were being produced.

Nicanor Kendall wasn't the only New England gunsmith producing boot pistols in quantity. Ethan

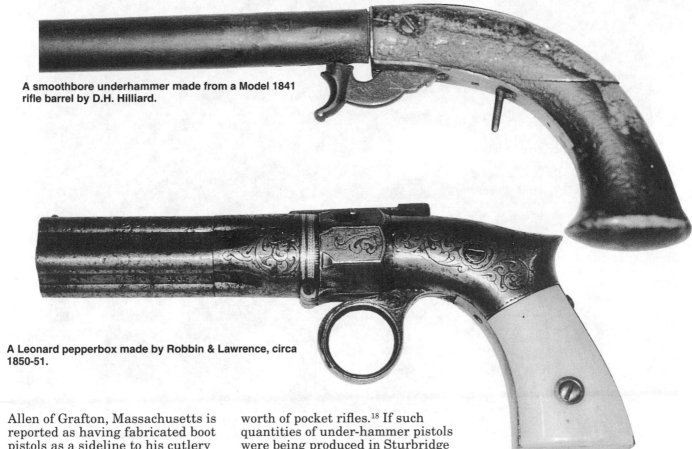

A smoothbore underhammer made from a Model 1841 rifle barrel by D.H. Hilliard.

A Leonard pepperbox made by Robbin & Lawrence, circa 1850-51.

Allen of Grafton, Massachusetts is reported as having fabricated boot pistols as a sideline to his cutlery business sometime between 1832 and 1834, but began his gun company with the introduction of the "Pocket Rifle" late in 1836, and soon followed with a second model with a shorter barrel in 1837.[17] These were the first production firearms made by this famous gunsmith and they continued to be produced until 1842. Gibbs, Tiffany & Co. of Sturbridge, Massachusetts was producing bootleg pistols in 1836 *(standard bulb grip, no guard, curved trigger, various calibers)* and as late as 1850 were still manufacturing this same style of handgun. Bacon & Company of Norwich, Connecticut was another famous gun manufacturer that began with the production of under-hammer pistols, although they're best known for their pepperboxes. In 1837 Sturbridge, Massachusetts had a thriving cottage industry that employed 36 people and produced $20,275

worth of pocket rifles.[18] If such quantities of under-hammer pistols were being produced in Sturbridge in 1837, how many were being made in Springfield, Massachusetts and Norwich, Connecticut, areas known for their gunsmiths and machine shops? Unfortunately, the answers to these questions remain to be discovered.

The widespread popularity of these under-hammer pistols was due to three significant factors: *1)* their streamlined form made them easy to carry in either boot or pocket; *2)* the simplicity of the lock mechanism was such that it didn't require a gunsmith to make repairs; and *3)* they were inexpensive.[19] Other reasons for their popularity: these pistols could be crafted in a day, were easily customized to fit the requirements of individual buyers, and were available in a wide range of calibers. All of these factors, coupled with the westward emigration of America's population, created

an unprecedented demand for these inexpensive non-martial arms.

Certainly not everyone who purchased a pistol was headed west to the frontier of Kansas or the unimaginably distant Oregon, but the sheer quantities of these pistols sold, along with isolated references, suggest that a large percentage of these guns were being taken West. Ethan Allen produced thousands of his "pocket-rifles"[20] and the quantity manufactured by N. Kendall & Company, while unknown, was considerable. Although the first manufacturers were concentrated primarily along the Connecticut

A D. H. Hilliard pistol based on a U.S Army musket barrel (21" barrel, 32" OAL). May have been a rifle prior to altering and adding a shoulder stock; similar to another original pistol. *Eldon Owens collection*

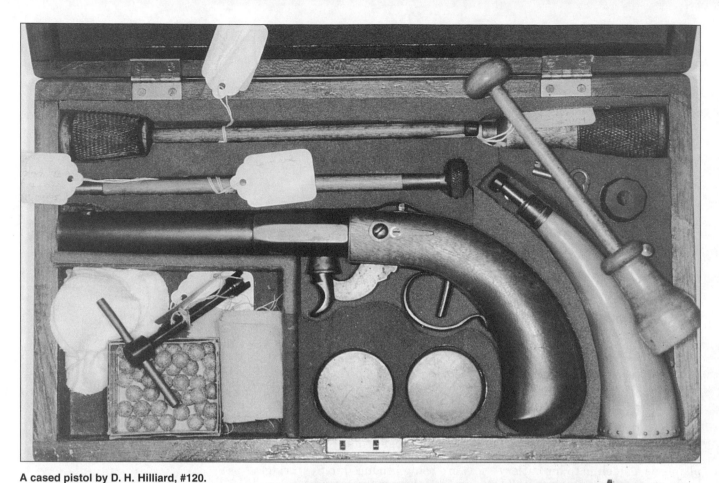

A cased pistol by D. H. Hilliard, #120.

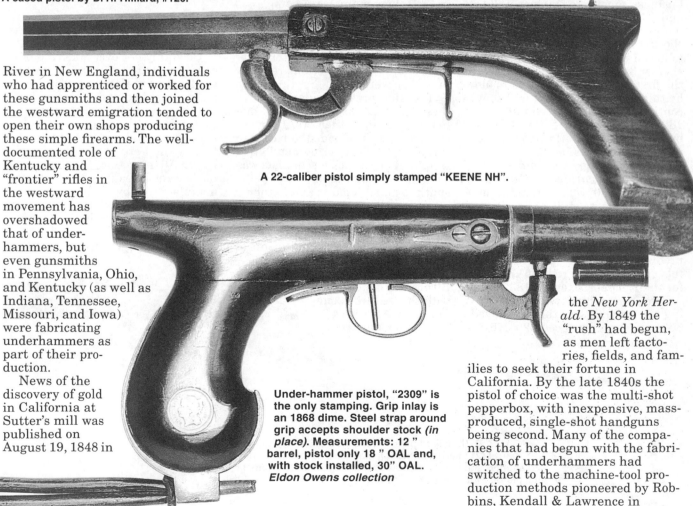

River in New England, individuals who had apprenticed or worked for these gunsmiths and then joined the westward emigration tended to open their own shops producing these simple firearms. The well-documented role of Kentucky and "frontier" rifles in the westward movement has overshadowed that of under-hammers, but even gunsmiths in Pennsylvania, Ohio, and Kentucky (as well as Indiana, Tennessee, Missouri, and Iowa) were fabricating underhammers as part of their production.

News of the discovery of gold in California at Sutter's mill was published on August 19, 1848 in

A 22-caliber pistol simply stamped "KEENE NH".

Under-hammer pistol, "2309" is the only stamping. Grip inlay is an 1868 dime. Steel strap around grip accepts shoulder stock *(in place)*. Measurements: 12 " barrel, pistol only 18 " OAL and, with stock installed, 30" OAL. *Eldon Owens collection*

the *New York Herald*. By 1849 the "rush" had begun, as men left factories, fields, and families to seek their fortune in California. By the late 1840s the pistol of choice was the multi-shot pepperbox, with inexpensive, mass-produced, single-shot handguns being second. Many of the companies that had begun with the fabrication of underhammers had switched to the machine-tool production methods pioneered by Robbins, Kendall & Lawrence in

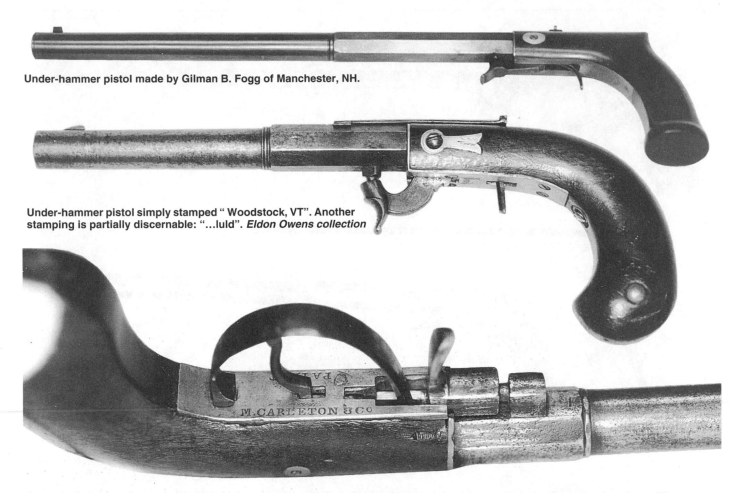

Under-hammer pistol made by Gilman B. Fogg of Manchester, NH.

Under-hammer pistol simply stamped " Woodstock, VT". Another stamping is partially discernable: "…luld". *Eldon Owens collection*

An under-hammer pistol (8" OAL) with "M. CARLETON & CO." and "PATENT" stamped on the brass lockplate by the trigger. The hammer travels horizontally. Carleton was from Haverill, NH or Newbury, VT. *Eldon Owens collection*

An under-hammer pistol made by Asa Story after 1838. The work is cruder than what was produced in the prison shops, so it probably dates after 1841. *Terry Tyler collection*

Windsor, Vermont and were producing more complicated firearms. But guns were an essential item for the "49ers" and demand became so high that almost anything that fired could be sold; even the new "American system"[21] of production couldn't keep up with the orders.

"*In manufacturing Government rifles [U.S. Model 1841], a loss of about thirty-eight percent was usual, these being condemned for poor material or workmanship. In 1849-50 the Great California Gold Rush excitement was raging, and guns were in such demand that we sold all our second quality work, with good mixed in — anything to make up a working gun — for the full good price. This was a great relief in every way and things looked very bright.*"
— memoirs of Richard S. Lawrence[22]

During this period, gun shops like D.H. Hilliard & Company[23] and many individual gunsmiths were kept working at full capacity manufacturing under-hammer guns, often purchasing second-grade parts (*especially the barrels*) from Robbins & Lawrence.[24]

By the time of the Civil War, under-hammer rifles and pistols were being made by gunsmiths as far south as Florida and as far west as California.

Almost no documentation of the use of under-hammer boot pistols exists for the Civil War, but it was a turning point for both under-hammer pistols and rifles. Besides the standard military issue rifle — Model 1861 "Springfields" — soldiers brought a variety of personal pistols onto the battlefields of this conflict. How many under-hammer boot pistols were carried to war is unknown, but they would have been a good personal choice since they used the

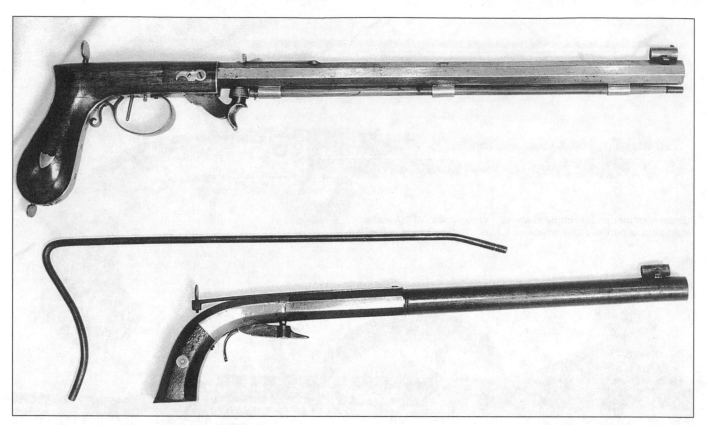

Two guns by Edward M. Glynn of East Clarendon VT, circa 1871-1885. The upper gun (a Kendall-style pistol) is marked; the lower is not. The iron rod is the shoulder stock for the upper gun and is held in position by the setscrew in the grip. *Terry Tyler collection*

same percussion caps and powder as the Springfield rifle. Smith & Wesson revolvers and a great variety of other small pistols using their 22-caliber cartridge, the lever-action rifles using Henry's 44-caliber cartridge, and the numerous breech-loading rifles produced during this era diminished the popularity of the under-hammer gun. In the aftermath of the war, the disillusioned and disenfranchised[25] created the second great wave of westward emigration; with a glut of firearms on the market probably very few under-hammers were carried into the American West of lore and legend. But not everyone went west.

The 1830s were truly the era of the underhammer. Yet in my opinion, many of the finest examples of these firearms were made in the 1850s and after the Civil War. Many gunsmiths, especially in Vermont and New Hampshire, continued to fabricate boot pistols and long arms in their traditional forms, while others brought these firearms to new artistic heights. Match-shooting competition was developing into a recognized sport in the 1850s, and in 1858 a group of enthusiasts formed The National Rifle Club, the oldest rifle club in the United States, in Framingham, Massachusetts. After the war similar clubs

were formed around the country and competition shooting became popular. Many of the finest gunsmiths of the era joined these clubs, and the prestige of winning was such that it reflected as much upon the gunmaker as upon the marksman. Match guns — rifles, pistols, underhammers, and sidehammers — were made by famous gunsmiths such as Norman Brockway, David Hall Hilliard, Artemus Leonard, and William Billinghurst.[26] Some gunsmiths, like Hilliard and Billinghurst, began their careers producing under-hammer guns; Norman Brockway and others, like Albert "Put" Gove of Lincoln, Vermont, had experience working for various armories and/or gun manufacturers, but chose to fabricate custom one-of-a-kind pieces instead.[27] Distinctive pistols, such as John Demeritt's,[28] with staghorn grips, and Edward Glynn's,[29] with a brass breech, found a ready market in an era of mass-produced handguns.

The term "boot" or "bootleg" pistol is not limited to under-hammer pistols, nor are under-hammer pistols limited to this category of firearm. These pistols are not easy to classify: they had a greater variety of grip styles of any firearm made before or since; barrel length varied from as little as 1 3/8-inches to over

20 inches[30] and were round, octagonal, or a combination of both; rifled bores ranged from at least 20 to 50 caliber. Fowling smoothbore barrels were larger; frames were generally made of cast steel, but also of wood and brass; and some had attachable shoulder stocks. Most were single-shot, muzzle-loading handguns, but a few multiple-shot varieties are known[31] and at least three breech-loading styles exist.[32] They were used for personal defense, hunting, sport, and warfare; mechanically they varied from simplistic to state-of-the-art; and artistically they ranged from crude endeavors to some of the most elegant firearms ever made. The under-hammer lock allowed creative gunsmiths to experiment with different concepts, many of which were essential to the development of modern firearms. Historically overshadowed by the works of Sharps, Colt, and Smith & Wesson, the role the underhammer played in the development of the machine-tool industry, the "American system" of manufacturing, and the opening of the far West has long been ignored. Perhaps a new look at these firearms will lead to a greater understanding of this era in American history. ●

Footnotes

1. The effects of nitrous oxide were discovered by Gardner Colton (from Georgia, Vermont), yet Dr. Horace Wells (from White River Junction, Vermont, but practicing in Boston), who learned the technique from Colton, was the first person to use laughing gas as an anesthetic for pulling teeth in 1844. Samuel Colt, a.k.a. "Doctor Coult" was a demonstrator and lecturer who promoted this new discovery in the years (1831 - 32) before he patented his revolver. From a letter from Hiram Powers (the famous Vermont-born sculptor) to his friend Samuel Colt, dated Sept. 10, 1851:

I have at last gotten possession of the wonderful 'revolver' which you have been so kind to send me.

And now let me thank you for this token of your kind remembrance. Our experience has been somewhat similar. Both of us have had some tough times in our day, we have passed through a variety of trying processes upwards to some distinction. But you have found pecuniary reward the soonest, and well have you merited it, and as well, the high reputation you now enjoy.

I shall never forget the gas at the old Museum [Western Museum of Cincinnati] nor your sly glances at the ropes stretched around the columns, when about to snatch the gas bag away from the huge blacksmith who glowered at you so threateningly while his steam was getting up, nor a moment after, his grab at your coat tails, when you froglike leaped between the ropes.

I remember you telling me in Washington, that at that very time you were elaborating in your mind the great invention you have since given to the world. But little did I then dream that in 1851 I should be in Italy, a sculptor, and fully employed. I had hopes for better things for the future, but they were faint indeed.

I have not forgotten my old mechanical pursuits, and I have a shop even here, a turning lathe, forge, etc., and I spend much of my leisure time in this way. I have invented several improvements in working marble and plaster of Paris. One of them you shall see one of these days, for it embraces much of your own art. It could not fail to be very useful even to you. It is not yet complete, but will be in a few months.

Johnathan is indeed taking a stand among the nations of the 'arth.' If his show at the Great Exhibition is meagre, he nevertheless beats all creation in his threshing machines, his steamers and yachts. John Bull don't like this from his rebellious son, but he chuckles at his being HIS son, after all.

Wishing you increased success in all your undertakings, I am, my dear friend,
Ever most sincerely yours,
Hiram Powers"

2. Oliver Winchester first became involved in the gun business when he purchased 80 shares of stock in the Volcanic Repeating Arms Company in June of 1855 for a sum of $2,000. On April 3, 1856 Oliver Winchester organized the New Haven Arms Company. On March 15, 1857 by order of the court, the entire assets of the Volcanic Company were assigned to Oliver Winchester for just over $39,000. Winchester had supplied loans and loan guarantees and had made arrangements with the heirs of the major stockholder, Nelson B. Gaston who had died in Dec. 1856.

3. The single-action Colt Frontier Model Revolver was the first Colt to use cartridges (the Smith & Wesson patent expired in 1872). One reason for its popularity was that it used the same cartridge (44-40-200 centerfire) as the Winchester Model 1873 rifle, thus reducing the need to carry two different types of ammunition; the caliber was later increased to 45/100.

4. The Model 1873 replaced the Model 1866; the ammunition was not compatible. The 44-caliber rimfire cartridge used by the Model 1866 contained only 28 grains of powder to propel the 200-grain bullet; the more powerful 44-caliber centerfire

A 40-caliber pistol with false muzzle and wood shoulder stock, by G.W. Green of Readsboro, VT circa 1870-1879. *Terry Tyler collection*

cartridge used by the Model 1873 contained 40 grains of powder to propel 200 grains of lead. The Model 1876 was essentially the same as the previous model, but used an even more powerful cartridge, the famous 45-caliber (75 grains of powder and 350 grains of lead; and the brass cartridge was reloadable).

5. Congress began selling 160-acre lots west of Wisconsin in 1840 for $1.25 per acre, provided that the settlers built a house and cultivated the land; the Oregon Trail was mapped by Lt. John Charles Frèmont in 1842; Brigham Young and his 15,000 followers headed west in 1846; and the so-called Mormon battalion under Lt. Col. Philip St. George Cook established the Santa Fe trail from New Mexico to San Diego, California in 1847.

6. The Henry Repeating Rifle was first made in 1858; the Spencer in 1860; the Ball in 1864.

7. The percussion cap was invented in England and there are numerous claims as to who was the first to do it. The United States patent for copper percussion caps was awarded to Joshua Shaw of Philadelphia, allegedly on June 19, 1822. The most thoroughly researched account of Joshua Shaw seems to have been done by Lewis Winant, who includes his research as a chapter in his book "*Early Percussion Firearms*" (Bonanza Books, NY 1959).

Joshua Shaw's claim to have invented the percussion cap in 1814 appears to have been a fabrication fostered by Shaw in his successful petition of 1846 (H.R. 206 of the 29th Congress) to obtain compensation from the U.S. Congress for use of his "invention." An important quote from a listing of patents in the 1829 issue of the "Journal of the Franklin Institute" reads: "For an improvement in Guns and Fire-arms, which improvement consists in a priming and giving them fire, by the means of percussion, fulminating or detonating powders: Joshua Shaw, Philadelphia. First issued June 19th, 1822, surrendered for the purpose of correcting the specification, and reissued May 7 [1829]."

The fact that Joshua Shaw surrendered his June 19, 1822 patent — and that it wasn't reissued until May 7, 1829 — would explain why percussion caps weren't available until around 1829. The original documentation was lost in the Patent Office fire of 1836, and the June 19, 1822 date was stated by Joshua Shaw (who conveniently left out the issue of surrendering the patent) in an affidavit by W.L. Ellsworth, Commissioner of Patents on December 1, 1844. This affidavit was used as evidence in his petition to Congress and the document referred to by historians in establishing the date of Joshua Shaw's patent.

8. In Herschel C. Logan's book "*The Pictorial History of Underhammer Guns*" he includes a description of pair of under-hammer flintlock pistols examined by Chester H. Johnson in an English shop. These pistols were engraved in small block letters on the top strap: CALDERWOOD — PHILADELPHIA. In "*American Firearms Makers*," A. Merwyn Carey has this listing: "Calderwood, William 1807-1819. Maker of flintlock Kentucky rifles and Army Model 1808 flintlock pistols. Shop located on Germantown Road, Philadelphia, Pennsylvania."

Herschel Logan also includes photos of an under-hammer flintlock rifle of German make, circa 1740, and a letter from the English owner W. Keith Neal.

An under-hammer matchlock musket (?) complete with a trigger guard and a full-stock is displayed in the armory room of the Doge's Palace in Venice, Italy and attributed to Persian manufacture in the 18th century (visually it appears like a late 19th century firearm). I hope to examine this firearm in detail in the near future, as it might be the earliest surviving example of an under-hammer lock.

These examples show that under-hammer locks were not a new concept — but flintlock underhammers certainly weren't common.

9. A treatise for the Co-operative Machine Department of the Windsor High

School and published by mimeograph by the Town School District of Windsor, Vermont.

10. Asahel Hubbard developed a rotary pump after witnessing a demonstration of Cooper's rotative piston pump (American Hydraulic Company) and observing its faults. Hubbard received a patent for his pump (which is still used in cars and fire engines) on April 28, 1828, and with the backing of Jabez Proctor and Zacharius Blood, incorporated the National Hydraulic Company on October 28, 1829.

11. My research shows that Asahel Hubbard and his family were living in Proctorsville at least from 1830 to 1833 and that Nicanor Kendall was also living in Proctorsville in 1833. I suspect that Kendall didn't produce his first under-hammer lock until at least 1832. Nicanor Kendall was married to Laura C. Hubbard, the "daughter of the house," on September 2, 1835.

12. It's generally believed that Asa Story and William B. Smith were two of the principals of the company and evidence seems to point to their continued involvement until sometime in 1841, although the exact nature of their involvement and business relationship is unknown.

13. Report by John H. Cotton, Superintendent Vermont State Prison, to the General Assembly of the State of Vermont, on October 13, 1835. ". . . a contract has been made with Messrs. N. Kendall and Company, for 18 to 20 convicts, employed at the manufacture of rifles; the company have been to considerable expense in machinery, in order to prosecute their business profitably. For the convicts, so employed in the rifle shop, the Superintendent receives an average price of 32 cents per day." As of September 30, 1835 the prison had received $907.29 in income for employment of convicts from N. Kendall & Company — over 2,800 man-hours.

14. Jedediah Caswell was granted one of the earliest U.S. patents for an underhammer lock (like most early patents, it was lost in the Patent Office fire of 1836 and never restored) and he was making boot pistols in the late 1820s: a pistol dated 1828 is known.

15. Measuring 7-1/2 inches overall with a 4-inch octagonal breech/round barrel and a 41-caliber bore, this pistol has a long arched hammer that looks like a modern trigger guard; an arched finger pull attached to the front of the hammer just below the head; and a flat trigger with a slight curve. The bulb grip is of walnut; the top strap, sides of the breech, and frame are lightly engraved; and a large oval panel in the center of the top strap is engraved in large bold script "LELAND." There are three large, fancy-shaped, solid silver inlays, each engraved with large, fancy letters "G.B.B. TO J.H.B." and lightly engraved on the handle and frame "T. Boyce." — #1690A N. Flayderman & Co. Inc. #112 1987

Although I have only examined a printed photograph, my opinion is that this gun appears more like those produced in the mid-1830s and later. The barrel, inlays, shape of the grip, the use of stamps for "T. Boyce," and the elaborate hammer and curved trigger are factors that suggest a later date than listed for this pistol.

16. I had the opportunity to examine a pistol made by M. Carleton in the collection of Eldon Owens. The action was exceptionally smooth — cocking the hammer was the easiest of any underhammer I've handled, and the balance of the pistol was ideal. The stamping on the pistol is "M. Carlton & Co. Patent" and, since other examples are known, I can only assume that this was a going concern — but how many were produced and during what years is unknown.

17. The double-action mechanism Allen patented in 1837 was applied to the frame of the second model Pocket Rifle, and the Allen & Thurber Tube Hammer Pistol was the result. *Flayderman's Guide to Antique American Firearms . . .and their values: 6th Edition*, by Norm Flayderman DBI Books, Inc., Northbrook, Ill, 1994, pg. 42

18. "The Pictorial History of the Under-hammer Gun" by Herschel C. Logan, Castle Books, NY, 1960, page 6. Logan is quoting from an earlier work, "Barber's Historical Collections" by John Warner Barber, Dorr, Howland & Company, Worcester, MA, 1839.

19. In 1847 a pair of Ethan Allen Pocket Rifles sold for $4.50; a Colt revolver was priced from $16.00 to $19.00.

20. The first product produced by this famous gunsmith was the "Pocket Rifle." Produced from 1836 to 1842 they were sold as matched (and numbered) pairs for around $4.50 in 1847. The term "pocket rifle" was used by several companies, but Ethan Allen was the first to coin it. This was one of two models of under-hammer pistols made by Ethan Allen/Allen & Thurber of Grafton, Massachusetts. Thurber was Allen's brother-in-law, and while the firm dates from 1838 to 1849, they stopped making under-hammer pistols after their move to Norwich, Connecticut in 1842.

21. The term "American system" was coined by Europeans to describe the new system of manufacturing employed in the United States and exemplified by the U.S. Model 1841 Rifle made by Robbins & Lawrence. Robbins & Lawrence demonstrated their achievement of mass-manufacturing a product whose parts were completely interchangeable at the "Crystal Palace" Exhibition of 1851 in London by having a representative completely disassemble six Model 1851 rifles, mix all the parts together, and then reassemble from the random parts six rifles that worked flawlessly. The other two American exhibitors were Samuel Colt, demonstrating his new Whitneyville-Walker revolvers, and Dr. Maynard, exhibiting his tape primer.

22. Windsor Industrial History, Part I by Guy Hubbard, privately published by the Windsor School District, Windsor, VT, 1922, pg. 64.

23. D.H. Hilliard worked as a gunsmith for N. Kendall & Company; his brother-in-law, William Smith, was one of the principal partners. N. Kendall & Company manufactured their guns in state-of-the-art shops located within the walls of the state prison at Windsor, using contracted convict labor from the spring of 1835 to December 1841. When the Vermont General Assembly voted in 1840 to terminate contract labor at the prison, a complicated contractual arrangement between Issac Watts Hubbard and the state prison was evoked, and the machinery — steam engine, foundry, machine tools, smithy, and more — jointly owned by Hubbard and the prison since 1834 (and freely used by N. Kendall & Company) became the property of the state in December of 1841. A few remaining under-hammer guns were assembled by two convicts under the supervision of Richard S. Lawrence until May 30, 1842. Asa Story returned to his West Windsor shop and D.H. Hilliard and William Smith moved across the Connecticut River to Hilliard's shop in Cornish, New Hampshire.

D.H. Hilliard & Company retained close ties with the Windsor armory and were the major purchasers of military rifle barrels that didn't pass government inspection. Hilliard then sold these and other parts to other regional gunsmiths.

24. Nicanor Kendall sold his interest in the company in December of 1847 after the completion of the first government contract and prior to the signing of the second one. The firm was renamed Robbins & Lawrence in 1848, became The Windsor Car & Rifle Company on November 7, 1849, and then reverted back to Robbins & Lawrence on November 6, 1850.

25. The social upheaval in the aftermath of the Civil War was not restricted to the "reconstruction" of the southern states. In Vermont three out of five men who went off to war didn't return; a postwar economic depression eventually lead to "Black Friday" on September 24, 1869; and severe floods in 1869 destroyed half the river mills in New England. Five years after the ending of the Civil War, Vermont's population had declined by over a third and numerous small villages were all but deserted.

26. David Hall Hilliard produced under-hammer match pistols and rifles from 1842 to 1877 (his son continued to produce guns under the D.H. Hilliard company until 1902); William Billinghurst of Rochester, New York crafted superb under-hammer match pistols and rifles during his career (1834 - 1861); Artemus Leonard of Saxtons River, Vermont hand-fabricated guns from 1843 to 1859; and Norman Brockway of Bellows Falls, Vermont, one of the most famous gunsmiths and match competitors of the era, was making guns from 1861 to 1900.

27. Albert (Put) Gove of Lincoln, Vermont (1830 - 1912) worked for the Remington Arms Company. Norman Brockway of Bellows Falls, Vermont (1841 - 1936) worked in the Springfield armory, for Norwich Arms Company, and for Smith & Wesson. — "Vermont's Gunsmiths & Gunmakers to 1900" by Harry Phillips and Terry Tyler, privately published, 2000

28. John Demeritt of Montpelier, Vermont produced guns from 1865 to 1892 and is best known for his under-hammer pistols, which, although made in various forms, all featured staghorn grips with the frame and barrel made from a single piece of steel.

29. Edgar Glynn produced guns from 1874 until 1889 in Clarendon, Vermont. Although he made various types and styles of firearms, he's best known for his aesthetic use of brass in his work.

30. A 20-caliber pistol with 1 3/8-inch round barrel made by R.W. Mitchell of West Lebanon, New Hampshire has the shortest barrel I know of, while, aside from cane guns, a fowling made by D.H. Hilliard of Cornish, New Hampshire, using a bored-out U.S. Model 1841 Musket Rifle barrel that didn't pass inspection, is the longest. This generalization doesn't include oddities such as the miniatures crafted by Alton J. Jones, cane guns, or pistols with standing breeches that would accept rifle barrels.

31. Bacon & Company, Blunt & Syms, E.B. White, and others produced pepperbox underhammers, but European gunsmiths produced this type of handgun in greater quantities. John Cochran's turret pistols were produced by C.B. Allen of Springfield, Massachusetts, but other examples, apparently based on his patent but made by European gunsmiths, exist. Over and under pistols whose barrels are revolved manually; Belgian double-action under-hammer pistols with a revolving cylinder; and a "harmonica" pistol are among the unusual under-hammer pistols that were developed.

32. William Billinghurst made at least one breech-loading match pistol; an unknown gunsmith made at least two examples (one pistol and a rifle) of an underhammer with a cylindrical breech operated by a lever; and the Model 1841 Danish Dragoon Pistol, whose barrel advanced forward and upwards exposing the breech, is another type.

Evolution Of The Modern High Performance Muzzleloader

by Toby Bridges

WHEN IT COMES to muzzle-loading, the age of innocence is at an end. Thanks to the advanced technology of the rifles, projectiles and modern powders we now shoot, the days of *"Gosh...By Golly...It went off!"* are long behind us. Some of today's newer rifle designs are as reliable as many centerfire cartridge rifles. And, when loaded with the latest fodder, some of these not-so-old-fashioned frontloaders will actually shoot as hard

and accurately as some popular centerfire big-game hunting rifles.

Scan through just about any of the current shooting publications and you're sure to come across muzzle-loading gun advertisements with headlines or sales copy claiming, *"The Most Powerful .50 cal. Muzzleloader in the World!"* or *"hard-hitting accuracy beyond 100 yards,"* or *"Muzzle*

energy equivalent to a 7mm Remington Mag".

There is no doubt that muzzle-loading has become a performance-driven sport, with a new breed of muzzle-loading hunter now demanding accuracy and knockdown power that – until now – had been impossible to obtain from a muzzle-loaded hunting rifle.

The Knight MK-85 was the rifle that began the mass exodus among

hunters from the traditional side-hammer muzzleloaders to a more efficient ignition system that positioned both the hammer and nipple squarely at the rear center of the barrel. With this system, fire from an exploding percussion cap has to travel only a fraction of an inch before contacting powder in the barrel. Ignition with the Knight in-line rifle was not only more positive; it was more spontaneous and reliable.

Knight Rifles is often credited with inventing the in-line percussion ignition system. However, there is enough evidence to establish that the concept was around during the early 1800s, and this writer had the opportunity to shoot and hunt with several modern-day in-line ignition rifles which pre-date the 1985 introduction of the MK-85. The earliest was a slick-looking little 45-caliber front loader known as the Eusopus Pacer, which I felt was 'way ahead of

▲ Early prototype of the Knight rifle, the in-line ignition muzzleloader that changed muzzleloading forever.

The Michigan Arms Wolverine could have been the first of the modern high-performance muzzleloaders, if only the maker had rifled it to shoot something other than the patched round ball. The rifle utilized hot No. 209 shotshell primers for ignition.

its time when shooting it back in 1972. Then there was the Michigan Arms Wolverine, an in-line ignition 50-caliber rifle that easily could have realized the success enjoyed by the Knight in-lines, if only the manufacturer had rifled the bore with a faster rate of twist for shooting hard-hitting conical bullets, rather than the patched round ball. The Wolverine preceded the Knight muzzleloader by three or four years, and was even built with an ignition system that utilized No. 209 primers.

The Eusopus Pacer was simply too advanced for the time it was introduced. Keep in mind that through the 1970s one of the biggest arguments among muzzle-loading shooters was whether the half-stock Thompson/Center "Hawken" was of traditional design, even though it featured a side-mounted hammer and exposed nipple. And by the time the Michigan Arms Wolverine hit the market during the early 1980s, muzzle-loading hunters were beginning to forsake the old patched round ball in favor of big conical bullets weighing twice as much and delivering nearly double the knock-down energy as the light spheres of soft, pure lead. The "round ball only" 1:66 rate of twist found in the bore of the Wolverine pretty well delivered the deathblow for this rifle. It was the beginning of a new era, in which optimum accuracy and big game stopping power suddenly took precedence over a muzzleloader of traditional styling. The round ball simply didn't cut it as a hunting projectile any longer.

What the Knight MK-85 brought to the muzzleloader market was the first modern in-line ignition muzzle-loading hunting rifle built with all of the features serious muzzle-loading hunters wanted – plus a few

many had never even thought of before! In addition to its fast, efficient in-line percussion ignition, the MK-85 featured great handling in a compact modern rifle design, easy scope mounting (*thanks to a receiver that came pre-drilled and tapped*), not one but two safeties, and a removable breech plug which made this rifle the easiest-to-clean muzzleloader ever offered. However, the great performance that the MK-85 became noted for didn't become a reality for several years.

In February of 1986 I received, from Tony Knight, MK-85 serial number *31*. The 50-caliber rifle was everything I could hope for in a muzzle-loading hunting rifle, and it's 1:48 rifling twist shot the then-new Buffalo Bullet Company heavy conical bullets better than anything I had shot them out of up to that time. However, the early MK-85 and its still relatively slow rifling twist only turned in so-so performance

with the brand new handgun bullet and sabot projectile system.

Fortunately, Tony Knight made several changes in the rate of rifling twist found in MK-85 barrels. In 1987, he changed the rate of twist to a faster 1:32 inches; then several years later stepped up the twist to 1:28 inches, the same twist found in Knight Rifle barrels today. With these rifling changes, the MK-85 and saboted handgun bullets became an unbeatable combination, one which quickly became a favorite with muzzle-loading hunters coast to coast. With a modern jacketed 250- to 300-grain bullet, a small plastic sabot and 100- to 120-grain charges of Pyrodex, the 24-inch barreled MK-85 would consistently group under 1 1/2-inches at 100 yards, and deliver the game-taking energy to cleanly drop deer at that distance – and slightly farther. This rifle was the first of today's high performance muzzleloaders, and paved the way for the dozens of other in-line ignition rifles that have followed.

Through the first half of the 1990s, the muzzleloading metamorphosis was in high gear. Knight Rifles, Thompson/Center Arms, Traditions, Connecticut Valley Arms, and a few other smaller muzzle-loading arms makers accelerated the in-line muzzleloader evolution: improving the design and performance of these rifles, while making them more affordable for the average muzzle-loading hunter. In the mid-1990s you could purchase, for under $250, an in-line percussion ignition rifle that would actually out-perform similarly styled in-line rifles that had carried $400 to $500 price tags during the late 1980s. The popularity of the in-line soared, to the point where the sales of these rifles easily accounted for 75 per-

The Knight MK-85 was the first modern in-line ignition design to give serious muzzleloading hunters all the features they demanded in a front-loading big game rifle. Shown is the author's early serial no. 31 50-caliber rifle.

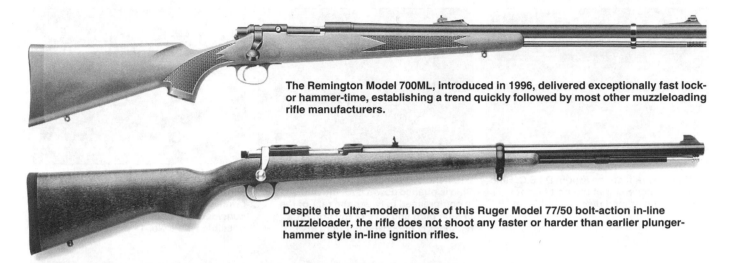

The Remington Model 700ML, introduced in 1996, delivered exceptionally fast lock- or hammer-time, establishing a trend quickly followed by most other muzzleloading rifle manufacturers.

Despite the ultra-modern looks of this Ruger Model 77/50 bolt-action in-line muzzleloader, the rifle does not shoot any faster or harder than earlier plunger-hammer style in-line ignition rifles.

The faster lock time of bolt-action in-line rifles, like the Traditions' Lightning shown here, can contribute to tighter groups. This model is now available with No. 11 percussion cap, musket cap or No. 209 primer ignition.

cent, or more, of the entire muzzleloader market. In 1995, Knight Rifles alone built and shipped more than 100,000 in-line ignition rifles, 90 percent of them in the popular 50-caliber.

Remington Arms Company took in-line ignition muzzle-loading design to a new level in 1996 with the introduction of their revered Model 700 bolt-action center-fire line in an all-new muzzle-loading configuration. Built around a modified Model 700 receiver and bolt, the Model 700ML gave shooters and hunters a front-loading rifle with a considerably faster hammer fall than possible with any of the plunger-hammer style in-line ignition systems. However, when it came to actual ballistics the Remington Model 700ML, and similarly styled "bolt-action" in-line ignition rifles which soon followed, did not shoot any faster, flatter or harder

than conventional plunger-hammer style in-line ignition rifles. However, shooters seemed to like the quicker lock time of a true bolt, and within a year or two of the Model 700ML introduction, Ruger entered the market with their bolt-action Model 77/50, Connecticut Valley Arms introduced their Firebolt and Accubolt models, Traditions brought out the now-popular Lightning model, and a new firm known as Austin & Halleck hit the market with an extremely classy looking bolt-action in-line percussion ignition muzzleloader. Again, the 50-caliber reigned in popularity.

Not to be outdone in this latest round of muzzleloader development, Knight Rifles took bolt-action in-line ignition design to yet another, higher level with the introduction of the Knight D.I.S.C. Rifle in early 1997. This unique bolt-action front-loader eliminated the nipple, and

instead of the standard No. 11 percussion cap, the D.I.S.C. Rifle relied on a much hotter No. 209 shotshell primer for putting more fire into the powder charge. The design of this system incorporates a small plastic disc, into which the primer is seated. This disc is then somewhat compressed between the face of the bolt and the rear of the breech plug. While some of the fire from the primer is lost between the fit of the plastic disc and the breech plug, the system still puts considerably more fire into the barrel than possible with a nipple and No. 11 cap.

A hotter flame reaching the powder charge means more sure-fire ignition, and Knight Rifles soon discovered that it also meant better consumption of heavier powder charges in this 50-caliber rifle. The company was one of the first to promote the use of "magnum" (three 50-grain Pyrodex Pellets [150 grains]) powder charges. Thompson/Center Arms quickly jumped on the magnum muzzleloader bandwagon with the introduction of the Encore 209x50 Magnum muzzleloader shortly after the Knight D.I.S.C. Rifle's début. Instead of a bolt-action, Thompson/Center chose to build their frontloading 50-caliber powerhouse on the break-open design of the popular single-shot handgun they also produce under the Encore name. The one thing this rifle has in common with the Knight bolt-action rifle is that it too relies on hotter No. 209 primers for ignition, and for a more complete burn of three 50-grain Pyrodex Pellets.

By the end of the 1990s, Connecticut Valley Arms, Traditions, Markesberry Muzzleloaders, and a few other companies began offering models with primer ignition systems. Suddenly a growing list of muzzle-loading rifle makers were promoting the use of "magnum" three 50-grain Pyrodex Pellet powder charges, some

Working the bolt on the Knight D.I.S.C. Rifle exposes an opening at the bolt face for inserting the primed disc.

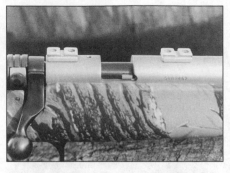

When the bolt handle of the Knight D.I.S.C. Rifle is pushed downward, the primed disc is compressed between the rear of the breech plug and face of the bolt for a reasonably good weather tight seal.

The plastic discs for the Knight D.I.S.C. Rifle allow some loss of fire from the No. 209 primer, but the system still puts considerably more fire into the barrel than possible with a No. 11 percussion cap.

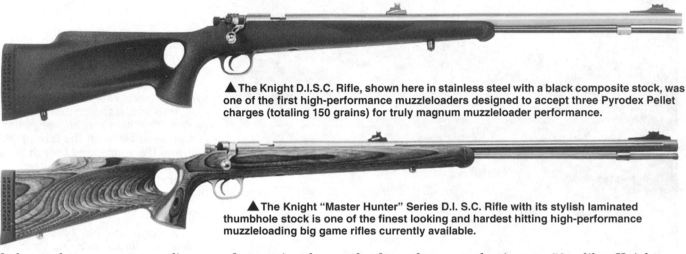

▲ The Knight D.I.S.C. Rifle, shown here in stainless steel with a black composite stock, was one of the first high-performance muzzleloaders designed to accept three Pyrodex Pellet charges (totaling 150 grains) for truly magnum muzzleloader performance.

▲ The Knight "Master Hunter" Series D.I. S.C. Rifle with its stylish laminated thumbhole stock is one of the finest looking and hardest hitting high-performance muzzleloading big game rifles currently available.

of whom only a year or two earlier emphatically stated in their owner's manuals that powder charges of 100 to 120 grains were "absolute" maximum charges for their rifles. The race was on to see who could build the fastest-shooting and hardest-hitting muzzle-loading big-game rifle.

A few of these companies began making some pretty outlandish claims about the velocities and energy levels produced by their rifles and the magnum powder charges behind saboted bullets. One very knowledgeable shooter I know, who has done considerable ballistics work with frontloaders, pretty well summed up much of the sales hype as "voodoo ballistics!" And,

after putting thousands of rounds across the screens of a chronograph, I have to agree with him.

Before getting into the ballistics of today's newer, hotter muzzleloading rifle designs, let's first take a look at the velocities and energy levels that *were* considered hot less than a decade ago.

Easily the most widely used powder charge out of the majority of older-style plunger-hammer in-line rifles was 100 grains of Pyrodex "RS" or "Select", the latter simply being a premium grade of "RS". When this powder charge is loaded behind a saboted 250-grain Hornady .452-inch XTP in the 24-inch barrel of a 1990

production run 50-caliber Knight MK-85, the load is good for right at 1620 fps at the muzzle. And this translates into just over 1450 ft/lbs (fpe) of energy. When the same rifle is loaded with two of the 50-grain Pyrodex Pellets (100-grain charge), a saboted 250-grain bullet leaves the muzzle at nearly 1675 fps, with about 1550 fpe. These same loads will basically produce the same ballistics out of any other No. 11 percussion cap-ignited in-line rifle with a 22- to 24-inch barrel, whether it was made by Knight, Remington, Thompson/Center, Traditions, Connecticut Valley Arms – or whoever.

When three of the 50-grain Pyrodex Pellets (150-grain charge) are loaded into my MK-85 behind a saboted 250-grain bullet, velocity jumps up to nearly 1850 fps, pushing muzzle energy to right at 1900 fpe of knockdown power. Now, this rifle utilizes a No. 11 cap for ignition,

◀ The modern muzzleloading hunter has found the familiar feel and handling characteristics of the latest bolt-action in-line muzzleloaders to their liking. With the right combination of powder charge and saboted bullet, some of these guns will shoot as accurately as many centerfire deer rifles.

which produces only a fraction of the fire possible with the hotter ignition systems that utilize a No. 209 primer. For comparison, I chronographed the same load out of a 50-caliber Knight D.I.S.C. Rifle with a 24-inch barrel. Thanks to the hotter fire from the No. 209 primers, my average velocity jumped to 1970 fps, which ups muzzle energy to slightly over 2150 fpe.

Thompson/Center Arms has advertised that

▼ Thompson/Center Arms' break-open Encore 209x50 Magnum muzzleloader is built on basically the same action as the firm's line of single-shot cartridge pistols also sold under the Encore name.

◄ Remove the ramrod and ramrod guide from the Savage Model 10ML, and this modem "smokeless pole" would look just like the Savage centerfire rifles. This is the first muzzleloader ever designed and built to shoot smokeless powders.

their Encore 209x50 Magnum is capable of producing *"Muzzle energy equal to a 7mm Rem. Mag."* by pushing a saboted 240-grain bullet out of the muzzle of the 26-inch barrel at 2203 fps. Now, according to my calculations, a bullet of this weight at that muzzle velocity would only be generating about 2580 fpe – not the 3100 to 3200 fpe produced by *most* factory 7mm Remington Magnum cartridges.

Shooting the .452-inch Hornady 240-grain XTP-MAG with the Muzzleload Magnum Products black high-pressure sabot and three 50-grain Pyrodex Pellets, my average velocity out of the 24-inch barreled Knight D.I.S.C. Rifle was about 1 990 fps. To more accurately compare my findings with Thompson/Center's published ballistics for a 240-grain saboted bullet and 150-grain three-pellet Pyrodex charge, I went to another 26-inch barreled and No. 209 primer-ignited muzzleloader, the Lenartz Rdi-50. While I did not have an Encore 209x50 Magnum on hand for these tests, I felt the ballistics should not be that different when the same load is fired from another 50-caliber rifle of the same length barrel, utilizing shotshell primers for ignition.

The Lenartz Rdi-50 is another of the "new wave" magnum frontload-

Bridges and a nice whitetail buck that was dropped in its tracks by a hot smokeless powder load from the Savage Model 10ML. This muzzleloader shoots fast, flat and hard.

The ignition system of the Rdi-50 is composed of three main components: a specially designed breech plug, rotating primer cover, and a plunger-style hammer with a firing pin on the face.

ers that will handle the 150-grain Pyrodex Pellet powder charges. The unique ignition system found on this well-built muzzle-loader is unlike any other on the market. The arrangement consists of a plunger-style hammer with a firing pin face, a rotating primer cover, and a removable breech plug with a cup-shaped primer seat at the rear. To prime this rifle, the shooter simply cocks the hammer back and places the handle in a safety notch, then lifts the handle of the cover upwards to expose a primer-shaped opening. A No. 209 primer is dropped in, and the cover handle

pushed downward to enclose the primer. With the hammer handle down and the side-safety in the forward *"off"* position, the rifle can be fired. To remove the spent primer, the shooter locks back the hammer, opens the cap cover and simply shakes the fired primer out of the opening.

The ignition system of this 50-caliber muzzleloader is very efficient, and very user-friendly. It puts plenty of fire into the barrel for full consumption of the magnum three-pellet 150-grain charges. With this much propellant behind a saboted 240-grain Hornady .452-inch XTP-MAG, this 26-inch barreled frontloader puts the bullet across the screens of my Shooting Chrony chronograph at just 2020 fps, and with 2175 fpe.

Easily the most efficient muzzle-loader ignition system I've ever fired has to be the system now found on the new Savage Model 10ML. This 50-caliber bolt-action in-line ignition muzzleloader incorporates a significantly modified version of the action found on the Savage Model 12FV single-shot centerfire varmint rifle. For ignition, this rifle relies on reusable stainless steel percussion ignition modules primed with No.

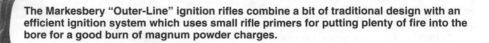

The Markesbery "Outer-Line" ignition rifles combine a bit of traditional design with an efficient ignition system which uses small rifle primers for putting plenty of fire into the bore for a good burn of magnum powder charges.

209 shotshell primers. These modules are chambered into a removable breech plug, which features a tiny .030-inch orifice running into the bore. When the bolt closes behind one of the modules, the only place that fire from the primer can go is forward and into the barrel. This is the only system that puts 100 percent of the fire from a shotshell primer into the powder charge. In fact, a primed module can be fired through an unloaded rifle and fire will shoot out the muzzle several feet. Now, that's ignition!

What really sets the new Savage Model 10ML apart from any other muzzleloader ever manufactured is that here - for the first time - is a frontloader that has been designed, engineered and built to be used with smokeless powders. It is, without doubt, the strongest muzzleloader ever commercially produced.

Savage Arms Inc., of Westfield, Massachusetts, sent a *second gener-ation* prototype of the rifle to me for evaluation several months before the gun made its official début in June 2000. My first loads through the rifle consisted of 46 grains of IMR-4227 behind a Hornady .452-inch 300-grain XTP, loaded with a new high-pressure sabot from Muzzleload Magnum Products. The first three-shot group fired with this rifle printed under an inch at 100 yards. And the vast majority of groups shot with that same load rarely opened

COPING WITH MUZZLELOADER TRAJECTORY

The ultramodern in-line ignition muzzleloaders that have become the first choice of today's muzzleloading hunter will definitely out-perform the traditional side-hammer designs from the past. Combined with the latest in saboted bullets, improved powders and with the hotter ignition of shotgun or rifle primers, these rifles are fully capable of producing *minute-of-angle* accuracy, and delivering increased knockdown power on big game. They do shoot faster, flatter and harder than front-loading hunting rifles of just a few decades ago, and muzzleloading rifle manufacturers have been making some very impressive claims about the effective game-taking range of these modernistic front-loaders.

So just what is the *maximum effective range* of today's newer high-performance muzzleloading rifles and loads? At what point is the shot *too far*? Well, for most of us the trajectory of the rifle and load—or in other words bullet *drop*, not bullet *energy*— dictates how far we should shoot.

While compiling much of the information for the accompanying article on today's high performance muzzleloading big game rifles, I did considerable shooting at 100, 150, 200—and even 300 yards—to determine bullet drop for even the hottest loads. In order to compare apples to apples, all of my shooting was done with the .452-inch diameter 250-grain Hornady XTP, loaded into the 50-caliber rifles with a Muzzleload Magnum Products high-pressure sabot. And all loads were first sighted dead-on at 100 yards before being fired at the longer ranges.

Pushed out of a 24-inch 50-caliber barrel by two 50-grain Pyrodex pellets (*a 100-grain charge*), average muzzle velocity was right at 1650 fps. At 150 yards, the bullet was down 6.9 inches. At 200 yards, it struck 19 inches low and at 300 yards, the 250-grain bullet hit the target paper a full 84 inches below point of aim.

Three of the 50-grain Pyrodex pellets (*a 150-grain charge*) upped average muzzle velocity to around 1983 fps. At 150 yards, the bullet hit 4.1 inches low and at 200 yards the bullet hit 10.8 inches below the aiming point. At 300 yards, shots landed 59 inches below the point of aim.

Shooting a variety of different smokeless powders and charges out of the Savage Model 10ML, I was able to determine the drop of the same bullet at 2100, 2200 and 2300 fps. Even at these higher velocities, the drop in trajectory is more than most of us can realistically calculate much past 200 yards. Even my hottest load of 44.4 grains of Vihtavouri N110 behind the 250-grain 45-caliber Hornady bullet, 2353 fps at the muzzle, produced a full 39 inches of drop at 300 yards. From 100 to 150, the load prints just 2.6 inches low, and at 200 yards it is only about 9 inches down. After that, gravity asserts itself and the bullet returns to Earth rather quickly.

At 250 yards, a 250-grain bullet that left the muzzle at just over 2300 fps would still be moving along at close to 1400 fps, with nearly 1100 ft/lbs (fpe) of energy. However, the bullet would be almost 16 inches low, making it extremely difficult for the average shooter to precisely place good hits on an average-sized deer at that distance. And with the slower near-2000 fps loads fired out of rifles like the Knight D.I.S.C. and T/C Encore 209x50 Magnum with three Pyrodex pellet loads, the drop at 250 yards would be somewhere around 20 to 22 inches, making shot placement even more difficult.

Jim Leatherwood, of Leatherwood Optics, has come up with something of a solution for this dilemma. Using the same concept he developed for producing *"bullet drop-compensating scopes"* for U.S. military snipers, he is now offering a similar self-adjusting scope that has been calibrated for the excessive drop common to all big game hunting muzzleloading rifles. The muzzleloader version of his "Sporter" 3x9 variable can be sighted to hit dead on at 100 yards, and then by simply reaching up and turning a "ranging ring" the scope will automatically compensate for bullet drop at 150...200...250...and even 300 yards. The cam, which precisely elevates the rear of the scope, can be adjusted to tailor the settings for 180- to 300-grain saboted bullets at velocities ranging from 1600 to 2300 fps.

I shot my favorite Savage Model 10ML with one of the Leatherwood scopes and was amazed at how well the arrangement allowed for bullet drop at the different distances. Sighted to print a 250-grain Hornady XTP *"on"* at 100 yards (at 2300 fps), I found that I could instantly turn to my 200-yard setting, hold dead on—and the bullet would impact at my point of aim. In fact, one three-shot group fired struck just 1.5 inches above dead-center, and clustered inside of 1-1/4 inches. Then I could turn to my 300-yard setting and, again holding dead on, keep my hits within a few inches of the 3-inch diameter bullseye. While testing the Leatherwood scope on the Savage Model 10ML, I shot my best 300-yard muzzleloader group ever. The three shots printed inside of 2-5/8 inches, right at the top of the bull.

Unfortunately, at that distance the 250-grain Hornady has slowed to the point where it is questionable whether it still has enough energy to cleanly bring down game as big as a whitetail. Velocity has slowed to around 1200 fps and remaining energy has dropped to less than 900 fpe. Also, once the bullet really begins to slow, the wind plays havoc with it. Just a 10 to 15 mph crosswind can push the bullet off to one side by 10 or 12 inches. But, that's another story.

For more details on the Leatherwood bullet drop-compensating scopes, visit their website at http://www.leatherwoodoptics.com.

The Savage Model 10ML relies on reusable stainless steel ignition modules and No. 209 shotshell primers for extremely reliable ignition. The heavy-walled construction of these modules contributes to the tremendous strength of this muzzleloader.

The uniquely shaped and light 175-grain DEVEL bullet proved to be exceptionally accurate when teamed up with the Muzzleload Magnum Products high-pressure sabot and fired out of the Savage Model 10ML. Even at velocities greater than 2300 fps, the bullet and smokeless powder loads still did not generate noticeable recoil.

past 1-1/2 inches. This load is good for 2080 fps at the muzzle, with 2880 fpe of game-taking punch.

The loads which I came to favor out of the Savage "smokeless pole" prototype – and another production run Model 10ML – have been 44 grains of Accurate Arms XMP-5744 behind either the 250- or 300-grain Hornady 45 XTPs, and 44.4 grains of Vihtavouri N110 behind either of the same bullets. With 44 grains of XMP-5744 and the saboted 250-grain XTP, the Savage muzzleloader is good for 2267 fps, with just over 2800 fpe. The same powder charge behind the 300-grain XTP bullet slows down slightly to 2218 fps, but produces an impressive 2940 fpe of knockdown power.

With 44.4 grains of Vihtavouri N110 (measured with a 3.7cc Lee plastic dipper), the Savage Model 10ML will push one of the 250-grain .452-inch Hornady XTPs from the

Today's modem in-line ignition rifles, improved powders and efficient saboted bullets are now delivering big game-taking performance unheard of just twenty years ago.

muzzle at an astounding 2353 fps for nearly 3075 fpe. And with the heavier 300-grain XTP, the rifle is good for 2227 fps and unbelievable 3300 fpe. Here, at last, is a muzzle-loading big-game hunting rifle that is fully capable of producing muzzle energies equivalent to those of a 7mm Remington Magnum; something this writer has found to be impossible when shooting Pyrodex or Pyrodex Pellets...in any quantity.

Last season, I managed to take several good whitetail bucks with the Savage Model 10ML, plus did my part for herd management and also harvested eight does. My largest buck was a big Midwestern 10-pointer which field-dressed nearly 300 pounds. Hit with one of the

Hornady 250-grain XTPs pushed out of the muzzle by 44.4 grains of Vihtavouri N110, the nearly 350 pounds-on-the-hoof whitetail standing at 80 yards never knew what hit him. That buck was dead before his legs ever began to fold beneath him. Again shooting the 250-grain XTP, but with 44 grains of Accurate Arms XMP-5744, I also managed to drop a good Nebraska 9-pointer at 156 yards. That deer went down on the spot, as well.

These two loads were also used to tag several does, but most of these were taken with a unique bullet design that's as new as the Savage smokeless muzzleloader – the DEVEL bullet from Leved Cartridge Ltd. of Georgetown, Texas. Two things set this projectile apart from any other I've ever shot from a muzzle-loading rifle. First, the bullet features five very distinct flutes, running back from the nose along the ogive, which forms a unique star-shaped nose. Second, this bullet is of the non-expanding variety, made of a copper-tin composite material that results in a light 175-grain 45-caliber projectile nearly as long as a 300-grain Hornady XTP. Loaded with a Muzzleload Magnum Products high-pressure sabot, the DEVEL bullet proved to be a real performer out of the Model 10ML with smokeless loads.

Loaded ahead of 45 grains of Accurate Arms XMP-5744, the 175-grain fluted bullet leaves the muzzle of the Savage frontloader at 2340 fps. Due to its light weight,

The majority of today's muzzleloading shooters are the hunters who have taken to the special muzzleloading seasons, and they're looking for hard-hitting big game performance from the muzzleloaders they carry to the woods, not a piece of history.

the bullet at this velocity develops only 2128 fpe, still nearly equal to the energy levels I found the three 50-grain Pyrodex Pellet charges to produce with a saboted 240-grain bullet out of the other primer-ignited in-line rifles. Accuracy with the load has been exceptional, and many three-shot hundred-yard groups result in all three holes in the target paper cutting one another. And as for recoil, there isn't any. This rifle, powder charge and bullet make up the perfect combination for any muzzleloading shooter or hunter who happens to be recoil sensitive, especially younger shooters and women with small frames.

From my very first shots with the DEVEL bullet, I was impressed with the outstanding accuracy and loved showing off every chance I got to knock over a woodchuck at 150 yards or 'explode' a small rock a hundred yards away. But having come from the old school of believing in an expanding bullet for transfer of energy to game, I had to wonder about the effectiveness of a non-expanding bullet. According to Charlie Kelsey, owner of Leved Cartridge Ltd., the uniquely-fluted nose

of the DEVEL bullet will create hydraulic shock waves much like the flattened nose of an expanding design; since this bullet does not deform upon impact, it results in superior penetration.

When an invitation arrived from Charlie to join him on a late August hunt for south Texas wild hogs, I jumped at the opportunity. Despite the 100-plus-degree heat, it was the opportunity I needed to witness the DEVEL bullet in action. In just three days, I managed to chalk up nine wild hogs with the Model 10ML and 175-grain DEVEL, shooting 45 grains of XMP-5744. The first of which happened to be the very first head of game ever taken with Savage's new front-loader. It and the other eight hogs, weighing 100 to 225 pounds, were all dropped right where they stood, whether they were at 30 yards or 130 yards. Not one ran, not one took another step. I was impressed with the performance of the bullet and the Model 10ML rifle.

Savage C.E.O. Ron Coburn and his staff were at the same time running extensive pressure tests to establish at what level the rifle would succumb to the high pressures of smokeless powders. They never did establish a 'destruct' point, and finally gave up trying when a 90-grain charge of Red Dot and three saboted bullets – one on top of the other – failed to damage the Model 10ML. *(Rifle fired from a remote location.)* Their tests told me I was shooting a muzzleloader stronger than any ever built, and I went back to the range to see just how much Pyrodex this system would consume and still shoot accurately.

My goal was to get a 240-grain bullet with Pyrodex Pellet loads up over 2200 fps. What I discovered is that it can't be done, not even in the super-efficient, exceptionally strong Savage Model 10ML muzzleloader. The three 50-grain pellet charges popular in the Knight D.I.S.C. Rifle and the Thompson/Center Encore 209x50 Magnum rifles would only push the 240-grain Hornady 45 XTP out of the Savage muzzle at a little over 1970 fps. Then I meticulously cut several of the 30-grain pellets in two, slowly trimming and weighing

one half to come up with a 15-grain wafer to increase my powder charge to 165 grains of the compressed propellant. My velocity only reached the lower 1990s. Then I loaded with three 50-grain pellets and one whole 30-grain pellet, or in other words a 180-grain pellet charge, and my velocity inched up to just 2014 fps. At that point, I decided to go all the way and load with four 50-grain Pyrodex Pellets for a full 200-grain powder charge. Recoil was excessive, almost to the point of being painful, and to my surprise velocity had gone backwards, possibly due to pushing a mostly-unburned fourth pellet up the barrel along with the sabot and bullet. Whatever the reason, the three shots I chronographed with four of the 50-grain pellets averaged just 1988 fps.

A couple of years ago, Knight Rifles introduced a 45-caliber version of their D.I.S.C. Rifle, promoting the use of saboted 40-caliber handgun bullets and 150-grain Pyrodex Pellet powder charges. According to the company, they have been able to top 2500 fps with light bullets like the 155-grain Hornady XTP hollow-point.

As impressive as this may sound, keep in mind that while a light projectile may get out of the muzzle quickly, it also loses that head of steam quickly. From the muzzle to 150 yards, such loads shoot extremely flat, and then really begin to drop - along with a dramatic loss in energy. At 2500 fps, a 155-grain bullet at the muzzle of a D.I.S.C. Rifle generates right at 2150 ft/lbs of energy. Downrange at 200 yards, it'll do good to retain half that energy.

Muzzleloading today is more performance-driven than at any other time in history. As we head on into the 21st century, more and more modern technology will find its way into this centuries-old shooting sport. No one really knows where all of this development will end. The consumer is the one in control and manufacturers generally respond to their demands. The muzzle-loading rifle maker who fails to bring to the market exactly what the muzzle-loading shooter and hunter wants won't be around for long. ●

NOTE: DO NOT ATTEMPT TO LOAD AND SHOOT MODERN SMOKELESS POWDERS IN ANY MUZZLELOADER OTHER THAN THE SAVAGE MODEL 10ML. IT IS CURRENTLY THE ONLY PRODUCTION MUZZLELOADER BUILT WHICH WILL WITHSTAND THE HIGHER PRESSURES CREATED BY THESE POWDERS.

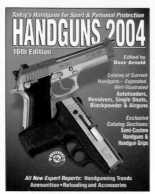

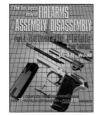   

THE MOST ACCLAIMED REVOLVER IN THE WORLD

FA

FREEDOM ARMS ®

FREEDOM ARMS INC.
P.O. BOX 150
FREEDOM, WYOMING 83120
307-883-2468

WEBSITE: WWW.FREEDOMARMS.COM
E-MAIL: FREEDOM@FREEDOMARMS.COM

Model 97 Premier Grade
Caliber's available
.45 Colt
   Optional cylinders in,
   .45 ACP
.41 Magnum
.357 Magnum
   Optional cylinder in,
   .38 Special
.22 Long Rifle
   Optional cylinder in:
   .22 Win. Mag.

Primary uses are Hunting,
Silhouette and Collecting.

Model 83 Premier and Field
Grade Caliber's available
.50 Action Express
.475 Linebaugh
454 Casull
   Optional cylinders in:
   .45 Colt
   .45 ACP
   .45 Win. Mag.
.44 Magnum
.41 Magnum
.357 Magnum
.22 Long Rifle
   Optional cylinder in:
   .22 Win. Mag.

These fine revolvers are
featured on the cover of
"Big Bore Handguns"
by John Taffin.
Get your copy today.

Too Many 45s?

by Lee Arten

THE PISTOL THAT started it all is an old Colt 45ACP with a World War I-vintage trigger, a flat mainspring housing and 'MODEL Of 1911' stamped on the slide. It sports a World War II-style hammer, and a thinning coat of gray Parkerizing.

I was just out of high school in 1969 when I talked my father into buying the pistol for $75, and later transferring it to me. The man who sold it to Dad had intended to make a target pistol out of the 45, so a set of Micro sights, a target bushing, three magazines and a Dwyer 'Group Gripper' came in the original deal. It wasn't long before I had a local gunsmith add the target sights and bushing to the pistol. I installed the 'Group Gripper' myself—it has been in the gun and working for 31 years.

I added black rubber Pachmayr grips in the 1980s but didn't have anything else done to the pistol until I started to shoot bullseye matches later that decade. The first few matches were shot indoors with a Colt 22 conversion kit installed on the gun. It took about two matches for me to decide the military trigger wasn't going to suffice. Shooting two-handed, I was able to manage the heavy trigger. One-handed match shooting was something else again, so I took the 45 to another gunsmith and had the trigger smoothed, and lightened by a pound or so.

Two or three years later, I was at the 1988 Second Chance Combat Shoot. I competed that match for the next 10 years and used the old 45 in about half of those matches. Even after I got a new custom 45, it came along as a backup gun.

At the 1988 match, the old 45 developed a dislike for the Blazer ammunition I brought. I remember thinking factory ammo would be a better bet than reloads but I shot poorly and cut myself on the rear sight clearing stoppages. As soon as

I stopped the bleeding, I took the 45 down to the Cylinder & Slide trailer near the end of Commercial Row and gave it to gunsmith Bill Laughridge from Fremont, Nebraska. He did a throating job on it and I fired my second event with reloads and without any jams. I had Bo-Mars

put on the gun when the sharp-edged Micro sights fell apart several years later.

I can't begin to guess how many thousands of rounds have gone through the old 45. At first, I didn't shoot it much since ammo was expensive and I didn't reload. In the

The 5 shots below the pistol in the nine- and ten-ring on this silhouette target were fired from 50 feet. The 5 in the five-and six-ring above the pistol were fired more quickly from seven yards. The author was happy with the perfomance of the Officer's ACP and his hardball-equivalent loads. *Isaac Arten photo*

The author's 45-caliber handguns include (*from the top*) the Model of 1911, a Model 1927, and Officer's ACP, an Ashabell Cook underhammer blackpowder 45, a Model 1991A1 Commander, the pin gun, a hybrid ported pistol with a Caspian slide and a Para Ordnance frame, and the target gun, a utilitarian bullseye pistol. These are just a good start, according to the author.

The pin gun with a target shot from 50 feet. The 'eight' was the author's fault, not that of the gun. *Isaac Arten photo*

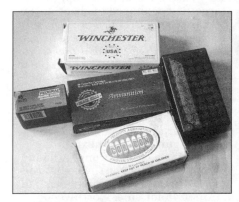

The pin gun has a Para Ordnance frame, and a hybrid slide and barrel from Caspian. The barrel has five ports that make compensated perfromance possible in a standard-size gun. The system controls recoil of heavy pin loads well, helping to cut time between shots in steel plate or bowling pin matchs.

early 1980s, after I got dies and a cheap box of bulk bullets, my 45 ACP consumption rose steadily. Practicing to shoot pin matches, I used to shoot up a hundred rounds one night, reload them the next and shoot them up again the night after. Later, I went on reloading binges every two or three months. By then, I had more brass and was making ammo for two 45s.

My standard 45 ACP load has become 5.8 grains of Unique and a 230-grain lead round-nose bullet, or the same amount of powder with a 230-grain full metal jacket slug. The load is accurate enough for pin shooting, International Defensive Pistol Association (IDPA) matches, steel matches, and plinking. I even used it in one 2700 match when I ran out of time to load target ammo. Accuracy was no problem but the brass bounced a long way down the range after being ejected from the Pin Gun. During breaks in the centerfire and 45 stages, other shooters

would come up to me and ask, *"What are you using in that thing?"*

I've also used 4.0 grains of Bullseye for target loads with 200-grain lead semi-wadcutters. Other loads I've tried have either been less accurate than my Unique or Bullseye loads; or they haven't functioned as well in my guns.

My second 45ACP handgun was a revolver. I'd come across a copy of *Shotgun News* and one of the display ads showed a Smith & Wesson 1917. In 1989 or '90, the Brazilians sold as surplus–at good prices–the revolvers they acquired from S&W in 1937 or '38. I'd always been fascinated by the S&W and Colt 1917 revolvers and so had a local dealer order me one of the returned Smiths from Southern Ohio Gun. I bought 100 full-moon clips from Ranch Products, and was ready to go.

The old revolver had a rough bore, skinny, oily stocks and a lot of holster and storage wear. It looked a little better after I wiped it down and cleaned the bore with FP10 and a lot of patches, and it shot much better than it looked. I put the old factory grips in a box and slipped rubber Pachmayr grips onto the gun. A few months later I added an Evans 'Wondersight' to the frame that allowed me to adjust the point of impact without having to resort to a file.

Later, after winning a certificate for some gun work at Second Chance, I had Cylinder & Slide check over and refinish the 1917. I had to send the gun to them for the work, instead of getting it done at the match. The old '17 came back in a few weeks with a report that said

The Target 45 with an 'X,' two tens, and a nine showing. The author hadn't shot bullseye for more than a year, but at least the gun remembered how.

Ammunition on hand for the author's 45s includes Winchester hardball, and Federal, Black Hills and Cor-Bon hollowpoints. The factory loads are backed up by lots of reloads, usually made with FMJs or LRN bullets.

the cylinder gap was slightly enlarged, but the revolver had passed the hammer push-off test. The 1917 also sported a new coat of black Parkerizing, looked handsomer than it had for many years—and shot just as well, too.

The old N-frame has served as a house gun, a backup gun in revolver events at pin matches, in PPC-type matches at local clubs and for small game hunting. I like to take it out at the end of small game season (*if the snow has melted enough*) and sneak around looking for cottontails or snowshoes. I once thought of cutting it down, but decided I liked it just as it was. Chronographing loads fired from the old S&W showed that, with the same loads, it produced higher velocities than my old 1911. It has almost a 1/2-inch longer barrel than my Government Model 45, but I had assumed the cylinder gap would drop velocities below those from an autopistol.

Although I did some conventional target shooting with rifles and pistols then, the biggest thing on my shooting calendar in the early 1990s was bowling pin shooting. Richard Davis, head of the Second Chance Body Armor Company, ran a very interesting and eclectic match. There were custom revolvers and autopistols made to suit almost any taste, and some of the people with the tricked-out guns could shoot them well, too. Carbines, shotguns and submachine guns were also in evidence and you could even try 30- and 50-caliber machineguns, and pay by the belt. My nearly stock

The long and the short of the author's 45s. At the top is the custom Para/Caspian P-14 with the larger grip, which accepts high-capacity magazines. Below is the Officer's ACP. It is about as accurate as the larger gun, but easier to conceal because it is smaller and thinner.

1911 sometimes looked like a Model A Ford at a modern drag race.

After meeting Charles Wooley and shooting his hybrid 45 on the practice range at Second Chance, I went into full plot-and-scheme mode. By 1992 I had a Para-Ordnance P-14 frame mated to a hybrid-ported Caspian slide. It was a slick setup, with a great trigger, and it would stack round-nose 230-grain bullets one on top of the other at eight yards, the distance from the firing line to the bowling pin tables. After I got some loading problems

Dillon's LTD holster nicely fits the author's carry 45s, the Officer's ACP and the 1991 Commander. It has carried both in matches. The Officer's ACP has ridden in it in the woods while the author was trout fishing.

worked out, I posted my best pin shooting times ever with that gun. Trivia was still my best event, but the Para definitely helped me improve in Five Pin.

I shot the Para in two steel matches at my club during the last two years, and managed to win both of them. The matches went by very quickly, but what stayed with me afterward was how the Para seemed to float smoothly from one 12-inch plate to another—and then go off at just the right time. After shooting pins, the plates seemed large and easy to hit. I knocked 12 plates off their steel racks in about 13 seconds. That isn't really fast, but it was fast enough to win that day.

The Para is heavy, too high-tech for IDPA matches, and I haven't hunted with it. It was fired in a few 2700 matches some years ago. In one, I posted the only 98 rapid-fire target I've managed to shoot in centerfire competition so far. (*The gun would have let me clean the target too, but I pulled one shot down into the eight ring.*) I haven't been able to make any bowling pin matches for the past two years, so I've been considering shooting the Para in the 'Centerfire' stage of bullseye again.

The Para/Casp is my most customized gun, but the next 45 I acquired is a close second. A friend told me that The Northwoods Trading Post in Hancock, Michigan had a target 45 for sale. Northwoods, run by a former cop, is one of my favorite gun stores so I was only too glad to stop by. When I got nose-to-nose with the handgun case, however, the target gun I thought I was

not much of a sight anymore, so I replaced it with a Tasco Pro-Point. This gun has been sitting, awaiting my return to bullseye competition. That return was "temporarily delayed" several years ago but the gun is ready, even if I'm not. With 4 grains of Bullseye and a locally cast 200-grain SWC, it would shoot slightly elongated one-hole groups at 25 yards when I was in training, or when shooting from bags.

The last 45 I got my hands on arrived in 1998. It is a stock Colt 1991A Commander that my brother, Jon, had before me. It has a matte black finish, high visibility sights

Uncle Mike's Sidekick #3 holster fits the Model 1917 quite well. It has carried the old revolver on rabbit hunts, in PPC-type matches, and in revolver stages at bowling pin matches.

looking for immediately took a back seat to a carry 45 that was also in the case.

The gun was a stainless Officer's ACP. (*Please don't call it an Officer's Model, which would make it a target 38 revolver.*) The ACP had a checkered front strap, a trigger job and a custom trigger, probably a Videki. It also had the best standard sights I'd ever seen on a 45. They were higher than the minuscule sights on my original 45, and sported white dots front and rear. I could have lived without the dots, but the high-visibility sights lined up quickly and impressed me.

I bought the Officer's ACP in the fall of 1994. The following June, in the Second Chance Trivia competition, I managed to come up with another certificate for gunsmithing. Using that, I had the factory bushing exchanged for one with less of a history of breaking and flying downrange at inopportune moments.

I intended to use the Officer's ACP as a concealed-carry piece, but found the custom trigger a bit light. I haven't had the trigger redone yet, and may not. In the meantime, I've used the little pistol in practical pistol matches, carried it in the open while fishing, and shot it at gongs and silhouette targets just for fun. It seems to be almost as accurate as the Para, and it is a favorite .45.

In 1996, for my 45th birthday, my wife gave me a target 45, complete with an old Aimpoint scope, an Elliason rear sight and rib, and extended front sight. The pistol appeared to have been made by a military armorer and is utilitarian, rather than decorative. The frontstrap was harshly stippled, and the frame and slide showed some wear. The old Aimpoint was usable but

The six 45 ACP handguns in the author's collection surround a 30-round group shot by the author's son Isaac. Isaac is left-handed and tends to shoot to the right with revolvers and the smaller semi-automatics. One shot was off the paper, but some groups from individual handguns weren't too bad.

and black plastic grips. It appears to have had a factory throating job and has usually been very reliable with hardball, hardball-equivalent reloads and target SWC reloads. It has also been accurate enough to hit a quart oil jug out to 60 yards.

The only time the gun has been unreliable was during an IDPA match. Because of a brain fade while packing my gear, I was short of magazines and had to shoot the match with one of my 10-round mags and one borrowed 8-rounder. The "Stage From Hell," as my squad quickly named it, started by requiring us to shoot right-handed around the left side of a barricade—and went downhill from there. One guy had his pistol jam so solidly he could barely work the action. Another shooter barked his knuckles severely and bled on the floor. I was lucky and just had a consistent second-to-last round stoppage with my 10-round magazine, and an occasional random stoppage with the borrowed one. The next week—same range, same gun, same ammo - but different magazines - I shot strong hand, weak hand, and from a barricade—with no stoppages at all.

I might have a little trigger work done on the 1991A1, but I don't think I'll do anything else to it. Except for that ill-fated IDPA match I haven't done any competition shooting with the 1991A1. I've done a little plinking and have considered it for a carry gun and a house gun. Some authorities on self-defense say that customized guns should not be used for self-defense. Unscrupulous attorneys have been known to paint owners of customized handguns as 'Rambo' wannabes or vigilantes. The 1991A1 is a stock gun's 'stock' gun, so I suppose it would be safe to defend myself with it.

I have another 45, a replica blackpowder 45-caliber under-hammer pistol. (*Early American gunsmith Ashabell Cook designed the original pistol.*) This replica was made in the 1980s by the Italian gunmaking firm of P. Bondini. I use a fired 45 ACP case filled with Pyrodex to load it.

One of the pin gun's best qualities is that it takes high-capacity magazines. Here it is with "not quite enough" 14-rounders.

The under-hammer design is supposed to be altogether American and that gives me a patriotic reason to like the Bondini replica. Another is that it is fun to shoot, and cleans up a lot easier than my other blackpowder firearms.

In my collection of 45 ACP pistols I have one for nostalgia: my 'starter' pistol, the 'MODEL Of 1911.'

There is a gun for bowling pins, steel shoots and some target shooting: the PARA/CASP P-14. It is my only real custom pistol and I'm very glad I got it before 1994, when high-capacity magazines were available and fairly cheap.

The S&W Model 1917 is available for PPC-type shooting, home defense, small game hunting and plinking.

When plinking palls, I have the utilitarian target 45 with the red-dot scope. I know that gun is going to make a good showing in bullseye someday; I just don't know when.

I also have two good carry guns. The Officer's ACP is one: stainless, small, powerful for its size and accurate. The 1991A1 Commander is the other carry piece. It is just 1/2-inch longer in barrel, slide and butt than the Officer's and can use the same holsters as all my other 45s with iron sights.

To remind me of how good 45 semi-autos really are, I have the under-hammer blackpowder single shot.

I think I've covered the 45ACP waterfront pretty well, but you never know what might turn up at Northwoods, or one of the other 'firearms emporiums' I frequent. The only 45 I'm actively seeking is a used Smith & Wesson 625. A modern 45 ACP revolver that uses full moon clips and loads as fast as my slightly tired 1917 would be just the thing for some of my shooting.

When I find a 625 on the same day I have the money, I will have eight 45s in the collection. That can be thought of as a lot of guns in one caliber—or just as a nice start. As the guys I shoot with like to say, "You can't have too many 45s." ●

The Backwoods Holster

by Bob Campbell

RECENTLY, I WAS asked what I did with my spare time now that I am no longer a peace officer. Running a business full time and looking after three children is more than enough, but I also love experimenting with handguns. I like to get into the woods when possible, the farther the better. If game presents itself, fine, if not I am just as happy if less well fed. I learned long ago that the secret to hunting is to be smarter than the game. If another of God's creatures outwits me that day I am sure the Good Man planned it that way!

I have carried a sidearm during most of my time afield, except when overseas. Regularly I have dealt with dangerous reptiles and the occasional feral dog. I have been fairly close to both bear and boar, without difficulty. It's just as well. It is possible to take large animals with a handgun—I have done it—but quite another to stop an attack with one. The only bear attack I have lived through was when a ragged old brownie scattered the first three rows at a third-rate circus. I leapt in

Above: **The 'Skelton rig' from Kirkpatrick.**

front of the children, my hand on the worn handles of my 45. The prayer on my lips served better.

The gun I carry in the woods is sometimes different from the gun I carry in self-defense, and sometimes not. The 45 auto is light, flat and powerful and will do anything I need done. On the other hand, the 22 rimfire revolver is lighter and handier.

There is nothing like a 357 Magnum for all-around utility and enjoyment. That is what shooting is all about, enjoyment! I also like to wander afield with a 4-inch barrel 44 Special, or even a 45 Auto Rim revolver. They suit me, and suit me better than most other guns for the kind of use they are put to. I like big, fat subsonic bullets. I occasionally fire a shot without ear protection when game shooting and these rounds are much less offensive than magnums.

Another gun I use afield fairly often is the 9mm auto. My personal Beretta is fitted with a KKM custom match-grade barrel. It is extremely accurate; accurate enough to 'bark' a squirrel. If you think this particular Beretta is among the last guns to carry afield, you are wrong. This gun is accurate, easy to shoot well, and easily used by other members of the family.

I have a son, now a police cadet sergeant, who seems destined to be issued the Beretta 9mm. I wanted him to have one to train with at home, and the gun grew on me. With 147-grain Hornady jacketed bullets over a light charge of Bullseye, I am realizing 880 fps and 1.25-inch 25-yard groups with the carefully fitted KKM barrel. It is a great small-game gun. If I loaded a 115-grain bullet to 1,300 fps (*the XTP will stay in 1.5 inches in this weight at that velocity from the KKM barrel*) I would have a dynamite predator/varmint gun.

When carrying in the field, I often carry a heavier gun most would consider a defense gun. It is true that the weight of a 40+-ounce handgun is a burden on long treks, but performance isn't free. I have tried several lighter field guns and, other than the 22 rimfire, they don't work for me.

For these field guns I need a comfortable, secure holster that satisfies a completely different set of criteria than those for service handguns carry systems.

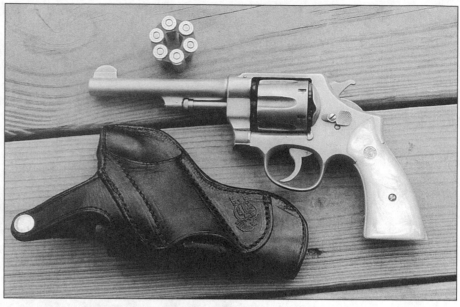

A good setup for spelunking. A Smith and Wesson Model 1917, a spare 'moon clip with six Silvertips, and a Schafer holster.

Hunter's '3 in 1'.

When we say secure in police terms, we mean secure from a gun grab. In field terms, we need a handgun safe from branches and brush that might sweep across it. A branch can pull a handgun's hammer back and—theoretically—fire the gun. When we sit or squat–and if the trek is long enough you'll be inclined to nap at times–there is the danger of the gun being tipped out of the holster. I have carried my defense handguns in open-top holsters for years, preferring to avoid 'suicide straps' on concealed-carry handguns. But handguns carried in the backwoods really need a thumb-snap or thumb-break. Tension isn't enough.

Full-flap holsters are ideal for protection, but slow. The first gunfighters, using ex-military flap holsters, simply cut the top off. When the Marines guarded the mail in the 1920s, the Commandant of the Marine Corps ordered Marines to fold the flap back, exposing the gun, and to carry the Colt cocked and locked, fully loaded. So, we know the flap holster is not for speed, although it does a fine job of protecting both the gun and shooter.

The question is, do we need a fast presentation from

Black Hills Leather's crossdraw. A good choice for traveling in brush.

El Paso's Austin, a wonderful investment in history.

the holster in a back-woods gun? Well, we shouldn't–but sometimes we do. I have drawn against snakes, timber rattlers and copperheads, on three occasions. I drew a 2-inch Military and Police on one occasion and it took two flat-points to settle the issue. On another occasion, I drew at a snake between my feet and a single 125-grain 357 (my deer load) made quite a mess of him. On another occasion, the children and I were checking out the ruins of an old mansion far off the beaten path when I called a halt. I smelled a snake close by.

I saw him coming through the leaves, drew my 45 and made a good shot. Three instances in 30 years isn't a lot but on no occasion would I have wished to draw from a pocket.

So, while we may not need the speed of a duty holster (*plenty of them are not fast*) we need a certain amount of speed. Thumb-breaks are fine but I still enjoy the rugged old carry strap. These straps, if long enough, can be swept away by the trigger finger. If you can use one, you can carry some pretty elegant holster wear.

Among my favorites is the El Paso Austin, one of the first duty

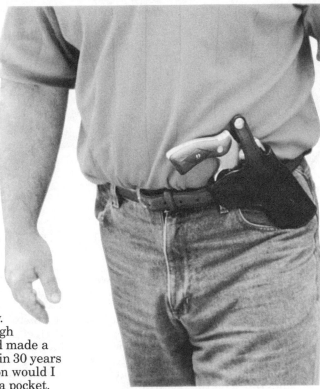

Schafer's crossdraw is handy, well-balanced.

holsters designed expressly for the Colt 1911. Yes, it is a Mexican loop holster but it is much more than a revolver holster with the cylinder bulge ironed out. The Austin holds a 1911 at a good draw angle and, with suede lining, offers plenty of protection. The security strap is long enough to give good purchase when making a fast draw.

I like this holster very much.

When carrying the 1911 in a crossdraw position, I sometimes forego the safety strap requirement. When the gun is in this position, and in a tightly-molded holster, such as those from Black Hills handgun leather, the chances of a limb brushing the gun's hammer are much less–and in any case the gun is carried cocked and locked. Rudy Lozano's crossdraw holster is well-stitched, with a strong welt at the upper lip of the holster for ease of re-holstering. That is important, especially if you are moving. You must be able to safely re-holster the gun with one hand, which means a tightly molded holster that will not collapse when the gun is removed.

I have carried the Beretta in a DeSantis 'Belt Scabbard' originally designed for the Postal Inspection Service. Mine was graciously delivered with the Postal Seal intact. This holster offers good adjustment and one of the fastest thumb-break action safety straps I have ever encountered. The hammer is fully covered and the design includes a tension screw adjustment.

When carrying the Magnum, I use Rusty Sherrick's crossdraw a great deal. I am not sure I have another belt holster for this gun! It works very well.

For the big guns, I have quite a few Tom Schafer holsters. He makes a

The Baird fast draw from a master leathermaker, Jerry Haugen.

IMA's full-flap holster. Very well made, historically correct, and rugged.

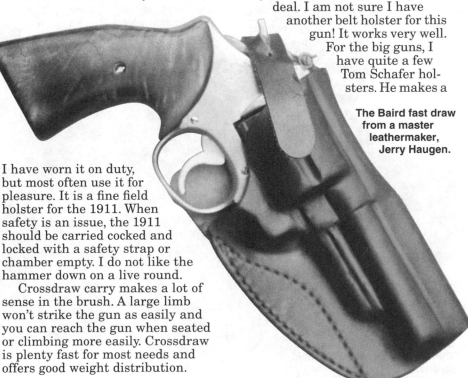

I have worn it on duty, but most often use it for pleasure. It is a fine field holster for the 1911. When safety is an issue, the 1911 should be carried cocked and locked with a safety strap or chamber empty. I do not like the hammer down on a live round.

Crossdraw carry makes a lot of sense in the brush. A large limb won't strike the gun as easily and you can reach the gun when seated or climbing more easily. Crossdraw is plenty fast for most needs and offers good weight distribution.

crossdraw that I find makes a great deal of sense. The holster has a thumb-break but it is a pull-through. In other words, a strong tug simply breaks the snap. I like this very much. When carrying cross-draw, you tend to draw across a target rather than into it, but small-game hunting requires accurate shooting and that means taking your time. This design is a winner.

Tom also makes grand cowboy holsters. I have adapted one of his single-action Colt holsters to a Smith and Wesson 44 Frontier. Sure, the Smith does not have an ejector rod, but in a pinch the holster works. The strap is unobtrusive, not likely to get hung up. I also use a Schafer holster for my Metal-ife-finished Smith and Wesson 45.

I once had a belt and holster made up by Kirkpatrick for a 4-inch barrel Smith and Wesson 44 Special. To my mind, there has been no better writer in this genre than Charles 'Skeeter' Skelton. Skeeter had practical experience in both the police and game field, and his writing showed it. His work was repeatable and verifiable. His conclusions have been borne out by modern scientific tests. His work in *Shooting Times* represented a high-water mark of shooting/police journalism. I wanted a gun like Skelton's and I had a nice Texas rig, belt and all, for the big magnum-

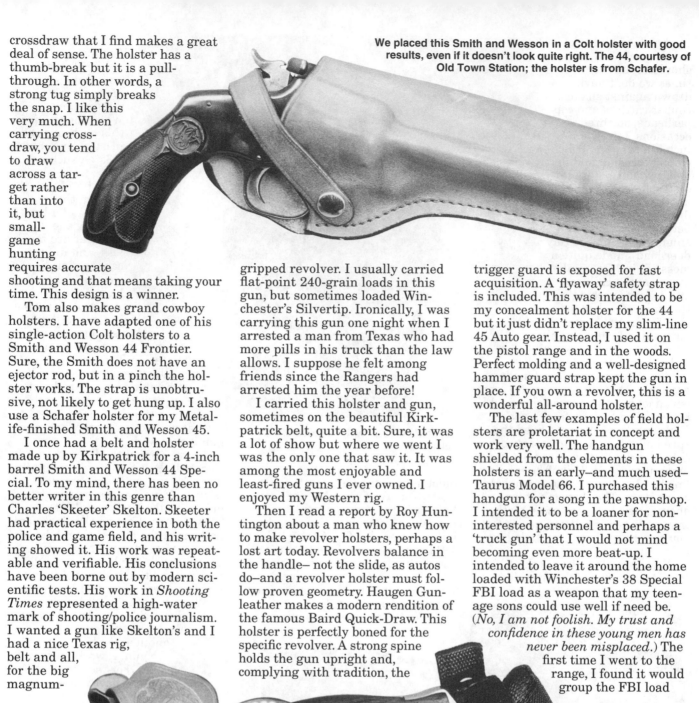

We placed this Smith and Wesson in a Colt holster with good results, even if it doesn't look quite right. The 44, courtesy of Old Town Station; the holster is from Schafer.

gripped revolver. I usually carried flat-point 240-grain loads in this gun, but sometimes loaded Winchester's Silvertip. Ironically, I was carrying this gun one night when I arrested a man from Texas who had more pills in his truck than the law allows. I suppose he felt among friends since the Rangers had arrested him the year before!

I carried this holster and gun, sometimes on the beautiful Kirkpatrick belt, quite a bit. Sure, it was a lot of show but where we went I was the only one that saw it. It was among the most enjoyable and least-fired guns I ever owned. I enjoyed my Western rig.

Then I read a report by Roy Huntington about a man who knew how to make revolver holsters, perhaps a lost art today. Revolvers balance in the handle— not the slide, as autos do—and a revolver holster must follow proven geometry. Haugen Gunleather makes a modern rendition of the famous Baird Quick-Draw. This holster is perfectly boned for the specific revolver. A strong spine holds the gun upright and, complying with tradition, the

trigger guard is exposed for fast acquisition. A 'flyaway' safety strap is included. This was intended to be my concealment holster for the 44 but it just didn't replace my slim-line 45 Auto gear. Instead, I used it on the pistol range and in the woods. Perfect molding and a well-designed hammer guard strap kept the gun in place. If you own a revolver, this is a wonderful all-around holster.

The last few examples of field holsters are proletariat in concept and work very well. The handgun shielded from the elements in these holsters is an early–and much used–Taurus Model 66. I purchased this handgun for a song in the pawnshop. I intended it to be a loaner for non-interested personnel and perhaps a 'truck gun' that I would not mind becoming even more beat-up. I intended to leave it around the home loaded with Winchester's 38 Special FBI load as a weapon that my teen-age sons could use well if need be. (*No, I am not foolish. My trust and confidence in these young men has never been misplaced.*) The first time I went to the range, I found it would group the FBI load

Magnolia Sports affordable, but durable, holster.

DeSantis offers custom quality with mass-production delivery. This belt scabbard is a fine field holster.

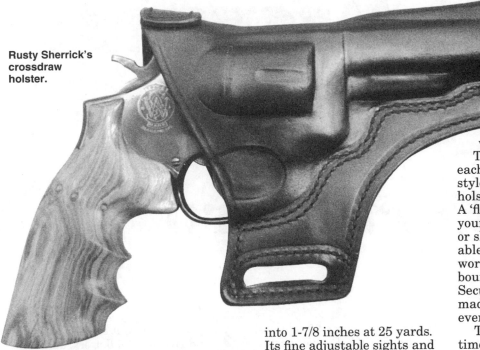

Rusty Sherrick's crossdraw holster.

holster's shape. The thumb-break and snap offer good adjustment. An outstanding field holster well suited to revolver use.

The holsters I have mentioned each fit a specific need and a certain style of handgun. A poorly designed holster can be a problem in the field. A 'flapping' holster that digs into your ribs each time you climb a hill, or shifts on the belt, is not acceptable. You can lose your gun–or worse. An acquaintance of mine bounded over a creek, but his Ruger Security Six fell out of a cheaply made holster halfway across. Wherever it fell, it is still there!

The main thing is enjoying your time afield. Choose quality gear, and rest easy.   •

into 1-7/8 inches at 25 yards. Its fine adjustable sights and smooth single-action trigger made it a prime candidate for a trail gun. I also found it was passing accurate with Winchester's powerful 145-grain Magnum Silvertip, although it rattled for a full minute after firing a cylinder-full!

One of the most useful holsters of all time is Hunter's '3 in 1'. This holster can be worn on a belt, as an inside-the-belt holster, or on a shoulder harness. I especially like the shoulder harness for outdoors work. It keeps the gun out of the way if you are cutting wood or other chores, and works well under a jacket in the winter. If you prefer thumb-break action, this holster has it. If you prefer a snap, unsnap the snap–either works.

I have used the Hunter holster a great deal. It wears well, if a bit bulkier than some concealment-designed shoulder holsters. It is easily thrown on, and can be conveniently hung on the bed or placed beside your sleeping bag.

Another holster that fits any budget is available from Magnolia Sports. These synthetic holsters are well designed and executed. I like them because they are available not only in the usual black, but brown as well. The holster is rigid, with reinforcements that keep the

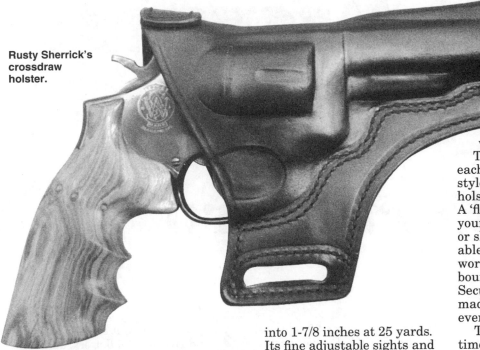

A very well-used Hunter full-flap holster for Colt 45–still useful.

Reference

Rusty Sherrick
   507 Mark Drive
   Elizabethtown PA 17022

Hunter Leather
   3300 W. 71st Avenue
   Westminster CO 80030

El Paso Saddlery
   PO 27194
   El Paso TX 79926

DeSantis Leather
   PO 2039
   49 Denton Avenue
   New Hyde Park NY 11040

Haugen Handgun Leather
   P O 6124
   Bismarck ND 58506

Tom Schafer
   948 Sandy Creek
   RoadDale TX 78616

Black Hills Leather
   410 W. Aurora
   Laredo TX 78041

Magnolia Sports
   211 W. Main St.
   Magnolia AR 71753

KirkPatrick Leather Co.
   PO 677
   Laredo TX 78042

KKM
   46 Alfonso 101
   Carson City NV 89706

International Military Antiques
   PO 256
   Millington NJ 07946

Short Magnums: Pro & Con

Part I: Pro

by Jon R. Sundra

IN CASE YOU haven't noticed, we've entered the age of the short magnum. I for one happen to like these stubby cartridges that have taken the country by storm, but before I tell you why, perhaps a little background is in order.

It's difficult to look back in time and say that this or that particular event was the start of a trend, but in this case, if I had to stick my neck out, I'd say the idea of a short cartridge matching the ballistics of a longer or standard-length one began in 1963 with the introduction of the 284 Winchester. If you want to split hairs, in that particular instance, it was a matter of trying to match the performance of the 270 Winchester —a cartridge requiring a standard-length action —with one that would cycle through a short-action rifle.

Two years later, Remington threw their hat into the arena with the 350 Magnum, followed the year after by the 6.5 Remington Magnum. But as with the 284 Winchester, both aspired to only match the per-

▲ John Lazzeroni's elegant L-2000-SA, a rifle designed from scratch around his own proprietary line of Short Action Magnums.

formance of longer, 30-06-based cartridges. In both instances, there were no commercial equivalents at that time against which to compare, but the wildcats 6.5-06 and 35 Whelen defined the targeted ballistics for these two Remington rounds.

Obviously, to match the performance of a longer cartridge with a shorter one, you have to somehow match its powder capacity æ or at least come close to it. The only way to accomplish that is by going to a fatter case. The 284 Winchester was unique in that it had a head diameter of 0.500-inch compared with the 0.472-inch of the 30-06 family. The two Remington "magnums" were derived by shortening the already shortened 7mm Remington Magnum to where they'd cycle through the 2 3/4-inch magazine of the short XP-100 action on which the Remington Model 600 Carbine was based. But again, the three aforementioned rounds were not of true magnum class, because their powder capacities were no greater than that of the basic 30-06 case.

The first genuine short magnums appeared without much fanfare in 1997, courtesy of John Lazzeroni. Three years prior, John had unveiled an entire 6-cartridge line of proprietary, hell-breathing super magnums based on two beltless

cases, one that closely matched the old British 404 Jeffery, and the other the 416 Rigby. There was actually a third case, the smallest of the three, that had the same 0.532-inch head diameter as the rim/belt of the H&H case, but that has since been discontinued.

Anyway, these were true magnum-length cartridges and as such required a 3.7-inch magazine. For what he calls his Short Action Magnums, John shortened the two parent cases on which his full-length magnums were based, and came up with six more cartridges ranging from 6mm to 416, all of which would fit magazines 2.8 inches in length.

The theory that short, fat powder columns are more conducive to accuracy was proven in the early 70s with the 22 and 6mm PPC, shown here flanking the 223 Remington for comparison.

Of course we all know what happened in 2000: Winchester Ammunition rolled out its 300 Short Magnum and the world of big-game rifles and cartridges hasn't been the same since. Six months later, in a rare mid-year introduction, Remington launched its 300 and 7mm Short Action Ultra Mags. Then, in late 2001, Winchester countered with its 270 and 7mm WSMs.

Over the five short years that all this has come about, I have personally used the 270 WSM; all three of the short 7mms of Remington, Winchester and Lazzeroni, and both the Remington and Winchester's short 30s to take a wide variety of game in Alaska, Arkansas, New Mexico, Wyoming, Montana, Labrador, South Africa, Patagonia, and Tanzania. So when I say I like them, it's based on more than mere cogitation.

Anyway, Lazzeroni may have started the short magnum ball rolling, but because his Short Action Magnums were proprietary and he had limited resources with which to promote them, they had negligible impact on the marketplace. However, once Winchester and Remington joined the fray, it was — and is — a whole 'nother ball game. Since that time you haven't been able to pick up a gun magazine that hasn't had at least one article dealing in some way with short magnums. It is truly a phenomenon the likes of which I haven't seen in the 35 years I've been writing about guns and hunting.

So what's the big deal? I mean, we all know these new short magnums don't launch bullets any faster than their belted counterparts. The 300 WSM and 300 Remington SAUM, for example, don't push their 150-, 165- or 180-grain payloads any faster than the tried and true 300 Winchester Magnum. It's the same with the 7mms; neither out-speed the 7mm Remington Mag that's been around since 1962. If indeed the only claim that could be made for the short mags was that

The author's first exposure to short magnums was with the Lazzeroni 7mm and 30-caliber versions. This custom Ruger No. 1 in 7.21 Tomahawk was used to take several species of plains game in Tanzania's Selous Reserve.

they could launch bullets just as fast as the belted, standard-length magnums, but do it with a rifle that was 1/2-inch shorter and about 4 oz. lighter, well, that's not a lot to hang one's hat on. I mean, even in this weight-conscious marketplace, that's hardly enough reason to sell or trade-in a perfectly good belted magnum just to be trendy.

Nope, there's got to be more to it. And there is.

For one thing, these short, fat cartridges are more efficient than ones of longer, more slender configuration. By more efficient, I mean they burn powder more efficiently so that less is needed to achieve the same velocities. This has to do with the

fact that a shorter, fatter powder column puts more of the powder charge closer to the primer flame, and combustion is completed closer to the chamber than with cases having longer powder columns. Consider, for example, the 7mm Winchester Short Magnum and the 7mm Remington Magnum. The latter's belted case holds approximately 86 grains of water by weight, the WSM about 81, for a difference of about 6 percent. Typically though, optimum loads for each will show the short case requiring as little as 8 percent less of the same powder to achieve the same velocities. Moreover, this more efficient combustion allows optimum velocities to be achieved with slightly faster-burning powders, which results in even lighter powder charges.

The differences are even more pronounced with the smaller Remington SAUM case, which holds only 76 grains of water or 12 percent less than the 7mm Remington Magnum, yet it too virtually matches the velocities of its belted big brother. The best illustration of this that I've seen appears in the new Swift reloading manual's data for the 7mm Remington SAUM and the 7mm Rem Mag. The exact same 9 propellants from three different manufacturers were used in developing the loading data for each cartridge behind the 150 gr. Swift Sirocco bullet. In both instances 24-inch Wiseman test barrels were used. The results show an average maximum powder charge for the 7mm Remington Mag. was 66.8 grains for an average maximum velocity of 3018 fps. For the 7mm SAUM with its 12 percent smaller case, the average maximum charge using those same 9 different powders was 62.3 grains; that's 7 percent less powder to achieve virtually the same average maximum velocity of 3015 fps!

Think that's a fluke? Then consider the data for the 300 Winchester Magnum and the 300 Winchester Short Magnum in that same Swift

When seated to factory specs, even medium-weight bullets like the 7mm/140 Barnes and 150/Scirocco in the center greatly intrude on powder space. At right is the 175/Barnes.

reloading manual. In that instance only 7 of the 9 powders used were the same: Hodgdon's 414, 4350 and 4831; Alliant's 15, 19 and 22; and IMR's 4350. Again, Bill Wiseman test barrels 24 inches in length were used for both. The results show the average maximum powder charge among the 7 propellants used for the 300 Winchester Magnum was 73.7 grains, for an average maximum velocity of 3191 fps; for the 12 percent smaller WSM case the average maximum powder charge was 69.6 grains or 6 percent less, for an average max velocity of 3195 fps!

I am currently handloading for five 7mm short magnums, three of Winchester persuasion, one Remington, and one Lazzeroni, and I can tell you my experiences accurately reflect Swift's data. In every case, I'm getting the same velocities with these smaller cases than I used to get in various 7mm Remington Magnums, and I'm doing it with 5-8 percent less powder.

Attendant with this combustion efficiency, which allows the use of lesser amounts of faster-burning powders, is less recoil. Not enough that you'd be able to discern between a short magnum and a belted magnum of identical weight and stock design, mind you, but less nonetheless. That's because with lighter charges of faster-burning powder, more of it is being burned within the barrel, so there's less ejecta. In other words, there's less unburned powder, if any, exiting the muzzle, which in turn decreases muzzle turbulence as

well as recoil. And the less muzzle turbulence a bullet encounters, the more it's likely to fly true. Many experts believe that was the primary reason why the short, squat cases of the 22 and 6mm PPC cartridges that appeared on the benchrest scene in the early 70s quickly came to dominate competitive shooting. To this day the PPC and similar squat cartridges are the ones to beat when it comes to trying to put every shot into the same hole.

As for the short magnums being inherently more accurate at the levels needed for big-game hunting, any claims in that regard are couched more in theory than in real-world results, because there are so many other factors affecting a given gun's grouping ability. Nevertheless, the fact remains that cases that headspace on a conical

shoulder tend to orient themselves in better coaxial alignment with the bore. With belted cases, the entire length of the cartridge forward of the datum line, i. e. from the front surface of the belt on a belted case, can assume any orientation that tolerances within the chamber allow. And there's no consistency to this misalignment because the chambered cartridge's orientation is determined by how perfectly the front surface of the belt matches the datum line at the rear of the chamber. These dimensional match-ups are rarely perfect, so if the front of the belt contacts its stop surface on one side of the case before the opposite side, the cartridge is tilted in that direction. Again, we're talking just a couple thousands of an inch at worst, but one of the most important factors in consistent accuracy is the coaxial alignment of the chambered cartridge with the bore.

And while there is no inherent disadvantage with belted cases with regard to case life, unless handloaders adjust their sizing dies to headspace on the shoulder rather

▲ This fine gemsbok was taken by Sundra using an H-S Precision rifle in 300 WSM.

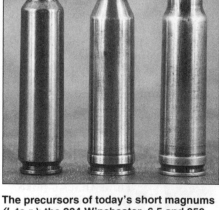

The precursors of today's short magnums (l. to r.): the 284 Winchester, 6.5 and 350 Remington Magnums of the mid-1960s. They, however, only aspired to match the performance standards of 30-06-based cartridges in a short-action rifle.

Today's short magnums (l. to r.): the 7mm and 300 Remington SAUMs; the 7.21 Lazzeroni Tomahawk and 7.82 Patriot; and the 270, 7mm and 300 WSMs.

than simply screwing them down tight against the shell holder, case head separations can occur in just a couple of reloadings. It goes without saying, of course, that if you use factory ammo, case life is something you needn't worry about.

As much as I like the short magnums, I would be remiss if I didn't mention the fact that their corpulence make them less than ideally suited to a lot of existing actions; actions that were never designed to handle cartridges larger in head diameter than the belted H&H case. The modifications required to achieve dead-reliable feeding of the .550-inch head diameter of Remington's SAUMs, the .555-inch of Winchester's WSMs, and especially the .580-inch of the Lazzeroni rounds, are tricky at best, not to mention that alterations must be made in the magazine follower and/or the magazine itself just to accommodate three rounds. Indeed, some actions like the '98 Mauser and commercial variations thereof, require such extensive modifications that it simply doesn't make economic sense to do so. If you want a short magnum, buy a factory rifle that's designed to handle it. Virtually all the major rifle makers now chamber for either the Remington or Winchester version, and some offer both.

▲ The short Winchester Model 70 is the best suited action for short magnums in that it has a magazine that's 3.1 inches æ long enough to seat all but the heaviest bullets flush with the base of the neck. Shown here is one of Jon's 7mm WSMs that was built by Mark Bansner, fitted with a Lilja barrel, in his own laid-up fiberglass stock.

and 350 mentioned at the outset, is that none of these new short magnums æ not Remington's, not Winchester's, not Lazzeroni's æ achieve their full ballistic potential with factory ammunition because bullets must be seated to where they seriously infringe on usable powder space. This is particularly true of the many "super bullets" now available as components and in factory ammunition, which have less lead and more copper, and are thus longer for their weight than bullets of more conventional construction. A 150-grain bullet, for example, is of only medium weight in the 7mm

for example, takes up almost 20 percent of usable powder space!

The best solution is to use an action that will allow bullets to be seated out where they belong, and to have the throat lengthened accordingly, but then you lose some of the most touted advantages claimed for the short magnums; namely, shorter stroke, shorter overall length, and lighter weight. Personally, a half-inch and a few ounces doesn't mean all that much to me, and most of my short magnum rifles are based on standard-length actions and throated accordingly, or on actions that have been modified to increase magazine length to 3 inches.

So you see, all is not perfect in Short Magnum Land. Not only are there some disadvantages, there is no one thing about the short mags that makes them significantly better than the belted magnums they're pitted against. Even when you add up all the little advantages we've discussed here æ some of which are admittedly more academic than real æ it still doesn't make a lot of sense to trade in or sell a perfectly good belted magnum to replace it with a stubby equivalent.

But what if you don't own a 270, 7mm or 300 Magnum and you're in the market for one, either in the form of a new rifle, or by way of having an existing action re-barreled? If indeed that's the case, I can't see how anyone could ignore all the little advantages the short, beltless magnums offer, because together they add up to a genuine improvement over the status quo. Not a quantum leap, mind you, but enough of step forward in ballistic technology that I, for one, refuse to be left behind. ●

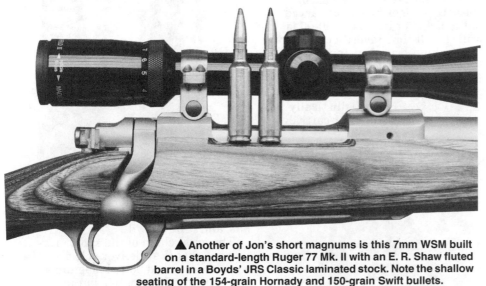

▲ Another of Jon's short magnums is this 7mm WSM built on a standard-length Ruger 77 Mk. II with an E. R. Shaw fluted barrel in a Boyds' JRS Classic laminated stock. Note the shallow seating of the 154-grain Hornady and 150-grain Swift bullets.

If you're thinking of having an action re-barreled, be sure you consult a competent gunsmith who's familiar with what's required and can tell you which actions are best suited to modification.

Another drawback, and one that goes back to the days of the 284 Winchester and Remington's 6.5

caliber, yet when bullets like the Barnes X or Swift's Scirocco are seated to factory overall lengths of roughly 2-3/4 inches, their bases are well below the shoulder of the case. It's like robbing the case of several grains of powder capacity. It's worse with 160-grain bullets, and forget 175s; a Barnes X-Bullet,

Short Magnums: Pro & Con

Part II: Con

by Terry Wieland

THE SHORT MAGNUMS are certainly good. I will concede that right off the bat.

As a group, they deliver higher velocity from a smaller case. From all accounts, they are sufficiently accurate, and they fit into a slightly shorter action.

Does this make them world-beaters? Does it mean the death of every other cartridge introduced since the 7x57 Mauser came on the scene in 1893 and set the standard for the next century? No, it does not. In fact, I would venture that only two or three of the rapidly expanding family of short magnums will still be with us in ten years, and even those will not make a significant dent in the popularity of favorites such as the 30-06, the 7mm Remington Magnum, and the 270 Winchester.

Here's why.

First, look at the 30-06. It is one hundred years old this year, if you date it from the birth of the original 30-03. During that time, it has survived every attempt to dethrone it. In 1925, the 270 Winchester was introduced, offering lighter bullets, flatter trajectory, and less recoil. In 1952, the 308 Winchester arrived, offering only slightly less power – but in a considerably smaller case. In 1962, the

The 284 Winchester beside the 300 WSM. The cartridges are so similar it is eerie. They are about the same length, are short, fat, with almost parallel walls and a rebated rim. The 284 was intended to provide 30-06-case ballistics in a shorter package. It never went anywhere.

7mm Remington Magnum came along, delivering greater velocity and flatter trajectory in a standard-length action, and the following year Winchester brought out its 300 Winchester Magnum, which offered greater power across the board.

The 30-06 survived every one of these challenges. While each of these cartridges has since carved out a niche for itself, the 30-06 is still the all-time favorite chambering for high-priced custom rifles – an excellent measure of its continuing popularity.

My point here is that the arrival of a ballistically superior cartridge does not spell doom for every other cartridge on the market. It never has, and it never will.

The great claim of the short magnums is that they deliver velocity equal to standard belted magnums, like the 7mm Remington, but in a shorter case. In theory, at least, this means they can be chambered in a

The 257 Weatherby is a typically superb short belted magnum, capable of handling animals as tough as a 600-pound zebra stallion, with the right bullets *(in this case, a 115-grain Trophy Bonded Bear Claw)*. Because the cartridge demands a long barrel for velocity and enough heft for accurate shooting, the so-called advantages of the short magnums are largely negated.

rifle with a commensurately shorter action, with a resulting reduction in overall length and weight.

But does it really mean this? Not that I can see.

For one thing, you need sufficient barrel length to consume the slow-burning powder necessary to impart the velocity. Does it make a huge difference if your rifle is 45-1/2 inches long instead of 46 inches? No.

As for accuracy, that requires a barrel that is stiff even if it is short – a heavy barrel, in other words. And that adds weight. The couple of ounces you might save on a shorter action are meaningless.

All of this assumes, of course, that these cartridges really do deliver the velocity they claim, and I have my doubts about that.

Now let's look at the downside of the short, fat cartridges.

First, there is magazine capacity. To accommodate a fatter cartridge, you need a wider box; otherwise you reduce your capacity by a cartridge or two. Second, you run the risk of feeding problems because the farther away you place the cartridge from the axis of the chamber, the more difficult it is to ensure smooth, reliable feeding. And finally, there is the question of longer, heavier bullets encroaching on the powder cavity, reducing capacity and therefore velocity.

I am not saying that all of these negatives will come to pass in any given rifle, merely that they are possibilities to consider.

Now let's consider a couple of other facts.

The 300 Weatherby handled this incoming brown bear at 17 yards, and dropped him on the third shot. Again, reliable feeding was the key, and power was secondary – although the 300 Weatherby has more than adequate power for the job. The cartridge's long neck allows the use of heavy bullets without encroaching on powder capacity, or making the cartridge too long for the action.

The firearms industry today is driven by new products. New rifles, new models, old models with new looks. The number of hunters and shooters has been in a steady decline for many years, which means more companies are competing for a share of a steadily shrinking pie.

By and large, rifles do not wear out. So the only way to get someone to buy a new rifle is by offering something bigger, faster, glitzier, or sexier. The rifle companies need to sell new rifles, otherwise they go out of business. I strongly suspect most new rifles are sold to people who already have at least one. Why are they buying another? Because they think it will be more powerful, more accurate, or because they will be the first in their club to have one.

The bottom line is that every firearms and ammunition company wants to come out with new cartridges or rifles that will excite the buying public. While many of these products are perfectly good, more than a few have their performance enhanced considerably by advertising and promotion, rather than by demonstrable ballistic superiority. Given the frenzy of short-magnum car-

tridge introductions taking place now, and the blizzard of press releases accompanying them, I suspect that a significant chunk of their performance is pure old-fashioned hype.

Still, I am willing to concede that they deliver slightly greater velocity in a slightly smaller case. But so what?

What I am NOT willing to concede is that they deliver enough velocity, or offer a sufficient saving in size, to make anyone forget the 30-06, the 7mm Remington, or the 300 Winchester.

Now let's look at some specific cartridges. Last time I looked, there were short magnums in 224, 243, 270, 7mm and 300, with others expected in 257, 264 and 338. Larger ones—375, 416 and 458—are reported to be in the offing. By the time you read this, all of these may have come to pass.

Which ones have a future? At a guess, I would say the 300 definitely, if only because 308-inch is our all-time favorite and any decent cartridge in that bore diameter will find a following. I can see a 224 and 243 doing well, but I suspect the 257 and 264 will wither. The 7mm could go either way, but to be honest I cannot see any diehard 7mm Rem-

The 30-06 spawned a large family of factory cartridges and wildcats based on its case simply necked up or down. Shown are two of the best – the 25-06 and 270 Winchester. Others include the 6.5-06, 280 Remington, 338-06, and 35 Whelen. The fact that so many of its offspring became solidly established shows the inherent balance of the 30-06, which is now 100 years old and still going very strong.

The 308 Winchester also spawned a large family, including *(from left)* the 243 Winchester, 260 Remington, 7mm-08, the 308 itself, and the 358 Winchester. The 308 does not deliver 30-06 ballistics, but it is a solid performer in shorter actions and lighter rifles, and lends itself to this application. The 300 WSM promises belted-magnum ballistics in a 308-length case, but delivers excessive recoil in light rifles, and lower velocities in shorter barrels. So what's the point?

ington fan abandoning that fine cartridge for the sake of saving a half-inch of action length.

In bores larger than 308, I doubt that any of the existing or projected short magnums have a future.

My general reason for this view has to do partly with recoil, partly with chamber pressure, and partly with feeding.

Once you get into the realm of cartridges used for dangerous game, factors other than velocity and accuracy become vital. Since the 338 is now widely carried in Alaskan bear country, these considerations apply to it just as they do to a 416 or 458.

A short, fat cartridge with almost parallel walls is likely to cause feeding problems, especially when loaded with flat- or round-nosed bullets, in wet or dirty conditions. As well, such a case has an alarming tendency to stick in the chamber, and lock up the bolt, when fired in extreme heat such as you have hunting Cape buffalo in Africa.

The real knock on these cartridges, though, has to do with recoil. Once you get into larger bores, you need a certain amount of rifle weight to tame the recoil. Buyers of larger bores are not nearly as concerned with overall weight as are buyers of mountain rifles. Nor are they overly concerned with length, since you can get excellent velocity – even from a 458 Lott – using a 22-inch barrel. Saving a half-inch on action length is at best a theoretical gain, whereas questionable feeding and reliability, and excessive

recoil, are definite negatives.

Proponents of the large-bore short magnums may argue that you get a shorter bolt throw, and that this means you are less likely to short-stroke the bolt in an emergency.

Since I have never found anyone who ever encountered such short-stroking in real life, regardless of the cartridge concerned, that argument is really grasping at straws.

Looking back over the last hundred years of cartridge development, since it was revolutionized by smokeless gunpowder, it is hard to counter the argument that the original designers, working from a relatively clean slate, essentially got it right. When they designed the 7x57 and the 30-06, and a little later the 375 H&H, they achieved an almost perfect balance of ballistic ability, and physical shape and size.

Since then, we have had several distinct waves of new-cartridge devel-

opment. First came the assault of the belted magnums – the Weatherby line in the 1940s, followed by the original short (belted) magnums of the 1960s. In theory, greater power should have sent the existing cartridges to the bone yard. They did not, because for every gain – actual or theoretical – there was an equal loss. If you don't need the muzzle blast, recoil, weight, and cost of a 300 Weatherby, why buy one instead of a nice Remington Model 700 30-06?

There were individual cartridges, too, which offered gains in specific calibers, or even promised to spawn whole families.

To wit: In 1963 – 40 years ago! – Winchester came out with the 284 Winchester, and if the sight of it does not give the short-magnum aficionados a fit of déjà vu, I don't know what would. The 284 is short (2.17 inches overall case length), fat, with almost parallel walls, and a rebated rim. Necked up to 308, it offers actual 30-06 performance from a case little longer than a 308. It has the rim diameter of a 30-06, but the body diameter of a belted magnum.

The 284 came and went so quickly that most rifle shooters have never even seen one, much less fired or owned one. Ahead of its time? Possibly. Or simply unnecessary, offering some gains but not enough to justify the expense. The anticipated family of cartridges based on the short, fat, rebated-rim case never came to pass.

Then we have the 350 Remington Magnum, and its little brother, the 6.5, vintage of 1965. They were gen-

With dangerous game like Cape buffalo, absolute reliability is more important than accuracy—or even power. This buffalo was killed with a souped-up 458 Winchester at a distance of four feet. The cartridges fed perfectly, which is why the author is still here.

uine belted magnums, cut off short to fit into the weird Remington Model 600 action. Ballistics were about what you would expect from a 35 or 264 based on the 30-06 case, but in a shorter, fatter package. The 350 offered 2700 fps with a 200-grain bullet (compared to 2600 fps in a 35 Whelen), while the 6.5 claimed 3200 fps with a 120-grain factory load (3175 fps for the wild-cat 6.5-06). Even assuming these numbers are real (*and that's a stretch*) there was not enough there to overcome the disadvantages: tooth-rattling recoil in the 350, and simple pointlessness in the 6.5.

Proponents may point to the 22 PPC and 6 PPC as examples of short, fat cartridges that did work, and I grant you they are superbly accurate and rule the benchrest roost. I have seen no evidence, however, that they are making any inroads whatever against the 223, 22-250 and 220 Swift among varmint hunters. Nor are they overthrowing the 243 Winchester. This is, I admit, an unfair comparison since neither PPC cartridge offers the power of the competing rounds I mention. Still, they are short, they fit into a tiny action, and there is no arguing with the accuracy, so they should have at least a niche following. If they

do, outside the benchrest world, I can't find it.

At the other end of the scale, we have the venerable 375 H&H – a cartridge introduced in 1912. On the surface, you would say it is inefficient and underpowered. It is long – 3.6 inches overall – and has, to a modern eye, far too much taper. The case could easily be blown out and more powder packed in to give greater velocity.

Well, folks, that has been done, more than once. Roy Weatherby did it with his original 375 Weatherby, which had walls blown out to the point where they were almost parallel. My good friend and short-magnum admirer Jon Sundra did much the same with his 375 JRS, which was intended to replace the 375 Weatherby after that company inexplicably killed its cartridge and stopped loading ammunition. A few companies chamber the 375 JRS, but nothing compared to the original 375 H&H.

How can that be, given the 375 JRS's undoubted ballistic advantages? Well, for one thing, the original with its excessive taper has two invaluable virtues when used for dangerous game in hot climates. It feeds beautifully (it is difficult even to deliberately create feeding problems with it) and it never sticks in the chamber when hot climates induce pressure spikes. The 375 Weatherby, on the other hand, with its red-hot factory load, was notorious for doing this.

Obviously, you can improve on the 375 H&H's ballistic performance, but not without taking away from its other, more valuable attributes.

While we are discussing cartridges at the larger end, we should mention the 425 Westley Richards, a forerunner of the 375 H&H. It was a fat, rimless cartridge with a rebated rim, introduced in 1909. Its rim was the size of a 30-06, so it would fit any standard bolt face. Reports of feeding problems because of the rebated rim, along with some oddities in the WR rifle (*such as a 28-inch barrel*) doomed the 425 WR, and all attempts to revive it have been stillborn. If you come across one, you can likely pick it up cheap.

Will the short magnums succeed where all of these cartridges failed? As I suggested earlier, some may achieve a lasting place. A really hot 224 to finally dethrone the Swift, and a

300 WSM beside a 220-grain bullet. Magnums really shine with heavy bullets, yet a 220-grain bullet would either cut excessively into the WSM's powder capacity, or be seated so far out it would negate the value of the cartridge's short overall length.

243 of genuine magnum capabilities, have real possibilities.

The 257 and 264, though, I just cannot see, nor even a 270. Anyone with a little cash could have had a 257 Weatherby (*a superb cartridge*) or a 264 Winchester Magnum (*likewise*) or a 270 Weatherby for half a century or more. Having eschewed those, why would we embrace the same caliber in the form of the new short magnums?

I admire the 338 Winchester, but I don't see the need for any other cartridge of that diameter, and apparently the shooting public at large sees no need at all for a big (*or small, for that matter*) 358. If it did, the 358 Winchester, 35 Whelen, and 358 Norma would have been world-beaters instead of unloved orphans, abandoned almost at birth.

Any serious large-bore, 416 and up, based on the short magnum case should be forgotten right now, before someone gets hurt.

As a breathless teenager, agog at the sight of belted magnums and believing the numbers I saw in ballistics tables, I witnessed the introduction of the 284 Winchester, the 300 Winchester Magnum and the 358 Norma, and wondered why anyone would buy a boring old 30-06 when those were available. Surely, thought I, the 30-06 is dead and almost gone.

Today, 40 years later and a couple of centuries wiser, I own a 30-06 and would never be without one. I also have a 257 Weatherby and various other hotshot rifles, so I am not a complete Luddite. It is just that in 40 years, if I have learned nothing else, it is to take the numbers published in ballistics tables with a grain of salt, and to look askance at all the supposed advantages promised by the ammunition companies.

In 1963, hype was in its infancy; today it is larger than life and twice as noisy. But it is hype, just the same. No one ever hyped the 30-06. No one ever needed to. ●

A mirror image: The 308 was touted as the ballistic equal of the 30-06, which it isn't, and was expected to displace it. While the 308 established itself as a fine cartridge, it damaged the 30-06 not at all. Whether the short magnums can do the same with the longer belted magnums remains to be seen, but even if they establish a niche for themselves, the belted magnums are here to stay.

THE TRUTH ABOUT THE 1903 PALMA

by Jim Foral

THE PALMA MATCH - the oldest international rifle shooting competition still fired - traces its origin to the excitement surrounding America's 100th birthday in 1876. Conceived by a fledgling National Rifle Association as part of the Centennial year celebration, a number of countries were invited to a long-range rifle competition. Four of England's colonies came to Creed- moor to be defeated by a strong American team shooting match rifles. A year later, the United States again issued a challenge for a second Palma meeting, the Championship of the World, as it was touted. Virtually every country with a rifle association or national club received an invitation. The muzzle-loading match rifle gave way to the newfangled breechloader that year. Shooting Remington and Sharp's rifles, the Americans out-Creed-moored the competition.

In 1878, the American team shot unopposed. Coinciding with a 20-year period of NRA inactivity, interest in the Palma trophy waned, and the prize was nearly forgotten. But the Spanish-American and the Boer Wars awakened an attraction to the rifle sports. In 1900, a revitalized

NRA wanted to resurrect the Palma, but no foreign team could be brought together on the short notice that was given.

The following year, America elected to host a Palma tournament to be held at Sea Girt in September. In April 1901, the American NRA was informed that the English reason for not supplying a team was that there were "not enough skilled men available for the contest". Seventeen countries were invited, one showed up. A Canadian team entered the competition against the Americans, and beat them in the first match restricted to the use of the military rifle of the representative nation. In 1902, the U.S. team attempted to regain possession of the trophy in a contest held at Rockcliffe, Canada, but had to be contented with second place. Great Britain won that year, defeating the U.S. and Canada.

The prospects of an annual Palma Match that everyone could look forward to gained momentum. More and more, nations prepared teams for the next competition. Riflemen around the world were hopeful that the series would continue, but it came real close to not working out that way. Let's go back.

Among the matters resolved at the March, 1903 meeting of the Executive Committee of the National Rifle Association had to do with sending a team of American military marksmen to England's Bisley range that summer to compete for the Palma trophy. Participation at Bisley was contingent upon the NRA raising the necessary funds. Eight thousand dollars was the earliest cost estimate, towards which eager National Guard units in New York and New Jersey immediately pledged a total of six hundred dollars.

On March 18, 1903, the British Embassy in Washington issued the official Palma invitation, outlining the match regulations and conditions, and briefly describing the program. The United States State Department received theirs a couple days later. Each nation's team was to consist of eight men, native-born citizens and residents of the country they represented. The British circular invitation went on to describe the legal rifle as simply: "The national military arm of the country the team represents." The match would be shot at the distances of 800, 900, and 1,000 yards. An entry fee of three pounds, five shillings, or $15.81 U.S. would be assessed each team.

For practice before the event, accommodations at Bisley would be placed at the disposal of competing teams and visitors were assured of convenient and comfortable arrangements. The earnest hope that as many nationalities as possible would take part in the match closed the British NRA proposition.

A strong showing of the world's best military shooters at the Bisley contest would stimulate and promote relations among the planet's riflemen's organizations. Unofficially, but very much on the record, it was the fervent desire of the global rifle-shooting fraternity that the 1903 shoot would continue to revitalize the lamentably declining interest in rifle marksmanship and the glory days of international competition.

In early April, Congress appropriated $2,500 for the purchase of a trophy and other prizes. At the same time, an effort was made to pull together the best rifle shots from the service branches and National Guard at a tryout for the coveted spots on the Palma team. In April, news of a May 18-20 qualifying competition was broadcast in the various military journals, and pinned to the bulletin boards of National Guard drill halls throughout New England.

On May 10, 1903, it was announced that NRA Secretary Lt. Albert E. Jones, along with Col. E.J. Dimmick, had made arrangements with the Army Ordinance Dept. for "new, carefully selected rifles" to be used by the team traveling to England. This action reportedly had the full blessing of the Secretary of War. The rifles alluded to were arsenal Krags specially re-barreled by Harry Pope, the most celebrated barrelmaker of the generation, during his 1901-06 association with the Stevens Arms and Tool Co.

Meanwhile, a panel for seven appointees selected the eight-man team from the personnel that competed for a position during the team trials. Guard units in four states and the District of Columbia sent representatives to the Sea Girt, New Jersey range to try out.

When the score sheets were turned in the afternoon of May 20, the selection committee eliminated all but the top eight men.

Twenty-nine year old Cpl. Charles B. Winder of the 6th Ohio National Guard fired the highest score in the team trials, assuring him a spot on the Palma squad.

Since 1889, Sgt. James "Jim" H. Keough frequented the famed Walnut Hill range, took up the Schuetzen games, and developed into a top-flight offhand rifleman. All of Sgt. Keough's military shooting prior to 1903 had been with the 45-caliber Springfield, but the Krag's newness didn't prevent him from firing well enough to earn a competitor's position. Sgt. Keough was with the Massachusetts Volunteer Militia. Cpl. William Byfield "Doc" Short was the pride of the 7th New York National Guard, and had been a member of regimental teams since 1896.

Representing the First Regiment, District of Columbia National Guard was accomplished long-range shooter Dr. George E. Cook. At the National Matches in 1902, his rank was listed as Private.

Without question, the best-recognized member of the 1903 squad was Lt. K.K.V. Casey, that era's Ty Cobb of long-distance riflery. "Long Range Casey", as he was well known, was a regular at Sea Girt, and had taken the Wimbledon Cup in 1902. Casey was an officer in the 71st New York National Guard, a unit which contributed two additional shooters to the 1903 Palma cause. Lt. Arthur E. Wells also made the cut. So did Sgt. George H. Doyle.

Only one man was able to brag to his grandchildren that he was the only United States Marine on the great 1903 Palma Team, and this was Leatherneck 2nd Lt. Thomas Holcomb. This clean-shaven, twenty-three-year-old was a seasoned competitor. He'd made the Marine Corps rifle team in 1901 and 1902. This was his second Palma. He'd shot at the one at Rockcliffe—the Canadian range—the year previously. Young Lt. Holcomb had been called from his station in the West Indies to try out for the 1903 team.

The team and coaches practiced industriously, isolated and improved their weaknesses, and demonstrated a noticeably high degree of raw talent and skill. The press was allowed to observe on occasion. The remarks of one reporter, a staffer for *FOREST AND STREAM*, gave the rifle-shooting community cause to share his expectations: *"Compared with the scores of prior teams, both American and British, the practice work of the American team is good warrant for a reasonable faith in their victory and the return of the Palma to America, where it lay undisturbed so many decades."*

In England, pre-match interest attached to the event was unexpectedly high. Many Americans, traveling abroad, had expressed their intention to be in attendance. King Edward, it was rumored, was a fan, and planned on personally presenting the Palma trophy to the winners at Mansion House in London.

By the first of June, the U.S. NRA was forced to revise upwards its Palma expense estimation to ten

The American team of riflemen practicing in England.

thousand dollars. Contributions had been slow and meager, a barometer of American excitement, it was feared. By mid-June, the total was still $3,000 short of the goal. A notice in *FOREST AND STREAM* for June 13, 1903 alerted the readership—many of whom were not in the pauper class—to the predicament in the hope of attracting a benefactor or two. The *F&S* correspondent didn't beat around the bush: *"Before the team sails, there is a hope that some gentlemen who are patriotic and wealthy will come to the front with the required subscriptions."*

The 1903 meeting for the Palma trophy would be the strongest one to date. Besides the U.S. and its perennial nemesis Great Britain, France would send over eight of its finest. A Norwegian team would come, too. England encouraged its colonies to assemble teams. Australian and Canadian teams would be firing their Enfields at Bisley. From Southern Africa, the little nation of Natal had committed its eight best snipers.

The broadened competition, by all accounts of the sporting weeklies, was expected to make for an interesting contest. Rhodesia, Switzerland, and Austria had also pledged to be there, but for one reason or another, didn't post. Four men from the expected Russian team showed up. Because they couldn't comply with the regulation requiring a team of eight members, they weren't permitted to shoot. The other half of the team — their comrades from Siberia — had not allowed for the thirteen day difference between the British and Julian calendar that the Russians were still using.

On Saturday June 13, 1903, the American team sailed to England on the steamer *Lucania*. Accompanying the team was an eleven-man entourage consisting of coaching, support, and administrative personnel. Lt. J.G. Ewing of the South Carolina Guard acted as the Quartermaster for the unit, and one must suppose that there was an armorer amongst the crew. Also boarding the Cunard liner that day was team captain Col. Leslie C. Bruce, a veteran international shooter from New York. The team's adjutant, Col. J.H. Wells, another of the 71st New York, also marched over *Lucania's* gangplank. Private Daniel C. Meyer of the 7th New York was part of this military embarkation. Pvt. Meyer had failed to make a place on the team during the Sea Girt tryouts, but had done some fine shooting over the previous six months, and on the strength of this was taken along as an alternate.

When the team and its escorts arrived at Bisley a few days later, they received their billeting assignments, drew their bedding, and proceeded straightaway to uncase their Krags and familiarize themselves with the new range. They spent the best part of the next three weeks dedicated to the task of practicing and preparing themselves for the all-important competition. As the foreign marksmen arrived from around the globe, the American Guardsmen and one Marine welcomed and fraternized with their strangely-uniformed peers as best their language barrier would allow.

The morning of July 11, 1903 brought a strong sunshine, a calm atmosphere, and good light. The 800-yard matches were shot under these favorable conditions.

The course of fire was fifteen shots per man at each range of 800, 900, and 1,000 yards. Each contestant was allowed to shoot from any position he chose, so long as it didn't involve an artificial rest. Each team was required to complete their firing in the one hundred and five minute time allotment.

The target was the standard National Rifle Assn. Target. It was twelve feet long by six feet high. The bull was three feet in diameter. Getting a bullet within its boundaries was worth five points. There was no **V** or **X** ring. A four and a half foot diameter circle surrounding the bull was referred to as the **center**. A competitor placing his shot in this ring was awarded four points. A six-foot square encasing the bullseye and center was known as the **Inner**. An inner shot, often called a "magpie", was worth three points on the scorecard. The two ends of the target, each side six by three feet, were designated the **Outers**. Any shot straying into the outer area only had a two-point value. Thus, the fifteen-shot course for each range had a maximum possible value of 75 points, or an aggregate of 225 points for the three distances. The teams fired in two four-man divisions, each completing their scores before the next went to the line. The Americans took one hour and fifteen minutes to complete their strings, the first team to finish at eight hundred.

Private Cook dropped just one point in a stellar performance, while Sgt. Keough held hard to register a

73, Cpl. Winder was in there with a 71, but Lt. Casey had trouble finding the range, winding up with a 69. Doyle and Holcomb each posted a 66. With his 65 points, Lt. Wells was by himself in the basement.

When the firing at the 800-yard line was completed, the British team was in the lead with a team total of 554, three points ahead of the Americans and eighteen points in front of the Canadians. Australia and tiny Natal finished fourth and fifth. Turning in a measly 441 points, six less than the Norwegians, the French were already in trouble.

Official match rules allowed shooting from any position that didn't incorporate a rest of some sort. The British all shot from prone, as did the Canadians with one exception, who shot from the back—or supine—position. Many considered this to be steadier than prone. Getting into this posture was accomplished by passing the rifle butt over the right shoulder and holding it with the left hand, which was placed behind the head. The trigger was pressed with the right thumb. Some of the Americans favored this position, too.

Long-distance shooting was unfamiliar to the team from Norway. They had made the trip to Bisley because they knew they could shoot. Their procedure was to fire right on, and as they went along, judge the wind and light effects as best they could collectively do by noting the result of the last shot. The practice of prone shooting was a foreign thought to the Norwegians. A nation of offhand shooters, they struggled to make the horizontal adjustment. Shooting from standing at the 800-yard practice sessions, they succeeded in impressing a small army of spectators. Under the circumstances, the Norwegian team did remarkably well at the new Palma game.

The Norwegians showed up with their military 6.5mm Krag-Jorgensen rifles. The front sight was equipped with a traversing movement, operated by a key. It is not clear if they had a special cartridge worked up for their guns or not. What is a matter of record is the powder charge: 34.3 grains of a coarse leaflet powder propellant. A .263-inch 155.3-grain projectile was separated from the powder charge by a small wisp of "cotton wool".

The ammunition provided the American competitive 30-caliber shooter prior to 1902 produced an irregular elevation. It was the source of endless frustration, and the consensus was that the 30-40 cartridge could tolerate some improvement. Dr. Walter Hudson contacted William Morgan Thomas, the highly regarded ballistic engineer at the Union Metallic Cartridge Co., and Thomas determined that the problem was with the bullet. He set about to develop a metal-cased bullet specifically for match shooting with the Krag cartridge. Reportedly, Dr. Hudson had some measure of influence in the bullet's design, and the 220-grain windbucker became famous, for a while, as the Hudson-Thomas bullet.

The U.S. team used them quite successfully in 1902, and it was these bullets, propelled by 36.2 grains of W.A. powder, that the 1903 team shot through their Krags at Bisley. The Pope-barreled Krags that the U.S. squad was issued had a special 1:8-inch twist. Numerous tests by the era's riflemen had shown that the standard ten-inch twist was insufficient to carry the 220-grain Krag bullet point foremost all the way to the 1,000-yard target. This difficulty could be overcome by using the more wind sensitive 200-grain projectile, but the service cartridge, and the 1903 Palma ammunition was loaded with the heavier bullets. Dr. Hudson wrote in January of 1903: *I had a barrel with an eight inch twist fitted to my Krag, and it seems to entirely remedy the wobbling tendency of bullets at the long range.*

Not all the service rifles of competing nations were blessed with rear battle sights suitable for a match-shooting application. In this regard, the Model 1901 Krag back sight was "exceptionally favored", as one reporter put it. The Krag was fitted with an aperture "peep hole" rear sight with a nice means of making minute adjustment for windage. An English columnist, writing at the time of the 1903 Match, conceded the advantage in rifle sighting to the Americans. The president of the French NRA considered the Krag with this sight, the envy of each foreign competitor on the firing line, to be a "match rifle less the spirit level."

The British team depended upon the intricate sight attached to the breech end of their Enfields. For elevation, a sliding bar could be microscopically adjusted with a Vernier. A combination of vertical white-painted lines provided references for making fine windage adjustments. The colonial teams from Canada, Australia, and Natal were issued the same equipment and ammunition that the English team was using.

The British recognized shortcomings in their own 303 ammunition, most notably its failure to maintain uniform velocities. This condition manifested itself most profoundly since the new long-range target was narrowed by two feet and not increased in height. Commercial firms of English ammunition loaders and armorers put their heads together in a united effort at improving the cartridge and thus increase the odds of keeping the Palma prize on the eastern side of the Atlantic. Some insisted that the powder charge be increased, improving upon the round's "feeble ballistics." Others maintained that a heavier bullet was more desirable.

The only point of agreement was that something needed to be done if British teams were to remain competitive. Experiments followed, and the new Palma 303 cartridge was the outcome. The Kings-Norton Metal Co., who produced the new long-range cartridge, provided the details on the round. Cordite was the propellant - 34.4 grains of it. Bullet weight was set forth at 225 grains. Mean velocities at the muzzle were measured at 2,023 fps, with a deviation of only 5.6 fps. For the 1903 match, the British had what they needed, an extraordinarily consistent match load.

The Frenchmen came to Bisley with their queer-looking, but rugged, Lebel Model 1886 8mm rifles. Without doubt, the Frenchmen were the worst served by way of rifle sights. The Lebel's sight was a primitive affair—even as a battle sight. Crudely notched, adjustable for elevation only, it was absolutely hopeless for long-distance match shooting, and the French shooters found themselves to be very much handicapped by the crudity their country's ordnance department had elected to supply them with. The front sight blade was broad enough to obliterate even the 900-yard target. One member spoke for the entire French team when he wrote: *We shot to hit an area represented by a target; the Americans and the English shot to hit a particular spot on the target.* The participation in the Bisley shoot convinced the French unit of the necessity for better sights. Shortly after the Match, they petitioned the French Minister in charge: *The morale of the troops will fall if equipment does not come up to scratch, particularly when it relates to sights on rifles.*

An unknown someone disassembled a French cartridge back in 1903 and provided us with the particulars on their loads. The specimen contained 42.5 grains of a coarse powder. Between powder and bullet were two wads; one of jute, the other of wax.

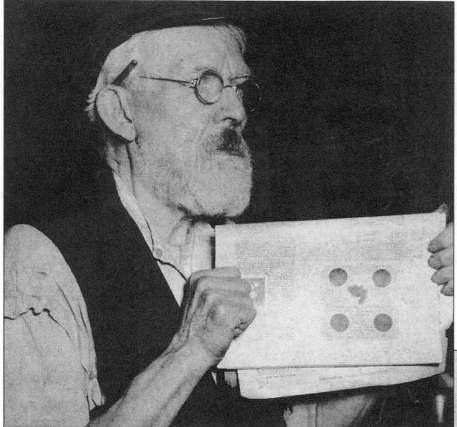

H.M. Pope, the barrel-maker. *Courtesy Michael Petrov.*

and intensity, for each individual shot. This procedure, a French competitor observed from a distance, always based each shot on the preceding one, and the British system would tend to accumulate errors, he theorized. Regardless, the British team was highly adept at their method.

It was maintained that the Americans were still comparatively green at the art of wind judging with a spotting scope, or telescope as they were referred to in 1903. The British were considered much more practiced at observing the drift of the mirage across the range, thought to be a much more reliable indicator of conditions affecting the flight of the bullet than the behavior of the wind flags. Experienced coaching was the specialty of the British team. Colonels Gibbs and Hopton continually peered through

Pope, an early photograph. *Courtesy Michael Petrov.*

The .321-inch bullet weighed 231.8 grains. Our dissector noted that the neck of the cartridge case was squeezed inordinately hard around the bullet, leaving a ring-shaped depression around it.

Before the planet's best rifle shooters walked back to their 900-yard firing points, the weather suddenly turned sour, and the competitors struggled to make allowances for the puffy wind that had come up. The wind's strength may have been variable, but its direction was constant. The Brits would have preferred a fickle breeze more familiar to them; blowing up- and down-range, then switching to one side or fishtailing to the other. Later it was written that this was a wind that favored the Americans. They were accustomed to mini-zephyrs such as this "genuine bit of American weather."

Coach Col. Bruce held his men for six seconds while he studied the tricky conditions. After careful observation, he gave the word. Sgt. Keough was the first to fire, and he sent six successive bullets through the five-point ring. Sgt. Keough shot a 69 to lead the U.S. team. Lt. Casey was a point behind him. Doyle and Short each contributed 66 points to the team aggregate. Pvt. Cook and Cpl. Winder added 63 points apiece. The Marine shot a 61. Low man again at 900 with a 59 was Lt. Wells.

When the dust had settled and the scores tallied, the Americans had taken over the lead with 1066 total points. Great Britain, still very much a contender, trailed by a mere eight points. Canada and Australia were in third and fourth places. Natal and Norway were hopelessly out of the picture but were contented that they wouldn't finish last. The French seemed to be destined to remain in that position.

The well-disciplined U.S. marksmen used a technique in dealing with the fickle forces of the wind, a trick picked up at the previous year's Palma, it was said. When there was a lull, the Americans shot into the bull as quickly as possible—one right after the other—as rapidly as the target marker would allow. When conditions were less uniform, the Guardsmen could afford to wait them out. At one point, they refrained from firing for a full ten minutes. The British team, in contrast, fired with a methodic regularity, doping each variance in the breezes' direction

their powerful telescopes and relayed their windage assessments to the firing line. On the other hand, the American coaches reported minimally with their men. It was inferred that the Guardsmen were all first-class individual marksmen, and were more than capable of coaching themselves and the team amongst themselves.

On the 1,000-yard range, there were concerns expressed that the possibility of collusion between shooters and scorers was a realistic threat and officials devised a scheme to safeguard against it. Teams drew lots for position, and the pit crews were not aware of which team they were scoring. The U.S. team was placed on the far right, next to the Norwegians. Successively to Norway's left were the French and the team from Natal. The rival English team was positioned on the extreme left of the range. The afternoon's shooting at 1,000 drew a fair number of spectators, many of whom were distinguished. The Naval Attaché of the British Embassy, Capt. Stockton, accompanied Ambassador and Mrs. Choate. Sir Aubrey Fletcher, President of the Army Rifle Assn., was also in the crowd.

On the long range, the men had to shoot from one hill to another, and the variable currents of wind needed to be gauged to a nicety. The French marksmen went on record as being at a disadvantage because they had never shot at targets that far way before. Their usual "long range" had always been 300 meters and their cartridge had been developed around this distance. In order to learn, even at the expense of not making a good global showing, the Frenchmen shot this portion of the match as naive apprentices. Apart from inexperience, there were other crosses for the French to bear. Retrospectively, the team would attribute its lackluster performance to poor training, poor organization, and poor equipment. The entire course of "training" had consisted of two half-days shooting at Maison's Lafitte. Bisley's translators managed only to confound the men as to the program and the match's rifle and ammunition restrictions. More importantly, the French Lebel rifles, competitive as they potentially were, had been furnished with that absurdly inadequate sighting arrangement. A small number of French bullets ricocheted into the scoring rings at the 1,000-yard mark. They were not counted as hits.

Lt. Wells, the weak sister at 800 and 900 yards, redeemed himself at 1,000. He and Pvt. Cook were tied for high man slot with a 68 each. The Corp's Lt. Holcomb was a point behind. Sgt. Keough shot a respectable 64. "Long Range Casey" we must assume, was disappointed with his 60-point effort. Three men with 59 points each shared last place at 1,000: Winder, Doyle, and Short.

Prior to the 1,000-yard segment of the match, the aggregates of the leading nations were so close together that the situation was far from being decisive. When the final tally was posted, however, the U.S. team had racked up a total of 1,570 points out of a possible 1,800, edging out the British sharpshooters by a scant 15 points. The Canadians, with 1,518 took home third place. The team from Down Under shot a not-so-bad 1,501 for fourth. The African riflemen from Natal were 101 points behind the Australians. With 1,241 points, the Norwegians were one notch out of the bottom of the list. 1,230 points, the score of the French team, incidentally, was held as an example of how far long-range riflery had progressed by 1903. Fifteen years prior, the point total that secured last place, would have won the Palma Match handily. Another remarkable point in the contest was the fact that this was the first Palma event in which the English and American teams did not miss the target once. This seems to be particularly significant when we consider that at the 1902 Palma, the English missed the target twelve times and the Americans seven.

Lt. A.S. Jones with the Ordnance Dept. of New Jersey and Secretary of the NRA was among the party accompanying the team to Bisley. Lt. Jones attributed the eight men's performance to teamwork. *"Our boys cannot be given enough credit for the way they overcame every known obstacle. They coached each other almost to perfection, and to this system of teamwork our victory is due. Before a man fired, the men on each side of him took careful observations of the wind and mirage, and when they seemed to agree the shooter let go, and the result was invariably first class."*

After the conclusion of the Match, Major General Lord Cheylesmore presented the Palma Trophy to the victorious American team, congratulating them on their skill and success. The award ceremony was conducted in conjunction with a banquet, at which the Duke of Cambridge, the President of the British Army Rifle Association, presided. It was a gala affair, highlighted by the cordial fraternizing amongst the opponents and guests. The victors were toasted, and their rifles, ammunition, and marksmanship were praised. Col. L.C. Bruce, spokesman for the American Palma team, responded that the best eight men in the United States had been required for triumph, and extended the team's thanks and appreciation for the

"fairness and courtesies" that had been extended during their stay.

A 1904 Palma, to be fired at Sea Girt, New Jersey, was already in the planning stages. Increasingly, there was talk that the once-in-a-while competition would work into an annual affair. An English spectator at Bisley, not short on finances apparently, volunteered to bankroll the Norwegians and presented them with $7,500 expense money to assure their participation the next year. England's team received $1,500, and each of the other competing nations was allowed the sum of $500. Ten teams were anticipated for the scheduled 1904 shoot. The *London Daily Telegraph* informed the American NRA that the paper would be pleased to provide a trophy.

Before the Americans left England, Lord Roberts cabled the following message: *"I am very sorry I have come too late to see you and congratulate your team on the splendid success at Bisley."* Lord Cheylesmore wired the team his wishes for a prosperous voyage. Col. Bruce responded with the following dispatch: *"The United States rifle team and myself are honored by the kind messages from the distinguished soldier Lord Roberts and Yourself. We leave our good English friends with hearts full of gratitude."* The American team departed from Liverpool, again sailing on the *Lucania*. In a pre-departure interview Col. Bruce was quoted as saying: *"Nothing that I could say would give the English proper credit for the splendid way they treated us. The result of the International shoot shows that the best marksmen outside America and Great Britain are from British South Africa, Canada, and Australia."*

The *Philadelphia Public Ledger* in August 1903 recorded that a committee representing the National Rifle Assn. met the home-comers. Brigadier General Bird W. Spencer led this illustrious group. There was a scattering of Colonels and Majors, and a couple of Captains, too. Also present was Dr. Walter G. Hudson, famed Schuetzen rifleman and an accomplished military rifle shooter in his own right. Four years later, Dr. Hudson would shoot with the U.S. Palma team. Winder and Casey would be among his teammates. General Spencer congratulated the champions and assured them that their victory had done a great deal to stimulate the dormant American interest in long-range rifle shooting. He promised a near-future gathering where the medals won at Bisley would be presented by Secretary of War Root.

The 1903 Palma U.S. Team. Just a few identified, as follows: *Front Row* - older man, seated in center, is L. C. Bruce. *Second Row* – fourth from left, with hands folded over rifle muzzle, is Lt. K. K. V. Casey. Second from right, with both hands on his Krag, looking into camera is C. B. Winder. *Third Row* – first on left, the young man looking to the left is U.S. Marine T. Holcomb.

Immediately before and during the match, doubts had arisen among certain members of the British executive staff as to whether the American team's Krags were strictly in conformity with the service rifle of the U.S. Army. There were strong grounds for believing that their privately-made barrels had more than four grooves, and that the twist was steeper than the known 1:10-inch pitch of the standard issue Krag rifle.

During the shoot, British officials seriously considered lodging a formal protest, but performing the proper measurements would have required special instruments, and a procedure not easily or tactfully done in the field. A fair amount of temerity to make the accusation, under the circumstances, would have likewise been necessary. The British didn't move hastily. They were aware that changes in the U.S. government service rifle were certainly pending, and they considered the probability that the interior of the team's barrels matched the bore specifications of the rifle recently approved as the new service Springfield 1903 rifle. Lacking the proof of deliberate non-compliance by the U.S. armorers to justify a formal protest, the English skeptics did the gentlemanly thing - they maintained their silence.

The British, already suspicious that all was not right, together with the rest of the literate English-speaking world, were alerted to an accusation that the American team actually shot a non-regulation arm at the Bisley matches. Foul play on the part of the American Team was charged in a newspaper article that appeared in the July 29, 1903 edition of the *Washington Evening Star*. It was authored, astonishingly enough, by a veteran Creedmoor shooter, winner of uncountable national and international marksmanship prizes including the 1880 Wimbledon Cup, the crack shot of the blackpowder era, Milton Farrow. Farrow's standing in the international community very likely lent a strong measure of credibility to the charges.

On October 26, 1903, Col. C.R. Crosse, the Secretary of the NRA of Great Britain, addressed a communication to the NRA of America, requesting explanations as to the Farrow article and demanding an answer to certain questions regarding the rifles the American team used in the contest. Under the circumstances, Col. Crosse's requirements were fairly diplomatically stated: "*I have to say that my council have no other object in view than to dispel the doubts which have arisen in connection with this match.*" On both sides of the ocean, the naturally following press comments on the subject kept the matter in a worldwide limelight. Anyone who paid attention to the considerable gossip could sense the tension, the incubating trouble and the inevitable trans-Atlantic head-butting brewing. The tremendous distances involved, the guarded consideration this delicate matter demanded from all parties, and the intervals between meetings of the separate Associations, thwarted any hope of a speedy resolution. The matter's progress prolonged well into the next year.

Col. Crosse's letter was read at an NRA Board of Director's meeting held January 19, 1904. NRA President General Spencer was instructed to reply. Spencer began his response by denying statements Farrow attributed to a Major Bell, concerning the rifles in question. Spencer's communication reminded the British NRA officials that two sets of Krag rifles were taken to Bisley. The first set, of course, was the government arsenal-standard Krags. Stevens-Pope barrels were screwed into receivers of the otherwise identical issue model of 1892 rifles that made up set #2.

UMC advertisement, August 1903.

The new service rifle, the Model of 1903, was officially adopted but unobtainable at the time. Cartridges for the new 30-caliber hadn't been perfected either. Gen. Spencer stressed the fact that Col. Bruce, the team captain, had been given strict instructions at the last moment before sailing that if the slightest objection was raised to the use of the specially barreled Krags, Set#2 was to be set aside and the match fired with the regular issue guns. At the January, 1904 NRA Director's meeting, Col. Bruce testified that the nature of the rifles was clearly understood by every team captain involved, and no objection had been raised. Prior to the match, the special Krags had been freely and publicly passed around to officers and members of the opposing teams for examination and trial if they desired. Col. Bruce proceeded to give a description of the rifles, and an explanation of the distinctive rifling pitch and form. He noted also that the rifles had been fully sanctioned by the U.S. NRA. Everyone associated with the Palma had been informed that the Americans intended to use the non-regula-

tion rifles with their special barrels, and that they openly and honestly invited opposition to that plan.

Curiously, when the U.S. decided to host a Palma at Sea Girt in 1901 - the first match in which target rifles were excluded - the NRA drafted a regulation restricting legal rifles to "the national military arm of the country they represent, without alteration of any kind."

Articles published in London's *SHOOTING TIMES* and *THE VOLUNTEER SERVICE GAZETTE* detailed how the entire matter had been gone over by selected committees of the Great Britain NRA, and these panels unanimously permitted the special Krag's use in the Bisley matches. In a letter to Col. Crosse, dated March 7, 1904, Gen. Spencer alleged that the 1:8-inch twist of the "special" service rifles was identical to the "present service arm of the U.S." According to Spencer, the new model 30-caliber Springfield adopted June 19,1903, had a 1:8-inch twist, which justified the non-standard pitch in the Palma Match Krags. Crosse fired back. He held that a rifle adopted June 19,1903 - three weeks before the con-

troversial match - could not possibly satisfy the rule which stated legal competition rifles were to be "of a pattern adopted and issued to the troops for service." Crosse's point, though worthy of the making, was a moot one. At that point in 1903, production of the 1903 Springfield had just been initiated. Had a need arisen to mobilize and arm the infantry, the troopers would have been issued the ready Krags in any event.

FOREST AND STREAM magazine was interested in determining and sharing the facts with its vast readership. In the spring of 1904, a representative of the publisher pried into the matter on his own accord. His letter to the Secretary of War posed these questions: *"In June of 1903, were specifications for a United States service rifle with eight grooves and an eight inch twist approved and adopted by the U.S. Government? If so, were any such rifles issued to the regular troops at any time in June of 1903, or subsequently. Would a rifle with an eight inch twist and eight grooves, made by a private maker, have been accepted by the United States Government in June 1903, or afterwards, as service rifles?"*

RIFLE RANGE, SEA GIRT, N. J.

Scene of the 1903 Palma tryouts.

Charged with spearing these questions was Col. Frank H. Phillips, Commander of Army Ordnance. He got right to the point: *"To all of which I reply, No."*

As an international courtesy, a specimen of the very latest M1903 Springfield service arm was shipped to the British War Office by the U.S. Dept. of War. The rifle was examined by a panel of experts who measured the rate of twist as one turn in ten inches, and agreed that they'd counted no more than four grooves.

The input of U.S. competitor Dr. W.B. Short was solicited and recorded in *FOREST AND STREAM* magazine for June 11, 1904. Two weeks before the match, England's Col. Crosse approached Dr. Short and asked if the competitor's equipment would match the arms troops would be issued, should they be "sent out on service". With a soldierly directness, Short replied that the rifle barrels provided by the Stevens Arms Co. were made according to the specifications governing the rifle adopted by the War Department for use by the United States Army. The ammunition, though loaded specially for the matches, was "made by the company furnishing ammunition to the government, and identical to it." Short turned the tables and posed the same questions to the Colonel. Crosse explained that a private firm had made the 303 barrels for the British team. Afterwards the barrels were sent to a government arsenal for "viewing", or inspection, proving, and stamping with the government mark. The British ammu-

nition had also been specially loaded by an outside concern.

None of the British marksmen at Bisley in 1903 had shot a rifle made in a government plant. While rifles and ammunition used by the English were not literally of service character, they were practically so. The same could be truthfully said of the equipment drawn by the American team. General Spencer wrote sometime later: *"The advantage we derived from having the barrels made in private works was a more careful workmanship, but in every way these barrels were constructed to conform to the government pattern. The reason we had them made was that we knew the British team would do the selfsame thing."* Lt. A.S. Jones, in cabling home the match results on July 11, 1903, admitted with no hidden enthusiasm; *"The truth of the matter is, we owe the victory mainly to the barrels and ammunition used." Jones' remark was never common knowledge.*

The *Washington Evening Post* recorded H.M. Pope's input into the overzealous British pronouncements that the U.S. barrels had been "excessively perfected." The *Post* had telegraphed Pope for his reply, which was printed in the June 3, 1904 edition. The solicitation of Mr. Pope's thoughts may have been prompted by Milton Farrow's published statement that the Stevens-Pope barrels were actually an enlarged 30-caliber bore measuring .311-inch.

External dimensions of the Stevens-Pope and arsenal-built barrels were identical, Pope explained.

Internally, he elaborated, there was "somewhat of a difference" dimensionally, and this "superior" difference rested on three points. Pope carefully cut eight grooves, rather than the government-standard four. Secondly, groove depth was a uniform .00275-inch compared to the customary .004-inch found in the issue Krag barrels. The shallower rifling of the Stevens-Pope barrel generated less internal friction and afforded a gas-tight fit. As a practical consequence, velocity was boosted by a presumably chronographed 30 fps over a conventionally rifled tube, resulting in a very slightly flatter trajectory. Finally, the service arms rate of twist was 1:10 inches. Pope gave his barrels a quicker 1:8 inch pitch. In addition, Pope purposefully finished off the corners of the grooves by very slightly rounding them, rather than making them angular. The ordinary Krag piece often left the machines with their lands shaped the same way, but this was due mainly to dulling of the cutting tools. The rounded edges kept the barrel from fouling, an important consideration, according to Harry Pope.

An *Evening Post*-Pope telephone conversation supplemented Harry's telegram, during which he leaked a little nugget that was not public knowledge in 1903. Two of the Krags shot at the Ottawa Palma the year before were of a special pattern. One of the experimental rifles had a barrel with two grooves, the other had four. The rate of twist in each was one turn in eight inches. It is believed that Dr. Hudson drew

The International Rifle Trophy.

"Through the courtesy of our contemporary The Spirit of the Times, we are enabled to present to our readers a remarkably handsome cut of the trophy contested for last week by the picked riflemen of Scotland, Ireland, Australia, Canada, and the United States.

"The design is a Roman banner, after the style of the battle flag of the Roman Legions, and was suggested by General Martin McMahon, Chairman of the Trophy Committee N.R.A. Messrs. Tiffany & Co., of Union Square, New York City, are the manufacturers, and Mr. J. H. Whitehouse the designer. The trophy is seven feet six inches high by twenty-four inches wide, and is composed of iron, steel, silver, and gold. To commence at the bottom, the staff is of iron, four inches wide, and is composed of iron, steel, silver, and gold. To commence at the bottom, the staff is of iron, with copper fillets; from this staff hangs the banner, made of solid iron, the front being inlaid with a tracing of gold over which the is the inscription, in incrusted silver, and partly raised, the bottom having a deep fringe of gold. Hanging in front, and surrounding this banner, is a series of copper and silver laurel garlands, on which to commemorate the date of the matches and names of the winners. The banner bar is of semi-bright copper, and represents the fasces of the Roman lectors, and as the trophy is an emblem of peace and good-will, the axe is dropped. To this bar is attached a smaller bar or plate of solid iron, copper edged, with the Latin motto Palma (crown of victory), in raised silver letters, while in front of the plate hangs pendant a large silver wreath. Immediately over this bar or plate stands an eagle of half-bright copper, resting on a Fulmen. On the face of the banner is the following inscription: "In the name of the United States of America, to the Riflemen of the World." The reverse of the banner is inlaid with the $, or mark of American Federation, after the manner of the Fleur-de-lis, on the banners of France." *Forest and Stream*

Milton Farrow in his prime.

one of these rifles. Everyone with the need to know was aware of this, yet no objection whatever had been made. These guns were not protested by the Englishmen, Pope theorized, "possibly because the British team won." Another disclosure that crackled across the telephone wires was that the contention that the Americans were in violation of the rules of the Palma had actually been initiated by officials with the Canadian team.

In a cable dated June 3, 1904, it was learned that Col. Crosse went on record that he absolutely denied that the question of the American barrels was ever brought before an official British NRA counsel or committee that he was associated with, at any time before or after the Bisley match. General Spencer responded that his information was derived from certain London sporting papers, which very clearly stated that the matter of the barrels had gone before a select committee of Britain's NRA, and by unanimous consent, this body permitted the U.S. team to use them in the competition. These periodicals had been the source of his quotations, he explained. Gen. Spencer summarized: *"The members of the British team knew before the Bisley*

Match that the Americans had these rifles, and furthermore, the character of the rifles. There is not the slightest doubt about that. But I want to reiterate that I have never made a statement that the American rifles had been inspected and approved by a committee of the British association; I merely quoted two English periodicals which stated this to be a fact."

A notice in *FOREST AND STREAM* for June 11, 1904 reviewed the high points of the May 31st meeting of Britain's NRA. Of special interest to the American riflemen were the details concerning the Palma question. Apparently, the meeting had been called for the purpose of clearing up the issue. President Lord Cheylesmore presided. The correspondence between Col. Crosse and Gen. Spencer, concerning "informal" objections to the Pope-barreled Krags was read and discussed. Spencer's efforts to make clear that the American team acted in good faith were convincing and successful. In the end, the British NRA agreed that no formal protest would be made. Lord Cheylesmore decreed that England's NRA had no desire to change the result of the 1903 Palma, or to evoke a bitterness that might endure. The Executive

Committee of the American NRA met in Washington on June 11, 1904 to consider the proper steps to finally resolve the issue. After carefully analyzing all the facts and correspondence in connection with the unpleasant controversy, they adopted a resolution that effectively stated the difference of opinion that had arisen and the negative publicity that was generated was regrettable. In addition, without a dissenting voice, it was agreed upon that the captain of the American team made no secret as to the character of the Pope-barreled rifles, and although he believed their use to be entirely proper, the difference of opinion would never have reached that present point had he *OFFICIALLY* submitted the guns for approval. Col. Bruce had been given explicit instructions, from the President of the NRA, to do so.

Most importantly, indefinitely prolonging the arguments of the Krag's conformity with regulations would serve no good purpose. Each panelist realized that, in the meantime, serious harm to competitive military rifle shooting the world over would be the inevitable result. By unanimous vote, the NRA committee agreed to return the Palma trophy immediately to the NRA of Great Britain. A telegram, sent to the New York location where the trophy was stored, ordered its packing and shipment back to England. Britain's NRA graciously accepted custody of the trophy and agreed to hold it until the victors of the next Palma earned the right to carry it home.

The most regrettable and tragic outcome of the meeting and the jumble of "whereases" that comprised the resulting resolution was the association's decision to withdraw the planned Palma competition from the NRA program for 1904. This action, of course, dealt a severe blow to the sport that the 1903 event was intended and expected to promote. Once the matter was disposed of, it was effectively opened for public discussion. Typically, *FOREST AND STREAM* magazine took an editorial stance on controversial and debatable issues such as this one, and the surrender of the Palma trophy was no exception. Days after the status of the trophy was officially settled, the journal's opinion was given the whole of Page One for the June 10, 1904 issue. Prior to this date, the *F&S* staff had restrained themselves from a rash judgment of the NRA. The kournal pointed its accusing finger at the officials heading that organization. To begin with, the association's censure of

Col. Bruce was wholly undeserved. The real pertinent mistake, the paper contended, was the sending of the Americans abroad with two superficially similar, but radically unlike, sets of rifles. The Pope-barreled Krag was either a service rifle, or it was not. If it was, Col. Bruce's order to submit it for approval was unnecessary. If it was not, the guns should have not been used at all. Furthermore, the specific instruction to retire the special set of Krags only if they were objected to as actually an admission of an irregularity that could not easily been evaded or excused. The NRA's official plea, offered to justify the use of the Pope barrels, was that no one objected to them. The F&S critic maintained that this reasoning, if swallowed as sound, would have permitted the use of any kind of rifle. Also broadcast here for the first time was the fact that no other team captain submitted their rifles for approval or disapproval, and none suggested a need for doing so.

This wasn't an issue confined between National Rifle Associations of two nations separated by an ocean, the editor intimated. He wrote: *"The real issue is between the British people and the American people. If the rifles were irregular, the American people have a right to know it fully, definitely, and conclusively. As the matter now stands, there is an evasiveness which by the world at large will be construed as guilt."* While the editorialist had written harshly regarding the U.S. NRA, he appeared to be sympathetic with the actions of the British, when he addressed the matter of the privately-made barrels of the British team: *"...while the British did have some special barrels, the British government had officially approved them as regular. Therefore, they are out of the controversy."* He snidely added: *"Even if the British had been wrong, it is a weak plea to justify wrongdoing by others."*

There was considerable gossip, in the press and on the street, rather freely alleging that the English were simply "bad losers". *FOREST AND STREAM* confronted the idle talk squarely: *"Such assertion is the weakest rant."* At Bisley, the paper pointed out, the British accepted defeat "manfully and pleasantly", and didn't hesitate to lavish sincere congratulations and honor upon the U.S. team. Subsequent developments on the service rifle question, here and at many points abroad, was the source of the trouble. *"The English had a perfect right to know the facts fully and freely,"* F&S defended. *"in all this,*

there is nothing to show a bad loser." That the F&S editorial reaction was overly critical of the NRA was a widely-held opinion throughout the summer of 1904.

The staff at widely circulated *OUTING* delved into the unhappy postmortem controversy. The British use of privately-made barrels on their Enfields, "viewed" or not, made England's peevish protest "a case of the pot calling the kettle black." Too, the magazine was overly critical of its scapegoat, Capt. Leslie Bruce. In a 1904 number, Bruce was publicly censured across the pages by Caspar Whitney, who wrote: *"Had Captain Bruce obeyed instructions, the first duty of an officer, he would have saved the association (NRA) from this controversy and spared America the slander of implied deceit."*

The publisher of *FIELD AND STREAM*, just getting established, editorialized a brief homespun solution far too simple to work. In essentials: *"Equip each team with the same rifle and re-shoot the match. The winner keeps the trophy."*

One of the few concerns to have profited from the ordeal was the ammunition contractor. The Union Metallic Cartridge Co. made promotional use of the U.S. "victory." In commemoration, the outfit offered a souvenir cartridge of the type used to win the match to any *FOREST AND STREAM* reader who would furnish the necessary stamp.

1903 was a good year for Cpl. C. B. Winder. He did well at Bisley and came home to win the Leech Cup in the same 12-month period. Winder's name became a familiar one to single-shot rifle buffs. As a Captain, he designed the Winder version of the Winchester Lo-Wall Musket. As a Lt. Colonel, Winder also made the 1907 Palma team.

Sgt. Keough continued to be a highly-skilled National Match competitor with the Massachusetts

Volunteers until 1911. As a Captain, he established a new range record at Sea Girt in 1912. In June of 1910, Keough traveled from his home in Wakefield, Mass. to London. Of 50 Americans at the International Small Bore Rifle Match, Keough, one point shy of a possible, was at the top of the winner's list.

Cpl. W.B. Short fired for the 7th New York for four more years, and as part of the N.Y. State team at the National Matches until Taft was out of the White House. He was high man at Creedmoor in 1906. Promoted to Lt. Short, he captured the Nevada Trophy in 1911. In so doing, he established a new record at the 1,200-yard match. Dr. Cook continued to shoot well. In 1904, he was able to put his name on the coveted Wimbledon Cup. Before he was finished, he won the Leech Cup too. In 1904, he placed first in the Long Range Aggregate Match at Sea Girt, and came in second in the Seabury and Spencer Matches.

Captain Kenyon K.V. Casey made the Palma team again in 1907, 1912, and 1913. In 1907, he went on to win the Wimbledon. In 1908, he competed with the Olympic team, won the Wimbledon again, and picked up the Leech Cup. A tireless experimenter, Casey went to work for Du Pont in 1905, heading up their smokeless powder division. In 1920, Major Casey was entrusted with the hand selection of the rifles for the U.S. Olympic team.

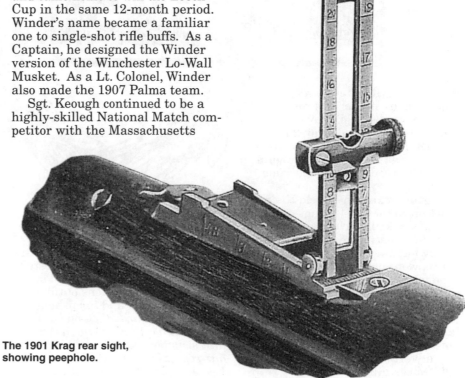

The 1901 Krag rear sight, showing peephole.

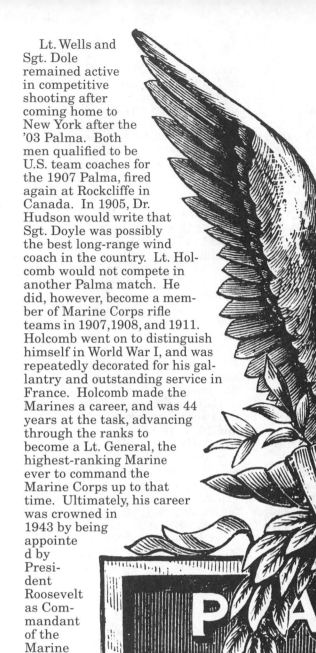

Lt. Wells and Sgt. Dole remained active in competitive shooting after coming home to New York after the '03 Palma. Both men qualified to be U.S. team coaches for the 1907 Palma, fired again at Rockcliffe in Canada. In 1905, Dr. Hudson would write that Sgt. Doyle was possibly the best long-range wind coach in the country. Lt. Holcomb would not compete in another Palma match. He did, however, become a member of Marine Corps rifle teams in 1907, 1908, and 1911. Holcomb went on to distinguish himself in World War I, and was repeatedly decorated for his gallantry and outstanding service in France. Holcomb made the Marines a career, and was 44 years at the task, advancing through the ranks to become a Lt. General, the highest-ranking Marine ever to command the Marine Corps up to that time. Ultimately, his career was crowned in 1943 by being appointed by President Roosevelt as Commandant of the Marine Corps.

General Bird W. Spencer, NRA President and central figure in the 1904 row, died the way he might have wanted to. He passed away, 28 July 1931, at the clubhouse of his beloved Sea Girt range. His funeral service was conducted in the same building.

Steven's executives held their reaction to the 1904 goings-on until all the smoke had cleared. When they did reflect, they came across as somewhat snappish, and by the evidence, were not above holding a grudge. During 1903, the institution had been unabashedly proud of their association with the Palma, and touted their barrel's instrumentality in the match's outcome. They noted the usefulness of the point and advertised it widely. But in 1908, a certain anonymous J. Stevens Arms and Tool Co. official

finally reacted as he editorialized in *FIELD AND STREAM*'s August number. At the time, the correspondent insisted that it was the men selected for the U.S. 1903 team that had requested to be equipped with Stevens-Pope barrels, and the Stevens outfit had dutifully obliged and furnished them. *"We regarded it"*, he wrote, *"and so did all Americans, as simple and sensible sportsmanship that our representatives should have the best equipment possible. There were Army etiquette reasons for adopting*

the Krag stock instead of ours. We accepted that situation and fitted our barrels onto the Krag stocks."* He went on: *"The American team won the trophy and carried it proudly home. The English felt sore, and were not sportsmanlike in their defeat. They put up a claim that each team was supposed to use the regular rifle adapted by its war department; that in this instance it was not the man behind the gun, but the gun itself that carried victory, and that the United States government had violated the unwritten law in seeking out a private factory where it was known that the best target barrel in the world was made."*

Wholly lost or disregarded during this entire misadventure was the well-established fact that the British government had, in 1903, signed contracts with two of the private arms manufacturers in Birmingham to build a great number of new rifles for use by the British Army. Securing the resources of private plants as an auxiliary to government arsenals was thought to be a good idea (*so long as the barrels of competition rifles didn't get monkeyed with*). Even our mutual Uncle Samuel recognized the wisdom of this plan, and adopted it shortly thereafter.

Despite what did or didn't happen at Bisley in July 1903, the spirit of Palma refused to yield. The wound of 1904 healed quickly enough that the great Palma tradition survived and was renewed in 1907. It developed into, and continues to be, a celebrated international institution of goodwill. And every three years, the finest marksmen on the planet still assemble to shoot the time-honored match, and to speak the universal language understood by long-range precision riflemen. •

Engraved & Custom Gun Review

By Tom Turpin

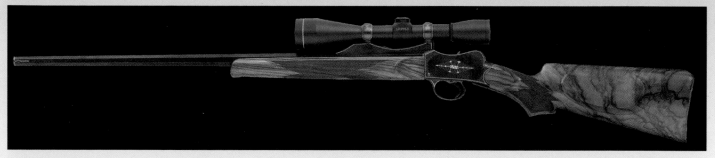

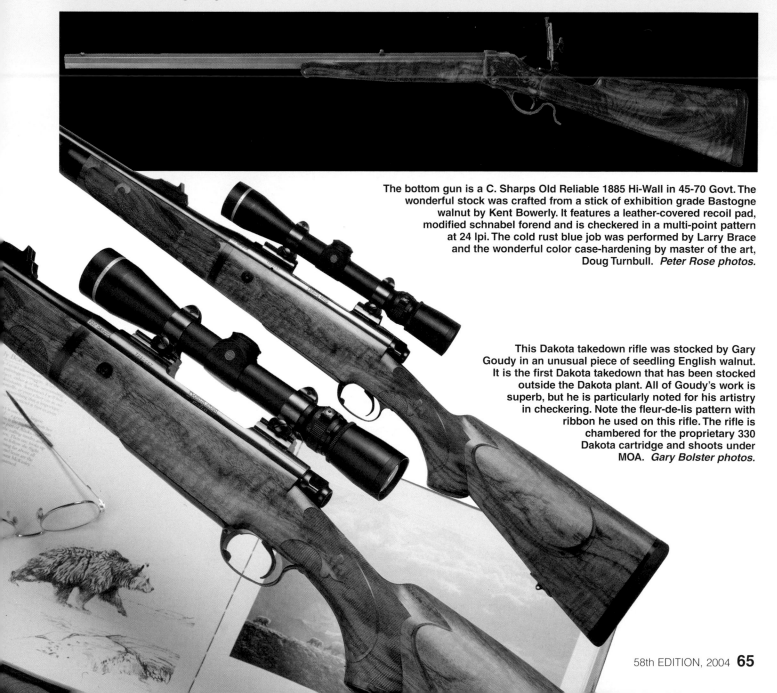

For single shot fans, two magnificent examples to whet the appetite. The top gun is a Martini Cadet. The metalwork on this rifle was executed by Robert Snapp who specializes in single shot rifles. Snapp also fitted the octagon barrel and chambered the rifle for the 223 Remington cartridge. The exhibition grade English walnut stock was crafted by Kent Bowerly. It features heel and toe plates with checkered butt, schuetzen-style grip, European-style cheekpiece, modified schnabel forend tip, and multi-point checkering, cut at 26 lpi. Robert Evans did the engraving.

The bottom gun is a C. Sharps Old Reliable 1885 Hi-Wall in 45-70 Govt. The wonderful stock was crafted from a stick of exhibition grade Bastogne walnut by Kent Bowerly. It features a leather-covered recoil pad, modified schnabel forend and is checkered in a multi-point pattern at 24 lpi. The cold rust blue job was performed by Larry Brace and the wonderful color case-hardening by master of the art, Doug Turnbull. *Peter Rose photos.*

This Dakota takedown rifle was stocked by Gary Goudy in an unusual piece of seedling English walnut. It is the first Dakota takedown that has been stocked outside the Dakota plant. All of Goudy's work is superb, but he is particularly noted for his artistry in checkering. Note the fleur-de-lis pattern with ribbon he used on this rifle. The rifle is chambered for the proprietary 330 Dakota cartridge and shoots under MOA. *Gary Bolster photos.*

Single shot rifles are very popular recipients of the gunmakers art. This Ruger No. 1 was worked over by Gary Goudy. He stocked the rifle with a superb stick of Turkish walnut and fitted heel and toe plates to the butt. He constructed a wooden plug to hide the access hole to the stock bolt and checkered the wood in-between the plates. The rifle was nicely engraved in a floral and scroll pattern by Charles Lee, and the metal finishing came from George Komadina. *Gary Bolster photos.*

Three views of a lovely custom rifle by Stephen Billeb. Starting with a '98 Mauser action, an Apex barrel, and a stock blank he acquired from fabled gunmaker Len Brownell many years ago, Billeb fashioned the components into this wonderful classic-styled 284 Winchester rifle. Steve is a charter member of the American Custom Gunmakers Guild and his wife Jan is the Executive Director of the Guild. *Courtesy Tom Alexander Photography.*

A beautiful custom Ruger No. 1 rifle stocked by Larry Amrine and engraved in an unusual but very attractive pattern by Barry Lee Hands. Chambered for my pet cartridge, the 270 Winchester, this rifle would be great in the hunting fields. *Courtesy Point Seven Studios.*

A Winchester High Wall 45-70 Express-style rifle, stocked with a piece of dense French walnut and a shape designed for offhand shooting. The rifle features an ebony forend tip and 2-leaf express sight. All work on the rifle was done by Steven Hughes. *Steven Dodd Hughes photo.*

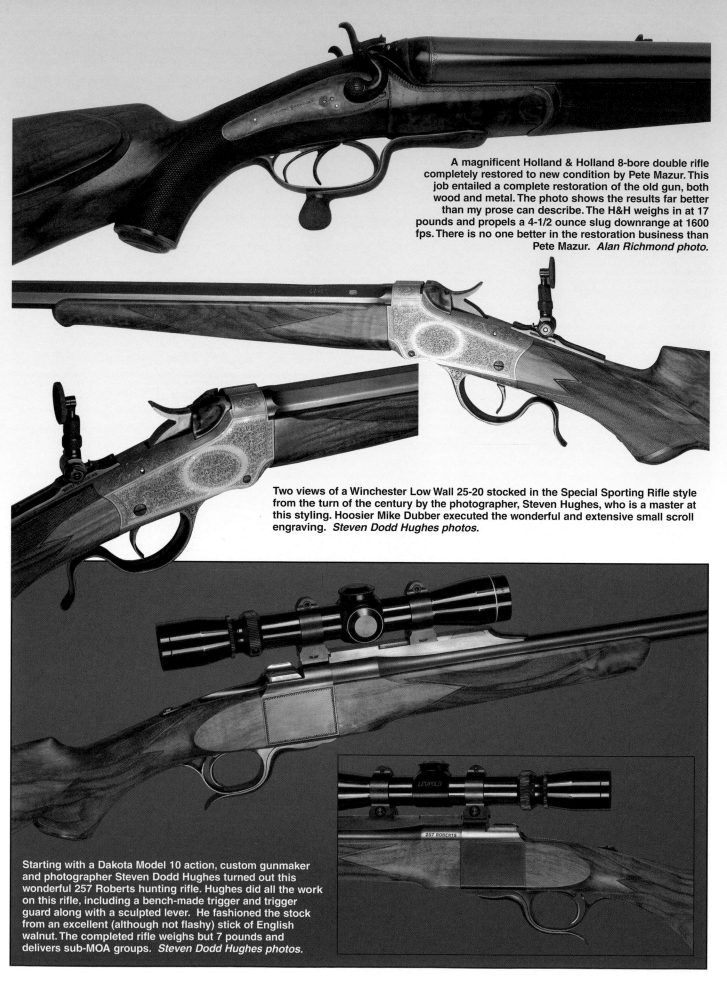

A magnificent Holland & Holland 8-bore double rifle completely restored to new condition by Pete Mazur. This job entailed a complete restoration of the old gun, both wood and metal. The photo shows the results far better than my prose can describe. The H&H weighs in at 17 pounds and propels a 4-1/2 ounce slug downrange at 1600 fps. There is no one better in the restoration business than Pete Mazur. *Alan Richmond photo.*

Two views of a Winchester Low Wall 25-20 stocked in the Special Sporting Rifle style from the turn of the century by the photographer, Steven Hughes, who is a master at this styling. Hoosier Mike Dubber executed the wonderful and extensive small scroll engraving. *Steven Dodd Hughes photos.*

Starting with a Dakota Model 10 action, custom gunmaker and photographer Steven Dodd Hughes turned out this wonderful 257 Roberts hunting rifle. Hughes did all the work on this rifle, including a bench-made trigger and trigger guard along with a sculpted lever. He fashioned the stock from an excellent (although not flashy) stick of English walnut. The completed rifle weighs but 7 pounds and delivers sub-MOA groups. *Steven Dodd Hughes photos.*

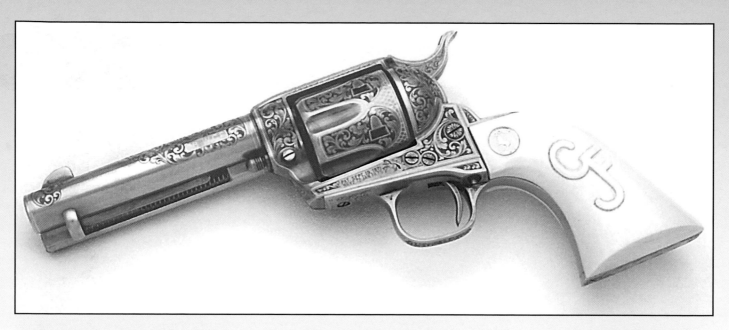

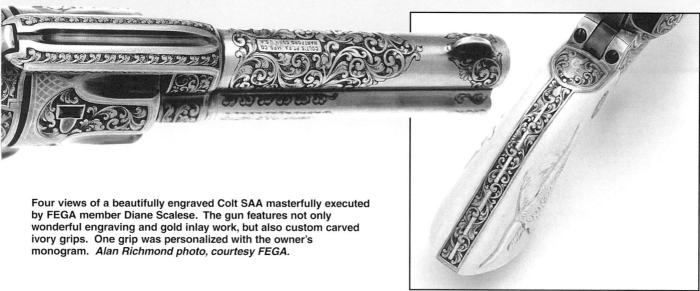

Four views of a beautifully engraved Colt SAA masterfully executed by FEGA member Diane Scalese. The gun features not only wonderful engraving and gold inlay work, but also custom carved ivory grips. One grip was personalized with the owner's monogram. *Alan Richmond photo, courtesy FEGA.*

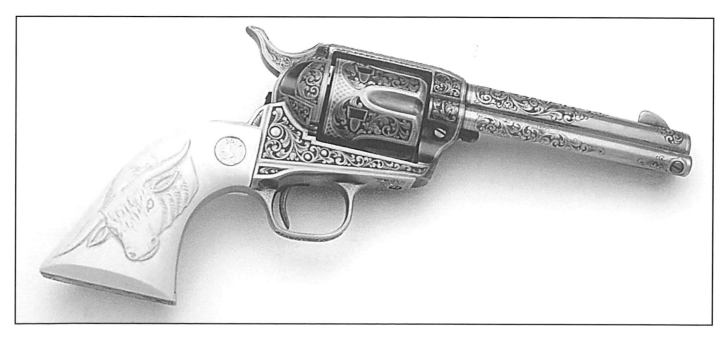

Two views of an outstandingly adorned Colt Commander Model handgun. It is sort of a rare bird as well as it is chambered for the 30 Luger cartridge. This exceptional pistol was engraved, gold inlaid and the ivory grips made and carved by my dear friend, the late Erich Boessler from Germany. *Erich Boessler photo.*

Another Colt Government Model 45 embellished in the shop of Ray Viramontez. This handgun was done to celebrate the Bicentennial of our American Revolution. *Ray Viramontez photo.*

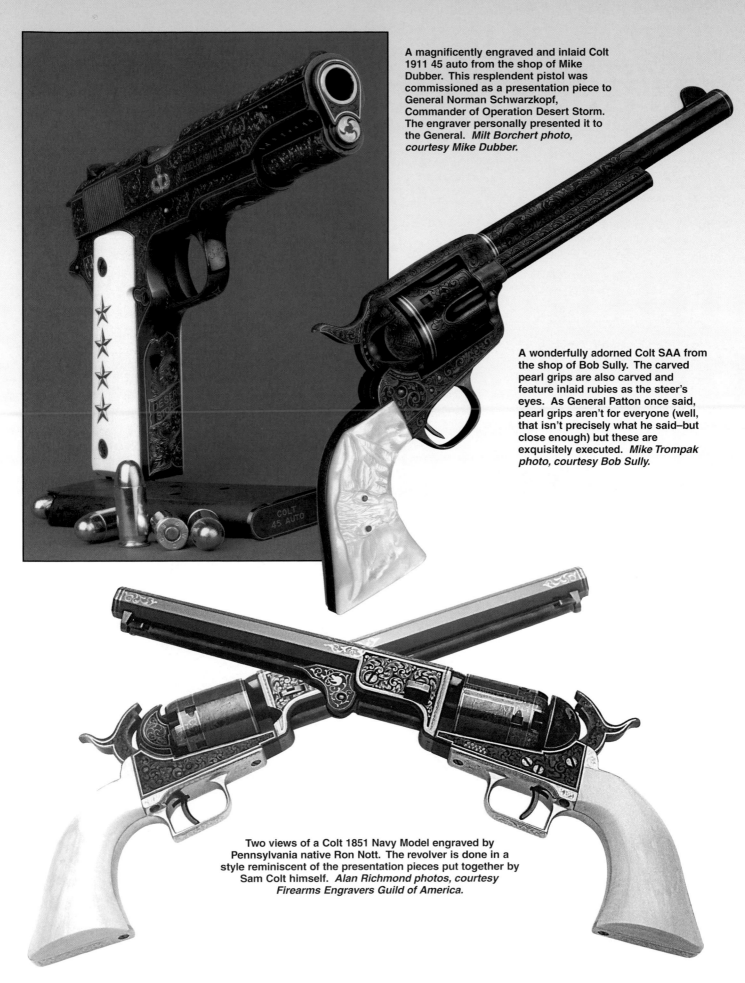

A magnificently engraved and inlaid Colt 1911 45 auto from the shop of Mike Dubber. This resplendent pistol was commissioned as a presentation piece to General Norman Schwarzkopf, Commander of Operation Desert Storm. The engraver personally presented it to the General. *Milt Borchert photo, courtesy Mike Dubber.*

A wonderfully adorned Colt SAA from the shop of Bob Sully. The carved pearl grips are also carved and feature inlaid rubies as the steer's eyes. As General Patton once said, pearl grips aren't for everyone (well, that isn't precisely what he said–but close enough) but these are exquisitely executed. *Mike Trompak photo, courtesy Bob Sully.*

Two views of a Colt 1851 Navy Model engraved by Pennsylvania native Ron Nott. The revolver is done in a style reminiscent of the presentation pieces put together by Sam Colt himself. *Alan Richmond photos, courtesy Firearms Engravers Guild of America.*

William Batterman Ruger

His destiny was to refine the gun trade in the United States

By John C. Dougan

Articles featuring Bill Ruger, his company and the products produced in his factories have appeared in almost every annual and monthly firearm publication for five decades. Thousands of pages have been penned by names that are forever woven into the fabric of American gun lore: Elmer Keith, Warren Page, Roger Barlow, Pete Kuhloff, Skeeter Skelton and John T. Amber, to name but a few. A comprehensive article could be written about the writers who promoted and tested Ruger products. Their stories portray Bill Ruger as an American icon, a genius, a living legend and Renaissance man. He has been compared to Henry Ford, Sam Colt and Enzo Ferrari; he was all of these and more.

He was intelligent and ethical, a man of vision and

passion. He loved vintage electric trains, antique automobiles and firearms. He enjoyed history and classic literature and was driven by an intense awareness of art and of order in all things; this is evident in his letters and drawings and is clearly manifested in the shapes of his gun designs.

Ruger was captivated by, and understood, mechanisms and the mechanisms that made them. He appreciated anything with moving parts and even designed and built some of his own machinery. It is only natural that he would have an affinity for automobiles and firearms.

Ruger collected antique cars designed by the engineers and coach makers of a bygone era: Stutz, Bentley, Bugatti, Rolls Royce, Packard and Duesenberg. He collected the great cars from Europe,

Britain and America. There were almost 30 cars in the collection. He even designed and built his own classic cars in the late 1960s.

Among Ruger's favorite trains was the Lionel set from his boyhood. There was over 350 feet of track to his train collection.

Ruger liked nice things, among which was an amazing and varied collection of nineteenth and twentieth century art. Over 200 beautiful paintings and sculptures by Schreyvogel, Bierstadt, Remington and others graced the walls and rooms of his offices and homes.

After the Hunt is a wonderful new book by Adrienne Ruger Conzelman that offers a first-hand account of Bill Ruger and his breathtaking art collection. He was also a patron of contemporary artists and engravers: Triggs, Kritz, Lantuch, and A.A. White.

Ruger was an ardent hunter and had an appetite for adventure and stories of adventure. Some of his favorite

The 1993 Copper State 1000; Bill Ruger "taking a breather" in front of Hubbel Trading Post at the border of Arizona and Utah. They are traveling in his 1928 Stutz Fishtail Speedster. *Courtesy Lyle Patterson*

guns were the classic double rifles taken on safari and used to hunt big game in far-off Africa or India, and single-shot target rifles from the late 19th century.

In a less complicated time when coffee was percolated, agreements were sealed with a handshake and a Coke was a nickel. Alexander Sturm and Bill Ruger established Sturm, Ruger & Co. At first they struggled, but overcame and began shipping 22LR semi-automatic pistols in October of 1949 from a small wooden shop across the street from the Southport, Connecticut train-station. By 1951 production of the Ruger Standard Auto was well under way and the possibility of producing a single-action revolver was being explored. Ruger began to work on preliminary designs for the famous Ruger Single-Six.

The company was making a profit and all was going well when tragedy struck. Ruger's friend and partner became ill, Alex Sturm died at age 29. Ruger never got over the loss.

Alone, Bill Ruger led his company to an unprecedented level in the American firearms industry. Early on, Colt and S&W were indifferent to Ruger's dream; they had been resting on their laurels for years and perceived themselves as invincible in their respective markets. Too late, they awoke to the realization that Ruger was a force to be reckoned with in the pistol and revolver markets. Ruger was the competition and he was formidable!

Eventually Ruger was presented with the opportunity to purchase these competitors: Colt, Smith & Wesson and later Winchester—each with a rich and illustrious tradition. Although Ruger had the financial ability, these companies were not acquired; this is an interesting irony, a milestone in the history of American arms making.

At the time of this writing Sturm, Ruger & Co., Inc. has designed and manufactured over twenty million pistols, revolvers, shotguns and rifles in all popular calibers. They have produced hundreds of models and sub-models under at least 115 U.S. and foreign patents.

In the pursuit of quality and efficiency of fabrication, Ruger utilized stampings and coil springs and pioneered and perfected the application of precision investment castings to small arms manufacturing. Whenever possible, component shapes were designed to fit generic tools and to conform to established fabrication techniques rather than require that special

"Edith" *(above)* was built in the Rolls Royce plant at Springfield, Massachusetts and originally purchased by Edith Archbald of New York; it is distinguished by the left-hand drive. The car was photographed at Ruger's townhouse in Prescott, Arizona. *Courtesy of John C. Dougan*

Ruger at home in Croydon, New Hampshire sitting below one of his favorite paintings *The Great Trees, Mariposa Grove* by Albert Bierstadt. This magnificent painting was completed in 1876 and was first exhibited in the Department of Art—United States Centennial Commission International Exhibition, Philadelphia, Pennsylvania in that same year. This photo is from Bill Ruger's 1989 Christmas card to lifelong friend Jack Behn. In 1997 Bill Ruger, grandson Alex Vogel, Lyle and Kathi Patterson drove from Monterey, California to Yosemite in "Edith," Ruger's 1928 Rolls Royce Phantom I Tilbury Sedan, to visit "Grizzly Giant" 121 years after Bierstadt set up his easel to paint this beautiful grove of trees. *Courtesy of John C. Dougan*

The first Ruger revolver shipped. Engraved by Cole Agee, gold and silver-plated and inscribed on the backstrap, "To John T. Amber With the Compliments of Col. Ruger". This historic Ruger single-action revolver graced the cover of the Gun Digest, 8th Edition in 1954, 50 years ago. *Courtesy John C. Dougan*

Aerial view of the "Red Barn" and shops where Ruger began. The company still maintains these historical buildings and, except for a paved parking lot, they have changed very little. The Southport train station is seen in the foreground, ca. 1956. *Courtesy Sturm, Ruger & Co.*

tooling be designed to produce the shapes.

Ruger believed that pricing for his products should be structured so that a typical customer could purchase one of his guns for a price equal to one week's pay. This manufacturing and marketing approach proved to be sound, and indeed, one week's pay

would purchase a gun and Ruger would still make a profit. Fifty years later this principal still holds true.

In 1996 Simon & Shuster released *Ruger and His Guns* by R.L.Wilson, an official biography that is an unprecedented window into Bill Ruger's life wherein the products and history of his factories are revealed in striking detail. Additionally, there are at least 20 well-researched and detailed reference books that explore specific models or groups of Ruger firearms

for purposes of collecting.

This writer can offer very little that has not been written about the man, the guns and his factories. What will be presented here is a comprehensive chronological outline of company history and product development, with insight into some of Bill Ruger's special accomplishments.

Shops in rear of the "Red Barn". A young firearms engraver named Charles H. Jerred and his wife drove their Oldsmobile from Fulton, New York to Southport, Connecticut to meet Bill Ruger and discuss the possibility of doing engraving work on the new Single-Six. They arrived during the night; since there was no hotel in town they were content to sleep in the car until the workers arrived early the following day. Ruger and Jerred spent most of the day together; Jerred went on to engrave 275 guns for Ruger, ca. 1954. *Courtesy John C. Dougan*

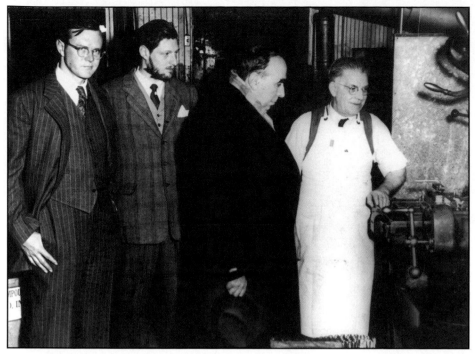

1916; Bill Ruger was born June 21st in Brooklyn, New York, son of Adolph Ruger and Mary Batterman Ruger.

Ruger attended public schools in Brooklyn. Enrolled in Salisbury Prep School, Salisbury, Connecticut and attended the University of North Carolina at Chapel Hill.

1938: Ruger met and married Mary Carolyn Thompson and left the university after two years to concentrate on gun designing. They moved to Hartford, Connecticut and Ruger took a job at a small shop that specialized in guns where he converted an 1899 lever-action Savage rifle to a semi-auto. The rifle and an article by William B. Ruger later appeared in the December, 1943 *American Rifleman*.

1939: William B. Ruger Jr. is born.

Ruger begins work at Springfield Armory for the U.S. Government.

1940: Auto Ordnance, at age 24 Ruger went to work in the engineering department to perfect the light machinegun he had developed a couple of years before. He spent the next four years there.

1941: Carolyn R. "Molly" Ruger is born.

1944: James Thompson "Tom" Ruger is born.

1946: Ruger and a partner opened the Ruger Corp. in Southport, Connecticut to manufacture a line of carpenter tools, some of which resemble pistols. Goes into receivership in 1949.

1949: Meets Alexander Sturm and proposes partnership. Establishes Sturm, Ruger & Co. to manufacture 22-caliber pistols in the same buildings that housed the Ruger Corp., on the same tooling. Shipments commence in October. One of the buildings is two stories and resembles a barn. All of the structures are painted barn red with white trim. This complex is affectionately referred to as *"The Red Barn"*.

1951: Introduced Mark I Automatic Pistol with adjustable sights and various barrel lengths. Proved to be a match winner and was adopted by the Army and Air Force as a training arm.

Alexander Sturm dies; returning in the fall from a hunting trip in Quebec, Ruger finds his partner in the hospital, seriously ill. Alex dies less than two weeks later.

1953: Began Manufacture of Single-Six, 22LR chambering. Styled after the Colt Peacemaker, it remained in production until 1973. An aluminum Lightweight Model and Engraved Model were introduced in 1956. A magnum model was introduced in 1959 chambered for the 22 WRM. A Super Single Six with adjustable sights was added to the Single-Six line in 1964.

Paulina Sturm, Alex's wife dies in January at age 31. She was Teddy Roosevelt's granddaughter.

1955: Introduces Blackhawk single-action revolvers: Initially offered in the 357 Magnum chambering; in 1956, the 44 Magnum; in 1965, the 41 Magnum; in 1967 the 30 Carbine caliber; and in 1971 the 45 Colt.

1958: The Bearcat Revolver, 22LR chambering. This small, aluminum-frame single-action revolver was reminiscent of Civil War-era Remington revolvers. In 1971 a Super Bearcat model with a steel frame was introduced. Both models

were discontinued in 1973. In 1993 introduces the New Bearcat, redesigned to employ the innovative "transfer bar" ignition system in use on all revolvers beginning in 1973.

The Red Barn closes, the original wooden structures where Alex Sturm and Bill Ruger began a decade before had become obsolete, business was very good and more space was needed for production. The tooling was relocated to a newly finished factory built specifically for firearms production.

Safari in Kenya, Ruger and George Rowbottom, six weeks, took a lion.

1959: The Lacey Place factory opens, moved and began production by January. More space was built in successive years as the demand for Ruger handguns grew. This plant produced over 3,000,000 guns and was becoming obsolete by the late 1980s due to lack of space to expand; it was closed in the summer of 1991 and now houses the corporate offices of Sturm, Ruger & Co., Inc.

The Super Blackhawk Revolver, 44 Magnum chambering. A redesigned and improved version of the earlier 44 Magnum Blackhawk, the Super Blackhawk proved to be a favorite of handgun hunters and sportsmen.

1960: The Deerstalker Carbine, 44 Magnum chambering. Ruger's first

Serial number 5112. One of only 22 engraved and cased Single-Six revolvers shipped to Spain for engraving in 1954. Additionally, 238 Single-Sixes were engraved by Charles H. Jerred of Fulton, New York 1954-1958. *Courtesy John C. Dougan*

rifle, this semi-automatic carbine met with wide acceptance as the ideal brush-country deer rifle. Name changed to 44 Carbine in 1962.

Safari in Uganda, Ruger and Pete Kuhloff took Deerstalker 44 Magnum carbine. Shot leopard, warthog, hyena, waterbuck and a record book reedbuck.

1963: The Hawkeye Pistol, 256 Winchester Magnum chambering. This unusual single-shot pistol featured a heavy manually rotating breechblock. Discontinued 1964.

Pine Tree Castings; foundry established at Newport, NH by

Sturm, Ruger & Co. as a source for precision investment castings for the firearms made by its parent company. Pine Tree has also become a reliable supplier to all industries requiring production lots of high-quality investment castings. Over the years, they have cast valve bodies, jet engine components, parts for gun manufacturers and other items too numerous to list. On several occasions additional space was added.

The Newport factory, separated from Pine Tree Castings by the Sugar River, was opened for gun production. This 200,000 square foot facility is self-reliant and is now one of the most advanced small arms plants in the world. Hundreds of workers make stocks, operate machines, make parts, polish, finish and assemble long guns and revolvers.

1964: The Model 10/22 Rifle, 22LR chambering. This autoloading rifle incorporated a unique 10-shot rotary magazine and has become one of the most popular firearms of its type in the world. It is still in production in many configurations.

1967: The Number One Single-Shot Rifle. Produced in a variety of chamberings from 22-250 to 458 Magnum, the Ruger Number One Rifle is used today by big-game

The Ruger team with Rhode Island Governor John Notte. They were there to present the Governor with an inscribed Ruger 44 Carbine, serial number 600. Standing (L–R): "Monty" Montenaro, Elaine "Lanie" Horelik, Peggy Montenaro, Mary Ruger, Bill Ruger and Michael Horelik. Seated is Governor Notte. *Courtesy Sturm, Ruger & Co.*

hunters in all parts of the world. In 1972, an "Americanized" version of this single-shot design was introduced as the Number 3 Carbine.

1968: The M-77 Bolt-Action Rifle. Offered in a variety of configurations and chamberings from 22-250 to 458 Magnum, the M-77 Rifle achieved unusual standing and great popularity among sportsmen.

1969-70: Ruger Tourers. Two prototype automobiles patterned after the Bentley Vanden Plas. Powered by a powerful 425 hp Ford engine. The car was never put into production. The prototypes are in the factory collection.

1971: The Security-Six, Police Service-Six and Speed-Six Double-Action Revolvers. Offered in 38 Special and 357 Magnum chamberings. The new double-action revolver design marked Ruger's entry into the law-enforcement field and has met with ever-increasing demand among sportsmen and law enforcement agencies. In 1975, stainless steel versions of all double-action models were offered. Beginning in 1986 these were replaced by the GP-100, SP-101, Redhawk and Super Redhawk revolvers. Chamberings range from 22LR to 480 Ruger in several frame sizes and finishes.

1972: The Old Army Revolver. Offered in 45-caliber percussion. Ruger's first offering for the blackpowder shooter. The Old Army Revolver, like the Single-Six model,

Successful hunting with the new No. 1 rifle at Corbin Park in the Blue Mountain Forest. (R-L) Ed Nolan (vice-president of marketing) and Bill Ruger; others unknown to author, ca. 1967. *Courtesy Sturm, Ruger & Co.*

was redolent of the guns of the Western frontier days. A stainless steel version was offered in 1975. Old Armies are still in production, with and without adjustable sights.

1973: The New Model Single-Six, New Model Blackhawk and New Model Super Blackhawk were introduced incorporating an entirely new, patented "transfer-bar" ignition system. All older model Ruger single-action revolvers were

discontinued at this time. In 1974, stainless models were introduced. These models are still being produced in all popular calibers. Collaboration with Remington in

Amid a forest of barrels, Bill Ruger inspects a newly completed 44 Magnum Carbine. Early 1960s; the Lacey Place factory in Southport, Connecticut. *Courtesy Sturm, Ruger & Co.*

Aerial view of the Lacey Place plant in Southport, Connecticut. This facility opened in 1959 and suspended operations in 1991. The corporate offices are still housed there. The large building in the foreground is Superior Manufacturing Co., ca. late 1960s. *Courtesy Sturm, Ruger & Co.*

1982 resulted in a 357 Maximum Blackhawk. In 1986 a Bisley version was introduced. 1n 1993 the Vaquero model came out featuring a topstrap akin to the Colt Peacemaker.

1975: The Mini-14 Rifle.
Chambered for the 223 Remington cartridge. The company released to the general market this model that had already enjoyed considerable success in government and law-enforcement markets. Many foreign governments and police forces have adopted a Government Model rifle in a variety of configurations. In 1978, stainless steel versions were being shipped. The Ranch Rifle, a model with integral scope mounts and the Mini-Thirty chambered for the 7.62x39mm cartridge was later introduced.

1977: The Over and Under Shotgun.
Although shotgun manufacturing represented a new area for Sturm, Ruger & Co., the new 20-gauge Red Label Over and Under shotgun demonstrated their expertise and originality in small arms design and manufacture. Later a 12- and 28-gauge were offered, and a .410 barrel liner to fit the 28-gauge could be ordered. The Red Label Over and Under is still being offered in various configurations and enjoys great popularity with hunters and competition shooters.

Titania, construction of Ruger's second yacht began at Robert Derektor's Boat Yard in Mamaroneck, NY. Schooled as a naval architect, Ruger designed the 88-foot boat himself. Derektor provided engineering, drawings and construction. It was completed in late 1979.

1979: The 30th Anniversary of Ruger Firearms.

Completes the 1,000,000th Standard Auto pistol.

1982: The Mark II Standard and Target Pistols,
22LR chambering. Upgrade of original pistol designs, specifically a different magazine and hold-open mechanism. Still in production in many configurations and finishes; the most popular pistol of its type.

Completes the 1,000,000th double-action revolver.

Free Conversion Kit Offer, to be factory-installed on "Old Model" single-action revolvers and older Bearcats made before 1973. The kit features another patented transfer bar similar to that of the New Model. Installation of the kit helps prevent accidental discharge and allows for loading of all six chambers. This free service is still offered.

1987: P85 Pistol,
9mm chambering. Ruger occupied a 9000 square foot building close to the airport in Prescott, AZ to build and ship the

ARMS MAKERS FOR RESPONSIBLE CITIZENS

Right: 1973 – Bill Ruger in his Southport, Connecticut office, discussing the merits of the new and innovative lockwork of the New Model Single-Six. *Courtesy Sturm, Ruger & Co.*

Lower Left: Bill Ruger and Chris Cashavelli at the drafting table in the engineering department at the Lacey Place plant in Southport, Connecticut ca. 1973. *Courtesy Sturm, Ruger & Co.*

Lower Right: Summer 1971 – In the stock-making department at the Newport, New Hampshire plant. Bill Ruger with Skeeter Skelton, Handgun Editor of *Shooting Times. Courtesy Sturm, Ruger & Co.*

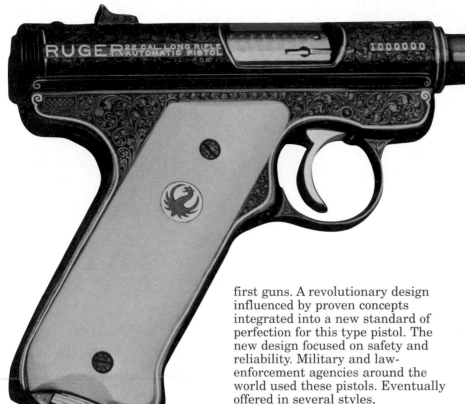

The One Millionth Ruger Standard Automatic Pistol. Pulled from the production line in 1979, then engraved and inlayed with gold by Master Engraver Ray Viramontez, this highly ornate pistol was auctioned to the highest bidder in connection with the 1980 NRA meetings. The proceeds went to the International Shooter Development Fund. *Courtesy Sturm, Ruger & Co., Inc.*

first guns. A revolutionary design influenced by proven concepts integrated into a new standard of perfection for this type pistol. The new design focused on safety and reliability. Military and law-enforcement agencies around the world used these pistols. Eventually offered in several styles, configurations, calibers, materials and finishes.

The One Millionth Ruger Double-Action Revolver. Pulled from the assembly line in 1983 and engraved and inlayed by Master Engraver Paul Lantuch, this stainless steel Security-Six was released from the collection of Sturm, Ruger & Co. to be auctioned to the highest bidder in connection with the 1985 SHOT Show. The proceeds went to the National Shooting Sports Foundation. *Courtesy Sturm, Ruger & Co.*

1989: The 40th Anniversary of Ruger Firearms.

Occupies Prescott Factory, an extensively renovated 200,000 square foot building near the airport in Prescott, AZ. Ruger Investment Casting is established to cast titanium components. Tooling is set and production of the P-series continues, slowly at first, but now all Ruger pistols are produced in this state-of-the-art plant. Later Ruger Investment Casting was expanded to accommodate the production of castings for outside customers. Ruger casts titanium golf club heads. They also market their own line of golf clubs.

Introduced the M-77 Mark II Rifle, an improved version of the original M-77 featuring a controlled-feed extractor and a three-position receiver safety. Today the M-77 MK II family includes over 100 rifles to meet any need, in all popular chamberings from 223 Remington to 458 Lott.

1991: Southport factory closes after 30 years of operation. Production of single-action revolvers and 22-caliber pistols was moved to the company's other two plants. The Company's corporate headquarters remain in the Southport facility.

Stephen Vogel dies, Ruger's son-in-law, VP of Ruger Export Corp. at Southport and later plant manager at the early Prescott operation.

1993: Tom Ruger dies, Ruger's younger son, was vice president of sales and marketing at the Southport operation.

Mary and Bill Ruger at home in the mid-1970s. *Courtesy Sturm, Ruger & Co.*

The *Titania*; a magnificent 88-foot yacht designed by and for Bill Ruger, engineered and built at Robert Derektor's Boat Yard at Mamaroneck, New York. Her distinctive profile is reminiscent of the rumrunners of the Prohibition Era. The *Titania* is not a small vessel; she has a 20-foot beam and features two 500-hp Caterpillar diesel engines. The hull is constructed of aluminum. Finished in 1979. *Courtesy Sturm, Ruger & Co.*

Bill Ruger in his office in Southport, Connecticut – 1987. *Courtesy Sturm, Ruger & Co.*

Right: Bill Ruger and friend Dave Crosby at Ruger's estate in Croydon, New Hampshire. The car is Ruger's 1914 Rolls Royce Alpine Tourer. *Courtesy Sturm, Ruger & Co.*

Aerial view of Pine Tree Casting and the plant at Newport, New Hampshire ca. 1975. *Courtesy Sturm, Ruger & Co.*

October 1996: Bill Ruger at his Prescott, Arizona plant. The magnificent bronze statue is *"An Honest Days Work"* by Fred Fellows. The beautiful automobile is a Ruger Sports Tourer, one of two built in 1968 – 1970. *Courtesy Sturm, Ruger & Co.*

1994: *Mrs. Ruger passes away*, on Thursday before Easter. Wife and companion for nearly 60 years.

Production of MP9, a selective-fire 9mm from Uzi Gal's M201. For law- enforcement and government sales only.

1996: *The M-96 Lever Action Rifle*, in 22LR and 44 Magnum chamberings. Popular with sportsmen and Cowboy Action Shooters.

1997: *Ruger Carbine*, 9mm and 40 S&W chamberings. Autoloader mounted in a black polymer stock. Uses 10-round Ruger pistol magazines.

1998: *77/50 Muzzleloading Rifle*, single shot, 50-caliber bolt-action percussion rifle for use with blackpowder during muzzle-loading hunting season.

Bill Ruger personally donates $1,000,000 to the National Firearms Museum.

Bill Ruger personally donates $1,000,000 to the Buffalo Bill Historical Center to establish the Cody Firearms Museum.

Bill Ruger is named Man-of-the-Year by the Shooting, Hunting & Outdoor Trade (S.H.O.T.). Featured in *SHOT BUSINESS* magazine.

1999: *The Golden Anniversary of Ruger Firearms*. Celebrated by dozens of 50th Anniversary memorabilia and special offerings.

2000: *Bill Ruger officially retires*, October 24, 2000. Becomes Chairman Emeritus.

Bill Ruger Jr. appointed CEO

2002: *Announces Gold Label Side-by-Side Shotgun* in 12-gauge, weighing only 6-1/2 pounds, made in the tradition of the finest European and British makers. Dickson-style selective ejectors, no visible pins or screws, back-bored with choke tubes.

The Gold Label is a work of art, to be cherished during your lifetime, and then passed on to another who exults in the joy of being afield on a crisp fall day.

With this gun Sturm, Ruger has reached the pinnacle of gunmaking.

William B. Ruger dies at home close to his factory in Prescott, Arizona. He was a pragmatist who understood and accepted the eventuality of life. On Saturday morning July 6, 2002, with mercy and grace God drew him to his bosom.

Ruger believed in his own ability. He enjoyed a long and sententious life on his own terms. He always knew that the American Dream existed and could be attained through vision and perseverance. His legacy is proof enough.

The time for grieving is at an end; a time to celebrate the memory of his life, his factories, the guns and his extraordinary achievements is now at hand. I knew Mr. Ruger and I believe this is how he would want to be remembered, and we shall remember him with fondness each time we admire a factory engraved Single-Six or shoulder a Gold Label and fill our game bag.

• • • • • • •

Guns & The Hunt
For Texas Killers
Bonnie & Clyde

by Jerry Burke

EASTER MORNING 1934 was a beauty in central Texas. Heat waves shimmered off a Ford sedan with custom yellow wheels parked on a dusty side road. Two men lounged inside the car while nearby, a young woman played with a white rabbit. The bunny was an Easter present for her mother. Two motorcycle cops arrived to investigate a report of loud drunken behavior. As the lawmen rolled within 25 feet of the sedan, neither expected trouble. In a flash, a tall man emerged from the vehicle, shattering the tranquil rural scene with a burst from his Browning Automatic Rifle (BAR). The impact of the jacketed 30-06 bullets pulverized Officer Wheeler's chest, killing him instantly. The second officer reached for a sawed-off shotgun strapped to his bike, but a small man rounded the car, downing him with 00-buckshot. Both officers lie in the dirt: one dead, the other dying. Placing the pet rabbit in the car, the slender woman with dyed red hair and deep blue eyes approached the severely wounded Officer Murphy. She pumped two shots into his head from her own sawed-off semi-auto shotgun. As she

climbed into the car, the redhead laughingly remarked how the lawman's head had jumped with each blast. The stolen V8 Ford sped away from the scene. Clyde Barrow, Bonnie Parker and an accomplice had just killed the first two Texas Highway Patrolmen to die in the line of duty.

The Principal Players

Simply put, Clyde Barrow was a piece-of-work. Born into serious poverty in the Dallas area, he and formal schooling parted company in the 5th grade. If there'd been a yearbook, Clyde's hobbies would have included swiping hubcaps and robbing houses. By the time he was 15, Clyde had more than 60 arrests to his "credit". At age 16, he was an accomplished car thief. Clyde then graduated to armed robbery, including the occasional U.S. Post Office heist. He cold-bloodedly killed anyone who got in his way. No more than five feet, seven

Bonnie Parker & Clyde Barrow hamming it up. Bonnie holds shotgun used to kill a Texas Highway Patrolmen. *Western History Collections, University of Oklahoma*

A Model 1928 Thompson submachine gun with 100-round drum magazine. Capable of single-shot or full-auto fire, the formidable weapon was employed by the Barrow Bunch and the lawmen who sought to end their lawlessness.

inches in height, weighing 125 pounds, Clyde Barrow was sensitive about his unimposing persona. He liked to dress professionally in an effort to compensate.

In a desperate fight with assassins, Frank Hamer's life was saved by an S&W 44-Special "Triple Lock" DA revolver. One side of stocks features a carved steer head with genuine ruby eyes.

Bonnie Parker with large-frame Colt DA revolver taken from kidnapped lawman. She loved her liquor but didn't really smoke stogies. *Institute of Texan Cultures*

Enter Bonnie Parker, who had a better start in life than Clyde Barrow. But by her early 20s, Bonnie was married to a man serving life-without-parole in Texas' Huntsville State Prison. No surprise, Bonnie had developed quite a passion for whisky. She was waitressing in a greasy diner when she met Clyde Barrow, and it was a match made in Hell. One of Bonnie's attributes Clyde loved was her diminutive four-foot, ten-inch frame; Bonnie made her man feel big and powerful. For Clyde, another plus was the double-heart-pierced-with-an-arrow tattoo her husband applied to the inside of her right thigh. Thus began a companionship which lasted little over two years, "til death did they part".

Frank Hamer was the absolute antithesis of Bonnie or Clyde. He stood 6' 3", and was 200 pounds of pure muscle. Raised a hard-working cowboy and blacksmith, his law enforcement career began as a horseback Ranger (circa. 1906) with State service continuing into the 1930s. His honesty and integrity were beyond reproach. In the line of duty, Hamer was on the winning side of more than 50 personal gunfights and hundreds of engagements. He was absolutely fearless. By his own account, Frank Hamer took a bullet at least 23 times and was left for dead more than once. However, Hamer was highly skilled in the use of hands and feet in resolving dangerous situations; firearms were a last resort. Black suits suited him, and he dispensed with wearing boots when he no longer rode a horse to work. Although one of the most notable Texas Rangers of the 20th century, bringing the Texas killers Clyde Barrow and Bonnie Parker to justice brought Capt. Hamer unsolicited national, as well as international, fame.

Colt semi-auto smuggled into a Waco, Texas jail by Bonnie Parker. Clyde Barrow soon used same to escape.

Ill-Gotten Firepower of The Devil's Duo

Clyde Barrow's first armed robbery was committed with a cut-down single-shot shotgun in the junk category. Bonnie Parker launched her firearm offenses with a stolen Colt 380 ACP semi-auto pistol. She slipped the Colt between her breasts and herself into a Waco jail to visit Clyde. Understandably, Clyde found it much easier to break out of jail while armed. Clyde only bought firearms once, and those illegal automatic weapons proved faulty. Thereafter, his motto was, "It is a far, far better thing to steal guns than pay for them". He loved shopping at National Guard armories in the middle of the night for BARs, Thompson submachine guns, Colt 45 ACP pistols, spare magazines all around and plenty of ammo. Another constant companion of the deadly Texas duo were semi-auto shotguns stuffed with 00-buck-shot. Specifically, Remington's Model 11A, a Browning look-alike.

As a military officer in the 1960s, I acquired considerable experience and respect for the BAR (*invented by the famous and prolific firearms designer John Moses Browning*), Thompson submachine gun and other firearms no longer in active U.S. inventory. One of my duties was training non-uniformed U. S. govt. intelligence personnel in this "Old Family" of weapons. The Browning caliber 30 Model 1918 gas-operated Automatic Rifle, with 24-inch barrel, fires the then Government-standard 30-06 cartridge from a 20-round staggered detachable box magazine. Fully loaded, the foot soldier was looking at lugging nearly 16 pounds of deadly destruction. If fed cartridges without interruption, a BAR can belch out 600 rounds-per-minute, but the wooden forearm can start to smolder under heavy use. The BAR is functionally reliable and devastatingly accurate in well-trained hands, with or without a bipod. Maximum effective range is about 800 yards. A horizontal operating handle on the left side of the receiver is used to cock the BAR. A vertical lever on the same side allows the operator to elect full-auto or single-shot functioning, as well as "safe". On full-auto, a loaded 20-round magazine can be emptied in 3 blinks of an eye. Making its debut in WWI, the BAR proved even more useful in WWII and the Korean War that followed. As the United States entered the conflict in Southeast Asia, the BAR was used both by American advisors and our allies in the region. The law enforcement version of the BAR sported a pistol-grip stock and muzzle compensator to aid in controlling the weapon during automatic fire.

The Thompson submachine gun first hit the market in 1921, the creation of General John T. Thompson, who also invented the term "submachine gun". Chicago bootleggers and similar types were the first to find the "Thompson" an attractive on-the-job tool. The military version was dubbed the Thompson Submachine Gun M1928. A Cutts compensator was affixed to the muzzle of the M1928 to control climb during automatic firing. As a plus, the Thompson fired the same round as the Pistol, caliber 45, M1911/M1911A1...the Government automatic. Available in a variety of configurations–from dual pistol grips to being devoid of buttstock–and featuring a shotgun-style fore grip, the Thompson provided devastating up-close firepower. Double-stack stick magazines in 20- and 30-round capacities were issued. Drum magazines taking 50 or 100 rounds were also available. The original Thompson product is easily identified by the cocking lever at the top of the receiver. In the later, simplified M1 version, the cocking lever was moved to the right side of the receiver. The Thompson lends itself to close-up targets when maneuverability is an asset as in

A young Texas Ranger Frank Hamer *(left)* in Del Rio, Texas *(circa 1906)* packing a Colt SAA and Winchester Model '92 carbine. *Western History Collections, University of Oklahoma*

urban fighting, cave clearing or easy toting in a vehicle. The 1928 Thompson was something of an armorer's nightmare, as critical parts had to be hand-fitted to a particular weapon. In addition, the drum magazines were tricky to load and subject to malfunctions. The loaded weight with 20-round magazine is approximately 11 pounds.

Little-Used Colts of A Legendary Texas Ranger

Frank Hamer owned and used a number of handguns in nearly three decades of upholding Texas law. Early in his horseback Rangering days, he carried a 45-caliber Colt Single Action Army Revolver with 7 1/2-inch barrel. His "cavalry"-length Colt was carried in a double-loop Mexican holster and matching gunbelt. While not nearly as handy as the shorter

In this 1908 image, Frank Hamer *(left)* still carries a Colt SAA revolver but had switched to the more powerful Winchester Model '95. *Western History Collections, University of Oklahoma*

factory barrel lengths, the 7 1/2-inch barrel improved the odds of connecting with a target while perched on a moving equine.

In 1918, Frank Hamer borrowed a "plain Jane" Colt SAA revolver with 5 1/2-inch barrel from fellow Ranger Captain W. W. Sterling. Hamer proceeded to provide onlookers with an astonishing exhibit of handgunning prowess. Years later, then Adjutant General Sterling presented the handgun to Hamer. Another blue and casehardened Colt 45 SAA with barrel reduced to between 4 3/4 inches and 5 1/2 inches, also saw Frank Hamer use. This was a common alteration when

the hog-leg was abundantly available, especially on a lawman's salary. Typically such work is not difficult to spot, as the reduced end of the barrel is usually flat in profile, not crowned (rounded-off) as on a factory-original.

In his early horseback Rangering days, Frank Hamer carried a Colt SAA with 7 1/2-inch barrel. Cavalry-length tube was a "plus" when shooting from a moving horse.

Frank Hamer's career-long favorite handgun was "Old Lucky" in the same configuration as this one, chambered for the 45 Colt cartridge and sporting a 4 3/4-inch barrel. "Old Lucky" was blued/casehardened on top of heavy engraving. Grip panels were standard hard rubber.

Late in his career, Capt. Hamer occasionally carried a "C"-engraved, nickel-plated Colt 45 single action with 4 3/4-inch barrel and carved grips with eagle head motif. Serial number 180260, the weapon was produced in 1898. The previous owner had taken at least one life with the Colt before Hamer acquired it. When Capt. Hamer parted with this six-gun, the document accompanying the sale stated that the handgun had been, "… carried by me [Frank Hamer] for a number of years while in the services as a peace officer."

Another Frank Hamer-marked revolver is a beautiful nickel-plated Colt New Service double-action, complete with butt swivel. The sideplate on the right side of the frame features the Texas Star, the legend, "Texas Rangers"; and, the date…"1939". "Frank Hamer" is engraved down the backstrap and gold-filled. Chambered in 45 Colt, the handgun is in unfired, as-new condition. Many an individual and organization tried to heap honors on Capt. Hamer, but he rejected most. While obviously Hamer-related, I am not certain Frank Hamer ever accepted this handsome gift of appreciation.

Regarding semi-auto pistols, now-deceased Texas Ranger Captain Clint Peoples…who participated in the hunt for Bonnie & Clyde…told me Frank Hamer gave the semi-auto pistol a try just once. Hamer informally test-fired a Colt Government Model 45, but the pistol jammed. According to Peoples, Hamer put the pistol down and never used another.

Clyde Barrow *(circa mid-1920s)*. Dirt-poor and poorly educated, he dressed professionally to appear successful. *Institute of Texan Cultures*

Author's son with cheap single-shot shotgun Clyde Barrow used in his first stick-up.

The story had become part of Ranger lore when recounted to me and unfortunately, Capt. Peoples had not witnessed the event.

Smith & Wesson Saves The Day

A 44 Special Smith & Wesson "Triple Lock" double-action revolver saved Frank Hamer's life in a hair-raising 1917 fight. Texas lawmen created quite a reputation for S&W's new "N"-frame, with aficionados…not the factory…labeling it the "Triple Lock". A Ft. Worth distributor placed a heady 3,500-unit factory order for the big six-guns. Introduced in 1908 to accommodate the 44 Special cartridge, a third lock-up point was added between the frame and swing-out cylinder. Also new with the "N" frame was a shroud underneath the barrel to protect the ejector rod. There were, in fact, three versions of the "Triple Lock", with only the first actually having the coveted 3rd locking point.

Frank Hamer was warned by friends not to testify in a major case, but he steadfastly refused to heed the advice. After the court proceedings, Frank, his brother Harrison (also a Texas Ranger) and Frank's wife Gladys stopped at a garage to have a flat tire repaired. Hamer smelled a rat, and strapped-on a Smith & Wesson "Triple Lock" in addition to the Colt SAA he was packing. Harrison Hamer went down the street on an errand; Gladys stayed in the car while Frank located the garage owner. When Capt. Hamer emerged from the office, he was confronted with a hired killer.

Hamer was fired on at pointblank range with a Colt Government Model 45 ACP semi-auto pistol. Apparently rattled by Hamer's heady reputation, the shot went wide of the mark, driving a piece of Hamer's watch chain into his left shoulder and disabling his primary gun hand. (*As was the fashion, Capt. Hamer ran his pocket watch chain through the buttonhole of his suit coat lapel.*) Hamer grabbed his assailant and deflected the Colt. The pistol discharged again, this time striking Hamer in the leg. Thankfully, the big 45 auto jammed.

As this desperate life-and-death struggle unfolded, Hamer's wife saw another man approaching, armed with a shotgun. Plucky Gladys, South Texas ranch born and raised, picked up a small-caliber Colt automatic and began shooting from the car. Gladys kept the second gunman pinned down until she ran the Colt dry. Seeing his accomplice approaching, the man Capt. Hamer was struggling with broke free to give his pal a clear shot. Again at pointblank range, Hamer received a near-miss shotgun blast that blew his hat off and knocked him to his knees. Not getting the job done, the hired guns fled down the street. Twice wounded, Capt. Hamer followed the gunmen. The shotgun-toting outlaw crouched nearby, ready to finish the job he'd been paid for. Frank Hamer drew his S&W "Triple Lock" and sent a hot spinning 44-caliber projectile through the killer's heart. The first shooter was cowering in a nearby doorway. Frank invited him to stand up and use his gun, but he wisely elected to high-tail it. Now on the scene, Harrison Hamer raised his rifle to nail the fleeing coward in the back, but Frank deflected his aim. As luck would have it, a grand jury watched the entire episode unfold from across the street. They immediately took up the matter just witnessed, clearing the Hamers as Frank was being stitched-up in the courtroom.

"Old Lucky", In A Class By Itself

Capt. Hamer's most-carried, most-cherished six-shooter was a heavily engraved Colt SAA with 4 3/4-inch barrel…serial number 314012…produced in 1910. Despite the extensive engraving, this historic Colt is finished in traditional blue with case-hardening and fitted with standard hard rubber grip panels. For the advanced Colt collector, the engraving has style elements of master craftsman Cunio Helfricht. Down the backstrap is the legend, "F. A. Hamer".

Clyde Barrow was partial to stolen hardware, and left nothing behind. Seen here, long-barreled Colt DA revolver with target sights.

County Attorney Conlo Spann of Navasota, Texas, presented young Frank Hamer with this six-gun in 1913. It first drew blood at Del Rio, Texas two years later, when a murderer was brought to justice. That Capt. Hamer called this Colt "Old Lucky" was well known to his men by 1918. He never parted with "Old Lucky" and when he died in bed in 1955, ownership passed to Frank Hamer, Jr.

I recall "Old Lucky" being on display in central Texas for a lengthy period, but in the early 1970s Hamer's son sold his father's carry gun. Frank Hamer, Jr. provided "Old Lucky's" new owner with a statement of fact. A few quotes from that document, not taken out-of-context, speak volumes. Hamer's son verified that…

"This weapon was the favorite handgun of my father throughout his career as a peace officer, and he used it in at least 52 individual gunfights…".

"My father referred to this gun as "Old Lucky"…". "This is the handgun that my father used,

except on very rare occasions, throughout his career."

"When he [Frank Hamer, Sr.] was transferred to Austin where he was Central Captain, he continued to carry this pistol."

"The last gunfight in which my father was engaged and in which he carried "Old Lucky" was on the morning of May 23, 1934, near Gibbsland, Louisiana, when he apprehended Bonnie Parker and Clyde Barrow."

Frank Hamer's Long Guns

Beginning with the very first Winchester product, Texas Rangers had a long-standing preference for the lever-action products of that company. Frank Hamer followed suit, packing Models 92 & 95 early in his career. However, he and other Rangers became partial to Remington semi-automatic rifles like the company's Model 8, available in several calibers. Being a renowned crack shot, Hamer was often asked to put on a demonstration of his skills. He was doing just that on the Tex-Mex border in the early 1920s for a group of soldiers, with an agent of the Remington Firearms Company in attendance. Months later, Hamer was notified by Petmeky's…Austin's most famous gun shop…that a shipment for him had arrived. Inside the crate was a fully engraved, 30-caliber Remington Model 8F rifle with presentation-grade stock and forend. The left side of the receiver features the engraved gold-filled legend, "Capt. Frank Hamer of The Texas Rangers". Both sides of the receiver featured scenes highlighting Capt. Hamer's early Rangering days. Inset in the right side of the stock is a gold seal of the State of Texas. The new rifle became his favorite. Hamer used the presentation Remington regularly, both as a duty weapon and for more pleasant tasks like deer hunting. Having personally handled Capt. Hamer's Remington on several occasions, I can

understand its appeal. In addition to providing reliable semi-automatic fire, it is well balanced…easy to shoulder and quick to get on-target.

On an especially dark night along the Rio Grande, Frank Hamer first put his prize Remington rifle to serious use. Hamer and his Rangers took fire from the Mexican side of the border as they had for more than 100 consecutive nights. Gunfire at night is spectacular, illuminating the shooter and his immediate environment with each shot. At a time when most Rangers were armed with lever-action Winchesters, Capt. Hamer let loose with a string of rapid-fire shots from his engraved Remington, dropping the bandit. Those who witnessed Hamer's feat described the rifle as his "pear burner", after a flame thrower-like contraption still used today to control prickly pear cactus in South Texas. As to scatterguns, Hamer was predisposed to Remington's Model 11 semi-automatic. He used a 12-gauge Model 11 as his "car gun".

Crime Without Punishment

An additional example of Bonnie & Clyde mayhem will serve to represent a score of deadly escapades and narrow escapes from the law. In 1933, while the heat was on in Texas, Clyde rented a garage apartment in Joplin, Missouri. In residence were Bonnie, Clyde's brother Buck, Buck's wife Blanche—plus Ray Hamilton. Armed with ever-present stolen hardware, the gang conducted a string of robberies in the area, using the same stolen getaway car. Armed with Thompson submachine guns and more, Missouri lawmen converged on the residence as Clyde returned to the scene. Before Clyde could close the garage door, one cop tried to force his way inside. Outlaw Remington semi-auto shotguns boomed with 00-buckshot. The hits severed the lawman's left arm, but he got off a shot that struck Buck Barrow in the right temple, exiting through the opposite side of his forehead. Disregarding his own safety, a fellow officer now plunged through the garage door. Another volley of lead exploded and the second officer fell mortally wounded.

As the remaining lawmen regrouped, Clyde stitched them with murderous fire from all three second-story windows. He'd had three 20-round BAR magazines welded together, significantly increasing his sustained firepower. Clyde's second-story fusillade was answered by the chatter of Thompsons from the lawmen. Every inanimate object inside the apartment

The big S&W "N" frame DA revolver was a favorite of both lawmen and outlaws. Clyde Barrow killed nine lawmen getting some of his handguns.

Close-up of Remington Model 8 receiver of heavily engraved rifle presented to Capt. Hamer after a shooting exhibition. Hamer later used the rifle to end the careers of Bonnie & Clyde.

Author with a Monitor, law enforcement version of the Browning Automatic Rifle. Firing the 30-06 cartridge, Clyde Barrow had 3 of the 20-round magazines welded together for increased firepower.

was destroyed in a hail of hot lead. Clyde ordered the gang down the interior stairway and into the vehicle. A wall of 45-caliber slugs now slammed into both garage doors, sending wood and rock fragments whistling through the air. Risking death, Clyde opened a garage door while Ray Hamilton rushed to remove a dead officer's body blocking the car. Still under intense fire, Clyde lurched the stolen car forward, pushing a police car out of the way. The getaway car careened down the street; Clyde kept going until he'd covered more than 500 miles. Startling photos from undeveloped film discovered in the garage apartment were widely distributed to aid in apprehending the Barrow Bunch.

The Hunt Is On

But the worm was about to turn. Plenty of heat was applied to state authorities to resolve the deadly crime spree. Texans had had quite enough of sensational newspaper headlines and radio bulletins warning them to lock their doors and windows signaling Bonnie & Clyde were on the prowl. Frank Hamer, who had resigned from active Ranger service due to corruption of the Governor's office by James and "Ma" Ferguson, accepted the task of nailing Bonnie & Clyde. Hamer's charge was to exterminate the killer

couple and, "everyone in sight" when they were cornered. To legitimize matters, Hamer was given a commission in the Texas Highway Patrol. Thus began a 102-day, non-stop manhunt. Hamer worked without public knowledge until his task was accomplished.

Frank Hamer picked up the killers' trail in Texarkana. Little-by-little, collecting information from criminal sources he never revealed, he closed in on the lawless pair. Like Bonnie & Clyde, Hamer drove a Ford sedan with the most powerful V-8 engine of the day. Outlaws and lawmen alike spent most of the ordeal sleeping in their cars. In addition to informants, Hamer tracked the criminal pair through purchases they made and remnants left at locations where they camped. Bonnie & Clyde enjoyed the comfort and support of their families, and remained in contact with them to the end. Through an informant, a criminal associate of Bonnie and Clyde, Frank Hamer had the couple's Louisiana "mail drop" relocated to a location well known to him. A "mail drop" in this context is identical to a "dead drop" used in the spy trade for exchanging information and cash on the sly. Frank Hamer never revealed the name of the snitch, but he was in fact Henry Methvin. The exact location was under a board near a big stump, deep in the piney woods. Capt. Hamer even managed to orchestrate when Bonnie & Clyde would visit the site, and developed his plan-of-action accordingly.

A Trap Of Brains, Steel & Lead

Arriving near the mail drop on May 23, 1934, Hamer's party included Texas Ranger Manny Gault, two Dallas County Sheriff's officers and a pair of Louisiana lawmen. With the stump-and-board drop on the west side of the road, Capt. Hamer selected a vantage point on the east side, at a slight elevation. Scrounging pine branches in the darkness, the six lawmen developed cover to screen them from view and spread out at 10-yard intervals to await developments. If the Texas killers would not surrender, everyone was prepared to do their duty. The ambush team was armed with BARs and semi-auto shotguns, as well as handguns. As noted above, Capt. Hamer was packing "Old Lucky", plus his engraved Remington rifle. Hours passed, and still they waited in silence; mosquitoes and chiggers attacked the lawmen with ferocity. They began to suspect the informant had been wrong or the wily Bonnie & Clyde had changed their plans.

By full daylight, only a few vehicles had passed the lonely stake-out. But at 9:10, they heard the unmistakable whine of a big V8 engine in the distance, coming on at high speed. Moments later, the killer's car came into view, slowing as it neared what appeared to be a disabled truck. The truck belonged to Henry Methvin's father, the informant who set up Bonnie & Clyde. They paused at the truck, their tension slightly eased by a face and a vehicle they knew well. In fact, Clyde had bought the truck for the senior Methvin. The sun was behind Hamer and his team. Everyone held their breath as the occupants of the car came closer. Hamer had never actually seen Bonnie Parker or Clyde Barrow before this moment, but there was no mistaking the smallish man and the slight female with dyed red hair. Both driver and passenger were looking intently toward the mail drop opposite the officer's position. Unbeknown to the lawmen, Clyde had a semi-auto scattergun on each side of his seat. Bonnie had a fully-loaded and cocked nickel-plated Colt 45 semi-auto pistol under a magazine on her lap.

Cause Of Death: Lead Poisoning

With "Old Lucky" on his left hip, Frank Hamer raised the presentation-grade Remington rifle to his shoulder. Texas Ranger Manny Gault did the same with another Remington owned by Hamer. In unison, the other four lawmen put BARs or semi-auto shotguns to their shoulders, forming a six-man skirmish line. If the deadly duo tried to flee, the BARs could burst the Ford's engine block. Capt. Hamer stated his exact words to the devilish pair were, "Stick 'em up"! Bonnie & Clyde both reached for weapons. The

six lawmen let loose a thunderous hail of lead and steel-jacketed slugs. Bonnie screamed like a panther; Clyde's body jolted from two hits to the head. The driver's side of the stolen Ford was peppered with bullets and the occupants riddled from head to toe. The vehicle rolled slowly forward into the side ditch as the lawmens' guns continued to blaze. And then it was over. Official records state Clyde Barrow received at least 29 bullet wounds, eight of which severed his spine. What had been the 90-pound Bonnie Parker was hit 30 times; her skull was burst and several fingers were shot off her right hand. It is important to remember, however, that the pair had killed 9 lawmen and a notably larger number of unarmed civilians. Capt. Hamer approached the death car with "Old Lucky" drawn. Seeing the threat had been neutralized, Hamer leaned his Remington against the Ford and opened the driver's door. The body that had been Clyde Barrow rolled onto the ground, along with a shotgun. Hamer's rifle fell on top of both. Bonnie's head was in her lap. The fancy red hat she'd been wearing was in a shambles in the back seat. They had vowed not to be taken alive, and got their wish. An absolute arsenal of stolen weapons was found in the vehicle. The inventory included three BARs, two sawed-off shotguns, seven Colt Govt. 45 ACP automatics, two small-caliber semi-autos, a large-frame Colt double-action revolver, 100 loaded BAR magazines and an additional 3,000 rounds of ammunition.

Guns In The Aftermath

The circus that followed the demise of Bonnie & Clyde began as soon as the gunsmoke cleared. A substantial crowd gathered quickly. Before flesh and metal could be properly secured, souvenir hunters snatched bits of broken glass and

clothing, including Bonnie's hat splattered with blood and brains. Pocketknives dug bullets from trees; onlookers restrained a man from cutting off Clyde's trigger finger. The death car was towed into town with the bodies still crumpled inside. Grateful authorities would award Capt. Hamer the captured weapons.

But the saga of Bonnie & Clyde's stolen firearms did not end there. Bonnie's mother was approached by a showman wanting to buy her daughter's body and turn it into a traveling attraction. He also coveted the stolen firearms Bonnie & Clyde had in their possession at the time of their demise. Smelling money, both the Parker and Barrow families brazenly wrote to Capt. Hamer, demanding return of the illegal weapons that "belonged" to their relatives. Capt. Hamer never responded to the ridiculous requests and retained the weapons for the remainder of his life.

As the reality of Bonnie Parker & Clyde Barrow faded over the decades, the killer couple achieved something of folk hero status. Glorified in print and on film, they have sometimes been portrayed as a couple of misguided, lovesick kids from the wrong side of the tracks who took a turn for the worse. I recall telling Senior Texas Ranger Captain/Executive U.S. Marshal Clint Peoples in 1989, that a smaller American handgun manufacturer had issued a brace of commemorative Bonnie & Clyde revolvers. It was the only time I saw him at a loss for words. To a lawman of the 1930s, a comparable event today would be offering American shooters an Osama Bin Laden commemorative AK-47. But, the deadly Texas duo continues to fire the imagination. Country Western star Travis Tritt included, "Modern Day Bonnie & Clyde" on a recent best-selling CD. Although done with a bit of humor, the recording and music video relay a clear message…crime doesn't pay!

The D.W. King Gunsight Company

by David W. Ploeger

IN THE 1930s, pistolsmithing came of age and by far the largest pistolsmithing company was the D.W. King Gunsight Co. of San Francisco, California. Mr. King, a nationally ranked rifleman holding many records, perceived a need for better rifle sights and, accordingly, the original King patented sights were rifle sights. The King sights were innovative in design, of good quality and early models were manufactured by subcontractors and marketed by King from Denver, Colorado. There were several other rifle sight manufacturers, such as Marble and Redfield. In the early 1930s, King relocated to San Francisco and began marketing handgun sights particularly suited for target shooting.

In the 1930s Americans were developing a growing interest in handgun target shooting and the sport was increasing in popularity, creating a demand for good guns—and better

King Cockeyed Hammer (and short action job) on a S&W K-frame chambered for the 38 Special cartridge.

sights. Although the rapid-fire stage in the NRA course of fire required 5 shots in 10 seconds, most guns used were double-action revolvers since many considered the auto-loading pistols inferior to a Colt or Smith & Wesson target revolver.

The most popular match was the centerfire match, shot primarily with 38 Special revolvers. The 22-rimfire match was important, but less significant to most shooters. The 45 service match was usually shot with the 1911 Government Model 45 ACP, although some shot it with revolvers chambered for the 45 ACP cartridge.

Colt revolvers were generally preferred as they were considered to have the better–and lighter–single-action trigger pull. Remember, these matches were shot single action (*double-action fire was not as accurate*) with the competitor cocking the gun for each shot. Competitors found they could maintain a more consistent hold in rapid fire with the Colt than with the Smith & Wesson with its heavier hammer spring.

This growth in competitive handgun shooting increased the demand for better guns. However, handgun options were limited: Colt or Smith & Wesson. The three frame sizes of double-action revolvers offered by each company were, of necessity, the predominant choice of the more skilled target shooters. Shooters began looking for modifications to their guns to improve their scores and gunsmiths started offering what the shooters wanted: Heavy barrels, better sights, short actions, better grips, better trigger pulls—anything and everything to improve scores.

Sights were the most obvious item to improve upon since the Colt and S&W sights of the 1920s and '30s left a lot to be desired. Sights—even on the best target guns—were narrow and rounded, and their adjustments were neither precise nor repeatable.

Back then, hammer fall was long, much longer than on today's Colt and S&W revolvers, and left lots of time for the sights to wander off-target after the trigger was squeezed. The old Colt and S&W actions were very smooth, thanks to the hand labor lavished on these guns—but the action designs themselves were already 30 to 40 years old.

Custom gunsmiths and competitors began customizing handguns early on, but the real demand started in the 1930s with rise in competitive handgun shooting. D.W. King already had the catalog with rifle sights and some handgun sights. King had the inventive mind to design the sights and pistol modifications the shooting public wanted and— by the 1930s—had the expertise and manufacturing skill to make parts and modify the guns.

The first accessory invented by D.W. King was the reflector ramp front sight. This was a large steel front sight that usually fit over the existing front sight. The top of the sight base had a small mirror, fit at a 45-degree angle in the rear of the base, to shine sunlight onto the face of a

King's ramp reflector front sight.

Patridge-type interchangeable blade—usually fitted with colored plastic inserts at the tip like the current S&W red ramp-type inserts (*in fact, this is where S&W got the idea*). The inserts were white, red, gold and plain black—and any other color desired, on special order. The light reflected was quite effective in making the insert and sight blade stand out. There were 1/10- to 1/4-inch Patridge front sight blades— and sizes in-between. The Keith long-range gold bar front sight was available. There was even a super police night sight, which was a very large white-faced bead sight. These inserts fit into a key slot atop the ramp and were attached by a screw through the side of the base.

Rear sights were not neglected. S&W and Colt rear sight blades were made in both the square-notch and rounded-notch designs so popular in the 1930s, and aperture models were also made. For the first time, a person could order from a catalog any type of sight standardized for each gun type and need. S&W offered the King sights as standard on their 357 Registered

Magnum in the 1930s. Other S&Ws— and some Colts—could be had from the factory with King sights.

The King Super Target Ramp was invented in the mid-1930s to increase the barrel weight of revolvers and utilize better sights. This full rib incorporated the King mirror ramp front sight and a truly adjustable rear sight. The rear sight had repeatable adjustments of 1 inch per click at 50 yards. The whole rib was attached by (only) two pins at the front sight base on the factory barrel, and the vented rib went back to the rear sight, with one threaded screw for rear sight elevation control drilled into the rear top of the frame. The rib in the frame area was milled almost flush with the top of the frame, thus moving weight to the front of the barrel where it was much needed—as well as providing good sights with repeatable adjustments. This 'super' target ramp design was very popular and target shooters flocked to King for this modification. This 'super ramp' combination could be fitted to any revolver or semi-auto pistol, and King's production department standardized them to fit most popular handguns.

The King Cockeyed Hammer was created to facilitate fast cocking of the revolver hammer in rapid-fire shooting events. This item involved a large hammer spur, usually on one side of the hammer, that enabled the thumb to grasp the hammer more easily, thus allowing the marksman to maintain a sure constant grip on the gun, so important to accurate shooting. The hammer spur could be lowered as well as lightened—and often was. The spur could be widened on one side or the other—or both sides. This was a trademark modification by King, and different employees made the hammer slightly different—but all were well done. The hammer spur was carefully built up with weld, then shaped and finely checkered. The hammers

Matched pair of Colt Officer's Model Match revolvers (38 Spl. & 22 rimfire) with King half-ribs, reflector front sights, cockeyed hammers, short action jobs, Fitz grips and trigger shoes.

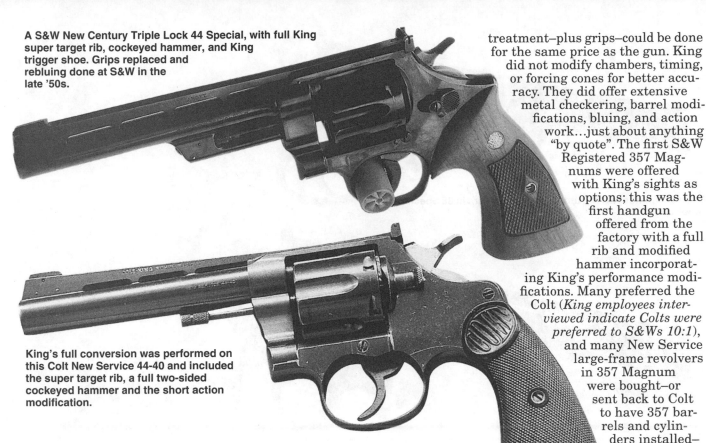

A S&W New Century Triple Lock 44 Special, with full King super target rib, cockeyed hammer, and King trigger shoe. Grips replaced and rebluing done at S&W in the late '50s.

King's full conversion was performed on this Colt New Service 44-40 and included the super target rib, a full two-sided cockeyed hammer and the short action modification.

treatment—plus grips—could be done for the same price as the gun. King did not modify chambers, timing, or forcing cones for better accuracy. They did offer extensive metal checkering, barrel modifications, bluing, and action work…just about anything "by quote". The first S&W Registered 357 Magnums were offered with King's sights as options; this was the first handgun offered from the factory with a full rib and modified hammer incorporating King's performance modifications. Many preferred the Colt (*King employees interviewed indicate Colts were preferred to S&Ws 10:1*), and many New Service large-frame revolvers in 357 Magnum were bought—or sent back to Colt to have 357 barrels and cylinders installed—and were then sent to King for installation of 'super' target ramp sights (which made a revolver similar to the S&W Registered Magnum and, to many, a better handgun).

By 1940, S&W had modified their K-22 to incorporate the short action, heavier ribbed barrel, micro-adjustable sights and larger hammer spur. After WWII, the whole S&W line incorporated these features. Colt made the barrel on the Officers Model larger in diameter, and improved the sights—but never equaled the new S&W sights, even after WWII. The Colt Python, of mid-1950s design, looks like a full conversion pre-war Officer's Model with a barrel weight that King did pre-WWII. The sights are almost exactly the same and King rear sight blades will fit in Colt post-WWII sights—and the adjustments are exactly the same

were then cyanide heat-treated to reharden and, in the case of S&W, to case-color the hammer. Colt hammers were extensively modified with lowered spurs, and lightened. Often the Colt actions were modified to deliver shorter hammer-fall, a procedure that entailed completely changing the timing of the gun. Many believed this contributed to better scores. Walter King, the shop foreman (no relation to D.W. King), originated the short action and standardized this modification for all types of revolvers. By the late 1930s, the King catalog ran to 82 pages of modifications and accessories.

By the mid-1930s, the King catalogs were mostly devoted to handguns and contained listings for all sorts of exotic grips, grip adapters, sights, the full S&W and Colt handgun lines, reloading and casting equipment—as well as cleaning supplies and targets. By the late 1930s, the King catalog included 82 pages of modifications and accessories.

per week at King's. Sights were sent all over the world and many outside gunsmiths used King parts for custom handgun projects.

Colt sold many more revolvers than S&W in pre-WWII America. The Officer's Model Target medium-frame Colt 38 and 22 were the preferred target and police handguns, and many of these were modified with full super target ramps, short action jobs and cockeyed hammers. The cost, in the late 1930s, for these modifications was $20.00 for the super target rib (installed), $5.00 for the King "Cockeyed" hammer; the King short-action job was $8.50 for Colts and $10.00 for S&Ws. A half-rib with rear sight was $10.00. A King red-ramp front sight, fitted over the existing front sight base, was $5.00 (installed). The Colt Officer's Model Target revolver was $45.75 in the late 1930s; the whole target

The D.W. King store and shop was on the 4th and 5th floor of a building (still standing) at 171-3 Second Street, and later King moved to Howard Street. In the late 1930s, the King company had 50 to 60 gunsmiths and employees. There were as many as 100 handguns modified

A 357 Magnum Colt New Service with full super target rib, cockeyed hammer, a short action job and Roper grips. Originally chambered for the 44 Special, this revolver was returned to Colt for the caliber conversion, then sent on to King for the rest of the work.

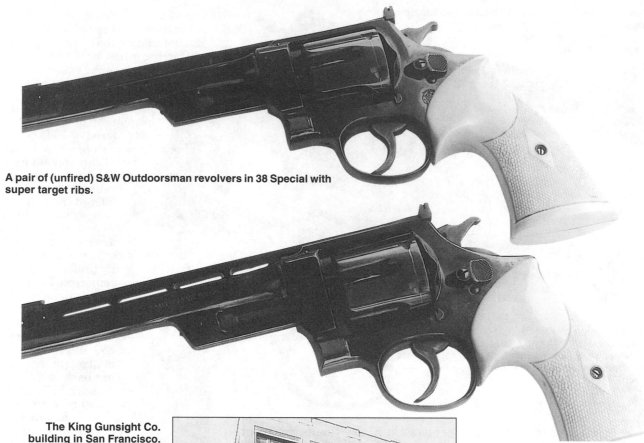

A pair of (unfired) S&W Outdoorsman revolvers in 38 Special with super target ribs.

The King Gunsight Co. building in San Francisco.

for the sights, right down to the size and location of the adjustments.

King did not neglect semi-automatic handguns, either. There was an extensive list of modifications for the Colt Government Model 45 Automatic, from tight bushings with ball bearings to tighten the barrel to spring-loaded ball bearings in the frame to tighten the slide-to-frame fit. There were trigger modifications and full 'super' target sight ribs, as well.

Towards the end of the 1930s, the 22 semi-autos were gaining favor with target shooters. The Colt Woodsman and the High Standard 22 autos were given the full treatment—full ribs and sights—as well. The thin, light barrels of these autos were given full-length hollow steel underlugs with adjustable weight systems featuring wood, aluminum, steel or lead inserts.

During WWII, no commercial work was done while King produced M1 carbine front sights and barrel bushings for Colt 45 autos to support the war effort. Mr. King died during WWII and Mrs. King took over operation of the business, with the help of a succession of managers. After the war, several key employees quit in a labor dispute and started the Micro Sight Company, which went on to become one of the major sight manufacturers and distributors on the West Coast.

Post-WWII production resumed at King and continued until 1952, when the company went out of business. By then, there was a great deal of competition in the custom firearms market and the factory handguns of this post-war era were incorporating many of the modifications pioneered by King. The company published the first catalog offering standardized modifications to handguns, did excellent work in high volume, and influenced the design of handguns to this day. Modern Ruger and Colt adjustable handgun rear sights are very similar to the King rear sights, and the King rear sight blades will fit modern Colts and Rugers. ●

COMBAT CARTRIDGES OF THE 20TH CENTURY

by Christopher R. Bartocci

The most influential military small arm calibers of the last century (*left to right*): 7.62x63mm, 7.62x54R, 7.92x57mm, 7.7x56mm (303 British), 7.62x33mm (30 Carbine), 7.92x33mm Kurz, 7.62x39mm, 7.62x45mm Czech, 7.62x51mm NATO, 7x43mm (280 British), 6mm SAW, 5.56x45mm, 5.45x39mm Soviet, 5.56x45mm NATO (Belgian SS109/ U.S. M885 Ball) and 4.85x49mm British.
Aaron Matson photo

MILITARY TECHNOLOGY HAS changed greatly in design as well as concept over the last 100 years. Perhaps the metallic cartridge and modern assault weapons have come to an evolutionary crossroads. The evolution of military assault rifles and cartridges have reached their peak of development. With the evolution from long-range bolt-action rifles to semi-automatic long-range guns to the submachine gun to the modern military assault rifles we can see how warfare has evolved and how technology evolved with it.

In the early 1900s, the bolt-action rifle was the main battle implement. In the United States, it was the M1903 Springfield rifle firing the legendary 30-06 (7.62x63mm) cartridge. The Soviet Union used the Model 1891 Mosin-Nagant bolt-action rifle firing the 7.62x54R cartridge. Germany used the 7.92x57mm round in their Mauser rifles and the British the 303 British cartridge in their Enfield rifles. At this time World War I was getting under way and the stalemate of trench warfare kept combat at greater distances where 500 meters-plus distances were commonplace. Individual marksmanship was in its prime and most military units subscribed to the "One Shot, One Kill" philosophy.

Towards the end of the 1930s, and the advent of World War II, Nazi Germany would forever change the way wars would be fought. The introduction of mechanized/maneuver warfare would call for new weapons and tactics. The rapid mobility and use of armored vehicles to transport troops into combat saw the need for rapid fire, as well as the new machine pistols. Higher volume of fire was desired to deal with combat at closer ranges, where engagements were normally occurred at less than 300 meters. Urban warfare would bring it still closer.

In the 1950s, NATO was looking to adopt an intermediate cartridge. Great Britain introduced the 280 British, but this would fall victim to the 7.62x51mm cartridge. With the war in Vietnam scaling-up in the 1960s, a totally new concept for the modern military caliber—as well as rifle—was introduced and would be a catalyst for a total re-thinking of the concept of the modern battle rifle. There was a changeover from intermediate-caliber rounds, such as the 7.92x33mm *Kurz* and the 7.62x39mm, to the high-velocity low-impulse 22-caliber 5.56x45mm round and the 5.45x39mm Soviet. Once again Great Britain would make an entry into the NATO competition for a small-caliber cartridge with their 4.85mm cartridge that was beaten out, and justly so, by the 5.56x45mm SS109/M855 Ball cartridge.

In this article we will explore the most influential small arms calibers of the last century and see the evolution from the full-power battle cartridges to the intermediate-range cartridges, as well as the arms that fire them.

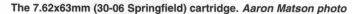

The 7.62x63mm (30-06 Springfield) cartridge. *Aaron Matson photo*

The 7.62x63mm (30-06 Springfield)

The 30-06 Springfield cartridge was adopted by the United States in 1906 for the M1903 Springfield bolt-action rifle and the M1917 machine-gun. The original loading for this rimless bottleneck cartridge called for a 220-grain bullet at approximately 2,585 feet per second (fps) and later changed to a 150-grain bullet at approximately 2740 fps. The 30-06 remained the primary rifle and machinegun cartridge for the U.S. military from 1906 to the mid-1950s. The bullet came in several forms; armor-piercing proved to be the most popular for U.S. forces during World War II.

During World War II, the United States military adapted the 30-06 cartridge as its primary small-arm caliber. It was employed in the M1903 Springfield, the M1 Garand, BAR (Browning Automatic Rifle), as well as the range of the M1919-series belt-fed general-purpose machineguns.

The 30-06 cartridge has little military use today, however it is still very popular in the commercial arena. It remains one of the most popular medium- to large-game cartridges in North America. It still is employed in both sniper and competition rifles.

The 7.62x63mm (30-06 Springfield) M1 Garand rifle was the first general issue semi-automatic rifle of the U.S. military. *Springfield Armory photo*

The Russian 7.62x54R cartridge. *Aaron Matson photo*

7.62x54R Russian

The oldest military cartridge still in service today. The 7.62x54R cartridge was adopted in 1891 in the Soviet Union for use in their bolt-action Mosin-Nagant rifles. In the original loading, the cartridge utilized a 211-grain round-nose bullet. The cartridge case was rimmed and early production was manufactured from brass, and later made of steel with either copper-washed or lacquered finish. Beginning in the 1960s the ammunition was often sealed at both the primer and mouth with lacquer. Prior to World War I, the bullet was changed from a round-nose bullet to a 148-grain spitzer firing at approximately 2800 fps.

The original rifle for this cartridge was the Mosin-Nagant bolt-action rifle. During World War II a semi-automatic rifle was developed to fire this cartridge. In 1938, the Simonov Model 1936 (AVS36) became the first semi-automatic rifle to be adopted by the Red Army. This was a gas-oper-ated rifle with the capability to fire both semi- and fully-automatic. The rifle and cartridge combination proved to be a very difficult weapon to fire due to excessive recoil and muzzle blast. In latter 1938 the AVS was replaced by the famous SVT30, or the Tokarev. This 8-pound rifle carried a 10-round detachable box magazine and served a very short stint with the Russian Army. In 1940 the SVT40 replaced the SVT38. This was merely a stronger-built version of the rifle and marked the last service rifle to utilize this cartridge.

Throughout the century, all of the Soviet general-purpose machine guns fired the 7.62x54mm cartridge. The Maxim 1910 was the first, followed by the Degtyarev DP, DT, and ShKas Air-craft guns. In 1943, the SG43 Goryunov was adopted to replace the Maxim (PM1910). With a few others down the road the Kalashnikov-designed PK and PKM were adopted as the Soviet Union's general-purpose machine gun and—to this day—it remains in that position with the Russian Army, as well as many others: The most reliable of any of the belt-fed 7.62x54R machineguns. Even with the complications in autoloading rifles and machineguns with rimmed cartridges, the Russians would not develop and implement a rimless cartridge for this purpose so it provided a challenge to all Russian machinegun and automatic weapon designers.

However, in 1963 a new sniper rifle was introduced into the Soviet Army; the SVD Dragunov rifle, based on the AK47/49 design. This semi-automatic-only sniper rifle utilizes the PSO-1 telescopic sight. The rifle has a 10-round detachable box magazine and is still in use today as one of the most respected semi-automatic sniper rifles in the world.

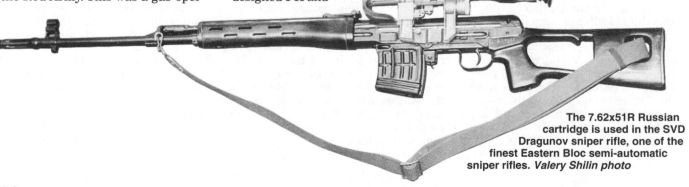

The 7.62x51R Russian cartridge is used in the SVD Dragunov sniper rifle, one of the finest Eastern Bloc semi-automatic sniper rifles. *Valery Shilin photo*

The German 7.92x57mm cartridge. *Aaron Matson photo*

The 7.92x57mm Mauser

The first 7.92x57mm cartridges were produced in 1888 by Germany. The initial military load called for a bullet diameter of 0.318-inch, with 226-grain round-nose bullet firing at a velocity of 293 fps. This was known as the 7.92x57mm J (*Infanterie*) cartridge. There was room for improvement ballistically for the cartridge and, in 1905, the German Army adopted the 7.92x57mm JS (*Infanterie Spitzer*) cartridge. The main difference–besides the shape– was that the bullet diameter was increased to 0.323-inch; the bullet would be a 154-grain spitzer bullet, with a pointed tip and flat base. The muzzle velocity was also increased

to 2880 fps. Since the introduction of the 7.92x57mm JS cartridge in 1905, all future German military weapons were chambered for the larger-diameter JS cartridge. There was an interchangeability issue, the S could be fired in the JS barrel but the larger-diameter JS could not be fired in an S barrel. This cartridge was standard with the German Army in both World War I and II.

The 7.92x57mm cartridge achieved great popularity throughout the world and is still in use in some countries today. Some of these countries that have produced the cartridge are China, Japan, Poland, Great Britain, Portugal and Spain.

Numerous variations of the bullet have been produced, depending on need and availability of resources. Some of the more popular weapons chambered for this cartridge are the Gewehr 88, Mauser K98/K98 K, FG42, MG38 and MG42. The cartridge was used until the end of World War II. With the split-up of Germany, the West German Army adopted the 7.62x51mm NATO, as well as the 5.56x45mm NATO, cartridges and East Germany went with the Warsaw Pact 7.62x54R, 7.62x39mm and 5.45x39mm Soviet cartridges. Currently the United Germany uses the NATO standard calibers.

The 7.63x56R (303 British) cartridge. *Aaron Matson photo.*

The 7.7x56R (303 British)

On February 20, 1889 the British Army officially adopted the 303 British cartridge. Its roots go back to the 7.5mm Swiss Rubin cartridge, which was also a rimmed cartridge. The cartridge was developed for the Lee Metford rifle, adopted in December of 1888. The British Army, at the turn of the century, was interested in replacing the 303 cartridge but two World Wars interrupted their research and development efforts. It was not until

the early 1950s–with the development of the 280 British– that they made a serious effort to replace the aging 303 cartridge. In the end the 7.62x51mm NATO cartridge would officially retire the 303 British cartridge in 1957. Numerous firearms were chambered for the 303 cartridge, such as the Lee-Enfield rifle; Lewis, Bren, Vickers-Maxim machinegun, to name a few.

Numerous configurations of the 303 cartridge were designed, imple-

mented and replaced throughout the cartridge's years of service. The original blackpowder load for the 303 British cartridge was a 215-grain round-nose ball cartridge delivering a muzzle velocity of 1850 fps. In 1892, the propellant was switched from blackpowder to smokeless powder, increasing the muzzle velocity to 1970 fps. The final military load adopted was a 174-grain flat-base pointed bullet firing at a muzzle velocity of 2440 fps.

The 7.62x33mm (30 Carbine) cartridge. *Aaron Matson photo.*

The 7.62x33mm (30 Carbine)

The 30 Carbine cartridge was adopted by the United States in October 23, 1941. This cartridge is classified more as a pistol cartridge than a full-power–or intermediate– rifle cartridge. The rimless cartridge case is tapered, and carries a 110-grain round-nose bullet fired at approximately 1950 fps.

During World War II, there was a requirement for a lightweight rifle that could be carried by personnel such as mortar crews, tankers, artillerymen, and machine-gunners who would normally carry

only the M1911A1 45 ACP pistol. This lightweight rifle would have greater range than a pistol. The rifle ultimately developed was the M1 Carbine. The semi-automatic-only M1 Carbine weighed a light 5 pounds, 7 ounces (unloaded) and carried a 15-round magazine. The lightweight and higher-capacity magazine, when compared to the M1 Garand, made the M1 Carbine very popular with troops in all areas. It became general-purpose issue and proved very popular. While effective in close-quarter

engagements, beyond 100 to 150 yards it was mostly ineffective.

By the time the Korean War came around, the M1 Carbine was updated to the M2 Carbine, the main difference being the M2 was selective fire. To accommodate the high rate of fire, a 30-round magazine was developed. Both M1 and M2 carbines are still in use today, throughout the world. In 1963, through the National Rifle Association, the military sold existing stocks of M1 Carbines to civilian sportsmen.

The Development Of Intermediate-Range Cartridges

The 7.92x33mm *Kurz*, the world's first issue intermediate cartridge developed for the world's first assault rifle, the StG 44, or "Storm Rifle". *Aaron Matson photo*

The 7.92x33mm *Kurz*

Towards the end of World War II, Nazi Germany was experimenting with many different types of weapons and concepts. There was a clear need for lightweight weapons with high-capacity magazines. Since most engagements took place under 400 yards, the long-range power of the 7.92x57mm cartridge was not utilized. Therefore, the intermediate cartridge delivered accuracy and power to the required distance with lower recoil and less weight. They implemented the submachine gun on a large scale, but it was seriously deficient in accuracy and range. The introduction of the FG42 was the first step towards a new concept for the modern battle rifle. This was a lightweight magazine-fed rifle capable of semi- as well as fully-automatic fire. The only problem was

that it was chambered for the full-powered 7.92x57mm cartridge. The rifle was nearly impossible to control on full automatic, and was basically employed in a semi-automatic role.

In 1941 a new cartridge was adopted called the 7.92x33mm *Kurz Patrone*, or 7.9 Short Cartridge, manufactured by Polte-Magdeburg. The cartridge utilizes a 125-grain bullet fired at a muzzle velocity of approximately 2247 fps. This decrease in weight enabled the soldier to carry significantly more ammunition for the same combat load-out.

The rifles designed to fire this new cartridge were the MP43, MP43/1, MP44 and–the most famous–the StG44 *Sturmgewehr*–or "Storm" Rifle. This rifle weighed approximately 11 pounds, carried a 30-round magazine

and was capable of both accurate and controllable automatic fire. It had a range up to 400 yards. This rifle and cartridge revolutionized the modern combat rifle and all future military rifles would adhere to the concept of light weight, high capacity and selective-fire.

The 7.92x33mm *Kurz* cartridge had a very short service life: no production rifles were made outside of the ones used by the Third Reich. Ammunition production halted after World War II. In the early 1960s, the former East Germany produced limited quantities of ammunition for export sales to nations who used wartime MP43, MP43/1, MP44 and StG44 rifles. No commercial rifles were ever chambered for this cartridge.

The world's first assault rifle. The 7.92x33mm *Kurz* StG44, or "Storm Rifle". All post-World War II military small arms would adhere to this concept of both weapon and ammunition. *Aaron Matson photo*

The 7.62x39mm Soviet cartridge. Developed for the AK47 and AKM assault rifles. *Aaron Matson photo*

The 7.62x39mm

With the trench warfare of World War I gone forever, the role of the combat rifle had to be re-thought. Nazi Germany was the true pioneer of the modern assault rifle. With the concept of an intermediate battle cartridge, a soldier could carry a lighter and more controllable selective-fire rifle with two to three times the amount of ammunition for the same combat weight. The assault rifle in concept derived from the StG44/MP43 rifles and their 7.92x33mm *Kurz* ammunition.

It has long been told that the origins of the 7.62x39mm cartridge derived from the 7.92x33mm *Kurz*

cartridge when in fact the cartridge was the German Vollmer 7.75x40mm (M35) intermediate cartridge of 1934 or 1935. The main issue for the Russians was the bullet; they required a 7.62mm-caliber projectile. The first attempt at a Soviet-made interme-

The evolution of the 7.62x39mm. The new Soviet intermediate cartridge was derived from the 7.75x40mm Vollmer *(left)*. The Soviet designers expanded the mouth to accept the desirable 7.62mm projectile, creating the experimental 7.62x41mm cartridge *(center)*. The final production led to the 7.62x39mm cartridge *(right)*. Woodin Laboratory photo

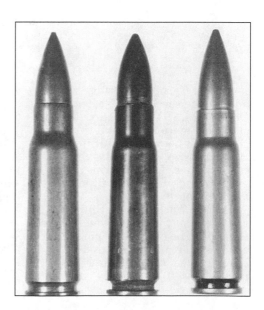

diate cartridge was the 7.62x41mm and early SKS rifles, as well as the original prototype AK47, were chambered for it. Due to some technical difficulties with the shortness of the bullet, it was necessary to shorten the neck of the cartridge case to the current 7.62x39mm dimensions. The

7.62x41mm cartridge never left the experimental stages.

The 7.62x39mm cartridge uses a 122/123-grain bullet, firing at approximately 2300 fps, which comes in numerous configurations including ball, tracer, armor-piercing, incendiary as well as blank ammunition. This cartridge is made

all over the world by Russia, China, Poland, Romania, Finland, Bulgaria, Cuba and Hungary to just name a few. The main weapons that fire this round are the SKS rifles, AK47/AKM, any AK-type clones, RPK and the RPD.

The 7.62x45mm Czech cartridge. *Aaron Matson photo*

The 7.62x45mm

The 7.62x45mm cartridge was independently developed in Czechoslovakia and put into service in 1952. It was developed for the Vz 52 semi-automatic rifle and machinegun.

The cartridge performed similar to the 7.62x39mm cartridge ballistically with approximately 100 yards more

effective range due to the extra powder capacity in the cartridge case. This new concept was brought up for consideration with the Soviet Union with no response. Due to the standardization of the Warsaw Pact countries, all 7.62x45mm rifles and machineguns were re-chambered for the M43

7.62x39mm cartridge, or decommissioned and sold off to other countries.

The Vz 52/57/58P/58V have a similar appearance to the AK47/AKM rifles; however, they are totally different inside. Instead of a rotating bolt, they use a tilting bolt with a swinging hammer.

The NATO Trials Of The Early 1950s

In 1950, the NATO trials began in an effort to standardize small arms ammunition and weapons for the new NATO allies. With the end of World War II and the introduction of the intermediate cartridge, Great Britain embraced the concept of the lightweight cartridge that would be

more controllable on full auto. However the other competitor, the United States, had not accepted the concept—or even considered development of their own intermediate cartridge. The United States was bent on keeping the full-power 30-caliber cartridge. The tests were politically

driven, and perhaps the best cartridge did not win. American influence has always weighed heavy in small arms testing and, oddly enough, it would be the United States who would break the NATO agreement and adopt another caliber during the war in Vietnam.

The 7.62x51mm cartridge, developed for the American M-14 rifle.
Aaron Matson photo

The 7.62x51mm

In the early 1950s, the United States military set out to replace all existing small arms ammunition with a single cartridge. They would have a single small arm that would replace the M1 Garand, M1 Carbine, Thompson submachine gun, M3 Grease Gun and the BAR. This new rifle was supposed to take the best attributes of each: the long range of the M1 Garand, light weight of the M1 Carbine, the high-capacity and controllability of full-auto fire of the Thompson and the M3 Grease Gun, and the firepower of the BAR. The general-purpose belt-fed machinegun would use this

same cartridge for interchangeability and logistical reasons.

The ammunition selected to base this upon was the newly developed "light-rifle" cartridge, which was merely a shortened version (from 63mm to 51mm) of the 7.62x63mm (30-06) cartridge. The rifle chosen was basically an improved M1 Garand. The 7.62x51mm cartridge would fire a 147- to 150-grain FMJ boattail bullet at a muzzle velocity of 2750 fps. The rifle would be selective fire and use a 20-round detachable box magazine. In 1957, the M-14

rifle was selected to be the next service rifle for the U.S. military, along with the M-60 general-purpose machinegun—both chambered for the new 7.62x51mm cartridge. The unfortunate reality was that the only weapon to be replaced in the series would be the M1 Garand. The new rifle was still heavy, uncontrollable when fired on full-auto, and there was little difference in recoil and the weight of the ammunition.

Although the 280 British cartridge was more advanced, being an intermediate caliber controllable on

The M14 was the first small arm to be chambered for the 7.65x51mm NATO cartridge. The M14 had the shortest service life of any U.S. military small arm with only six years of service. *Springfield Armory photo*

full-auto and with a reasonable effective range, the 7.62x51mm cartridge was adopted as the new NATO cartridge in January of 1954. Without a doubt, the United States influence had pushed this caliber on NATO, putting it a step behind the Warsaw Pact countries in the area of small arms development. It would not be until the war in Vietnam that the United States would realize they had made a mistake. The future of military small arms was seen to be in intermediate and small-caliber battle cartridges. This would lead to the short six-year service life for the M-14 and rushing the underdeveloped 5.56x45mm AR-15/M-16 rifle into service to equip the troops in Vietnam.

The British intermediate caliber 7x43mm (280 British). This cartridge was developed for the Enfield EM-2. *Aaron Matson photo*

The 7x43mm (280 British)

Following the end of World War II, the British Army began a program to replace their old and outdated bolt-action 303 rifles with a new advanced lightweight autoloading rifle. However, the British were not satisfied that any of the current cartridges–including the U.S. 7.62x63mm (30-06 Springfield), the German 7.92x57mm Mauser or the Russian 7.62x54R–were the proper choices for their new rifle. They had seen the advantages the 7.92x33mm *Kurz* cartridge had given the Germans, but felt it was underpowered. Following the war, in 1945 the Small Arms Caliber Panel (SACP) was established with the sole responsibility of determining the best and most ideal caliber for this new lightweight autoloading rifle. In March of 1947 they issued their finding recommending the smallest possible caliber. This would decrease the weight of the ammunition, thereby allowing larger quantities to be carried for the same combat weight. They believed the ideal should be 270-caliber, with a minimum of 250-caliber.

In Great Britain during 1947, the specifications were approved for the 276 cartridge and later the name was changed to the 280. This helped distinguish the cartridge from others with similar specifications. The bullet was to weigh approximately 100 grains with an armor-piercing core and be fired at a velocity between 2750 and 2900 fps. Later that year a second cartridge was developed utilizing a smaller 270-caliber bullet. By late 1948, the 270-caliber

cartridge was discontinued in favor of the 280-caliber.

As development went on, the 280-caliber cartridge specifications called for a 130-grain bullet traveling at 2450 fps with muzzle energy of 1680 fpe. The ammunition was manufactured by Royal Ordnance Factory Radway Green and Imperial Chemical Industries Ltd. Production included ball, tracer, armor-piercing, and incendiary ammunition. The next significant change was made to the rim; it was increased from .458-inch to the same diameter as the American 7.62x63mm cartridge (.469-inch) in anticipation of the NATO trials where it would compete against the U.S. 7.62x51mm cartridge. The modified cartridge was called the 280/30-caliber. By changing the rim, the cartridge could be easily adapted to any currently produced 30-caliber rifle, including the FN FAL and the M-14.

As trials in Great Britain continued, a deficiency was found in the penetration test. By requirement, the bullet must penetrate a steel helmet at 2000 yards and the original loading failed to do so. As a result, a 140-grain bullet was introduced and the specification was decreased to 1600 yards.

The rifle designed to fire this cartridge was the new EM-2 (Enfield Model-2), an unconventional bullpup design, where the magazine was behind the trigger. The rifle was selective fire and utilized a 20-round detachable box magazine. Also, FN FAL prototypes were made to fire the 280/30 cartridge.

In 1950 the NATO trials began. It was mainly the 280/30-caliber against the American 30-caliber light rifle cartridge. The main deficiency noted was that the 280/30 had a higher trajectory than the American cartridge. But, the bottom line was that the U.S. Army would not drop below 30-caliber, and their recommendation was to adopt their cartridge as the new 7.62x51mm NATO cartridge. There were two different concepts for the cartridges. The 280/30 British cartridge was developed as an intermediate cartridge, not a full-power rifle cartridge. The intermediate caliber would lack long-range penetration. The U.S. Army was not willing to decrease their range and penetration specifications and reduce power any further, and would not revisit this issue until the war in Vietnam.

The British realized that the testing went in favor of the 7.62x51mm, rightly or not. All parties involved knew the sole purpose of the NATO trials was for standardization. However, the British still felt they had the better cartridge and they needed to get on with production to rearm the British military. In August of 1951, Great Britain went against NATO and adopted the 280/30 cartridge (SA, Ball, 7mm Mk 1 Z) as the official cartridge of the British Army, along with the EM-2 rifle.

In 1952, through all the political turmoil, Great Britain reversed its decision and halted production on both the EM-2 and the 280/30 ammunition in favor of the 7.62x51mm NATO cartridge and

The highly advanced British EM-2 (Enfield Model – 2) rifle was developed to fire the 280 British intermediate cartridge. This rifle and ammunition combination fell victim to the NATO trials and was passed over for the heavier, full-powered 7.62x51mm NATO cartridge. *Collector Grade Publications photo*

the FN FAL rifle. The British Army did not support this decision, but politics prevailed and Britain went with the NATO decision. Unfortu- nately, Great Britain was left with a full-power battle cartridge in a heavy rifle that was less effective on automatic fire than their EM-2.

This was the exact opposite of what they were trying to accomplish. Progress took another step back.

The 6x45mm (6mm SAW) cartridge. *Aaron Matson photo*

The 6mm SAW

The 6mm SAW (XM732 Ball), or 6x45mm cartridge, never left the experimental stage although signifi- cant quantities of ammunition were produced. In the late 1960s to early 1970s the U.S. military initiated a project to develop a new SAW (Squad Automatic Weapon), and the 6mm cartridge was earmarked to be the most optimal military caliber. At the time of its introduction, the 5.56x45mm and the 7.62x51mm cartridge were in U.S. service. The 6mm SAW cartridge utilized a 105- grain FMJ boattail bullet firing at a muzzle velocity of 2520 fps.

The purpose of the SAW project was to develop a new light machine- gun that would replace the M-60 as a general-purpose machinegun. At the conclusion of the trials in 1976, it was decided that it would not be advisable to enter a new caliber into general issue and the 6mm project was dropped and, instead, atten- tion was focused on the newly devel- oped/updated 5.56x45mm NATO cartridge. The SAW project contin- ued, eventually leading to the adop- tion of the 5.56mm FN MINIMI M249 SAW in 1982.

The Development Of Small-Caliber (Low-Impulse) Cartridges

The 5.56x45mm cartridge. This cartridge was developed for the ArmaLite AR15, which went on to be the American M-16 and M-16A1 assault rifles. *Aaron Matson photo*

The 5.56x45mm

From 1953 to 1956 the U.S. Army conducted the SALVO field trials testing various types of 22-caliber loads, multiple-ball loads and flech- ette loads for possible military use. This test was to go along with the SPIW (Special Purpose Individual Weapon); this was the project that was supposed to succeed the M-14 and the early M-16 rifles. Particular interest went to the 22-caliber car- tridges. An M2 carbine was modi- fied to accept the 22 Gustafson cartridge *(the 30 Carbine necked down to 22-caliber)*. Testing of this cartridge showed it to be superior in every way to the 7.62x33mm (30 Carbine) cartridge.

In February of 1957, ArmaLite was given the results of the SALVO field trials. At this point, they knew the AR-10 had no future with the Army after the offi- cial adoption of the M-14. General Wyman, who was impressed with the AR-10, which he saw demonstrated in 1956, went to see Gene Stoner, briefed him on the SALVO field trials and asked about scaling down the AR-10 to fit this requirement.

The first attempt ArmaLite made was scaling down the AR-10 to fire the commercial 222 Remington car- tridge. There were many benefits to this rifle and ammunition combina- tion; with the in-line stock and the heavy weight of the recoiling parts, the rifle was incredibly accurate and controllable during full-auto fire. ArmaLite now focused on their new AR-15 rifle and its 22-caliber car- tridge. In 1957, Gene Stoner went to Fort Benning to get the desired char- acteristics for this new cartridge.

He designed a 22-caliber 55-grain FMJ bullet and had it manufactured by the Sierra Bullet Company. The cartridge case was lengthened to allow a heavier powder charge and loaded with commercial IMR propel- lant. This new cartridge was called the 222 Special.

The 222 Special/223 Remington cartridge was in fact designed for the AR-15/M-16 rifle. With the adop- tion of the AR-15 by the U.S. Air Force in 1963 and the U.S. Army in 1967, the cartridge was called the M193 Ball cartridge. This cartridge remained in service until the adop- tion of the 5.56x45mm NATO M885/ SS109 ball cartridge in October of 1980, following the NATO trials.

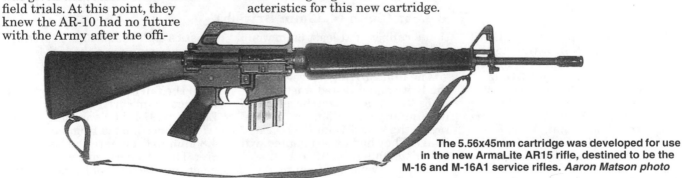

The 5.56x45mm cartridge was developed for use in the new ArmaLite AR15 rifle, destined to be the M-16 and M-16A1 service rifles. *Aaron Matson photo*

The 5.45x39mm Soviet cartridge was the Soviet Union's answer to the 5.56x45mm and M-16 series rifle. *Aaron Matson photo*

The 5.45x39mm Soviet

As a result of being on the receiving end of the new 5.56x45mm cartridge in the Vietnam War, the Soviet Union was forced to rethink their battle rifle and cartridge. The Soviet Union wanted to develop its own low impulse high velocity cartridge. Mikhail Kalashnikov, who was charged with developing the new rifle to fire it, was adamantly opposed to small-caliber weapons; he had felt the Soviet Army was much better off with the 7.62x39mm.

In the late 1960s, a small team of ammunition experts was created to develop this new cartridge. All samples and experimental cartridges would be compared to the American 5.56x45mm. The projectile chosen was a 0.221-inch FMJ bullet with a steel core weighing 52 to 54 grains. The bullet has a long profile with an empty space in the tip between the lead plug that encapsulated the steel core and the jacket. The bullet

has a muzzle velocity of approximately 2950 fps. In 1974 the cartridge was officially adopted as the 5.45x39mm (M74) cartridge.

When tested by the U.S. Army, the 5.45x39mm cartridge was found to be extremely effective in causing traumatic wounds. The empty space in the bullet's tip, between the lead plug and the jacket, caused the bullet to destabilize (tumble) on impact with soft tissue. The lead core shifted forward on impact, contributing to the effect.

The rifle designed to fire this new cartridge was the Kalashnikov-designed AK74 rifle, merely an AKM modified to fire the 5.45x39mm cartridge. Added to the rifle was a new muzzlebrake. The barrel had a faster twist of 1:9.25 inches to stabilize the new cartridge. The AK74 utilized a Bakelite (polymer) 30-round magazine. This new rifle and cartridge were first put to the test in the Soviet war in

Afghanistan. Western intelligence would learn of this advancement through a journalist from *Soldier of Fortune* magazine, Galen Geer.

The 5.45x39mm cartridge remains today as the main Russian battle cartridge. Currently the Russians employ AKS74 *(side-folding stock)* rifles as well as the standard AK74 *(fixed stock)* and the AKSU-74 *(short-barreled with side-folding stock)* rifles. The AK74 is now being slowly replaced by the new AN94 assault rifle designed by Gennady Nikonov. This rifle utilizes a new operating system called 'Blow Back Shifted Pulse', a combination of both recoil and gas operation. The AN94 is said to be significantly more accurate and reliable than the AK74. The 5.45x39mm cartridge was adopted in numerous former Warsaw Pact countries, such as Poland, Romania, Bulgaria and the former East Germany.

The Second Round Of NATO Trials

From 1977 to 1980, NATO held their second round of trials for further acceptance of NATO ammunition. This go-around was primarily focused on small-caliber high-velocity ammunition. The competitors included the British 4.85mm, and the 5.56x45mm, *(the United States XM777 ball cartridge and the XM778 tracer, the Belgian SS109 ball cartridge and L110 tracer)*, West German 4.7x21mm caseless ammunition–as well as some

French 5.56x45mm ammunition. The ammunition standard was the U.S. 5.56x45mm M193 ball cartridge and the West German 7.62x51mm NATO ball cartridge.

The United States and the Belgian 5.56x45mm entries were various types of armor-piercing/penetrator ammunition. At the conclusion of the trials there was little difference in performance of the 4.85mm and the 5.56mm. Due to the potential of severe barrel erosion

with the 4.85mm cartridge, the Belgium SS109 and L110 tracer were the combination chosen as the future small arms caliber for NATO. The final combination was the 5.56x45mm individual weapon backed up by a 7.62x51mm medium support weapon that still exists today. The 7.62x51mm cartridge has been slowly phased out in favor of a 5.56x45mm medium support weapon, such as the U.S. M249 SAW.

The 4.85x49mm cartridge (4.85mm British). *Aaron Matson photo*

The 4.85x49mm (4.85mm British)

The results of the last NATO trials left Great Britain with a heavy rifle with full-powered ammunition. Due the recoil of the 7.62x51mm NATO cartridge, the rifle was not effective on automatic fire. With the introduction of the 5.56x45mm cartridge, the Royal Small Arms Factory at Enfield Lock carried out an investigation into low-impulse, small-caliber high-velocity ammunition in 1969. The study concluded

that a caliber of at least 6mm would be optimal for the new generation of small-caliber British weapons.

The first cartridge developed by the British and tested was the 6.25x43mm cartridge, chosen due to its similar penetration characteristics to the 7.62x51mm NATO cartridge. They had experimented with bullet weights from 91 to 100 grains, at a velocity of approximately 2680 fps. The design charac-

teristics of the 6.25x43mm cartridge were very similar to the U.S. 6mm SAW cartridge. Experimentation with the 6.25mm cartridge lasted until the fall of 1971 when tests of a reduced 5mm cartridge began. Later in 1972 the name of the cartridge was changed from 5mm to 4.85mm to designate the bore diameter. The new cartridge was able to meet the standard of hit probability established by West Germany.

There were numerous versions of the 4.85mm-caliber cartridge during the experimentation phases. The original version had a case length of 44mm (4.85x44mm). This initial attempt was basically a necked-down 5.56x45mm cartridge case. In August of 1972 the cartridge case neck was lengthened and the new round was called the 4.85x49mm cartridge. The rationale was that due to larger case capacity, higher velocity could be achieved, therefore improving penetration characteristics. The first large quantities were manufactured by Radway Green in April of 1973 and were sent to Enfield for testing. Some earlier cases were made from fired 5.56x45mm blank cartridge cases. The main bullet used was a 56-grain FMJ.

The rifle developed to fire the new 4.85x49mm cartridge was the XL64E5. Like the EM-2, this was a bullpup design with the magazine behind the pistol grip. It was a selective-fire rifle with optics mounted. This rifle was eventually chambered for the 5.56x45mm NATO cartridge and adopted as the L85A1.

The 5.56x45mm NATO cartridge (Belgian SS109) was utilized in the M16A2 assault rifles and many others. *Aaron Matson photo*

The Belgian SS109 5.56x45mm (M855 Ball)

The U.S. M-16/M-16A1 rifle in 5.56x45mm had numerous desirable characteristics of combat effectiveness of both weapon and ammunition, although there was room for improvement to optimize the 5.56x45mm cartridge—particularly regarding its effective range and penetration.

The FN/Belgium-made SS109 cartridge was a 5.56x45mm cartridge case loaded with a 62-grain FMJ boattail bullet with a mild steel penetrator core in the tip, firing at a muzzle velocity of 3100 fps. In order to stabilize this bullet, a change had to be made in the barrel's rifling rate from a slower 1:12 inches to a much faster 1:7 inches. The bullet profile was slightly different from the standard 55-grain FMJ boattail bullet; the SS109 has a much sharper point. These improvements led to higher retained velocity and improved accuracy at ranges beyond 400 meters. With the mild steel penetrator core, penetration increased–in all conditions–over the original loading. Numerous tests have shown the penetration of the SS109 is very similar to that of the U.S. M80 7.62x51mm ball cartridge.

When the NATO trials concluded, it was officially announced on October 24, 1980 that the SS109 was selected as the new 5.56x45mm NATO cartridge and would serve in numerous allied countries including the United States, Canada, Belgium, Portugal, Israel, Great Britain, France and Germany, to name a few. Some of the main weapons to be chambered in the 5.56 NATO cartridge include the M-16A2/M4 rifles, Canadian C7/C8 rifles, Heckler & Koch 93 and G36 rifles, Israeli Galil, British L85A1, French FA MAS rifles and the FN MINIMI (M249) squad automatic weapon.

Conclusions

There has been—without doubt––a total change in thought and purpose of the battle cartridge and the weapons that fire them. An unfortunate truth is that when it comes to selecting small arms and ammunition, the decisions made are sometimes more political rather than objective. It is sometimes difficult to obtain truly impartial evaluations of new concepts, more so in the United States. The United States military has always been deeply rooted in tradition, which sometimes clouds their judgment. Several major advancements were available to the U.S. Ordnance Corps over the last century but were shunned as being too new or too radical. Those in power have gone as far as to rig tests to keep with tradition. This was the case with the 7.62x51mm-chambered AR-10, and later the AR-15/M-16 series rifles and 5.56x45mm ammunition. Unfortunately, that lack of vision has a lot of weight and overpowering influence behind it. Bypassing the more practical 280 British in favor of the 7.62x51mm cartridge was a clear example, causing NATO to fall behind in small arms advancement vs. the Warsaw Pact countries.

Perhaps we are at a crossroads in small arms and ammunition development; that is, until a replacement is found for the standard metallic cartridge. Over the last 20 years, there has been little change in ammunition. Small arms are refined, made more reliable—but remain basically the same. Perhaps the next major advancement will be a laser plasma blaster! We will just have to wait and see. •

Acknowledgements

I would like to thank George Kass of Forensic Ammunition Service and Bill Woodin of Woodin Laboratory for their technical assistance and support for this article.

Modernizing the 30-30—

The 30-30 Ackley Improved

by David Ward

THE 30-30 IS over 100 years old. Without a doubt, it has been one of the most popular medium-range, medium-power deer cartridges ever developed. And for good reason: When used within the proper parameters by a reasonably efficient marksman, it will take deer with monotonous regularity.

Still, it is more than a century old, and consequently it carries along with it some dated baggage, especially when it comes to handloading. Now, if you could make a good cartridge even better by maybe increasing the velocity, most likely increasing accuracy, and certainly increasing case life and loading versatility – all with only a modest amount of cost and effort – would you do it? I would, and I did. Here's what happened:

Let's start with a brief history of the 30-30 *(and I do mean brief, since it's been done so many times before)*. Introduced in 1895 as one of the first smokeless cartridges from Winchester and chambered for

their Model 1894 lever action, the combination was an instant success and has been ever since. The reason is simple: It does the job it was designed to do – kill medium- and sometimes even large game at modest ranges efficiently. No doubt, many companies today would be delighted to introduce a product that performs its intended job so well. Consequently, numerous rifles, and in recent years quite a number of handguns, have been chambered for the 30-30. It is the deer rifle that many youngsters east of the Missouri River learned to hunt with, as well as the saddle gun that most Westerners grew up with. There are literally millions of 30-30s out there.

Marlin 336 SC and 3x Weaver scope used for the conversion from 30-30 Win. to 30-30 AckleyImproved. Marlin is a good, strong action, but nearly any 30-30 Win. is a good candidate for the conversion. Have any rifle checked thoroughly by a competent gunsmith before rechambering.

I have two of them. One is an old Model 94 with a half-magazine and a crescent steel buttplate. Somewhere along the way, someone in his infinite wisdom cut the barrel back to 20-1/2 inches *(no crown, thank you; just a trim)* and then reblued the whole package. Fortunately, they did not overbuff, and the original markings are easily readable. It shoots nicely and is stamped 30 WCF. My other rifle is a nice Marlin 336 with a three-quarter magazine and walnut pistol-grip stock. It sports a Weaver 3x scope on its solid-top receiver. It also shoots well, and I smile every time I look at it standing in the rack because of the exceptional deal I made on it a few years back at a local gun show.

I was surprised to find that the 30-30 is a popular number for handloading. My initial thought was that the many hunters who use a 30-30 Winchester instead of a double-whammy, smoke-'em-out-the-bore *modern* cartridge wouldn't be much into handloading. Just buy a box of factory ammo at the start of the deer season, touch a few off just to make sure Old Betsy's still on, and then head into the woods.

I was wrong. The 30-30 is a consistent and popular seller when it comes to reloading dies, staying in or around the top 10, and its popularity is further noted by the number of flat-nosed offerings in 30 caliber by the various bullet manufacturers. I suspect that many hunters are loading their own smokeless rounds because factory ammo is expensive, and handloading is not complicated–and relatively inexpensive. Also, of course, for those prone to experiment a bit, handloading offers a chance to squeeze a tad more in accuracy out of rifles not exactly known as tack drivers.

In one of the modern single-shot or magazine-fed bolt-action pistols, the 30-30 becomes something more than a minor-league player. Loaded with a pointed 125- or 130-grain bullet, we now have a solid performer out to about 200 yards. It is also a player in silhouette shooting.

For my purposes here, I will deal with rifles, although any loading data presented should be useable in the stronger pistols. What you get with a handloaded 30-30 is about 2200 to 2300 fps out of a 20-inch barrel with a 150-grain bullet. The requirement of a flat-nosed bullet in a tubular magazine rifle and the open sights found on most lever rifles limit the effective range to about 150 yards. A 125-grain bullet gains about 100 to 150 fps, and the 170-grainer loses about 100 fps to the 150-grain load. Effective range stays about the same, still limited primarily by open sights and type of timbered or brushy country generally hunted with the 30-30.

And what is wrong with those numbers? Nothing at all. The approximately one bazillion deer dispatched with those loads over the last hundred years can testify to that. Why, then, would anyone want to literally improve an already successful cartridge that does exactly what it was designed to do?

Before and after. Old-timer 30-30 Win. loaded round and case *(left)* and 30-30 AI conversion. Designed around the turn of the century, the 30-30 Win. has a long neck and gently sloping shoulder and sides that contribute to case stretch and eventual head separation. The more modern 30-30 AI has straight-sided case walls and sharp 40-degree shoulder, making it more suitable for reloading.

By far the most common reason to wildcat and or improve a cartridge is to increase its ballistic performance. Sometimes it works quite well, transforming a modest performer into a go-getter. For instance, the 250 Ackley Improved from the 250 Savage (see author's article, "The 250 Ackley Improved Works," *Handloader's Digest*, 12th Edition), the 257 Ackley Improved from 257 Roberts, the 22 K-Hornet, and many others show significant performance increases. All with the relatively

simple process of boring out the chamber to straighten the case sides and increase the shoulder angle, and then fireforming the cases.

Wildcatting doesn't always produce such worthwhile results. It can be, as one editor put it, "a useless exercise in gun-nuttery." Working to upgrade the performance of, say, the 257 Weatherby Magnum, an already overbore cartridge, is simply a reason to help fill your friendly gunsmith's bank account.

There are other reasons for wildcatting. One is to fill a gap in the commercial cartridge lineup. Very few gaps are left to be filled these days, however, since most manufacturers are acutely aware of what the consumer wants and needs. Items like a 270/308 offer good potential if you just have to have 270 performance from a short action.

And, of course, some people just like to tinker.

One of the best reasons to go through the trouble of rechambering a perfectly good rifle to a nonstandard cartridge is to modernize it. We are handloaders already, so whether it is one case or another doesn't really make a difference to us. But if wildcatting makes a particular case easier to work with or

Bullets used for loading *(from left)*: Speer 100-grain Plinker, Speer 110-grain Hollow Point, Sierra 125-grain Flat Nose, Speer 150-grain FN, and Speer 170-grain FN. The 30-30 AI can be a versatile cartridge used for anything from varmints up to medium-large big game.

Empty 30-30 AI case, hunting bullets, and loaded 30-30 AI. Bullets *(from left)*: 125-grain Sierra FN, 150-grain Speer FN, and 170-grain Speer FN. These are, in the author's opinion, the most useful bullets for the 30-30 AI. The 125- and 150-grainers are mostly for deer and the 170-grain bullet is for elk or black bear.

more flexible in loading – and maybe offers some increase in performance thrown in for good measure – then the project is worth some scrutiny.

That is exactly why the 30-30 Ackley Improved is worth doing. The idea is not to turn your brush gun into a lever-action 30-06 or 308. If you had wanted one of those, you would probably have gotten one by now. The 30-30 AI makes the dated 30-30 case modern and infinitely more reloadable by taking out the taper in the case wall that was so much in vogue at the turn of the century. At the same time, it eliminates that long sloping shoulder and substitutes one of 40 degrees. The process increases the volume of the case by about 10 percent, but more importantly, it all but eliminates that major cause of 30-30 case retirement – case stretch leading to head separation. The minimum-taper case also allows higher pressures in the relatively weak lockup of the lever action.

When loading 30-30 brass in the past, trimming was required after two or three full-power loads. Most cases did not make it past five reloads. Having worked with the 250 Ackley Improved and seen that the straight-walled case design did virtually eliminate stretch in that instance, I began to look seriously at the 30-30 AI. Believe me, I was

hesitant to send the Marlin off to the gunsmith and have the chamber reamed for the new cartridge. Once done, it's done, and the new chambering would affect the rifle's collector's value. It then occurred to me that this rifle was not particularly a collector's piece. What the heck.

Because my gunsmith could not lay his hands on a reamer, I talked with the folks at Clymer Manufac-

turing Co. and discovered that the 30-30 AI is a standard, or in-stock item. That meant delivery time was just a few days away, and the price was quite reasonable.

Then I talked to Jay Postman at RCBS about reloading dies. Jay is a master at solving those sometimes not so small reloading problems. He said RCBS had the dies as a standard stock item. This was sounding like it would be easier than I thought, which is rarely the case.

Clymer's reamer arrived promptly, and I took it and the Marlin to my gunsmith in Denver. While they had the rifle, the dies arrived, and I set about loading up some new Winchester cases.

A caution here about loading the 30-30: The case walls are thin. Mine from Winchester miked .012 inch. A 308 Win.case mikes out at .015 inch – a 25 percent increase in thickness. Practically speaking, that means be gentle with the case when reloading. Put the muscle to it and it will buckle or stretch or collapse the case mouth. Go easy on the case lube when resizing and those annoying little dents in the case walls won't plague you. Also, a slight chamfer on the inside of the case mouth helps to start the bullet during seating. Remember these few hints and you'll keep a lot more cases for handloading and toss fewer casualties in the trashcan.

Since the new chamber would be about 10 percent larger in volume, and during fireforming the new case would expand into that space, I decided to load the standard 30-30 cases with a 110-grain round-nose bullet and 31 grains of 3031 powder.

Some of the components and dies used for reloading the 30-30 AI. More modern design makes for longer case life and less case stretch while giving higher velocities.

sures in the Marlin – more than .003-inch case head expansion and cratered and flattened primers. Somewhat disappointed, I backed off another 10 percent and began again. Pressures were fine there, but the experience left me very cautious on published loads. It could have been my particular batch of powder, too. I don't know, although problems did not arise while working with the same batch of 4198 on another project. For the 125 FP and 3031, Ackley listed 39 grains. I stopped at 37 grains, noting indications of excessive pressure above that amount in the Marlin. It was the same situation for the 150-grainers. Published loads were too high for my rifle.

I was initially disappointed. But then I reminded myself that the idea here was not to make an '06 out of this brush gun, but to make the cartridge more flexible and user friendly. Maybe I should write that in big capital letters on a piece of poster board and put it right above my portable loading table so I can't miss it. It is always a temptation to push loads to the absolute maximum when in real-life application, the extra velocity is rarely necessary.

The accompanying table shows the final results of the maximum-load testing, and overall I was quite pleased with what came about. Loads were chronographed on my Competition Electronics Pro-Tach with the muzzle of the rifle about 10 feet from the screens. As can be seen, several powders gave excellent results, but different powders performed better with different bullet weights.

For the light 110-grain bullets (*just the ticket for you lever-actioned varminters out there*) IMR 3031 was the velocity champ at 2750 fps when bumped by 39 grains of propellant. Second at 2678 fps was 40 grains of BL-C2. A distant third was 37.5 grains of 4064, making 2539 fps. In the 125-grain category, 3031 was still the leader with 37 grains giving 2552 fps, but close behind was IMR 4198 with Winchester's 748 and Hodgdon's BL-C2 close to them. Moving up to the 150-grain weight, 3031 is still No. 1 in velocity with 36 grains dishing up 2404 fps. Second place goes to 748 and third to IMR 4895. For the heavy 170-grain bullets, the leader is 4198 at 2210 fps with the remaining powders all giving velocities in the 2050 fps range.

What does all this tell us? First, that, yes, we can improve on the standard 30-30 velocities by a usable 200 fps or so. That would be logical since the case capacity increases by about 10 percent in the

Author and his two 30-caliber lever guns. At left is the Marlin converted from 30-30 Win. to 30-30 AI, while at right is a half-magazine Model 94 Winchester with the 20 1/2-inch barrel. The latter rifle was not rechambered because of its age.

That is almost a full-power load, about 1 grain less than maximum. I load fairly hot loads for fireforming for two reasons: First is to ensure a complete forming of the new case. Using reduced loads in the past, I found many cases were not fully formed into the new chamber. Grab any powder/bullet combination out of a loading manual and reduce it about 1 grain below max, and the fireforming process will produce a perfectly formed case each time. Second, by having 50 or 100 full-power rounds to expend, a trip to the country allows a complete familiarization with the project rifle. After that much shooting, you learn most of the weapon's little idiosyncrasies – trigger pull, feeding, sights, or whatever. Besides, some practice at targets at varying

ranges never hurts. No sense in just wasting all those shots.

With the rifle back from the gunsmith and the new cases uneventfully fireformed, it was time to get down to the serious business of working up some loads for the Improved case. P.O. Ackley's *Handbook for Shooters and Reloaders, Volume I*, was the obvious place to start. He lists several loads for the 30-30 AI, working mainly with 3031 and 4198. Hoping for more flexibility, I began there and added BL-C2, H-380, IMR 4064, and 4895, and finally Winchester's 748. Immediately, I hit a snag. For the Sierra 125-grain FP, I reduced Ackley's max 4198 load of 35 grains by 10 percent (*as one should ALWAYS do when working up new loads*) and still got indications of high pres-

fireforming process. It would also be logical in that the new straight-walled case allows the weaker lever actions to operate at higher pressures. Great. Whether or not any deer might notice the velocity difference at normal operating distances of 150 yards or less where this lever gun is used, well that's another question.

So why bother to convert to the 30-30 Ackley Improved? Two reasons – versatility in loading, and extended case life. Look at it this way: With the Ackley conversion, the handloader now has an extra 200 fps or so to experiment with in finding that best load for his before he is back down to the maximum velocities for the standard 30-30. That's quite a window to work within, and we all know that rarely does the most accurate load coincide with the highest velocity. And with all of that load experimentation going on, case loss will be at a minimum. Case stretch is virtually nonexistent, and consequently, cases keep going in and coming out, getting used again and again. I have

In spite of the sharper shoulder on the 30-30 AI, the author experienced no feeding problems with the Marlin 336.

eight and 10 loads on this brass without a loss, and only recently a trim. Such exceptional performance is not obtainable with standard 30-30 brass.

If you like the handy rifles that shoot the old 30-30 but are frustrated having to load a case designed over a hundred years ago, take a look at the 30-30 Ackley Improved. It is an easy conversion that makes a good old cartridge even better. ●

BULLET	POWDER	MAX. LOAD (gr.)	VELOCITY (fps)
110 gr.	IMR 3031	39.0	2750
	IMR 4895	39.0	2509
	IMR 4064	37.5	2539
	BL-C2	40.0	2678
125 gr.	IMR 3031	37.0	2552
	IMR 4895	38.0	2369
	IMR 4064	37.5	2368
	BL-C2	38.5	2498
	748	41.0	2512
	IMR 4198	30.0	2521
150 gr.	IMR 3031	36.0	2404
	IMR 4895	36.0	2339
	IMR 4064	35.0	2242
	BL-C2	36.0	2215
	H-380	41.0	2281
	748	39.5	2375
	IMR 4198	29.5	2284
170 gr.	IMR 3031	32.5	2050
	IMR 4198	28.5	2210
	BL-C2	33.0	2021
	H-380	36.0	2061
	748	35.0	2072

The results of too much force during the loading process. Lack of a gentle touch produced this bent lip and crumpled shoulder on the case at right during bullet seating. Brass used in 30-30 cases is thin, so be careful.

Velocities measured on Competition Electronics Pro-Tach 10 feet from the muzzle and based on a 10-shot average. Primers were all CCI 200. Cases of Winchester manufacture. Temperature: 81 degrees F.
WARNING: Loads tested here were safe in the author's rifle. They may not be safe in yours. When testing your own loads, start with a minimum charge reduction of 10 percent and work up from there.

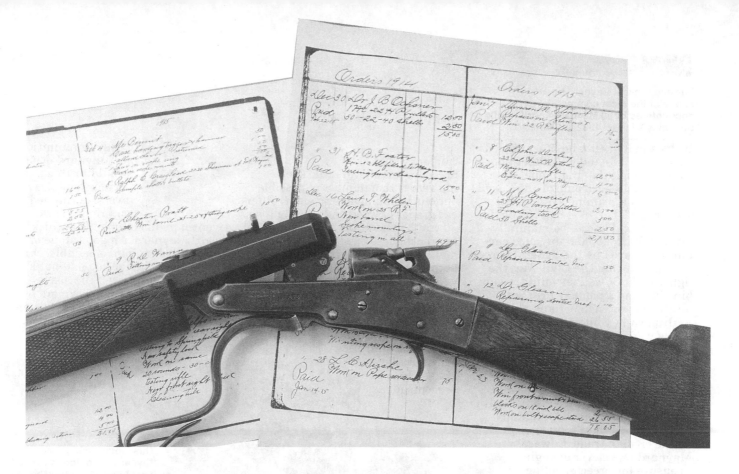

The Maynard Single-Shot Rifle...

19th Century Practicality At Its Best

by George J. Layman

BORN IN THE prelude years of the American Civil War, the Maynard breech-loader went on to become one of the most practical single-shot rifles—and held that distinction for over 30 years.

Throughout the 1860s, single-shot rifle design became one of the liveliest fields in United States arms development from the standpoint of creativeness. More different types of breech-loading rifles and pistols–both single-shot and repeating–made their mark within this violent decade. Perhaps it was the Civil War, followed by Western expansion during the remainder of that decade, which stimulated scores of inventors to deliver their best. One highly skilled and gifted inventor, whose patents stretched back to the mid-1840s, was a Washington D.C.-based dentist named Dr. Edward Maynard. He was an internationally recognized doctor of dental surgery whose achievements ranged from the discovery of dental fevers to being designated court dentist to Emperor Nicholas I of Russia. Maynard, while maintaining professional skills, nonetheless became deeply involved in the field of arms and ammunition design.

Dr. Maynard's first step into the ordnance arena was his September 1845 patent of his "tape primer" principle, intended to speed up the reloading process of the muzzleloading military arms. The idea was clever and the system was adopted for limited use by the U.S. military, but it was discovered the device performed poorly in wet weather or

This is a Second Generation Maynard that Niedner rebarreled to 22-rimfire Maynard and straightened the hammer. The rifle lies over two photocopied pages of Niedner's work records *(from 1914-15, when the work was performed)* that include two entries *(without serial numbers)* regarding work on 22s.

areas of high humidity. Maynard did not stop his inventive pursuits with the tape primer system as, in a few short years, he would receive his first patent on the idea of a breech-loading rifle.

On May 27, 1851 Dr. Maynard was granted U.S. patent #8,126 essentially for a lever-action, single-shot breech-loading firearm that used a metallic cartridge ignited by a percussion cap. By 1857, Maynard had won a U.S. government contract for about 400 pieces. The Massachusetts Arms Company of Chicopee Falls, Massachusetts began a lifelong relationship with the Maynard breechloader, becoming the major manufacturer of this arm from the pre-Civil War period until the company's demise between 1891 to 1894. Know for its peculiar, oversize-rimmed cartridge, the Maynard–from 1857 through the early 1870s–was chambered for car-

The economical Maynard No. 9 is one of the most commonly encountered of all Maynard sporting rifles. Shown is a Model 1882 in 35-30.

tridges in 35-, 40- and 50-caliber, as well as the 55- and 64-caliber shotshell. Though the first model breech-loading carbine of 1857 used the tape roll priming system, the second model of 1863 had the device removed, and had to be manually primed. With 20,002 Maynard carbines procured by the Federal Government during the Civil War, the lightweight 50-caliber military carbine became a popular arm with military men and civilians alike.

Ironically, while military contracts were being fulfilled, the Maynard was manufactured concurrently in commercial sporting models as well. At war's end, several manufacturers with lucrative military contracts found themselves with no market for their output. Many had to unload their large inventories on the civilian trade. Edward Maynard was clever enough to ensure his breech-loading rifle would not suffer such an economic disaster. In the immediate post-war period, he advertised the Maynard was available in a number of newly-introduced sporting configurations and noted that with only one frame, extra interchangeable rifle and shotgun barrels of various

calibers would make for a truly versatile sporting arm with a number of possible options including a tang sight, different grades of wood and loading tools.

As the end of the 1860s approached, several self-contained metallic cartridge arms appeared—both single-shot and repeating—which were a sign of the times as far as cartridge development was concerned. During this period, the Maynard was still a caplock arm—an ignition system fast becoming obsolete. Edward Maynard did not see his breechloader

This Model 1865 percussion Maynard is equipped with a 64-caliber Maynard shotgun barrel. A large number of post-war Maynards were built up from leftover parts from government contract overruns.

enter the conventional cartridge era as quickly as the Sharps, but on February 18, 1873 he received U.S. patent #135,928, which covered the design of his first fixed metallic cartridge rifle. As noted previously, the trademark characteristic of the Maynard percussion breech-loading rifle was the large rim on its cartridges.

The introduction of the Model 1873 family of centerfire cases differed somewhat from their earlier percussion ancestors. In contrast to the older, thin-rimmed Maynard cases with a flash hole at the base, the new Berdan-primed cartridges had extremely thick rims. As a result, the Maynard 1873 action had a gap of almost 1/8-inch between the barrel's standing breech and the frame.

Only ammunition of Maynard design would fit this particular action. The oversize rimmed cartridges were eventually nicknamed the "thick head" Maynard. An advantage of these peculiar, but reloadable, cartridges was the Parker patent slotted base that allowed the easy decapping of the spent primers by the Hadley Cap Picker, listed as an accessory in the Maynard catalog.

The Model 1873 set this breechloader on a progressive path which led to fifteen different rifle and three shotgun models, in seven rifle and two shotgun chamberings, offered by the end of the 1870s. The Maynard action is uniquely sturdy and had a reputation as being hand-fit during manufacture to assure the closest tolerances possible. The barrel is mounted on a strong, transverse pivot at the front of the frame. The bottom of the barrel adjacent to the breech has a large lug connected by a toggle-link to an underlever, which itself is mounted on its own frame pivot that also serves as the trigger guard. The serpentine-shaped takedown lever is located on the right frame. Rotating this lever, with the action open, allows it to be pulled out, releasing the barrel from the frame. It was this feature—primarily—that made the Maynard a success with outdoorsmen and target shooters, enabling them to quickly and easily change barrels of different calibers, while utilizing the same frame.

Maynard barrels were serial numbered just beneath the chamber and many are found with numbers that appear to have been stamped upon polished bare metal. The small numbers above the serial number indicate the rate of twist.

Massachusetts Arms Co. barrels chambered for the 22-rimfire cartridge. *(Top)* This shows the countersunk chambering method wherein the cartridge rim fit flush with an external alignment ring that snugged up to the face of the standing breech. *(Below)* An earlier adaptation; the rear of the chamber had an extended face to fill the wide breech gap when using an 1873 frame. Regardless of rimfire chamber modification, the rimfire firing pin had to be changed if a centerfire barrel was installed.

Among the primary shortcomings of the Model 1873 Maynard was cartridge availability. Most storekeepers didn't keep a regular stock of all Maynard calibers because they appealed only to certain groups of shooters. Thus, 1873 Maynard owners usually had to special-order extra brass cases and other accessories directly out of the Maynard catalog.

A most cleverly conceived invention, allowing the 1873 Maynard to effectively use conventional rimfire ammunition, was the Hadley Device. Invented and patented by George W. Hadley on October 5, 1880 this attachment consisted of a circular cap and firing pin disc and was mounted to the front of the frame by two small screws. The free-floating disc inside the cap had a

protrusion that served as the firing pin and crushed the rim of the cartridge at ignition. The Hadley Device was a standard feature on the Maynard Number One, Two and Three, regularly catalogued for either the 22- or 32-caliber rimfire cartridges,

respectively. For a $3.00 fee, the factory would install the device, thus converting the rifle to a convertible rimfire/centerfire configuration. When the use of the centerfire ammunition was desired, removal of the two screws allowed the cap to be taken off and replacing the centerfire firing pin was all that was required.

Because of the odd dimensions of the 1873 series of Maynard cartridges *(which couldn't be used in other types of firearms)* it must be presumed that both Dr. Maynard and the Massachusetts Arms Company eventually felt modification of the Maynard rifle was inevitable. In late 1881 the action was redesigned

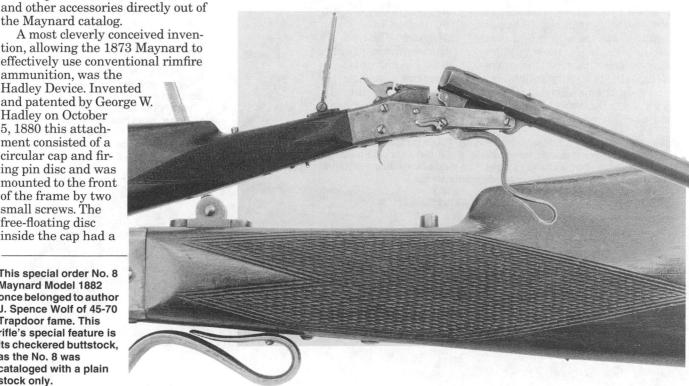

This special order No. 8 Maynard Model 1882 once belonged to author J. Spence Wolf of 45-70 Trapdoor fame. This rifle's special feature is its checkered buttstock, as the No. 8 was cataloged with a plain stock only.

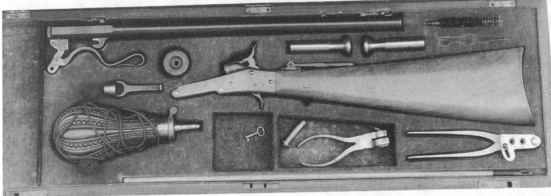

This No. 13 Mid-Range Model 1873 was a complete special order specimen, equipped with the No. 14-style Creedmoor buttstock and *(now missing)* lever pistol grip. The rifle barrel (installed) is chambered for the 40-60 Maynard; the extra barrel for the 64 Maynard shotshell cartridge. *(J. C. Devine photo)*

Probably the best-known cased Maynard set is this example, now owned by the author and featured in James Grant's second book, *More Single Shot Rifles, (1959).* The rifle appears to be an early No. 8 Maynard Sporting Rifle and, along with its accessories, is in pristine condition indicting it may have been a salesman's sample.

by bringing the standing breech closer to the frame, and lengthening the chamber area altogether. With reduction of the gap between the face of the breech and the receiver to about 1/12-inch, the Maynard could finally accept conventional, thin-rimmed Boxer-primed cartridges. Christened the Model 1882, the new rifle saw six additional cartridges join the line over the next five years. Also at the time, another Maynard rifle appeared in the factory literature. The deluxe and well-configured No. 16 became an immediate sensation and would go on to become the most popular Maynard sporting rifle ever introduced. With its highly polished fancy walnut checkered stock and forend, nickeled Swiss buttplate, and fine mid-range patent Vernier sights, it was an extremely well liked target rifle. Chambered for such new cartridges as the 32/35 and 38/50 Maynard, the rifle made rapid inroads with renowned single-shot match shooters, such as F.J. Rabbeth and O.M. Jewell, who scored high with the No. 16 at the Walnut Hill range in Woburn, Massachusetts through the 1880s.

With efficient, powerful cartridges such as the 40/60 and 40/70 Maynard 1882, the requirements of hunters and outdoorsmen were at last satisfied in that they could purchase many of the lesser-grade Maynards in their favorite big-game cartridges having the more conventional Boxer primer *(a great boon to reloading, in contrast to the earlier 1873 Berdan-primed case)*. The Model 1882 was also advertised in a No. 3 Shotgun, available in 20 gauge, cataloged as able to handle paper shotshells. This particular Maynard was tagged the "Sportsman's Favorite" because of its practicality in interchanging with 1882 rifle barrels.

The 1873 Maynard remained in production, alongside the 1882, until manufacture terminated in the early 1890s. Among the last new cartridges chambered for

For $3, the factory would install the Hadley device to convert the early percussion Maynard to a rimfire or centerfire cartridge gun. This specimen has a Winchester tang sight and brass Swiss buttplate—apparently factory-installed on special order.

Cased Maynard sets are always interesting. This example, based on a Model 1873 rifle, includes four matching barrels, a complete set of reloading tools and bullet moulds, and an extra tang sight. The leather case has an inletted border to hold cartridge cases for the various chamberings.

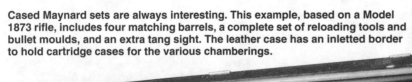

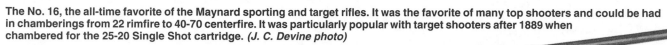
The No. 16, the all-time favorite of the Maynard sporting and target rifles. It was the favorite of many top shooters and could be had in chamberings from 22 rimfire to 40-70 centerfire. It was particularly popular with target shooters after 1889 when chambered for the 25-20 Single Shot cartridge. *(J. C. Devine photo)*

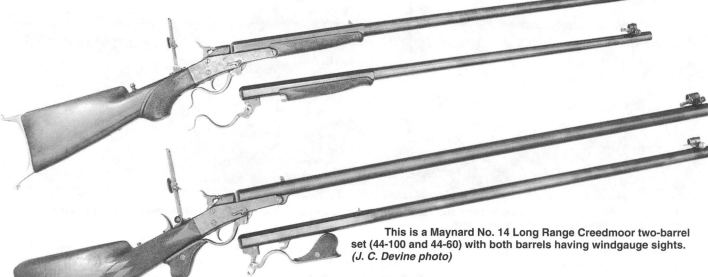
This is a Maynard No. 14 Long Range Creedmoor two-barrel set (44-100 and 44-60) with both barrels having windgauge sights. *(J. C. Devine photo)*

the Model 1882, and those with the Hadley Device, was the 25 Stevens rimfire. The author has viewed several examples of Maynards, *(serial numbers in the 12-20,000 range)* found with 25-caliber barrels and frames with matching numbers. Pinpointing exact production quantities of the Maynard, from the early 1870s through the final years, is difficult. Dr. Maynard, an astute businessman, was known to keep very close track of sales of his rifles and other patented items of his design. Serial numbers appear to have some overlap at different times. When an updated model or a new variant was added to the line, Maynard kept a listing and, at times, made certain the Massachusetts Arms Company started a separate serial number range. Total combined production of the 1873 and 1882 Maynard is estimated *(without the factory ledgers)* around 35,000 units, possibly fewer.

An interesting area that collectors frequently address is the serialization of the later Maynard rifles and

The No. 15 Maynard was a classy target rifle, just one notch beneath the all-time favorite No. 16, and remained popular to the closure of the Massachusetts Arms Co. in 1891.

shotguns. Often cased sets are found with two or more barrels that have the identical serial number as the frame. A common occurrence is the discovery of Maynard barrels that have the serial number stamped in an area devoid of finish — "in the white". The bottom of the barrel adjacent to the lug seems to be stamped after the barrel was blued. In a more detailed perspective, it must be remembered that outside the common Maynard patent markings and stampings of "1873" or "1882", none of these carried model numbers—or any such identification—on barrels or receivers. Markings such as "No. 9 Improved

Hunters Rifle" or "Maynard No. 16", etc. were not found on any of these rifles to aid in their identification. The customer simply ordered the Maynard out of the catalog by chambering, barrel length, sights, and the grade of wood under the heading of Numbers 1 through 16, and received the arm in this configuration.

This was an extremely efficient and convenient arrangement for the Massachusetts Arms Company, as well as an excellent means of inventory record-keeping. Example: the Maynard Numbers 1, 3, 5 and 7 had open, non-adjustable rear sights; whereas the Numbers 2, 4, 6, 8, 9, and 10 had elevating rear sights. By maintaining a quantity of frames

that could be matched to any number of barrels to make up a particular rifle, all that needed to be done was select one chambered for the customer's choice of cartridge, and stamp the barrel with the number of the frame. Thus, an inventory of barrels of various calibers–without serial numbers–would also have to be kept. It seems that some barrels, previously serial-numbered, may

have had the existing number ground off and were subsequently re-stamped to match the serial number on a frame. This would be highly economical; using barrels from a standing universal inventory by simply grinding a clean surface, then re-stamping a new number— instead of producing an entirely new barrel.

A Model 1873 No. 8 I once owned showed evidence of this since it was serial numbered in the 20,000 range, which is well beyond the high-water mark serial range of the '73 Maynard. The arm was probably ordered sometime in the late 1880s or early 1890s, and its new-like condition reflected this—along with the barrel's serial number being stamped over a bare, previously ground area. In any case, the theory of re-stamping serial numbers on Maynard barrels after final finish or bluing has been applied, is a fairly logical explanation to barrels being found with an "in the white" patch in this area.

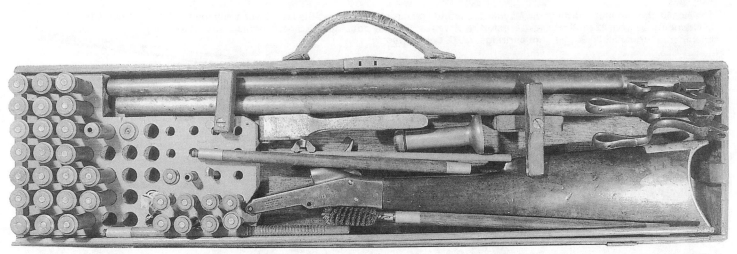

A Maynard two-barrel set, complete with tools and spare cartridge cases, based upon the Model 1865 frame converted to use the 1873 thick-head centerfire cases. *(J. C. Devine photo)*

Maynard collectors occasionally notice that some particular rifles do not match any of those in Maynard catalogs or early factory literature. Examination of the 1880, 1885, or the 1890 catalogs shows a broad selection of accoutrements and extras were offered. Citing an example, in the 1885 edition one could purchase 30 different barrels in 44 different calibers, with a total of 38 varying barrel lengths. Along with walnut stocks of numerous grades and several types of hammers, levers, and other equipment, one could literally create a unique Maynard sporting rifle and assign a personal number to it. Customers in the last century undoubtedly took advantage of this large selection of additional components, resulting in today's confusion over the discovery of many undecipherable Maynards.

The author has owned several that appeared completely alien and were definitely not "catalog correct". One of them had plain walnut stocks that, with the basic mid-range Vernier tang sight, allowed the gun to meet the specifications for any of six different versions. Add

a 32-inch barrel with a nine-inch octagonal breech in 38-50 Maynard, and you have a Maynard not covered by a factory designation. If serial numbers on barrel and frame match on such specimens, they may indeed be considered special-order pieces.

The Maynard Model 1873 and 1882 were among the most popular target and match rifles of their day, and are still in use today by some dedicated groups of shooters, although they are not seen on the firing line as often as the Ballard, Sharps, or the Remington Rolling Block.

Another area of Maynard collecting or shooting involves those rifles modified or custom-built by some of the famous riflesmiths of the last century who could take a 'stock' Maynard rifle and transform it into a work of art–or a 'tackdriver' for the range. This group of single-shot rifles, rebuilt by early gunsmiths,

has become known as the Second Generation category and has a special following by modern collectors. Once the name of Harry Pope, Adolph Niedner, or Schoyen shows up on one of these at an auction or gun show, you can be certain the collecting fraternity experiences an excitement difficult to describe!

For the antique collector who has chosen the Maynard specialty, the challenge of obtaining one of each specimen is a boundless task, especially if the ultimate objective is to obtain a specimen of each version from One to Sixteen, in both the 1873 and 1882 models. Even here, the total would amount to a generous 32 pieces in all. In Maynard collecting, the endless list of variations seems to be the trademark of this family of firearms, but we must always remember that there are only so many units of any one antique firearm in existence. The thrill of finding that prize Maynard helps make this fine single-shot breechloader very interesting. ●

References:

A Guide to the Maynard Breechloader George J. Layman, Ayer, MA 1993 & Pioneer Press, Union City, TN 1998 (revised edition).

The Rifle in America, Philip B. Sharpe, Funk & Wagnalls, NY, NY 1938, 1958. Maynard Catalogs of 1880, 1885, and 1890—original publications of the Massachusetts Arms Company.

Another Second Generation Maynard modified by Merton S. Hendricks, a gunsmith active in Aurora, Illinois, from 1895 to 1915. This rifle, with characteristics of a No. 16, is chambered for the 25-21 Stevens cartridge and topped with a 6x scope by L. C. Cummins of Montpelier, VT. Note the triple inlays at the rear of the chambers.

The Lost Sport Of Dump Rat Shooting

by Michael Kluever and Illustrated by Boots Reynolds

NOW DON'T GET me wrong, I really am for progress, improved environments and healthier people. There are times though, when I think we may have gone to far. It's great that we have computers, jet planes, cleaner air and all forms of pills to make us feel better. Great as these may be, there are some things that are gone and that I truly miss. One of them is shooting rats at the local dump.

For those who don't know what a dump is, let me fill you in. The clos-est thing we have today is called a landfill. Each day waste products picked up at our front door are deli-cately deposited in a landfill. By nightfall these are sanitarily bur-ied deep beneath the earth. A dump is (or was) a place anyone could come and "dump" anything from old tires to a kitchen sink. Of course, there were other things dumped as well—including a great deal of good old-fashioned pure rotting garbage *(a gourmet favorite of rats)*. Every now or then, the local government

would come around and bury some of it. You could always tell when you were near a dump by the delicate change of air quality.

I was never good at hitting a baseball and I didn't appreciate someone trying to yank my head off to get a football. Golf seemed dull and tennis much too repetitive. My folks were really concerned that I would never find an outdoor sports niche. Imagine how delighted they were when I took up shooting rats at the dump! Dad said it showed a real pioneering spirit and mom felt that I was making the world a better place for everyone *(except, of course, for rats)*.

Growing up in central Wisconsin in the late Fifties, a gun was as common as changing underwear twice a week. My shooting career began early in life. I lived—and frequently slept—with my Daisy Red Ryder lever-action BB gun *(...my blankie mysteriously disappeared at the tender age of six)*. Like many boys my age, I was also a major purchaser of baseball cards. While many cherished these as collector items that their mothers would eventually

taking his pride and joy, a 1949 yellow Nash, to the dump. That car was always in pristine shape despite the salt-infested roadways of a Wisconsin winter. *Don's greatest dream was to be able to take the "sexmobile" (the front seats folded down into beds) cruising. Mr. Bronk, on the other hand, was determined not to rush being a grandfather—and thus another of Don's dreams was dashed.*

My car, in contrast, was a deep green decorated with numerous rust patches, which gave it the appearance of being camouflaged. "The rats will never know its there," his

explained. "It will give you a great limited field of fire."

"Limited field of fire?"

"Yeah, you shoot only between that burned-out '39 Dodge and the busted Kohler toilet."

"How come?" I asked.

" 'Cause Don and me don't tolerate 22 wounds much," he responded. "And don't worry about those three million flies buzzing around your head. Come near sunset they will disappear. Of course, then come those pesky gnats. Try not to breath in or swallow any. It might not be real healthy. And keep the shirt sleeves rolled down to minimize the

Winchester Model 74.

Remington Model 512A.

throw away, I purchased them for their target appeal. I particularly valued the New York Yankee cards. A couple of weeks ago I was at a neighbor's house and he brought out part of his baseball card collection.

"You see this Mickey Mantle," he said admiringly, "this card is really rare. It cost me a couple of hundred bucks!"

"Gee," I commented, "I blasted the hell out of a bunch of those as a kid."

My neighbor hasn't spoken to me since. I don't know what he's so upset about. Thanks to me, that card of his will probably continue to grow in value. He might even be able to retire on its value, thanks to my Red Ryder and me. And on top of all that, I don't have to hate my mother for throwing away my valuable baseball card collection.

I have to thank my school buddy Don Bronk and his dad for introducing me to the sport of dump rat shooting. Don introduced me to the excitement and adventure he and his dad experienced at the dump. After much pleading—plus agreement that we would take my 1950 Studebaker *("Torpedo, the shape of things to come")*, they agreed to take me. I was unaware at the time, but Mr. Bronk had no intention of

dad would always say when I suggested we take his vehicle. "Hell, they will see us coming before we get out of Wausau if we take the Nash."

In anticipation, I surgically cleaned my Model 74 Winchester semiautomatic 22 rifle, a present on my sixteenth birthday. My gun had a tendency to jam and did it's best when fed only 22 Long Rifle cartridges.

"Sunset isn't until 8:30 PM," Don warned, "but we want to get there early."

"You mean to get a good shooting position?"

"Naw, to look for hidden treasures first," Don explained.

They say location is everything. Don was uncommonly lucky. He lived near a dump. One summer he and I built a three-room completely furnished tree house out of treasures found at the dump. The only hang-up came from *(predominately downwind)* neighbors who complained of obnoxious odors.

Once we had gathered our treasures and loaded them into my car's trunk, Don's dad took me to a particularly high heap of assorted garbage. Carefully removing a nicely browned banana skin from the sole of his boot he advised, "This will be your shooting position," he

chance of an getting an infectious disease from those blood-sucking mosquitoes"

As I loaded my trusted 22, Don walked over.

"Where are your rubber bands?" he asked. "You don't want any rats running up your pant legs."

"Aw, that's one of those urban legends," I replied.

"Hey dad, show him the scars on your right leg!"

"Oh my God!"

Fortunately, Don and his dad each carried a spare rubber band and I was thus protected. *(After all, you never know when one of the rubber bands is going to break—kind of like shoestrings.)*

"And," Don continued, "next time wear heavy-soled shoes or boots. Step on a nail sticking out of a board or the jagged edge of a glass bottle and it's going right through those PF Flyers. You wouldn't want to ruin tonight's hunt with a hospital visit."

As the sun began to set, a rustling could be heard from all around us. My heart began to beat wildly. Sweat began to form across my forehead. My right thumb was on the safety, ready to release it the moment a rat appeared. I soon learned a dump rat shooter had to have the patience of a fisherman and the keen sight of a

.400 baseball hitter. And a stuffed-up nose is certainly a plus.

"You know what would be neat," I called to across Don while fending off a swarm of gnats.

"What?"

"For every rat we kill, we should paint a picture of a rat on our gunstocks. You know like the fighter pilots do, when they shoot down an enemy plane."

Of course, we never did that. If we had, I would have had half a rat on my stock. The only time I recall possibly hitting a rat was some weeks later when Don's dad and I both fired at the same time at the same rat. The creature somersaulted high in the air, disappearing behind a large Hills Brothers two-pound coffee can. Neither of us could confirm the fatal bullet. Ballistic analysis was still in its infancy then.

With my semiautomatic, I pumped off five shots to his bolt-action's one. I have always been a proponent of massive firepower as opposed to the disciplined fire of the more purist shooter. Don and his dad preferred Remington bolt actions, specifically the Model 512 with the tubular magazine.

"You can always count on a bolt action to fire," his dad was fond of saying quite often, "damn semi-autos jam at the most critical moment."

Oh sure, there were some drawbacks to dump rat shooting. It's primarily a male-oriented sport. I remember one time Don and I were taking a couple of girls home from school. While Beefy Bev and Crazy Judy were not prom queens, they were girls—and we could not be especially selective. As luck would have it, the route took us past a dump that we had never shot—or even explored. Well, how could anyone pass up an opportunity like that? To our amazement, the girls refused to leave the car to accompany us on our reconnaissance of the area. They even refused to help us load our newfound priceless treasures into the car's trunk. That was the last time any of the school's girls ever accepted a ride home from Don or me. That even included the now well-documented Blizzard of '56 and the Devastating Flood of '59.

The sport of dump rat shooting probably lost all hope of survival when television failed to recognize its true potential. After sleeping through golf and finding no love in tennis telecasts, it could have bridged the gap created by the lesser, boring sports. I can see it now:

"We're live from the Town of Maine dump located near beautiful Wausau, Wisconsin for the inaugural presentation of Man versus Rat.

The rat has been man's greatest enemy since time immemorial, causing millions of anguished deaths through its vile sanitary habits. As the sun begins to set we find the Bronks, accompanied by Mike Kluever, versus the ferocious Town of Maine Rodents. "John, how do you see tonight's match up?"

"Pat, what the hell are we doing sitting in the back of this dump truck? I've got a call into my agent. This is …disgusting."

"John, once the match begins, you'll thank your lucky stars that you're surrounded by 3-inch steel. Flick the flies off that pizza and get ready for what looks like a really close match."

"It's getting near sunset, Pat, shouldn't something be happening?"

"Listen, do you hear that? That rustling sound means that the rats are making their way onto the, ah, field. Bronk senior is lifting his gun. He is pointing it toward the dead cow in right field. He fires a shot. Look at that, John. That's a goner for sure!"

"Yeah, when you see a rat do a triple somersault in the air like that, you can figure it a point for the Bronk team. Hey, what's that noise in front of our truck?"

"John, it appears to be two rats trying to make an end run toward the broken mayonnaise jars. Kluever sees them. He's clicked

the safety off his rifle and is zeroing in on those varmints."

"Pat, I believe he has elevated his rifle a bit too high to get a hit."

"Right. That point goes to the rats that are now hungrily lapping up the mayonnaise. It's now 1 to 1. And now a brief word from our sponsors."

Come on now, that's got to be better than watching a lousy golf ball bouncing across the grass or some guy in shorts pounding a tennis ball into a net.

The dumps are now long gone, as are Don and his dad. The rats have moved on to less challenging encounters with mankind. I guess rat shooting would never have become a TV sport even if the dumps had survived. It's weird how you look back on memorable events in your past, and yearn to return. I suppose some folk won't be able to relate to the joys of being knee-deep in piles of garbage, surrounded by big ugly rats and millions of buzzing flies and gnats—with people shooting guns in all directions. But just maybe it's that youthful dump rat shooting experience that's helped me survive in the business world of today.

•

The Hudson - Krag Handloads

by Jim Foral

1901 MAY NOT have been a good year for Queen Victoria or William McKinley, but it was a banner year for America's military marksmen. Sparked by the Boer and Spanish-American Wars, the world was enjoying a revival of interest in rifle shooting. Dormant and impotent for two decades, the National Rifle Association was renewing itself into a significant, strong force. Shooting the U.S. service arm, the 30-40 Krag-Jorgensen, suddenly and solidly fell into fashion about 1899.

Participating in this newly-popular pastime required practice to attain any degree of proficiency at the 600-800 yard ranges, and practice shooting with the Krag was fraught with a daunting assortment of obstacles. To begin with, suitably safe military ranges for the flat-shooting 30-40 were scattered and in short supply. Those available weren't generally accessible to this era's less mobile shooter.

Further discouraging rifle practice was the short life of the Krag barrel, caused by the extraordinarily erosive effects of the primitive nitroglycerin-rich smokeless powders in use at the time. Useful barrel life was generally put at 1,000-1,200 rounds, but Lt. Townsend Whelen recorded in 1905 that 1,400 shots was just as realistic.

Inherently accurate as it was, the Krag rifle was handicapped by abysmally inaccurate ammunition. In 1900, no match loads had been worked up for it, and the standard 220-grain metal-cased bullet simply couldn't be relied upon to place its shots closer than the 3-ring at 800 yards.

Most importantly though, the Defense Department hadn't budgeted for supplying center-fire cartridges for something as petty and seemingly unproductive as shooting paper targets. Each trooper was issued a small annual allotment of cartridges for this purpose, and when those were gone, there was no more. The most avid and competitive service rifle marksmen, the New England National Guardsmen, were most affected by the Army's inflexible ammunition distribution edicts. Abandoned, they felt, by the powers at Army Ordnance, the Guardsmen resigned themselves to providing their own practice ammunition. The problem was discussed at armory ranges, drill halls, or wherever the citizen-soldier assembled in 1899. The commercial ammunition option was briefly considered and dismissed as both unaffordable and unworkable. In the end, an inexpensive cast bullet handload was determined to be the most logical alternative.

Among the first to conceptualize a solution to the 30-caliber lead bullet dilemma was St. Louis librarian and widely-published columnist Horace Kephart. At some point in 1898, Mr. Kephart found himself in the need of a small-game bullet for his Winchester Hi-Wall 30-40 that would also double as a military sharpshooter's practice load. Better known for his writings on camping and woodcraft subjects, Kephart tried his hand at bullet design.

The front end of what came to be well known as the Kephart bullet embodied characteristics its originator considered to be essential. A groove at the base of the nose insured that the bullet lubricant would precede the body of the bullet on its trip down the bore. The squared edge of the forward band acted as a dirt-scraper, the traditional black-powder feature not easily dispensed with in these early transitional years. The nose of the Kephart bullet was sufficiently sub-bore diameter so that this function was not interfered with.

To withstand the torque of the 30-40's quick ten-inch twist, and the hot smokeless powder gas at the base, the bullet should have a band that was broad and strong, he reasoned. In addition, Kephart realized that the best of bullets could be ruined in a sizing chamber or die, and he insisted upon an as-cast diameter of .308-inch with a specified 1:10 tin-lead alloy. Kephart submitted a sketch of the proposed bullet to John Barlow at Ideal Manufacturing, who had the cherries shaped for both a two-banded 125-grain and three-banded 165-grain version, and assigned the mould number #308206 to the Kephart design. Loads were worked up during the summer of 1899, and by January 1900, readers of *Outing* and *Shooting and Fishing*

United States Rifle Team of 1902

1st Row—Doctor S.I. Scott (Coach), Dist. of Columbia; *Capt. Frank L. Graham (Team Adjutant), U.S. Army; Brig Gen B.W. Spencer, (Team Captain), I.G.R.P. State of New Jersey; Colonel S.C. Bruce, Old Guard, New York; William Hayes, Esq., (Coach), New Jersey.

2nd Row—Sub. Major G.B. Young, 1st Regt. Infy., D.C. N.G.; Corp. Kellog K.V. Casey, 71st Regt. Infy., New York N.G.; Capt. W.B. Martin, 2nd Regt., New Jersey N.G.; Sub. Lieut. W.W. Cookson, 2nd Regt. Infy., D.C. N.G.; *Pte. W.G. Hudson, Sig. Corps Infy., New Jersey N.G.

3rd Row—*Pte. H.H.Laizear, 6th regt, Infy., Penna. N.F.; Pte. Horace M. Bell, 1stRegt. Infy., New Jersey N.G.; *Pte.M.w. Parker, 1st Corps Cadets, Mass. Vol. Militia; *Lieut. Thos. Holcomb, Y.s. Marine corps; *Pte. G.E. Cook, 1st Regt. Infy., D.C. N.G.

Shot in the Match.

were learning how close Mr. Kephart had come to achieving the goal. Kephart loaded his shells with enough of Du Pont's or Laflin and Rand's most primitive smokeless powders to generate muzzle velocities estimated in the 1,200-1,500 fps neighborhood. At these speeds, either the long or short #308206 variation, lubed with a homemade ozocerite-based wax, could be depended upon to place 20 shots into a 2.5/3-inch circle at 100 yards.

The Kephart bullet appeared to have some promise, and Ideal Manufacturing did what they could to promote the projectile and foster an interest in the cause.

The Kephart bullet and its possibilities attracted its fair share of attention. By the time it was fresh news in the magazines, Kephart's New York City associate and correspondent Dr. Walter G. Hudson was very much aware of the tests at the range in St. Louis. Dr. Hudson was the unquestioned turn-of-the-century authority on rifle shooting and ballistic matters. A natural-born rifle shooter, he ranked among America's most notable and accomplished Schuetzen riflemen of the 1890s. "The Human Machine Rest," as he was known, Hudson was considered by many to be the most highly skilled competitor of the 200-yard offhand match era.

Strangely, something about the Krag magazine rifle and the long-range 30-caliber shooting craze appealed to Dr. Hudson. He became absorbed with the new and unfamiliar discipline, pursued it with a passion and his usual determination to excel at the game. In 1900, Hudson abandoned the single-shot target rifle almost entirely and took up competitive shooting with the Krag, a move some fellow Schuetzen shooters felt was a degrading activity.

Dr. Hudson possessed an analytical turn of mind. His contemporaries agreed that, by nature, he was an investigative sort of individual. When Hudson disclosed his inclination to perfect a mid-range cast bullet load for the Krag rifle, military rifleman knew instinctively that a better-qualified man for the task would be hard to find. Apart from Hudson's characteristic thoroughness, the most important facet of his make-up was the man's intense level of self-application. Early in 1900, Hudson directed his considerable energy toward a cast bullet handload for the U.S. Krag rifle.

An influential and well-connected person, Dr. Hudson was promised unrestricted material and technical support from Laflin and Rand, Du Pont, and Union Metallic Cartridge Co. John Barlow at Ideal stood willing to produce any and all moulds the doctor should need in his undertak-

Ideal #308279 Hudson with 15 grains of Marksman.

Ideal #308334 with 25 grains of Lightning, Hudson's '06 load.

ing. Laflin and Rand provided special tubular powders, while the ballistic crew at U.M.C. volunteered to furnish non-mercuric primers that were unavailable to the general public.

Fundamentally, Dr. Hudson's mission was to develop a simple cast bullet, working within the restrictions of the holdover blackpowder plain-base bullet concept, which would be accurate to 600 yards.

When Hudson exchanged views on the matter with other National Guardsmen, the 1900 shooter consensus concluded that the lube grooves should ideally be contained in the cartridge neck. If the handload was to magazine well, an important rapid-fire consideration, it should more or less externally resemble the arsenal full-patch cartridge.

As unfamiliar as the veteran breechseater was with fixed ammunition, Hudson was forced to deal with this additional military-related requirement.

At first, bullet design wasn't a major hurdle. Hudson elected to use what was available to him. Initial efforts centered upon an early projectile dreamed up by William M. Cooper before 1898. Catalogued in turn-of-the-century Ideal handbooks as #3081, this flat-nosed 30-caliber was more familiarly known as the Cooper bullet. In its four-banded 200-grain form, #3081 looked as if it should fit Dr. Hudson's general length and weight requirements. Prudent enough not to introduce an uncontrollable number of variables, Hudson systematically tested the 200-grain Cooper, sized to .308-inch and as-cast to .311-inch in a variety of tin/lead alloys. Muzzle velocities in the 1,300-1,500 fps range were obtained by burning the most up-to-date smokeless propellants from Laflin and Rand and Du Pont, and King's semi-smokeless powders.

The cast #3081s were fired from a 30-40 Winchester High Wall, secured in a machine rest, directed at the 200-yard military target. Dr. Hudson recorded scores of ten-shot groups. His days were spent on the range, and spare time invested in compiling and evaluating data. The first combinations delivered, by Hudson's standards, unacceptable accuracy. The 200-yard groups ranged from eight inches to over two feet. Accompanying the mediocre accuracy was a pronounced tendency for these bullets to stagger, or keyhole. This tipping varied in degree. Hudson theorized the Cooper bullet's point put it badly out of balance, in spite of the Winchester's quick ten-inch twist. He thought that increasing the velocity a bit might solve the problem, but might make the load unnecessarily powerful.

More encouraging were the results with an unsized, vaguely described experimental bullet, cast of hard type metal and weighing 165 grains. John Barlow had furnished Hudson a mould of the Perfection pattern, adjustable for a variety of weights. The shank of the bullet measured .308-inch. Up front was a .310/.312-inch band to act as a dirt scraper and to prevent the entire bullet from slipping back into the unsized shell. To move the bullet's center of gravity forward, a hollow concavity was formed at the base. At the target, groups were strikingly tighter—ten shots in four inches in one instance. However, combustion of the powder charges were usually incomplete, a serious flaw in Hudson's opinion. More importantly, the persistent instability troubles still had not been overcome. Hudson freely admitted that this design was not an improvement over the Cooper. Dr. Hudson's cartridges, incidentally, were prepared with washed and unresized Frankford Arsenal shells, and loaded on either a Winchester 1894 tool or the Hudson-preferred Ideal tong tool.

Dr. Hudson gave the 175-grain Kephart bullet fair trial, too. To meet the cartridge's length restrictions, the Kephart needed to be seated out so far that one lubricant-filled groove protruded beyond the case mouth, a clear disadvantage from a military standpoint. Accuracy, in Hudson's High Wall and an issue Krag, was disappointing. Two hundred-yard groups averaged a not so good ten to twelve inches. The dirt scraper feature may have had some appeal, but if Walter Hudson felt that if Kephart's .275-inch diameter nose was a good design feature, he never let on. All in all, the 175-grain Kephart #308206, for Hudson's purposes, had little to recommend it.

In 1900, the Union Metallic Cartridge Co., hopeful of capitalizing on the Guardsmen's predicament, tried to remedy things very simply by introducing a reduced velocity loading with a 180-grain full-jacketed bullet. These inexpensive factory loads would group into four to five inches at 200 yards, and were still wonderfully accurate to 800 yards, Hudson reported. On the downside, they were needlessly powerful. A 180-grain reduced load would still pass through 12-1/2 pine boards, the industry gauge of comparative "power." (*The 220-grain service load would penetrate four feet.*) Based on this alone, the U.M.C. load, good as it was, was out of the question, and Hudson was forced to abandon it.

In his 1900 tests, detailed in *Shooting and Fishing* late that year, Hudson had compiled enough data to conclude that he was a long ways from having perfected the Krag reduced load. As he prepared for another set of experiments, he drew up a mental blueprint of the ideal 30-caliber cast bullet, combining the good points of the Kephart

and Cooper bullets and the Frankford Arsenal full-patch 220-grain service bullets.

Determined to improve on the balance of the Cooper bullet, Hudson reasoned out the first of his own mould designs. By the winter of 1901, he was prepared to report on the progress of that summer's shooting season.

The rounded point of what became cataloged as Ideal #308223 was, not coincidentally, formed very similar to the Krag service bullet. The sharp-cornered dirt scraper feature that Dr. Hudson incorporated eliminated the possibility of a bore-riding forward section. The nose diameter measured .290-inch. Ideal #308223 was distributed in three weight variations: 150, 175, and 200 grains. The three-groove 175-grain version performed best in Hudson's test rifles. Either 9 grains of Laflin and Rand's Sharpshooter, 8 grains of L&R's Infallible, or 12 grains of Du Pont #2 were the charges advised for up to 200-yard target shooting and practice. Each load would produce a velocity estimated to be 1,200 fps. Though accurate enough at 200 yards, #308223 didn't qualify as a realistic 500-yard bullet, at least at the moderate velocity it would tolerate. 1,200 fps

was the practical limit before fusion and gas cutting reared their heads.

After a considerable amount of experimenting with alloys, Hudson arrived at the conclusion that these bullets should be hardened entirely with elemental antimony. 84 parts of pure lead needed to be blended with 16 parts of antimony, an alloy with the hardness of about 19 BHN. He felt the harder alloy was the way to avert the continuing difficulties he'd experienced with fusion. The *Ideal Handbook #15*, circulated in 1903, described how to properly melt this hard-to-prepare alloy.

Hudson warned against undersized bullets and explained the gas-cutting consequences of the slightest leak. Further, he stressed that the bullet-to-bore relationship was critical and that an absolutely gas-tight fit was essential. With this hard antimony-bearing alloy, riflemen could no longer rely on upsettage or obturation to seal the bore. The bullets, dropped from Ideal mould #308223 and cast of Hudson's alloy, measured an amply snug .312-inch.

Gallery shooting was a way of maintaining the guardsmen's competitive form during the winter months. On the whole, it was hard to keep the troops interested in shooting the 22 rimfire, and they were much more

Ideal #308284 gas-check load with 22 grains of Lightning.

The #308206 Kephart bullets.

inclined to practice with the service rifle, if special ammunition could be prepared for it. In addition, distribution of the lightly regarded government gallery practice rounds for the Krag was not what it might have been. In New York, Dr. Hudson's unit tried out chamber bushings, or cartridge adaptors of the Winchester type, firing 32-caliber smokeless pistol cartridges. Apart from the bullet's two-inch free-bored leap into the rifling, there was considerable gas leakage past the projectile involved. Terrible gas-cutting and leading were the direct results.

In about 1900, Dr. Hudson invented what he viewed as an improvement over the bushing principle. His implement held the pistol bullet in the neck of the rifle's chamber, very close to the throat. A partially split base allowed insertion of the cartridge and removal of the spent case, and an auxiliary firing pin transmitted the firing pin's blow to the primer. Hudson himself had no interest in profiting from his device, and turned the rights over to a fellow New Yorker by the name of Brayton, who marketed it for a time. The Marble Safety Axe Co. eventually took over manufacture and promotion. Quite scarce today, the Hudson/Brayton/

Marble adaptor was an essential part of each National Guard rifleman's shooting kit. By all accounts, and Hudson's candid admission, this adaptor with pistol bullets "shot very well at gallery ranges." The principle drawback, of course, was that the cost of 32-caliber centerfire cartridges was many times that of the cheap rimfire.

Again, a mild lead-bullet handload appeared to be in order, and Dr. Hudson took on this secondary project. From 1900-1902, Dr. Hudson was recommending the 125-grain Kephart bullet for use at armory ranges, which were often up to 80 yards long. The powder charge was less specific - five to eight grains of "almost any quick-burning smokeless powder." The indoor alloy was 1:10 tin/lead.

By 1900, it had become clear that his high-antimony alloys were as out of place in the inadequately ventilated drill hall ranges as a snapping turtle in a petting zoo. The brittle bullets pulverized upon impacting the steel deflecting plates of the bullet stops. Antimony dust filled the air and was inhaled by firers and markers, several of whom

came down ill enough to require hospitalization. The doctor was able to diagnose the mysterious ailment as antimonial poisoning.

By 1904, Hudson was willing to make some recommendations based on the experiences of gallery Krag shooters. For indoor and basement ranges or backyard varminting, he advised the 77-grain Ideal #308252, the 32 Colt Auto lead bullet. Two and a-half grains of Laflin and Rand's Unique, "Bullseye," or Infallible" got it out of the barrel. For 25-80 yards, a shooter needed a longer, heavier bullet, Hudson insisted. Both the 87-grain #308245 Ideal bullet or the 125-grain version of #308241, in front of 3-5 grains of these same L&R powders, filled the bill at these short distances.

These loads were used widely by the Marine Corps and U.S. Army Guardsmen throughout America.

This system was found to be so consistently accurate that, as late as 1907, Dr. Hudson had no reason to experiment further in this direction.

In the spring of 1902, Hudson made the cut for the U.S. 1902 Palma squad. Preparation for, and participation in the September Match in Ottawa, Canada, limited the time he was able to devote to the cast bullet mission. The greatest obstacle still confronting Dr. Hudson in 1903 was to get a bullet to work at a velocity generating sufficient energy to be practical and useful at the 500-600 yard mid-ranges. The most serious barrier to this objective was fusion of the fragile bullet base when driven to the necessary speeds.

After the powder gas had flame-cut a passage through the bullet base, Hudson discovered the leakage often extended up the side of the projectile. Depending on the severity of this action, leading and out-of-balance bullets were the more noticeable consequences. Too, extreme variations in pressure, accompanied by irregular elevations were a direct result. In the end, it all printed on the target. Assisted by John Barlow, Hudson designed a three-bullet series in the hopes of obtaining more power and range. #308256, #308259, and #308268 were developed in 1903 and explained to those who bought the 1904 *Ideal Handbook*. One of the common characteristics was a greatly oversized forward band that, upon chambering and closing the bolt, plugged the breech against gas. At .327-inch diameter, the tapered

Krag gallery stuff. *L to R:* Arsenal round-ball gallery load; F.A. 107-grain gallery load; Winchester 30-40 cartridge adapter; Hudson/Brayton/Marble's adapter.

front band of #308359 would have corked up an 8mm bore. The 200-grainers, #308268 and #308256, both had a square-sided bore-sealing band of .319-inch. Each new Hudson bullet had snug bore-riding, self-centering .300/.302-inch noses. Most importantly, the third feature was a much broader base for the prevention of gas escape. Hudson's reasoning was that the mass of the base bands would conduct the heat of the powder gases before the jet of flame could liquefy the base and leak to the forward bands. The conspicuously wide base of #308268 most emphatically illustrates this principle.

The smallest of the lot, the #308256, was intended for the minority of arsenal Krags with standard .308-inch bores. For the bulk of these rifles with oversized barrels, the .312-inch diameter #308259 was the sensible solution. #308268, in terms of application, was the happy medium—and the best all-around

Two ancient handloads from the era. On the left is a head-stamped F.A. 1902 with the Hudson #308223. The other is a 1905 head-stamped shell with the #308284 gas-check bullet.

30-40 medium-charge bullet in the eyes of its designer.

These improved cast bullets allowed practical velocities of over 1,300 fps without undue fusion, leading, or keyholing. They all grouped well out to 500 yards, but not as well as the advanced full-jacketed bullets that had been brought to a much higher standard by 1903. 14-15 grains of Marksman powder produced a chronographed 1,380 fps for the 200-grainer. In the course of developing these Ideal numbers, Hudson announced a switch in favored alloys, without disclosing the reason for the change of mind. Reportedly, complaints concerning the 16% antimony alloy being pesky to melt and difficult to cast perfect bullets with, were fairly widespread. At that point, Hudson supported the use of a harder and more agreeable 80-10-10 blend (BHN 23) and an 86-7-7 (BHN 20) alloy that was just as easy to handle. Despite the success of the 1903 alloy bullet designs, there was room for improvement. Dr. Hudson recognized and acknowledged the need for devising a bullet with the capability to withstand 1,500 fps.

In the meantime, Guard personnel ladled molten alloy into eight-cavity Ideal Armory moulds, metered out Marksman from Ideal #1 measures, and assembled the Hudson-bulleted handloads on Ideal #3 Special handtools. The largest units often purchased the Ideal Armory Loading Outfit, the earliest available press-type tool. And National Guard marksmen continued to shoot outstanding practice scores with the Hudson-approved cast bullet loads.

In 1904, Dr. Hudson, together with the crew at Ideal, came up with an improved #308268. In essentials, Ideal #308279 was not dissimilar to its predecessors, apart from the shape of its nose. To give the new bullet increased length and long-range stability the bore-dimensioned nose of the newest Hudson bullet tapered sharply to a domed point, a feature inspired by the proven Hudson-Thomas jacketed Krag match bullet. It also better fit the Krag's inordinately long throat better than the bullets it superseded.

To combat the persistent threat of gas-cutting, the .312-inch diameter rear band

was made broader yet. The gas-sealing square-edged front band, a bit larger than the body of the bullet, was a fixture on Hudson's bullets by now.

By 1905, Hudson was recommending a load for the new bullet. The correct charge for the 195-grain #308279 was once again 14-15 grains of the quick-burning bulk Marksman, for a velocity of 1,300-1,350 fps.

But enough of the hot Marksman-generated gas burned through the reinforced band of #308279 that eventually Dr. Hudson realized that the 500-yard accuracy he'd sought so devoutly wasn't going to happen. However optimistic Dr. Hudson may have been about the potential of his latest and most popular of the series, 1,500 fps remained an elusive goal with the class of cast bullet he was working with. A level of 1,300 fps with the plain base was as high as he could realistically hope for.

#308279 was said to be the most accurate of the doctor's designs. Accounts vary, and most are not particularly meaningful as they were expressed in terms of scores rather than group size. The indications are, however, that ten-shot 200-yard groups were routinely fired that could be covered by a three-inch disk. Good enough, for practice ammunition certainly, but a cure for the fusion needed to be worked out.

In the main, Dr. Hudson worked independently and unaided on his pet project. Updates of his progress were posted periodically in the rifle-man's press. Once other shooters became aware, the mood to create a workable reduced Krag handload became a contagious one. Along the way, other clear-thinking Krag enthusiasts rallied in support of the movement's guiding spirit and stepped in to offer fresh insights, new ideas, and changes in direction. The worthiness of this input varied in degree. Some recommended a harder or softer alloy. Many tried wads of varying descriptions, and still others filled the empty space ahead of the powder charge with inert cotton, asbestos, or sawdust.

James H. Keough, a top-flight rifleman and a 1903 Palma team member, came up with a commendable suggestion. Keough was a three-striper with the Massachusetts Volunteers. Fill the air space with Cream of Wheat and firewall the base band in this fashion, Sgt. Keough offered. He had tried it, and it worked for him. At the 1904 National Matches held in Fort Riley, KS, he shared his discovery with the other competitors, and the news circulated quickly. In addition to this, Keough is believed to be the

Hudson-recommended gallery load with Ideal #308245. Case head stamped F.A. '05.

brains behind Ideal #308280. Sgt. George Doyle, another Palma man and a 71st New York Guardsman, made a significant contribution. Sgt. Doyle produced a well-balanced 200-grain wide-banded bullet modeled after the successful Hudson-Thomas jacketed match bullet. Ideal assigned Doyle's bullet cherry number 308274. An illustration of an extraordinarily tight group, published in *Outdoor Life*, showed clearly what #308274 was capable of. Sgt. Doyle used 14-15 grains of fast-burning Sharpshooter powder, and the velocity was measured at 1,450 fps. Two hundred-yard accuracy was rated as "good," and grouping at 500 yards was what Hudson termed as "fairly good." Dr. Hudson thought enough of it to write in July of 1905: "Doyle's bullet is probably the best of any so far brought out." The small quantity of smokeless powder left a considerable amount of air space in the shell, and a cereal filler was funneled in, *ala* Keough, up to the case-neck level. Tested for pressure at the Du Pont labs, the Doyle load was found to generate pressures actually in excess of the full-power service load.

Still, the idea appealed to Hudson, who resolved to try slower-burning powders, such as L&R's Lightning and W.A., in combination with the Cream of Wheat. Twenty grains of Lightning were burned behind the Doyle bullet. Projectiles recovered from an armory water tank showed a total absence of fusion—the cereal

had prevented it. Minor stripping was evident, which became more marked when the charge was increased by two grains. Over the chronograph, the 20-grain Lightning load clocked at 1,600 fps. Machine-rest test groups were into four inches (ten shots) at 200 yards. Very good accuracy, coupled with freedom from fusion, was a long-awaited combination. Just as importantly, the velocity increase that was made possible promised better results at the 500-600 yard targets. Hudson considered the Doyle system, with 20 grains Lightning, at least initially, to be a distinct advance. A major setback occurred when the unspecified ballistic lab reported back with the pressure figures. Mean pressures were just under 40,000 psi with a maximum set at 44,700 psi. The Cream of Wheat added to the total weight of the ejecta, which, in turn, had its not totally expected effect on chamber pressure. The volume of the cereal also decreased the case capacity. Face to face with the bottom line, Hudson realized that he couldn't prudently recommend these cereal-incorporating loads for the single-lugged Krag rifle. The powder companies quickly issued statements declaring their products weren't designed to be used in conjunction with fillers, and if some inept or unlucky investigator were to blow himself up, they couldn't be held responsible. Hudson published these cautions, along with his project's update, in the July, 1905 number of *Outdoor Life*. At this time, he was recommending a mid-range load using 15-16 grains of Marksman and a good bullet in the 200-grain class, preferably #308268, #308274, or #308279. But no cereal, please.

The battle with fusion was a hard-fought one. In his earliest endeavors, Dr. Hudson tried loose asbestos wads beneath the bullets to protect the bullet's base from the hot gas. He used them plain, pasted on, or sandwiched between cardboard discs, in conjunction with felt, and in all manner of ways. Still, the gas got by them all, and the troublesome fusion persisted. Base band melting had occurred where the cardboard wads weren't even scorched. Hudson scratched his head, and approached the problem from a different angle. He fashioned wads from sheet copper, or layers of copper wire gauze, loaded beneath the bases of his unjacketed bullets, and began to notice a decided improvement. When bullets were recovered and inspected, Hudson could see that the fusion was largely eliminated. The doc-

tor theorized that this success was due to the metal acting as a heat sink, rather than as a shield. As early as 1902, Hudson had studied methods to deal with the gas-cutting and solicited the cooperation of Union Metallic Cartridge Co. personnel. They made for him some copper wafers that he used, presumably unattached to the bullet base. Hudson alluded to these "copper gas checks" in the *Ideal Handbook* released in 1903.

What we know and take for granted today as the gas check, evolved rapidly and directly from Dr. Hudson's simple discovery, and it was a long step in a forward direction. History and the U.S. Patent Office officially credit the copper gas check cup to John Barlow of Ideal in 1907. The truth, however, is recorded in an obscure and forgotten location. In *Outers Book* for September of 1908, we find this nugget straight from the doctor's typewriter: "These experiments, in fact, which I did in conjunction with Mr. Barlow of the Ideal Manufacturing Co. led to the production by that company of their copper gas-check bullet."

Both men realized that a positive and secure attachment of a gas-checking device called for the redesign of the bullet base. The first bullet to incorporate the new cup was the still-familiar #308284. The design, attributed to Ideal, clearly came about through the solicited input of Walter G. Hudson, M.D. As a practical matter, the gas-checked bullet became the solution to the dreaded and ongoing fusion difficulty. Its use allowed an increase in muzzle velocities to 1,700 fps before other restricting complications arose. This gain in velocity and rotational speed minimized or eliminated the irritating troubles with bullet stability.

Ideal #308241, long and short.

Hudson gallery load with bullets (*l to r*) # 308252; 125-gr. #308206 Kephart; 125-gr. Ideal #30821...and four grains of Unique.

The Doyle handload: Ideal #308274, 15 grains of Sharpshooter, Cream of Wheat filler.

Military rifle shooters instantly embraced the new 207-grain projectile. Then Lt. Townsend Whelen and others demonstrated its potential by shooting near-possibles at Sea Girt in the fall of 1905. Hudson broadcast his choice of midrange loads, which consisted of 22-23 grains of Lightning behind the #308284. Shooters were further advised that the bullet needed to be moulded from the 80-10-10 or 86-7-7 smokeless alloy. 600-yard accuracy of this handload, Hudson was delighted to report, was as good as the improved ball cartridges Frankford Arsenal and its contractors produced.

The men of the 71st New York used thousands of these handloads for 600-yard practice during the 1906 season.

The troopers of the 7th New York were perhaps the most active and competitive guardsmen/riflemen in New England at the time. In 1906, they put their heads together and concocted a design that seemed to combine the good features of the various Hudson styles in one package. In some circles, it had enough merit to cause John Barlow to form a cherry for this 195-grain bullet and assign it number 308287. In the face of the gas-checked #308284's popularity, the committee-formed bullet never really caught on at more than a regional level.

The days of the Krag, as it was turning out, were severely numbered. The 1903 Springfield superseded the old 1892 30-caliber, and as it became better distributed and more and more popular, the Krag was retired and relegated to surplus status. The 1907 Palma, fired with the Krag, was the last major competition where these rifles were seen on the firing line. This end of an era, incidentally, also marks Walter Hudson's second and final participation in the international contest.

Ironically, when the cast lead bullet was in its 1908 state of perfection, there was no longer much need for it. The Krags had all but been put away, and the powers at the Defense Department had been shown the benefits of soldiers burning up a few practice rounds. Springfield shooters discovered that Army Ordnance was much less miserly when it passed out '06 ammunition.

When it came time to abandon the 30-40, the Hudson Krag handload principle transferred appropriately, directly, and successfully to the 30-1906 cartridge. The doctor's prescription for Springfield riflemen was the new gas-checked semi-pointed 190-grain #308334 and 25 grains of Lightning, which produced not only a sizzling 1,750 fps, but stellar 600-yard grouping as well.

As an achievement, Hudson was successful in perfecting and providing his fellow Krag riflemen what he'd determined they needed. As an advancement, Dr. Hudson laid the foundation for the present-day cast bullet when he revolutionized deeply-rooted alloy bullet attitudes with his groundbreaking exploration and discoveries that would remain unexampled in significance until Col. E.H. Harrison happened onto the cast bullet scene a half-century later.

One simply cannot appreciate the modern alloy bullet until one recognizes the effort, inspiration, range time and sleepless nights that went into it.

After nearly a century, there still exists a niche for Walter Hudson's class of 30-40 loads. Nowadays, it's just as much fun to shoot a Krag as it was when the first Roosevelt was in the White House, and this sort of load will still perform at the midranges. And stretching out prone with tightly-drawn sling, sighting at a black bull over a long Krag barrel, nostrils full of leather, Alox, and burnt powder smells, is a grand way to hearken back to the glory days of the competition Krag, when the eastern National Guard units dominated at the ranges of Wimbledon, Creedmoor and Sea Girt. ●

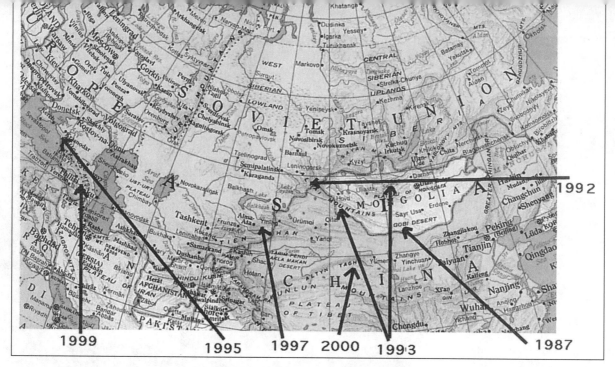

1999   1995   1997   2000   1993   1987   1992

Map showing approximate hunting locales.

Random Observations On Privately Owned Firearms In The Communist Bloc

by Clarence E. "Doc" Ellis

OVER THE PAST 13 years I have been privileged to hunt in several areas of the former Communist bloc, both before and after the dissolution of the Soviet Union. Most recently I hunted in China. Most of the people who have hunted these countries are avid hunters, but only moderately interested in firearms for their own sake. I, on the other hand, spent 10 years as a professional gunsmith before becoming a professional in the science of geology, while maintaining my interest in firearms. Thus I am trained to use my eyes, and not my ears, to gather information since rocks are not known for their verbal propensity. This is just as well, since on earlier hunts the interpreters obviously avoided some subjects, gave questionable information or, at times, they just plain lied. It seems to be a habit that still crops up, usually for no logical reason. Most times while actually hunting you are accompanied only by a guide, and maybe an

assistant or two—none of who speak English. This works remarkably well unless you happen to be a compulsive talker.

Back in my younger days I was led to believe that firearms ownership in communist countries was strictly forbidden to all but the hierarchy. It turns out that exceptions existed, at least in the remote Asian regions of the communist empire. The same regions also must have had considerable illegal firearms ownership.

Photos used here were taken to record the hunt, and are not ideally suited for the purpose at hand. I will relate observations chronologically, restrict my comments to firearms and their use, and leave conclusions to someone else.

1987: Mongolia, Gobi Desert

Mongolia was a communist country at that time.

Enroute from Dalanzahgdad to the hunting camp, our caravan of

two Russian jeeps gave a lift to a couple going to a "tourist camp".

Left to right: A 30-06, 7.62x54R, 8mm Mongol Magnum (with a .323-inch 230-grain bullet seated to the base of the neck), and the 300 Winchester Magnum.

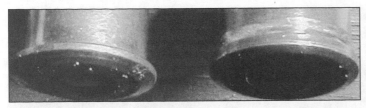

The 7.62x54R (*left*) and the Mongol Magnum have the same rim diameter (.563-inch), and similar bevels, but are not parent and child.

Benchrest technique in Kazahkstan; zeroing a shotgun that just had a badly bent barrel straightened by the man in the light cap. This is a herders' camp. The structure is a *ger* (yurt).

Altai Mountains, Kazahkstan; the rifle is a Russian bolt-action 22, slung muzzle up.

When we arrived we took time to sight in our rifles. While rummaging behind the rear seat I observed a crudely-sporterized Mosin-Nagant, which I never saw when we unloaded the jeep at hunting camp.

The first day hunting in a barren range of low mountains, while stopped to glass for sheep, I spied three tarnished shell casings in a pile almost at my feet. I brought one back, and have tried to identify it since, with no success. At first glance it looked to be derived from the 7.62x54R used in the Mosin-Nagant, having a beveled rim, and the same rim diameter. However, the case is too long, and the base too large.

Rim: .564-inch; Base: .524-inch; Shoulder: .460-inch; Neck: .376-inch; Length: 2.62 inches; Rim thickness: .055-inch

A .323-inch bullet fits snugly in the neck, so it probably fired a .318-inch bullet. With over a thousand rifle cartridges in my collection, and nine cartridge collector books in my library, I haven't found it or a parent, so I'll call it the 8mm Mongol Magnum. Given the climate in the Gobi Desert, it could easily predate communism.

While touring the Wildlife Museum in Ulan Bator I saw a beautifully sporterized semi-auto rifle which was most likely a 1938 or 1940 Tokarev (I handled only one of these unsuccessful military rifles, *and that was many years previously, so I could be mistaken*). As nearly as

The base of the 7.62x54R case is .484-inch, while Mongol's measures .524-inch. The rim thickness on the 7.62x54R runs .062/.067-inch, while the Mongol measure .050/.055-inch. The 300 Holland & Holland Super 30 is similar, but has a longer case. The 280 Ross is closer, but rimless, while I consider the Mongol semi-rimmed.

I could tell through the display case, the workmanship and artistry were both excellent.

1992: Altai Mountains, Kazahkstan

The Soviet Union had only recently dissolved, and Kazahkstan was now independent. Our hunting area was near the boundary junction of Mongolia, China, Russia, and Kazahkstan. We wandered across the Russia-Kazahkstan border (*completely unmarked*) on a daily basis. We got to base camp in a 4-wheel-drive vehicle. Further travel was by horse.

Our head guide had a Russian 22-rimfire bolt-action rifle; the same as was written up in the "Dope Bag" of the *American Rifleman* magazine. He did not have the magazine. He was the regional predator control officer, charged with controlling the population of wolves and grizzly bears. He once related (*in sign language*) the problems he had loading a round in the chamber (*it kept falling through the magazine well*) when confronted by a grizzly! Having experienced the difficulties any guy with big fingers has in accomplishing said task, without the elevated stress level, I could well appreciate the tale.

Desiring to take advantage of my 338 to eliminate a cattle-killing grizzly, we joined with a group of local herdsmen for a driven bear hunt. Prior to the hunt a couple of single-barrel, break-open 20-gauge shotguns—of utilitarian design and workmanship—were produced by the half-dozen or so assembled herdsmen. Both guns were well used but sound, except that one had a badly bent barrel. Proving his versatility, the head guide retired to the woodpile and proceeded to straighten the barrel by the same means I used while in the trade. The next step was to target the gun—but first, ammunition must be loaded.

Out came a little leather satchel with the loading kit. Brass shells were used, tarnished black. Depriming the Berdan primers was with a tool like a small awl, and presented no difficulty. They were just pried out. Primer pockets may have been loose from long use. Priming was with a small hammer (*cringe!*). A new-looking can of powder displayed Cyrillic markings and a picture of a bird. A measured charge of flake powder was followed by a couple wads torn from a pamphlet, and topped with a cast round ball, and more wads. All in all, it was a practiced operation with the equivalent of a Lee Loader. The powder had to be Russian-made, intended for handloading, and they'd obviously been doing this for many years.

Using a stump for a rest, the repaired gun was fired at another stump about 30 yards distant. Three shots by two different guys gave three hits. There was probably little or no choke in the barrel.

My hunting partners on this trip were Austrian and German, and their rifles carried monster scopes appropriate to their type of hunting. The local guides all had military experience and, in trying our various rifles, the unanimous opinion was that the German and Austrian rifles were too heavy, and poorly balanced, but my 7-pound 338 with a 4x scope was *NICE*.

1993: Mongolia, Altai Mountains

Mongolia was barely behind Poland in declaring itself non-communist.

On the way from Hovd to the first hunting camp, we paused at a river crossing to rebuild the Russian jeep's fuel pump. A couple heavy trucks were parked for similar purposes. I was engaged in conversation by a young fellow who wanted to practice his English, and immediately recognized I was not a Mongol. It turned out he made his living shooting marmots, and selling the pelts in Russia for fur hats. He claimed 400-percent profit. Capitalism obviously was not a difficult concept for the younger folks to grasp.

While hunting one day we encountered a couple guys on camel-back, out marmot hunting. One of the guides in elk camp spent middays stalking marmots. The rifles used were the Russian 22-rimfire bolt actions.

My guide for ibex owned a well-used Czech BRNO sporter. I never got close enough to it while wearing my bifocals to read the chambering, but based on bore size and action

Mongolia: I spent the whole evening in this *ger* (yurt) and never noticed the revolver until I got the photo.

Caucasus Mountains, Russia; the SKS certainly has sporting value if it's all you have.

length I estimated it was a 7x64mm. I found an empty casing in my *ger* (yurt) that was a new 7mm Remington Magnum of Yugoslav manufacture (*Prvi Partizanm Titovo Uzice, if it matters*). Hunters in Mongolia are predominantly American, German, and Austrian—none of who would seem likely to use Yugoslav ammo.

During the course of the ibex hunt I was privileged to be the honored guest at a wedding in the camp just down the creek. I never noticed it at the time, but some of my photos revealed a revolver tucked above a roof pole. Other than city dwellers, nearly all Mongolians are

Caucasus Mountains, Russia: the ubiquitous SKS and my Ruger 77.

nomads who take their flocks and herds where the grazing is good. With no motor vehicles, their routes are limited only by the agility of their pack animals, which include camels, yaks, and horses.

Is a picture emerging?

Match-grade Mosin-Nagant.

Tien Shan Mountains, Kazahkstan: the local guides carried their rifles slung muzzle down when on horseback. Match-grade Mosin Nagant shown. The saddlebags are full of ibex meat.

This Kazak guide carries an SKS, slung muzzle up because of the brush.

Kazak guide with his match-grade Mosin Nagant and roe buck.

1995: Caucasus Mountains, Russia

My guide on this trip carried an SKS, and had only military ball ammunition. With sign language and scratching on rocks it was learned that his SKS cost virtually the same as my Ruger 77 Mk II (less scope): $400. I should point out that the Russians preferred payment and tips be in U.S. dollars, even over Deutsche marks, and certainly not rubles, so he definitely understood dollars. This is true everywhere I have hunted. Even in the year 2000, in Communist China, in one of the most remote parts of that country, U.S. dollars are preferred.

We flew into our high camp in a Mi-8 transport helicopter in the company of an anti-poaching patrol armed with AK-47s (*according to the interpreter*). Their guns, as well as the guide's SKS, were cased and kept out of sight when anyone else might be around. When we returned to the guide's home he made sure his canvas gun case stayed out of sight.

1997: Tien Shan Mountains, Kazahkstan

We had five hunters in camp, so we had five guides. An SKS was shared by a couple of guides. At least they had come up with soft-point ammo from somewhere. Two other guides had somewhat similar Mosin-Nagants; not, to my knowledge, reported anywhere. Both rifles had pistol-grip stocks and barrels in the 24-26 inch range. One mounted a PS01 sniper scope, supposedly in current use on the Dragunov, and had a non-laminated stock of dark-colored hardwood.

The other had a laminated stock and match-grade sights. The front sight was a hooded post, but higher than on the 1891/30. The rear sight was a micrometer peep sight with Cyrillic markings. Both rifles were well made, the only crude workmanship being the relocation of sling swivels to the side, instead of the bottom, of the stocks. They had no softpoint ammunition for the 7.62x54R cartridge, however.

In Asia I never saw saddle scabbards. Most guides carried their rifles slung muzzle up across their back, and we visiting hunters had to do the same. In this particular region the guides all carried their rifles slung muzzle down, even the short SKS.

Tea (lunch) time in the Tien Shan Mountains, Kazahkstan. Mosin-Nagant with PSO1 scope.

Azerbaijan: Author's Ruger Model 77 in 300 Winchester Magnum next to a 12-gauge double. Obviously long barrels are not in.

Caucasus Mountains, Azerbaijan: members of the hunters' association.

A lot of hunters complain that their guides want them to shoot at ridiculously long ranges, apparently believing that a scope of, say, 4X increases the effective range by four times. Maybe they are all used to the 7.62x39 cartridge, and anything from 30-06 on up therefore seems very powerful. In any event, I never had any such pressure put on me. Most shots were in the 200-300 meter ballpark; the longest may have crowded 400 meters.

1999: Caucasus Mountains, Azerbaijan

The locals preferred driving game past a hunter in a blind instead of the "spot and stalk" hunting style preferred in most other places I've been. The beaters were members of the local hunters' association, which numbered about 1,000 members. The beaters carried an assortment of shotguns in 12 and 20 gauge. The 20-gauge shotguns were all single-barrel break-open guns of the same pattern I observed in the Altai Mountains of Kazahkstan in 1992. The 12-gauge guns included the same single-barrel model and a couple of side-by-side doubles with exposed hammers. The doubles showed a higher grade of workmanship. Although not top-quality guns, they were not strictly utilitarian. Loads appeared to be round ball, as the wadding looked too sloppy to hold birdshot. Brass cases were used, and I suspect the loading tools used were very similar to those I saw used in Kazahkstan in 1992.

2000: Altyn Shan Mountains, China

China is still a communist country. I was one of a party of four blue sheep hunters. In base camp I found a fired 22 Long Rifle cartridge. The head-stamp is attributed by two references to Factory No. 10 in China, although the references both show that factory produces only centerfire cartridges with numbers indicating date of manufacture. Given that the Chinese were, or are, exporting their copy of the Russian 22-caliber bolt-action rifle, it is only logical that they manufacture their own ammunition for said rifle at one or more of their ordnance factories. No firearms were seen except for those we brought.

It was interesting to note that on our return to camp on a partially-sunny afternoon (*base camp was over 13,000 ft. elevation, and this was March in northern China*), three guys we'd never seen before emerged from a yurt to take pictures of our bag of Tibetan gazelles with some fairly jazzy 35mm single-lens reflex cameras. There were no vehicles around except the two we arrived in, and these guys were not local herders. I'll bet they were worse on horseback than I am. Definitely city boys.

It is tempting to draw conclusions based on even such limited evidence as this. I am a scientist. I won't. Somebody with considerable knowledge of the culture, economics, and politics of these various remote regions might be able to reach some valid conclusions. For the rest of us, it's just interesting to learn what goes on in parts of the world about which we know little.

On several of these hunts there was a guide or camp manager who was essentially the same age as I. Invariably there is an initial recognition by both parties that we were once classified as enemies. They were in the armed forces of the Soviet Union when I was in the armed forces of the United States, during the peak of the Cold War. Without exception, when we parted, it was as friends, grateful that we'd had the opportunity to meet on the terms we did—and we sure didn't need an interpreter to make those feelings clear to each other! ●

Weatherby Sub-MOA Mark V Rifle and Nosler AccuBond Bullet

by Layne Simpson

WEATHERBY HAS LONG guaranteed the Mark V rifle capable of shooting three bullets into a 1/1-2 inch group at 100 yards. While such a level of precision is most certainly acceptable for big-game hunting, some hunters are willing to dig deeper into their pockets for an even more accurate rifle. Weatherby's answer to the accuracy question is to offer the Mark V Accumark and Super VarmintMaster rifles with sub-minute-of-angle guarantees. Weatherby is accomplishing this by routing a rifle through the company's custom shop where it is fine-tuned and tested with a variety of factory loads. After a magic load is found, the rifle is shipped to the customer's dealer along with test targets and information on the ammunition used to fire the groups. The rifle is identified from standard-production rifles by a distinctive "Sub-MOA" engraving on the body of its bolt.

Back in January I had the opportunity to be the first person outside of the Nosler company to shoot something besides paper with that company's new bonded-core, polymer-tipped AccuBond bullet. Bob Nosler invited me to join him and his son John on a hunt for nilgai on the King Ranch in south Texas and I couldn't say *yes* quickly enough. Bob and I have shared several campfires together through the years and spending time in the field with him is always a treat. As hunting seasons come and go the AccuBond family will grow but for now our choices are 270/140-grain, 7mm/160-grain, 30/200-grain, 338/225-grain and 375/260-grain. All come with extremely high ballistic coefficients. At a BC of .588 the 30-caliber Accu-

Bond is completely off the ballistics chart in Nosler's latest handloading manual and, as far as I know, it is higher than any other big-game bullet. To describe the AccuBond in a nutshell, it looks like a Ballistic Tip, shoots as accurately as the Ballistic Tip and it penetrates as deeply as the Nosler Partition.

During the final development stages of his new bullet, Bob Nosler told me that in its various calibers it had proven to be capable of squeezing into groups measuring as small as half an inch when fired from a machine rest. Four groups I saw were fired with a barrel in 300 Weatherby Magnum; they measured 0.52, 0.67, 0.42 and 0.25, for an average of 0.47-inch. The handload used by the Nosler technicians who fired those groups consisted of the Remington case, Federal 215 primer and the 200-grain AccuBond seated atop 78.0 grains of Reloder 22. Average muzzle velocity was 3051 fps. Weight retention of the

The Mark V Sub-MOA wears a synthetic stock.

The two 30-caliber, 200-grain AccuBond bullets shown beside the unfired bullet expanded to 58-caliber and retained close to 70 percent of their original weight, even when fired into heavy bone.

I was the first person outside the Weatherby and Nosler companies to shoot something other than paper with the Mark V Sub-MOA rifle and the AccuBond bullet; both worked fine on this Texas nilgai antelope.

AccuBond averages 60 to 70 percent when it is fired into animal glue, a material that's much tougher on bullets than the ballistic gelatin used for test purposes by some of the other companies. The dozens of Partition bullets I have recovered from big game through the years have averaged around 60 percent.

Since the Nosler crew had proven the new AccuBond bullet capable of snuggling together into groups small enough to win matches, I figured the thing to do would be to hunt nilgai with a rifle capable of delivering the same level of precision. Which gets me back to the new Sub-MOA version of the Weatherby Mark V. Included in the package with the rifle I received were four three-shot groups fired at 100 yards by Weatherby technicians Greg King and Jim Beck. They measured 0.56, 0.99, 0.85 and 0.89 for an average of 0.82-inch. They also sent a couple of boxes of the same Weatherby ammo the groups were fired with; it was loaded with the Nosler 180-grain Ballistic Tip. After attaching a Zeiss 3-9X Diavari V/T scope to the Mark V, I headed to the rifle range. The first five groups I fired with the Weatherby factory load measured 1.16, 0.86, 0.52, 1.07 and 0.67-inch for an of 0.87-inch. Virtually the same as the fellows in sunny California had averaged with the same rifle and ammo—and not bad for a country boy on a rather windy day. Just for the fun of it, I shifted to the 300-yard target and squeezed off a couple of groups; they measured 2.26 and 2.74 inches. Just as the guys at Weatherby had told me to do, I allowed the barrel to cool down completely between groups.

After shooting those tiny groups with factory ammo in the Mark V, I figured a super-accurate handload with the 200-grain AccuBond would come easy. Wrong. I started out by seating the bullet to an overall cartridge length of 3.69 inches, which was as long as the magazine box of the rifle would allow. Since the

Seeing the new Nosler AccuBond bullet average less than an inch when fired from the Sub-MOA variation of the Weatherby Mark V came as no surprise.

Mark V in 300 magnum has a free-bored chamber I just knew it would shoot best with bullets seated out as close as possible to the rifling. Wrong again. Three-shot groups were considerably larger than an inch. After trying six different powders I was just about ready to throw in the towel when I noticed how deeply the bullet was seated in Weatherby's factory ammo. So I made up small test batches of handloads with the 200-grain AccuBond seated progressively deeper in the case in .010-inch increments. Once I reached an overall length of 3.59 inches (.025-inch longer than the Weatherby 180-grain factory load)

good things began to happen. My first three shots with the 200-grain bullet pushed along at an average velocity of 3031 fps by 85.0 grains of Reloder 25 squeezed into a 0.72-inch group. I fired four more groups and not a single one exceeded an inch with the smallest measuring 0.52-inch. When I zeroed the rifle three inches high at 100 yards the 200-grain AccuBond landed a couple of inches below my aiming point at 300 yards and about 12 inches low at 400. None of the groups I fired at 400 yards were larger than six inches and I might have done better in less wind.

You can get your own Weatherby AccuMark on the standard or magnum action. Both have a blued steel receiver, a stainless steel barrel and a synthetic stock, the latter replete with CNC-machined aluminum bedding block and Pachmayr Decelerator recoil pad. Rifles built on the standard action have 24-inch barrels chambered for nine standard cartridges from 223 Remington to 30-06, plus the 240 Weatherby Magnum. Those built on the larger magnum action have 26-inch barrels in all the Weatherby magnum calibers plus the 7mm Remington Magnum, 7mm STW and 300 Winchester Magnum. The standard-action rifle is rated at 7-1/4 pounds. The Weatherby catalog says 8-3/4 pounds for the rifle with the magnum-size action but I'm not sure that's correct; the one in 300 Weatherby Magnum I hunted with pushed the pointer on my postal scale to 9-3/4 pounds and that with the Weatherby two-piece mount and a 15-ounce Zeiss scope. The trigger was great; it pulled an average of 58 ounces on my RCBS scale with a pull-to-pull variation of only two ounces. Creep was nonexistent and while any trigger that also serves as the bolt stop/release as does the one on the Mark V is sure to have a bit of overtravel, I did not notice it when I dropped a nilgai bull at a laser-ranged 311 yards with a single shot to the shoulder.

After pulverizing the onside shoulder of the nilgai, the Nosler AccuBond ended up against the hide on the opposite side. It had expanded to 58-caliber and retained 67 percent of its original weight. Since it left the muzzle of my 300 Magnum at 3000 fps its impact velocity at 300 yards was around 2550 fps, about what can be expected at the muzzle of a rifle in 30-06 when it is loaded to maximum speed with a 200-grain bullet. Mark V AccuMark, 300 Weatherby Magnum, Nosler AccuBond, Zeiss scope; a winning foursome if I have ever seen and used one. •

Thompson/Center

22 Classic

by C. Rodney James

MANY OF US have longed for the return of those classic-style 22 autoloading rifles like the Winchester 63 or Weatherby Mark XXII, with the accuracy of those rifles Grandpa told us about. If properly engineered, autoloaders can be tack drivers. This has been demonstrated by outfits such as Volquartsen Custom Ltd., whose custom 10/22 Rugers shoot as well as many bolt-action target rifles.

Thompson/Center, long famous for their precision single-shot pistols,

carbines and muzzleloaders now offers their version of such a rifle. The Classic features all blued steel, beautifully finished. The stock is fine straight-grained black walnut with a dull finish. The look is reminiscent of 50s and 60s rifles, such as the H & R 800 and the Ithaca Lightning. Wood-to-metal fit is equal to the best.

The Classic also contains many features those older rifles never had. The practical iron sights are clean and crisp with green (*rear*) and red (*front*) fiber-optic inserts that give illumination in low light conditions. They are the best open sights I've seen. The rifle has a last shot hold-open feature, as all autoloaders should have. Bolt closure is a simple pull-back on the open bolt

to unlock it, then allowing the bolt to snap closed, chambering a round––which it did every time, quick and simple. The bolt is cushioned by a synthetic rubber recoil pad at the rear of the receiver preventing the problem of metal-on-metal battering, or fully compressed springs. This should keep the action tight for a long shooting life. The barrel is pretty close to match quality, finely finished inside and out. The bore is button rifled, six-grooves right with a slightly faster than normal 1:15-inch twist.

The magazine is extruded steel, featuring a one-piece body with a removable floorplate for cleaning. The rugged design is close to indestructible, compared to those stamped steel ones that dent easily and occasionally come apart. This magazine fed perfectly with all the Long Rifle ammunition put through it. The magazine release is a trigger-shaped piece of metal fitted neatly in the front of the trigger guard —easy to reach yet not liable to be accidentally bumped off—a great improvement over those tiny levers and catches on many autoloaders. The magazine pops out freely, no pulling needed.

The excellent trigger breaks cleanly at an ounce over 3-1/2 pounds. Both the trigger and the hooked M1-style operating handle are highly polished.

As of this writing, test reports have been published by *American Rifleman* and *Gun Week*. The latter tested the rifle at 50 feet. It functioned just fine and delivered very

Magazine release is positive, easy to reach and of excellent design.

small groups, but then most guns larger than a derringer will do that at 50 feet. The *Rifleman* ran tests indoors at 50 yards with four types of Federal match ammunition, producing five-shot groups averaging between 0.67- to 0.88-inch. The choice of ammunition seemed curious since this is a sporter, not a target arm, but the selection was based on factory test results.

With this in mind, we began our testfire project. The weather gods were with us in the form of a January thaw that blessed central Ohio with two days of calm sunny afternoons. Temperatures were in the low 40s, with calm conditions and breeze only occasionally running to about 3 m.p.h.

A 6x K-series Weaver was mounted on the rifle. The test session began with a 100-yard benchmark group from a bull-barrel Winchester 52C target gun. It printed 0.55-inch with Winchester Power Points, which is as good as that ammunition ever shoots in dead calm.

Since the T/C Classic is a sporter, we tried seven kinds of Long Rifle—four hunting brands, two match brands and one competition brand. All functioned perfectly. Not too surprisingly the hunting cartridges performed the best. After shooting five-shot groups at 50 yards, the target was backed off to 75 yards to see how the best performers would do at this extended range. Here are the results:

These are reasonably good groups, better than most lower-end autoloaders, *BUT* I feel they could have been—should have been—better. Why weren't they better? Maybe some readers remember that those classic 22 autoloaders of the '50s and '60s shared a common problem—bullet damage in the feeding process. I've had a lot of experience with 22 autoloaders—much of it bad.** An important test (*certainly before you buy one*) is to load the magazine and run several cartridges through the action, snapping the bolt quickly to chamber them, then ejecting them carefully, and making a close examination. If they don't look like they did when they came out of the box—try another gun. All the various types of ammunition tested were given this test, and the "acid test" of cycling rounds through the action by firing and examining the last one in the magazine to see how it survived the trip through that magazine into the chamber.

Unfortunately, all were damaged to some degree. Not too surprisingly, those with the least damage were better shooters. CCI Mini-Mag hollow-points, when cycled by firing, were

dented on one side to the point the bullets were bent in the case. We saw no point in firing these for record.

It might be argued that some damage is no big deal. That is why I fired a series

Rear sight is fully adjustable with fiber-optic inserts.

Outdoor Accuracy Test Results

Five-shot groups @ 50 yards, sandbag rest.

Ammunition	Group
Winchester T-22	.9"
Winchester Super Silhouette	.7"
Winchester Power Point	.65"
Remington HVHP	.6"
CCI Stinger	1.25" (4 in .9")
PMC Match	1.3"
Federal Gold Medal Match	1.1"

Five-shot groups @75 yards, sandbag rest.

Ammunition	Group
Remington HVHP	2.7"
Winchester Super Silhouette	1.75"
CCI Stinger	1.2"
WW Power PT	1.0", 1.4", .75" (*hand-fed*)

Temp 40-43F. Wind 0-3 mph. Bright sun on snow.

All cartridges fed through the Classic's action sustained some damage. Worst was with the CCI Mini-Mag HP – the two examples on the right.

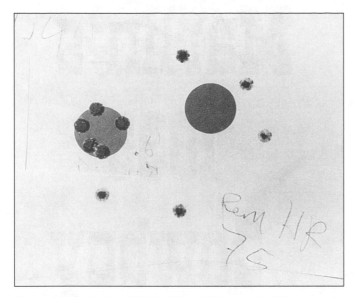

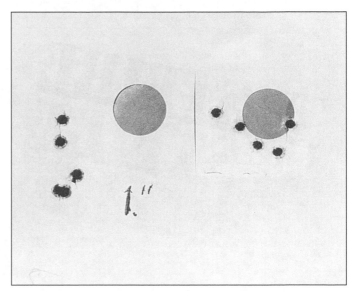

Groups of Remington HVHP at 50 and 75 yards. Bullet damage was the likely cause for the considerable expansion of group size at the longer range.

Either of these 75-yard groups made with the Winchester Power Point would equal five dead woodchucks. Hand-fed groups were even better!

of hand-loaded cartridges (*as they came from the box*). This shaved a quarter-inch off the best auto-loaded group and 1/2-inch off the worst at 75 yards. I consider that significant.

In the process of ejecting rounds for inspection, I encountered this rifle's second major problem – the extractor hook failed to extract live rounds about half the time, or more. This necessitated tapping the butt on the floor or shoe top until the round dropped clear. A few had to be poked out with a cleaning rod.

The ejection problem may have had something to do with the following statement in the owner's manual that came with the rifle. Viz: *"Never use 22 'Stinger' cartridges in your T/C 22 LR Classic rifle. Stinger cartridges have a longer case than 22 LR cartridges loaded to U.S. industry specifications. They are prone to stick in tight chambers, which can result in a ruptured case and release hot powder gases and brass when fired. This can be hazardous to the shooter or bystanders."*

The Stinger ammunition I tried worked just fine, so long as I did not try to extract a loaded round. They were (*perhaps*) more difficult to remove than standard Long Rifles. Needless to say, I did not try any ammunition with a heavy grease lubricant, or I would likely still be trying to extract it. Chamber fouling would certainly exacerbate this problem if Stingers were introduced after firing a number of standard-length cartridges, with the front of the longer case lying in an area of heavier fouling. The same problem would occur with other extended-length cases, such as the Agulia Super Max and MPB Quik-Shok. Examination of fired Stinger cases

Magazine is compact and of a semi-staggered design. With a tweaking of the lip design and a softer spring, bullet damage problems could be eliminated. Stamped, steel Winchester magazine shown for comparison.

revealed no evidence of head swelling that would indicate they were fired slightly out of battery. Stingers are within SAAMI specs. They go into and out of the chamber of a Winchester 52 match rifle; I have fired hundreds with no problem.

The final annoyance was the heavy spring in the magazine. This made loading difficult. Getting the last round in was like fitting a size 10 foot into a size 8 shoe. There is no need for that much spring. A 10-round magazine is in the works and may well be available by the time this article is in print.

In conclusion I feel T/C has made a fine, accurate rifle, potentially the most accurate out-of-the-box auto-loader available—and without doubt one of the best looking. Unfortunately, it suffers from magazine, feeding, and extraction problems. These appear to stem from an extractor hook that is too shallow and needs to be flatter on the end engaging the breech face so that it hooks firmly on the cartridge rim *before* the cartridge is fired. The

notch in the magazine should be farther back so that the cartridge is disengaged from the magazine lips before the bearing surface of the bullet enters the chamber. As it is, the bullet enters the chamber at an angle and gets bent as it is rammed home. Ruger, among others, solved the magazine feed problem with their rotary magazine (*the best rimfire magazine ever*), eliminating bullet damage. Even the little Phoenix HP-22 pistol, selling for under a hundred dollars, has a feed system that is virtually foolproof.*** With some relatively minor tweaking, the T/C Classic could become a first-class rifle in all respects —very likely the best ever built outside of those from a custom shop. With their demonstrated high standards, we fully expect this to happen. ●

* "Dope Bag" *American Rifleman* January, 2001
** *GUN DIGEST 1994*, "Autoloader Classics." By C. Rodney James
*** *GUN DIGEST 1999*, "Testfire Phoenix HP 22." By C. Rodney James

Marlin's 1895 Cowboy

by R.H. VanDenburg

Marlin 1895CB Cowboy - *Courtesy the Marlin Firearms Company*

MOST GUN MANUFAC-TURERS these days seem to be spending their time introducing new calibers within their existing product lines. The Marlin Firearms Company, on the other hand, has been busy introducing new models, for the most part, on their existing line of calibers. The trend began in 1994 with the introduction of the 1894 CLMD, a variation on their 1894 lever-action rifle celebrating the 100th anniversary of its original introduction. The 1894 has a short action ideally suited for handgun cartridges. This was followed by a series of 1894 Cowboy models in 45 Colt, 44-40 WCF, 357 Magnum and 44 Magnum. All had straight-grip stocks and octagonal barrels. The next year saw the 100th anniversary of the 1895 model in 45-70 Govt. with a pistol grip stock and 24-inch, half-octagonal barrel. Then came the very popular "Guide" gun in 45-70 and "Outfitter" in 444 Marlin with shortened, 18-1/2 inch, ported barrels and half-magazines. I really began to take notice in 1999 when Marlin announced the 336 Cowboy, with its straight-gripped stock and 24-inch octagonal barrel in 30-30 Winchester and 38-55.

However, it was 2001 when the company introduced the 1895 Cow-boy that it got my full attention. The model number is the 1895CB, in 45-70 Govt., of course. Following the western theme it has a straight-gripped walnut stock without check-ering. A hard rubber buttplate carries the Marlin name. The barrel is tapered octagonal, 26 inches in length, and topped with Marble iron sights: (*a brass bead front and semi-buckhorn rear*). The receiver is drilled and tapped for auxiliary iron or scope sights. All metal parts are blued; a full-length magazine holds nine rounds. Weight is nominally given as eight pounds. By the spring of the year I had one of the first guns off the assembly line.

The 1895 model, as most Marlin fans know, is currently built on the company's justly famous 336 action. Originally offered from 1895 to 1916, it was re-introduced in 1972 and remains in the catalog in a variety of guises. Early in 1972, 1895 barrels had eight grooves but by 1973, the company had changed to a 12-groove "Micro-Groove" barrel, a Marlin trademark.

Not everyone was pleased with that change. Shooters who used only factory ammunition or hand-loaded only jacketed bullets felt no imposition. Those of us who were students of the 45-70 cartridge, however, and appreciated its marvelous history wanted to shoot cast bullets. "Micro-Groove" barrels and cast bullets, in the eyes of many, are not a good marriage. Fortunately, not only did Marlin change the rifling on its Cowboy series of rifles, but in the current catalog all 1895 models, including the 444 in 444 Marlin and the 1895M in the new 450 Marlin, have six groove, "deep-cut Ballard-type rifling."

While it was obvious from looking at the barrel, my new gun had six lands and grooves, I set out to determine exactly what was Ballard or Ballard-type rifling. After some searching I found that Ballard rifling was known for grooves that were both wider and deeper than normal. Also, I found that the Marlin Fire

Semi-buckhorn rear sight is in keeping with the cartridge and the rifle style

Arms company, and before it, John M. Marlin, had manufactured the Ballard line of breech-loading, single-shot rifles from 1875 to 1890. As a result, Marlin had traditionally used the term "Ballard" or "Ballard-type" to describe its rifling. More recently, however, the term "Ballard-type" has been used to distinguish its traditional rifling from its "Micro-Groove" rifling. That said, I was able to determine that the current "Ballard-type" rifling is indeed cut rifling; "Micro-Groove" rifling is formed using the button-rifling technique. With today's recognition of the tolerances required in manufacturing, groove width of Marlin's 45-70 barrels is given as .141 +/ .002 inch, with six grooves, 1:20, right-hand twist. What's left becomes the lands. On average, a groove width becomes .141-inch, lands, .094-inch. Groove diameter is .456/458-inch; bore diameter, .450/.452-inch. This means the rifling depth is nominally .003-inch. Interestingly, these dimensions are almost exactly the same as for the original 1895 barrels.

After receiving my gun, a good cleaning became the first order of the day, along with re-familiarizing myself with the action and operation. One of the advantages of the Marlin lever action is that the barrel can be cleaned from the breech end. Removing one screw that secures the lever to the frame allows the bolt to be slid out the rear making cleaning a snap. The ejector fits in a hole in the left side of the receiver and is held there by the bolt. With the bolt removed for cleaning, the ejector is free to fall out and care must be taken to ensure the ejector is in place as the bolt is re-installed. Most lever actions seem to take a bit of cycling of the action for things to smooth out. I was pleasantly surprised to find how smoothly this Marlin operated from the beginning, although it continues to become smoother with use. Even the trigger pull is far better than what we've come to expect in this litigious age, about 7-1/2 pounds. The balance point, depending on the number of rounds in the magazine, is right at the front of the action. It is very comfortable to carry.

My plan was to shoot a couple hundred jacketed bullets through the barrel as a breaking-in process. The effort would not only serve to smooth out any burrs in the barrel but allow me to develop suitable hand-loads and find the appropriate sight settings. Next would come cast bullets along with, perhaps, round ball or "collar button" loads. In addition to laying in a supply of 300- and 405-grain jacketed bullets and 300- and 400-grain cast, I was able to persuade Ed Schmitt of Lyman to scrounge around and find one of the last of the Lyman 457130 "collar button" bullet moulds. This style of bullet for small game and gallery shooting is as old as the cartridge but perhaps not as appreciated as it once was. Next will be Lyman's #457122, the famous 45-330 Gould Express, a 330-grain hollow point, designed by the legendary John Barlow, founder of the Ideal Manufacturing Company, for the equally well-known A.C. Gould, editor of *Shooting and Fishing* magazine, of a century ago. For folks like me, the ability to stretch the limits of the cartridge as well as recreate a moment of times past, such moulds are a godsend.

Handloaders will note that the current SAAMI-approved overall cartridge length of the 45-70 of 2.550 inches—as well as the Marlin action length—preclude the use of the traditional military rifle bullet 500-grain. Actually such a round can be loaded through the ejection port and chambered but once the extractor engages the case rim, the cartridge cannot be ejected. Firing it in a 7-1/2 pound rifle isn't a lot of fun, either. Traditional bullets these days are of 300, 350 and 400/405 grains and quite in keeping with this rifle. The Speer 350-grain Hot-Core flat nose is also unusable as it creates a round that exceeds the overall length restrictions of the action. Other 350-grain bullets such as the Hornady, work quite well.

At the range I found it was quite possible to push 300-grain bullets to 2500 fps but even with the rear sight at its lowest position, bullet impact was a full two feet above point of aim at 100 yards. In the end it was obvious this new 1895 was designed to operate at modern factory pressures and velocities, in spite of the greater potential of the action. The same was true of other bullet weights. Accuracy was a marvelous surprise with several loads turning in excellent groups in the 2-inch range at 100 yards with suitable targets. I mention this latter point as I found the front brass bead difficult to see at times. A dab of white paint sufficed but an ivory bead is in the cards.

One of the hallmarks of success in the firearms industry is the appearance of aftermarket parts and services. A cottage industry is growing up around the Marlin lever actions, in particular the 1895. Firms such as Wild West Guns of Anchorage, Alaska specialize in these guns and my first after-market acquisition was one of Wild West's tuned ejectors. The completely satisfactory factory part now serves as a spare.

All in all, I'm extremely pleased with my new 1895CB Marlin. I could take advantage of the rifle's inherent strength and step up bullet velocities if I changed the sights or added a scope. I suspect I won't. For hunting the way I like to hunt and shooting the way I like to shoot, it suits me just fine as-is. •

by JOHN MALLOY

HANDGUNS TODAY:

AUTOLOADERS

*T*HERE IS SO much going on that it is difficult to quickly summarize the situation as it pertains to autoloading handguns. At the February 2003 SHOT Show, a surprising number of prototypes and pre-production specimens were exhibited. Although there was a great variety of new pistols, the largest number of recent new model introductions have been for the 45 ACP, and most were based on the 1911 design.

It is hard to believe that the 45 ACP (Automatic Colt Pistol) cartridge, introduced in 1905, and the Colt/Browning 1911 pistol design are just a short time shy of their 100th birthdays. Yet, they remain among the most popular cartridge and pistol choices available today.

The big-bore spotlight does not belong exclusively to the 45 ACP, however. Two other new 45-caliber cartridges have been recently introduced. In addition, smaller-caliber bottleneck centerfire pistol cartridges have entered the scene and are gaining recognition. The 22 Long Rifle (22 LR) remains ever popular, and new pistols—and conversion kits to adapt existing centerfire pistols to 22—are offered. The 17-caliber rimfire made an amazing debut in the rifle field last year, and a new 17-caliber cartridge—and new 17-caliber semiautomatic pistols adapted for it—are now being offered.

Autoloading handguns are acquired by ordinary people for personal protection, for competition, for hunting, for plinking and fun and relaxation; and to some degree, for collecting—or just pride of ownership. With the threat of terrorism now never far from our minds, perhaps defense of our families and ourselves plays an even larger role than before. The personal protection aspect is important, and most of the autoloading pistols offered are suitable for such use.

Politics continues to influence the world of autoloading handguns. The elections of November 2002 were encouraging, but did not stanch the flow of anti-gun efforts. Some firearms manufacturers have gone out of business, due in part to restrictive legislation, or to litigation. States such as California, Maryland, Massachusetts and New Jersey make their own rules as to what handguns can and cannot be sold within their borders. Gunmakers must decide whether or not to redesign and retool to conform to these rules. Substantial expense is required to change a pistol design, with no guarantee it will be approved. Some companies just resign themselves to not selling in restrictive states. Nevertheless, more manufacturers are incorporating lock and safety mechanisms into their pistols in an effort to comply with at least some of these restrictions.

Guns have been prominent in the news in the past year or so. The "DC Sniper" killings of October 2002 brought predictable calls for more gun control. However, many people saw, instead, the advantage of ordinary citizens being armed. After a series of murders of women in the Baton Rouge area of Louisiana, the Governor of that state made a public statement that people should become licensed and then carry pistols for personal protection. Airline pilots, after a long uphill fight, were finally authorized by Congress to carry firearms. Or were they? Bureaucratic restrictions were so onerous that at the time of this writing, not a single pilot has been legally armed.

In early 2003, as pressure mounted for war against Iraq, new threats of terrorist activities increased, and the country was put on Orange Alert. Government officials made announcements concerning preparations for a terrorist attack. Although such advice never mentioned firearms (but recommended duct tape), many people read between the lines. They realized they were ultimately responsible for their safety, and that of their loved ones. Another firearm (or a first firearm, for some) seemed like a good idea. Pistols, especially, were favored to be available in case of an emergency.

High-capacity pistols are still being introduced, even though they are limited to 10-round magazines unless sold to police or military. There is a logical reason for this continued interest in high-capacity handguns by people who cannot acquire the high-capacity magazines. Just a short distance down the road lies September 2004. At that time, the so-called "Assault Weapons" law of September 1994 is due to expire. One provision that affected autoloading pistol shooters was the ban on magazines that hold more than 10 rounds. It will be good when this restriction is gone. This provision has created two classes of citizens in the United States—ordinary people who could not be "trusted" with more than 10 shots, and agents of the government who could have more than 10. This provision has

Stainless-steel firearms made under the AMT name are no longer available. Galena Industries, the manufacturer, went out of business in 2002. AMT handguns tended to be innovative and eye-catching. Here, Malloy shoots an AMT Long Slide Hardballer, a 1911-style pistol with an impressive 7-inch barrel.

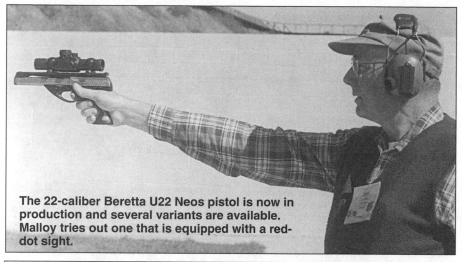

The 22-caliber Beretta U22 Neos pistol is now in production and several variants are available. Malloy tries out one that is equipped with a red-dot sight.

The new "Special Duty" specimens of the Beretta 92 and 96 pistols have an integral accessory rail, a heavier "Brigadier" slide and other features.

The new Beretta 92G-SD is an updated version of the original Beretta 92. Here, the new 9mm is fired by Clo Malloy, the writer's sister-in-law.

A deluxe version of the 22-caliber NEOS pistol has been added, with optional grip frames and sights. 7-1/2-inch barrels and Inox (stainless) finishes are also available.

driven a wedge between law enforcement and the armed citizen, who is traditionally the greatest ally of the police. This situation should not be allowed to continue. However, anti-gun forces are campaigning to extend the law past its end time.

These are some of the factors influencing the world of autoloading handguns. With all this in mind, let's take a look at what the companies are doing:

AMT

The innovative stainless-steel pistols made under the AMT name are no longer available. The AMT trademark appeared on a number of "firsts" in the firearms industry. The company was the first to make an all-stainless 1911-type pistol, and first to offer a subcompact 380. They marketed semiautomatic pistols in calibers from 22 Long Rifle (22 LR) to 50 Action Express (50 AE). In 1998, Galena Industries acquired the right to produce most of the AMT-developed firearms. Within a few years, the company moved from restrictive California to Sturgis, South Dakota, for a new start. Somehow, it did not work out. The final remaining assets of the company were sold at auction in August 2002. Parts are still available from Numrich Gun Parts and Jack First, but shooters will miss the variety of pistols offered under the AMT name.

Arms Moravia

The on-again, off-again importation of the striking-looking Arms Moravia CZ-G2000 seems to have stabilized. Anderson Arms of Fort Worth, TX will import the pistol. Introduced in 1999, the polymer-frame pistol is now available in all-black or two-tone (nickel slide and black frame) variants. Chambering options are 9mm and 40 S&W. Arms Moravia also makes a nifty little miniature 380 pistol, the ZP 98, which uses a gas-delayed blowback system. However, it is too small to be imported into the United States under the restrictions of the Gun Control Act of 1968 (GCA 68).

Beretta

The new 22-caliber pistol, the U22 Neos, introduced last year, is now in production. It is the first Beretta pistol 100-percent designed and manufactured in the United States. In case you were wondering, "Neos" is from the Greek, meaning "new." This new Beretta has a replaceable polymer grip frame and comes in 4-1/2-inch and 6-inch barrel lengths.

A deluxe (DLX) version has also been added. Optional grip frames with blue or gray rubber inlays are furnished. Also, black, red and white front sights come with each pistol. Three rear sight blades (color-outlined red and white–as well as black) allow the shooter to mix-and-match the sights to suit his preference. 7-1/2-inch barrels and Inox (stainless) finish are also available on the DLX variants.

All the Neos pistols have their sights set into a mounting rib that allows easy installation of optical or electronic sights.

The modular construction of the U22 pistol has led to speculation that a light carbine, based on the same operating mechanism, might be introduced. Such a carbine is under development, but is not now available.

In the centerfire line, the new models 92- and 96G-SD (92 indicates 9mm, 96 indicates 40-caliber) have been introduced. To further break the code, **G** denotes a de-cocker mechanism, and SD represents "Special Duty." The pistols might be seen as a modernized alternative to the original 92. The new SD guns have an accessory rail integral with the frame, a "Brigadier" heavy reinforced slide, and 3-dot tritium night sights. The frame is checkered front and back, and the magazine well is beveled.

Your writer had the opportunity to shoot a new 9mm 92G-SD. Standing at the short-range line of a police range, I faced a standard silhouette target that had been liberally sprinkled by other shooters. Looking for an untouched spot, I chose the left ear. The pistol put nine shots in a cluster on the ear, with only one slightly out of the group. I think it is safe to say that shooters will find the Beretta SD pistols acceptably accurate.

The Beretta B-LOK locking device is being phased in on pistols in the company's line.

Bernardelli

Gone from the handgun scene for some time, the Bernardelli name returned last year, reintroducing much of its previous pistol line. Since then, the company has also added a series of pistols based on the CZ-75 design.

Now, a new design has entered the Bernardelli line. The new pistols are polymer-frame guns using the basic CZ-75 mechanism. To say this is a colorful line is something of an understatement. Frames are available in black, blue, yellow, red, white and purple. Should that array not offer enough choices, slides are available in black or silver finish. The new polymer-frame Bernardelli pistols are designated Model 2000. They entered production in early 2003.

Bersa

The Argentine Bersa firm is noted for their compact blowback pocket pistols. A departure for the company was the introduction of a double-action locked-breech 45-caliber arm in 2003.

The new Bersa, designated the Thunder 45 Ultra Compact, is a nice-looking pistol that feels good in the hand. It has a conventional double-action trigger mechanism, that is, double-action for the first shot, single-action for succeeding shots. The barrel length is 3.6 inches. The pistol measures 4.9 inches high by 6.7 inches long, which neatly puts it into the compact category (5x7). Weight is 27 ounces. The magazine holds 7 rounds, giving the pistol a 7+1 capacity.

▶ The new Bersa Thunder 45 is a compact double-action pistol chambered for the 45 ACP cartridge.

Finishes are offered as matte black, Duo-tone and satin nickel. Availability of the Thunder 45 was scheduled for Spring 2003, from Eagle Imports.

Bond

Bond Arms, a long-time maker of double derringers, has entered the semi-auto field with their own 1911-style pistol. The Bond pistol has many of the features in vogue with today's shooters. It is not just a newcomer to the pack, however, as it is designed for its own unique cartridge—the 450 Autobond.

The 450 Autobond round is an interesting concept. Externally of about the same dimensions as the 45 ACP, the Autobond cartridge uses a very light 100-grain bullet pushed to the impressive speed of 2300 feet per second

▶ Bond Arms, long-time manufacturer of double derringers, has joined the list of companies making 1911-style 45 pistols. The difference is that this one is designed for a new high-velocity cartridge—the 45 Autobond.

Performance Plus Platinum
450 AUTOBOND
100 gr. Total Fragmenting Soft Point

◀ The bullet of the 450 Autobond cartridge (*nearest the cartridge box*) is a light 100-grain fragmenting soft-point pushed to 2300 fps from the Autobond pistol. A 230-grain 45 ACP bullet is shown for comparison.

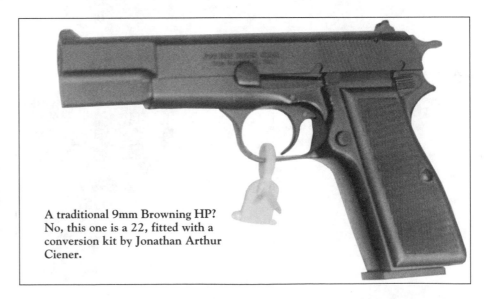

A traditional 9mm Browning HP? No, this one is a 22, fitted with a conversion kit by Jonathan Arthur Ciener.

Browning has introduced a new polymer-frame double-action pistol in 9mm and 40 S&W calibers. This is the Pro-9, in 9mm, with a dual-tone finish.

(fps) from a 5-inch barrel. Not since the 1904 appearance of the Danish Schouboe pistol has this approach been tried for a 45-caliber pistol. The Schouboe cartridge used an extremely light 63-grain bullet pushed to 1600 fps, an impressive speed for a handgun of those days. The Schouboe, however, used the light bullet to keep pressures within the capabilities of its blowback action. The Bond pistol was designed for very different circumstances.

The Bond uses the traditional tilting-barrel locking system of the 1911 design. The cartridge case is a reinforced version of the 45 ACP case, and is designed to be used in a fully-supported chamber. Thus, the cartridge is not recommended for use in pistols other than the Bond. The bullet is a frangible one that, in Bond's words, "resists over-penetration." Recoil is reported to be only slightly greater than that of a standard 45 ACP 230-grain load. Those who choose the Bond pistol can make the recoil comparison for themselves. The Autobond can use standard 45 ACP cartridges as well as the special 450 round.

Browning

New for Browning are polymer-frame pistols in 9mm and 40 S&W. The frames of the new PRO-9 and PRO-40 pistols have integral accessory rails and interchangeable backstrap inserts.

Trigger action is conventional double action, with single-action shots after the first. A cocked hammer can be lowered by a decocking lever. In this case, from either side, as the ambidextrous design has a decocking lever on both sides of the frame. The plugged magazines hold, for ordinary Americans, ten rounds of either cartridge.

Browning celebrated its 125th anniversary in 2003, taking the company's history back to 1878, when John M. Browning introduced his famous single-shot rifle. In commemoration, four famous firearms that have carried the Browning name were made as limited editions. The four guns were the Single-Shot, the 22 autoloading rifle, the Superposed shotgun, and—representing the Browning pistols—the 9mm Hi-Power. Only 125 of the Belgian-made commemorative 9mm pistols were to be made. They will have scroll engraving, gold highlights and select walnut grips.

The standard Hi-Power is mysteriously absent from the 2003 Browning master catalog. This situation has led to rumors that Browning has—or plans to—discontinue the Hi-Power. A Browning representative told your writer that this was not so, but was at a loss to explain the absence.

Century

Century International Arms' line of 1911-style 45 pistols, introduced in 2001, has been well-received. The guns are made in the Philippines by SAM (Shooters Arms Manufacturing, Inc.) and include traditional and enhanced variants.

Introduced in 2003 were several new models. The Blue Thunder Commodore is a 4 1/4-inch barrel version of the original striking-looking full-size Blue Thunder. The Commodore 1911 is a 4 1/4-inch enhanced pistol without the distinctive trigger guard and sculptured grip of the Blue Thunder.

The SAM Chief is mechanically the same as the original Blue Thunder, but has a matte finish rather than the original's polished blue. The SAM GI is a more-or-less traditional 1911 design, but with a 4 1/4-inch barrel.

Perhaps the most interesting is the Falcon pistol—a full-size high-capacity pistol *(which now comes with a 10-round magazine)*. It is built with a steel, rather than polymer, frame. Small separate grip panels are attached. The Falcon has a squared trigger guard and extended controls, including an extended magazine release.

Browning HP ("Hi-Power") pistol, a 9mm single-action design. It has the early burr-type hammer spur, but some modern niceties—extended safety lever, ball & bar type express sights, and Uncle Mike's rubber grip panels—have been added. Availability was scheduled for the first quarter of 2003.

Ciener

The 22 Long Rifle (22 LR) conversions of Jonathan Arthur Ciener are especially popular in localities that limit the number of handguns a person may possess. They are not additional firearms, but are kits that may be quickly installed or removed by the shooter. Even without such restrictions, shooters can save ammunition money, get in more practice, and get one gun to serve several purposes. The pistol conversion kits have been available for 1911-type pistols, Beretta and Taurus models, and various Glocks.

Newly introduced is a conversion kit for the Browning Hi-Power and derivative pistols. Availability was scheduled for May 2003.

The kits are available with fixed or adjustable sights, and in matte, high polish or silver finishes. This variety lets shooters match the conversion to the gun's original finish, or create a two-tone effect. Says Ciener, "I don't want to give anyone an excuse to not get a conversion kit."

Cobra

Cobra Enterprises, which took over the defunct Republic, Talon and Davis pistol designs last year, has made improvements and has also added a new line.

Here is a key to the Cobra line: Pistols in the Patriot series are double-action-only (DAO) and have black polymer frames and stainless-steel slide. Chamberings are 45, 9mm and 380. The 45 is the former Republic 45. The 9mm and 380 are improved Talon designs.

The Freedom series comprises 32- and 38-caliber metal-frame pistols. The CA32 and CA380 are modified Davis pistols. New this year are modifications

▲ Charles Daly is offering the new M-5 high-capacity polymer-frame 1911-style pistols, in several variants. Shown here is the Commander version.

Charles Daly

Charles Daly / KBI has discontinued its line of double-action polymer-frame pistols to concentrate on its single-action line. New are the Daly M-5 polymer-frame high-capacity 1911 pistols. Built by BUL in Israel, the pistols feature beavertail grip safeties and ambidextrous manual safeties. Variants are Government, Commander and IPSC models, scheduled for Spring 2003, and the smaller M-5 Ultra-X, coming later.

The newest pistol in the Charles Daly lineup is the Daly HP. Not surprisingly, it is basically a copy of the original

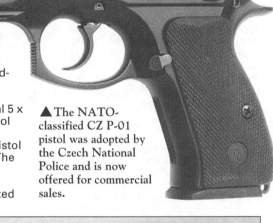

▶ It looks like a brand new Colt Model 1911—because it really is. Colt is bringing back the original 1911 design of the World War I period, complete with original markings. This prototype is serial number 1002X.

of the old Lorcin design in 32 and 380. Many people liked the Lorcins, and the company sold a lot of guns in years gone by; the design gives Cobra an addition to their line of larger pistols in 32- and 38-calibers.

Many shooters did not like the situation in which misguided legislation and litigation were able to drive legitimate manufacturers out of business. It is good that updates of these affordable designs are again available.

Colt

Colt continues to explore the roots of its semi-auto pistol line. Recall that about two years ago, the company brought out its recreation of the Model 1911A1 as produced at the beginning of World War II. Now it will offer the original Model 1911 as made in the 1918 period. A prototype, serial number 1002X, was displayed at the February 2003 SHOT Show. This will be an authentic 1911, complete to the unrelieved frame, lanyard loop, narrow-slot grip screws and original markings. All required "modern" markings will be on the frame under the grips.

About 3000 of the 1911A1 recreations were made, and it is no longer in production. Note that the serial numbers had a "WMK" prefix *(for Colt's head, Lt. Gen. William M. Keys, who authorized the project)*. The new 1911 pistols will use "WMK" as a serial number suffix. Availability was scheduled for May 2003.

Colt also offers the reproduction of the Series 70 Government Model—a recreation of the pistol produced during the 1970s. The only difference I could spot is the "big diamond" rosewood grips, which the original pistols did not have.

To prove they do not dwell in the past, Colt also has introduced its Gunsite pistol. The pistol was built incorporating ideas from Colt and the Gunsite training facility in Arizona. Features include a "palm swell" beavertail grip safety, Heinie front and Novak rear sights, Wilson extended safety lever, McCormick hammer and sear, and two 8-round Wilson magazines. The gun comes with a $100 coupon good toward training at Gunsite. The Gunsite pistol will be available in blue or stainless-steel finishes.

CZ

Two new CZ pistols are being offered.

The CZ P-01 was accepted last year by the Czech National Police. It has also been rated as a NATO-classified pistol. During testing, the number of stoppages was seven during a total of 15,000 rounds fired. The pistol can probably be considered reliable. The P-01 is chambered for the 9mm Parabellum cartridge. It has an aluminum frame with an integral accessory rail and a lanyard loop. It features a decocker, checkered rubber grips and front-and-rear slide serrations. With a 3.8-inch barrel, the pistol measures 5.3 x 7.2 inches, just a hair over the traditional 5 x 7 measurement for the compact pistol category.

Also new is the CZ 75 Tactical pistol sold with a CZ-logo folding knife. The pistol is a CZ 75B with low-profile sights, checkered rubber grips, a lanyard loop and a green poly-coated

frame. Only 1000 Tactical combos were scheduled for production in 2003.

Dan Wesson

The Dan Wesson "Patriot" pistol, introduced last year, is now in full production. Recall that the Patriot is a modification of the 1911 design that uses an external extractor.

In the year 2000, Dan Wesson changed from being a revolver-only company to one that produces revolvers and 45-caliber 1911-type autoloaders. Their line has expanded to cover a number of niches. A special limited-quantity run of 10mm semiautos was scheduled for production in 2003.

DPMS / Panther Arms

Last year, DPMS (Defense Procurement Manufacturing Services) introduced a prototype 1911-type 45 pistol, and production was tentatively scheduled for November 2002.

Latest information from a DPMS representative is that the project has been put on hold. DPMS is a maker of AR-15 style rifles and accessories, and

▲ The NATO-classified CZ P-01 pistol was adopted by the Czech National Police and is now offered for commercial sales.

Mike Lott of FNH USA *(left)* points out the operation of the new Hi-Power SFS (Safe Fast Shooting) system to Malloy.

at this time will not add the 45-caliber pistol to their line.

EAA

EAA (European American Armory) is offering two new models in its Witness line.

A polymer-frame Witness will be available with a full-size frame and compact slide. The high-capacity frame will provide a capacity of 10+1. A bull barrel is fitted to this short slide, which carries low-profile sights. The pistol was so new it had not yet been given a name at the February 2003 SHOT Show.

Some localities permit a 45-caliber or 10mm pistol for big-game hunting if it is equipped with a barrel of six inches or longer. To fill this niche, the Witness Hunter is made with a 6-inch barrel chambered in 45 ACP and 10mm. It is offered with blue or camo finishes, and a scope rail is available.

All right, EAA also has an item that really isn't a semi-auto pistol, but it is related, and so interesting I must mention it. The "Thor" is a conversion unit that can be mounted on a 1911 frame to form a breakopen single-shot hunting pistol. It is offered in 45-70 only now, with other calibers planned for later.

FNH

Recall that FNH USA is the American subsidiary arm of FN Herstal in Belgium. They offer the HP series, commonly thought of as the "Browning Hi-Power." One new HP pistol has been introduced, the HP-SFS. The last three letters stand for "Safe Fast Shooting" and the mechanism combines features of both single-action and double-action systems. When the hammer is cocked and a shot is not to be made, the hammer can simply be pushed forward. This action engages the manual safety, locks the sear and locks the slide. When the safety is pushed down, the hammer rises to its cocked position, and the pistol is ready to fire again.

A new polymer-frame hammer-fired pistol is the FNP 9. The trigger mechanism is conventional double-action, that is, double-action (DA) for the first shot, then single-action (SA) for succeeding shots. Introduced first in 9mm, a 40-caliber version was also scheduled for late in 2003. With a 4-inch barrel, the pistol is 7 inches long and weighs 25 ounces. Magazine capacity for the 9mm is 16 for law enforcement, 10 for us common folk.

The unusual Five-seveN pistol, introduced last year for the special 5.7 x 28mm cartridge, now has an adjustable-sight model added to the line. The new version has a 10-round magazine and a magazine safety. It will be marketed to individual active-duty police officers. Now that there are two versions, the original version has to be called something to differentiate it, so it is now the "Tactical" version.

Glock

Glock has introduced the new Glock 37, a 45-caliber pistol, but not a 45 ACP. The company's previous offering of the Model 21 gave the market a big Glock 45 ACP pistol, and it was subsequently shortened into the 30 and the single-column 36.

Ah—Glock engineers apparently reasoned—it would be possible to produce a full-capacity 45 in the smaller frame size—if only the 45 cartridge were smaller. Accordingly, they created their own cartridge. The new 45 Glock round is smaller than the 45 ACP, with an overall length of 1.10 inches. *(The 45 ACP OAL is 1.28 inches)*. Two 45 Glock loads are planned—a 185-grain bullet at 1100 fps, and a 200-grain bullet at 984 fps.

The Glock 37 pistol has a 4-inch barrel, is 1.18 inches wide and weighs 22 ounces (without magazine). The capacity is 10 + 1.

Heckler & Koch

HK has introduced two new pistols. The P 2000 GPM (German Police Model) is a compact (5x7 inches) polymer-frame 9mm pistol designed for the German Police. The trigger mechanism is HK's LEM (Law Enforcement Modification), in which part of the mechanism is pre-cocked by

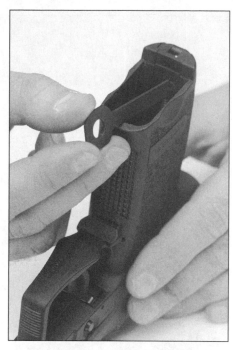

Heckler & Koch is adding a new lockout device to all production pistols.

the slide, allowing a light DA pull for most of the trigger motion, then a short pull of about 7 pounds to fire. In case of a misfire, the trigger has "second snap" capabilities, but the pull is heavy all the way through. The pistol has a 3.62-inch barrel and features ambidextrous slide releases. Interchangeable rear grip inserts are provided to allow the shooter to fit the pistol to his hand. Magazine capacity is 10 rounds, with larger-capacity magazines now available for law enforcement and military users. A 40 S&W variant is also being planned.

The USP Elite is a new longer variant of the popular USP pistol. Chambered for 9mm and 45 ACP, the

◄ The old RamLine polymer pistol is now the Hi-Standard Plinker, offered in both 22 Long Rifle and 17 High Standard calibers.

▲ The new 17 High Standard (*left*) will work in 22 LR Hi-Standard pistols by simply replacing the barrel. For comparison, the 17 Hornady Magnum Rimfire (*with its parent, the 22 Winchester Magnum Rimfire*) was introduced last year in rifles and the Volquartsen Cheetah pistol.

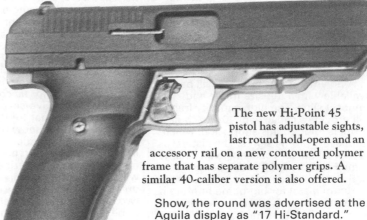

The new Hi-Point 45 pistol has adjustable sights, last round hold-open and an accessory rail on a new contoured polymer frame that has separate polymer grips. A similar 40-caliber version is also offered.

Near a modest-size enlargement of the new 17 High Standard cartridge, Alan Aronstein of High Standard (*left*) points out to Malloy that only a barrel change was necessary to convert this Hi-Standard Citation to the new 17-caliber cartridge.

Elite has a substantially longer 6.2-inch barrel and elongated 9 1/2-inch slide to match. It has the HK O-ring barrel-positioning system and adjustable target sights. The trigger mechanism is conventional DA, and the trigger has a trigger stop. It has a decocker, but can also be carried cocked-and-locked.

A lock-out device is being added to all HK production pistols now.

HIGH STANDARD

High Standard's big news is the 17 caliber. Last year, the 17-rimfire cartridge caught on like wildfire, and a number of companies chambered rifles for the new 17 Hornady Magnum Rimfire (17 HMR) cartridge. Only one semi-auto handgun, however, the Volquartsen Cheetah, was able to handle the 17.

Now, that has changed. High Standard Manufacturing Company now has several Hi-Standard semiautomatic pistols chambered for a new 17-rimfire cartridge—the 17 High Standard!

A similar cartridge was introduced a year or so ago—at least in concept—as the 17 Aguila. Reportedly, no specimens were actually available at the time of introduction. The 17 Aguila was to be based on the 22 LR case necked down to 17 caliber. The concept interested High Standard as a possibility for use in pistols designed for the 22 LR cartridge. Digging into old company history, High Standard's Alan Aronstein was surprised to learn the company had actually developed a 17-caliber cartridge based on the 22 LR back in 1940, and had made at least one pistol in that chambering. World War II apparently stopped developmental work, and the project lay forgotten.

With this background, High Standard and Aguila got together on the project. Reportedly, the 1940 round was only slightly different in dimension from the specifications of the 17 Aguila. Slight modifications were made, and the cartridge was introduced in January 2003 as the 17 High Standard. With a 20-grain bullet, the pressure is balanced to that of the 22 LR, so that any Hi-Standard pistol can be converted to 17 by simply changing the barrel. This swap also works for removable-barrel rifles, such as the AR-7 Explorer.

High Standard now offers all its target pistols in 17 High Standard as well as 22 LR. From an 18-inch test barrel, the cartridge produced a muzzle velocity of 1830 fps. The 10-inch barrel Hi-Standard Citation pistol reportedly tops 1700 fps.

High Standard has also acquired the rights to the discontinued polymer RamLine pistol, and is also planning to offer it—in 22 LR and 17 High Standard—as the Hi-Standard Plinker. Delivery was scheduled for Fall 2003. The new pistol will resurrect the "Plinker" name and will expand the company's offerings.

Lest someone think I am not consistent, let me mention that the new 17 cartridge was introduced on January 20, 2003 as the "17 High Standard," and I have used that nomenclature. However, at the February 2003 SHOT Show, the round was advertised at the Aguila display as "17 Hi-Standard." Both spellings have long been appropriate in different contexts. The company has always been called "High Standard," and the pistol models have been "Hi-Standard." With the predicted popularity of the new 17 cartridge, the terminology should soon become, shall we say, "standardized."

Also, recall that High Standard introduced its own 45-caliber 1911 pistol line in 2000, and offers variants with 4-1/2, 5- and 6-inch barrels. In 2003, the company introduced a new Custom line of 1911 pistols.

Hi-Point

Without much fanfare, Hi-Point has introduced two new big-bore pistols. The new polymer-frame handguns are a new 45, and a new 40 S&W. In keeping with Hi-Point's concept of phasing in features, the new guns have push-button magazine release, last round hold-open,

Kahr Arms' Randall Casseday displays a prototype of the new Thompson Custom 1911 pistol, an enhanced version of the Auto-Ordnance line of 1911-style pistols. This specimen carries serial number 0002.

3-dot adjustable sights and frame accessory rails. Magazine safeties *(the gun won't fire with the magazine out)* have also been added. A trigger lock comes with each gun.

The new guns have 4-1/2-inch barrels and weigh 32 ounces. The contoured polymer frame feels good in the hand and, unlike most polymer-frame pistols, the grip panels are separate pieces. The 45 uses a 9-shot magazine, and the 40 variant has a 10-rounder. The magazines are different than those previously used in Hi-Point pistols, and are similar in construction to those used in the company's popular 9mm carbine. It is probably not overly speculative to surmise that Hi-Point, looking to the future, plans 40- and 45-caliber carbines and wants magazines to interchange between their pistols and carbines.

The Hi-Points are simple blowbacks, but are "+P" rated, and have a good reputation for functioning. Repair policy is lifetime, with no questions asked. With a suggested retail price of $169, the new Hi-bore pistols are the least expensive big-bore pistols available.

Kahr

The Kahr PM 9, introduced last year, is in full production, and a new variant has been added. The new Kahr has a blackened stainless-steel slide on a black polymer frame. Availability for this variant is scheduled for May 2003. The PM 9 is Kahr's smallest and lightest 9mm pistol, sporting a 3-inch barrel and weighing less than a pound. Small as it is, it is rated for +P and +P+ ammunition. Two magazines—a six-rounder with a flush base and a

▶Kahr's new little 9mm, the polymer-frame PM9, was introduced last year with a two-tone finish. Now the pistol is in full production, and a new all-black variant has been added.

7-round version with a grip extension—are furnished.

The new, larger T9, seen in somewhat different prototype last year, is now a production pistol with two variants. The "Tactical 9" has a 4-inch barrel, and a larger grip frame that accommodates checkered wood grips and an 8-round single-column magazine. The construction of frame and slide is matte-finish stainless steel. The pistol measures about 6-1/2 inches by 5 inches and weighs 28 ounces. Sights are Novak low-profile, with tritium night-sight inserts. The "Target 9" is basically the same pistol with an MMC adjustable rear sight.

Also, a TP 9 was introduced, as a polymer-frame pistol with a 4-inch barrel. This new Kahr did not make it in to the company's 2003 catalog, but has a slightly shorter grip frame than the T9, using a 7-round magazine.

Recall that Kahr also offers the Auto-Ordnance line of 45-caliber pistols, in

Standard, Deluxe and WWII Parkerized versions. Now, Kahr is offering a custom 1911. The new Custom pistol will be in stainless steel, with extended safety lever, beveled magazine well, "big diamond" grips, and Chip McCormick trigger and sights.

Kel-Tec

The Florida firm of Kel-Tec comes up with some innovative firearms, both rifles and pistols. The big pistol news is the introduction of their little P-3AT pistol. Sound it out and the name tells its caliber—38. I had to chuckle out loud when I first read the model number.

The new 380 was developed from the popular P-32 (32 ACP) pistol. The clever design makes the P-3AT almost visually indistinguishable from the P-32. It is only about .080-inch longer, and weighs about a half-ounce more.

Thus, the new 380 is about 3.5 inches high by 5.2 inches long, and weighs about 7.2 ounces. Amazingly, the new

Kel-Tec's Renee Goldman displays the small size of the company's new 38 ACP pistol, the P-3AT. Diagrams showing the pistol's operation are in the background.

Kel-Tec's new offering is the 380 ACP polymer-frame P-3AT. There are very slight dimensional differences, but the little gun is visually indistinguishable from the firm's 32-caliber P-32.

Here is a first peek at Kimber's new 1911 rimfire pistol, introduced at the February 2003 SHOT Show.

▶The Kimber TLE (Tactical Law Enforcement) pistol is identical, except for markings, to the sidearm chosen by the Los Angeles Police Department's SWAT Team.

relatively high power of the 40 S&W round could lead to problems when the gun was "limp-wristed" by the shooter.

Kimber

Kimber has been busy in the handgun field. Let's start with the 45-caliber 1911 USA Shooting Team pistol. The distinctive pistol will be used for practice shooting by our rapid-fire pistol team. The gun is offered to the shooting public as the Kimber Team Match II, and for each pistol sold, Kimber is donating $100 to the shooting team. By mid-February 2003, over $50,000 had been raised.

The TLE (Tactical Law Enforcement) pistol is identical to the full-size pistol chosen by the Los Angeles Police Department SWAT team. The Tactical series is a modified 1911 design with an external extractor. Tactical pistols come in custom (5"), Pro (4") and Ultra (3") variants. A Kimber representative said that, in the future, all Kimber pistols may use the external extractor of the Tactical series.

The Ultra Ten CDP II is a polymer-frame 45 with a machined aluminum insert in the frame. Capacity is 10+1. Kimber Custom Shop features include a "meltdown" treatment *(edges rounded)* and night sights. The new Tactical series extractor and loaded chamber indicator are now standard on Ten II pistols.

The greatest departure from the traditional Kimber line is the new 1911 in 22 LR. The blowback 22s will be offered in variants of two models—the Rimfire Target (adjustable sights) and the Rimfire Custom (fixed sights). Each model will be available in black or silver finishes. Frames and slides of the rimfire pistols are of aluminum alloy. A conversion kit to convert existing 45-caliber pistols will also be offered.

Korth

The Korth semiautomatic pistol was introduced in 1989 for the 9mm Parabellum cartridge. Since then, it has also been offered in 9x21, 40 S&W and 357 SIG.

At the February 2003 SHOT Show, a new prototype of a Korth pistol in 45 ACP was exhibited. It uses the same basic Korth mechanism, enlarged to handle the dimensions of the 45 cartridge. The magazine is of single-

gun is still only 3/4 of an inch wide. Mechanically, the internal slide stop has been omitted in the P-3AT, and *(because of the larger-diameter cartridge)* the magazine capacity is reduced to 6 rounds. The nifty little 380 has created a lot of interest, and availability was scheduled for May 2003.

The P-40 pistol has been out of production for a couple of years, and I missed reporting that. A Kel-Tec representative said the pistol worked fine, but the light weight of the gun and the

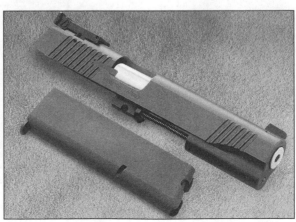

Kimber is also offering a conversion kit to make 1911-type pistols into 22 Long Rifle conversions.

Kimber is now offering 1911 pistols in 22 Long Rifle.

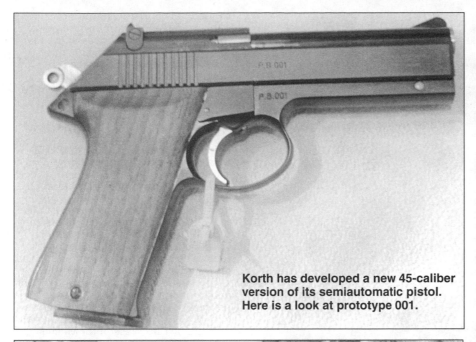

Korth has developed a new 45-caliber version of its semiautomatic pistol. Here is a look at prototype 001.

Wes Ripley proudly exhibits a specimen of Lone Star Armament's new line of 1911-style pistols.

Korth's Silke Musik demonstrates the new Korth 45 ACP prototype to Malloy.

column type and holds 8 rounds. A silenced version of the 45 will be available to law enforcement. As with other Korth pistols, the price is high, but the materials and the workmanship are unsurpassed.

Les Baer

Les Baer Custom was approached by Clint Smith, head of the Thunder

Ranch training center in Texas, about a pistol built to his specifications. The result was the Baer 1911 Thunder Ranch Special, a "working" 45 that has features thought desirable by Smith and other shooters. The pistol comes with night sights, extended safety lever and checkered front strap and mainspring housing. The Thunder Ranch logo appears on the slide and

grips. For those who like to look at their pistols a lot, a special engraved model with ivory grips is available.

Lone Star

A new series of 1911 pistols has been introduced by Lone Star Armament of Stephenville, Texas. Lone Star makes the slides and frames, then the pistols are assembled by Nowlin Manufacturing, using Nowlin barrels and Chip McCormick parts. Guns are made to shoot inside 1-1/2 inches at 25 yards. The guns are offered in Lawman (5") and Ranger (4") series. "Match" variants with adjustable sights are available in either series.

Magnum Research

Magnum Research displayed a prototype of the IMI (Israeli Military Industries) Barak 45 pistol last year. Now the gun is in production, and has been designated the SP-21.

The pistol has a polymer frame with an integral accessory rail, and the trigger mechanism is conventional double-action. The gun is hammer-fired, and the locking system is tilting-barrel. The barrel has polygonal rifling. Controls comprise an ambidextrous manual safety, a slide release and a decocker on the top of the slide. An internal locking mechanism for times of non-use is included.

The magazine release is reversible for right- or left-hand shooters. The magazines themselves are interchangeable with those of Magnum Research's Baby Eagle pistols—a nice touch. The SP-21 is now offered in 9mm and 40 S&W as well as 45 ACP.

The rear sight is shielded within the raised panel at the rear of the slide.

Lone Star Armament has introduced a new line of 1911 pistols. This is the Lawman, with a 5-inch barrel.

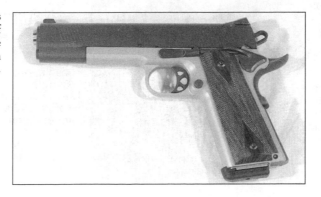

▲ The new polymer-frame SP-21 from IMI is being offered by Magnum Research. Available in 9mm, 40 and 45 calibers, the new pistols use the same magazines as the company's Baby Eagle pistols.

▲ The Mitchell name has returned to the world of 1911-type 45 pistols with the Mitchell Gold Series '03. Here is a look at the first prototype, serial number EXPMA 1.

◄ Mitchell offers restored original Luger pistols as cased sets, with historical information. A reproduction of the Blue Max medal is on the lid of each presentation case.

This is one of the "Gas Gun" variations offered by NCG (Network Custom Guns). The pistols use forward gas pressure to control rearward recoil. Complete pistols and kits for converting 1911-type pistols are offered.

Night sights and adjustable sights are options. A small but important point: there are plenty of grooves at the rear of the slide, and they cover a lot of area. This arrangement makes operating the slide easier, especially under adverse conditions.

Mitchell

It has been a number of years since the Mitchell name has appeared on a 45 automatic. At the February 2003 SHOT Show, three prototypes of a new Mitchell Arms 1911 pistol were exhibited. Pistols numbered EXPMA-1, EXPMA-2 and EXPMA-3 arrived just in time for the opening of the show. Called the Mitchell Gold Series '03 pistols, they are full-size arms with 5-inch barrels. They include some of the niceties today's shooters seem to prefer, such as extended manual safety, beavertail grip safety, skeletonized hammer and trigger and front-and-rear slide serrations. They are cataloged in 40 S&W and 9mm, as well as 45 ACP. Reportedly, the guns will be built by Dan Wesson for Mitchell. Commercial availability was scheduled for Spring 2003.

Mitchell has been doing business as Mitchell's Mausers, and the company has offered rebuilt historical arms. Artisans in Germany are now rebuilding and refinishing original Luger (Parabellum) pistols. Mitchell is offering them, cased, along with the book, *The P08 Luger Pistol* and a History Channel videotape concerning the Luger. Models offered are the Army (4" barrel), Navy (6" barrel) and Artillery (8" barrel) versions.

NCG

NCG (Network Custom Guns) came into our consciousness as a part of KG Industries. KG makes a line of lubrication and cleaning products for firearms owners. Late in 2001, KG became associated with NCG for the purpose of producing a gas-operated recoil control system for the 1911 design. The design was from NCG's John Adkins, who developed a system that could be added to an existing 1911 pistols. It uses an under-barrel gas piston to retard the rearward movement of the slide. The company now offers conversion kits and complete pistols under the "Gas Gun" tradename.

North American

North American Arms' new Guardian 32 NAA Guardian, introduced last year, has become a hot item in the world of small pocket pistols. Recall that the cartridge case is basically formed by necking a 380 case to 32-caliber. The new cartridge, called appropriately enough the 32 NAA, has been approved by the Sporting Arms & Ammunition Manufacturers Association (SAAMI). Now that standards have been set, any ammunition manufacturer may decide to produce the cartridges. At present, Cor-Bon makes the ammunition, which pushes a 60-grain bullet out at over 1200 fps from the Guardian's 2 1/2-inch

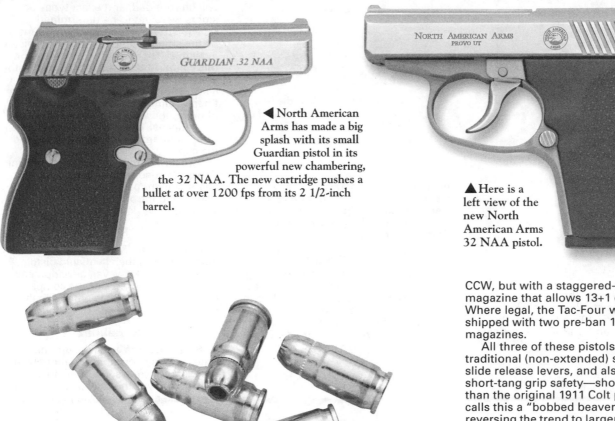

◀ North American Arms has made a big splash with its small Guardian pistol in its powerful new chambering, the 32 NAA. The new cartridge pushes a bullet at over 1200 fps from its 2 1/2-inch barrel.

▲ Here is a left view of the new North American Arms 32 NAA pistol.

▲ The new high-velocity 32 NAA cartridge has now been standardized by SAAMI.

barrel. Consider that the 2 1/2 inches includes the chamber, so the bullet has less than two inches of bore in which to get up to speed. Pretty impressive.

North American never hesitates to hook up with the good ideas of other companies. They have added the Taurus-design key-locking system to the Guardian 32 and 380 pistols. Now the little pocket pistols are California-compliant, as this device is acceptable as a manual safety.

Olympic

Olympic Arms has introduced an eye-catching addition to its 45-caliber 1911 line. The new "Westerner" features a case-color finish on both frame and slide. Various types of grips can be fitted, but the light-colored ones show the "Westerner" logo well. It is an attractive combination of an Old-West appearance on an up-to-date self-loading pistol.

Para-Ordnance

Para-Ordnance Manufacturing, Inc. has been using the shorter name "Para" more and more lately. Because it uses fewer letters, let's use it here.

The company created quite a stir when it introduced its innovative LDA (Light Double Action) trigger system a few years ago, in 1999. Now, almost all of the Para pistols use this trigger. In

February 2003, three new variants were introduced, all in 45 ACP.

The Para CCW pistol (4 1/4-inch barrel) and the Para Companion – Carry Option (3 1/2-inch barrel) are similar except for barrel length and related slide length. They are stainless-steel guns with spurless hammers and the LDA trigger. Capacity is 7+1, and "big diamond" cocobolo grips are fitted. Tritium night sights are standard.

The new Tac-Four is a high-capacity pistol similar to the Para

CCW, but with a staggered-column magazine that allows 13+1 capacity. Where legal, the Tac-Four will be shipped with two pre-ban 13-round magazines.

All three of these pistols have traditional (non-extended) safety and slide release levers, and also have a short-tang grip safety—shorter even than the original 1911 Colt part. Para calls this a "bobbed beavertail", reversing the trend to larger and longer beavertail tangs. The result is a more compact, more concealable package to carry for personal protection.

It is a small thing, but Para still cuts slide grooves straight up-and-down, as on the original Colt 1911 and 1911A1 models. Most other companies angle the grooves for appearance. They all seem to work just fine, but the reality of physics is that the more they are slanted, the less purchase the grooves provide for retracting the slide. It is nice that Para is employing the original configuration.

Pardini

The Italian Pardini firm has produced a 45-caliber competition pistol, the Pardini GT 45. The new pistol is available with either a 5- or 6-inch barrel. With a 5-incher, the gun

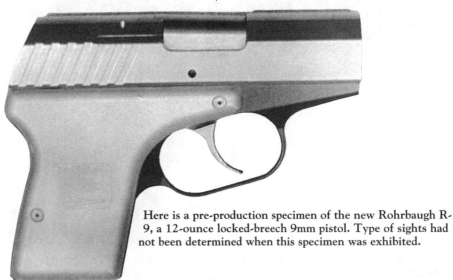

Here is a pre-production specimen of the new Rohrbaugh R-9, a 12-ounce locked-breech 9mm pistol. Type of sights had not been determined when this specimen was exhibited.

Here is a first look at the new Sarsilmaz pistol, which is based on the CZ-75 mechanism. This specimen is serial number 1.

weighs 39 ounces; the 6-inch version tips the scales at 42 ounces. The magazine holds 10 rounds, and the Pardini is suited for IPSC or Practical pistol shooting. Extras, such as a frame-mounted scope base and a German red-dot sight, are also available from the importer, Nygord Precision Products.

Rohrbaugh

Introduced last year, the Rohrbaugh R-9 9mm pistol had its own production facility by February 2003, and deliveries were scheduled for June 2003. Some changes in final production specifications were to be made. Edges will be rounded, and exact types of sights were yet to be determined.

The little Rohrbaugh pistol claims to be the smallest and lightest 9mm pistol available. There is good evidence for this claim. At 3.6 x 4.9 inches, the pistol will almost hide under a 3x5 index card. Grip choices are polymer, carbon fiber or aluminum. Depending on type of grips, the weight ranges from 12 to 12.7 ounces. The Rohrbaugh pistol uses standard 9mm ammunition, and the capacity is 6+1.

The new company is already looking down the road. Within about 1-1/2 years, they hope to offer a laser-sight option and introduce a 40-caliber version.

Ruger

Sturm, Ruger & Company offered nothing new in their semiauto pistol lines this year. However, developments may be coming soon, as the company is evaluating the need to conform to the requirements of certain restrictive states.

Sarsilmaz

Sarsilmaz, the Turkish company noted for its shotguns, is definitely in the pistol business. Founded in 1880, the company is the only private Turkish armsmaker. Last year, the pistol line was announced, but the pistols themselves were held up in Customs. They became available early in 2003. Specimens numbered 01 and 02 were displayed at the 2003 SHOT Show. The Sarsilmaz pistols are based on the CZ-75, and are available in 9mm. Variants are Kilinc (full-size) and Hancer (compact) models.

SIGARMS

Only small changes in the pistol line for SIGARMS, apparently all to their 45-caliber pistols. The full-size P 220 now is available with an accessory rail in the stainless version. Both 7- and 8-shot magazines are available for the P 220.

The downsized P 245 comes with a 6-round magazine, but now an "ErgoGrip" extender can be added to let the smaller pistol use the 8-round magazine. The extender simply snaps over the 8-round magazine. I suspect P 245 owners may want to continue to carry the pistol with the original 6-round magazine, but if a spare is carried, it makes sense to choose the optional 8-rounder.

Smith & Wesson

S&W really introduced a lot of new things at the February 2002 SHOT Show. Without much doubt, the star of their show was a revolver—the big 500 Magnum. That said, you'll have to read about it in the proper place. Here, let us go over the interesting new autoloaders that were almost upstaged by the big revolver.

After years of contending that S&W 45 autos were as good or better than the 1911 design, the company finally entered the fray, and has introduced its own 1911 pistol. The new SW1911 has a few modifications to the original, such as an external extractor. It has an

S&W has entered the 1911 market with its new SW1911 pistol. For now, the new pistol is offered only in a 5-inch, stainless steel version.

S&W's polymer-frame SW99, previously available in 9mm and 40 S&W, is now offered in 45 ACP.

Springfield has introduced a 3-inch barrel version of its new XD polymer-frame pistol. Springfield's Terra Davis displays a specimen in 9mm.

internal drop safety that is disengaged by the grip safety, not the trigger. Other parts interchange, allowing use of 1911 aftermarket parts. However, there may be few that S&W has not already included. The SW1911 uses Wolff springs, Chip McCormick hammer and safety, Wilson beavertail and magazines, Novak sights and Briley barrel bushing. The pistol is offered now in only one version, with a 5-inch barrel, and in stainless steel only.

The polymer-frame SW99 is now available in a new chambering—45 ACP. Barrel length of the new, big SW99 is 4-1/4 inches, with a weight of 25.6 ounces. Capacity is 9+1. A more compact variant of the original 9mm and 40-caliber SW99 is now available

with a shortened grip frame. Magazine capacity is still 10 rounds for the 9mm, but reduced to 8 for the 40 S&W.

The new Smith & Wesson Model 4040PD is the first scandium-frame semiautomatic pistol. Caliber is 40 S&W. The pistol uses a single-column magazine that holds 7 rounds. With a 3-1/2-inch barrel, the pistol weighs 25.6 ounces.

S&W's Performance Center handguns are now available to all distributors. Thus, limited-edition products such as the Model 945 *(still considered by S&W as the top-of-the-line 45 single-action auto)* and the Model 952 *(the 9mm target pistol)* can be ordered.

Springfield

Springfield made a big splash last year with the introduction of its polymer-frame XD pistol. Now, a new 9mm "Sub-Compact" version, with a 3-inch barrel, is offered. The new XD has a shortened grip, but still carries a 10-round magazine made of stainless steel *(two are furnished with each pistol)*. Short as it is, the new XD has a stubby accessory rail at the forward part of its frame, and Springfield has a special XML light to fit. Weight of the small XD is 20-1/2 ounces, and the sights are 3 dot, dovetailed front and rear.

In just a year, the XD has expanded into an entire line of pistols. They are now available with 3-, 4-, and 5-inch barrels, in 9mm, 40S&W and 357 SIG. Frames are black or OD green, and

slides are black or silver. Sights may be white dot, several choices of night sights, or fiber optic type. All this presents a lot of possibilities for mixing or matching.

A number of new variants have also been introduced in the 1911-A1 line. One is a 3-inch barrel version with an accessory rail, which will also take the XML light. Two striking-looking pistols are 3-inch and 5-inch pistols made of stainless steel, blackened, then with the sides polished bright. Springfield calls this treatment "Black Stainless."

Steyr

Last year, I reported that Steyr firearms were scheduled to be imported by Dynamit Nobel RWS. Well, that is half-true. The Nobel firm will import Steyr long guns, but not pistols. By press time, I was unable to learn about the status of the Steyr pistols.

STI

STI International is introducing their "Duty One" pistol, a single-column 45 with an extended frame "dust cover" that carries an accessory rail. The 5-inch bull barrel is ramped, and the chamber fully supported. Delivery was scheduled for third quarter 2003. Finish was planned as flat blue metal, with rosewood grips.

Taurus

The 22-caliber PT 922 introduced last year has changed considerably.

STI has introduced its DUTY ONE pistol, a single-column 45 with an extended forward frame that includes an accessory rail.

▲ Taurus' new Millenium Pro series is an updated version of the original Millenium design. This PT 145 has an all-black finish.

▶ More finish options are offered for Taurus pistols. Here is a dual-tone version of the new Millenium Pro 45-caliber pistol.

The prototype of 2002 had a metal frame and looked just a bit like a Walther P38. The 2003 version had a polymer frame and looked just a bit like a Colt Woodsman. Even though it was included in the 2003 catalog, Taurus' Eddy Fernandez said it is still under development. This version looked and felt good, and it would be nice to see it finalized.

In the polymer-frame Millenium line, the Millenium "Pro" series has been introduced. This is an updating of the original Millenium design, with pronounced grip checkering, enlarged and smoother-working controls, easier takedown and 3-dot sights. These are some of the subtle, but visible changes. Internally, a captive recoil spring has been added, and the magazine release, trigger pull and internal firing pin lock have been improved.

Tired of all polymer-frame guns having flat black grips? Apparently some people are, for Taurus has

▶ Taurus' PT 922, introduced in prototype last year, has already undergone changes in design and appearance. It is now a polymer-frame 22 pistol that is shaped just a bit like the old Colt Woodsman.

Linda Moore, Wildey's president, holds one of the big Wildey gas-operated pistols, now available in 44 Auto Mag chambering. The 44 Auto Mag cartridge started the trend to magnum autoloaders.

brought out the Millenium Deluxe. The new pistols have wood or "pearl" grip inserts added to spruce up the polymer frames.

Valtro

Valtro has added a hard-chrome version to its line of Italian-made 1911-style pistols. The basic pistol is their 1998A1, with many variations made on a custom and semi-custom basis. All Valtro pistols have many of the niceties that modern shooters seem to prefer. The company claims the pistols are machined to the tightest standards in the industry, resulting in accuracy of less than three inches at 50 yards. A Valtro representative said some guns achieve groups of about one inch at that distance, fired from a stationary fixture.

Vektor

Vektor USA, the United States subsidiary of the South African Vektor firm, no longer exists. The only remnant

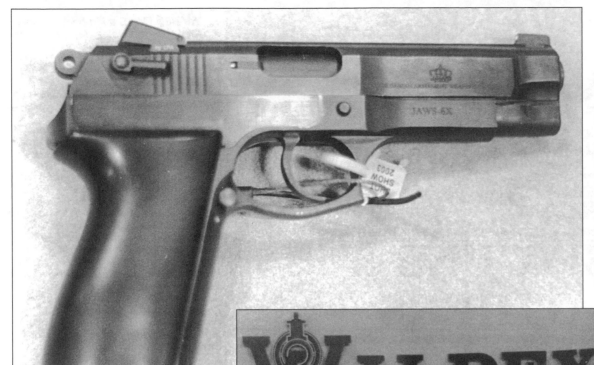

Here is a peek at prototype number 6 of the new JAWS (Jordanian Armament Weapon Systems) multi-caliber pistol. The new gun can be a 9mm, 40 or 45 by changing three parts.

Wildey is now handling the JAWS service pistol, made in Jordan.

in America is a Vektor Special Projects Office, formed to handle a recall for the Vektor CP-1 series of pistols. The recall was scheduled to end in 2003, so owners of such pistols should call 877-831-8313 as soon as possible.

Volquartsen

The Volquartsen Cheetah, the first *(and apparently still the only)* semiautomatic pistol chambered for the 17 HMR (17 Hornady Magnum Rimfire) cartridge, was introduced last year and is now in production. It is also offered in 22 Long Rifle and 22 Winchester Magnum Rimfire.

Wildey

The big Wildey gas-operated pistol is now available in a new chambering, the 44 Auto Mag. Well, the cartridge isn't exactly new, as it was the original magnum semiauto pistol cartridge–designed for the old Auto Mag pistol–and dates back prior to 1970. However, the round has not been commercially chambered in a factory production pistol since the demise of the Auto Mag in the early 1980s. There was a demand for a new pistol using this cartridge, and Wildey added it for 2003. It joins the original Wildey chambering, the 45 Winchester Magnum, and the subsequent 45 and 475 Wildey Magnum offerings.

There are lots of hunters who believe that big pistol cartridges are plenty good as ammunition for a handy carbine. For them, Wildey has introduced the Wildey Carbine, based on the pistol mechanism. It has an 18-inch barrel and a skeletonized stock and forearm, both made of walnut. The

Wildey Carbine is offered in the same four chamberings as the Wildey pistols.

The company is adding a new line, a big departure for them. Wildey will now also handle a new service-type pistol, chambered for 45 ACP, 40 S&W and 9mm cartridges. The pistol is manufactured in Jordan by Jordanian Armament Weapons Systems, and will be marketed under the logical *(and catchy)* acronym, "JAWS." It is of tilting-barrel locking system, with a conventional double-action trigger mechanism. A special feature is its ability to change calibers simply by changing the barrel, a breechblock in the slide, and an insert in the magazine. JAWS prototype number 6 was exhibited at the February 2003 SHOT Show.

Wilson

Wilson Combat has introduced a Tactical Super Grade Compact pistol. The new handgun is similar to their top-of-the-line 1911-style "Super Grade," but is made with a 4.1-inch barrel. It has many of the features

desired today, such as an ambidextrous extended-lever safety, beavertail grip safety and tactical combat sights. Each pistol comes with six magazines *(a nice touch)* and an instructional video, along with other extras. The new pistol has an accuracy guarantee of one inch at 25 yards.

In 2003, Wilson celebrated its 25th year in the custom firearms business. Congratulations!

POSTSCRIPT

It is well to be reminded that anti-gun forces do not want Americans to possess autoloading handguns. They welcomed the passage of the federal "Assault Weapons" bill of 1994 in part because it also restricted pistol magazine capacity. Now, the law is due to expire in September 2004. There is political agitation to continue the restrictions past the sunset date. It would be wise to contact our Senators and Representatives; we should ask for their support in letting this misguided legislation die at the appointed time. ●

by **JOHN TAFFIN**

SIXGUNS & OTHERS

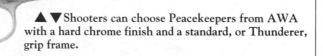

▲▼Shooters can choose Peacekeepers from AWA with a hard chrome finish and a standard, or Thunderer, grip frame.

WHEN I WAS a kid back in those dinosaur pre-television days, one of the most famous newscasters on radio was a man by the name of Gabriel Heater. He would always come on with the phrase: "Ah, there's good news tonight!" If he were alive he would be the perfect lead-in to announce what is going on in the world of six-guns. There really is good news–and lots of it–for shooters. Dozens of new models are coming out, including those that are entirely original, and others that are simply upgrades-or slightly different versions-of existing six-guns.

Not only do we have new six-guns to talk about, but we also have both the smallest and largest revolver cartridges ever commercially produced being introduced in new six-guns this year. Those two cartridges are the 17 HMR (Hornady Magnum Rimfire) and the 500 S&W Magnum. The former is now being chambered in revolvers from Ruger, Smith & Wesson, and Taurus; the latter–at least for now–is found only in the new Model 500 X-Frame from Smith & Wesson.

Competition among the major manufacturers is exceptionally fierce to see who can get there "fustest with the mostest." This, of course, is great news for consumers as we reap the benefit of a wide range of both large and small six-guns for virtually any application. Not only in this going to be another great year for handgunners in general, and six-gunners in particular, I speculate that – in the words of the late Al Jolson, that great entertainer from the first half of the 20th century – "You ain't seen nothing yet." If we can continue to hold the anti-gunners at bay, the future will be both exciting and enjoyable. Let us take an alphabetical journey through many of the manufacturers viewing some of the models they are offering.

American Western Arms

American Western Arms (AWA) offers two replica Single-Action Armies known as the Longhorn and the Peacekeeper. The former is their standard-finished Single Action available in 45 Colt, 44-40, 44 Special, 38-40, and 357 Magnum. The Peacekeeper has the same chamberings; however, it is specially tuned, exquisitely finished, and also fitted with checkered rubber grips instead of the one-piece style found on the Longhorn. The Peacekeeper is as beautiful a Single-Action Army replica as one is ever going to find anywhere. The top-of-the-line model Peacekeeper, in addition to a factory-tuned action, has an 11-degree forcing cone, 1st Generation-style cylinder flutes, and bone/charcoal case-hardened frame.

◄▲AWA's top-of-the-line Peacekeeper, here shown in a 7 1/2-inch 44-40 and 4 3/4-inch 45 Colt, exhibits a deep blue finish, brilliant case colors, and eagle-style rubber grips.

The Bond Texas Cowboy features easily interchangeable barrel assemblies, shown here are 45 Colt and 32 Magnum barrels.

left side of the frame of the Cowboy Derringer is a spring-loaded camming lever that, when pushed down, unlatches the barrel assembly allowing it to move upwards to be unloaded and reloaded. Each barrel assembly has its own built-in spring-loaded ejector. The Bond Cowboy Texas Defender Model is stainless steel and comes with grips of an impregnated laminated rosewood that are small, but they nestle comfortably in the hand. The hammer is of the rebounding type and a cross-bolt safety is found on the Bond and should–that is SHOULD–always be applied if the Bond is carried loaded. The Bond Cowboy/Texas Defender Derringer comes in 32 Magnum, 357 Maximum, 9mm, 45ACP, 44 Special/44 Magnum, 40 S&W, 38 Special/357 Magnum, 45 Colt, and 45 Colt/.410.

The Bond Derringer is quality, and unlike some derringers on the market, is easy to operate one-handed. The trigger pull is not overly heavy and the hammer is easy to cock with the thumb of the shooting hand and, for all practical purposes for which such a little gun should be used, point of impact with both barrels is close enough.

Both models feature a beveled ejector rod housing to keep the metal from digging into the leather on a tight holster, and both models can be had in nickel finish, while the Peacekeeper can also be ordered with the "blackpowder frame", distinctive because an angled screw in the front of the frame – rather than the spring-loaded cross-pin retainer – holds the cylinder pin in place. It is also available in a satin hard chrome finish that not only looks great, but also cleans up easily for those using blackpowder loads.

American Western Arms cylinders have virtually no end play or side-to-side movement; the one-piece walnut stocks on the Longhorn, and black rubber American Eagle grips on the Peacekeeper are individually fitted with no overlapping of grip or frame. AWA is now fitting their single actions with a coil mainspring. These are more reliable, and give a more even hammer pull and faster hammer fall than the old-style flat mainspring. The coil springs are available in three weights: 15#, 17#, and 19# and can be fitted to older six-guns by filing a small area behind the trigger guard part of the grip frame and using a coil-spring holding shelf that screws into the hole used for the original flat mainspring.

Bond Arms

Several years ago I tested the first Bond Derringer and discovered it was a good, strong two-shooter with two problems. The trigger pull was very heavy, and the changing of barrel and shims took three hands, or more, to accomplish. That is all past. The Cowboy Derringer is exceptionally easy to use. Changing barrels *(each frame accepts all caliber barrels)* takes about one minute to accomplish, using an Allen wrench of the proper size. On the

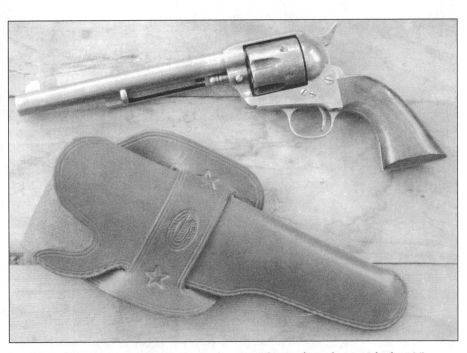

Available in either the standard finish *(shown)* or original finish, Cimarron's Wyatt Earp Buntline is an excellent shooter. Shield in the right grip commemorates the presentation of the Buntline Special to Earp.

It is a brand-new six-gun from Cimarron; however this 7 1/2-inch 44-40 looks 125 years old due to its 'original' finish. Period leather is by Will Ghormley.

Cimarron offers both the 45 New Thunderer *(top)*, and 38 Lightning Model. Custom grips are by Buffalo Brothers.

Jamie Harvey of Cimarron Firearms shows off the new stainless steel Model P 45 Colt.

▲ Cimarron brings back a short but important time in history with their 1871-72 Open-Top, chambered in 44 Colt. Carved eagle grips are by Buffalo Brothers.

Cimarron Firearms

Cimarron is now providing brand-new six-guns in what they call an original finish. This finish is actually what a six-gun would look like after much usage on a daily basis, after hundreds and hundreds of times being drawn and replaced in a leather holster. My original 1879-vintage Colt Frontier Six-Shooter, *(as the early Colts chambered in 44-40 were called)* with one-piece stocks and a 7 1/2-inch barrel has a finish earned with over 100 years of service. The new 'original' finish of the Cimarron Model P perfectly matches with what is left on my old Six-Shooter. The Cimarron's finish is not simply an in-the-white six-gun with no bluing. Instead it has age marks, blemishes—and even a small spot or two with a brownish patina. The one-piece stocks are also appropriately distressed. CFA also offers the Wyatt Earp Buntline Special 10-inch barrel 45 Colt in either blue/case color or original finish. Either way, it fairly reeks of history and, for most six-gunners, is also easy to shoot well due to the long barrel and great distance between sights.

Cowboy Action Shooting has been responsible for the availability of replicas of most of the great single actions of the past, not only the well known Colt Single-Action Army and Remington Model 1875, but also the Richards Conversion, the Richards-Mason Conversion, and the 1871-72 Open-Top. Cimarron has offered all three of these, and currently offers the Richards-Mason and the Open-Top. While attending Range War in Fredericksburg, Texas I had the opportunity to visit the Cimarron

Firearms facility—and came home with a pair of consecutively-numbered 1871-72 Open-Tops, chambered in 44 Colt.

The modern 44 Colt is simply a 44 Special cartridge case that has been slightly shortened, with the diameter of the rim turned down to allow six rounds to fit in the 1860 Army-sized cylinders of the Colt cartridge conversions. Open-Tops, with their connection to the past and mild recoil, are such a pleasure that it seemed reasonable to have them fitted with custom stocks. For grips I called upon Buffalo Brothers. They specialize in molded, antique-looking polymer grips for all the old six-guns, and their replicas. Using old-style patterns and modern coloring techniques, Buffalo Brothers offers ten different shades of historical antique coloring molded into the grip, as well as carvings such as those found on single actions in the middle of the 19th-century. For the Open-Tops I chose ivory grips with a carved Eagle symbol. They really set off these Open-Tops and make them extremely attractive.

Cimarron's newest offering is a Model P in stainless steel. These six-guns are made by Uberti and, as you read this, will be available in both 357 Magnum and 45 Colt in the three standard barrel lengths of 4-3/4, 5-1/2, and 7-1/2 inches. For the first time, those that pack a traditional single action in all kinds of weather will have the advantage of stainless steel's ability to withstand the elements. A bonus, for those shooting blackpowder, is that they are much easier to clean and maintain.

Colt's Manufacturing Company, Inc.

More good news from Colt this year. Two years ago the retail price of the Colt Single Action Army was $1,968. Last year this dropped by $438 to $1,530, and now Colt continues the trend with a new MSRP of $1,380. Some replicas are already running as high as $1,100 or more, so this may cause some six-gunners to take another look at the original Single Action Army. Colt has two advantages over the replicas: First, they are genuine Colts—no other single action can make that statement. Second, the Colt Single Action has more than a century and one-half of history behind it. Again, no other single action can make that claim.

A second piece of good news from Colt is that the Single Action Army is once again offered in the original 1873 Cavalry Model 7 1/2-inch barrel length. It has probably been a decade since shooters could have anything except 4 3/4- and 5 1/2-inch Single Actions from Colt. Now all three standard barrel lengths are available in 357 Magnum, 44-40, and 45 Colt. There is a downside, however, as the nickel-plate finish has been dropped from the catalog; now only the standard blued finish with a casehardened frame is offered. Grips are a checkered black

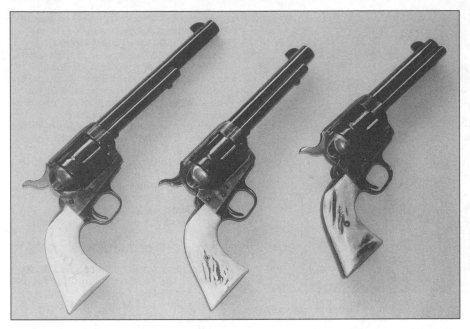

The classic Colt Single Action Army has not only been lowered in price by nearly $600 over the past two years, it is now offered in all three standard barrel lengths. Custom stocks are extra.

composite with the rampant colt emblem at the top and the American Eagle at the bottom.

Colt also continues to offer their answer to Ruger's Vaquero—the Cowboy—in 45 Colt only and a choice of 4 3/4- and 5 1/2-inch barrel lengths. This six-gun is also offered only in the blued/casehardened finish. To round out their six-gun offerings, Colt continues to offer a stainless steel 44 Magnum Anaconda in barrel lengths of 4, 6, and 8 inches, as well as the 357 Python Elite in either of blue or stainless, and a barrel length choice of 4 or 6 inches. All double-action models feature adjustable sights with a red ramp front and white outline rear sight. Anacondas come equipped with finger-grooved rubber grips, while the Python Elite is the only Colt revolver currently offered with wooden stocks (finger-grooved combat-style walnut).

Early & Modern Firearms (EMF)

EMF imports a full line of quality revolvers and offers them under the Hartford label. In the past many of their replica six-guns have been manufactured by Armi San Marco, however they have now turned to Pietta to produce a new lineup of single-action six-guns that bear the Great Western name. Although labeled Great Western, these new six-guns are not replicas of the original replica, the Great Western, having the traditional Colt-style firing pin instead of the original frame-mounted firing pin of the original Great Western. Forty years after the demise of the Great Western Frontier Revolver, EMF is offering the Great Western II in nickel, satin nickel, full blue, or blue with a beautifully case-colored frame. Another version, known as The Californian, is offered with a standard finish. I have had the opportunity to test two 4 3/4-inch 45s; one a satin nickel Great Western II with one-piece polymer ivory stocks, the other a Californian with one-piece wood stocks. The less expensive Californian has the best-looking wooden stocks I have yet to find on any Italian replica. They are perfectly fitted and finished, and performed and shot well.

◄ New from EMF this year is the Great Western II, here shown in both the Californian and the satin nickel versions.

◄ ► EMF offers both the 1875 Remington and 1890 Remington in 45 Colt. Stocks are by Buffalo Brothers.

Forty-fours from Freedom Arms: Model 83 *(top)* chambered in 44 Magnum, and the new Model 97 set up for the 44 Special.

Freedom Arms newest offering is the mid-framed Model 97, a five-shot 44 Special. This could well be the finest factory-manufactured 44 Special ever.

Freedom Arms is now delivering the Model 97 22LR/22 WMR. This may well be most accurate 22 revolver ever offered to shooters.

EMF also offers excellent copies of the Remington single actions. It has been my pleasure to test both a 7 1/2-inch Model 1875 and a 5 1/2-inch Model 1890, both chambered in 45 Colt. Cylinders lock up tightly, and I do mean tightly, and both are timed better than the average Italian replica. Actions are smooth, and mainsprings are also much lighter than found on Remington replicas from two decades ago. The Model 1875 is blued with a case-colored frame and hammer, while the 1890 is fully blued. The Model 1890 also has a round lanyard ring in the butt. Both six-guns proved to be well above average in the accuracy department for this type of revolver.

Freedom Arms

Freedom Arms full-sized five-shot revolver, the Model 83, continues to be produced in 454 Casull, 44 Magnum, 357 Magnum, 41 Magnum, 475 Linebaugh and 50AE. There is even a 22 LR version. These are simply the finest six-guns ever to come from a factory being, in fact, custom-built. Seven years ago, Freedom Arms introduced their mid-frame six-gun, the Model 97. The Model 97 is built exactly the same way as the larger Model 83, using the same materials and the same strict attention to tight tolerances and precision fitting. Although the Model 83 is available with both a Field Grade and Premier Grade finish, the Model 97 is thus far offered only in Premier Grade. Pricewise, the Model 97 costs about 12 percent less than a comparable Model 83 due to less material being used for the smaller gun, rather than any shortcuts or difference in manufacturing. The cylinders on the little gun are still line-bored as they are on the big gun.

Last year Freedom Arms introduced the Model 97 in 22 Long Rifle with an extra 22 Magnum cylinder. I have now had a chance to thoroughly test this grand little 22 and I can say the Model 97 22/22 Magnum really shoots! The performance of this Model 97 is superb with both cylinders using either 22 Long Rifle or 22 Magnum Rimfire ammunition resulting in groups of less than one-third of an inch for five shots at 25 yards. CCI's Mini-Mag Hollow Points, Remington's Yellow Jackets, and Winchester's High Velocity Hollow Points all came in well under one-third of an inch with the 22 Long Rifle cylinder in place, while CCI's Maxi-Mag Hollow Points delivered the same results with the 22 Magnum cylinder in use.

New for this year is the Model 97 chambered in 44 Special. Most dedicated and knowledgeable six-gunners agree the first 44 Special, the Smith & Wesson 1st Model Hand Ejector of 1907 is not only the finest double-action six-gun ever built, it is also the grandest of 44 Specials. Until now. The old Triple-Lock has met its match with the new Freedom Arms 44 Special.

I've been a connoisseur of 44 Specials since my first Smith & Wesson Model 1950 Target was acquired in 1959. I've had just about every 44

Kelly Baker of Freedom Arms displays the new Model 97 44 Special.

Special ever manufactured: Smith & Wesson Triple-Lock, Model 1926, 1950 Military, 1950 Target, Model 24, and Model 624; Colt New Service, Single Action Army, and New Frontier; Great Western Frontier Model; Texas Longhorn Arms South Texas Army and Flat-Top Target; and many custom 44s built on Ruger 357 Magnum Blackhawk Flat-Tops and Three-Screws. None can surpass the Freedom Arms Model 97 for quality, accuracy, and portability. Many cannot understand the deep appreciation for the 44 Special, a cartridge that has been "surpassed" by so many big-bore magnums. For those that do understand, no explanation is necessary; for those that don't, no explanation is possible. It is a spiritual thing with many six-gunners.

Magnum Research

Magnum Research has long been known for the semi-automatic Desert Eagle. However, in recent years they have been offering the BFR *(Biggest Finest Revolver),* an all stainless-steel revolver offered in two frame sizes. The standard frame and cylinder *(they call it the Short Cylinder)* is chambered in 454 Casull, 22 Hornet, and 475 Linebaugh–which also handles the 480 Ruger. The Long Cylinder version handles the 45-70, 444 Marlin, 450 Marlin, or a 45 Colt version that also handles .410 shot shells.

This past year I have been shooting one of the Short Cylinder versions with a 6 1/2-inch barrel chambered in 480/475 Linebaugh. Instead of adjustable sights, it came from the factory fitted with a mounted scope and no iron sights whatsoever. The rubber grips supplied are not pretty but they certainly help in handling felt recoil. With a suggested retail price of $999, the BFR is the most affordable way to own a quality single-action revolver chambered in many large calibers.

The standard BFR rear sight is fully adjustable, and mated with an interchangeable front sight. Barrels are cut-rifled, barrel/cylinder gaps are held to less than 0.005-inch, and cylinders are freewheeling; that is, when the loading gate is opened the cylinder can be rotated clockwise or counterclockwise. A nice touch usually found only on custom revolvers.

Navy Arms

Val Forgett, founder of Navy Arms and the Father of the Replica Firearms Industry passed away this past year at the age of 72. Navy Arms continues under the leadership of his son, Val Forgett III. We now have available a replica of virtually every single-action revolver from the 19th century, thanks to the efforts of several individuals. However, it all started back in the 1950s with Forgett introducing a copy of the 1851 Colt Navy. Forgett and Navy Arms were directly responsible for the introduction of Smith & Wesson single actions, beginning with the 1875 Schofield and followed by the Model #3 Russian.

New models from Navy Arms this year include two new Schofields. First is a Founders Model with a color-casehardened receiver, polymer ivory grips, 7 1/2-inch barrel, and chambered in 45 Colt. The 38 Special Schofield joins the 45 Colt and 44-40 in both the 7 1/2-inch Cavalry and 5 1/2-inch Wells Fargo models.

Those who prefer Colt replicas have not been forgotten. Navy Arms' 1873 Single Actions are now offered as a Gunfighter Series with all standard springs replaced by custom Wolff springs, a nickel-plated backstrap and trigger guard, and black checkered grips. These are offered in the three standard barrel lengths of 4 inches, 5 1/2 inches, and 7 1/2 inches in 357 Magnum, 44-40, and 45 Colt. For the first time, Navy Arms is also offering a stainless steel 1873 Single Action Army with the same black checkered grips and Wolff springs in all three barrel lengths, chambered in 357 Magnum or 45 Colt.

Finally from Navy Arms comes a Deluxe Model 1873 Single Action Army in 32-20. When the West was wild the most popular chamberings were 45 Colt, 44-40, and 38-40. However, as

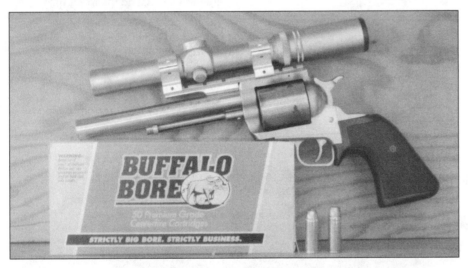

The BFR revolver from Magnum Research has proven to be an extremely accurate six-gun when using either 480 Ruger or 475 Linebaugh ammunition.

Navy Arms is now offering the Schofield Model chambered for 38 Special or 38 Long Colt. Grips are by Buffalo Brothers.

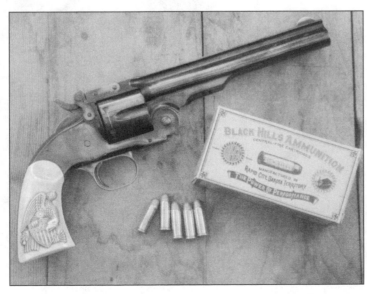

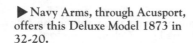

▶Navy Arms, through Acusport, offers this Deluxe Model 1873 in 32-20.

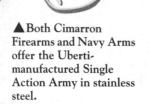

▲Both Cimarron Firearms and Navy Arms offer the Uberti-manufactured Single Action Army in stainless steel.

things began to settle down, around the turn-of-the-century, the 32-20 became very popular so is altogether fitting that Navy Arms would choose this chambering for their Deluxe Model. This version features a color-casehardened receiver and loading gate; charcoal- or fire-blue barrel, cylinder, and grip frame; hand-rubbed walnut stocks, and Wolff springs.

Savage

Savage not only produces some of the finest rifles available, they are also part of the handgunner's world with their Striker bolt-action pistol. All of these superbly accurate handguns have a left-handed bolt and a black ambidextrous synthetic stock, with a finger-groove pistol grip. Centerfire models are offered in both blue and stainless, a magazine capacity of two rounds and chambered in 243 Winchester, 7-08 and 308, while the 223 version is offered in blued steel only. For fanciers of the new short cartridges, a stainless-steel Striker is cataloged, chambered for the 270, 7mm, and 300 WSM. All centerfire Strikers have 14-inch barrels.

For those who prefer to hunt varmints with a rimfire, the Striker is available chambered in 22 WMR and 17 HMR with a 10-inch barrel and five-round magazine, while a 10-shot version can be had for everyone's favorite cartridge for plinking and relaxing, 22 Long Rifle. All Strikers come with scope bases already installed and button-rifled, free-floating barrels.

Dale Donough of SIGARMS shows off the new Blaser 93 bolt-action pistol.

SIGARMS

No I'm not going to report on any semi-automatics from SIG. John Malloy handles that pleasant chore quite well. However, SIGARMS is offering a handgun that fits into my section. It is the Blaser R93 bolt-action hunting handgun. And a beauty it is! It is a straight-pull, bolt-action pistol built on the same action as the Blaser 93 Rifle, with free-floating interchangeable barrels. Barrels are hammer-forged, 14 inches in length; the stock is beautifully-figured walnut; and the forearm is furnished with a sling swivel for the attachment of a Harris bipod. Chambering options currently include the 223 Remington, 243 Winchester, 6mm BR, 270 Winchester, 308 Winchester, 30/06, 7-08, 7mm Remington Magnum, and the new 300WSM. With a price tag in the $2650 to $2800 range, only serious handgun hunters need apply.

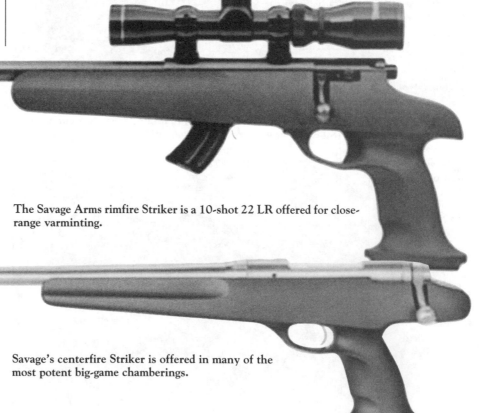

The Savage Arms rimfire Striker is a 10-shot 22 LR offered for close-range varminting.

Savage's centerfire Striker is offered in many of the most potent big-game chamberings.

Smith & Wesson

Smith & Wesson reclaims the title of King of the Magnum Six-guns with the introduction of the 500 S&W Magnum cartridge, and the X-frame Model 500 revolver to handle it. From the 1930s the 1960s it was all Smith & Wesson, as far as magnum chamberings were concerned, as they introduced *(in succession)* the 357 Magnum, the 44 Magnum, and the 41 Magnum. After that, the game plan changed as other companies and individuals introduced the 454 Casull, the 475 and 500 Linebaugh, the 357, 375, 445, 475, and 500 Maximums/SuperMags, and the 480 Ruger. Now Smith & Wesson is back on top of the mountain with the 500 Magnum.

When the 357 Magnum was introduced in 1935, there was no way it could ever be surpassed. It was, however, with the 44 Magnum introduction in 1955, which could never be challenged. Then came the 454 in the 1970s, and then the…. Well, you get the picture. With every new cartridge we felt we were at the top. We certainly have reached it now! I cannot see how we could come up with a more powerful cartridge for a handheld six-gun than the 500 that is, by the way, a slightly modified version of John Linebaugh's original 500 Maximum. The latter uses a 1.610-inch cartridge case with a 0.511-inch bullet, while Smith & Wesson's version has a 1.625-inch case and a true 0.500-inch bullet.

The standard Model 500 has an 8 3/8-inch ported barrel, stretched frame and cylinder to fit the longer cartridge, heavy underlug barrel, felt recoil-reducing rubber grips, stainless-steel finish, and a weight of 4 pounds that will be welcomed by most shooters. The Performance Center will be offering a 10-inch Model 500 with sling swivels and a scope mount base, and Smith & Wesson is at least contemplating an easy-packing 3-inch barrel version. Cor-Bon has three loads for the 500 S&W: a 275-grain Barnes X-Bullet at 1665 fps with a muzzle energy of 1688 ft/lbs; a 400-grain SP at 1675 fps and 2500 ft/lbs; and a 440-grain Hard Cast, 1625 fps

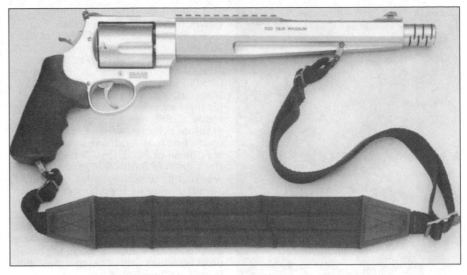

In addition to the standard Model 500, Smith & Wesson also offers this Performance Center model complete with built-in scope mount, sling swivels, and carrying strap.

Big—that is B-I-G—news from Smith & Wesson is the Model 500 X-Frame chambered in the new 500 S&W.

From the Smith & Wesson Performance Center comes this exceptionally businesslike 2-inch barrel, short-cylinder Model 625 in 45 ACP.

The lightest 44 Magnum ever offered; the S&W329PD weighs in at 26 ounces. It will pack like a dream and kick like a nightmare!

This year's Mountain Gun offering from S&W is a blued 4-inch Model 29 in 44 Magnum.

Jim Rae of the Smith & Wesson Performance Center with a new S&W Model 500 Hunter Model.

and 2580 ft/lbs! This is incredible power in a handheld revolver.

As stout as recoil of the Model 500 will be, it may be overshadowed by the second offering from Smith & Wesson––the 44 Magnum Model 329PD. We are used to titanium and scandium 357 Magnums, now it's time to get ready for light versions in 44 Magnum. The Model 329PD has a scandium frame, titanium cylinder, 4-inch barrel, black matte finish, Hi-Viz front sight, and weighs all of 26 ounces! When I asked Herb Belin of Smith & Wesson why it was equipped with wooden grips, he admitted after he fired it rubber grips were more appropriate. So this Smith & Wesson comes with two pair of grips: Ahrends finger-groove wood and a Hogue rubber Monogrip. One will be able to tell what type of loads are being used by which grip is being employed. Recoil will be HEAVY.

Several other revolvers of note: Smith & Wesson is now chambering

the 17 HMR in the medium-frame Model 647, with a companion Model 648 in 22 WMR. Both are 6-inch stainless steel six-guns with heavy underlug barrels. From the Performance Center we have the return of the blued Model 29 in a Mountain Gun version with a 4-inch tapered barrel. I have always felt the 357 Magnum Model 27 with a 3 1/2-inch barrel was the most serious-looking double-action revolver around. Now the rather strange-looking Performance Center Model 625, with a 2-inch barrel and a shortened cylinder to accommodate the 45 ACP, has surpassed it. Since much of the barrel is in the frame and extends to the front of the cylinder, only a small nub protrudes in front of the frame. Now that six-gun really looks serious!

Sturm, Ruger & Co.

In 1999, Ruger celebrated the 50th anniversary of the founding of their

Shooters now have a choice of six-guns chambered for the largest: 500 S&W, and smallest: 17HMR.

Ruger celebrates fifty years of fine single actions with this Anniversary Model 22 Single-Six 22LR/22WMR.

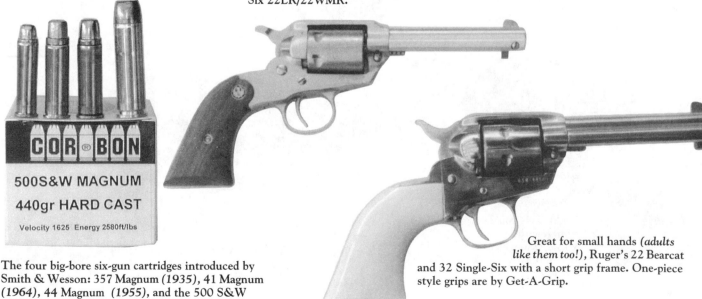

The four big-bore six-gun cartridges introduced by Smith & Wesson: 357 Magnum (*1935*), 41 Magnum (*1964*), 44 Magnum (*1955*), and the 500 S&W (*2003*).

Great for small hands (*adults like them too!*), Ruger's 22 Bearcat and 32 Single-Six with a short grip frame. One-piece style grips are by Get-A-Grip.

company by issuing an Anniversary Commemorative Model Red Eagle 22 semi-auto pistol. Now, four years later, it is time for the Ruger Single-Six 50th Anniversary Model. Bill Ruger correctly read the shooting public and resurrected the single-action revolver in 1953. He very wisely maintained the Colt grip shape, while scaling down the rest of the revolver to 22 rimfire size. The price in 1953 was a very affordable $63.25 and a whole box of 22s could be had for well under 50 cents. Single-Sixes have been favored by shooters ever since. The 50th Anniversary Model will feature a New Model Single-Six with a 4 5/8-inch barrel that will be marked "50 Years of Single-Six 1953 to 2003". Grips will be of coco bola and, for the first time ever, will have red eagle medallions. An extra cylinder chambered in 22 MRF will be included.

Last year Ruger reintroduced the 44 Magnum Super Blackhawk Hunter model, which I consider the greatest bargain available to the handgun hunter. With its 7 1/2-inch barrel, stainless-steel construction, and full-length barrel rib cut for the Ruger scope rings (included), a handgun hunter gets just about everything he needs. Now Ruger has made the Hunter Model even more attractive by providing a Bisley version. Most shooters find the Bisley grip frame handles felt recoil better than any other grip frame configuration. A great bargain just got better.

Ruger's Old Army, which is without doubt the finest cap and ball revolver ever produced, is now being offered in an easier-to-carry 5 1/2-inch version. It should find great favor with cowboy action shooters who prefer blackpowder. Cowboy action shooters will also appreciate that the 4 5/8-inch Bird's Head Vaquero is now offered in 357 Magnum. Last year Ruger introduced several rifles chambered in the new 17 HMR. They are followed with a 6 1/2-inch Single-Six chambered in this smallest of rimfires.

Two six-guns that were announced last year are now coming through regularly. Those two are the Bearcat in 22 rimfire and the Single-Six in 32 Magnum with a shorter grip frame—both in stainless steel. For these two small six-guns I used some of my grandkids as the field-testers and expert panel of judges to report upon their merits. Elyse (17), Laura (16), and Brian John (10), joined me to test the newest Ruger single actions. The Bearcat has a very small grip frame that fits the smallest hands, and the newest 32 Magnum features a grip frame approximately 1/4-inch shorter (top to bottom) than the standard Blackhawk grip frame. The kids liked the way this grip frame fit their relatively small hands. They work pretty well for the rest of us, too.

Taylor's & Co.

Taylor's has producing a line of quality replicas for several years. However, the big news is that Taylor's is now distributing R&D conversion

Ruger's standard model Old Army is now joined by a 5 1/2-inch version. Gunfighter grips are by Eagle grips, auxiliary 45 Colt cylinders are from Taylor's.

cylinders for both Remington replicas and Ruger Old Army percussion revolvers. I mentioned above the fact Ruger was now offering the Old Army in a 5 1/2-inch version. A pair of these was ordered in stainless steel, along with R&D 45 Colt conversion cylinders from Taylor's. The cylinders are not offered in stainless steel. However, one has a choice of blue or nickel finish, with the latter nicely matching the Ruger stainless-steel finish.

I was very impressed with the quality and workmanship of the cylinders and the fact that they work not only in these two Old Armies, but two older versions as well. To put these cylinders to use, the conversion ring is removed from the back, five cartridges are loaded in the six-shot cylinder, the conversion ring is replaced (lining up the pin hole with the corresponding pin on the cylinder), the cylinder is then replaced carefully (with the empty chamber under the hammer), and the Ruger Old Army cap-and-ball revolver is converted to use 45 Colt cartridges. I intend to use these guns and cylinders to shoot both Frontier Cartridge and Plainsman in cowboy action shooting matches.

Taurus

This company just continues to amaze—they not let any grass grow under their feet. For the new 17 Hornady Magnum Rimfire they have not only chambered their pump-action rifle, they now are offering shooters 10 six-gun choices. Shooters have a choice of both blue and stainless eight-shooters, or the new Model 17SS12. The "12" of this model number

Taylor's & Co. now offers the R&D 45 Colt Conversion Cylinder for Ruger's Old Army, here shown in the new 5 1/2-inch stainless steel model fitted with Eagle's checkered buffalo horn Gunfighter grips.

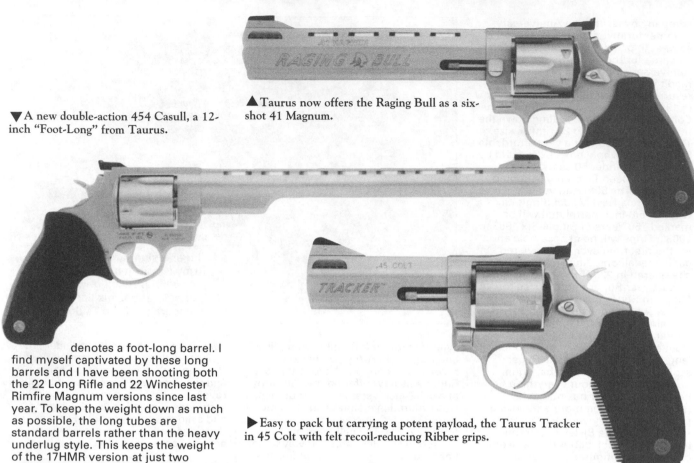

▲Taurus now offers the Raging Bull as a six-shot 41 Magnum.

▼A new double-action 454 Casull, a 12-inch "Foot-Long" from Taurus.

▶Easy to pack but carrying a potent payload, the Taurus Tracker in 45 Colt with felt recoil-reducing Ribber grips.

denotes a foot-long barrel. I find myself captivated by these long barrels and I have been shooting both the 22 Long Rifle and 22 Winchester Rimfire Magnum versions since last year. To keep the weight down as much as possible, the long tubes are standard barrels rather than the heavy underlug style. This keeps the weight of the 17HMR version at just two ounces over three pounds. Taurus calls this the "Perfect Gun and Ammunition Match for Coyote, Rabbit, Squirrel, Crow and Other Small Game Hunting." They could well be right and to further ensure this they include a free scope mount base with each foot-long 17.

The 17HMR, 22LR, and 22WMR 12-inch six-guns are now joined by centerfire versions in both 357 Magnum and 218 Bee, as well as two big-game hunting models chambered in 44 Magnum and 454 Casull. All have a vent-ribbed standard barrel, fully adjustable rear sight, Patridge front sight, cushioned rubber grips, and a weight of 3 pounds. The 44 is a standard six-shot revolver, while the 454 is a five-shooter. Taurus also offers an optional arm support that attaches to the grip and wraps around the forearm. It can be bent to give the required tension and has been given the *OK* by ATF.

Taurus' very popular Raging Bull has been offered in 44 Magnum, 454 Casull, and 480 Ruger. The connoisseur's other cartridge, the 41 Magnum has now been added to the line. Raging Bull's feature heavy underlug barrels, four ports on each side of the front sight, fully adjustable rear sight, Patridge front sight, and cushioned rubber grips. Scope mount bases are also offered. The Raging Bulls have now been joined by three other Raging Models, the Raging Hornet (22 Hornet), the Raging Bee (218 Bee), and the Raging Thirty (30 Carbine). These are all eight-shooters weighing two ounces over

three pounds with their 10-inch barrels. Scope mounts are also available for these varmint pistols.

For those that are looking for an easy-to-pack but potent six-gun, Taurus offers four 4-inch, five-shot Trackers chambered in 357 Magnum, 41 Magnum, 45 ACP, and 45 Colt. All of these feature heavy underlug barrels and the felt recoil-reducing wraparound "Ribber" grips. All but the 41 are also offered in a 6 1/2-inch vent rib model. This latter version also comes in 17HMR and 218 Bee. Taurus of course continues to offer a full line of revolvers for concealed carry, including the 2-inch CIA and Protector, in 38 Special and 357 Magnum, including Total Titanium versions in 38. The CIA is a hammerless, DAO five-shooter, while the

Protector has just enough of the hammer spur showing to allow cocking for single-action fire. Both models feature finger-grooved rubber grips.

Thompson/Center

T/C's Contender opened up new vistas for the handgun hunter more than three decades ago. The standard Contender frame was replaced last year with the new G2 Contender featuring an easier-to-open action, more room for the hand between the back of the trigger guard and front of the grip, and a hammer-block safety that does not require the action be re-opened if the shooter decides to lower the hammer, and then re-cock. On the old models, once the hammer was lowered, the

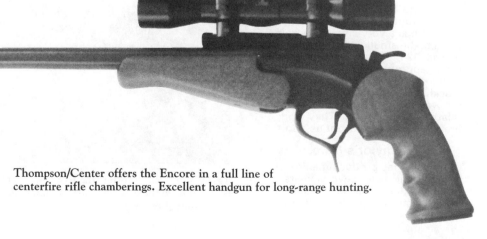

Thompson/Center offers the Encore in a full line of centerfire rifle chamberings. Excellent handgun for long-range hunting.

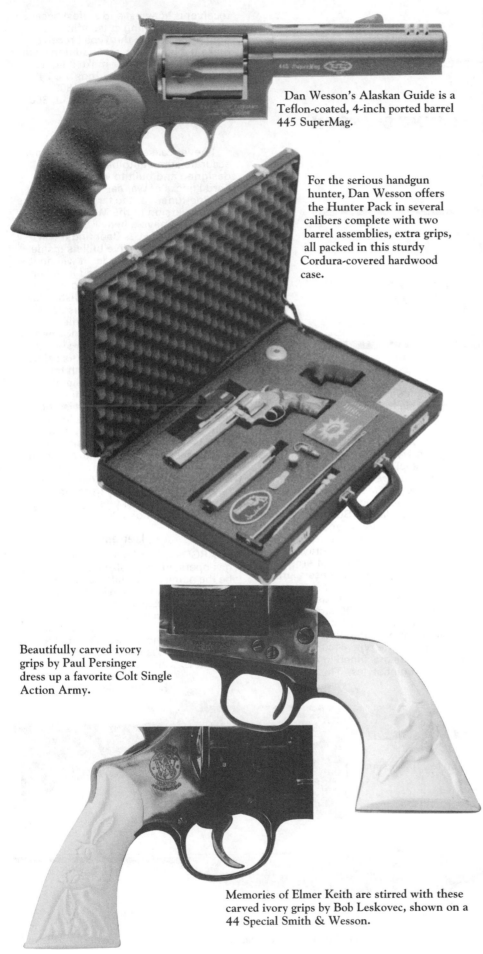

Dan Wesson's Alaskan Guide is a Teflon-coated, 4-inch ported barrel 445 SuperMag.

For the serious handgun hunter, Dan Wesson offers the Hunter Pack in several calibers complete with two barrel assemblies, extra grips, all packed in this sturdy Cordura-covered hardwood case.

Beautifully carved ivory grips by Paul Persinger dress up a favorite Colt Single Action Army.

Memories of Elmer Keith are stirred with these carved ivory grips by Bob Leskovec, shown on a 44 Special Smith & Wesson.

action had to be opened before it could be re-cocked. The G2 will accept all original Contender barrels; however, the grip frame is different and requires use of the new grip. As of this writing, G2s continue to be in short supply.

The G2 may be in short supply but the Encore is not. This stronger version of the Contender allows the use of high-pressure rifle cartridges above the level of the 44 Magnum/30-30 Contender. The Encore is offered in both 12-inch and 15-inch easy opening models in such chamberings as 454 Casull, 480 Ruger, 22-250 Remington, 25-06, 7-08, 308, 30-06, 45-70, and 450 Marlin and is also used for a whole range of wildcat cartridges from SSK Industries and Reeder Custom Guns. Thompson/Center continues to build the single-shot pistols by which all others are judged.

Wesson Firearms

Dan Wesson has been concentrating on introducing their Pointman series of semi-automatic 45s the past year, however they continue to offer the superbly accurate revolver created by Dan Wesson in 1968. All Dan Wesson revolvers feature easily interchangeable barrels and are offered in several versions—all in stainless steel with fully adjustable sights and finger-grooved rubber grips. The Small Frame is available in 22LR, 32 Magnum, 32-20, and 357 Magnum. Moving up to the Large Frame, we find 360DW, 41 Magnum, 44 Magnum, and 45 Colt. Wesson introduced the SuperMag cartridges designed by Elgin Gates in the 1980s and their SuperMag revolver is now offered in 445 SuperMag and 357 SuperMag. This revolver is also offered, with special sights, as the Super Ram Silhouette.

The Alaskan Guide Series is a special 445 SuperMag with a compensated 4-inch VH (Vent Heavy) barrel and the entire gun coated in the Teflon-based Yukon Coat to protect it from harsh weather. Other special offerings from Wesson Firearms include ported barrels; The Pistol Pack, featuring a revolver with three or four extra barrel assemblies; The Hunter Pack with two barrel assemblies, one scoped. Both Packs come packaged in a high-quality, foam-lined, Cordura-covered, locking hardwood case.

Carved Ivory Grips

I am one who likes to add a fancy touch to special six-guns in the form of custom grips. There is no better way to do this than with carved ivory.

For great carved ivory grips for single actions, Paul Persinger can be reached at 915-821-7541. Bob Leskovec offers excellent ivories for double actions, single actions, and semi-autos. He is found at 724-449-8360. We earlier mentioned Buffalo Brothers cast polymer grips for virtually every single action ever offered. They are at 480-986-7858 and are also on the web at www.buffalobrothers.net.

Have a great six-gunnin' year.

by LAYNE SIMPSON

RIFLE REVIEW

Anschutz

Julias Gottfried Anschutz started the company back in 1856 and one of his first products was a pocket pistol chambered for a brand new cartridge we now know as the 22 Short. A number of new products have been added to the catalog for 2003. Two are built around the Model 54 action and called 1710KL Monte Carlo and 1712 Silhouette Sporter. Both are in 22 Long Rifle and both are available with stocks classified as semi-fancy and Mastergrade. As you might not have guessed, neither is available in 17 HMR although the 1717D Classic and 1717D KL Monte Carlo are. Same goes for rifles on the Model 64 action; 1517D Classic, 1416D Heavy-Barrel Classic, 1517D Monte Carlo and 1517MPR Multi-Purpose with its heavy 25-1/2 inch barrel, high-comb buttstock and beavertail forearm. A 10-shot group I saw measured about .400-inch. It was shot at 55 yards with the 17-caliber Model 1517MPR/M-P.

DSA Incorporated

The lineup of civilian versions of the FN/FAL rifle from DSA keeps getting longer. I count fourteen SA58 variations ranging from the Tactical Carbine with a 16 1/4-inch barrel to the Gray Wolf with a 21-inch barrel. Blued carbon steel and stainless steel are available, as are synthetic and wood stocks. Some models come with scope mount and iron sights; others come only with the latter. Some models are fitted with a carrying handle; others are not. The finish is called Duracoat and it comes in Olive Drab and gray solid colors, as well as camo patterns such as Mossy Oak Breakup, desert, urban, winter twig, underbrush (my favorite), woodland, Belgian and tiger stripe. My favorites? I like the OD stock and handguard with blued steel. I also like the underbrush camo finish over the entire rifle. The type 4140 steel receivers are machined in America in three different styles. The standard

receiver is heaviest and stiffest because it has no lightening cuts. Minor lightening cuts in the Type I receiver make it a bit lighter, and additional cuts in the Type II receiver make it lighter still. Standard chamberings are 243 Winchester, 260 Remington, 308 Winchester and believe it or not, 300 WSM.

Les Baer

I never cease to be amazed at how accurate some autoloading rifles designed and built to withstand the hard knocks of war can be when they are fine-tuned for the target range. The civilian version of the M16 is a good example. I have a heavy-barrel AR-15 put together by Les Baer and it will consistently shoot five bullets inside half an inch at 100 yards. It will do it with several handloads and it will do it with Federal Premium ammo loaded with the Nosler 55-grain Ballistic Tip. Upon my suggestion, Les has decided to offer his super-accurate rifle in 6x45mm. The case is easily formed by necking up 223 brass for 6mm bullets. I have an old Kimber rifle in this caliber. When loaded to 2900 fps with the Nosler 85-grain Partition bullet the 6x45 is quite effective on whitetails out to 200 yards or so and recoil is not enough to notice. Load it to 3300 fps with the 55-grain Ballistic Tip and the 6x45 is not a bad varmint cartridge. The very latest from Baer is a tactical-style rifle called the Thunder Ranch. I have not shot this particular rifle but I have been to the place from which it gets its name and if you haven't you are missing out on a lot of fun.

Benelli

ARGO is short for auto-regulating, gas-operated and it also just happens to be the name a new autoloading rifle from Benelli goes by in Europe. In America it is called the R1, which also makes sense since it is Benelli's first rifle. To operate the action, propellant gas is tapped from the barrel closer to the chamber than is usually seen on other gas guns. The result, according to a Benelli spokesman, is less residue buildup inside the

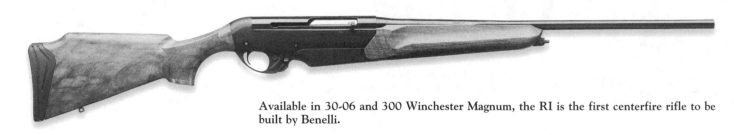

The SA58 rifle comes in a variety of weights, styles, finishes and calibers, including 300 WSM.

Available in 30-06 and 300 Winchester Magnum, the RI is the first centerfire rifle to be built by Benelli.

action. Three locking lugs on the rotating bolt head engage recesses in the barrel extension. The barrel is free-floating, compliments of a receiver-attached forearm. As I write this, two versions should be headed this way on the boat from Italy, one with a blued receiver in 30-06 and 300 Winchester Magnum, the other with its receiver covered with nickel plating and in 30-06 only. Regardless of which way you go, you end up with a rifle weighing around 7-1/4 pounds. The receiver is actually two-piece in design. The upper shell houses the bolt and is attached to the barrel. It is also drilled and tapped for scope mounting. The lower receiver houses everything else. The cryogenically treated barrel is 20-1/2 inches long. Shims included with the rifle can be used to adjust drop dimensions of the stock. Two types of detachable magazines are optional; one detaches like the magazine on a Remington Model 7400; the other will remind you of the Browning BAR. I carried a R1 carbine with a 20-inch barrel in 300 Magnum while hunting stag, boar and bear in the Transylvania mountains of Romania. The one issued to me there had the battue-style open sights that are still quite popular among the French, who take shots at driven game. As for me, I'd rather have had a good variable-power scope with either 1X or 1.5X at the lower end of its magnification range. I seldom hunt with autoloading centerfire rifles but if ever I decide to, the R1 might just be the one I will carry.

Blaser

The S2 Safari from Blaser is a double-barrel rifle with a rather unusual locking block. It is available in several elephant-stopping Nitro Express chamberings such as the 470 and 500. A scaled-down version is chambered for an old classic called the 9.3x74mm rimmed.

Browning

The new lightweight version of Browning's BLR leveraction is slated for availability in all the regular chamberings, plus 450 Marlin and 358 Winchester. I am happy to see someone once again offer a rifle chambered for the latter cartridge. I still own a 35-caliber Winchester Model

88 and I would take on any game animal in North America inside 200 yards with it. My favorite handload with either H4895 or IMR-4895 powder pushes the 225-grain Nosler Partition or Swift A-Frame bullet along at close to 2500 fps. The A-Bolt rifle is now available in a super-short action built especially for the 223 and 224 Winchester super-short magnums it is now chambered for.

Ed Brown

Ed Brown's new Model 702 Denali is a lighter version of the rifle he has been offering for several years. The match-grade barrel is hand-lapped and available in 23-inch lightweight or 22-inch super lightweight configuration. The action is glass-bedded in a McMillan synthetic stock. Available chamberings include all the popular numbers, including Remington's new 7mm and 300 Short Action Ultra Mag. Among other things, the Denali has a steel trigger guard/floorplate assembly, three-position safety and its receiver is drilled and tapped for 8-40 screws. It is rated at 6-3/4 pounds. Even lighter at 6-1/4 pounds is the Ozark. It has a shorter action, a slimmer 21-inch barrel and its synthetic stock is copied after the stock of the Remington Model Seven.

Cimarron

According to a Cimarron representative, the Sharps Rifle Company built only 36 rifles for the Texas Rangers and the 1863TR is a reproduction thereof. Offered in 45-70 and 50-70, its 22-inch barrel has six-groove rifling with a twist rate of 1:22 inches. Sights consist of a plain-blade front and a windage-adjustable rear.

CZ USA

Sometime back I wrote an article describing how much fun I had been having with a CZ 527 rifle in 7.62x39mm Russian. As luck would have it, CZ management decided to drop that chambering just as my story was published. But not for long. After receiving about a zillion requests from those who read my report, the decision-makers decided to bring back the 30-caliber Russian in 2003. It is a jewel of a little rifle with a miniature

Mauser action. They say it will also be available in another of my favorites, the 221 Remington Fire Ball.

Daisy

Since we do not have an air gun editor I don't believe I will be scolded for mentioning that Daisy is bringing back its copy of the Winchester Model 94. It holds 15 of those once-precious golden BBs. As it was for most kids who grew up in the 1950s, my first rifle was a Daisy. Branded on the side of its buttstock were Red Ryder and his sidekick, Little Beaver, both caught in mid-gallop as they headed to the pass to cut off the bad bunch. Like Ralphie's mother in "A Christmas Story" my mom was always warning me about "shooting out your eye with that thing", but I never did. What I did do was make life miserable for every English sparrow in the neighborhood. When combined with just a pinch of childhood imagination the Daisy was also just the ticket for transforming an old tree stump in the yard into a charging grizzly and for bouncing BBs off a tin can that looked for all the world like a ten-point buck.

European American Armory

Latest from this importer of economy-grade firearms is a Russian-made single shot with its own decocking system. Also built by Baikal is a combination gun with 22 rimfire barrel up top and a 410-bore barrel below deck.

A problem with the double-barrel rifle is you may not be able to find ammunition that shoots to the correct points of impact for which its barrels were regulated at the factory. According to management at EAA, the engineers at Baikal who designed the MP221 solved that potential problem by making one of its barrels regulation-adjustable. You simply zero the fixed barrel of the rifle with the ammunition you intend to use and then bring bullet point of impact of the other barrel to the same zero by adjusting it in the desired direction. Other features include automatic tang safety, double triggers, adjustable open sights, scope-mounting rail, extractors and walnut stock and forearm. The barrels are chrome-lined for rust resistance.

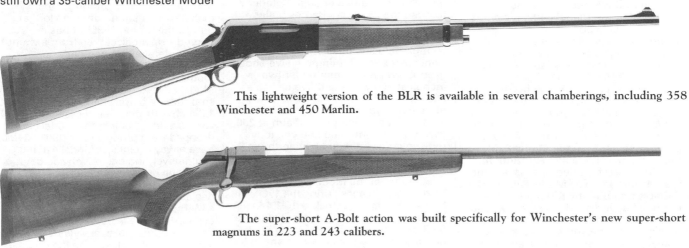

This lightweight version of the BLR is available in several chamberings, including 358 Winchester and 450 Marlin.

The super-short A-Bolt action was built specifically for Winchester's new super-short magnums in 223 and 243 calibers.

Also new from EAA is a Baikal single-shot rifle built on a beefed-up shotgun receiver. Among its features are an internal hammer, cocking indicator, hammer-forged and chrome-lined barrel, trigger-block safety, walnut stock and a very interesting decocking system. Chambering options are not available as I write this but my guess is they will at the very least include the 223, 308, 30-06 and several other popular numbers.

Henry Repeating Arms Co.

The name Big Boy sounds more appropriate for a cheeseburger with bacon, lettuce, tomato, onion and all the other trimmings than for a lever-action rifle but that's what somebody at Henry Repeating Arms decided to call the company's latest. Chambered for the 44 Magnum cartridge, it has a 20-inch octagon barrel with 1:38-inch rifling twist, weighs 8-3/4 pounds and measures 38-1/2 inches overall. The receiver, buttplate and barrel band are polished brass while the stock is walnut. Its sights are from Marble: brass-colored bead at the muzzle and a full-adjustable semi buckhorn out back. Come cowboy action-shooting time, I wouldn't be surprised to see a cowpoke or two gallop into town, slide to a screeching halt in a boil of dust and pull one of these from Old Paint's saddle scabbard. Henry has also added the 17 HMR to the list of options for its lever-action rimfire rifle.

High Tech Gun Works

George Vais has introduced a new muzzle brake and while I have not gotten round to giving it a try, he says muzzle blast perceived by the shooter is increased by only three decibels on a rifle in 300 Weatherby Magnum. As I write this, his brakes are available for all calibers up to 30 but larger calibers are in the works. You can contact George by calling 208-323-7674 or by writing to High Tech Gun Works, 182 South Cole Rd., Boise, ID 83708.

Kimber

Biggest news from Kimber for 2003 is the introduction of a scaled-up version of the Model 84M centerfire rifle. Called the Model 8400, it weighs 6-3/4 pounds (a pound heavier than the Model 84M) and is chambered for the 270, 7mm and 300 WSM cartridges. Four variations are available; Classic, Classic Left Hand, SuperAmerica and Montana. All have 24-inch barrels. Kimber's second synthetic-stocked rifle (the Model 84M Longmaster was first), the Model 8400 Montana is rated at six pounds, two ounces. This is about a pound heavier than the Model 82M Montana, which is also new. Both have stainless steel barreled actions, another first for Kimber. The Model 8400 CLH is the first rifle built by Kimber to have a left-hand action and I am sure it will not be the last. Kimber, by the way, is making its own synthetic stocks and I really like the way they look and feel.

Legacy Sports

Seems like everybody who is anybody is chambering rifles for the 300 WSM and Legacy Sports is no exception. This particular company is also offering the 270 and 7mm WSM chamberings. The Howa Model 1500WSM has a 24-inch barrel and is available in blued or stainless steel and with various stock options. Also new from Legacy is the Model 1500 Thumbhole Varminter Supreme in 223, 22-250 and 308 Winchester. In addition to the thumbhole styling the laminated wood stock has a palm swell, a straight, rollover comb and a ventilated forearm. Sure to get your undivided attention with the first squeeze of its trigger is the Brazilian-built Puma Model 92, a lever-action hammer gun in 454 Casull or 480 Ruger. It has a hardwood stock and (let us hope) a very thick and soft recoil pad.

Marlin

I have just about lost count of the number of black bears I have taken through the years but I will never forget the one I bagged on Vancouver Island in June of 2002. That hunt was special for two reasons; I was hunting with good friends and I was hunting with a rifle that brought my bear hunting days back full circle. The first bear I ever killed and one of the best I have taken fell victim during the early 1960s to my old Marlin Model 336 Sporting Carbine in 35 Remington. It wore its original factory iron sights. That bruin weighed 411 pounds on a local farmer's cotton scale—and that's big for my neck of the woods. My most recent bear was also taken with a Marlin but it was a 336CB in 38-55 Winchester. I made the hunt even more fun by leaving all my scopes at home and equipping the rifle with a Marble's tang sight sent to me by Frank Brownell. That bear was not quite as large as my first one but it was one of the biggest I have taken. Never in a thousand years will it happen again but I shot the 38th bear my guide Fred Lackey and I spotted. I'd like to say I shot the bear at 55 yards but the actual truth is, it was 43 yards away when I pulled the trigger. *Brer* bruin dropped in its tracks and never moved again. My handload contained enough Reloder 7 to push the 255-grain Barnes bullet along at just over 1800 fps, which comes close to duplicating the old 38-55 high-velocity loads once offered by Winchester and Remington. Five-shot groups averaged a hair under two inches at 100 yards and five inches at 200. With the rifle zeroed two inches high at 100 yards those big, fat bullets landed dead on my point of aim at 200 yards. Try it sometime and you may rediscover as I did that having to get close before you pull the trigger is as much fun as it used to be.

Remember the Model 336 Marauder sold by Marlin back during the 1960s? It had a straight-grip stock, a 16 1/4-inch barrel and it was available in 30-30 and 35 Remington. A friend of mine by the name of Jimmy Davis owned one in 35

caliber and I really liked it. (At the time I hunted with a Model 336SC in the same caliber.) At any rate, Marlin's new Spikehorn variation of America's favorite deer rifle has a 16 1/2-inch barrel and except for its curved grip, it reminds me a lot of my old deer-hunting partner's Marauder. I used to hunt black bear with hounds in some of the steepest, roughest country the mountains in my neck of the woods had to offer and if I were to do it again, the Spikehorn in 35 Remington is the medicine I would carry if I didn't tote a handgun. It weighs a feathery 6-1/2 pounds, and at 34 inches it is not much longer than your arm.

Marlin is now offering the 45 Colt chambering in its Model 1894 Cowboy Competition and, while it obviously is aimed at the cowboy action shooting market, my guess is more will be bought by deer hunters. When handloaded to its true potential the old Colt cartridge is more effective on whitetails at woods ranges than the 44 Magnum, or so say a couple of friends of mine. Both hunt with 45-caliber Ruger Blackhawks in country where deer season is over four months long and there is no bag limit on bucks, so they should know. The 1894CBC has a straight-grip stock, a 20-inch octagon barrel with Ballard-style rifling and its magazine holds 10 rounds. The case-colored receiver really looks nice. Since its action is slicked-up by hand before it leaves the factory the lever travels to and fro like it is riding on oil-suspended roller bearings. The grand old firm of Marble's makes the sights, a fully-adjustable semibuckhorn at the back and a blade up front. Another new Model 1894 variation is called the PG (which is short for pistol-grip stock?). Available in 44 Magnum (also uses 44 Special ammo), its 20-inch barrel has Ballard-style rifling. And if all that isn't enough to make lever-gun fans occupied for the next 12 months, Marlin has also brought back the 41 Magnum chambering in the Model 1894.

I thought the 450 Marlin was a good idea because it is a way for those who do not handload to enjoy the power those of us who do handload have, for many years, been squeezing from the old 45-70 Government cartridge. I consider the 450 an even better idea now that Marlin is offering it in a 22-inch barrel. In addition to its longer barrel, the Model 1895MR has a curved-grip stock carved from a walnut tree, replete with recoil pad.

Back in 1929 Marlin introduced the Model 410 shotgun, a variation of the Model 93 lever-action rifle with a smoothbore barrel chambered for the 2 1/2-inch .410 shotshell. Less than 10,000 were produced before the model was dropped from production in 1932. If you have always wanted a Model 410 but could never find one or you could not afford the one you did find, you need to pay another visit to your local Marlin dealer. There, sitting on his shelf, will be a Model 410 built on the Model 336 action. It will have a 22-inch smoothbore barrel with no choke, or Cylinder Bore as it is commonly called. Like the original

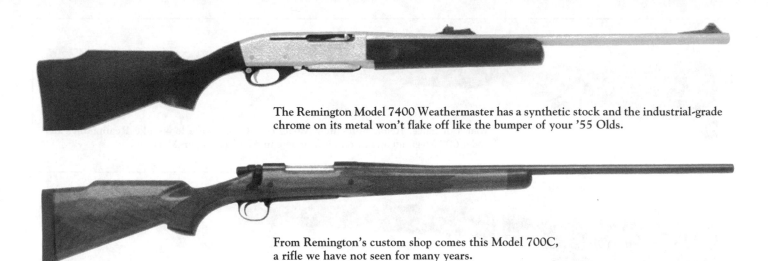

The Remington Model 7400 Weathermaster has a synthetic stock and the industrial-grade chrome on its metal won't flake off like the bumper of your '55 Olds.

From Remington's custom shop comes this Model 700C, a rifle we have not seen for many years.

Model 410, it is chambered for the 2 1/2-inch shell and its magazine holds four of them. In addition to its cut-checkered walnut stock, the gun has rifle-style sights, fully adjustable rear and a beaded ramp up front replete with a snap-on fiber optic sight. Come September, I will be hunting caribou in the Northwest Territories and plan to take a Model 410 along. Who knows, I might bump into a ptarmigan or something.

Merkel

One of the rifles I would like to have brought home from the SHOT Show was the Merkel single-shot stalking rifle. Both variations are built on the Franz Jager break-open action. The Model K-1 is the standard version with modest checkering on the sides of its boxlock action. Moving up to quite a bit more money is the Model K-2 with octagon barrel, express-style rear sight and ornate engraving on its sideplates. Both models come with scope mounting rings in your choice of one inch or 30mm. Nominal weight is only 5-1/2 pounds. To cock the rifle you simply push its tang safety slide all the way forward, same as the safety on the Krieghoff double-barrel rifle. Pulling the safety to the rear decocks the firing pin and places the rifle on safe. Rifles imported to America will be in 243 Winchester, 270 Winchester, 7x57R, 308 Winchester, 30-06, 7mm Remington Magnum, 300 Winchester Magnum and 9.3x74mm. What a great sheep rifle this one in 270 would make. When fitted out with a lightweight leather carrying sling and a Burris or Leupold 3-9X compact scope, the entire rig would weigh about seven pounds.

M.O.A. Corporation

The M.O.A. single-shot pistol with its falling-block action has long been available in a rifle version with buttstock and longer barrel. The tangs on the latest version of the receiver are machined at a different angle and the added beef in the buttstock makes it more resistant to breakage. Through the years I have shot M.O.A. handguns

and rifles in various chamberings and all were capable of shooting five bullets inside an inch at 100 yards. Only recently I shot a heavy-barrel gun in 260 Remington and it averaged 0.72-inch with 45.0 grains of Reloder 19 and the Nosler 120-grain Ballistic Tip. I plan to try the 6.5-284 Norma in this gun. Name a rimfire or centerfire cartridge and chances are good M.O.A. chambers for it. To name but a few more: 17 Remington, 17 HMR, 22 Long Rifle, 220 Swift, 243 Winchester, 25-06, 280 Remington, 308 Winchester, 338-06, 350 Remington Magnum, 375 H&H Magnum and 454 Casull.

Navy Arms

The "Cowboy Combo" from Navy Arms includes two guns, both chambered for the grand old 32-20 Winchester cartridge. One is a single-action revolver and the other is a copy of the Winchester Model 92 lever gun. Buy one of these packages along with a second revolver, a Winchester '97 shotgun and a couple thousand dollars worth of costume and you will be ready to out-cowboy the best of them.

New England Firearms

I recently examined two versions of the Harrington & Richardson single-shot rifle offered by New England Arms and was impressed. The Buffalo Classic is chambered for the 45-70, weighs eight pounds and has a 32-inch barrel. About a half-pound lighter, the Target Model has a 28-inch barrel in 38-55 Winchester. The guns have case-coloring on their receivers and cut checkering on their walnut stocks. Both wear a Williams receiver sight at the rear and a globe-style target sight with eight interchangeable aperture inserts up front. Last but certainly not least from New England, the 7mm-08 Remington chambering is now available in standard and youth versions of the Handi-Rifle. Respective lengths of pull of the hardwood stocks are 14-1/4 and 11-3/4 inches. The stocks wear recoil pads and carrying sling swivels.

Remington

From a distance Remington's new Model 673 Guide Rifle looks a lot like my old Model 600 carbine. Both are in 350 Remington Magnum, both have laminated wood stocks and both have ventilated ribs replete with fully adjustable sights sitting atop their barrels. The Model 673 has even inherited the shark fin-style front sight of the Model 600. Up close it is easier to see that the Model 673 is built around the Model Seven action, which is basically an improved version of the Model 600 action that was a repeating version of the XP-100 pistol action. Got that straight? Back in August of 2002 I managed to get my hands on the only Model 673 in existence at the time and I was greatly impressed by the quality and workmanship. Wood to metal fit was excellent, as were the wood and metal finishes. With a Burris 3-9X compact scope it weighed exactly 8-3/4 pounds. This compares to 7-1/2 pounds for my Model 600 and its Weaver 1.5X scope. The 22-inch barrel of the Model 673 is 3-1/2 inches longer and it has a heavier contour. This, plus the fact that its barrel rib is steel as opposed to the synthetic rib of the Model 600, explains most of the weight difference. That first Model 673 was not quite as accurate as my old Model 600 but it was accurate enough for shooting a brown bear as far away as should be attempted. My favorite handload for the 350 Magnum— Remington case, Remington 9-1/2 primer, 59.0 grains of W748 and the Nosler 225-grain Partition produced five-shot groups averaging 1.8 inches at 100 yards. Velocity was just over 2700 fps. A few months later I tried Remington's new 200-grain factory load in another Model 673 and, while I did not have an opportunity to check out velocity, it averaged 1.3 inches at 100 yards.

As far as I know, Remington has offered the 300 Savage chambering in more different rifles than any other company. I once owned a Model 722 in that caliber and still own a Model 81. Early on, the Model 760 pump gun was also available in 300 Savage. Add one more to the list as the limited edition

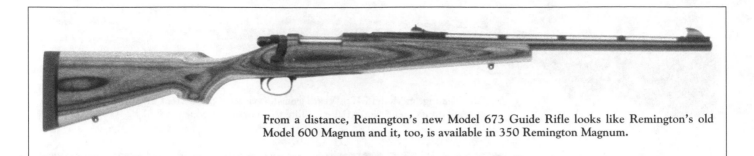

From a distance, Remington's new Model 673 Guide Rifle looks like Remington's old Model 600 Magnum and it, too, is available in 350 Remington Magnum.

The 24-inch barrel of this Remington Model 700 BDL is now chambered to 7mm and 300 Short Action Ultra Mag.

Model 700 Classic with a 24-inch barrel will be chambered for the 300 Savage during 2003. The one I shot averaged 1.55 inches overall for five-shot groups at 100 yards with three handloads and five factory loads. Remington's 180-grain roundnose Core-Lokt loading won the factory ammo contest with an average of 1.4 inches at a velocity of 2412 fps. The most accurate handload at 1.1 inches consisted of the Remington case, Remington 9-1/2 primer and 40.0 grains of Reloder 7 pushing the 125-grain Nosler Ballistic Tip along at an average muzzle velocity of 3048 fps. I really like that bullet and powder combination for shooting whitetails and pronghorn antelope at ranges exceeding 100 yards with the 300 Savage. With the charge weight of RL-7 reduced to 38.0 grains my old Savage Model 99 averages 2829 fps and 2.1 inches at 100 yards. That same combination delivers 2862 fps and groups averaging 1.7 inches in my Remington Model 81. Both guns wear iron sights.

Remington's highly successful 7mm and 300 Short Action Ultra Mag chamberings are now available in the Model 700 BDL/SS and the Model 700 Sendero SF. As you may have already correctly guessed, the former is the original Model 700 BDL with a synthetic stock and a stainless steel barreled action. It has a 24-inch barrel. Also a combination of synthetic and stainless steel, the Model 700 Sendero SF has a 26-inch fluted barrel. Both rifles have hinged floorplates and a magazine capacity of three rounds. I shot the Sendero in 300 Short Action Ultra Mag with Remington ammo loaded with the new 150-grain Core-Lokt Ultra bullet and five-shot groups averaged just about dead on an inch at 100 yards.

Remington officials have long refused to chamber a Remington rifle for any cartridge not loaded at its Lonoke, Arkansas ammunition plant so it comes as no surprise to see the company introduce a 17 HMR factory load along with Model 597 rifles chambered for it. I believe this makes Remington first to offer an autoloading rifle chambered for

this close-range varmint cartridge. Called the Model 597 Magnum LS, it weighs six pounds, has a gray laminated wood stock, a 20-inch button-rifled barrel and measures 40 inches overall. Barrel and action have a satin blue finish. The detachable magazine holds eight rounds. I shot one down in Florida and it averaged just under 1-1/4 inches for five shots at 100 yards.

The third annual limited-edition Model 700 Remington is building for the Rocky Mountain Elk Foundation is chambered for the 300 Short Action Ultra Mag. The synthetic stock has the Realtree Hardwoods Gray camo finish with the RMEF logo laser-etched into its right-hand side. All metal is stainless steel, including the 24-inch barrel. This rifle will be available only during 2003 and each will come with a paid membership in the RMEF. Remington also plans to donate a portion of the sales to the foundation.

Considering how popular synthetics and rust-resisting metals have become among American hunters, it comes as no surprise to see the Model 7400 autoloader wearing both. The Model 7400 Weathermaster (great name) has a black synthetic stock and forearm and all metal is covered with an industrial grade nickel that won't chip or flake like the plating did on the bumpers of your old '55 Oldsmobile. For now it is available in the world's two most popular big-game cartridges, 30-06 Springfield and 270 Winchester. The one I shot was in 270 and it averaged less than two inches for five shots with Remington's 130-grain Bronze Point load. Due to its weight of about 8-1/2 pounds (with scope) and its gas-operated action, it was extremely comfortable to shoot. Phyllis enjoys shooting it so well Remington may never get it back. Incidentally, if "Weathermaster" rings a bell to some of you old-timers out there it is because Remington has given other rifles similar names in the past. I still own a Model 81 Woodsmaster in 300 Savage and once owned a Model 141 Gamemaster in 30 Remington. Just

thinking about those old names brings back memories of times and places none of us will ever again see.

During the mid-1960s Remington started building a rifle called the Model 700 Custom. It was basically the Model 700 BDL with an oil finish and cut checkering on its stock, all with a price tag of $334.95. At the time, the standard Model 700 BDL had a plastic finish and impressed checkering on its stock and it sold for $144.95. I believe the 700C also had a rosewood forend and grip cap. The original Model 700C was discontinued years ago but those clever craftsmen in Remington's custom shop are bringing it back in 2003. Everything the old one had is seen in the new one, including figured walnut with satin finish, cut checkering, rosewood forend and grip cap, and hinged floorplate. Barrel lengths are 26 inches for the Ultra Mags and 24 inches for everything else.

The R3 recoil pad from Remington is darned amazing. As one of Remington's engineers put it, the new recoil pad incorporates a decay time modification system that displaces shock on a broadband spectrum to ensure maximum relief from recoil. In language you and I can better understand, the thing reduces perceived recoil better than any pad I have tried–and I have tried them all. Beginning in 2003 the R3 will be available on eight Remington firearms, all with synthetic stocks; Model 700 BDL/SS, Model 700 BDL/SS/DM, Model 11-87 Special Purpose Synthetic, Model 11-87 Super Magnum SPS, Model 870 SPS, Model 870 Super Magnum SPS, Model SP-10 Magnum Synthetic and Model 1100 Competition Match synthetic. It will also be available as an accessory for retrofitting to various synthetic-stocked versions of the Model 710, Model 700 (ADL and BDL), Model 700 ML, Model 7600, Model 11-87, Model 1100 and Model 870.

Rogue Rifle Co.

The Chipmunk, a lightweight, scaled-down, 2-1/2 pound rifle made just for kids is now available in a number of variations, including walnut or laminated-wood stock and standard-weight or varmint-weight barrel. Its chamberings are 22 Long Rifle, 22 WMR and, new for 2003, the 17 HMR. Santas who buy rifles chambered for the latter cartridge for hiding beneath the Christmas tree should remember to include a few boxes of the equally new Remington and CCI ammunition.

Rossi

The 17 HMR bandwagon becomes even more crowded with the introduction of Rossi's single-shot rifle for this cartridge. One version has a shortened length of pull for kids or anybody else with short arms.

Ruger

Ruger is now offering the 17 HMR chambering in two variations of its Model 77 bolt-action rifle, and in the Model 96 lever action as well. The Model 77/17 Varmint has a heavy 24-inch barrel and a black laminated hardwood stock. It weighs seven pounds. The stainless steel barreled action has Ruger's attractive "Target Grey" finish. Weighing a pound less, the standard Model 77/17 has a sporter-weight 22-inch barrel and a synthetic stock. As far as I know, the Model 96/17 is the first lever-action rifle to become available in 17 HMR. An aluminum receiver brings its weight down to a feathery 5-1/4 pounds. The stock is hardwood. All three rifles utilize the same excellent nine-round rotary magazine. Also new from Ruger are the 458 Lott and 405 Winchester chamberings in the No. 1 single-shot rifle.

Savage

Savage rifles have long had a reputation for excellent mechanical accuracy, but poor trigger quality has often made them difficult to shoot to their true potential. The new AccuTrigger being offered on several variations of the Model 110 rifle should

take care of that. Using a special tool that comes with the rifle, the trigger is easily adjusted to a pull weight as light as 1-1/2 pounds, yet its design resists accidental discharge should the rifle be jarred or dropped. This is due to the fact that sear travel is blocked until the shooter pulls the AccuRelease lever resting alongside the trigger fingerpiece. Sounds complicated but it is quite simple and should work very well. Savage is also expanding the lineup of chambering options in its Model 110 rifles by adding Remington's short and long Ultra Mags in 7mm and 300 calibers. Savage is also adding the 17 HMR chambering to several of its rimfire rifles, including the Model 93 and Model 30R.

Schuerman Arms Ltd.

Remember how smooth the bolts were on the Colt Sauer or perhaps that old sporterized Krag-Jorgensen you once hunted with? I surely do and sliding the bolt of the Schuerman Arms SA40 to and fro reminded me of those rifles. Like the Colt rifle, the SA40 has pivoting locking lugs but they are located close to the front of the bolt rather than at the rear. Placing the locking lugs up front minimizes receiver stretch and practically eliminates bolt compression during firing. The result is longer case life for the handloader. Other features include a recessed bolt face, firing pin cocking indicator, match-grade trigger, extremely quick locktime and center-feed detachable magazine. Chambering options range from the 7mm STW to the 416 Remington Magnum.

SIGARMS

The new S2 Safari from SIGARMS is a double-barrel rifle with a manual cocking system. A list of available chamberings is not available as I write this.

Taurus

Taurus has expanded its line of Brazilian-made Winchester Model 62 and Model 63 reproductions. The

Model 62 pump gun is available in stainless or blued steel and in 22 Long Rifle, 22 WMR and 17 HMR chamberings. You can also get the carbon steel gun with a blued or case-colored receiver finish. Rifles with 23-inch barrels and carbines with 16 1/2-inch barrels are available. Nominal weights are 4-1/2 pounds for the former and 5 pounds for the latter. Tubular magazine capacities range from 10 to 13 depending on the cartridge. Button-rifled barrels and fully adjustable sights are standard. Extra-cost options include a folding tang sight, barrel-attached scope mounting base and a plastic carrying case. Then we have the 4-1/2 pound Model 63 autoloader with a 23-inch barrel in the same three chamberings. Like the original built by Winchester from 1933 to 1958, it has a 10-round tubular magazine in its buttstock. Unlike the original, the Taurus rifle has a lock on its bolt that prevents the gun from being fired by anyone except those who hold its key. Taurus offers a folding tang sight for this one as well. Remember the speed loaders used by hawkers at the county fair to fill the magazines of gallery rifles? A plastic version of the old reloading tube is now available from Taurus and it works on any 22 rimfire rifle with a tubular magazine.

Thompson/Center

The 22-caliber autoloader from T/C is now available in a heavy-barrel version called the Classic Match. Of laminated wood, the stock has a high Monte Carlo-style comb and a beavertail forearm. The 18-inch barrel has a blued finish, as does the receiver. The detachable magazine holds 10 Long Rifle cartridges. Then we have the G2 Contender, a single-shot rifle built on the latest version of the Contender handgun action and with 23-inch interchangeable barrels. Stock and forearm are American walnut and neither is checkered. Optional chamberings for now are 17 HMR, 22 Long Rifle Match, 223 Remington,

You rainy weather hunters out there can now buy a Weatherby Vanguard with synthetic stock and stainless steel barreled action.

Once sold only at "mart" stores, the Weatherby Vanguard *(in a special edition)* is now available at your friendly neighborhood gun shop.

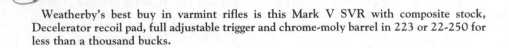

Weatherby's best buy in varmint rifles is this Mark V SVR with composite stock, Decelerator recoil pad, full adjustable trigger and chrome-moly barrel in 223 or 22-250 for less than a thousand bucks.

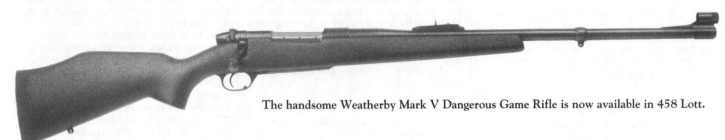

The handsome Weatherby Mark V Dangerous Game Rifle is now available in 458 Lott.

30-30 Winchester and 45-70 Government. The 45-caliber muzzleloader barrel uses #209 shotshell primers for ignition. Overall length is a compact 37 inches and weight is less than 5-1/2 pounds. Carbine barrels made for the old Contender will fit this one as well. T/C has also added the 375 Holland & Holland Magnum chambering to the list of options for its Encore rifle line.

Tikka

The T3 rifle from Tikka is now available with a wood or synthetic stock and in stainless or blued steel. Its chamberings include 223, 22-250, 243, 25-06, 7mm Remington Magnum, 270 WSM and 300 WSM.

USRAC

The 17 HMR is now available in two USRAC rifles. One, called the Model 94/17 is nothing less than the Winchester 94/22 with a smaller diameter hole through its barrel. Another is the neat little Model 1885 Winchester single-shot Low Wall rifle.

Quite sometime back USRAC added a transverse safety button to the receiver of the Winchester Model 94 rifle. It has now been replaced by a sliding button on the upper tang. The new safety works great and, while it is more convenient to operate than the old safety, it might not be quite as foolproof. Members of the Rocky Mountain Elk Foundation are excited about a new Model 70 rifle to be built during 2003 just for them. Called the Super Grade Stainless, it is chambered in 300 Winchester Magnum.

Volquartsen

I own three of Tom Volquartsen's incredibly accurate autoloading rifles and all are favorites. One is in 22 Long Rifle, another is in 22 WMR and the other, called the Firefly, is in 22 Short. Last summer I had a ball shooting prairie dogs out to 150 yards or so with the rifle in 22 WMR. It shot inside 3/4-inch at 100 yards with two loads, Remington 33-grain green tip and Federal Premium loaded with the Speer 30-grain TNT hollowpoint. That same

rifle is now available with interchangeable barrels in 22 WMR and 17 WMR. I plan to get one, if for no other reason than to once again prove something I discovered years ago while shooting the 17 Hornet—the 17 HMR is actually inferior to the 22 WMR in the varmint field.

Weatherby

During the past few years the Weatherby Vanguard has been available only in a "mart" version and sold through discount houses across the nation, but real gun shops run by people who know a thing or two about guns now have versions that will be available only from them. They are the Synthetic and Synthetic Stainless versions in a lineup of selected chamberings that includes the 300 WSM. Among other things, the Vanguard has an injection-molded stock made by Butler Creek, forged receiver, 24-inch hammer-forged barrel, hinged floorplate with release button inside the trigger guard, an easy-to-see cocking indicator and fully adjustable trigger. Each rifle comes from the factory with its own three-shot group measuring 1-1/2 inches or less. All of this at a suggested retail price of less than $500 for the Synthetic.

Latest edition of the Weatherby Mark V is the Special Varmint Rifle with a 22-inch, medium-heavy, chrome-moly barrel in 223 or 22-250. Its hand-laminated composite stock consists of Aramid fibers combined with unidirectional graphite and glass fibers and it is finished in black with gray spiderwebbing. The stock also wears a Pachmayr Decelerator recoil pad. While the barrel is free-floating, the action rests in a CNC-machined aluminum bedding block in the stock. Other features include six locking lugs, 54-degree bolt lift and a weight of 7-1/4 pounds.

For many years Weatherby has guaranteed 1-1/2 inch accuracy for three shots at 100 yards with good ammo in its rifles and, while most I have shot did better than that, you can now own a Mark V capable of shooting three bullets into an inch. Accumark

As the engraving on its bolt indicates, this Weatherby Mark V is guaranteed to shoot three bullets inside an inch at 100 yards.

The new drop box magazine from Weatherby is easily installed and it increases cartridge capacity of the Mark V rifle to four for the big boys (30-378 through 460 Magnums), five for magnums from 257 Weatherby to 458 Lott and seven for chamberings such as the 270 Winchester and 30-06.

and Super VarmintMaster versions of the Mark V are guaranteed to average less than minute-of-angle with specified factory ammo are now available from Weatherby's custom shop. As I explain in my "Testfire" report included elsewhere in this edition of GUN DIGEST, each rifle will have "Sub-Moa" engraved on its bolt.

Equally new from Weatherby's custom shop is the 458 Lott chambering in the Dangerous Game Rifle. Built around the Mark V action, the DGR in this caliber has a Monte Carlo-style synthetic stock, 25-inch chrome-moly barrel, Decelerator recoil pad, express-style rear sight with gold-filled shallow "V", hooded barrel-band style front sight with large gold bead, black oxide metal finish and front sling swivel post-mounted out on the barrel as it should be on any rifle chambered for a hard-kicking cartridge. Also available in other

Weatherby magnum chamberings such as the 375, 416 and 460, the DGR weighs 8-3/4 pounds and comes in black, desert camo and snow camo.

Another great idea from Atascadero is a drop-box magazine that increases the capacity of Mark V rifles chambered for Weatherby's 30-378, 338-378, 416 and 460 Magnum cartridges to four rounds with one in the chamber. The magazine I tried worked without a hitch and you can bet my 416 will soon wear one. Easily retrofitted to both Japanese- and American-built Mark Vs, it increases the capacity of rifles chambered for smaller magnums such as the 257 Weatherby and 458 Lott to a total of five cartridges. Rifles in standard calibers like the 30-06 and 338-06 will hold a total of seven cartridges,

with one up the spout. Suggested retail is $150. From what I see, anyone owning a small wood chisel and having less than 10 thumbs should be able to install the new magazine but those who had rather not do it themselves can have the custom shop do it for an additional $25.

Weatherby Performance Wool Clothing

Since we have no clothing editor I believe it would not be inappropriate for me to mention how impressed I have been with the Performance Wool clothing lineup introduced last year by Weatherby. In lieu of a wool/cotton blend as seen in wool garments from other manufacturers, Wade Krinke, Weatherby's director of soft goods, decided to incorporate a viscose synthetic fiber for increased tear resistance and to make the garments more shrink-resistant during laundering. A hydrophobic synthetic lining traps heat from the body while wicking moisture away from the skin and into the outer wool shell for rapid evaporation and drying. In laymen's terms, the stuff keeps you warm when it is cold without boiling you in your own sweat when the weather warms up at mid-day. Other features include articulated elbows for comfort, two durable layers of fabric at knees and elbows, heavy-duty zippers that work every time and suspenders included with the pants. It all works, too. I wore the parka, double-yoke shirt, cargo pant and ice cap while hunting for bear and stag in the frigid Transylvania mountains of Romania and stayed warm as toast even at an average daily temperature of about 20 degrees Fahrenheit. My only complaint is the clothing can be too good at times. While it is great for sitting or standing still with the thermometer bottomed out, it is a bit too warm for a lot of walking. This is why I am happy to see the same high quality in a lighter 14-ounce fabric ready for a 2003 introduction. The color options are Late Season Gray and High Desert Brown. ●

Layne's new 325-page book, *Rifles and Cartridges For Large Game,* is in hardback, 8-1/2x11" format and is illustrated with over 150 color photos. Autographed copies are available for $39.95 plus $5 for shipping and handling from High Country Press, 306 Holly Park Lane, Dept. GD, Simpsonville, SC 29681.

Weatherby's new line of wool clothing proved to be just the ticket for a cold-weather hunt in the Transylvania mountains of Romania.

THE 2004 GUN DIGEST WEB DIRECTORY

by Holt Bodinson

WE ARE BECOMING a world of "e-citizens" involved in a World Wide Web of "e-commerce." The pace of this new electronic technology is dramatic. Consider the fact that after electricity was introduced in the U.S., it took 46 years for 30 percent of homes to be wired while the Internet took only seven years to penetrate 30 percent of American households.

In the latest research by the Pew Charitable Trusts, 70 percent of American parents have used the Internet while fully 75 percent of American youths under 18 have Internet access. More importantly, 80 percent of Internet users expect a business to have a web site.

Still, Verizon Communications reports that nearly 70 percent of the 5.6 million small businesses in the U.S., the engines of the economy, still don't maintain a web site. This may be true in the broader picture, but the firearms industry is doing just fine on the Internet.

The Gun Digest Web Directory is in its fifth year of publication. The trend is clear. More and more firearm related businesses are striking out and creating their own discrete web pages, and it's never been easier with the inexpensive software programs now available.

The Internet is a dynamic environment and since our last edition, there have been numerous changes. Companies have consolidated and adopted a new owner's web site address. New companies have appeared and old companies have disappeared. Search engines are now more powerful than ever and seem to root out even the most obscure reference to a product name or manufacturer.

The following index of current web addresses is offered to our readers as a convenient jumping-off point. Half the fun is just exploring what's out there. Considering that most of the web pages have hot links to other firearm-related web pages, the Internet trail just goes on-and-on once you've taken the initial step to go online.

Here are a few pointers:

If the web site you desire is not listed, try using the full name of the company or product, typed without spaces, between www.-and-.com, for example, www.krause.com. Probably 95 percent of current Web sites are based on this simple, self-explanatory format.

Try a variety of search engines like Microsoft Internet Explorer, Metacrawler, GoTo.com, Yahoo, HotBot, AltaVista, Lycos, Excite, InfoSeek, Looksmart, Google, and WebCrawler while using key words such as gun, firearm, rifle, pistol, blackpowder, shooting, hunting—frankly, any word that relates to the sport. Each search engine seems to comb through the World Wide Web in a different fashion and produces different results. We find Google to be among the best. Accessing the various search engines is simple. Just type www.google.com for example, and you're on your way.

Welcome to the digital world of firearms. Enjoy our Directory!

WEB DIRECTORY

AMMUNITION AND COMPONENTS

3-D Ammunition www.3dammo.com
Accurate Arms Co. Inc www.accuratepowder.com
ADCO/Nobel Sport Powder www.adcosales.com
Aguila Ammunition www.aguilaammo.com
All Purpose Ammunition www.dragonbreath.com
Alliant Powder www.alliantpowder.com
American Ammunition www.a-merc.com
Ammo Depot www.ammodepot.com
Arizona Ammunition, Inc. www.arizonaammunition.com
A-Zoom Ammo www.a-zoom.com
Ballistic Products,Inc. www.ballisticproducts.com
Barnes Bullets www.barnesbullets.com
Baschieri & Pellagri www.baschieri-pellagri.com
Beartooth Bullets www.beartoothbullets.com
Bell Brass www.bellbrass.com
Berger Bullets, Ltd. www.bergerbullets.com
Berry's Mfg., Inc. www.berrysmfg.com
Big Bore Bullets of Alaska www.awloo.com/bbb/index.htm
Big Bore Express www.bigbore.com
Bismuth Cartridge Co. www.bismuth-notox.com
Black Hills Ammunition, Inc. www.black-hills.com
Brenneke of America Ltd. www.brennekeusa.com
Buffalo Arms www.buffaloarms.com
Bull-X inc. www.bull-x.com
Calhoon, James, Bullets www.jamescalhoon.com
Cartuchos Saga www.saga.es
Cast Performance Bullet www.castperformance.com
CCI www.cci-ammunition.com
Century Arms www.centuryarms.com
Cheaper Than Dirt www.cheaperthandirt.com
Cheddite France www.cheddite.com
Claybuster Wads www.claybusterwads.com
Clean Shot Powder www.cleanshot.com
Cole Distributing www.cole-distributing.com
Combined Tactical Systems www.less-lethal.com
Cor-Bon/Glaser www.cor-bon.com
Denver Bullet Co. denbullets@aol.com
Dillon Precision www.dillonprecision.com
DKT, Inc. www.dktinc.com
Dynamit Nobel RWS Inc. www.dnrws.com
Elephant/Swiss Black Powder www.elephantblackpowder.com
Eley Ammunition www.remington.com
Eley Hawk Ltd. www.eleyhawk.com
Eley Limited www.eley.co.uk
Estate Cartridge www.estatecartridge.com
Extreme Shock Munitions www.extremeshockusa.com
Federal Cartridge Co. www.federalcartridge.com
Fiocchi of America www.fiocchiusa.com
Fowler Bullets www.benchrest.com/fowler
Garrett Cartridges www.garrettcartridges.com
Gentner Bullets www.benchrest.com/gentner/
Glaser Safety Slug, Inc. www.corbon.com
GOEX Inc. www.goexpowder.com
Graf & Sons www.grafs.com
Hawk Bullets www.hawkbullets.com
Hevi.Shot www.hevishot.com
Hi-Tech Ammunition www.iidbs.com/hitech
Hodgdon Powder www.hodgdon.com
Hornady www.hornady.com
Hull Cartridge www.hullcartridge.com
Huntington Reloading Products www.huntingtons.com
Impact Bullets www.impactbullets.com
IMR Smokeless Powders www.imrpowder.com
International Cartridge Corp www.internationalcartridgecorp.com
Israel Military Industries www.imisammo.co.il

ITD Enterprise www.itdenterpriseinc.com
Kent Cartridge America www.kentgamebore.com
Knight Bullets www.benchrest.com/knight/
Kynoch Ammunition www.kynochammunition.com
Lapua www.lapua.com
Lawrence Brand Shot www.metalico.com
Lazzeroni Arms Co. www.lazzeroni.com
Liberty Shooting Supplies www.libertyshootingsupplies.com
Lightfield Ammunition Corp www.lightfield-ammo.com
Lomont Precision Bullets www.klomont.com/kent
Lost River Ballistic Technologies,Inc. www.lostriverballistic.com
Lyman www.lymanproducts.com
Magnus Bullets www.magnusbullets.com
MagSafe Ammunition www.realpages.com/magsafeammo
Magtech www.magtechammunition.com
Mast Technology www.bellammo.com
Masterclass Bullet Co. www.mastercast.com
Meister Bullets www.meisterbullets.com
Midway USA www.midwayusa.com
Miltex,Inc. www.miltexusa.com
Mitchell Mfg. Co. www.mitchellsales.com
MK Ballistic Systems www.mkballistics.com
Mullins Ammunition www.mullinsammunition.com
National Bullet Co. www.nationalbullet.com
Nobel Sport www.adcosales.com
Nobel Sport www.snpe.com
Norma www.norma.cc
Nosler Bullets Inc www.nosler.com
Old Western Scrounger www.ows-ammunition.com
Oregon Trail/Trueshot Bullets www.trueshotbullets.com
Pattern Control www.patterncontrol.com
PMC-Eldorado Cartridge www.pmcammo.com
Polywad www.polywad.com
PowerBelt Bullets www.powerbeltbullets.com
Precision Ammunition www.precisionammo.com
Pro Load Ammunition www.proload.com
Rainier Ballistics www.rainierballistics.com
Ram Shot Powder www.ramshot.com
Reloading Specialties Inc. www.reloadingspecialties.com
Remington www.remington.com
Roc Imports (GPA bullets) www.roc-import.com
Sellier & Bellot USA inc. www.sb-usa.com
Shilen www.shilen.com
Sierra www.sierrabullets.com
Speer Bullets www.speer-bullets.com
Sporting Supplies Int'l Inc. www.ssiintl.com
Starline www.starlinebrass.com
Triton Cartridge www.tritonammo.com
Trueshot Bullets www.trueshotbullets.com
Tru-Tracer www.trutracer.com
Vihtavuori Lapua www.lapua.com
West Coast Bullets www.westcoastbullet.com
Western Powders Inc. www.westernpowders.com
Widener's Reloading & Shooters Supply www.wideners.com
Winchester Ammunition www.winchester.com
Wolf Ammunition www.wolfammo.com
Woodleigh Bullets www.woodleighbullets.com.au
Zanders Sporting Goods www.gzanders.com

CASES, SAFES, GUN LOCKS, AND CABINETS

Ace Case Co. www.acecase.com
AG English Sales Co. www.agenglish.com
All Americas' Outdoors www.innernet.net/gunsafe
Alpine Cases www.alpinecases.com
Aluma Sport by Dee Zee www.deezee.com
American Security Products www.amsecusa.com
Americase www.americase.com

WEB DIRECTORY

Avery Outdoors, Inc. www.averyoutdoors.com
Bear Track Cases www.beartrackcases.com
Boyt Harness Co. www.boytharness.com
Bulldog Gun Safe Co. www.gardall.com
Cannon Safe Co. www.cannonsafe.com
CCL Security Products www.cclsecurity.com
Concept Development Corp. www.saf-t-blok.com
Doskocil Mfg. Co. www.doskocilmfg.com
Fort Knox Safes www.ftknox.com
Franzen Security Products www.securecase.com
Frontier Safe Co. www.frontiersafe.com
Granite Security Products www.granitesafe.com
Gunlocker Phoenix USA Inc. www.gunlocker.com
GunVault www.gunvault.com
Hakuba USA Inc. www.hakubausa.com
Heritage Safe Co. www.heritagesafecompany.com
Hide-A-Gun www.hide-a-gun.com
Homak Safes www.homak.com
Hunter Company www.huntercompany.com
Kalispel Case Line www.kalispelcaseline.com
Knouff & Knouff, Inc. www.kkair.com
Knoxx Industries www.knoxx.com
Kolpin Mfg. Co. www.kolpin.com
Liberty Safe & Security www.libertysafe.com
New Innovative Products www.starlightcases
Noble Security Systems Inc. www.noble.co.ll
Phoenix USA Inc. www.gunlocker.com
Plano Molding Co. www.planomolding.com
Rhino Gun Cases www.rhinoguns.com
Safe Tech, Inc. www.safrgun.com
Saf-T-Hammer www.saf-t-hammer.com
Saf-T-Lok Corp. www.saf-t-lok.com
San Angelo All-Aluminum Products Inc. sasptuld@x.netcom.com
Securecase www.securecase.com
Shot Lock Corp. www.shotlock.com
Smart Lock Technology Inc. www.smartlock.com
Sportsmans Steel Safe Co. www.sportsmansteelsafes.com
Stack-On Products Co. www.stack-on.com
Sun Welding www.sunwelding.com
T.Z. Case Int'l www.tz-case.com
Versatile Rack Co. www.versatilegunrack.com
V-Line Industries www.vlineind.com
Winchester Safes www.fireking.com
Ziegel Engineering www.ziegeleng.com
Zonetti Armor www.zonettiarmor.com

CHOKE DEVICES, RECOIL REDUCERS, AND ACCURACY DEVICES

100 Straight Products www.100straight.com
Answer Products Co. www.answerrifles.com
Briley Mfg www.briley.com
Carlson's www.carlsonschokes.com
Colonial Arms www.colonialarms.com
Comp-N-Choke www.comp-n-choke.com
Hastings www.hastingsbarrels.com
Kick's Industries www.kicks-ind.com
Mag-Na-Port Int'l Inc. www.magnaport.com
Sims Vibration Laboratory www.limbsaver.com
Truglo www.truglo.com

CHRONOGRAPHS AND BALLISTIC SOFTWARE

Barnes Ballistic Program www.barnesbullets.com
Competitive Edge Dynamics www.cedhk.com
Hodgdon Shotshell Program www.hodgdon.com
Lee Shooter www.leeprecision.com
Load From A Disk www.loadammo.com

Oehler Research Inc. www.oehler-research.com
PACT www.pact.com
ProChrony www.competitionelectronics.com
Quickload www.neconos.com
RCBS Load www.rcbs.com
Shooting Chrony Inc www.chrony.ca
Sierra Infinity Ballistics Program www.sierrabullets.com

CLEANING PRODUCTS

Accupro www.accupro.com
Ballistol USA www.ballistol.com
Birchwood Casey www.birchwoodcasey.com
Bore Tech www.boretech.com
Break-Free, Inc. www.break-free.com
Bruno Shooters Supply www.brunoshooters.com
Butch's Bore Shine www.lymanproducts.com
C.J. Weapons Accessories www.cjweapons,com
Clenzoil www.clenzoil.com
Corrosion Technologies www.corrosionx.com
Dewey Mfg. www.deweyrods.com
Eezox Inc. www.xmission.com
G 96 www.g96.com
Hoppes www.hoppes.com
Hydrosorbent Products www.dehumidify.com
Iosso Products www.iosso.com
KG Industries www.kgcoatings.com
Kleen-Bore Inc. www.kleen-bore.com
L&R Mfg. www.lrultrasonics.com
Mpro7 Gun Care www.mp7.com
Otis Technology, Inc. www.otisgun.com
Outers www.outers-guncare.com
Ox-Yoke Originals Inc. www.oxyoke.com
Parker-Hale Ltd. www.parker-hale.com
Prolix Lubricant www.prolixlubricant.com
ProShot Products www.proshotproducts.com
ProTec Lubricants www.proteclubricants.com
Rusteprufe Labs www.rusteprufe.com
Sagebrush Products www.sagebrushproducts.com
Sentry Solutions Ltd. www.sentrysolutions.com
Shooters Choice Gun Care www.shooters-choice.com
Silencio www.silencio.com
Slip 2000 www.slip2000.com
Stony Point Products www.stoneypoint.com
Tetra Gun www.tetraproducts.com
World's Fastest Gun Bore Cleaner www.michaels-oregon.com

FIREARM MANUFACTURERS AND IMPORTERS

AAR, Inc. www.iar-arms.com
Accuracy Int'l North America www.accuracyinternational.org
Accuracy Rifle Systems www.mini-14.net
Ace Custom 45's www.acecustom45.com
Advanced Weapons Technology www.AWT-Zastava.com
AIM www.aimsurplus.com
AirForce Airguns www.airforceairguns.com
Airguns of Arizona www.airgunsofarizona.com
Airgun Express www.airgunexpress.com
Alchemy Arms www.alchemyltd.com
Alexander Arms www.alexanderarms.com
American Derringer Corp. www.amderringer.com
Anics Corp. www.anics.com
Answer Products Co. www.answerrifles.com
AR-7 Industries,LLC www.ar-7.com
Armalite www.armalite.com
Armsco www.armsco.net
Armscorp USA Inc. www.armscorpusa.com
Arnold Arms www.arnoldarms.com
Arsenal USA www.arsenalusa.com

WEB DIRECTORY

Arthur Brown Co. www.eabco.com
Austin & Halleck www.austinhalleck.com
Autauga Arms,Inc. www.autaugaarms.com
Auto-Ordnance Corp. www.tommygun.com
AWA Int'l www.awaguns.com
Axtell Rifle Co. www.riflesmith.com
Aya www.aya-fineguns.com
Baikal www.baikalinc.ru/eng/
Ballard Rifle & Cartridge LLC www.ballardrifles.com
Barrett Firearms Mfg. www.barrettrifles.com
Beeman Precision Airguns www.beeman.com
Benelli USA Corp. www.benelliusa.com
Benjamin Sheridan www.crosman.com
Beretta U.S.A. Corp. www.berettausa.com
Bernardelli www.bernardelli.com
Bill Hanus Birdguns www.billhanusbirdguns.com
Bleiker www.bleiker.ch
Bond Arms www.bondarms.com
Borden's Rifles, Inc. www.bordensrifles.com
Boss & Co. www.bossguns.co.uk
Bowen Classic Arms www.bowenclassicarms.com
Briley Mfg www.briley.com
BRNO Arms www.zbrojovka.com
Brown, David McKay www.mckaybrown.com
Brown, Ed Products www.brownprecision.com
Browning www.browning.com
BSA Guns www.bsaguns.com
BUL Ltd. www.bultransmark.com
Bushmaster Firearms/Quality Parts www.bushmaster.com
BWE Firearms www.bwefirearms.com
Cape Outfitters www.doublegun.com
Carbon 15 www.professional-ordnance.com
Caspian Arms, Ltd. www.caspianarmsltd.8m.com
Casull Arms Corp. www.casullarms.com
Century Arms www.centuryarms.com
Chadick's Ltd. www.chadicks-ltd.com
Champlin Firearms www.champlinarms.com
Chapuis Arms www.doubleguns.com/chapuis.htm
Charles Daly www.charlesdaly.com
Charter2000, Inc. www.charterfirearms.com
Christensen Arms www.christensenarms.com
Cimarron Firearms Co. www.cimarron-firearms.com
Clark Custom Guns www.clarkcustomguns.com
Cobra Enterprises www.cobrapistols.com
Cogswell & Harrison www.cogswell.co.uk/home.htm
Colt Mfg Co. www.colt.com
Compasseco, Inc. www.compasseco.com
Connecticut Valley Arms www.cva.com
Cooper Firearms www.cooperfirearms.com
Crosman www.crosman.com
Crossfire, L.L.C. www.crossfirelle.com
C. Sharps Arms Co. www.csharpsarms.com
CZ USA www.cz-usa.com
Daisy Mfg Co. www.daisy.com
Dakota Arms Inc. www.dakotaarms.com
Dan Wesson Firearms www.danwessonfirearms.com
Davis Industries www.davisindguns.com
Dixie Gun Works www.dixiegun.com
Dlask Arms Corp. www.dlask.com
D.S. Arms, Inc. www.dsarms.com
Dumoulin www.dumoulin-herstal.com
Dynamit Noble www.dnrws.com
Eagle Imports,Inc. www.bersa-llama.com
EDM Arms www.edmarms.com
E.M.F. Co. www.emf-company.com
Enterprise Arms www.enterprise.com
European American Armory Corp. www.eaacorp.com

Evans, William www.williamevans.com
Fabarm www.fabarm.com
Falcon Pneumatic Systems www.falcon-airguns.com
Fausti Stefano www.faustistefanoarms.com
Firestorm www.firestorm-sgs.com
Flodman Guns www.flodman.com
FN Herstal www.fnherstal.com
FNH USA www.fnhusa.com
Franchi www.franchiusa.com
Freedom Arms www.freedomarms.com
Gambo Renato www.renatogamba.it
Gamo www.gamo.com
Gary Reeder Custom Guns www.reeder-customguns.com
Gazelle Arms www.gazellearms.com
Gibbs Rifle Company www.gibbsrifle.com
Glock www.glock.com
Griffin & Howe www.griffinhowe.com
Grizzly Big Boar Rifle www.largrizzly.com
GSI Inc. www.gsifirearms.com
Hammerli www.hammerli.com
Hatsan Arms Co. www.hatsan.com.tr
Heckler and Koch www.hecklerkoch-usa.com
Henry Repeating Arms Co. www.henryrepeating.com
Heritage Mfg. www.heritagemfg.com
Heym www.heym-waffenfabrik.de
High Standard Mfg. www.highstandard.com
Hi-Point Firearms www.hi-pointfirearms.com
Holland & Holland www.hollandandholland.com
H&R Firearms www.marlinfirearms.com
H-S Precision www.hsprecision.com
IAR Inc. www.iar-arms.com
Imperial Miniature Armory www.1800miniature.com
Interarms www.interarms.com
Inter Ordnance www.interordnance.com
Intrac Arms International LLC www.hsarms.com
Israel Arms www.israelarms.com
Ithaca Gun Co. www.ithacagun.com
Izhevsky Mekhanichesky Zavod www.baikalinc.ru
Jarrett Rifles,Inc. www.jarrettrifles.com
Johannsen Express Rifle www.johannsen-jagd.de
JP Enterprises, Inc. www.jpar15.com
Kahr Arms/Auto-Ordnance www.kahr.com
K.B.I. www.kbi-inc.com
Kel-Tec CNC Ind., Inc. www.kel-tec.com
Kifaru www.kifaru.net
Kimber www.kimberamerica.com
Knight's Armament Co. www.knightsarmament.com
Knight Rifles www.knighttrifles.com
Korth www.korthwaffen.com and www.korthusa.com
Krieghoff GmbH www.krieghoff.de
Krieghoff Int'l www.krieghoff.com
L.A.R Mfg www.largrizzly.com
Lazzeroni Arms Co. www.lazzeroni.com
Legacy Sports International www.legacysports.com
Les Baer Custom, Inc. www.lesbaer.com
Linebaugh Custom Sixguns www.sixgunner.com/linebaugh
Ljutic www.ljuticgun.com
Lone Star Rifle Co. www.lonestarrifle.com
Magnum Research www.magnumresearch.com
Markesbery Muzzleloaders www.markesbery.com
Marksman Products www.marksman.com
Marlin www.marlinfirearms.com
Mauser www.mauserwaffen.de
McMillan Bros Rifle Co. www.mcfamily.com
Meacham Rifles www.meachamrifles.com
Merkel www.gsifirearms.com
Miltech www.miltecharms.com

WEB DIRECTORY

Miltex, Inc. www.miltexusa.com
MK Ballistic Systems www.mkballistics.com
M-Mag www.mmag.com
Montana Rifle Co. www.montanarifleman.com
Navy Arms www.navyarms.com
Nesika Actions www.nesika.com
New England Arms Corp. www.newenglandarms.com
New England Custom Gun Svc, Ltd. www.newenglandcustomgun.com
New England Firearms www.hr1871.com
New Ultra Light Arms www.newultralight.com
North American Arms www.naaminis.com
Nowlin Mfg. Inc. www.nowlinguns.com
O.F. Mossberg & Sons www.mossberg.com
Olympic Arms www.olyarms.com
Panther Arms www.dpmsinc.com
Para-Ordnance www.paraord.com
Pedersoli Davide & Co. www.davide-pedersoli.com
Perazzi www.perazzi.com
Power Custom www.powercustom.com
Purdey & Sons www.purdey.com
Remington www.remington.com
Republic Arms Inc. www.republicarmsinc.com
Rigby www.johnrigbyandco.com
Rizzini Di Rizzini www.rizzini.it
Robar Companies, Inc. www.robarguns.com
Robinson Armament Co. www.robarm.com
Rock River Arms, Inc. www.rockriverarms.com
Rogue Rifle Co. Inc. www.chipmunkrifle.com
Rohrbaugh Firearms www.rohrbaughfirearms.com
Rossi Arms www.rossiusa.com
RPM www.rpmxlpistols.com
RWS www.dnrws.com
Sabatti SPA www.sabatti.com
Saco Defense www.sacoinc.com
Safari Arms www.olyarms.com
Sako www.berettausa.com
Samco Global Arms Inc. www.samcoglobal.com
Sarco Inc. www.sarcoinc.com
Savage Arms Inc. www.savagearms.com
Scattergun Technologies Inc. www.wilsoncombat.com
Searcy Enterprises www.searcyent.com
SIG Arms,Inc. www.sigarms.com
Simpson Ltd. www.simpsonltd.com
SKB Shotguns www.skbshotguns.com
Smith & Wesson www.smith-wesson.com
Sphinx System www.sphinxarms.com
Springfield Armory www.springfield-armory.com
SSK Industries www.sskindustries.com
Steyr Mannlicher www.gsifirearms.com
STI Int'l sales@sti-guns.com
Strayer-Voigt Inc. www.sviguns.com
Sturm,Ruger & Company www.ruger-firearms.com
Tar-Hunt Slug Guns, Inc. www.tar-hunt.com
Taser Int'l www.taser.com
Taurus www.taurususa.com
Tennessee Guns www.tennesseeguns.com
The 1877 Sharps Co. www.1877sharps.com
Thompson Center Arms www.tcarms.com
Tikka www.berettausa.com
Traditions www.traditionsfirearms.com
Uberti www.stoegerindustries.com
U.S. Firearms Mfg. Co. www.usfirearms.com
U.S. Repeating Arms Co. www.winchester-guns.com
Valkyrie Arms www.valkyriearms.com
Vektor Arms www.vektorarms.com
Volquartsen Custom Ltd. www.volquartsen.com
Walther USA www.waltheramerica.com

Weatherby www.weatherby.com
Webley and Scott Ltd. www.webley.co.uk
Westley Richards www.westleyrichards.com
Widley www.widleyguns.com
Wild West Guns www.wildwestguns.com
William Larkin Moore & Co. www.doublegun.com
Wilson's Gun Shop Inc. www.wilsoncombat.com
Winchester Firearms www.winchester-guns.com

GUN PARTS, BARRELS, AFTER-MARKET ACCESSORIES

300 Below www.300below.com
Accuracy International of North America www.accuracyinternational.org
Accuracy Speaks, Inc. www.accuracyspeaks.com
Advanced Barrel Systems www.carbonbarrels.com
AK-USA www.ak-103.com
American Spirit Arms Corp. www.gunkits.com
AMT Gun Parts www.amt-gunparts.com
Badger Barrels, Inc. www.badgerbarrels.com
Bar-Sto Precision Machine www.barsto.com
Battenfeld Technologies www.battenfeldtechnologies.com
Belt Mountain Enterprises www.beltmountain.com
Brownells www.brownells.com
Buffer Technologies www.buffertech.com
Bullberry Barrel Works www.bullberry.com
Bushmaster Firearms/Quality Parts www.bushmaster.com
Butler Creek Corp www.butler-creek.com
Cape Outfitters Inc. www.capeoutfitters.com
Caspian Arms Ltd. www.caspianarmsltd.8m.com
Cheaper Than Dirt www.cheaperthandirt.com
Chesnut Ridge www.chestnutridge.com/
Chip McCormick Corp www.chipmccormickcorp.com
Colonial Arms www.colonialarms.com
Comp-N-Chokc www.comp-n-choke.com
Cylinder & Slide Shop www.cylinder-slide.com
Digi-Twist www.fmtcorp.com
Dixie Gun Works www.dixiegun.com
Douglas Barrels www.benchrest.com/douglas/
DPMS www.dpmsinc.com
D.S.Arms,Inc. www.dsarms.com
Ed Brown Products www.edbrown.com
EFK Marketing/Fire Dragon Pistol Accessories www.flmfire.com
Federal Arms www.fedarms.com
Forrest Inc. www.gunmags.com
Gemtech www.gem-tech.com
Gentry, David www.gentrycustom.com
Gun Parts Corp. www.e-gunparts.com
Harris Barrels wwharris@msn.com
Hart Rifle Barrels www.hartbarrels.com
Hastings Barrels www.hastingsbarrels.com
Heinie Specialty Products www.heinie.com
100 Straight Products www.100straight.com
I.M.A. www.ima-usa.com
Jarvis, Inc. www.jarvis-custom.com
J&T Distributing www.jtdistributing.com
Jonathan Arthur Ciener, Inc. www.22lrconversions.com
JP Enterprises www.jpar15.com
King's Gunworks www.kingsgunworks.com
Knoxx Industries www.knoxx.com
Krieger Barrels www.kriegerbarrels.com
Les Baer Custom, Inc. www.lesbaer.com
Lilja Barrels www.riflebarrels.com
Lone Star Rifle Co. www.lonestarrifles.com
Lone Wolf Dist. www.lonewolfdist.com
Lothar Walther Precision Tools Inc. www.lothar-walther.de
M&A Parts, Inc. www.m-aparts.com

WEB DIRECTORY

MAB Barrels www.mab.com.au
Marvel Products, Inc. www.marvelprod.com
MEC-GAR SrL www.mec-gar.com
Michaels of Oregon Co. www.michaels-oregon.com
North Mfg. Co. www.rifle-barrels.com
Numrich Gun Parts Corp. www.e-gunparts.com
Pachmayr www.pachmayr.com
Pac-Nor Barrels www.pac-nor.com
Para Ordinance Pro Shop www.ltms.com
Point Tech Inc. pointec@ibm.net
Promag Industries www.promagindustries.com
Power Custom, Inc. www.powercustom.com
Red Star Arms www.redstararms.com
Rocky Mountain Arms www.rockymountainarms.com
Royal Arms Int'l www.royalarms.com
R.W. Hart www.rwhart.com
Sarco Inc. www.sarcoinc.com
Scattergun Technologies Inc. www.wilsoncombat.com
Schuemann Barrels www.schuemann.com
Seminole Gunworks Chamber Mates www.chambermates.com
Shilen www.shilen.com
Sims Vibration Laboratory www.limbsaver.com
Smith & Alexander Inc. www.smithandalexander.com
Speed Shooters Int'l www.shooternet.com/ssi
Sprinco USA Inc. sprinco@primenet.com
S&S Firearms www.ssfirearms.com
SSK Industries www.sskindustries.com
Sunny Hill Enterprises www.sunny-hill.com
Tapco www.tapco.com
Trapdoors Galore www.trapdoors.com
Triple K Manufacturing Co. Inc. www.triplek.com
U.S.A. Magazines Inc. www.usa-magazines.com
Verney-Carron SA www.verney-carron.com
Volquartsen Custom Ltd. www.volquartsen.com
W.C. Wolff Co. www.gunsprings.com
Waller & Son www.wallerandson.com
Weigand Combat Handguns www.weigandcombat.com
Western Gun Parts www.westerngunparts.com
Wilson Arms www.wilsonarms.com
Wilson Combat www.wilsoncombat.com
Wisner's Inc. www.gunpartsspecialist.com
Z-M Weapons www.zmweapons.com/home.htm

GUNSMITHING SUPPLIES AND INSTRUCTION

American Gunsmithing Institute www.americangunsmith.com
Battenfeld Technologies www.battenfeldtechnologies.com
Brownells, Inc. www.brownells.com
B-Square Co. www.b-square.com
Clymer Mfg. Co. www.clymertool.com
Craftguard Metal Finishing crftgrd@aol.com
Dem-Bart www.dembartco.com
Du-Lite Corp. www.dulite.com
Dvorak Instruments www.dvorakinstruments.com
Gradiant Lens Corp. www.gradientlens.com
Gunline Tools www.gunline.com
JGS Precision Tool Mfg. LLC www.jgstools.com
Mag-Na-Port International www.magnaport.com
Manson Precision Reamers www.mansonreamers.com
Midway www.midwayusa.com
Olympus America Inc. www.olympus.com
Trinidad State Junior College www.trinidadstate.edu

HANDGUN GRIPS

Ajax Custom Grips, Inc. www.ajaxgrips.com
Altamont Co. www.altamontco.com
Badger Grips www.pistolgrips.com
Barami Corp. www.hipgrip.com

Crimson Trace Corp. www.crimsontrace.com
Eagle Grips www.eaglegrips.com
Falcon Industries www.ergogrips.net
Hogue Grips www.getgrip.com
Lett Custom Grips www.lettgrips.com
Nill-Grips USA www.nill-grips.com
Pachmayr www.pachmayr.com
Pearce Grips www.pearcegrip.com
Trausch Grips Int.Co. www.trausch.com
Uncle Mike's: www.uncle-mikes.com

HOLSTERS AND LEATHER PRODUCTS

Akah www.akah.de
Aker Leather Products www.akerleather.com
Alessi Distributor R&F Inc. www.alessiholsters.com
Alfonso's of Hollywood www.alfonsogunleather.com
Armor Holdings www.holsters.com
Bagmaster www.bagmaster.com
Bianchi International www.bianchi-int.com
Blackhills Leather www.blackhillsleather.com
BodyHugger Holsters www.nikolais.com
Boyt Harness Co. www.boytharness.com
Brigade Gun Leather www.brigadegunleather.com
Chimere www.chimere.com
Classic Old West Styles www.cows.com
Conceal It www.conceal-it.com
Concealment Shop Inc. www.theconcealmentshop.com
Coronado Leather Co. www.coronadoleather.com
Creedmoor Sports, Inc. www.creedmoorsports.com
Custom Leather Wear www.customleatherwear.com
Defense Security Products www.thunderwear.com
Dennis Yoder www.yodercustomleather.com
DeSantis Holster www.desantisholster.com
Dillon Precision www.dillonprecision.com
Don Hume Leathergoods, Inc. www.donhume.com
Ernie Hill International www.erniehill.com
Fist www.fist-inc.com
Fobus USA www.fobusholster.com
Front Line Ltd. frontlin@internet-zahav.net
Galco www.usgalco.com
Gilmore's Sports Concepts www.gilmoresports.com
Gould & Goodrich www.goulduse.com
Gunmate Products www.gun-mate.com
Hellweg Ltd. www.hellwegltd.com
Hide-A-Gun www.hide-a-gun.com
Holsters.Com www.holsters.com
Horseshoe Leather Products www.horseshoe.co.uk
Hunter Co. www.huntercompany.com
Kirkpatrick Leather Company www.kirkpatrickleather.com
KNJ www.knjmfg.com
Kramer Leather www.kramerleather.com
Law Concealment Systems www.handgunconcealment.com
Levy's Leathers Ltd. www.levysleathers.com
Michaels of Oregon Co. www.michaels-oregon.com
Milt Sparks Leather www.miltsparks.com
Mitch Rosen Extraordinary Gunleather www.mitchrosen.com
Old World Leather www.gun-mate.com
Pager Pal www.pagerpal.com
Phalanx Corp. www.phalanxarms.com
PWL www.pwlusa.com
Rumanya Inc. www.rumanya.com
S.A. Gunleather www.elpasoleather.com
Safariland Ltd. Inc. www.safariland.com
Shooting Systems Group Inc. www.shootingsystems.com
Strictly Anything Inc. www.strictlyanything.com
Strong Holster Co. www.strong-holster.com
The Belt Co. www.conceal-it.com

WEB DIRECTORY

The Leather Factory Inc. lflandry@flash.net
The Outdoor Connection www.outdoorconnection.com
Top-Line USA inc. www.toplineusa.com
Triple K Manufacturing Co. www.triplek.com
Wilson Combat www.wilsoncombat.com

MISCELLANEOUS SHOOTING PRODUCTS

10X Products Group www.10Xwear.com
Aero Peltor www.aearo.com
Beartooth www.beartoothproducts.com
Dalloz Safety www.cdalloz.com
Deben Group Industries Inc. www.deben.com
Decot Hy-Wyd Sport Glasses www.sportyglasses.com
E.A.R., Inc. www.earinc.com
First Choice Armor www.firstchoicearmor.com
Howard Leight Hearing Protectors www.howardleight.com
Hunters Specialities www.hunterspec.com
Johnny Stewart Wildlife Calls www.hunterspec.com
North Safety Products www.northsafety-brea.com
Pro-Ears www.pro-ears.com
Second Chance Body Armor Inc. www.secondchance.com
Silencio www.silencio.com
Smart Lock Technologies www.smartlock.com
Surefire www.surefire.com
Walker's Game Ear Inc. www.walkersgameear.com

MUZZLELOADING FIREARMS AND PRODUCTS

Austin & Halleck, Inc. www.austinhalleck.com
CVA www.cva.com
Davis, Vernon C. & Co. www.mygunroom/vcdavis&co/
Dixie Gun Works, Inc. www.dixiegun.com
Elephant/Swiss Black Powder www.elephantblackpowder.com
Goex Black Powder www.goexpowder.com
Jedediah Starr Trading Co. www.jedediah-starr.com
Jim Chambers Flintlocks www.flintlocks.com
Kahnke Gunworks www.powderandbow.com/kahnke/
Knight Rifles www.knightrifles.com
Log Cabin Shop www.logcabinshop.com
Lyman www.lymanproducts.com
Millennium Designed Muzzleloaders www.mdm-muzzleloaders.com
Mountain State Muzzleloading www.mtnstatemuzzleloading.com
MSM, Inc. www.msmfg.com
Muzzleloading Technologies, Inc. www.mtimuzzleloading.com
Navy Arms www.navyarms.com
October Country Muzzleloading www.oct-country.com
Ox-Yoke Originals Inc. www.oxyoke.com
Palmetto Arms www.palmetto.it
Rightnour Mfg. Co. Inc. www.rmcsports.com
The Rifle Shop trshoppe@aol.com
Thompson Center Arms www.tcarms.com
Traditions Performance Muzzleloading www.traditionsfirearms.com

PUBLICATIONS, VIDEOS, AND CDs

Airgun Letter www.airgunletter.com
American Firearms Industry www.amfire.com
American Handgunner www.americanhandgunner.com
American Hunter www.americanhunter.org
American Shooting Magazine www.americanshooting.com
Blacksmith bcbooks@glasscity.net
Blackpowder Hunting www.blackpowderhunting.org
Black Powder Journal www.blackpowderjournal.com
Blue Book Publications www.bluebookinc.com
Combat Handguns www.combathandguns.com
Countrywide Press www.countrysport.com
DBI Books/Krause Publications www.krause.com
Delta Force www.infogo.com/delta
Discount Gun Books www.discountgunbooks.com

Gun List www.gunlist.com
Gun Video www.gunvideo.com
GUNS Magazine www.gunsmagazine.com
Guns & Ammo www.gunsandammomag.com
Gunweb Magazine WWW Links www.imags.com
Gun World www.gunworld.com
Harris Publications www.harrispublications.com
Heritage Gun Books www.gunbooks.com
Krause Publications www.krause.com
Moose Lake Publishing MooselakeP@aol.com
Munden Enterprises Inc. www.bob-munden.com
Outdoor Videos www.outdoorvideos.com
Precision Shooting www.precisionshooting.com
Rifle and Handloader Magazines www.riflemagazine.com
Safari Press Inc. www.safaripress.com
Shoot! Magazine www.shootmagazine.com
Shooters News www.shootersnews.com
Shooting Industry www.shootingindustry.com
Shooting Sports Retailer ssretailer@ad.com
Shotgun News www.shotgunnews.com
Shotgun Report www.shotgunreport.com
Shotgun Sports Magazine www.shotgun-sports.com
Small Arms Review www.smallarmsreview.com
Sporting Clays Web Edition www.sportingclays.com
Sports Afield www.sportsafield.com
Sports Trend www.sportstrend.com
Sportsmen on Film www.sportsmenonfilm.com
The Gun Journal www.shooters.com
The Shootin Iron www.off-road.com/4x4web/si/si.html
The Single Shot Exchange Magazine singleshot@earthlink.net
Voyageur Press www.voyageurpress.com
VSP Publications www.gunbooks.com
Vulcan Outdoors Inc. www.vulcanpub.com

RELOADING TOOLS AND SUPPLIES

Ballisti-Cast Mfg. www.ballisti-cast.com
Bruno Shooters Supply www.brunoshooters.com
CH Tool & Die www.cdhd.com
Corbin Mfg & Supply Co. www.corbins.com
Dillon Precision www.dillonprecision.com
Forster Precision Products www.forsterproducts.com
Hanned Line www.hanned.com
Harrell's Precision www.harrellsprec.com
Hornady www.hornady.com
Huntington Reloading Products www.huntingtons.com
J & J Products Co. www.jandjproducts.com
Load Data www.loaddata.com
Lee Precision,Inc. www.leeprecision.com
Littleton Shotmaker www.leadshotmaker.com
Lyman www.lymanproducts.com
Magma Engineering www.magmaengr.com
Mayville Engineering Co. (MEC) www.mecreloaders.com
Midway www.midwayusa.com
Moly-Bore www.molybore.com
MTM Case-Guard www.mtmcase-guard.com
NECO www.neconos.com
Neil Jones Custom Products www.neiljones.com
Ponsness/Warren www.reloaders.com
Ranger Products www.pages.prodigy.com/rangerproducts.home.htm
Rapine Bullet Mold Mfg Co. www.customloads.com/rapine.html
RCBS www.rcbs.com
Redding Reloading Equipment www.redding-reloading.com
Russ Haydon's Shooting Supplies www.shooters-supply.com
Sinclair Int'l Inc. www.sinclairintl.com
Stoney Point Products Inc www.stoneypoint.com
Thompson Bullet Lube Co. www.thompsonbulletlube.com
Wilson(L.E. Wilson) www.lewilson.com

WEB DIRECTORY

RESTS— BENCH, PORTABLE, ATTACHABLE

Bench Master www.bench-master.com
B-Square www.b-square.com
Bullshooter www.bullshootersightingin.com
Desert Mountain Mfg. www.bench-master.com
Harris Engineering Inc. www.cyberteklabs.com/harris/main/htm
Kramer Designs www.snipepod.com
L Thomas Rifle Support www.ltsupport.com
Level-Lok www.levellok.com
Midway www.midwayusa.com
Ransom International www.ransom-intl.com
R.W. Hart www.rwhart.com
Sinclair Intl, Inc. www.sinclairintl.com
Stoney Point Products www.stoneypoint.com
Target Shooting www.targetshooting.com
Varmint Masters www.varmintmasters.com
Versa-Pod www.versa-pod.com

SCOPES, SIGHTS, MOUNTS AND ACCESSORIES

Accusight www.accusight.com
ADCO www.shooters.com/adco/index/htm
Adirondack Opitcs www.adkoptics.com
Aimpoint www.aimpoint.com
Aim Shot, Inc. www.miniosprey.com
Aimtech Mount Systems www.aimtech-mounts.com
Alpec Team, Inc. www.alpec.com
Alpen Outdoor Corp. www.alpenoutdoor.com
American Technologies Network, Corp. www.atncorp.com
AmeriGlo, LLC www.ameriglo.net
AO Sight Systems Inc. www.aosights.com
Ashley Outdoors, Inc. www.ashleyoutdoors.com
ATN www.atncorp.com
BSA Optics www.bsaoptics.com
B-Square Company, Inc. www.b-square.com
Burris www.burrisoptics.com
Bushnell Performance Optics www.bushnell.com
Carl Zeiss Optical Inc. www.zeiss.com
Carson Optical www.carson-optical.com
C-More Systems www.cmore.com
Conetrol Scope Mounts www.conetrol.com
Crimson Trace Corp. www.crimsontrace.com
Crossfire L.L.C. www.amfire.com/hesco/html
DCG Supply Inc. www.dcgsupply.com
EasyHit, Inc. www.easyhit.com
EAW www.eaw.de
Electro-Optics Technologies www.eotechmdc.com/holosight
Europtik Ltd. www.europtik.com
Fujinon, Inc. www.fujinon.com
Gilmore Sports www.gilmoresports.com
Hakko Co. Ltd. www.hakko-japan.co.jp
Hesco www.hescosights.com
Hitek Industries www.nightsight.com
HIVIZ www.hivizsights.com
Horus Vision www.horusvision.com
Hunter Co. www.huntercompany.com
Innovative Weaponry,Inc. www.ptnightsights.com
Ironsighter Co. www.ironsighter.com
ITT Night Vision www.ittnightvision.com
Kahles www.kahlesoptik.com
Kowa Optimed Inc. www.kowascope.com
Laser Bore Sight www.laserboresight.com
Laser Devices Inc. www.laserdevices.com
Lasergrips www.crimsontrace.com
LaserLyte www.laserlyte.com
LaserMax Inc. www.lasermax-inc.com
Laser Products www.surefire.com

Leapers, Inc. www.leapers.com
Leatherwood www.leatherwoodoptics.com
Leica Camera Inc. www.leica-camera.com/usa
Leupold www.leupold.com
LightForce/NightForce USA www.nightforcescopes.com
Lyman www.lymanproducts.com
Lynx www.b-square.com
Marble's Outdoors www.marblesoutdoors.com
MDS,Inc. www.mdsincorporated.com
Meprolight www.kimberamerica.com
Micro Sight Co. www.microsight.com
Millett www.millettsights.com
Miniature Machine Corp. www.mmcsight.com
Montana Vintage Arms www.montanavintagearms.com
Mounting Solutions Plus www.mountsplus.com
NAIT www.nait.com
Newcon International Ltd. newconsales@newcon-optik.com
Night Owl Optics www.nightowloptics.com
Nikon Inc. www.nikonusa.com
North American Integrated Technologies www.nait.com
O.K. Weber, Inc. www.okweber.com
Pentax Corp. www.pentaxlightseeker.com
Premier Reticle www.premierreticles.com
Redfield www.redfieldoptics.com
R&R Int'l Trade www.nightoptic.com
Schmidt & Bender www.schmidt-bender.com
Scopecoat www.scopecoat.com
Scopelevel www.scopelevel.com
Segway Industries www.segway-industries.com
Shepherd Scope Ltd. www.shepherdscopes.com
Sightron www.sightron.com
Simmons www.simmonsoptics.com
S&K www.scopemounts.com
Springfield Armory www.springfield-armory.com
Sure-Fire www.surefire.com
Swarovski/Kahles www.swarovskioptik.com
Swift Instruments Inc. www.swift-optics.com
Talley Mfg. Co. www.talleyrings.com
Tasco www.tascosales.com
Trijicon Inc. www.trijicon-inc.com
Truglo Inc. www.truglo.com
US Night Vision www.usnightvision.com
U.S. Optics Technologies Inc. www.usoptics.com
Valdada-IOR Optics www.valdada.com
Warne www.warnescopemounts.com
Weaver Scopes www.weaveroptics.com
Wilcox Industries Corp www.wilcoxind.com
Williams Gun Sight Co. wwwwilliamsgunsight.com
Zeiss www.zeiss.com

SHOOTING ORGANIZATIONS, SCHOOLS AND RANGES

Amateur Trapshooting Assoc. www.shootata.com
American Custom Gunmakers Guild www.acgg.org
American Gunsmithing Institute www.americangunsmith.com
American Pistolsmiths Guild www.americanpistol.com
American Shooting Sports Council www.assc.com
Assoc. of Firearm & Tool Mark Examiners www.afte.org
BATF www.atf.ustreas.gov
Blackwater Lodge and Training Center www.blackwaterlodge.com
Boone and Crockett Club www.boone-crockett.org
Buckmasters, Ltd. www.buckmasters.com
Citizens Committee for the Right to Keep & Bear Arms www.ccrkba.org
Civilian Marksmanship Program www.odcmp.com
Colorado School of Trades www.gunsmith-school.com
Ducks Unlimited www.ducks.org

WEB DIRECTORY

Fifty Caliber Shooters Assoc. www.fcsa.org
Firearms Coalition www.nealknox.com
Front Sight Firearms Training Institute www.frontsight.com
German Gun Collectors Assoc. www.germanguns.com
Gun Clubs www.associatedgunclubs.org
Gun Owners' Action League www.goal.org
Gun Owners of America www.gunowners.org
Gun Trade Asssoc. Ltd. www.brucepub.com/gta
Gunsite Training Center,Inc. www.gunsite.com
Hunting and Shooting Sports Heritage Fund www.hsshf.org
International Defense Pistol Assoc. www.idpa.com
International Handgun Metallic Silhouette Assoc. www.ihmsa.org
International Hunter Education Assoc. www.ihea.com
Jews for the Preservation of Firearms Ownership www.jpfo.org
Murray State College(gunsmithing)darnold@msc.cc.ok.us
National 4-H Shooting Sports www.4-hshootingsports.org
National Benchrest Shooters Assoc. www.benchrest.com
National Muzzle Loading Rifle Assoc. www.nmlra.org
National Reloading Manufacturers Assoc www.reload-nrma.com
National Rifle Assoc. www.nra.org
National Rifle Assoc. ILA www.nraila.org
National Shooting Sports Foundation www.nssf.org
National Skeet Shooters Association www.nssa-nsca.com
National Sporting Clays Assoc. www.nssa-nsca.com
National Wild Turkey Federation www.nwtf.com
North American Hunting Club www.huntingclub.com
Pennsylvania Gunsmith School www.pagunsmith.com
Quail Unlimited www.qu.org
Right To Keep and Bear Arms www.rkba.org
Rocky Mountain Elk Foundation www.rmef.org
SAAMI www.saami.org
Second Amendment Foundation www.saf.org
Second Amendment Sisters www.2asisters.org
Shooting Ranges Int'l www.shootingranges.com
Single Action Shooting Society www.sassnet.com
S&W Academy and Nat'l Firearms Trng. Center www.sw-academy.com
Tactical Defense Institute www.tdiohio.com
Ted Nugent United Sportsmen of America www.tnugent.com
Thunder Ranch www.thunderranchinc.com
Trapshooters Homepage www.trapshooters.com
Trinidad State Junior College www.trinidadstate.edu
U.S. Int'l Clay Target Assoc. www.usicta.com
United States Fish and Wildlife Service www.fws.gov
U.S. Practical Shooting Assoc. www.uspsa.org
USA Shooting www.usashooting.com
Varmint Hunters Assoc. www.varminthunter.org
U.S. Sportsmen's Alliance www.ussportsmen.org
Women Hunters www.womanhunters.com
Women's Shooting Sports Foundation www.wssf.org

STOCKS

Advanced Technology www.atigunstocks.com
Bell & Carlson, Inc. www.bellandcarlson.com
Boyd's Gunstock Industries, Inc. www.boydboys.com
Butler Creek Corp www.butler-creek.com
Calico Hardwoods, Inc. www.calicohardwoods.com
Choate Machine www.riflestock.com
Elk Ridge Stocks www.reamerrentals.com/elk_ridge.htm
Fajen www.battenfeldtechnologies.com
Great American Gunstocks www.gunstocks.com
Herrett's Stocks www.herrettstocks.com
Lone Wolf www.lonewolfriflestocks.com
McMillan Fiberglass Stocks www.mcmfamily.com
MPI Stocks www.mpistocks.com
Ram-Line- Blount Inc. www.blount.com
Rimrock Rifle Stock www.rimrockstocks.com
Royal Arms Gunstocks www.imt.net/~royalarms

Speedfeed, Inc. www.speedfeedinc.com
Tiger-Hunt Curly Maple Gunstocks www.gunstockwood.com
Wenig Custom Gunstocks Inc. www.wenig.com

TARGETS AND RANGE EQUIPMENT

Action Target Co. www.actiontarget.com
Advanced Interactive Systems www.ais-sim.com
Birchwood Casey www.birchwoodcasey.com
Caswell Detroit Armor Companies www.caswellintl.com
Laser Shot www.lasershot.com
MTM Products www.mtmcase-gard.com
Natiional Target Co. www.nationaltarget.com
Newbold Target Systems www.newboldtargets.com
Porta Target,Inc. www.portatarget.com
Range Management Services Inc. www.casewellintl.com
Range Systems www.shootingrangeproducts.com
Reactive Target Systems Inc. chrts@primenet.com
ShatterBlast Targets www.daisy.com
Super Trap Bullet Containment Systems www.supertrap.com
Thompson Target Technology www.thompsontarget.com
Visible Impact Targets www.crosman.com
White Flyer www.whiteflyer.com

TRAP AND SKEET SHOOTING
EQUIPMENT AND ACCESSORIES

Auto-Sporter Industries www.auto-sporter.com
10X Products Group www.10Xwear.com
Claymaster Traps www.claymaster.com
Do-All Traps, Inc. www.do-alltraps.com
Laporte USA www.laporte-shooting.com
Outers www.outers-guncare.com
Trius Products Inc. www.triustraps.com
White Flyer www.whiteflyer.com

TRIGGERS

Brownells www.brownells.com
Shilen www.shilen.com
Timney Triggers www.timneytrigger.com

MAJOR SHOOTING WEB SITES AND LINKS

Alphabetic Index of Links www.gunsgunsguns.com
Auction Arms www.auctionarms.com
Benchrest Central www.benchrest.com
Bullseye Pistol www.bullseyepistol.com
For The Hunt www.forthehunt.com
Gun Broker Auctions www.gunbroker.com
Gun Index www.gunindex.com
Gun Industry www.gunindustry.com
GunLinks www.gunlinks.com
Gun Nuts www.gunuts.com
Guns For Sale www.gunsamerica.com
Gun Show Auction www.gunshowauction.com
GunXchange www.gunxchange.com
Hunting Digest www.huntingdigest.com
Hunting Information(NSSF) www.huntinfo.org
Hunting Network www.huntingnetwork.com
Outdoor Yellow Pages www.outdoorsyp.com
Real Guns www.realguns.com/links/glinks.htm
Rec.Guns www.recguns.com
Shooters' Gun Calendar www.guncalendar.com/index.cfm
Shooter's Online Services www.shooters.com
Shooters Search www.shooterssearch.com
Shotgun Sports Resource Guide www.shotgunsports.com
Sixgunner www.sixgunner.com
Sportsman's Web www.sportsmansweb.com
Where To Shoot www.wheretoshoot.com

by JOHN HAVILAND

SHOTGUN REVIEW

FOR YEARS WOMEN who hunted birds were given a .410 and patted on the head. Now women, the only growing segment of shotgun shooters, want a shotgun tailored to their needs. My wife is a perfect example. For years, Gail took the only shotgun left in the gun cabinet to shoot clay targets and hunt upland birds. Lately, she said she wanted her own gun, and not a .410 or a clunky 12 gauge.

Proper shotguns for women can be autoloaders, pumps or double guns, as long as they are lightweight. An autoloading shotgun spreads recoil over a longer time to reduce felt recoil, which is a plus for kick-sensitive shooters. Eight-time American and world champion sporting clays shooter Linda Joy shoots an over/under in competition. *"But if I was starting out again I'd go with an autoloader for the lighter kick,"* she says. *"For hunting I'd definitely go with an autoloader because they're so quick to point and light to carry all day,"* she says.

However, many women are put off by an auto's complex operation. Cathy Williams, of Beretta USA, says she shoots an over/under because it is uncomplicated and easy to load. *"I drop in two shells, fire them, open the action and the empties pop out,"* she says.

Pump guns are simple to operate because each back-and-forth cycling of the forearm lets the shooter know when an empty is ejected and a new shell is chambered. Because the shooter works the action, pump-action guns reliably cycle all shells no matter how light the load.

Joy prefers 30-inch barrels on an over/under and a 28-inch barrel on an autoloader. *"You need that length to keep your swing smooth,"* she says. Those barrel lengths also provide an extended sight radius for more precise aim on long shots. A somewhat shorter barrel is better for point-and-shoot shots, like ruffed grouse in a thicket.

Last summer, my wife Gail handled and shot several shotguns in her search for a new grouse gun. She hefted a Remington 870 12-gauge three-inch magnum and immediately put it down. A Remington 870 20-gauge that weighed 6 lbs. 10 oz. felt much better in her hands and she regularly dusted clay pigeons with it, firing Winchester's loading of 3/4-oz. of #7 1/2s. A Browning Gold Hunter autoloader with a 26-inch barrel and rubber butt pad weighed 6 lbs. 11 oz. and took a lot of the sting out of the kick of heavy 1- and 1-1/8 oz. loads. The lighter recoil also permitted a fast second shot. The Gold Hunter was the gun Gail chose for shooting heavy loads at waterfowl and pheasants.

Gail did her best shooting with a Browning and a Beretta over/under. The guns' slender wrists helped Gail control the guns, and the high, full stock combs instantly brought her eye into alignment with the barrel ribs, and then out to the target.

The Browning Feather, with 26-inch barrels and a plastic buttplate, weighed 5 lbs. 10 oz. The Beretta Whitewing with 28-inch barrels and GEL-TEK recoil pad weighed 6 lbs. 2 oz., and was her ultimate choice since the recoil pad with the silicone gel core soaked up a considerable amount of recoil. She knew she would appreciate the light weight on mountain hikes for blue grouse.

During September Gail hunted ruffed grouse in the creek bottoms and blue grouse in the foothills of timbered draws and springs surrounded by mountain maples. Even on the steep uphills the Beretta remained ready in her hands, so when grouse flushed she knocked them down. She's definitely not going back to a clunky old 12 gauge.

Gail must think like a lot of hunters because this year companies have introduced a whole bunch of light, smaller-gauge guns.

Charles Daly

The Field Hunter VR-MC 20-gauge autoloading shotgun is now available in a youth model. The gun has a 22-inch barrel with three interchangeable chokes. The length of pull has also been shortened by 1 5/8 inches, but can be lengthened to full size.

The Field Hunter 12 gauge has also been fully covered with Advantage camouflage. This camo pattern joins several other camo patterns and the black synthetic stock and forearm on other Field Hunter guns.

The 28 gauge has also joined the Field Hunter line. The gun has 24-, 26- or 28-inch ported barrels and screw-in chokes.

Benelli

The Sport II is Benelli's newest all-around competition 12-gauge based on its Inertia System, comprised of a stiff spring between the bolt body and bolt head which begins to compress when the gun moves back during recoil. Benelli states the system is adaptable to almost any sort of ammunition. About the only way to stop a Benelli from cycling is to put the butt against a brick wall, because the shotgun must be free to move back slightly for the bolt spring to compress.

The Sport II traits include cryogenically-treated 28- or 30-inch barrels. Benelli states the cryogenic treatment relieves stresses left over from hammer-forging, and thus delivers a shorter shot string and more evenly distributed patterns. The barrel has a ventilated rib that steps up from the breech. Extra-long choke tubes constrict the shot charge more gradually to lessen pellet damage and keep more of pellets in the pattern. Choke tubes include Cylinder, Improved Cylinder, Improved Modified and Full.

The Sport II has a two-piece receiver that rides steel on steel like the Legacy model autoloading shotguns. The sweeping contour of the lower receiver blends into the gun's trigger guard and the checkered walnut stock completes the gun's good looks. Plastic shims supplied with the gun fit between the rear of its receiver and the buttstock wrist to adjust cast, drop of comb and length of pull.

For those who shake like a leaf when a turkey gobbler struts into view, Benelli has added a vertical pistol grip to its Black Eagle and M1 turkey guns. The grip allows you to hold a gun more steady while waiting for a gobbler to take those last few steps into sure range, and directs some of the hefty recoil from turkey loads into your hand.

The awesome hitting power—and recoil—of new slug loads like Remington's Copper Solid and Winchester's Partition Gold have convinced many shooters that these 12-gauge loads are too much for deer. The high velocity and good bullets of these sabot slug loads, though, have made the 20 gauge entirely adequate for deer and hogs. In line with that thinking, Benelli's M1 Field Slug Gun is also now available in 20 gauge.

Light weight and easy kick are the main features women want in an upland bird gun, like this 20-gauge Beretta Whitewing over/under.

The autoloader comes with a black or Advantage Timber HD camouflage synthetic stock. The gun's 24-inch barrel has a 1:28-inch twist for shooting sabot slugs and is fitted with open sights. The receiver is drilled and tapped to accept scope mounts.

The M1 Practical 12 gauge is ready for you to take out your aggression on bowling pins and the three-gun matches in IPSC shooting. The Practical comes with a 26-inch compensated barrel, oversized controls and a nine-round magazine. Both ghost ring sights and a Picatinny rail provide a range of sighting options.

The Benelli Nova Pump is also available in 20 gauge with a rifled bore. The Nova has the same stock options, barrel length and rifling twist, sights and scope mounting as the M1 slug gun. My son's friend has been dragging a Nova Pump across the swamps and fields for several years now. Teenagers are known to be a bit hard on equipment, but the Nova has taken everything the young fellow has dished out.

The Nova Pump in 3 1/2-inch 12 gauge is also available in a Tactical version for law enforcement. Sight choices are either open sights or ghost-ring aperture sights.

Beretta

Beretta has upgraded some of its existing autoloader and over/under guns.

The Onyx over/under Pro Series has the X-Tra Wood finish featuring a film and sealant that waterproofs the stock and produces a rich grain pattern. The film is protected by a tough semi-gloss lacquer. The process does partially fill in checkering grooves and covers the sharp points. The Pro Series also comes with a TRUGLO Tru-Bead fiber optic front bead, extended choke tubes, fluted beavertail forearm and Gel-Tek recoil pad. A molded carry case includes five chokes and an assortment of accessories. The gun is chambered for 12, 20, and 28 gauge. A 12-gauge 3 1/2-inch version features a non-reflective matte black finish on the barrels and receiver.

The new White Onyx features a nickel-alloy receiver machined with a Dura-Jewel pattern. A schnabel forearm and "two-point" cut checkering highlight the walnut stock on this 6.8 pound 12-gauge gun. A molded carrying case includes five chokes and an assortment of accessories.

The Silver Pigeon IV over/under is designed for the American market. The black-finish receiver is completely covered in scroll engraving and features gold-filled mallards and pheasants on the 12-gauge model; quail and grouse on the 20- and 28-gauge guns. A gold-filled "three-arrow" Beretta logo rests on the receiver base. A Gel-Tek recoil pad completes the oil-finished walnut stock and beavertail forearm. A TRUGLO fiber-optic bead provides the gun's sight. A hard case and all the chokes and goodies are included.

The side-by-side barrels of the 471 Silver Hawk have been laser-fused to its monoblock. The gun's Optima-Choke tubes have a longer constriction taper to treat pellets kindly and improve patterns. A switch inside the forearm selects either automatic ejection or manual extraction of fired cases. A nickel finish protects the floral engraving.

The 12-gauge Ringneck and 20-gauge Covey join the 686 over/under lineup. The 12 gauge features three gold-filled flushing pheasants to honor the conservation organization Pheasants Forever. The 20 gauge includes a scene on the receiver of flushing quail for the Quail Unlimited conservation organization.

The autoloading AL391 Covey and Ringneck receive the same treatment.

The AL391 Teknys are further refined 391s. The 12- and 20-gauge guns feature a nickel receiver, with polished sides and an anti-glare top.

Its TRUGLO fiber-optic front sight comes in two colors. Stocks on the Teknys have been treated with X-Tra Wood to waterproof and improve their appearance. The stock on the 12-gauge model also accepts Beretta's recoil reducer, an 8 1/2-ounce device adapted from the Spring-Mass recoil reduction system on the AL391 Xtremea 3 1/2-inch gun. All 12-gauge guns come standard with Optima-Bore overbored barrels and Optima-Choke Plus tubes. The guns come in a hard case that includes stock adjustment spacers, magazine reducer, grip cap, sling swivels, five choke tubes and wrench and a gas valve disassembly tool.

The AL391 Teknys Gold and Gold Sporting guns include all those features. But select walnut has been used instead of the X-Tra Wood covering. The receiver flats also feature engraved hunting scenes and colored enamel inserts that continue into the grip sides.

The A391 Xtrema 3-1/2 has been in hunters' hands for nearly a year and it is the closest gun yet to an all-around shotgun, if there is such a gun. The Xtrema cycles all my 12-gauge 1 1/8-ounce loads and nearly all my 1-ounce target loads. Plus its in-stock recoil reducer, Gel-Tek recoil pad and rubber inlays in the grip and forearm take a lot of the sting out of 3 1/2-inch magnum shells. I fired 60 magnum shells through it one after another, then a box of target loads at clay pigeons. The gun cycled flawlessly and stood ready for more.

The 3901 is a no-frills autoloading 12- or 20-gauge gun derived from the AL390 Silver Mallard. This year the line has been expanded to include the 3901 Camo with full coverage of Mossy Oak New Break-Up and New Shadowgrass.

Gail Haviland with her 20-gauge Beretta and ruffed grouse.

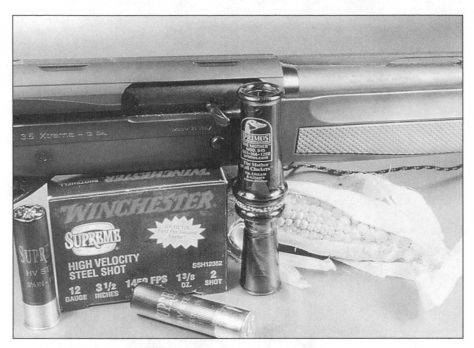

The 3 1/2-inch, 12-gauge Beretta Extreme has been in the field for a year now and comes close to being the all-around gun.

The 3901 RL (reduced length) in 20 gauge has a shorter 13 1/2-inch length of pull, and a one-inch spacer for when the kids grow up.

Circling ducks will have a more difficult time spotting the ES100 autoloader with its complete covering of Realtree Hardwoods HD camo.

The Sporting version of the EELL Diamond Pigeon 12 gauge has an Optima-Bore and five flush-fitting Optima-Chokes.

Browning

The 28 gauge and .410 bore have been added to the Citori 525 Field, Sporting and Golden Clays over/unders. These smaller gauge guns actually weigh 6 to 12 ounces more than the same model gun in 20 gauge.

A Golden Clays version is now available in the BT-99 single-barrel 12-gauge trap gun. It has an adjustable comb and a GraCoil recoil reduction system. Its engraving is accented with 24-karat gold and there is a brighter finish on its wood.

Browning has also added its Dura-Touch armor-coating finish to the stock and forearm of its Gold and BPS shotguns with Mossy Oak camouflage.

Also standard on Gold and BPS turkey shotguns is the HiViz TriViz fiber-optic sight. The triangular-shaped rear portion of the sight contains two fiber optic beads. The front bead, mounted at the muzzle, aligns between the two rear beads.

EAA Corporation

European American Armory Corporation of Sharpes, Florida, imports a full line of guns from Russia, from BB guns and target rifles to handguns and shotguns.

A couple of their new guns are the autoloading 12-gauge MP153 SYN with a black synthetic stock and forend, and the IZH18 Sporting single-barrel with a nickel receiver.

EAA's best accessory is rifle barrel inserts for its cowboy IZH43KH side-by-side hammer shotgun. The inserts are chambered in 45-70, 30-06, 308 Winchester, 222 and 223 Remington. The inserts are held in the 12-gauge bore with a lock at the breech, and by the threads of the screw-in chokes at the muzzle. It is a pretty solid gun to contain the pressure of a 308.

FABARM

Gold Lion Mark II has been replaced with the Gold Lion Mark III. The Mark III has a new gas system to reliably cycle all 12-gauge shells—from light target loads to 3-inch goose killers. The Mark III also features nicer walnut in its stock and forearm, as well as scroll engraving and gold inlays on the receiver flats.

The H368 autoloader is now available in a left-hand version. Also added is a polymer stock with a "soft-touch" coating for a sure grip.

Cosmetic changes have been made to several shotguns. Color case-hardening adds a subdued look to the Sporting Clays Max Lion over/under and Lion Elite side-by-side. A black and silver finish highlights the receiver of the Rex Lion autoloader

New sights grace the FABARM law enforcement shotguns. A ghost ring rear aperture makes for quick sighting. A Picatinny rail accepts scopes and other sights.

Ithaca

Making some internal parts of synthetic material has allowed Ithaca to introduce three lower-cost pump shotguns based on its Model 37. The Deerslayer II Storm has a 24-inch rifled barrel with a 1:35 twist. The gun has open sights and its receiver top is drilled and tapped for scope mounts. The Turkeyslayer Storm 12 gauge has a 24-inch barrel. TRUGLO fiber-optic front and rear sight help aim in low light. Realtree Hardwood Green camo covers the entire gun. The Waterfowler Storm 12 gauge wears a black synthetic stock and forearm with a removable 28-inch barrel and a Raybar front sight. Both bird guns have screw-in choke tubes.

All three have Parkerized finishes on metal parts. A Sims LimbSaver recoil pad helps tame recoil.

For Model 37 shotguns with serial numbers above 855,000, Ithaca is offering a Turkey Retro Fit Kit. The Kit includes a camouflaged turkey barrel, stock and forearm and Sims LimbSaver recoil pad. The made-over gun stores in a supplied hard case.

The Ithaca folks say the 16-gauge Model 37 continues to sell very well.

The autoloading 20-gauge Browning gold was Gail Haviland's choice for harder-kicking waterfowl and pheasant loads.

Marlin

Perhaps spurred by the success of Winchester's Model 9410, Marlin now chambers its 1985 lever action in the .410 2 1/2-inch shell and calls it, naturally, the Model 410. This fun little gun has a 22-inch barrel with no choke and a tube magazine that holds four rounds. Sights include an open folding rear, brass-bead front, or a snap-on green fiber-optic front sight. The receiver is ready for scope mounts, in case you want to shoot slugs at chicken-stealing varmints.

Marlin made pretty much the same Model 410 between 1929 and 1932. It was based on the Marlin Model 93 lever action, which was also chambered for the 25-36 Marlin, 30-30, 32 Special, 32-40 and 38-55. What was old is now new.

Mossberg

Mossberg has camouflaged more of its guns and added a few more variations to its Model 500 pump gun.

The new 500 models include the .410 Slugster and .410 Bantam Slugster. Both guns have 24-inch cylinder bore barrels topped with adjustable fiber-optic sights. Both are equipped with black synthetic stocks and forearms and swivel studs to attach slings. The Bantam has a 13-inch length of pull, and a grip contour that places small hands closer to the trigger.

The 500 line now includes the 20-gauge Bantam Turkey with Mossy Oak Treestand-camoed stock and forearm. It also has a 13-inch length of pull, tighter grip and EZ-Reach forearm that brings the pump forend closer to the shooter.

Guns receiving camouflage covering include: SSI-ONE Turkey and Slug with Mossy Oak New Break-Up; Bantam Turkey 20 gauge with Woodlands camo, or Parkerized metal with a Mossy Oak Treestand stock and forearm; 835 Ulti-Mag pump in Realtree Hardwoods HD Green, Mossy Oak New Break-Up, Forest Floor and Shadow Grass. These guns come with a molded hard case and cable lock.

Perazzi

For those who cannot decide whether to drive the Bentley or Hummer to the country estate to hunt woodcock and ruffed grouse, Perazzi has a set of four Game Shotguns. The 12-, 20-, 28-gauge, and .410 over/unders can be made with 26 3/4- to 29 1/2-inch barrels, and a straight- or curved-grip stock of beautifully marbled walnut, plus your choice of several dozen engraving patterns, all meticulously magnificent.

The Model MX8 and MX2000/8 12-gauge competition guns come with an extra set of lighter barrels that accept gauge-reduction tubes.

RCBS' The Grand

Ever since reloading shotshells on RCBS' new The Grand progressive shotshell press, I no longer need to sweep up inadvertently spilled powder and shot because The Grand only dispenses powder and shot when a

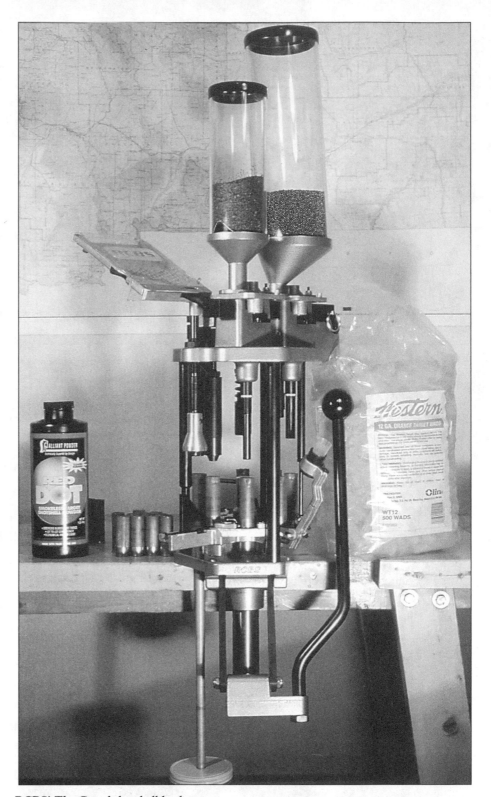

RCBS' *The Grand* shotshell loader.

shell is present to accept it. That's just one of The Grand's features that make loading shotshells easy and fast.

The Grand comes fully assembled, except for the shot and powder hoppers and spent primer catcher. Those require only a couple minutes to install. After weighing the dispensed shot and powder to make sure they were correct, every pull of the handle kicked out a finished shell. All I had to do was insert a hull in the first station and a wad in the fourth station.

The press weighs nearly forty pounds and its heavy frame, steel rod assembly, 1.5-inch diameter ram and compound leverage system make it sturdy and powerful enough to effortlessly load shells. Each pull of the handle completes eight reloading steps from resizing a case to eject a finished shell. On the down stroke, cases rotate to the next reloading step. At every station, cases are easily removed for inspection. In addition to the lockout feature that prevented a mess of spilled powder and shot, the priming system worked flawlessly and the tilt-out wad guide made inserting wads fast and easy. Each station is easily adjusted by loosening a lock nut and screwing the tools up or down to accommodate different style hulls and wads that require varying amounts of pressure to seat primers and wads and crimp the shell mouths. Switching from Federal to Winchester cases took all of one minute.

Changing the powder and shot bushings involved only removing a pin, sliding out the charge bar and inserting bushings. Additional lead shot and powder bushings are available from RCBS. Midway (1-800-243-3220) also lists them at $4.99 each and states Hornady powder bushings are interchangeable. Shot bushings range from 7/8-ounce of #9s to 1 ⌡ ounces of #6 lead shot. Bushings for harder nontoxic shots, like steel, are not yet available.

I loaded 100 12-gauge rounds in about 20 minutes. When I finished, I turned the powder and shot hoppers to the "empty" positions and drained the powder and shot back into their containers. Once again, no mess.

The one thing I didn't like about The Grand is the finished shotshells are ejected at the left rear of the press. I had to stretch around to catch each shell as it kicked out or let them pile up on the bench top and then pack them in a box. One solution would be to mount the press on an optional riser stand that raises the press four inches above the bench. Then shells will fall into a container. Also, a three-inch diameter hole can be drilled through the bench top for the shells to fall through into a container beneath the bench, if you don't mind a big hole in your bench. However, letting the shells pile up is a minor inconvenience, considering how smooth and fast The Grand produces shotshells.

The press is available in 12 or 20 gauge. An optional conversion kit switches gauges.

Remington

The 16-gauge Remington Model 870 sold so well during the last year that Remington is back with more models in this middle gauge. Remington calls the 16-gauge Model 1100 Classic Field "the

TRUGLO fiber-optic sights are the hottest sights on shotguns.

ultimate upland autoloader." The 16-gauge version is based on the 12-gauge receiver with an American walnut stock and forearm. The walnut has white line spacers between the wood and plastic grip cap and buttplate, reminiscent of the 16-gauge 1100 of 30-some years ago. Metal finish is polished blue and a mid-rib aiming bead reminds you to keep your cheek planted on the stock comb. The Synthetic Field has a black plastic stock and black matte finish on its metal. Barrels for both models are 26 or 28 inches, with a ventilated rib and interchangeable chokes.

The Model 1100 Competition Master 12 gauge is Remington's entry for three-gun matches in practical shooting sports. Its stock and forearm are flat-gray synthetic. A Sims R3 recoil pad soaks up recoil. The metal is finished in matte-black. The 22-inch vent-ribbed barrel accepts interchangeable chokes and has a fiber-optic front bead. An eight-round magazine attaches to the barrel and a receiver-mounted ammo carrier holds an extra seven shells. An extended carrier release button and extra large bolt handle helps speed loading.

The Model 1100 Tournament Skeet 12 gauge features American walnut stock and forearm, and polished blued receiver and barrel. The stock dimensions are slightly different from standard models, with a slightly longer 14 3/16-inch length of pull and 1/4-inch less drop at heel compared to Model 1100 Sporting guns. For those who forget what they are doing, "Tournament Skeet" is roll-marked on the barrel. The barrel is 26 inches with a light contour to shave some weight, and a white front bead and mid-rib steel bead. Extended Skeet and Improved Cylinder choke tubes complete the outfit.

Many turkey hunters have found a boxcar full of shot from a 10- or 12-gauge magnum isn't required to kill a turkey. The three-inch 20 gauge with 1 1/4-ounces of shot is plenty to roll over a gobbler, and the recoil won't knock you out from under your camo cap. Model 870 Express Youth Turkey Camo and Model 1100 Youth Synthetic Turkey Camo 20-gauge guns have been outfitted in Skyline Excel Camouflage. Their 21-inch barrels and 13-inch length of pull are just right for young hunters. The Model 870 SPS-T 20 gauge is made to fit grown-up hunters. It has TRUGLO fiber-optic sights, synthetic stock and forearm, an extended turkey Super Full choke tube and a compete covering of Mossy Oak Break-up camouflage.

The Model 870 Express Turkey Camo gun also has its stock and forearm covered in Skyline Excel Camouflage. The 870 Express Super Magnum Turkey is completely covered in Skyline Excel.

As a tribute to NASCAR legend Dale Earnhardt, Remington has issued a limited edition Model 11-87 Premier Dale Earnhardt. It has a 12-gauge 28-inch light contour barrel and an American walnut stock and forearm. The blued receiver is engraved with

Earnhardt's likeness, gold signature and "7 time Winston Cup Champion" banner.

Stevens/Savage

Al Kasper, of Savage/Stevens, says his company has always been associated with value-priced shotguns, like the Savage 330 over/under and Stevens 311 side-by-side. The new Stevens Model 411 Upland Sporter side-by-side in 12, 20 and .410 continues that tradition.

The gun is made in Imz, Russia in a factory that used to supply the Russian military. "But with the Cold War over, the factories had thousands of employees standing around with nothing to do," Kasper says. "Now they're starting to turn their resources to commercial ventures."

When Savage was considering the shotgun, Savage's president, Ron Coburn, traveled to Russia to help the Russians include the fit and features Americans want. Coburn got it right, and at a retail price of $395 for the 12-gauge gun.

A sample gun handled very well with a thin wrist to its checkered grip, one-inch drop between the comb and heel, and nice balance between the stock and splinter forearm of its 26-inch barrels. The 12 gauge weighs 6 3/4 pounds, the 20 gauge and .410 a half-pound less. The gun has chrome-lined bores threaded to accept Full, Modified and Improved Cylinder choke tubes. The gun also has a single selective trigger, automatic ejectors and a tang-mounted safety that returns to *safe* when the action is opened. Laser engraving shows a dog flushing a duck on one sideplate and a dog flushing a pheasant on the other. Engraving also adorns the trigger guard and forearm iron. A brass middle bead and red fluorescent front bead point the way to the target.

Stoeger

Barrels, a slug gun and a hammerless hinge action are new from Stoeger.

The barrels fit the Model 2000 autoloader. The 26-inch field barrel has a ventilated rib and front white bead. The slug barrel is a 24-inch smooth bore with adjustable sights and screw-in Cylinder choke. Take your pick of black or Advantage Timber HD camo.

The Model 2000 Slug Synthetic has the same barrel with, as the name implies, a black synthetic stock and forearm.

The Single Barrel Hunter is hammerless and its hinge action opens by squeezing the trigger guard up and in. The gun comes in 12, 20 or .410 with four screw-in chokes. The barrel has a ventilated rib and fiber-optic front bead. A youth model in 20 and .410 has a 13-inch length of pull. It's a perfect gun for potting grouse along the trail.

Traditions

Tradition's Fausti Stefano shotguns, produced in Brescia, Italy, have introduced two new models of its Elite side-by-sides and three Field over/unders and Emilio Rizzini side-by-side and over/under guns.

The Fausti Field III 20 has a ventilated rib and 26- or 28-inch barrels, three screw-in chokes, automatic ejectors, single triggers, and gold engraved receiver. Weights are 7 1/4 to 7 1/2 pounds. All that comes packaged in a hard case. The Field Hunter Silver is a slightly plainer version in 12 and 20 gauge. The Sporting Clay III 20 gauge weighs 3/4 of a pound more. Barrels are 28 or 30 inches. Extra features include four chokes, ported barrels, front target bead and 3/8-inch wide rib.

The side-by-side Elite Hunter ST Silver and Elite I DT join the established Elite I ST. The DT has double triggers, fixed chokes and a straight grip. Gauges are 12, 20, 28 and .410 bore. Very retro. But how nice, at 5 3/4 pounds in the 28 gauge, to carry in a ruffed grouse bottom. The ST Silver 12 and 20 have a matte silver receiver and screw-in chokes, single trigger and a curved grip. The 26-inch-barreled 20 gauge weighs 5 3/4 pounds. Very forward thinking.

The 12-gauge Emilio Rizzini over/under Gold Wing includes the III, SL III, II Silver, III Silver and SL III Silver. The Silver grades are made with silver-colored receivers engraved with game birds. The regular Golds have color case-hardened receivers with engraving and gold-filled game birds. All the guns weigh 7 1/2 pounds with a single trigger, 28-inch barrels and screw-in chokes. Walnut stocks have checkered, curved grips and matching forearms.

The Emilion Rizzini Uplander Series includes 12- and 20-gauge side-by-sides in three grades. All the guns have three-inch chambers and 28- or 26-inch ventilated rib barrels, threaded muzzles to accept various choke tubes, and straight-grip stocks and splinter forearms. The Uplander II has double triggers, tang safety and a limited amount of engraving on the receiver. The Uplander III is a step up, with a single trigger and engraved silver receiver featuring a gold-inlayed woodcock. The Uplander V has extended sideplates that, along with the receiver, are completely engraved and include a scene of a gold-inlayed flushing duck.

Tristar

Marty Fajen's father-in-law was Reinhart Fajen, who owned the Fajen gunstock company for decades. After the company was sold Marty decided to open her own company, Tristar, importing shotguns, rifles, revolvers and shooting accessories.

Tristar imports Emilio Rizzini shotguns from Italy. They include over/unders, side-by-sides and semi-auto guns in a wide range of styles, for flying game from geese to quail. Gauges include the 12, 16, 20, 28 and .410 bore. There's even a 12-gauge over/under chambered for the 12-gauge 3 1/2-inch shell, although why anyone would voluntarily take such a sledgehammer blow to the head is a mystery.

Verona

B.C. Outdoors' Verona has brought out new competition, sporting and hunting guns.

The LX980 Top Competition includes the Trap, Sporting and Skeet/Sporting 12 gauge over/unders. All three have 2 3/4-inch chambers; four locking, ported barrels that accept four Briley Spectrum choke tubes, TRUGLO fiber-optic front bead, and plain bead on the middle of the ventilated rib. A hard case protects the Turkish walnut stock from dings and scratches. The Trap model has 32-inch barrels and an adjustable comb. The stock comb is also adjustable on the Skeet/Sporting, which wears 30-inch barrels. The Sporting wears a standard stock and 30-inch barrels.

The Verona LX692 Gold Competition superposed guns are now available in smaller bores, with two- and three-barrel sets. The LX692GCSK-20/28 is chambered in 20 and 28 with 30-inch barrels, complete with forearms. The LX692GCSK-28/410 comes in 28 and .410 and the LX692GC-Trio in 20, 28 and .410 bore. The 20- and 28-gauge barrels include five screw-in chokes, while the .410 has Skeet and Skeet chokes. All combinations weigh about 6 1/4 pounds and come with a hard case.

Bernardelli in Italy makes the LX801 Sporting and Competition/Sporting semiautomatics. These gas-operated guns include a ported 28- or 30-inch barrel, 9mm-width ventilated rib and TRUGLO front bead and four Trulock screw-in chokes. Stocks have a Monte Carlo hump.

The LX1001 Express Combo is for days when the country holds both furred and feathered game. The over/under has a 28-inch barrel set in 20 gauge. The twin barrels for rifles are chambered for 223, 243, 270, 308 or 30-06. A 30-06/20-gauge set is for grouse and big game during the same hike. Rifle sights are a **V** at the rear on a quarter-rib; at the front a fiber-optic pipe atop a blade. A sling swivel hangs below the bottom rifle barrel.

How did hunters ever kill game without using camouflaged guns? Game won't have an inkling what hit them because the Verona semi-auto 12-gauge SX405 is covered with specific camo patterns for different animals. The SX405 Camo for waterfowl hunters is cloaked with Real Tree Wetland or Hardwood camo. The SX405T Camo for turkey hunters is shrouded in Real Tree Hardwood. The gun has a 24-inch barrel, with front and rear TRUGLO sights. The SX405Slug has a 22-inch rifled barrel and TRUGLO front and rear sights—all hidden under the Hardwood pattern. The SX405 Combo has the same slug barrel, and a 26-inch smoothbore for birds, with a plain black synthetic stock and forearm.

Weatherby

Weatherby's Italian-made Semi-Auto Shotgun (SAS) is decked out in different styles for sporting clays, upland game to waterfowl. Now the SAS is made in a slug gun configuration. The gas-operated 12-gauge, 3-inch gun has a 22-inch rifled barrel with a cantilever scope base that extends back over the receiver. The hump of the Monte Carlo comb says *Weatherby*, and raises the eye to line up with a scope. Shims fit between the receiver and front of the grip to adjust drop and cast.

Winchester

Winchester had such a hit with its Model 9410 in .410 bore that it has added the Invector-Plus Choke System, with Full, Improved Modified, Modified and Skeet tubes, to its Packer and Packer Compact models. All five 9410 models have the new top tang safety.

The Supreme Select Elegance, Sporting and Field 12-gauge guns are Winchester's next generation of over/under guns. Winchester states balance is their best feature, derived from lighter and slimmer barrels, low-profile receiver and a "well-executed stock." The guns have two locking lugs along the lower sides of the top barrel. The lugs can be adjusted to compensate for wear over the years. A third fixed lug under the barrels reduces wear. Barrels are back-bored and include the Invector-Plus choke tubes.

The Field features a scene of flushing game birds engraved on the receiver flats, and blued barrels to match. Barrel lengths are 26 or 28 inches and come with chrome-plated, three-inch chambers. Its walnut is the plainest of the three models, yet full panels of checkering cover the grip and forearm.

The Elegance is the fancy model and has flushing pheasants engraved on its grayed receiver and Grade III walnut, checkered in a point pattern on the grip and forearm. Barrel choices are 26 or 28 inches, with three-inch chambers. For some reason the butt wears a hard plate.

Probably because the Sporting will be shot more, it has a ribbed recoil pad and ported barrels. A swoop of dark gray on the receiver sides contrasts well with the brushed silver receiver. A trigger shoe easily adjusts length of pull. Barrels are 28 or 30 inches, with 2 3/4-inch chambers.

The Dura-Touch armor coating has been added to more Super X2 shotguns. The coating has a soft feel and provides a sure grip in all the foul weather a waterfowl hunter endures during a season. In addition, the coating protects the finish on the stock and forearm. The finish has been added to the Practical MK II, Signature Red Sporting, Composite, 3 1/2-inch Composite and camouflage models.

The red hardwood stock makes the Super X2 Signature Red Sporting stand out in any rack of guns in the clubhouse. The gun includes shims to adjust the stock's cast and comb height, five choke tubes and two gas pistons that help the gun cycle all sporting loads. ●

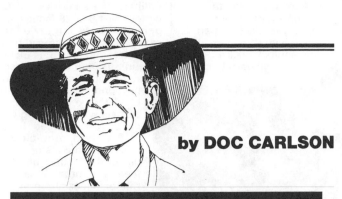

by DOC CARLSON

BLACKPOWDER REVIEW

*F*OR MANY YEARS, the only folks shooting blackpowder were those interested in traditional muzzle-loading firearms. Hunting was usually done during regular centerfire seasons with the traditional side-hammer flint or percussion firearm. The reproduction guns on the market catered to this interest, and the relative few who were into "reenacting" usually were Civil War re-enactors, or buckskinners who relived the pre-1840 period.

Then the muzzleloading hunting craze hit and the market responded by offering the "in-line" rifle. These guns, while muzzleloaders, duplicated the look and feel of the modern, bolt-action rifle familiar to most hunters. Traditional sidelock guns dwindled in market share.

Then the blackpowder cartridge interest developed, kindled by interest in blackpowder cartridge silhouette, cowboy action shooting and Creedmoor long-range shooting with the old blackpowder cartridge firearms. The marketplace again responded and soon new guns appeared to shoot the blackpowder cartridges of yesteryear.

Today, we have a well-balanced market that offers a wide range of all types of blackpowder firearms. There's something for everyone, regardless of the field of interest.

Traditions Performance Firearms

Traditions Performance Firearms is one of the early companies involved in the rebirth of interest in blackpowder. Their first offerings were purely traditional side-hammer guns, but over time their product line expanded to all phases of the blackpowder sport, and now includes modern shotguns as well.

New this year from Traditions are the Evolution and Thunder Bolt series of rifles. These are bolt-action in-line guns. The Evolution features a new, stainless steel bolt system designed to operation smoothly. The striker cocks on lifting of the oversize bolt handle designed to give a firm grip with cold, or gloved fingers. a cocking indicator at the rear of the bolt indicates–by sight or touch–whether the gun is cocked or not. The 24-inch tapered

barrel is available in either blued or stainless steel, in 50-caliber with a 1:28-inch twist or 54-caliber with a 1:48-inch spiral. All barrels feature the Positive Alignment System (PAS), a recessed muzzle to ease starting the bullet in perfect alignment with the bore. Projectile alignment is essential to good accuracy and the recessed muzzle eases reloading in the field.

The Evolution rifle is offered in several stock styles including black synthetic, synthetic with a camo finish, beech wood and New X-Wood—which is a coating on a beech stock that looks more like very high-grade walnut than the real thing. The tapered barrel makes these guns balance and shoulder well. Sights are steel fiber optic and the ramrod is aluminum. Ignition is by 209 shotgun primers.

An Evolution LD (Long Distance) is offered with an extended barrel to give more velocity. This one will be available in 45- and 50-caliber, with an internally-ported barrel to handle heavier charges with lower recoil. The Evolution Premier will have all the bells and whistles of the Evolution, plus a ported, fluted barrel.

The Thunder Bolt is a modified, economical version of the Evolution featuring the same bolt system etc., in blued steel only. It is available in 45- or 50-caliber with plastic fiber optic sights and a synthetic ramrod. It is available with either a black or camo synthetic stock and either blued or stainless steel barrel. A youth-size model with black synthetic stock in 50-caliber is available also.

Both the Evolution and Thunder Bolt guns are drilled and tapped for scope mounts and carry sling swivel studs.

Traditions also offers a full line of traditional muzzleloaders–both rifles and pistols–as well as blackpowder cartridge rifles and pistols.

Rossi Firearms

Rossi Firearms is a well recognized as a maker of cartridge pistols, revolvers and rifles. They are now in the muzzle-loading game with a top-break in-line type rifle that resembles the single-shot shotgun familiar to all.

Traditions Evolution with camo stock.

Traditions Evolution with the Real Wood stock coating that looks more like high-grade walnut than the real thing.

Rossi's three-barrel, do-anything rifle.

This gun features a center-hung hammer with a hammer-block safety. The easily removable breech plug takes #209 shotgun primers. The 50-caliber barrel is 23 inches long and available in either matte stainless or blued finish. Sights are Tru-Glo fiber optic and a brass and wood collapsible ramrod that tucks under the barrel and into the forend is supplied. The gun is drilled and tapped for scope mounting, if you wish, and a hammer extension is available for ease of cocking under a scope. The stocks are wood and the buttstock is supplied with a rubber recoil pad. A breech plug wrench is included with these rifles, as well as a trigger lock. The Rossi is a good quality rifle at a reasonable price.

The icing on the cake is availability of these rifles in combination sets. The muzzle-loading rifle can be had with interchangeable barrels in 20-gauge *(cartridge, with a Modified choke)* and 243 Winchester, or as a three-barrel set with the 50-caliber muzzleloader combined with two of the hottest new cartridges: the 270 Winchester Short Magnum (WSM) and the 17 HMR. These combination sets come with extra forends for their respective barrels and a custom nylon carrying case with a shoulder strap that fits either the carrying case or the guns. A nice set-up, at a very reasonable price, for the all-season hunter and shooter— and a great starter outfit for the beginning shooter.

Winchester Firearms/USRAC

Winchester introduced a bolt-action in-line muzzleloader a couple of years ago and have now added another rifle to the Winchester muzzle-loading

Knight Rifle's Master Hunter Disc Extreme rifle.

line. Called the Apex Magnum, this new offering features a drop-block action. The trigger guard is dropped down, which rotates a breechblock backward and downward to clear the breech plug area of the rifle. A #209 shotgun primer is inserted into the breech plug, the trigger guard is pulled back into position, rotating the breechblock back up behind the breech plug, and the hammer is cocked. When the trigger is pulled, the hammer falls, firing the gun. The dropping block clears the breech plug for ease of installing the #209 primers or removal of the breech plug for cleaning. When closed, the breechblock provides a weather-tight seal, very important when hunting on a wet, snowy day. These guns feature a typical Monte Carlo stock with palm swell and beavertail forend–in either black fleck or Mossy Oak Break Up synthetic–and are fitted with a magnum recoil pad and sling swivels. Barrel and action finish can be either blue or stainless. Fiber-optic sights are installed on the fluted 30-inch barrel and are guaranteed for life against breakage.

Calibers offered are 45 and 50, both with a twist of 1:28 inches and a bullet-guiding, recessed muzzle for loading ease. A synthetic ramrod hangs under the barrel and a sling is included with all guns. Trigger pull is preset at the factory at 3 pounds and the rebounding hammer features a block that keeps the hammer from contact with the firing pin unless the trigger is pulled.

The short, drop-block action on this new Winchester gun allows the use of the 30-inch barrel with no feeling of muzzle-heaviness. The rifle balances and points very well.

Knight Rifles

Knight Rifles continues to add to their line and upgrade their products for the muzzle-loading hunter. Their newest rifle, the Master Hunter Disc Extreme, incorporates the latest upgrades and design advances found in the Knight line, and features the full plastic jacket ignition system that encloses the #209 shotgun primer. The jacket is then slipped on a nipple at the rear of the breech plug and the bolt is closed, sealing the whole system weather-tight. The Knight folks have submerged this breech/primer system in water for a full hour with no leakage or failure to fire, so it should work OK in rain or snow, I imagine.

The schnabel forend, thumbhole-style stock is made of laminated wood with a high gloss finish. The gun is shipped with a spare synthetic stock that can be used in the hunting field, if one wishes one stock to admire and another one to rattle around in the pickup. Stocks are supplied with recoil pad and sling swivel studs. The fluted

The Knight Full Plastic Jacket System.

Knight's new disc that takes #11 percussion caps.

fiber optic, ramrod is of a synthetic near-unbreakable material and the receiver is, of course, drilled and tapped for scope bases.

Knight has added a modified priming disc, to be used in their standard disc rifles, that takes #11 caps. This allows these guns to be used in states that require the use of percussion caps and ban the #209 shotgun primer.

Rightnour Manufacturing Inc.

Along a more traditional line but with a touch of modern, we have the RMC Accusporter Rifles by Rightnour Manufacturing Inc. This half-stock flintlock rifle (in either right- or left-hand) is set into a laminated wood stock (brown or green camo) usually found on a modern in-line action rifle, not a flintlock. The stock style is a shotgun configuration with a flat butt that points and handles recoil well. The 28-inch Green Mountain barrel carries a 1:48 or 1:28 twist for either patched round ball or sabots and bullet-type projectiles. The flintlock itself is made

by the L & R Lock Company, well known for quality flint and percussion locks, whose locks are used on many of the custom muzzle-loading guns made by the better-known makers. The rifles are set up for hunting, with fiber-optic sights (standard) and a single trigger. Hardware and barrel are blued. They are available in either right or left hand.

For those with something else in mind, barrel-wise, the lock/stock assembly can also be purchased, sans barrel. You can then add any of the standard "drop-in" barrels that fit the T/C Hawken, Lyman Deerstalker or Trade Rifle, Traditions Hawken & Deerhunter, or similar guns. This allows selection of any caliber and barrel length, as long as you stay with 15/16-inch barrels. A nice idea, and not offered anywhere else, to my knowledge.

For those who shoot flint guns because they'd rather—or for those who must, due to game laws in their state—this RMC Accusporter is a well-made, fast-handling little rifle with top quality components.

Thompson/Center

An old friend is back. A few years ago Thompson/Center dropped their Renegade series rifles from production. I really missed the little rifle, a workhorse hunting rifle of a traditional, side-hammer percussion design. My wife has had one in 54-caliber for some years and has killed a fair amount of

stainless barrel is available in 50- or 45-caliber with 1:30 and 1:28 twists, respectively. The stainless barrel is cryogenically accurized by exposure to a controlled heating and freezing process for two days to stabilize the barrel at the molecular level by relieving stresses in the barrel steel. The result is a barrel that has little or no tendency to warp when exposed to the heat of firing, thus delivering superior accuracy, something that the centerfire shooters have known for some time.

The bolt (and those of all Knight rifles) has been updated so that it can be disassembled without tools, eliminating the need to carry a special tool afield or to the range. Sights are

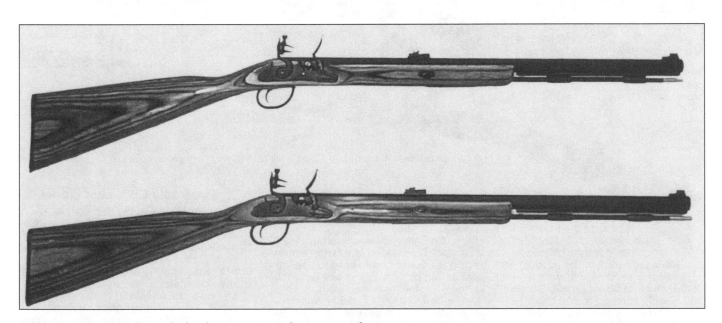

RMC's Accusporter rifle stocked in brown- or green-laminate wood.

The Thompson/Center Renegade Hunter—an old friend.

The Thompson/Center Renegade is a world-class hunting rifle.

hardened. As an added bonus, the gun is available in both right- and left-hand versions.

Welcome back, Renegade. The muzzle-loading hunters of this country will be glad to see you again.

T/C has also added a 45-caliber option to their very successful Omega series drop block in-line rifles. At present, the 45-caliber version of the Omega is available only with a synthetic stock, and either stainless or blued-steel barrel.

Austin & Halleck

The Mountain Rifle, a very traditional half-stock rifle from Austin & Halleck, is available with rifling twists of 1:66 for round ball and 1:28 for bullets. The 32-inch 50-caliber browned barrel of these rifles is 1 inch across the flats and topped with buckhorn rear and silver blade front sights. The sights are fixed *(non-adjustable),* as were most originals. The double-set, double-throw triggers are enclosed in a scroll trigger guard. All hardware is iron, except the barrel key escutcheons, which appear to be German silver.

The maple stock, a typical southern mountain half-stock style, is available in select grade with a great deal of figure; really beautiful wood. The guns are available in either flintlock or percussion, depending on your preference. These rifles are getting a well-deserved reputation for quality and good looks. They would be equally at home on the hunting trail or at Rendezvous.

Austin & Halleck Mountain Rifle; very traditional, very good quality.

game with it in the U.S. and Africa. I've enjoyed shooting the little rifle— when she would let me. The good news is that T/C has put the Renegade back in the product line.

Available in 50-caliber with a 1-inch, 1:48-inch twist blued barrel, the rifle will handle patched round ball, sabotted bullets or slugs with equal aplomb. The QLA (Quick Load Accurizor) recessed muzzle feature *(eases loading of either patched round ball or conical projectiles)* will be appreciated by hunters

everywhere. The reliable percussion lock has the same coil-spring innards found in the well-known T/C Hawken series of rifles.

The Renegade's single hunting trigger is enclosed in a large, roomy trigger guard that is easy to use while wearing gloves. Sights are typical of the T/C bloodline, a fully adjustable rear coupled with a bead front. The sights are fairly coarse; intended for hunting, not precision target shooting. The half-stock is good, close-grained American walnut, with plain forend and recoil pad. All hardware is blued except the lockplate, which is case-

Pedersoli/ Dixie Gun Works

Another gun—new this year— undoubtedly of interest to the pre-1830 crowd, is the Indian Trade Gun, made by Pedersoli and imported by Dixie Gun Works. This is a pretty close copy of the trade guns made in the 1700s by many makers: Chance, Barnett, Tryon, Deringer, Lehman and Henry come to mind. These musket-like guns were a major item of trade with companies like the Hudson Bay Co., Northwest Co., American Fur Co., and others who traded for the furs and robes of the American wilderness.

Pedersoli/Dixie Indian Trade Gun.

The smoothbore 20-gauge (62-cal.) barrel is just a tad over 36 inches, typical of the breed. The dark-stained, European walnut stock has lines appropriate for this style of

The Gibbs Target Rifle from Dixie.

gun. The large flintlock is the familiar Lott lock that has been seen on reproduction guns for many years. It's a heavily sprung, good-sparking lock that can be relied upon to ignite the large pan every time, if the shooter does his part. The large, typical trigger guard and trigger are iron *(browned)* and the wooden ramrod is held under the full-stock forend in brass ferrules. The left side of the stock has the obligatory brass dragon sideplate that carries the lock screws. A brass front sight and brass buttplate complete the picture. There is no rear sight; again, typical of these firearms. Given the interest in the Fur Trade era of American history, I expect Dixie will have a lot of success with this latest offering from Italy.

Over the years there has been a lot of interest in the English rifles, made for hunting and target shooting, by such makers as Manton, Egg, and Gibbs. The English style of rifle is patterned similarly to modern stock styles, although these guns date back to the 1700s. They shoulder, point and handle recoil well. The feel of these guns is similar to a well-fitting, modern shotgun. The Brits definitely knew how to make a rifle. The problem has been that, up to now, the only sources of

these fine rifles has been either an original through the collectors' market or a custom creation—both expensive.

Dixie has again teamed up with Pedersoli to bring one of these fine rifles to the muzzleloader shooter, a copy of an English target rifle made in 1865 by George Gibbs. The pistol grip half-stock is of European walnut, oil-finished and hand-checkered on both pistol grip and forend. It sports a horn buttplate, grip cap and forend tip, as did the original gun. The blued steel barrel is a bit over 35 inches long and goes from an octagon-shaped patent breech area to a tapered round configuration, similar to what is found on most originals. It makes this gun "hang" well for offhand shooting.

The percussion lock is of top quality, as one would expect on a target gun. The trigger mechanism is a simple single trigger with a good let-off. I've always been partial to the English style of gun and this one duplicates the look and feel of the originals pretty well.

The sights supplied with the gun include a precision Creedmoor rear, coupled with a windage-adjustable front that takes inserts, 18 of which are supplied with the rifle. The Creedmoor rear has adjustment for windage and almost 3 inches of height adjustment.

There is an oval escutcheon of German silver *(for the owner's initials)* on the underside of the buttstock, forward of the toe. Sling swivels complete the stock furniture.

The rifle is offered in both 40- and 451-caliber with a twist of 1:23-5/8 inches and 5 lands and grooves. Each rifle is shipped with a sizer to size and lubricate cast bullets to fit the barrel. Dixie carries the correct Pedersoli molds.

This rifle handles and points very well and, while it is called a target rifle, there is certainly no reason it wouldn't perform well in the hunting field. This one definitely deserves a look.

Hodgdon Powder Company

Last year Hodgdon Powder Company brought out their new replica blackpowder called 777. Subsequently, it has made a name for itself among shooters for the absence of fouling and plain water cleanup. There is no sulfur so the "rotten egg" smell is gone, allowing the blackpowder shooter to mingle in polite society without causing olfactory alarm. New for this year, Hodgdon has figured out how to pelletize Triple Seven, which is now available in 50-grain pellets

Hodgdon's Triple Seven now available in pellets for 50-caliber.

A new blackpowder from Germany–Scheutzen.

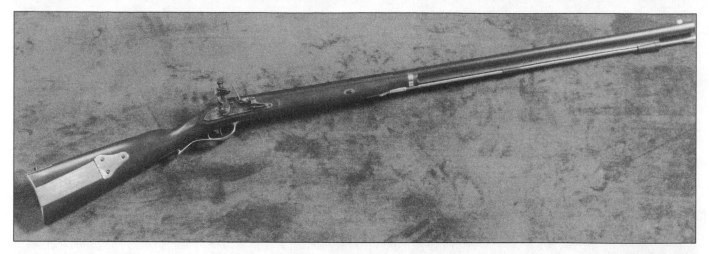

Navy's 1803 Harpers Ferry Lewis and Clark Commemorative Rifle.

for 50-caliber in-lines using #209 primers. The maximum load recommended is two of the 50-grain pellets. This new powder is very consistent, and accuracy has been very good in tests.

The new pellets should be well received by hunters since they eliminate the need to carry flasks, measures and the like. Just drop a pellet or two down the barrel, seat a bullet, prime with a #209—and shoot. One of these days someone is going to figure out how to hook a bullet onto these pellets *(maybe even a primer)* and have the complete load in one package.

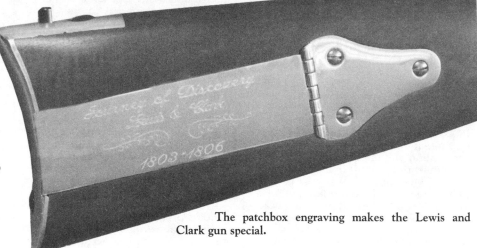

The patchbox engraving makes the Lewis and Clark gun special.

Petro-Explo, Inc.

Blackpowder shooters and hunters now have another brand of blackpowder to use. Petro-Explo, Inc., the folks that import Elephant and Swiss blackpowder, are bringing in a new powder from Germany called Schuetzen. Manufactured by the Wano Schwartzpulver factory using the much sought-after alder charcoal, this new blackpowder will be available in the standard granulations and should be priced with other powders on the market. The Petro-Explo folks have spent considerable time in the German factory to assure the quality and consistency of this powder is top-notch. German powders have a good reputation and, hopefully, this new powder will enhance it.

American Pioneer Powder Company

American Pioneer Powder Company is marketing a loose, granular powder designed to be a sulfurless blackpowder replacement. It is currently available in two granulations––3Fg and 2Fg—and can be used as a volume-for-volume replacement for conventional blackpowder. The manufacturer's published load data show this new powder is slightly hotter than blackpowder, delivering velocities approximately 10 percent above

equivalent loads of blackpowder. It is reported to leave little or no fouling in the bore and, according to the manufacturer, requires no wiping between shots or lubrication of the bullet. It cleans up with plain water.

In addition to the loose granulations, the American Pioneer Powder is available in 50-grain equivalent compressed charges for 50-caliber firearms. The compressed charges are square and are simply pushed down the barrel, followed by the bullet. They have no blackpowder "booster charge" added to facilitate ignition, the manufacturer claiming none is needed. Soon to follow are compressed 50-grain equivalent charges for 45-caliber.

The preceding, along with Goex and KIK blackpowder, and Pyrodex and Clean Shot replacement blackpowder, indicate there will be a good supply of fodder to feed your blackpowder firearm. The many choices available in the marketplace should assure the shooter of finding the right combination of powder and bullet to work best in whatever blackpowder gun is involved, be it muzzleloader or cartridge gun.

Navy Arms Co.

Last year the blackpowder fraternity lost one of its founding fathers, Val Forgett, founder of Navy Arms Co. Navy Arms was one of the first to begin making replica firearms for blackpowder shooters and is, I am happy to say, alive and well and carrying on Val's legacy.

In keeping with the upcoming bicentennial of the Lewis and Clark Expedition, Navy is offering a Model 1803 Harpers Ferry rifle to commemorate the event. The 54-caliber rifle features a half-round, half-octagon browned barrel and an upgraded oil-finished walnut stock. The brass patchbox is engraved "Lewis & Clark Journey of Discovery 1803-1806". Included with each rifle is an exact replica of the Thomas Jefferson Peace Medal or Friendship Medal minted for Lewis & Clark to give to the Indians encountered along the way. This rifle would be a nice memento of the expedition, whether hanging on the wall or being carried afield or to the range.

Enjoy!

by **WAYNE VAN ZWOLL**

SCOPES AND MOUNTS

"THEY DON'T LOOK much different than they did 40 years ago. But they sure cost a lot more." I had to agree with the plaid-clad veteran. He finished wiping down the old Model 70, then ran the rag over its Weaver K4. "You wouldn't believe I paid $49 for that scope." Actually, I did. My first 2.5x Bushnell cost even less. These days, scopes still amount to glass lenses in metal tubes. But if you look *through* them, not just *at* them, you'll see brighter, sharper images and truer colors. You'll see tighter groups on target when you change magnification on variables. And you'll see reticles that don't move off center when you twist adjustment knobs. Some of those reticles help you determine and compensate for range. Some glow in the dark. You might rue rising prices, but you probably don't miss all the features of early scopes: Fogging, for example, or parallax that moved point of impact. Or even adjustment dials that required a screwdriver or a coin.

Binoculars and spotting scopes have undergone similar changes – more substantive than cosmetic, despite continuing efforts to make them look different than their forebears. And now the optics umbrella covers laser rangefinders, which hadn't even entered military service when Weaver K4s first listed for $49.

Annual updates of new hunting optics are seldom complete. Mercifully. Because in a field as broad and competitive as this, you'll find more than you really want to read about. I'll mention here what seem to be the most innovative and useful new optics.

Innovative? It's hard to upstage the new Smart Scope from Adirondack Optics. It's a 3-9x44 with fully multi-coated optics in a 1-inch alloy tube. It has standard quarter-minute adjustments, 3 1/2-inch eye relief. What's different is the integral digital camera. The viewfinder on the ocular housing, and the beefy turret, do nothing for the scope's profile, but it's remarkable that a camera can be included at all in a rifle scope of traditional design! Capture the animal on a SmartMedia memory card before you shoot. Or take the photo instead of a shot. Save it in JPG format to bring up on your computer later. The Smart Scope uses three AAA batteries. You can also select from the Mountain Man scope series: a 1.5-6x44, 3-10x or 4-17x44, all with 30mm tubes (800-815-6814).

If a camera in a scope tests your definition of versatility, there are plenty of other options. Like a military-style scope from United States Optics Technologies. Heavy and costly, these scopes are also very bright and very rugged. The 1-4x SN-4 is properly compact. Other variables, the 1.8-10x, 3.2-17x and 3.8-22x, offer a wide power range and range-compensating reticle options. Prices: from $1905. The 10x,

17x and 22x fixed-powers appeal to me. For extra-long shooting, consider the 3.8-22x SN-9 with an external adjustment that gives you 300 minutes of elevation (usoptics.com).

Horus Vision also looks to the growing market in high-power variables, with a 4-16x scope that boasts the range-finding grid designed by Dennis Sammut for military use. The scope has a turret-mounted parallax adjustment – but that's not all. It comes with a Palm PDA and software that allows you to plot any bullet's trajectory and determine the correct hold for any range or wind condition! Used with the complex and sophisticated reticle, it entertains for hours. Sight pictures never told you so much (horusvision.com).

What does the Sammut reticle look like and how does it work? Well, it incorporates a crosswire with calibrated hashmarks above, below and to the sides of the intersection about a third of the way to the edge of the field. There are 13 crossbars on the lower wire. These vary in length, and are themselves hash-marked. They also have mil-dots. In the upper left quadrant is a rangefinding grid with stadia wires for more precise rangefinding. On windy days, you hold off, using a tic on a horizontal wire as your aiming point. Horizontal wires are longer near the bottom of the field because as range increases and you elevate, you'll get more drift. The Sammut reticle in Schmidt & Bender scopes has evidently been used to shoot Australian vermin at ranges exceeding 1100 yards. Using an S&B scope on a Savage 110 tactical rifle, I was soon planting 185-grain Berger Match bullets near target centers at 700 yards. But it's not a reticle for quick shooting. The spiderweb effect takes some getting used to.

Mil-dot reticles draw lots of attention these days. "Mil" is an abbreviation for *milliradian*, 1/6400 of a degree in angular measurement. That's 3.6 inches at 100 yards, or 3 feet at l000. In a reticle, a mil is the space between

Cabela's offers its own brand of optics, including riflescopes, binoculars and spotting scopes.

3/4-minute dots, strung vertically *(and usually horizontally)* along a crosswire. To use this reticle as a rangefinder, divide target height in mils at 100 yards by the number of spaces subtending it. The result is range in hundreds of yards. For example, a deer 3 feet at the shoulder (10 mils at 100 yards) appears in your scope to stand two dots high. Divide 2 into 10, and you come up with 5; the buck is 500 yards away. You can also divide target size in yards (in this case, 1) by the number of mils subtended (2) and multiply by 1000 to get range in yards. Mil-dot reticles must be calibrated for a single magnification. In variable scopes, that's usually the top-end setting or 10x, but some sights with very high magnification are calibrated at other power settings.

A booklet describing the fine points of long shooting is available from Lou Schwiebert. Called *Mil Dot Master*, it complements Schwiebert's own Ballisticard. The card is a pocket-size ballistics table featuring your favorite load. You specify the bullet you're using, and how fast it leaves the rifle. With the help of sophisticated computer programs, Schwiebert delivers an all-weather laminated 3x5 card with the data you'll need for long-range hits. A three-card set has red, blue and green headings. The green card contains "baseline" data. The red card covers the same bullet shot 100 fps faster, as might be the case if you hunted in hot weather. The blue card shows flight for that bullet driven 100 fps slower: a cold-weather card. Ballisticards show bullet drop (and quarter-minute click values to compensate) at 50-yard intervals from 0 to 500 yards. They include lead values for running game, as well as drift data and corrections for vertical shot angles of 15, 30 and 45 degrees.

Hunters may not have time to consult cards when they see game, but Schwiebert points out that "On stand they can prepare for a shot by ranging objects where the game might appear and by doping wind. That's how tactical shooters operate." Lou can factor in the effects of elevation, temperature and humidity where you hunt. Ballisticards for a couple of my loads are right on the money. They cost about $30 each, with duplicate (800-378-2174).

Hitting at long range can be done quickly if you learn how to use simple rangefinding reticles like those comprising two horizontal stadia wires. The space between subtends a specified measure at a given range. Stadia wires might, for example, subtend the 27-inch depth of a bull elk's chest at 100 yards. If an elk fills half the space, he is roughly 200 yards off. Of course, you'll have to measure subtention before season. Mark paper targets with a felt pen at 3-inch vertical intervals, and examine the paper through your scope at 100 yards. Remember that most variable scopes sold in the U.S. feature reticles in the rear focal plane, so target subtention changes as you change magnification. Reticles in the front focal plane

This inexpensive 8x40 Remington binocular performs like mid-priced glass.

Red-dot sights, like this Smith & Wesson on a new S&W 500 revolver, help you shoot fast.

Bushnell's new Firefly lighted reticle is available in several Elite variable scopes.

Opti-Logic's new rangefinder, like the latest Pentax, can tell you the horizontal component of target distance – useful if you're shooting at steep angles.

Leupold's scope line continues to grow. Wayne mounted this 35x target model on an H-S rifle.

The Minox 8x32 and 10x32 binoculars marketed by Leica make sense for long carries.

in the front focal plane and one in the rear. They are superimposed, appearing as one. You get an aiming reticle that doesn't change size, but a rangefinding reticle *(a series of circles that does not interfere with the aiming reticle)* that changes size with power. You can still get reticles with stadia wires. The Ballistic Plex in Burris Fullfield II scopes is both a rangefinding and range-compensating device. The thin wire beneath the center of the plex-like reticle is a little longer than the other three wires (so the bottom post is shorter). There are three short hash marks on that lower wire, each gap bigger than the one above it, so you get four subtensions at any magnification. Find one or two that are most useful at the power setting you favor on the hunt, and memorize them. The differential spacing of the tics also reflect the parabolic trajectory of bullets. Zero at 100 yards with a 180-grain 30-06 bullet, and you'll hit at the first hash mark (3 inches low) at 200 yards, the second mark (13 inches low) at 300 and the third tic (30 inches low) at 400. At 500 yards, the bullet strikes near the top of the bottom post. Faster bullets zeroed at 200 yards hit near the center wire to 250 yards. At 300 yards your bullet will land about 5 inches low, or close to the first hash mark. At 400 it will strike near the second, 18 inches low. The third tic serves as an aiming point at 500 yards (- 38 inches). You'll hit 66 inches below center at 600, at the top of the post. I've used this Burris reticle for long-range target shooting and hunting. I like its simplicity. Apparently it is selling very well. Burris has incorporated the Ballistic Plex with the mil dot reticle. Result: the Ballistic Mil Dot, now in 6.5-20x Fullfield II, and in 4-16x, 6-24x, and 8x32x Signature and Black Diamond scopes (burrisoptics.com).

New **Burris** products include a "semi-compact" Signature binocular. Choose an 8x32 or 10x32. Minimum advertised prices (MAP): $227 and $244. MAP figures, incidentally, are much lower than retail, something to keep in mind when comparing. Burris now includes aluminum hard cases with Signature and Landmark spotting scopes and has assembled a "comp kit" with the 20x50 spotter announced last year, plus window mount and tripod, and an 8x26 or 10x25 binocular. Priced at $270 retail and $158 MAP (with the 10x25), the kit is already popular. You'll also see new shotgun/muzzleloader scopes: a 2.5x Fullfield and 1-4x XER. The unique (and useful!) 4-12x Compact riflescope now wears a Ballistic Plex reticle. There's a 6x32 Compact Hunter Benchrest Fullfield II with superfine crosshair – and a new reticle, the European #4, for the popular 3-9x40. The Signature 1.75-5x has a new Fast Plex reticle for dangerous game. Burris, which was recently bought by Beretta, has added to its 30mm Black Diamond series, which now includes a 2.5-10x44, 4-16x50, 6-24x50 and 8x32x50. MAP prices: from $521 to $658. The 2.5-10x is available with European #4 reticle; others have

(popular in Europe) change apparent size with power shift, *but stay in constant relationship with the target.* Hunters Stateside like the rear-plane reticle because it covers less of the target at high power, for greater precision, and it is easy to see at low power, when you're taking quick aim at game close up. Front-plane reticles get super-slim at low magnification and thick when you crank the power up.

Redfield once had a rangefinding reticle designed to read accurately at any power. You bracketed the target between the stadia wires by changing power, then read the range on a vertical scale at the bottom of the scope field. Shepherd scopes have two reticles, one

Aimpoint made the first red-dot sight; its Model 7000 still defines the state of the art.

Burris came out with this sub-compact scope last year. Leupold offers one for 2003.

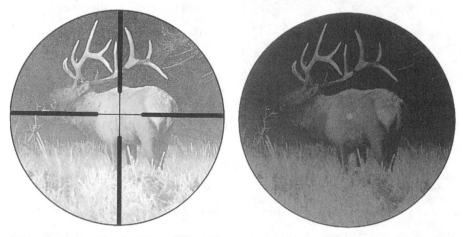

Lighted reticles, like this Burris Electro-Dot, remain popular. They can't make targets brighter!

turret-mounted parallax adjustment. Lighted reticles appear in Fullfield II 3-9x40 and 3.5-10x50 sights, as well as on the Signature 1.75-5x. Yes, you can get a lighted Ballistic Plex.

The TDS Tri-Factor reticle is similar to the Ballistic Plex. First cataloged in Swarovski scopes, It has four horizontal range-marker bars laddering the lower vertical bar. For 2003, **Kahles** (a Swarovski-owned company) has installed the TDS range-compensating reticule in two more scopes: the American Hunter 2-7x36 and 3.5-10x50. The AH 3-9x42 already offers the TDS DS-equipped scopes. They list for about $80 more than those with standard reticles – $620 for the new 2-7x, $743 for the 3.5-10x. Kahles is a very old Austrian company but only recently began a strong marketing campaign in the U.S. It builds very good scopes that are also good bargains.

The world is full of scopes whose names have rarely appeared in popular reviews Stateside. One is **KAPS**. Karl Kaps, GmbH & Co.KG is, you guessed it, a German firm. The plant in Asslar/Wetzlar has been turning out scopes for sportsmen and soldiers for 50 years. Current models, all with 30mm tubes, include a 4x36, 6x42, 8x56 and five variables: 1-4x22, 1.5-6x42, 2-8x42, 2.5-10x50 and 2.5-10x56. The most powerful two variables and the 8x56 are available with illuminated scopes. It appears to me that these are top-quality scopes, and they're now being imported (kaps-optik.de or 304-574-1779).

A more familiar name to many outdoorsmen is **Brunton**. Think compasses and, more recently, a line of modestly priced binoculars. This year Brunton has vaulted into the ring with Leica, Zeiss, Nikon and Swarovski to maul for market share with a top-end binocular. The new Brunton Epoch is a roof-prism instrument with 43mm objectives. Choose 7.5x or 10.5x. Naturally, you get fully multi-coated, phase-corrected optics, along with what Brunton calls SF glass. Fields of view: 37 and 29 feet at 100 yards. The magnesium alloy frame keeps weight to a manageable 25 and 26 ounces. Eyecups pull out in steps. One intriguing feature is the variable-speed focus, finer and slower from 30 feet in than from 30 feet out. Buy an Epoch, and you get removable *(but, like most lens caps, marginally serviceable)* "optivisors." Also included: a doubler that easily attaches to one ocular housing to turn your binocular into a spotting scope. Of course, there's a tripod attachment. And a neck strap. The Epoch and its accoutrements come in a sturdy Pelican hard case, which, like the binocular, is waterproof. I've examined but not tested this glass. It looks good, retails for $1450 (brunton.com).

Chief among the new Brunton's competition is the **Nikon** LX (8x42 and 10x42). That binocular line now has two new members. The Mini LX 8x20 and 10x25 are center-focus, roof-prism, phase-coated glasses with twist-out rubber eyecups and generous eye relief – nearly inch. They weigh 9.7 and 10.9 ounces, respectively and focus down to

Better spotting scopes from Leica, Swarovski and Nikon have saved hunters miles of walking!

The new Zeiss 12x56 is one of the sharpest, most brilliant binoculars available.

8 and 10 feet. Fields of view: 356 and 282 feet at 1000 yards. The new Mini LXs retail for $349 and $379. Nikon also lists new scopes in its 2003 catalog. The 1.5-6x42, 2.5-10x50 and 2.5-10x56 have 30mm tubes (Nikon's first) and the European-style fast-focus eyepieces that became standard on the company's scopes mid-year 2002. The 2.5-10x models also have turret-mounted parallax dials. All three offer Nikoplex and German #4 reticles. My friend Pat Mundy, who represents Nikon, tells me there's a full 80 minutes of adjustment in the 2.5-10x tubes, and 120 minutes in the 1.5-6x (nikonusa.com).

BSA, importer of affordable optics for sportsmen, lists several new scopes for 2003. Sweet 17 is the series name for 4x32 and 2-7x32 scopes with a range-compensating elevation adjustment calibrated to the arc of a 17 HMR bullet. The BSA folks don't actually say these scopes will ensure hits to 350 yards, the dial's maximum range. I suspect you'll find 200 yards a stretch for the 17, even if the wind is

down. Prices for these waterproof 1-inch scopes are certainly reasonable: $80 and $110. New rimfire scopes with quarter-minute adjustments include 4x32 and 3-9x32 versions. They come, with rings, in silver or black finish: $40 and $90. For big game hunters, BSA offers a new Huntsman series, the scopes ranging in price from $90 to $172. It includes three 3-9 variables, a 6-18 AO, plus other variables and fixed-power models, two with 50mm objectives. An expanded line of red dot sights completes BSA's new-product listings. The two latest have 30mm tubes, 5-minute dots. They come with rings and retail for $90 (bsaoptics.com).

If you want a red dot sight, however, you must consider the **Aimpoint** 7000. Unlike others of its kind, this sight has compound front glass that corrects for parallax. The "doublet" brings the dot to your eye *in a line parallel with the optical axis of the sight*, whatever your eye position. The reflective path of any *single*-lens sight varies with eye position. Result: If the dot isn't centered, you get parallax error. With an Aimpoint, you always hit where you see the dot.

Besides, the 7000's 3-volt battery gives you *20,000 hours* of operation. That's 20 times the life of previous red dot sights, even those from Aimpoint, which sold the first to a local Swedish hunter in 1975. To use the early model, you found the dot with one eye, and the target with the other. You couldn't look *through* the sight at all! Improvements followed. By 1978 Aimpoint was selling sights in the U.S. The new 7000 is available in short (6.3 inches) and long (7.9 inches) versions, with 1x or 2x magnification. A 4.7-inch Comp (competition) model gives you more than 140 inches of windage and elevation adjustment in -minute increments. A new 7000SC combines features of the Comp and S. All sights weigh less than 8 ounces. While Aimpoint 7000s are not nitrogen-filled, they're certified fog-proof – with the caps off! I carried one in day-long rain; no fogging.

Aimpoint sights impose almost no limits on eye relief. You can shoot with

both eyes open – and accurately enough for 200-yard hits. A 2x Aimpoint 7000 gave me 1 1/2-inch groups at 100 yards. In woods too dark for iron sights, I used it to kill two moose. Keeping the brightness dial at a low setting gave me a distinct aiming point with no halo. The company's heavy-duty sights feature band-pass coatings on front lenses, so they work with military night-vision equipment. Military accounts generate about 75 percent of Aimpoint's sales, but the firm exports hunting sights to 40 countries. One of 10 Swedish hunters carrying optical sights owns an Aimpoint. Retail prices for the 7000 range from $298 to $521 (877-246-7646).

Steiner, a German manufacturer noted for its military binoculars, has recently worked to design and build binoculars that appeal to sportsmen. The roof-prism Predator line has earned a modest following – and deserves a look if you're after a serviceable mid-priced glass. Now, though, Steiner has a high-end binocular. It's called the Peregrine and comes in 8x42 and 10x42 versions. They weigh 24 ounces, deliver fields of 367 and 294 feet at 1000 yards. Prices: $849 and $899. I've compared these roof-prism glasses to the Predator and can testify that they're brighter. The other new binocular from Steiner this year is an 8x56 Big Horn. This 44-ounce Porro instrument has the individual-focus design of traditional Steiner military models. Unfortunately, its angled eyecups turn when you focus so they're no longer angled to the side. A bit bulky for hunting, this 8x56 qualifies as a camp glass. It lists for $549 (800-257-7742).

Jeremy Ashmore, who designs packaging for Redfield, Simmons and Weaver, has been waiting to see what 2003 would bring to these three lines. Last fall, they'd just been sold by Alliant Tech Systems to **Meade**, a big optics firm in Irvine, California. "ATK really wasn't in the optics business; we've survived a maintenance budget." Jeremy said. Oh, ATK has money, but its focus had traditionally been on munitions, rockets and space programs. The optics package it got with the purchase of Blount didn't fit its mission as well as did the Federal Cartridge, RCBS, Speer/CCI and other projectile-oriented divisions.

I spoke with Meade's vice president Robert Davis at the 2003 SHOT show. He told me **Simmons** and **Weaver** would get strong promotion, but that a marketing program for **Redfield** had yet to be finalized. One of the most popular scopes when I was young, Redfield lost market share to Leupold. When Weaver's line expanded to include the new Grand Slam series a few years ago, it began edging into Redfield territory – and staking claim to it. Expect few changes in the Redfield line this year. Simmons is getting an overdue trim. "Too many subdivisions by price point," agreed a colleague the other day. "Some of those Simmons scopes are great bargains, but the catalogs are confusing." Meade has a

The Zeiss Conquest line now includes a 6.5-20x variable. Price: $799.

long and solid reputation marketing telescopes (meade.com).

Bushnell is another company with a wide range of products, from inexpensive to costly. The lists fill more pages than you'll find in my town's telephone directory. Even thicker catalogs may result from Bushnell's recent purchase of the Tasco brand. Among the most innovative of new Bushnell offerings is the Yardage Pro Quest, which features BaK4 prisms in an 8x36 Porro binocular that weighs 34 ounces and incorporates a laser rangefinding unit that reads from 15 to 1300 yards. A 9-volt battery is good for up to 10,000 readings. This center-focus binocular has long eye relief, fold-down eyecups and a 340-foot field at 1000 yards. List price: $600. Bushnell has also developed a waterproof laser rangefinder *(the only one at this writing)*. The new Yardage Pro Legend will even float! It's pocket-size and weighs just 7 ounces, but reads accurately from 10 to 930 yards in favorable conditions. A 6x eyepiece helps you distinguish targets. Scan mode allows you to track moving targets. In Zip mode, you eliminate interference at close range. An automatic battery switch shuts the instrument off after 30 seconds of non-use, so you should get 8000 reads from a battery. The new Yardage Pro Legend retails for $400.

Another new Bushnell development is the Firefly, a scope reticle you "ignite" by hitting it with the beam of a flashlight for a minute. After a brief glow, the reticle fades to black. But as shooting light dims, the Firefly brightens to a luminescent green. Perhaps best of all, there's no battery to die, or battery bubble to spoil the sleek lines of your scope. The Firefly is available in four Elite 3200 scopes: 1.5-4.5x32, 3-9x40 and two 3-9x50s. New scopes from Bushnell include the 3-9x40, 3-9x50 and 5-15x40 Legends, one price point below Elite models. They feature fully multi-coated lenses and fast-focus eyepieces (bushnell.com).

Germany's **Schmidt & Bender** has announced two new high-quality 30mm scopes for the first half of 2003. The Zenith 2.5-10x56 and 3.5-12x50 come with or without illuminated reticles. While a Schmidt & Bender scope is costly, it's also one of the best you can get. Anywhere. The line doesn't change a great deal from year to year because each new item is carefully planned and engineered for a specific market and purpose. In 2002, S&B expanded its tactical line. I applaud the firm for continuing to offer high-quality fixed-power scopes for hunters, like the 4x36 in my rack (schmidt-bender.de).

Leica optics, also from *Deutschland*, have long been celebrated as some of the best available. The firm's 62mm spotting scopes, technically a 2002 introduction, are just now being shipped in quantity. So too the 12x52 Minox binocular, announced mid-year. Leica is also adding a new Duovid to its line. Like the 8 and 12x42 announced in 2002, this 10 and 15x50 binocular gives you a choice of two magnifications in a top-quality instrument. I've used the 8/12 and am impressed. It's easier to use than a binocular with a doubler, while affording you the field of an 8x and the reach of a 12. The 10/15 should appeal to hunters in open country. List: $1795 (800-222-1118).

From **Swarovski** comes yet another spotting scope, a big brother to the ATS/STS 65 introduced in 2002. A couple of inches shorter and about 15 percent lighter than the 80mm scope it will supplant, the ATS/STS 80 is, according to my information, the lightest, most compact high-quality, full-size scope you can buy. It features both angled and straight eyepieces and attractive rubber armor. The big focusing ring is easy to grab with gloves and gives you a close-focus limit of just 16 feet. A small removable sighting tube helps you find game quickly. Choose 20x, 30x, 45x or 20-60x eyepieces, all of which also work on the ATS/STS 65mm Swarovski. "Magnification won't change either," says Robert Thiem, who works at the Absam plant near Innsbruck, Austria. "That's because the focal lengths of the two scope bodies are the same." Both have filter threads up front and a bayonet-style camera adapter at the eyepiece. The body of this new waterproof scope can be rotated on its axis for comfortable viewing (800-426-3089).

Perhaps no company has felt the impact of Swarovski in the U.S. more keenly than **Leupold**. This year, the Beaverton, Oregon firm continues to show its competitive, progressive spirit with the introduction of three new tactical "M1" scopes in 2003: 4.5-14x50, 6.5-20x50 and 8.5-32x50. Illuminated reticles will be dropped from scopes with 1-inch tubes, but they'll still be offered in selected 30mm models. New in the binocular line are top-quality phase-

Swarovski's big news is an 80mm spotting scope. The 8x20 pocket binocular deserves a look, too!

coated 42mm glasses, 8x and 10x, under the series name of "Pinnacle." An overhaul of the Wind River binocular line gave every sub-series the moniker of a wilderness area: In decreasing price order under Pinnacle, you'll find Olympic, Cascade and Mesa glasses. The Olympic binos include 8x42, 10x50 and 12x50 models, and 8x25 and 10x25 Compacts. Cascade 8x42s and 10x42s are also of roof prism design. The 8x42 and 10x50 Mesas, and 8x23 and 10x23 Mesa Compacts have Porro prisms. To complement its expanded binocular line, Leupold now catalogs a super-compact Golden Ring 10-20x40mm spotting scope that weighs only 16 ounces (just under half the heft of most 60mm scopes). It focuses to an incredibly close 5 feet; field of view at 100 yards ranges from 19 to 13 feet. The traditional Wind River 60mm Sequoia spotting scope gets a 45-degree eyepiece for 2003, and longer eye relief.

The most unusual new product from this conservative firm is the Wind River RB800 and RB800C range-finding binocular. An 8x32 roof prism glass, it doesn't hinge like conventional binoculars. Instead, you change the interpupillary distance by sliding the barrels across a 58 to 72mm range. A 31-foot field of view at 100 yards compares favorably with that of ordinary binoculars. But the Leupold RB800 is hardly ordinary. The laser rangefinder inside shows you exact distances to targets as far as 850 yards away. Even animals in the shadows can be "read" beyond rifle range. A scan mode helps you follow moving game. At 35 ounces, the RB800 is much lighter than Leica's Geovid, for years the only viable bino/rangefinder. It's also a lot more affordable (leupold.com).

Sightron has three new SI scopes for the 2003 lineup: 3-9x40, 2.5-10x44 and

The Swarovski ATS/STS 80 (*shown*) accepts lenses from the 65mm model. Same magnification.

Pentax Lightseeker and Whitetails Unlimited lines now share catalogs with the 3-9x40 Pioneer.

distinguish three new scopes. The 1.5-6x40, 3-9x40 and 4-12x50 are waterproof models with multi-coated lenses. A lithium battery (included) lights up the reticle centers. An 11-position dial controls brightness. Look for Swift Instruments to command more attention from shooters! (swiftoptics.com).

Mid-year's debut of the 6.5-20x Conquest scope kept **Zeiss** in the news. Now there's a Varipoint VM/V 2.5-10x50 T* for the headlines. It features a lighted dot in the second (rear) image plane. Unlike reticles up front, this reticle won't vary in size with changes in magnification. The dot is available alone or with first-plane horizontal bars. T* coating ensures superior light transmission in the blue light of dawn and dusk. The waterproof scope has a constant eye relief of 3.5 inches. Zeiss has also added a binocular to its Victory series. The new 12x56 has T* lens coating on lead-free, arsenic-free glass. There's also a P* (phase-correction) film on its four-element lens system. The diopter dial has click detents; you push or pull eyecups to adjust eye relief. A 270-foot field at 1000 yards, and a weight of 46 ounces, make this glass less versatile than more compact Victory models. Expect bright images in poor light; twilight factor figures out to a whopping 26. The new Zeiss 12x56 retails for $1700 – though as with most optics, "street price" is considerably less. Zeiss has made a strong bid for the U.S. hunter's dollar of late, with useful products reasonably priced. I'm impressed by the company's newest compact binoculars. You'll find that many compacts (*with objectives smaller than 30mm*) deliver less brightness than you'd like when you're glassing into the shadows as the sun sinks. The Zeiss compacts I examined recently were remarkably bright – and tack-sharp (zeiss.com).

Pentax has a new entry-level scope: the Pioneer. Complementing its Whitetails Unlimited and top-drawer Lightseeker lines, the Pioneer comes only in popular 3-9x40 form, with plex reticle. It weighs just 13 ounces, features fully-coated optics and a one-piece tube. Other new scopes from Pentax

3.5-10x50. The 3-9x features a mil dot reticle. Like other SI scopes announced last season, these are waterproof, with finger-adjustable dials and a lifetime replacement warranty. They all list for less than $265. In the SII line, you'll find illuminated reticles for the 3-9x42 and 4.5-14x42MD (mil dot) at $504 and $689. Sightron has also decided to re-introduce its ESD, or Electronic Sighting Device, in both black and stainless finish. An 11-position rheostat and four available reticles add versatility. The waterproof ESD lists for $296. New in the binocular line are top-quality phase-coated 42mm glasses, 8x and 10x. Three SII binoculars – 8x42, 10x42 and 12x42 – feature BaK4 prisms, twist-up eyecups and modest price tags: $136, $151 and $163. I've used Sightron optics for three years now; they

perform like optics that cost a lot more (sightron.com).

The **Swift** name has long been known among birders and hobbyist astronomers, but hunters didn't have a lot to do with it until recently, when the company began offering more rifle scopes and emphasizing their low prices. Illuminated reticles

Steiner's biggest Nighthunter, like the new 12x56 Big Horn, is a Porro prism glass with individual focus. More popular: Steiner's roof prism Predator. The new Peregrine should flourish too.

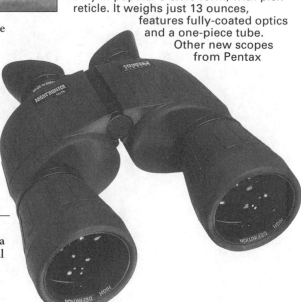

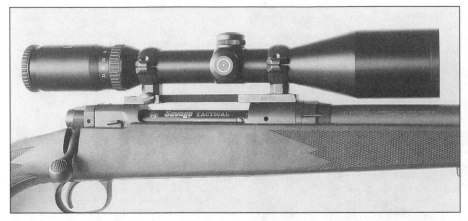

Schmidt & Bender scopes, like the variable on this Savage, feature first-class lenses and coatings.

This vintage Weaver K4 is still serviceable. New isn't always better. It's usually more expensive.

Good optics are a worthwhile investment. Smart shopping can also give you a good buy.

include a pair of Lightseekers: a 1-inch 4-16x50 and a 30mm 8.5-32x50. The 8.5x32 is lighter and shorter than its parent sight and boasts a turret-mounted parallax adjustment. There's also a Whitetails Unlimited 3.5-10x50 with a lighted Ballistic Plex reticle. More news at Pentax comes with an improved line of laser rangefinders. If you'd like to know the horizontal distance to a target that's above or below you, carry the AC500WP, or an 800- or 1000-yard model. All three give you the correct read for accurate aim on steeply angled shots. Get these units in black or camo finish. At 12 ounces, they're easy to carry, and the single 9-volt battery lasts for 1000 reads. You'll find the 8x magnification useful on distant targets (pentaxlightseeker.com).

There are other names to look for if you're in the market for optics. Like **Remington**. No, it's not the same company as the firearms maker. It imports binoculars from China and Japan. Some have little to recommend them, but the better models are still inexpensive. I found an 8x40 that seemed an incredible bargain. It delivered the image of binoculars listing for several hundred dollars. It retails for $80. You'll also want to find a Cabela's catalog. Besides offering optics from many well-known makers, **Cabela's** has its own lines. I've used the Alaskan Guide and Big Sky 42mm binoculars – armored roof-prism binoculars priced under $550 and $440 respectively (for the 10x; less if you choose the 8x). Cabela's also offers more affordable Pine Ridge models. The Alaskan Guide rifle scope line includes the 4x44 and 6x44 fixed-power sights I've used on my rifles, plus 3.5-10x, 4.5-14x and 6.5-20x variables, all with adjustable objectives. A 3-12x52 has a 30mm tube. Rangefinding reticles are available in the 3.5-10x and 4.5-14x versions. You'll find 5x, 2-7x and 3-12x compact scopes, and a Pine Ridge line with double-digit pricing (cabela's.com).

Back when Weaver K4s cost $49, it was easy to spotlight new optics. Now any sportsmen keen to learn about all current offerings must commit to a lot of reading. Indeed, the number of new items in any given year exceeds the number of *total* optics listings for sportsmen 40 years ago! Not all that's trotted out has merit. Some products are too heavy or bulky for field use. Some are too fragile or complex. Many fill a narrow market slot but lack versatility. Others qualify, charitably, as gadgets. Some optics just cost too much. But among the hastily conceived, poorly designed and optimistically priced are scopes, binoculars, spotting scopes and rangefinders that will enhance your outdoors experience. They'll help you find more game and make more accurate shots. If you're in the market for new glass, a few hours perusing catalogs is time well spent. Optics have improved markedly in the past four decades. Just remember that the best of outdoor gear does not quickly become obsolete.

by CHARLES E. PETTY

HANDLOADING UPDATE

IN THE PAST this space has focused primarily on new product reports—but I gotta tell you that this year we'd be hard-pressed to get more than a page or two that way. Instead I'd like to look at how things have evolved to make our hobby easier, more scientific and safer. That covers a lot of ground and, along the way, we'll get to the new stuff–and the best stuff–even if it ain't precisely new.

Reflecting now it dawns on me that I have been involved in reloading almost for fifty years and witnessed what amounts to a revolution in the hobby. Few of you would even recognize the gear I started with. Antique loading tools are prized for something other than churning out ammo these days. They were simple things: a Redding scale, Lyman powder measure and a Lyman Tru-line Jr. press. Today I've got a new turret press from Redding, a new progressive from RCBS, my old standby Dillon 550B and a compact little single-stage from Frankford Arsenal. Scales are electronic and there are powder dispensers from PACT, RCBS and Lyman that will trickle out precise powder charges with the push of a button. The stuff I use today doesn't look much like the old gear but does exactly the same job–just faster and more efficiently.

Major milestones have fed on one another and driven the entire market to where it is today. Some examples: the availability of carbide sizing dies, bulk brass, progressive reloading tools, and high-volume shooting sports such as practical shooting. In turn those have created other markets. Before we had bulk brass, nobody needed plastic ammo boxes. The number of available bullets and powders has been multiplied many times. In short, we've got lots of goodies to work with these days. And we're always on the lookout for improvements.

So with that in mind the industry flocks to the SHOT Show– this year held in Orlando, Florida–to check out new stuff. "New" is a badly abused word and I can't say that I found much that fits the strict definition of the word but there are quite a few things that make our work easier or safer.

One of the real big advances in reloading comes from the electronics industry, for small microprocessors make it possible for the average shooter to have a level of technical information not even dreamt of a generation ago. A great example, and a new product, is the Lyman 1200-grain Digital Powder System. Electronic dispensers have been around awhile and have proven their utility–but must be re-calibrated every time you change to a different powder. The Lyman system will store up to 20 loads in its memory and keep them even if the power is turned off. The unit is a scale and powder trickler in a single package. There's a keyboard for data entry or the scale can be used by itself. It looks to be well designed.

One of the cleverest new products also comes from Lyman: a thoughtfully designed combination weighing pan and powder funnel. There's a little spout on one side and all you have to do is pour right into the case. No separate funnel is needed. This is one of those things that make you mad at yourself for not thinking of it long ago.

The electronics advances have made it possible for anyone who wants one to have a chronograph. And anyone who considers himself a serious handloader who doesn't have one is truly flying blind. The loading manuals give us good general information, but if you want to know what's really happening in your gun you need a chronograph. There aren't any new ones this year and cost is much more a factor of convenience features and accessories than relating to the simple job of timing how long it takes a bullet to cover a known distance. You can have a very functional chronograph for less than $100.

To go a step further, I'd like to mention the Oehler Model 43 Personal Ballistics Laboratory. This isn't new either–although the software continually improves–but it is such a powerful tool that it allows the hobbyist to do much the same sort of work that is done in multimillion-dollar laboratories. With it and a laptop computer you can do all sorts of neat stuff. A strain gauge glued to the barrel

Lyman 1200 digital powder system.

Dr. Ken Oehler demonstrates the Model 43 Personal Ballistics Laboratory.

The RCBS digital micrometer.

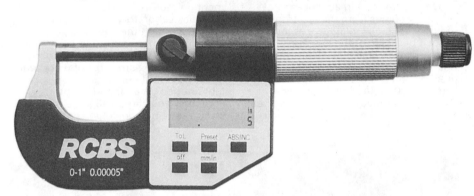

shows us the numbers. There's no need to interpolate–a fancy word for "guess" and somebody with less than 20-15 vision can still get it right.

The same basic technology–the strain gauge–that makes the Oehler system work also gives us digital powder scales. They provide the same benefit as other digital gear–we just read the numbers–but that level of sophistication is not without cost. We must be vigilant to insure that no environmental factor, such as temperature, messes up the accuracy of the scale. To me routine calibration and frequent use of check weights is a

will give approximations of chamber pressure that are remarkably consistent with those obtained by standard methods. An accessory acoustic target will record and measure groups without so much as a piece of paper and you can also get accurate downrange velocities and true ballistic coefficients calculated for individual loads.

A big advance from electronics influences how we measure things. Reloaders need to do a lot of that. There are lots of length and diameter numbers we need to know and, over the years, I've found it to be increasingly difficult to read the fine graduations of calipers and micrometers. The electronics advances have brought us digital readouts for calipers and micrometers and the big numbers sure are easier to see, but there's another more important benefit. The digital display eliminates a potential source of error. With micrometers we have to count graduations and then look at three or four different scales to come up with a measurement. The digital display just

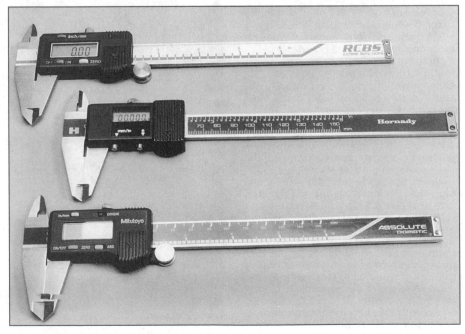

Digital calipers are easier to read.

The PACT digital scale and powder dispenser.

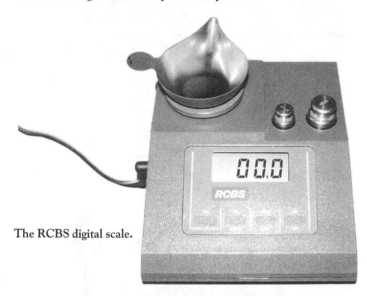

The RCBS digital scale.

Computer software from Sierra, Quick Load and AccuLoad.

small price to pay for the improved precision. Electronic scales are not more accurate than our old beam balances *(both are usually plus or minus one tenth of a grain)* but we don't have to adjust weights or watch swings—we just read the number when the display stabilizes, which is quicker than a beam balance anyhow.

Little microprocessors or integrated circuits are doing some pretty cool stuff. The PACT and RCBS powder dispenser is an example. It's an extremely glorified powder trickler run by a small digital computer. There is real-time communication between the scale and dispenser via an infrared data port and, as the scale nears the set charge weight, the dispenser adjusts the speed of the trickle tubes. The new Lyman 1200 DPS (digital powder system) is a compact unit that does both jobs in a single unit with the added ability to store up to 20 "standard" loads that can be recalled without the need for re-calibration.

The computer revolution helps shooters, too. They can quickly calculate trajectory information for specific bullets and velocities. External ballistic calculations for drop and wind drift can be done in an instant with any number of software programs. The latest of these is version 5.0 of Sierra's Infinity Suite. A ballistic calculator is included in the software of PACT's Professional Chronograph and with the advent of pocket-sized computers you can take them anywhere. But to me the more interesting new computer programs give us the ability to look at internal ballistics without a degree in thermodynamics. There are two software packages, "Quickload" and "AccuLoad" that allow us to look at bullet and powder combinations without putting guns or people at risk. Both have large databases of cartridges, bullets and powders and let us play "what if" games for pressure and velocity results.

Single-Stage Presses

One of the perennial questions from folks getting started in reloading is what type of press to buy. My feeling is that–with very few exceptions–a beginner should learn on a single-stage press. Don't misunderstand, I like progressive tools and use them all the time, but when there are several operations happening at the same time it's easier to lose track of where you are

The PACT Professional Chronograph.

The updated RCBS Rock Chucker.

and make a mistake. But there's another equally good reason: Reloading is a hobby that almost always grows on you, so even if at first the beginner only intends to load a single handgun cartridge it is reasonable to expect the time will come to load a box of ammo for the hunting rifle. That's where the progressive may have a drawback.

Of all the single-stage presses on the market today my vote for the longest-lived goes to the RCBS Rockchucker. They've been around nearly forever and after all those years it has finally gotten an update: no major revisions, just stuff to keep it in step with the times where extra-long rifle cartridges are becoming more popular. The press opening has been enlarged to handle almost anything short of the 50 BMG. There's a new primer catcher that looks just great and there are two holes for the handle to make it ambidextrous. Redding has done something similar by increasing the size of their "Boss" single-stage press. The new version is called the Big Boss. It's enlarged overall to better deal with magnum cartridges.

Progressive Loaders

If we were to pick the most significant development in reloading in the last half of the 20th century, the

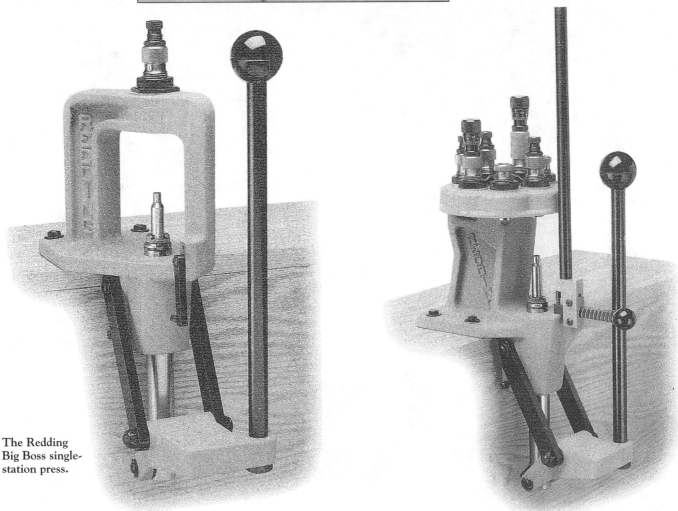

The Redding Big Boss single-station press.

Redding's T-7 Turret Press.

Allan Jernigan of RCBS demonstrates the Pro 2000.

wide distribution of progressive loaders would be high on the list. Without them, none of the high-volume shooting sports such as IPSC or Cowboy Action could have grown at the rate they did. Without doubt, the leader in this area is Dillon's ubiquitous 550B. The most recent competitor to emerge is the RCBS Pro 2000. It uses the RCBS APS (advanced priming system) that feeds primers in a plastic strip that advances with each stroke of the press. There are no tubes to fill or any need to handle primers at all. This also makes it possible to change primer sizes in a matter of seconds by simply screwing out one assembly and replacing it with another.

Dies

I bet you'd have to try pretty hard to find a set of plain steel dies for any straight-walled pistol cartridge these days. Carbide sizing dies make the progressive loaders practical but are old news now. In fact, loading dies do exactly the same thing they always have. But there's an interesting paradox. Before carbide dies we had to lube each case individually, usually with lanolin. Today's modern spray lubricants do a great job and aren't messy at all. A lot of shooters used to avoid cartridges like the 32-20, 38-40 or 44-40 because their bottlenecks effectively eliminated carbide dies, but with the much-improved lubes available now they are a piece of cake to load.

Precision Reloading

There really is a whole different category of loading equipment and practice that goes far beyond what most of us consider standard. These are the things that benchrest and competitive shooters do to wring the last possible thousandth of an inch of accuracy out of their gun/ammo combination. Almost everything they use is special. A great example is the Forster Co-Ax press. This isn't new–actually it has been around for ages–but the idea is to avoid possible run-out. Instead of a central ram, the Forster press uses two precision-ground guide rods and a special shellholder to ensure the case goes in and out of the die in a straight line. We hear lots of people talk about "benchrest" equipment. It's a term almost everyone uses and generally means stuff made to tighter tolerances.

One of the basic goals of reloading is to reduce the amount we work the brass. Neck-sizing is old hat, but some wrinkles have come along such as bushing neck-sizing dies that let us control sizing to within a thousandth of an inch. Micrometer adjustments have been added to both sizing and seating dies. When we load ammo for most bolt-action target or varmint rifles all you really need is enough sizing to hold the bullet in place for loading. Redding's precision neck-sizing dies work with interchangeable bushings to allow control of sizing to the nearest

Hornady has added an automatic case feeder to their progressive loader.

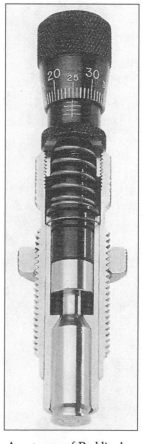

A cutaway of Redding's competition bushing neck-sizing die.

Forster's Co-Ax Press.

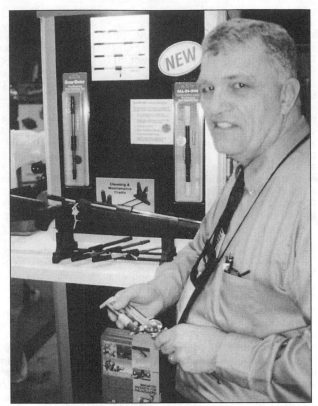

Tom Peterson of Stoney Point with their new overall-length gauge.

thousandth. They couple a bushing with a micrometer adjustment, which permits control of the amount of the neck sized. It isn't necessary to size all of it and my experience suggests that between 25 to 50 percent delivers the best results. Several companies have seating dies with the same sort of adjustment. Sometimes small changes in overall length can have a big effect on accuracy and with them you can find exactly what works best in each rifle.

Another very important factor in accuracy is the overall length of the cartridge and the relation of the bullet in the chamber to the origin of the rifling. Simply fiddling with the overall length of the cartridge can produce dramatic accuracy changes. The position of the bullet in relation to the start of the rifling can be important and precise control is almost always helpful. And of course we need some way to determine when the bullet actually touches the rifling. There are lots of ways to do this but the easiest I've found is with the Stoney Point overall length gauge. It uses a modified dummy cartridge case that lets you put a bullet in and push it up until it stops on the rifling. That way you can find the overall length needed to touch the rifling and adjust accordingly. Differences in bullet shape make it necessary to measure with any bullet you want to shoot and re-check now and then to keep track of bore wear.

One of the real secrets to best accuracy is to turn case necks to a uniform thickness. There are a number of neck-turning tools, both manual and power-driven; if you plan on turning very many necks power is a big help. I use an adapter from Sinclair that fits a special shellholder into a cordless screwdriver. Most benchrest rifles are chambered to a specific neck diameter and all you do is turn the brass to a couple of thousandths less. But variation in wall thickness can also be an issue. It isn't unusual for a difference of a few thousandths of an inch in wall thickness from one side to another to have a measurable effect on accuracy. The idea is, as chamber pressure builds and the bullet begins to push through the neck, the thinner side will release the bullet more easily and give it an uneven start down the bore. Frankford Arsenal has just developed a digital neck-thickness gauge that is very

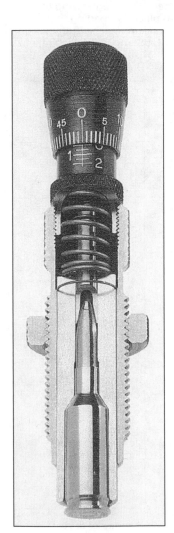

A cutaway of Redding's competition seating die.

Sinclair neck-turning tool, with adapter to a cordless screwdriver.

The Sinclair fixture for precision adjustment of neck-turning tools.

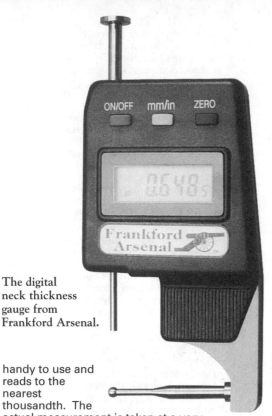

The digital neck thickness gauge from Frankford Arsenal.

New loading manuals from Sierra and Nosler.

handy to use and reads to the nearest thousandth. The actual measurement is taken at a very small spot so it is possible to take a number of readings around the circumference of the case as well as 1.5 inches down into the body.

Everything Old Is New Again

The terrific growth of cowboy-style shooting events has breathed new life into a whole series of guns and cartridges that were formerly thought to be dead, or nearly so. Most of those have their origins back in blackpowder days, but have made the transition to smokeless without much trouble. The availability of old Winchester lever actions and Colt SAAs—and copies thereof—have gotten shooters interested in cartridges that have "dashes" in their names such as: 32-20, 38-40, 44-40 and a whole host of others. Most have enjoyed limited availability of factory ammo to service the old guns out there, but large-scale shooting of these chamberings is relatively new. RCBS, for example, has an entire line of "Cowboy" dies with dimensions geared specifically toward working with cast bullets.

Starline brass gets lots of credit for producing high quality, reasonably priced cases for most of the old cartridges. The other positive influence is the increase in demand for lead alloy bullets. The hobbyist has always had access to everything needed to make his own bullets, but the bigger change has come in the growth of regional suppliers of cast bullets. To be sure there is some national distribution from companies like Oregon Trail Bullet Co. or through large mail-order houses—Midway USA or Cabela's, to name just two. But if you go to almost any gun show you'll find somebody there selling cast bullets. When you consider the high cost of freight for heavy stuff like lead, buying from a local source just makes sense.

Loading Manuals

Up-to-date data is the lifeblood of any reloader. The speed with which new components and cartridges arrive conspires to make manuals incomplete by the time they reach the shelves. This isn't a criticism; it's just a reality of any publishing endeavor that discusses an ever-changing subject. The past year has brought us the fifth edition of the *Nosler Reloading Guide* and the *Sierra Rifle and Handgun Reloading Data, 5th Edition* manual is just out. It follows the past loose-leaf format that is so handy and now combines both rifle and pistol data into a single volume. Hodgdon has adopted a new format with their *Annual Manual* that has a "magazine look" and combines feature stories with updated loading data. It replaces the hardbound book they've done in the past. A new edition of the *Hornady Handbook* will be available when you read this.

Stuff To Come

This year saw the introduction of at least three new cartridges from mainstream companies and a few more that still are wildcats. But the hot news is Winchester's pair of Super Short Magnums in 22 and 6mm, derived from the WSM cases in that the body and rim diameters are the same but the case is a bunch shorter. The 223 WSSM is reported to approximate the 22-250 in a much shorter case. The 243 WSSM may be even more spectacular. Factory ammo will have a 55-grain Ballistic Silvertip bullet at a published velocity of 4060 fps to outdo the fabled 220 Swift for pure speed and also a 95-grain Ballistic Silvertip at 3250 fps, which exceeds the speed of the same bullet in the 243 Winchester case by 150 fps.

The efficiency of short, fat cases is well established and the vast assortment of powders and bullets that will be suitable is going to make it both feast and challenge for the handloader. But until folks gain some experience loading this new family of cases, we'll have to wait and see. I am pretty sure that we'll end up using powders that differ a bunch from those we're used to with the 22-250 or 243. In the case of the 243 WSSM, the great variety of 6mm bullets on the market makes it suitable for both varmint and deer-sized big game.

The other newcomer is the 500 S&W Magnum. S&W says it's the most powerful "production" handgun and that is an important distinction. No more can Eastwood say, "This is the world's most powerful handgun..." because there are some wildcats or semi-production cartridges that may have a tad more power—but at those levels an energy pound or two really doesn't matter. Initially there will be three loads produced by CorBon: a 275-grain solid copper hollowpoint @ 1665 fps, a 400-grain JSP @ 1625 fps and a 440-grain lead flat point @ 1625 fps.

For the handloader components may be the biggest obstacle at first, for choices in 50-caliber bullets are limited. If the cartridge takes off as most expect it to, more component choices will follow quickly. Powder selection probably won't be tough, though, since a bunch of H-110 or WW 296 is almost sure to work. There may be others to emerge as we go along, but it's 'way too early to tell.

The Good Old Days

It really isn't rare to hear someone lament the sorry state of things and talk about how much better it was 'way back when. If anyone starts that line about today's reloading you can be sure they are woefully uninformed. Sure, we could still turn out ammo that would go "bang" using really old gear and components—and there is something appealing about retro stuff—but we have come a long way, with every aspect of handloading having benefited from advances of science, manufacturing and electronics.

●

by **RAYMOND CARANTA**

THE GUNS OF EUROPE

The Private Collection of Christian Ducros

REGULAR GUN DIGEST readers may recall (*53rd edition, page 124; 54th edition, page 142*) Christian Ducros is a young French artist practicing arms design of a futuristic nature. However, living in a rural area of France along the Lozere River and dining regularly on boar meat, trout, mushrooms and chestnuts, he could hardly do other than be faithful to his hunting sports heritage.

This pioneer of modern art applied to gunsmithing has gathered, beginning in his apprenticeship in Saint-Etienne, more than 100 shotguns and rifles he considers to be masterpieces of arms design from the 19th and 20th centuries.

As he used to say, "*the gun makers of these dazzling periods reached the apex of their art and, as far as fine shotgun design, workmanship and engraving are concerned, they will never be exceeded, because they had the passion and, for them, time did not matter. This is why I have chosen to dedicate my life to modernity...*"

The Christian Ducros Collection

This gun collection is not organized around intended uses, mechanical systems, or national origins of the models included— rather, strictly on the artist's fancy–without consideration of expense–in a true "*Belle Epoque*" spirit.

Upon the thick river stone walls of Ducros' 21st-century building are hung, in random fashion, vintage express rifles and shotguns by Holland & Holland, Westley Richards, Gastinne-Renette, Parker Bros., Francotte, Lefaucheux, Darne, Ideal, John Rigby, Jeannot, Tolley, Lebeau-Courally, Devisme, Lepage-Moutier, Jeffery, Greener, etc., mingled with numerous modern doubles from Mario Abbiatico, Fratelli Gamba, Ferlach, Brno, Ijhevsk, Suhl, Browning, as well as Swiss Martini rifles, two personal guns of Ettore Bugatti, a turn-of-the-century Sjogren Danish automatic shotgun, as well as common Russian folding-bayonet Mosin-Nagants.

Christian Ducros holding his pet Westley Richards "Long Range Large Game Rifle" and the J&W Tolley double express.

Our Selection

From this hodgepodge of gun-making wonders, I have selected some curiosities, such as a top-quality drilling with two 16-gauge smoothbore barrels and the rifled barrel chambered in 351 Winchester (!), two French fixed-barrel side-by-sides in the Darne style: one with removable lockplates, the other with an Anson & Deeley trigger mechanism.

Also, my fancy was caught by a Lebeau-Courally side-by-side No. 78 "Prince Kourakine" with custom removable ejector; a Jeffery hammerless double featuring tapered smoothbore barrels; a pinfire Westley Richards finished by Gastinne-Renette in Paris, and several French "Ideal" turn of the century side-by-sides, with custom spare barrels of different calibers fitted to the same action—an option never listed in Manufrance catalogs.

Ducros meticulously disassembled many of his guns to study their designs and found one of his 12-gauge blackpowder "Ideal" shotguns had a rare 3-inch chambering, while another had short 26-inch barrels with extra-long 3.15-inch (80mm) chambers. Obviously, the "Magnum" concept was not born only yesterday...

Another rarity is a Lepage 20-gauge side-by-side muzzleloader, with the V-type mainsprings "bridged" to accommodate the lockplates' transverse attaching screws.

These guns constitute the personal collection of an artistic designer, gathered for the purpose of studying their action designs and workmanship.

▲ This is the Darne Model 1908 "Rotary" double hammerless shotgun (fewer than 1,000 made), which was the final descendant of the original external hammer prototype of 1879 (about 15,000 made in 30 years, for all variations). The 12-gauge barrels measure a short 25-1/2 inches. The stock is of straight-grain walnut and the engraving is of a floral design.

▲ The Darne 1908 rotating-barrel shotgun opened for loading; it was easily field-stripped into two parts for cleaning.

Ducros, also involved for many years in the restoration and repair of luxury arms, has reconditioned some and all vary from "very good" to "excellent" and–rarely–"mint."

For their proud owner, they are an endless source of inspiration from bygone days.

Christian Ducros
Promenade Saint-Paul
Rue Tranquille
30130 Saint-Paulet-De Caisson
FRANCE
e-mail: ducros.atelier@wanadoo.fr

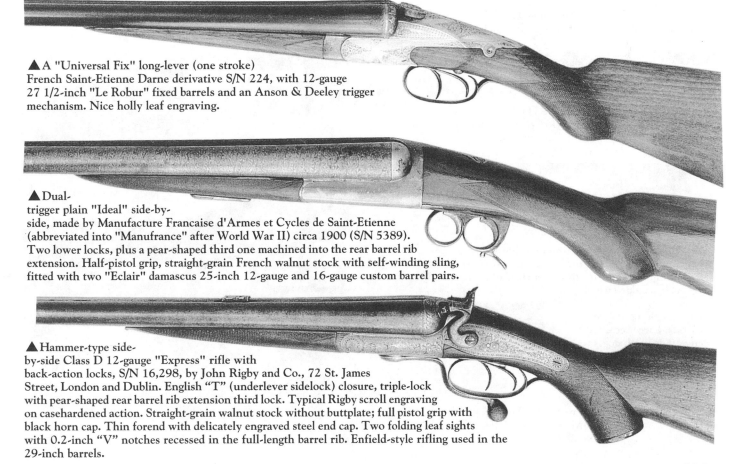

▲ A "Universal Fix" long-lever (one stroke) French Saint-Etienne Darne derivative S/N 224, with 12-gauge 27 1/2-inch "Le Robur" fixed barrels and an Anson & Deeley trigger mechanism. Nice holly leaf engraving.

▲ Dual-trigger plain "Ideal" side-by-side, made by Manufacture Francaise d'Armes et Cycles de Saint-Etienne (abbreviated into "Manufrance" after World War II) circa 1900 (S/N 5389). Two lower locks, plus a pear-shaped third one machined into the rear barrel rib extension. Half-pistol grip, straight-grain French walnut stock with self-winding sling, fitted with two "Eclair" damascus 25-inch 12-gauge and 16-gauge custom barrel pairs.

▲ Hammer-type side-by-side Class D 12-gauge "Express" rifle with back-action locks, S/N 16,298, by John Rigby and Co., 72 St. James Street, London and Dublin. English "T" (underlever sidelock) closure, triple-lock with pear-shaped rear barrel rib extension third lock. Typical Rigby scroll engraving on casehardened action. Straight-grain walnut stock without buttplate; full pistol grip with black horn cap. Thin forend with delicately engraved steel end cap. Two folding leaf sights with 0.2-inch "V" notches recessed in the full-length barrel rib. Enfield-style rifling used in the 29-inch barrels.

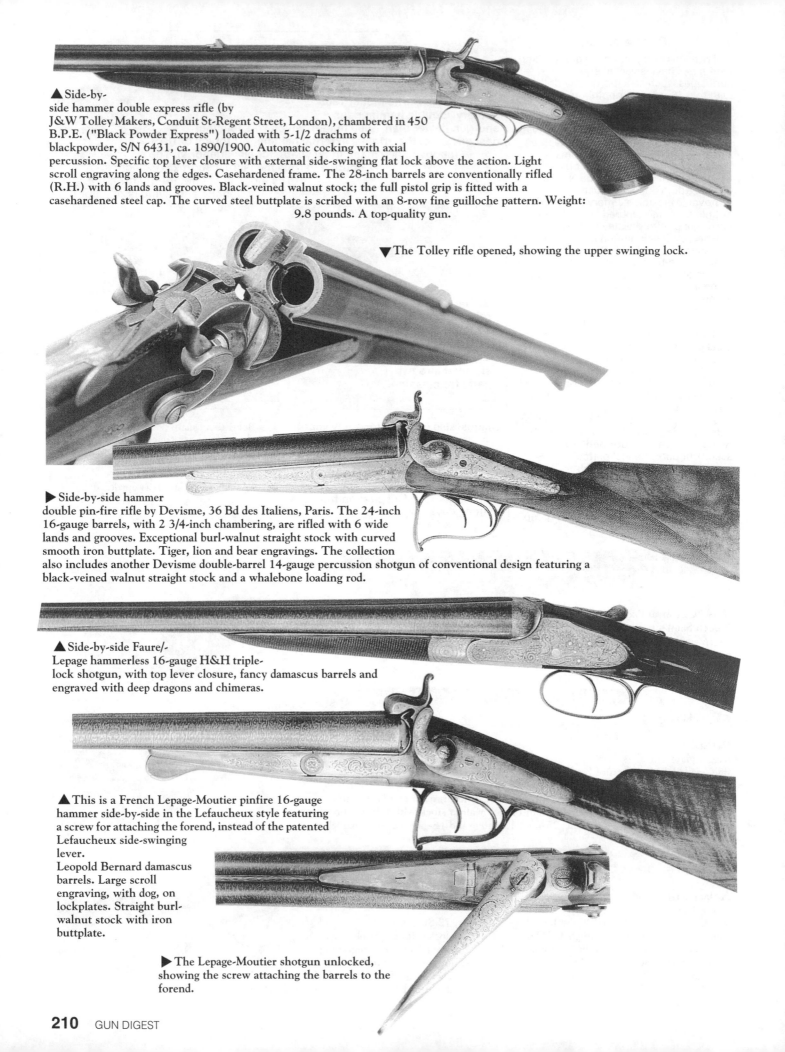

▲Side-by-
side hammer double express rifle (by
J&W Tolley Makers, Conduit St-Regent Street, London), chambered in 450
B.P.E. ("Black Powder Express") loaded with 5-1/2 drachms of
blackpowder, S/N 6431, ca. 1890/1900. Automatic cocking with axial
percussion. Specific top lever closure with external side-swinging flat lock above the action. Light
scroll engraving along the edges. Casehardened frame. The 28-inch barrels are conventionally rifled
(R.H.) with 6 lands and grooves. Black-veined walnut stock; the full pistol grip is fitted with a
casehardened steel cap. The curved steel buttplate is scribed with an 8-row fine guilloche pattern. Weight:
9.8 pounds. A top-quality gun.

▼The Tolley rifle opened, showing the upper swinging lock.

▶Side-by-side hammer
double pin-fire rifle by Devisme, 36 Bd des Italiens, Paris. The 24-inch
16-gauge barrels, with 2 3/4-inch chambering, are rifled with 6 wide
lands and grooves. Exceptional burl-walnut straight stock with curved
smooth iron buttplate. Tiger, lion and bear engravings. The collection
also includes another Devisme double-barrel 14-gauge percussion shotgun of conventional design featuring a
black-veined walnut straight stock and a whalebone loading rod.

▲Side-by-side Faure/-
Lepage hammerless 16-gauge H&H triple-
lock shotgun, with top lever closure, fancy damascus barrels and
engraved with deep dragons and chimeras.

▲This is a French Lepage-Moutier pinfire 16-gauge
hammer side-by-side in the Lefaucheux style featuring
a screw for attaching the forend, instead of the patented
Lefaucheux side-swinging
lever.
Leopold Bernard damascus
barrels. Large scroll
engraving, with dog, on
lockplates. Straight burl-
walnut stock with iron
buttplate.

▶The Lepage-Moutier shotgun unlocked,
showing the screw attaching the barrels to the
forend.

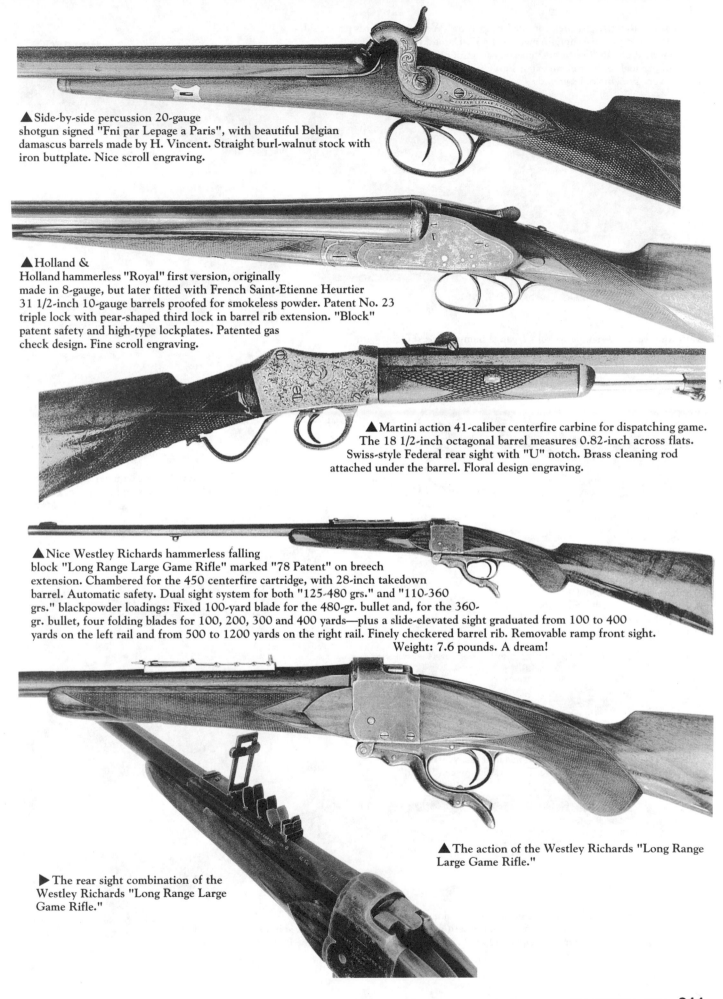

▲ Side-by-side percussion 20-gauge
shotgun signed "Fni par Lepage a Paris", with beautiful Belgian
damascus barrels made by H. Vincent. Straight burl-walnut stock with
iron buttplate. Nice scroll engraving.

▲ Holland &
Holland hammerless "Royal" first version, originally
made in 8-gauge, but later fitted with French Saint-Etienne Heurtier
31 1/2-inch 10-gauge barrels proofed for smokeless powder. Patent No. 23
triple lock with pear-shaped third lock in barrel rib extension. "Block"
patent safety and high-type lockplates. Patented gas
check design. Fine scroll engraving.

▲ Martini action 41-caliber centerfire carbine for dispatching game.
The 18 1/2-inch octagonal barrel measures 0.82-inch across flats.
Swiss-style Federal rear sight with "U" notch. Brass cleaning rod
attached under the barrel. Floral design engraving.

▲ Nice Westley Richards hammerless falling
block "Long Range Large Game Rifle" marked "78 Patent" on breech
extension. Chambered for the 450 centerfire cartridge, with 28-inch takedown
barrel. Automatic safety. Dual sight system for both "125-480 grs." and "110-360
grs." blackpowder loadings: Fixed 100-yard blade for the 480-gr. bullet and, for the 360-
gr. bullet, four folding blades for 100, 200, 300 and 400 yards—plus a slide-elevated sight graduated from 100 to 400
yards on the left rail and from 500 to 1200 yards on the right rail. Finely checkered barrel rib. Removable ramp front sight.
Weight: 7.6 pounds. A dream!

▲ The action of the Westley Richards "Long Range
Large Game Rifle."

▶ The rear sight combination of the
Westley Richards "Long Range Large
Game Rifle."

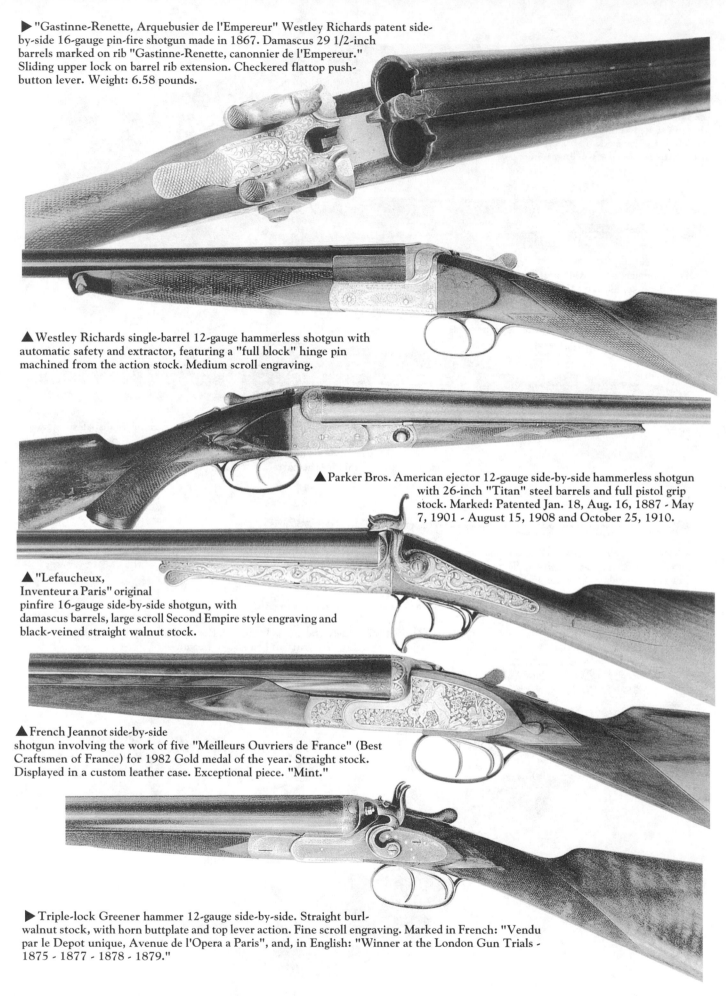

▶ "Gastinne-Renette, Arquebusier de l'Empereur" Westley Richards patent side-by-side 16-gauge pin-fire shotgun made in 1867. Damascus 29 1/2-inch barrels marked on rib "Gastinne-Renette, canonnier de l'Empereur." Sliding upper lock on barrel rib extension. Checkered flattop push-button lever. Weight: 6.58 pounds.

▲ Westley Richards single-barrel 12-gauge hammerless shotgun with automatic safety and extractor, featuring a "full block" hinge pin machined from the action stock. Medium scroll engraving.

▲ Parker Bros. American ejector 12-gauge side-by-side hammerless shotgun with 26-inch "Titan" steel barrels and full pistol grip stock. Marked: Patented Jan. 18, Aug. 16, 1887 - May 7, 1901 - August 15, 1908 and October 25, 1910.

▲ "Lefaucheux, Inventeur a Paris" original pinfire 16-gauge side-by-side shotgun, with damascus barrels, large scroll Second Empire style engraving and black-veined straight walnut stock.

▲ French Jeannot side-by-side shotgun involving the work of five "Meilleurs Ouvriers de France" (Best Craftsmen of France) for 1982 Gold medal of the year. Straight stock. Displayed in a custom leather case. Exceptional piece. "Mint."

▶ Triple-lock Greener hammer 12-gauge side-by-side. Straight burl-walnut stock, with horn buttplate and top lever action. Fine scroll engraving. Marked in French: "Vendu par le Depot unique, Avenue de l'Opera a Paris", and, in English: "Winner at the London Gun Trials - 1875 - 1877 - 1878 - 1879."

by HOLT BODINSON

AMMUNITION, BALLISTICS & COMPONENTS

*T*HE MAGNUMS JUST keep getting shorter. Winchester's launch of the 223 and 243 Super Short Magnums caught us all off guard. There will be more to follow. By whom? That's the question.

Smith & Wesson surprised us a bit as well. The company who has given us the 357, 41, and 44 magnums upped the ante with the release of their 500 S&W Magnum, and a behemoth of a revolver to handle it.

Bonded-core bullets have had a relatively small niche in commercial ammunition and component lines. No longer. Remington has added bonded cores to its Core-Lokt bullet design. Nosler has introduced a new line of bonded-core "Accubond" projectiles, and Hornady has done the same under its "InterBond" label. Think of that. Three new sources of bonded-core bullets in one year. The price of bonded-core hunting bullets is heading down!

Non-toxic projectiles are the rage. We see more signs of "green" bullets in the rifle and handgun ammunition lines each year. This year Lapua brings us the "Naturalis" bullet, naturally.

Lots of great new reloading manuals are out in print, and most include data on the latest short magnums. Look for further information under Hodgdon, Hornady, Lee Precision, Lyman, Nosler, Sierra, and Swift.

Ballistic software is finally becoming more sophisticated and user-friendly. See the latest offerings under Lee Precision, Load from a Disk and Sierra.

It's been an intriguing year in ammunition, ballistics and components.

A-Square Co.

To the many who have asked for the current address of the reconstituted company, it is: A-Square Co., 205 Fairview Ave., Jeffersonville, IN 47130. (812) 283-0577.

Alliant

The focus this year is on shotgun powders and there are two new formulations that fill some gaps in Alliant's lineup. Simply called "410," the new powder is a clean-burning flake powder designed specifically for .410 skeet and field loads. Next, "E3" powder is being introduced with a

Alliant's new "410" powder is a clean-burning flake powder formulated for .410 skeet and field loads.

burning rate roughly equivalent to 700-X. E3 should prove ideal for 1-1/8 oz. trap and skeet loads in the 12-gauge, light loads in the 10- and 16-gauges, and with possibly some application in handgun cartridges and in reduced lead bullet loads in centerfire calibers. Finally, attention you 223 Remington fans who have found Reloader 10X so useful and accurate. Alliant warns that one of their earlier published loads—34.5 grs. of Reloader 10X with the 45-grain Speer SP bullet—should read, "24.5 grs." of Reloader 10X. www.alliantpowder.com

Ballistic Products

If you hanker to try your hand at loading Hevi-Shot, send for Ballistic Product's new catalog and their brand new reloading manual on Hevi-Shot that contains extensive data for the 20, 12 and 10 gauges. The company currently stocks Hevi-Shot in shot sizes B, 2,4,6,7.5, and #9-plus they offer a variety of new wads and Mylar wrappers designed specifically for Hevi-Shot. Noting the increasing interest in the 16-gauge, they have designed a Multi-Metal 16-gauge Field wad that can handle any shot type and is provided in an unslit condition with optional Mylar wrappers to protect the bore when slits are cut. Always a proponent of the 10-gauge Magnum for waterfowling, the company has added a new wad for that beloved cannon, the Deci-Max. The Deci-Max is a cushioned wad designed for the smaller shot sizes, such as #4 and #6 in steel or Hevi-Shot. They always seem to have a good supply of Federal 10-gauge 31/2-inch, and 12 gauge 3- and 31/2-inch hulls in stock and have added a new line of straight-walled, plastic base wad hulls in 12, 16 and .410 from Nobel Sport. See them at www.ballisticproducts.com

Barnes

Barnes is introducing a refined version of their X-Bullet called the "Triple-Shock." Featuring three relief grooves around the shank of the bullet that reportedly reduce pressure and increase accuracy, the Triple-Shock is available in a variety of weights in 6mm, 270, 7mm, and 308 calibers. New, too, is a line of uncoated, super explosive, and competitively priced varmint bullets labeled, "Varmin-A-Tor." The new line is available in 40- and 50-grain .224-inch, 58- and 72-grain 6mm and is available in boxes of 100 or 250 units. www.barnesbullets.com

Berger Bullets

Is the 20-caliber making a comeback? Not since the 5mm Rem. Rimfire Magnum have we seen such interest in this intermediate 0.204-inch bore diameter. Berger has decided to fill the niche with 30-, 35-, 36-, 40-, and 50-grain bullets being offered this year. www.bergerbullets.com

Black Hills has created a true small deer/antelope loading for the 223 Remington featuring a 60-grain Nosler Partition at 3150 fps.

Using a 140-grain Barnes-X bullet, the optimum weight for 7mm, Black Hills has created a fast, deeply penetrating big game load for the 7mm Remington Magnum.

Combining the accuracy of the 100-grain Ballistic Tip and a velocity of 3200 fps, Black Hills' new 25-06 load is suitable for varmints through light big game.

Remington topped with a 60-grain Nosler Partition at 3150 fps. During load development, this interesting combination produced almost match-level accuracy in even standard twist barrels. The 38-55 Win. has been a neglected round for many years and typically has been offered with an undersized .375-inch diameter jacketed bullet. No longer. Black Hills has added a proper sized 255-grain lead bullet at 1250 fps to its Cowboy line. Two perennial favorites are new to the company's Gold line—the 25-06 Rem. with a 115-grain Barnes-X pill at 2975 fps plus a 100-grain Nosler Ballistic Tip at 3200 fps; and the 7mm Rem. Mag. with either a 140-grain Barnes-X or a 140-grain Nosler Ballistic Tip at a respectable 3150 fps. Black Hills has earned an enviable reputation for producing some of the most consistently accurate ammunition being loaded in the industry. Nice folks, too.

Brenneke

Keeping right up with the rifled bores and sabot slugs, Brenneke is fielding a heavy 1-3/8 oz. slug with a muzzle velocity of 1502 fps for the 3-inch 12-gauge. The slug is designed for smoothbores and sports an attractive black coating called "CleanSpeed" that minimizes bore leading. Brenneke claims 2-inch groups at 50 yards and 3-inch groups at 100 yards—from a smoothbore, no less.
www.brennekeusa.com

Burgess Bullets

Remember the Littleton Shotmaker? Burgess Bullets has bought the company and improved the product. Capable of turning out 45 pounds of high antimony #6 thru #9 shot per hour

from melted wheel weights, the Littleton machine is indeed remarkable. It even produces those hard-to-get shot sizes--#7 and #8. It's a regular little household shot tower and not expensive.
www.littletonshotmaker.com

Cabela's

Look in their catalog for a new, competitively priced shotgun ammunition line loaded by Federal. Lots of interesting 12-gauge offerings in the turkey and steel shot arenas as well as extra-hard shot upland loads for the 12 and 20. www.cabelas.com

CCI-SPEER

CCI's extensive, sintered copper/tin, frangible bullet line just got bigger. New this year under the Blazer label is a 140-grain 45 ACP load clocking 1200 fps; a 90-grain 9mm load at 1350 fps; and a 105-grain 40 S&W loading at 1380 fps. Speer is introducing a 250-grain loading for that old stalwart, the 45 Colt, with a respectable velocity of 900 fps. In their component line, Speer has added a 210-grain 44 Magnum Gold Dot HP bullet and 185- and 200-grain Totally Metal Jacket bullets designed for 45 ACP velocities.
www.cci-ammunition.com
www.speer-bullets.com

Cor-Bon

When Smith & Wesson went looking for a new magnum handgun cartridge, Cor-Bon jumped at the chance to design the 500 S&W Magnum cartridge. The brass is being drawn right there in Sturgis, ND by Jamison International and the completed ammunition is being loaded by Cor-Bon. Initially, three different 500 S&W loads are being offered: a 275-grain Barnes X bullet at 1665 fps; a 400-grain SP at 1675 fps; and a wrist-shocking 440-grain gas-checked LBT "wide flat nose" pill at 1625 fps. At the other end of the ballistic scale, Cor-Bon has

Loaded with a soft bullet sized to 0.377-inch, Black Hills' 38-55 ammunition will accommodate the variety of bore sizes found in old rifles.

Black Hills Ammunition

A bunch of new loads from the Black Hills of South Dakota. Can the 223 Remington be considered a light big-game cartridge? Winchester thought so ten years ago and gave us the 64-grain deer bullet loading that also proved adequate for antelope–if all game ranges were kept under 200 yards. This year Black Hills introduces the 223

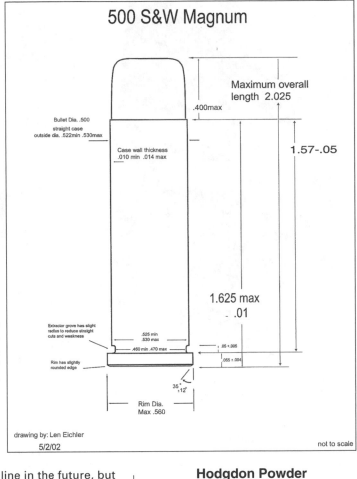

Smith&Wesson decided to capture the high ground with the release of their 500 S&W Magnum.

teamed up with North American Arms (NAA) and created the 32NAA. The 32NAA is a bottlenecked 32-caliber cartridge based on a necked down 380 ACP case that fits in NAA's little pocket automatic, the Guardian. The resulting ballistics from the Guardian's 2.5-inch barrel are impressive. The 32NAA loaded with a 60-grain bullet achieves 1200 fps. Cor-Bon and NAA are now working on the 25NAA that will be a based on a 32ACP case. Stay tuned! www.corbon.com

Environ Metal

Environ Metal is the manufacturer of Hevi-Shot products. New offerings include Hevi-Shot 00 buck *(currently loaded by Remington)* as well as shotguns slugs, 40-caliber frangible bullets and 30-caliber rifle bullets made from their proprietary, non-toxic alloy. www.hevishot.com

Federal

The 300 Winchester Short Magnum is taking off under the Federal Premium label with a 180-grain Nosler Partition at 2970 fps and a 150-grain Nosler BT at 3300 fps. Priced slightly lower in their Classic cartridge series is a 180-grain Hi-Shok loading at 2970 fps.

Urban geese and other varmints are successfully being taken on with Federal's sub-sonic 12-gauge ammunition. The "Metro Sub-Sonic Tungsten-Iron" 3-inch loading features 1-1/8 oz. of BBs at a lethargic 850 fps, while the 2 3/4-inch "Metro Sub-Sonic Field Load" does slightly better with 1-1/8 oz. of #7-1/2 shot at 900 fps. There are a number of new Trophy Bonded Bear Claw loadings in the Premium centerfire line and a Premium Grand Slam Turkey 2 3/4-inch load with 1-1/2 oz. of copper-plated #4, 5, and 6 shot at 1315 fps. www.federalcartridge.com

GOEX

Clear Shot, Goex's popular, non-corrosive blackpowder replacement, is currently out of production. They hope

The 1.57-inch case length of S&W's new 500 illustrates how big this new cartridge really is.

to get it back on line in the future, but in the meantime, stock up on it. Several of their distributors still have it. www.goexpowder.com

GPA Bullets

North American distribution of this new line of monolithic, copper alloy rifle bullets has been arranged through Rock Enterprise LLC headquartered in Flagstaff, AZ. The line now includes every decimal and metric caliber from 6mm to 600 Nitro.

www.rockenterprise.com

Graf & Sons

Great news for everyone who enjoys shooting the military warhorses. Graf has contracted with Hornady to produce Boxer-primed brass and loaded ammunition in 6.5x52 Carcano, 6.5x50 Jap, 7.7x58 Jap, 8x56R Mannlicher, 7.5x54 MAS, 7.65x53 Argentine, 7.5x55 Swiss, and 7.62x54 Russian. Initial headstamps will read "Frontier," later "Graf." Graf also offers a unique 123-grain V-Max bullet for the 7.62x39 and a 160-grain round-nose bullet for the 6.5 Carcano. www.grafs.com

Hodgdon Powder

Good, old slow-burning H870 is gone, but if you've missed Winchester's 540 and 571 series, they're back. Hodgdon is reintroducing them as HS-6 and HS-7, respectfully. Hodgdon offers new loading data—or one can use original 540 and 571 data. Triple Seven, Hodgdon's high energy, blackpowder substitute, has been pelletized as 50-caliber/50-grain charges designed for in-lines with #209 shotshell ignition. The traditional

Hodgdon's pelletized Triple Seven is increasingly being used to load metallic cartridges.

Muzzleloaders will be pleased with Hodgdon's new 54-caliber Pyrodex pellet.

Hornady's two-volume reloading manual contains vital information on their new bullets and cartridge lines.

Pyrodex pellet line has been expanded to include 45-caliber/50-grain, 50-caliber/50-grain, 50-caliber/30-grain, and 54-caliber/60-grain loadings. There's a brand new Pyrodex brochure at your dealers that provides interesting loading data for metallic cartridges and shotshells, as well as muzzleloaders. Speaking about interesting reloading data, Hodgdon has issued "reduced" loading data for the most popular rifle and shotgun calibers to assist beginning shooters, youths, and informal target shooters. There's a new "annual" reloading manual available that includes data for the latest short magnums plus 5000 other loads and some great articles from the past by Skeeter Skelton and Bob Milek. www.hodgdon.com www.pyrodex.com

Hornady

Bonded bullets are really in this year. Hornady has taken its successful SST design and bonded the jacket and core. Called "InterBond," the new line of bullets retains 90% of its mass, is available in Hornady-brand ammunition as well as components, and will be competitively priced. Initially, the line will feature a 130-grain/270-caliber; 139- and 145-grain/7mm, and 150- and 165-grain/30-caliber bullets. The standard SST design is being introduced in the muzzleloading sabot line. Look for some very streamlined 200-grain 45-caliber, and 250- and 300-grain 50-caliber sabots. Need some 20-caliber bullets for your 20 Squirrel? Look no further. Hornady makes a 33-grain V-Max bullet in .204-inch diameter.

There's a lot of fresh loading data available in Hornady's new, two-volume reloading manual for many of the short magnums and other recent cartridge introductions. See Graf and Huntington listings for additional products. www.hornady.com

Huntington

If you need brass, or bullets, or RCBS products, Huntington is the first stop. They are particularly strong in the rare and obsolete caliber department. For example, this year they're adding brass for the 5.6x35R Verling, 280 Ross, 8mm Lebel, 11.2x72 Schuler, 450 NE thin rim, 450 #2, 475 #2, 475 NE, 476 WR, and 500 NE 3-inch. They're the only source for 8mm Nambu bullets and carry the full Woodleigh line. How about 7mm-TCU, 220 Russian, 5.6x61 Vom Hofe, 6mm Remington Benchrest, or 500 Linebaugh brass? Huntington has them—plus they offer a unique service for cartridge collectors and handloaders. They will sell you a single case in every conceivable caliber for a very reasonable price. See their extensive catalog at www.huntington.com

Lapua

Lead-free is in at Lapua with the introduction of their "Naturalis" bullet in 6.5mm, 308 and 9.3mm. It's a monolithic hunting bullet with a plastic point capping a hollow cavity. The new bullet is available in loaded

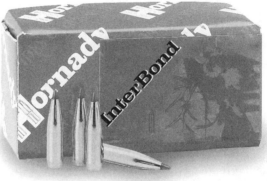

Hornady new core-bonded bullet is based on the streamlined SST design.

ammunition as well as a component. Under their Aficionado + line of competitive target ammunition are new loadings in 223 Rem. and 308 Win. featuring their highly acclaimed Scenar HPBT match bullets. www.lapua.com www.kaltron.com

Lazzeroni

The father of the short magnums is stretching out in the other direction with the production of the 30-caliber "Battlestar" cartridge. Design characteristics for this super non-belted magnum call for a 180-grain bullet at 3700 fps! New, too, is a proprietary plated, monolithic bullet with relief grooves cut into the shank. Named the "LazerHead," the projectile is available in 120-grain/7mm; 150-grain/30-caliber; and a non-grooved version in 185-grain/338-caliber. www.lazzeroni.com

Lyman Reloading Handbook, 48th Edition.

"Guardian Gold" is the label given Magtech's latest line of JHP ammunition for law enforcement and personal protection.

custom-sized to order. Liberty bullets are quality products. www.libertyshooting supplies.com

Load From A Disk

An upgraded and expanded Version #4 of this popular program is now available. www.loadammo.com/upgrade.htm

LYMAN

Lyman has just released the 48th Edition of its "*Reloading Handbook.*" Advertised as the "world's most comprehensive reloading manual," it lives up to its reputation. Packed with lots of new data and powders and informative articles, the new manual has returned to the practice of indicating the potentially most accurate load. This is a "must have" reloading manual.

Magtech

"Guardian Gold" is the label for Magtech's latest line of jacketed hollowpoint ammunition for law enforcement and personal defense. The new loading is available in 380, 38 Special, 357, 9mm, 40 S&W and 45 Auto. Also new is their "Clean Range" line—in 380, 38 Special, 9mm and 40 S&W—that features a fully encapsulated bullet and lead-free primer. www.magtechammuniti on.com

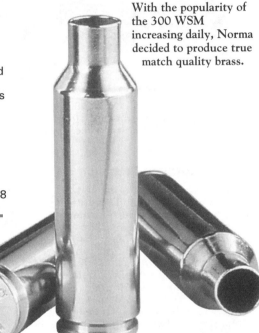

With the popularity of the 300 WSM increasing daily, Norma decided to produce true match quality brass.

Lee Precision

The father of the most affordable and unique reloading equipment line in the world, Richard Lee, has just released the 2nd edition of his book, *Modern Reloading.* This is the most personal and refreshingly written reloading manual in the field. Within its 720 pages is a complete description of the history, theory and practice of reloading that includes original chapters on bullet casting, reduced loads, measuring powder by volume, pressure, and, of course, a full description of the design and function of Lee tools. There is loading data for cartridges not normally covered in other manuals and the case diagrams indicate the year of introduction and the capacity of the case in cc's. Released, too, this year is a brand new software program called "Lee Shooter." Contained in the program are detailed logs for storing and printing out your handloading data and firearm collection information; trajectory, energy, recoil, wind drift calculators; printable targets; the complete loading manuals of Accurate Arms, Alliant, Hodgdon, IMR and VihtaVuori—plus the Lee Precision catalog. Priced at only $19.98 plus postage, it's another great Lee bargain. www.leeprecision.com

Liberty Shooting Supplies

Liberty's a great source for hard-to-find cast bullet designs. Recent introductions include bullets for the 22 WCF, 32 Colt (heeled), 351 Win. and 44 Evans (.423"). Then there are old standbys like 22 Hi-Power, 310 Cadet, 348 Win., 38-55 (.379"), 41 Swiss, and 43 Spanish and Mauser–plus all standard calibers. Many bullets can be

Nosler's new .224-inch 77-grain match bullet is designed for AR 15s and 16s with a 1:8 twist.

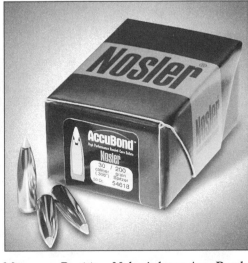

Move over Partition, Nolser's latest AccuBond hunting bullet features a bonded core.

Norma

With the popularity of the 300 WSM increasing daily, Norma is offering a match-grade case for the new caliber. www.norma.cc

Northern Precision

Imagine a bonded core, spitzer bullet for the 454 Casull that fits in a Freedom Arms cylinder. Northern Precision has them in weights from 300 to 375 grains. A 300-grain/ 308 bullet short enough to function in standard cases and actions? They've done it by using a powdered tungsten core. There's a new 250-grain, bonded-core bullet for the 356 Win., and a 400-grain/416 Sabre Star bullet designed to open up quickly. Just right for woodchucks. Call for their very unique catalog. (315) 493-1711

Nosler's new 728-page reloading manual includes fresh data on the short magnums as well as on the latest Nosler and Combined Technology bullets.

Nosler

Move over Partition. This year Nosler's gone bonded core with a line called "AccuBond". These boattail, polymer-tipped bullets cover the caliber spectrum with a 270/140-grain, 7mm/160-grain, 308/200-grain, 338/225-grain and a 375/260-grain being offered. The 270 WSM, with its attendant higher velocities, has had some influence at Nosler with two, heavier 270-caliber bullets making their appearance—a 140-grain Partition and a 150-grain Ballistic Silvertip. Responding to the almost universal use of the 223 Remington as an across-the-board match cartridge, Nosler has designed a 77-grain boattail, hollowpoint with a high ballistic coefficient of .340. The new bullet is designed to function through the magazines of semi-automatic service rifles. Finally, Nosler has released a new 728-page reloading manual with lots of new data and new bullets. The graphic displays of loading density, as well as technical footnotes, make this manual a must. www.nosler.com

Old Western Scrounger

What do you do when you have 600,000 rounds of 5mm Rem. Rimfire Magnum back-ordered from your customers? You go make it, right? Well, the Old Western Scrounger has done just that. He's contracted with Aguila to make a run of 2 million rounds. Hold on to your Remington Models 591 and 592. Ammo is on the way. www.ows-ammunition.com

Remington

Did I say bonded core was in? Remington has taken their superb Core-Lokt design and added a bonded core. The new Premier

Remington's new AccuTip bullets are designed for sub minute-of-angle accuracy, flat trajectories, and high down-range energy.

Core-Lokt Ultra bullet design is available in the 243 Win., 270 Win., 7mm Rem. Mag., 7mm Rem. Ultra Mag., 7mm Rem. SA Ultra Mag., 308 Win., 30-06, 300 Win., 300 Rem. Ultra Mag. and 300 Rem. SA Ultra Mag.

And there's another new rifle bullet at Big Green–a highly accurate, polymer-tipped Premier AccuTip that will be loaded in eight calibers from 243 through 300 Win. Mag. There are three new additions to the metallic cartridge line: the 17 Hornady Magnum Rimfire with a 17-grain V-Max pill; the 454 Casull with a 300-grain bonded-core JHP; and the return of the 350 Rem. Mag. with a 200-grain Core-Lokt SP. Building on their Hevi-Shot relationship, Remington is fielding a Hevi-Shot 00 buckshot loading in the 2 3/4-inch/12-gauge case and much requested Hevi-Shot Magnum Turkey loads in the 3 1/2-inch /10 gauge and 3-inch/20 gauge. Speaking about the 20 gauge, there's a new 260-grain Core-Lokt Ultra Bonded slug for the 2 3/4-inch/20-gauge case with a muzzle velocity of 1900 fps. Accommodating 2 3/4-inch/12-gauge sluggers, Remington has added a BuckHammer Attached-Sabot 1-1/4 oz. soft lead slug to its lineup that is not only accurate but offers tremendous expansion. Finally, going for speed, there's a 7/8 oz. Foster-type rifled slug for the 2 3/4-inch /12 gauge with a velocity of 1800 fps. www.remington.com

Schroeder Bullets

Here's a small firm that specializes in old and odd size bullets and brass. Need some 22 Cooper Centerfire Magnum or 7.92x33mm *Kurz* brass? Schroeder makes it. His latest creation is 25 Stevens centerfire brass. Interesting catalog. (619) 423-3523

Featuring a 1-1/4 oz. slug with an attached sabot, Remington's Express BuckHammer offers accuracy with tremendous expansion.

Remington's Core-Lokt Ultra Bullets provide controlled 1.8X expansion with deep penetration and 85% weight retention.

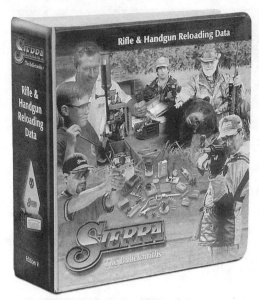

Sierra's 5th Edition reloading manual includes the latest cartridges and powders and is bound in a single volume.

Sellier & Bellot

NONTOX primers combined with TFMJ bullets are being offered in 9mm and 38 Special this year. www.sb-usa.com

Sierra Bullets

Sierra's 5th Edition *Rifle & Handgun Reloading Manual* has been released and it's better than ever. Lots of new powders and cartridges. The exterior ballistics chapter has been condensed and rewritten so that the whole 1149-page manual now fits in one binder.

Released in concert with the new manual is Sierra's "INFINITY" Version 5.0 exterior ballistics software

SSK's 14.5mm JDJ cartridge takes 235 grains of powder and an 1173-grain bullet.

program. The program has been expanded to include the bullets of all major manufacturers and ammunition companies. A Windows format makes it user-friendly and flexible. No new bullets, but some great Sierra match-grade bullet jackets in 22, 6mm and 30 caliber are now available. www.sierrabullets.com

Ssk Industries

What takes 235 grains of 5010 powder and a 1173-grain bullet? J.D. Jones' latest creation—the 14.5mm JDJ. Based on a necked-up and blown-out 50 BMG case, and fired from a 50-caliber rifle, the 14.5mm JDJ was designed for folks who consider the 50 BMG just a bit wimpy. After the appearance of the 500 S&W case, it didn't take JD long to create two new rounds for the Encore. Using the S&W basic case, he's necked it down to form the 475/500 and 458/500 JDJ Woodswalkers. SSK is also busy converting and chambering the AR10T for the 270, 7mm, and 300 WSM. www.sskindustries.com

The 500 S&W has been wildcatted already as evidenced by SSK's 458/500 and 475/500 Woodswalkers, pictured here with the parent 500.

Starline

Some interesting new brass this year—50 Alaskan, 50 Beowulf, 50-110, 480 Ruger, 41 Colt, 32 S&W and a special run of 475 Wildey–for Wildey. In the planning stages are the 38-55, 45 Auto Rim, some hard-to-find metrics. www.starlinebrass.com

Swift

Kudos to Swift for producing the highest quality handloading manual to date. Swift's hardbound *Reloading Manual Number One* is simply gorgeous. I laid my copy out on our coffee table. It offers extensive coverage of 49 rifle and pistol cartridges loaded with Swift's premium A-Frame and Scirocco bullets. The trajectory charts are adjacent to the loading data, and each cartridge is highlighted with an artist's rendering of a game animal commonly associated with the caliber. It's a real collector's item. (785) 754-3959.

West Coast Bullets

How do you tell duty ammunition from frangible target ammo? West Coast produces non-toxic, sintered iron-tin-copper bullets for all popular handgun calibers–plus the 223 Winchester. To ensure none of their loaded frangible bullets are accidentally carried while an officer is on duty, they color their bullets purple, green; in fact, just about any color you want.

www.westcoastbullets.com

Winchester Ammunition

Catching all of us by surprise, Winchester created their new "Super Short Magnum" series in 223 and 243. Designed to equal or exceed the velocities of the 22/250 and 240 Weatherby respectfully, the 223 WSSM and 243 WSSM are being teamed with super short-action Winchester Model 70s and Browning A Bolts. Having taken several whitetail this past fall using the 223 WSSM loaded with Winchester's 64-grain deer bullet at 3600 fps, I can report that the 223 WSSM is impressive. The 243 WSSM should be spectacular. The 223 WSSM

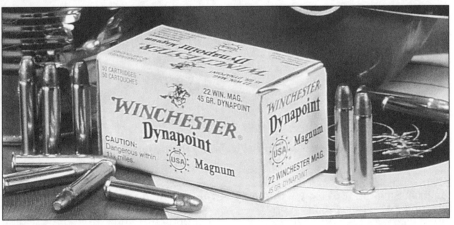

With the success of the Dyna Point design in the LR, Winchester is now loading a new Dyna Point in the 22 Rimfire Magnum.

Winchester's Supreme 20-gauge Platinum Tip slug makes the 20-gauge a serious deer and bear gun.

Sporting clays shooters will find Winchester's new hard shot, high-velocity loads in 28 and .410 gauges ideal.

41 Magnum shooters will be delighted with Winchester's new 240-grain Platinum Tip loading in the handgun line.

Winchester surprised the shooting world with the release of their hot, little 223 and 243 Super Short Magnums.

The 22 WRF is being returned to the Winchester rimfire line.

is currently loaded with a 55-grain Ballistic Silvertip (BST) in the Supreme line and a 55-grain soft point and 64-grain Power-Point in the Super-X line. 243 WSSM loadings feature a 55-grain BST and 95-grain BST in the Supreme line and a 100-grain Power-Point in the Super-X. Building on the strength of their existing short magnums, Winchester is giving the 270 WSM a 150-grain BST and Power-Point loading at 3150 fps that should prove ideal on larger big game. Similarly, the 300 WSM is getting a 180-grain BST

loading this year. The Supreme Varmint line has been expanded to include 55-grain BST loadings for the 223 Remington and 22-250 Remington.

The old 22 WRF is back in the line, while the 22 Rimfire Magnum sports a new bullet, the 45-grain Dynapoint at 1550 fps. Will 41 Rem. Mag. fans be happy! Winchester is introducing a 240-grain Platinum Tip loading at 1250 fps. The 28 and .410 gauges are getting the new High Strength AA hull and extra hard shot in the Super Sport line. The 28 gauge will feature 3/4 oz. of #7-1/2 and #8-1/2 while the .410 will carry 1/2 oz. of #8-1/2. All three new loads have a muzzle velocity of 1300 fps. And speaking of shot, #8-1/2 is being brought back to the 12-gauge AA Light and Xtra Lite target lines. There's a new 260-grain Platinum Tip Sabot Slug for the 20-gauge with a velocity of 1700 fps. Even the muzzlestuffers are getting something new this year—a 200-grain Platinum Sabot round for the 45-caliber ML and a 400-grain model for the 54-caliber ML. Finally, controlling the cost of non-toxic waterfowl loads, Winchester is adding a 3-inch/20-gauge steel shot loading of #2 and #4 to its Xpert line.
www.winchester.com

Many manufacturers do not supply suggested retail prices. Others did not get their pricing to us before press time. All pricing can vary dependent on the exact brand and style of ammo selected and/or the retail outlet from which you make your purchase. Pricing has been rounded to the nearest dollar and represents our best estimate of average pricing. An * after the cartridge means these loads are available with Nosler Partition or Swift A-Frame bullets. Listed pricing may or may not reflect this bullet type. ** = these are packed 50 to box, all others are 20 to box. Wea. Mag.= Weatherby Magnum. Spfd. = Springfield. A-A-Sq. = A-Square. N.E.=Nitro Express.

Cartridge	Bullet Weight Grains	VELOCITY (fps)					ENERGY (ft. lbs.)					TRAJ. (in.)				Est. Price/box
		Muzzle	100 yds.	200 yds.	300 yds.	400 yds.	Muzzle	100 yds.	200 yds.	300 yds.	400 yds.	100 yds.	200 yds.	300 yds.	400 yds.	
17 Remington	25	4040	3284	2644	2086	1606	906	599	388	242	143	+2.0	+1.7	-4.0	-17.0	$17
221 Fireball	50	2800	2137	1580	1180	988	870	507	277	155	109	+0.0	-7.0	-28.0	NA	$14
22 Hornet	34	3050	2132	1415	1017	852	700	343	151	78	55	+0.0	-6.6	-15.5	-29.9	NA
22 Hornet	35	3100	2278	1601	1135	929	747	403	199	100	67	+2.75	0	-16.9	-60.4	NA
22 Hornet	45	2690	2042	1502	1128	948	723	417	225	127	90	+0.0	-7.7	-31.0	NA	$27**
218 Bee	46	2760	2102	1550	1155	961	788	451	245	136	94	+0.0	-7.2	-29.0	NA	$46**
222 Remington	40	3600	3117	2673	2269	1911	1151	863	634	457	324	++1.07	0.0	-6.13	-18.9	
222 Remington	50	3140	2602	2123	1700	1350	1094	752	500	321	202	++2.0	-0.4	-11.0	-33.0	$11
222 Remington	55	3020	2562	2147	1773	1451	1114	801	563	384	257	+2.0	-0.4	-11.0	-33.0	$12
22 PPC	52	3400	2930	2510	2130	NA	1335	990	730	525	NA	+2.0	1.4	-5.0	NA	NA
223 Remington	40	3650	3010	2450	1950	1530	1185	805	535	340	265	+2.0	+1.0	-6.0	-22.0	$14
223 Remington	40	3800	3305	2845	2424	2044	1282	970	719	522	371	0.84	0.0	-5.34	-16.6	NA
223 Remington	50	3300	2874	2484	2130	1809	1209	917	685	504	363	1.37	0.0	-7.05	-21.8	NA
223 Remington	52/53	3330	2882	2477	2106	1770	1305	978	722	522	369	+2.0	+0.6	-6.5	-21.5	$14
223 Remington	55	3240	2748	2305	1906	1556	1282	922	649	444	296	+2.0	-0.2	-9.0	-27.0	$12
223 Remington	60	3100	2712	2355	2026	1726	1280	979	739	547	397	+2.0	+0.2	-8.0	-24.7	$16
223 Remington	64	3020	2621	2256	1920	1619	1296	977	723	524	373	+2.0	-0.2	-9.3	-23.0	$14
223 Remington	69	3000	2720	2460	2210	1980	1380	1135	925	750	600	+2.0	+0.8	-5.8	-17.5	$15
223 Remington	75	2790	2554	2330	2119	1926	1296	1086	904	747	617	2.37	0.0	-8.75	-25.1	NA
223 Remington	77	2750	2584	2354	2169	1992	1293	1110	948	804	679	1.93	0.0	-8.2	-23.8	NA
223 WSSM	55	3850	3438	3064	2721	2402	1810	1444	1147	904	704	0.7	0	-4.4	-13.6	NA
223 WSSM	64	3600	3144	2732	2356	2011	1841	1404	1061	789	574	1.0	0	-5.7	-17.7	NA
222 Rem. Mag.	55	3240	2748	2305	1906	1556	1282	922	649	444	296	+2.0	-0.2	-9.0	-27.0	$14
225 Winchester	55	3570	3066	2616	2208	1838	1556	1148	836	595	412	+2.0	+1.0	-5.0	-20.0	$19
224 Wea. Mag.	55	3650	3192	2780	2403	2057	1627	1244	943	705	516	+2.0	+1.2	-4.0	-17.0	$32
22-250 Rem.	40	4000	3320	2720	2200	1740	1420	980	660	430	265	+2.0	+1.8	-3.0	-16.0	$14
22-250 Rem.	50	3725	3264	2641	2455	2103	1540	1183	896	669	491	0.89	0.0	-5.23	-16.3	NA
22-250 Rem.	52/55	3680	3137	2656	2222	1832	1654	1201	861	603	410	+2.0	+1.3	-4.0	-17.0	$13
22-250 Rem.	60	3600	3195	2826	2485	2169	1727	1360	1064	823	627	+2.0	+2.0	-2.4	-12.3	$19
220 Swift	40	4200	3678	3190	2739	2329	1566	1201	904	666	482	+0.51	0.0	-4.0	-12.9	NA
220 Swift	50	3780	3158	2617	2135	1710	1586	1107	760	506	325	+2.0	+1.4	-4.4	-17.9	$20
220 Swift	50	3850	3396	2970	2576	2215	1645	1280	979	736	545	0.74	0.0	-4.84	-15.1	NA
220 Swift	55	3800	3370	2990	2630	2310	1765	1390	1090	850	650	0.8	0.0	-4.7	-14.4	NA
220 Swift	55	3650	3194	2772	2384	2035	1627	1246	939	694	506	+2.0	+2.0	-2.6	-13.4	$19
220 Swift	60	3600	3199	2824	2475	2156	1727	1364	1063	816	619	+2.0	+1.6	-4.1	-13.1	$19
22 Savage H.P.	71	2790	2340	1930	1570	1280	1225	860	585	390	190	+2.0	-1.0	-10.4	-35.7	NA
6mm BR Rem.	100	2550	2310	2083	1870	1671	1444	1185	963	776	620	+2.5	-0.6	-11.8	NA	$22
6mm Norma BR	107	2822	2667	2517	2372	2229	1893	1690	1506	1337	1181	+1.73	0.0	-7.24	-20.6	NA
6mm PPC	70	3140	2750	2400	2070	NA	1535	1175	895	665	NA	+2.0	+1.4	-5.0	NA	NA
243 Winchester	55	4025	3597	3209	2853	2525	1978	1579	1257	994	779	+0.6	0.00	-4.0	-12.2	NA
243 Winchester	60	3600	3110	2660	2260	1890	1725	1285	945	680	475	+2.0	+1.8	-3.3	-15.5	$17
243 Winchester	70	3400	3040	2700	2390	2100	1795	1435	1135	890	685	1.1	0.0	-5.9	-18.0	NA
243 Winchester	75/80	3350	2955	2593	2259	1951	1993	1551	1194	906	676	+2.0	+0.9	-5.0	-19.0	$16
243 Winchester	85	3320	3070	2830	2600	2380	2080	1770	1510	1280	1070	+2.0	+1.2	-4.0	-14.0	$18
243 Winchester	90	3120	2871	2635	2411	2199	1946	1647	1388	1162	966	1.4	0.0	-6.4	-18.8	NA
243 Winchester*	100	2960	2697	2449	2215	1993	1945	1615	1332	1089	882	+2.5	+1.2	-6.0	-20.0	$16
243 Winchester	105	2920	2689	2470	2261	2062	1988	1686	1422	1192	992	+2.5	+1.6	-5.0	-18.4	$21
243 Light Mag.	100	3100	2839	2592	2358	2138	2133	1790	1491	1235	1014	+1.5	0.0	-6.8	-19.8	NA
243 WSSM	55	4060	3628	3237	2880	2550	2013	1607	1280	1013	794	0.6	0	-3.9	-12	NA
243 WSSM	95	3250	3000	2763	2538	2325	2258	1898	1610	1359	1140	1.2	0	-5.7	-16.9	NA
243 WSSM	100	3110	2838	2583	2341	2112	2147	1789	1481	1217	991	1.4	0	-6.6	-19.7	NA
6mm Remington	80	3470	3064	2694	2352	2036	2139	1667	1289	982	736	+2.0	+1.1	-5.0	-17.0	$16
6mm Remington	100	3100	2829	2573	2332	2104	2133	1777	1470	1207	983	+2.5	+1.6	-5.0	-17.0	$16
6mm Remington	105	3060	2822	2596	2381	2177	2105	1788	1512	1270	1059	+2.5	+1.1	-3.3	-15.0	$21
6mm Rem. Light Mag.	100	3250	2997	2756	2528	2311	2345	1995	1687	1418	1186	1.59	0.0	-6.33	-18.3	NA
6.17(.243) Spitfire	100	3350	3122	2905	2698	2501	2493	2164	1874	1617	1389	2.4	3.20	0	-8	NA
240 Wea. Mag.	87	3500	3202	2924	2663	2416	2366	1980	1651	1370	1127	+2.0	+2.0	-2.0	-12.0	$32
240 Wea. Mag.	100	3395	3106	2835	2581	2339	2559	2142	1785	1478	1215	+2.5	+2.8	-2.0	-11.0	$43

17
22

6mm (24)

Cartridge	Bullet Weight Grains	VELOCITY (fps)					ENERGY (ft. lbs.)					TRAJ. (in.)				Est. Price/box
		Muzzle	100 yds.	200 yds.	300 yds.	400 yds.	Muzzle	100 yds.	200 yds.	300 yds.	400 yds.	100 yds.	200 yds.	300 yds.	400 yds.	
25-20 Win.	86	1460	1194	1030	931	858	407	272	203	165	141	0.0	-23.5	NA	NA	$32**
25-35 Win.	117	2230	1866	1545	1282	1097	1292	904	620	427	313	+2.5	-4.2	-26.0	NA	$24
250 Savage	100	2820	2504	2210	1936	1684	1765	1392	1084	832	630	+2.5	+0.4	-9.0	-28.0	$17
257 Roberts	100	2980	2661	2363	2085	1827	1972	1572	1240	965	741	+2.5	-0.8	-5.2	-21.6	$20
257 Roberts+P	117	2780	2411	2071	1761	1488	2009	1511	1115	806	576	+2.5	-0.2	-10.2	-32.6	$18
257 Roberts+P	120	2780	2560	2360	2160	1970	2060	1750	1480	1240	1030	+2.5	+1.2	-6.4	-23.6	$22
257 Roberts	122	2600	2331	2078	1842	1625	1831	1472	1169	919	715	+2.5	0.0	-10.6	-31.4	$21
257 Light Mag.	117	2940	2694	2460	2240	2031	2245	1885	1572	1303	1071	+1.7	0.0	-7.6	-21.8	NA
25-06 Rem.	87	3440	2995	2591	2222	1884	2286	1733	1297	954	686	+2.0	+1.1	-2.5	-14.4	$17
25-06 Rem.	90	3440	3043	2680	2344	2034	2364	1850	1435	1098	827	+2.0	+1.8	-3.3	-15.6	$17
25-06 Rem.	100	3230	2893	2580	2287	2014	2316	1858	1478	1161	901	+2.0	+0.8	-5.7	-18.9	$17
25-06 Rem.	117	2990	2770	2570	2370	2190	2320	2000	1715	1465	1246	+2.5	+1.0	-7.9	-26.6	$19
25-06 Rem.*	120	2990	2730	2484	2252	2032	2382	1985	1644	1351	1100	+2.5	+1.2	-5.3	-19.6	$17
25-06 Rem.	122	2930	2706	2492	2289	2095	2325	1983	1683	1419	1189	+2.5	+1.8	-4.5	-17.5	$23
257 Wea. Mag.	87	3825	3456	3118	2805	2513	2826	2308	1870	1520	1220	+2.0	+2.7	-0.3	-7.6	$32
257 Wea. Mag.	100	3555	3237	2941	2665	2404	2806	2326	1920	1576	1283	+2.5	+3.2	0.0	-8.0	$32
257 Scramjet	100	3745	3450	3173	2912	2666	3114	2643	2235	1883	1578	+2.1	+2.77	0.0	-6.93	NA
6.5x50mm Jap.	139	2360	2160	1970	1790	1620	1720	1440	1195	985	810	+2.5	-1.0	-13.5	NA	NA
6.5x50mm Jap.	156	2070	1830	1610	1430	1260	1475	1155	900	695	550	+2.5	-4.0	-23.8	NA	NA
6.5x52mm Car.	139	2580	2360	2160	1970	1790	2045	1725	1440	1195	985	+2.5	0.0	-9.9	-29.0	NA
6.5x52mm Car.	156	2430	2170	1930	1700	1500	2045	1630	1285	1005	780	+2.5	-1.0	-13.9	NA	NA
6.5x55mm Light Mag.	129	2750	2549	2355	2171	1994	2166	1860	1589	1350	1139	+2.0	0.0	-8.2	-23.9	NA
6.5x55mm Swe.	140	2550	NA	NA	NA	NA	2020	NA	NA	NA	NA	NA	NA	NA	NA	$18
6.5x55mm Swe.*	139/140	2850	2640	2440	2250	2070	2525	2170	1855	1575	1330	+2.5	+1.6	-5.4	-18.9	$18
6.5x55mm Swe.	156	2650	2370	2110	1870	1650	2425	1950	1550	1215	945	+2.5	0.0	-10.3	-30.6	NA
260 Remington	125	2875	2669	2473	2285	2105	2294	1977	1697	1449	1230	1.71	0.0	-7.4	-21.4	NA
260 Remington	140	2750	2544	2347	2158	1979	2351	2011	1712	1448	1217	+2.2	0.0	-8.6	-24.6	NA
6.5-284 Norma	142	3025	2890	2758	2631	2507	2886	2634	2400	2183	1982	1.13	0.0	-5.7	-16.4	NA
6.71 (264) Phantom	120	3150	2929	2718	2517	2325	2645	2286	1969	1698	1440	+1.3	0.0	-6.0	-17.5	NA
6.5 Rem. Mag.	120	3210	2905	2621	2353	2102	2745	2248	1830	1475	1177	+2.5	+1.7	-4.1	-16.3	Disc.
264 Win. Mag.	140	3030	2782	2548	2326	2114	2854	2406	2018	1682	1389	+2.5	+1.4	-5.1	-18.0	$24
6.71 (264) Blackbird	140	3480	3261	3053	2855	2665	3766	3307	2899	2534	2208	+2.4	+3.1	0.0	-7.4	NA
270 Winchester	100	3430	3021	2649	2305	1988	2612	2027	1557	1179	877	+2.0	+1.0	-4.9	-17.5	$17
270 Winchester	130	3060	2776	2510	2259	2022	2702	2225	1818	1472	1180	+2.5	+1.4	-5.3	-18.2	$17
270 Win. Supreme	130	3150	2881	2628	2388	2161	2865	2396	1993	1646	1348	1.3	0.0	-6.4	-18.9	NA
270 Winchester	135	3000	2780	2570	2369	2178	2697	2315	1979	1682	1421	+2.5	+1.4	-6.0	-17.6	$23
270 Winchester*	140	2940	2700	2480	2260	2060	2685	2270	1905	1590	1315	+2.5	+1.8	-4.6	-17.9	$20
270 Win. Light Magnum	130	3215	2998	2790	2590	2400	2983	2594	2246	1936	1662	1.21	0.0	-5.83	-17.0	NA
270 Winchester*	150	2850	2585	2336	2100	1879	2705	2226	1817	1468	1175	+2.5	+1.2	-6.5	-22.0	$17
270 Win. Supreme	150	2930	2693	2468	2254	2051	2860	2416	2030	1693	1402	1.7	0.0	-7.4	-21.6	NA
270 WSM	130	3275	3041	2820	2609	2408	3096	2669	2295	1564	1673	1.1	0.00	-5.5	-16.1	
270 WSM	140	3125	2865	2619	2386	2165	3035	2559	2132	1769	1457	1.4	0.00	-6.5	-19.0	
270 WSM	150	3120	2923	2734	2554	2380	3242	2845	2490	2172	1886	1.3	0.0	-5.9	-17.2	NA
270 Wea. Mag.	100	3760	3380	3033	2712	2412	3139	2537	2042	1633	1292	+2.0	+2.4	-1.2	-10.1	$32
270 Wea. Mag.	130	3375	3119	2878	2649	2432	3287	2808	2390	2026	1707	+2.5	-2.9	-0.9	-9.9	$32
270 Wea. Mag.*	150	3245	3036	2837	2647	2465	3507	3070	2681	2334	2023	+2.5	+2.6	-1.8	-11.4	$47
7mm BR	140	2216	2012	1821	1643	1481	1525	1259	1031	839	681	+2.0	-3.7	-20.0	NA	$23
7mm Mauser*	139/140	2660	2435	2221	2018	1827	2199	1843	1533	1266	1037	+2.5	0.0	-9.6	-27.7	$17
7mm Mauser	145	2690	2442	2206	1985	1777	2334	1920	1568	1268	1017	+2.5	+0.1	-9.6	-28.3	$18
7mm Mauser	154	2690	2490	2300	2120	1940	2475	2120	1810	1530	1285	+2.5	+0.8	-7.5	-23.5	$17
7mm Mauser	175	2440	2137	1857	1603	1382	2313	1774	1340	998	742	+2.5	-1.7	-16.1	NA	$17
7x57 Light Mag.	139	2970	2730	2503	2287	2082	2722	2301	1933	1614	1337	+1.6	0.0	-7.2	-21.0	NA
7x30 Waters	120	2700	2300	1930	1600	1330	1940	1405	990	685	470	+2.5	-0.2	-12.3	NA	$18
7mm-08 Rem.	120	3000	2725	2467	2223	1992	2398	1979	1621	1316	1058	+2.0	0.0	-7.6	-22.3	$18
7mm-08 Rem.*	140	2860	2625	2402	2189	1988	2542	2142	1793	1490	1228	+2.5	+0.8	-6.9	-21.9	$18
7mm-08 Rem.	154	2715	2510	2315	2128	1950	2520	2155	1832	1548	1300	+2.5	+1.0	-7.0	-22.7	$23
7mm-08 Light Mag.	139	3000	2790	2590	2399	2216	2777	2403	2071	1776	1515	+1.5	0.0	-6.7	-19.4	NA
7x64mm Bren.	140				Not Yet Announced											$17
7x64mm Bren.	154	2820	2610	2420	2230	2050	2720	2335	1995	1695	1430	+2.5	+1.4	-5.7	-19.9	NA
7x64mm Bren.*	160	2850	2669	2495	2327	2166	2885	2530	2211	1924	1667	+2.5	+1.6	-4.8	-17.8	$24
7x64mm Bren.	175				Not Yet Announced											$17
284 Winchester	150	2860	2595	2344	2108	1886	2724	2243	1830	1480	1185	+2.5	+0.8	-7.3	-23.2	$24
280 Remington	120	3150	2866	2599	2348	2110	2643	2188	1800	1468	1186	+2.0	+0.6	-6.0	-17.9	$17

Side tabs: **25**, **6.5**, **27**, **7mm**

Cartridge	Bullet Weight Grains	VELOCITY (fps)					ENERGY (ft. lbs.)					TRAJ. (in.)				Est. Price/ box
		Muzzle	100 yds.	200 yds.	300 yds.	400 yds.	Muzzle	100 yds.	200 yds.	300 yds.	400 yds.	100 yds.	200 yds.	300 yds.	400 yds.	
280 Remington	140	3000	2758	2528	2309	2102	2797	2363	1986	1657	1373	+2.5	+1.4	-5.2	-18.3	$17
280 Remington*	150	2890	2624	2373	2135	1912	2781	2293	1875	1518	1217	+2.5	+0.8	-7.1	-22.6	$17
280 Remington	160	2840	2637	2442	2556	2078	2866	2471	2120	1809	1535	+2.5	+0.8	-6.7	-21.0	$20
280 Remington	165	2820	2510	2220	1950	1701	2913	2308	1805	1393	1060	+2.5	+0.4	-8.8	-26.5	$17
7x61mm S&H Sup.	154	3060	2720	2400	2100	1820	3200	2520	1965	1505	1135	+2.5	+1.8	-5.0	-19.8	NA
7mm Dakota	160	3200	3001	2811	2630	2455	3637	3200	2808	2456	2140	+2.1	+1.9	-2.8	-12.5	NA
7mm Rem. Mag.*	139/140	3150	2930	2710	2510	2320	3085	2660	2290	1960	1670	+2.5	+2.4	-2.4	-12.7	$21
7mm Rem. Hvy Mag	139	3250	3044	2847	2657	2475	3259	2860	2501	2178	1890	1.1	0	-5.5	-16.2	NA
7mm Rem. Mag.	150/154	3110	2830	2568	2320	2085	3221	2667	2196	1792	1448	+2.5	+1.6	-4.6	-16.5	$21
7mm Rem. Mag.*	160/162	2950	2730	2520	2320	2120	3090	2650	2250	1910	1600	+2.5	+1.8	-4.4	-17.8	$34
7mm Rem. Mag.	165	2900	2699	2507	2324	2147	3081	2669	2303	1978	1689	+2.5	+1.2	-5.9	-19.0	$28
7mm Rem Mag.	175	2860	2645	2440	2244	2057	3178	2718	2313	1956	1644	+2.5	+1.0	-6.5	-20.7	$21
7mm Rem. SA ULTRA MAG	140	3175	2934	2707	2490	2283	3033	2676	2277	1927	1620	1.3	0.00	-6	-17.7	
7mm Rem. SA ULTRA MAG	150	3110	2828	2563	2313	2077	3221	2663	2188	1782	1437	2.5	2.10	-3.6	-15.8	
7mm Rem. SA ULTRA MAG	160	2960	2762	2572	2390	2215	3112	2709	2350	2029	1743	2.6	2.20	-3.6	-15.4	
7mm Rem. WSM	140	3225	3008	2801	2603	2414	3233	2812	2438	2106	1812	1.2	0.00	-5.6	-16.4	
7mm Rem. WSM	160	2990	2744	2512	2081	1883	3176	2675	2241	1864	1538	1.6	0	-7.1	-20.8	
7mm Wea. Mag.	140	3225	2970	2729	2501	2283	3233	2741	2315	1943	1621	+2.5	+2.0	-3.2	-14.0	$35
7mm Wea. Mag.	154	3260	3023	2799	2586	2382	3539	3044	2609	2227	1890	+2.5	+2.8	-1.5	-10.8	$32
7mm Wea. Mag.*	160	3200	3004	2816	2637	2464	3637	3205	2817	2469	2156	+2.5	+2.7	-1.5	-10.6	$47
7mm Wea. Mag.	165	2950	2747	2553	2367	2189	3188	2765	2388	2053	1756	+2.5	+1.8	-4.2	-16.4	$43
7mm Wea. Mag.	175	2910	2693	2486	2288	2098	3293	2818	2401	2033	1711	+2.5	+1.2	-5.9	-19.4	$35
7.21(.284) Tomahawk	140	3300	3118	2943	2774	2612	3386	3022	2693	2393	2122	2.3	3.20	0.0	-7.7	NA
7mm STW	140	3325	3064	2818	2585	2364	3436	2918	2468	2077	1737	+2.3	+1.8	-3.0	-13.1	NA
7mm STW Supreme	160	3150	2894	2652	2422	2204	3526	2976	2499	2085	1727	1.3	0.0	-6.3	-18.5	NA
7mm Rem. Ultra Mag.	140	3425	3184	2956	2740	2534	3646	3151	2715	2333	1995	1.7	1.60	-2.6	-11.4	NA
7mm Firehawk	140	3625	3373	3135	2909	2695	4084	3536	3054	2631	2258	+2.2	+2.9	0.0	-7.03	NA
7.21 (.284) Firebird	140	3750	3522	3306	3101	2905	4372	3857	3399	2990	2625	1.6	2.4	0.0	-6	NA
30 Carbine	110	1990	1567	1236	1035	923	977	600	373	262	208	0.0	-13.5	NA	NA	$28**
303 Savage	190	1890	1612	1327	1183	1055	1507	1096	794	591	469	+2.5	-7.6	NA	NA	$24
30 Remington	170	2120	1822	1555	1328	1153	1696	1253	913	666	502	+2.5	-4.7	-26.3	NA	$20
7.62x39mm Rus.	123/125	2300	2030	1780	1550	1350	1445	1125	860	655	500	+2.5	-2.0	-17.5	NA	$13
30-30 Win.	55	3400	2693	2085	1570	1187	1412	886	521	301	172	+2.0	0.0	-10.2	-35.0	$18
30-30 Win.	125	2570	2090	1660	1320	1080	1830	1210	770	480	320	-2.0	-2.6	-19.9	NA	$13
30-30 Win.	150	2390	1973	1605	1303	1095	1902	1296	858	565	399	+2.5	-3.2	-22.5	NA	$13
30-30 Win. Supreme	150	2480	2095	1747	1446	1209	2049	1462	1017	697	487	0.0	-6.5	-24.5		NA
30-30 Win.	160	2300	1997	1719	1473	1268	1879	1416	1050	771	571	+2.5	-2.9	-20.2	NA	$18
30-30 PMC Cowboy	170	1300	1198	1121			638	474				0.0	-27.0			NA
30-30 Win.*	170	2200	1895	1619	1381	1191	1827	1355	989	720	535	+2.5	-5.8	-23.6	NA	$13
300 Savage	150	2630	2354	2094	1853	1631	2303	1845	1462	1143	886	+2.5	-0.4	-10.1	-30.7	$17
300 Savage	180	2350	2137	1935	1754	1570	2207	1825	1496	1217	985	+2.5	-1.6	-15.2	NA	$17
30-40 Krag	180	2430	2213	2007	1813	1632	2360	1957	1610	1314	1064	+2.5	-1.4	-13.8	NA	$18
7.65x53mm Arg.	180	2590	2390	2200	2010	1830	2685	2280	1925	1615	1345	+2.5	0.0	-27.6	NA	NA
307 Winchester	150	2760	2321	1924	1575	1289	2530	1795	1233	826	554	+2.5	-1.5	-13.6	NA	Disc.
307 Winchester	180	2510	2179	1874	1599	1362	2519	1898	1404	1022	742	+2.5	-1.6	-15.6	NA	$20
7.5x55 Swiss	180	2650	2450	2250	2060	1880	2805	2390	2020	1700	1415	+2.5	+0.6	-8.1	-24.9	NA
308 Winchester	55	3770	3215	2726	2286	1888	1735	1262	907	638	435	-2.0	+1.4	-3.8	-15.8	$22
308 Winchester	150	2820	2533	2263	2009	1774	2648	2137	1705	1344	1048	+2.5	+0.4	-8.5	-26.1	$17
308 Winchester	165	2700	2440	2194	1963	1748	2670	2180	1763	1411	1199	+2.5	0.0	-9.7	-28.5	$20
308 Winchester	168	2680	2493	2314	2143	1979	2678	2318	1998	1713	1460	+2.5	0.0	-8.9	-25.3	$18
308 Winchester	178	2620	2415	2220	2034	1857	2713	2306	1948	1635	1363	+2.5	0.0	-9.6	-27.6	$23
308 Winchester*	180	2620	2393	2178	1974	1782	2743	2288	1896	1557	1269	+2.5	-0.2	-10.2	-28.5	$17
308 Light Mag.*	150	2980	2703	2442	2195	1964	2959	2433	1986	1606	1285	+1.6	0.0	-7.5	-22.2	NA
308 Light Mag.	165	2870	2658	2456	2263	2078	3019	2589	2211	1877	1583	+1.7	0.0	-7.5	-21.8	NA
308 High Energy	165	2870	2600	2350	2120	1890	3020	2485	2030	1640	1310	+1.8	0.0	-8.2	-24.0	NA
308 Light Mag.	168	2870	2658	2456	2263	2078	3019	2589	2211	1877	1583	+1.7	0.0	-7.5	-21.8	NA
308 High Energy	180	2740	2550	2370	2200	2030	3000	2600	2245	1925	1645	+1.9	0.0	-8.2	-23.5	NA
30-06 Spfd.	55	4080	3485	2965	2502	2083	2033	1483	1074	764	530	+2.0	+1.9	-2.1	-11.7	$22
30-06 Spfd.	125	3140	2780	2447	2138	1853	2736	2145	1662	1279	953	+2.0	+1.0	-6.2	-21.0	$17
30-06 Spfd.	150	2910	2617	2342	2083	1853	2820	2281	1827	1445	1135	+2.5	+0.8	-7.2	-23.4	$17
30-06 Spfd.	152	2910	2654	2413	2184	1968	2858	2378	1965	1610	1307	+2.5	+1.0	-6.6	-21.3	$23

Cartridge	Bullet Weight Grains	Muzzle	100 yds.	200 yds.	300 yds.	400 yds.	Muzzle	100 yds.	200 yds.	300 yds.	400 yds.	100 yds.	200 yds.	300 yds.	400 yds.	Est. Price/box
		VELOCITY (fps)					ENERGY (ft. lbs.)					TRAJ. (in.)				
30-06 Spfd.*	165	2800	2534	2283	2047	1825	2872	2352	1909	1534	1220	+2.5	+0.4	-8.4	-25.5	$17
30-06 Spfd.	168	2710	2522	2346	2169	2003	2739	2372	2045	1754	1497	+2.5	+0.4	-8.0	-23.5	$18
30-06 Spfd.	178	2720	2511	2311	2121	1939	2924	2491	2111	1777	1486	+2.5	+0.4	-8.2	-24.6	$23
30-06 Spfd.*	180	2700	2469	2250	2042	1846	2913	2436	2023	1666	1362	-2.5	0.0	-9.3	-27.0	$17
30-06 Spfd.	220	2410	2130	1870	1632	1422	2837	2216	1708	1301	988	+2.5	-1.7	-18.0	NA	$17
30-06 Light Mag.	150	3100	2815	2548	2295	2058	3200	2639	2161	1755	1410	+1.4	0.0	-6.8	-20.3	NA
30-06 Light Mag.	180	2880	2676	2480	2293	2114	3316	2862	2459	2102	1786	+1.7	0.0	-7.3	-21.3	NA
30-06 High Energy	180	2880	2690	2500	2320	2150	3315	2880	2495	2150	1845	+1.7	0.0	-7.2	-21.0	NA
300 REM SA ULTRA MAG	150	3200	2901	2622	2359	2112	3410	2803	2290	1854	1485	1.3	0.00	-6.4	-19.1	
300 REM SA ULTRA MAG	165	3075	2792	2527	2276	2040	3464	2856	2339	1898	1525	1.5	0.00	-7	-20.7	
300 REM SA ULTRA MAG	180	2960	2761	2571	2389	2214	3501	3047	2642	2280	1959	2.6	2.20	-3.6	-15.4	
7.82 (308) Patriot	150	3250	2999	2762	2537	2323	3519	2997	2542	2145	1798	+1.2	0.0	-5.8	-16.9	NA
300 WSM	150	3300	3061	2834	2619	2414	3628	3121	2676	2285	1941	1.1	0.0	-5.4	-15.9	NA
300 WSM	180	2970	2741	2524	2317	2120	3526	3005	2547	2147	1797	1.6	0.0	-7.0	-20.5	NA
300 WSM	180	3010	2923	2734	2554	2380	3242	2845	2490	2172	1886	1.3	0	-5.9	-17.2	NA
308 Norma Mag.	180	3020	2820	2630	2440	2270	3645	3175	2755	2385	2050	+2.5	+2.0	-3.5	-14.8	NA
300 Dakota	200	3000	2824	2656	2493	2336	3996	3542	3131	2760	2423	+2.2	+1.5	-4.0	-15.2	NA
300 H&H Magnum*	180	2880	2640	2412	2196	1990	3315	2785	2325	1927	1583	+2.5	+0.8	-6.8	-21.7	$24
300 H&H Magnum	220	2550	2267	2002	1757	NA	3167	2510	1958	1508	NA	-2.5	-0.4	-12.0	NA	NA
300 Peterson	180	3500	3319	3145	2978	2817	4896	4401	3953	3544	3172	+2.3	+2.9	0.0	-6.8	NA
300 Win. Mag.	150	3290	2951	2636	2342	2068	3605	2900	2314	1827	1424	+2.5	+1.9	-3.8	-15.8	$22
300 Win. Mag.	165	3100	2877	2665	2462	2269	3522	3033	2603	2221	1897	+2.5	+2.4	-3.0	-16.9	$24
300 Win. Mag.	178	2900	2760	2568	2375	2191	3509	3030	2606	2230	1897	+2.5	+1.4	-5.0	-17.6	$29
300 Win. Mag.*	180	2960	2745	2540	2344	2157	3501	3011	2578	2196	1859	+2.5	+1.2	-5.5	-18.5	$22
300 W.M. High Energy	180	3100	2830	2580	2340	2110	3840	3205	2660	2190	1790	+1.4	0.0	-6.6	-19.7	NA
300 W.M. Light Mag.	180	3100	2879	2668	2467	2275	3840	3313	2845	2431	2068	+1.39	0.0	-6.45	-18.7	NA
300 Win. Mag.	190	2885	1691	2506	2327	2156	3511	3055	2648	2285	1961	+2.5	+1.2	-5.7	-19.0	$26
300 W.M. High Energy	200	2930	2740	2550	2370	2200	3810	3325	2885	2495	2145	+1.6	0.0	-6.9	-20.1	NA
300 Win. Mag.*	200	2825	2595	2376	2167	1970	3545	2991	2508	2086	1742	-2.5	+1.6	-4.7	-17.2	$36
300 Win. Mag.	220	2680	2448	2228	2020	1823	3508	2927	2424	1993	1623	+2.5	0.0	-9.5	-27.5	$23
300 Rem. Ultra Mag.	150	3450	3208	2980	2762	2556	3964	3427	2956	2541	2175	1.7	1.5	-2.6	-11.2	NA
300 Rem. Ultra Mag.	180	3250	3037	2834	2640	2454	4221	3686	3201	2786	2407	2.4		-3.0	-12.7	NA
300 Rem. Ultra Mag.	200	3025	2826	2636	2454	2279	4063	3547	3086	2673	2308	2.4	0.0	-3.4	-14.6	NA
300 Wea. Mag.	100	3900	3441	3038	2652	2305	3714	2891	2239	1717	1297	+2.0	+2.6	-0.6	-8.7	$32
300 Wea. Mag.	150	3600	3307	3033	2776	2533	4316	3642	3064	2566	2137	+2.5	+3.2	0.0	-8.1	$32
300 Wea. Mag.	165	3450	3210	3000	2792	2593	4360	3796	3297	2855	2464	+2.5	+3.2	0.0	-7.8	NA
300 Wea. Mag.	178	3120	2902	2695	2497	2308	3847	3329	2870	2464	2104	+2.5	-1.7	-3.6	-14.7	$43
300 Wea. Mag.	180	3330	3110	2910	2710	2520	4430	3875	3375	2935	2540	+1.0	0.0	-5.2	-15.1	NA
300 Wea. Mag.	190	3030	2830	2638	2455	2279	3873	3378	2936	2542	2190	+2.5	+1.6	-4.3	-16.0	$38
300 Wea. Mag.	220	2850	2541	2283	1964	1736	3967	3155	2480	1922	1471	+2.5	+0.4	-8.5	-26.4	$35
300 Warbird	180	3400	3180	2971	2772	2582	4620	4042	3528	3071	2664	+2.59	+3.25	0.0	-7.95	NA
300 Pegasus	180	3500	3319	3145	2978	2817	4896	4401	3953	3544	3172	+2.28	+2.89	0.0	-6.79	NA
32-20 Win.	100	1210	1021	913	834	769	325	231	185	154	131	0.0	-32.3	NA	NA	$23**
303 British	150	2685	2441	2210	1992	1787	2401	1984	1627	1321	1064	+2.5	+0.6	-8.4	-26.2	$18
303 British	180	2460	2124	1817	1542	1311	2418	1803	1319	950	687	+2.5	-1.8	-16.8	NA	$18
303 Light Mag.	150	2830	2570	2325	2094	1884	2667	2199	1800	1461	1185	+2.0	0.0	-8.4	-24.6	NA
7.62x54mm Rus.	146	2950	2730	2520	2320	NA	2820	2415	2055	1740	NA	+2.5	+2.0	-4.4	-17.7	NA
7.62x54mm Rus.	180	2580	2370	2180	2000	1820	2650	2250	1900	1590	1100	+2.5	0.0	-9.8	-28.5	NA
7.7x58mm Jap.	180	2500	2300	2100	1920	1750	2490	2105	1770	1475	1225	+2.5	0.0	-10.4	-30.2	NA
8x57mm JS Mau.	165	2850	2520	2210	1930	1670	2965	2330	1795	1360	1015	+2.5	+1.0	-7.7	NA	NA
32 Win. Special	170	2250	1921	1626	1372	1175	1911	1393	998	710	521	+2.5	-3.5	-22.9	NA	$14
8mm Mauser	170	2360	1969	1622	1333	1123	2102	1464	993	671	476	+2.5	-3.1	-22.2	NA	$18
8mm Rem. Mag.	185	3080	2761	2464	2186	1927	3896	3131	2494	1963	1525	+2.5	+1.4	-5.5	-19.7	$30
8mm Rem. Mag.	220	2830	2581	2346	2123	1913	3912	3254	2688	2201	1787	+2.5	+0.6	-7.6	-23.5	Disc.
338-06	200	2750	2553	2364	2184	2011	3358	2894	2482	2118	1796	+1.9	0.0	-8.22	-23.6	NA
330 Dakota	250	2900	2719	2545	2378	2217	4668	4103	3595	3138	2727	+2.3	+1.3	-5.0	-17.5	NA
338 Lapua	250	2963	2795	2640	2493	NA	4842	4341	3881	3458	NA	+1.9	0.0	-7.9	NA	NA
338 Win. Mag.	200	2960	2658	2375	2110	1862	3890	3137	2505	1977	1539	+2.5	+1.0	-6.7	-22.3	$27
338 Win. Mag.*	210	2830	2590	2370	2150	1940	3735	3130	2610	2155	1760	+2.5	+1.4	-6.0	-20.9	$33
338 Win. Mag.*	225	2785	2517	2266	2029	1808	3871	3165	2565	2057	1633	+2.5	+0.4	-8.5	-25.9	$27
338 W.M. Heavy Mag.	225	2920	2678	2449	2232	2027	4259	3583	2996	2489	2053	+1.75	0.0	-7.65	-22.0	NA
338 W.M. High Energy	225	2940	2690	2450	2230	2010	4320	3610	3000	2475	2025	+1.7	0.0	-7.5	-22.0	NA

Cartridge	Bullet Weight Grains	VELOCITY (fps) Muzzle	100 yds.	200 yds.	300 yds.	400 yds.	ENERGY (ft. lbs.) Muzzle	100 yds.	200 yds.	300 yds.	400 yds.	TRAJ. (in.) 100 yds.	200 yds.	300 yds.	400 yds.	Est. Price/box
338 Win. Mag.	230	2780	2573	2375	2186	2005	3948	3382	2881	2441	2054	+2.5	+1.2	-6.3	-21.0	$40
338 Win. Mag.*	250	2660	2456	2261	2075	1898	3927	3348	2837	2389	1999	+2.5	+0.2	-9.0	-26.2	$27
338 W.M. High Energy	250	2800	2610	2420	2250	2080	4350	3775	3260	2805	2395	+1.8	0.0	-7.8	-22.5	NA
338 Ultra Mag.	250	2860	2645	2440	2244	2057	4540	3882	3303	2794	2347	1.7	0.0	-7.6	-22.1	NA
8.59(.338) Galaxy	200	3100	2899	2707	2524	2347	4269	3734	3256	2829	2446	3	3.80	0.0	-9.3	NA
340 Wea. Mag.*	210	3250	2991	2746	2515	2295	4924	4170	3516	2948	2455	+2.5	+1.9	-1.8	-11.8	$56
340 Wea. Mag.*	250	3000	2806	2621	2443	2272	4995	4371	3812	3311	2864	+2.5	+2.0	-3.5	-14.8	$56
338 A-Square	250	3120	2799	2500	2220	1958	5403	4348	3469	2736	2128	+2.5	+2.7	-1.5	-10.5	NA
338-378 Wea. Mag.	225	3180	2974	2778	2591	2410	5052	4420	3856	3353	2902	3.1	3.80	0.0	-8.9	NA
338 Titan	225	3230	3010	2800	2600	2409	5211	4524	3916	3377	2898	+3.07	+3.80	0.0	-8.95	NA
338 Excalibur	200	3600	3361	3134	2920	2715	5755	5015	4363	3785	3274	+2.23	+2.87	0.0	-6.99	NA
338 Excalibur	250	3250	2922	2618	2333	2066	5863	4740	3804	3021	2370	+1.3	0.0	-6.35	-19.2	NA
348 Winchester	200	2520	2215	1931	1672	1443	2820	2178	1656	1241	925	+2.5	-1.4	-14.7	NA	$42
357 Magnum	158	1830	1427	1138	980	883	1175	715	454	337	274	0.0	-16.2	-33.1	NA	$25**
35 Remington	150	2300	1874	1506	1218	1039	1762	1169	755	494	359	+2.5	-4.1	-26.3	NA	$16
35 Remington	200	2080	1698	1376	1140	1001	1921	1280	841	577	445	+2.5	-6.3	-17.1	-33.6	$16
356 Winchester	200	2460	2114	1797	1517	1284	2688	1985	1434	1022	732	+2.5	-1.8	-15.1	NA	$31
356 Winchester	250	2160	1911	1682	1476	1299	2591	2028	1571	1210	937	+2.5	-3.7	-22.2	NA	$31
358 Winchester	200	2490	2171	1876	1619	1379	2753	2093	1563	1151	844	+2.5	-1.6	-15.6	NA	$31
358 STA	275	2850	2562	2292	2039	NA	4958	4009	3208	2539	NA	+1.9	0.0	-8.6	NA	NA
350 Rem. Mag.	200	2710	2410	2130	1870	1631	3261	2579	2014	1553	1181	+2.5	-0.2	-10.0	-30.1	$33
35 Whelen	200	2675	2378	2100	1842	1606	3177	2510	1958	1506	1145	+2.5	-0.2	-10.3	-31.1	$20
35 Whelen	225	2500	2300	2110	1930	1770	3120	2650	2235	1870	1560	+2.6	0.0	-10.2	-29.9	NA
35 Whelen	250	2400	2197	2005	1823	1652	3197	2680	2230	1844	1515	+2.5	-1.2	-13.7	NA	$20
358 Norma Mag.	250	2800	2510	2230	1970	1730	4350	3480	2750	2145	1655	+2.5	+1.0	-7.6	-25.2	NA
358 STA	275	2850	2562	229*2	2039	1764	4959	4009	3208	2539	1899	+1.9	0.0	-8.58	-26.1	NA
9.3x57mm Mau.	286	2070	1810	1590	1390	1110	2710	2090	1600	1220	955	+2.5	-2.6	-22.5	NA	NA
9.3x62mm Mau.	286	2360	2089	1844	1623	NA	3538	2771	2157	1670	1260	+2.5	-1.6	-21.0	NA	NA
9.3x64mm	286	2700	2505	2318	2139	1968	4629	3984	3411	2906	2460	+2.5	+2.7	-4.5	-19.2	NA
9.3x74Rmm	286	2360	2089	1844	1623	NA	3538	2771	2157	1670	NA	+2.5	-2.0	-11.0	NA	NA
38-55 Win.	255	1320	1190	1091	1018	963	987	802	674	587	525	0.0	-23.4	NA	NA	$25
375 Winchester	200	2200	1841	1526	1268	1089	2150	1506	1034	714	527	+2.5	-4.0	-26.2	NA	$27
375 Winchester	250	1900	1647	1424	1239	1103	2005	1506	1126	852	676	+2.5	-6.9	-33.3	NA	$27
376 Steyr	225	2600	2331	2078	1842	1625	3377	2714	2157	1694	1319	2.5	0.0	-10.6	-31.4	NA
376 Steyr	270	2600	2372	2156	1951	1759	4052	3373	2787	2283	1855	2.3	0.0	-9.9	-28.9	NA
375 Dakota	300	2600	2316	2051	1804	1579	4502	3573	2800	2167	1661	+2.4	0.0	-11.0	-32.7	NA
375 N.E. 2-1/2"	270	2000	1740	1507	1310	NA	2398	1815	1362	1026	NA	+2.5	-6.0	-30.0	NA	NA
375 Flanged	300	2450	2150	1886	1640	NA	3998	3102	2369	1790	NA	+2.5	-2.4	-17.0	NA	NA
375 H&H Magnum	250	2670	2450	2240	2040	1850	3955	3335	2790	2315	1905	+2.5	-0.4	-10.2	-28.4	NA
375 H&H Magnum	270	2690	2420	2166	1928	1707	4337	3510	2812	2228	1747	+2.5	0.0	-10.0	-29.4	$28
375 H&H Magnum*	300	2530	2245	1979	1733	1512	4263	3357	2608	2001	1523	+2.5	-1.0	-10.5	-33.6	$28
375 H&H Hvy. Mag.	270	2870	2628	2399	2182	1976	4937	4141	3451	2150	1845	+1.7	0.0	-7.2	-21.0	NA
375 H&H Hvy. Mag.	300	2705	2386	2090	1816	1568	4873	3793	2908	2195	1637	+2.3	0.0	-10.4	-31.4	NA
375 Rem. Ultra Mag.	270	2900	2558	2241	1947	1678	5041	3922	3010	2272	1689	1.9	2.7	-8.9	-27	NA
375 Rem. Ultra Mag.	300	2760	2505	2263	2035	1822	5073	4178	3412	2759	2210	2.0	0.0	-8.8	-26.1	NA
375 Wea. Mag.	300	2700	2420	2157	1911	1685	4856	3901	3100	2432	1891	+2.5	-.04	-10.7	-	NA
378 Wea. Mag.	270	3180	2976	2781	2594	2415	6062	5308	4635	4034	3495	+2.5	+2.6	-1.8	-11.3	$71
378 Wea. Mag.	300	2929	2576	2252	1952	1680	5698	4419	3379	2538	1881	+2.5	+1.2	-7.0	-24.5	$77
375 A-Square	300	2920	2626	2351	2093	1850	5679	4594	3681	2917	2281	+2.5	+1.4	-6.0	-21.0	NA
38-40 Win.	180	1160	999	901	827	764	538	399	324	273	233	0.0	-33.9	NA	NA	$42**
405 WIN	300	2200	1851	1545	1296		3224	2282	1589	1119		4.6	0.00	-19.5		
450/400-3"	400	2150	1932	1730	1545	1379	4105	3316	2659	2119	1689	+2.5	-4.0	-9.5	-30.0	NA
416 Dakota	400	2450	2294	2143	1998	1859	5330	4671	4077	3544	3068	+2.5	-0.2	-10.5	-29.4	NA
416 Taylor	400	2350	2117	1896	1693	NA	4905	3980	3194	2547	NA	+2.5	-1.2	15.0	NA	NA
416 Hoffman	400	2380	2145	1923	1718	1529	5031	4087	3285	2620	2077	+2.5	-1.0	-14.1	NA	NA
416 Rigby	350	2600	2449	2303	2162	2026	5253	4661	4122	3632	3189	+2.5	-1.8	-10.2	-26.0	NA
416 Rigby	400	2370	2210	2050	1900	NA	4990	4315	3720	3185	NA	+2.5	-0.7	-12.1	NA	NA
416 Rigby	410	2370	2110	1870	1640	NA	5115	4050	3165	2455	NA	+2.5	-2.4	-17.3	NA	$110
416 Rem. Mag.*	350	2520	2270	2034	1814	1611	4935	4004	3216	2557	2017	+2.5	-0.8	-12.6	-35.0	$82
416 Rem. Mag.*	400	2400	2175	1962	1763	1579	5115	4201	3419	2760	2214	+2.5	-1.5	-14.6	NA	$80
416 Wea. Mag.*	400	2700	2397	2115	1852	1613	6474	5104	3971	3047	2310	+2.5	0.0	-10.1	-30.4	$96
10.57 (416) Meteor	400	2730	2532	2342	2161	1987	6621	5695	4874	4147	3508	+1.9	0.0	-8.3	-24.0	NA
404 Jeffrey	400	2150	1924	1716	1525	NA	4105	3289	2614	2064	NA	+2.5	-4.0	-22.1	NA	NA
425 Express	400	2400	2160	1934	1725	NA	5115	4145	3322	2641	NA	+2.5	-1.0	-14.0	NA	NA
44-40 Win.	200	1190	1006	900	822	756	629	449	360	300	254	0.0	-33.3	NA	NA	$36**
44 Rem. Mag.	210	1920	1477	1155	982	880	1719	1017	622	450	361	0.0	-17.6	NA	NA	$14

33

34
35

9.3 mm

375

40
41

425
44

Cartridge	Bullet Weight Grains	VELOCITY (fps)					ENERGY (ft. lbs.)					TRAJ. (in.)				Est. Price/box
		Muzzle	100 yds.	200 yds.	300 yds.	400 yds.	Muzzle	100 yds.	200 yds.	300 yds.	400 yds.	100 yds.	200 yds.	300 yds.	400 yds.	
44 Rem. Mag.	240	1760	1380	1114	970	878	1650	1015	661	501	411	0.0	-17.6	NA	NA	$13
444 Marlin	240	2350	1815	1377	1087	941	2942	1753	1001	630	472	+2.5	-15.1	-31.0	NA	$22
444 Marlin	265	2120	1733	1405	1160	1012	2644	1768	1162	791	603	+2.5	-6.0	-32.2	NA	Disc.
444 Marlin Light Mag	265	2335	1913	1551	1266		3208	2153	1415	943		2	-4.90	-26.5		
45-70 Govt.	300	1810	1497	1244	1073	969	2182	1492	1031	767	625	0.0	-14.8	NA	NA	$21
45-70 Govt. Supreme	300	1880	1558	1292	1103	988	2355	1616	1112	811	651	0.0	-12.9	-46.0	-105	NA
45-70 Govt. CorBon	350	1800	1526	1296			2519	1810	1307			0.0	-14.6			NA
45-70 Govt.	405	1330	1168	1055	977	918	1590	1227	1001	858	758	0.0	-24.6	NA	NA	$21
45-70 Govt. PMC Cowboy	405	1550	1193				1639	1280				0.0	-23.9			NA
45-70 Govt. Garrett	415	1850					3150					3.0	-7.0			NA
45-70 Govt. Garrett	530	1550	1343	1178	1062	982	2828	2123	1633	1327	1135	0.0	-17.8			NA
450 Marlin	350	2100	1774	1488	1254	1089	3427	2446	1720	1222	922	0.0	-9.7	-35.2		NA
458 Win. Magnum	350	2470	1990	1570	1250	1060	4740	3065	1915	1205	870	+2.5	-2.5	-21.6	NA	$43
458 Win. Magnum	400	2380	2170	1960	1770	NA	5030	4165	3415	2785	NA	+2.5	-0.4	-13.4	NA	$73
458 Win. Magnum	465	2220	1999	1791	1601	NA	5088	4127	3312	2646	NA	+2.5	-2.0	-17.7	NA	NA
458 Win. Magnum	500	2040	1823	1623	1442	1237	4620	3689	2924	2308	1839	+2.5	-3.5	-22.0	NA	$61
458 Win. Magnum	510	2040	1770	1527	1319	1157	4712	3547	2640	1970	1516	+2.5	-4.1	-25.0	NA	$41
450 Dakota	500	2450	2235	2030	1838	1658	6663	5544	4576	3748	3051	+2.5	-0.6	-12.0	-33.8	NA
450 N.E. 3-1/4"	465	2190	1970	1765	1577	NA	4952	4009	3216	2567	NA	+2.5	-3.0	-20.0	NA	NA
450 N.E. 3-1/4"	500	2150	1920	1708	1514	NA	5132	4093	3238	2544	NA	+2.5	-4.0	-22.9	NA	NA
450 No. 2	465	2190	1970	1765	1577	NA	4952	4009	3216	2567	NA	+2.5	-3.0	-20.0	NA	NA
450 No. 2	500	2150	1920	1708	1514	NA	5132	4093	3238	2544	NA	+2.5	-4.0	-22.9	NA	NA
458 Lott	465	2380	2150	1932	1730	NA	5848	4773	3855	3091	NA	+2.5	-1.0	-14.0	NA	NA
458 Lott	500	2300	2062	1838	1633	NA	5873	4719	3748	2960	NA	+2.5	-1.6	-16.4	NA	NA
450 Ackley Mag.	465	2400	2169	1950	1747	NA	5947	4857	3927	3150	NA	+2.5	-1.0	-13.7	NA	NA
450 Ackley Mag.	500	2320	2081	1855	1649	NA	5975	4085	3820	3018	NA	+2.5	-1.2	-15.0	NA	NA
460 Short A-Sq.	500	2420	2175	1943	1729	NA	6501	5250	4193	3319	NA	+2.5	-0.8	-12.8	-	NA
460 Wea. Mag.	500	2700	2404	2128	1869	1635	8092	6416	5026	3878	2969	+2.5	+0.6	-8.9	-28.0	$72
500/465 N.E.	480	2150	1917	1703	1507	NA	4926	3917	3089	2419	NA	+2.5	-4.0	-22.2	-	NA
470 Rigby	500	2150	1940	1740	1560	NA	5130	4170	3360	2695	NA	+2.5	-2.8	-19.4	NA	NA
470 Nitro Ex.	480	2190	1954	1735	1536	NA	5111	4070	3210	2515	NA	+2.5	-3.5	-20.8	NA	NA
470 Nitro Ex.	500	2150	1890	1650	1440	1270	5130	3965	3040	2310	1790	+2.5	-4.3	-24.0	NA	$177
475 No. 2	500	2200	1955	1728	1522	NA	5375	4243	3316	2573	NA	+2.5	-3.2	-20.9	NA	NA
505 Gibbs	525	2300	2063	1840	1637	NA	6166	4922	3948	3122	NA	+2.5	-3.0	-18.0	NA	NA
500 N.E.-3"	570	2150	1928	1722	1533	NA	5850	4703	3752	2975	NA	+2.5	-3.7	-22.0	NA	NA
500 N.E.-3"	600	2150	1927	1721	1531	NA	6158	4947	3944	3124	NA	+2.5	-4.0	-22.0	NA	NA
495 A-Square	570	2350	2117	1896	1693	NA	5850	4703	3752	2975	NA	+2.5	-1.0	-14.5	NA	NA
495 A-Square	600	2280	2050	1833	1635	NA	6925	5598	4478	3562	NA	+2.5	-2.0	-17.0	NA	NA
500 A-Square	600	2380	2144	1922	1766	NA	7546	6126	4920	3922	NA	+2.5	-3.0	-17.0	NA	NA
500 A-Square	707	2250	2040	1841	1567	NA	7947	6530	5318	4311	NA	+2.5	-2.0	-17.0	NA	NA
500 BMG PMC	660	3080	2854	2639	2444	2248	13688		500 yd. zero			+3.1	+3.90	+4.7	+2.8	Est.
577 Nitro Ex.	750	2050	1793	1562	1360	NA	6990	5356	4065	3079	NA	+2.5	-5.0	-26.0	NA	box
577 Tyrannosaur	750	2400	2141	1898	1675	NA	9591	7633	5996	4671	NA	+3.0	0.0	-12.9	NA	NA
600 N.E.	900	1950	1680	1452	NA	NA	7596	5634	4212	NA	NA	+5.6	0.0	NA	NA	NA
700 N.E.	1200	1900	1676	1472	NA	NA	9618	7480	5774	NA	NA	+5.7	0.0	NA	NA	NA

Side index tabs: 425, 44, 45, 475, 50, 58, 600, 700

CENTERFIRE HANDGUN CARTRIDGES — BALLISTICS & PRICES

Notes: Blanks are available in 32 S&W, 38 S&W and 38 Special. "V" after barrel length indicates test barrel was vented to produce ballistics similar to a revolver with a normal barrel-to-cylinder gap. Ammo prices are per 50 rounds except when marked with an ** which signifies a 20 round box; *** signifies a 25-round box. Not all loads are available from all ammo manufacturers. Listed loads are those made by Remington, Winchester, Federal, and others. DISC. is a discontinued load. Prices are rounded to nearest whole dollar and will vary with brand and retail outlet. † = new bullet weight this year; "c" indicates a change in data.

Cartridge	Bullet Wgt. Grs.	VELOCITY (fps)			ENERGY (ft. lbs.)			Mid-Range Traj. (in.)		Bbl. Lgth. (in.)	Est. Price/ box
		Muzzle	50 yds.	100 yds.	Muzzle	50 yds.	100 yds.	50 yds.	100 yds.		
221 Rem. Fireball	50	2650	2380	2130	780	630	505	0.2	0.8	10.5"	$15
25 Automatic	35	900	813	742	63	51	43	NA	NA	2"	$18
25 Automatic	45	815	730	655	65	55	40	1.8	7.7	2"	$21
25 Automatic	50	760	705	660	65	55	50	2.0	8.7	2"	$17
7.5mm Swiss	107	1010	NA	NA	240	NA	NA	NA	NA	NA	NEW
7.62mmTokarev	87	1390	NA	NA	365	NA	NA	0.6	NA	4.5"	NA
7.62 Nagant	97	1080	NA	NA	350	NA	NA	NA	NA	NA	NEW
7.63 Mauser	88	1440	NA	NA	405	NA	NA	NA	NA	NA	NEW
30 Luger	93†	1220	1110	1040	305	255	225	0.9	3.5	4.5"	$34
30 Carbine	110	1790	1600	1430	785	625	500	0.4	1.7	10"	$28
30-357 AeT	123	1992	NA	NA	1084	NA	NA	NA	NA	10"	NA
32 S&W	88	680	645	610	90	80	75	2.5	10.5	3"	$17
32 S&W Long	98	705	670	635	115	100	90	2.3	10.5	4"	$17
32 Short Colt	80	745	665	590	100	80	60	2.2	9.9	4"	$19
32 H&R Magnum	85	1100	1020	930	230	195	165	1.0	4.3	4.5"	$21
32 H&R Magnum	95	1030	940	900	225	190	170	1.1	4.7	4.5"	$19
32 Automatic	60	970	895	835	125	105	95	1.3	5.4	4"	$22
32 Automatic	60	1000	917	849	133	112	96			4"	NA
32 Automatic	65	950	890	830	130	115	100	1.3	5.6	NA	NA
32 Automatic	71	905	855	810	130	115	95	1.4	5.8	4"	$19
8mm Lebel Pistol	111	850	NA	NA	180	NA	NA	NA	NA	NA	NEW
8mm Steyr	112	1080	NA	NA	290	NA	NA	NA	NA	NA	NEW
8mm Gasser	126	850	NA	NA	200	NA	NA	NA	NA	NA	NEW
380 Automatic	60	1130	960	NA	170	120	NA	1.0	NA	NA	NA
380 Automatic	85/88	990	920	870	190	165	145	1.2	5.1	4"	$20
380 Automatic	90	1000	890	800	200	160	130	1.2	5.5	3.75"	$10
380 Automatic	95/100	955	865	785	190	160	130	1.4	5.9	4"	$20
38 Super Auto +P	115	1300	1145	1040	430	335	275	0.7	3.3	5"	$26
38 Super Auto +P	125/130	1215	1100	1015	425	350	300	0.8	3.6	5"	$26
38 Super Auto +P	147	1100	1050	1000	395	355	325	0.9	4.0	5"	$26
9x18mm Makarov	95	1000	NA	NA	NA	NA	NA	NA	NA	NA	NEW
9x18mm Ultra	100	1050	NA	NA	240	NA	NA	NA	NA	NA	NEW
9x23mm Largo	124	1190	1055	966	390	306	257	0.7	3.7	4"	NA
9x23mm Win.	125	1450	1249	1103	583	433	338	0.6	2.8	NA	NA
9mm Steyr	115	1180	NA	NA	350	NA	NA	NA	NA	NA	NEW
9mm Luger	88	1500	1190	1010	440	275	200	0.6	3.1	4"	$24
9mm Luger	90	1360	1112	978	370	247	191	NA	NA	4"	$26
9mm Luger	95	1300	1140	1010	350	275	215	0.8	3.4	4"	NA
9mm Luger	100	1180	1080	NA	305	255	NA	0.9	NA	4"	NA
9mm Luger	115	1155	1045	970	340	280	240	0.9	3.9	4"	$21
9mm Luger	123/125	1110	1030	970	340	290	260	1.0	4.0	4"	$23
9mm Luger	140	935	890	850	270	245	225	1.3	5.5	4"	$23
9mm Luger	147	990	940	900	320	290	265	1.1	4.9	4"	$26
9mm Luger +P	90	1475	NA	NA	437	NA	NA	NA	NA	NA	NA
9mm Luger +P	115	1250	1113	1019	399	316	265	0.8	3.5	4"	$27
9mm Federal	115	1280	1130	1040	420	330	280	0.7	3.3	4"V	$24
9mm Luger Vector	115	1155	1047	971	341	280	241	NA	NA	4"	NA
9mm Luger +P	124	1180	1089	1021	384	327	287	0.8	3.8	4"	NA
38 S&W	146	685	650	620	150	135	125	2.4	10.0	4"	$19
38 Short Colt	125	730	685	645	150	130	115	2.2	9.4	6"	$19
39 Special	100	950	900	NA	200	180	NA	1.3	NA	4"V	NA
38 Special	110	945	895	850	220	195	175	1.3	5.4	4"V	$23
38 Special	110	945	895	850	220	195	175	1.3	5.4	4"V	$23
38 Special	130	775	745	710	175	160	120	1.9	7.9	4"V	$22

Notes: Blanks are available in 32 S&W, 38 S&W and 38 Special. "V" after barrel length indicates test barrel was vented to produce ballistics similar to a revolver with a normal barrel-to-cylinder gap. Ammo prices are per 50 rounds except when marked with an ** which signifies a 20 round box; *** signifies a 25-round box. Not all loads are available from all ammo manufacturers. Listed loads are those made by Remington, Winchester, Federal, and others. DISC. is a discontinued load. Prices are rounded to nearest whole dollar and will vary with brand and retail outlet. † = new bullet weight this year; "c" indicates a change in data.

Cartridge	Bullet Wgt. Grs.	VELOCITY (fps)			ENERGY (ft. lbs.)			Mid-Range Traj. (in.)		Bbl. Lgth. (in).	Est. Price/ box
		Muzzle	50 yds.	100 yds.	Muzzle	50 yds.	100 yds.	50 yds.	100 yds.		
38 Special Cowboy	140	800	767	735	199	183	168			7.5" V	NA
38 (Multi-Ball)	140	830	730	505	215	130	80	2.0	10.6	4"V	$10**
38 Special	148	710	635	565	165	130	105	2.4	10.6	4"V	$17
38 Special	158	755	725	690	200	185	170	2.0	8.3	4"V	$18
38 Special +P	95	1175	1045	960	290	230	195	0.9	3.9	4"V	$23
38 Special +P	110	995	925	870	240	210	185	1.2	5.1	4"V	$23
38 Special +P	125	975	929	885	264	238	218	1	5.2	4"	NA
38 Special +P	125	945	900	860	250	225	205	1.3	5.4	4"V	#23
38 Special +P	129	945	910	870	255	235	215	1.3	5.3	4"V	$11
38 Special +P	130	925	887	852	247	227	210	1.3	5.50	4"V	NA
38 Special +P	147/150(c)	884	NA	NA	264	NA	NA	NA	NA	4"V	$27
38 Special +P	158	890	855	825	280	255	240	1.4	6.0	4"V	$20
357 SIG	115	1520	NA	NA	593	NA	NA	NA	NA	NA	NA
357 SIG	124	1450	NA	NA	578	NA	NA	NA	NA	NA	NA
357 SIG	125	1350	1190	1080	510	395	325	0.7	3.1	4"	NA
357 SIG	150	1130	1030	970	420	355	310	0.9	4.0	NA	NA
356 TSW	115	1520	NA	NA	593	NA	NA	NA	NA	NA	NA
356 TSW	124	1450	NA	NA	578	NA	NA	NA	NA	NA	NA
356 TSW	135	1280	1120	1010	490	375	310	0.8	3.50	NA	NA
356 TSW	147	1220	1120	1040	485	410	355	0.8	3.5	5"	NA
357 Mag., Super Clean	105	1650									NA
357 Magnum	110	1295	1095	975	410	290	230	0.8	3.5	4"V	$25
357 (Med.Vel.)	125	1220	1075	985	415	315	270	0.8	3.7	4"V	$25
357 Magnum	125	1450	1240	1090	585	425	330	0.6	2.8	4"V	$25
357 (Multi-Ball)	140	1155	830	665	420	215	135	1.2	6.4	4"V	$11**
357 Magnum	140	1360	1195	1075	575	445	360	0.7	3.0	4"V	$25
357 Magnum	145	1290	1155	1060	535	430	360	0.8	3.5	4"V	$26
357 Magnum	150/158	1235	1105	1015	535	430	360	0.8	3.5	4"V	$25
357 Mag. Cowboy	158	800	761	725	225	203	185				NA
357 Magnum	165	1290	1189	1108	610	518	450	0.7	3.1	8-3/8"	NA
357 Magnum	180	1145	1055	985	525	445	390	0.9	3.9	4"V	$25
357 Magnum	180	1180	1088	1020	557	473	416	0.8	3.6	8"V	NA
357 Mag. CorBon F.A.	180	1650	1512	1386	1088	913	767	1.66	0.0		NA
357 Mag. CorBon	200	1200	1123	1061	640	560	500	3.19	0.0		NA
357 Rem. Maximum	158	1825	1590	1380	1170	885	670	0.4	1.7	10.5"	$14**
40 S&W	135	1140	1070	NA	390	345	NA	0.9	NA	4"	NA
40 S&W	155	1140	1026	958	447	362	309	0.9	4.1	4"	$14***
40 S&W	165	1150	NA	NA	485	NA	NA	NA	NA	4"	$18***
40 S&W	180	985	936	893	388	350	319	1.4	5.0	4"	$14***
40 S&W	180	1015	960	914	412	368	334	1.3	4.5	4"	NA
400 Cor-Bon	135	1450	NA	NA	630	NA	NA	NA	NA	5"	NA
10mm Automatic	155	1125	1046	986	436	377	335	0.9	3.9	5"	$26
10mm Automatic	170	1340	1165	1145	680	510	415	0.7	3.2	5"	$31
10mm Automatic	175	1290	1140	1035	650	505	420	0.7	3.3	5.5"	$11**
10mm Auto. (FBI)	180	950	905	865	361	327	299	1.5	5.4	4"	$16**
10mm Automatic	180	1030	970	920	425	375	340	1.1	4.7	5"	$16**
10mm Auto H.V.	180†	1240	1124	1037	618	504	430	0.8	3.4	5"	$27
10mm Automatic	200	1160	1070	1010	495	510	430	0.9	3.8	5"	$14**
10.4mm Italian	177	950	NA	NA	360	NA	NA	NA	NA	NA	NEW
41 Action Exp.	180	1000	947	903	400	359	326	0.5	4.2	5"	$13**
41 Rem. Magnum	170	1420	1165	1015	760	515	390	0.7	3.2	4"V	$33
41 Rem. Magnum	175	1250	1120	1030	605	490	410	0.8	3.4	4"V	$14**

Notes: Blanks are available in 32 S&W, 38 S&W and 38 Special. "V" after barrel length indicates test barrel was vented to produce ballistics similar to a revolver with a normal barrel-to-cylinder gap. Ammo prices are per 50 rounds except when marked with an ** which signifies a 20 round box; *** signifies a 25-round box. Not all loads are available from all ammo manufacturers. Listed loads are those made by Remington, Winchester, Federal, and others. DISC. is a discontinued load. Prices are rounded to nearest whole dollar and will vary with brand and retail outlet. † = new bullet weight this year; "c" indicates a change in data.

Cartridge	Bullet Wgt. Grs.	VELOCITY (fps)			ENERGY (ft. lbs.)			Mid-Range Traj. (in.)		Bbl. Lgth. (in).	Est. Price/ box
		Muzzle	50 yds.	100 yds.	Muzzle	50 yds.	100 yds.	50 yds.	100 yds.		
41 (Med. Vel.)	210	965	900	840	435	375	330	1.3	5.4	4"V	$30
41 Rem. Magnum	210	1300	1160	1060	790	630	535	0.7	3.2	4"V	$33
41 Rem. Magnum	240	1250	1151	1075	833	706	616	0.8	3.3	6.5V	NA
44 S&W Russian	247	780	NA	NA	335	NA	NA	NA	NA	NA	NA
44 S&W Special	180	980	NA	NA	383	NA	NA	NA	NA	6.5"	NA
44 S&W Special	180	1000	935	882	400	350	311	NA	NA	7.5"V	NA
44 S&W Special	200†	875	825	780	340	302	270	1.2	6.0	6"	$13**
44 S&W Special	200	1035	940	865	475	390	335	1.1	4.9	6.5"	$13**
44 S&W Special	240/246	755	725	695	310	285	265	2.0	8.3	6.5"	$26
44-40 Win. Cowboy	225	750	723	695	281	261	242				NA
44 Rem. Magnum	180	1610	1365	1175	1035	745	550	0.5	2.3	4"V	$18**
44 Rem. Magnum	200	1400	1192	1053	870	630	492	0.6	NA	6.5"	$20
44 Rem. Magnum	210	1495	1310	1165	1040	805	635	0.6	2.5	6.5"	$18**
44 (Med. Vel.)	240	1000	945	900	535	475	435	1.1	4.8	6.5"	$17
44 R.M. (Jacketed)	240	1180	1080	1010	740	625	545	0.9	3.7	4"V	$18**
44 R.M. (Lead)	240	1350	1185	1070	970	750	610	0.7	3.1	4"V	$29
44 Rem. Magnum	250	1180	1100	1040	775	670	600	0.8	3.6	6.5"V	$21
44 Rem. Magnum	250	1250	1148	1070	867	732	635	0.8	3.3	6.5"V	NA
44 Rem. Magnum	275	1235	1142	1070	931	797	699	0.8	3.3	6.5"	NA
44 Rem. Magnum	300	1200	1100	1026	959	806	702	NA	NA	7.5"	$17
44 Rem. Magnum	330	1385	1297	1220	1406	1234	1090	1.83	0.00	NA	NA
440 CorBon	260	1700	1544	1403	1669	1377	1136	1.58	NA	10"	NA
450 Short Colt/450 Revolver	226	830	NA	NA	350	NA	NA	NA	NA	NA	NEW
45 S&W Schofield	180	730	NA	NA	213	NA	NA	NA	NA	NA	NA
45 S&W Schofield	230	730	NA	NA	272	NA	NA	na		NA	NA
45 Automatic	165	1030	930	NA	385	315	NA	1.2	NA	5"	NA
45 Automatic	185	1000	940	890	410	360	325	1.1	4.9	5"	$28
45 Auto. (Match)	185	770	705	650	245	204	175	2.0	8.7	5"	$28
45 Auto. (Match)	200	940	890	840	392	352	312	2.0	8.6	5"	$20
45 Automatic	200	975	917	860	421	372	328	1.4	5.0	5"	$18
45 Automatic	230	830	800	675	355	325	300	1.6	6.8	5"	$27
45 Automatic	230	880	846	816	396	366	340	1.5	6.1	5"	NA
45 Automatic +P	165	1250	NA	NA	573	NA	NA	NA	NA	NA	NA
45 Automatic +P	185	1140	1040	970	535	445	385	0.9	4.0	5"	$31
45 Automatic +P	200	1055	982	925	494	428	380	NA	NA	5"	NA
45 Super	185	1300	1190	1108	694	582	504	NA	NA	5"	NA
45 Win. Magnum	230	1400	1230	1105	1000	775	635	0.6	2.8	5"	$14**
45 Win. Magnum	260	1250	1137	1053	902	746	640	0.8	3.3	5"	$16**
45 Win. Mag. CorBon	320	1150	1080	1025	940	830	747	3.47			NA
455 Webley MKII	262	850	NA	NA	420	NA	NA	NA	NA	NA	NA
45 Colt	200	1000	938	889	444	391	351	1.3	4.8	5.5"	$21
45 Colt	225	960	890	830	460	395	345	1.3	5.5	5.5"	$22
45 Colt + P CorBon	265	1350	1225	1126	1073	884	746	2.65	0.0		NA
45 Colt + P CorBon	300	1300	1197	1114	1126	956	827	2.78	0.0		NA
45 Colt	250/255	860	820	780	410	375	340	1.6	6.6	5.5"	$27
454 Casull	250	1300	1151	1047	938	735	608	0.7	3.2	7.5"V	NA
454 Casull	260	1800	1577	1381	1871	1436	1101	0.4	1.8	7.5"V	NA
454 Casull	300	1625	1451	1308	1759	1413	1141	0.5	2.0	7.5"V	NA
454 Casull CorBon	360	1500	1387	1286	1800	1640	1323	2.01	0.0		NA
475 Linebaugh	400	1350	1217	1119	1618	1315	1112	NA	NA	NA	NA
480 Ruger	325	1350	1191	1076	1315	1023	835	2.6	0.0	7.5"	NA
50 Action Exp.	325	1400	1209	1075	1414	1055	835	0.2	2.3	6"	$24**
500 S&W	275	1665	1392	1183	1693	1184	854	1.5	NA	8.375	NA
500 S&W	400	1675	1472	1299	2493	1926	1499	1.3	NA	8.375	NA
500 S&W	440	1625	1367	1169	2581	1825	1337	1.6	NA	8.375	NA

40, 10mm

44

45, 50

Note: The actual ballistics obtained with your firearm can vary considerably from the advertised ballistics. Also, ballistics can vary from lot to lot with the same brand and type load.

Cartridge	Bullet Wt. Grs.	Velocity (fps) 22-1/2" Bbl.		Energy (ft. lbs.) 22-1/2" Bbl.		Mid-Range Traj. (in.)	Muzzle Velocity 6" Bbl.
		Muzzle	100 yds.	Muzzle	100 yds.	100 yds.	
17 Aguila	20	1850	NA	NA	NA	NA	NA
17 HMR	17	2550	1902	245	136	NA	NA
22 Short Blank	—	—	—	—	—	—	—
22 Short CB	29	727	610	33	24	NA	706
22 Short Target	29	830	695	44	31	6.8	786
22 Short HP	27	1164	920	81	50	4.3	1077
22 Colibri	20	375	183	6	1	NA	NA
22 Super Colibri	20	500	441	11	9	NA	NA
22 Long CB	29	727	610	33	24	NA	706
22 Long HV	29	1180	946	90	57	4.1	1031
22 LR Ballistician	25	1100	760	65	30	NA	NA
22 LR Pistol Match	40	1070	890	100	70	4.6	940
22 LR Sub Sonic HP	38	1050	901	93	69	4.7	NA
22 LR Standard Velocity	40	1070	890	100	70	4.6	940
22 LR HV	40	1255	1016	140	92	3.6	1060
22 LR Silhoutte	42	1220	1003	139	94	3.6	1025
22 SSS	60	950	802	120	86	NA	NA
22 LR HV HP	40	1280	1001	146	89	3.5	1085
22 Velocitor GDHP	40	1435	0	0	0	NA	NA
22 LR Hyper HP	32/33/34	1500	1075	165	85	2.8	NA
22 LR Stinger HP	32	1640	1132	191	91	2.6	1395
22 LR Hyper Vel	30	1750	1191	204	93	NA	NA
22 LR Shot #12	31	950	NA	NA	NA	NA	NA
22 WRF LFN	45	1300	1015	169	103	3	NA
22 Win. Mag.	30	2200	1373	322	127	1.4	1610
22 Win. Mag. V-Max BT	33	2000	1495	293	164	0.60	NA
22 Win. Mag. JHP	34	2120	1435	338	155	1.4	NA
22 Win. Mag. JHP	40	1910	1326	324	156	1.7	1480
22 Win. Mag. FMJ	40	1910	1326	324	156	1.7	1480
22 Win. Mag. Dyna Point	45	1550	1147	240	131	2.60	NA
22 Win. Mag. JHP	50	1650	1280	300	180	1.3	NA
22 Win. Mag. Shot #11	52	1000	—	NA	—	—	NA

SHOTSHELL LOADS & PRICES

NOTES: * = 10 rounds per box. ** = 5 rounds per box. Pricing variations and number of rounds per box can occur with type and brand of ammunition. Listed pricing is the average nominal cost for load style and box quantity shown. Not every brand is available in all shot size variations. Some manufacturers do not provide suggested list prices. All prices rounded to nearest whole dollar. The price you pay will vary dependent upon outlet of purchase. # = new load spec this year; "C" indicates a change in data.

Dram Equiv.	Shot Ozs.	Load Style	Shot Sizes	Brands	Avg. Price/box	Velocity (fps)
10 Gauge 3-1/2" Magnum						
4-1/2	2-1/4	premium	BB, 2, 4, 5, 6	Win., Fed., Rem.	$33	1205
Max	2	premium	4, 5, 6	Fed., Win.	NA	1300
4-1/4	2	high velocity	BB, 2, 4	Rem.	$22	1210
4-1/2	2-1/4	duplex	4x6	Rem.	$14*	1205
Max	18 pellets	premium	00 buck	Fed., Win.	$7**	1100
Max	1-7/8	hevi. shot	4, 5, 6	Rem.	NA	1225
Max	1-7/8	Bismuth	BB, 2, 4	Win., Bis.	NA	1225
Max	1-3/4	Tungsten-Polymer	4, 6	Fed.	NA	1325
Max	1-3/4	hevi. shot	2, 4	Rem.	NA	1300
4-1/4	1-3/4	steel	TT, T, BBB, BB, 1, 2, 3	Win., Rem.	$27	1260
Mag	1-5/8	steel	T, BBB	Win.	$27	1285
4-5/8	1-5/8	steel	F, T, BBB	Fed.	$26	1350
Max	1-5/8	Tungsten - Iron	BBB, BB, 2, 4	Fed.		1300
Max	1-5/8	Bismuth	BB, 2, 4	Bismuth	NA	1375
Max	1-1/2	Tungsten - Iron & steel	2xBB	Fed.	NA	1375
Max	1-3/4	steel	T, BBB, BB, 2	Fed., Win.	NA	1450
Max	1-3/8	Tungsten - Iron	BBB, BB, 2, 4	Fed.	NA	1450
Max	1-3/4	slug, rifled	slug	Fed.	NA	1280
Max	24 pellets	Buckshot	1 Buck	Fed.	NA	1100
Max	54 pellets	Super-X	4 Buck	Win.	NA	1150
12 Gauge 3-1/2" Magnum						
Max	2-1/4	premium	4, 5, 6	Fed., Rem., Win.	$13*	1150
Max	2	Lead	4, 5, 6	Fed.	NA	1275
Max	2	Copper plated turkey	4, 5	Rem.	NA	1300
Max	18 pellets	premium	00 buck	Fed., Win., Rem.	$7**	1100
Max	1-7/8	Bismuth	BB, 2, 4	Win., Bis.	NA	1225
Max	1-3/4	Tungsten-Polymer	4, 6	Fed.	NA	1275
Max	1-5/8	hevi. shot	2, 4, 6	Rem.	NA	1350
4-1/8	1-9/16	steel	TT, F, T, BBB, BB, 1, 2	Rem., Win., Fed.	$22	1335
Max	1-1/2	hevi. shot	2, 4, 6	Rem.	NA	1400
Max	1-3/8	steel	T, BBB, BB, 2, 4	Fed., Win., Rem.	NA	1450
Max	1-3/8	Tungsten - Iron	BBB, BB, 2, 4	Fed.	NA	1450
Max	1-3/8	Tungsten - Iron & steel	2xBB	Fed.	NA	1375
Max	24 pellets	Premium	1 Buck	Fed.	NA	1100
Max	54 pellets	Super-X	4 Buck	Win.	NA	1050
12 Gauge 3" Magnum						
4	2	premium	BB, 2, 4, 5, 6	Win., Fed., Rem.	$9*	1175
4	2	duplex	4x6	Rem.	$10	1175
4	1-7/8	premium	BB, 2, 4, 6	Win., Fed., Rem.	$19	1210
4	1-7/8	duplex	4x6	Rem., Fio.	$9*	1210
Max	1-3/4	turkey	4, 5, 6	Fed., Fio., Win., Rem.	NA	1300
4	1-3/4	duplex	2x4, 4x6	Fio.	NA	1150
4	1-5/8	premium	2, 4, 5, 6	Win., Fed., Rem.	$18	1290
Max	1-5/8	Bismuth	BB, 2, 4, 5, 6	Win., Bis.	NA	1250
Max	1-3/8	hevi. shot	2, 4, 6	Rem.	NA	1450
Max	1-1/4	hevi. shot	2, 4, 6	Rem.	NA	1450
4	24 pellets	buffered	1 buck	Win., Fed., Rem.	$5**	1040
4	15 pellets	buffered	00 buck	Win., Fed., Rem.	$6**	1210
4	10 pellets	buffered	000 buck	Win., Fed., Rem.	$6**	1225
4	41 pellets	buffered	4 buck	Win., Fed., Rem.	$6**	1210
Max	1-3/8	Tungsten - Polymer	4, 6	Fed.	NA	1330

Dram Equiv.	Shot Ozs.	Load Style	Shot Sizes	Brands	Avg. Price/box	Velocity (fps)
12 Gauge 3" Magnum (cont.)						
Max	1-3/8	Tungsten-Iron	4	Fed.	NA	1300
Max	1-1/4	Tungsten - Iron & steel	4x2, 4x4	Fed.	NA	1400
Max	1-3/8	slug	slug	Bren.	NA	1476
Max	1-1/4	slug, rifled	slug	Fed.	NA	1600
Max	1-3/16	saboted slug	copper slug	Rem.	NA	1500
Max	7/8	slug, rifled	slug	Rem.	NA	1875
Max	1-1/8	Tungsten - Iron	BBB, BB, 2, 4	Fed.	NA	1400
Max	1	steel	4, 6	Fed.		1330
Max	1	slug, rifled	slug, magnum	Win., Rem.	$5**	1760
Max	1	saboted slug	slug	Rem., Win., Fed.	$10**	1550
3-5/8	1-3/8	steel	TT, F, T, BBB, BB, 1, 2, 3, 4	Win., Fed., Rem.	$19	1275
Max	1-1/8	steel	BB, 2, 4	Rem.	NA	1500
Max	1-1/8	steel	T, BBB, BB, 2, 4, 5, 6	Fed., Win.	NA	1450
Max	1-1/8	steel	BB, 2	Fed.	NA	1400
4	1-1/4	steel	TT, F, T, BBB, BB, 1, 2, 3, 4, 6	Win., Fed., Rem.	$18	1375
Max	1-1/4	Tungsten-Iron and Steel	4x2	Fed.	NA	1400
Max	1-1/8	Tungsten-Polymer	4, 6	Fed.	NA	1375
Max	1-3/8	Tungsten-Polymer	4, 6	Fed.	NA	1330
12 Gauge 2-3/4"						
Max	1-5/8	magnum	4, 5, 6	Win., Fed.	$8*	1250
Max	1-3/8	turkey	4, 5, 6	Fio.	NA	1250
Max	1-3/8	duplex	2x4, 4x6	Fio.	NA	1200
Max	1-3/8	Bismuth	BB, 2, 4, 5, 6	Win., Bis.	NA	1280
Max	1-3/8	hevi. shot	4, 5, 6	Rem.	NA	1250
3-3/4	1-1/2	magnum	BB, 2, 4, 5, 6	Win., Fed., Rem.	$16	1260
3-3/4	1-1/2	duplex	BBx4, 2x4, 4x6	Rem., Fio.	$9*	1260
Max	1-1/4	Supreme H-V	4, 5, 6, 7-1/2	Win. Rem.	NA	1400
3-3/4	1-1/4	high velocity	BB, 2, 4, 5, 6, 7-1/2, 8, 9	Win., Fed., Rem., Fio.	$13	1330
Max	1-1/4	Tungsten - Polymer	4, 6	Fed.	NA	1330
Max	1-1/4	hevi. shot	4, 6, 7-1/2	Rem.	NA	1325
3-1/2	1-1/4	mid-velocity	7, 8, 9	Win.	Disc.	1275
3-1/4	1-1/4	standard velocity	6, 7-1/2, 8, 9	Win., Fed., Rem., Fio.	$11	1220
Max	1-1/4	Bismuth	4, 6	Win.		1220
3-1/4	1-1/8	standard velocity	4, 6, 7-1/2, 8, 9	Win., Fed., Rem., Fio.	$9	1255
Max	1	steel	BB, 2	Fed.	NA	1450
Max	1	Tungsten - Iron	BB, 2, 4	Fed.	NA	1450
3-1/4	1	standard velocity	6, 7-1/2, 8	Rem., Fed., Fio., Win.	$6	1290
3-1/4	1-1/4	target	7-1/2, 8, 9	Win., Fed., Rem.	$10	1220
3	1-1/8	spreader	7-1/2, 8-1/2, 9	Fio.	NA	1200
3	1-1/8	target	7-1/2, 8, 9, 7-1/2x8	Win., Fed., Rem., Fio.	$7	1200
2-3/4	1-1/8	target	7-1/2, 8, 8-1/2, 9, 7-1/2x8	Win., Fed., Rem., Fio.	$7	1145
2-3/4	1-1/8	low recoil	7-1/2, 8	Rem.	NA	1145
2-1/2	26 grams	low recoil	8	Win.	NA	980
2-1/4	1-1/8	target	7-1/2, 8, 8-1/2, 9	Rem., Fed.	$7	1080
Max	1	spreader	7-1/2, 8, 8-1/2, 9	Fio.	NA	1300
3-1/4	28 grams (1 oz)	target	7-1/2, 8, 9	Win., Fed., Rem., Fio.	$8	1290
3	1	target	7-1/2, 8, 8-1/2, 9	Win., Fio.	NA	1235
2-3/4	1	target	7-1/2, 8, 8-1/2, 9	Fed., Rem., Fio.	NA	1180

Shotshell Loads & Prices, *continued*

12 Gauge 2-3/4" (cont.)

Dram Equiv.	Shot Ozs.	Load Style	Shot Sizes	Brands	Avg. Price/box	Velocity (fps)
3-1/4	24 grams	target	7-1/2, 8, 9	Fed., Win., Fio.	NA	1325
3	7/8	light	8	Fio.	NA	1200
3-3/4	8 pellets	buffered	000 buck	Win., Fed., Rem.	$4**	1325
4	12 pellets	premium	00 buck	Win., Fed., Rem.	$5**	1290
3-3/4	9 pellets	buffered	00 buck	Win., Fed., Rem., Fio.	$19	1325
Max	9 pellets	hevi. shot	00 buck	Rem.	NA	1325
3-3/4	12 pellets	buffered	0 buck	Win., Fed., Rem.	$4**	1275
4	20 pellets	buffered	1 buck	Win., Fed., Rem.	$4**	1075
3-3/4	16 pellets	buffered	1 buck	Win., Fed., Rem.	$4**	1250
4	34 pellets	premium	4 buck	Fed., Rem.	$5**	1250
3-3/4	27 pellets	buffered	4 buck	Win., Fed., Rem., Fio.	$4**	1325
Max	1	saboted slug	slug	Win., Fed., Rem.	$10**	1450
Max	1-1/4	slug, rifled	slug	Fed.	NA	1520
Max	1-1/4	slug	slug	Lightfield		1440
Max	1-1/4	saboted slug	attached sabot	Rem.	NA	1550
Max	1	slug, rifled	slug, magnum	Rem., Fio.	$5**	1680
Max	1	slug, rifled	slug	Win., Fed., Rem.	$4**	1610
Max	1	sabot slug	slug	Sauvestre		1640
Max	7/8	slug, rifled	slug	Rem.	NA	1800
Max	400	plat. tip	sabot slug	Win.	NA	1700
Max	385 grains	Partition Gold Slug	slug	Win.	NA	1900
Max	385 grains	Core-Lokt bonded	sabot slug	Rem.	NA	1900
Max	325 grains	Barnes Sabot	slug	Fed.	NA	1900
3	1-1/8	steel target	6-1/2, 7	Rem.	NA	1200
2-3/4	1-1/8	steel target	7	Rem.	NA	1145
3	1#	steel	7	Win.	$11	1235
3-1/2	1-1/4	steel	T, BBB, BB, 1, 2, 3, 4, 5, 6	Win., Fed., Rem.	$18	1275
3-3/4	1-1/8	steel	BB, 1, 2, 3, 4, 5, 6	Win., Fed., Rem., Fio.	$16	1365
3-3/4	1	steel	2, 3, 4, 5, 6, 7	Win., Fed., Rem., Fio.	$13	1390
Max	7/8	steel	7	Fio.	NA	1440

16 Gauge 2-3/4"

Dram Equiv.	Shot Ozs.	Load Style	Shot Sizes	Brands	Avg. Price/box	Velocity (fps)
3-1/4	1-1/4	magnum	2, 4, 6	Fed., Rem.	$16	1260
3-1/4	1-1/8	high velocity	4, 6, 7-1/2	Win., Fed., Rem., Fio.	$12	1295
Max	1-1/8	Bismuth	4, 5	Win., Bis.	NA	1200
2-3/4	1-1/8	standard velocity	6, 7-1/2, 8	Fed., Win., Fio.	$9	1185
2-1/2	1	dove	6, 7-1/2, 8, 9	Fio., Win.	NA	1165
2-3/4	1		6, 7-1/2, 8	Fio.	NA	1200
Max	15/16	steel	2, 4	Fed., Rem.	NA	1300
Max	7/8	steel	2, 4	Win.	$16	1300
3	12 pellets	buffered	1 buck	Win., Fed., Rem.	$4**	1225
Max	4/5	slug, rifled	slug	Win., Fed., Rem.	$4**	1570
Max	.92	sabot slug	slug	Sauvestre		1560

20 Gauge 3" Magnum

Dram Equiv.	Shot Ozs.	Load Style	Shot Sizes	Brands	Avg. Price/box	Velocity (fps)
3	1-1/4	premium	2, 4, 5, 6, 7-1/2	Win., Fed., Rem.	$15	1185
Max	1-1/4	Tungsten-Polymer	4, 6	Fed.	NA	1185
3	1-1/4	turkey	4, 6	Fio.	NA	1200
Max	1-1/4	hevi. shot	4, 5, 6	Rem.	NA	1175
Max	1-1/8	hevi. shot	4, 6, 7-1/2	Rem.	NA	1300
Max	18 pellets	buck shot	2 buck	Fed.	NA	1200
Max	24 pellets	buffered	3 buck	Win.	$5**	1150

20 Gauge 3" Magnum (cont.)

Dram Equiv.	Shot Ozs.	Load Style	Shot Sizes	Brands	Avg. Price/box	Velocity (fps)
2-3/4	20 pellets	buck	3 buck	Rem.	$4**	1200
3-1/4	1	steel	1, 2, 3, 4, 5, 6	Win., Fed., Rem.	$15	1330
Max	7/8	steel	2, 4	Win.	MA	1300
Max	1-1/16	Bismuth	2, 4, 5, 6	Bismuth	NA	1250
Max	7/8	Tungsten - Iron	2, 4	Fed.	NA	1375
Mag	5/8	saboted slug	275 gr.	Fed.	NA	1450

20 Gauge 2-3/4"

Dram Equiv.	Shot Ozs.	Load Style	Shot Sizes	Brands	Avg. Price/box	Velocity (fps)
2-3/4	1-1/8	magnum	4, 6, 7-1/2	Win., Fed., Rem.	$14	1175
Max	1-1/8	Tungsten-Polymer	4, 6	Fed.	NA	1175
2-3/4	1	high velocity	4, 5, 6, 7-1/2, 8, 9	Win., Fed., Rem., Fio.	$12	1220
Max	1	Bismuth	4, 6	Win., Bis.	NA	1200
Max	1	hevi-shot	4, 6, 7-1/2	Rem.	NA	1275
Max	1	Supreme H-V	4, 6, 7-1/2	Win. Rem.	NA	1300
Max	7/8	Steel	2, 3, 4	Fio.	NA	1500
2-1/2	1	standard velocity	6, 7-1/2, 8	Win., Rem., Fed., Fio.	$6	1165
2-1/2	7/8	clays	8	Rem.	NA	1200
2-1/2	7/8	promotional	6, 7-1/2, 8	Win., Rem., Fio.	$6	1210
2-1/2	1	target	8, 9	Win., Rem.	$8	1165
Max	7/8	clays	7-1/2, 8	Win.	NA	1275
2-1/2	7/8	target	8, 9	Win., Fed., Rem.	$8	1200
2-1/2	7/8	steel - target	7	Rem.		1200
Max	5/8	Saboted Slug	Copper Slug	Rem.	NA	1500
Max	20 pellets	buffered	3 buck	Win., Fed.	$4	1200
Max	5/8	slug, saboted	slug	Win.,	$9**	1400
2-3/4	5/8	slug, rifled	slug	Rem.	$4**	1580
Max	3/4	saboted slug	copper slug	Fed., Rem.	NA	1450
Max	3/4	slug, rifled	slug	Win., Fed., Rem., Fio.	$4**	1570
Max	.9	sabot slug	slug	Sauvestre		1480
Max	260 grains	Partition Gold Slug	slug	Win.	NA	1900
Max	260 grains	Core-Lokt Ultra	slug	Rem.	NA	1900
Max	260 grains	saboted slug	platinum tip	Win.	NA	1700
Max	3/4	steel	2, 3, 4, 6	Win., Fed., Rem.	$14	1425
Max	1/2	rifled, slug	slug	Rem.	NA	1800

28 Gauge 2-3/4"

Dram Equiv.	Shot Ozs.	Load Style	Shot Sizes	Brands	Avg. Price/box	Velocity (fps)
2	1	high velocity	6, 7-1/2, 8	Win.	$12	1125
2-1/4	3/4	high velocity	6, 7-1/2, 8, 9	Win., Fed., Rem., Fio.	$11	1295
2	3/4	target	8, 9	Win., Fed., Rem.	$9	1200
Max	3/4	sporting clays	7-1/2, 8-1/2	Win.	NA	1300
Max	5/8	Bismuth	4, 6	Win., Bis.	NA	1250

410 Bore 3"

Dram Equiv.	Shot Ozs.	Load Style	Shot Sizes	Brands	Avg. Price/box	Velocity (fps)
Max	11/16	high velocity	4, 5, 6, 7-1/2, 8, 9	Win., Fed., Rem., Fio.	$10	1135
Max	9/16	Bismuth	4	Win., Bis.	NA	1175

410 Bore 2-1/2"

Dram Equiv.	Shot Ozs.	Load Style	Shot Sizes	Brands	Avg. Price/box	Velocity (fps)
Max	1/2	high velocity	4, 6, 7-1/2	Win., Fed., Rem.	$9	1245
Max	1/5	slug, rifled	slug	Win., Fed., Rem.	$4**	1815
1-1/2	1/2	target	8, 8-1/2, 9	Win., Fed., Rem., Fio.	$8	1200
Max	1/2	sporting clays	8-1/2	Win.	NA	1300

SHOOTER'S MARKETPLACE

INTERESTING PRODUCT NEWS
FOR THE ACTIVE SHOOTING SPORTSMAN

The companies represented on the following pages will be happy to provide additional information – feel free to contact them.

This Book Could Save Your Life!

The Gun Digest® Book of Combat Handgunnery

5th Edition

by Massad Ayoob

Learn essential survival techniques to defend yourself, your loved ones, and your property with a handgun. All tactics and techniques are described in detail, including concealed carry. You'll be shown how to choose the right handgun and how to build and test the necessary handling skills, as well as where to find additional training. This reference will also help you avoid common mistakes and accidents.

Softcover • 8½x11 • 256 pages • 350 b&w photos

Item# COM5 • $22.95

To order call **800-258-0929** Offer DAB3

Krause Publications, Offer DAB3
P.O. Box 5009, Iola WI 54945-5009 • **www.krausebooks.com**

Please add $4.00 for shipping & handling to U.S. addresses.
Non-U.S. addresses please add $20.95.
Residents of CA, IA, IL, KS, NJ, PA, SD, TN, WI please add appropriate sales tax.

QUALITY GUNSTOCK BLANKS

Cali'co Hardwoods has been cutting superior-quality shotgun and rifle blanks for more than 31 years. Cali'co supplies blanks to many of the major manufacturers—Browning, Weatherby, Ruger, Holland & Holland, to name a few—as well as custom gunsmiths the world over.

Profiled rifle blanks are available, ready for inletting and sanding. Cali'co sells superior California hardwoods in Claro walnut, French walnut, Bastogne, maple and myrtle.

Cali'co offers good, serviceable blanks and some of the finest exhibition blanks available. Satisfaction guaranteed.

Color catalog, retail and dealer price list (FFL required) free upon request.

CALI'CO HARDWOODS, INC.

3580 Westwind Blvd., Santa Rosa, CA 95403
Phone: 707-546-4045 • Fax: 707-546-4027

NYLON COATED GUN CLEANING RODS

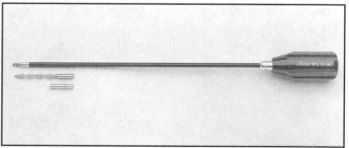

J. Dewey cleaning rods have been used by the U.S. Olympic shooting team and the benchrest community for over 20 years. These one-piece, spring-tempered, steel-base rods will not gall delicate rifling or damage the muzzle area of front-cleaned firearms. The nylon coating elliminates the problem of abrasives adhering to the rod during the cleaning operation. Each rod comes with a hard non-breakable plastic handle supported by ball-bearings, top and bottom, for ease of cleaning.

The brass cleaning jags are designed to pierce the center of the cleaning patch or wrap around the knurled end to keep the patch centered in the bore.

Coated rods are available from 17-caliber to shotgun bore size in several lengths to meet the needs of any shooter. Write for more information.

J. DEWEY MFG. CO., INC.

P.O. Box 2014, Southbury, CT 06488
Phone: 203-264-3064 • Fax: 203-262-6907
Web: www.deweyrods.com

SHOOTER'S MARKETPLACE

ULTIMATE 500

MTM Case-Gard introduces 13 new products to make your shooting experience more organized and productive. Riflemen, shotgun, muzzleloaders and reloaders will find hundreds of items in their line of shooting products they can use.

Send $2.00 for a full-size catalog or look them up on their web site.

MTM MOLDED PRODUCTS COMPANY
P.O. Box 14117, Dayton, OH. 45414
Web: www.mtmcase-gard.com

COMBINATION RIFLE AND OPTICS REST

The Magna-Pod weighs less than two pounds, yet firmly supports more than most expensive tripods. It will hold 50 pounds at its low 9-inch height and over 10 pounds extended to 17 inches. It sets up in seconds where there is neither time nor space for a tripod and keeps your expensive equipment safe from knock-overs by kids, pets, pedestrians, or even high winds. It makes a great mono-pod for camcorders, etc., and its carrying box is less than 13" x 13" x 3 1/4" high for easy storage and access.

Attached to its triangle base it becomes an extremely stable table pod or rifle bench rest. The rifle yoke pictured in photo is included.

It's 5 pods in 1: Magna-Pod, Mono-Pod, Table-Pod, Shoulder-Pod and Rifle Rest. Send for free catalog.

SHEPHERD ENTERPRISES, INC.
Box 189, Waterloo, NE 68069
Phone: 402-779-2424 • Fax: 402-779-4010
E-mail: shepherd@shepherdscopes.com • Web: www.shepherdscopes.com

PREMIER HUNTING

John X Safaris offers premier hunting on a wide range of terrain that spans over 3,000,000 acres in South Africa. The leader in Plains Game hunting for over 20 years their clients have taken "eight" of the new or pending SCI top ten Kudu including #1 & 3, the # 1 and #6 Steenbuck, #8 Red Lechwe, #10 Eland as well as dozens more top twenty record book species. Their accommodations are rated four star and our chefs award winning. Their hunting areas are Malaria "FREE" and politically stable. Their package hunts currently run $3,450 for a seven day 5 animal package or $4,200 for a ten day six animal package. For more information visit their web site www.johnxsafaris.com or phone 901-409-1218 and speak to Dave Harwood.

LASERMAX
YOUR NEW SECURITY SYSTEM

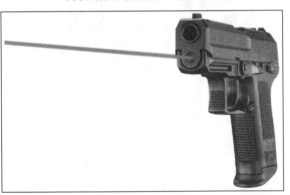

Rugged. Reliable. Consistent. Totally internal. Always stays aligned. User installed, with no gunsmithing. Use with any tactical lights. Fits all holsters. Ambidextrous switch at the take-down lever. Point-of-aim/impact is center of mass from 0 to 20 yds. Features pulsating beam more noticeable to the eye. Sights for all Glocks and most Sigs, including the P239 and P245. Available now: the HK USP Compact 40. Other models include M1911s, Berettas, Taurus and S&W. **LaserMax** offers law enforcement discounts and training programs.

LASERMAX, INC.
3495 Winton Place, Bldg. B, Rochester, NY 14623-2807
Toll-free Phone: (800) LASER-03 • Fax: (585) 272-5427
E-mail: customerservice@lasermax-inc.com
Web: www.lasermax-inc.com

SHOOTER'S MARKETPLACE

FINE GUN STOCKS

Manufacturing custom and production gunstocks for hundreds of models of rifles and shotguns—made from the finest stock woods and available in all stages of completion.

Visit www.gunstocks.com to view their bargain list of fine custom gunstocks. Each displayed in full color.

GREAT AMERICAN GUNSTOCK COMPANY

3420 Industrial Drive
Yuba City, CA 95993
Phone: 530-671-4570
Fax: 530-671-3906
Gunstock Hotline: 800-784-GUNS (4867)
Web: www.gunstocks.com
E-mail: gunstox@syix.com

BORDER CLASSIC

Gary Reeder Custom Guns, builder of full custom guns including hunting handguns, custom Encores, large caliber hunting rifles and over 20 different series of cowboy guns, including our Border Classic, shown. This beauty is the first ever snubbie Schofield, and can be built on any current Schofield. Fully engraved, round butted, with their Black Chromex finish and a solid silver Mexican coin for the front sight, this one is truly a masterpiece. See them all at their website, or call for a brochure.

GARY REEDER CUSTOM GUNS

2601 E. 7th Avenue, Flagstaff, AZ 86004
Phone: 928-527-4100 or 928-526-3313
Website: www.reedercustomguns.com

NEW CATALOG!

Catalog #25 is Numrich's latest edition! This 1,200 page catalog features more than 500 schematics for use in identifying obsolete and current commercial, military, antique and foreign guns. Edition #25 contains 180,000 items from their inventory of over 650 million parts and accessories and is a necessity for any true gunsmith or hobbyist. It has been the industry's leading reference book for firearm parts and identification for over 50 years!

Order Item #YP-25 $12.95
U.S. Orders: Bulk mail, shipping charges included
Foreign Orders: Air mail, 30-day delivery; or surface, 90-day delivery. Shipping charges additional.

NUMRICH GUN PARTS CORPORATION

226 Williams Lane, P.O. Box 299, West Hurley, NY 12491
Orders Toll-Free: 866-NUMRICH (866-686-7424)
Customer Service: (845) 679-4867
Toll-Free Fax: (877) GUNPART
Web: e-GunParts.com • E-mail: info@gunpartscorp.com

HIGH QUALITY OPTICS

One of the best indicators of quality is a scope's resolution number. The smaller the number, the better. Our scope has a resolution number of 2.8 seconds of angle. This number is about 20% smaller (better) than other well-known scopes costing much more. It means that two .22 caliber bullets can be a hair's breadth apart and edges of each still be clearly seen. With a Shepherd at 800 yards, you will be able to tell a four inch antler from a four inch ear and a burrowing owl from a prairie dog. Bird watchers will be able to distinguish a Tufted Titmouse from a Ticked-Off Field Mouse. Send for free catalog.

SHEPHERD ENTERPRISES, INC.

Box 189, Waterloo, NE 68069
Phone: 402-779-2424 • Fax: 402-779-4010
E-mail: shepherd@shepherdscopes.com • Web: www.shepherdscopes.com

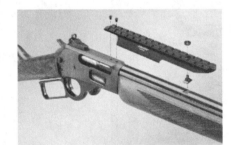

SHOOTER'S MARKETPLACE

PRECISION RIFLE REST

Bald Eagle Precision Machine Co. offers a rifle rest perfect for the serious benchrester or dedicated varminter.

"The Slingshot" or Next Generation has 60° front legs. The rest is constructed of aircraft-quality aluminum or fine grain cast iron and weighs 12 to 20 lbs. The finish is 3 coats of Imron clear. Primary height adjustments are made with a rack and pinion gear. Secondary adjustment uses a mariner wheel with thrust bearings for smooth operation. A hidden fourth leg allows for lateral movement on the bench.

Bald Eagle offers approximately 150 rest combinations to choose from, including windage adjustable, right or left hand, cast aluminum or cast iron.

Prices: $175.00 to $345.00

BALD EAGLE PRECISION MACHINE CO.
101-K Allison Street, Lock Haven, PA 17745
Phone: 570-748-6772 — Fax: 570-748-4443
Web: www.baldeaglemachine.com

FOLDING BIPODS

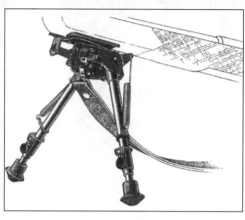

Harris Bipods clamp securely to most stud-equipped bolt-action rifles and are quick-detachable. With adapters, they will fit some other guns. On all models except the Model LM, folding legs have completely adjustable spring-return extensions. The sling swivel attaches to the clamp. This time-proven design is manufactured with heat-treated steel and hard alloys and has a black anodized finish.

Series S Bipods rotate 35° for instant leveling on uneven ground. Hinged base has tension adjustment and buffer springs to eliminate tremor or looseness in crotch area of bipod. They are otherwise similar to non-rotating Series 1A2.

Thirteen models are available from Harris Engineering; literature is free.

HARRIS ENGINEERING INC.
Dept: GD54, Barlow, KY 42024
Phone: 270-334-3633 • Fax: 270-334-3000

6x18x40 VARMINT/TARGET SCOPE

Send for
Free Catalog

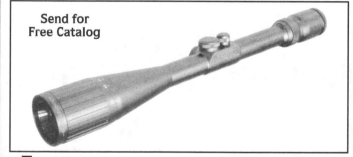

The Shepherd 6x18x40 Varmint/Target Scope makes long-range varmint and target shooting child's play. Just pick the ranging circle that best fits your target (be it prairie dogs, coyotes or paper varmints) and Shepherd's exclusive, patented Dual Reticle Down Range System does the rest. You won't believe how far you can accurately shoot, even with rimfire rifles.

Shepherd's superior lens coating mean superior light transmission and tack-sharp resolution.

This new shockproof, waterproof scope features 1/4 minute-of-angle clicks on the ranging circles and friction adjustments on the crosshairs that allows fine-tuning to 0.001 MOA. A 40mm adjustable objective provides a 5.5-foot field of view at 100 yards (16x setting). 16.5 FOV @ 6X.

SHEPHERD ENTERPRISES, INC.
Box 189, Waterloo, NE 68069
Phone: 402-779-2424 • Fax: 402-779-4010
Email: shepherd@shepherdscopes.com • Web: www.shepherdscopes.com

CUSTOM RESTORATION/CASE COLORING

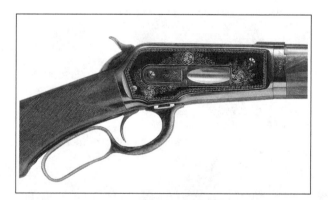

Doug Turnbull Restoration continues to offer bone charcoal case hardening work, matching the original case colors produced by Winchester, Colt, Marlin, Parker, L.C. Smith, Fox and other manufacturers. Also available is charcoal blue, known as Carbona or machine blue, a prewar finish used by most makers. "Specializing in the accurate recreation of historical metal finishes on period firearms, from polishing to final finishing. Including Bone Charcoal Color Case Hardening, Charcoal Bluing, Rust Blue, and Nitre Blue".

DOUG TURNBULL RESTORATION
P.O. Box 471, 6680 Rt 5&20, Dept SM2003
Bloomfield, New York 14469 • Phone/Fax: 585-657-6338
E-mail: turnbullrest@mindspring.com
Web: www.turnbullrestoration.com

SHOOTER'S MARKETPLACE

ULTIMATE 500

Gary Reeder Custom Guns, builder of full custom guns for over 25 years, and with over 50 different series of custom hunting handguns, cowboy guns, custom Encores and large caliber hunting rifles, has a free brochure for you. Or visit their website. One of the most popular is their Ultimate 500, chambered in the 500 S&W Magnum. This beefy 5-shot revolver is for the serious handgun hunter and is one of several series of large caliber handguns, such as 475 Linebaugh and 475 Maximum, 500 Linebaugh and 500 Maximum. For more information, contact:

GARY REEDER CUSTOM GUNS
2601 E. 7th Avenue, Flagstaff, AZ 86004
Phone: 928-527-4100 or 928-526-3313
Website: www.reedercustomguns.com

BLACK HILLS GOLD AMMUNITION

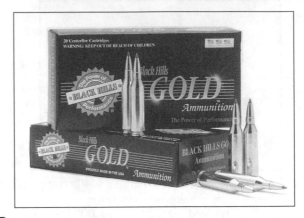

Black Hills Ammunition has introduced a new line of premium performance rifle ammunition. Calibers available in the Black Hills Gold Line are .243, .270, .308, .30-06, and .300 Win Mag. This line is designed for top performance in a wide range of hunting situations. Bullets used in this ammunition are the Barnes X-Bullet with XLC coating and the highly accurate Nosler Ballistic-Tip™.

Black Hills Ammunition is sold dealer direct. The Gold line is packaged in 20 rounds per box, 10 boxes per case. Black Hills pays all freight to dealers in the continental United States. Minimum dealer order is only one case.

BLACK HILLS AMMUNITION
P.O. Box 3090, Rapid City, SD 57709
Phone: 1-605-348-5150 • Fax: 1-605-348-9827
Web: www.black-hills.com

BEAR TRACK CASES

Designed by an Alaskan bush pilot! Polyurethane coated, zinc plated corners and feet, zinc plated— spring loaded steel handles, stainless steel hinges, high density urethane foam inside with a neoprene seal. Aluminum walls are standard at .070 with riveted ends. Committed to quality that will protect your valuables regardless of the transportation method you use. Exterior coating also protects other items from acquiring "aluminum black."

Many styles, colors and sizes available. Wheels come on large cases and special orders can be accommodated. Call for a brochure or visit online.

Bear Track Cases when top quality protection is a must.

BEAR TRACK CASES
314 Highway 239, Freedom, WY 83120
Phone: 307-883-2468 • Fax: 307-883-2005
Web: www.beartrackcases.com

DETACHABLE RINGS & BASES

A.R.M.S.® #22 Throw Lever Rings

All steel 30mm ring, secured with A.R.M.S.® dovetail system to an extruded aluminum platform. Built in no-mar patented buffer pads. Available in Low, Medium, and High height. Low height measures .925". Medium height measures 1.150". High height measures 1.450". Height is measured from the center of the optic to the bottom of the base.

Sugg. Retail $99.00
U.S. Patent No. 5,276,988 & 4,845,871
Item #37 to convert 30mm to 1",
    Suggested Retail $29.00

Call for dealer or distributor in your area.

A.R.M.S., INC.
230 W. Center St., West Bridgewater, MA 02379
Phone: (508) 584-7816 • Fax: (508) 588-8045
E-mail: sales@armsmounts • Web: www.armsmounts.com

SHOOTER'S MARKETPLACE

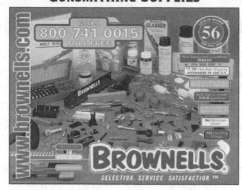

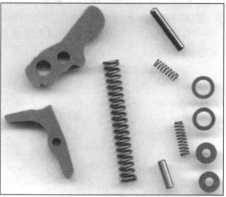

SHOOTER'S MARKETPLACE

A NEW TREND IN GUN COLLECTING: GUNS THAT CAN'T SHOOT!

INTERNATIONAL MILITARY ANTIQUES, INC. of New Jersey, the company that supplied the machine guns used in "Saving Private Ryan", "Band of Brothers," and many other World War II block buster movies, has introduced a new trend in gun collecting. Historically significant NON-FIRING machine guns constructed from original G.I. military parts to BATF specifications, making them legally unrestricted by federal law and unconvertible to firing condition.

Previously unavailable, these original weapons can complete any 20th century military collection without the extremely high cost, extensive paperwork and security measures that comes with operational machine gun ownership.

Spanning from the WWI water-cooled Maxim and Vickers guns through the myriad of weapons developed by many countries during two World Wars, including the legendary Nazi era MG34 and MG42 series light machine guns, I.M.A. has developed a range of some of the most famous and infamous weapons that forged the modern world we know today.

In addition, I.M.A. offers a vast range of other military-related materials, both original and high quality reproduction. Military holsters, complete with replicated markings together with belts, pouches, swords, helmets, and accoutrements from over 300 years of history cater to the requirements of the collector and reenactor alike. With its parent company Fire-Power International, Ltd. of England supplying the lion's share of the ex-military equipment, I.M.A.'s offerings are often unique to the U.S. market.

A mail order company operating from a 25,000 sq. ft. facility in New Jersey, the depth and scope of its inventory provides something for everyone. The often humorous but always highly accurate detailed cartoon illustrations by the renowned military artist SCOTT NOVZEN make I.M.A.'s advertisements and catalogs, or a visit to their website an added treat. Take a light hearted look at military history.

For further information contact:

INTERNATIONAL MILITARY ANTIQUES, INC.

Box 256, Millington, New Jersey 07946, U.S.A.
Phone: 908-903-1200 • Fax: 908-903-0106
www.ima-usa.com

2004
GUN DIGEST
Complete Compact
CATALOG

 GUNDEX

 HANDGUNS

 RIFLES

 SHOTGUNS

 BLACKPOWDER

 AIRGUNS

 ACCESSORIES

 REFERENCE

 DIRECTORY OF THE ARMS TRADE

GUNDEX

GUNDEX

GUNDEX

GUNDEX

GUNDEX

Includes models suitable for several forms of competition and other sporting purposes.

Accu-Tek HC-380

Accu-Tek XL-9

Auto-Ordnance 1911A1 Standard

Baer Custom Carry

Baer Premium II

Auto-Ordnance Deluxe

ACCU-TEK MODEL HC-380 AUTO PISTOL

Caliber: 380 ACP, 10-shot magazine. **Barrel:** 2.75". **Weight:** 26 oz. **Length:** 6" overall. **Grips:** Checkered black composition. **Sights:** Blade front, rear adjustable for windage. **Features:** External hammer; manual thumb safety with firing pin and trigger disconnect; bottom magazine release. Stainless steel construction. Introduced 1993. Price includes cleaning kit and gun lock. Made in U.S.A. by Accu-Tek.
Price: Satin stainless $249.00

ACCU-TEK XL-9 AUTO PISTOL

Caliber: 9mm Para., 5-shot magazine. **Barrel:** 3". **Weight:** 24 oz. **Length:** 5.6" overall. **Grips:** Black pebble composition. **Sights:** Three-dot system; rear adjustable for windage. **Features:** Stainless steel construction; double-action-only mechanism. Introduced 1999. Price includes cleaning kit and gun lock, two magazines. Made in U.S.A. by Accu-Tek.
Price: $267.00

AMERICAN DERRINGER LM-5 AUTOMATIC PISTOL

Caliber: 25 ACP, 5-shot magazine. **Barrel:** 2-1/4". **Weight:** 15 oz. **Length:** NA. **Grips:** Wood. **Sights:** Fixed. **Features:** Compact, stainless, semi-auto, single-action hammerless design. Hand assembled and fitted.
Price: $425.00

AUTO-ORDNANCE 1911A1 AUTOMATIC PISTOL

Caliber: 45 ACP, 7-shot magazine. **Barrel:** 5". **Weight:** 39 oz. **Length:** 8-1/2" overall. **Grips:** Checkered plastic with medallion. **Sights:** Blade front, rear adjustable for windage. **Features:** Same specs as 1911A1 military guns—parts interchangeable. Frame and slide blued; each radius has non-glare finish. Made in U.S.A. by Auto-Ordnance Corp.
Price: 45 ACP, blue $511.00
Price: 45 ACP, Parkerized $515.00
Price: 45 ACP Deluxe (three-dot sights, textured rubber wraparound grips) $525.00

AUTAUGA 32 AUTO PISTOL

Caliber: 32 ACP, 6-shot magazine. **Barrel:** 2". **Weight:** 11.3 oz. **Length:** 4.3" overall. **Grips:** Black polymer. **Sights:** Fixed. **Features:** Double-action-only mechanism. Stainless steel construction. Uses Winchester Silver Tip ammunition.
Price: . . . . NA

BAER 1911 CUSTOM CARRY AUTO PISTOL

Caliber: 45 ACP, 7- or 10-shot magazine. **Barrel:** 5". **Weight:** 37 oz. **Length:** 8.5" overall. **Grips:** Checkered walnut. **Sights:** Baer improved ramp-style dovetailed front, Novak low-mount rear. **Features:** Baer forged NM frame, slide and barrel with stainless bushing; fitted slide to frame; double serrated slide (full-size only); Baer speed trigger with 4-lb. pull; Baer deluxe hammer and sear, tactical-style extended ambidextrous safety, beveled magazine well; polished feed ramp and throated barrel; tuned extractor; Baer extended ejector, checkered slide stop; lowered and flared ejection port, full-length recoil guide rod; recoil buff. Partial listing shown. Made in U.S.A. by Les Baer Custom, Inc.
Price: Standard size, blued $1,640.00
Price: Standard size, stainless $1,690.00
Price: Comanche size, blued $1,640.00
Price: Comanche size, stainless $1,690.00
Price: Comanche size, aluminum frame, blued slide $1,923.00
Price: Comanche size, aluminum frame, stainless slide $1,995.00

BAER 1911 PREMIER II AUTO PISTOL

Caliber: 9x23, 38 Super, 400 Cor-Bon, 45 ACP, 7- or 10-shot magazine. **Barrel:** 5". **Weight:** 37 oz. **Length:** 8.5" overall. **Grips:** Checkered rosewood, double diamond pattern. **Sights:** Baer dovetailed front, low-mount Bo-Mar rear with hidden leaf. **Features:** Baer NM forged steel frame and barrel with stainless bushing; slide fitted to frame; double serrated slide; lowered, flared ejection port; tuned, polished extractor; Baer extended ejector, checkered slide stop, aluminum speed trigger with 4-lb. pull, deluxe Commander hammer and sear, beavertail grip safety with pad, beveled magazine well, extended ambidextrous safety; flat mainspring housing; polished feed ramp and throated barrel; 30 lpi checkered front strap. Made in U.S.A. by Les Baer Custom, Inc.
Price: Blued $1,428.00
Price: Stainless $1,558.00
Price: 6" model, blued, from $1,595.00

BAER 1911 S.R.P. PISTOL

Caliber: 45 ACP. **Barrel:** 5". **Weight:** 37 oz. **Length:** 8.5" overall. **Grips:** Checkered walnut. **Sights:** Trijicon night sights. **Features:** Similar to the F.B.I. contract gun except uses Baer forged steel frame. Has Baer match barrel with supported chamber, Wolff springs, complete tactical action job. All parts Mag-na-fluxed; deburred for tactical carry. Has Baer Ultra Coat finish. Tuned for reliability. Contact Baer for complete details. Introduced 1996. Made in U.S.A. by Les Baer Custom, Inc.
Price: Government or Comanche length $2,240.00

Beretta 92 Billennium

Beretta 96

Beretta M8000/8040 Cougar

BERETTA MODEL 92 BILLENNIUM LIMITED EDITION

Caliber: 9mm. **Grips:** Carbon fiber. **Sights:** 3 dot. **Features:** Single action. Semiauto. Steel frame, frame mounted safety. Only 2000 made worldwide.
Price: **$1,429.00**

BERETTA MODEL 92FS PISTOL

Caliber: 9mm Para., 10-shot magazine. **Barrel:** 4.9". **Weight:** 34 oz. **Length:** 8.5" overall. **Grips:** Checkered black plastic. **Sights:** Blade front, rear adjustable for windage. Tritium night sights available. **Features:** Double action. Extractor acts as chamber loaded indicator, squared trigger guard, grooved front and backstraps, inertia firing pin. Matte or blued finish. Introduced 1977. Made in U.S.A. and imported from Italy by Beretta U.S.A.
Price: With plastic grips **$691.00**
Price: Vertec with access rail **$726.00**
Price: Vertec Inox **$776.00**

Beretta Model 92FS/96 Brigadier Pistols

Similar to the Model 92FS/96 except with a heavier slide to reduce felt recoil and allow mounting removable front sight. Wrap-around rubber grips. Three-dot sights dovetailed to the slide, adjustable for windage. Weighs 35.3 oz. Introduced 1999.
Price: 9mm or 40 S&W, 10-shot **$748.00**
Price: Inox models (stainless steel) **$798.00**

Beretta Model 92FS Compact and Compact Type M Pistol

Similar to the Model 92FS except more compact and lighter: overall length 7.8"; 4.3" barrel; weighs 30.9 oz. Has Bruniton finish, chrome-lined bore, combat trigger guard, ambidextrous safety/decock lever. Single column 8-shot magazine (Type M), or double column 10-shot (Compact), 9mm only. Introduced 1998. Imported from Italy by Beretta U.S.A.
Price: Compact (10-shot) **$691.00**
Price: Compact Type M (8-shot) **$691.00**
Price: Compact Inox (stainless) **$748.00**
Price: Compact Type M Inox (stainless) **$748.00**

BERETTA MODEL 96 PISTOL

Same as the Model 92FS except chambered for 40 S&W. Ambidextrous safety mechanism with passive firing pin catch, slide safety/decocking lever, trigger bar disconnect. Has 10-shot magazine. Available with three-dot sights. Introduced 1992.
Price: Model 96, plastic grips **$691.00**
Price: Stainless, rubber grips **$798.00**
Price: Vertec with access rail **$726.00**
Price: Vertec Inox **$776.00**

BERETTA MODEL 80 CHEETAH SERIES DA PISTOLS

Caliber: 380 ACP, 10-shot magazine (M84); 8-shot (M85); 22 LR, 7-shot (M87). **Barrel:** 3.82". **Weight:** About 23 oz. (M84/85); 20.8 oz. (M87). **Length:** 6.8" overall. **Grips:** Glossy black plastic (wood optional at extra cost). **Sights:** Fixed front, drift-adjustable rear. **Features:** Double action, quick takedown, convenient magazine release. Introduced 1977. Imported from Italy by Beretta U.S.A.
Price: Model 84 Cheetah, plastic grips **$599.00**
Price: Model 85 Cheetah, plastic grips, 8-shot **$563.00**
Price: Model 87 Cheetah, wood, 22 LR, 7-shot **$599.00**
Price: Model 87 Target, plastic grips **$682.00**

Beretta Model 86 Cheetah

Similar to the 380-caliber Model 85 except has tip-up barrel for first-round loading. Barrel length is 4.4", overall length of 7.33". Has 8-shot magazine, walnut grips. Introduced 1989.
Price: **$599.00**

Beretta Model 21 Bobcat Pistol

Similar to the Model 950 BS. Chambered for 22 LR or 25 ACP. Both double action. Has 2.4" barrel, 4.9" overall length; 7-round magazine on 22 cal.; 8 rounds in 25 ACP, 9.9 oz., available in nickel, matte, engraved or blue finish. Plastic grips. Introduced in 1985.
Price: Bobcat, 22 or 25, blue **$292.00**
Price: Bobcat, 22, stainless **$315.00**
Price: Bobcat, 22 or 25, matte **$259.00**

BERETTA MODEL 3032 TOMCAT PISTOL

Caliber: 32 ACP, 7-shot magazine. **Barrel:** 2.45". **Weight:** 14.5 oz. **Length:** 5" overall. **Grips:** Checkered black plastic. **Sights:** Blade front, drift-adjustable rear. **Features:** Double action with exposed hammer; tip-up barrel for direct loading/unloading; thumb safety; polished or matte blue finish. Imported from Italy by Beretta U.S.A. Introduced 1996.
Price: Blue **$379.00**
Price: Matte **$349.00**
Price: Stainless **$428.00**
Price: Titanium **$589.00**
Price: With Tritium sights **$420.00**

BERETTA MODEL 8000/8040/8045 COUGAR PISTOL

Caliber: 9mm Para., 10-shot, 40 S&W, 10-shot magazine; 45 ACP, 8-shot. **Barrel:** 3.6". **Weight:** 33.5 oz. **Length:** 7" overall. **Grips:** Checkered plastic. **Sights:** Blade front, rear drift adjustable for windage. **Features:** Slide-mounted safety; rotating barrel; exposed hammer. Matte black Bruniton finish. Announced 1994. Imported from Italy by Beretta U.S.A.
Price: **$709.00**
Price: D model, 9mm, 40 S&W **$709.00**
Price: D model, 45 ACP **$764.00**

BERETTA MODEL 9000S COMPACT PISTOL

Caliber: 9mm Para., 40 S&W; 10-shot magazine. **Barrel:** 3.4". **Weight:** 26.8 oz. **Length:** 6.6". **Grips:** Soft polymer. **Sights:** Windage-adjustable white-dot rear, white-dot blade front. **Features:** Glass-reinforced polymer frame; patented tilt-barrel, open-slide locking system; chrome-lined barrel; external serrated hammer; automatic firing pin and manual safeties. Introduced 2000. Imported from Italy by Beretta USA.
Price: 9000S Type F (single and double action, external hammer) **$558.00**
Price: 9000S Type D (double-action only, no external hammer or safety) **$558.00**

Beretta Model 8000/8040/8045 Mini Cougar

Similar to the Model 8000/8040 Cougar except has shorter grip frame and weighs 27.6 oz. Introduced 1998. Imported from Italy by Beretta U.S.A.
Price: 9mm or 40 S&W **$709.00**
Price: 9mm or 40 S&W, DAO **$709.00**
Price: 45 ACP DAO **$764.00**

Beretta U22 Neos

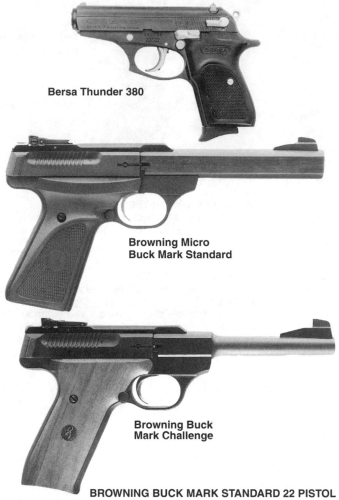

Bersa Thunder 380

Browning Micro Buck Mark Standard

Browning Buck Mark Challenge

BERETTA MODEL U22 NEOS

Caliber: 22 LR, 10-shot magazine. **Barrel:** 4.2"; 6". **Weight:** 32 oz.; 36 oz. **Length:** 8.8"; 10.3". **Sights:** Target. **Features:** Integral rail for standard scope mounts, light, perfectly weighted, 100% American made by Beretta.

Price:	$265.00
Price: Inox	$315.00
Price: DLX	$336.00
Price: Inox	$386.00

BERSA THUNDER 380 AUTO PISTOLS

Caliber: 380 ACP, 7-shot (Thunder 380 Lite), 9-shot magazine (Thunder 380 DLX). **Barrel:** 3.5". **Weight:** 23 oz. **Length:** 6.6" overall. **Grips:** Black polymer. **Sights:** Blade front, notch rear adjustable for windage; three-dot system. **Features:** Double action; firing pin and magazine safeties. Available in blue, nickel, or duo tone. Introduced 1995. Distributed by Eagle Imports, Inc.

Price: Thunder 380, 7-shot, deep blue finish	$266.95
Price: Thunder 380 Deluxe, 9-shot, satin nickel	$299.95
Price: Thunder 380 Gold, 7-shot	$299.95

BERSA THUNDER 45 ULTRA COMPACT PISTOL

NEW!

Similar to the Bersa Thunder 380 except in 45 ACP. Available in three finishes. Introduced 2003. Imported from Argentina by Eagle Imports, Inc.

Price: Thunder 45, matte blue	$400.95
Price: Thunder 45, Duotone	$424.95
Price: Thunder 45, Satin nickel	$441.95

BLUE THUNDER/COMMODORE 1911-STYLE AUTO PISTOLS

Caliber: 45 ACP, 7-shot magazine. **Barrel:** 4-1/4", 5". **Weight:** NA. **Length:** NA. **Grips:** Checkered hardwood. **Sights:** Blade front, drift-adjustable rear. **Features:** Extended slide release and safety, spring guide rod, skeletonized hammer and trigger, magazine bumper, beavertail grip safety. Imported from the Philippines by Century International Arms Inc.

Price:	$464.80 to $484.80

BROWNING HI-POWER 9mm AUTOMATIC PISTOL

Caliber: 9mm Para.,10-shot magazine. **Barrel:** 4-21/32". **Weight:** 32 oz. **Length:** 7-3/4" overall. **Grips:** Walnut, hand checkered, or black Polyamide. **Sights:** 1/8" blade front; rear screw-adjustable for windage and elevation. Also available with fixed rear (drift-adjustable for windage). **Features:** External hammer with half-cock and thumb safeties. A blow on the hammer cannot discharge a cartridge; cannot be fired with magazine removed. Fixed rear sight model available. Includes gun lock. Imported from Belgium by Browning.

Price: Fixed sight model, walnut grips	$680.00
Price: Fully adjustable rear sight, walnut grips	$730.00
Price: Mark III, standard matte black finish, fixed sight, moulded grips, ambidextrous safety	$662.00

Browning Hi-Power Practical Pistol

Similar to the standard Hi-Power except has silver-chromed frame with blued slide, wrap-around Pachmayr rubber grips, round-style serrated hammer and removable front sight, fixed rear (drift-adjustable for windage). Available in 9mm Para. Includes gun lock. Introduced 1991.

Price:	$717.00

BROWNING BUCK MARK STANDARD 22 PISTOL

Caliber: 22 LR, 10-shot magazine. **Barrel:** 5-1/2". **Weight:** 32 oz. **Length:** 9-1/2" overall. **Grips:** Black moulded composite with checkering. **Sights:** Ramp front, Browning Pro Target rear adjustable for windage and elevation. **Features:** All steel, matte blue finish or nickel, gold-colored trigger. Buck Mark Plus has laminated wood grips. Includes gun lock. Made in U.S.A. Introduced 1985. From Browning.

Price: Buck Mark Standard, blue	$286.00
Price: Buck Mark Nickel, nickel finish with contoured rubber grips	$338.00
Price: Buck Mark Plus, matte blue with laminated wood grips	$350.00
Price: Buck Mark Plus Nickel, nickel finish, laminated wood grips	$383.00

Browning Buck Mark Camper

Similar to the Buck Mark except 5-1/2" bull barrel. Weight is 34 oz. Matte blue finish, molded composite grips. Introduced 1999. From Browning.

Price:	$258.00
Price: Camper Nickel, nickel finish, molded composite grips	$287.00

Browning Buck Mark Challenge

Similar to the Buck Mark except has a lightweight barrel and smaller grip diameter. Barrel length is 5-1/2", weight is 25 oz. Introduced 1999. From Browning.

Price:	$320.00

Browning Buck Mark Micro

Same as the Buck Mark Standard and Buck Mark Plus except has 4" barrel. Available in blue or nickel. Has 16-click Pro Target rear sight. Introduced 1992.

Price: Micro Standard, matte blue finish	$286.00
Price: Micro Nickel, nickel finish	$338.00
Price: Buck Mark Micro Plus, matte blue, lam. wood grips	$350.00
Price: Buck Mark Micro Plus Nickel	$383.00

HANDGUNS

Charles Daly M-1911-A1P

Cobra FS380

Cobra Patriot

Cobra CA32

Colt 1991 Model O

Colt 1991 Model O Commander

Colt XSE Model O Commander

Browning Buck Mark Bullseye

Same as the Buck Mark Standard except has 7-1/4" fluted barrel, matte blue finish. Weighs 36 oz.
Price: Bullseye Standard, molded composite grips **$420.00**
Price: Bullseye Target, contoured rosewood grips **$541.00**

Browning Buck Mark 5.5

Same as the Buck Mark Standard except has a 5-1/2" bull barrel with integral scope mount, matte blue finish.
Price: 5.5 Field, Pro-Target adj. rear sight,
contoured walnut grips **$459.00**
Price: 5.5 Target, hooded adj. target sights, contoured walnut grips
. . . . **$459.00**

Buck Mark Commemorative

Same as the Buck Mark Standard except has a 6-3/4" Challenger-style barrel, matte blue finish and scrimshaw-style, bonded ivory grips. Includes pistol rug. Limited to 1,000 guns.
Price: Commemorative **$437.00**

CHARLES DALY M-1911-A1P AUTOLOADING PISTOL

Caliber: 45 ACP, 7- or 10-shot magazine. **Barrel:** 5". **Weight:** 38 oz. **Length:** 8-3/4" overall. **Grips:** Checkered. **Sights:** Blade front, rear drift adjustable for windage; three-dot system. **Features:** Skeletonized combat hammer and trigger; beavertail grip safety; extended slide release; oversize thumb safety; Parkerized finish. Introduced 1996. Imported from the Philippines by K.B.I., Inc.
Price: **$469.95**

COBRA ENTERPRISES FS380 AUTO PISTOL

NEW! **Caliber:** 380 ACP, 7-shot magazine. **Barrel:** 3.5". **Weight:** 2.1 lbs. **Length:** 6-3/8" overall. **Grips:** Black composition. **Sights:** Fixed. **Features:** Choice of bright chrome, satin nickel or black finish. Introduced 2002. Made in U.S.A. by Cobra Enterprises.
Price: **$98.00**

Cobra Enterprises FS32 AUTO PISTOL

NEW! **Caliber:** 32 ACP, 8-shot magazine. **Barrel:** 3.5". **Weight:** 2.1 lbs. **Length:** 6-3/8" overall. **Grips:** Black composition. **Sights:** Fixed. **Features:** Choice of black, satin nickel or bright chrome finish. Introduced 2002. Made in U.S.A. by Cobra Enterprises.
Price: **$107.00**

Cobra Industries Patriot Pistol

NEW! **Caliber:** .380ACP, 9mm Luger,6-shot magazine. **Barrel:** 3.3". **Weight:** 20 oz. **Length:** 6" overall. **Grips:** Checkered polymer. **Sights:** Fixed. **Features:** Stainless steel slide with load indicator; double-action-only trigger system. Introduced 2002. Made in U.S.A. by Cobra Enterprises, Inc.
Price: . . . . About **$325.00**

Cobra Industries CA32, CA380

Caliber: 32ACP, 380 ACP. **Barrel:** 2.8" **Weight:** 22 oz. **Length:** 5.4". **Grips:** Laminated wood (CA32); Black molded synthetic (CA380). **Sights:** Fixed. **Features:** True pocket pistol size and styling without bulk. Made in U.S.A. by Cobra Enterprises.
Price: . . . . **NA**

COLT MODEL 1991 MODEL O AUTO PISTOL

Caliber: 45 ACP, 7-shot magazine. **Barrel:** 5". **Weight:** 38 oz. **Length:** 8.5" overall. **Grips:** Checkered black composition. **Sights:** Ramped blade front, fixed square notch rear, high profile. **Features:** Matte finish. Continuation of serial number range used on original G.I. 1911 A1 guns. Comes with one magazine and moulded carrying case. Introduced 1991.
Price: **$645.00**
Price: Stainless **$800.00**

Colt Model 1991 Model O Commander Auto Pistol

Similar to the Model 1991 A1 except has 4-1/4" barrel. Overall length is 7-3/4". Comes with one 7-shot magazine, molded case.
Price: Blue **$645.00**
Price: Stainless steel **$800.00**

COLT XSE SERIES MODEL O AUTO PISTOLS

Caliber: 45 ACP, 8-shot magazine. **Barrel:** 4.25", 5". **Grips:** Checkered, double diamond rosewood. **Sights:** Drift-adjustable three-dot combat. **Features:** Brushed stainless finish; adjustable, two-cut aluminum trigger; extended ambidextrous thumb safety; upswept beavertail with palm swell; elongated slot hammer; beveled magazine well. Introduced 1999. From Colt's Manufacturing Co., Inc.
Price: XSE Government (5" barrel) **$950.00**
Price: XSE Commander (4.25" barrel) **$950.00**

Colt XSE Lightweight Commander

Colt Defender

Colt Series 70

Colt 38 Super

Colt Gunsite

CZ 75B 9mm

CZ 75B Decocker

COLT XSE LIGHTWEIGHT COMMANDER AUTO PISTOL

Caliber: 45 ACP, 8-shot. **Barrel:** 4-1/4". **Weight:** 26 oz. **Length:** 7-3/4" overall. **Grips:** Double diamond checkered rosewood. **Sights:** Fixed, glare-proofed blade front, square notch rear; three-dot system. **Features:** Brushed stainless slide, nickeled aluminum frame; McCormick elongated-slot enhanced hammer, McCormick two-cut adjustable aluminum hammer. Made in U.S.A. by Colt's Mfg. Co., Inc.
Price: 45, stainless **$950.00**

COLT DEFENDER

Caliber: 40 S&W, 45 ACP, 7-shot magazine. **Barrel:** 3". **Weight:** 22-1/2 oz. **Length:** 6-3/4" overall. **Grips:** Pebble-finish rubber wraparound with finger grooves. **Sights:** White dot front, snag-free Colt competition rear. **Features:** Stainless finish; aluminum frame; combat-style hammer; Hi Ride grip safety, extended manual safety, disconnect safety. Introduced 1998. Made in U.S.A. by Colt's Mfg. Co.
Price: **$773.00**
Price: 41 Magnum Model, from. **$825.00**

COLT SERIES 70
NEW!

Caliber: 45 ACP. **Barrel:** 5". **Weight:** NA **Length:** NA **Grips:** Rosewood with double diamond checkering pattern. **Sights:** Fixed. **Features:** A custom replica of the Original Series 70 pistol with a Series 70 firing system, original rollmarks. Introduced 2002. Made in U.S.A. by Colt's Manufacturing.
Price: . . . . **NA**

COLT 38 SUPER
NEW!

Caliber: 38 Super **Barrel:** 5" **Weight:** NA. **Length:** 8-1/2" **Grips:** Checkered rubber (Stainless and blue models); Wood with double diamond checkering pattern (Bright stainless model). **Sights:** 3-dot. **Features:** Beveled magazine well, standard thumb safety and service-style grip safety. Introduced 2003. Made in U.S.A. by Colt's Mfg. Co.
Price: . . . . (Blue) **$864.00** (Stainless steel) **$943.00**
Price: . . . . (Bright stainless steel) **$1,152.00**

COLT GUNSITE PISTOL
NEW!

Caliber: 45 ACP **Barrel:** 5". **Weight:** NA. **Length:** NA. **Grips:** Rosewood. **Sights:** Heinie, front; Novak, rear. **Features:** Contains most all of the Gunsite school recommended features such as Series 70 firing system, Smith & Alexander metal grip safety w/palm swell, serrated flat mainspring housing, dehorned all around. Available in blue or stainless steel. Introduced 2003. Made in U.S.A. by Colt's Mfg. Co.
Price: . . . . **NA**

CZ 75B AUTO PISTOL

Caliber: 9mm Para., 40 S&W, 10-shot magazine. **Barrel:** 4.7". **Weight:** 34.3 oz. **Length:** 8.1" overall. **Grips:** High impact checkered plastic. **Sights:** Square post front, rear adjustable for windage; three-dot system. **Features:** Single action/double action design; firing pin block safety; choice of black polymer, matte or high-polish blue finishes. All-steel frame. Imported from the Czech Republic by CZ-USA.
Price: Black polymer **$472.00**
Price: Glossy blue. **$486.00**
Price: Dual tone or satin nickel **$486.00**
Price: 22 LR conversion unit. **$279.00**

CZ 75B Decocker

Similar to the CZ 75B except has a decocking lever in place of the safety lever. All other specifications are the same. Introduced 1999. Imported from the Czech Republic by CZ-USA.
Price: 9mm, black polymer **$467.00**
Price: 40 S&W **$481.00**

CZ 75B Compact Auto Pistol

Similar to the CZ 75 except has 10-shot magazine, 3.9" barrel and weighs 32 oz. Has removable front sight, non-glare ribbed slide top. Trigger guard is squared and serrated; combat hammer. Introduced 1993. Imported from the Czech Republic by CZ-USA.
Price: 9mm, black polymer **$499.00**
Price: Dual tone or satin nickel **$513.00**
Price: D Compact, black polymer **$526.00**

CZ 85

CZ 97B

CZ 75/85 Kadet

CZ 100

**Dan Wesson Firearms
Pointman Major**

CZ 75M IPSC Auto Pistol

Similar to the CZ 75B except has a longer frame and slide, slightly larger grip to accommodate new heavy-duty magazine. Ambidextrous thumb safety, safety notch on hammer; two-port in-frame compensator; slide racker; frame-mounted Firepoint red dot sight. Introduced 2001. Imported from the Czech Republic by CZ USA.

Price: 40 S&W, 10-shot mag. **$1,551.00**
Price: CZ 75 Standard IPSC (40 S&W, adj. sights) **$1,038.00**

CZ 85B Auto Pistol

Same gun as the CZ 75 except has ambidextrous slide release and safety-levers; non-glare, ribbed slide top; squared, serrated trigger guard; trigger stop to prevent overtravel. Introduced 1986. Imported from the Czech Republic by CZ-USA.

Price: Black polymer. **$483.00**
Price: Combat, black polymer. **$540.00**
Price: Combat, dual tone **$487.00**
Price: Combat, glossy blue. **$499.00**

CZ 85 Combat

Similar to the CZ 85B (9mm only) except has an adjustable rear sight, adjustable trigger for overtravel, free-fall magazine, extended magazine catch. Does not have the firing pin block safety. Introduced 1999. Imported from the Czech Republic by CZ-USA.

Price: 9mm, black polymer **$540.00**
Price: 9mm, glossy blue **$566.00**
Price: 9mm, dual tone or satin nickel **$586.00**

CZ 83B DOUBLE-ACTION PISTOL

Caliber: 9mm Makarov, 32 ACP, 380 ACP, 10-shot magazine. **Barrel:** 3.8". **Weight:** 26.2 oz. **Length:** 6.8" overall. **Grips:** High impact checkered plastic. **Sights:** Removable square post front, rear adjustable for windage; three-dot system. **Features:** Single action/double action; ambidextrous magazine release and safety. Blue finish; non-glare ribbed slide top. Imported from the Czech Republic by CZ-USA.

Price: Blue **$378.00**
Price: Nickel **$397.00**

CZ 97B AUTO PISTOL

Caliber: 45 ACP, 10-shot magazine. **Barrel:** 4.85". **Weight:** 40 oz. **Length:** 8.34" overall. **Grips:** Checkered walnut. **Sights:** Fixed. **Features:** Single action/double action; full-length slide rails; screw-in barrel bushing; linkless barrel; all-steel construction; chamber loaded indicator; dual transfer bars. Introduced 1999. Imported from the Czech Republic by CZ-USA.

Price: Black polymer. **$625.00**
Price: Glossy blue. **$641.00**

CZ 75/85 KADET AUTO PISTOL

Caliber: 22 LR, 10-shot magazine. **Barrel:** 4.88". **Weight:** 36 oz. **Grips:** High impact checkered plastic. **Sights:** Blade front, fully adjustable rear. **Features:** Single action/double action mechanism; all-steel construction. Duplicates weight, balance and function of the CZ 75 pistol. Introduced 1999. Imported from the Czech Republic by CZ-USA.

Price: Black polymer. **$486.00**

CZ 100 AUTO PISTOL

Caliber: 9mm Para., 40 S&W, 10-shot magazine. **Barrel:** 3.7". **Weight:** 24 oz. **Length:** 6.9" overall. **Grips:** Grooved polymer. **Sights:** Blade front with dot, white outline rear drift adjustable for windage. **Features:** Double action only with firing pin block; polymer frame, steel slide; has laser sight mount. Introduced 1996. Imported from the Czech Republic by CZ-USA.

Price: 9mm Para. **$405.00**
Price: 40 S&W **$424.00**

DAN WESSON FIREARMS POINTMAN MAJOR AUTO PISTOL

Caliber: 45 ACP. **Barrel:** 5". **Grips:** Rosewood checkered. **Sights: Features:** Blued or stainless steel frame and serrated slide; Chip McCormick match-grade trigger group, sear and disconnect; match-grade barrel; high-ride beavertail safety; checkered slide release; high rib; interchangeable sight system; laser engraved. Introduced 2000. Made in U.S.A. by Dan Wesson Firearms.

Price: Model PM1-B (blued) **$799.00**
Price: Model PM1-S (stainless) **$799.00**

Dan Wesson Firearms Pointman Seven Auto Pistols

Similar to Pointman Major, dovetail adjustable target rear sight and dovetail target front sight. Available in blued or stainless finish. Introduced 2000. Made in U.S.A. by Dan Wesson Firearms.

Price: PM7 (blued frame and slide) **$999.00**
Price: PM7S (stainless finish). **$1,099.00**

Dan Wesson Firearms Pointman Guardian Auto Pistols

Similar to Pointman Major, more compact frame with 4.25" barrel. Avaiable in blued or stainless finish with fixed or adjustable sights. Introduced 2000. Made in U.S.A. by Dan Wesson Firearms.

Price: PMG-FS, all new frame (fixed sights) **$769.00**
Price: PMG-AS (blued frame and slide, adjustable sights) **$799.00**
Price: PMGD-FS Guardian Duce, all new frame (stainless frame and blued slide, fixed sights) **$829.00**
Price: PMGD-AS Guardian Duce (stainless frame and blued slide, adj. sights) **$799.00**

Dan Wesson Firearms Major Aussie

Dan Wesson Firearms Patriot Marksman

Desert Baby Eagle

Desert Eagle Mark XIX

Dan Wesson Firearms Major Tri-Ops Packs

Similar to Pointman Major. Complete frame assembly fitted to 3 match grade complete slide assemblied (9mm, 10mm, 40 S&W). Includes recoil springs and magazines that come in hard cases fashioned after high-grade European rifle case. Constructed of navy blue cordura stretched over hardwood with black leather trim and comfortable black leather wrapped handle. Brass corner protectors, dual combination locks, engraved presentation plate on the lid. Inside, the Tri-Ops Pack components are nested in precision die-cut closed cell foam and held sercurely in place by convoluted foam in the inside of the lid. Introduced 2002. Made in U.S.A. by Dan Wesson Firearms.

Price: TOP1B (blued), TOP1-S (stainless) **$2.459.00**

Dan Wesson Firearms Major Aussie

Similar to Pointman Major. Available in 45 ACP. Features Bomar-style adjustable rear target sight, unique slide top configuration exclusive to this model (features radius from the flat side surfaces of the slide to a narrow flat on top and then a small redius and reveal ending in a flat, low (1/16" high) sight rib 3/8" wide with lengthwise serrations). Clearly identified by the Southern Cross flag emblem laser engraved on the sides of the slide (available in 45 ACP only). Introduced 2002. Made in U.S.A. by Dan Wesson Firearms.

Price: PMA-B (blued) **$999.00**
Price: PMA-S (stainless) **$1,099.00**

Dan Wesson Firearms Pointman Minor Auto Pistol

Similar to Pointman Major. Full size (5") entry level IDPA or action pistol model with blued carbon alloy frame and round top slide, bead blast matte finish on frame and slide top and radius, satin-brushed polished finish on sides of slide, chromed barrel, dovetail mount fixed rear target sight and tactical/target ramp front sight, match trigger, skeletonized target hammer, high ride beavertail, fitted extractor, serrations on thumb safety, slide release and mag release, lowered and relieved ejection port, beveled mag well, exotic hardwood grips, serrated mainspring housing, laser engraved. Introduced 2000. Made in U.S.A. by Dan Wesson Firearms.

Price: Model PM2-P **$599.00**

Dan Wesson Firearms Pointman Hi-Cap Auto Pistol

Similar to Pointman Minor, full-size high-capacity (10-shot) magazine with 5" chromed barrel, blued finish and dovetail fixed rear sight. Match adjustable trigger, ambidextrous extended thumb safety, beavertail safety. Introduced 2001. From Dan Wesson Firearms.

Price: PMHC (Pointman High-Cap) **$689.00**

Dan Wesson Firearms Pointman Dave Pruitt Signature Series

Similar to other full-sized Pointman models, customized by Master Pistolsmith and IDPA Grand Master Dave Pruitt. Alloy carbon-steel with black oxide bluing and bead-blast matte finish. Front and rear chevron cocking serrations, dovetail mount fixed rear target sight and tactical/target ramp front sight, ramped match barrel with fitted match bushing and link, Chip McCormick (or equivalent) match grade trigger group, serrated ambidextrous tactical/carry thumb safety, high ride beavertail, serrated slide release and checkered mag release, match grade sear and hammer, fitted extractor, lowered and relieved ejection port, beveled mag well, full length 2-piece recoil spring guide rod, cocobolo double diamond checkered grips, serrated steel mainspring housing, special laser engraving. Introduced 2001. From Dan Wesson Firearms.

Price: PMDP (Pointman Dave Pruitt) **$899.00**

DAN WESSON FIREARMS PATRIOT 1911 PISTOL

Caliber: 45 ACP. **Grips:** Exotic exhibition grade cocobolo, double diamond hand cut checkering. **Sights:** New innovative combat/carry rear sight that completely encloses the dovetail. **Features:** The new Patriot Expert and Patriot Marksman are full size match grade series 70 1911s machined from steel forgings. Available in blued chome moly steel or stainless steel. Beveled mag well, lowered and flared ejection port, high sweep beavertail safety. Delivery begins in June 2002.

Price: Model PTM-B (blued) **$797.00**
Price: Model PTM-S (stainless) **$898.00**
Price: Model PTE-B (blued) **$864.00**
Price: Model PTE-S (stainless) **$971.00**

DESERT EAGLE MARK XIX PISTOL

Caliber: 357 Mag., 9-shot; 44 Mag., 8-shot; 50 Magnum, 7-shot. **Barrel:** 6", 10", interchangeable. **Weight:** 357 Mag.—62 oz.; 44 Mag.—69 oz.; 50 Mag.— 72 oz. **Length:** 10-1/4" overall (6" bbl.). **Grips:** Polymer; rubber available. **Sights:** Blade on ramp front, combat-style rear. Adjustable available. **Features:** Interchangeable barrels; rotating three-lug bolt; ambidextrous safety; adjustable trigger. Military epoxy finish. Satin, bright nickel, hard chrome, polished and blued finishes available. 10" barrel extra. Imported from Israel by Magnum Research, Inc.

Price: 357, 6" bbl., standard pistol **$1,199.00**
Price: 44 Mag., 6", standard pistol **$1,199.00**
Price: 50 Magnum, 6" bbl., standard pistol **$1,199.00**

DESERT BABY EAGLE PISTOLS

Caliber: 9mm Para., 40 S&W, 45 ACP, 10-round magazine. **Barrel:** 3.5", 3.7", 4.72". **Weight:** NA. **Length:** 7.25" to 8.25" overall. **Grips:** Polymer. **Sights:** Drift-adjustable rear, blade front. **Features:** Steel frame and slide; polygonal rifling to reduce barrel wear; slide safety; decocker. Reintroduced in 1999. Imported from Israel by Magnum Research Inc.

Price: Standard (9mm or 40 cal.; 4.72" barrel, 8.25" overall) **$499.00**
Price: Semi-Compact (9mm, 40 or 45 cal.; 3.7" barrel,
7.75" overall) **$499.00**
Price: Compact (9mm or 40 cal.; 3.5" barrel, 7.25" overall) **$499.00**
Price: Polymer (9mm or 40 cal; polymer frame; 3.25" barrel,
7.25" overall) **$499.00**

EAA Witness

Ed Brown Commander Bobtail

Ed Brown Kobra Carry

Entréprise Elite P500

Entréprise Boxer P500

Entréprise Tactical 500

EAA WITNESS DA AUTO PISTOL

Caliber: 9mm Para., 10-shot magazine; 38 Super, 40 S&W, 10-shot magazine; 45 ACP, 10-shot magazine. **Barrel:** 4.50". **Weight:** 35.33 oz. **Length:** 8.10" overall. **Grips:** Checkered rubber. **Sights:** Undercut blade front, open rear adjustable for windage. **Features:** Double-action trigger system; round trigger guard; frame-mounted safety. Introduced 1991. Imported from Italy by European American Armory.

Price: 9mm, blue.	$449.00
Price: 9mm, Wonder finish	$459.00
Price: 9mm Compact, blue, 10-shot	$449.00
Price: As above, Wonder finish	$459.60
Price: 40 S&W, blue	$449.60
Price: As above, Wonder finish	$459.60
Price: 40 S&W Compact, 9-shot, blue	$449.60
Price: As above, Wonder finish	$459.60
Price: 45 ACP, blue	$449.00
Price: As above, Wonder finish	$459.60
Price: 45 ACP Compact, 8-shot, blue	$449.00
Price: As above, Wonder finish	$459.60

EAA EUROPEAN MODEL AUTO PISTOLS

Caliber: 32 ACP or 380 ACP, 7-shot magazine. **Barrel:** 3.88". **Weight:** 26 oz. **Length:** 7-3/8" overall. **Grips:** European hardwood. **Sights:** Fixed blade front, rear drift-adjustable for windage. **Features:** Chrome or blue finish; magazine, thumb and firing pin safeties; external hammer; safety-lever takedown. Imported from Italy by European American Armory.

Price: Blue	$132.60
Price: Wonder finish	$163.80

EAA/BUL 1911 AUTO PISTOL

Caliber: 45 ACP. **Barrel:** 3", 4", 5". **Weight:** 24-30 oz. **Length:** 7-10". **Grips:** Full checkered. **Sights:** Tactical rear, dove tail front. **Features:** Lightweight polymer frame, extended beavertail, skeletonized trigger and hammer, beveled mag well.

Price: Blue	$559.00
Price: Chrome	$599.00

ED BROWN COMMANDER BOBTAIL

Caliber: 45 ACP, 400 Cor-Bon, 40 S&W, 357 SIG, 38 Super, 9mm Luger, 7-shot magazine. **Barrel:** 4.25". **Weight:** 34 oz. **Grips:** Hogue exotic wood. **Sights:** Customer preference front; fixed Novak low-mount, rear. Optional night inserts available. **Features:** Checkered forestrap and bobtailed mainspring housing. Other options available.

Price:	$2,300.00

ED BROWN KOBRA, KOBRA CARRY

Caliber: 45 ACP, 7-shot magazine. **Barrel:** 5" (Kobra); 4.25" (Kobra Carry). **Weight:** 39 oz. (Kobra); 34 oz. (Kobra Carry). **Grips:** Hogue exotic wood. **Sights:** Ramp, front; fixed Novak low-mount night sights, rear. **Features:** Has snakeskin pattern serrations on forestrap and mainspring housing, denorned edges, beavertail grip safety.

Price:	**$1,795.00** (Kobra); **$1,995.00** (Kobra Carry)

ENTRÉPRISE ELITE P500 AUTO PISTOL

Caliber: 45 ACP, 10-shot magazine. **Barrel:** 5". **Weight:** 40 oz. **Length:** 8.5" overall. **Grips:** Black ultra-slim, double diamond, checkered synthetic. **Sights:** Dovetailed blade front, rear adjustable for windage; three-dot system. **Features:** Reinforced dust cover; lowered and flared ejection port; squared trigger guard; adjustable match trigger; bolstered front strap; high grip cut; high ride beavertail grip safety; steel flat mainspring housing; extended thumb lock; skeletonized hammer, match grade sear, disconnector; Wolff springs. Introduced 1998. Made in U.S.A. by Entréprise Arms.

Price:	$739.90

Entréprise Boxer P500 Auto Pistol

Similar to the Medalist model except has adjustable Competizione "melded" rear sight with dovetailed Patridge front; high mass chiseled slide with sweep cut; machined slide parallel rails; polished breech face and barrel channel. Introduced 1998. Made in U.S.A. by Entréprise Arms.

Price:	$1,399.00

Entréprise Medalist P500 Auto Pistol

Similar to the Elite model except has adjustable Competizione "melded" rear sight with dovetailed Patridge front; machined slide parallel rails with polished breech face and barrel channel; front and rear slide serrations; lowered and flared ejection port; full-length one-piece guide rod with plug; National Match barrel and bushing; stainless firing pin; tuned match extractor; oversize firing pin stop; throated barrel and polished ramp; slide lapped to frame. Introduced 1998. Made in U.S.A. by Entréprise Arms.

Price: 45 ACP	$979.00
Price: 40 S&W	$1,099.00

Entréprise Tactical P500 Auto Pistol

Similar to the Elite model except has Tactical2 Ghost Ring sight or Novak lo-mount sight; ambidextrous thumb safety; front and rear slide serrations; full-length guide rod; throated barrel, polished ramp; tuned match extractor; fitted barrel and bushing; stainless firing pin; slide lapped to frame; dehorned. Introduced 1998. Made in U.S.A. by Entréprise Arms.

Price:	$979.90
Price: Tactical Plus (full-size frame, Officer's slide)	$1,049.00

FEG PJK-9HP

Felk MTF 450

Firestorm Mini

Firestorm 45 Gov't

Glock 17C

Glock 22

ERMA KGP68 AUTO PISTOL

Caliber: 32 ACP, 6-shot, 380 ACP, 5-shot. **Barrel:** 4". **Weight:** 22-1/2 oz. **Length:** 7-3/8" overall. **Grips:** Checkered plastic. **Sights:** Fixed. **Features:** Toggle action similar to original "Luger" pistol. Action stays open after last shot. Has magazine and sear disconnect safety systems.
Price: **$499.95**

FEG PJK-9HP AUTO PISTOL

Caliber: 9mm Para., 10-shot magazine. **Barrel:** 4.75". **Weight:** 32 oz. **Length:** 8" overall. **Grips:** Hand-checkered walnut. **Sights:** Blade front, rear adjustable for windage; three dot system. **Features:** Single action; polished blue or hard chrome finish; rounded combat-style serrated hammer. Comes with two magazines and cleaning rod. Imported from Hungary by K.B.I., Inc.
Price: Blue **$259.95**
Price: Hard chrome. **$259.95**

FEG SMC-380 AUTO PISTOL

Caliber: 380 ACP, 6-shot magazine. **Barrel:** 3.5". **Weight:** 18.5 oz. **Length:** 6.1" overall. **Grips:** Checkered composition with thumbrest. **Sights:** Blade front, rear adjustable for windage. **Features:** Patterned after the PPK pistol. Alloy frame, steel slide; double action. Blue finish. Comes with two magazines, cleaning rod. Imported from Hungary by K.B.I., Inc.
Price: **$224.95**

FELK MTF 450 AUTO PISTOL

Caliber: 9mm Para. (10-shot); 40 S&W (8-shot); 45 ACP (9-shot magazine). **Barrel:** 3.5". **Weight:** 19.9 oz. **Length:** 6.4" overall. **Grips:** Checkered. **Sights:** Blade front; adjustable rear. **Features:** Double-action-only trigger, striker fired; polymer frame; trigger safety, firing pin safety, trigger bar safety; adjustable trigger weight; fully interchangeable slide/barrel to change calibers. Introduced 1998. Imported by Felk Inc.
Price: **$395.00**
Price: 45 ACP pistol with 9mm and 40 S&W slide/barrel assemblies **$999.00**

FIRESTORM AUTO PISTOL

Features: 7 or 10 rd. double action pistols with matte, duotone or nickel finish. Distributed by SGS Importers International.
Price: 22 LR 10 rd, 380 7 rd. matte. **$264.95**
Price: Duotone **$274.95**
Price: Mini 9mm, 40 S&W, 10 rd. matte **$383.95**
Price: Duotone **$391.95**
Price: Nickel **$408.95**
Price: Mini 45, 7 rd. matte. **$383.95**

Price: Duotone 45. . . . . **$399.95**
Price: Nickel 45. . . . . **$416.95**
Price: 45 Government, Compact, 7 rd. matte **$324.95**
Price: Duotone **$333.95**
Price: Extra magazines. **$29.95-49.95**

GLOCK 17 AUTO PISTOL

Caliber: 9mm Para., 10-shot magazine. **Barrel:** 4.49". **Weight:** 22.04 oz. (without magazine). **Length:** 7.32" overall. **Grips:** Black polymer. **Sights:** Dot on front blade, white outline rear adjustable for windage. **Features:** Polymer frame, steel slide; double-action trigger with "Safe Action" system; mechanical firing pin safety, drop safety; simple takedown without tools; locked breech, recoil operated action. Adopted by Austrian armed forces 1983. NATO approved 1984. Imported from Austria by Glock, Inc.
Price: Fixed sight, with extra magazine, magazine loader, cleaning kit **$641.00**
Price: Adjustable sight **$671.00**
Price: Model 17L (6" barrel) **$800.00**
Price: Model 17C, ported barrel (compensated) **$646.00**

Glock 19 Auto Pistol

Similar to the Glock 17 except has a 4" barrel, giving an overall length of 6.85" and weight of 20.99 oz. Magazine capacity is 10 rounds. Fixed or adjustable rear sight. Introduced 1988.
Price: Fixed sight **$641.00**
Price: Adjustable sight **$671.00**
Price: Model 19C, ported barrel **$646.00**

Glock 20 10mm Auto Pistol

Similar to the Glock Model 17 except chambered for 10mm Automatic cartridge. Barrel length is 4.60", overall length is 7.59", and weight is 26.3 oz. (without magazine). Magazine capacity is 10 rounds. Fixed or adjustable rear sight. Comes with an extra magazine, magazine loader, cleaning rod and brush. Introduced 1990. Imported from Austria by Glock, Inc.
Price: Fixed sight **$700.00**
Price: Adjustable sight **$730.00**

Glock 21 Auto Pistol

Similar to the Glock 17 except chambered for 45 ACP, 10-shot magazine. Overall length is 7.59", weight is 25.2 oz. (without magazine). Fixed or adjustable rear sight. Introduced 1991.
Price: Fixed sight **$700.00**
Price: Adjustable sight **$730.00**

Glock 26

Glock 30

Glock 31

Glock 35

Hammerli Trailside

Glock 22 Auto Pistol

Similar to the Glock 17 except chambered for 40 S&W, 10-shot magazine. Overall length is 7.28", weight is 22.3 oz. (without magazine). Fixed or adjustable rear sight. Introduced 1990.

Price: Fixed sight	**$641.00**
Price: Adjustable sight	**$671.00**
Price: Model 22C, ported barrel	**$646.00**

Glock 23 Auto Pistol

Similar to the Glock 19 except chambered for 40 S&W, 10-shot magazine. Overall length is 6.85", weight is 20.6 oz. (without magazine). Fixed or adjustable rear sight. Introduced 1990.

Price: Fixed sight	**$641.00**
Price: Model 23C, ported barrel	**$646.00**
Price: Adjustable sight	**$671.00**

GLOCK 26, 27 AUTO PISTOLS

Caliber: 9mm Para. (M26), 10-shot magazine; 40 S&W (M27), 9-shot magazine. **Barrel:** 3.46". **Weight:** 21.75 oz. **Length:** 6.29" overall. **Grips:** Integral. Stippled polymer. **Sights:** Dot on front blade, fixed or fully adjustable white outline rear. **Features:** Subcompact size. Polymer frame, steel slide; double-action trigger with "Safe Action" system, three safeties. Matte black Tenifer finish. Hammer-forged barrel. Imported from Austria by Glock, Inc. Introduced 1996.

Price: Fixed sight	**$641.00**
Price: Adjustable sight	**$671.00**

GLOCK 29, 30 AUTO PISTOLS

Caliber: 10mm (M29), 45 ACP (M30), 10-shot magazine. **Barrel:** 3.78". **Weight:** 24 oz. **Length:** 6.7" overall. **Grips:** Integral. Stippled polymer. **Sights:** Dot on front, fixed or fully adjustable white outline rear. **Features:** Compact size. Polymer frame steel slide; double-recoil spring reduces recoil; Safe Action system with three safeties; Tenifer finish. Two magazines supplied. Introduced 1997. Imported from Austria by Glock, Inc.

Price: Fixed sight	**$700.00**
Price: Adjustable sight	**$730.00**

Glock 31/31C Auto Pistols

Similar to the Glock 17 except chambered for 357 Auto cartridge; 10-shot magazine. Overall length is 7.32", weight is 23.28 oz. (without magazine). Fixed or adjustable sight. Imported from Austria by Glock, Inc.

Price: Fixed sight	**$641.00**
Price: Adjustable sight	**$671.00**
Price: Model 31C, ported barrel	**$646.00**

Glock 32/32C Auto Pistols

Similar to the Glock 19 except chambered for the 357 Auto cartridge; 10-shot magazine. Overall length is 6.85", weight is 21.52 oz. (without magazine). Fixed or adjustable sight. Imported from Austria by Glock, Inc.

Price: Fixed sight	**$616.00**
Price: Adjustable sight	**$644.00**
Price: Model 32C, ported barrel	**$646.00**

Glock 33 Auto Pistol

Similar to the Glock 26 except chambered for the 357 Auto cartridge; 9-shot magazine. Overall length is 6.29", weight is 19.75 oz. (without magazine). Fixed or adjustable sight. Imported from Austria by Glock, Inc.

Price: Fixed sight	**$641.00**
Price: Adjustable sight	**$671.00**

GLOCK 34, 35 AUTO PISTOLS

Caliber: 9mm Para. (M34), 40 S&W (M35), 10-shot magazine. **Barrel:** 5.32". **Weight:** 22.9 oz. **Length:** 8.15" overall. **Grips:** Integral. Stippled polymer. **Sights:** Dot on front, fully adjustable white outline rear. **Features:** Polymer frame, steel slide; double-action trigger with "Safe Action" system; three safeties; Tenifer finish. Imported from Austria by Glock, Inc.

Price: Model 34, 9mm	**$770.00**
Price: Model 35, 40 S&W	**$770.00**

GLOCK 36 AUTO PISTOL

Caliber: 45 ACP, 6-shot magazine. **Barrel:** 3.78". **Weight:** 20.11 oz. **Length:** 6.77" overall. **Grips:** Integral. Stippled polymer. **Sights:** Dot on front, fully adjustable white outline rear. **Features:** Polymer frame, steel slide; double-action trigger with "Safe Action" system; three safeties; Tenifer finish. Imported from Austria by Glock, Inc.

Price: Fixed sight	**$700.00**
Price: Adj. sight	**$730.00**

HAMMERLI "TRAILSIDE" TARGET PISTOL

Caliber: 22 LR. **Barrel:** 4.5", 6". **Weight:** 28 oz. **Grips:** Synthetic. **Sights:** Fixed. **Features:** 10-shot magazine. Imported from Switzerland by Sigarms. Distributed by Hammerli U.S.A.

Price:	**$579.00**

HECKLER & KOCH USP AUTO PISTOL

Caliber: 9mm Para., 10-shot magazine, 40 S&W, 10-shot magazine. **Barrel:** 4.25". **Weight:** 28 oz. (USP40). **Length:** 6.9" overall. **Grips:** Non-slip stippled black polymer. **Sights:** Blade front, rear adjustable for windage. **Features:** New HK design with polymer frame, modified Browning action with recoil reduction system, single control lever. Special "hostile environment" finish on all metal parts. Available in SA/DA, DAO, left- and right-hand versions. Introduced 1993. Imported from Germany by Heckler & Koch, Inc.

Price: Right-hand	**$827.00**
Price: Left-hand	**$852.00**
Price: Stainless steel, right-hand	**$888.00**
Price: Stainless steel, left-hand	**$913.00**

Heckler & Koch
USP Compact

Heckler & Koch USP45

Heckler & Koch
USP45 Compact

Heckler & Koch
USP45 Tactical

Heckler & Koch
Elite

Heckler & Koch
Mark 23 Special Operations

Heckler & Koch P7M8

HECKLER & KOCH USP COMPACT AUTO PISTOL

Similar to the USP except has 3.58" barrel, measures 6.81" overall, and weighs 1.60 lbs. (9mm). Available in 9mm Para. 357 SIG or 40 S&W with 10-shot magazine. Introduced 1996. Imported from Germany by Heckler & Koch, Inc.

Price: Blue $786.00
Price: Blue with control lever on right $821.00
Price: Same as USP Compact DAO, enhanced trigger
    performance $821.00

Heckler & Koch USP45 Auto Pistol

Similar to the 9mm and 40 S&W USP except chambered for 45 ACP, 10-shot magazine. Has 4.13" barrel, overall length of 7.87" and weighs 30.4 oz. Has adjustable three-dot sight system. Available in SA/DA, DAO, left- and right-hand versions. Introduced 1995. Imported from Germany by Heckler & Koch, Inc.

Price: Right-hand $827.00
Price: Left-hand $862.00
Price: Stainless steel right-hand $888.00
Price: Stainless steel left-hand $923.00

Heckler & Koch USP45 Compact

Similar to the USP45 except has stainless slide; 8-shot magazine; modified and contoured slide and frame; extended slide release; 3.80" barrel, 7.09" overall length, weighs 1.75 lbs.; adjustable three-dot sights. Introduced 1998. Imported from Germany by Heckler & Koch, Inc.

Price: With control lever on left, stainless $909.00
Price: As above, blue $857.00
Price: With control lever on right, stainless $944.00
Price: As above, blue $892.00

HECKLER & KOCH USP45 TACTICAL PISTOL

Caliber: 45 ACP, 10-shot magazine. **Barrel:** 4.92". **Weight:** 2.24 lbs. **Length:** 8.64" overall. **Grips:** Non-slip stippled polymer. **Sights:** Blade front, fully adjustable target rear. **Features:** Has extended threaded barrel with rubber O-ring; adjustable trigger; extended magazine floorplate; adjustable trigger stop; polymer frame. Introduced 1998. Imported from Germany by Heckler & Koch, Inc.

Price: $1,124.00

HECKLER & KOCH MARK 23 SPECIAL OPERATIONS PISTOL

Caliber: 45 ACP, 10-shot magazine. **Barrel:** 5.87". **Weight:** 43 oz. **Length:** 9.65" overall. **Grips:** Integral with frame; black polymer. **Sights:** Blade front, rear drift adjustable for windage; three-dot. **Features:** Polymer frame; double action; exposed hammer; short recoil, modified Browning

action. Civilian version of the SOCOM pistol. Introduced 1996. Imported from Germany by Heckler & Koch, Inc.

Price: $2,444.00

HECKLER & KOCH USP EXPERT PISTOL

Combines features of the USP Tactical and HK Mark 23 pistols with a new slide design. Chambered for 45 ACP, .40 S&W & 9mm; 10-shot magazine. Has adjustable target sights, 5.20" barrel, 8.74" overall length, weighs 1.87 lbs. Match-grade single- and double-action trigger pull with adjustable stop; ambidextrous control levers; elongated target slide; barrel O-ring that seals and centers barrel. Suited to IPSC competition. Introduced 1999. Imported from Germany by Heckler & Koch, Inc.

Price: $1,533.00

HECKLER & KOCH ELITE

A long slide version of the USP combining features found on standard-sized and specialized models of the USP. Most noteworthy is the 6.2-inch barrel, making it the most accurate of the USP series. In 9mm and .45 ACP. Imported from Germany by Heckler & Koch, Inc. Introduced 2003.

Price: $1,533.00

HECKLER & KOCH P7M8 AUTO PISTOL

Caliber: 9mm Para., 8-shot magazine. **Barrel:** 4.13". **Weight:** 29 oz. **Length:** 6.73" overall. **Grips:** Stippled black plastic. **Sights:** Blade front, adjustable rear; three dot system. **Features:** Unique "squeeze cocker" in frontstrap cocks the action. Gas-retarded action. Squared combat-type trigger guard. Blue finish. Compact size. Imported from Germany by Heckler & Koch, Inc.

Price: P7M8, blued $1,472.00

Hi-Point 9MM Comp

Kahr K9

Kahr MK40

Kel-Tec P-11

NEW!

HECKLER & KOCH P2000 GPM PISTOL

Caliber: 9mmx19; 10-shot magazine. 13- or 16-round law enforcment/military magazines. **Barrel:** 3.62". **Weight:** 21.87 ozs. **Length:** 7". **Grips:** Interchangeable panels. **Sights:** Fixed partridge style, drift adjustable for windage, standard 3-dot. **Features:** German Pistol Model incorporating features of the HK USP Compact such as the pre-cocked hammer system which combines the advantages of a cocked striker with the double action hammer system. Introduced 2003. Imported from Germany by Heckler & Koch, Inc.
Price: .... **NA**

HI-POINT FIREARMS 9MM COMP PISTOL

Caliber: 9mm, Para., 10-shot magazine. **Barrel:** 4". **Weight:** 39 oz. **Length:** 7.72" overall. **Grips:** Textured acetal plastic. **Sights:** Adjustable; low profile. **Features:** Single-action design. Scratch-resistant, non-glare blue finish, alloy frame. Muzzle brake/compensator. Compensator is slotted for laser or flashlight mounting. Introduced 1998. From MKS Supply, Inc.
Price: Matte black **$159.00**

HI-POINT FIREARMS MODEL 9MM COMPACT PISTOL

Caliber: 9mm Para., 8-shot magazine. **Barrel:** 3.5". **Weight:** 29 oz. **Length:** 6.7" overall. **Grips:** Textured acetal plastic. **Sights:** Combat-style adjustable three-dot system; low profile. **Features:** Single-action design; frame-mounted magazine release; polymer or alloy frame. Scratch-resistant matte finish. Introduced 1993. Made in U.S.A. by MKS Supply, Inc.
Price: Black, alloy frame **$137.00**
Price: With polymer frame (29 oz.), non-slip grips **$137.00**
Price: Aluminum with polymer frame **$137.00**

Hi-Point Firearms Model 380 Polymer Pistol

Similar to the 9mm Compact model except chambered for 380 ACP, 8-shot magazine, adjustable three-dot sights. Weighs 29 oz. Polymer frame. Introduced 1998. Made in U.S.A. by MKS Supply.
Price: **$109.00**

Hi-Point Firearms 380 Comp Pistol

Similar to the 380 Polymer Pistol except has a 4" barrel with muzzle compensator; action locks open after last shot. Includes a 10-shot and an 8-shot magazine; trigger lock. Introduced 2001. Made in U.S.A. by MKS Supply Inc.
Price: **$125.00**
Price: With laser sight **$190.00**

Hi-Point Firearms 45 Polymer Frame

NEW!
Caliber: .45 ACP, 9-shot. **Barrel:** 4.5". **Weight:** 35 oz. **Sights:** Adjustable 3-dot. **Features:** Last round lock-open, grip mounted magazine release, magazine disconnect safety, integrated accessory rail. Introduced 2002. Made in U.S.A. by MKS Supply Inc.
Price: **$169.00**

IAI M-2000 PISTOL

Caliber: 45 ACP, 8-shot. **Barrel:** 5", (Compact 4.25"). **Weight:** 36 oz. **Length:** 8.5", (6" Compact). **Grips:** Plastic or wood. **Sights:** Fixed. **Features:** 1911 Government U.S. Army-style. Steel frame and slide parkerized. GI grip safety. Beveled feed ramp barrel. By IAI, Inc.
Price: **$465.00**

KAHR K9, K40 DA AUTO PISTOLS

Caliber: 9mm Para., 7-shot, 40 S&W, 6-shot magazine. **Barrel:** 3.5". **Weight:** 25 oz. **Length:** 6" overall. **Grips:** Wrap-around textured soft polymer. **Sights:** Blade front, rear drift adjustable for windage; bar-dot combat style. **Features:** Trigger-cocking double-action mechanism with passive firing pin block. Made of 4140 ordnance steel with matte black finish. Contact maker for complete price list. Introduced 1994. Made in U.S.A. by Kahr Arms.
Price: E9, black matte finish **$425.00**
Price: Matte black, night sights 9mm **$668.00**
Price: Matte stainless steel, 9mm...................... **$638.00**
Price: 40 S&W, matte black **$580.00**
Price: 40 S&W, matte black, night sights **$668.00**
Price: 40 S&W, matte stainless **$638.00**
Price: K9 Elite 98 (high-polish stainless slide flats, Kahr combat trigger), from **$694.00**
Price: As above, MK9 Elite 98, from.................... **$694.00**
Price: As above, K40 Elite 98, from **$694.00**
Price: Covert, black, stainless slide, short grip........ **$599.00**
Price: Covert, black, tritium nite sights **$689.00**

Kahr K9 9mm Compact Polymer Pistol

Similar to K9 steel frame pistol except has polymer frame, matte stainless steel slide. Barrel length 3.5"; overall length 6"; weighs 17.9 oz. Includes two 7-shot magazines, hard polymer case, trigger lock. Introduced 2000. Made in U.S.A. by Kahr Arms.
Price: **$599.00**

Kahr MK9/MK40 Micro Pistol

Similar to the K9/K40 except is 5.5" overall, 4" high, has a 3" barrel. Weighs 22 oz. Has snag-free bar-dot sights, polished feed ramp, dual recoil spring system, DA-only trigger. Comes with 6- and 7-shot magazines. Introduced 1998. Made in U.S.A. by Kahr Arms.
Price: Matte stainless **$638.00**
Price: Elite 98, polished stainless, tritium night sights **$791.00**

KAHR PM9 PISTOL

Caliber: 9x19. **Barrel:** 3", 1:10 twist. **Weight:** 15.9 oz. **Length:** 5.3" overall. **Features:** Lightweight black polymer frame, polygonal rifling, stainless steel slide, DAO with passive striker block, trigger lock, hard case, 6 and 7 rd. mags.
Price: Matte stainless slide............................ **$622.00**
Price: Tritium night sights **$719.00**

KEL-TEC P-11 AUTO PISTOL

Caliber: 9mm Para., 10-shot magazine. **Barrel:** 3.1". **Weight:** 14 oz. **Length:** 5.6" overall. **Grips:** Checkered black polymer. **Sights:** Blade front, rear adjustable for windage. **Features:** Ordnance steel slide, aluminum frame. Double-action-only trigger mechanism. Introduced 1995. Made in U.S.A. by Kel-Tec CNC Industries, Inc.
Price: Blue **$314.00**
Price: Hard chrome..................................... **$368.00**
Price: Parkerized **$355.00**

HANDGUNS

Kel-Tec P-32

Kimber Custom II

Kimber Pro Carry II

Kimber Ultra Carry II

Kimber Ten II High Capacity Polymer

Kimber Gold Match II

KEL-TEC P-32 AUTO PISTOL

Caliber: 32 ACP, 7-shot magazine. **Barrel:** 2.68". **Weight:** 6.6 oz. **Length:** 5.07" overall. **Grips:** Checkered composite. **Sights:** Fixed. **Features:** Double-action-only mechanism with 6-lb. pull; internal slide stop. Textured composite grip/frame. Now available in 380 ACP. Made in U.S.A. by Kel-Tec CNC Industries, Inc.

Price: Blue **$300.00**
Price: Hard chrome. $340.00
Price: Parkerized $355.00

KIMBER CUSTOM II AUTO PISTOL

Caliber: 45 ACP, 40 S&W, .38 Super. **Barrel:** 5", match grade, .40 S&W, .38 Super barrels ramped. **Weight:** 38 oz. **Length:** 8.7" overall. **Grips:** Checkered black rubber, walnut, rosewood. **Sights:** Dovetail front and rear, Kimber adjustable or fixed three dot (green) Meptrolight night sights. **Features:** Slide, frame and barrel machined from steel or stainless steel forgings. Match grade barrel, chamber and trigger group. Extended thumb safety, beveled magazine well, beveled front and rear slide serrations, high ride beavertail grip safety, checkered flat mainspring housing, kidney cut under trigger guard, high cut grip, match grade stainless steel berrel bushing, polished breech face, Commander-style hammer, lowered and flared ejection port, Wolff springs, bead blasted black oxide finish. Introduced in 1996. Made in U.S.A. by Kimber Mfg., Inc.

Price: Custom $730.00
Price: Custom Walnut (double-diamond walnut grips) $752.00
Price: Custom Stainless $832.00
Price: Custom Stainless 40 S&W $870.00
Price: Custom Stainless Target 45 ACP (stainless, adj. sight) . . . $945.00
Price: Custom Stainless Target 38 Super $974.00

Kimber Custom II Auto Pistol

Similar to Compact II, 4" bull barrel fitted directly to the stainless steel slide without a bushing, grip is .400" shorter than standard, no front serrations. Weighs 34 oz. 45 ACP only. Introduced in 1998. Made in U.S.A. by Kimber Mfg., Inc.

Price: $870.00

Kimber Pro Carry II Auto Pistol

Similar to Custom II, has aluminum frame, 4" bull barrel fitted directly to the slide without bushing. HD with stainless steel frame. Introduced 1998. Made in U.S.A. by Kimber Mfg., Inc.

Price: 45 ACP $773.00
Price: HD II $879.00
Price: Pro Carry HD II Stainless 45 ACP $845.00
Price: Pro Carry HD II Stainless 38 Spec. $917.00

Kimber Ultra Carry II Auto Pistol

Similar to Compact Stainless II, lightweight aluminum frame, 3" match grade bull barrel fitted to slide without bushing. Grips .400" shorter. Special slide stop. Low effort recoil. Weighs 25 oz. Introduced in 1999. Made in U.S.A. by Kimber Mfg., Inc.

Price: $767.00
Price: Stainless. $841.00
Price: Stainless 40 S&W $884.00

Kimber Ten II High Capacity Polymer Pistol

Similar to Custom II, Pro Carry II and Ultra Carry II depending on barrel length. Ten-round magazine capacity (double stack and flush fitting). Polymer grip frame molded over stainless steel or aluminum (Ultra Ten II only) frame insert. Checkered front strap and belly of trigger guard. All models have fixed sights except Gold Match Ten II, which has adjustable sight. Frame grip dimensions approximate that of the standard 1911 for natural aiming and better recoil control. Ultra Ten II weight is 24 oz. Others 32-34 oz. Additional 14-round magazines available where legal. Much-improved version of the Kimber Polymer series. Made in U.S.A. by Kimber Mfg., Inc.

Price: Ultra Ten II $850.00
Price: Pro Carry Ten II $828.00
Price: Stainless Ten II $812.00

Kimber Gold Match II Auto Pistol

Similar to Custom II models. Includes stainless steel barrel with match grade chamber and barrel bushing, ambidextrous thumb safety, adjustable sight, premium aluminum trigger, hand-checkered double diamond rosewood grips. Barrel hand-fitted to bushing and slide for target accuracy. Made in U.S.A. by Kimber Mfg., Inc.

Price: Gold Match II $1,169.00
Price: Gold Match Stainless II 45 ACP $1,315.00
Price: Gold Match Stainless II 40 S&W $1,345.00

Kimber Gold Match Ten II Polymer Auto Pistol

Similar to Stainless Gold Match II. High capacity polymer frame with ten-round magazine. No ambi thumb safety. Polished flats add elegant look. Introduced 1999. Made in U.S.A. by Kimber Mfg., Inc.

Price: $1,118.00

Kimber Gold Match II

Kimber Gold Combat II

Kimber CDP II

Kimber Eclipse II

Kimber Eclipse Pro II

Kimber LTP II

Llama Micromax 380

Kimber Gold Combat II Auto Pistol

Similar to Gold Match II except designed for concealed carry. Extended and beveled magazine well, Meprolight tritium night sights; premium aluminum trigger; 30 lpi front strap checkering; special Custom Shop markings; Kim Pro premium finish. Introduced 1999. Made in U.S.A. by Kimber Mfg., Inc.

Price: 45 ACP **$1,682.00**
Price: Gold Combat Stainless (satin-finished stainless frame
and slide, special Custom Shop markings). **$1,623.00**

Kimber CDP II Series Auto Pistol

Similar to Custom II, but designed for concealed carry. Aluminum frame. Standard features include stainless steel slide, Meprolight tritium three dot (green) dovetail-mounted night sights, match grade barrel and chamber, 30 LPI front strap checkering, two tone finish, ambidextrous thumb safety, hand-checkered double diamond rosewood grips. Introduced in 2000. Made in U.S.A. by Kimber Mfg., Inc.

Price: Ultra CDP II 40 S&W **$1,120.00**
Price: Ultra CDP II (3 barrel, short grip) **$1,084.00**
Price: Compact CDP II (4 barrel, short grip). **$1,084.00**
Price: Pro CDP II (4 barrel, full length grip) **$1,084.00**
Price: Custom CDP II (5 barrel, full length grip) **$1,084.00**

Kimber Eclipse II Series Auto Pistol

Similar to Custom II and other stainless Kimber pistol.s Stainless slide and frame, black anodized, two tone finish. Gray/black laminated grips. 30 LPI front strap checkering. All have night sights, with Target versions having Meprolight adjustable Bar/Dot version. Made in U.S.A. by Kimber Mfg., Inc.

Price: Eclipse Ultra II (3 barrel, short grip) **$1,052.00**
Price: Eclipse Pro II (4 barrel, full length grip) **$1,052.00**
Price: Eclipse Pro Target II (4 barrel, full length grip,
adjustable sight) **$1,153.00**
Price: Eclipse Custom II (5 barrel, full length grip) **$1,071.00**
Price: Eclipse Target II (5 barrel, full length grip,
adjustable sight) **$1,153.00**

Kimber LTP II Polymer Auto Pistol

Similar to Gold Match II. Built for Limited Ten competition. First Kimber pistol with new, innovative Kimber external extractor. KimPro premium finish. Stainless steel match grade barrel. Extended and beveled magazine well. Checkered front strap and trigger guard belly. Tungsten full length guide rod. Premium aluminum trigger. Ten-round single stack magazine. Wide ambidextrous thumb safety. Made in U.S.A. by Kimber Mfg., Inc.

Price: **$2,036.00**

Kimber Super Match II Auto Pistol

Similar to Gold Match II. Built for target and action shotting competition. Tested for accuracy. Target included. Stainless steel barrel and chamber. KimPro finish on stainless steel slide. Stainless steel frame. 30 LPI checkered front strap, premium aluminum trigger, Kimber adjustable sight. Introduced in 1999.

Price: **$1,926.00**

KORTH PISTOL

Caliber: .40 S&W, .357 SIG (9-shot); 9mm Para, 9x21 (10-shot). **Barrel:** 4" (standard), 5" (optional). Trigger **Weight:** 3.3 lbs. (single Action), 11 lbs. (double action). **Sights:** Fully adjustable. **Features:** All parts of surface-hardened steel; recoil-operated action, mechanically-locked via large pivoting bolot block maintaining parallel positioning of barrel during the complete cycle. Accessories include sound suppressor for qualified buyers. A masterpiece of German precision. Imported by Korth USA.

Price: **$5,413.00**

LLAMA MICROMAX 380 AUTO PISTOL

Caliber: 32 ACP, 8-shot, 380 ACP, 7-shot magazine. **Barrel:** 3-11/16". **Weight:** 23 oz. **Length:** 6-1/2" overall. **Grips:** Checkered high impact polymer. **Sights:** 3-dot combat. **Features:** Single-action design. Mini custom extended slide release; mini custom extended beavertail grip safety; combat-style hammer. Introduced 1997. Distributed by Import Sports, Inc.

Price: Matte blue. **$281.95**
Price: Satin chrome (380 only) **$298.95**

Llama Minimax

Llama Max-1
Government Deluxe

North American
Arms Guardian

Para-Ordnance P12.45

Para-Ordnance LDA

LLAMA MINIMAX SERIES

Caliber: 40 S&W, 7-shot; 45 ACP, 6-shot magazine. **Barrel:** 3-1/2". **Weight:** 35 oz. **Length:** 7-1/3" overall. **Grips:** Checkered rubber. **Sights:** Three-dot combat. **Features:** Single action, skeletonized combat-style hammer, extended slide release, cone-style barrel, flared ejection port. Introduced 1996. Distributed by Import Sports, Inc.

Price: Blue **$333.95**
Price: Duo-Tone finish (45 only) **$342.95**
Price: Satin chrome **$349.95**

Llama Minimax Sub-Compact Auto Pistol

Similar to the Minimax except has 3.14" barrel, weighs 31 oz.; 6.8" overall length; has 10-shot magazine with finger extension; beavertail grip safety. Introduced 1999. Distributed by Import Sports, Inc.

Price: 45 ACP, matte blue **$349.95**
Price: As above, satin chrome **$367.95**
Price: Duo-Tone finish (45 only) **$358.95**

LLAMA MAX-I AUTO PISTOLS

Caliber: 45 ACP, 7-shot. **Barrel:** 5-1/8". **Weight:** 36 oz. **Length:** 8-1/2" overall. **Grips:** Polymer. **Sights:** Blade front; three-dot system. **Features:** Single-action trigger; skeletonized combat-style hammer; steel frame; extended manual and grip safeties, matte finish. Introduced 1995. Distributed by Import Sports, Inc.

Price: 45 ACP, 7-shot, Government model **$324.95**

NORTH AMERICAN ARMS GUARDIAN PISTOL

Caliber: 32 ACP, 380 ACP, 32NAA, 6-shot magazine. **Barrel:** 2.1". **Weight:** 13.5 oz. **Length:** 4.36" overall. **Grips:** Black polymer. **Sights:** Fixed. **Features:** Double-action-only mechanism. All stainless steel construction; snag-free. Introduced 1998. Made in U.S.A. by North American Arms.

Price: .... **$408.00 to $449.00**

OLYMPIC ARMS OA-96 AR PISTOL

Caliber: 223. **Barrel:** 6", 8", 4140 chrome-moly steel. **Weight:** 5 lbs. **Length:** 15-3/4" overall. **Grips:** A2 stowaway pistol grip; no buttstock or receiver tube. **Sights:** Flat-top upper receiver, cut-down front sight base. **Features:** AR-15-type receivers with special bolt carrier; short aluminum hand guard; Vortex flash hider. Introduced 1996. Made in U.S.A. by Olympic Arms, Inc.

Price: **$858.00**

Olympic Arms OA-98 AR Pistol

Similar to the OA-93 except has removable 7-shot magazine, weighs 3 lbs. Introduced 1999. Made in U.S.A. by Olympic Arms, Inc.

Price: **$990.00**

PARA-ORDNANCE P-SERIES AUTO PISTOLS

Caliber: 9mm Para., 40 S&W, 45 ACP, 10-shot magazine. **Barrel:** 3", 3-1/2", 4-1/4", 5". **Weight:** From 24 oz. (alloy frame). **Length:** 8.5" overall. **Grips:** Textured composition. **Sights:** Blade front, rear adjustable for windage. High visibility three-dot system. **Features:** Available with alloy, steel or stainless steel frame with black finish (silver or stainless gun). Steel and stainless steel frame guns weigh 40 oz. (P14.45), 36 oz. (P13.45), 34 oz. (P12.45). Grooved match trigger, rounded combat-style hammer. Beveled magazine well. Manual thumb, grip and firing pin lock safeties. Solid barrel bushing. Contact maker for full details. Introduced 1990. Made in Canada by Para-Ordnance.

Price: Steel frame................................... **$795.00**
Price: Alloy frame **$765.00**
Price: Stainless steel **$865.00**

Para-Ordnance Limited Pistols

Similar to the P-Series pistols except with full-length recoil guide system; fully adjustable rear sight; tuned trigger with overtravel stop; beavertail grip safety; competition hammer; front and rear slide serrations; ambidextrous safety; lowered ejection port; ramped match-grade barrel; dovetailed front sight. Introduced 1998. Made in Canada by Para-Ordnance.

Price: 9mm, 40 S&W, 45 ACP .... **$945.00 to $999.00**

Para-Ordnance LDA Auto Pistols

Similar to P-series except has double-action trigger mechanism. Steel frame with matte black finish, checkered composition grips. Available in 9mm Para., 40 S&W, 45 ACP. Introduced 1999. Made in Canada by Para-Ordnance.

Price: **$775.00**

Para-Ordnance LDA Limited Pistols

Similar to LDA, has ambidextrous safety, adjustable rear sight, front slide serrations and full-length recoil guide system. Made in Canada by Para-Ordnance.

Price: Black finish **$975.00**
Price: Stainless................................... **$1,049.00**

PARA-ORDNANCE C5 45 LDA PARA CARRY

Caliber: 45 ACP. **Barrel:** 3", 6+1 shot. **Weight:** 30 oz. **Length:** 6.5". **Grips:** Double diamond checkered Cocobolo. **Features:** Stainless finish and receiver, "world's smallest DAO 45 auto." Para LDA trigger system and safeties.

Price: **$899.00**

Para-Ordnance C5
45 LDA Para Carry

Para-Ordnance C7
45 LDA Para Companion

Peters Stahl High Capacity

Peters Stahl Trophy Master

Peters Stahl Millenium

Phoenix
Arms HP22

Rock River Standard Match

Ruger P89

Ruger P90

PARA-ORDNANCE C7 45 LDA PARA COMPANION

Caliber: 45 ACP. **Barrel:** 3.5", 7+1 shot. **Weight:** 32 oz. **Length:** 7". **Grips:** Double diamond checkered Cocobolo. **Features:** Para LDA trigger system with Para LDA 3 safeties (slide lock, firing pin block and grip safety). Lightning speed, full size capacity.
Price: **$899.00**

PETERS STAHL AUTOLOADING PISTOLS

Caliber: 9mm Para., 45 ACP. **Barrel:** 5" or 6". **Grips:** Walnut or walnut with rubber wrap. **Sights:** Fully adjustable rear, blade front. **Features:** Stainless steel extended slide stop, safety and extended magazine release button; speed trigger with stop and approx. 3-lb. pull; polished ramp. Introduced 2000. Imported from Germany by Phillips & Rogers.
Price: High Capacity (accepts 15-shot magazines in 45 cal.; includes 10-shot magazine) **$1,695.00**
Price: Trophy Master (blued or stainless, 7-shot in 45,
8-shot in 9mm) **$1,995.00**
Price: Millenium Model (titanium coating on receiver and slide). **$2,195.00**

PHOENIX ARMS HP22, HP25 AUTO PISTOLS

Caliber: 22 LR, 10-shot (HP22), 25 ACP, 10-shot (HP25). **Barrel:** 3". **Weight:** 20 oz. **Length:** 5-1/2" overall. **Grips:** Checkered composition. **Sights:** Blade front, adjustable rear. **Features:** Single action, exposed hammer; manual hold-open; button magazine release. Available in satin nickel, polished blue finish. Introduced 1993. Made in U.S.A. by Phoenix Arms.
Price: With gun lock and cable lanyard. **$130.00**
Price: HP Rangemaster kit with 5" bbl., locking case
and assessories **$171.00**
Price: HP Deluxe Rangemaster kit with 3" and 5" bbls.,
2 mags., case **$210.00**

ROCK RIVER ARMS STANDARD MATCH AUTO PISTOL

Caliber: 45 ACP. **Barrel:** NA. **Weight:** NA. **Length:** NA. **Grips:** Cocobolo, checkered. **Sights:** Heine fixed rear, blade front. **Features:** Chrome-moly steel frame and slide; beavertail grip safety with raised pad; checkered slide stop; ambidextrous safety; polished feed ramp and extractor; aluminum speed trigger with 3.5 lb. pull. Made in U.S.A. From Rock River Arms.
Price: **$1,025.00**

ROCKY MOUNTAIN ARMS PATRIOT PISTOL

Caliber: 223, 10-shot magazine. **Barrel:** 7", with muzzle brake. **Weight:** 5 lbs. **Length:** 20.5" overall. **Grips:** Black composition. **Sights:** None furnished. **Features:** Milled upper receiver with enhanced Weaver base; milled lower receiver from billet plate; machined aluminum National Match handguard. Finished in DuPont Teflon-S matte black or NATO green. Comes with black nylon case, one magazine. Introduced 1993. From Rocky Mountain Arms, Inc.
Price: With A-2 handle top . . . . **$2,500.00 to $2,800.00**
Price: Flat top model. . . . . **$3,000.00 to $3,500.00**

RUGER P89 AUTOLOADING PISTOL

Caliber: 9mm Para., 10-shot magazine. **Barrel:** 4.50". **Weight:** 32 oz. **Length:** 7.84" overall. **Grips:** Grooved black synthetic composition. **Sights:** Square post front, square notch rear adjustable for windage, both with white dot inserts. **Features:** Double action, ambidextrous slide-mounted safety-levers. Slide 4140 chrome-moly steel or 400-series stainless steel, frame lightweight aluminum alloy. Ambidextrous magazine release. Blue, stainless steel. Introduced 1986; stainless 1990.
Price: P89, blue, extra mag and mag loader, plastic case locks . **$475.00**
Price: KP89, stainless, extra mag and mag loader,
plastic case locks **$525.00**

Ruger P93D

Ruger KP94D

Ruger KP95DAO

Ruger KMK 4

Ruger P89D Decocker Autoloading Pistol

Similar to standard P89 except has ambidextrous decocking levers in place of regular slide-mounted safety. Decocking levers move firing pin inside slide where hammer can not reach, while simultaneously blocking firing pin from forward movement—allows shooter to decock cocked pistol without manipulating trigger. Conventional thumb decocking procedures are therefore unnecessary. Blue, stainless steel. Introduced 1990.
Price: P89D, blue, extra mag and mag loader, plastic case locks **$475.00**
Price: KP89D, stainless, extra mag and mag loader,
plastic case locks **$525.00**

Ruger P89 Double-Action-Only Autoloading Pistol

Same as KP89 except operates only in double-action mode. Has spurless hammer, gripping grooves on each side of rear slide; no external safety or decocking lever. Internal safety prevents forward movement of firing pin unless trigger is pulled. Available 9mm Para., stainless steel only. Introduced 1991.
Price: Lockable case, extra mag and mag loader **$525.00**

RUGER P90 MANUAL SAFETY MODEL AUTOLOADING PISTOL

Caliber: 45 ACP, 8-shot magazine. **Barrel:** 4.50". **Weight:** 33.5 oz. **Length:** 7.75" overall. **Grips:** Grooved black synthetic composition. **Sights:** Square post front, square notch rear adjustable for windage, both with white dot. **Features:** Double action ambidextrous slide-mounted safety-levers move firing pin inside slide where hammer can not reach, simultaneously blocking firing pin from forward movement. Stainless steel only. Introduced 1991.
Price: KP90 with extra mag, loader, case and gunlock. **$565.00**
Price: P90 (blue). . . . . :. . **$525.00**

Ruger KP90 Decocker Autoloading Pistol

Similar to the P90 except has a manual decocking system. The ambidextrous decocking levers move the firing pin inside the slide where the hammer can not reach it, while simultaneously blocking the firing pin from forward movement—allows shooter to decock a cocked pistol without manipulating the trigger. Available only in stainless steel. Overall length 7.75", weighs 33.5 oz. Introduced 1991.
Price: KP90D with case, extra mag and mag loading tool **$565.00**

RUGER P93 COMPACT AUTOLOADING PISTOL

Caliber: 9mm Para., 10-shot magazine. **Barrel:** 3.9". **Weight:** 31 oz. **Length:** 7.25" overall. **Grips:** Grooved black synthetic composition. **Sights:** Square post front, square notch rear adjustable for windage. **Features:** Front of slide crowned with convex curve; slide has seven finger grooves; trigger guard bow higher for better grip; 400-series stainless slide, lightweight alloy frame; also blue. Decocker-only or DAO-only. Includes hard case and lock. Introduced 1993. Made in U.S.A. by Sturm, Ruger & Co.
Price: KP93DAO, double-action-only **$575.00**
Price: KP93D ambidextrous decocker, stainless **$575.00**
Price: P93D, ambidextrous decocker, blue **$495.00**

Ruger KP94 Autoloading Pistol

Sized midway between full-size P-Series and compact P93. 4.25" barrel, 7.5" overall length, weighs about 33 oz. KP94 manual safety model; KP94DAO double-action-only (both 9mm Para., 10-shot magazine); KP94D is decocker-only in 40-caliber with 10-shot magazine. Slide gripping grooves roll over top of slide. KP94 has ambidextrous safety-levers; KP94DAO has no external safety, full-cock hammer position or decocking

lever; KP94D has ambidextrous decocking levers. Matte finish stainless slide, barrel, alloy frame. Also blue. Includes hard case and lock. Introduced 1994. Made in U.S.A. by Sturm, Ruger & Co.
Price: P94, P944, blue (manual safety) **$495.00**
Price: KP94 (9mm), KP944 (40-caliber) (manual
safety-stainless) **$575.00**
Price: KP94DAO (9mm), KP944DAO (40-caliber) **$575.00**
Price: KP94D (9mm), KP944D (40-caliber)-decock only **$575.00**

RUGER P95 AUTOLOADING PISTOL

Caliber: 9mm Para., 10-shot magazine. **Barrel:** 3.9". **Weight:** 27 oz. **Length:** 7.25" overall. **Grips:** Grooved; integral with frame. **Sights:** Blade front, rear drift adjustable for windage; three-dot system. **Features:** Moulded polymer grip frame, stainless steel or chrome-moly slide. Suitable for +P+ ammunition. Safety model, decocker or DAO. Introduced 1996. Made in U.S.A. by Sturm, Ruger & Co. Comes with lockable plastic case, spare magazine, loader and lock.
Price: P95 DAO double-action-only **$425.00**
Price: P95D decocker only **$425.00**
Price: KP95D stainless steel decocker only **$475.00**
Price: KP95DAO double-action only, stainless steel. **$475.00**
Price: KP95 safety model, stainless steel. **$475.00**
Price: P95 safety model, blued finish **$425.00**

RUGER P97 AUTOLOADING PISTOL

Caliber: 45ACP 8-shot magazine. **Barrel:** 4-1/8". **Weight:** 30-1/2 oz. **Length:** 7-1/4" overall. Grooved: Integral with frame. **Sights:** Blade front, rear drift adjustable for windage; three dot system. **Features:** Moulded polymer grip frame, stainless steel slide. Decocker or DAO. Introduced 1997. Made in U.S.A. by Sturm, Ruger & Co. Comes with lockable plastic case, spare magaline, loading tool.
Price: KP97D decocker only. **$495.00**
Price: KP97DAO double-action only **$495.00**
Price: P97D decocker only, blued **$460.00**

RUGER MARK II STANDARD AUTOLOADING PISTOL

Caliber: 22 LR, 10-shot magazine. **Barrel:** 4-3/4" or 6". **Weight:** 35 oz. (4-3/4" bbl.). **Length:** 8-5/16" (4-3/4" bbl.). **Grips:** Checkered composition grip panels. **Sights:** Fixed, wide blade front, fixed rear. **Features:** Updated design of original Standard Auto. New bolt hold-open latch. 10-shot magazine, magazine catch, safety, trigger and new receiver contours. Introduced 1982.
Price: Blued (MK 4, MK 6) **$289.00**
Price: In stainless steel (KMK 4, KMK 6) **$379.00**

Ruger 22/45-P4

Ruger KP512

SIG Sauer P220

Ruger 22/45 Mark II Pistol

Similar to other 22 Mark II autos except has grip frame of Zytel that matches angle and magazine latch of Model 1911 45 ACP pistol. Available in 4" bull, 4-3/4" standard and 5-1/2" bull barrels. Comes with extra magazine, plastic case, lock. Introduced 1992.

Price: P4, 4" bull barrel, adjustable sights **$275.00**
Price: KP 4 (4-3/4" barrel), stainless steel, fixed sights **$305.00**
Price: KP512 (5-1/2" bull barrel), stainless steel, adj. sights **$359.00**
Price: P512 (5-1/2" bull barrel, all blue), adj. sights **$275.00**

SAFARI ARMS ENFORCER PISTOL

Caliber: 45 ACP, 6-shot magazine. **Barrel:** 3.8", stainless. **Weight:** 36 oz. **Length:** 7.3" overall. **Grips:** Smooth walnut with etched black widow spider logo. **Sights:** Ramped blade front, LPA adjustable rear. **Features:** Extended safety, extended slide release; Commander-style hammer; beavertail grip safety; throated, polished, tuned. Parkerized matte black or satin stainless steel finishes. Made in U.S.A. by Safari Arms.
Price: **$630.00**

SAFARI ARMS GI SAFARI PISTOL

Caliber: 45 ACP, 7-shot magazine. **Barrel:** 5", 416 stainless. **Weight:** 39.9 oz. **Length:** 8.5" overall. **Grips:** Checkered walnut. **Sights:** G.I.-style blade front, drift-adjustable rear. **Features:** Beavertail grip safety; extended thumb safety and slide release; Commander-style hammer. Parkerized finish. Reintroduced 1996.
Price: **$439.00**

SAFARI ARMS CARRIER PISTOL

Caliber: 45 ACP, 7-shot magazine. **Barrel:** 6", 416 stainless steel. **Weight:** 30 oz. **Length:** 9.5" overall. **Grips:** Wood. **Sights:** Ramped blade front, LPA adjustable rear. **Features:** Beavertail grip safety; extended controls; full-length recoil spring guide; Commander-style hammer. Throated, polished and tuned. Satin stainless steel finish. Introduced 1999. Made in U.S.A. by Safari Arms, Inc.
Price: **$714.00**

SAFARI ARMS COHORT PISTOL

Caliber: 45 ACP, 7-shot magazine. **Barrel:** 3.8", 416 stainless. **Weight:** 37 oz. **Length:** 8.5" overall. **Grips:** Smooth walnut with laser-etched black widow logo. **Sights:** Ramped blade front, LPA adjustable rear. **Features:** Combines the Enforcer model, slide and MatchMaster frame. Beavertail grip safety; extended thumb safety and slide release; Commander-style hammer. Throated, polished and tuned. Satin stainless finish. Introduced 1996. Made in U.S.A. by Safari Arms, Inc.
Price: **$654.00**

SAFARI ARMS MATCHMASTER PISTOL

Caliber: 45 ACP, 7-shot. **Barrel:** 5" or 6", 416 stainless steel. **Weight:** 38 oz. (5" barrel). **Length:** 8.5" overall. **Grips:** Smooth walnut. **Sights:** Ramped blade, LPA adjustable rear. **Features:** Beavertail grip safety; extended controls; Commander-style hammer; throated, polished and tuned.

Parkerized matte-black or satin stainless steel. Made in U.S.A. by Olympic Arms, Inc.
Price: 5" barrel **$594.00**
Price: 6" barrel **$654.00**

Safari Arms Carry Comp Pistol

Similar to the Matchmaster except has Wil Schueman-designed hybrid compensator system. Made in U.S.A. by Olympic Arms, Inc.
Price: **$1,067.00**

SEECAMP LWS 32 STAINLESS DA AUTO

Caliber: 32 ACP Win. Silvertip, 6-shot magazine. **Barrel:** 2", integral with frame. **Weight:** 10.5 oz. **Length:** 4-1/8" overall. **Grips:** Glass-filled nylon. **Sights:** Smooth, no-snag, contoured slide and barrel top. **Features:** Aircraft quality 17-4 PH stainless steel. Inertia-operated firing pin. Hammer fired double-action-only. Hammer automatically follows slide down to safety rest position after each shot—no manual safety needed. Magazine safety disconnector. Polished stainless. Introduced 1985. From L.W. Seecamp.
Price: **$425.00**

SEMMERLING LM-4 SLIDE-ACTION PISTOL

Caliber: 45 ACP, 4-shot magazine. **Barrel:** 2". **Weight:** 24 oz. **Length:** NA. **Grips:** NA. **Sights:** NA. **Features:** While outwardly appearing to be a semi-automatic, the Semmerling LM-4 is a unique and super compact pistol employing a thumb activated slide mechanism (the slide is manually retracted between shots). Hand-built and super reliable, it is intended for professionals in law enforcement and for concealed carry by licensed and firearms knowledgeable private citizens. From American Derringer Corp.
Price: **$2,635.00**

SIG SAUER P220 SERVICE AUTO PISTOL

Caliber: 45 ACP, (7- or 8-shot magazine). **Barrel:** 4-3/8". **Weight:** 27.8 oz. **Length:** 7.8" overall. **Grips:** Checkered black plastic. **Sights:** Blade front, drift adjustable rear for windage. Optional Siglite nightsights. **Features:** Double action. Decocking lever permits lowering hammer onto locked firing pin. Squared combat-type trigger guard. Slide stays open after last shot. Imported from Germany by SIGARMS, Inc.
Price: Blue SA/DA or DAO **$790.00**
Price: Blue, Siglite night sights **$880.00**
Price: K-Kote or nickel slide **$830.00**
Price: K-Kote or nickel slide with Siglite night sights **$930.00**

SIG Sauer P220 Sport Auto Pistol

Similar to the P220 except has 4.9" barrel, ported compensator, all-stainless steel frame and slide, factory-tuned trigger, adjustable sights, extended competition controls. Overall length is 9.9", weighs 43.5 oz. Introduced 1999. From SIGARMS, Inc.
Price: **$1,320.00**

SIG Sauer P245 Compact

SIG Sauer Pro 2009

SIG Sauer P229 Sport

SIG Sauer P232

Smith & Wesson 457 TDA

SIG Sauer P245 Compact Auto Pistol

Similar to the P220 except has 3.9" barrel, shorter grip, 6-shot magazine, 7.28" overall length, and weighs 27.5 oz. Introduced 1999. From SIG-ARMS, Inc.

Price: Blue $780.00
Price: Blue, with Siglite sights. $850.00
Price: Two-tone $830.00
Price: Two-tone with Siglite sights. $930.00
Price: With K-Kote finish $830.00
Price: K-Kote with Siglite sights $930.00

SIG Sauer P229 DA Auto Pistol

Similar to the P228 except chambered for 9mm Para., 40 S&W, 357 SIG. Has 3.86" barrel, 7.08" overall length and 3.35" height. Weight is 30.5 oz. Introduced 1991. Frame made in Germany, stainless steel slide assembly made in U.S.; pistol assembled in U.S. From SIGARMS, Inc.

Price: $795.00
Price: With nickel slide $890.00
Price: Nickel slide Siglite night sights $935.00

SIG PRO AUTO PISTOL

Caliber: 9mm Para., 40 S&W, 10-shot magazine. **Barrel:** 3.86". **Weight:** 27.2 oz. **Length:** 7.36" overall. **Grips:** Composite and rubberized one-piece. **Sights:** Blade front, rear adjustable for windage. Optional Siglite night sights. **Features:** Polymer frame, stainless steel slide; integral frame accessory rail; replaceable steel frame rails; left- or right-handed magazine release. Introduced 1999. From SIGARMS, Inc.

Price: SP2340 (40 S&W) $596.00
Price: SP2009 (9mm Para.) $596.00
Price: As above with Siglite night sights $655.00

SIG Sauer P226 Service Pistol

Similar to the P220 pistol except has 4.4" barrel, and weighs 28.3 oz. 357 SIG or 40 S&W. Imported from Germany by SIGARMS, Inc.

Price: Blue SA/DA or DAO $830.00
Price: With Siglite night sights $930.00
Price: Blue, SA/DA or DAO 357 SIG. $830.00
Price: With Siglite night sights $930.00
Price: K-Kote finish, 40 S&W only or nickel slide $830.00
Price: K-Kote or nickel slide Siglite night sights $930.00
Price: Nickel slide 357 SIG $875.00
Price: Nickel slide, Siglite night sights $930.00

SIG Sauer P229 Sport Auto Pistol

Similar to the P229 except available in 357 SIG only; 4.8" heavy barrel; 8.6" overall length; weighs 40.6 oz.; vented compensator; adjustable

target sights; rubber grips; extended slide latch and magazine release. Made of stainless steel. Introduced 1998. From SIGARMS, Inc.

Price: $1,320.00

SIG SAUER P232 PERSONAL SIZE PISTOL

Caliber: 380 ACP, 7-shot. **Barrel:** 3-3/4". **Weight:** 16 oz. **Length:** 6-1/2" overall. **Grips:** Checkered black composite. **Sights:** Blade front, rear adjustable for windage. **Features:** Double action/single action or DAO. Blow-back operation, stationary barrel. Introduced 1997. Imported from Germany by SIGARMS, Inc.

Price: Blue SA/DA or DAO $505.00
Price: In stainless steel $545.00
Price: With stainless steel slide, blue frame $525.00
Price: Stainless steel, Siglite night sights, Hogue grips $585.00

SIG SAUER P239 PISTOL

Caliber: 9mm Para., 8-shot, 357 SIG 40 S&W, 7-shot magazine. **Barrel:** 3.6". **Weight:** 25.2 oz. **Length:** 6.6" overall. **Grips:** Checkered black composite. **Sights:** Blade front, rear adjustable for windage. Optional Siglite night sights. **Features:** SA/DA or DAO; blackened stainless steel slide, aluminum alloy frame. Introduced 1996. Made in U.S.A. by SIGARMS, Inc.

Price: SA/DA or DAO $620.00
Price: SA/DA or DAO with Siglite night sights. $720.00
Price: Two-tone finish $665.00
Price: Two-tone finish, Siglite sights $765.00

SMITH & WESSON MODEL 22A SPORT PISTOL

Caliber: 22 LR, 10-shot magazine. **Barrel:** 4", 5-1/2", 7". **Weight:** 29 oz. **Length:** 8" overall. **Grips:** Two-piece polymer. **Sights:** Patridge front, fully adjustable rear. **Features:** Comes with a sight bridge with Weaver-style integral optics mount; alloy frame; .312" serrated trigger; stainless steel slide and barrel with matte blue finish. Introduced 1997. Made in U.S.A. by Smith & Wesson.

Price: 4" $264.00
Price: 5-1/2" $292.00
Price: 7" $331.00

SMITH & WESSON MODEL 457 TDA AUTO PISTOL

Caliber: 45 ACP, 7-shot magazine. **Barrel:** 3-3/4". **Weight:** 29 oz. **Length:** 7-1/4" overall. **Grips:** One-piece Xenoy, wrap-around with straight backstrap. **Sights:** Post front, fixed rear, three-dot system. **Features:** Aluminum alloy frame, matte blue carbon steel slide; bobbed hammer; smooth trigger. Introduced 1996. Made in U.S.A. by Smith & Wesson.

Price: $591.00

Smith & Wesson 908

Smith & Wesson 4013 TSW

Smith & Wesson 410 DA

Smith & Wesson 910 DA

Smith & Wesson 3913 LadySmith

Smith & Wesson 4006

SMITH & WESSON MODEL 908 AUTO PISTOL

Caliber: 9mm Para., 8-shot magazine. **Barrel:** 3-1/2". **Weight:** 26 oz. **Length:** 6-13/16". **Grips:** One-piece Xenoy, wrap-around with straight backstrap. **Sights:** Post front, fixed rear, three-dot system. **Features:** Aluminum alloy frame, matte blue carbon steel slide; bobbed hammer; smooth trigger. Introduced 1996. Made in U.S.A. by Smith & Wesson.
Price: **$535.00**

SMITH & WESSON MODEL 4013, 4053 TSW AUTOS

Caliber: 40 S&W, 9-shot magazine. **Barrel:** 3-1/2". **Weight:** 26.4 oz. **Length:** 6-7/8" overall. **Grips:** Xenoy one-piece wrap-around. **Sights:** Novak three-dot system. **Features:** Traditional double-action system; stainless slide, alloy frame; fixed barrel bushing; ambidextrous decocker; reversible magazine catch, equipment rail. Introduced 1997. Made in U.S.A. by Smith & Wesson.
Price: Model 4013 TSW **$886.00**
Price: Model 4053 TSW, double-action-only **$886.00**

Smith & Wesson Model 22S Sport Pistols

Similar to the Model 22A Sport except with stainless steel frame. Available only with 5-1/2" or 7" barrel. Introduced 1997. Made in U.S.A. by Smith & Wesson.
Price: 5-1/2" standard barrel **$358.00**
Price: 5-1/2" bull barrel, wood target stocks with thumbrest **$434.00**
Price: 7" standard barrel **$395.00**
Price: 5-1/2" bull barrel, two-piece target stocks with thumbrest . **$353.00**

SMITH & WESSON MODEL 410 DA AUTO PISTOL

Caliber: 40 S&W, 10-shot magazine. **Barrel:** 4". **Weight:** 28.5 oz. **Length:** 7.5 oz. **Grips:** One-piece Xenoy, wrap-around with straight backstrap. **Sights:** Post front, fixed rear; three-dot system. **Features:** Aluminum alloy frame; blued carbon steel slide; traditional double action with left-side slide-mounted decocking lever. Introduced 1996. Made in U.S.A. by Smith & Wesson.
Price: Model 410 . . . . **$591.00**
Price: Model 410, HiViz front sight **$612.00**

SMITH & WESSON MODEL 910 DA AUTO PISTOL

Caliber: 9mm Para., 10-shot magazine. **Barrel:** 4". **Weight:** 28 oz. **Length:** 7-3/8" overall. **Grips:** One-piece Xenoy, wrap-around with straight backstrap. **Sights:** Post front with white dot, fixed two-dot rear. **Features:** Alloy frame, blue carbon steel slide. Slide-mounted decocking lever. Introduced 1995.
Price: Model 910 . . . . **$535.00**
Price: Model 410, HiViz front sight **$535.00**

SMITH & WESSON MODEL 3913 TRADITIONAL DOUBLE ACTION

Caliber: 9mm Para., 8-shot magazine. **Barrel:** 3-1/2". **Weight:** 26 oz. **Length:** 6-13/16" overall. **Grips:** One-piece Delrin wrap-around, textured surface. **Sights:** Post front with white dot, Novak LoMount Carry with two dots. **Features:** Aluminum alloy frame, stainless slide (M3913) or blue steel slide (M3914). Bobbed hammer with no half-cock notch; smooth .304" trigger with rounded edges. Straight backstrap. Equipment rail. Extra magazine included. Introduced 1989.
Price: **$760.00**

Smith & Wesson Model 3913-LS LadySmith Auto

Similar to the standard Model 3913 except has frame that is upswept at the front, rounded trigger guard. Comes in frosted stainless steel with matching gray grips. Grips are ergonomically correct for a woman's hand. Novak LoMount Carry rear sight adjustable for windage, smooth edges for snag resistance. Extra magazine included. Introduced 1990.
Price: **$782.00**

Smith & Wesson Model 3953 DAO Pistol

Same as the Model 3913 except double-action-only. Model 3953 has stainless slide with alloy frame. Overall length 7"; weighs 25.5 oz. Extra magazine included. Equipment rail. Introduced 1990.
Price: **$760.00**

Smith & Wesson Model 3913TSW/3953TSW Auto Pistols

Similar to the Model 3913 and 3953 except TSW guns have tighter tolerances, ambidextrous manual safety/decocking lever, flush-fit magazine, delayed-unlock firing system; magazine disconnector. Compact alloy frame, stainless steel slide. Straight backstrap. Introduced 1998. Made in U.S.A. by Smith & Wesson.
Price: Single action/double action **$760.00**
Price: Double action only **$760.00**

SMITH & WESSON MODEL 4006 TDA AUTO

Caliber: 40 S&W, 10-shot magazine. **Barrel:** 4". **Weight:** 38.5 oz. **Length:** 7-7/8" overall. **Grips:** Xenoy wrap-around with checkered panels. **Sights:** Replaceable post front with white dot, Novak LoMount Carry fixed rear with two white dots, or micro. click adjustable rear with two white dots. **Features:** Stainless steel construction with non-reflective finish. Straight backstrap, quipment rail. Extra magazine included. Introduced 1990.
Price: With adjustable sights **$944.00**
Price: With fixed sight **$907.00**
Price: With fixed night sights **$1,040.00**
Price: With Saf-T-Trigger, fixed sights **$927.00**

Smith & Wesson 4566 TSW

Smith & Wesson Sigma SW40V

Smith & Wesson 99

SMITH & WESSON MODEL 4006 TSW

Caliber: 40, 10-shot. **Barrel:** 4". **Grips:** Straight back strap grip. **Sights:** Fixed Novak LoMount Carry. **Features:** Traditional double action, ambidextrous safety, Saf-T-Trigger, equipment rail, satin stainless.
Price: **$927.00**

Smith & Wesson Model 4043, 4046 DA Pistols

Similar to the Model 4006 except is double-action-only. Has a semi-bobbed hammer, smooth trigger, 4" barrel; Novak LoMount Carry rear sight, post front with white dot. Overall length is 7-1/2", weighs 28 oz. Model 4043 has alloy frame, equipment rail. Extra magazine included. Introduced 1991.
Price: Model 4043 (alloy frame) **$886.00**
Price: Model 4046 (stainless frame) **$907.00**
Price: Model 4046 with fixed night sights **$1,040.00**

SMITH & WESSON MODEL 4500 SERIES AUTOS

Caliber: 45 ACP, 8-shot magazine. **Barrel:** 5" (M4506). **Weight:** 41 oz. (4506). **Length:** 8-1/2" overall. **Grips:** Xenoy one-piece wrap-around, arched or straight backstrap. **Sights:** Post front with white dot, adjustable or fixed Novak LoMount Carry on M4506. **Features:** M4506 has serrated hammer spur, equipment rail. All have two magazines. Contact Smith & Wesson for complete data. Introduced 1989.
Price: Model 4566 (stainless, 4-1/4", traditional DA, ambidextrous
safety, fixed sight) **$942.00**
Price: Model 4586 (stainless, 4-1/4", DA only) **$942.00**
Price: Model 4566 (stainless, 4-1/4" with Saf-T-Trigger,
fixed sight) **$961.00**

SMITH & WESSON MODEL 4513TSW/4553TSW PISTOLS

Caliber: 45 ACP, 7-shot magazine. **Barrel:** 3-3/4". **Weight:** 28 oz. (M4513TSW). **Length:** 6-7/8 overall. **Grips:** Checkered Xenoy; straight backstrap. **Sights:** White dot front, Novak LoMount Carry 2-Dot rear. **Features:** Model 4513TSW is traditional double action, Model 4553TSW is double action only. TSW series has tighter tolerances, ambidextrous manual safety/decocking lever, flush-fit magazine, delayed-unlock firing system; magazine disconnector. Compact alloy frame, stainless steel slide, equipment rail. Introduced 1998. Made in U.S.A. by Smith & Wesson.
Price: Model 4513TSW. **$924.00**
Price: Model 4553TSW. **$924.00**

SMITH & WESSON MODEL 4566 TSW

Caliber: 45 ACP. **Barrel:** 4-1/4", 8-shot . **Grips:** Straight back strap grip. **Sights:** Fixed Novak LoMount Carry. **Features:** Ambidextrous safety, equipment rail, Saf-T-Trigger, satin stainless finish. Traditional double action.
Price: **$961.00**

SMITH & WESSON MODEL 5900 SERIES AUTO PISTOLS

Caliber: 9mm Para., 10-shot magazine. **Barrel:** 4". **Weight:** 28-1/2 to 37-1/2 oz. (fixed sight); 38 oz. (adjustable sight). **Length:** 7-1/2" overall. **Grips:** Xenoy wrap-around with curved backstrap. **Sights:** Post front with white dot, fixed or fully adjustable with two white dots. **Features:** All stainless, stainless and alloy or carbon steel and alloy construction. Smooth .304" trigger, .260" serrated hammer. Equipment rail. Introduced 1989.
Price: Model 5906 (stainless, traditional DA, adjustable sight,
ambidextrous safety) **$904.00**
Price: As above, fixed sight. **$841.00**

Price: With fixed night sights. **$995.00**
Price: With Saf-T-Trigger. **$882.00**
Price: Model 5946 DAO (as above, stainless frame and slide)... **$863.00**

SMITH & WESSON ENHANCED SIGMA SERIES DAO PISTOLS

Caliber: 9mm Para., 40 S&W, 10-shot magazine. **Barrel:** 4". **Weight:** 26 oz. **Length:** 7.4" overall. **Grips:** Integral. **Sights:** White dot front, fixed rear; three-dot system. Tritium night sights available. **Features:** Ergonomic polymer frame; low barrel centerline; internal striker firing system; corrosion-resistant slide; Teflon-filled, electroless-nickel coated magazine, equipment rail. Introduced 1994. Made in U.S.A. by Smith & Wesson.
Price: SW9E, 9mm, 4" barrel, black finish, fixed sights **$447.00**
Price: SW9V, 9mm, 4" barrel, satin stainless, fixed night sights.. **$447.00**
Price: SW9VE, 4" barrel, satin stainless, Saf-T-Trigger,
fixed sights **$466.00**
Price: SW40E, 40 S&W, 4" barrel, black finish, fixed sights **$657.00**
Price: SW40V, 40 S&W, 4" barrel, black polymer, fixed sights ... **$447.00**
Price: SW40VE, 4" barrel, satin stainless, Saf-T-Trigger,
fixed sights **$466.00**

SMITH & WESSON MODEL CS9 CHIEF'S SPECIAL AUTO

Caliber: 9mm Para., 7-shot magazine. **Barrel:** 3". **Weight:** 20.8 oz. **Length:** 6-1/4" overall. **Grips:** Hogue wrap-around rubber. **Sights:** White dot front, fixed two-dot rear. **Features:** Traditional double-action trigger mechanism. Alloy frame, stainless or blued slide. Ambidextrous safety. Introduced 1999. Made in U.S.A. by Smith & Wesson.
Price: Blue or stainless. **$680.00**

Smith & Wesson Model CS40 Chief's Special Auto

Similar to CS9, chambered for 40 S&W (7-shot magazine), 3-1/4" barrel, weighs 24.2 oz., measures 6-1/2" overall. Introduced 1999. Made in U.S.A. by Smith & Wesson.
Price: Blue or stainless. **$717.00**

Smith & Wesson Model CS45 Chief's Special Auto

Similar to CS40, chambered for 45 ACP, 6-shot magazine, weighs 23.9 oz. Introduced 1999. Made in U.S.A. by Smith & Wesson.
Price: Blue or stainless. **$717.00**

SMITH & WESSON MODEL 99

Caliber: 9mm Para. 4" barrel; 40 S&W 4-1/8" barrel; 10-shot, adj. sights. **Features:** Traditional double action satin stainless, black polymer frame, equipment rail, Saf-T-Trigger.
Price: 4" barrel **$648.00**
Price: 4-1/8" barrel **$648.00**

SPRINGFIELD, INC. FULL-SIZE 1911A1 AUTO PISTOL

Caliber: 9mm Para., 9-shot; 38 Super, 9-shot; 40 S&W, 9-shot; 45 ACP, 7-shot. **Barrel:** 5". **Weight:** 35.6 oz. **Length:** 8-5/8" overall. **Grips:** Cocobolo. **Sights:** Fixed three-dot system. **Features:** Beveled magazine well; lowered and flared ejection port. All forged parts, including frame, barrel, slide. All new production. Introduced 1990. From Springfield, Inc.
Price: Mil-Spec 45 ACP, Parkerized **$559.00**
Price: Standard, 45 ACP, blued, Novak sights **$824.00**
Price: Standard, 45 ACP, stainless, Novak sights **$828.00**
Price: Lightweight 45 ACP (28.6 oz., matte finish, night sights).. **$877.00**
Price: 40 S&W, stainless **$860.00**
Price: 9mm, stainless **$837.00**

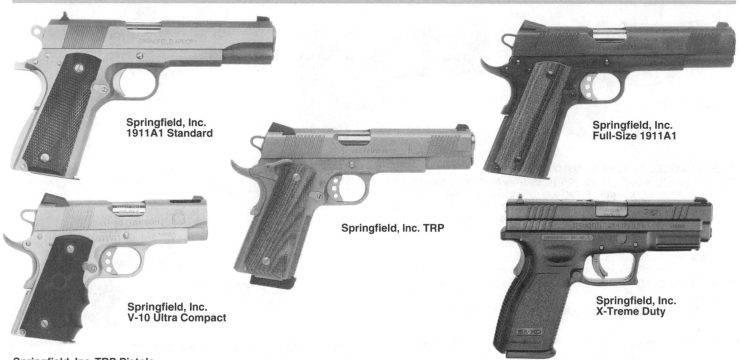

Springfield, Inc.
1911A1 Standard

Springfield, Inc. TRP

Springfield, Inc.
Full-Size 1911A1

Springfield, Inc.
V-10 Ultra Compact

Springfield, Inc.
X-Treme Duty

Springfield, Inc. TRP Pistols

Similar to 1911A1 except 45 ACP only, checkered front strap and main-spring housing, Novak Night Sight combat rear sight and matching dovetailed front sight, tuned, polished extractor, oversize barrel link; lightweight speed trigger and combat action job, match barrel and bushing, extended ambidextrous thumb safety and fitted beavertail grip safety. Carry bevel on entire pistol; checkered cocobolo wood grips, comes with two Wilson 7-shot magazines. Frame is engraved "Tactical," both sides of frame with "TRP." Introduced 1998. From Springfield, Inc.

Price: Standard with Armory Kote finish **$1,395.00**
Price: Standard, stainless steel **$1,370.00**
Price: Standard with Operator Light Rail Armory Kote **$1,473.00**

Springfield, Inc. 1911A1 High Capacity Pistol

Similar to Standard 1911A1, available in 45 ACP with 10-shot magazine. Commander-style hammer, walnut grips, beveled magazine well, plastic carrying case. Can accept higher-capacity Para Ordnance magazines. Introduced 1993. From Springfield, Inc.

Price: Mil-Spec 45 ACP **$756.00**
Price: 45 ACP Ultra Compact (3-1/2" bbl.) **$909.00**

Springfield, Inc. 1911A1 V-Series Ported Pistols

Similar to standard 1911A1, scalloped slides with 10, 12 or 16 matching barrel ports to redirect powder gasses and reduce recoil and muzzle flip. Adjustable rear sight, ambi thumb safety, Videki speed trigger, and beveled magazine well. Checkered walnut grips standard. Available in 45 ACP, stainless or bi-tone. Introduced 1992.

Price: V-16 Long Slide, stainless **$1,121.00**
Price: Target V-12, stainless **$878.00**
Price: V-10 (Ultra-Compact, bi-tone) **$853.00**
Price: V-10 stainless **$863.00**

Springfield, Inc. 1911A1 Champion Pistol

Similar to standard 1911A1, slide is 4". Novak Night Sights. Delta hammer and cocobolo grips. Available in 45 ACP only; Parkerized or stainless. Introduced 1989.

Price: Stainless **$849.00**

Springfield Inc. Ultra Compact Pistol

Similar to 1911A1 Compact, shorter slide, 3.5" barrel, beavertail grip safety, beveled magazine well, Novak Low Mount or Novak Night Sights, Videki speed trigger, flared ejection port, stainless steel frame, blued slide, match grade barrel, rubber grips. Introduced 1996. From Springfield, Inc.

Price: Parkerized 45 ACP, Night Sights **$589.00**
Price: Stainless 45 ACP, Night Sights **$849.00**
Price: Lightweight, 9mm, stainless **$837.00**

Springfield Inc. Compact Lightweight

Mates a Springfield Inc. Champion length slide with the shorter Ultra-Compact forged alloy frame for concealability. In 45 ACP.

Price: **$733.00**

Springfield Inc. Long Slide 1911 A1 Pistol

Similar to Full Size model, 6" barrel and slide for increased sight radius and higher velocity, fully adjustable sights, muzzle-forward weight distribution for reduced recoil and quicker shot-to-shot recovery. From Springfield Inc.

Price: Target, 45 ACP, stainless with Night Sights **$1,049.00**
Price: Trophy Match, stainless with adj. sights **$1,452.00**
Price: V-16 stainless steel **$1,121.00**

SPRINGFIELD, INC. MICRO-COMPACT 1911A1 PISTOL

Caliber: 45 ACP, 40 S&W 6+1 capacity. **Barrel:** 3" 1:16 LH. **Weight:** 24 oz. **Length:** 5.7". **Sights:** Novak LoMount tritium. Dovetail front. **Features:** Forged frame and slide, ambi thumb safety, extreme carry bevel treatment, lockable plastic case, 2 magazines.

Price: . . . . **$993.00 to $1,021.00**

SPRINGFIELD, INC. X-TREME DUTY

Caliber: 9mm, 40 S&W, 357 Sig. **Barrel:** 4.08". **Weight:** 22.88 oz. **Length:** 7.2". **Sights:** Dovetail front and rear. **Features:** Lightweight, ultra high-impact polymer frame. Trigger, firing pin and grip safety. Two 10-rod steel easy glide magazines. Imported from Croatia.

Price: . . . . **$489.00 to $1,099.00**

STEYR M & S SERIES AUTO PISTOLS

Caliber: 9mm Para., 40 S&W, 357 SIG; 10-shot magazine. **Barrel:** 4" (3.58" for Model S). **Weight:** 28 oz. (22.5 oz. for Model S). **Length:** 7.05" overall (6.53" for Model S). **Grips:** Ultra-rigid polymer. **Sights:** Drift-adjustable, white-outline rear; white-triangle blade front. **Features:** Polymer frame; trigger-drop firing pin, manual and key-lock safeties; loaded chamber indicator; 5.5-lb. trigger pull; 111-degree grip angle enhances natural pointing. Introduced 2000. Imported from Austria by GSI Inc.

Price: Model M (full-sized frame with 4" barrel) **$609.95**
Price: Model S (compact frame with 3.58" barrel) **$609.95**
Price: Extra 10-shot magazines (Model M or S) **$39.00**

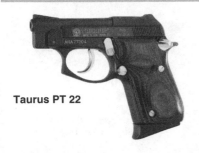

Taurus PT 22

Taurus PT-911

Taurus PT-938

Taurus PT-940

TAURUS MODEL PT 22/PT 25 AUTO PISTOLS

Caliber: 22 LR, 8-shot (PT 22); 25 ACP, 9-shot (PT 25). **Barrel:** 2.75". **Weight:** 12.3 oz. **Length:** 5.25" overall. **Grips:** Smooth rosewood or mother-of-pearl. **Sights:** Fixed. **Features:** Double action. Tip-up barrel for loading, cleaning. Blue, nickel, duotone or blue with gold accents. Introduced 1992. Made in U.S.A. by Taurus International.

Price: 22 LR, 25 ACP, blue, nickel or with duo-tone finish
with rosewood grips **$219.00**

Price: 22 LR, 25 ACP, blue with gold trim, rosewood grips **$234.00**

Price: 22 LR, 25 ACP, blue, nickel or duotone finish with checkered
wood grips **$219.00**

Price: 22 LR, 25 ACP, blue with gold trim, mother of pearl grips . **$250.00**

TAURUS MODEL PT24/7

NEW!

Caliber: 9mm, 10+1 shot; .40 Cal., 10+1 shot. **Barrel:** 4". **Weight:** 27.2 oz. **Length:** 7-18". **Grips:** RIBBER rubber-finned overlay on polymer. **Sights:** Adjustable. **Features:** Accessory rail, four safeties, blue or stainless finish, consistent trigger pull weight and travel. Introduced 2003. Imported from Brazil by Taurus Int'l. Manufacturing.

Price: 9mm **$578.00**

Price: .40 Cal. **$594.00**

TAURUS MODEL PT92 AUTO PISTOL

Caliber: 9mm Para., 10-shot mag. **Barrel:** 5". **Weight:** 34 oz. **Length:** 8.5" overall. **Grips:** Checkered rubber, rosewood, mother-of-pearl. **Sights:** Fixed notch rear. Three-dot sight system. Also offered with micrometer-click adjustable night sights. **Features:** Double action, ambidextrous 3-way hammer drop safety, allows cocked & locked carry. Blue, stainless steel, blue with gold highlights, stainless steel with gold highlights, forged aluminum frame, integral key-lock. .22 LR conversion kit available. Imported from Brazil by Taurus International Manufacturing.

Price: Blue .... **$578.00 to $672.00**

Taurus Model PT99 Auto Pistol

Similar to PT92, fully adjustable rear sight.

Price: Blue .... **$575.00 to $670.00**

Price: 22 Conversion kit for PT 92 and PT99 (includes barrel and slide)
.... **$266.00**

TAURUS MODEL PT-100/101 AUTO PISTOL

Caliber: 40 S&W, 10-shot mag. **Barrel:** 5". **Weight:** 34 oz. **Length:** 8-1/2". **Grips:** Checkered rubber, rosewood, mother-of-pearl. **Sights:** 3-dot fixed or adjustable; night sights available. **Features:** Single/double action with three-position safety/decocker. Re-introduced in 2001. Imported by Taurus International.

Price: PT100. .... **$578.00 to $672.00**

Price: PT101. .... **$594.00 to $617.00**

TAURUS MODEL PT-111 MILLENNIUM PRO AUTO PISTOL

Caliber: 9mm Para., 10-shot mag. **Barrel:** 3.25". **Weight:** 18.7 oz. **Length:** 6-1/8" overall. **Grips:** Polymer. **Sights:** 3-dot fixed; night sights available. Low profile, three-dot combat. **Features:** Double action only, polymer frame, matte stainless or blue steel slide, manual safety, integral key-lock. Deluxe models with wood grip inserts. Now issued in a third generation series with many cosmetic and internal improvements.

Price: .... **$445.00 to $539.00**

Taurus Model PT-111 Millennium Titanium Pistol

Similar to PT-111, titanium slide, night sights.

Price: **$586.00**

TAURUS PT-132 MILLENIUM PRO AUTO PISTOL

Caliber: 32 ACP, 10-shot mag. **Barrel:** 3.25". **Weight:** 18.7 oz. **Grips:** Polymer. **Sights:** 3-dot fixed; night sights available. **Features:** Double action only, polymer frame, matte stainless or blue steel slide, manual safety, integral key-lock action. Introduced 2001.

Price: .... **$445.00 to $461.00**

TAURUS PT-138 MILLENIUM PRO SERIES

Caliber: 380 ACP, 10-shot mag. **Barrel:** 3.25". **Weight:** 18.7 oz. **Grips:** Polymer. **Sights:** Fixed 3-dot fixed. **Features:** Double action only, polymer frame, matte stainless or blue steel slide, manual safety, integral key-lock.

Price: .... **$445.00 to $461.00**

TAURUS PT-140 MILLENIUM PRO AUTO PISTOL

Caliber: 40 S&W, 10-shot mag. **Barrel:** 3.25". **Weight:** 18.7 oz. **Grips:** Checkered polymer. **Sights:** 3-dot fixed; night sights available. **Features:** Double-action only; matte stainless or blue steel slide, black polymer frame, manual safety, integral key-lock action. From Taurus International.

Price: .... **$484.00 to $578.00**

TAURUS PT-145 MILLENIUM AUTO PISTOL

Caliber: 45 ACP, 10-shot mag. **Barrel:** 3.27". **Weight:** 23 oz. **Stock:** Checkered polymer. **Sights:** 3-dot fixed; night sights available. **Features:** Double-action only, matte stainless or blue steel slide, black polymer frame, manual safety, integral key-lock. From Taurus International.

Price: .... **$484.00 to $578.00**

TAURUS MODEL PT-911 AUTO PISTOL

Caliber: 9mm Para., 10-shot mag. **Barrel:** 4". **Weight:** 28.2 oz. **Length:** 7" overall. **Grips:** Checkered rubber, rosewood, mother-of-pearl. **Sights:** Fixed, three-dot blue or stainless; night sights optional. **Features:** Double action, semi-auto ambidextrous 3-way hammer drop safety, allows cocked and locked carry. Blue, stainless steel, blue with gold highlights, or stainless steel with gold highlights, forged aluminum frame, integral key-lock.

Price: .... **$523.00 to $617.00**

TAURUS MODEL PT-938 AUTO PISTOL

Caliber: 380 ACP, 10-shot mag. **Barrel:** 3.72". **Weight:** 27 oz. **Length:** 6.5" overall. **Grips:** Checkered rubber. **Sights:** Fixed, three-dot. **Features:** Double action, ambidextrous 3-way hammer drop allows cocked & locked carry. Forged aluminum frame. Integral key-lock. Imported by Taurus International.

Price: Blue **$516.00**

Price: Stainless. **$531.00**

Taurus PT-945

Taurus PT-957

Walther PPK/S

Walther PPK

Walther P99

Walther P22

Wilkinson Sherry

TAURUS MODEL PT-940 AUTO PISTOL

Caliber: 40 S&W, 10-shot mag. **Barrel:** 3-5/8". **Weight:** 28.2 oz. **Length:** 7" overall. **Grips:** Checkered rubber, rosewood or mother-of-pearl. **Sights:** Fixed, three-dot blue or stainless; night sights optional. **Features:** Double action, semi-auto ambidextrous 3-way hammer drop safety, allows cocked & locked carry. Blue, stainless steel, blue with gold highlights, or stainless steel with gold hightlights, forged aluminum frame, integral key-lock.
Price: .... $523.00 to $617.00

TAURUS MODEL PT-945 SERIES

Caliber: 45 ACP, 8-shot mag. **Barrel:** 4.25". **Weight:** 28.2/29.5 oz. **Length:** 7.48" overall. **Grips:** Checkered rubber, rosewood or mother-of-pearl. **Sights:** Fixed, three-dot; night sights optional. **Features:** Double-action with ambidextrous 3-way hammer drop safety allows cocked & locked carry. Forged aluminum frame, PT-945C has poarted barrel/slide. Blue, stainless, blue with gold highlights, stainless with gold highlights, integral key-lock. Introduced 1995. Imported by Taurus International.
Price: .... $563.00 to $641.00

TAURUS MODEL PT-957 AUTO PISTOL

Caliber: 357 SIG, 10-shot mag. **Barrel:** 4". **Weight:** 28 oz. **Length:** 7" overall. **Grips:** Checkered rubber, rosewood or mother-of-pearl. **Sights:** Fixed, three-dot blue or stainless; night sights optional. **Features:** Double-action, blue, stainless steel, blue with gold accents or stainless with gold accents, ported barrel/slide, three-position safety with decocking lever and ambidextrous safety. Forged aluminum frame, integral key-lock. Introduced 1999. Imported by Taurus International.
Price: .... $525.00 to $620.00
Price: Non-ported .... $525.00 to $535.00

TAURUS MODEL 922 SPORT PISTOL

NEW! **Caliber:** .22 LR, 10-shot magazine. **Barrel:** 6". **Weight:** 24.8 oz. **Length:** 9-1/8". **Grips:** Polymer. **Sights:** Adjustable. **Features:** Matte blue steel finish, machined target crown, polymer frame, single and double action, easy disassembly for cleaning.
Price: .... (blue) $310.00
Price: .... (stainless) $328.00

WALTHER PPK/S AMERICAN AUTO PISTOL

Caliber: 380 ACP, 7-shot magazine. **Barrel:** 3.27". **Weight:** 23-1/2 oz. **Length:** 6.1" overall. **Stocks:** Checkered plastic. **Sights:** Fixed, white markings. **Features:** Double action; manual safety blocks firing pin and drops hammer; chamber loaded indicator on 32 and 380; extra finger rest magazine provided. Made entirely in the United States. Introduced 1980.
Price: 380 ACP only, blue................................ $540.00
Price: As above, 32 ACP or 380 ACP, stainless $540.00

Walther PPK American Auto Pistol

Similar to Walther PPK/S except weighs 21 oz., has 6-shot capacity. Made in the U.S. Introduced 1986.
Price: Stainless, 32 ACP or 380 ACP $540.00
Price: Blue, 380 ACP only $540.00

WALTHER P99 AUTO PISTOL

Caliber: 9mm Para., 9x21, 40 S&W,10-shot magazine. **Barrel:** 4". **Weight:** 25 oz. **Length:** 7" overall. **Grips:** Textured polymer. **Sights:** Blade front (comes with three interchangeable blades for elevation adjustment), micrometer rear adjustable for windage. **Features:** Double-action mechanism with trigger safety, decock safety, internal striker safety; chamber loaded indicator; ambidextrous magazine release levers; polymer frame with interchangeable backstrap inserts. Comes with two magazines. Introduced 1997. Imported from Germany by Carl Walther USA.
Price: $799.00

Walther P990 Auto Pistol

Similar to the P99 except is double action only. Available in blue or silver tenifer finish. Introduced 1999. Imported from Germany by Carl Walther USA.
Price: $749.00

WALTHER P22 PISTOL

Caliber: 22 LR. **Barrel:** 3.4", 5". **Weight:** 19.6 oz. (3.4"), 20.3 oz. (5"). **Length:** 6.26", 7.83". **Grips:** NA. **Sights:** Interchangeable white dot, front, 2-dot adjustable, rear. **Features:** A rimfire version of the Walther P99 pistol, available in nickel slide with black frame, or green frame with black slide versions. Made in Germany and distributed in the U.S. by Smith & Wesson.
Price: .... NA

WILKINSON SHERRY AUTO PISTOL

Caliber: 22 LR, 8-shot magazine. **Barrel:** 2-1/8". **Weight:** 9-1/4 oz. **Length:** 4-3/8" overall. **Grips:** Checkered black plastic. **Sights:** Fixed, groove. **Features:** Cross-bolt safety locks the sear into the hammer. Available in all blue finish or blue slide and trigger with gold frame. Introduced 1985.
Price: $280.00

WILKINSON LINDA AUTO PISTOL

Caliber: 9mm Para. **Barrel:** 8-5/16". **Weight:** 4 lbs., 13 oz. **Length:** 12-1/4" overall. **Grips:** Checkered black plastic pistol grip, walnut forend. **Sights:** Protected blade front, aperture rear. **Features:** Fires from closed bolt. Semi-auto only. Straight blowback action. Cross-bolt safety. Removable barrel. From Wilkinson Arms.
Price: $675.00

Includes models suitable for several forms of competition and other sporting purposes.

Baer 1911 Ultimate Master

Baer 1911 Bullseye Wadcutter

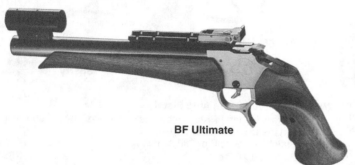

BF Ultimate

Browning Buck Mark Target 5.5

BAER 1911 ULTIMATE MASTER COMBAT PISTOL

Caliber: 9x23, 38 Super, 400 Cor-Bon 45 ACP (others available), 10-shot magazine. **Barrel:** 5", 6"; Baer NM. **Weight:** 37 oz. **Length:** 8.5" overall. **Grips:** Checkered rosewood. **Sights:** Baer dovetail front, low-mount Bo-Mar rear with hidden leaf. **Features:** Full-house competition gun. Baer forged NM blued steel frame and double serrated slide; Baer triple port, tapered cone compensator; fitted slide to frame; lowered, flared ejection port; Baer reverse recoil plug; full-length guide rod; recoil buff; beveled magazine well; Baer Commander hammer, sear; Baer extended ambidextrous safety, extended ejector, checkered slide stop, beavertail grip safety with pad, extended magazine release button; Baer speed trigger. Made in U.S.A. by Les Baer Custom, Inc.

Price: Compensated, open sights. **$2,476.00**
Price: 6" Model 400 Cor-Bon **$2,541.00**

BAER 1911 NATIONAL MATCH HARDBALL PISTOL

Caliber: 45 ACP, 7-shot magazine. **Barrel:** 5". **Weight:** 37 oz. **Length:** 8.5" overall. **Grips:** Checkered walnut. **Sights:** Baer dovetail front with undercut post, low-mount Bo-Mar rear with hidden leaf. **Features:** Baer NM forged steel frame, double serrated slide and barrel with stainless bushing; slide fitted to frame; Baer match trigger with 4-lb. pull; polished feed ramp, throated barrel; checkered front strap, arched mainspring housing; Baer beveled magazine well; lowered, flared ejection port; tuned extractor; Baer extended ejector, checkered slide stop; recoil buff. Made in U.S.A. by Les Baer Custom, Inc.

Price: **$1,335.00**

Baer 1911 Bullseye Wadcutter Pistol

Similar to National Match Hardball except designed for wadcutter loads only. Polished feed ramp and barrel throat; Bo-Mar rib on slide; full-length recoil rod; Baer speed trigger with 3-1/2-lb. pull; Baer deluxe hammer and sear; Baer beavertail grip safety with pad; flat mainspring housing checkered 20 lpi. Blue finish; checkered walnut grips. Made in U.S.A. by Les Baer Custom, Inc.

Price: From **$1,495.00**
Price: With 6" barrel, from. **$1,690.00**

BF ULTIMATE SILHOUETTE HB SINGLE SHOT PISTOL

Caliber: 7mm U.S., 22 LR Match and 100 other chamberings. **Barrel:** 10.75" Heavy Match Grade with 11-degree target crown. **Weight:** 3 lbs.,

15 oz. **Length:** 16" overall. **Grips:** Thumbrest target style. **Sights:** Bo-Mar/Bond ScopeRib I Combo with hooded post front adjustable for height and width, rear notch available in .032", .062", .080" and .100" widths; 1/2-MOA clicks. **Features:** Designed to meet maximum rules for IHMSA Production Gun. Falling block action gives rigid barrel-receiver mating. Hand fitted and headspaced. Etched receiver; gold-colored trigger. Introduced 1988. Made in U.S.A. by E. Arthur Brown Co. Inc.

Price: **$669.00**

BF Classic Hunting Pistol

Similar to BF Ultimate Silhouette HB Single Shot Pistol, except no sights; drilled and tapped for scope mount. Barrels from 8" to 15". Variety of options offered. Made in U.S.A. by E. Arthur Brown Co. Inc.

Price: **$599.00**

BROWNING BUCK MARK SILHOUETTE

Caliber: 22 LR, 10-shot magazine. **Barrel:** 9-7/8". **Weight:** 53 oz. **Length:** 14" overall. **Grips:** Smooth walnut stocks and forend, or finger-groove walnut. **Sights:** Post-type hooded front adjustable for blade width and height; Pro Target rear fully adjustable for windage and elevation. **Features:** Heavy barrel with .900" diameter; 12-1/2" sight radius. Special sighting plane forms scope base. Introduced 1987. Made in U.S.A. From Browning.

Price: **$448.00**

Browning Buck Mark Target 5.5

Same as Buck Mark Silhouette, 5-1/2" barrel with .900" diameter. Hooded sights mounted on scope base that accepts optical or reflex sight. Rear sight is Browning fully adjustable Pro Target, front sight is adjustable post that customizes to different widths, can be adjusted for height. Contoured walnut grips with thumbrest, or finger-groove walnut. Matte blue finish. Overall length is 9-5/8", weighs 35-1/2 oz. Has 10-shot magazine. Introduced 1990. From Browning.

Price: **$425.00**
Price: Target 5.5 Gold (as above with gold anodized frame and
top rib) **$477.00**
Price: Target 5.5 Nickel (as above with nickel frame
and top rib) **$477.00**

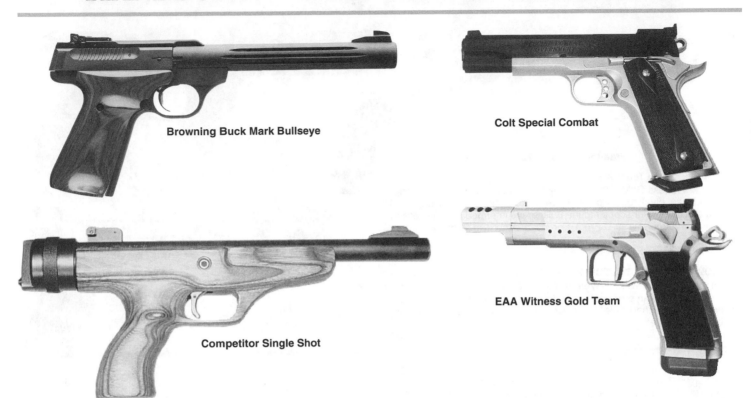

Browning Buck Mark Bullseye

Colt Special Combat

Competitor Single Shot

EAA Witness Gold Team

Browning Buck Mark Field 5.5

Same as Target 5.5, hoodless ramp-style front sight and low profile rear sight. Matte blue finish, contoured or finger-groove walnut stocks. Introduced 1991.

Price: **$425.00**

Browning Buck Mark Bullseye

Similar to Buck Mark Silhouette, 7-1/4" heavy barrel with three flutes per side; trigger adjusts from 2-1/2 to 5 lbs.; specially designed rosewood target or three-finger-groove stocks with competition-style heel rest, or with contoured rubber grip. Overall length 11-5/16", weighs 36 oz. Introduced 1996. Made in U.S.A. From Browning.

Price: With ambidextrous moulded composite stocks. **$389.00**
Price: With rosewood stocks, or wrap-around finger groove..... **$500.00**

COLT GOLD CUP MODEL O PISTOL

Caliber: 45 ACP, 8-shot magazine. **Barrel:** 5", with new design bushing. **Weight:** 39 oz. **Length:** 8-1/2". **Grips:** Checkered rubber composite with silver-plated medallion. **Sights:** Patridge-style front, Bomar-style rear adjustable for windage and elevation, sight radius 6-3/4". **Features:** Arched or flat housing; wide, grooved trigger with adjustable stop; ribbed-top slide, hand fitted, with improved ejection port.

Price: Blue **$1,050.00**
Price: Stainless.. **$1,116.00**

COLT SPECIAL COMBAT GOVERNMENT

Caliber: 45 ACP. **Barrel:** 5" **Weight:** NA. **Length:** 8-1/2" **Grips:** Rosewood w/double diamond checkering pattern. **Sights:** Clark dovetail, front; Bomar adjustable, rear. **Features:** A competition ready pistol with enhancements such as skeletonized trigger, upswept grip safety, custom tuned action, polished feed ramp. Blue or satin nickel finish. Introduced 2003. Made in U.S.A. by Colt's Mfg. Co.

Price: **$1,640.00**

COMPETITOR SINGLE SHOT PISTOL

Caliber: 22 LR through 50 Action Express, including belted magnums. **Barrel:** 14" standard; 10.5" silhouette; 16" optional. **Weight:** About 59 oz. (14" bbl.). **Length:** 15.12" overall. **Grips:** Ambidextrous; synthetic (standard) or laminated or natural wood. **Sights:** Ramp front, adjustable rear. **Features:** Rotary canon-type action cocks on opening; cammed ejector; interchangeable barrels, ejectors. Adjustable single stage trigger, sliding thumb safety and trigger safety. Matte blue finish. Introduced 1988. From Competitor Corp., Inc.

Price: 14", standard calibers, synthetic grip **$414.95**
Price: Extra barrels, from **$159.95**

CZ 75 CHAMPION COMPETITION PISTOL

Caliber: 9mm Para., 9x21, 40 S&W, 10-shot mag. **Barrel:** 4.49". **Weight:** 35 oz. **Length:** 9.44" overall. **Grips:** Black rubber. **Sights:** Blade front, fully adjustable rear. **Features:** Single-action trigger mechanism; three-port compensator (40 S&W, 9mm have two port) full-length guide rod; extended magazine release; ambidextrous safety; flared magazine well; fully adjustable match trigger. Introduced 1999. Imported from the Czech Republic by CZ USA.

Price: 9mm Para., 9x21, 40 S&W, dual-tone finish.......... **$1,551.00**

CZ 75 ST IPSC AUTO PISTOL

Caliber: 40 S&W, 10-shot magazine. **Barrel:** 5.12". **Weight:** 2.9 lbs. **Length:** 8.86" overall. **Grips:** Checkered walnut. **Sights:** Fully adjustable rear. **Features:** Single-action mechanism; extended slide release and ambidextrous safety; full-length slide rail; double slide serrations. Introduced 1999. Imported from the Czech Republic by CZ-USA.

Price: Dual-tone finish **$1,038.00**

EAA/BAIKAL IZH35 AUTO PISTOL

Caliber: 22 LR, 5-shot mag. **Barrel:** 6". **Grips:** Walnut; fully adjustable right-hand target-style. **Sights:** Fully adjustable rear, blade front; detachable scope mount. **Features:** Hammer-forged target barrel; machined steel receiver; adjustable trigger; manual slide hold back, grip and manual trigger-bar disconnect safeties; cocking indicator. Introduced 2000. Imported from Russia by European American Armory.

Price: Blued finish...................................... **$539.00**

EAA WITNESS GOLD TEAM AUTO

Caliber: 9mm Para., 9x21, 38 Super, 40 S&W, 45 ACP. **Barrel:** 5.1". **Weight:** 41.6 oz. **Length:** 9.6" overall. **Grips:** Checkered walnut, competition style. **Sights:** Square post front, fully adjustable rear. **Features:** Triple-chamber cone compensator; competition SA trigger; extended safety and magazine release; competition hammer; beveled magazine well; beavertail grip. Hand-fitted major components. Hard chrome finish. Match-grade barrel. From E.A.A. Custom Shop. Introduced 1992. From European American Armory.

Price: **$2,150.00**

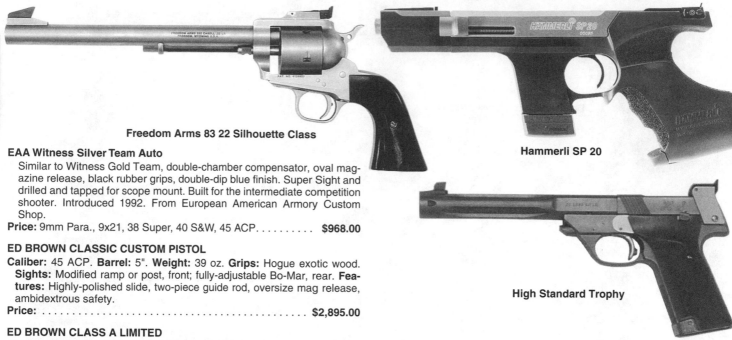

Freedom Arms 83 22 Silhouette Class

Hammerli SP 20

High Standard Trophy

EAA Witness Silver Team Auto
Similar to Witness Gold Team, double-chamber compensator, oval magazine release, black rubber grips, double-dip blue finish. Super Sight and drilled and tapped for scope mount. Built for the intermediate competition shooter. Introduced 1992. From European American Armory Custom Shop.
Price: 9mm Para., 9x21, 38 Super, 40 S&W, 45 ACP **$968.00**

ED BROWN CLASSIC CUSTOM PISTOL
Caliber: 45 ACP. **Barrel:** 5". **Weight:** 39 oz. **Grips:** Hogue exotic wood. **Sights:** Modified ramp or post, front; fully-adjustable Bo-Mar, rear. **Features:** Highly-polished slide, two-piece guide rod, oversize mag release, ambidextrous safety.
Price: **$2,895.00**

ED BROWN CLASS A LIMITED
Caliber: 45 ACP, 400 Cor-Bon, 10mm, 40 S&W, 357 SIG, 38 Super, 9x23, 9mm Luger, 7-shot magazine. **Barrel:** 4.25", 5". **Weight:** 34 to 39 oz. **Grips:** Hogue exotic wood. **Sights:** Customer preference, front; fixed Novak low-mount or fully-adjustable Bo-Mar, rear. **Features:** Checkered forestrap and mainspring housing, matte finished top sighting surface. Many options available.
Price: **$2,250.00**

ENTRÉPRISE TOURNAMENT SHOOTER MODEL I
Caliber: 45 ACP, 10-shot mag. **Barrel:** 6". **Weight:** 40 oz. **Length:** 8.5" overall. **Grips:** Black ultra-slim double diamond checkered synthetic. **Sights:** Dovetailed Patridge front, adjustable Competizione "melded" rear. **Features:** Oversized magazine release button; flared magazine well; fully machined parallel slide rails; front and rear slide serrations; serrated top of slide; stainless ramped bull barrel with fully supported chamber; full-length guide rod with plug; stainless firing pin; match extractor; polished ramp; tuned match extractor; black oxide. Introduced 1998. Made in U.S.A. by Entréprise Arms.
Price: **$2,300.00**
Price: TSMIII (Satin chrome finish, two-piece guide rod) **$2,700.00**

EXCEL INDUSTRIES CP-45, XP-45 AUTO PISTOL
Caliber: 45 ACP, 6-shot & 10-shot mags. **Barrel:** 3-1/4". **Weight:** 31 oz. & 25 oz. **Length:** 6-3/8" overall. **Grips:** Checkered black nylon. **Sights:** Fully adjustable rear. **Features:** Stainless steel frame and slide; single action with external hammer and firing pin block, manual thumb safety; last-shot hold open. Includes gun lock and cleaning kit. Introduced 2001. Made in U.S.A. by Excel Industries Inc.
Price: CP-45 . . . . **$425.00**
Price: XP-45 . . . . **$465.00**

FEINWERKEBAU AW93 TARGET PISTOL
Caliber: 22. **Barrel:** 6". **Grips:** Fully adjustable orthopaedic. **Sights:** Fully adjustable micrometer. **Features:** Advanced Russian design with German craftmanship. Imported from Germany by Nygord Precision Products.
Price: **$1,495.00**

FREEDOM ARMS MODEL 83 22 FIELD GRADE SILHOUETTE CLASS
Caliber: 22 LR, 5-shot cylinder. **Barrel:** 10". **Weight:** 63 oz. **Length:** 15.5" overall. **Grips:** Black Micarta. **Sights:** Removable patridge front blade; Iron Sight Gun Works silhouette rear, click adjustable for windage and elevation (optional adj. front sight and hood). **Features:** Stainless steel, matte finish, manual sliding-bar safety system; dual firing pins, lightened hammer for fast lock time, pre-set trigger stop. Introduced 1991. Made in U.S.A. by Freedom Arms.

Price: Silhouette Class **$1,901.75**
Price: Extra fitted 22 WMR cylinder **$264.00**

FREEDOM ARMS MODEL 83 CENTERFIRE SILHOUETTE MODELS
Caliber: 357 Mag., 41 Mag., 44 Mag.; 5-shot cylinder. **Barrel:** 10", 9" (357 Mag. only). **Weight:** 63 oz. (41 Mag.). **Length:** 15.5", 14-1/2" (357 only). **Grips:** Pachmayr Presentation. **Sights:** Iron Sight Gun Works silhouette rear sight, replaceable adjustable front sight blade with hood. **Features:** Stainless steel, matte finish, manual sliding-bar safety system. Made in U.S.A. by Freedom Arms.
Price: Silhouette Models **$1,634.85**

GAUCHER GP SILHOUETTE PISTOL
Caliber: 22 LR, single shot. **Barrel:** 10". **Weight:** 42.3 oz. **Length:** 15.5" overall. **Grips:** Stained hardwood. **Sights:** Hooded post on ramp front, open rear adjustable for windage and elevation. **Features:** Matte chrome barrel, blued bolt and sights. Other barrel lengths available on special order. Introduced 1991. Imported by Mandall Shooting Supplies.
Price: **$425.00**

HAMMERLI SP 20 TARGET PISTOL
Caliber: 22 LR, 32 S&W. **Barrel:** 4.6". **Weight:** 34.6-41.8 oz. **Length:** 11.8" overall. **Grips:** Anatomically shaped synthetic Hi-Grip available in five sizes. **Sights:** Integral front in three widths, adjustable rear with changeable notch widths. **Features:** Extremely low-level sight line; anatomically shaped trigger; adjustable JPS buffer system for different recoil characteristics. Receiver available in red, blue, gold, violet or black. Introduced 1998. Imported from Switzerland by SIGARMS, Inc and Hammerli Pistols USA.
Price: Hammerli 22 LR **$1,668.00**
Price: Hammerli 32 S&W **$1,743.00**

HAMMERLI X-ESSE SPORT PISTOL
An all-steel .22 LR target pistol with a Hi-Grip in a new anatomical shape and an adjustable hand rest. Made in Switzerland. Introduced 2003.
Price: **$710.00**

HARRIS GUNWORKS SIGNATURE JR. LONG RANGE PISTOL
Caliber: Any suitable caliber. **Barrel:** To customer specs. **Weight:** 5 lbs. **Stock:** Gunworks fiberglass. **Sights:** None furnished; comes with scope rings. **Features:** Right- or left-hand benchrest action of titanium or stainless steel; single shot or repeater. Comes with bipod. Introduced 1992. Made in U.S.A. by Harris Gunworks, Inc.
Price: **$2,700.00**

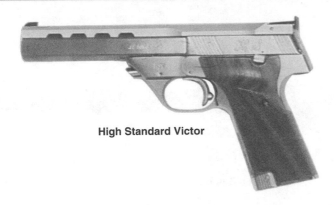

High Standard Victor

Ruger Mark II Target

HIGH STANDARD TROPHY TARGET PISTOL

Caliber: 22 LR, 10-shot mag. **Barrel:** 5-1/2" bull or 7-1/4" fluted. **Weight:** 44 oz. **Length:** 9.5" overall. **Stock:** Checkered hardwood with thumbrest. **Sights:** Undercut ramp front, frame-mounted micro-click rear adjustable for windage and elevation; drilled and tapped for scope mounting. **Features:** Gold-plated trigger, slide lock, safety-lever and magazine release; stippled front grip and backstrap; adjustable trigger and sear. Barrel weights optional. From High Standard Manufacturing Co., Inc.

Price: 5-1/2", scope base **$540.00**
Price: 7.25" **$689.00**
Price: 7.25", scope base **$625.00**

HIGH STANDARD VICTOR TARGET PISTOL

Caliber: 22 LR, 10-shot magazine. **Barrel:** 4-1/2" or 5-1/2"; push-button takedown. **Weight:** 46 oz. **Length:** 9.5" overall. **Stock:** Checkered hardwood with thumbrest. **Sights:** Undercut ramp front, micro-click rear adjustable for windage and elevation. Also available with scope mount, rings, no sights. **Features:** Stainless steel construction. Full-length vent rib. Gold-plated trigger, slide lock, safety-lever and magazine release; stippled front grip and backstrap; polished slide; adjustable trigger and sear. Comes with barrel weight. From High Standard Manufacturing Co., Inc.

Price: 4-1/2" scope base. **$564.00**
Price: 5-1/2", sights. **$625.00**
Price: 5-1/2" scope base. **$564.00**

KIMBER SUPER MATCH AUTO PISTOL

Caliber: 45 ACP, 7-shot magazine. **Barrel:** 5". **Weight:** 38 oz. **Length:** 18.7" overall. **Sights:** Blade front, Kimber fully adjustable rear. **Features:** Guaranteed to have shot 3" group at 50 yards. Stainless steel frame, black KimPro slide; two-piece magazine well; premium aluminum match-grade trigger; 30 lpi front strap checkering; stainless match-grade barrel; ambidextrous safety; special Custom Shop markings. Introduced 1999. Made in U.S.A. by Kimber Mfg., Inc.

Price: **$1,927.00**

KORTH MATCH REVOLVER

Caliber: .357 Mag., .38 Special, .32 S&W Long, 9mm Para., .22 WMR, .22 LR. **Barrel:** 5 π", 6". **Grips:** Adjustable match of oiled walnut with matte finish. **Sights:** Fully adjustable with rear sight leaves (wide th of sight notch: 3.4 mm, 3.5 mm, 3.6 mm), rear; undercut partridge, front. **Trigger:** Equipped with completely machined trigger shoe. Interchangeable caliber cylinders available as well as a variety of finishes. Made in Germany.

Price: . . . . From **$5,442.00**

MORINI MODEL 84E FREE PISTOL

Caliber: 22 LR, single shot. **Barrel:** 11.4". **Weight:** 43.7 oz. **Length:** 19.4" overall. **Grips:** Adjustable match type with stippled surfaces. **Sights:** Interchangeable blade front, match-type fully adjustable rear. **Features:** Fully adjustable electronic trigger. Introduced 1995. Imported from Switzerland by Nygord Precision Products.

Price: **$1,450.00**

PARDINI MODEL SP, HP TARGET PISTOLS

Caliber: 22 LR, 32 S&W, 5-shot magazine. **Barrel:** 4.7". **Weight:** 38.9 oz. **Length:** 11.6" overall. **Grips:** Adjustable; stippled walnut; match type. **Sights:** Interchangeable blade front, interchangeable, fully adjustable rear. **Features:** Fully adjustable match trigger. Introduced 1995. Imported from Italy by Nygord Precision Products.

Price: Model SP (22 LR). **$995.00**
Price: Model HP (32 S&W). **$1,095.00**

PARDINI GP RAPID FIRE MATCH PISTOL

Caliber: 22 Short, 5-shot magazine. **Barrel:** 4.6". **Weight:** 43.3 oz. **Length:** 11.6" overall. **Grips:** Wrap-around stippled walnut. **Sights:** Interchangeable post front, fully adjustable match rear. Introduced 1995. Imported from Italy by Nygord Precision Products.

Price: Model GP **$1,095.00**
Price: Model GP-E Electronic, has special parts **$1,595.00**

PARDINI K22 FREE PISTOL

Caliber: 22 LR, single shot. **Barrel:** 9.8". **Weight:** 34.6 oz. **Length:** 18.7" overall. **Grips:** Wrap-around walnut; adjustable match type. **Sights:** Interchangeable post front, fully adjustable match open rear. **Features:** Removable, adjustable match trigger. Toggle bolt pushes cartridge into chamber. Barrel weights mount above the barrel. New upgraded model introduced in 2002. Imported from Italy by Nygord Precision Products.

Price: **$1,295.00**

PARDINI GT45 TARGET PISTOL

Caliber: 45, 9mm, 40 S&W. **Barrel:** 5", 6". **Grips:** Checkered fore strap. **Sights:** Interchangeable post front, fully adjustable match open rear. **Features:** Ambi-safeties, trigger pull adjustable. Fits Helweg Glock holsters for defense shooters. Imported from Italy by Nygord Precision Products.

Price: 5" **$1,050.00**
Price: 6" **$1,125.00**
Price: Frame mount available . . . . **$75.00 extra**
Price: Slide mount available . . . . **$35.00 extra**

PARDINI/NYGORD "MASTER" TARGET PISTOL

Caliber: 22 cal. **Barrel:** 5-1/2". **Grips:** Semi-wrap-around. **Sights:** Micrometer rear and red dot. **Features:** Elegant NRA "Bullseye" pistol. Superior balance of Pardini pistols. Revolutionary recirpcating internal weight barrel shroud. Imported from Italy by Nygord Precision Products.

Price: **$1,145.00**

RUGER MARK II TARGET MODEL AUTOLOADING PISTOL

Caliber: 22 LR, 10-shot magazine. **Barrel:** 6-7/8". **Weight:** 42 oz. **Length:** 11-1/8" overall. **Grips:** Checkered composition grip panels. **Sights:** .125" blade front, micro-click rear, adjustable for windage and elevation. Sight radius 9-3/8". Plastic case with lock included.

Features: Introduced 1982.
Price: Blued (MK-678) **$349.00**
Price: Stainless (KMK-678) **$439.00**

Ruger Mark II Government Target Model

Same gun as Mark II Target Model except has 6-7/8" barrel, higher sights and is roll marked "Government Target Model" on right side of receiver below rear sight. Identical in all aspects to military model used for training U.S. Armed Forces except for markings. Comes with factory test target, also lockable plastic case. Introduced 1987.

Price: Blued (MK-678G) **$425.00**
Price: Stainless (KMK-678G) **$509.00**

Ruger Mark II Government Target

Ruger Mark II Bull Barrel - MK10

Safari Arms Big Deuce

Smith & Wesson Model 41

Springfield, Inc. 1911A1 Bullseye Wadcutter

Ruger Stainless Competition Model Pistol

Similar to Mark II Government Target Model stainless pistol, 6-7/8" slab-sided barrel; receiver top is fitted with Ruger scope base of blued, chrome moly steel; has Ruger 1" stainless scope rings for mounting variety of optical sights; checkered laminated grip panels with right-hand thumbrest. Blued open sights with 9-1/4" radius. Overall length 11-1/8", weight 45 oz. Case and lock included. Introduced 1991.

Price: KMK-678GC **$529.00**

Ruger Mark II Bull Barrel

Same gun as Target Model except has 5-1/2" or 10" heavy barrel (10" meets all IHMSA regulations). Weight with 5-1/2" barrel is 42 oz., with 10" barrel, 51 oz. Case with lock included.

Price: Blued (MK-512) **$349.00**
Price: Blued (MK-10) **$357.00**
Price: Stainless (KMK-10) **$445.00**
Price: Stainless (KMK-512) **$439.00**

SAFARI ARMS BIG DEUCE PISTOL

Caliber: 45 ACP, 7-shot magazine. **Barrel:** 6", 416 stainless steel. **Weight:** 40.3 oz. **Length:** 9.5" overall. **Grips:** Smooth walnut. **Sights:** Ramped blade front, LPA adjustable rear. **Features:** Beavertail grip safety; extended thumb safety and slide release; Commander-style hammer. Throated, polished and tuned. Parkerized matte black slide with satin stainless steel frame. Introduced 1995. Made in U.S.A. by Safari Arms, Inc.

Price: **$714.00**

SMITH & WESSON MODEL 41 TARGET

Caliber: 22 LR, 10-shot clip. **Barrel:** 5-1/2", 7". **Weight:** 44 oz. (5-1/2" barrel). **Length:** 9" overall (5-1/2" barrel). **Grips:** Checkered walnut with modified thumbrest, usable with either hand. **Sights:** 1/8" Patridge on ramp base; micro-click rear adjustable for windage and elevation. **Features:** 3/8" wide, grooved trigger; adjustable trigger stop drilled and tapped.

Price: S&W Bright Blue, either barrel **$958.00**

SMITH & WESSON MODEL 22A TARGET PISTOL

Caliber: 22 LR, 10-shot magazine. **Barrel:** 5-1/2" bull. **Weight:** 38.5 oz. **Length:** 9-1/2" overall. **Grips:** Dymondwood with ambidextrous thumbrests and flared bottom or rubber soft touch with thumbrest. **Sights:** Patridge front, fully adjustable rear. **Features:** Sight bridge with Weaver-style integral optics mount; alloy frame, stainless barrel and slide; blue finish. Introduced 1997. Made in U.S.A. by Smith & Wesson.

Price: **$367.00**
Price: HiViz front sight **$387.00**

Smith & Wesson Model 22S Target Pistol

Similar to the Model 22A except has stainless steel frame. Introduced 1997. Made in U.S.A. by Smith & Wesson.

Price: **$434.00**
Price: HiViz front sight **$453.00**

SPRINGFIELD, INC. 1911A1 BULLSEYE WADCUTTER PISTOL

Caliber: 38 Super, 45 ACP. **Barrel:** 5". **Weight:** 45 oz. **Length:** 8.59" overall (5" barrel). **Grips:** Checkered walnut. **Sights:** Bo-Mar rib with undercut blade front, fully adjustable rear. **Features:** Built for wadcutter loads only. Has full-length recoil spring guide rod, fitted Videki speed trigger with 3.5-lb. pull; match Commander hammer and sear; beavertail grip safety; lowered and flared ejection port; tuned extractor; fitted slide to frame; recoil buffer system; beveled and polished magazine well; checkered front strap and steel mainspring housing (flat housing standard); polished and throated National Match barrel and bushing. Comes with two magazines with slam pads, plastic carrying case, test target. Introduced 1992. From Springfield, Inc.

Price: **$1,499.00**

HANDGUNS

Springfield, Inc. Expert

Springfield, Inc. Distinguished

Springfield, Inc. N.M. Hardball

Springfield, Inc. 1911A1 Trophy Match

Springfield, Inc. Basic Competition Pistol

Has low-mounted Bo-Mar adjustable rear sight, undercut blade front; match throated barrel and bushing; polished feed ramp; lowered and flared ejection port; fitted Videki speed trigger with tuned 3.5-lb. pull; fitted slide to frame; recoil buffer system; checkered walnut grips; serrated, arched mainspring housing. Comes with two magazines with slam pads, plastic carrying case. Introduced 1992. From Springfield, Inc.

Price: 45 ACP, blue, 5" only **$1,295.00**

Springfield, Inc. Expert Pistol

Similar to the Competition Pistol except has triple-chamber tapered cone compensator on match barrel with dovetailed front sight; lowered and flared ejection port; fully tuned for reliability; fitted slide to frame; extended ambidextrous thumb safety, extended magazine release button; beavertail grip safety; Pachmayr wrap-around grips. Comes with two magazines, plastic carrying case. Introduced 1992. From Springfield, Inc.

Price: 45 ACP, Duotone finish **$1,724.00**
Price: Expert Ltd. (non-compensated) **$1,624.00**

Springfield, Inc. Distinguished Pistol

Has all the features of the 1911A1 Expert except is full-house pistol with deluxe Bo-Mar low-mounted adjustable rear sight; full-length recoil spring guide rod and recoil spring retainer; checkered frontstrap; S&A magazine well; walnut grips. Hard chrome finish. Comes with two magazines with slam pads, plastic carrying case. From Springfield, Inc.

Price: 45 ACP **$2,445.00**
Price: Distinguished Limited (non-compensated) **$2,345.00**

Springfield, Inc. 1911A1 N.M. Hardball Pistol

Has Bo-Mar adjustable rear sight with undercut front blade; fitted match Videki trigger with 4-lb. pull; fitted slide to frame; throated National Match barrel and bushing; polished feed ramp; recoil buffer system; tuned extractor; Herrett walnut grips. Comes with two magazines, plastic carrying case, test target. Introduced 1992. From Springfield, Inc.

Price: 45 ACP, blue **$1,336.00**

Springfield, Inc. Leatham Legend TGO Series Pistols

Three models of 5" barrel, .45 ACP 1911 pistols built for serious competition. TGO 1 has deluxe low mount BoMar rear sight, Dawson fiber optics front sight, 3.5 lb. trigger pull. TGO 2 has BoMar low mount adjustable rear sight, Dawson fiber optic front sight, 4.5 to 5 lb. trigger pull. TGO 3 has Springfield Armory fully adjustable rear sight with low mount BoMar cut Dawson fiber optic front sight, 4.5 to 5 lb. trigger.

Price: TGO 1 . . . . **$2,999.00**
Price: TGO 2 . . . . **$1,899.00**
Price: TGO 3 . . . . **$1,295.00**

Springfield, Inc. Trophy Match Pistol

Similar to Springfield, Inc.'s Full Size model, but designed for bullseye and action shooting competition. Available with a Service Model 5" frame with matching slide and barrel in 5" and 6" lengths. Fully adjustable sights, checkered frame front strap, match barrel and bushing. In 45 ACP only. From Springfield Inc.

Price: **$1,248.00**

STI EAGLE 5.0, 6.0 PISTOL

Caliber: 9mm, 9x21, 38 & 40 Super, 40 S&W, 10mm, 45 ACP, 10-shot magazine. **Barrel:** 5", 6" bull. **Weight:** 34.5 oz. **Length:** 8.62" overall. **Grips:** Checkered polymer. **Sights:** STI front, Novak or Heine rear. **Features:** Standard frames plus 7 others; adjustable match trigger; skeletonized hammer; extended grip safety with locator pad; match-grade fit of all parts. Many options available. Introduced 1994. Made in U.S.A. by STI International.

Price: . . . . (5.0 Eagle) **$1,794.00**, (6.0 Eagle) **$1,894.00**

STI Executive Pistol

Caliber: 40 S&W. **Barrel:** 5" bull. **Weight:** 39 oz. **Length:** 8-5/8". **Grips:** Gray polymer. **Sights:** Dawson fiber optic, front; STI adjustable rear. **Features:** Stainless mag. well, front and rear serrations on slide. Made in U.S.A. by STI.

Price: **$2,389.00**

STI Trojan

Caliber: 9mm, 38 Super, 40S&W, 45 ACP. **Barrel:** 5", 6". **Weight:** 36 oz. **Length:** 8.5". **Grips:** Rosewood. **Sights:** STI front with STI adjustable rear. **Features:** Stippled front strap, flat top slide, one-piece steel guide rod.

Price: (Trojan 5") **$1,024.00**
Price: (Trojan 6", not available in 38 Super) **$1,232.50**

WALTHER GSP MATCH PISTOL

Caliber: 22 LR, 32 S&W Long (GSP-C), 5-shot magazine. **Barrel:** 4.22". **Weight:** 44.8 oz. (22 LR), 49.4 oz. (32). **Length:** 11.8" overall. **Grips:** Walnut. **Sights:** Post front, match rear adjustable for windage and elevation. **Features:** Available with either 2.2-lb. (1000 gm) or 3-lb. (1360 gm) trigger. Spare magazine, barrel weight, tools supplied. Imported from Germany by Nygord Precision Products.

Price: GSP, with case **$1,495.00**
Price: GSP-C, with case **$1,595.00**

HANDGUNS — DOUBLE ACTION REVOLVERS, SERVICE & SPORT

Includes models suitable for hunting and competitive courses of fire, both police and international.

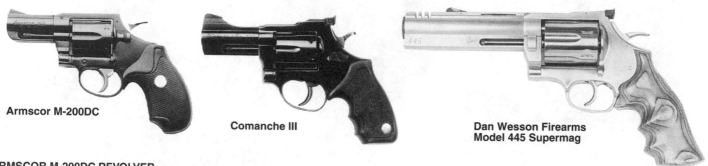

Armscor M-200DC

Comanche III

Dan Wesson Firearms Model 445 Supermag

ARMSCOR M-200DC REVOLVER
Caliber: 38 Spec., 6-shot cylinder. **Barrel:** 2-1/2", 4". **Weight:** 22 oz. (2-1/2" barrel). **Length:** 7-3/8" overall (2-1/2" barrel). **Grips:** Checkered rubber. **Sights:** Blade front, fixed notch rear. **Features:** All-steel construction; floating firing pin, transfer bar ignition; shrouded ejector rod; blue finish. Reintroduced 1996. Imported from the Philippines by K.B.I., Inc.
Price: 2-1/2" **$199.99**
Price: 4" **$205.00**

ARMSPORT MODEL 4540 REVOLVER
Caliber: 38 Special. **Barrel:** 4". **Weight:** 32 oz **Length:** 9" overall. **Sights:** Fixed rear, blade front. **Features:** Ventilated rib; blued finish. Imported from Argentina by Armsport Inc.
Price: **$140.00**

COMANCHE I, II, III DA REVOLVERS
Features: Adjustable sights. Blue or stainless finish. Distributed by SGS Importers.
Price: I 22 LR, 6" bbl, 9-shot, blue **$236.95**
Price: I 22LR, 6" bbl, 9-shot, stainless **$258.95**
Price: II 38 Special, 3", 4" bbl, 6-shot, blue. **$219.95**
Price: II 38 Special, 4" bbl, 6-shot, stainless. **$236.95**
Price: III 357 Mag, 3", 4", 6" bbl, 6-shot, blue **$253.95**
Price: III 357 Mag, 3", 4", 6" bbl, 6-shot, stainless **$274.95**
Price: II 38 Special, 3" bbl, 6-shot, stainless steel **$236.95**

DAN WESSON FIREARMS MODEL 722 SILHOUETTE REVOLVER
Caliber: 22 LR, 6-shot. **Barrel:** 10", vent heavy. **Weight:** 53 oz. **Grips:** Combat style. **Sights:** Patridge-style front, .080" narrow notch rear. **Features:** Single action only. Satin brushed stainless finish. Reintroduced 1997. Made in U.S.A. by Dan Wesson Firearms.
Price: 722 VH10 (vent heavy 10" bbl.) **$888.00**
Price: 722 VH10 SRS1 (Super Ram Silhouette, Bo-Mar sights, front hood, trigger job). **$1,164.00**

DAN WESSON FIREARMS MODEL 3220/73220 TARGET REVOLVER
Caliber: 32-20, 6-shot. **Barrel:** 2.5", 4", 6", 8", 10" standard vent, vent heavy. **Weight:** 47 oz. (6" VH). **Length:** 11.25" overall. **Grips:** Hogue Gripper rubber (walnut, exotic hardwoods optional). **Sights:** Red ramp interchangeable front, fully adjustable rear. **Features:** Bright blue (3220) or stainless (73220). Reintroduced 1997. Made in U.S.A. by Dan Wesson Firearms.
Price: 3220 VH2.5 (blued, 2.5" vent heavy bbl.) **$643.00**
Price: 73220 VH10 (stainless 10" vent heavy bbl.) **$873.00**

DAN WESSON FIREARMS MODEL 40/740 REVOLVERS
Caliber: 357 Maximum, 6-shot. **Barrel:** 4", 6", 8", 10". **Weight:** 72 oz. (8" bbl.). **Length:** 14.3" overall (8" bbl.). **Grips:** Hogue Gripper rubber (walnut or exotic hardwood optional). **Sights:** 1/8" serrated front, fully adjustable rear. **Features:** Blue or stainless steel. Made in U.S.A. by Dan Wesson Firearms.
Price: Blue, 4". **$702.00**
Price: Blue, 6". **$749.00**

Price: Blue, 8" **$795.00**
Price: Blue, 10". **$858.00**
Price: Stainless, 4" **$834.00**
Price: Stainless, 6" **$892.00**
Price: Stainless, 8" slotted **$1,024.00**
Price: Stainless, 10" **$998.00**
Price: 4", 6", 8" Compensated, blue . . . . **$749.00 to $885.00**
Price: As above, stainless. . . . . **$893.00 to $1,061.00**

Dan Wesson Firearms Model 414/7414 and 445/7445 SuperMag Revolvers
Similar size and weight as Model 40 revolvers. Chambered for 414 SuperMag or 445 SuperMag cartridge. Barrel lengths of 4", 6", 8", 10". Contact maker for complete price list. Reintroduced 1997. Made in the U.S. by Dan Wesson Firearms.
Price: 4", vent heavy, blue or stainless **$904.00**
Price: 8", vent heavy, blue or stainless **$1,026.00**
Price: 10", vent heavy, blue or stainless **$1,103.00**
Price: Compensated models . . . . **$965.00 to $1,149.00**

DAN WESSON FIREARMS MODEL 22/722 REVOLVERS
Caliber: 22 LR, 22 WMR, 6-shot. **Barrel:** 2-1/2", 4", 6", 8" or 10"; interchangeable. **Weight:** 36 oz. (2-1/2"), 44 oz. (6"). **Length:** 9-1/4" overall (4" barrel). **Grips:** Hogue Gripper rubber (walnut, exotic woods optional). **Sights:** 1/8" serrated, interchangeable front, white outline rear adjustable for windage and elevation. **Features:** Built on the same frame as the Wesson 357; smooth, wide trigger with over-travel adjustment, wide spur hammer, with short double-action travel. Available in blue or stainless steel. Reintroduced 1997. Contact Dan Wesson Firearms for complete price list.
Price: 22 VH2.5/722 VH2.5 (blued or stainless 2-1/2" bbl.) **$551.00**
Price: 22VH10/722 VH10 (blued or stainless 10" bbl.) **$750.00**

Dan Wesson 722M Small Frame Revolver
Similar to Model 22/722 except chambered for 22 WMR. Blued or stainless finish, 2-1/2", 4", 6" or 10" barrels.
Price: Blued or stainless finish . . . . **$643.00 to $873.00**

DAN WESSON FIREARMS MODEL 15/715 and 32/732 REVOLVERS
Caliber: 32-20, 32 H&R Mag. (Model 32), 357 Mag. (Model 15). **Barrel:** 2-1/2", 4", 6", 8" (M32), 2-1/2", 4", 6", 8", 10" (M15); vent heavy. **Weight:** 36 oz. (2-1/2" barrel). **Length:** 9-1/4" overall (4" barrel). **Grips:** Checkered, interchangeable. **Sights:** 1/8" serrated front, fully adjustable rear. **Features:** New Generation Series. Interchangeable barrels; wide, smooth trigger, wide hammer spur; short double-action travel. Available in blue or stainless. Reintroduced 1997. Made in U.S.A. by Dan Wesson Firearms. Contact maker for full list of models.
Price: Model 15/715, 2-1/2" (blue or stainless) **$551.00**
Price: Model 15/715, 8" (blue or stainless) **$612.00**
Price: Model 15/715, compensated . . . . **$704.00 to $827.00**
Price: Model 32/732, 4" (blue or stainless) **$674.00**
Price: Model 32/732, 8" (blue or stainless) **$766.00**

Dan Wesson Firearms Model 744 VH8

**Dan Wesson Firearms
Super Ram Silhouette**

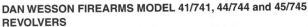

**Dan Wesson Firearms
Alaskan Guide Special**

DAN WESSON FIREARMS MODEL 41/741, 44/744 and 45/745 REVOLVERS

Caliber: 41 Mag., 44 Mag., 45 Colt, 6-shot. **Barrel:** 4", 6", 8", 10"; interchangeable; 4", 6", 8" Compensated. **Weight:** 48 oz. (4"). **Length:** 12" overall (6" bbl.) **Grips:** Smooth. **Sights:** 1/8" serrated front, white outline rear adjustable for windage and elevation. **Features:** Available in blue or stainless steel. Smooth, wide trigger with adjustable over-travel, wide hammer spur. Available in Pistol Pac set also. Reintroduced 1997. Contact Dan Wesson Firearms for complete price list.

Price: 41 Mag., 4", vent heavy (blue or stainless). **$643.00**
Price: 44 Mag., 6", vent heavy (blue or stainless). **$689.00**
Price: 45 Colt, 8", vent heavy (blue or stainless) **$766.00**
Price: Compensated models (all calibers) . . . . **$812.00 to $934.00**

DAN WESSON FIREARMS LARGE FRAME SERIES REVOLVERS

Caliber: 41, 741/41 Magnum; 44, 744/44 Magnum; 45, 745/45 Long Colt; 360, 7360/357; 460, 7460/45. **Barrel:** 2"-10". **Weight:** 49 oz.-69 oz. **Grips:** Standard, Hogue rubber Gripper Grips. **Sights:** Standard front, serrated ramp with color insert. Standard rear, adustable wide notch. Other sight options available. **Features:** Available in blue or stainless steel. Smooth, wide trigger with overtravel, wide hammer spur. Double and single action.

Price: . . . . **$769.00 to $889.00**

DAN WESSON FIREARMS MODEL 360/7360 REVOLVERS

Caliber: 357 Mag. **Barrel:** 4", 6", 8", 10"; vent heavy. **Weight:** 64 oz. (8" barrel). **Grips:** Hogue rubber finger groove. **Sights:** Interchangeable ramp or Patridge front, fully adjustable rear. **Features:** New Generation Large Frame Series. Interchangeable barrels and grips; smooth trigger, wide hammer spur. Blue (360) or stainless (7360). Introduced 1999. Made in U.S.A. by Dan Wesson Firearms.

Price: 4" bbl., blue or stainless **$735.00**
Price: 10" bbl., blue or stainless **$873.00**
Price: Compensated models . . . . **$858.00 to $980.00**

DAN WESSON FIREARMS MODEL 460/7460 REVOLVERS

Caliber: 45 ACP, 45 Auto Rim, 45 Super, 45 Winchester Magnum and 460 Rowland. **Barrel:** 4", 6", 8", 10"; vent heavy. **Weight:** 49 oz. (4" barrel). **Grips:** Hogue rubber finger groove; interchangeable. **Sights:** Interchangeable ramp or Patridge front, fully adjustable rear. **Features:** New Generation Large Frame Series. Shoots five cartridges (45 ACP, 45 Auto Rim, 45 Super, 45 Winchester Magnum and 460 Rowland; six half-moon

clips for auto cartridges included). Interchangeable barrels and grips. Available with non-fluted cylinder and Slotted Lightweight barrel shroud. Introduced 1999. Made in U.S.A. by Dan Wesson Firearms.

Price: 4" bbl., blue or stainless **$735.00**
Price: 10" bbl., blue or stainless **$888.00**
Price: Compensated models . . . . **$919.00 to $1,042.00**

DAN WESSON FIREARMS STANDARD SILHOUETTE REVOLVERS

Caliber: 357 SuperMag/Maxi, 41 Mag., 414 SuperMag, 445 SuperMag. **Barrel:** 8", 10". **Weight:** 64 oz. (8" barrel). **Length:** 14.3" overall (8" barrel). **Grips:** Hogue rubber finger groove; interchangeable. **Sights:** Patridge front, fully adjustable rear. **Features:** Interchangeable barrels and grips, fluted or non-fluted cylinder, satin brushed stainless finish. Introduced 1999. Made in U.S.A. by Dan Wesson Firearms.

Price: 357 SuperMag/Maxi, 8" **$1,057.00**
Price: 41 Mag., 10" **$888.00**
Price: 414 SuperMag., 8" **$1,057.00**
Price: 445 SuperMag., 8" **$1,057.00**

Dan Wesson Firearms Super Ram Silhouette Revolver

Similar to Standard Silhouette except has 10 land and groove Laser Coat barrel, Bo-Mar target sights with hooded front, special laser engraving. Fluted or non-fluted cylinder. Introduced 1999. Made in U.S.A. by Dan Wesson Firearms.

Price: 357 SuperMag/Maxi, 414 SuperMag., 445 SuperMag., 8", blue or stainless **$1,364.00**
Price: 41 Magnum, 44 Magnum, 8", blue or stainless **$1,241.00**
Price: 41 Magnum, 44 Magnum, 10", blue or stainless **$1,333.00**

DAN WESSON FIREARMS ALASKAN GUIDE SPECIAL

Caliber: 445 SuperMag, 44 Magnum. **Barrel:** Compensated 4" vent heavy barrel assembly. **Features:** Stainless steel with baked on, non-glare, matte black coating, special laser engraving.

Price: Model 7445 VH4C AGS **$995.00**
Price: Model 744 VH4C AGS **$855.00**

EAA STANDARD GRADE REVOLVERS

Caliber: 38 Spec., 6-shot; 357 magnum, 6-shot. **Barrel:** 2", 4". **Weight:** 38 oz. (22 rimfire, 4"). **Length:** 8.8" overall (4" bbl.). **Grips:** Rubber with finger grooves. **Sights:** Blade front, fixed or adjustable on rimfires; fixed only on 32, 38. **Features:** Swing-out cylinder; hammer block safety; blue finish. Introduced 1991. Imported from Germany by European American Armory.

Price: 38 Special 2" **$249.00**
Price: 38 Special, 4" **$259.00**
Price: 357 Magnum, 2" **$259.00**
Price: 357 Magnum, 4" **$279.00**

KORTH COMBAT REVOLVER

Caliber: .357 Mag., .32 S&W Long, 9mm Para., .22 WMR, .22 LR. **Barrel:** 3", 4", 5 π", 6", 8". **Sights:** Fully-adjustable, rear; Baughman ramp, front. **Grips:** Walnut (checkered or smooth). Also available as a Target model in .22 LR, .38 Spl., .32 S&W Long, .357 Mag. with undercut partridge front sight; fully-adjustable rear. Made in Germany. Imported by Korth USA.

Price: . . . . From **$5,442.00**

Medusa Model 47   Ruger GP-161   Ruger KGP-141

Ruger KSP-331X

NEW! **KORTH TROJA REVOLVER**

Caliber: .357 Mag. **Barrel:** 6". **Finish:** Matte blue. **Grips:** Smooth, over-sized finger contoured walnut. **Features:** Maintaining all of the precision German craftsmanship that has made this line famous, the final surface finish is not as finely polished as the firm's other products – thus the lower price. Introduced 2003. Imported from Germany by Korth USA.
Price: . . . . From **$3,995.00**

MEDUSA MODEL 47 REVOLVER

Caliber: Most 9mm, 38 and 357 caliber cartridges; 6-shot cylinder. **Barrel:** 2-1/2", 3", 4", 5", 6"; fluted. **Weight:** 39 oz. **Length:** 10" overall (4" barrel). **Grips:** Gripper-style rubber. **Sights:** Changeable front blades, fully adjustable rear. **Features:** Patented extractor allows gun to chamber, fire and extract over 25 different cartridges in the .355 to .357 range, without half-moon clips. Steel frame and cylinder; match quality barrel. Matte blue finish. Introduced 1996. Made in U.S.A. by Phillips & Rogers, Inc.
Price: **$899.00**

ROSSI MODEL 351/352 REVOLVERS

Caliber: 38 Special +P, 5-shot. **Barrel:** 2". **Weight:** 24 oz. **Length:** 6-1/2" overall. **Grips:** Rubber. **Sights:** Blade front, fixed rear. **Features:** Patented key-lock Taurus Security System; forged steel frame handles +P ammunition. Introduced 2001. Imported by BrazTech/Taurus.
Price: Model 351 (blued finish) **$298.00**
Price: Model 352 (stainless finish) **$345.00**

ROSSI MODEL 461/462 REVOLVERS

Caliber: 357 Magnum +P, 6-shot. **Barrel:** 2". **Weight:** 26 oz. **Length:** 6-1/2" overall. **Grips:** Rubber. **Sights:** Fixed. **Features:** Single/double action. Patented key-lock Taurus Security System; forged steel frame handles +P ammunition. Introduced 2001. Imported by BrazTech/Taurus.
Price: Model 461 (blued finish) **$298.00**
Price: Model 462 (stainless finish) **$345.00**

ROSSI MODEL 971/972 REVOLVERS

Caliber: 357 Magnum +P, 6-shot. **Barrel:** 4", 6". **Weight:** 40-44 oz. **Length:** 8-1/2" or 10-1/2" overall. **Grips:** Rubber. **Sights:** Fully adjustable. **Features:** Single/double action. Patented key-lock Taurus Security System; forged steel frame handles +P ammunition. Introduced 2001. Imported by BrazTech/Taurus.
Price: Model 971 (blued finish, 4" barrel) **$345.00**
Price: Model 972 (stainless steel finish, 6" barrel) **$391.00**

Rossi Model 851

Similar to Model 971/972, chambered for 38 Special +P. Blued finish, 4" barrel. Introduced 2001. From BrazTech/Taurus.
Price: **$298.00**

RUGER GP-100 REVOLVERS

Caliber: 38 Spec., 357 Mag., 6-shot. **Barrel:** 3", 3" full shroud, 4", 4" full shroud, 6", 6" full shroud. **Weight:** 3" barrel—35 oz., 3" full shroud—36 oz., 4" barrel—37 oz., 4" full shroud—38 oz. **Sights:** Fixed; adjustable on 4" full shroud, all 6" barrels. **Grips:** Ruger Santoprene Cushioned Grip with Goncalo Alves inserts. **Features:** Uses action, frame incorporating improvements and features of both the Security-Six and Redhawk revolvers. Full length, short ejector shroud. Satin blue and stainless steel.
Price: GP-141 (357, 4" full shroud, adj. sights, blue) **$499.00**
Price: GP-160 (357, 6", adj. sights, blue) **$499.00**
Price: GP-161 (357, 6" full shroud, adj. sights, blue), 46 oz. **$499.00**
Price: GPF-331 (357, 3" full shroud) **$495.00**

Price: GPF-340 (357, 4") **$495.00**
Price: GPF-341 (357, 4" full shroud) **$495.00**
Price: KGP-141 (357, 4" full shroud, adj. sights, stainless) **$555.00**
Price: KGP-160 (357, 6", adj. sights, stainless), 43 oz. **$555.00**
Price: KGP-161 (357, 6" full shroud, adj. sights, stainless) 46 oz. **$555.00**
Price: KGPF-330 (357, 3", stainless) **$555.00**
Price: KGPF-331 (357, 3" full shroud, stainless) **$555.00**
Price: KGPF-340 (357, 4", stainless), KGPF-840 (38 Special) . . . **$555.00**
Price: KGPF-341 (357, 4" full shroud, stainless) **$555.00**
Price: KGPF-840 (38 Special, 4", stainless) **$555.00**

Ruger SP101 Double-Action-Only Revolver

Similar to standard SP101 except double-action-only with no single-action sear notch. Spurless hammer for snag-free handling, floating firing pin and Ruger's patented transfer bar safety system. Available with 2-1/4" barrel in 357 Magnum. Weighs 25 oz., overall length 7.06". Natural brushed satin, high-polish stainless steel. Introduced 1993.
Price: KSP321XL (357 Mag.) **$495.00**

RUGER SP101 REVOLVERS

Caliber: 22 LR, 32 H&R Mag., 6-shot; 38 Spec. +P, 357 Mag., 5-shot. **Barrel:** 2-1/4", 3-1/16", 4". **Weight:** (38 & 357 mag models) 2-1/4"—25 oz.; 3-1/16"—27 oz. **Sights:** Adjustable on 22, 32, fixed on others. **Grips:** Ruger Cushioned Grip with inserts. **Features:** Incorporates improvements and features found in the GP-100 revolvers into a compact, small frame, double-action revolver. Full-length ejector shroud. Stainless steel only. Introduced 1988.
Price: KSP-821X (2-1/4", 38 Spec.) **$495.00**
Price: KSP-831X (3-1/16", 38 Spec.) **$495.00**
Price: KSP-241X (4" heavy bbl., 22 LR), 34 oz. **$495.00**
Price: KSP-3231X (3-1/16", 32 H&R), 30 oz. **$495.00**
Price: KSP-321X (2-1/4", 357 Mag.) **$495.00**
Price: KSP-331X (3-1/16", 357 Mag.) **$495.00**
Price: KSP-3241X (32 Mag., 4" bbl) **$495.00**

CONSULT
SHOOTER'S MARKETPLACE
Page 233, This Issue

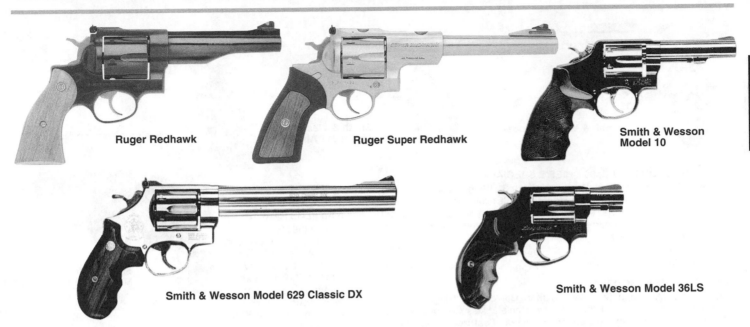

Ruger Redhawk

Ruger Super Redhawk

Smith & Wesson
Model 10

Smith & Wesson Model 629 Classic DX

Smith & Wesson Model 36LS

RUGER REDHAWK

Caliber: 44 Rem. Mag., 45 Colt, 6-shot. **Barrel:** 5-1/2", 7-1/2". **Weight:** About 54 oz. (7-1/2" bbl.). **Length:** 13" overall (7-1/2" barrel). **Grips:** Square butt cushioned grip panels. **Sights:** Interchangeable Patridge-type front, rear adjustable for windage and elevation. **Features:** Stainless steel, brushed satin finish, blued ordnance steel. 9-1/2" sight radius. Introduced 1979.
Price: Blued, 44 Mag., 5-1/2" RH-445, 7-1/2" RH-44 . . . . **$585.00**
Price: Blued, 44 Mag., 7-1/2" RH44R, with scope mount, rings . . **$625.00**
Price: Stainless, 44 Mag., KRH445, 5-1/2", 7-1/2" KRH-44 . . . . . **$645.00**
Price: Stainless, 44 Mag., 7-1/2", with scope mount, rings KRH-44R. **$685.00**
Price: Stainless, 45 Colt, KRH455, 5-1/2", 7-1/2" KRH-45 . . . . . . **$645.00**
Price: Stainless, 45 Colt, 7-1/2", with scope mount and rings KRH-45R. **$685.00**

Ruger Super Redhawk Revolver

Similar to standard Redhawk except has heavy extended frame with Ruger Integral Scope Mounting System on wide topstrap. Also available 454 Casull and 480 Ruger. Wide hammer spur lowered for better scope clearance. Incorporates mechanical design features and improvements of GP-100. Choice of 7-1/2" or 9-1/2" barrel, both ramp front sight base with Redhawk-style Interchangeable Insert sight blades, adjustable rear sight. Comes with Ruger "Cushioned Grip" panels with wood panels. Target gray stainless steel. Introduced 1987.
Price: KSRH-7 (7-1/2"), KSRH-9 (9-1/2"), 44 Mag **$685.00**
Price: KSRH-7454 (7-1/2") 454 Casull, 9-1/2 KSRH-9454 . . . . . . **$775.00**
Price: KSRH-7480 (7-1/2") 480 Ruger **$775.00**
Price: KSRH-9480 (9-1/2") 480 Ruger **$775.00**

SMITH & WESSON MODEL 10 M&P HB REVOLVER

Caliber: 38 Spec., 6-shot. **Barrel:** 4". **Weight:** 33.5 oz. **Length:** 9-5/16" overall. **Grips:** Uncle Mike's Combat soft rubber; square butt. **Sights:** Fixed; ramp front, square notch rear.
Price: Blue **$496.00**

SMITH & WESSON COMMEMORATIVE MODEL 29

Features: Reflects original Model 29: 6-1/2" barrel, four-screw side plate, over-sized target grips, red vamp front and black blade rear sights, 150th Anniversary logo, engraved, gold-plated, blue, in wood presentation case. Limited.
Price: . . . . **NA**

SMITH & WESSON MODEL 629 REVOLVERS

Caliber: 44 Magnum, 44 S&W Special, 6-shot. **Barrel:** 5", 6", 8-3/8". **Weight:** 47 oz. (6" bbl.). **Length:** 11-3/8" overall (6" bbl.). **Grips:** Soft rubber; wood optional. **Sights:** 1/8" red ramp front, white outline rear, internal lock, adjustable for windage and elevation.
Price: Model 629, 4" **$717.00**
Price: Model 629, 6" **$739.00**
Price: Model 629, 8-3/8" barrel. **$756.00**

Smith & Wesson Model 629 Classic Revolver

Similar to standard Model 629, full-lug 5", 6-1/2" or 8-3/8" barrel, chamfered front of cylinder, interchangeable red ramp front sight with adjustable white outline rear, Hogue grips with S&W monogram, frame is drilled and tapped for scope mounting. Factory accurizing and endurance packages. Overall length with 5" barrel is 10-1/2"; weighs 51 oz. Introduced 1990.
Price: Model 629 Classic (stainless), 5", 6-1/2" **$768.00**
Price: As above, 8-3/8" **$793.00**
Price: Model 629 with HiViz front sight. **$814.00**

Smith & Wesson Model 629 Classic DX Revolver

Similar to Model 629 Classic, offered only with 6-1/2" or 8-3/8" full-lug barrel, five front sights: red ramp, black Patridge, black Patridge with gold bead, black ramp, black Patridge with white dot, white outline rear sight, adjustable sight, internal lock. Hogue combat-style and wood round butt grip. Introduced 1991.
Price: Model 629 Classic DX, 6-1/2". **$986.00**
Price: As above, 8-3/8" **$1,018.00**

SMITH & WESSON MODEL 37 CHIEF'S SPECIAL & AIRWEIGHT

Caliber: 38 Spec. +P, 5-shot. **Barrel:** 1-7/8". **Weight:** 19-1/2 oz. (2" bbl.); 13-1/2 oz. (Airweight). **Length:** 6-1/2" (round butt). **Grips:** Round butt soft rubber. **Sights:** Fixed, serrated ramp front, square notch rear. Glass beaded finish.
Price: Model 37. . . . . **$523.00**

Smith & Wesson Model 637 Airweight Revolver

Similar to the Model 37 Airweight except has alloy frame, stainless steel barrel, cylinder and yoke; rated for 38 Spec. +P; Uncle Mike's Boot Grip. Weighs 15 oz. Introduced 1996. Made in U.S.A. by Smith & Wesson.
Price: **$548.00**

Smith & Wesson Model 36LS, 60LS LadySmith

Caliber: .38 S&W Special +P, 5-shot. **Barrel:** 1-7/8". **Weight:** 20 oz. **Length:** 6-5/16 overall (1-7/8" barrel). **Grips:** Combat Dymondwood® grips with S&W monogram. **Sights:** Serrated ramp front, fixed notch rear. **Features:** Speedloader cutout. Comes in a fitted carry/storage case. Introduced 1989.
Price: Model 36LS **$518.00**
Price: Model 60LS, 2-1/8" barrel stainless, 357 Magnum. **$566.00**

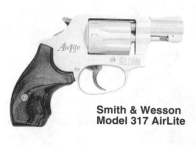

Smith & Wesson Model 65LS

Smith & Wesson Model 65LS

Smith & Wesson Model 317 AirLite

Smith & Wesson Model 625

Smith & Wesson Model 340 PD Airlite Sc

SMITH & WESSON MODEL 60 CHIEF'S SPECIAL

Caliber: 357 Magnum, 5-shot. **Barrel:** 2-1/8" or 3". **Weight:** 24 oz. **Length:** 7-1/2 overall (3" barrel). **Grips:** Rounded butt synthetic grips. **Sights:** Fixed, serrated ramp front, square notch rear. **Features:** Stainless steel construction. 3" full lug barrel, adjustable sights, internal lock. Made in U.S.A. by Smith & Wesson.

Price: 2-1/8" barrel **$541.00**
Price: 3" barrel **$574.00**

SMITH & WESSON MODEL 65

Caliber: 357 Mag. and 38 Spec., 6-shot. **Barrel:** 4". **Weight:** 34 oz. **Length:** 9-5/16" overall (4" bbl.). **Grips:** Uncle Mike's Combat. **Sights:** 1/8" serrated ramp front, fixed square notch rear. **Features:** Heavy barrel. Stainless steel construction. Internal lock.

Price: **$531.00**

SMITH & WESSON MODEL 317 AIRLITE, 317 LADYSMITH REVOLVERS

Caliber: 22 LR, 8-shot. **Barrel:** 1-7/8" 3". **Weight:** 9.9 oz. **Length:** 6-3/16" overall. **Grips:** Dymondwood Boot or Uncle Mike's Boot. **Sights:** Serrated ramp front, fixed notch rear. **Features:** Aluminum alloy, carbon and stainless steels, and titanium construction. Short spur hammer, smooth combat trigger. Clear Cote finish. Introduced 1997. Made in U.S.A. by Smith & Wesson.

Price: With Uncle Mike's Boot grip **$550.00**
Price: With DymondWood Boot grip, 3" barrel, HiViz front sight, internal lock **$600.00**
Price: Model 317 LadySmith (DymondWood only, comes with display case) **$596.00**

SMITH & WESSON MODEL 64 STAINLESS M&P

Caliber: 38 Spec. +P, 6-shot. **Barrel:** 2", 3", 4". **Weight:** 34 oz. **Length:** 9-5/16" overall. **Grips:** Soft rubber. **Sights:** Fixed, 1/8" serrated ramp front, square notch rear. **Features:** Satin finished stainless steel, square butt.

Price: 2" **$522.00**
Price: 3", 4" **$532.00**

SMITH & WESSON MODEL 65LS LADYSMITH

Caliber: 357 Magnum, 38 Spec. +P, 6-shot. **Barrel:** 3". **Weight:** 31 oz. **Length:** 7.94" overall. **Grips:** Rosewood, round butt. **Sights:** Serrated ramp front, fixed notch rear. **Features:** Stainless steel with frosted finish. Smooth combat trigger, service hammer, shrouded ejector rod. Comes with case. Introduced 1992.

Price: **$584.00**

SMITH & WESSON MODEL 66 STAINLESS COMBAT MAGNUM

Caliber: 357 Mag. and 38 Spec. +P, 6-shot. **Barrel:** 2-1/2", 4", 6". **Weight:** 36 oz. (4" barrel). **Length:** 9-9/16" overall. **Grips:** Soft rubber. **Sights:** Red ramp front, micro-click rear adjustable for windage and elevation. **Features:** Satin finish stainless steel. Internal lock.

Price: 2-1/2" **$590.00**
Price: 4" **$579.00**
Price: 6" **$608.00**

SMITH & WESSON MODEL 67 COMBAT MASTERPIECE

Caliber: 38 Special, 6-shot. **Barrel:** 4". **Weight:** 32 oz. **Length:** 9-5/16" overall. **Grips:** Soft rubber. **Sights:** Red ramp front, micro-click rear adjustable for windage and elevation. **Features:** Stainless steel with satin finish. Smooth combat trigger, semi-target hammer. Introduced 1994.

Price: **$585.00**

Smith & Wesson Model 686 Magnum PLUS Revolver

Similar to the Model 686 except has 7-shot cylinder, 2-1/2", 4" or 6" barrel. Weighs 34-1/2 oz., overall length 7-1/2" (2-1/2" barrel). Hogue rubber grips. Internal lock. Introduced 1996. Made in U.S.A. by Smith & Wesson.

Price: 2-1/2" barrel **$631.00**
Price: 4" barrel **$653.00**
Price: 6" barrel **$663.00**

SMITH & WESSON MODEL 625 REVOLVER

Caliber: 45 ACP, 6-shot. **Barrel:** 5". **Weight:** 46 oz. **Length:** 11.375" overall. **Grips:** Soft rubber; wood optional. **Sights:** Patridge front on ramp, S&W micrometer click rear adjustable for windage and elevation. **Features:** Stainless steel construction with .400" semi-target hammer, .312" smooth combat trigger; full lug barrel. Glass beaded finish. Introduced 1989.

Price: 5" **$745.00**
Price: 4" with internal lock. **$745.00**

SMITH & WESSON MODEL 640 CENTENNIAL DA ONLY

Caliber: 357 Mag., 38 Spec. +P, 5-shot. **Barrel:** 2-1/8". **Weight:** 25 oz. **Length:** 6-3/4" overall. **Grips:** Uncle Mike's Boot Grip. **Sights:** Serrated ramp front, fixed notch rear. **Features:** Stainless steel. Fully concealed hammer, snag-proof smooth edges. Internal lock. Introduced 1995 in 357 Magnum.

Price: **$599.00**

SMITH & WESSON MODEL 617 K-22 MASTERPIECE

Caliber: 22 LR, 6- or 10-shot. **Barrel:** 4", 6", 8-3/8". **Weight:** 42 oz. (4" barrel). **Length:** NA. **Grips:** Soft rubber. **Sights:** Patridge front, adjustable rear. Drilled and tapped for scope mount. **Features:** Stainless steel with satin finish; 4" has .312" smooth trigger, .375" semi-target hammer; 6" has either .312" combat or .400" serrated trigger, .375" semi-target or .500" target hammer; 8-3/8" with .400" serrated trigger, .500" target hammer. Introduced 1990.

Price: 4" **$644.00**
Price: 6", target hammer, target trigger **$625.00**
Price: 6", 10-shot **$669.00**
Price: 8-3/8", 10 shot **$679.00**

SMITH & WESSON MODEL 610 CLASSIC HUNTER REVOLVER

Caliber: 10mm, 40 S&W, 6-shot cylinder. **Barrel:** 6-1/2" full lug. **Weight:** 52 oz. **Length:** 12" overall. **Grips:** Hogue rubber combat. **Sights:** Interchangeable blade front, micro-click rear adjustable for windage and elevation. **Features:** Stainless steel construction; target hammer, target trigger; unfluted cylinder; drilled and tapped for scope mounting. Introduced 1998.

Price: **$785.00**

SMITH & WESSON MODEL 340 PD AIRLITE Sc CENTENNIAL

Caliber: 357 Magnum, 38 Spec. +P, 5-shot. **Barrel:** 1-7/8". **Grips:** Rounded butt grip. **Sights:** HiViz front. **Features:** Synthetic grip, internal lock. Blue.

Price: **$799.00**

Smith & Wesson Model 360 PD Airlite SC Chief's Special

Smith & Wesson Model 386 PD Airlite SC

Smith & Wesson Model 442

Smith & Wesson Model 696

Smith & Wesson Model 500

SMITH & WESSON MODEL 360 PD AIRLITE Sc CHIEF'S SPECIAL

Caliber: 357 Magnum, 38 Spec. +P, 5-shot. **Barrel:** 1-7/8". **Grips:** Rounded butt grip. **Sights:** Fixed. **Features:** Synthetic grip, internal lock. Stainless.

Price: Red ramp front $767.00
Price: HiViz front $781.00

SMITH & WESSON MODEL 386 PD AIRLITE Sc

Caliber: 357 Magnum, 38 Spec. +P, 7-shot. **Barrel:** 2-1/2". **Grips:** Rounded butt grip. **Sights:** Adjustable, HiViz front. **Features:** Synthetic grip, internal lock.

Price: Blue $815.00

SMITH & WESSON MODEL 331, 332 AIRLITE Ti REVOLVERS

Caliber: 32 H&R Mag., 6-shot. **Barrel:** 1-7/8". **Weight:** 11.2 oz. (with wood grip). **Length:** 6-15/16" overall. **Grips:** Uncle Mike's Boot or Dymondwood Boot. **Sights:** Black serrated ramp front, fixed notch rear. **Features:** Aluminum alloy frame, barrel shroud and yoke; titanium cylinder; stainless steel barrel liner. Matte finish. Introduced 1999. Made in U.S.A. by Smith & Wesson.

Price: Model 331 Chiefs $716.00
Price: Model 332, internal lock $734.00

SMITH & WESSON MODEL 337 CHIEF'S SPECIAL AIRLITE Ti

Caliber: 38 Spec. +P, 5-shot. **Barrel:** 1-7/8". **Weight:** 11.2 oz. (Dymondwood grips). **Length:** 6-5/16" overall. **Grips:** Uncle Mike's Boot or Dymondwood Boot. **Sights:** Black serrated front, fixed notch rear. **Features:** Aluminum alloy frame, barrel shroud and yoke; titanium cylinder; stainless steel barrel liner. Matte finish. Introduced 1999. Made in U.S.A. by Smith & Wesson.

Price: $716.00

SMITH & WESSON MODEL 342 CENTENNIAL AIRLITE Ti

Caliber: 38 Spec. +P, 5-shot. **Barrel:** 1-7/8". **Weight:** 11.3 oz. (Dymondwood stocks). **Length:** 6-15/16" overall. **Grips:** Uncle Mike's Boot or Dymondwood Boot. **Sights:** Black serrated ramp front, fixed notch rear. **Features:** Aluminum alloy frame, barrel shroud and yoke; titanium cylinder; stainless steel barrel liner. Shrouded hammer. Matte finish. Internal lock. Introduced 1999. Made in U.S.A. by Smith & Wesson.

Price: $734.00

Smith & Wesson Model 442 Centennial Airweight

Similar to Model 640 Centennial, alloy frame giving weighs 15.8 oz. Chambered for 38 Special +P, 1-7/8" carbon steel barrel; carbon steel cylinder; concealed hammer; Uncle Mike's Boot grip. Fixed square notch rear sight, serrated ramp front. DA only, glass beaded finish. Introduced 1993.

Price: Blue $547.00

SMITH & WESSON MODEL 638 AIRWEIGHT BODYGUARD

Caliber: 38 Spec. +P, 5-shot. **Barrel:** 1-7/8". **Weight:** 15 oz. **Length:** 6-15/16" overall. **Grips:** Uncle Mike's Boot grip. **Sights:** Serrated ramp front, fixed notch rear. **Features:** Alloy frame, stainless cylinder and barrel; shrouded hammer. Glass beaded finish. Introduced 1997. Made in U.S.A. by Smith & Wesson.

Price: With Uncle Mike's Boot grip $564.00

Smith & Wesson Model 642 Airweight Revolver

Similar to Model 442 Centennial Airweight, stainless steel barrel, cylinder and yoke with matte finish; Uncle Mike's Boot Grip; DA only; weighs 15.8 oz. Introduced 1996. Made in U.S.A. by Smith & Wesson.

Price: $571.00

Smith & Wesson Model 642LS LadySmith Revolver

Same as Model 642 except has smooth combat wood grips, comes with deluxe soft case; Dymondwood grip; aluminum alloy frame, stainless cylinder, barrel and yoke; frosted matte finish. Weighs 15.8 oz. Introduced 1996. Made in U.S.A. by Smith & Wesson.

Price: 1-7/8" $597.00

SMITH & WESSON MODEL 649 BODYGUARD REVOLVER

Caliber: 357 Mag., 38 Spec. +P, 5-shot. **Barrel:** 2-1/8". **Weight:** 20 oz. **Length:** 6-5/16" overall. **Grips:** Uncle Mike's Combat. **Sights:** Black pinned ramp front, fixed notch rear. **Features:** Stainless steel construction; shrouded hammer; smooth combat trigger. Internal lock. Made in U.S.A. by Smith & Wesson.

Price: $594.00

SMITH & WESSON MODEL 657 REVOLVER

Caliber: 41 Mag., 6-shot. **Barrel:** 7-1/2" full lug. **Weight:** 48 oz. **Grips:** Soft rubber. **Sights:** Pinned 1/8" red ramp front, micro-click rear adjustable for windage and elevation. Target hammer, drilled and tapped, unfluted cylinder. **Features:** Stainless steel construction.

Price: $706.00

SMITH & WESSON MODEL 696 REVOLVER

Caliber: 44 Spec., 5-shot. **Barrel:** 3". **Weight:** 35.5 oz. **Length:** 8-1/4" overall. **Grips:** Uncle Mike's Combat. **Sights:** Red ramp front, click adjustable white outline rear. **Features:** Stainless steel construction; round butt frame; satin finish. Introduced 1997. Made in U.S.A. by Smith & Wesson.

Price: $620.00

SMITH & WESSON MODEL 500

Caliber: .50. **Barrel:** 8-3/8". **Weight:** 72.5 oz. **Length:** NA. **Grips:** Rubber. **Sights:** Interchangeable blade, front, adjustable rear. **Features:** Built on the massive, new X-Frame, recoil compensator, ball detent cylinder latch. Made in U.S.A. by Smith & Wesson.

Price: .... NA

Taurus Model 82

Taurus Model 85

Taurus Model 94 UL

Taurus Model 22H Raging Hornet

Taurus Model 44

TAURUS SILHOUETTE REVOLVERS

Available in calibers from .22 LR through 454 Casull, the common trait is a 12" vent rib barrel. An optional arm support that wraps around the forearm is available.
Price: . . . . **$414.00 to $859.00**

TAURUS MODEL 17 "TRACKER"

Caliber: 17 HMR, 7-shot. **Barrel:** 6-1/2". **Weight:** 45.8 oz. **Grips:** Rubber. **Sights:** Adjustable. **Features:** Double action, matte stainless, integral key-lock.
Price: . . . . **$430.00 to $438.00**

TAURUS MODEL 17-12 TARGET "SILHOUETTE"

Caliber: 17 HMR, 7-shot. **Barrel:** 12". **Weight:** 57.8 oz. **Grips:** Rubber. **Sights:** Adjustable. **Features:** Vent rib, double action, adjustable main spring and trigger stop. Matte stainless, integral key-lock.
Price: **$430.00**

TAURUS MODEL 17-C SERIIES

Similar to the Models 17 Tracker and Silhouette series but 8-shot cylinder, 2", 4" or 5" barrel, blue or stainless finish and regular (24 oz.) or UltraLite (18.5 oz.) versions available. All models have target crown for enhanced accuracy.
Price: . . . . **$359.00 to $391.00**

TAURUS MODEL 63

Caliber: 22 LR, 10 + 1 shot. **Barrel:** 23". **Weight:** 97.9 oz. **Grips:** Premium hardwood. **Sights:** Adjustable. **Features:** Auto loading action, round barrel, manual firing pin block, integral security system lock, trigger guard mounted safety, blue or stainless finish.
Price: . . . . **$295.00 to $310.00**

TAURUS MODEL 65 REVOLVER

Caliber: 357 Mag., 6-shot. **Barrel:** 4". **Weight:** 38 oz. **Length:** 10-1/2" overall. **Grips:** Soft rubber. **Sights:** Fixed. **Features:** Double action, integral key-lock. Imported by Taurus International.
Price: Blue or matte stainless . . . . **$375.00 to $422.00**

TAURUS MODEL 66 REVOLVER

Similar to Model 65, 4" or 6" barrel, 7-shot cylinder, adjustable rear sight. Integral key-lock action. Imported by Taurus International.
Price: Blue or matte stainless . . . . **$422.00 to $469.00**

TAURUS MODEL 66 SILHOUETTE REVOLVER

Similar to Model 6, 12" barrel, 7-shot cylinder, adjustable sight. Integral key-lock action, blue or matte stainless steel finish, rubber grips. Introduced 2001. Imported by Taurus International.
Price: . . . . **$414.00 to $461.00**

TAURUS MODEL 82 HEAVY BARREL REVOLVER

Caliber: 38 Spec., 6-shot. **Barrel:** 4", heavy. **Weight:** 36.5 oz. **Length:** 9-1/4" overall (4" bbl.). **Grips:** Soft black rubber. **Sights:** Serrated ramp front, square notch rear. **Features:** Double action, solid rib, integral key-lock. Imported by Taurus International.
Price: Blue or matte stainless . . . . **$352.00 to $398.00**

TAURUS MODEL 85 REVOLVER

Caliber: 38 Spec., 5-shot. **Barrel:** 2". **Weight:** 17-24.5 oz., titanium 13.5-15.4 oz. **Grips:** Rubber, rosewood or mother-of-pearl. **Sights:** Ramp front, square notch rear. **Features:** Blue, matte stainless, blue with gold accents, stainless with gold accents; rated for +P ammo. Integral key-lock. Introduced 1980. Imported by Taurus International.
Price: . . . . **$375.00 to $547.00**
Price: Total Titanium **$531.00**

TAURUS MODEL 94 REVOLVER

Caliber: 22 LR, 9-shot cylinder. **Barrel:** 2", 4", 5". **Weight:** 18.5-27.5 oz. **Grips:** Soft black rubber. **Sights:** Serrated ramp front, click-adjustable rear. **Features:** Double action, integral key-lock. Introduced 1989. Imported by Taurus International.
Price: Blue **$325.00**
Price: Matte stainless **$375.00**
Price: Model 94 UL, forged aluminum alloy, 18-18.5 oz. **$365.00**
Price: As above, stainless **$410.00**

TAURUS MODEL 22H RAGING HORNET REVOLVER

Caliber: 22 Hornet, 8-shot. **Barrel:** 10". **Weight:** 50 oz. **Length:** 6.5" overall. **Grips:** Soft black rubber. **Sights:** Fully adjustable, scope mount base included. **Features:** Ventilated rib, stainless steel construction with matte finish. Double action, integral key-lock. Introduced 1999. Imported by Taurus International.
Price: **$898.00**

TAURUS MODEL 30C RAGING THIRTY

Caliber: 30 carbine, 8-shot. **Barrel:** 10". **Weight:** 72.3 oz. **Grips:** Soft black rubber. **Sights:** Adjustable. **Features:** Double action, ventilated rib, matte stainless, comes with five "Stellar" full-moon clips, integral key-lock.
Price: **$898.00**

TAURUS MODEL 44 REVOLVER

Caliber: 44 Mag., 6-shot. **Barrel:** 4", 6-1/2", 8-3/8". **Weight:** 44-3/4 oz. **Grips:** Rubber. **Sights:** Adjustable. **Features:** Double action, integral key-lock. Introduced 1994. New Model 44S12 has 12" vent rib barrel. Imported from Brazil by Taurus International Manufacturing, Inc.
Price: Blue or stainless steel . . . . **$445.00 to $602.00**

Taurus Model 415

Taurus Model 608

Taurus Model 450

Taurus Model 454 Raging Bull

TAURUS MODEL 217 TARGET "SILHOUETTE"
Caliber: 218 Bee, 8-shot. **Barrel:** 12". **Weight:** 52.3 oz. **Grips:** Rubber. **Sights:** Adjustable. **Features:** Double action, ventilated rib, adjustable mainspring and trigger stop, matte stainless, integral key-lock.
Price: **$461.00**

TAURUS MODEL 218 RAGING BEE
Caliber: 218 Bee, 7-shot. **Barrel:** 10". **Weight:** 74.9 oz. **Grips:** Rubber. **Sights:** Adjustable rear. **Features:** Ventilated rib, adjustable action, matte stainless, integral key-lock. Also Available as Model 218SS6 Tracker with 6-1/2" vent rib barrel.
Price: . . . . (Raging Bee) **$898.00**
Price: . . . . (Tracker) **$406.00**

TAURUS MODEL 415 REVOLVER
Caliber: 41 Mag., 5-shot. **Barrel:** 2-1/2". **Weight:** 30 oz. **Length:** 7-1/8" overall. **Grips:** Rubber. **Sights:** Fixed. **Features:** Stainless steel construction; matte finish; ported barrel. Double action. Integral key-lock. Introduced 1999. Imported by Taurus International.
Price: **$508.00**
Price: Total Titanium **$602.00**

TAURUS MODEL 425/627 TRACKER REVOLVERS
Caliber: 357 Mag., 7-shot; 41 Mag., 5-shot. **Barrel:** 4" and 6". **Weight:** 28.8-40 oz. (titanium) 24.3-28. (6"). **Grips:** Rubber. **Sights:** Fixed front, adjustable rear. **Features:** Double action stainless steel, Shadow Gray or Total Titanium; vent rib (steel models only); integral key-lock action. Imported by Taurus International.
Price: . . . . **$508.00 to $516.00**
Price: Total Titanium **$688.00**

TAURUS MODEL 445
Caliber: 44 Special, 5-shot. **Barrel:** 2". **Weight:** 20.3-28.25 oz. **Length:** 6-3/4" overall. **Grips:** Rubber. **Sights:** Ramp front, notch rear. **Features:** Blue or stainless steel. Standard or DAO concealed hammer, optional porting. Introduced 1997. Imported by Taurus International.
Price: . . . . **$345.00 to $500.00**
Price: Total Titanium 19.8 oz. **$600.00**

TAURUS MODEL 455 "STELLAR TRACKER"
Caliber: 45 ACP, 5-shot. **Barrel:** 2", 4", 6". **Weight:** 28/33/38.4 oz. **Grips:** Rubber. **Sights:** Adjustable. **Features:** Double action, matte stainless, includes five "Stellar" full-moon clips, integral key-lock.
Price: **$523.00**

TAURUS MODEL 460 "TRACKER"
Caliber: 45 Colt, 5-shot. **Barrel:** 4" or 6". **Weight:** 33/38.4 oz. **Grips:** Rubber. **Sights:** Adjustable. **Features:** Double action, ventilated rib, matte stainless steel, comes with five "Stellar" full-moon clips.
Price: **$516.00**
Price: . . . . (Shadow gray, Total Titanium) **$688.00**

TAURUS MODEL 605 REVOLVER
Caliber: 357 Mag., 5-shot. **Barrel:** 2". **Weight:** 24 oz. **Grips:** Rubber. **Sights:** Fixed. **Features:** Double action, blue or stainless, concealed hammer models DAO, porting optional, integral key-lock. Introduced 1995. Imported by Taurus International.
Price: . . . . **$375.00 to $438.00**

TAURUS MODEL 731 REVOLVER
Similar to the Taurus Model 605, except in .32 Magnum.
Price: . . . . **$438.00 to $531.00**

TAURUS MODEL 608 REVOLVER
Caliber: 357 Mag. 38 Spec., 8-shot. **Barrel:** 4", 6-1/2", 8-3/8". **Weight:** 44-57 oz. **Length:** 9-3/8" overall. **Grips:** Soft black rubber. **Sights:** Adjustable. **Features:** Double action, integral key-lock action. Available in blue or stainless. Introduced 1995. Imported by Taurus International.
Price: . . . . **$469.00 to $547.00**

TAURUS MODEL 44 SERIES REVOLVER
Similar to Taurus Model 60 series, but in .44 Rem. Mag. With six-shot cylinder, blue and matte stainless finishes.
Price: . . . . **$500.00 to $578.00**

TAURUS MODEL 650CIA REVOLVER
Caliber: 357 Magnum, 5-shot. **Barrel:** 2". **Weight:** 24.5 oz. **Grips:** Rubber. **Sights:** Ramp front, square notch rear. **Features:** Double-action only, blue or matte stainless steel, integral key-lock, internal hammer. Introduced 2001. From Taurus International.
Price: . . . . **$406.00 to $453.00**

TAURUS MODEL 651 CIA REVOLVER
Caliber: 357 Magnum, 5-shot. **Barrel:** 2". **Weight:** 17-24.5 oz. **Grips:** Rubber. **Sights:** Fixed. **Features:** Concealed single action/double action design. Shrouded cockable hammer, blue, matte stainless, Shadow Gray, Total Titanium, integral key-lock. Made in Brazil. Imported by Taurus International Manufacturing, Inc.
Price: . . . . **$406.00 to $578.00**

TAURUS MODEL 450 REVOLVER
Caliber: 45 Colt, 5-shot. **Barrel:** 2". **Weight:** 21.2-22.3 oz. **Length:** 6-5/8" overall. **Grips:** Rubber. **Sights:** Ramp front, notch rear. **Features:** Double action, blue or stainless, ported, integral key-lock. Introduced 1999. Imported from Brazil by Taurus International.
Price: **$492.00**
Price: Ultra-Lite (alloy frame) **$523.00**
Price: Total Titanium, 19.2 oz. **$600.00**

TAURUS MODEL 444/454/480 RAGING BULL REVOLVERS
Caliber: 44 Mag., 45 LC, 454 Casull, 480 Ruger, 5-shot. **Barrel:** 5", 6-1/2", 8-3/8". **Weight:** 53-63 oz. **Length:** 12" overall (6-1/2" barrel). **Grips:** Soft black rubber. **Sights:** Patridge front, adjustable rear. **Features:** Double action, ventilated rib, ported, integral key-lock. Introduced 1997. Imported by Taurus International.
Price: Blue . . . . **$578.00 to $797.00**
Price: Matte stainless . . . . **$641.00 to $859.00**

Taurus Raging Bull Model 416

Taurus Model 817

Taurus Model 941

Taurus Model 970 Tracker

Taurus Model 980 Silhouette

Taurus Model 905

TAURUS RAGING BULL MODEL 416
Caliber: 41 Magnum, 6-shot. **Barrel:** 6-1/2". **Weight:** 61.9 oz. **Grips:** Rubber. **Sights:** Adjustable. **Features:** Double action, ported, ventilated rib, matte stainless, integral key-lock.
Price: $641.00

TAURUS MODEL 617 REVOLVER
Caliber: 357 Magnum, 7-shot. **Barrel:** 2". **Weight:** 28.3 oz. **Length:** 6-3/4" overall. **Grips:** Soft black rubber. **Sights:** Fixed. **Features:** Double action, blue, shadow gray, bright spectrum blue or matte stainless steel, integral key-lock. Available with porting, concealed hammer. Introduced 1998. Imported by Taurus International.
Price: . . . . $391.00 to $453.00
Price: Total Titanium, 19.9 oz. $602.00

TAURUS MODEL 445 SERIES REVOLVER
Similar to Taurus Model 617 series except in .44 Spl. with 5-shot cylinder.
Price: . . . . $389.00 to $422.00

TAURUS MODEL 617ULT REVOLVER
Similar to Model 617 except aluminum alloy and titanium components, matte stainless finish, integral key-lock action. Weighs 18.5 oz. Available ported or non-ported. Introduced 2001. Imported by Taurus International.
Price: (5-shot cylinder) . . . . $530.00 to $545.00

TAURUS MODEL 817 ULTRA-LITE REVOLVER
Caliber: 38 Spec., 7-shot. **Barrel:** 2". **Weight:** 21 oz. **Length:** 6-1/2" overall. **Grips:** Soft rubber. **Sights:** Fixed. **Features:** Double action, integral key-lock. Rated for +P ammo. Introduced 1999. Imported from Brazil by Taurus International.
Price: Blue $375.00
Price: Blue, ported $395.00
Price: Matte, stainless. $420.00
Price: Matte, stainless, ported $440.00

TAURUS MODEL 850CIA REVOLVER
Caliber: 38 Special, 5-shot. **Barrel:** 2". **Weight:** 17-24.5 oz. **Grips:** Rubber. **Sights:** Ramp front, square notch rear. **Features:** Double action only, blue or matte stainless steel, rated for +P ammo, integral key-lock, internal hammer. Introduced 2001. From Taurus International.
Price: . . . . $406.00 to $453.00
Price: Total Titanium $578.00

TAURUS MODEL 851CIA REVOLVER
Caliber: 38 Spec., 5-shot. **Barrel:** 2". **Weight:** 17-24.5 oz. **Grips:** Rubber. **Sights:** Fixed-UL/ULT adjustable. **Features:** Concealed single action/double action design. Shrouded cockable hammer, blue, matte

stainless, Total Titanium, blue or stainless UL and ULT, integral key-lock. Rated for +P ammo.
Price: . . . . $406.00 to $578.00

TAURUS MODEL 94, 941 REVOLVER
Caliber: 22 LR (Mod. 94), 22 WMR (Mod. 941), 8-shot. **Barrel:** 2", 4", 5". **Weight:** 27.5 oz. (4" barrel). **Grips:** Soft black rubber. **Sights:** Serrated ramp front, rear adjustable. **Features:** Double action, integral key-lock. Introduced 1992. Imported by Taurus International.
Price: Blue . . . . $328.00 to $344.00
Price: Stainless (matte) . . . . $375.00 to $391.00
Price: Model 941 Ultra Lite,
forged aluminum alloy, 2" . . . . $359.00 to $375.00
Price: As above, stainless. $406.00 to $422.00

TAURUS MODEL 970/971 TRACKER REVOLVERS
Caliber: 22 LR (Model 970), 22 Magnum (Model 971); 7-shot. **Barrel:** 6". **Weight:** 53.6 oz. **Grips:** Rubber. **Sights:** Adjustable. **Features:** Double barrel, heavy barrel with ventilated rib; matte stainless finish, integral key-lock. Introduced 2001. From Taurus International.
Price: . . . . $391.00 to $406.00

TAURUS MODEL 980/981 SILHOUETTE REVOLVERS
Caliber: 22 LR (Model 980), 22 Magnum (Model 981); 7-shot. **Barrel:** 12". **Weight:** 68 oz. **Grips:** Rubber. **Sights:** Adjustable. **Features:** Double action, heavy barrel with ventilated rib and scope mount, matte stainless finish, integral key-lock. Introduced 2001. From Taurus International.
Price: (Model 980) $398.00
Price: (Model 981) $414.00

TAURUS MODEL 905, 405, 455 PISTOL CALIBER REVOLVERS
Caliber: 9mm, .40, .45 ACP, 5-shot. **Barrel:** 2", 4", 6-1/2". **Weight:** 21 oz. to 40.8 oz. **Grips:** Rubber. **Sights:** Fixed, adjustable on Model 455SS6 in .45 ACP. **Features:** Produced as a backup gun for law enforcement officers who desire to carry the same caliber ammunition in their back-up revolver as they do in their service sidearm. Introduced 2003. Imported from Brazil by Taurus International Manufacturing, Inc.
Price: . . . . $383.00 to $523.00

Both classic six-shooters and modern adaptations for hunting and sport.

Century Model 100

Cimarron Lightning

Cimarron Model P

Cimarron Model P
New Sheriff

Cimarron Bisley

Cimarron Roughrider

CABELA'S MILLENNIUM REVOLVER
Caliber: 45 Colt. **Barrel:** 4-3/4". **Weight:** NA. **Length:** 10" overall. **Grips:** Hardwood. **Sights:** Blade front, hammer notch rear. **Features:** Matte black finish; unpolished brass accents. Introduced 2001. From Cabela's.
Price: **$229.99**

CENTURY GUN DIST. MODEL 100 SINGLE-ACTION
Caliber: 30-30, 375 Win., 444 Marlin, 45-70, 50-70. **Barrel:** 6-1/2" (standard), 8", 10". **Weight:** 6 lbs. (loaded). **Length:** 15" overall (8" bbl.). **Grips:** Smooth walnut. **Sights:** Ramp front, Millett adjustable square notch rear. **Features:** Highly polished high tensile strength manganese bronze frame, blue cylinder and barrel; coil spring trigger mechanism. Contact maker for full price information. Introduced 1975. Made in U.S.A. From Century Gun Dist., Inc.
Price: 6-1/2" barrel, 45-70. . . . . **$2,000.00**

CIMARRON LIGHTNING SA
Caliber: 38 Colt, 38 Special. **Barrel:** 3-1/2", 4-3/4", 5-1/2". **Grips:** Smooth or checkered walnut. **Sights:** Blade front. **Features:** Replica of the Colt 1877 Lightning DA. Similar to Cimarron Thunderer™, except smaller grip frame to fit smaller hands. Standard blue, charcoal blue or nickel finish with forged, old model, or color case hardened frame. Introduced 2001. From Cimarron F.A. Co.
Price: . . . . **$489.00 to $554.00**

CIMARRON MODEL P
Caliber: 32 WCF, 38 WCF, 357 Mag., 44 WCF, 44 Spec., 45 Colt. **Barrel:** 4-3/4", 5-1/2", 7-1/2". **Weight:** 39 oz. **Length:** 10" overall (4" barrel). **Grips:** Walnut. **Sights:** Blade front, fixed or adjustable rear. **Features:** Uses "old model" blackpowder frame with "Bullseye" ejector or New Model frame. Imported by Cimarron F.A. Co.
Price: . . . . **$499.00 to $549.00**
Price: New Sheriff . . . . **$499.00 to $564.00**

Cimarron Bisley Model Single-Action Revolvers
Similar to 1873 Model P, special grip frame and trigger guard, knurled wide-spur hammer, curved trigger. Available in 357 Mag., 44 WCF, 44 Spl., 45 Colt. Introduced 1999. Imported by Cimarron F.A. Co.
Price: **$519.00**

Cimarron Flat Top Single-Action Revolvers
Similar to 1873 Model P, flat top strap with windage-adjustable rear sight, elevation-adjustable front sight. Available in 44 WCF, 45 Colt; 7-1/2" barrel. Introduced 1999. Imported by Cimarron F.A. Co.
Price: **$519.00**

CIMARRON MODEL "P" JR.
Caliber: 38 Special. **Barrel:** 3-1/2", 4-3/4", 5-1/2". **Grips:** Checkered walnut. **Sights:** Blade front. **Features:** Styled after 1873 Colt Peacemaker, except 20 percent smaller. Blue finish with color-case hardened frame; Cowboy Comp® action. Introduced 2001. From Cimarron F.A. Co.
Price: . . . . **$419.00 to $479.00**

CIMARRON ROUGHRIDER ARTILLERY MODEL SINGLE-ACTION
Caliber: 45 Colt. **Barrel:** 5-1/2". **Weight:** 39 oz. **Length:** 11-1/2" overall. **Grips:** Walnut. **Sights:** Fixed. **Features:** U.S. markings and cartouche, case-hardened frame and hammer; 45 Colt only. Imported by Cimarron F.A. Co.
Price: . . . . **$549.00 to $599.00**

HANDGUNS

Cimarron Thunderer

Colt Cowboy

Colt Single-Action Army

EAA Bounty Hunter

EMF Hartford

EMF 1894 Bisley

CIMARRON 1872 OPEN TOP REVOLVER
Caliber: 38, 44 Special, 45 S&W Schofield. **Barrel:** 5-1/2" and 7-1/2". **Grips:** Walnut. **Sights:** Blade front, fixed rear. **Features:** Replica of first cartridge-firing revolver. Blue, charcoal blue, nickel or Original® finish; Navy-style brass or steel Army-style frame. Introduced 2001 by Cimarron F.A. Co.
Price: . . . . $529.00 to $599.00

CIMARRON THUNDERER REVOLVER
Caliber: 357 Mag., 44 WCF, 44 Spl, 45 Colt, 6-shot. **Barrel:** 3-1/2", 4-3/4", 5-1/2", 7-1/2", with ejector. **Weight:** 38 oz. (3-1/2" barrel). **Grips:** Smooth walnut. **Sights:** Blade front, notch rear. **Features:** Thunderer grip; color case-hardened frame with balance blued. Introduced 1993. Imported by Cimarron F.A. Co.
Price: 3-1/2", 4-3/4", smooth grips . . . . $519.00 to $549.00
Price: As above, checkered grips . . . . $564.00 to $584.00
Price: 5-1/2", 7-1/2", smooth grips . . . . $519.00 to $549.00
Price: As above, checkered grips . . . . $564.00 to $584.00

COLT COWBOY SINGLE-ACTION REVOLVER
Caliber: 45 Colt, 6-shot. **Barrel:** 5-1/2". **Weight:** 42 oz. **Grips:** Black composition, first generation style. **Sights:** Blade front, notch rear. **Features:** Dimensional replica of Colt's original Peacemaker with medium-size color case-hardened frame; transfer bar safety system; half-cock loading. Introduced 1998. From Colt's Mfg. Co.
Price: About $670.00

COLT SINGLE-ACTION ARMY REVOLVER
Caliber: 44-40, 45 Colt, 6-shot. **Barrel:** 4-3/4", 5-1/2", 7-1/2". **Weight:** 40 oz. (4-3/4" barrel). **Length:** 10-1/4" overall (4-3/4" barrel). **Grips:** Black Eagle composite. **Sights:** Blade front, notch rear. **Features:** Available in full nickel finish with nickel grip medallions, or Royal Blue with color case-hardened frame, gold grip medallions. Reintroduced 1992.
Price: $1,380.00

EAA BOUNTY HUNTER SA REVOLVERS
Caliber: 22 LR/22 WMR, 357 Mag., 44 Mag., 45 Colt, 6-shot. **Barrel:** 4-1/2", 7-1/2". **Weight:** 2.5 lbs. **Length:** 11" overall (4-5/8" barrel). **Grips:** Smooth walnut. **Sights:** Blade front, grooved topstrap rear. **Features:** Transfer bar safety; three position hammer; hammer forged barrel. Introduced 1992. Imported by European American Armory.

Price: Blue or case-hardened $369.00
Price: Nickel $399.00
Price: 22LR/22WMR, blue $269.00
Price: As above, nickel $299.00

EMF HARTFORD SINGLE-ACTION REVOLVERS
Caliber: 357 Mag., 32-20, 38-40, 44-40, 44 Spec., 45 Colt. **Barrel:** 4-3/4", 5-1/2", 7-1/2". **Weight:** 45 oz. **Length:** 13" overall (7-1/2" barrel). **Grips:** Smooth walnut. **Sights:** Blade front, fixed rear. **Features:** Identical to the original Colts with inspector cartouche on left grip, original patent dates and U.S. markings. All major parts serial numbered using original Colt-style lettering, numbering. Bullseye ejector head and color case-hardening on frame and hammer. Introduced 1990. From E.M.F.
Price: $500.00
Price: Cavalry or Artillery $390.00
Price: Nickel plated, add. $125.00
Price: Casehardened New Model frame. $365.00

EMF 1894 Bisley Revolver
Similar to the Hartford single-action revolver except has special grip frame and trigger guard, wide spur hammer; available in 38-40 or 45 Colt, 4-3/4", 5-1/2" or 7-1/2" barrel. Introduced 1995. Imported by E.M.F.
Price: Casehardened/blue $400.00
Price: Nickel $525.00

EMF Hartford Pinkerton Single-Action Revolver
Same as the regular Hartford except has 4" barrel with ejector tube and birds head grip. Calibers: 357 Mag., 45 Colt. Introduced 1997. Imported by E.M.F.
Price: $375.00

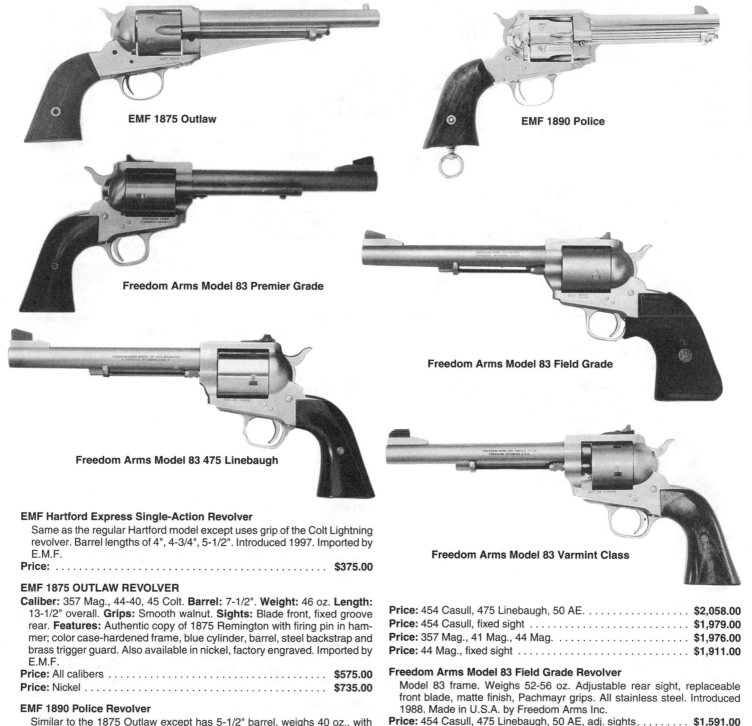

EMF 1875 Outlaw

EMF 1890 Police

Freedom Arms Model 83 Premier Grade

Freedom Arms Model 83 Field Grade

Freedom Arms Model 83 475 Linebaugh

Freedom Arms Model 83 Varmint Class

EMF Hartford Express Single-Action Revolver
Same as the regular Hartford model except uses grip of the Colt Lightning revolver. Barrel lengths of 4", 4-3/4", 5-1/2". Introduced 1997. Imported by E.M.F.
Price: **$375.00**

EMF 1875 OUTLAW REVOLVER
Caliber: 357 Mag., 44-40, 45 Colt. **Barrel:** 7-1/2". **Weight:** 46 oz. **Length:** 13-1/2" overall. **Grips:** Smooth walnut. **Sights:** Blade front, fixed groove rear. **Features:** Authentic copy of 1875 Remington with firing pin in hammer; color case-hardened frame, blue cylinder, barrel, steel backstrap and brass trigger guard. Also available in nickel, factory engraved. Imported by E.M.F.
Price: All calibers **$575.00**
Price: Nickel **$735.00**

EMF 1890 Police Revolver
Similar to the 1875 Outlaw except has 5-1/2" barrel, weighs 40 oz., with 12-1/2" overall length. Has lanyard ring in butt. No web under barrel. Calibers 357, 44-40, 45 Colt. Imported by E.M.F.
Price: All calibers **$590.00**
Price: Nickel **$750.00**

FREEDOM ARMS MODEL 83 PREMIER GRADE REVOLVER
Caliber: 357 Mag., 41 Mag., 44 Mag., 454 Casull, 475 Linebaugh, 50 AE, 5-shot. **Barrel:** 4-3/4", 6", 7-1/2", 9" (357 Mag. only), 10". **Weight:** 52.8 oz. **Length:** 13" (7-1/2" bbl.). **Grips:** Impregnated hardwood. **Sights:** Blade front, notch or adjustable rear. **Features:** All stainless steel construction; sliding bar safety system. Lifetime warranty. Made in U.S.A. by Freedom Arms, Inc.

Price: 454 Casull, 475 Linebaugh, 50 AE. **$2,058.00**
Price: 454 Casull, fixed sight **$1,979.00**
Price: 357 Mag., 41 Mag., 44 Mag. **$1,976.00**
Price: 44 Mag., fixed sight **$1,911.00**

Freedom Arms Model 83 Field Grade Revolver
Model 83 frame. Weighs 52-56 oz. Adjustable rear sight, replaceable front blade, matte finish, Pachmayr grips. All stainless steel. Introduced 1988. Made in U.S.A. by Freedom Arms Inc.
Price: 454 Casull, 475 Linebaugh, 50 AE, adj. sights. **$1,591.00**
Price: 454 Casull, fixed sights. **$1,553.00**
Price: 357 Mag., 41 Mag., 44 Mag. **$1,527.00**

FREEDOM ARMS MODEL 83 VARMINT CLASS REVOLVERS
Caliber: 22 LR, 5-shot. **Barrel:** 5-1/8, 7-1/2". **Weight:** 58 oz. (7-1/2" bbl.). **Length:** 11-1/2" (7-1/2" bbl.). **Grips:** Impregnated hardwood. **Sights:** Steel base adjustable "V" notch rear sight and replaceable brass bead front sight. **Features:** Stainless steel, matte finish, manual sliding-bar system, dual firing pins, pre-set trigger stop. One year limited wararanty to original owner. Made in U.S.A. by Freedom Arms, Inc.
Price: Varmint Class **$1,828.00**
Price: Extra fitted 22 WMR cylinder **$264.00**

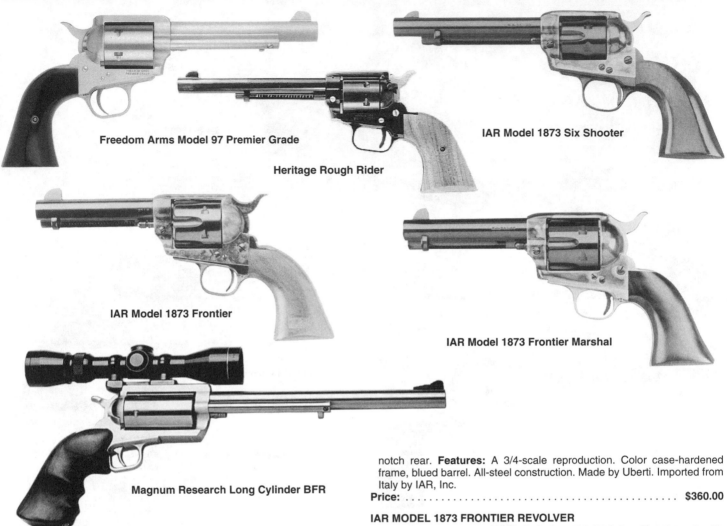

Freedom Arms Model 97 Premier Grade

Heritage Rough Rider

IAR Model 1873 Six Shooter

IAR Model 1873 Frontier

IAR Model 1873 Frontier Marshal

Magnum Research Long Cylinder BFR

FREEDOM ARMS MODEL 97 PREMIER GRADE REVOLVER

Caliber: 22 LR, 357 Mag., 41 Mag., 44 Special, 45 Colt, 5-shot. **Barrel:** 4-1/2", 5-1/2", 7-1/2", 10". **Weight:** 37 oz. (45 Colt 5-1/2"). **Length:** 10-3/4" (5-1/2" bbl.). **Grips:** Impregnated hardwood. **Sights:** Adjustable rear, replaceable blade front. **Features:** Stainless steel, brushed finish, automatic transfer bar safety system. Introduced in 1997. Made in U.S.A. by Freedom Arms.

Price: 357 Mag., 41 Mag., 45 Colt **$1,668.00**
Price: 357 Mag., 45 Colt, fixed sight **$1,576.00**
Price: Extra fitted cylinders 38 Special, 45 ACP **$264.00**
Price: 22 LR with sporting chambers **$1,732.00**
Price: Extra fitted 22 WMR cylinder **$264.00**
Price: Extra fitted 22 LR match grade cylinder **$476.00**
Price: 22 match grade chamber instead of 22 LR sport chamber
. . . . **$214.00**

HERITAGE ROUGH RIDER REVOLVER

Caliber: 22 LR, 22 LR/22 WMR combo, 6-shot. **Barrel:** 2-3/4", 3-1/2", 4-3/4", 6-1/2", 9". **Weight:** 31 to 38 oz. **Length:** NA. **Grips:** Exotic hardwood, laminated wood or mother of pearl; bird's head models offered. **Sights:** Blade front, fixed rear. Adjustable sight on 6-1/2" only. **Features:** Hammer block safety. High polish blue or nickel finish. Introduced 1993. Made in U.S.A. by Heritage Mfg., Inc.

Price: . . . . **$184.95 to $239.95**

IAR MODEL 1873 SIX SHOOTER

Caliber: 22 LR/22 WMR combo. **Barrel:** 5-1/2". **Weight:** 36-1/2" oz. **Length:** 11-3/8" overall. **Grips:** One-piece walnut. **Sights:** Blade front, notch rear. **Features:** A 3/4-scale reproduction. Color case-hardened frame, blued barrel. All-steel construction. Made by Uberti. Imported from Italy by IAR, Inc.

Price: **$360.00**

IAR MODEL 1873 FRONTIER REVOLVER

Caliber: 22 RL, 22 LR/22 WMR. **Barrel:** 4-3/4". **Weight:** 45 oz. **Length:** 10-1/2" overall. **Grips:** One-piece walnut with inspector's cartouche. **Sights:** Blade front, notch rear. **Features:** Color case-hardened frame, blued barrel, black nickel-plated brass trigger guard and backstrap. Bright nickel and engraved versions available. Introduced 1997. Imported from Italy by IAR, Inc.

Price: **$380.00**
Price: Nickel-plated **$425.00**
Price: 22 LR/22WMR combo **$420.00**

IAR MODEL 1873 FRONTIER MARSHAL

Caliber: 357 Mag., 45 Colt. **Barrel:** 4-3/4", 5-1/2, 7-1/2". **Weight:** 39 oz. **Length:** 10-1/2" overall. **Grips:** One-piece walnut. **Sights:** Blade front, notch rear. **Features:** Bright brass trigger guard and backstrap, color case-hardened frame, blued barrel and cylinder. Introduced 1998. Imported from Italy by IAR, Inc.

Price: **$395.00**

MAGNUM RESEARCH BFR SINGLE-ACTION REVOLVER

(Long cylinder) Caliber: 45/70 Government, 444 Marlin, 45 LC/410, 450 Marlin, .500 S&W. **Barrel:** 7.5", 10". **Weight:** 4 lbs., 4.36 lbs. **Length:** 15", 17.5".
(Short cylinder) Caliber: 454 Casull, 22 Hornet, BFR 480/475. **Barrel:** 6.5", 7.5", 10". **Weight:** 3.2 lbs., 3.5 lbs., 4.36 lbs. (10"). **Length:** 12.75 (6"), 13.75", 16.25"
Sights: All have fully adjustable rear, black blade ramp front. **Features:** Stainless steel construction, rubber grips, all 5-shot capacity. Barrels are stress-relieved and cut rifled. Made in U.S.A. From Magnum Research, Inc.

Price: **$999.00**

Navy Arms Flat Top

Navy Arms Bisley

Navy Arms 1875 Schofield

Navy Arms 1873

Navy Arms 1851 Navy

Navy Arms New Model Russian

MAGNUM RESEARCH BFR REVOLVER
Caliber: 22 Hornet, 444 Marlin, 45 LC/410, 450 Marlin, 454 Casull, 45/70, 480 Ruger/475 Linebaugh. **Barrel:** 6-1/2", 7-1/2", 10". **Weight:** 3.2-4.36 lbs. **Length:** 12.75"-17.5". **Grips:** Rubber. **Sights:** Ramp front, adjustable rear. **Features:** Single action, stainless steel construction. Announced 1998. Made in U.S.A. from Magnum Research.
Price: **$999.00**

NAVY ARMS FLAT TOP TARGET MODEL REVOLVER
Caliber: 45 Colt, 6-shot cylinder. **Barrel:** 7-1/2". **Weight:** 40 oz. **Length:** 13-1/4" overall. **Grips:** Smooth walnut. **Sights:** Spring-loaded German silver front, rear adjustable for windage. **Features:** Replica of Colt's Flat Top Frontier target revolver made from 1888 to 1896. Blue with color case-hardened frame. Introduced 1997. Imported by Navy Arms.
Price: **$450.00**

NAVY ARMS BISLEY MODEL SINGLE-ACTION REVOLVER
Caliber: 44-40 or 45 Colt, 6-shot cylinder. **Barrel:** 4-3/4", 5-1/2", 7-1/2". **Weight:** 40 oz. **Length:** 12-1/2" overall (7-1/2" barrel). **Grips:** Smooth walnut. **Sights:** Blade front, notch rear. **Features:** Replica of Colt's Bisley Model. Polished blue finish, color case-hardened frame. Introduced 1997. Imported by Navy Arms.
Price: . . . . **$425.00 to $460.00**

NAVY ARMS 1873 SINGLE-ACTION REVOLVER
Caliber: 357 Mag., 44-40, 45 Colt, 6-shot cylinder. **Barrel:** 4-3/4", 5-1/2", 7-1/2". **Weight:** 36 oz. **Length:** 10-3/4" overall (5-1/2" barrel). **Grips:** Smooth walnut. **Sights:** Blade front, notch rear. **Features:** Blue with color case-hardened frame. Introduced 1991. Imported by Navy Arms.
Price: **$405.00**

NAVY ARMS 1875 SCHOFIELD REVOLVER
Caliber: 44-40, 45 Colt, 6-shot cylinder. **Barrel:** 3-1/2", 5", 7". **Weight:** 39 oz. **Length:** 10-3/4" overall (5" barrel). **Grips:** Smooth walnut. **Sights:** Blade front, notch rear. **Features:** Replica of Smith & Wesson Model 3 Schofield. Single-action, top-break with automatic ejection. Polished blue finish. Introduced 1994. Imported by Navy Arms.
Price: Hideout Model, 3-1/2" barrel. **$695.00**
Price: Wells Fargo, 5" barrel **$695.00**
Price: U.S. Cavalry model, 7" barrel, military markings **$695.00**

NAVY ARMS NEW MODEL RUSSIAN REVOLVER
Caliber: 44 Russian, 6-shot cylinder. **Barrel:** 6-1/2". **Weight:** 40 oz. **Length:** 12" overall. **Grips:** Smooth walnut. **Sights:** Blade front, notch rear. **Features:** Replica of the S&W Model 3 Russian Third Model revolver. Spur trigger guard, polished blue finish. Introduced 1999. Imported by Navy Arms.
Price: **$769.00**

NAVY ARMS 1851 NAVY CONVERSION REVOLVER
Caliber: 38 Spec., 38 Long Colt. **Barrel:** 5-1/2", 7-1/2". **Weight:** 44 oz. **Length:** 14" overall (7-1/2" barrel). **Grips:** Smooth walnut. **Sights:** Bead front, notch rear. **Features:** Replica of Colt's cartridge conversion revolver. Polished blue finish with color case-hardened frame, silver plated trigger guard and backstrap. Introduced 1999. Imported by Navy Arms.
Price: **$165.00**

NavyArms 1860 Army

North American Mini

North American Mini-Master

North American Black Widow

Ruger "Bird's Head" Single Six

Ruger Blackhawk

Ruger SSMBH-4F

Ruger Bisley Single-Action

NAVY ARMS 1860 ARMY CONVERSION REVOLVER

Caliber: 38 Spec., 38 Long Colt. **Barrel:** 5-1/2", 7-1/2". **Weight:** 44 oz. **Length:** 13-1/2" overall (7-1/2" barrel). **Grips:** Smooth walnut. **Sights:** Blade front, notch rear. **Features:** Replica of Colt's conversion revolver. Polished blue finish with color case-hardened frame, full-size 1860 Army grip with blued steel backstrap. Introduced 1999. Imported by Navy Arms.
Price: **$190.00**

NORTH AMERICAN MINI REVOLVERS

Caliber: 22 Short, 22 LR, 22 WMR, 5-shot. **Barrel:** 1-1/8", 1-5/8". **Weight:** 4 to 6.6 oz. **Length:** 3-5/8" to 6-1/8" overall. **Grips:** Laminated wood. **Sights:** Blade front, notch fixed rear. **Features:** All stainless steel construction. Polished satin and matte finish. Engraved models available. From North American Arms.
Price: 22 Short, 22 LR . . . . **$186.00 to $221.00**
Price: 22 WMR, 1-1/8" or 1-5/8" bbl. **$205.00**
Price: 22 WMR, 1-1/8" or 1-5/8" bbl. with extra 22 LR cylinder. . . **$245.00**

NORTH AMERICAN MINI-MASTER

Caliber: 22 LR, 22 WMR, 17 HMR, 5-shot cylinder. **Barrel:** 4". **Weight:** 10.7 oz. **Length:** 7.75" overall. **Grips:** Checkered hard black rubber. **Sights:** Blade front, white outline rear adjustable for elevation, or fixed. **Features:** Heavy vent barrel; full-size grips. Non-fluted cylinder. Introduced 1989.
Price: Adjustable sight, 22 WMR, 17 HMR or 22 LR **$304.00**
Price: As above with extra WMR/LR cylinder **$343.00**
Price: Fixed sight, 22 WMR, 17 HMR or 22 LR **$286.00**
Price: As above with extra WMR/LR cylinder **$324.00**

North American Black Widow Revolver

Similar to Mini-Master, 2" heavy vent barrel. Built on 22 WMR frame. Non-fluted cylinder, black rubber grips. Available with Millett Low Profile fixed sights or Millett sight adjustable for elevation only. Overall length 5-7/8", weighs 8.8 oz. From North American Arms.
Price: Adjustable sight, 22 LR, 17 HMR or 22 WMR **$274.00**

Price: As above with extra WMR/LR cylinder **$312.00**
Price: Fixed sight, 22 LR, 17 HMR or 22 WMR **$256.00**
Price: As above with extra WMR/LR cylinder **$294.00**

RUGER NEW MODEL SINGLE SIX REVOLVER

Caliber: 32 H&R. **Barrel:** 4-5/8", 6-shot. **Grips:** Black Micarta "birds head", rosewood with color case. **Sights:** Fixed. **Features:** Instruction manual, high impact case, gun lock standard.
Price: Stainless, KSSMBH-4F, birds head **$576.00**
Price: Color case, SSMBH-4F, birds head **$576.00**
Price: Color case, SSM-4F-S, rosewood **$576.00**

RUGER NEW MODEL BLACKHAWK AND BLACKHAWK CONVERTIBLE

Caliber: 30 Carbine, 357 Mag./38 Spec., 41 Mag., 45 Colt, 6-shot. **Barrel:** 4-5/8" or 5-1/2", either caliber; 7-1/2" (30 Carbine and 45 Colt). **Weight:** 42 oz. (6-1/2" bbl.). **Length:** 12-1/4" overall (5-1/2" bbl.). **Grips:** American walnut. **Sights:** 1/8" ramp front, micro-click rear adjustable for windage and elevation. **Features:** Ruger transfer bar safety system, independent firing pin, hardened chrome-moly steel frame, music wire springs throughout. Case and lock included.
Price: Blue 30 Carbine, 7-1/2" (BN31) **$435.00**
Price: Blue, 357 Mag., 4-5/8", 6-1/2" (BN34, BN36). **$435.00**
Price: As above, stainless (KBN34, KBN36) **$530.00**
Price: Blue, 357 Mag./9mm Convertible, 4-5/8", 6-1/2" (BN34X, BN36X) includes extra cylinder. **$489.00**
Price: Blue, 41 Mag., 4-5/8", 6-1/2" (BN41, BN42) **$435.00**
Price: Blue, 45 Colt, 4-5/8", 5-1/2", 7-1/2" (BN44, BN455, BN45) **$435.00**
Price: Stainless, 45 Colt, 4-5/8", 7-1/2" (KBN44, KBN45) **$530.00**
Price: Blue, 45 Colt/45 ACP Convertible, 4-5/8", 5-1/2" (BN44X, BN455X) includes extra cylinder **$489.00**

Ruger Super Blackhawk Hunter

Ruger Vaquero

Ruger New Bearcat

Ruger Bisley-Vaquero

Ruger Single-Six

Ruger Bisley Single-Action Revolver

Similar to standard Blackhawk, hammer is lower with smoothly curved, deeply checkered wide spur. The trigger is strongly curved with wide smooth surface. Longer grip frame has hand-filling shape. Adjustable rear sight, ramp-style front. Unfluted cylinder and roll engraving, adjustable sights. Chambered for 357, 44 Mags. and 45 Colt; 7-1/2" barrel; overall length of 13"; weighs 48 oz. Plastic lockable case. Introduced 1985.
Price: RB-35W, 357Mag, RBD-44W, 44Mag, RB-45W, 45 Colt . . **$535.00**

RUGER NEW MODEL SUPER BLACKHAWK

Caliber: 44 Mag., 6-shot. Also fires 44 Spec. **Barrel:** 4-5/8", 5-1/2", 7-1/2", 10-1/2" bull. **Weight:** 48 oz. (7-1/2" bbl.), 51 oz. (10-1/2" bbl.). **Length:** 13-3/8" overall (7-1/2" bbl.). **Grips:** American walnut. **Sights:** 1/8" ramp front, micro-click rear adjustable for windage and elevation. **Features:** Ruger transfer bar safety system, fluted or un-fluted cylinder, steel grip and cylinder frame, round or square back trigger guard, wide serrated trigger, wide spur hammer. With case and lock.
Price: Blue, 4-5/8", 5-1/2", 7-1/2" (S458N, S45N, S47N) **$519.00**
Price: Blue, 10-1/2" bull barrel (S411N) **$529.00**
Price: Stainless, 4-5/8", 5-1/2", 7-1/2" (KS458N, KS45N, KS47N) **$535.00**
Price: Stainless, 10-1/2" bull barrel (KS411N) **$545.00**

RUGER NEW MODEL SUPER BLACKHAWK HUNTER

Caliber: 44 Mag., 6-shot. **Barrel:** 7-1/2", full-length solid rib, unfluted cylinder. **Weight:** 52 oz. **Length:** 13-5/8". **Grips:** Black laminated wood. **Sights:** Adjustable rear, replaceable front blade. **Features:** Reintroduced Ultimate SA revolver. Includes instruction manual, high-impact case, set 1" medium scope rings, gun lock, ejector rod as standard.
Price: **$639.00**

RUGER VAQUERO SINGLE-ACTION REVOLVER

Caliber: 357 Mag., 44-40, 44 Mag., 45 LC, 6-shot. **Barrel:** 4-5/8", 5-1/2", 7-1/2". **Weight:** 38-41 oz. **Length:** 13-1/8" overall (7-1/2" barrel). **Grips:** Smooth rosewood with Ruger medallion. **Sights:** Blade front, fixed notch rear. **Features:** Uses Ruger's patented transfer bar safety system and loading gate interlock with classic styling. Blued model color case-hardened finish on frame, rest polished and blued. Stainless has high-gloss. Introduced 1993. From Sturm, Ruger & Co.

Price: 357 Mag. BNV34, KBNV34 (4-5/8"), BNV35, KBNV35 (5-1/2") **$535.00**
Price: 44-40 BNV40, KBNV40 (4-5/8"). BNV405, KBNV405 (5-1/2"). BNV407, KBNV407 (7-1/2") **$535.00**
Price: 44 Mag., BNV474, KBNV474 (4-5/8"). BNV475, KBNV475 (5-1/2"). BNV477, KBNV477 (7-1/2") **$535.00**
Price: 45 LC, BN444, KBNV44 (4-5/8"). BNV455, KBNV455 (5-1/2"). BNV45, KBNV45 (7-1/2") **$535.00**
Price: 45 LC, BNVBH453, KBNVBH453 3-3/4" with "birds head" grip **$576.00**
Price: 357 Mag., RBNV35 (5-1/2") **$535.00**; KRBNV35 (5-1/2") . **$555.00**
Price: 45 LC, RBNV44 (4-5/8"), RBNV455 (5-1/2") **$535.00**
Price: 45 LC, KRBNV44 (4-5/8"), KRBNV455 (5-1/2") **$555.00**

Ruger Bisley-Vaquero Single-Action Revolver

Similar to Vaquero, Bisley-style hammer, grip and trigger, available in 357 Magnum, 44 Magnum and 45 LC only, 4-5/8" or 5-1/2" barrel. Smooth rosewood grips with Ruger medallion. Roll-engraved, unfluted cylinder. Introduced 1997. From Sturm, Ruger & Co.
Price: Color case-hardened frame, blue grip frame, barrel and cylinder, RBNV-475, RBNV-474, 44 Mag. **$535.00**
Price: High-gloss stainless steel, KRBNV-475, KRBNV-474 . . . . **$555.00**
Price: For simulated ivory grips add . . . . **$41.00 to $44.00**

RUGER NEW BEARCAT SINGLE-ACTION

Caliber: 22 LR, 6-shot. **Barrel:** 4". **Weight:** 24 oz. **Length:** 8-7/8" overall. **Grips:** Smooth rosewood with Ruger medallion. **Sights:** Blade front, fixed notch rear. **Features:** Reintroduction of the Ruger Bearcat with slightly lengthened frame, Ruger patented transfer bar safety system. Available in blue only. Introduced 1993. With case and lock. From Sturm, Ruger & Co.
Price: SBC4, blue **$379.00**
Price: KSBC-4, ss **$429.00**

RUGER MODEL SINGLE-SIX REVOLVER

Caliber: 32 H&R Magnum. **Barrel:** 4-5/8", 6-shot. **Weight:** 33 oz. **Length:** 10-1/8". **Grips:** Blue, rosewood, stainless, simulated ivory. **Sights:** Blade front, notch rear fixed. **Features:** Transfer bar and loading gate interlock safety, instruction manual, high impact case and gun lock.
Price: **$576.00**
Price: Blue, SSM4FS **$576.00**
Price: SS, KSSM4FSI **$576.00**

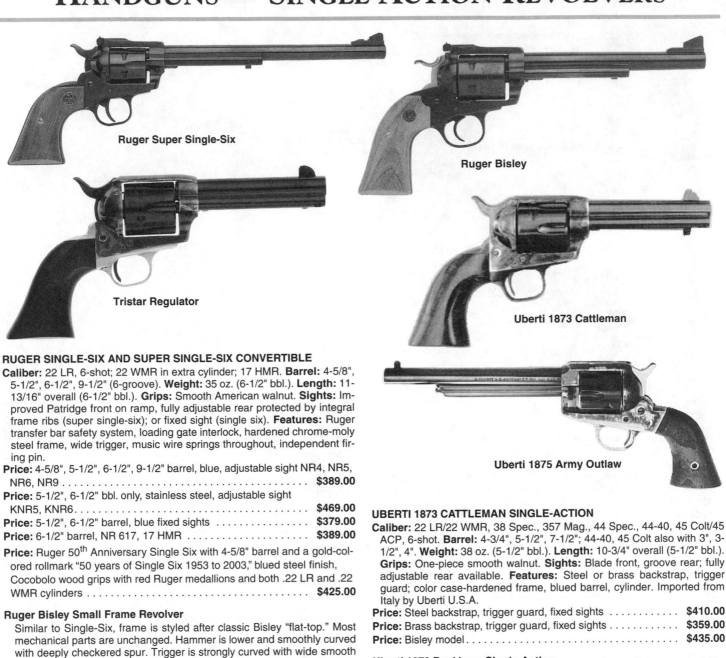

Ruger Super Single-Six

Ruger Bisley

Tristar Regulator

Uberti 1873 Cattleman

Uberti 1875 Army Outlaw

RUGER SINGLE-SIX AND SUPER SINGLE-SIX CONVERTIBLE
Caliber: 22 LR, 6-shot; 22 WMR in extra cylinder; 17 HMR. **Barrel:** 4-5/8", 5-1/2", 6-1/2", 9-1/2" (6-groove). **Weight:** 35 oz. (6-1/2" bbl.). **Length:** 11-13/16" overall (6-1/2" bbl.). **Grips:** Smooth American walnut. **Sights:** Improved Patridge front on ramp, fully adjustable rear protected by integral frame ribs (super single-six); or fixed sight (single six). **Features:** Ruger transfer bar safety system, loading gate interlock, hardened chrome-moly steel frame, wide trigger, music wire springs throughout, independent firing pin.
Price: 4-5/8", 5-1/2", 6-1/2", 9-1/2" barrel, blue, adjustable sight NR4, NR5, NR6, NR9 . . . . **$389.00**
Price: 5-1/2", 6-1/2" bbl. only, stainless steel, adjustable sight KNR5, KNR6 . . . . **$469.00**
Price: 5-1/2", 6-1/2" barrel, blue fixed sights **$379.00**
Price: 6-1/2" barrel, NR 617, 17 HMR **$389.00**
Price: Ruger 50th Anniversary Single Six with 4-5/8" barrel and a gold-colored rollmark "50 years of Single Six 1953 to 2003," blued steel finish, Cocobolo wood grips with red Ruger medallions and both .22 LR and .22 WMR cylinders **$425.00**

Ruger Bisley Small Frame Revolver
Similar to Single-Six, frame is styled after classic Bisley "flat-top." Most mechanical parts are unchanged. Hammer is lower and smoothly curved with deeply checkered spur. Trigger is strongly curved with wide smooth surface. Longer grip frame designed with hand-filling shape, and trigger guard is a large oval. Adjustable dovetail rear sight; front sight base accepts interchangeable square blades of various heights and styles. Unfluted cylinder and roll engraving. Weighs 41 oz. Chambered for 22 LR, 6-1/2" barrel only. Plastic lockable case. Introduced 1985.
Price: RB-22AW **$422.00**

SMITH & WESSON COMMEMORATIVE MODEL 2000
Caliber: 45 S&W Schofield. **Barrel:** 7". **Features:** 150th Anniversary logo, engraved, gold-plated, walnut grips, blue, original style hammer, trigger, and barrel latch. Wood presentation case. Limited.
Price: . . . . **NA**

TRISTAR/UBERTI REGULATOR REVOLVER
Caliber: 45 Colt. **Barrel:** 4-3/4", 5-1/2". **Weight:** 32-38 oz. **Length:** 8-1/4" overall (4-3/4" bbl.) **Grips:** One-piece walnut. **Sights:** Blade front, notch rear. **Features:** Uberti replica of 1873 Colt Model "P" revolver. Color-case hardened steel frame, brass backstrap and trigger guard, hammer-block safety. Imported from Italy by Tristar Sporting Arms.
Price: Regulator **$335.00**
Price: Regulator Deluxe (blued backstrap, trigger guard) **$367.00**

UBERTI 1873 CATTLEMAN SINGLE-ACTION
Caliber: 22 LR/22 WMR, 38 Spec., 357 Mag., 44 Spec., 44-40, 45 Colt/45 ACP, 6-shot. **Barrel:** 4-3/4", 5-1/2", 7-1/2"; 44-40, 45 Colt also with 3", 3-1/2", 4". **Weight:** 38 oz. (5-1/2" bbl.). **Length:** 10-3/4" overall (5-1/2" bbl.). **Grips:** One-piece smooth walnut. **Sights:** Blade front, groove rear; fully adjustable rear available. **Features:** Steel or brass backstrap, trigger guard; color case-hardened frame, blued barrel, cylinder. Imported from Italy by Uberti U.S.A.
Price: Steel backstrap, trigger guard, fixed sights **$410.00**
Price: Brass backstrap, trigger guard, fixed sights **$359.00**
Price: Bisley model **$435.00**

Uberti 1873 Buckhorn Single-Action
A slightly larger version of the Cattleman revolver. Available in 44 Magnum or 44 Magnum/44-40 convertible, otherwise has same specs.
Price: Steel backstrap, trigger guard, fixed sights **$410.00**

UBERTI 1875 SA ARMY OUTLAW REVOLVER
Caliber: 357 Mag., 44-40, 45 Colt, 45 Colt/45 ACP convertible, 6-shot. **Barrel:** 5-1/2", 7-1/2". **Weight:** 44 oz. **Length:** 13-3/4" overall. **Grips:** Smooth walnut. **Sights:** Blade front, notch rear. **Features:** Replica of the 1875 Remington S.A. Army revolver. Brass trigger guard, color case-hardened frame, rest blued. Imported by Uberti U.S.A.
Price: **$483.00**
Price: 45 Colt/45 ACP convertible **$525.00**

UBERTI 1890 ARMY OUTLAW REVOLVER
Caliber: 357 Mag., 44-40, 45 Colt, 45 Colt/45 ACP convertible, 6-shot. **Barrel:** 5-1/2", 7-1/2". **Weight:** 37 oz. **Length:** 12-1/2" overall. **Grips:** American walnut. **Sights:** Blade front, groove rear. **Features:** Replica of the 1890 Remington single-action. Brass trigger guard, rest is blued. Imported by Uberti U.S.A.
Price: **$483.00**

Uberti 1890 Army Outlaw

Uberti Russian

Uberti 1875 Schofield

Uberti Bisley

Uberti Bisley Flat Top

UBERTI NEW MODEL RUSSIAN REVOLVER

Caliber: 44 Russian, 6-shot cylinder. **Barrel:** 6-1/2". **Weight:** 40 oz. **Length:** 12" overall. **Grips:** Smooth walnut. **Sights:** Blade front, notch rear. **Features:** Repica of the S&W Model 3 Russian Third Model revolver. Spur trigger guard, polished blue finish. Introduced 1999. Imported by Uberti USA.
Price: **$800.00**

UBERTI 1875 SCHOFIELD-STYLE BREAK-TOP REVOLVER

Caliber: 44-40, 45 Colt, 6-shot cylinder. **Barrel:** 5", 7". **Weight:** 39 oz. **Length:** 10-3/4" overall (5" barrel). **Grips:** Smooth walnut. **Sights:** Blade front, notch rear. **Features:** Replica of Smith & Wesson Model 3 Schofield. Single-action, top-break with automatic ejection. Polished blue finish. Introduced 1994. Imported by Uberti USA.
Price: **$750.00**

UBERTI BISLEY MODEL SINGLE-ACTION REVOLVER

Caliber: 38-40, 357 Mag., 44 Spec., 44-40 or 45 Colt, 6-shot cylinder. **Barrel:** 4-3/4", 5-1/2", 7-1/2". **Weight:** 40 oz. **Length:** 12-1/2" overall (7-1/2" barrel). **Grips:** Smooth walnut. **Sights:** Blade front, notch rear. **Features:** Replica of Colt's Bisley Model. Polished blue finish, color case-hardened frame. Introduced 1997. Imported by Uberti USA.
Price: **$435.00**

Uberti Bisley Model Flat Top Target Revolver
Similar to standard Bisley model, flat top strap, 7-1/2" barrel only, spring-loaded German silver front sight blade, standing leaf rear sight adjustable for windage. Polished blue finish, color case-hardened frame. Introduced 1998. Imported by Uberti USA.
Price: **$435.00**

U.S. FIRE-ARMS SINGLE ACTION ARMY REVOLVER

Caliber: 45 Colt (standard); .32 WCF, .38 WCF, .38 S&W, .41 Colt, .44WCF, .44 S&W (optional, additional charge), 6-shot cylinder. **Barrel:** 4-3/4", 5-1/2", 7-1/2". **Weight:** 37 oz. **Length:** NA. **Grips:** Hard rubber. **Sights:** Blade front, notch rear. **Features:** Recreation of original guns; 3" and 4" have no ejector. Available with all-blue, blue with color case-hardening, or full nickel-plate finish. Made in U.S.A. by United States Fire-Arms Mfg. Co.
Price: Blue/cased-colors. **$1,250.00**
Price: Carbonal blue/case-colors **$1,400.00**
Price: Nickel **$1,450.00**

U.S. Fire-Arms "China Camp" Cowboy Action Revolver

Similar to Single Action Army revolver, available in Silver Steel finish only. Offered in 4-3/4", 5-1/2", 7-1/2" barrels. Made in U.S.A. by United States Fire-Arms Mfg. Co.
Price: **$1,200.00**

U.S. FIRE-ARMS RODEO COWBOY ACTION REVOLVER

Caliber: 45 Colt. **Barrel:** 4-3/4", 5-1/2". **Grips:** Rubber. **Features:** Historically correct armory bone case hammer, blue satin finish, transfer bar safety system, correct solid firing pin. Entry level basic cowboy SASS gun for beginner or expert.
Price: **$550.00**

U.S. FIRE-ARMS UNITED STATES PRE-WAR

Caliber: .45 Colt, other caliber available. **Barrel:** 4-3/4", 5-1/2", 7-1/2". **Grips:** Hard rubber. **Features:** Armory bone case/Armory blue finish standard, cross-pin or black powder frame. Introduced 2002. Made in U.S.A. by United States Firearms Manufacturing Co.
Price: **$1,525.00**

Specially adapted single-shot and multi-barrel arms.

American Derringer Model 1

American Derringer Model 4

American Derringer Model 6

American Derringer Model 7

American Derringer Lady Derringer

American Derringer DA 38

AMERICAN DERRINGER MODEL 1

Caliber: 22 LR, 22 WMR, 30 Carbine, 30 Luger, 30-30 Win., 32 H&R Mag., 32-20, 380 ACP, 38 Super, 38 Spec., 38 Spec. shotshell, 38 Spec. +P, 9mm Para., 357 Mag., 357 Mag./45/410, 357 Maximum, 10mm, 40 S&W, 41 Mag., 38-40, 44-40 Win., 44 Spec., 44 Mag., 45 Colt, 45 Win. Mag., 45 ACP, 45 Colt/410, 45-70 single shot. **Barrel:** 3". **Weight:** 15-1/2 oz. (38 Spec.). **Length:** 4.82" overall. **Grips:** Rosewood, Zebra wood. **Sights:** Blade front. **Features:** Made of stainless steel with high-polish or satin finish. Two-shot capacity. Manual hammer block safety. Introduced 1980. Available in almost any pistol caliber. Contact the factory for complete list of available calibers and prices. From American Derringer Corp.

Price: 22 LR	$320.00
Price: 38 Spec.	$320.00
Price: 357 Maximum	$345.00
Price: 357 Mag.	$335.00
Price: 9mm, 380	$320.00
Price: 40 S&W	$335.00
Price: 44 Spec.	$398.00
Price: 44-40 Win.	$398.00
Price: 45 Colt	$385.00
Price: 30-30, 45 Win. Mag.	$460.00
Price: 41, 44 Mags.	$470.00
Price: 45-70, single shot	$387.00
Price: 45 Colt, 410, 2-1/2"	$385.00
Price: 45 ACP, 10mm Auto	$340.00

American Derringer Model 4

Similar to the Model 1 except has 4.1" barrel, overall length of 6", and weighs 16-1/2 oz.; chambered for 357 Mag., 357 Maximum, 45-70, 3" 410-bore shotshells or 45 Colt or 44 Mag. Made of stainless steel. Manual hammer block safety. Introduced 1980.

Price: 3" 410/45 Colt	$425.00
Price: 45-70	$560.00
Price: 44 Mag. with oversize grips	$515.00
Price: Alaskan Survival model (45-70 upper barrel, 410 or 45 Colt lower)	$475.00

American Derringer Model 6

Similar to the Model 1 except has 6" barrel chambered for 3" 410 shotshells or 22 WMR, 357 Mag., 45 ACP, 45 Colt; rosewood stocks; 8.2" o.a.l. and weighs 21 oz. Shoots either round for each barrel. Manual hammer block safety. Introduced 1980.

Price: 22 WMR	$440.00
Price: 357 Mag.	$440.00
Price: 45 Colt/410	$450.00
Price: 45 ACP	$440.00

American Derringer Model 7 Ultra Lightweight

Similar to Model 1 except made of high strength aircraft aluminum. Weighs 7-1/2 oz., 4.82" o.a.l., rosewood stocks. Available in 22 LR, 22 WMR, 32 H&R Mag., 380 ACP, 38 Spec., 44 Spec. Introduced 1980.

Price: 22 LR, WMR	$325.00
Price: 38 Spec.	$325.00
Price: 380 ACP	$325.00
Price: 32 H&R Mag/32 S&W Long	$325.00
Price: 44 Spec.	$565.00

American Derringer Model 10 Ultra Lightweight

Similar to the Model 1 except frame is of aluminum, giving weight of 10 oz. Stainless barrels. Available in 38 Spec., 45 Colt or 45 ACP only. Matte gray finish. Introduced 1980.

Price: 45 Colt	$385.00
Price: 45 ACP	$330.00
Price: 38 Spec.	$305.00

American Derringer Lady Derringer

Same as the Model 1 except has tuned action, is fitted with scrimshawed synthetic ivory grips; chambered for 32 H&R Mag. and 38 Spec.; 357 Mag., 45 Colt, 45/410. Deluxe Grade is highly polished; Deluxe Engraved is engraved in a pattern similar to that used on 1880s derringers. All come in a French fitted jewelry box. Introduced 1989.

Price: 32 H&R Mag.	$375.00
Price: 357 Mag.	$405.00
Price: 38 Spec.	$360.00
Price: 45 Colt, 45/410	$435.00

American Derringer Texas Commemorative

A Model 1 Derringer with solid brass frame, stainless steel barrel and rosewood grips. Available in 38 Spec., 44-40 Win., or 45 Colt. Introduced 1980.

Price: 38 Spec.	$365.00
Price: 44-40	$420.00
Price: Brass frame, 45 Colt	$450.00

AMERICAN DERRINGER DA 38 MODEL

Caliber: 22 LR, 9mm Para., 38 Spec., 357 Mag., 40 S&W. **Barrel:** 3". **Weight:** 14.5 oz. **Length:** 4.8" overall. **Grips:** Rosewood, walnut or other hardwoods. **Sights:** Fixed. **Features:** Double-action only; two-shots. Manual safety. Made of satin-finished stainless steel and aluminum. Introduced 1989. From American Derringer Corp.

Price: 22 LR	$435.00
Price: 38 Spec.	$460.00
Price: 9mm Para.	$445.00
Price: 357 Mag.	$450.00
Price: 40 S&W	$475.00

ANSCHUTZ MODEL 64P SPORT/TARGET PISTOL

Caliber: 22 LR, 22 WMR, 5-shot magazine. **Barrel:** 10". **Weight:** 3 lbs., 8 oz. **Length:** 18-1/2" overall. **Stock:** Choate Rynite. **Sights:** None furnished; grooved for scope mounting. **Features:** Right-hand bolt; polished blue finish. Introduced 1998. Imported from Germany by AcuSport.

Price: 22 LR	$455.95
Price: 22 WMR	$479.95

Bond Arms Texas Defender

Bond Arms Century 2000 Defender

Cobra Big Bore

Cobra D-Series

HANDGUNS

Comanche Super Single Shot

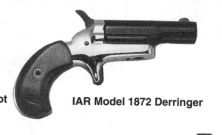

Downsizer WSP Single Shot

IAR Model 1872 Derringer

Gaucher GN1 Silhouette

BOND ARMS DEFENDER DERRINGER

Caliber: 410 Buckshot or slug, 45 Colt/45 Schofield (2.5" chamber), 45 Colt (only), 450 Bond Super/45 ACP/45 Super, 44 Mag./44 Special/44 Russian, 10mm, 40 S&W, 357 SIG, 357 Maximum/357 Mag./38 Special, 357 Mag/38 Special & 38 Long Colt, 38 Short Colt, 9mm Luger (9x19), 32 H&R Mag./38 S&W Long/32 Colt New Police, 22 Mag., 22 LR., 38-40, 44-40. **Barrel:** 3", 3-1/2". **Weight:** 20-21 oz. **Length:** 5"-5-1/2". **Grips:** Exotic woods or animal horn. **Sights:** Blade front, fixed rear. **Features:** Interchangeable barrels, retractingand rebounding firing pins, cross-bolt safety, automatic extractor for rimmed calibers. Stainless steel construction. Right or left hand.
Price: Texas (with TG) 3" bbl. **$359.00**
Price: Super (with TG) 3" bbl., 450 Bond Super and 45 ACP ... **$359.00**
Price: Cowboy (no TG) **$359.00**
Price: Century 2000 (with TG), Cowboy Century 2000 (no TG), 3-1/2" bbls., 410/45 Colt **$379.00**
Price: additional calibers available separately

BROWN CLASSIC SINGLE SHOT PISTOL

Caliber: 17 Ackley Hornet through 45-70 Govt. **Barrel:** 15" airgauged match grade. **Weight:** About 3 lbs., 7 oz. **Grips:** Walnut; thumbrest target style. **Sights:** None furnished; drilled and tapped for scope mounting. **Features:** Falling block action gives rigid barrel-receiver mating; hand-fitted and headspaced. Introduced 1998. Made in U.S.A. by E.A. Brown Mfg.
Price: **$499.00**

COBRA BIG BORE DERRINGERS

Caliber: 22 WMR, 38 Spec., 9mm Para. **Barrel:** 2.75". **Weight:** 11.5 oz. **Length:** 4.65" overall. **Grips:** Textured black synthetic. **Sights:** Blade front, fixed notch rear. **Features:** Alloy frame, steel-lined barrels, steel breech block. Plunger-type safety with integral hammer block. Chrome or black Teflon finish. Introduced 2002. Made in U.S.A. by Cobra Enterprises.
Price: **$98.00**
Price: 9mm Para. **$104.00**

COBRA LONG-BORE DERRINGERS

Caliber: 22 WMR, 38 Spec., 9mm Para. **Barrel:** 3.5". **Weight:** 13 oz. **Length:** 5.65" overall. **Grips:** Textured black synthetic. **Sights:** Fixed. **Features:** Chrome or black Teflon finish. Larger than Davis D-Series models. Introduced 2002. Made in U.S.A. by Cobra Enterprises.
Price: **$104.00**
Price: 9mm Para. **$110.00**
Price: Big-Bore models (same calibers, 3/4" shorter barrels)..... **$98.00**

COBRA D-SERIES DERRINGERS

Caliber: 22 LR, 22 WMR, 25 ACP, 32 ACP. **Barrel:** 2.4". **Weight:** 9.5 oz. **Length:** 4" overall. **Grips:** Laminated wood or pearl. **Sights:** Blade front, fixed notch rear. **Features:** Choice of black Teflon or chrome finish; spur trigger. Introduced 2002. Made in U.S.A. by Cobra Enterprises.
Price: **$99.50**

COMANCHE SUPER SINGLE SHOT PISTOL

Caliber: 45 LC, 410 ga. **Barrel:** 10". **Sights:** Adjustable. **Features:** Blue finish, not available for sale in CA, MA. Distributed by SGS Importers International, Inc.
Price: **$174.95**
Price: Satin nickel **$191.95**
Price: Duo tone **$185.95**

DOWNSIZER WSP SINGLE SHOT PISTOL

Caliber: 357 Magnum, 45 ACP. **Barrel:** 2.10". **Weight:** 11 oz. **Length:** 3.25" overall. **Grips:** Black polymer. **Sights:** None. **Features:** Single shot, tip-up barrel. Double action only. Stainless steel construction. Measures .900" thick. Introduced 1997. From Downsizer Corp.
Price: **$499.00**

GAUCHER GN1 SILHOUETTE PISTOL

Caliber: 22 LR, single shot. **Barrel:** 10". **Weight:** 2.4 lbs. **Length:** 15.5" overall. **Grips:** European hardwood. **Sights:** Blade front, open adjustable rear. **Features:** Bolt action, adjustable trigger. Introduced 1990. Imported from France by Mandall Shooting Supplies.
Price: About **$525.00**
Price: Model GP Silhouette **$425.00**

IAR MODEL 1872 DERRINGER

Caliber: 22 Short. **Barrel:** 2-3/8". **Weight:** 7 oz. **Length:** 5-1/8" overall. **Grips:** Smooth walnut. **Sights:** Blade front, notch rear. **Features:** Gold or nickel frame with blue barrel. Reintroduced 1996 using original Colt designs and tooling for the Colt Model 4 Derringer. Made in U.S.A. by IAR, Inc.
Price: **$109.00**
Price: Single cased gun **$125.00**
Price: Double cased set **$215.00**

IAR MODEL 1866 DOUBLE DERRINGER

Caliber: 38 Special. **Barrel:** 2-3/4". **Weight:** 16 oz. **Grips:** Smooth walnut. **Sights:** Blade front, notch rear. **Features:** All steel construction. Blue barrel, color case-hardened frame. Uses original designs and tooling for the Uberti New Maverick Derringer. Introduced 1999. Made in U.S.A. by IAR, Inc.
Price: **$395.00**

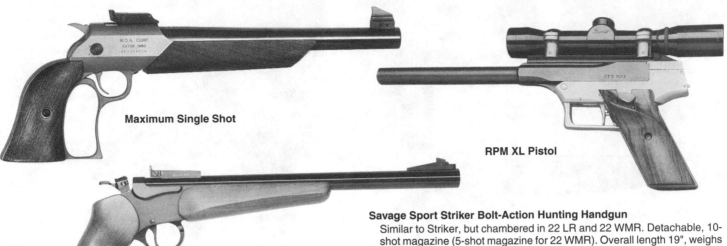

Maximum Single Shot

RPM XL Pistol

Thompson/Center C2 Contender

MAXIMUM SINGLE SHOT PISTOL

Caliber: 22 LR, 22 Hornet, 22 BR, 22 PPC, 223 Rem., 22-250, 6mm BR, 6mm PPC, 243, 250 Savage, 6.5mm-35M, 270 MAX, 270 Win., 7mm TCU, 7mm BR, 7mm-35, 7mm INT-R, 7mm-08, 7mm Rocket, 7mm Super-Mag., 30 Herrett, 30 Carbine, 30-30, 308 Win., 30x39, 32-20, 350 Rem. Mag., 357 Mag., 357 Maximum, 358 Win., 375 H&H, 44 Mag., 454 Casull. **Barrel:** 8-3/4", 10-1/2", 14". **Weight:** 61 oz. (10-1/2" bbl.); 78 oz. (14" bbl.). **Length:** 15", 18-1/2" overall (with 10-1/2" and 14" bbl., respectively). **Grips:** Smooth walnut stocks and forend. Also available with 17" finger groove grip. **Sights:** Ramp front, fully adjustable open rear. **Features:** Falling block action; drilled and tapped for M.O.A. scope mounts; integral grip frame/receiver; adjustable trigger; Douglas barrel (interchangeable). Introduced 1983. Made in U.S.A. by M.O.A. Corp.

Price: Stainless receiver, blue barrel	**$799.00**
Price: Stainless receiver, stainless barrel	**$883.00**
Price: Extra blued barrel	**$254.00**
Price: Extra stainless barrel	**$317.00**
Price: Scope mount	**$60.00**

RPM XL SINGLE SHOT PISTOL

Caliber: 22 LR through 45-70. **Barrel:** 8", 10-3/4", 12", 14". **Weight:** About 60 oz. **Grips:** Smooth Goncalo Alves with thumb and heel rests. **Sights:** Hooded front with interchangeable post, or Patridge; ISGW rear adjustable for windage and elevation. **Features:** Barrel drilled and tapped for scope mount. Visible cocking indicator. Spring-loaded barrel lock, positive hammer-block safety. Trigger adjustable for weight of pull and over-travel. Contact maker for complete price list. Made in U.S.A. by RPM.

Price: XL Hunter model (action only)	**$1,045.00**
Price: Extra barrel, 8" through 10-3/4"	**$407.50**
Price: Extra barrel, 12" through 14"	**$547.50**
Price: Muzzle brake	**$160.00**
Price: Left hand action, add	**$50.00**

SAVAGE STRIKER BOLT-ACTION HUNTING HANDGUN

Caliber: 223, 243, 7mm-08, 308, 300 WSM 2-shot mag. **Barrel:** 14". **Weight:** About 5 lbs. **Length:** 22-1/2" overall. **Stock:** Black composite ambidextrous mid-grip; grooved forend; "Dual Pillar" bedding. **Sights:** None furnished; drilled and tapped for scope mounting. **Features:** Short left-hand bolt with right-hand ejection; free-floated barrel; uses Savage Model 110 rifle scope rings/bases. Introduced 1998. Made in U.S.A. by Savage Arms, Inc.

Price: Model 510F (blued barrel and action)	**$425.00**
Price: Model 516FSS (stainless barrel and action)	**$462.00**
Price: Model 516FSAK (stainless, adjustable muzzle brake)	**$512.00**
Price: Model 516FSAK black stock (ss, aMB, 300WSM)	**$588.00**

Savage Sport Striker Bolt-Action Hunting Handgun

Similar to Striker, but chambered in 22 LR and 22 WMR. Detachable, 10-shot magazine (5-shot magazine for 22 WMR). Overall length 19", weighs 4 lbs. Ambidextrous fiberglass/graphite composite rear grip. Drilled and tapped, scope mount installed. Introduced 2000. Made in U.S.A. by Savage Arms Inc.

Price: Model 501F (blue finish, 22LR)	**$216.00**
Price: Model 501FXP with soft case, 1.25-4x28 scope	**$258.00**
Price: Model 502F (blue finish, 22 WMR)	**$238.00**

SPRINGFIELD M6 SCOUT PISTOL

Caliber: 22 LR/45 LC/.410, 22 Hornet, 45 LC/.410, **Barrel:** 10". **Weight:** NA. **Length:** NA. **Grip:** NA. **Sights:** NA. **Features:** Adapted from the U.S. Air Force M6 Survival Rifle, it is also available as a carbine with 16" barrel.

Price:	**$169.00 to $197.00**
Price: Pistol/Carbine	**$183.00 to $209.00**

THOMPSON/CENTER ENCORE PISTOL

Caliber: 22-250, 223, 260 Rem., 7mm-08, 243, 308, 270, 30-06, 44 Mag., 454 Casull, 480 Ruger, 444 Marlin single shot, 450 Marlin with muzzle tamer, no sights. **Barrel:** 12", 15", tapered round. **Weight:** NA. **Length:** 21" overall with 12" barrel. **Grips:** American walnut with finger grooves, walnut forend. **Sights:** Blade on ramp front, adjustable rear, or none. **Features:** Interchangeable barrels; action opens by squeezing the trigger guard; drilled and tapped for scope mounting; blue finish. Announced 1996. Made in U.S.A. by Thompson/Center Arms.

Price:	**$582.00 to $588.00**
Price: Extra 12" barrels	**$258.00**
Price: Extra 15" barrels	**$263.00**
Price: 45 Colt/410 barrel, 12"	**$282.00**
Price: 45 Colt/410 barrel, 15"	**$297.00**

Thompson/Center Stainless Encore Pistol

Similar to blued Encore, made of stainless steel, available with 15" barrel in 223, 22-250, 243 Win., 7mm-08, 308, 30/06 Sprgfld., 45/70 Gov't., 45/410 VR. With black rubber grip and forend. Made in U.S.A. by Thompson/Center Arms.

Price:	**$622.00 to $644.00**

Thompson/Center G2 Contender Pistol

A second generation Contender pistol maintaining the same barrel interchangeability with older Contender barrels and their corresponding forends (except Herrett forend). The G2 frame will not accept old-style grips due to the change in grip angle. Incorporates an automatic hammer block safety with built-in interlock. Features include trigger adjustable for overtravel, adjustable rear sight; ramp front sight blade, blued steel finish.

Price:	**$566.75**

UBERTI ROLLING BLOCK TARGET PISTOL

Caliber: 22 LR, 22 WMR, 22 Hornet, 357 Mag., 45 Colt, single shot. **Barrel:** 9-7/8", half-round, half-octagon. **Weight:** 44 oz. **Length:** 14" overall. **Stock:** Walnut grip and forend. **Sights:** Blade front, fully adjustable rear. **Features:** Replica of the 1871 rolling block target pistol. Brass trigger guard, color case-hardened frame, blue barrel. Imported by Uberti U.S.A.

Price:	**$410.00**

Both classic arms and recent designs in American-style repeaters for sport and field shooting.

Armalite M15A2

Armalite AR-10A4

Armalite AR-180B

Auto-Ordnance 1927 A-1 Thompson

ARMALITE M15A2 CARBINE

Caliber: 223, 7-shot magazine. **Barrel:** 16" heavy chrome lined; 1:9" twist. **Weight:** 7 lbs. **Length:** 35-11/16" overall. **Stock:** Green or black composition. **Sights:** Standard A2. **Features:** Upper and lower receivers have push-type pivot pin; hard coat anodized; A2-style forward assist; M16A2-type raised fence around magazine release button. Made in U.S.A. by ArmaLite, Inc.

Price: Green **$930.00**
Price: Black **$945.00**

ARMALITE AR-10A4 SPECIAL PURPOSE RIFLE

Caliber: 308 Win., 10-shot magazine. **Barrel:** 20" chrome-lined, 1:12" twist. **Weight:** 9.6 lbs. **Length:** 41" overall **Stock:** Green or black composition. **Sights:** Detachable handle, front sight, or scope mount available; comes with international style flattop receiver with Picatinny rail. **Features:** Proprietary recoil check. Forged upper receiver with case deflector. Receivers are hard-coat anodized. Introduced 1995. Made in U.S.A. by ArmaLite, Inc.

Price: Green **$1,383.00**
Price: Black **$1,383.00**
Price: Green or black with match trigger **$1,483.00**
Price: Green or Black with match trigger and stainless barrel . . **$1,583.00**

Armalite AR-10(T)

Similar to the Armalite AR-10A4 but with stainless steel, barrel, machined tool steel, two-stage National Match trigger group and other features.

Price: AR-10(T) Rifle **$2,080.00**
Price: AR-10(T) Carbine **$2,080.00**

Armalite AR-10A2

Utilizing the same 20" double-lapped, heavy barrel as the Armalite AR-10A4 Special Purpose Rifle, the AR-10A2 has a clamping front sight base allowing the removeable front sight to be rotated to zero the front sight. This assures the rear sight is centered and full left and right windage movement is available when shooting in strong winds. Offered in 308 caliber only. Made in U.S.A. by Armalite, Inc.

Price: AR-10A2 Rifle or Carbine. **$1,435.00**
Price: AR-10A2 Rifle or Carbine with match trigger **$1,535.00**
Price: AR-10A2 Rifle with stainless steel barrel **$1,535.00**

ARMALITE AR-180B RIFLE

Caliber: 223, 10-shot magazine. **Barrel:** 19.8" **Weight:** 6 lbs. **Length:** 38". **Stock:** Synthetic. **Sights:** Rear sight adjustable for windage, small and large apertures. **Features:** Lower receiver made of polymer, upper formed of sheet metal. Uses standard AR-15 magazines. Made in U.S.A. by Armalite. **Price:** **$650.00**
Price: With match trigger **$750.00**

ARSENAL USA SSR-56

Caliber: 7.62x39mm **Barrel:** 16.25" **Weight:** 7.4 lbs. **Length:** 35.5" **Stock:** Black polymer. **Sights:** Adjustable rear. **Features:** An AK-47 style rifle built on a hardened Hungarian FEG receiver with the required six U.S. made parts to make it legal for use with all extra-capacity magazines. From Arsenal I, LLC.

Price: **$565.00**

Barrett Model 82A-1

Browning Mark II Safari

ARSENAL USA SSR-74-2
Caliber: 5.45x39mm **Barrel:** 16.25" **Weight:** 7 lbs. **Length:** 36.75" **Stock:** Polymer or wood. **Sights:** Adjustable. **Features:** Built with parts from an unissued Bulgarian AK-74 rifle, it has a Buffer Technologies recoil buffer, and enough U.S.-made parts to allow pistol grip stock, and use with all extra-capacity magazines. Assembled in U.S.A. From Arsenal I, LLC.
Price: **$499.00**

ARSENAL USA SSR-85C-2
Caliber: 7.62x39mm **Barrel:** 16.25" **Weight:** 7.1 lbs. **Length:** 35.5" **Stock:** Polymer or wood. **Sights:** Adjustable rear calibrated to 800 meters. **Features:** Built from parts obtained from unissued Polish AK-47 rifles, the gas tube is vented and the receiver cover is plain. Rifle contains enough U.S.-sourced parts to allow pistol grip stock and use with all extra-capacity magazines. Assembled in U.S.A. by Arsenal USA I, LLC.
Price: **$499.00**

AUTO-ORDNANCE 1927 A-1 THOMPSON
Caliber: 45 ACP. **Barrel:** 16-1/2". **Weight:** 13 lbs. **Length:** About 41" overall (Deluxe). **Stock:** Walnut stock and vertical forend. **Sights:** Blade front, open rear adjustable for windage. **Features:** Recreation of Thompson Model 1927. Semi-auto only. Deluxe model has finned barrel, adjustable rear sight and compensator; Standard model has plain barrel and military sight. From Auto-Ordnance Corp.
Price: Deluxe **$950.00**
Price: 1927A1C Lightweight model (9-1/2 lbs.) **$950.00**

Auto-Ordnance Thompson M1/M1-C
Similar to the 1927 A-1 except is in the M-1 configuration with side cocking knob, horizontal forend, smooth unfinned barrel, sling swivels on butt and forend. Matte black finish. Introduced 1985.
Price: M1 semi-auto carbine **$950.00**
Price: M1-C lightweight semi-auto **$925.00**

Auto-Ordnance 1927A1 Commando
Similar to the 1927A1 except has Parkerized finish, black-finish wood butt, pistol grip, horizontal forend. Comes with black nylon sling. Introduced 1998. Made in U.S.A. by Auto-Ordnance Corp.
Price: **$950.00**

BARRETT MODEL 82A-1 SEMI-AUTOMATIC RIFLE
Caliber: 50 BMG, 10-shot detachable box magazine. **Barrel:** 29". **Weight:** 28.5 lbs. **Length:** 57" overall. **Stock:** Composition with energy-absorbing recoil pad. **Sights:** Scope optional. **Features:** Semi-automatic, recoil operated with recoiling barrel. Three-lug locking bolt; muzzle brake. Adjustable bipod. Introduced 1985. Made in U.S.A. by Barrett Firearms.
Price: From. **$7,200.00**

BENELLI RI RIFLE
Caliber: 300 Win. Mag., 30-06 Springfield. **Barrel:** 20", 22", 24". **Weight:** 7.1 lbs. **Length:** 43.75" **Stock:** Select satin walnut. **Sights:** None. **Features:** Auto-regulating gas-operated system, three-lugged rotary bolt, interchangeable barrels. Introduced 2003. Imported from Italy by Benelli USA.
Price: . . . . **$1065.00 to $1,080.00**

BROWNING BAR MARK II SAFARI SEMI-AUTO RIFLE
Caliber: 243, 25-06, 270, 30-06, 308, 270 WSM, 7mm WSM. **Barrel:** 22" round tapered. **Weight:** 7-3/8 lbs. **Length:** 43" overall. **Stock:** French walnut pistol grip stock and forend, hand checkered. **Sights:** Gold bead on hooded ramp front, click adjustable rear, or no sights. **Features:** Has new bolt release lever; removable trigger assembly with larger trigger guard; redesigned gas and buffer systems. Detachable 4-round box magazine. Scroll-engraved receiver is tapped for scope mounting. BOSS barrel vibration modulator and muzzle brake system available only on models without sights. Mark II Safari introduced 1993. Imported from Belgium by Browning.
Price: Safari, with sights **$833.00**
Price: Safari, no sights **$815.00**
Price: Safari, 270 and 30-06, no sights, BOSS **$891.00**

Browning BAR Mark II Lightweight Semi-Auto
Similar to the Mark II Safari except has lighter alloy receiver and 20" barrel. Available in 243, 308, 270, 30-06, 7mm Rem. Mag., 300 Win. Mag., 338 Win. Mag. Weighs 7 lbs., 2 oz.; overall length 41". Has dovetailed, gold bead front sight on hooded ramp, open rear click adjustable for windage and elevation. Introduced 1997. Imported from Belgium by Browning.
Price: 243, 308, 270, 30-06 . . . . **$833.00**
Price: 7mm Rem. Mag., 300 Win. Mag., 338 Win. Mag **$909.00**

Browning BAR Mark II Safari Rifle in magnum calibers
Same as the standard caliber model, except weighs 8-3/8 lbs., 45" overall, 24" bbl., 3-round mag. Cals. 7mm Mag., 300 Win. Mag., 338 Win. Mag. BOSS barrel vibration modulator and muzzle brake system available only on models without sights. Introduced 1993.
Price: Safari, with sights. **$909.00**
Price: Safari, no sights **$890.00**
Price: Safari, no sights, BOSS **$967.00**

NEW!

RIFLES

Bushmaster M17S Bullpup

Bushmaster XM15 E2S Carbine

Bushmaster Varminter

Colt Match Target Lightweight

Browning BAR High-Grade Auto Rifles

Similar to BAR Mark II Safari model except has grayed receiver with big-game scenes framed in gold with select walnut stock and forearm. Furnished with no sights. Introduced 2001.

Price: 270, 30-06 (whitetail and mule deer scenes) **$1,820.00**
Price: 7mm Rem. Mag., 300 Win. Mag. (moose and elk scenes)
. . . . **$1,876.00**

BROWNING BAR STALKER AUTO RIFLES

Caliber: 243, 308, 270, 30-06, 7mm Rem. Mag., 300 Win. Mag., 338 Win. Mag., 270 WSM< 7mm WSM. **Barrel:** 20", 22" and 24". **Weight:** 6 lbs., 12 oz. (243) to 8 lbs., 2 oz. (magnum cals.) **Length:** 41" to 45" overall. **Stock:** Black composite stock and forearm. **Sights:** Hooded front and adjustable rear or none. **Features:** Optional BOSS (no sights); gas-operated action with seven-lug rotary bolt; dual action bars; 3- or 4-shot magazine (depending on caliber). Introduced 2001. Imported by Browning.

Price: BAR Stalker, open sights (243, 308, 270, 30-06) **$809.00**
Price: BAR Stalker, open sights (7mm, 300 Win. Mag.,
338 Win. Mag.) **$883.00**
Price: BAR Stalker, BOSS (7mm, 300 Win. Mag., 338 Win. Mag.) **$941.00**

BUSHMASTER M17S BULLPUP RIFLE

Caliber: 223, 10-shot magazine. **Barrel:** 21.5", chrome lined;1:9" twist. **Weight:** 8.2 lbs. **Length:** 30" overall. **Stock:** Fiberglass-filled nylon. **Sights:** Designed for optics—carrying handle incorporates scope mount rail for Weaver-type rings; also includes 25-meter open iron sights. **Features:** Gas-operated, short-stroke piston system; ambidextrous magazine release. Introduced 1993. Made in U.S.A. by Bushmaster Firearms, Inc./Quality Parts Co.

Price: **$765.00**

BUSHMASTER SHORTY XM15 E2S CARBINE

Caliber: 223,10-shot magazine. **Barrel:** 16", heavy; 1:9" twist. **Weight:** 7.2 lbs. **Length:** 34.75" overall. **Stock:** A2 type; fixed black composition. **Sights:** Fully adjustable M16A2 sight system. **Features:** Patterned after Colt M-16A2. Chrome-lined barrel with manganese phosphate finish. "Shorty" handguards. Has forged aluminum receivers with push-pin. Made in U.S.A. by Bushmaster Firearms Inc.

Price: . . . . (A2) **$985.00**
Price: (A3) **$1,085.00**

Bushmaster XM15 E2S Dissipator Carbine

Similar to the XM15 E2S Shorty carbine except has full-length "Dissipator" handguards. Weighs 7.6 lbs.; 34.75" overall; forged aluminum receivers with push-pin style takedown. Made in U.S.A. by Bushmaster Firearms, Inc.

Price: . . . . (A2 type) **$995.00**
Price: (A3 type) **$1,095.00**

Bushmaster XM15 E25 AK Shorty Carbine

Similar to the XM15 E2S Shorty except has 14.5" barrel with an AK muzzle brake permanently attached giving 16" barrel length. Weighs 7.3 lbs. Introduced 1999. Made in U.S.A. by Bushmaster Firearms, Inc.

Price: . . . . (A2 type) **$1,005.00**
Price: (A3 type) **$1,105.00**

Bushmaster M4/M4A3 Post-Ban Carbine

Similar to the XM15 E2S except has 14.5" barrel with Mini Y compensator, and fixed tele-stock. MR configuration has fixed carry handle; M4A3 has removeable carry handle.

Price: (M4) **$1,065.00**
Price: (M4A3) **$1,165.00**

BUSHMASTER VARMINTER RIFLE

Caliber: 223 Rem., 5-shot. **Barrel:** 24", 1:9" twist, fluted, heavy, stainless. **Weight:** 8/3/4 lbs. **Length:** 42-1/4". **Stock:** Rubberized pistol grip. **Sights:** 1/2" scope risers. **Features:** Gas-operated, semi-auto, 2 stage trigger, slotted free floater forend, lockable hard case.

Price: **$1,245.00**

COLT MATCH TARGET RIFLE

Caliber: 223 Rem., 5-shot magazine. **Barrel:** 16.1" or 20". **Weight:** 7.1 to 8-1/2 lbs. **Length:** 34-1/2" to 39" overall. **Stock:** Composition stock, grip, forend. **Sights:** Post front, rear adjustable for windage and elevation. **Features:** 5-round detachable box magazine, flash suppressor, sling swivels. Forward bolt assist included. Introduced 1991. Made in U.S.A. by Colt's Manufacturing Co. Inc.

Price: Colt Light Rifle **$779.00**
Price: Match Target HBAR, from **$1,194.00**

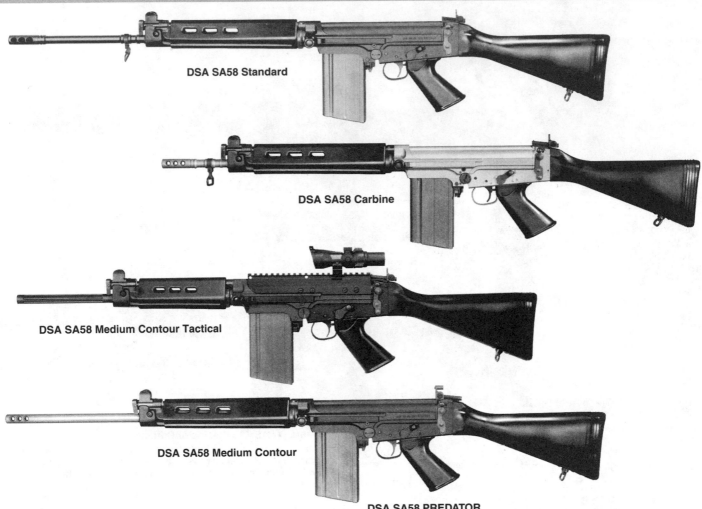

DSA SA58 Standard

DSA SA58 Carbine

DSA SA58 Medium Contour Tactical

DSA SA58 Medium Contour

DPMS PANTHER ARMS A-15 RIFLES

Caliber: 223 Rem., 7.62x39. **Barrel:** 16" to 24". **Weight:** 7-3/4 to 11-3/4 lbs. **Length:** 34-1/2 to 42-1/4" overall. **Stock:** Black Zytel® composite. **Sights:** Square front post, adjustable A2 rear. **Features:** Steel or stainless steel heavy or bull barrel; hard-coat anodized receiver; aluminum free-float tube handguard; many options. From DPMS Panther Arms.
Price: Panther Bull A-15 (20" stainless bull barrel). **$915.00**
Price: Panther Bull Twenty-Four (24" stainless bull barrel) **$945.00**
Price: Bulldog (20" stainless fluted barrel, flat top receiver). . . . **$1,219.00**
Price: Panther Bull Sweet Sixteen (16" stainless bull barrel) **$885.00**
Price: DCM Panther (20" stainless heavy bbl., n.m. sights). . . . **$1,099.00**
Price: Panther 7.62x39 (20" steel heavy barrel). **$849.00**

DSA SA58 CONGO, PARA CONGO

Caliber: 308 Win. **Barrel:** 18" w/short muzzle brake. **Weight:** 8.6 lbs. (Congo); 9.85 lbs. (Para Congo). **Length:** 39.75" **Stock:** Synthetic w/military grade furniture (Congo); Synthetic with non-folding steel para stock (Para Congo). **Sights:** Post, front, windage adjustable peep, rear (Congo); Belgian style para flip peep, rear (Para Congo). **Features:** Fully-adjustable gas system, high-grade steel upper receiver with carry handle. Made in U.S.A. by DSA, Inc.
Price: . . . . **$1,695.00** (Congo); **$1,995.00** (Para Congo)

DSA SA58 GRAY WOLF

Caliber: 308 Win., 300 WSM. **Barrel:** 21" match-grade bull w/target crown. **Weight:** 13 lbs. **Length:** 41.75" **Stock:** Synthetic. **Sights:** Elevation adjustable post, front; windage adjustable match peep, rear. **Features:** Fully-adjustable gas system, high-grade steel upper receiver, Picatinny scope mount, DuraCoat finish. Made in U.S.A. by DSA, Inc.
Price: **$2,120.00**

DSA SA58 PREDATOR

Caliber: 260 Rem., 243 Win., 308 Win. **Barrel:** 16" and 19" w/target crown. **Weight:** 9 to 9.3 lbs. **Length:** 36.25" to 39.25". **Stock:** Synthetic. **Sights:** Elevation adjustable post, front; windage adjustable match peep, rear. **Features:** Fully-adjustable gas system, high-grade steel upper receiver, Picatinny scope mount, DuraCoat solid and camo finishes.
Price: . . . . **$1,595.00** (308 win.); **$1,695.00** (243 Win., 260 Rem.)

DSA SA58 T48

Caliber: 308 Win. **Barrel:** 16.25" with Browning replica flash hider. **Weight:** 9.3 lbs. **Length:** 44.5". **Stock:** European walnut. **Sights:** Adjustable post front, adjustable rear peep. **Features:** Gas-operated semi-auto with fully adjustable gas system, high grade steel upper receiver. DuraCoat finishes. Made in U.S.A. by DSA, Inc.
Price: **$1,795.00**

DSA SA58 GI

Similar to the SA58 T48, except has steel bipod cut handguard with haardwood stock and synthetic pistol grip, original GI steel lower receiver with GI bipod. Made in U.S.A. by DSA, Inc.
Price: **$1,695.00**

DSA SA58 TACTICAL CARBINE, CARBINE

Caliber: 308 Win., limited 243 and 260. **Barrel:** 16.25" with integrally machined muzzle brake. **Weight:** 8.75 lbs. **Length:** 38.25". **Stock:** Fiberglass reinforced synthetic handguard. **Sights:** Adjustable post front, adjustable rear peep. **Features:** Gas-operated semi-auto with fully adjustable gas system, high grade steel or 416 stainless upper receiver. In variety of camo finishes. Made in U.S.A. by DSA, Inc.
Price: Tactical Fluted bbl. **$1,475.00**
Price: Carbine stainless steel bbl. **$1,645.00**
Price: Carbine high-grade steel bbl. **$1,395.00**

DSA SA58 Bull

DSA SA58 T48 Replica

DSA SA58 OSW

EAA/Saiga 380

RIFLES

DSA SA58 MEDIUM CONTOUR

Caliber: 308 Win., limited 243 and 260. **Barrel:** 21" with integrally machined muzzle brake. **Weight:** 9.75 lbs. **Length:** 43". **Stock:** Fiberglass reinforced synthetic handguard. **Sights:** Adjustable post front with match rear peep. **Features:** Gas-operated semi-auto with fully adjustable gas system, high grade steel or 416 stainless upper receiver. In variety of camo finishes. Made in U.S.A. by DSA, Inc.
Price: chrome moly. **$1,475.00**
Price: stainless steel. **$1,725.00**

DSA SA58 21" OR 24" BULL BARREL RIFLE

Caliber: 308 Win., 300 WSM. **Barrel:** 21" or 24". **Weight:** 11.1 and 11.5 lbs. **Length:** 41.5" and 44.5". **Stock:** Synthetic, free floating handguard. **Sights:** Elevation adjustable protected post front, match rear peep. **Features:** Gas-operated semi-auto with fully adjustable gas system, high grade steel or stainless upper receiver. Made in U.S.A. by DSA, Inc.
Price: 21", 24" **$1,745.00**
Price: 24" fluted bbl. **$1,795.00**

DSA SA58 MINI OSW

Caliber: 7.62 NATO. **Barrel:** 11" or 13" with muzzle brake. **Weight:** 9 to 9.35 lbs. **Length:** 33". **Stock:** Synthetic. **Features:** Gas-operated semi-auto or select fire with fully adjustable short gas system, optional FAL Rail Interface Handguard, SureFire Vertical Foregrip System, EOTech HOLOgraphic Sight and ITC Cheekrest. Made in U.S.A. by DSA, Inc.
Price: **$1,525.00**

EAA/SAIGA SEMI-AUTO RIFLE

Caliber: 7.62x39, 308, 223. **Barrel:** 20.5", 22", 16.3". **Weight:** 7 to 8-1/2 lbs. **Length:** 43". **Stock:** Synthetic or wood. **Sights:** Adjustable, sight base. **Features:** Based on AK Combat rifle by Kalashnikov. Imported from Russia by EAA Corp.
Price: 7.62x39 (syn.) **$239.00**
Price: 308 (syn. or wood) **$429.00**
Price: 223 (syn.) **$389.00**

EAGLE ARMS AR-10 RIFLE

Caliber: 308. **Barrel:** 20", 24". **Weight:** NA **Length:** NA **Stock:** Synthetic. **Sights:** Adjustable A2, front, Std. A2, rear; Flat top and Match Rifle have no sights but adjustable Picatinny rail furnished. **Features:** A product of the latest in manufacturing technology to provide a quality rifle at a reasonable price. Introduced 2003. Made in U.S.A. by Eagle Arms.
Price: AR-10 Service Rifle **$1,055.00**
Price: AR-10 Flat Top Rifle **$999.95**
Price: AR-10 Match Rifle **$1,480.00**

EAGLE ARMS M15 RIFLE

Caliber: 223. **Barrel:** 16", 20". **Weight:** NA **Length:** NA **Stock:** Synthetic. **Sights:** Adjustable A2, front; Std. A2, rear; Flat Top Rifle & Carbine versions, no sights furnished. **Features:** Available in 4 different configurations, the latest manufacturing technology has been employed to keep the price reasonable. Introduced 2003. Made in U.S.A. by Eagle Arms.
Price: A2 Rifle **$795.00**
Price: A2 Carbine **$795.00**
Price: Flat Top Rifle **$835.00**
Price: Flat Top Carbine **$835.00**

Heckler & Koch SLB 2000

Heckler & Koch SL8-1

Heckler & Koch USC

Hi-Point Carbine

HECKLER & KOCH SLB 2000 RIFLE

Caliber: 30-06; 2-, 5- and 10-shot magazines. **Barrel:** 19.7". **Weight:** 8 lb. **Length:** 41.3". **Stock:** Oil-finished, checkered walnut. **Sights:** Ramp front, patridge rear. **Features:** Short-stroke, piston-actuated gas operation; modular steel and polymer construction; free-floating barrel; pistol grip angled for natural feel. Introduced 2001. From H&K.
Price: **$1,299.00**

HECKLER & KOCH SL8-1 RIFLE

Caliber: 223; 10-shot magazine. **Barrel:** 17.7". **Weight:** 8.6 lbs. **Length:** 38.6" overall. **Stock:** Polymer thumbhole. **Sights:** Blade front with integral hood; fully adjustable rear diopter. Picatinny rail. **Features:** Based on German military G36 rifle. Uses short-stroke piston-actuated gas operation; almost entirely constructed of carbon fiber-reinforced polymer. Free-floating heavy target barrel. Introduced 2000. From H&K.
Price: **$1,249.00**

HECKLER & KOCH USC CARBINE

Caliber: 45 ACP, 10-shot magazine. **Barrel:** 16". **Weight:** 8.6 lb. **Length:** 35.4" overall. **Stock:** Skeletonized polymer thumbhole. **Sights:** Blade front with integral hood, fully adjustable diopter. **Features:** Based on German UMP submachine gun. Blowback operation; almost entirely constructed of carbon fiber-reinforced polymer. Free-floating heavy target barrel. Introduced 2000. From H&K.
Price: **$1,249.00**

HI-POINT 9MM CARBINE

Caliber: 9mm Para., 40 S&W, 10-shot magazine. **Barrel:** 16-1/2" (17-1/2" for 40 S&W). **Weight:** 4-1/2 lbs. **Length:** 31-1/2" overall. **Stock:** Black polymer, camouflage. **Sights:** Protected post front, aperture rear. Integral scope mount. **Features:** Grip-mounted magazine release. Black or chrome finish. Sling swivels. Available with laser or red dot sights. Introduced 1996. Made in U.S.A. by MKS Supply, Inc.
Price: Black or chrome, 9mm **$199.00**
Price: 40 S&W **$225.00**
Price: Camo stock **$210.00**

IAI M-333 M1 GARAND

Caliber: 30-06, 8-shot clip. **Barrel:** 24". **Weight:** 9-1/2 lbs. **Length:** 43.6" overall. **Stock:** Hardwood. **Sights:** Blade front, aperture adjustable rear. **Features:** Parkerized finish; gas-operated semi-automatic; remanufactured to military specifications. From IAI.
Price: **$971.75**

IAI M-888 M1 CARBINE SEMI-AUTOMATIC RIFLE

Caliber: 22, 30 Carbine. **Barrel:** 18"-20". **Weight:** 5-1/2 lbs. **Length:** 35"-37" overall. **Stock:** Laminate, walnut or birch. **Sights:** Blade front, adjustable rear. **Features:** Gas-operated, air cooled, manufactured to military specifications. 10/15/30 rnd. mag. scope available. From IAI.
Price: 30 cal. .... **$556.00 to $604.00**
Price: 22 cal. .... **$567.00 to $654.00**

Intrac Arms IAI-65 Rifle

A civilian-legal version of the original HKM rifle manufactured in Hungary. Manufactured by Gordon Technologies using an original AMD-65 matching parts kit built on an AKM receiver. The original wire stock is present, but it is welded in the open position as per BATF regulations. Furnished with a 12.6" barrel with large weld-in-place muzzle brake to bring its length over the 16" federal minimum. This rifle accepts all 7.62x39mm magazines and drums. Introduced 2002. From Intrac Arms International, Inc.
Price: **$799.00**

Remington Model 7400

Ruger Deerfield 99/44 Carbine

Ruger PC4 Carbine

Ruger Ranch Mini 14/5R

RIFLES

LES BAER CUSTOM ULTIMATE AR 223 RIFLES

Caliber: 223. **Barrel:** 18", 20", 22", 24". **Weight:** 7-3/4 to 9-3/4 lb. **Length:** NA. **Stock:** Black synthetic. **Sights:** None furnished; Picatinny-style flat top rail for scope mounting. **Features:** Forged receiver; Ultra single-stage trigger (Jewell two-stage trigger optional); titanium firing pin; Versa-Pod bipod; chromed National Match carrier; stainless steel, hand-lapped and cryo-treated barrel; guaranteed to shoot 1/2 or 3/4 MOA, depending on model. Made in U.S.A. by Les Bear Custom Inc.
Price: Super Varmint Model **$1,989.00**
Price: M4 Flattop Model **$2,195.00**
Price: IPSC Action Model **$2,195.00**

LR 300 SR LIGHT SPORT RIFLE

Caliber: 223. **Barrel:** 16-1/4"; 1:9" twist. **Weight:** 7.2 lbs. **Length:** 36" overall (extended stock), 26-1/4" (stock folded). **Stock:** Folding, tubular steel, with thumbhold-type grip. **Sights:** Trijicon post front, Trijicon rear. **Features:** Uses AR-15 type upper and lower receivers; flattop receiver with weaver base. Accepts all AR-15/M-16 magazines. Introduced 1996. Made in U.S.A. from Z-M Weapons.
Price: **$2,550.00**

OLYMPIC ARMS CAR-97 RIFLES

Caliber: 223, 7-shot; 9mm Para., 45 ACP, 40 S&W, 10mm, 10-shot. **Barrel:** 16". **Weight:** 7 lbs. **Length:** 34.75" overall. **Stock:** A2 stowaway grip, telescoping-look butt. **Sights:** Post front, fully adjustable aperature rear. **Features:** Based on AR-15 rifle. Post-ban version of the CAR-15. Made in U.S.A. by Olympic Arms, Inc.
Price: 223 . . . . **$780.00**
Price: 9mm Para., 45 ACP, 40 S&W, 10mm **$840.00**
Price: PCR Eliminator (223, full-length handguards) **$803.00**

OLYMPIC ARMS PCR-4 RIFLE

Caliber: 223, 10-shot magazine. **Barrel:** 20". **Weight:** 8 lbs., 5 oz. **Length:** 38.25" overall. **Stock:** A2 stowaway grip, trapdoor buttstock. **Sights:** Post front, A1 rear adjustable for windage. **Features:** Based on the AR-15 rifle. Barrel is button rifled with 1:9" twist. No bayonet lug. Introduced 1994. Made in U.S.A. by Olympic Arms, Inc.
Price: **$792.00**

OLYMPIC ARMS PCR-6 RIFLE

Caliber: 7.62x39mm (PCR-6), 10-shot magazine. **Barrel:** 16". **Weight:** 7 lbs. **Length:** 34" overall. **Stock:** A2 stowaway grip, trapdoor buttstock.

Sights: Post front, A1 rear adjustable for windage. **Features:** Based on the CAR-15. No bayonet lug. Button-cut rifling. Introduced 1994. Made in U.S.A. by Olympic Arms, Inc.
Price: **$845.00**

REMINGTON MODEL 7400 AUTO RIFLE

Caliber: 243 Win., 270 Win., 308 Win., 30-06, 4-shot magazine. **Barrel:** 22" round tapered. **Weight:** 7-1/2 lbs. **Length:** 42-5/8" overall. **Stock:** Walnut, deluxe cut checkered pistol grip and forend. Satin or high-gloss finish. **Sights:** Gold bead front sight on ramp; step rear sight with windage adjustable. **Features:** Redesigned and improved version of the Model 742. Positive cross-bolt safety. Receiver tapped for scope mount. Introduced 1981.
Price: **$624.00**
Price: Carbine (18-1/2" bbl., 30-06 only) **$624.00**
Price: With black synthetic stock, matte black metal,
rifle or carbine. **$520.00**
Price: Weathermaster, nickel-plated w/synthetic stock and forend,
270, 30-06 . . . . **$624.00**

ROCK RIVER ARMS STANDARD A2 RIFLE

Caliber: 45 ACP. **Barrel:** NA. **Weight:** 8.2 lbs. **Length:** NA. **Stock:** Thermoplastic. **Sights:** Standard AR-15 style sights. **Features:** Two-stage, national match trigger; optional muzzle brake. Made in U.S.A. From River Rock Arms.
Price: **$925.00**

RUGER DEERFIELD 99/44 CARBINE

Caliber: 44 Mag., 4-shot rotary magazine. **Barrel:** 18-1/2". **Weight:** 6-1/4 lbs. **Length:** 36-7/8" overall. **Stock:** Hardwood. **Sights:** Gold bead front, folding adjustable aperture rear. **Features:** Semi-automatic action; dual front-locking lugs lock directly into receiver; integral scope mount; push-button safety; includes 1" rings and gun lock. Introduced 2000. Made in U.S.A. by Sturm, Ruger & Co.
Price: **$675.00**

RUGER PC4, PC9 CARBINES

Caliber: 9mm Para., 40 cal., 10-shot magazine. **Barrel:** 16.25". **Weight:** 6 lbs., 4 oz. **Length:** 34.75" overall. **Stock:** Black high impact synthetic checkered grip and forend. **Sights:** Blade front, open adjustable rear; integral Ruger scope mounts. **Features:** Delayed blowback action; manual push-button cross bolt safety and internal firing pin block safety automatic slide lock. Introduced 1997. Made in U.S.A. by Sturm, Ruger & Co.
Price: PC9, PC4, (9mm, 40 cal.) **$605.00**
Price: PC4GR, PC9GR, (40 auto, 9mm, post sights, ghost ring) **$628.00**

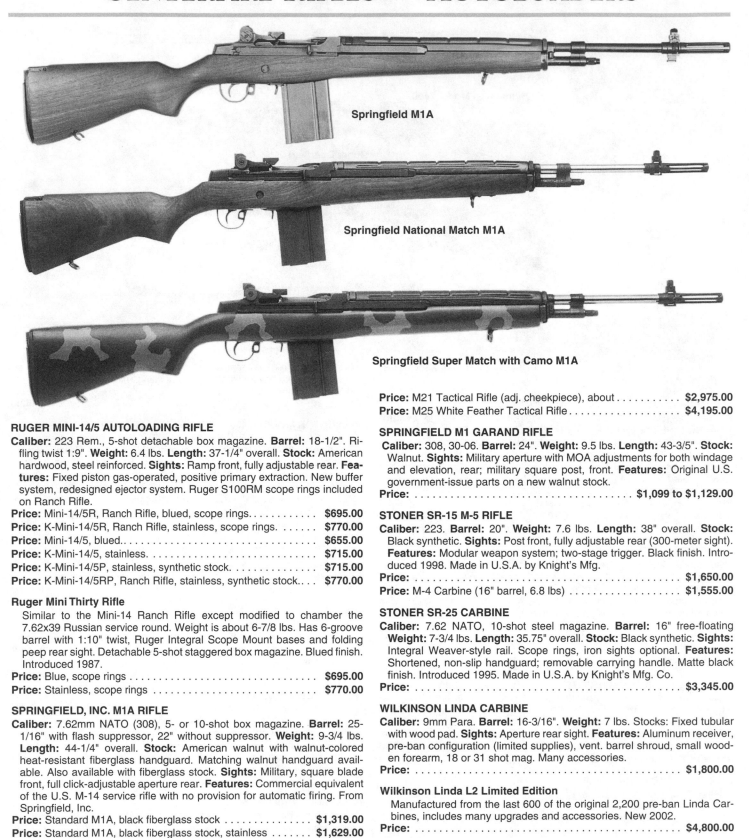

Springfield M1A

Springfield National Match M1A

Springfield Super Match with Camo M1A

RUGER MINI-14/5 AUTOLOADING RIFLE

Caliber: 223 Rem., 5-shot detachable box magazine. **Barrel:** 18-1/2". Rifling twist 1:9". **Weight:** 6.4 lbs. **Length:** 37-1/4" overall. **Stock:** American hardwood, steel reinforced. **Sights:** Ramp front, fully adjustable rear. **Features:** Fixed piston gas-operated, positive primary extraction. New buffer system, redesigned ejector system. Ruger S100RM scope rings included on Ranch Rifle.

Price: Mini-14/5R, Ranch Rifle, blued, scope rings. **$695.00**
Price: K-Mini-14/5R, Ranch Rifle, stainless, scope rings. **$770.00**
Price: Mini-14/5, blued. **$655.00**
Price: K-Mini-14/5, stainless. **$715.00**
Price: K-Mini-14/5P, stainless, synthetic stock. **$715.00**
Price: K-Mini-14/5RP, Ranch Rifle, stainless, synthetic stock. . . . **$770.00**

Ruger Mini Thirty Rifle

Similar to the Mini-14 Ranch Rifle except modified to chamber the 7.62x39 Russian service round. Weight is about 6-7/8 lbs. Has 6-groove barrel with 1:10" twist, Ruger Integral Scope Mount bases and folding peep rear sight. Detachable 5-shot staggered box magazine. Blued finish. Introduced 1987.

Price: Blue, scope rings **$695.00**
Price: Stainless, scope rings **$770.00**

SPRINGFIELD, INC. M1A RIFLE

Caliber: 7.62mm NATO (308), 5- or 10-shot box magazine. **Barrel:** 25-1/16" with flash suppressor, 22" without suppressor. **Weight:** 9-3/4 lbs. **Length:** 44-1/4" overall. **Stock:** American walnut with walnut-colored heat-resistant fiberglass handguard. Matching walnut handguard available. Also available with fiberglass stock. **Sights:** Military, square blade front, full click-adjustable aperture rear. **Features:** Commercial equivalent of the U.S. M-14 service rifle with no provision for automatic firing. From Springfield, Inc.

Price: Standard M1A, black fiberglass stock **$1,319.00**
Price: Standard M1A, black fiberglass stock, stainless **$1,629.00**
Price: Standard M1A, black stock, carbon barrel **$1,379.00**
Price: Standard M1A, Mossy Oak stock, carbon barrel **$1,443.00**
Price: Scout Squad M1A . . . . **$1,529 to $1,639.00**
Price: National Match . . . . **$1,995.00 to $2,040.00**
Price: Super Match (heavy premium barrel), about **$2,449.00**

Price: M21 Tactical Rifle (adj. cheekpiece), about **$2,975.00**
Price: M25 White Feather Tactical Rifle **$4,195.00**

SPRINGFIELD M1 GARAND RIFLE

Caliber: 308, 30-06. **Barrel:** 24". **Weight:** 9.5 lbs. **Length:** 43-3/5". **Stock:** Walnut. **Sights:** Military aperture with MOA adjustments for both windage and elevation, rear; military square post, front. **Features:** Original U.S. government-issue parts on a new walnut stock.

Price: . . . . **$1,099 to $1,129.00**

STONER SR-15 M-5 RIFLE

Caliber: 223. **Barrel:** 20". **Weight:** 7.6 lbs. **Length:** 38" overall. **Stock:** Black synthetic. **Sights:** Post front, fully adjustable rear (300-meter sight). **Features:** Modular weapon system; two-stage trigger. Black finish. Introduced 1998. Made in U.S.A. by Knight's Mfg.

Price: **$1,650.00**
Price: M-4 Carbine (16" barrel, 6.8 lbs) **$1,555.00**

STONER SR-25 CARBINE

Caliber: 7.62 NATO, 10-shot steel magazine. **Barrel:** 16" free-floating **Weight:** 7-3/4 lbs. **Length:** 35.75" overall. **Stock:** Black synthetic. **Sights:** Integral Weaver-style rail. Scope rings, iron sights optional. **Features:** Shortened, non-slip handguard; removable carrying handle. Matte black finish. Introduced 1995. Made in U.S.A. by Knight's Mfg. Co.

Price: **$3,345.00**

WILKINSON LINDA CARBINE

Caliber: 9mm Para. **Barrel:** 16-3/16". **Weight:** 7 lbs. **Stocks:** Fixed tubular with wood pad. **Sights:** Aperture rear sight. **Features:** Aluminum receiver, pre-ban configuration (limited supplies), vent. barrel shroud, small wooden forearm, 18 or 31 shot mag. Many accessories.

Price: **$1,800.00**

Wilkinson Linda L2 Limited Edition

Manufactured from the last 600 of the original 2,200 pre-ban Linda Carbines, includes many upgrades and accessories. New 2002.

Price: **$4,800.00**

WILKINSON TERRY CARBINE

Caliber: 9mm Para. **Barrel:** 16-3/16". **Weight:** 7 lbs. **Stocks:** Black or maple. **Sights:** Adjustable. **Features:** Blowback semi-auto action, 31 shot mag., closed breech.

Price: . . . . **NA**

RIFLES

Both classic arms and recent designs in American-style repeaters for sport and field shooting.

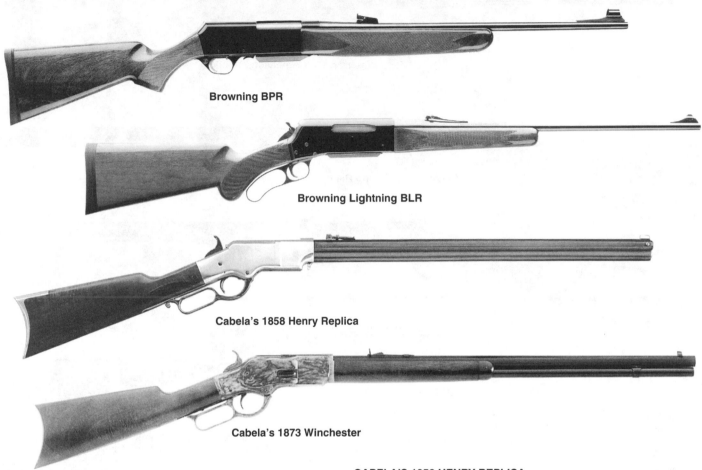

Browning BPR

Browning Lightning BLR

Cabela's 1858 Henry Replica

Cabela's 1873 Winchester

BROWNING BPR PUMP RIFLE
Caliber: 243, 308 (short action); 270, 30-06, 7mm Rem. Mag., 300 Win. Mag., 4-shot magazine (3 for magnums). **Barrel:** 22"; 24" for magnum calibers. **Weight:** 7 lbs., 3 oz. **Length:** 43" overall (22" barrel). **Stock:** Select walnut with full pistol grip, high gloss finish. **Sights:** Gold bead on hooded ramp front, open click adjustable rear. **Features:** Slide-action mechanism cams forend down away from the barrel. Seven-lug rotary bolt; cross-bolt safety behind trigger; removable magazine; alloy receiver. Introduced 1997. Imported from Belgium by Browning.
Price: Standard calibers **$718.00**
Price: Magnum calibers **$772.00**

BROWNING LIGHTNING BLR LEVER-ACTION RIFLE
Caliber: 22-250, 243, 7mm-08, 308 Win., 270 WSM, 7mm WSM, 300 WSM, 358, 450 Marlin, 270 Win., 30-06 Sprg., 7mm Rem. Mag., 300 Win. Mag. 4-shot detachable magazine. **Barrel:** 20" round tapered. **Weight:** 6 lbs., 8 oz. **Length:** 39-1/2" overall. **Stock:** Walnut. Checkered grip and forend, high-gloss finish. **Sights:** Gold bead on ramp front; low profile square notch adjustable rear. **Features:** Wide, grooved trigger; half-cock hammer safety; fold-down hammer. Receiver tapped for scope mount. Recoil pad installed. Introduced 1996. Imported from Japan by Browning.
Price: **$649.00**

Browning Lightning BLR Long Action
Similar to the standard Lightning BLR except has long action to accept 30-06, 270, 7mm Rem. Mag. and 300 Win. Mag. Barrel lengths are 22" for 30-06 and 270, 24" for 7mm Rem. Mag. and 300 Win. Mag. Has six-lug rotary bolt; bolt and receiver are full-length fluted. Fold-down hammer at half-cock. Weighs about 7 lbs., overall length 42-7/8" (22" barrel). Introduced 1996.
Price: **$686.00**

CABELA'S 1858 HENRY REPLICA
Caliber: 44-40, 45 Colt. **Barrel:** 24-1/4". **Weight:** 9.3 lbs. **Length:** 43.75" overall. **Stock:** American walnut. **Sights:** Bead front, open adjustable rear. **Features:** Brass receiver and buttplate. Uses original Henry loading system. Faithful to the original rifle. Introduced 1994. Imported by Cabela's.
Price: **$999.99**

CABELA'S 1866 WINCHESTER REPLICA
Caliber: 44-40, 45 Colt. **Barrel:** 24-1/4". **Weight:** 9 lbs. **Length:** 43" overall. **Stock:** European walnut. **Sights:** Bead front, open adjustable rear. **Features:** Solid brass receiver, buttplate, forend cap. Octagonal barrel. Faithful to the original Winchester '66 rifle. Introduced 1994. Imported by Cabela's.
Price: **$799.99**

CABELA'S 1873 WINCHESTER REPLICA
Caliber: 44-40, 45 Colt. **Barrel:** 24-1/4", 30". **Weight:** 8.5 lbs. **Length:** 43-1/4", 50" overall. **Stock:** European walnut. **Sights:** Bead front, open adjustable rear; globe front, tang rear. **Features:** Color case-hardened steel receiver. Faithful to the original Model 1873 rifle. Introduced 1994. Imported by Cabela's.
Price: Sporting model, 30" barrel, 44-40, 45 Colt. **$999.99**
Price: Sporting model, 24" or 25" barrel **$899.99**

CIMARRON 1860 HENRY REPLICA
Caliber: 44 WCF, 13-shot magazine. **Barrel:** 24-1/4" (rifle), 22" (carbine). **Weight:** 9-1/2 lbs. **Length:** 43" overall (rifle). **Stock:** European walnut. **Sights:** Bead front, open adjustable rear. **Features:** Brass receiver and buttplate. Uses original Henry loading system. Faithful to the original rifle. Introduced 1991. Imported by Cimarron F.A. Co.
Price: **$1,029.00**

Cimarron 1866 Winchester Replica

Cimarron 1873 Long Range

Dixie 1873

IAR 1873
Revolver Carbine

CIMARRON 1866 WINCHESTER REPLICAS
Caliber: 22 LR, 22 WMR, 38 Spec., 44 WCF. **Barrel:** 24-1/4" (rifle), 19" (carbine). **Weight:** 9 lbs. **Length:** 43" overall (rifle). **Stock:** European walnut. **Sights:** Bead front, open adjustable rear. **Features:** Solid brass receiver, buttplate, forend cap. Octagonal barrel. Faithful to the original Winchester '66 rifle. Introduced 1991. Imported by Cimarron F.A. Co.
Price: Rifle $839.00
Price: Carbine. $829.00

CIMARRON 1873 SHORT RIFLE
Caliber: 357 Mag., 38 Spec., 32 WCF, 38 WCF, 44 Spec., 44 WCF, 45 Colt. **Barrel:** 20" tapered octagon. **Weight:** 7.5 lbs. **Length:** 39" overall. **Stock:** Walnut. **Sights:** Bead front, adjustable semi-buckhorn rear. **Features:** Has half "button" magazine. Original-type markings, including caliber, on barrel and elevator and "Kings" patent. From Cimarron F.A. Co.
Price: . . . . $949.00 to $999.00

CIMARRON 1873 LONG RANGE RIFLE
Caliber: 44 WCF, 45 Colt. **Barrel:** 30", octagonal. **Weight:** 8-1/2 lbs. **Length:** 48" overall. **Stock:** Walnut. **Sights:** Blade front, semi-buckhorn ramp rear. Tang sight optional. **Features:** Color case-hardened frame; choice of modern blue-black or charcoal blue for other parts. Barrel marked "Kings Improvement." From Cimarron F.A. Co.
Price: . . . . $999.00 to $1,199.00

Cimarron 1873 Sporting Rifle
Similar to the 1873 Short Rifle except has 24" barrel with half-magazine.
Price: . . . . $949.00 to $999.00

DIXIE ENGRAVED 1873 RIFLE
Caliber: 44-40, 11-shot magazine. **Barrel:** 20", round. **Weight:** 7-3/4 lbs. **Length:** 39" overall. **Stock:** Walnut. **Sights:** Blade front, adjustable rear. **Features:** Engraved and case-hardened frame. Duplicate of Winchester 1873. Made in Italy. From 21 Gun Works.
Price: $1,350.00
Price: Plain, blued carbine $850.00

E.M.F. 1860 HENRY RIFLE
Caliber: 44-40 or 45 Colt. **Barrel:** 24.25". **Weight:** About 9 lbs. **Length:** About 43.75" overall. **Stock:** Oil-stained American walnut. **Sights:** Blade

IAR 1873
Revolver Carbine

front, rear adjustable for elevation. **Features:** Reproduction of the original Henry rifle with brass frame and buttplate, rest blued. From E.M.F.
Price: Brass frame $850.00
Price: Steel frame. $950.00

E.M.F. 1866 YELLOWBOY LEVER ACTIONS
Caliber: 38 Spec., 44-40. **Barrel:** 19" (carbine), 24" (rifle). **Weight:** 9 lbs. **Length:** 43" overall (rifle). **Stock:** European walnut. **Sights:** Bead front, open adjustable rear. **Features:** Solid brass frame, blued barrel, lever, hammer, buttplate. Imported from Italy by E.M.F.
Price: Rifle $690.00
Price: Carbine. $675.00

E.M.F. HARTFORD MODEL 1892 LEVER-ACTION RIFLE
Caliber: 45 Colt. **Barrel:** 24", octagonal. **Weight:** 7-1/2 lbs. **Length:** 43" overall. **Stock:** European walnut. **Sights:** Blade front, open adjustable rear. **Features:** Color case-hardened frame, lever, trigger and hammer with blued barrel, or overall blue finish. Introduced 1998. Imported by E.M.F.
Price: Standard. $590.00

E.M.F. MODEL 1873 LEVER-ACTION RIFLE
Caliber: 32/20, 357 Mag., 38/40, 44-40, 44 Spec., 45 Colt. **Barrel:** 24". **Weight:** 8 lbs. **Length:** 43-1/4" overall. **Stock:** European walnut. **Sights:** Bead front, rear adjustable for windage and elevation. **Features:** Color case-hardened frame (blue on carbine). Imported by E.M.F.
Price: Rifle $865.00
Price: Carbine, 19" barrel $865.00

IAR MODEL 1873 REVOLVER CARBINE
Caliber: 357 Mag., 45 Colt. **Barrel:** 18". **Weight:** 4 lbs., 8 oz. **Length:** 34" overall. **Stock:** One-piece walnut. **Sights:** Blade front, notch rear. **Features:** Color case-hardened frame, blue barrel, backstrap and triggerguard. Introduced 1998. Imported from Italy by IAR, Inc.
Price: Standard. $490.00

RIFLES

Marlin 336C

Marlin 336 Cowboy

Marlin 336Y Spikehorn

Marlin 444P Outfitter

MARLIN MODEL 336C LEVER-ACTION CARBINE

Caliber: 30-30 or 35 Rem., 6-shot tubular magazine. **Barrel:** 20" Micro-Groove®. **Weight:** 7 lbs. **Length:** 38-1/2" overall. **Stock:** Checkered American black walnut, capped pistol grip. Mar-Shield® finish; rubber butt pad; swivel studs. **Sights:** Ramp front with Wide-Scan hood, semi-buck-horn folding rear adjustable for windage and elevation. **Features:** Hammer-block safety. Receiver tapped for scope mount, offset hammer spur; top of receiver sandblasted to prevent glare. Includes safety lock.
Price: **$529.00**

Marlin Model 336 Cowboy

Similar to the Model 336C except chambered for 38-55 Win., 24" tapered octagon barrel with deep-cut Ballard-type rifling; straight-grip walnut stock with hard rubber buttplate; blued steel forend cap; weighs 7-1/2 lbs.; 42-1/2" overall. Introduced 1999. Includes safety lock. Made in U.S.A. by Marlin.
Price: **$735.00**

Marlin Model 336A Lever-Action Carbine

Same as the Marlin 336C except has cut-checkered, walnut-finished hardwood pistol grip stock with swivel studs, 30-30 only, 6-shot. Hammer-block safety. Adjustable rear sight, brass bead front. Includes safety lock.
Price: **$451.00**
Price: With 4x scope and mount. **$501.00**

Marlin Model 336CC Lever-Action Carbine

Same as the Marlin 336A except has Mossy Oak® Break-Up camouflage stock and forearm. 30-30 only, 6-shot; receiver tapped for scope mount or receiver sight. Introduced 2001. Includes safety lock. Made in U.S.A. by Marlin.
Price: **$503.00**

Marlin Model 336SS Lever-Action Carbine

Same as the 336C except receiver, barrel and other major parts are machined from stainless steel. 30-30 only, 6-shot; receiver tapped for scope. Includes safety lock.
Price: **$640.00**

Marlin Model 336W Lever-Action Rifle

Similar to the Model 336CS except has walnut-finished, cut-checkered Maine birch stock; blued steel barrel band has integral sling swivel; no front sight hood; comes with padded nylon sling; hard rubber butt plate. Introduced 1998. Includes safety lock. Made in U.S.A. by Marlin.
Price: **$457.00**
Price: With 4x scope and mount. **$506.00**

Marlin Model 336 Y "Spikehorn"

Similar to the Models in the 336 series except in a compact format with 16-1/2" barrel measuring only 34" in overall length. Weight is 6-1/2 lbs., length of pull 12-1/2". Blued steel barrel and receiver. Chambered for 30/30 cartridge. Introduced 2003.
Price: **$536.00**

MARLIN MODEL 444 LEVER-ACTION SPORTER

Caliber: 444 Marlin, 5-shot tubular magazine. **Barrel:** 22" deep cut Ballard rifling. **Weight:** 7-1/2 lbs. **Length:** 40-1/2" overall. **Stock:** Checkered American black walnut, capped pistol grip, rubber rifle butt pad. Mar-Shield® finish; swivel studs. **Sights:** Hooded ramp front, folding semi-buckhorn rear adjustable for windage and elevation. **Features:** Hammer-block safety. Receiver tapped for scope mount; offset hammer spur. Includes safety lock.
Price: **$618.00**

Marlin Model 444P Outfitter Lever-Action

Similar to the 444SS with deep-cut Ballard-type rifling; weighs 6-3/4 lbs.; overall length 37". Available only in 444 Marlin. Introduced 1999. Includes safety lock. Made in U.S.A. by Marlin.
Price: **$631.00**

MARLIN MODEL 1894 LEVER-ACTION CARBINE

Caliber: 44 Spec./44 Mag., 10-shot tubular magazine. **Barrel:** 20" Ballard-type rifling. **Weight:** 6 lbs. **Length:** 37-1/2" overall. **Stock:** Checkered American black walnut, straight grip and forend. Mar-Shield® finish. Rubber rifle butt pad; swivel studs. **Sights:** Wide-Scan hooded ramp front, semi-buckhorn folding rear adjustable for windage and elevation. **Features:** Hammer-block safety. Receiver tapped for scope mount, offset hammer spur, solid top receiver sand blasted to prevent glare. Includes safety lock.
Price: **$544.00**

NEW!

Marlin 1894PG

Marlin 1894 Cowboy

Marlin 1894SS

Marlin 1895

Marlin 1895GS

Marlin Model 1894PG/1894FG

Pistol-gripped versions of the Model 1894. Model 1894PG is chambered for .44 Magnum; Model 1894FG is chambered for .41 Magnum.
Price: (Model 1894PG) $610.00
Price: (Model 1894FG) $610.00

Marlin Model 1894C Carbine

Similar to the standard Model 1894S except chambered for 38 Spec./357 Mag. with full-length 9-shot magazine, 18-1/2" barrel, hammer-block safety, hooded front sight. Introduced 1983. Includes safety lock.
Price: $556.00

MARLIN MODEL 1894 COWBOY

Caliber: 357 Mag., 44 Mag., 45 Colt, 10-shot magazine. Barrel: 20" except .45 Colt which has a 24" tapered octagon, deep cut rifling. Weight: 7-1/2 lbs. Length: 41-1/2" overall. Stock: Straight grip American black walnut, hard rubber buttplate, Mar-Shield® finish. Sights: Marble carbine front, adjustable Marble semi-buckhorn rear. Features: Squared finger lever; straight grip stock; blued steel forend tip. Designed for Cowboy Shooting events. Introduced 1996. Includes safety lock. Made in U.S.A. by Marlin.
Price: $820.00

Marlin Model 1894 Cowboy Competition Rifle

Similar to Model 1894 except 20" barrel, 37-1/2" long, weighs only 6 lbs., antique finish on receiver, lever and bolt. Factory-tuned for competitive cowboy action shooting.Available in .38 Spl. And .45 Colt.
Price: $986.00

Marlin Model 1894SS

Similar to Model 1894 except has stainless steel barrel, receiver, lever, guard plate, magazine tube and loading plate. Nickel-plated swivel studs.
Price: $680.00

MARLIN MODEL 1895 LEVER-ACTION RIFLE

Caliber: 45-70, 4-shot tubular magazine. Barrel: 22" round. Weight: 7-1/2 lbs. Length: 40-1/2" overall. Stock: Checkered American black walnut, full pistol grip. Mar-Shield® finish; rubber butt pad; quick detachable swivel studs. Sights: Bead front with Wide-Scan hood, semi-buckhorn folding rear adjustable for windage and elevation. Features: Hammer-block safety. Solid receiver tapped for scope mounts or receiver sights; offset hammer spur. Includes safety lock.
Price: $631.00

Marlin Model 1895G Guide Gun Lever-Action Rifle

Similar to Model 1895 with deep-cut Ballard-type rifling; straight-grip walnut stock. Overall length is 37", weighs 7 lbs. Introduced 1998. Includes safety lock. Made in U.S.A. by Marlin.
Price: $646.00

Marlin Model 1895GS Guide Gun

Similar to Model 1895G except receiver, barrel and most metal parts are machined from stainless steel. Chambered for 45-70, 4-shot, 18-1/2" barrel. Overall length is 37", weighs 7 lbs. Introduced 2001. Includes safety lock. Made in U.S.A. by Marlin.
Price: $760.00

Marlin Model 1895 Cowboy Lever-Action Rifle

Similar to Model 1895 except has 26" tapered octagon barrel with Ballard-type rifling, Marble carbine front sight and Marble adjustable semi-buckhorn rear sight. Receiver tapped for scope or receiver sight. Overall length is 44-1/2", weighs about 8 lbs. Introduced 2001. Includes safety lock. Made in U.S.A. by Marlin.
Price: $802.00

Marlin Model 1895M Lever-Action Rifle

Similar to Model 1895 except has an 18-1/2" barrel with Ballard-type cut rifling. New Model 1895MR variant has 22" barrel, pistol grip. Chambered for 450 Marlin. Includes safety lock.
Price: (Model 1895M)................................... $695.00
Price: (Model 1895MR) $761.00

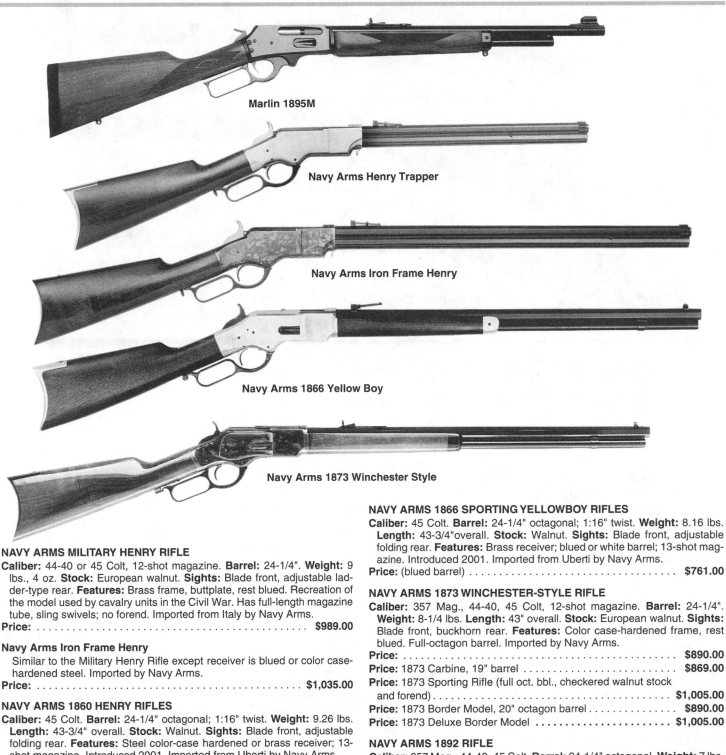

Marlin 1895M

Navy Arms Henry Trapper

Navy Arms Iron Frame Henry

Navy Arms 1866 Yellow Boy

Navy Arms 1873 Winchester Style

NAVY ARMS MILITARY HENRY RIFLE

Caliber: 44-40 or 45 Colt, 12-shot magazine. **Barrel:** 24-1/4". **Weight:** 9 lbs., 4 oz. **Stock:** European walnut. **Sights:** Blade front, adjustable ladder-type rear. **Features:** Brass frame, buttplate, rest blued. Recreation of the model used by cavalry units in the Civil War. Has full-length magazine tube, sling swivels; no forend. Imported from Italy by Navy Arms.
Price: **$989.00**

Navy Arms Iron Frame Henry

Similar to the Military Henry Rifle except receiver is blued or color case-hardened steel. Imported by Navy Arms.
Price: **$1,035.00**

NAVY ARMS 1860 HENRY RIFLES

Caliber: 45 Colt. **Barrel:** 24-1/4" octagonal; 1:16" twist. **Weight:** 9.26 lbs. **Length:** 43-3/4" overall. **Stock:** Walnut. **Sights:** Blade front, adjustable folding rear. **Features:** Steel color-case hardened or brass receiver; 13-shot magazine. Introduced 2001. Imported from Uberti by Navy Arms.
Price: (steel color-case hardened receiver) **$984.00**
Price: (brass receiver) **$1,035.00**

NAVY ARMS 1866 YELLOW BOY RIFLE

Caliber: 38 Spec., 44-40, 45 Colt, 12-shot magazine. **Barrel:** 20" or 24", full octagon. **Weight:** 8-1/2 lbs. **Length:** 42-1/2" overall. **Stock:** Walnut. **Sights:** Blade front, adjustable ladder-type rear. **Features:** Brass frame, forend tip, buttplate, blued barrel, lever, hammer. Introduced 1991. Imported from Italy by Navy Arms.
Price: **$761.00**
Price: Carbine, 19" barrel **$746.00**

NAVY ARMS 1866 SPORTING YELLOWBOY RIFLES

Caliber: 45 Colt. **Barrel:** 24-1/4" octagonal; 1:16" twist. **Weight:** 8.16 lbs. **Length:** 43-3/4" overall. **Stock:** Walnut. **Sights:** Blade front, adjustable folding rear. **Features:** Brass receiver; blued or white barrel; 13-shot magazine. Introduced 2001. Imported from Uberti by Navy Arms.
Price: (blued barrel) **$761.00**

NAVY ARMS 1873 WINCHESTER-STYLE RIFLE

Caliber: 357 Mag., 44-40, 45 Colt, 12-shot magazine. **Barrel:** 24-1/4". **Weight:** 8-1/4 lbs. **Length:** 43" overall. **Stock:** European walnut. **Sights:** Blade front, buckhorn rear. **Features:** Color case-hardened frame, rest blued. Full-octagon barrel. Imported by Navy Arms.
Price: **$890.00**
Price: 1873 Carbine, 19" barrel **$869.00**
Price: 1873 Sporting Rifle (full oct. bbl., checkered walnut stock and forend) **$1,005.00**
Price: 1873 Border Model, 20" octagon barrel **$890.00**
Price: 1873 Deluxe Border Model **$1,005.00**

NAVY ARMS 1892 RIFLE

Caliber: 357 Mag., 44-40, 45 Colt. **Barrel:** 24-1/4" octagonal. **Weight:** 7 lbs. **Length:** 42" overall. **Stock:** American walnut. **Sights:** Blade front, semi-buckhorn rear. **Features:** Replica of Winchester's early Model 1892 with octagonal barrel, forend cap and crescent buttplate. Blued or color case-hardened receiver. Introduced 1998. Imported by Navy Arms.
Price: **$545.00**

Navy Arms 1892 Stainless Carbine

Similar to the 1892 Rifle except stainless steel, has 20" round barrel, weighs 5-3/4 lbs., and is 37-1/2" overall. Introduced 1998. Imported by Navy Arms.
Price: **$585.00**

Navy Arms 1892 Rifle

Navy Arms 1892 Short Rifle

Puma Model 92

Remington 7600 Rifle

Ruger Model 96/44

Navy Arms 1892 Short Rifle

Similar to the 1892 Rifle except has 20" octagonal barrel, weighs 6-1/4 lbs., and is 37-3/4" overall. Replica of the rare, special order 1892 Winchester nicknamed the "Texas Special." Blued or color case-hardened receiver and furniture. Introduced 1998. Imported by Navy Arms.

Price: **$545.00**
Price: (stainless steel, 20" octagon barrel) **$585.00**

NAVY ARMS 1892 STAINLESS RIFLE

Caliber: 357 Mag., 44-40, 45 Colt. **Barrel:** 24-1/4" octagonal. **Weight:** 7 lbs. **Length:** 42". **Stock:** American walnut. **Sights:** Brass bead front, semi-buckhorn rear. **Features:** Designed for the Cowboy Action Shooter. Stainless steel barrel, receiver and furniture. Introduced 2000. Imported by Navy Arms.

Price: **$585.00**

PUMA MODEL 92 RIFLES & CARBINES

Caliber: 38 Spec./357 Mag., 44 Mag., 45 Colt, 454 Casull (20" carbine only), 480 Ruger. **Barrel:** 20" round, 24"octagonal. **Weight:** 6.1-7.7 lbs. **Stock:** Walnut-stained hardwood. **Sights:** Open, buckhorn front & rear available. **Features:** Blue, case-hardened, stainless steel and brass receivers, matching buttplates. Blued, stainless steel barrels, full-length magazines. Thumb safety on top of both. 454 Casull carbine loads through magazine tube, has rubber recoil pad. 45 Colt brass-framed, saddle-ring rifle and 454 Casull carbine introduced 2002. The 480 Ruger version was introduced in 2003. Imported from Brazil by Legacy Sports International.

Price: Octagonal barrel. . . . . **$500.00 to $561.00**
Price: Round barrel. . . . . **$407.00 to $549.00**

REMINGTON MODEL 7600 PUMP ACTION

Caliber: 243, 270, 30-06, 308. **Barrel:** 22" round tapered. **Weight:** 7--1/2 lbs. **Length:** 42-5/8" overall. **Stock:** Cut-checkered walnut pistol grip and forend, Monte Carlo with full cheekpiece. Satin or high-gloss finish. **Sights:** Gold bead front sight on matted ramp, open step adjustable sporting rear. **Features:** Redesigned and improved version of the Model 760. Detachable 4-shot clip. Cross-bolt safety. Receiver tapped for scope mount. Introduced 1981.

Price: **$588.00**
Price: Carbine (18-1/2" bbl., 30-06 only) **$588.00**
Price: With black synthetic stock, matte black metal, rifle or
carbine **$484.00**

RUGER MODEL 96/44 LEVER-ACTION RIFLE

Caliber: 44 Mag., 4-shot rotary magazine. **Barrel:** 18-1/2". **Weight:** 5-7/8 lbs. **Length:** 37-5/16" overall. **Stock:** American hardwood. **Sights:** Gold bead front, folding leaf rear. **Features:** Solid chrome-moly steel receiver. Manual cross-bolt safety, visible cocking indicator; short-throw lever action; integral scope mount; blued finish; color case-hardened lever. Introduced 1996. Made In U.S. by Sturm, Ruger & Co.

Price: 96/44M, 44 Mag **$525.00**

TRISTAR/UBERTI 1873 SPORTING RIFLE

Caliber: 44-40, 45 Colt. **Barrel:** 24-1/4", 30", octagonal. **Weight:** 8.1 lbs. **Length:** 43-1/4" overall. **Stock:** Walnut. **Sights:** Blade front adjustable for windage, open rear adjustable for elevation. **Features:** Color case-hardened frame, blued barrel, hammer, lever, buttplate, brass elevator. Imported from Italy by Tristar Sporting Arms Ltd.

Price: 24-1/4" barrel **$925.00**
Price: 30" barrel **$969.00**

RIFLES

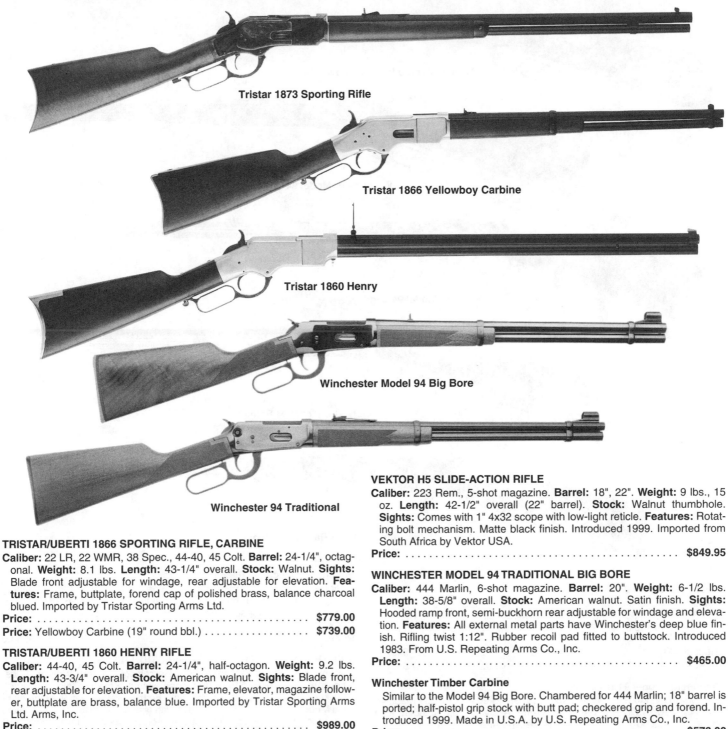

Tristar 1873 Sporting Rifle

Tristar 1866 Yellowboy Carbine

Tristar 1860 Henry

Winchester Model 94 Big Bore

Winchester 94 Traditional

TRISTAR/UBERTI 1866 SPORTING RIFLE, CARBINE
Caliber: 22 LR, 22 WMR, 38 Spec., 44-40, 45 Colt. **Barrel:** 24-1/4", octagonal. **Weight:** 8.1 lbs. **Length:** 43-1/4" overall. **Stock:** Walnut. **Sights:** Blade front adjustable for windage, rear adjustable for elevation. **Features:** Frame, buttplate, forend cap of polished brass, balance charcoal blued. Imported by Tristar Sporting Arms Ltd.
Price: **$779.00**
Price: Yellowboy Carbine (19" round bbl.) **$739.00**

TRISTAR/UBERTI 1860 HENRY RIFLE
Caliber: 44-40, 45 Colt. **Barrel:** 24-1/4", half-octagon. **Weight:** 9.2 lbs. **Length:** 43-3/4" overall. **Stock:** American walnut. **Sights:** Blade front, rear adjustable for elevation. **Features:** Frame, elevator, magazine follower, buttplate are brass, balance blue. Imported by Tristar Sporting Arms Ltd. Arms, Inc.
Price: **$989.00**

Tristar/Uberti 1860 Henry Trapper Carbine
Similar to the 1860 Henry Rifle except has 18-1/2" barrel, measures 37-3/4" overall, and weighs 8 lbs. Introduced 1999. Imported from Italy by Tristar Sporting Arms Ltd.
Price: Brass frame, blued barrel **$989.00**

U.S. FIRE-ARMS LIGHTNING MAGAZINE RIFLE
NEW! **Caliber:** .45 Colt, .44 WCF, .44 Spl., .38 WCF, .32 WCF, 15-shot. **Barrel:** 26" (rifle); 20" carbine, round or octagonal. **Stock:** Oiled walnut. **Finish:** Dome blue. Introduced 2002. Made in U.S.A. by United States Fire Arms Manufacturing Co.
Price: **$995.00**

VEKTOR H5 SLIDE-ACTION RIFLE
Caliber: 223 Rem., 5-shot magazine. **Barrel:** 18", 22". **Weight:** 9 lbs., 15 oz. **Length:** 42-1/2" overall (22" barrel). **Stock:** Walnut thumbhole. **Sights:** Comes with 1" 4x32 scope with low-light reticle. **Features:** Rotating bolt mechanism. Matte black finish. Introduced 1999. Imported from South Africa by Vektor USA.
Price: **$849.95**

WINCHESTER MODEL 94 TRADITIONAL BIG BORE
Caliber: 444 Marlin, 6-shot magazine. **Barrel:** 20". **Weight:** 6-1/2 lbs. **Length:** 38-5/8" overall. **Stock:** American walnut. Satin finish. **Sights:** Hooded ramp front, semi-buckhorn rear adjustable for windage and elevation. **Features:** All external metal parts have Winchester's deep blue finish. Rifling twist 1:12". Rubber recoil pad fitted to buttstock. Introduced 1983. From U.S. Repeating Arms Co., Inc.
Price: **$465.00**

Winchester Timber Carbine
Similar to the Model 94 Big Bore. Chambered for 444 Marlin; 18" barrel is ported; half-pistol grip stock with butt pad; checkered grip and forend. Introduced 1999. Made in U.S.A. by U.S. Repeating Arms Co., Inc.
Price: **$573.00**

WINCHESTER MODEL 94 TRADITIONAL-CW
Caliber: 30-30 Win., 6-shot; 44 Mag., 11-shot tubular magazine. **Barrel:** 20". **Weight:** 6-1/2 lbs. **Length:** 37-3/4" overall. **Stock:** Straight grip checkered walnut stock and forend. **Sights:** Hooded blade front, semi-buckhorn rear. Drilled and tapped for scope mount. Post front sight on Trapper model. **Features:** Solid frame, forged steel receiver; side ejection, exposed rebounding hammer with automatic trigger-activated transfer bar. Introduced 1984.
Price: 30-30 . . . . **$440.00**
Price: 44 Mag. **$463.00**
Price: Traditional (no checkering, 30-30 only) **$407.00**

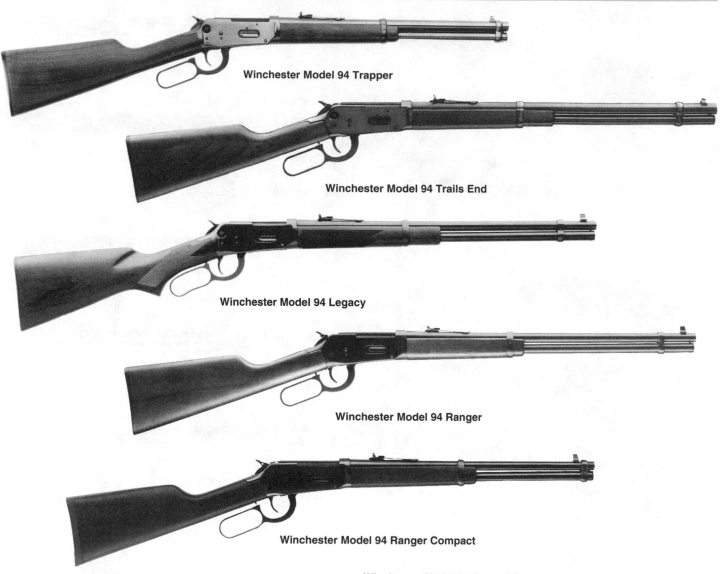

Winchester Model 94 Trapper

Winchester Model 94 Trails End

Winchester Model 94 Legacy

Winchester Model 94 Ranger

Winchester Model 94 Ranger Compact

Winchester Model 94 Trapper
Similar to Model 94 Traditional except has 16" barrel, 5-shot magazine in 30-30, 9-shot in 357 Mag., 44 Magnum/44 Special, 45 Colt. Has stainless steel claw extractor, saddle ring, hammer spur extension, smooth walnut wood.
Price: 30-30 . . . . **$407.00**
Price: 44 Mag., 357 Mag., 45 Colt **$431.00**

Winchester Model 94 Trails End
Similar to the Model 94 Walnut except chambered only for 357 Mag., 44-40, 44 Mag., 45 Colt; 11-shot magazine. Available with standard lever loop. Introduced 1997. From U.S. Repeating Arms Co., Inc.
Price: With standard lever loop. **$445.00**

Winchester Model 94 Legacy
Similar to the Model 94 Traditional-CW except has half-pistol grip walnut stock, checkered grip and forend. Chambered for 30-30, 357 Mag., 44 Mag., 45 Colt; 24" barrel. Introduced 1995. Made in U.S.A. by U.S. Repeating Arms Co., Inc.
Price: With 24" barrel **$457.00**

Winchester Model 94 Ranger
Similar to the Model 94 Traditional except has a hardwood stock, post-style front sight and hammer-spur extension.
Price: (20" barrel) **$355.00**

Winchester Model 94 Ranger Compact
Similar to the Model 94 Ranger except has 16" barrel and 12-1/2" length of pull, rubber recoil pad, post front sight. Introduced 1998. Made in U.S.A. by U.S. Repeating Arms Co., Inc.
Price: 357 Mag. **$378.00**
Price: 30-30 . . . . **$355.00**

WINCHESTER MODEL 1895 LEVER-ACTION RIFLE
Caliber: 405 Win, 4-shot magazine. **Barrel:** 24", round. **Weight:** 8 lbs. **Length:** 42" overall. **Stock:** American walnut. **Sights:** Gold bead front, buckhorn rear adjustable for elevation. **Features:** Recreation of the original Model 1895. Polished blue finish with Nimschke-style scroll engraving on receiver. Scalloped receiver, two-piece cocking lever, Schnabel forend, straight-grip stock. Introduced 1995. From U.S. Repeating Arms Co., Inc.
Price: Grade I **$1,045.00**
Price: High Grade **$1,532.00**

WINCHESTER MODEL 1886 EXTRA LIGHT LEVER-ACTION RIFLE
Caliber: 45-70, 4-shot magazine. **Barrel:** 22", round tapered. **Weight:** 7-1/4 lbs. **Length:** 40-1/2" overall. **Stock:** Smooth walnut. **Sights:** Bead front, ramp-adjustable buckhorn-style rear. **Features:** Recreation of the Model 1886. Polished blue finish; crescent metal butt plate; metal forend cap; pistol grip stock. Reintroduced 1998. From U.S. Repeating Arms Co., Inc.
Price: Grade I **$1,152.00**
Price: High Grade **$1,440.00**

RIFLES

CENTERFIRE RIFLES — BOLT ACTION

Includes models for a wide variety of sporting and competitive purposes and uses.

Anschutz 1733D

Barrett Model 95

Blaser R93 Classic

ANSCHUTZ 1743D BOLT-ACTION RIFLE
Caliber: 222 Rem., 3-shot magazine. **Barrel:** 19.7". **Weight:** 6.4 lbs. **Length:** 39" overall. **Stock:** European walnut. **Sights:** Hooded blade front, folding leaf rear. **Features:** Receiver grooved for scope mounting; single stage trigger; claw extractor; sling safety; sling swivels. Imported from Germany by AcuSport Corp.
Price: **$1,588.95**

ANSCHUTZ 1740 MONTE CARLO RIFLE
Caliber: 22 Hornet, 5-shot clip; 222 Rem., 3-shot clip. **Barrel:** 24". **Weight:** 6-1/2 lbs. **Length:** 43.25" overall. **Stock:** Select European walnut. **Sights:** Hooded ramp front, folding leaf rear; drilled and tapped for scope mounting. **Features:** Uses match 54 action. Adjustable single stage trigger. Stock has roll-over Monte Carlo cheekpiece, slim forend with Schnabel tip, Wundhammer palm swell on grip, rosewood gripcap with white diamond insert. Skip-line checkering on grip and forend. Introduced 1997. Imported from Germany by AcuSport Corp.
Price: From **$1,439.00**
Price: Model 1730 Monte Carlo, as above except in
22 Hornet **$1,439.00**

Anschutz 1733D Rifle
Similar to the 1740 Monte Carlo except has full-length, walnut, Mannlicher-style stock with skip-line checkering, rosewood Schnabel tip, and is chambered for 22 Hornet. Weighs 6.4 lbs., overall length 39", barrel length 19.7". Imported from Germany by AcuSport Corp.
Price: **$1,588.95**

BARRETT MODEL 95 BOLT-ACTION RIFLE
Caliber: 50 BMG, 5-shot magazine. **Barrel:** 29". **Weight:** 22 lbs. **Length:** 45" overall. **Stock:** Energy-absorbing recoil pad. **Sights:** Scope optional. **Features:** Bolt-action, bullpup design. Disassembles without tools; extendable bipod legs; match-grade barrel; high efficiency muzzle brake. Introduced 1995. Made in U.S.A. by Barrett Firearms Mfg., Inc.
Price: From. **$4,950.00**

BLASER R93 BOLT-ACTION RIFLE
Caliber: 22-250, 243, 6.5x55, 270, 7x57, 7mm-08, 308, 30-06, 257 Wea. Mag., 7mm Rem. Mag., 300 Win. Mag., 300 Wea. Mag., 338 Win Mag., 375 H&H, 416 Rem. Mag. **Barrel:** 22" (standard calibers), 26" (magnum). **Weight:** 7 lbs. **Length:** 40" overall (22" barrel). **Stock:** Two-piece European walnut. **Sights:** None furnished; drilled and tapped for scope mounting. **Features:** Straight pull-back bolt action with thumb-activated safety slide/cocking mechanism; interchangeable barrels and bolt heads. Introduced 1994. Imported from Germany by SIGARMS.
Price: R93 Classic **$3,680.00**
Price: R93 LX. **$1,895.00**
Price: R93 Synthetic (black synthetic stock) **$1,595.00**
Price: R93 Safari Synthetic (416 Rem. Mag. only). **$1,855.00**
Price: R93 Grand Lux. **$4,915.00**
Price: R93 Attaché **$5,390.00**

BRNO 98 BOLT-ACTION RIFLE
Caliber: 7x64, 243, 270, 308, 30-06, 300 Win. Mag., 9.3x62. **Barrrel:** 23.6". **Weight:** 7.2 lbs. **Length:** 40.9" overall. **Stock:** European walnut. **Sights:** Blade on ramp front, open adjustable rear. **Features:** Uses Mauser 98-type action; polished blue. Announced 1998. Imported from the Czech Republic by Euro-Imports.
Price: Standard calibers **$507.00**
Price: Magnum calibers **$547.00**
Price: With set trigger, standard calibers **$615.00**
Price: As above, magnum calibers **$655.00**
Price: With full stock, set trigger, standard calibers **$703.00**
Price: As above, magnum calibers. **$743.00**
Price: 300 Win. Mag., with BOSS. **$933.00**

BROWNING A-BOLT RIFLES
Caliber: 223, 22-250, 243, 7mm-08, 308, 25-06, 260, 270, 30-06, 260 Rem., 7mm Rem. Mag., 300 Win. Short Mag., 300 Win. Mag., 338 Win. Mag., 375 H&H Mag, 223 WSSM, 243 WSSM, 270 WSM, 7mm WSM, 300 WSM. **Barrel:** 22" medium sporter weight with recessed muzzle; 26" on mag. cals. **Weight:** 6-1/2 to 7-1/2 lbs. **Length:** 44-3/4" overall (magnum and standard); 41-3/4" (short action). **Stock:** Classic style American walnut; recoil pad standard on magnum calibers. **Features:** Short-throw (60°) fluted bolt, three locking lugs, plunger-type ejector; adjustable trigger is grooved and gold-plated. Hinged floorplate, detachable box magazine (4 rounds std. cals., 3 for magnums). Slide tang safety. BOSS barrel vibration modulator and muzzle brake system not available in 375 H&H. Introduced 1985. Imported from Japan by Browning.
Price: Hunter, no sights **$620.00**
Price: Hunter, no sights, magnum calibers. **$646.00**
Price: For BOSS add **$80.00**

Browning A-Bolt Hunter

Browning A-Bolt Medallion

Browning A-Bolt White Gold Medallion

Browning A-Bolt Eclipse M-1000

Browning A-Bolt Medallion

Similar to standard A-Bolt except has glossy stock finish, rosewood grip and forend caps, engraved receiver, high-polish blue, no sights. New calibers include 223 WSSM, 243 WSSM< 270 WSM, 7mm WSM.

Price: Short-action calibers. $730.00
Price: Long-action calibers $756.00
Price: Medallion, 375 H&H Mag., open sights $767.00
New! **Price:** 300 Win. Short Magnum $756.00
New! **Price:** 300 Rem. Ultra Mag., 338 Rem. Ultra Mag. $756.00
Price: For BOSS, add $80.00

Browning A-Bolt Medallion Left-Hand

Same as the Medallion model A-Bolt except has left-hand action and is available in 270, 30-06, 7mm Rem. Mag., 300 Win. Mag. Introduced 1987.

Price: 270, 30-06 (no sights) $758.00
Price: 7mm Mag., 300 Win. Mag. (no sights) $784.00
Price: For BOSS, add $80.00

Browning A-Bolt White Gold Medallion

Similar to the standard A-Bolt except has select walnut stock with brass spacers between rubber recoil pad and between the rosewood gripcap and forend tip; gold-filled barrel inscription; palm-swell pistol grip, Monte Carlo comb, 22 lpi checkering with double borders; engraved receiver flats. In 270, 30-06, 7mm Rem. Mag. and 300 Win. Mag. Introduced 1988.

Price: 270, 30-06 . . . . $1,046.00
Price: 7mm Rem. Mag, 300 Win. Mag.. . . . . $1,072.00
Price: For BOSS, add $76.00

Browning A-Bolt Custom Trophy Rifle

Similar to the A-Bolt Medallion except has select American walnut stock with recessed swivel studs, octagon barrel, skeleton pistol gripcap, gold highlights, shadowline cheekpiece. Calibers 270, 30-06, 7mm Rem. Mag., 300 Win. Mag. Introduced 1998. Imported from Japan by Browning.

Price: $1,360.00

Browning A-Bolt Eclipse Hunter

Similar to the A-Bolt II except has gray/black laminated, thumbhole stock, BOSS barrel vibration modulator and muzzle brake. Available in long and short action with heavy barrel. In 270 Win., 30-06, 7mm Rem. Mag. Introduced 1996. Imported from Japan by Browning.

Price: 270, 30-06, with BOSS. $1,017.00
Price: 7mm Rem. Mag, with BOSS $1,043.00

Browning A-Bolt Eclipse M-1000

Similar to the A-Bolt II Eclipse except has long action and heavy target barrel. Chambered only for 300 Win. Mag. Adjustable trigger, bench-style forend, 3-shot magazine; laminated thumbhold stock; BOSS system standard. Introduced 1997. Imported for Japan by Browning.

Price: $1,048.00

Browning A-Bolt Micro Hunter

Similar to the A-Bolt II Hunter except has 13-5/16" length of pull, 20" barrel, and comes in 260 Rem., 243, 308, 7mm-08, 223, 22-250, 22 Hornet, 270 WSM, 7mm WSM, 300 WSM. Weighs 6 lbs., 1 oz. Introduced 1999. Imported by Browning.

Price: (no sights) $614.00

Browning A-Bolt Classic Hunter

Similar to the A-Bolt unter except has low-luster bluing and walnut stock with Monte Carlo comb, pistol grip palm swell, double-border checkering. Available in 270, 30-06, 7mm Rem. Mag., 300 Win. Mag, 223 WSSM, 243 WSSM. Introduced 1999. Imported by Browning.

Price: 270, 30-06 . . . . $698.00
Price: 7mm Mag., 300 Mag. $724.00

RIFLES

CENTERFIRE RIFLES — BOLT ACTION

Browning A-Bolt Stalker

Charles Daly Superior

CZ 527 Lux

CZ 550 Lux

Browning A-Bolt Stainless Stalker

Similar to the Hunter model A-Bolt except receiver and barrel are made of stainless steel; the rest of the exposed metal surfaces are finished with a durable matte silver-gray. Graphite-fiberglass composite textured stock. No sights are furnished. Available in 260, 243, 308, 7mm-08, 270, 280, 30-06, 7mm Rem. Mag., 300 WSM, 300 Rem. Ultra Mag., 338 Win. Mag., 338 Rem. Ultra Mag., 375 H&H, 223 WSSM, 243 WSSM, 270 WSM, 7mm WSM. Introduced 1987.

Price: Short-action calibers. $813.00
Price: Magnum calibers $839.00
New! **Price:** 300 Win. Short Magnum $839.00
New! **Price:** 300 Rem. Ultra Mag., 338 Rem. Ultra Mag. $839.00
Price: For BOSS, add. $80.00
Price: Left-hand, 270, 30-06. . . . . $838.00
Price: Left-hand, 7mm, 300 Win. Mag., 338 Win. Mag. $864.00
Price: Left-hand, 375 H&H, with sights. $864.00
Price: Left-hand, for BOSS, add. $80.00
Price: Carbon-fiber barrel, 22-250 . . . . $1,750.00
Price: Carbon-fiber barrel, 300 Win. Mag. $1,776.00

Browning A-Bolt Composite Stalker

Similar to the A-Bolt Hunter except has black graphite-fiberglass stock with textured finish. Matte blue finish on all exposed metal surfaces. Available in 223, 22-250, 243, 7mm-08, 308, 30-06, 270, 280, 25-06, 7mm Rem. Mag., 300 WSM, 300 Win. Mag., 338 Win. Mag, 223 WSSM, 243 WSSM, 270 WSM, 7mm WSM. BOSS barrel vibration modulator and muzzle brake system offered in all calibers. Introduced 1994.

Price: Standard calibers, no sights. $639.00
Price: Magnum calibers, no sights $665.00
Price: For BOSS, add. $77.00

CARBON ONE BOLT-ACTION RIFLE

Caliber: 22-250 to 375 H&H. **Barrel:** Up to 28". **Weight:** 5-1/2 to 7-1/4 lbs. **Length:** Varies. **Stock:** Synthetic or wood. **Sights:** None furnished. **Features:** Choice of Remington, Browning or Winchester action with free-floated Christensen graphite/epoxy/steel barrel, trigger pull tuned to 3 to 3-1/2 lbs. Made in U.S.A. by Christensen Arms.

Price: Carbon One Hunter Rifle, 6-1/2 to 7 lbs. $1,499.00
Price: Carbon One Custom, 5-1/2 to 6-1/2 lbs., Shilen trigger . . $2,750.00
Price: Carbon Ranger, 50 BMG, 5-shot repeater $4,750.00
Price: Carbon Ranger, 50 BMG, single shot $3,950.00

CHARLES DALY SUPERIOR BOLT-ACTION RIFLE

Caliber: 22 Hornet, 5-shot magazine. **Barrel:** 22.6". **Weight:** 6.6 lbs. **Length:** 41.25" overall. **Stock:** Walnut-finished hardwood with Monte Carlo comb and cheekpiece. **Sights:** Ramped blade front, fully adjustable open rear. **Features:** Receiver dovetailed for tip-off scope mount. Introduced 1996. Imported by K.B.I., Inc.

Price: $364.95

Charles Daly Empire Grade Rifle

Similar to the Superior except has oil-finished American walnut stock with 18 lpi hand checkering; black hardwood gripcap and forend tip; highly polished barreled action; jewelled bolt; recoil pad; swivel studs. Imported by K.B.I., Inc.

Price: $469.95

CZ 527 LUX BOLT-ACTION RIFLE

Caliber: 22 Hornet, 222 Rem., 223 Rem., detachable 5-shot magazine. **Barrel:** 23-1/2"; standard or heavy barrel. **Weight:** 6 lbs., 1 oz. **Length:** 42-1/2" overall. **Stock:** European walnut with Monte Carlo. **Sights:** Hooded front, open adjustable rear. **Features:** Improved mini-Mauser action with non-rotating claw extractor; single set trigger; grooved receiver. Imported from the Czech Republic by CZ-USA.

Price: $566.00
Price: Model FS, full-length stock, cheekpiece. $658.00

CZ 527 American Classic Bolt-Action Rifle

Similar to the CZ 527 Lux except has classic-style stock with 18 l.p.i. checkering; free-floating barrel; recessed target crown on barrel. No sights furnished. Introduced 1999. Imported from the Czech Republic by CZ-USA.

Price: 22 Hornet, 222 Rem., 223 Rem. . . . . **$586.00 to $609.00**

CZ 550 LUX BOLT-ACTION RIFLE

Caliber: 22-250, 243, 6.5x55, 7x57, 7x64, 308 Win., 9.3x62, 270 Win., 30-06. **Barrel:** 20.47". **Weight:** 7.5 lbs. **Length:** 44.68" overall. **Stock:** Turkish walnut in Bavarian style or FS (Mannlicher). **Sights:** Hooded front, adjustable rear. **Features:** Improved Mauser-style action with claw extractor, fixed ejector, square bridge dovetailed receiver; single set trigger. Imported from the Czech Republic by CZ-USA.

Price: Lux . . . . **$566.00 to $609.00**
Price: FS (full stock) $706.00

RIFLES

CZ 550 American Classic

CZ 550 Magnum

Dakota 76 Classic

Dakota 76 Safari

CZ 550 American Classic Bolt-Action Rifle

Similar to CZ 550 Lux except has American classic-style stock with 18 l.p.i. checkering; free-floating barrel; recessed target crown. Has 25.6" barrel; weighs 7.48 lbs. No sights furnished. Introduced 1999. Imported from the Czech Republic by CZ-USA.

Price: . . . .$586.00 to $609.00

CZ 550 Medium Magnum Bolt-Action Rifle

Similar to the CZ 550 Lux except chambered for the 300 Win. Mag. and 7mm Rem. Mag.; 5-shot magazine. Adjustable iron sights, hammer-forged barrel, single-set trigger, Turkish walnut stock. Weighs 7.5 lbs. Introduced 2001. Imported from the Czech Republic by CZ USA.

Price: $621.00

CZ 550 Magnum Bolt-Action Rifle

Similar to CZ 550 Lux except has long action for 300 Win. Mag., 375 H&H, 416 Rigby, 458 Win. Mag. Overall length is 46.45"; barrel length 25"; weighs 9.24 lbs. Hooded front sight, express rear with one standing, two folding leaves. Imported from the Czech Republic by CZ-USA.

Price: 300 Win. Mag. $717.00
Price: 375 H&H. $756.00
Price: 416 Rigby $809.00
Price: 458 Win. Mag. $744.00

CZ 700 M1 SNIPER RIFLE

Caliber: 308 Winchester, 10-shot magazine. **Barrel:** 25.6". **Weight:** 11.9 lbs. **Length:** 45" overall. **Stock:** Laminated wood thumbhole with adjustable buttplate and cheekpiece. **Sights:** None furnished; permanently attached Weaver rail for scope mounting. **Features:** 60-degree bolt throw; oversized trigger guard and bolt handle for use with gloves; full-length equipment rail on forend; fully adjustable trigger. Introduced 2001. Imported from the Czech Republic by CZ USA.

Price: $2,097.00

DAKOTA 76 TRAVELER TAKEDOWN RIFLE

Caliber: 257 Roberts, 25-06, 7x57, 270, 280, 30-06, 338-06, 35 Whelen (standard length); 7mm Rem. Mag., 300 Win. Mag., 338 Win. Mag., 416 Taylor, 458 Win. Mag. (short magnums); 7mm, 300, 330, 375 Dakota Magnums. **Barrel:** 23". **Weight:** 7-1/2 lbs. **Length:** 43-1/2" overall. **Stock:** Medium fancy-grade walnut in classic style. Checkered grip and forend; solid butt pad. **Sights:** None furnished; drilled and tapped for scope mounts. **Features:** Threadless disassembly—no threads to wear or stretch, no interrupted cuts, and headspace remains constant. Uses modified Model 76 design with many features of the Model 70 Winchester. Left-hand model also available. Introduced 1989. Made in U.S.A. by Dakota Arms, Inc.

Price: Classic $4,495.00
Price: Safari $5,495.00
Price: Extra barrels. . . . . $1,650.00 to $1,950.00

DAKOTA 76 CLASSIC BOLT-ACTION RIFLE

Caliber: 257 Roberts, 270, 280, 30-06, 7mm Rem. Mag., 338 Win. Mag., 300 Win. Mag., 375 H&H, 458 Win. Mag. **Barrel:** 23". **Weight:** 7-1/2 lbs. **Length:** 43-1/2" overall. **Stock:** Medium fancy grade walnut in classic style. Checkered pistol grip and forend; solid butt pad. **Sights:** None furnished; drilled and tapped for scope mounts. **Features:** Has many features of the original Model 70 Winchester. One-piece rail trigger guard assembly; steel gripcap. Model 70-style trigger. Many options available. Left-hand rifle available at same price. Introduced 1988. From Dakota Arms, Inc.

Price: $3,595.00

DAKOTA 76 SAFARI BOLT-ACTION RIFLE

Caliber: 270 Win., 7x57, 280, 30-06, 7mm Dakota, 7mm Rem. Mag., 300 Dakota, 300 Win. Mag., 330 Dakota, 338 Win. Mag., 375 Dakota, 458 Win. Mag., 300 H&H, 375 H&H, 416 Rem. **Barrel:** 23". **Weight:** 8-1/2 lbs. **Length:** 43-1/2" overall. **Stock:** XXX fancy walnut with ebony forend tip; point-pattern with wrap-around forend checkering. **Sights:** Ramp front, standing leaf rear. **Features:** Has many features of the original Model 70 Winchester. Barrel band front swivel, inletted rear. Cheekpiece with shadow line. Steel gripcap. Introduced 1988. From Dakota Arms, Inc.

Price: Wood stock $4,595.00

Dakota Longbow

Dakota 97 Lightweight Hunter

Dakota Hunter

Ed Brown 702 Savanna

Dakota African Grade

Similar to 76 Safari except chambered for 338 Lapua Mag., 404 Jeffery, 416 Rigby, 416 Dakota, 450 Dakota, 4-round magazine, select wood, two stock cross-bolts. 24" barrel, weighs 9-10 lbs. Ramp front sight, standing leaf rear. Introduced 1989.

Price: **$4,995.00**

DAKOTA LONGBOW TACTICAL E.R. RIFLE

Caliber: 300 Dakota Magnum, 330 Dakota Magnum, 338 Lapua Magnum. **Barrel:** 28", .950" at muzzle **Weight:** 13.7 lbs. **Length:** 50" to 52" overall. **Stock:** Ambidextrous McMillan A-2 fiberglass, black or olive green color; adjustable cheekpiece and buttplate. **Sights:** None furnished. Comes with Picatinny one-piece optical rail. **Features:** Uses the Dakota 76 action with controlled-round feed; three-position firing pin block safety, claw extractor; Model 70-style trigger. Comes with bipod, case tool kit. Introduced 1997. Made in U.S.A. by Dakota Arms, Inc.

Price: **$4,250.00**

DAKOTA 97 LIGHTWEIGHT HUNTER

Caliber: 22-250 to 330. **Barrel:** 22"-24". **Weight:** 6.1-6.5 lbs. **Length:** 43" overall. **Stock:** Fiberglass. **Sights:** Optional. **Features:** Matte blue finish, black stock. Right-hand action only. Introduced 1998. Made in U.S.A. by Dakota Arms, Inc.

Price: **$1,995.00**

DAKOTA LONG RANGE HUNTER RIFLE

Caliber: 25-06, 257 Roberts, 270 Win., 280 Rem., 7mm Rem. Mag., 7mm Dakota Mag., 30-06, 300 Win. Mag., 300 Dakota Mag., 338 Win. Mag., 330 Dakota Mag., 375 H&H Mag., 375 Dakota Mag. **Barrel:** 24", 26", match-quality; free-floating. **Weight:** 7.7 lbs. **Length:** 45" to 47" overall. **Stock:** H-S Precision black synthetic, with one-piece bedding block system. **Sights:** None furnished. Drilled and tapped for scope mounting. **Features:** Cylindrical machined receiver controlled round feed; Mauser-style extractor; three-position striker blocking safety; fully adjustable match trigger. Right-hand action only. Introduced 1997. Made in U.S.A. by Dakota Arms, Inc.

Price: **$1,995.00**

ED BROWN MODEL 702, SAVANNA

Caliber: (long action) 25-06, 270 Win., 280 Rem., 7mm Rem. Mag., 7STW, 30-06, 300 Win. Mag., 300 Weatherby, 338 Win. Mag. (Short action) 223, 22-250, 243, 6mm, 260 Rem. 7mm-08, 308, 300 WSM, 270 WSM, 7mm WSM. **Barrel:** 23" (standard calibers) light weight #3 contour; medium weight 24", 26" with #4 contour on medium calibers. **Weight:** 8 to 8.5-lbs. **Stock:** Fully glass-bedded McMillan fiberglass sporter. **Sights:** None furnished. Talley scope mounts utilzing heavy duty 8-40 screws. **Features:** Custom action with machined steel trigger guard and hinged floor plate. Available in left-hand version.

Price: From **$2,800.00**

Ed Brown 702 Ozark

Ed Brown 702 Bushveld

Ed Brown 702 Varmint

Harris Gunworks Alaskan

Ed Brown Model 702 Denali, Ozark

Similar to the Ed Brown Model 702 Savanna but the Denali is a lighter weight rifle designed specifically for mountain hunting, especially suited to the 270 and 280 calibers. Right hand only. Weighs about 7.75 lbs. The Model 702 Ozark is another lighter weight rifle made on a short action with a very light weight stock. Ozark calibers are 223, 243, 6mm, 260 Rem., 7mm-08, 308. Weight 6.5 lbs.
Price: From (either model) **$2,800.00**

ED BROWN MODEL 702 BUSHVELD

Caliber: 338 Win. Mag., 375 H&H, 416 Rem. Mag., 458 Win. Mag. And all Ed Brown Savanna long action calibers. **Barrel:** 24" medium or heavy weight. **Weight:** 8.25 lbs. **Stock:** Fully bedded McMillan fiberglass with Monte Carlo style cheekpiece, Pachmayr Decelerator recoil pad. **Sights:** None furnish. Talley scope mounts utilizing heavy duty 8-40 screws. **Features:** A dangerous game rifle with options including left-hand action, stainless steel barrel, additional calibers, iron sights.
Price: From **$2,900.00**

ED BROWN MODEL 702 VARMINT

Caliber: 223, 22-250, 220 Swift, 243, 6mm, 308. **Barrel:** Medium weight #5 contour 24"; heavy weight #17 contour 24"; 26" optional. **Weight:** 9 lbs. **Stock:** Fully glass-bedded McMillan fiberglass with recoil pad. **Sights:** None furnished. Talley scope mounts with heavy duty 8-40 screws. **Features:** Fully-adjustable trigger, steel trigger guard and floor plate, many options available.
Price: From **$2,500.00**

HARRIS GUNWORKS SIGNATURE CLASSIC SPORTER

Caliber: 22-250, 243, 6mm Rem., 7mm-08, 284, 308 (short action); 25-06, 270, 280 Rem., 30-06, 7mm Rem. Mag., 300 Win. Mag., 300 Wea. (long action); 338 Win. Mag., 340 Wea., 375 H&H (magnum action). **Barrel:** 22", 24", 26". **Weight:** 7 lbs. (short action). **Stock:** Fiberglass in green, beige, brown or black. Recoil pad and 1" swivels installed. Length of pull up to 14-1/4". **Sights:** None furnished. Comes with 1" rings and bases. **Features:** Uses right- or left-hand action with matte black finish. Trigger pull set at 3 lbs. Four-round magazine for standard calibers; three for magnums. Aluminum floorplate. Wood stock optional. Introduced 1987. From Harris Gunworks, Inc.
Price: **$2,700.00**

Harris Gunworks Signature Classic Stainless Sporter

Similar to Signature Classic Sporter except action is made of stainless steel. Same calibers, in addition to 416 Rem. Mag. Fiberglass stock, right- or left-hand action in natural stainless, glass bead or black chrome sulfide finishes. Introduced 1990. From Harris Gunworks, Inc.
Price: **$2,900.00**

Harris Gunworks Signature Alaskan

Similar to Classic Sporter except match-grade barrel with single leaf rear sight, barrel band front, 1" detachable rings and mounts, steel floorplate, electroless nickel finish. Wood Monte Carlo stock with cheekpiece, palm-swell grip, solid butt pad. Chambered for 270, 280 Rem., 30-06, 7mm Rem. Mag., 300 Win. Mag., 300 Wea., 358 Win., 340 Wea., 375 H&H. Introduced 1989.
Price: **$3,800.00**

Harris Gunworks Signature Titanium Mountain

Harris Gunworks Signature Super Varminter

Harris Gunworks Talon Safari

Howa Lightning

Harris Gunworks Signature Titanium Mountain Rifle
Similar to Classic Sporter except action made of titanium alloy, barrel of chrome-moly steel. Stock is graphite reinforced fiberglass. Weight is 5-1/2 lbs. Chambered for 270, 280 Rem., 30-06, 7mm Rem. Mag., 300 Win. Mag. Fiberglass stock optional. Introduced 1989.
Price: **$3,300.00**
Price: With graphite-steel composite light weight barrel. **$3,700.00**

Harris Gunworks Signature Varminter
Similar to Signature Classic Sporter except has heavy contoured barrel, adjustable trigger, field bipod and special hand-bedded fiberglass stock. Chambered for 223, 22-250, 220 Swift, 243, 6mm Rem., 25-06, 7mm-08, 7mm BR, 308, 350 Rem. Mag. Comes with 1" rings and bases. Introduced 1989.
Price: **$2,700.00**

HARRIS GUNWORKS TALON SAFARI RIFLE
Caliber: 300 Win. Mag., 300 Wea. Mag., 300 Phoenix, 338 Win. Mag., 30/378, 338 Lapua, 300 H&H, 340 Wea. Mag., 375 H&H, 404 Jeffery, 416 Rem. Mag., 458 Win. Mag. (Safari Magnum); 378 Wea. Mag., 416 Rigby, 416 Wea. Mag., 460 Wea. Mag. (Safari Super Magnum). **Barrel:** 24". **Weight:** About 9-10 lbs. **Length:** 43" overall. **Stock:** Gunworks fiberglass Safari. **Sights:** Barrel band front ramp, multi-leaf express rear. **Features:** Uses Harris Gunworks Safari action. Has quick detachable 1" scope mounts, positive locking steel floorplate, barrel band sling swivel. Match-grade barrel. Matte black finish standard. Introduced 1989. From Harris Gunworks, Inc.
Price: Talon Safari Magnum. **$3,900.00**
Price: Talon Safari Super Magnum **$4,200.00**

HARRIS GUNWORKS TALON SPORTER RIFLE
Caliber: 22-250, 243, 6mm Rem., 6mm BR, 7mm BR, 7mm-08, 25-06, 270, 280 Rem., 284, 308, 30-06, 350 Rem. Mag. (long action); 7mm Rem. Mag., 7mm STW, 300 Win. Mag., 300 Wea. Mag., 300 H&H, 338 Win. Mag., 340 Wea. Mag., 375 H&H, 416 Rem. Mag. **Barrel:** 24" (standard). **Weight:** About 7-1/2 lbs. **Length:** NA. **Stock:** Choice of walnut or fiberglass. **Sights:** None furnished; comes with rings and bases. Open sights optional. **Features:** Uses pre-'64 Model 70-type action with cone breech, controlled feed, claw extractor and three-position safety. Barrel and action are of stainless steel; chrome-moly optional. Introduced 1991. From Harris Gunworks, Inc.
Price: **$2,900.00**

HOWA LIGHTNING BOLT-ACTION RIFLE
Caliber: 223, 22-250, 243, 6.5x55, 270, 308, 30-06, 7mm Rem. Mag., 300 Win. Mag., 338 Win. Mag, 300 WSM, 7mm WSM, 270 WSM. **Barrel:** 22", 24" magnum calibers. **Weight:** 7-1/2 lbs. **Length:** 42" overall (22" barrel). **Stock:** Black Bell & Carlson Carbelite composite with Monte Carlo comb; checkered grip and forend. **Sights:** None furnished. Drilled and tapped for scope mounting. **Features:** Sliding thumb safety; hinged floorplate; polished blue/black finish. Introduced 1993. From Legacy Sports International.
Price: Blue, standard calibers. **$479.00**
Price: Blue, magnum calibers. **$502.00**
Price: Stainless, standard calibers **$585.00**
Price: Stainless, magnum calibers **$612.00**

Howa M-1500 Hunter Bolt-Action Rifle
Similar to Lightning Model except has walnut-finished hardwood stock. Polished blue finish or stainless steel. Introduced 1999. From Legacy Sports International.
Price: Blue, standard calibers. **$539.00**
Price: Stainless, standard calibers **$638.00**
Price: Blue, magnum calibers. **$560.00**
Price: Stainless, magnum calibers **$662.00**

RIFLES

Howa M-1500 Hunter

Howa M-1500 Ultralight

Howa M-1500 Varmint Supreme

Kimber 84M Classic

Kimber 84M Varmint

Howa M-1500 Supreme Rifles

Similar to Howa M-1500 Lightning except stocked with JRS Classic or Thumbhole Sporter laminated wood stocks in Nutmeg (brown/black) or Pepper (gray/black) colors. Barrel 22"; 24" magnum calibers. Weights are JRS stock 8 lbs., THS stock 8.3 lbs. Introduced 2001. Imported from Japan by Legacy Sports International.

Price: Blue, standard calibers, JRS stock. **$616.00**
Price: Blue, standard calibers, THS stock **$668.00**
Price: Blue, magnum calibers, JRS stock **$638.00**
Price: Blue, magnum calibers, THS stock **$638.00**
Price: Stainless, standard calibers, JRS stock **$720.00**
Price: Stainless, standard calibers, THS stock **$771.00**
Price: Stainless, magnum calibers, JRS stock **$720.00**
Price: Stainless, magnum calibers, THS stock **$742.00**

Howa M-1500 Ultralight

Similar to Howa M-1500 Lightning except receiver milled to reduce weight, tapered 22" barrel; 1-10" twist. Chambered for 243 Win. Stocks are black texture-finished hardwood. Weighs 6.4 lbs. Length 40"overall.
Price: Blued **$511.00**

Howa M-1500 Varmint and Varmint Supreme Rifles

Similar to M-1500 Lightning except has heavy 24" hammer-forged barrel. Chambered for 223, 22-250, 308. Weighs 9.3 lbs.; overall length 44.5". Introduced 1999. Imported from Japan by Interarms/Howa.

Varminter Supreme has heavy barrel, target crown muzzle. Heavy 24" barrel, laminated wood with raised comb stocks, rollover cheekpiece, vented beavertail forearm; available in 223 Rem., 22-250 Rem., 308 Win. Weighs 9.9 lbs. Introduced 2001. Imported from Japan by Legacy Sports International.

Price: Varminter, blue, polymer stock **$517.00**
Price: Varminter, stainless, polymer stock **$626.00**
Price: Varminter, blue, wood stock **$575.00**
Price: Varminter, stainless, wood stock **$677.00**
Price: Varminter Supreme, blued . . . . **$612.00 to $641.00**
Price: Varminter Supreme, stainless . . . . **$714.00 to $743.00**

KIMBER MODEL 84M BOLT-ACTION RIFLE

Caliber: 22-250, 243, 260 Rem., 7mm-08, 308, 5-shot. **Barrel:** 22", 24", 26". **Weight:** 5 lbs., 10 oz. to 10 lbs. **Length:** 41"-45". **Stock:** Claro walnut, checkered with steel grip cap or gray laminate. **Sights:** None; drilled and tapped for bases. **Features:** Mauser claw extractor, two-position wing safety, action bedded on aluminum pillars, free-floated barrel, match-grade trigger set at 4 lbs., matte blue finish. Includes cable lock. Introduced 2001. Made in U.S.A. by Kimber Mfg. Inc.
Price: Classic (243, 260, 7mm-08, 308) **$917.00**
Price: Varmint (22-250) **$1,001.00**

RIFLES

L.A.R. Grizzly

Legacy Sports International M-1500

Legacy Sports International Texas Safari

Legacy Sports International Mauser 98

L.A.R. GRIZZLY 50 BIG BOAR RIFLE

Caliber: 50 BMG, single shot. **Barrel:** 36". **Weight:** 30.4 lbs. **Length:** 45.5" overall. **Stock:** Integral. Ventilated rubber recoil pad. **Sights:** None furnished; scope mount. **Features:** Bolt-action bullpup design, thumb and bolt stop safety. All-steel construction. Unsurpassed accuracy and impact. Introduced 1994. Made in U.S.A. by L.A.R. Mfg., Inc.

Price: **$2,195.00**

LEGACY SPORTS INTERNATIONAL M-1500 CUSTOM RIFLES

Caliber: 300 WSM, 300 Win. Mag.; 3 plus 1 in chamber. **Weight:** 7.6-8.3 lbs. **Length:** 42.5" overall. **Stock:** Black polymer, laminated wood. **Features:** Built on Howa M-1500 stainless steel short-action, 3-position thumb safety, hinged floorplate, drilled and tapped for standard scope mounts. 300 WSM has stainless steel short action, 22 bbl. 300 Win. Mag. has blued long action, 24" bbl. with integral ported muzzle brake by Bill Wiseman. Introduced 2001 by Legacy Sports International.

Price: JRS Classic Pepper stock **$995.00**
Price: Thumbhole Pepper stock **$1,035.00**
Price: 300 WSM, polymer stock **$895.00**
Price: 300 Win. Mag., JRS Nutmeg stock **$855.00**

LEGACY SPORTS INTERNATIONAL TEXAS SAFARI RIFLES

Caliber: 270 Win., 300 Win. Mag. 270 Win.: 5 plus 1 in chamber; 300 Mag., 3 plus 1 in chamber. **Weight:** 7.8 lbs. **Length:** 42.5" overall; 44.5" in 300 Win. Mag. **Stock:** Brown/black laminated wood. **Features:** Built on Howa M-1500 action customized by Bill Wiseman, College Station, TX; Wiseman-designed 3-position thumb safety and bolt-release, hinged floorplate, drilled and tapped for standard scope mounts. Action glass-bedded, farrel free floated. 300 Win. Mag. has integral muzzle brake. Introduced 2001 by Legacy Sports International.

Price: 270 Win. **$1,522.00**
Price: 300 Win. Mag. **$1,753.00**

LEGACY SPORTS INTERNATIONAL MAUSER 98 RIFLE

Caliber: 300 Win. Mag. **Barrel:** 24", 1-10" twist. **Weight:** 8.4 lbs. **Length:** 45" overall. **Stock:** Premium American walnut. **Sights:** None. **Features:** Square-bridge Mauser 98 action dovetailed for ring mounts (scope and rings not included). 3-position thumb safety, hinged floorplate, adjustable trigger. Introduced 2001. Imported from Italy by Legacy Sports International.

Price: **$955.00**

MAGNUM RESEARCH MAGNUM LITE TACTICAL RIFLE

Caliber: 223 Rem., 22-250, 308 Win., 300 Win. Mag., 300 WSM. **Barrel:** 26" Magnum Lite™ graphite. **Weight:** 8.3 lbs. **Length:** NA. **Stock:** H-S Precision™ tactical black synthetic. **Sights:** None furnished; drilled and tapped for scope mount. **Features:** Accurized Remington 700 action; adjustable trigger; adjustable comb height. Tuned to shoot 1/2" MOA or better. Introduced 2001. From Magnum Research Inc.

Price: **$2,400.00**

Magnum Research Tactical

Raptor Bolt-Action

Remington 673 Guide

Remington 700 Classic

Remington 700 ADL Synthetic

MOUNTAIN EAGLE MAGNUM LITE RIFLE

Caliber: 22-250, 223 Rem. (Varmint); 280, 30-06 (long action); 7mm Rem. Mag., 300 Win. Mag., (magnum action). **Barrel:** 24", 26", free floating. **Weight:** 7 lbs., 13 oz. **Length:** 44" overall (24" barrel). **Stock:** Kevlar-graphite with aluminum bedding block, high comb, recoil pad, swivel studs; made by H-S Precision. **Sights:** None furnished; accepts any Remington 700-type base. **Features:** Special Sako action with one-piece forged bolt, hinged steel floorplate, lengthened receiver ring; adjustable trigger. Krieger cut-rifled benchrest barrel. Introduced 1996. From Magnum Research, Inc.

Price: Magnum Lite (graphite barrel) **$2,295.00**

NEW ULTRA LIGHT ARMS BOLT-ACTION RIFLES

Caliber: 17 Rem. to 416 Rigby (numerous calibers available). **Barrel:** Douglas, length to order. **Weight:** 4-3/4 to 7-1/2 lbs. **Length:** Varies. **Stock:** Kevlar®/ graphite composite, variety of finishes. **Sights:** None furnished; drilled and tapped for scope mount. **Features:** Timney trigger, hand-lapped action, button-rifled barrel, hand-bedded action, recoil pad, sling-swivel studs, optional Jewell Trigger. Made in U.S.A. by New Ultra Light Arms.

Price: Model 20 (short action) **$2,500.00**
Price: Model 24 (long action) **$2,600.00**
Price: Model 28 (magnum action) **$2,900.00**

Price: Model 40 (300 Wea. Mag., 416 Rigby) **$2,900.00**
Price: Left-hand models, add **$100.00**

RAPTOR BOLT-ACTION RIFLE

Caliber: 270, 30-06, 243, 25-06, 308; 4-shot magazine. **Barrel:** 22". **Weight:** 7 lbs., 6 oz. **Length:** 42.5" overall. **Stock:** Black synthetic, fiberglass reinforced; checkered grip and forend; vented recoil pad; Monte Carlo cheekpiece. **Sights:** None furnished; drilled and tapped for scope mounts. **Features:** Rust-resistant "Taloncote" treated barreled action; pillar bedded; stainless bolt with three locking lugs; adjustable trigger. Announced 1997. Made in U.S.A. by Raptor Arms Co., Inc.

Price: **$249.00**

Remington Model 673 Guide Rifle

Available in 350 Rem. Mag., 300 Rem. SAUM with 22" magnum contour barrel with machined steel ventilated rib, iron sights, wide laminate stock.

Price: **$825.00**

REMINGTON MODEL 700 CLASSIC RIFLE

Caliber: 300 Savage. **Barrel:** 24". **Weight:** About 7-1/4 lbs. **Length:** 44-1/2" overall. **Stock:** American walnut, 20 lpi checkering on pistol grip and forend. Classic styling. Satin finish. **Sights:** None furnished. Receiver drilled and tapped for scope mounting. **Features:** A "classic" version of the BDL with straight comb stock. Fitted with rubber recoil pad. Sling swivel studs installed. Hinged floorplate. Limited production in 2003 only.

Price: **$683.00**

RIFLES

NEW!

NEW!

Remington 700 BDL

Remington 700 BDL Left Hand

Remington 700 BDL SS

Remington 700 BDL SS DM

RIFLES

REMINGTON MODEL 700 ADL DELUXE RIFLE
Caliber: 270, 30-06. **Barrel:** 22" round tapered. **Weight:** 7-1/4 lbs. **Length:** 41-5/8" overall. **Stock:** Walnut. Satin-finished pistol grip stock with fine-line cut checkering, Monte Carlo. **Sights:** Gold bead ramp front; removable, step-adjustable rear with windage screw. **Features:** Side safety, receiver tapped for scope mounts.
Price: **$580.00**

Remington Model 700 ADL Synthetic
Similar to the 700 ADL except has a fiberglass-reinforced synthetic stock with straight comb, raised cheekpiece, positive checkering, and black rubber butt pad. Metal has matte finish. Available in 22-250, 223, 243, 270, 308, 30-06 with 22" barrel, 300 Win. Mag., 7mm Rem. Mag. with 24" barrel. Introduced 1996.
Price: From . . . . **$500.00 to $527.00**

Remington Model 700 ADL Synthetic Youth
Similar to the Model 700 ADL Synthetic except has 1" shorter stock, 20" barrel. Chambered for 243, 308. Introduced 1998.
Price: **$500.00**

Remington Model 700 BDL Custom Deluxe Rifle
Same as 700 ADL except chambered for 222, 223 (short action, 24" barrel), 7mm-08, 280, 22-250, 25-06. (short action, 22" barrel), 243, 270, 30-06, skip-line checkering, black forend tip and gripcap with white line spacers. Matted receiver top, quick-release floorplate. Hooded ramp front sight, quick detachable swivels.
Price: **$683.00**

Also available in 17 Rem., 7mm Rem. Mag., 7mm Rem. Ultra Mag., 300 Win. Mag. (long action, 24" barrel); 300 Rem. Ultra Mag. (26" barrel). Overall length 44-1/2", weight about 7-1/2 lbs.
Price: . . . . **$709.00 to $723.00**

Remington Model 700 BDL Left Hand Custom Deluxe
Same as 700 BDL except mirror-image left-hand action, stock. Available in 270, 30-06, 7mm Rem. Mag., 300 Rem. Ultra Mag, 338 Rem. Ultra Mag., 7mm Rem. Ultra Mag.
Price: . . . . **$709.00 to $749.00**

Remington Model 700 BDL DM Rifle
Same as 700 BDL except detachable box magazine (4-shot, standard calibers, 3-shot for magnums). Glossy stock finish, open sights, recoil pad, sling swivels. Available in 270, 30-06, 7mm Rem. Mag., 300 Win. Mag. Introduced 1995.
Price: From . . . . **$749.00 to $776.00**

Remington Model 700 BDL SS Rifle
Similar to 700 BDL rifle except hinged floorplate, 24" standard weight barrel in all calibers; magnum calibers have magnum-contour barrel. No sights supplied, but comes drilled and tapped. Corrosion-resistant follower and fire control, stainless BDL-style barreled action with fine matte finish. Synthetic stock has straight comb and cheekpiece, textured finish, positive checkering, plated swivel studs. Calibers—270, 30-06; magnums—7mm Rem. Mag., 7mm Rem. UltraMag., 300 Rem. Ultra Mag. (26" barrel) 300 Win. Mag., 338 Rem. Ultra Mag., 7mm Rem. SAUM, 300 Rem. SAUM. Weighs 7-3/8 to 7-1/2 lbs. Introduced 1993.
Price: From . . . . **$735.00 to $775.00**

Remington Model 700 BDL SS DM Rifle
Same as 700 BDL SS except detachable box magazine. Barrel, receiver and bolt made of #416 stainless steel; black synthetic stock, fine-line engraving. Available in 270, 30-06, 7mm Rem. Mag., 300 Win. Mag. Introduced 1995.
Price: From . . . . **$801.00 to $828.00**

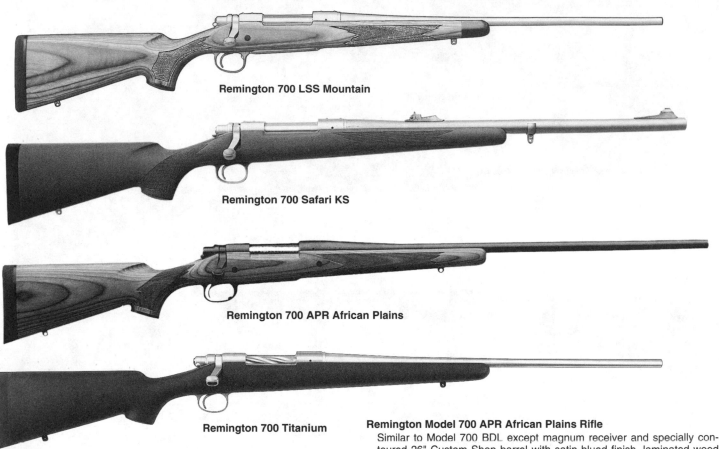

Remington 700 LSS Mountain

Remington 700 Safari KS

Remington 700 APR African Plains

Remington 700 Titanium

Remington Model 700 Custom KS Mountain Rifle

Similar to 700 BDL except custom finished with aramid fiber reinforced resin synthetic stock. Available in left- and right-hand versions. Chambered 270 Win., 280 Rem., 30-06, 7mm Rem. Mag., 7mm STW, 300 Rem. Ultra Mag., 338 Rem. Ultra Mag., 300 Win. Mag., 300 Wea. Mag., 35 Whelen, 338 Win. Mag., 8mm Rem. Mag., 375 H&H, with 24" barrel (except 300 Rem. Ultra Mag., 26"), 7mm RUM, 375 RUM. Weighs 6 lbs., 6 oz. Introduced 1986.

Price: Right-hand **$1,314.00**
Price: Left-hand **$1,393.00**
Price: Stainless. . . . . **$1,500 to $1,580.00**

Remington Model 700 LSS Mountain Rifle

Similar to Model 700 Custom KS Mountain Rifle except stainless steel 22" barrel and two-tone laminated stock. Chambered in 260 Rem., 7mm-08, 270 Winchester and 30-06. Overall length 42-1/2", weighs 6-5/8 oz. Introduced 1999.

Price: **$800.00**

Remington Model 700 Safari Grade

Similar to 700 BDL aramid fiber reinforced fiberglass stock, blued carbon steel bbl. and action, or stainless, w/cheekpiece, custom finished and tuned. In 8mm Rem. Mag., 375 H&H, 416 Rem. Mag. or 458 Win. Mag. calibers only with heavy barrel. Right- and left-hand versions.

Price: Safari KS . . . . **$1,520.00 to $1,601.00**
Price: Safari KS (stainless right-hand only) **$1,697.00**

Remington Model 700 AWR Alaskan Wilderness Rifle

Similar to the 700 BDL except has stainless barreled action finishBlack Teflon 24" bbl. 26" Ultra Mag raised cheekpiece, magnum-grade black rubber recoil pad. Chambered for 7mm RUM., 375 RUM, 7mm STW, 300 Rem. Ultra Mag., 300 Win. Mag., 300 Wea. Mag., 338 Rem. Ultra Mag., 338 Win. Mag., 375 H&H. Aramid fiber reinforced fiberglass stock. Introduced 1994.

Price: . . . . **$1,593.00** (right-hand); **$1,673.00** (left-hand)

Remington Model 700 APR African Plains Rifle

Similar to Model 700 BDL except magnum receiver and specially contoured 26" Custom Shop barrel with satin blued finish, laminated wood stock with raised cheekpiece, satin finish, black butt pad, 20 lpi cut checkering. Chambered for 7mm Rem. Mag., 7mm RUM, 375 RUM, 300 Rem. Ultra Mag., 300 Win. Mag., 300 Wea. Mag., 338 Win. Mag., 338 Rem. Ultra Mag., 375 H&H. Introduced 1994.

Price: **$1,716.00**

Remington Model 700 LSS Rifle

Similar to 700 BDL except stainless steel barreled action, gray laminated wood stock with Monte Carlo comb and cheekpiece. No sights furnished. Available in (RH) 7mm Rem. Mag., 300 Win. Mag., 300 RUM, 338 RUM, 7mm Rem. Ultra Mag., 375 Rem. Ultra Mag., (LH) 7mm Rem. Ultra Mag., 300 Rem. Ultra Mag., and 338 Rem. RUM. Introduced 1996.

Price: From. . . . .(Right-hand) **$820.00 to $840.00**; (LH) **$867.00**

Remington Model 700 MTN DM Rifle

Similar to 700 BDL except weighs 6-1/2 to 6-5/8 lbs., 22" tapered barrel. Redesigned pistol grip, straight comb, contoured cheekpiece, hand-rubbed oil stock finish, deep cut checkering, hinged floorplate and magazine follower, two-position thumb safety. Chambered for 260 Rem., 270 Win., 7mm-08, 25-06, 280 Rem., 30-06, 4-shot detachable box magazine. Overall length is 41-5/8"-42-1/2". Introduced 1995.

Price: **$728.00**

Remington Model 700 Titanium

Similar to 700 BDL except has titanium receiver, spiral-cut fluted bolt, skeletonized bolt handle and carbon-fiber and aramid fiber reinforced stock with sling swivel studs. Barrel 22"; weighs 5-1/4 lbs. (short action) or 5-1/2 lbs. (long action). Satin stainless finish. 260 Rem., 270 Win., 7mm-08, 30-06, 308 Win. Introduced 2001.

Price: **$1,239.00**

Remington Model 700 VLS Varmint Laminated Stock

Similar to 700 BDL except 26" heavy barrel without sights, brown laminated stock with beavertail forend, gripcap, rubber butt pad. Available in 223 Rem., 22-250, 6mm, 243, 308. Polished blue finish. Introduced 1995.

Price: From. **$705.00**

Remington 700 VLS

Remington 700 VS

Remington 700 VS SF

Remington 700 Sendero SF

Remington Seven LS

Remington Model 700 VS Varmint Synthetic Rifles

Similar to 700 BDL Varmint Laminated except composite stock reinforced with aramid fiber reinforced, fiberglass and graphite. Aluminum bedding block that runs full length of receiver. Free-floating 26" barrel. Metal has black matte finish; stock has textured black and gray finish and swivel studs. Available in 223, 22-250, 308. Right- and left-hand. Introduced 1992.

Price: . . . . **$811.00 to $837.00**

Remington Model 700 VS SF Rifle

Similar to Model 700 Varmint Synthetic except satin-finish stainless barreled action with 26" fluted barrel, spherical concave muzzle crown. Chambered for 223, 220 Swift, 22-250. Introduced 1994.

Price: **$976.00**

Remington Model 700 EtronX VSSF Rifle

Similar to Model 700 VS SF except features battery-powered ignition system for near-zero lock time and electronic trigger mechanism. Requires ammunition with EtronX electrically fired primers. Aluminum-bedded 26" heavy, stainless steel, fluted barrel; overall length 45-7/8"; weight 8 lbs., 14 oz. Black, Kevlar-reinforced composite stock. Light-emitting diode display on grip top indicates fire or safe mode, loaded or unloaded chamber, battery condition. Introduced 2000.

Price: 220 Swift, 22-250 or 243 Win. **$1,332.00**

Remington Model 700 Sendero SF Rifle

Similar to 700 Sendero except stainless steel action and 26" fluted stainless barrel. Weighs 8-1/2 lbs. Chambered for 7mm Rem. SAUM, 300 Rem. SAUM, 7mm Rem. Mag., 7mm STW, 300 Rem. Ultra Mag., 338 Rem. Ultra Mag., 300 Win. Mag., 7mm Rem. Ultra Mag. Introduced 1996.

Price: . . . . **$1,003.00 to $1,016.00**

REMINGTON MODEL 700 RMEF

Caliber: 300 Rem. SAUM. **Barrel:** 26". **Weight:** 7-5/8 lbs. **Length:** 46.5". **Stock:** Synthetic, Realtree Hardwoods HD finish. **Sights:** None; drilled and tapped. **Features:** Special Edition (sold one year only), Rocky Mountain Elk Foundation rifle, 416 stainless bolt, varrel, receiver. Portion of proceeds to RMEF.

Price: **$835.00**

REMINGTON MODEL 710 BOLT-ACTION RIFLE

Caliber: 270 Win., 30-06. **Barrel:** 22". **Weight:** 7-1/8 lbs. **Length:** 42-1/2" overall. **Stock:** Gray synthetic. **Sights:** Bushnell Sharpshooter 3-9x scope mounted and bore-sighted. **Features:** Unique action locks bolt directly into barrel; 60-degree bolt throw; 4-shot dual-stack magazine; key-operated Integrated Security System locks bolt open. Introduced 2001. Made in U.S.A. by Remington Arms Co.

Price: **$425.00**

REMINGTON MODEL SEVEN LS

Caliber: 223 Rem., 243 Win., 7mm-08 Rem., 308 Win. **Barrel:** 20". **Weight:** 6-1/2 lbs. **Length:** 39-1/4" overall. **Stock:** Brown laminated, satin finished. **Features:** Satin finished carbone steel barrel and action, 4-round magazine, hinged magazine floorplate. Furnished with iron sights and sling swivel studs, drilled and tapped for scope mounts.

Price: **$701.00**
Price: 7mmRSAUM, 300RSAUM, LS Magnum, 22" bbl. **$741.00**

Remington Model Seven SS

Similar to Model Seven LS except stainless steel barreled action and black synthetic stock, 20" barrel. Chambered for 243, 260 Rem., 7mm-08, 308. Introduced 1994.

Price: **$729.00**
Price: 7mmRSAUM, 300RSAUM, Model Seven SS

Magnum, 22" bbl. **$769.00**

RIFLES

Remington Model Seven LS Mag

Remington Model Seven SS Mag

Remington Model Seven Custom MS

Remington Seven Custom KS

Ruger Magnum

Ruger 77/22 Hornet Varmint

Remington Model Seven Custom MS Rifle

Similar to Model Seven LS except full-length Mannlicher-style stock of laminated wood with straight comb, solid black recoil pad, black steel forend tip, cut checkering, gloss finish. Barrel length 20", weighs 6-3/4 lbs. Available in 222 Rem., 223, 22-250, 243, 6mm Rem., 260 Rem., 7mm-08 Rem., 308, 350 Rem. Mag. Calibers 250 Savage, 257 Roberts, 35 Rem. Polished blue finish. Introduced 1993. From Remington Custom Shop.
Price: From **$1,332.00**

Remington Model Seven Youth Rifle

Similar to Model Seven LS except hardwood stock, 1" shorter length of pull, chambered for 223, 243, 260 Rem., 7mm-08. Introduced 1993.
Price: **$547.00**

Remington Model Seven Custom KS

Similar to Model Seven LS except gray aramid fiber reinforced stock with 1" black rubber recoil pad and swivel studs. Blued satin carbon steel barreled action. No sights on 223, 260 Rem., 7mm-08, 308; 35 Rem. and 350 Rem. have iron sights.
Price: **$1,314.00**

RUGER MAGNUM RIFLE

Caliber: 375 H&H, 416 Rigby, 458 Lott. **Barrel:** 23". **Weight:** 9-1/2 to 10-1/4 lbs. **Length:** 44". **Stock:** AAA Premium Grade Circassian walnut with live-rubber recoil pad, metal grip cap, and studs for mounting sling swivels. **Sights:** Blade, front; V-notch rear express sights (one stationary, two folding) drift-adjustable for windage. **Features:** Patented floorplate latch secures the hinged floorplate against accidental dumping of cartridges; one-piece bolt has a non-rotating Mauser-type controlled-feed extractor; fixed-blade ejector.
Price: M77RSMMKII **$1,695.00**

RUGER 77/22 HORNET BOLT-ACTION RIFLE

Caliber: 22 Hornet, 6-shot rotary magazine. **Barrel:** 20". **Weight:** About 6 lbs. **Length:** 39-3/4" overall. **Stock:** Checkered American walnut, black rubber butt pad. **Sights:** Brass bead front, open adjustable rear; also available without sights. **Features:** Same basic features as rimfire model except slightly lengthened receiver. Uses Ruger rotary magazine. Three-position safety. Comes with 1" Ruger scope rings. Introduced 1994.
Price: 77/22RH (rings only) **$589.00**
Price: 77/22RSH (with sights) **$609.00**
Price: K77/22VHZ Varmint, laminated stock, no sights **$625.00**

RIFLES

Ruger M77 Mark II

Ruger KM77RLFP MKII

Ruger KM77RSFP MKII

Ruger KM77RFP MKII

Ruger 77/44

RUGER M77 MARK II RIFLE

Caliber: 223, 220 Swift, 22-250, 243, 6mm Rem., 257 Roberts, 25-06, 6.5x55 Swedish, 270, 7x57mm, 260 Rem., 280 Rem., 308, 30-06, 7mm Rem. Mag., 7mm Rem. Short Ultra Mag., 300 Rem. Short Ultra Mag., 300 WSM, 300 Win. Mag., 338 Win. Mag., 4-shot magazine. **Barrel:** 20", 22"; 24" (magnums). **Weight:** About 7 lbs. **Length:** 39-3/4" overall. **Stock:** Synthetic American walnut; swivel studs, rubber butt pad. **Sights:** None furnished. Receiver has Ruger integral scope mount base, Ruger 1" rings. Some with iron sights. **Features:** Short action with new trigger, 3-position safety. Steel trigger guard. Left-hand available. Introduced 1989.
Price: M77RMKII (no sights). **$675.00**
Price: M77RSMKII (open sights) **$759.00**
Price: M77LRMKII (left-hand, 270, 30-06, 7mm Rem. Mag.,300 Win. Mag.) **$675.00**
Price: KM77REPMKII (Shorts) **$675.00**

Ruger M77RSI International Carbine

Same as standard Model 77 except 18" barrel, full-length International-style stock, steel forend cap, loop-type steel sling swivels. Integral-base receiver, open sights, Ruger 1" steel rings. Improved front sight. Available in 243, 270, 308, 30-06. Weighs 7 lbs. Length overall is 38-3/8".
Price: M77RSIMKII. **$769.00**

Ruger M77 Mark II All-Weather and Sporter Model Stainless Rifle

Similar to wood-stock M77 Mark II except all metal parts are stainless steel, has an injection-moulded, glass-fiber-reinforced polymer stock. Laminated wood stock. Chambered for 223, 243, 270, 308, 30-06, 7mm Rem. Mag., 300 Win. Mag., 338 Win. Mag. Fixed-blade-type ejector, 3-position safety, new trigger guard with patented floorplate latch. Integral Scope Base Receiver, 1" Ruger scope rings, built-in sling swivel loops. Introduced 1990.

Price: K77RFPMKII **$675.00**
Price: K77RLFPMKII Ultra-Light, synthetic stock, rings, no sights **$675.00**
Price: K77LRBBZMKII, left-hand, rings, no sights, laminated stock. **$729.00**
Price: K77RSFPMKII, synthetic stock, open sights **$759.00**
Price: K77RBZMKII, no sights, laminated wood stock, 223, 22/250, 243, 270, 280 Rem., 7mm Rem. Mag., 30-06, 308, 300 Win. Mag., 338 Win. Mag.. . . . . **$729.00**
Price: K77RSBZMKII, open sights, laminated wood stock, 243, 270, 7mm Rem. Mag., 30-06, 300 Win. Mag., 338 Win. Mag.. . . **$799.00**
Price: KM77RFPMKII (Shorts), M77RMKII **$675.00**

Ruger M77RL Ultra Light

Similar to standard M77 except weighs 6 lbs., chambered for 223, 243, 308, 270, 30-06, 257 Roberts, barrel tapped for target scope blocks, 20" Ultra Light barrel. Overall length 40". Ruger's steel 1" scope rings supplied. Introduced 1983.
Price: M77RLMKII **$729.00**

Ruger M77 Mark II Compact Rifles

Similar to standard M77 except reduced 16-1/2" barrel, weighs 5-3/4 lbs. Chambered for 223, 243, 260 Rem., 308, and 7mm-08.
Price: M77CR MKII (blued finish, walnut stock) **$675.00**
Price: KM77CRBBZ MkII (stainless finish, black laminated stock) **$729.00**

RUGER 77/44 BOLT-ACTION RIFLE

Caliber: 44 Magnum, 4-shot magazine. **Barrel:** 18-1/2". **Weight:** 6 lbs. **Length:** 38-1/4" overall. **Stock:** American walnut with rubber butt pad and swivel studs or black polymer (stainless only). **Sights:** Gold bead front, folding leaf rear. Comes with Ruger 1" scope rings. **Features:** Uses same action as the Ruger 77/22. Short bolt stroke; rotary magazine; three-position safety. Introduced 1997. Made in U.S.A. by Sturm, Ruger & Co.
Price: Blue, walnut, 77/44RS **$605.00**
Price: Stainless, polymer, stock, K77/44RS **$605.00**

Ruger M77VT Target

Sako TRG-S

Sako 75 Hunter

Sako 75 Stainless Hunter

Sako 75 Deluxe

RUGER M77VT TARGET RIFLE

Caliber: 22-250, 220 Swift, 223, 243, 25-06, 308. **Barrel:** 26" heavy stainless steel with target gray finish. **Weight:** 9-3/4 lbs. **Length:** Approx. 44" overall. **Stock:** Laminated American hardwood with beavertail forend, steel swivel studs; no checkering or gripcap. **Sights:** Integral scope mount bases in receiver. **Features:** Ruger diagonal bedding system. Ruger steel 1" scope rings supplied. Fully adjustable trigger. Steel floorplate and trigger guard. New version introduced 1992.
Price: K77VTMKII $819.00

SAKO TRG-S BOLT-ACTION RIFLE

Caliber: 338 Lapua Mag., 30-378 Weatherby, 3-shot magazine. **Barrel:** 26". **Weight:** 7.75 lbs. **Length:** 45.5" overall. **Stock:** Reinforced polyurethane with Monte Carlo comb. **Sights:** None furnished. **Features:** Resistance-free bolt with 60-degree lift. Recoil pad adjustable for length. Free-floating barrel, detachable magazine, fully adjustable trigger. Matte blue metal. Introduced 1993. Imported from Finland by Beretta USA.
Price: $896.00

Sako TRG-42 Bolt-Action Rifle

Similar to TRG-S except 5-shot magazine, fully adjustable stock and competition trigger. Offered in 338 Lapua Mag. and 300 Win. Mag. Imported from Finland by Beretta USA.
Price: $2,829.00

SAKO 75 HUNTER BOLT-ACTION RIFLE

Caliber: 17 Rem., 222, 223, 22-250, 243, 7mm-08, 308 Win., 25-06, 270, 280, 30-06; 270 Wea. Mag., 7mm Rem. Mag., 7mm STW, 7mm Wea. Mag., 300 Win. Mag., 300 Wea. Mag., 338 Win. Mag., 340 Wea. Mag., 375 H&H, 416 Rem. Mag. **Barrel:** 22", standard calibers; 24", 26" magnum calibers. **Weight:** About 6 lbs. **Length:** NA. **Stock:** European walnut with matte lacquer finish. **Sights:** None furnished; dovetail scope mount rails.

Features: New design with three locking lugs and a mechanical ejector, key locks firing pin and bolt, cold hammer-forged barrel is free-floating, 2-position safety, hinged floorplate or detachable magazine that can be loaded from the top, short 70 degree bolt lift. Five action lengths. Introduced 1997. Imported from Finland by Beretta USA.
Price: Standard calibers $1,129.00
Price: Magnum Calibers $1,163.00

Sako 75 Stainless Synthetic Rifle

Similar to 75 Hunter except all metal is stainless steel, synthetic stock has soft composite panels moulded into forend and pistol grip. Available in 22-250, 243, 308 Win., 25-06, 270, 30-06 with 22" barrel, 7mm Rem. Mag., 7mm STW, 300 Win. Mag., 338 Win. Mag. and 375 H&H Mag. with 24" barrel and 300 Wea. Mag., 300 Rem.Ultra Mag. with 26" barrel. Introduced 1997. Imported from Finland by Beretta USA.
Price: Standard calibers $1,212.00
Price: Magnum calibers $1,246.00

Sako 75 Deluxe Rifle

Similar to 75 Hunter except select wood rosewood gripcap and forend tip. Available in 17 Rem., 222, 223, 25-06, 243, 7mm-08, 308, 25-06, 270, 280, 30-06; 270 Wea. Mag., 7mm Rem. Mag., 7mm STW, 7mm Wea. Mag., 300 Win. Mag., 300 Wea. Mag., 338 Win. Mag., 340 Wea. Mag., 375 H&H, 416 Rem. Mag. Introduced 1997. Imported from Finland by Beretta USA.
Price: Standard calibers $1,653.00
Price: Magnum calibers $1,688.00

Sako 75 Varmint Stainless Laminated Rifle

Similar to Sako 75 Hunter except chambered only for 222, 223, 22-250, 22 PPC USA, 6mm PPC, heavy 24" barrel with recessed crown, all metal is stainless steel, laminated wood stock with beavertail forend. Introduced 1999. Imported from Finland by Beretta USA.
Price: $1,448.00

Sako 75 Varmint

Savage 110GXP3

Savage 111FXP3

Savage 111FCXP3

Sako 75 Varmint Rifle
Similar to Model 75 Hunter except chambered only for 17 Rem., 222 Rem., 223 Rem., 22-250 Rem., 22 PPC and 6mm PPC, 24" heavy barrel with recessed crown, beavertail forend. Introduced 1998. Imported from Finland by Beretta USA.
Price: **$1,337.00**

SAUER 202 BOLT-ACTION RIFLE
Caliber: Standard—243, 6.5x55, 270 Win., 308 Win., 30-06; magnum—7mm Rem. Mag., 300 Win. Mag., 300 Wea. Mag., 375 H&H. **Barrel:** 23.6" (standard), 26" (magnum). **Weight:** 7.7 lbs. (standard). **Length:** 44.3" overall (23.6" barrel). **Stock:** Select American Claro walnut with high-gloss epoxy finish, rosewood grip and forend caps; 22 lpi checkering. Synthetic also available. **Sights:** None furnished; drilled and tapped for scope mounting. **Features:** Short 60" bolt throw; detachable box magazine; six-lug bolt; quick-change barrel; tapered bore; adjustable two-stage trigger; firing pin cocking indicator. Introduced 1994. Imported from Germany by Sigarms, Inc.
Price: Standard calibers, right-hand **$1,035.00**
Price: Magnum calibers, right-hand **$1,106.00**
Price: Standard calibers, synthetic stock **$985.00**
Price: Magnum calibers, synthetic stock **$1,056.00**

SAVAGE MODEL 10GXP3, 110GXP3 PACKAGE GUNS
Caliber: 223 Rem., 22-250 Rem., 243 Win., 7mm-08 Rem., 308 Win., 300 WSM (10GXP3). 25-06 Rem., 270 Win., 30-06 Spfld., 7mm Rem. Mag., 300 Win. Mag., 300 Rem. Ultra Mag. (110GXP3). **Barrel:** 22" 24", 26". **Weight:** 7.5 lbs. average. **Length:** 43"-47". **Stock:** Walnut Monte Carlo with checkering. **Sights:** 3-9X40mm scope, mounted & bore sighted. **Features:** Blued, free floating and button rifled, internal box magazines, swivel studs, leather sling. Left-hand available.
Price: **$495.00**

SAVAGE MODEL 11FXP3, 111FXP3, 111FCXP3, 11FYXP3 (Youth) PACKAGE GUNS
Caliber: 223 Rem., 22-250 Rem., 243 Win., 308 Win., 300 WSM (11FXP3). 270 Win., 30-06 Spfld., 25-06 Rem., 7mm Rem. Mag., 300 Win. Mag., 338 Win. Mag., 300 Rem. Ultra Mag. (11FCXPE & 111FXP3). **Barrel:** 22"-26". **Weight:** 6.5 lbs. **Length:** 41"-47". **Stock:** Synthetic checkering, dual pillar bed. **Sights:** 3-9X40mm scope, mounted & bore sighted. **Features:** Blued, free floating and button rifled, Top loading internal box mag (except 111FXCP3 has detachable box mag.). Nylon sling and swivel studs. Some left-hand available.
Price: Model 11FXP3 . . . . **$505.00**
Price: Model 111FCXP3 . . . . **$425.00**
Price: Model 11FYXP3, 243 Win., 12.5" pull (youth) **$471.00**

Savage 11FYXP3

Savage 16FXP3

Savage 10FM Sierra Ultra Light

Savage 10FCM Scout Ultra Light

Savage Model 10FP

SAVAGE MODEL 16FXP3, 116FXP3 SS ACTION PACKAGE GUNS
Caliber: 223 Rem., 243 Win., 308 Win., 300 WSM, 270 Win., 30-06 Spfld., 7mm Rem. Mag., 300 Win. Mag., 338 Win. Mag., 375 H&H, 7mm S&W, 7mm Rem. Ultra Mag., 300 Rem. Ultra Mag. **Barrel:** 22", 24", 26". **Weight:** 6.75 lbs. average. **Length:** 41"-46". **Stock:** Synthetic checkering, dual pillar bed. **Sights:** 3-9X40mm scope, mounted & bore sighted. **Features:** Free floating and button rifled. Internal box mag., nylon sling and swivel studs.
Price: **$556.00**

SAVAGE MODEL 10FM SIERRA ULTRA LIGHT RIFLE
Caliber: 223, 243, 308. **Barrel:** 20". **Weight:** 6 lbs. **Length:** 41-1/2". **Stock:** "Dual Pillar" bedding in black synthetic stock with silver medallion in grip-cap. **Sights:** None furnished; drilled and tapped for scope mounting. **Features:** True short action. Comes with sling and quick-detachable swivels. Introduced 1998. Made in U.S.A. by Savage Arms, Inc.
Price: **$495.00**

SAVAGE MODEL 10FCM SCOUT ULTRA LIGHT RIFLE
Caliber: 7mm-08 Rem., 308 Win. **Barrel:** 20", 4-shot. **Weight:** 6.25 lbs. **Length:** 39.75" overall. **Stock:** Synthetic checkering, dual pillar bed. **Sights:** Ghost ring rear, gold bead front. **Features:** Blued, detachable box magazine, Savage shooting sling/carry strap. Quick detach swivels.
Price: **$581.00**

SAVAGE MODEL 10/110FP LONG RANGE RIFLE
Caliber: 223, 25-06, 308, 30-06, 300 Win. Mag., 7mm Rem. Mag., 4-shot magazine. **Barrel:** 24", heavy; recessed target muzzle. **Weight:** 8-1/2 lbs. **Length:** 45.5" overall. **Stock:** Black graphite/fiberglass composition; positive checkering. **Sights:** None furnished. Receiver drilled and tapped for scope mounting. **Features:** Pillar-bedded stock. Black matte finish on all metal parts. Double swivel studs on the forend for sling and/or bipod mount. Right or left-hand. Introduced 1990. From Savage Arms, Inc.
Price: Right- or left-hand **$558**

Savage Model 10FP Tactical Rifle
Similar to the Model 110FP except has true short action, chambered for 223, 308; black synthetic stock with "Dual Pillar" bedding. Introduced 1998. Made in U.S.A. by Savage Arms, Inc.
Price: **$558.00**
Price: Model 10FLP (left-hand) **$558.00**
Price: Model 10FP-LE1 (20"), 10FPLE2 (26") **$566.00**
Price: Model 10FPXP-LE w/Burris 3.5-10X50 scope,
Harris bipod package **$1,632.00**

Savage Model 10FP-LE1A Tactical Rifle
Similar to the Model 110FP except weighs 10.75 lbs. and has overall length of 39.75". Chambered for 223 Rem., 308 Win. Black synthetic Choate™ adjustable stock with accessory rail and swivel studs.
Price: **$684.00**

CENTERFIRE RIFLES — BOLT ACTION

Savage Model 10FPLE1

Savage Model 10FPXP-LE

Savage Model 111F

Savage Hunter 111G

Savage Model 11F

Savage Hunter 11G

SAVAGE MODEL 111 CLASSIC HUNTER RIFLES
Caliber: 25-06 Rem., 270 Win., 30-06 Spfld., 7mm Rem. Mag, 300 Win. Mag., 7mm RUM, 300 RUM. **Barrel:** 22", 24", 26" (magnum calibers). **Weight:** 6.5 to 7.5 lbs. **Length:** 42.75" to 47.25". **Stock:** Walnut-finished hardwood (M111G, GC); graphite/fiberglass filled composite. **Sights:** Ramp front, open fully adjustable rear; drilled and tapped for scope mounting. **Features:** Three-position top tang safety, double front locking lugs, free-floated button-rifled barrel. Comes with trigger lock, target, ear puffs. Introduced 1994. Made in U.S.A. by Savage Arms, Inc.
Price: Model 111F (270 Win., 30-06 Spfld., 7mm Rem. Mag., 300 win. Mag.) **$411.00**
Price: Model 111F (25-06 Rem., 338 Win. Mag., 7mm Rem. Ultra Mag, 300 Rem. Ultra Mag.) **$461.00**

Price: Model 111G
(wood stock, top-loading magazine, right- or left-hand) **$436.00**
Price: Model 111GNS (wood stock,
top-loading magazine, no sights, right-hand only) **$428.00**

Savage Model 11 Classic Hunter Rifles, Short Action
Similar to the Model 111F except has true short action, chambered for 22-250, Rem., 243 Win., 7mm-08 Rem., 308 Win.; black synthetic stock with "Dual Pillar" bedding, positive checkering. Introduced 1998. Made in U.S.A. by Savage Arms, Inc.
Price: Model 11F **$461.00**
Price: Model 11FL (left-hand)............................ **$461.00**
Price: Model 11FNS (right-hand, no sights) **$453.00**
Price: Model 11G (wood stock) **$436.00**
Price: Model 11GL (as above, left-hand) **$436.00**
Price: Model 11FC (right hand, open sights) **$487.00**

Savage Model 10GY

Savage Model 114U

Savage Model 12FV

Savage Model 12VSS Varminter

Savage Model 10GY

Similar to the Model 111G except weighs 6.3 lbs., is 42-1/2" overall, and the stock is scaled for ladies, small-framed adults and youths. Chambered for 223, 243, 308. Ramp front sight, open adjustable rear; drilled and tapped for scope mounts. Made in U.S.A. by Savage Arms, Inc.

Price: Model 10GY (short action, calibers 223, 243, 308) **$436.00**

SAVAGE MODEL 114U ULTRA RIFLE

Caliber: 270 Win., 30-06 Spfld., 7mm Rem. Mag., 7mm STW, 300 Win. Mag. **Barrel:** 22"-24". **Weight:** 7-7.5 lbs. **Length:** 43.25"-45.25" overall. **Stock:** Ultra high gloss American walnut with black tip and custom cut checkering. **Sights:** None furnished; drilled and tapped for scope mounting. **Features:** High-luster blued barrel action, internal box magazine.

Price: **$552.00**

SAVAGE MODEL 112 LONG RANGE RIFLES

Caliber: 22-250, 223, 5-shot magazine. **Barrel:** 26" heavy. **Weight:** 8.8 lbs. **Length:** 47.5" overall. **Stock:** Black graphite/fiberglass filled composite with positive checkering. **Sights:** None furnished; drilled and tapped for scope mounting. **Features:** Pillar-bedded stock. Blued barrel with recessed target-style muzzle. Double front swivel studs for attaching bipod. Introduced 1991. Made in U.S.A. by Savage Arms, Inc.

Price: Model 112FVSS (cals. 223, 22-250, 25-06, 7mm Rem. Mag., 300 Win. Mag., stainless barrel, bolt handle, trigger guard), right- or left-hand **$626.00**

Price: Model 112FVSS-S (as above, single shot) **$675.00**

Price: Model 112BVSS (heavy-prone laminated stock with high comb, Wundhammer swell, fluted stainless barrel, bolt handle, trigger guard) **$675.00**

Price: Model 112BVSS-S (as above, single shot) **$675.00**

Savage Model 12 Long Range Rifles

Similar to the Model 112 Long Range except with true short action, chambered for 223, 22-250, 308. Models 12FV, 12FVSS have black synthetic stocks with "Dual Pillar" bedding, positive checkering, swivel studs; model 12BVSS has brown laminated stock with beavertail forend, fluted stainless barrel. Introduced 1998. Made in U.S.A. by Savage Arms, Inc.

Price: Model 12FV (223, 22-250, 243 Win., 308 Win., blue) **$515.00**

Price: Model 12FVSS (blue action, fluted stainless barrel) **$626.00**

Price: Model 12FLVSS (as above, left-hand) **$626.00**

Price: Model 12FVSS-S (blue action, fluted stainless barrel, single shot) **$934.00**

Price: Model 12BVSS (laminated stock) **$675.00**

Price: Model 12BVSS-S (as above, single shot) **$675.00**

Price: Model 12BVSS-XP (hard case, Burris 6-18X37) **$1,100.00**

Savage Model 12VSS Varminter Rifle

Similar to other Model 12s except blue/stainless steel action, fluted stainless barrel, Choate full pistol-grip, adjustable synthetic stock, Sharp Shooter trigger. Overall length 47-1/2 inches, weighs appx. 15 lbs. No sights; drilled and tapped for scope mounts. Chambered in 223, 22-250, 308 Win. Made in U.S.A. by Savage Arms Inc.

Price: **$934.00**

SAVAGE MODEL 116SE SAFARI EXPRESS RIFLE

Caliber: 458 Win. Mag. **Barrel:** 24". **Weight:** 8.5 lbs. **Length:** 45.5" overall. **Stock:** Classic-style select walnut with ebony forend tip, deluxe cut checkering. Two cross bolts; internally vented recoil pad. **Sights:** Bead on ramp front, three-leaf express rear. **Features:** Controlled-round feed design; adjustable muzzle brake; one-piece barrel band stud. Satin-finished stainless steel barreled action. Introduced 1994. Made in U.S.A. by Savage Arms, Inc.

Price: **$1,013.00**

RIFLES

Savage Model 116SE Safari Express

Savage Model 116SE Safari Express

Savage Model 16FSS

Savage Model 116FSAK

Sigarms SHR 970

Steyr Mannlicher SBS

SAVAGE MODEL 116 WEATHER WARRIORS

Caliber: 375 H&H, 300 Rem. Ultra Mag., 308 Win., 300 Rem. Ultra Mag., 300 WSM, 7mm Rem. Ultra Mag., 7mm Rem. Short Ultra Mag., 7mm S&W, 7mm-08 Rem. **Barrel:** 22", 24" for 7mm Rem. Mag., 300 Win. Mag., 338 Win. Mag. (M116FSS only). **Weight:** 6.25 to 6.5 lbs. **Length:** 41"-47". **Stock:** Graphite/fiberglass filled composite. **Sights:** None furnished; drilled and tapped for scope mounting. **Features:** Stainless steel with matte finish; free-floated barrel; quick-detachable swivel studs; laser-etched bolt; scope bases and rings. Left-hand models available in all models, calibers at same price. Model 116FSS introduced 1991; 116FSAK introduced 1994. Made in U.S.A. by Savage Arms, Inc.
Price: Model 116FSS (top-loading magazine) **$520.00**
Price: Model 116FSAK (top-loading magazine, Savage Adjustable Muzzle Brake system). **$601.00**
Price: Model 16BSS (brown laminate, 24") **$668.00**
Price: Model 116BSS (brown laminate, 26") **$668.00**

Savage Model 16FSS Rifle

Similar to Model 116FSS except true short action, chambered for 223, 243, 22" free-floated barrel; black graphite/fiberglass stock with "Dual

Pillar" bedding. Also left-hand. Introduced 1998. Made in U.S.A. by Savage Arms, Inc.
Price: **$520.00**

SIGARMS SHR 970 SYNTHETIC RIFLE

Caliber: 270, 30-06. **Barrel:** 22". **Weight:** 7.2 lbs. **Length:** 41.9" overall. **Stock:** Textured black fiberglass or walnut. **Sights:** None furnished; drilled and tapped for scope mounting. **Features:** Quick takedown; interchangeable barrels; removable box magazine; cocking indicator; three-position safety. Introduced 1998. Imported by Sigarms, Inc.
Price: Synthetic stock. **$499.00**
Price: Walnut stock. **$550.00**

STEYR CLASSIC MANNLICHER SBS RIFLE

Caliber: 243, 25-06, 308, 6.5x55, 6.5x57, 270, 7x64 Brenneke, 7mm-08, 7.5x55, 30-06, 9.3x62, 6.5x68, 7mm Rem. Mag., 300 Win. Mag., 8x685, 4-shot magazine. **Barrel:** 23.6" standard; 26" magnum; 20" full stock standard calibers. **Weight:** 7 lbs. **Length:** 40.1" overall. **Stock:** Hand-checkered fancy European oiled walnut with standard forend. **Sights:** Ramp front adjustable for elevation, V-notch rear adjustable for windage. **Features:** Single adjustable trigger; 3-position roller safety with "safe-bolt" setting; drilled and tapped for Steyr factory scope mounts. Introduced 1997. Imported from Austria by GSI, Inc.
Price: Full-stock, standard calibers **$1,749.00**

Steyr SBS Forester

Steyr SBS Prohunter

Steyr Scout Rifle

Tikka Whitetail Hunter

STEYR SBS FORESTER RIFLE

Caliber: 243, 25-06, 270, 7mm-08, 308 Win., 30-06, 7mm Rem. Mag., 300 Win. Mag. Detachable 4-shot magazine. **Barrel:** 23.6", standard calibers; 25.6", magnum calibers. **Weight:** 7.5 lbs. **Length:** 44.5" overall (23.6" barrel). **Stock:** Oil-finished American walnut with Monte Carlo cheekpiece. Pachmayr 1" swivels. **Sights:** None furnished. Drilled and tapped for Browning A-Bolt mounts. **Features:** Steyr Safe Bolt systems, three-position ambidextrous roller tang safety, for Safe, Loading Fire. Matte finish on barrel and receiver; adjustable trigger. Rotary cold-hammer forged barrel. Introduced 1997. Imported by GSI, Inc.

Price: Standard calibers $799.00
Price: Magnum calibers $829.00

Steyr SBS Prohunter Rifle

Similar to the SBS Forester except has ABS synthetic stock with adjustable butt spacers, straight comb without cheekpiece, palm swell, Pachmayr 1" swivels. Special 10-round magazine conversion kit available. Introduced 1997. Imported by GSI.

Price Standard calibers $769.00
Price Magnum calibers $799.00

STEYR SCOUT BOLT-ACTION RIFLE

Caliber: 308 Win., 5-shot magazine. **Barrel:** 19", fluted. **Weight:** NA. **Length:** NA. **Stock:** Gray Zytel. **Sights:** Pop-up front & rear, Leupold M8 2.5x28 IER scope on Picatinny optic rail with Steyr mounts. **Features:** luggage case, scout sling, two stock spacers, two magazines. Introduced 1998. From GSI.

Price: From $1,969.00

STEYR SSG BOLT-ACTION RIFLE

Caliber: 308 Win., detachable 5-shot rotary magazine. **Barrel:** 26" **Weight:** 8.5 lbs. **Length:** 44.5" overall. **Stock:** Black ABS Cycolac with spacers for length of pull adjustment. **Sights:** Hooded ramp front adjustable for elevation, V-notch rear adjustable for windage. **Features:** Sliding safety; NATO rail for bipod; 1" swivels; Parkerized finish; single or double-set triggers. Imported from Austria by GSI, Inc.

Price: SSG-PI, iron sights **$1,699.00**
Price: SSG-PII, heavy barrel, no sights **$1,699.00**
Price: SSG-PIIK, 20" heavy barrel, no sights **$1,699.00**
Price: SSG-PIV, 16.75" threaded heavy barrel with flash hider . **$2,659.00**

TIKKA WHITETAIL HUNTER LEFT-HAND BOLT-ACTION RIFLE

Caliber: 22-250, 223, 243, 7mm-08, 25-06, 270, 308, 30-06, 7mm Rem. Mag., 300 Win. Mag., 338 Win. Mag. **Barrel:** 22-1/2" (std. cals.), 24-1/2" (magnum cals.). **Weight:** 7-1/8 lbs. **Length:** 43" overall (std. cals.). **Stock:** European walnut with Monte Carlo comb, rubber butt pad, checkered grip and forend. **Sights:** None furnished. **Features:** Detachable four-shot magazine (standard calibers), three-shot in magnums. Receiver dovetailed for scope mounting. Reintroduced 1996. Imported from Finland by Beretta USA.

Price: Left-hand $710.00

CONSULT

SHOOTER'S MARKETPLACE

Page 233, This Issue

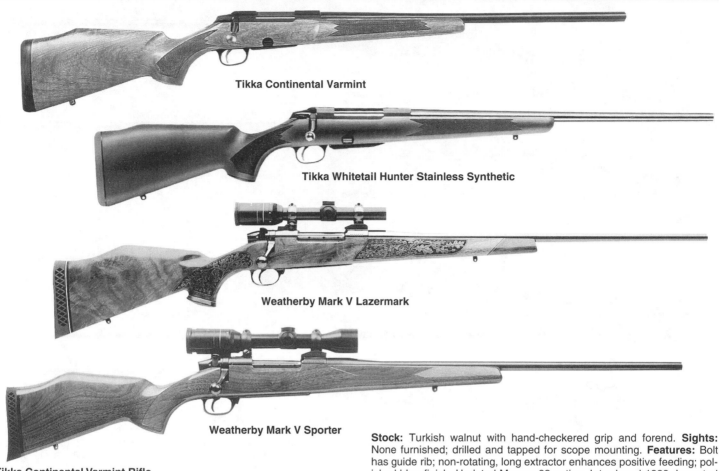

Tikka Continental Varmint

Tikka Whitetail Hunter Stainless Synthetic

Weatherby Mark V Lazermark

Weatherby Mark V Sporter

Tikka Continental Varmint Rifle

Similar to the standard Tikka rifle except has 26" heavy barrel, extra-wide forend. Chambered for 17 Rem., 22-250, 223, 308. Reintroduced 1996. Made in Finland by Sako. Imported by Beretta USA.

Price: **$720.00**

Tikka Continental Long Range Hunting Rifle

Similar to the Whitetail Hunter except has 26" heavy barrel. Available in 25-06, 270 Win., 7mm Rem. Mag., 300 Win. Mag. Introduced 1996. Imported from Finland by Beretta USA.

Price: 25-06, 270 Win. **$720.00**
Price: 7mm Rem. Mag., 300 Win. Mag. **$750.00**

Tikka Whitetail Hunter Stainless Synthetic

Similar to the Whitetail Hunter except all metal is of stainless steel, and it has a black synthetic stock. Available in 22-250, 223, 243, 7mm-08, 25-06, 270, 308, 30-06, 7mm Rem. Mag., 300 Win. Mag., 338 Win. Mag. Introduced 1997. Imported from Finland by Beretta USA.

Price: Standard calibers **$775.00**
Price: Magnum calibers **$745.00**

VEKTOR BUSHVELD BOLT-ACTION RIFLE

Caliber: 243, 308, 7x57, 7x64 Brenneke, 270 Win., 30-06, 300 Win. Mag., 300 H&H, 9.3x62. **Barrel:** 22"-26". **Weight:** NA. **Length:** NA. **Stock:** Turkish walnut with wrap-around hand checkering. **Sights:** Blade on ramp front, fixed standing leaf rear. **Features:** Combines the best features of the Mauser 98 and Winchester 70 actions. Controlled-round feed; Mauser-type extractor; no cut-away through the bolt locking lug; M70-type three-position safety; Timney-type adjustable trigger. Introduced 1999. Imported from South Africa by Vektor USA.

Price: . . . . **$1,595.00 to $1,695.00**

VEKTOR MODEL 98 BOLT-ACTION RIFLE

Caliber: 243, 308, 7x57, 7x64 Brenneke, 270 Win., 30-06, 300 Win. Mag., 300 H&H, 375 H&H, 9.3x62. **Barrel:** 22"-26". **Weight:** NA. **Length:** NA.

Stock: Turkish walnut with hand-checkered grip and forend. **Sights:** None furnished; drilled and tapped for scope mounting. **Features:** Bolt has guide rib; non-rotating, long extractor enhances positive feeding; polished blue finish. Updated Mauser 98 action. Introduced 1999. Imported from South Africa by Vektor USA.

Price: . . . . **$1,149.00 to $1,249.00**

WEATHERBY MARK V DELUXE BOLT-ACTION RIFLE

Caliber: All Weatherby calibers plus 22-250, 243, 25-06, 270 Win., 280 Rem., 7mm-08, 30-06, 308 Win. **Barrel:** 24" barrel on standard calibers. **Weight:** 8-1/2 to 10-1/2 lbs. **Length:** 46-5/8" to 46-3/4" overall. **Stock:** Walnut, Monte Carlo with cheekpiece; high luster finish; checkered pistol grip and forend; recoil pad. **Sights:** None furnished. **Features:** Cocking indicator; adjustable trigger; hinged floorplate, thumb safety; quick detachable sling swivels. Made in U.S.A. From Weatherby.

Price: 257, 270, 7mm. 300, 340 Wea. Mags., 26" barrel **$1,767.00**
Price: 416 Wea. Mag. with Accubrake, 28" barrel **$2,079.00**
Price: 460 Wea. Mag. with Accubrake, 28" barrel **$2,443.00**
Price: 24" barrel **$1,715.00**

Weatherby Mark V Lazermark Rifle

Same as Mark V Deluxe except stock has extensive oak leaf pattern laser carving on pistol grip and forend. Introduced 1981.

Price: 257, 270, 7mm Wea. Mag., 300, 340, 26" **$1,923.00**
Price: 378 Wea. Mag., 28" **$2,266.00**
Price: 416 Wea. Mag., 28", Accubrake. **$2,266.00**
Price: 460 Wea. Mag., 28", Accubrake. **$2,661.00**

Weatherby Mark V Sporter Rifle

Same as the Mark V Deluxe without the embellishments. Metal has low-luster blue, stock is Claro walnut with matte finish, Monte Carlo comb, recoil pad. Introduced 1993. From Weatherby.

Price: 22-250, 243, 240 Wea. Mag., 25-06, 7mm-08, 270 WCF, 280, 30-06, 308; 24" **$1,091.00**
Price: 257 Wea., 270, 7 mm Wea., 7mm Rem., 300 Wea., 300 Win., 340 Wea., 338 Win. Mag., 26" barrel for Wea. Calibers; 24" for non-Wea. Calibers. **$1,143.00**

Weatherby Mark V Euromark

Weatherby Mark V Stainless

Weatherby Mark V Synthetic

Weatherby Mark V Accumark

Weatherby Mark V Euromark Rifle

Similar to the Mark V Deluxe except has raised-comb Monte Carlo stock with hand-rubbed oil finish, fine-line hand-cut checkering, ebony grip and forend tips. All metal has low-luster blue. Right-hand only. Uses Mark V action. Introduced 1995. Made in U.S.A. From Weatherby.

Price: 257, 270, 7mm, 300, 340 Wea. Mags., 26" barrel **$1,819.00**
Price: 7mm Rem. Mag., 300 Win. Mag., 338 Win. Mag.,
375 H&H, 24" barrel **$1,819.00**
Price: 378 Wea. Mag., 416 Wea. Mag., 28" barrel **$2,131.00**

Weatherby Mark V Stainless Rifle

Similar to the Mark V Deluxe except made of 410-series stainless steel. Also available in 30-378 Wea. Mag. Has lightweight injection-moulded synthetic stock with raised Monte Carlo comb, checkered grip and forend, custom floorplate release. Right-hand only. Introduced 1995. Made in U.S.A. From Weatherby.

Price: 22-250 Rem., 243 Win., 240 Wby. Mag., 25-06 Rem., 270 Win.,
280 Rem., 7mm-08 Rem., 30-06 Spfld., 308 Win., 24" barrel . **$1,018.00**
Price: 257, 270, 7mm, 300, 340 Wby. Mag., 26" barrel **$1,070.00**
Price: 7mm Rem. Mag., 300 Win. Mag., 338 Win. Mag.,
375 H&H Mag., 24" barrel. **$1,070.00**

Weatherby Mark V Eurosport Rifle

Similar to the Mark V Deluxe except has raised-comb Monte Carlo stock with hand-rubbed satin oil finish, low-luster blue metal. No gripcap or forend tip. Right-hand only. Introduced 1995. Made in U.S.A. From Weatherby.

Price: 257, 270, 7mm, 300, 340 Wea. Mags., 26" barrel **$1,143.00**
Price: 7mm Rem. Mag., 300, 338 Win. Mags., 24" barrel **$1,143.00**
Price: 375 H&H, 24" barrel **$1,143.00**

Weatherby Mark V Synthetic

Similar to the Mark V Stainless except made of matte finished blued steel. Injection moulded synthetic stock. Weighs 6-1/2 lbs., 24" barrel. Available in 22-250, 240 Wea. Mag., 243, 25-06, 270, 7mm-08, 280, 30-06, 308. Introduced 1997. Made in U.S.A. From Weatherby.

Price: **$923.00**
Price: 257, 270, 7mm, 300, 340 Wea. Mags., 26" barrel **$975.00**
Price: 7mm STW, 7mm Rem. Mag., 300, 338 Win. Mags **$975.00**
Price: 375 H&H, 24" barrel **$975.00**
Price: 30-378 Wea. Mag., 338-378 Wea 28" barrel.. . . . . **$1,151.00**

WEATHERBY MARK V ACCUMARK RIFLE

Caliber: 257, 270, 7mm, 300, 340 Wea. Mags., 338-378 Wea. Mag., 30-378 Wea. Mag., 7mm STW, 7mm Rem. Mag., 300 Win. Mag. **Barrel:** 26", 28". **Weight:** 8-1/2 lbs. **Length:** 46-5/8" overall. **Stock:** Bell & Carlson with full length aluminum bedding block. **Sights:** None furnished. Drilled and tapped for scope mounting. **Features:** Uses Mark V action with heavy-contour stainless barrel with black oxidized flutes, muzzle diameter of .705". Introduced 1996. Made in U.S.A. From Weatherby.

Price: 26" **$1,507.00**
Price: 30-378 Wea. Mag., 338-378 Wea. Mag., 28",
Accubrake. **$1,724.00**
Price: 223, 22-250, 243, 240 Wea. Mag., 25-06, 270,
280 Rem., 7mm-08, 30-06, 308; 24" **$1,455.00**
Price: Accumark Left-Hand 257, 270, 7mm, 300, 340 Wea.
Mag., 7mm Rem. Mag., 7mm STW, 300 Win. Mag. **$1,559.00**
Price: Accumark Left-Hand 30-378, 333-378 Wea. Mags. **$1,788.00**

Weatherby Mark V Accumark Ultra Lightweight Rifles

Similar to the Mark V Accumark except weighs 5-3/4 lbs, 6-3/4 lbs. in Mag. calibers.; 24", 26" fluted barrel with recessed target crown; hand-laminated stock with CNC-machined aluminum bedding plate and faint gray "spider web" finish. Available in 257, 270, 7mm, 300 Wea. Mags., (26"); 243, 240 Wea. Mag., 25-06, 270 Win., 280 Rem., 7mm-08, 7mm Rem. Mag., 30-06, 338-06 A-Square, 308, 300 Win. Mag. (24"). Introduced 1998. Made in U.S.A. by Weatherby.

Price: . . . . **$1,459.00 to $1,517.00**
Price: Left-hand models **$1,559.00**

Weatherby Mark V SVR

Weatherby Mark V Fibermark

Weatherby Mark V Dangerous Game Rifle

Wilderness Explorer

Weatherby Mark V Special Varmint Rifle (SVR)

A new entrant in the Mark V series similar to the Super VarmintMaster and Accumark with 22", #3 contour chrome moly 4140 steel Krieger Criterion botton-rifled barrel with 1-degree target crown and hand-laminated composite stock. Available in .223 Rem. (5+1 magazine capacity) and .22-250 Rem. (4+1 magazine capacity) in right-hand models only.
Price: **$999.00**

Weatherby Mark V SVM/SPM Rifles

Similar to the Mark V Accumark except has 26" fluted (SVM) or 24" fluted Krieger barrel, spiderweb-pattern tan laminated synthetic stock. SVM has a fully adjustable trigger. Chambered for 223, 22-250, 220 Swift (SVM only), 243, 7mm-08 and 308. Made in U.S.A. by Weatherby.
Price: SVM (Super VarmintMaster), repeater or single-shot . . . **$1,517.00**
New! **Price:** SPM (Super PredatorMaster) **$1,459.00**

Weatherby Mark V Fibermark Rifles

Similar to other Mark V models except has black Kevlar® and fiberglass composite stock and bead-blast blue or stainless finish. Chambered for 19 standard and magnum calibers. Introduced 1983; reintroduced 2001. Made in U.S.A. by Weatherby.
Price: Fibermark . . . . **$1,070.00 to $1,347.00**
Price: Fibermark Stainless . . . . **$1,165.00 to $1,390.00**

WEATHERBY MARK V DANGEROUS GAME RIFLE

Caliber: 375 H&H, 375 Wea. Mag., 378 Wea. Mag., 416 Rem. Mag., 416 Wea. Mag., 458 Win. Mag., .458 Lott, 460 Wea. Mag. 300 Win. Mag., 300 Wby., Mag., 338 Win. Mag., 340 Wby. Mag., 24" only **Barrel:** 24" or 26". **Weight:** 8-3/4 to 9-1/2 lbs. **Length:** 44-5/8" to 46-5/8" overall. **Stock:** Kevlar® and fiberglass composite. **Sights:** Barrel-band hooded front with large gold bead, adjustable ramp/shallow "V" rear. **Features:** Designed for dangerous-game hunting. Black oxide matte finish on all metalwork; Pachmayr Decelerator™ recoil pad, short-throw Mark V action. Introduced 2001. Made in U.S.A. by Weatherby.
Price: . . . . **$2,703.00 to $2,935.00**

WEATHERBY MARK V SUPER BIG GAMEMASTER DEER RIFLE

Caliber: 240 Wby. Mag., 25-06 Rem., 270 Win., 280 Rem., 30-06 Spfld., 257 Wby. Mag., 270 Wby. Mag., 7mm Rem., Mag., 7mm Wby. Mag., 338-06 A-Square, 300 Win. Mag., 300 Wby. Mag. **Barrel:** 26", target crown. **Weight:** 5-3/4 lbs., (6-3/4 lbs. Magnum). **Stock:** Raised comb Monte Carlo composite. **Features:** Fluted barrel, aluminum bedding block, Pachmayr decelerator, 54-degree bolt lift, adj. trigger.
Price: **$1,459.00**
Price: Magnum **$1,517.00**

WEATHERBY MARK V ROYAL CUSTOM RIFLE

Caliber: 257, 270, 7mm, 300, 340 all Wby. Mags. Other calibers available upon request. **Barrel:** 26". **Stock:** Monte Carlo hand-checkered claro walnut with high gloss finish. **Features:** Bolt and follower are damascened with checkered knob. Engraved receiver, bolt sleeve and floorplate sport scroll pattern. Animal images on floorplate optional. High gloss blue, 24-karat gold and nickel-plating. Made in U.S.A. From Weatherby.
Price: **$5,831.00**

WEATHERBY THREAT RESPONSE RIFLES (TRR) SERIES

Caliber: TRR 223 Rem., 300 Win. TRR Magnum and Magnum Custom 300 Win. Mag., 300 Wby. Mag., 30-378 Wby. Mag., 328-378 Wby. Mag. **Barrel:** 22", 26", target crown. **Stock:** Hand-laminated composite. TTR & TRR Magnum have raised comb Monte Carlo style. TRR Magnum Custom adjustable ergonomic stock. **Features:** Adjustable trigger, aluminum bedding block, beavertail forearms dual tapered, flat-bottomed. "Rocker Arm" lockdown scope mounting. 54 degree bolt. Pachmayr decelerator pad. Made in U.S.A.
Price: TRR Magnum Custom 300 . . . . **$2,699.00**
Price: 30-378, 338-378 with accubrake **$2,861.00**

WILDERNESS EXPLORER MULTI-CALIBER CARBINE

Caliber: 22 Hornet, 218 Bee, 44 Magnum, 50 A.E. (interchangeable). **Barrel:** 18", match grade. **Weight:** 5.5 lbs **Length:** 38-1/2" overall. **Stock:** Synthetic or wood. **Sights:** None furnished; comes with Weaver-style mount on barrel. **Features:** Quick-change barrel and bolt face for caliber switch. Removable box magazine; adjustable trigger with side safety; detachable swivel studs. Introduced 1997. Made in U.S.A. by Phillips & Rogers, Inc.
Price: **$995.00**

Winchester Model 70 Classic

Winchester Model 70 Classic Stainless

Winchester Model 70 Classic Featherweight

Winchester Model 70 Classic Compact

Winchester Model 70 Black Shadow

WINCHESTER MODEL 70 CLASSIC SPORTER LT

Caliber: 25-06, 270 Win., 30-06, 7mm STW, 7mm Rem. Mag., 300 Win. Mag., 338 Win. Mag., 3-shot magazine; 5-shot for 25-06, 270 Win., 30-06. **Barrel:** 24", 26" for magnums. **Weight:** 7-3/4 to 8 lbs. **Length:** 46-3/4" overall (26" bbl.). **Stock:** American walnut with cut checkering and satin finish. Classic style with straight comb. **Sights:** None furnished. Drilled and tapped for scope mounting. **Features:** Uses pre-64-type action with controlled round feeding. Three-position safety, stainless steel magazine follower; rubber butt pad; epoxy bedded receiver recoil lug. From U.S. Repeating Arms Co.

Price: 25-06, 270, 30-06 . . . . $727.00
Price: Other calibers $756.00
Price: Left-hand, 270 or 30-06 . . . . $762.00
Price: Left-hand, 7mm Rem. Mag or 300 Win. Mag. $793.00

Winchester Model 70 Classic Stainless Rifle

Same as Model 70 Classic Sporter except stainless steel barrel and pre-64-style action with controlled round feeding and matte gray finish, black composite stock impregnated with fiberglass and graphite, contoured rubber recoil pad. No sights (except 375 H&H). Available in 270 Win., 30-06, 7mm STW, 7mm Rem. Mag., 300 Win. Mag., 300 Ultra Mag., 338 Win. Mag., 375 H&H Mag. (24" barrel), 3- or 5-shot magazine. Weighs 7-1/2 lbs. Introduced 1994.

Price: 270, 30-06 . . . . $800.00
Price: 375 H&H Mag., with sights $924.00
Price: Other calibers $829.00

Winchester Model 70 Classic Featherweight

Same as Model 70 Classic except action bedded in standard-grade walnut stock. Available in 22-250, 243, 6.5x55, 308, 7mm-08, 270 Win., 30-06. Drilled and tapped for scope mounts. Weighs 7 lbs. Introduced 1992.

Price: $726.00

Winchester Model 70 Classic Compact

Similar to Classic Featherweight except scaled down for smaller shooters. 20" barrel, 12-1/2" length of pull. Pre-'64-type action. Available in 243, 308 or 7mm-08. Introduced 1998. Made in U.S.A. by U. S. Repeating Arms Co.

Price: $740.00

Winchester Model 70 Black Shadow

Similar to Model 94 Ranger except black composite stock, matte blue barrel and action. Push-feed bolt design; hinged floorplate. Available in 270, 30-06, 7mm Rem. Mag., 300 Win. Mag. Made in U.S.A. by U.S. Repeating Arms Co.

Price: 270, 30-06 . . . . $523.00
Price: 7mm Rem. Mag., 300 Win. Mag. $553.00

Winchester Model 70 Coyote

Winchester Model 70 Stealth

Winchester Model 70 Classic Super Grade

Winchester Model 70 Safari Express

Winchester Model 70 WSM

Winchester Model 70 Coyote

Similar to Model 70 Black Shadow except laminated wood stock, 24" medium-heavy stainless steel barrel Available in223 Rem., 22-250 Rem., 243 Win., or 308 Win.

Price: **$705.00**

WINCHESTER MODEL 70 STEALTH RIFLE

Caliber: 223, 22-250, 308 Win. **Barrel:** 26". **Weight:** 10-3/4 lbs. **Length:** 46" overall. **Stock:** Kevlar/fiberglass/graphite Pillar Plus Accu-Block with full-length aluminum bedding block. **Sights:** None furnished. **Features:** Push-feed bolt design; matte finish. Introduced 1999. Made in U.S.A. by U.S. Repeating Arms Co.

Price: **$785.00**

WINCHESTER MODEL 70 CLASSIC SUPER GRADE

Caliber: 25-06, 270, 30-06, 5-shot magazine; 7mm Rem. Mag., 300 Win. Mag., 338 Win. Mag., 3-shot magazine. **Barrel:** 24", 26" for magnums. **Weight:** 7-3/4 lbs. to 8 lbs. **Length:** 44-1/2" overall (24" bbl.) **Stock:** Walnut with straight comb, sculptured cheekpiece, wrap-around cut checkering, tapered forend, solid rubber butt pad. **Sights:** None furnished; comes with scope bases and rings. **Features:** Controlled round feeding with stainless steel claw extractor, bolt guide rail, three-position safety; all steel bottom metal, hinged floorplate, stainless magazine follower. Introduced 1994. From U.S. Repeating Arms Co.

Price: 25-06, 270, 30-06............................... **$995.00**
Price: Other calibers................................. **$1,024.00**

WINCHESTER MODEL 70 CLASSIC SAFARI EXPRESS

Caliber: 375 H&H Mag., 416 Rem. Mag., 458 Win. Mag., 3-shot magazine. **Barrel:** 24". **Weight:** 8-1/4 to 8-1/2 lbs. **Stock:** American walnut with Monte Carlo cheekpiece. Wrap-around checkering and finish. **Sights:** Hooded ramp front, open rear. **Features:** Controlled round feeding. Two steel cross bolts in stock for added strength. Front sling swivel stud mounted on barrel. Contoured rubber butt pad. From U.S. Repeating Arms Co.

Price: **$1,124.00**
Price: Left-hand, 375 H&H only **$1,163.00**

WINCHESTER MODEL 70 WSM RIFLES

Caliber: 300 WSM, 3-shot magazine. **Barrel:** 24". **Weight:** 7-1/4 to 7-3/4 lbs. **Length:** 44" overall. **Stock:** Checkered walnut, black synthetic or laminated wood. **Sights:** None. **Features:** Model 70 designed for the new 300 Winchester Short Magnum cartridge. Short-action receiver, three-position safety, knurled bolt handle. Introduced 2001. From U.S. Repeating Arms Co.

Price: Classic Featherweight WSM (checkered walnut stock and forearm)....................................... **$769.00**
Price: Classic Stainless WSM (black syn. stock, stainless steel bbl.).................................. **$829.00**
Price: Classic Laminated WSM (laminated wood stock) **$793.00**

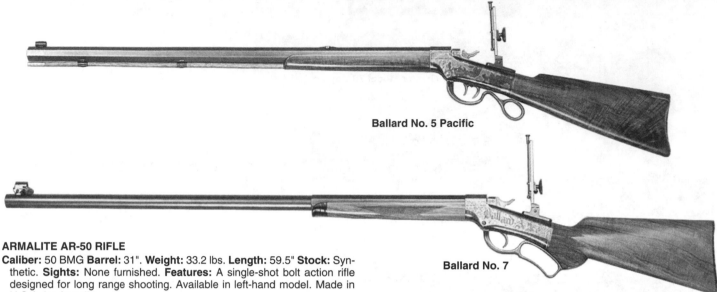

Ballard No. 5 Pacific

Ballard No. 7

ARMALITE AR-50 RIFLE

Caliber: 50 BMG **Barrel:** 31". **Weight:** 33.2 lbs. **Length:** 59.5" **Stock:** Synthetic. **Sights:** None furnished. **Features:** A single-shot bolt action rifle designed for long range shooting. Available in left-hand model. Made in U.S.A. by Armalite.
Price: **$2,745.00**

ARMSPORT 1866 SHARPS RIFLE, CARBINE

Caliber: 45-70. **Barrel:** 28", round or octagonal. **Weight:** 8.10 lbs. **Length:** 46" overall. **Stock:** Walnut. **Sights:** Blade front, folding adjustable rear. Tang sight set optionally available. **Features:** Replica of the 1866 Sharps. Color case-hardened frame, rest blued. Imported by Armsport.
Price: **$865.00**
Price: With octagonal barrel **$900.00**
Price: Carbine, 22" round barrel **$850.00**

BALLARD NO. 1 3/4 FAR WEST RIFLE

Caliber: 22 LR, 32-40, 38-55, 40-65, 40-70, 45-70, 45-110, 50-70, 50-90. **Barrel:** 30" std. or heavyweight. **Weight:** 10-1/2 lbs. (std.) or 11-3/4 lbs. (heavyweight bbl.) **Length:** NA. **Stock:** Walnut. **Sights:** Blade front, Rocky Mountain rear. **Features:** Single or double-set triggers, S-lever or ring-style lever; color case-hardened finish; hand polished and lapped Badger barrel. Made in U.S.A. by Ballard Rifle & Cartridge Co.
Price: **$2,250.00**

BALLARD NO. 4 PERFECTION RIFLE

Caliber: 22 LR, 32-40, 38-55, 40-65, 40-70, 45-70, 45-90, 45-110, 50-70, 50-90. **Barrel:** 30" or 32" octagon, standard or heavyweight. **Weight:** 10-1/2 lbs. (standard) or 11-3/4 lbs. (heavyweight bbl.). **Length:** NA. **Stock:** Smooth walnut. **Sights:** Blade front, Rocky Mountain rear. **Features:** Rifle or shotgun-style buttstock, straight grip action, single or double-set trigger, "S" or right lever, hand polished and lapped Badger barrel. Made in U.S.A. by Ballard Rifle & Cartridge Co.
Price: **$2,250.00**

BALLARD NO. 5 PACIFIC SINGLE-SHOT RIFLE

Caliber: 32-40, 38-55, 40-65, 40-90, 40-70 SS, 45-70 Govt., 45-110 SS, 50-70 Govt., 50-90 SS. **Barrel:** 30", or 32" octagonal. **Weight:** 10-1/2 lbs. **Length:** NA. **Stock:** High-grade walnut; rifle or shotgun style. **Sights:** Blade front, Rocky Mountain rear. **Features:** Standard or heavy barrel; double-set triggers; under-barrel wiping rod; ring lever. Introduced 1999. Made in U.S.A. by Ballard Rifle & Cartridge Co.
Price: **$2,575.00**

BALLARD NO. 7 LONG RANGE RIFLE

Caliber: 32-40, 38-55, 40-65, 40-70 SS, 45-70 Govt., 45-90, 45-110. **Barrel:** 32", 34" half-octagon. **Weight:** 11-3/4 lbs. **Length:** NA. **Stock:** Walnut; checkered pistol grip shotgun butt, ebony forend cap. **Sights:** Globe front. **Features:** Designed for shooting up to 1000 yards. Standard or heavy barrel; single or double-set trigger; hard rubber or steel buttplate. Introduced 1999. Made in U.S.A. by Ballard Rifle & Cartridge Co.
Price: From **$2,475.00**

BALLARD NO. 8 UNION HILL RIFLE

Caliber: 22 LR, 32-40, 38-55, 40-65 Win., 40-70 SS. **Barrel:** 30" half-octagon. **Weight:** About 10-1/2 lbs. **Length:** NA. **Stock:** Walnut; pistol grip butt with cheekpiece. **Sights:** Globe front. **Features:** Designed for 200-yard offhand shooting. Standard or heavy barrel; double-set triggers; full loop lever; hook Schuetzen buttplate. Introduced 1999. Made in U.S.A. by Ballard Rifle & Cartridge Co.
Price: From **$2,500.00**

BALLARD MODEL 1885 HIGH WALL SINGLE SHOT RIFLE

Caliber: 17 Bee, 22 Hornet, 218 Bee, 219 Don Wasp, 219 Zipper, 22 Hi-Power, 225 Win., 25-20 WCF, 25-35 WCF, 25 Krag, 7mmx57R, 30-30, 30-40 Krag, 303 British, 33 WCF, 348 WCF, 35 WCF, 35-30/30, 9.3x74R, 405 WCF, 50-110 WCF, 500 Express, 577 Express. **Barrel:** Lengths to 34". **Weight:** NA. **Length:** NA. **Stock:** Straight-grain American walnut. **Sights:** buckhorn or flat top rear, blade front. **Features:** Faithful copy of original Model 1885 High Wall; parts interchange with original rifles; variety of options available. Introduced 2000. Made in U.S.A. by Ballard Rifle & Cartridge LLC.
Price: From **$2,255.00**
Price: With single set trigger from **$2,355.00**

BARRETT MODEL 99 SINGLE SHOT RIFLE

Caliber: 50 BMG. **Barrel:** 33". **Weight:** 25 lbs. **Length:** 50.4" overall. **Stock:** Anodized aluminum with energy-absorbing recoil pad. **Sights:** None furnished; integral M1913 scope rail. **Features:** Bolt action; detachable bipod; match-grade barrel with high-efficiency muzzle brake. Introduced 1999. Made in U.S.A. by Barrett Firearms.
Price: From **$3,000.00**

BROWN MODEL 97D SINGLE SHOT RIFLE

Caliber: 17 Ackley Hornet through 45-70 Govt. **Barrel:** Up to 26", air gauged match grade. **Weight:** About 5 lbs., 11 oz. **Stock:** Sporter style with pistol grip, cheekpiece and Schnabel forend. **Sights:** None furnished; drilled and tapped for scope mounting. **Features:** Falling block action gives rigid barrel-receiver matting; polished blue/black finish. Hand-fitted action. Many options. Made in U.S.A. by E. Arthur Brown Co. Inc.
Price: From **$699.00**

BROWNING MODEL 1885 HIGH WALL SINGLE SHOT RIFLE

Caliber: 22-250, 30-06, 270, 7mm Rem. Mag., 454 Casull, 45-70. **Barrel:** 28". **Weight:** 8 lbs., 12 oz. **Length:** 43-1/2" overall. **Stock:** Walnut with straight grip, Schnabel forend. **Sights:** None furnished; drilled and tapped for scope mounting. **Features:** Replica of J.M. Browning's high-wall falling block rifle. Octagon barrel with recessed muzzle. Imported from Japan by Browning. Introduced 1985.
Price: **$1,027.00**

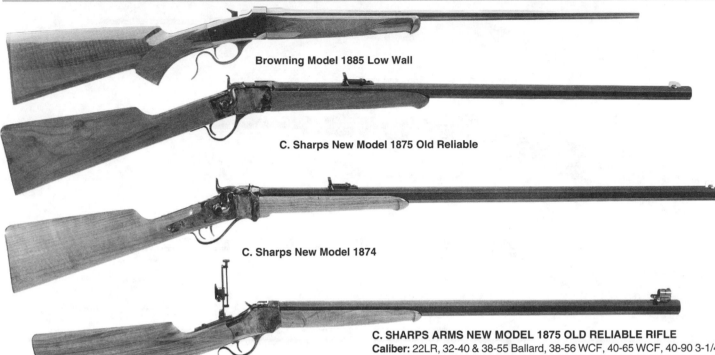

Browning Model 1885 Low Wall

C. Sharps New Model 1875 Old Reliable

C. Sharps New Model 1874

C. Sharps New Model 1885

Browning Model 1885 BPCR Rifle

Similar to the 1885 High Wall rifle except the ejector system and shell deflector have been removed; chambered only for 40-65 and 45-70; color case-hardened full-tang receiver, lever, buttplate and gripcap; matte blue 30" part octagon, part round barrel. The Vernier tang sight has indexed elevation, is screw adjustable windage, and has three peep diameters. The hooded front sight has a built-in spirit level and comes with sight interchangeable inserts. Adjustable trigger. Overall length 46-1/8", weighs about 11 lbs. Introduced 1996. Imported from Japan by Browning.
Price: **$1,766.00**

Browning Model 1885 Low Wall Traditional Hunter

Similar to the Model 1885 Low Wall except chambered for 357 Mag., 44 Mag. and 45 Colt; steel crescent buttplate; 1/16" gold bead front sight, adjustable buckhorn rear, and tang-mounted peep sight with barrel-type elevation adjuster and knob-type windage adjustments. Barrel is drilled and tapped for a Browning scope base. Oil-finished select walnut stock with swivel studs. Introduced 1997. Imported for Japan by Browning.
Price: **$1,289.00**

Browning Model 1885 Low Wall Rifle

Similar to the Model 1885 High Wall except has trimmer receiver, thinner 24" octagonal barrel. Forend is mounted to the receiver. Adjustable trigger. Walnut pistol grip stock, trim Schnabel forend with high-gloss finish. Available in 22 Hornet and 260 Rem. Overall length 39-1/2", weighs 6 lbs., 11 oz. Rifling twist rates: 1:16" (22 Hornet); 1:9" (260). Polished blue finish. Introduced 1995. Imported from Japan by Browning.
Price: **$997.00**

BRNO ZBK 110 SINGLE SHOT RIFLE

Caliber: 222 Rem., 5.6x52R, 22 Hornet, 5.6x50 Mag., 6.5x57R, 7x57R, 8x57JRS. **Barrel:** 23.6". **Weight:** 5.9 lbs. **Length:** 40.1" overall. **Stock:** European walnut. **Sights:** None furnished; drilled and tapped for scope mounting. **Features:** Top tang opening lever; cross-bolt safety; polished blue finish. Announced 1998. Imported from The Czech Republic by Euro-Imports.
Price: Standard calibers **$223.00**
Price: 7x57R, 8x57JRS **$245.00**
Price: Lux model, standard calibers **$311.00**
Price: Lux model, 7x57R, 8x57JRS **$333.00**

C. SHARPS ARMS NEW MODEL 1875 OLD RELIABLE RIFLE

Caliber: 22LR, 32-40 & 38-55 Ballard, 38-56 WCF, 40-65 WCF, 40-90 3-1/4", 40-90 2-5/8", 40-70 2-1/10", 40-70 2-1/4", 40-70 2-1/2", 40-50 1-11/16", 40-50 1-7/8", 45-90, 45-70, 45-100, 45-110, 45-120. Also available on special order only in 50-70, 50-90, 50-140. **Barrel:** 24", 26", 30" (standard), 32", 34" optional. **Weight:** 8-12 lbs. **Stock:** Walnut, straight grip, shotgun butt with checkered steel buttplate. **Sights:** Silver blade front, Rocky Mountain buckhorn rear. **Features:** Recreation of the 1875 Sharps rifle. Production guns will have case colored receiver. Available in Custom Sporting and Target versions upon request. Announced 1986. From C. Sharps Arms Co.
Price: 1875 Sporting Rifle (30" tapered oct. bbl.) **$1,185.00**

C. Sharps Arms 1875 Classic Sharps

Similar to New Model 1875 Sporting Rifle except 26", 28" or 30" full octagon barrel, crescent buttplate with toe plate, Hartford-style forend with cast German silver nose cap. Blade front sight, Rocky Mountain buckhorn rear. Weighs 10 lbs. Introduced 1987. From C. Sharps Arms Co.
Price: **$1,470.00**

C. Sharps Arms New Model 1875 Target & Long Range

Similar to New Model 1875 in all listed calibers except 22 LR; 34" tapered octagon barrel; globe with post front sight, Long Range Vernier tang sight with windage adjustments. Pistol grip stock with cheek rest; checkered steel buttplate. Introduced 1991. From C. Sharps Arms Co.
Price: **$1,549.50**

C. SHARPS ARMS NEW MODEL 1874 OLD RELIABLE

Caliber: 40-50, 40-70, 40-90, 45-70, 45-90, 45-100, 45-110, 45-120, 50-70, 50-90, 50-140. **Barrel:** 26", 28", 30" tapered octagon. **Weight:** About 10 lbs. **Length:** NA. **Stock:** American black walnut; shotgun butt with checkered steel buttplate; straight grip, heavy forend with Schnabel tip. **Sights:** Blade front, buckhorn rear. Drilled and tapped for tang sight. **Features:** Recreation of the Model 1874 Old Reliable Sharps Sporting Rifle. Double set triggers. Reintroduced 1991. Made in U.S.A. by C. Sharps Arms.
Price: **$1,584.00**

C. SHARPS ARMS NEW MODEL 1885 HIGHWALL RIFLE

Caliber: 22 LR, 22 Hornet, 219 Zipper, 25-35 WCF, 32-40 WCF, 38-55 WCF, 40-65, 30-40-Krag, 40-50 ST or BN, 40-70 ST or BN, 40-90 ST or BN, 45-70 2-1/10" ST, 45-90 2-4/10" ST, 45-100 2-6/10" ST, 45-110 2-7/8" ST, 45-120 3-1/4" ST. **Barrel:** 26", 28", 30", tapered full octagon. **Weight:** About 9 lbs., 4 oz. **Length:** 47" overall. **Stock:** Oil-finished American walnut; Schnabel-style forend. **Sights:** Blade front, buckhorn rear. Drilled and tapped for optional tang sight. **Features:** Single trigger; octagonal receiver top; checkered steel buttplate; color case-hardened receiver and buttplate, blued barrel. Many options available. Made in U.S.A. by C. Sharps Arms Co
Price: From **$1,439.00**

RIFLES

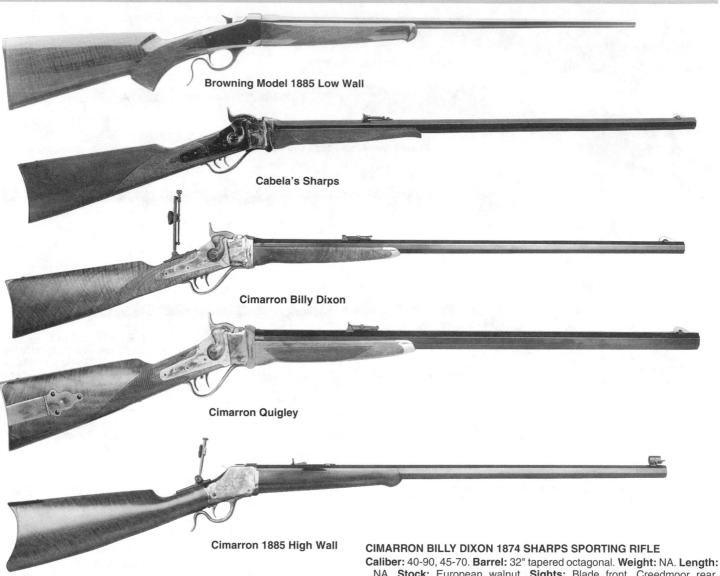

Browning Model 1885 Low Wall

Cabela's Sharps

Cimarron Billy Dixon

Cimarron Quigley

Cimarron 1885 High Wall

C. SHARPS ARMS CUSTOM NEW MODEL 1877 LONG RANGE TARGET RIFLE

Caliber: 44-90 Sharps/Rem., 45-70, 45-90, 45-100 Sharps. **Barrel:** 32", 34" tapered round with Rigby flat. **Weight:** Appx. 10 lbs. **Stock:** Walnut checkered. Pistol grip/forend. **Sights:** Classic long range with windage. **Features:** Elegant single shot, limited to custom production only.
Price: . . . . **$5,550.00 and up**

CABELA'S SHARPS BASIC RIFLE

Caliber: .45-70. **Barrel:** 28" tapered round. **Weight:** 8.7 lbs. **Length:** 44" overall. **Stock:** European walnut. **Sights:** Buckhorn rear, blade front. **Features:** Utilitarian look of the original with single trigger and 1-in-18 twist rate. Imported by Cabela's.
Price: **$799.99**

CABELA'S SHARPS SPORTING RIFLE

Caliber: 45-70, 45-120, .45-110, .50-70. **Barrel:** 32", tapered octagon. **Weight:** 9 lbs. **Length:** 47-1/4" overall. **Stock:** Checkered walnut. **Sights:** Blade front, open adjustable rear. **Features:** Color case-hardened receiver and hammer, rest blued. Introduced 1995. Imported by Cabela's.
Price: **$949.99**
Price: (Deluxe engraved Sharps, .45-70) **$1,599.99**
Price: (Heavy target Sharps, 45-70, 45-120, .50-70) **$1,099.99**
Price: (Quigley Sharps, 45-70, 45-120, 45-110) **$1,399.99**

CIMARRON BILLY DIXON 1874 SHARPS SPORTING RIFLE

Caliber: 40-90, 45-70. **Barrel:** 32" tapered octagonal. **Weight:** NA. **Length:** NA. **Stock:** European walnut. **Sights:** Blade front, Creedmoor rear. **Features:** Color case-hardened frame, blued barrel. Hand-checkered grip and forend; hand-rubbed oil finish. Introduced 1999. Imported by Cimarron F.A. Co.
Price: **$1,525.00**

CIMARRON QUIGLEY MODEL 1874 SHARPS SPORTING RIFLE

Caliber: 45-70, 45-90, 45-120. **Barrel:** 34" octagonal. **Weight:** NA. **Length:** NA. **Stock:** Checkered walnut. **Sights:** Blade front, adjustable rear. **Features:** Blued finish; double set triggers. From Cimarron F.A. Co.
Price: **$1,625.00**

CIMARRON SILHOUETTE MODEL 1874 SHARPS SPORTING RIFLE

Caliber: 45-70. **Barrel:** 32" octagonal. **Weight:** NA. **Length:** NA. **Stock:** Walnut. **Sights:** Blade front, adjustable rear. **Features:** Pistol-grip stock with shotgun-style butt plate; cut-rifled barrel. From Cimarron F.A. Co.
Price: **$1,299.00**

CIMARRON MODEL 1885 HIGH WALL RIFLE

Caliber: 38-55, 40-65, 45-70, 45-90, 45-120. **Barrel:** 30" octagonal. **Weight:** NA. **Length:** NA. **Stock:** European walnut. **Sights:** Bead front, semi-buckhorn rear. **Features:** Replica of the Winchester 1885 High Wall rifle. Color case-hardened receiver and lever, blued barrel. Curved butt-plate. Optional double set triggers. Introduced 1999. Imported by Cimarron F.A. Co.
Price: **$995.00**
Price: With pistol grip **$1,175.00**

Cumberland Mountain Plateau

Dakota Single Shot

Dixie 1874 Sharps Silhouette

H&R Ultra Hunter

CUMBERLAND MOUNTAIN PLATEAU RIFLE

Caliber: 40-65, 45-70. **Barrel:** Up to 32"; round. **Weight:** About 10-1/2 lbs. (32" barrel). **Length:** 48" overall (32" barrel). **Stock:** American walnut. **Sights:** Marble's bead front, Marble's open rear. **Features:** Falling block action with underlever. Blued barrel and receiver. Stock has lacquer finish, crescent buttplate. Introduced 1995. Made in U.S.A. by Cumberland Mountain Arms, Inc.
Price: **$1,085.00**

DAKOTA MODEL 10 SINGLE SHOT RIFLE

Caliber: Most rimmed and rimless commercial calibers. **Barrel:** 23". **Weight:** 6 lbs. **Length:** 39-1/2" overall. **Stock:** Medium fancy grade walnut in classic style. Checkered grip and forend. **Sights:** None furnished. Drilled and tapped for scope mounting. **Features:** Falling block action with under-lever. Top tang safety. Removable trigger plate for conversion to single set trigger. Introduced 1990. Made in U.S.A. by Dakota Arms.
Price: **$3,595.00**
Price: Barreled action **$2,095.00**
Price: Action only **$1,850.00**
Price: Magnum calibers **$3,595.00**
Price: Magnum barreled action. **$2,050.00**
Price: Magnum action only **$1,675.00**

DIXIE 1874 SHARPS BLACKPOWDER SILHOUETTE RIFLE

Caliber: 45-70. **Barrel:** 30"; tapered octagon; blued; 1:18" twist. **Weight:** 10 lbs., 3 oz. **Length:** 47-1/2" overall. **Stock:** Oiled walnut. **Sights:** Blade front, ladder-type hunting rear. **Features:** Replica of the Sharps #1 Sporter. Shotgun-style butt with checkered metal buttplate; color case-hardened receiver, hammer, lever and buttplate. Tang is drilled and tapped for tang sight. Double-set triggers. Meets standards for NRA blackpowder cartridge matches. Introduced 1995. Imported from Italy by Dixie Gun Works.
Price: **$1,025.00**

Dixie 1874 Sharps Lightweight Hunter/Target Rifle

Same as the Dixie 1874 Sharps Blackpowder Silhouette model except has a straight-grip buttstock with military-style buttplate. Based on the 1874 military model. Introduced 1995. Imported from Italy by Dixie Gun Works.
Price: **$995.00**

E.M.F. 1874 METALLIC CARTRIDGE SHARPS RIFLE

Caliber: 45-70, 45/120. **Barrel:** 28", octagon. **Weight:** 10-3/4 lbs. **Length:** NA. **Stock:** Oiled walnut. **Sights:** Blade front, flip-up open rear. **Features:** Replica of the 1874 Sharps Sporting rifle. Color case-hardened lock; double-set trigger; blued finish. Imported by E.M.F.
Price: From. **$700.00**
Price: With browned finish **$1,000.00**
Price: Military Carbine **$650.00**

HARRINGTON & RICHARDSON ULTRA VARMINT RIFLE

Caliber: 223, 243. **Barrel:** 24", heavy. **Weight:** About 7.5 lbs. **Stock:** Hand-checkered laminated birch with Monte Carlo comb. **Sights:** None furnished. Drilled and tapped for scope mounting. **Features:** Break-open action with side-lever release, positive ejection. Scope mount. Blued receiver and barrel. Swivel studs. Introduced 1993. From H&R 1871, Inc.
Price: **$332.00**

Harrington & Richardson Ultra Hunter Rifle

Similar to Ultra Varmint rifle except chambered for 25-06 with 26" barrel, or 308 Win., 450 Marlin with 22" barrel. Stock and forend are of cinnamon-colored laminate; hand-checkered grip and forend. Introduced 1995. Made in U.S.A. by H&R 1871, LLC.
Price: **$332.00**

Harrington & Richardson Ultra Comp Rifle

Similar to Ultra Varmint except chambered for 270 or 30-06; compensator to reduce recoil; camo-laminate stock and forend; blued, highly polished frame; scope mount. Made in U.S.A. by H&R 1871, LLC.
Price: **$376.00**

CENTERFIRE RIFLES — SINGLE SHOT

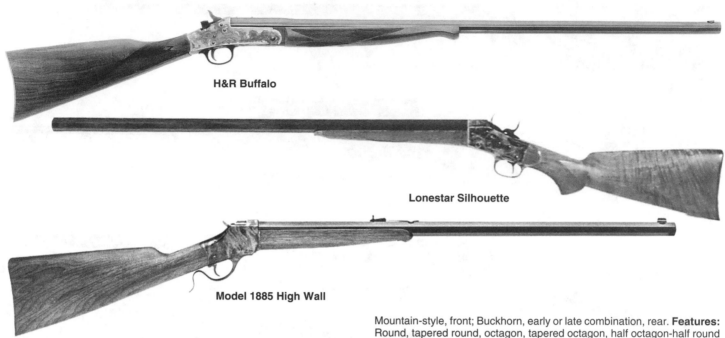

H&R Buffalo

Lonestar Silhouette

Model 1885 High Wall

HARRINGTON & RICHARDSON BUFFALO CLASSIC RIFLE
Caliber: 45-70. **Barrel:** 32" heavy. **Weight:** 8 lbs. **Length:** 52" overall. **Stock:** American black walnut. **Sights:** Williams receiver sight; Lyman target front sight with 8 aperture inserts. **Features:** Color case-hardened Handi-Rifle action with exposed hammer; color case-hardened crescent buttplate; 19th century checkering pattern. Introduced 1995. Made in U.S.A. by H&R 1871, LLC.
Price: About $418.00

Harrington & Richardson 38-55 Target Rifle
Similar to the Buffalo Classic rifle except chambered for 38-55 Win., has 28" barrel. The barrel, steel trigger guard and forend spacer, are highly polished and blued. Color case-hardened receiver and buttplate. Williams receiver sight; Lyman target front sight with 8 aperture inserts. Introduced 1998. Made in U.S.A. by H&R 1871, LLC.
Price: $418.00

HARRIS GUNWORKS ANTIETAM SHARPS RIFLE
Caliber: 40-65, 45-75. **Barrel:** 30", 32", octagon or round, hand-lapped stainless or chrome-moly. **Weight:** 11.25 lbs. **Length:** 47" overall. **Stock:** Choice of straight grip, pistol grip or Creedmoor with Schnabel forend; pewter tip optional. Standard wood is A Fancy; higher grades available. **Sights:** Montana Vintage Arms #111 Low Profile Spirit Level front, #108 mid-range tang rear with windage adjustments. **Features:** Recreation of the 1874 Sharps sidehammer. Action is color case-hardened, barrel satin black. Chrome-moly barrel optionally blued. Optional sights include #112 Spirit Level Globe front with windage, #107 Long Range rear with windage. Introduced 1994. Made in U.S.A. by Harris Gunworks.
Price: $2,400.00

KRIEGHOFF HUBERTUS SINGLE-SHOT RIFLE
Caliber: 222, 243, 270, 308, 30-06, 5.6x50R Mag., 5.6x52R, 6x62R Freres, 6.5x57R, 6.5x65R, 7x57R, 7x65R, 8x57JRS, 8x75RS, 7mm Rem. Mag., 300 Win. Mag. **Barrel:** 23-1/2". **Weight:** 6-1/2 lbs. **Length:** NA. **Stock:** High-grade walnut. **Sights:** Blade front, open rear. **Features:** Break-loading with manual cocking lever on top tang; take-down; extractor; Schnabel forearm; many options. Imported from Germany by Krieghoff International Inc.
Price: Hubertus single shot, from $5,850.00
Price: Hubertus, magnum calibers $6,850.00

LONE STAR NO. 5 REMINGTON PATTERN ROLLING BLOCK RIFLE
Caliber: 25-35, 30-30, 30-40 Krag. **Barrel:** 26" to 34". **Weight:** NA. **Length:** NA **Stock:** American walnut. **Sights:** Beech style, Marble bead, Rocky

Mountain-style, front; Buckhorn, early or late combination, rear. **Features:** Round, tapered round, octagon, tapered octagon, half octagon-half round barrels; bone-pack color case-hardened actions; single, single set, or double set triggers. Made in U.S.A. by Lone Star Rifle Co., Inc.
Price: $1,595.00

Lone Star Cowboy Action Rifle
Similar to the Lone Star No. 5 rifle, but designed for Cowboy Action Shooting with 28-33" barrel, buckhorn rear sight.
Price: $1,595.00

Lone Star Standard Silhouette Rifle
Similar to the Lone Star No. 5 rifle but designed for silhouette shooting with 30-34" barrel.
Price: $1,595.00

MEACHAM HIGHWALL SILHOUETTE RIFLE
Caliber: 40-65 Match, 45-70 Match. **Barrel:** 30", 34" octagon. **Stock:** Black walnut with cheekpiece. **Weight:** 11.5 to 11.9 lbs. **Sights:** None. Tang drilled for Win. base, 3/8" dovetail notch, front. Length of pull: 13-5/8". **Features:** Parts interchangeable copy of '85 Winchester. Available with single trigger, single set trigger, or Schuetzen-style double set triggers. Color case-hardened action. Introduced 2002. From Meacham T&H, Inc.
Price: $2,999.00

MERKEL K-1 MODEL LIGHTWEIGHT STALKING RIFLE
Caliber: 243 Win., 270 Win., 7x57R, 308 Win., 30-06, 7mm Rem. Mag., 300 Win. Mag., 9.3x74R. **Barrel:** 23.6". **Weight:** 5.6 lbs. unscoped. **Stock:** Satin-finished walnut, fluted and checkered; sling-swivel studs. **Sights:** None (scope base furnished). **Features:** Franz Jager single-shot break-open action, cocking/uncocking slide-type safety, matte silver receiver, selectable trigger pull weights, integrated, quick detach 1" or 30mm optic mounts (optic not included). Imported from Germany by GSI.
Price: Standard, simple border engraving $3,795.00
Price: Premium, light arabesque scroll. $3,795.00
Price: Jagd, fine engraved hunting scenes $4,395.00

MODEL 1885 HIGH WALL RIFLE
Caliber: 30-40 Krag, 32-40, 38-55, 40-65 WCF, 45-70. **Barrel:** 26" (30-40), 28"-30" all others. Douglas Premium #3 tapered octagon. **Weight:** 9 lbs, 4 oz. **Length:** 47" overall. **Stock:** Premium American black walnut. **Sights:** Marble's standard ivory bead front, #66 long blade top rear with reversible notch and elevator. **Features:** Receiver with octagon top, thick-wall High Wall with coil spring action. Tang drilled, tapped for High Wall tang sight. Receiver, lever, hammer and breechblock color case-hardened. Available from Montana Armory, Inc.
Price: $1,350.00

Mossberg SSi-One Sporter

Mossberg SSi-One Varminter

Navy Arms 1874 Sharps Cavalry Carbine

Navy Arms 1874 Sharps Plains

Navy Arms 1874 Sharps Sporting

RIFLES

MOSSBERG SSi-ONE SINGLE SHOT RIFLE

Caliber: 223 Rem., 22-250 Rem., 243 Win., 270 Win., 308 Rem., 30-06. **Barrel:** 24". **Weight:** 8 lbs. **Length:** 40". **Stock:** Satin-finished walnut, fluted and checkered; sling-swivel studs. **Sights:** None (scope base furnished). **Features:** Frame accepts interchangeable barrels, including 12-gauge, fully rifled slug barrel and 12 ga., 3-1/2" chambered barrel with Ulti-Full Turkey choke tube. Lever-opening, break-action design; single-stage trigger; ambidextrous, top-tang safety; internal eject/extract selector. Introduced 2000. From Mossberg.

Price: SSi-One Sporter (standard barrel) or 12 ga., 3-1/2" chamber **$459.00**

Price: SSi-One Varmint (bull barrel, 22-250 Rem. only; weighs 10 lbs.) **$480.00**

Price: SSi-One 12-gauge Slug (fully rifled barrel, no sights, scope base) **$480.00**

NAVY ARMS 1873 SHARPS "QUIGLEY"

Caliber: 45/70. Barrel: 34" heavy octagonal. Stock: Walnut. Features: Case-hardened receiver and military patchbox. Exact reproduction from "Quigley Down Under."

Price: **$1,390.00**

NAVY ARMS 1873 SHARPS NO. 2 CREEDMOOR RIFLE

Caliber: 45/70. **Barrel:** 30" tapered round. **Stock:** Walnut. **Sights:** Front globe, "soule" tang rear. **Features:** Nickel receiver and action. Lightweight sporting rifle.

Price: **$1,300.00**

NAVY ARMS 1874 SHARPS CAVALRY CARBINE

Caliber: 45-70. **Barrel:** 22". **Weight:** 7 lbs., 12 oz. **Length:** 39" overall. **Stock:** Walnut. **Sights:** Blade front, military ladder-type rear. **Features:** Replica of the 1874 Sharps military carbine. Color case-hardened receiver and furniture. Imported by Navy Arms.

Price: **$1,000.00**

NAVY ARMS 1874 SHARPS BUFFALO RIFLE

Caliber: 45-70, 45-90. **Barrel:** 28" heavy octagon. **Weight:** 10 lbs., 10 oz. **Length:** 46" overall. **Stock:** Walnut; checkered grip and forend. **Sights:** Blade front, ladder rear; tang sight optional. **Features:** Color case-hardened receiver, blued barrel; double-set triggers. Imported by Navy Arms.

Price: **$1,160.00**

Navy Arms Sharps Plains Rifle

Similar to Sharps Buffalo rifle except 45-70 only, 32" medium-weight barrel, weighs 9 lbs., 8 oz., and is 49" overall. Imported by Navy Arms.

Price: **$1,125.00**

Navy Arms Sharps Sporting Rifle

Same as the Navy Arms Sharps Plains Rifle except has pistol grip stock. Introduced 1997. Imported by Navy Arms.

Price: 45-70 only **$1,160.00**

NAVY ARMS 1885 HIGH WALL RIFLE

Caliber: 45-70; others available on special order. **Barrel:** 28" round, 30" octagonal. **Weight:** 9.5 lbs. **Length:** 45-1/2" overall (30" barrel). **Stock:** Walnut. **Sights:** Blade front, vernier tang-mounted peep rear. **Features:** Replica of Winchester's High Wall designed by Browning. Color case-hardened receiver, blued barrel. Introduced 1998. Imported by Navy Arms.

Price: 28", round barrel, target sights **$920.00**

Price: 30" octagonal barrel, target sights **$995.00**

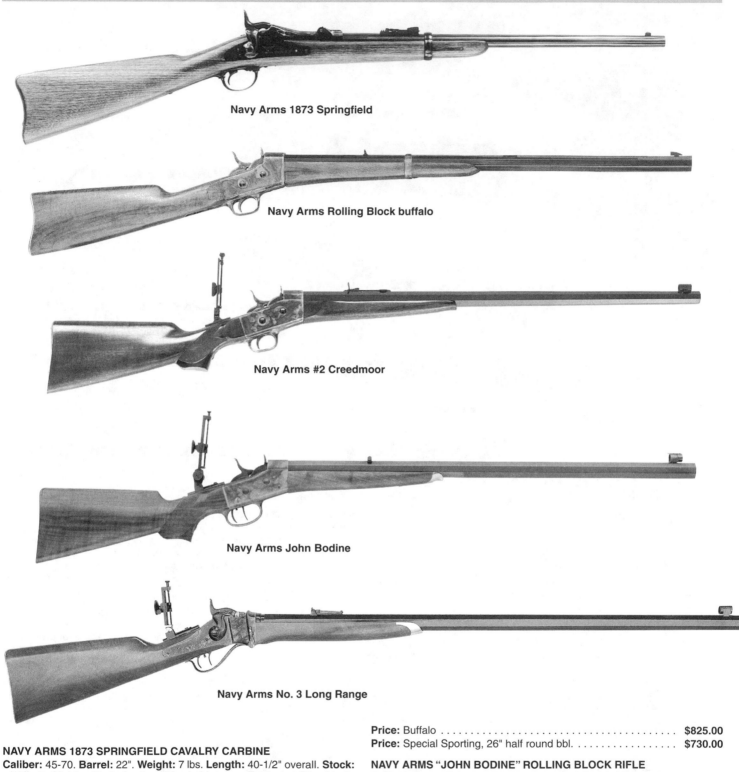

Navy Arms 1873 Springfield

Navy Arms Rolling Block buffalo

Navy Arms #2 Creedmoor

Navy Arms John Bodine

Navy Arms No. 3 Long Range

NAVY ARMS 1873 SPRINGFIELD CAVALRY CARBINE
Caliber: 45-70. **Barrel:** 22". **Weight:** 7 lbs. **Length:** 40-1/2" overall. **Stock:** Walnut. **Sights:** Blade front, military ladder rear. **Features:** Blued lockplate and barrel; color case-hardened breechblock; saddle ring with bar. Replica of 7th Cavalry gun. Imported by Navy Arms.
Price: $930.00

NAVY ARMS ROLLING BLOCK RIFLE
Caliber: 45-70. **Barrel:** 26", 30". **Stock:** Walnut. **Sights:** Blade front, adjustable rear. **Features:** Reproduction of classic rolling block action. Available with full-octagon or half-octagon-half-round barrel. Color case-hardened action, steel fittings. From Navy Arms.

Price: Buffalo $825.00
Price: Special Sporting, 26" half round bbl. $730.00

NAVY ARMS "JOHN BODINE" ROLLING BLOCK RIFLE
Caliber: 45-70. **Barrel:** 30" heavy octagonal. **Stock:** Walnut. **Sights:** Globe front, "soule" tang rear. **Features:** Double set triggers.
Price: $1,385.00

NAVY ARMS SHARPS NO. 3 LONG RANGE RIFLE
Caliber: 45-70, 45-90. **Barrel:** 34" octagon. **Weight:** 10 lbs., 12 oz. **Length:** 51-1/2". **Stock:** Deluxe walnut. **Sights:** Globe target front and match grade rear tang. **Features:** Shotgun buttplate, German silver forend cap, color case hardenend receiver. Imported by Navy Arms.
Price: $1,885.00

**New England
Firearms Handi-Rifle**

New England Firearms Super Light

New England Firearms Survivor

Remington No. 1 Mid-Range

NEW ENGLAND FIREARMS HANDI-RIFLE

Caliber: 22 Hornet, 223, 243, 30-30, 270, 280 Rem., 308, 30-06, 357 Mag., 44 Mag., 45-70. **Barrel:** 22", 24"; 26" for 280 Rem. **Weight:** 7 lbs. **Stock:** Walnut-finished hardwood; black rubber recoil pad. **Sights:** Ramp front, folding rear (22 Hornet, 30-30, 45-70). Drilled and tapped for scope mount; 223, 243, 270, 280, 30-06 have no open sights, come with scope mounts. **Features:** Break-open action with side-lever release. The 223, 243, 270 and 30-06 have recoil pad and Monte Carlo stock for shooting with scope. Swivel studs on all models. Blue finish. Introduced 1989. From New England Firearms.

Price: **$270.00**
Price: 280 Rem., 26" barrel **$270.00**
Price: Synthetic Handi-Rifle (black polymer stock and forend, swivels, recoil pad) **$281.00**
Price: Handi-Rifle Youth (223, 243) **$270.00**
Price: Stainless Handi-Rifle (223 Rem., 243 Rem.) **$337.00**

New England Firearms Super Light Rifle

Similar to Handi-Rifle except new barrel taper, shorter 20" barrel with recessed muzzle, special lightweight synthetic stock and forend. No sights furnished on 223 and 243 versions, but have factory-mounted scope base and offset hammer spur; Monte Carlo stock; 22 Hornet has ramp front, fully adjustable open rear. Overall length 36", weight is 5.5 lbs. Introduced 1997. Made in U.S.A. by New England Firearms.
Price: 22 Hornet, 223 Rem. or 243 Win. **$281.00**

NEW ENGLAND FIREARMS SURVIVOR RIFLE

Caliber: 223, 308 Win., single shot. **Barrel:** 22". **Weight:** 6 lbs. **Length:** 36" overall. **Stock:** Black polymer, thumbhole design. **Sights:** None furnished; scope mount provided. **Features:** Receiver drilled and tapped for scope mounting. Stock and forend have storage compartments for ammo, etc.; comes with integral swivels and black nylon sling. Introduced 1996. Made in U.S.A. by New England Firearms.
Price: Blue finish. **$284.00**

REMINGTON NO. 1 ROLLING BLOCK MID-RANGE SPORTER

Caliber: 45-70. **Barrel:** 30" round. **Weight:** 8-3/4 lbs. **Length:** 46-1/2" overall. **Stock:** American walnut with checkered pistol grip and forend. **Sights:** Beaded blade front, adjustable center-notch buckhorn rear. **Features:** Recreation of the original. Polished blue metal finish. Many options available. Introduced 1998. Made in U.S.A. by Remington.
Price: **$1,450.00**
Price: Silhouette model with single-set trigger, heavy barrel . . . **$1,560.00**

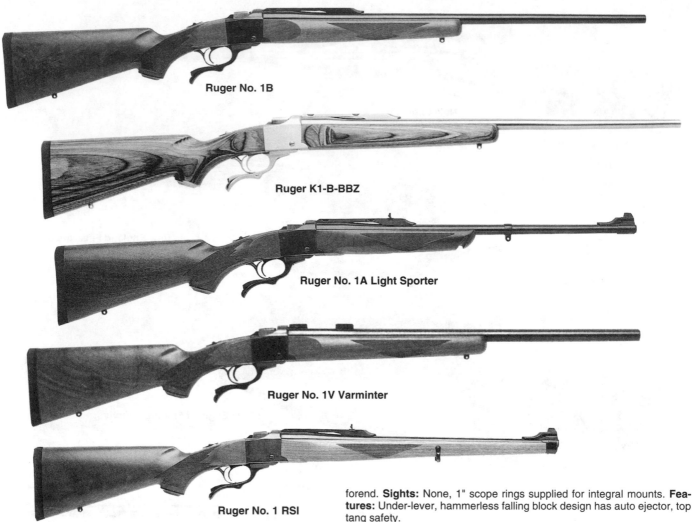

Ruger No. 1B

Ruger K1-B-BBZ

Ruger No. 1A Light Sporter

Ruger No. 1V Varminter

Ruger No. 1 RSI

ROSSI SINGLE SHOT CENTERFIRE RIFLE

Caliber: 308 Win., 270 Win., 30-06 Spfld., 223 Rem., 243 Win. **Barrel:** 23". **Weight:** 6-6.5 lbs. **Stock:** Monte carlo, exotic woods, walnut finish & swivels with white line space and recoil pad. **Sights:** None, scope rails and hammer extension included. **Features:** Break Open, positive ejection, internal transfer bar mechanism and manual external safety. Trigger block system included.
Price: **$179.95**

ROSSI CENTERFIRE/SHOTGUN "MATCHED PAIRS"

Caliber: 12 ga./223 Rem., full size, 20 ga./223 Rem. full & youth, 12 ga./342 Win. full, 20 ga./243 Win., full & youth, 12 ga./308 Win. full, 20 ga./308 Win. full & youth, 12 ga./30-06 Spfld. full, 20 ga./30-06 Spfld. full, 12 ga./270 Win. full, 20 ga./270 Win. full. **Barrel:** 28"/23" full, 22"/22" youth. **Weight:** 5-7 lbs. **Stock:** Straight, exotic woods, walnut finish and swivels wtih white line space and recoil pad. **Sights:** Bead front shotgun, fully adjustable rifle, drilled and tapped. **Features:** Break Open, positive ejection, internal transfer bar mechanism and manual external safety. Trigger block system included.
Price: 350.00

RUGER NO. 1B SINGLE SHOT

Caliber: 218 Bee, 22 Hornet, 220 Swift, 22-250, 223, 243, 6mm Rem., 25-06, 257 Roberts, 270, 280, 30-06, 7mm Rem. Mag., 300 Win. Mag., 308 Win., 338 Win. Mag., 270 Wea., 300 Wea. **Barrel:** 26" round tapered with quarter-rib; with Ruger 1" rings. **Weight:** 8 lbs. **Length:** 42-1/4" overall. **Stock:** Walnut, two-piece, checkered pistol grip and semi-beavertail

forend. **Sights:** None, 1" scope rings supplied for integral mounts. **Features:** Under-lever, hammerless falling block design has auto ejector, top tang safety.
Price: 1B. **$875.00**
Price: Barreled action **$600.00**
Price: K1-B-BBZ Stainless steel, laminated stock 25-06, 7MM mag, 7MM STW, 300 Win Mag., 243 Win., 30-06, 308 Win. **$910.00**

Ruger No. 1A Light Sporter

Similar to the No. 1B Standard Rifle except has lightweight 22" barrel, Alexander Henry-style forend, adjustable folding leaf rear sight on quarter-rib, dovetailed ramp front with gold bead. Calibers 243, 30-06, 270 and 7x57. Weighs about 7-1/4 lbs.
Price: No. 1A **$875.00**
Price: Barreled action **$600.00**

Ruger No. 1V Varminter

Similar to the No. 1B Standard Rifle except has 24" heavy barrel. Semi-beavertail forend, barrel ribbed for target scope block, with 1" Ruger scope rings. Calibers 22-250, 220 Swift, 223, 25-06, 6mm Rem. Weight about 9 lbs.
Price: No. 1V **$875.00**
Price: Barreled action **$600.00**
Price: K1-V-BBZ stainless steel, laminated stock 22-250 . . . . . . **$910.00**

Ruger No. 1 RSI International

Similar to the No. 1B Standard Rifle except has lightweight 20" barrel, full-length International-style forend with loop sling swivel, adjustable folding leaf rear sight on quarter-rib, ramp front with gold bead. Calibers 243, 30-06, 270 and 7x57. Weight is about 7-1/4 lbs.
Price: No. 1 RSI **$890.00**
Price: Barreled action **$600.00**

RIFLES

CENTERFIRE RIFLES — SINGLE SHOT

Ruger No. 1H Tropical

Ruger No. 1S Medium Sporter

Shiloh 1874 Long Range Express

Shiloh 1874 Quigley

Shiloh 1874 Saddle

Ruger No. 1H Tropical Rifle

Similar to the No. 1B Standard Rifle except has Alexander Henry forend, adjustable folding leaf rear sight on quarter-rib, ramp front with dovetail gold bead, 24" heavy barrel. Calibers 375 H&H, 416 Rem. Mag., 416 Rigby, and 458 Win. Mag. (weighs about 9 lbs.).

Price: No. 1H $875.00
Price: Barreled action $600.00
Price: K1-H-BBZ, S/S, 375 H&H, 416 Rigby $910.00

Ruger No. 1S Medium Sporter

Similar to the No. 1B Standard Rifle except has Alexander Henry-style forend, adjustable folding leaf rear sight on quarter-rib, ramp front sight base and dovetail-type gold bead front sight. Calibers 218 Bee, 7mm Rem. Mag., 338 Win. Mag., 300 Win. Mag. with 26" barrel, 45-70 with 22" barrel. Weighs about 7-1/2 lbs. In 45-70.

Price: No. 1S $875.00
Price: Barreled action $600.00
Price: K1-S-BBZ, S/S, 45-70 .... $910.00

SHILOH RIFLE CO. SHARPS 1874 LONG RANGE EXPRESS

Caliber: 40-50 BN, 40-70 BN, 40-90 BN, 45-70 ST, 45-90 ST, 45-110 ST, 50-70 ST, 50-90 ST, 38-55, 40-70 ST, 40-90 ST. **Barrel:** 34" tapered octagon. **Weight:** 10-1/2 lbs. **Length:** 51" overall. **Stock:** Oil-finished semi-fancy walnut with pistol grip, shotgun-style butt, traditional cheek rest,

Schnabel forend. **Sights:** Globe front, sporting tang rear. **Features:** Recreation of the Model 1874 Sharps rifle. Double set triggers. Made in U.S.A. by Shiloh Rifle Mfg. Co.

Price: $1,796.00
Price: Sporting Rifle No. 1 (similar to above except with 30" bbl., blade front, buckhorn rear sight). $1,706.00
Price: Sporting Rifle No. 3 (similar to No. 1 except straight-grip stock, standard wood) $1,504.00
Price: 1874 Hartford (Hartford collar, pewter tip) $1,702.00
Price: 1874 Sporter #1 (30" bbl, blade, buckhorn sights)..... $1,706.00
Price: 1874 Sporter #3 (walnut, shotgun or military stock)..... $1,504.00

SHILOH RIFLE CO. SHARPS 1874 QUIGLEY

Caliber: 45-70, 45-110. **Barrel:** 34" heavy octagon. **Stock:** Military-style with patch box, standard grade American walnut. **Sights:** Semi buckhorn, interchangeable front and midrange vernier tang wight with windage. **Features:** Gold inlay initials, pewter tip, hartford collar, case color or antique finish. Double set triggers.

Price: $2,860.00

SHILOH RIFLE CO. SHARPS 1874 SADDLE RIFLE

Caliber: 38-55, 40-50 BN, 40-65 Win., 40-70 BN, 40-70 ST, 40-90 BN, 40-90 ST, 44-77 BN, 44-90 BN, 45-70 ST, 45-90 ST, 45-100 ST, 45-110 ST, 45-120 ST, 50-70 ST, 50-90 ST. **Barrel:** 26" full or h alf octagon. **Stock:** Semi fancy American walnut. Shotgun style with cheekrest. **Sights:** Buckhorn and blade. **Features:** Double set trigger, numerous custom features can be added.

Price: $1,504.00

Shiloh 1874 Montana Roughrider

Shiloh 1874 Creedmoor

Thompson/Center Encore

Thompson/Center Encore "Katahdin"

Thompson/Center Encore

SHILOH RIFLE CO. SHARPS 1874 MONTANA ROUGHRIDER

Caliber: 38-55, 40-50 BN, 40-65 Win., 40-70 BN, 40-70 ST, 40-90 BN, 40-90 ST, 44-77 BN, 44-90 BN, 45-70 ST, 45-90 ST, 45-100 ST, 45-110 ST, 45-120 ST, 50-70 ST, 50-90 ST. **Barrel:** 30" full or half octagon. **Stock:** American walnut in shotgun or military style. **Sights:** Buckhorn and blade. **Features:** Double set triggers, numerous custom features can be added.
Price: **$1,504.00**

SHILOH RIFLE CO. SHARPS CREEDMOOR TARGET

Caliber: 38-55, 40-50 BN, 40-65 Win., 40-70 BN, 40-70 ST, 40-90 BN, 40-90 ST, 44-77 BN, 44-90 BN, 45-70 ST, 45-90 ST, 45-100 ST, 45-110 ST, 45-120 ST, 50-70 ST, 50-90 ST. **Barrel:** 32", half round-half octagon. **Stock:** Extra fancy American walnut. Shotgun style with pistol grip. **Sights:** Customer's choice. **Features:** Single trigger, AA finish on stock, polished barrel and screws, pewter tip.
Price: **$2,442.00**

THOMPSON/CENTER ENCORE RIFLE

Caliber: 22-250, 223, 243, 25-06, 270, 7mm-08, 308, 30-06, 7mm Rem. Mag., 300 Win. Mag. **Barrel:** 24", 26". **Weight:** 6 lbs., 12 oz. (24" barrel). **Length:** 38-1/2" (24" barrel). **Stock:** American walnut. Monte Carlo style; Schnabel forend or black composite. **Sights:** Ramp-style white bead front, fully adjustable leaf-type rear. **Features:** Interchangeable barrels; action opens by squeezing trigger guard; drilled and tapped for T/C scope

mounts; polished blue finish. Introduced 1996. Made in U.S.A. by Thompson/Center Arms.
Price: . . . . **$599 to $632.00**
Price: Extra barrels **$270.00**

Thompson/Center Stainless Encore Rifle

Similar to blued Encore except stainless steel with blued sights, black composite stock and forend. Available in 22-250, 223, 7mm-08, 30-06, 308. Introduced 1999. Made in U.S.A. by Thompson/Center Arms.
Price: . . . . **$670.00 to $676.00**

THOMPSON/CENTER ENCORE "KATAHDIN" CARBINE

Caliber: 45-70 Gov't., 444 Marlin, 450 Marlin. **Barrel:** 18" with muzzle tamer. **Stock:** Composite.
Price: **$619.00**

Thompson/Center G2 Contender Rifle

Similar to the G2 Contender pistol, but in a compact rifle format. **Features:** interchangeable 23" barrels, chambered for .17 HMR, .22LR, .223 Rem., 30/30 Win. and .45/70 Gov't; plus a .45 Cal. Muzzleloading barrel. All of the 16-1/4" and 21" barrels made for the old style Contender will fit. **Weight:** 5-1/2 lbs. Introduced 2003. Made in U.S.A. by Thompson/Center Arms.
Price: . . . . **$592.40 to $607.00**

RIFLES

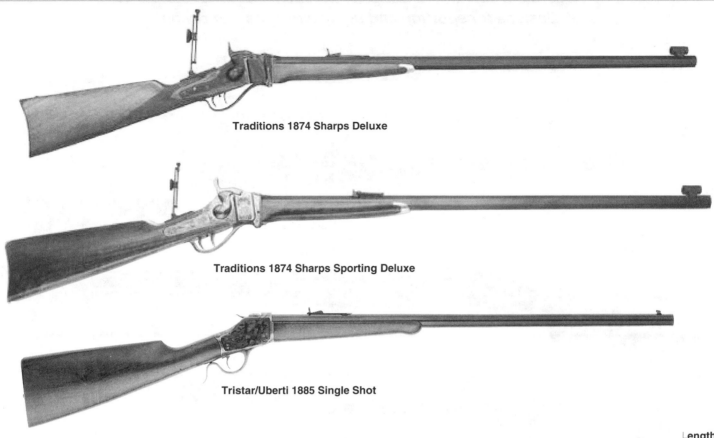

Traditions 1874 Sharps Deluxe

Traditions 1874 Sharps Sporting Deluxe

Tristar/Uberti 1885 Single Shot

RIFLES

TRADITIONS 1874 SHARPS DELUXE RIFLE

Caliber: 45-70. **Barrel:** 32" octagonal; 1:18" twist. **Weight:** 11.67 lbs. **Length:** 48.8" overall. **Stock:** Checkered walnut with German silver nose cap and steel butt plate. **Sights:** Globe front, adjustable creedmore rear with 12 inserts. **Features:** Color-case hardened receiver; double-set triggers. Introduced 2001. Imported from Pedersoli by Traditions.
Price: **$999.00**

Traditions 1874 Sharps Sporting Deluxe Rifle

Similar to Sharps Deluxe but custom silver engraved receiver, European walnut stock and forend, satin finish, set trigger, fully adjustable.
Price: **$1,999.00**

Traditions 1874 Sharps Standard Rifle

Similar to 1874 Sharps Deluxe Rifle, except has blade front and adjustable buckhorn-style rear sight. Weighs 10.67 pounds. Introduced 2001. Imported from Pedersoli by Traditions.
Price: **$769.00**

TRADITIONS ROLLING BLOCK SPORTING RIFLE

Caliber: 45-70. **Barrel:** 30" octagonal; 1:18" twist. **Weight:** 11.67 lbs. **Length:** 46.7" overall. **Stock:** Walnut. **Sights:** Blade front, adjustable rear. **Features:** Antique silver, color-case hardened receiver, drilled and tapped for tang/globe sights; brass butt plate and trigger guard. Introduced 2001. Imported from Pedersoli by Traditions.
Price: **$769.00**

TRADITIONS ROLLING BLOCK SPORTING RIFLE IN 30-30 WINCHESTER

Caliber: 45-70. **Barrel:** 28" round, blued. **Weight:** 8.25 lbs. **Stock:** Walnut. **Sights:** Fixed front, adjustable rear. **Features:** For hunting like in the Old West. Steel butt plate, trigger guard, barrel band. Classic reproduction.
Price: **$769.00**

Length: 44.5" overall. **Stock:** Walnut. **Sights:** Dovetail front, adjustable rear. **Features:** Cut checkering, case colored frame finish.
Price: **$795.00**

TRISTAR/UBERTI 1885 SINGLE SHOT

Caliber: 45-70. **Barrel:** 28". **Weight:** 8.75 lbs. **Length:** 44.5" overall. **Stock:** European walnut. **Sights:** Bead on blade front, open step-adjustable rear. **Features:** Recreation of the 1885 Winchester. Color case-hardened receiver and lever, blued barrel. Introduced 1998. Imported from Italy by Tristar Sporting Arms Ltd.
Price: **$765.00**

UBERTI BABY ROLLING BLOCK CARBINE

Caliber: 22 LR, 22 WMR, 22 Hornet, 357 Mag., single shot. **Barrel:** 22". **Weight:** 4.8 lbs. **Length:** 35-1/2" overall. **Stock:** Walnut stock and forend. **Sights:** Blade front, fully adjustable open rear. **Features:** Resembles Remington New Model No. 4 carbine. Brass trigger guard and buttplate; color case-hardened frame, blued barrel. Imported by Uberti USA Inc.
Price: **$490.00**
Price: Baby Rolling Block Rifle, 26" bbl. **$590.00**

Designs for sporting and utility purposes worldwide.

Beretta Express SSO

Beretta Model 455 SxS

Charles Daly Superior

Charles Daly Empire Combo

RIFLES

BERETTA EXPRESS SSO O/U DOUBLE RIFLES
Caliber: 375 H&H, 458 Win. Mag., 9.3x74R. **Barrel:** 25.5". **Weight:** 11 lbs. **Stock:** European walnut with hand-checkered grip and forend. **Sights:** Blade front on ramp, open V-notch rear. **Features:** Sidelock action with color case-hardened receiver (gold inlays on SSO6 Gold). Ejectors, double triggers, recoil pad. Introduced 1990. Imported from Italy by Beretta U.S.A.
Price: SSO6 . . . . **$21,000.00**
Price: SSO6 Gold **$23,500.00**

BERETTA MODEL 455 SxS EXPRESS RIFLE
Caliber: 375 H&H, 458 Win. Mag., 470 NE, 500 NE 3", 416 Rigby. **Barrel:** 23-1/2" or 25-1/2". **Weight:** 11 lbs. **Stock:** European walnut with hand-checkered grip and forend. **Sights:** Blade front, folding leaf V-notch rear. **Features:** Sidelock action with easily removable sideplates; color case-hardened finish (455), custom big game or floral motif engraving (455EELL). Double triggers, recoil pad. Introduced 1990. Imported from Italy by Beretta U.S.A.
Price: Model 455. . . . . **$36,000.00**
Price: Model 455EELL **$47,000.00**

BRNO 500 COMBINATION GUNS
Caliber/Gauge: 12 (2-3/4" chamber) over 5.6x52R, 5.6x50R, 222 Rem., 243, 6.x55, 308, 7x57R, 7x65R, 30-06. **Barrel:** 23.6". **Weight:** 7.6 lbs. **Length:** 40.5" overall. **Stock:** European walnut. **Sights:** Bead front, V-notch rear; grooved for scope mounting. **Features:** Boxlock action; double set trigger; blue finish with etched engraving. Announced 1998. Imported from The Czech Republic by Euro-Imports.
Price: **$1,023.00**
Price: O/U double rifle, 7x57R, 7x65R, 8x57JRS. **$1,125.00**

BRNO ZH 300 COMBINATION GUN
Caliber/Gauge: 22 Hornet, 5.6x50R Mag., 5.6x52R, 7x57R, 7x65R, 8x57JRS over 12, 16 (2-3/4" chamber). **Barrel:** 23.6". **Weight:** 7.9 lbs. **Length:** 40.5" overall. **Stock:** European walnut. **Sights:** Blade front, open adjustable rear. **Features:** Boxlock action; double triggers; automatic safety. Announced 1998. Imported from The Czech Republic by Euro-Imports.
Price: **$724.00**

BRNO ZH Double Rifles
Similar to ZH 300 combination guns except double rifle barrels. Available in 7x65R, 7x57R and 8x57JRS. Announced 1998. Imported from The Czech Republic by Euro-Imports.
Price: **$1,125.00**

CHARLES DALY SUPERIOR COMBINATION GUN
Caliber/Gauge: 12 ga. over 22 Hornet, 223 Rem., 22-250, 243 Win., 270 Win., 308 Win., 30-06. **Barrel:** 23.5", shotgun choked Imp. Cyl. **Weight:** About 7.5 lbs. **Stock:** Checkered walnut pistol grip buttstock and semi-beavertail forend. **Features:** Silvered, engraved receiver; chrome-moly steel barrels; double triggers; extractors; sling swivels; gold bead front sight. Introduced 1997. Imported from Italy by K.B.I. Inc.
Price: **$1,249.95**

Charles Daly Empire Combination Gun
Same as the Superior grade except has deluxe wood with European-style comb and cheekpiece; slim forend. Introduced 1997. Imported from Italy by K.B.I., Inc.
Price: **$1,789.95**

CZ 584 SOLO COMBINATION GUN
Caliber/Gauge: 7x57R; 12, 2-3/4" chamber. **Barrel:** 24.4". **Weight:** 7.37 lbs. **Length:** 45.25" overall. **Stock:** Circassian walnut. **Sights:** Blade front, open rear adjustable for windage. **Features:** Kersten-style double lump locking system; double-trigger Blitz-type mechanism with drop safety and adjustable set trigger for the rifle barrel; auto safety, dual extractors; receiver dovetailed for scope mounting. Imported from the Czech Republic by CZ-USA.
Price: **$851.00**

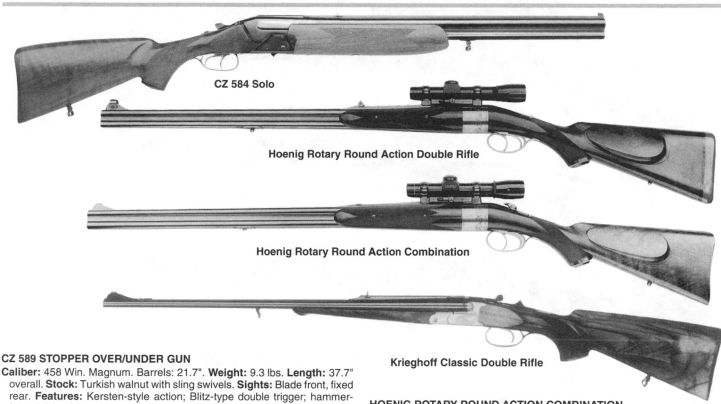

CZ 584 Solo

Hoenig Rotary Round Action Double Rifle

Hoenig Rotary Round Action Combination

Krieghoff Classic Double Rifle

CZ 589 STOPPER OVER/UNDER GUN

Caliber: 458 Win. Magnum. **Barrels:** 21.7". **Weight:** 9.3 lbs. **Length:** 37.7" overall. **Stock:** Turkish walnut with sling swivels. **Sights:** Blade front, fixed rear. **Features:** Kersten-style action; Blitz-type double trigger; hammer-forged, blued barrels; satin-nickel, engraved receiver. Introduced 2001. Imported from the Czech Republic by CZ USA.

Price: **$2,999.00**
Price: Fully engraved model......................... **$3,999.00**

DAKOTA DOUBLE RIFLE

Caliber: 470 Nitro Express, 500 Nitro Express. **Barrel:** 25". **Stock:** Exhibition-grade walnut. **Sights:** Express. **Features:** Round action; selective ejectors; recoil pad; Americase. From Dakota Arms Inc.

Price: **$25,000.00**

EAA/BAIKAL IZH-94 COMBINATION GUN

Caliber/Gauge: 12, 3" chamber; 222 Rem., 223, 5.6x50R, 5.6x55E, 7x57R, 7x65R, 7.62x39, 7.62x51, 308, 7.62x53R, 7.62x54R, 30-06. **Barrel:** 24", 26"; imp., mod. and full choke tubes. **Weight:** 7.28 lbs. **Stock:** Walnut; rubber butt pad. **Sights:** Express style. **Features:** Hammer-forged barrels with chrome-lined bores; machined receiver; single-selective or double triggers. Imported by European American Armory.

Price: Blued finish............................. **$549.00**
Price: 20 ga./22 LR, 20/22 Mag, 3" **$629.00**

GARBI EXPRESS DOUBLE RIFLE

Caliber: 7x65R, 9.3x74R, 375 H&H. **Barrel:** 24-3/4". **Weight:** 7-3/4 to 8-1/2 lbs. **Length:** 41-1/2" overall. **Stock:** Turkish walnut. **Sights:** Quarter-rib with express sight. **Features:** Side-by-side double; H&H-pattern sidelock ejector with reinforced action, chopper lump barrels of Boehler steel; double triggers; fine scroll and rosette engraving, or full coverage ornamental; coin-finished action. Introduced 1997. Imported from Spain by Wm. Larkin Moore.

Price: **$19,900.00**

HOENIG ROTARY ROUND ACTION DOUBLE RIFLE

Caliber: Most popular calibers from 225 Win. to 9.3x74R. **Barrel:** 22"-26". **Stock:** English Walnut; to customer specs. **Sights:** Swivel hood front with button release (extra bead stored in trap door gripcap), express-style rear on quarter-rib adjustable for windage and elevation; scope mount. **Features:** Round action opens by rotating barrels, pulling forward. Inertia extractor system, rotary safety blocks strikers. single lever quick-detachable scope mount. Simple takedown without removing forend. Introduced 1997. Made in U.S.A. by George Hoenig.

Price: **$24,975.00**

HOENIG ROTARY ROUND ACTION COMBINATION

Caliber: 28 ga. **Barrel:** 26". **Weight:** 7 lbs. **Stock:** English Walnut to customer specs. **Sights:** Front ramp with button release blades. Foldable aperture tang sight windage and elevation adjustable. Quarter rib with scope mount. **Features:** Round action opens by rotating barrels, pulling forward. Inertia extractor; rotary safety blocks strikers. Simple takedown without removing forend. Made in U.S.A. by George Hoenig.

Price: **$24,975.00**

KRIEGHOFF CLASSIC DOUBLE RIFLE

Caliber: 7x65R, 308 Win., 30-06, 8x57 JRS, 8x75RS, 9.3x74R. **Barrel:** 23.5". **Weight:** 7.3 to 8 lbs. **Stock:** High grade European walnut. Standard has conventional rounded cheekpiece, Bavaria has Bavarian-style cheekpiece. **Sights:** Bead front with removable, adjustable wedge (375 H&H and below), standing leaf rear on quarter-rib. **Features:** Boxlock action; double triggers; short opening angle for fast loading; quiet extractors; sliding, self-adjusting wedge for secure bolting; Purdey-style barrel extension; horizontal firing pin placement. Many options available. Introduced 1997. Imported from Germany by Krieghoff International.

Price: With small Arabesque engraving **$7,850.00**
Price: With engraved sideplates....................... **$9,800.00**
Price: For extra barrels.............................. **$4,500.00**
Price: Extra 20-ga., 28" shotshell barrels **$3,200.00**

Krieghoff Classic Big Five Double Rifle

Similar to the standard Classic excpet available in 375 Flanged Mag. N.E., 500/416 N.E., 470 N.E., 500 N.E. 3". Has hinged front trigger, non-removable muzzle wedge (larger than 375-caliber), Universal Trigger System, Combi Cocking Device, steel trigger guard, specially weighted stock bolt for weight and balance. Many options available. Introduced 1997. Imported from Germany by Krieghoff International.

Price: **$9,450.00**
Price: With engraved sideplates....................... **$11,400.00**

LEBEAU - COURALLY EXPRESS RIFLE SxS

Caliber: 7x65R, 8x57JRS, 9.3x74R, 375 H&H, 470 N.E. **Barrel:** 24" to 26". **Weight:** 7-3/4 to 10-1/2 lbs. **Stock:** Fancy French walnut with cheekpiece. **Sights:** Bead on ramp front, standing left express rear on quarter-rib. **Features:** Holland & Holland-type sidelock with automatic ejectors; double triggers. Built to order only. Imported from Belgium by Wm. Larkin Moore.

Price: **$41,000.00**

Merkel 96K Engraved

Merkel 140-1

Rizzini Express

Savage 24F Combination

Springfield M6 Scout

MERKEL DRILLINGS
Caliber/Gauge: 12, 20, 3" chambers, 16, 2-3/4" chambers; 22 Hornet, 5.6x50R Mag., 5.6x52R, 222 Rem., 243 Win., 6.5x55, 6.5x57R, 7x57R, 7x65R, 308, 30-06, 8x57JRS, 9.3x74R, 375 H&H. **Barrel:** 25.6". **Weight:** 7.9 to 8.4 lbs. depending upon caliber. **Stock:** Oil-finished walnut with pistol grip; cheekpiece on 12-, 16-gauge. **Sights:** Blade front, fixed rear. **Features:** Double barrel locking lug with Greener cross-bolt; scroll-engraved, case-hardened receiver; automatic trigger safety; Blitz action; double triggers. Imported from Germany by GSI.
Price: Model 96K (manually cocked rifle system), from **$7,495.00**
Price: Model 96K Engraved (hunting series on receiver) **$8,595.00**

Merkel Boxlock Double Rifles
Similar to the Model 160 double rifle except with Anson & Deely boxlock action with cocking indicators, double triggers, engraved color case-hardened receiver. Introduced 1995. Imported from Germany by GSI.
Price: Model 140-1, from **$6,695.00**
Price: Model 140-1.1 (engraved silver-gray receiver), from **$7,795.00**

RIZZINI EXPRESS 90L DOUBLE RIFLE
Caliber: 30-06, 7x65R, 9.3x74R. **Barrel:** 24". **Weight:** 7-1/2 lbs. **Length:** 40" overall. **Stock:** Select European walnut with satin oil finish; English-style cheekpiece. **Sights:** Ramp front, quarter-rib with express sight. **Features:** Color case-hardened boxlock action; automatic ejectors; single selective trigger; polished blue barrels. Extra 20-gauge shotshell barrels available. Imported for Italy by Wm. Larkin Moore.
Price: With case **$3,850.00**

SAVAGE 24F PREDATOR O/U COMBINATION GUN
Caliber/Gauge: 22 Hornet, 223, 30-30 over 12 (24F-12) or 22 LR, 22 Hornet, 223, 30-30 over 20-ga. (24F-20); 3" chambers. Action: Takedown, low rebounding visible hammer. Single trigger, barrel selector spur on hammer. **Barrel:** 24" separated barrels; 12-ga. has mod. choke tubes, 20-ga. has fixed Mod. choke. **Weight:** 8 lbs. **Length:** 40-1/2" overall. **Stock:** Black Rynite composition. **Sights:** Blade front, rear open adjustable for elevation. **Features:** Introduced 1989.
Price: 24F-12 . . . . **$586.00**
Price: 24F-20 . . . . **$556.00**

SPRINGFIELD, INC. M6 SCOUT RIFLE/SHOTGUN
Caliber/Gauge: 22 LR or 22 Hornet over 410-bore. **Barrel:** 18.25". **Weight:** 4 lbs. **Length:** 32" overall. **Stock:** Folding detachable with storage for 15 22 LR, four 410 shells. **Sights:** Blade front, military aperture for 22; V-notch for 410. **Features:** All-metal construction. Designed for quick disassembly and minimum maintenance. Folds for compact storage. Introduced 1982; reintroduced 1996. Imported from the Czech Republic by Springfield, Inc.
Price: Parkerized **$185.00**
Price: Stainless steel **$219.00**

Designs for hunting, utility and sporting purposes, including training for competition

Armscor M-20C Carbine

Browning Buck Mark Target

Browning Semi-Auto 22

Charles Daly
Superior Grade

RIFLES

AR-7 EXPLORER CARBINE

Caliber: 22 LR, 8-shot magazine. **Barrel:** 16". **Weight:** 2-1/2 lbs. **Length:** 34-1/2" / 16-1/2" stowed. **Stock:** Moulded Cycolac; snap-on rubber butt pad. **Sights:** Square blade front, aperture rear. **Features:** Takedown design stores barrel and action in hollow stock. Light enough to float. Reintroduced 1999. From AR-7 Industries, LLC.
Price: Black matte finish **$150.00**
Price: AR-20 Sporter (tubular stock, barrel shroud) **$200.00**
New! **Price:** AR-7 camo- or walnut-finish stock **$164.95**

ARMSCOR MODEL AK22 AUTO RIFLE

Caliber: 22 LR, 10-shot magazine. **Barrel:** 18.5". **Weight:** 7.5 lbs. **Length:** 38" overall. **Stock:** Plain mahogany. **Sights:** Adjustable post front, leaf rear adjustable for elevation. **Features:** Resembles the AK-47. Matte black finish. Introduced 1987. Imported from the Philippines by K.B.I., Inc.
Price: About **$219.95**

ARMSCOR M-1600 AUTO RIFLE

Caliber: 22 LR, 10-shot magazine. **Barrel:** 18.25". **Weight:** 6.2 lbs. **Length:** 38.5" overall. **Stock:** Black finished mahogany. **Sights:** Post front, aperture rear. **Features:** Resembles Colt AR-15. Matte black finish. Introduced 1987. Imported from the Philippines by K.B.I., Inc.
Price: About **$199.95**

ARMSCOR M-20C AUTO CARBINE

Caliber: 22 LR, 10-shot magazine. **Barrel:** 18.25". **Weight:** 6.5 lbs. **Length:** 38" overall. **Stock:** Walnut-finished mahogany. **Sights:** Hooded front, rear adjustable for elevation. **Features:** Receiver grooved for scope mounting. Blued finish. Introduced 1990. Imported from the Philippines by K.B.I., Inc.
Price: **$154.95**

BROWNING BUCK MARK SEMI-AUTO RIFLES

Caliber: 22 LR, 10-shot magazine. **Barrel:** 18" tapered (Sporter), heavy bull (Target), or carbon composite barrel (Classic Carbon). **Weight:** 4 lbs., 2 oz. (Sporter) or 5 lbs., 4 oz. (Target). **Length:** 34" overall. **Stock:** Walnut stock and forearm with full pistol grip. **Sights:** Hi-Viz adjustable (Sporter).

Features: A rifle version of the Buck Mark Pistol; straight blowback action; machined aluminum receiver with integral rail scope mount; recessed muzzle crown; manual thumb safety. Introduced 2001. From Browning.
Price: Sporter (adj. sights) **$518.00**
Price: Target (heavy bbl., no sights) **$518.00**

BROWNING SEMI-AUTO 22 RIFLE

Caliber: 22 LR, 11-shot. **Barrel:** 19-1/4". **Weight:** 5 lbs., 3 oz. **Length:** 37" overall. **Stock:** Checkered select walnut with pistol grip and semi-beavertail forend. **Sights:** Gold bead front, folding leaf rear. **Features:** Engraved receiver with polished blue finish; cross-bolt safety; tubular magazine in buttstock; easy takedown for carrying or storage. Imported from Japan by Browning.
Price: Grade I **$479.00**

Browning Semi-Auto 22, Grade VI

Same as the Grade I Auto-22 except available with either grayed or blued receiver with extensive engraving with gold-plated animals: right side pictures a fox and squirrel in a woodland scene; left side shows a beagle chasing a rabbit. On top is a portrait of the beagle. Stock and forend are of high-grade walnut with a double-bordered cut checkering design. Introduced 1987.
Price: Grade VI, blue or gray receiver **$1,028.00**

BRNO ZKM 611 AUTO RIFLE

Caliber: 22 WMR, 6- or 10-shot magazine. **Barrel:** 20.4". **Weight:** 5.9 lbs. **Length:** 38.9" overall. **Stock:** European walnut. **Sights:** Hooded blade front, open adjustable rear. **Features:** Removable box magazine; polished blue finish; cross-bolt safety; grooved receiver for scope mounting; easy takedown for storage. Imported from The Czech Republic by Euro-Imports.
Price: **$475.00**

CHARLES DALY FIELD GRADE AUTO RIFLE

Caliber: 22 LR, 10-shot magazine. **Barrel:** 20-3/4". **Weight:** 6.5 lbs. **Length:** 40-1/2" overall. **Stock:** Walnut-finished hardwood with Monte Carlo. **Sights:** Hooded front, adjustable open rear. **Features:** Receiver grooved for scope mounting; blue finish; shell deflector. Introduced 1998. Imported by K.B.I.
Price: **$124.00**
Price: Superior Grade (cut checkered stock, fully adjustable sight) **$199.00**

CZ 511 Auto

Henry U.S. Survival

Marlin Model 60

Marlin Model 60SSK

Marlin Model 70PSS

Charles Daly Empire Grade Auto Rifle

Similar to the Field Grade except has select California walnut stock with 24 l.p.i. hand checkering, contrasting forend and gripcaps, damascened bolt, high-polish blue. Introduced 1998. Imported by K.B.I.

Price: **$369.00**

CZ 511 AUTO RIFLE

Caliber: 22 LR, 8-shot magazine. **Barrel:** 22.2". **Weight:** 5.39 lbs. **Length:** 38.6" overall. **Stock:** Walnut with checkered pistol grip. **Sights:** Hooded front, adjustable rear. **Features:** Polished blue finish; detachable magazine; sling swivel studs. Imported from the Czech Republic by CZ-USA.

Price: **$351.00**

HENRY U.S. SURVIVAL RIFLE .22

Caliber: 22 LR, 8-shot magazine. **Barrel:** 16" steel lined. **Weight:** 2.5 lbs. **Stock:** ABS plastic. **Sights:** Blade front on ramp, aperture rear. **Features:** Takedown design stores barrel and action in hollow stock. Light enough to float. Silver, black or camo finish. Comes with two magazines. Introduced 1998. From Henry Repeating Arms Co.

Price: **$165.00**

MAGTECH MT 7022 AUTO RIFLE

Caliber: 22 LR, 10-shot magazine. **Barrel:** 18". **Weight:** 4.8 lbs. **Length:** 37" overall. **Stock:** Brazilian hardwood. **Sights:** Hooded blade front, fully adjustable open rear. **Features:** Cross-bolt safety; last-shot bolt hold-open; alloy receiver is drilled and tapped for scope mounting. Introduced 1998. Imported from Brazil by Magtech Ammunition Co.

Price: **$100.00**

MARLIN MODEL 60 AUTO RIFLE

Caliber: 22 LR, 14-shot tubular magazine. **Barrel:** 19" round tapered. **Weight:** About 5-1/2 lbs. **Length:** 37-1/2" overall. **Stock:** Press-checkered, walnut-finished Maine birch with Monte Carlo, full pistol grip; MarShield® finish. **Sights:** Ramp front, open adjustable rear. **Features:** Matted receiver is grooved for scope mount. Manual bolt hold-open; automatic last-shot bolt hold-open. Model 60C is similar except has hardwood MonteCarlo stock with Mossy Oak Break-Up camouflage pattern. From Marlin.

Price: **$185.00**
Price: With 4x scope **$193.00**
Price: (Model 60C) $220.00

Marlin Model 60SS Self-Loading Rifle

Same as the Model 60 except breech bolt, barrel and outer magazine tube are made of stainless steel; most other parts are either nickel-plated or coated to match the stainless finish. Monte Carlo stock is of black/gray Maine birch laminate, and has nickel-plated swivel studs, rubber butt pad. Introduced 1993. From Marlin.

Price: **$297.00**
Price: Model 60SSK (black fiberglass-filled stock) **$257.00**
Price: Model 60SB (walnut-finished birch stock) **$235.00**
Price: Model 60SB with 4x scope **$251.00**

MARLIN 70PSS PAPOOSE STAINLESS RIFLE

Caliber: 22 LR, 7-shot magazine. **Barrel:** 16-1/4" stainless steel, MicroGroove® rifling. **Weight:** 3-1/4 lbs. **Length:** 35-1/4" overall. **Stock:** Black fiberglass-filled synthetic with abbreviated forend, nickel-plated swivel studs, moulded-in checkering. **Sights:** Ramp front with orange post, cutaway Wide Scan® hood; adjustable open rear. Receiver grooved for scope mounting. **Features:** Takedown barrel; cross-bolt safety; manual bolt hold-open; last shot bolt hold-open; comes with padded carrying case. Introduced 1986. Made in U.S.A. by Marlin.

Price: **$304.00**

Marlin 7000

Marlin 795

Marlin 552 BDL Speedmaster

Remington 597

Ruger 10/22 International

RIFLES

MARLIN MODEL 7000 AUTO RIFLE

Caliber: 22 LR, 10-shot magazine **Barrel:** 18" heavy target with 12-groove Micro-Groove® rifling, recessed muzzle. **Weight:** 5-1/2 lbs. **Length:** 37" overall. **Stock:** Black fiberglass-filled synthetic with Monte Carlo combo, swivel studs, moulded-in checkering. **Sights:** None furnished; comes with ring mounts. **Features:** Automatic last-shot bolt hold-open, manual bolt hold-open; cross-bolt safety; steel charging handle; blue finish, nickel-plated magazine. Introduced 1997. Made in U.S.A. by Marlin Firearms Co.
Price: **$249.00**

Marlin Model 795 Auto Rifle

Similar to Model 7000 except standard-weight 18" barrel with 16-groove Micro-Groove rifling. Ramp front sight with brass bead, screw adjustable open rear. Receiver grooved for scope mount. Introduced 1997. Made in U.S.A. by Marlin Firearms Co.
Price: **$176.00**

Marlin Model 795SS Auto Rifle

Similar to Model 795 except stainless steel barrel. Most other parts nickel-plated. Adjustable folding semi-buckhorn rear sights, ramp front high-visibility post and removeable cutaway wide scan hood.
Price: **$235.00**

REMINGTON MODEL 552 BDL DELUXE SPEEDMASTER RIFLE

Caliber: 22 S (20), L (17) or LR (15) tubular mag. **Barrel:** 21" round tapered. **Weight:** 5-3/4 lbs. **Length:** 40" overall. **Stock:** Walnut. Checkered grip and forend. **Sights:** Big game. **Features:** Positive cross-bolt safety, receiver grooved for tip-off mount.
Price: **$393.00**

REMINGTON 597 AUTO RIFLE

Caliber: 22 LR, 10-shot clip. **Barrel:** 20". **Weight:** 5-1/2 lbs. **Length:** 40" overall. **Stock:** Black synthetic. **Sights:** Big game. **Features:** Matte black finish, nickel-plated bolt. Receiver is grooved and drilled and tapped for scope mounts. Introduced 1997. Made in U.S.A. by Remington.
Price: **$169.00**
Price: Model 597 Magnum, 22 WMR, 8-shot clip **$335.00**
Price: Model 597 LSS (laminated stock, stainless) **$279.00**
Price: Model 597 SS
(22 LR, stainless steel, black synthetic stock) **$224.00**
Price: Model 597 LS Heavy Barrel (22 LR, laminated stock) **$265.00**
Price: Model 597 Magnum LS Heavy Barrel
(22 WMR, lam. stock) **$399.00**
Price: Model 597 Magnum 17 HMR, 8-shot clip. **$361.00**

RUGER 10/22 AUTOLOADING CARBINE

Caliber: 22 LR, 10-shot rotary magazine. **Barrel:** 18-1/2" round tapered. **Weight:** 5 lbs. **Length:** 37-1/4" overall. **Stock:** American hardwood with pistol grip and barrel band or synthetic. **Sights:** Brass bead front, folding leaf rear adjustable for elevation. **Features:** Detachable rotary magazine fits flush into stock, cross-bolt safety, receiver tapped and grooved for scope blocks or tip-off mount. Scope base adaptor furnished with each rifle.
Price: Model 10/22 RB (blue) **$239.00**
Price: Model K10/22RB (bright finish stainless barrel) **$279.00**
Price: Model 10/22RPF (blue, synthetic stock) **$239.00**

Ruger 10/22 International Carbine

Similar to the Ruger 10/22 Carbine except has full-length International stock of American hardwood, checkered grip and forend; comes with rubber butt pad, sling swivels. Reintroduced 1994.
Price: Blue (10/22RBI) **$279.00**
Price: Stainless (K10/22RBI) **$299.00**

Ruger 10/22 Deluxe Sporter

Ruger 10/22 Target

Ruger 10/22 International

Savage Model 64FV

Ruger 10/22 Deluxe Sporter
Same as 10/22 Carbine except walnut stock with hand checkered pistol grip and forend; straight buttplate, no barrel band, has sling swivels.
Price: Model 10/22 DSP **$299.00**

Ruger 10/22T Target Rifle
Similar to the 10/22 except has 20" heavy, hammer-forged barrel with tight chamber dimensions, improved trigger pull, laminated hardwood stock dimensioned for optical sights. No iron sights supplied. Introduced 1996. Made in U.S.A. by Sturm, Ruger & Co.
Price: 10/22T **$425.00**
Price: K10/22T, stainless steel **$485.00**

Ruger K10/22RPF All-Weather Rifle
Similar to the stainless K10/22/RB except has black composite stock of thermoplastic polyester resin reinforced with fiberglass; checkered grip and forend. Brushed satin, natural metal finish with clear hardcoat finish. Weighs 5 lbs., measures 36-3/4" overall. Introduced 1997. From Sturm, Ruger & Co.
Price: **$279.00**

RUGER 10/22 MAGNUM AUTOLOADING CARBINE
Caliber: 22 WMR, 9-shot rotary magazine. **Barrel:** 18-1/2". **Weight:** 6 lbs. **Length:** 37-1/4" overall. **Stock:** Birch. **Sights:** Gold bead front, folding rear. **Features:** All-steel receiver has integral Ruger scope bases for the included 1" rings. Introduced 1999. Made in U.S.A. by Sturm, Ruger & Co.
Price: 10/22RBM **$499.00**

SAVAGE MODEL 64G AUTO RIFLE
Caliber: 22 LR, 10-shot magazine. **Barrel:** 20", 21". **Weight:** 5-1/2 lbs. **Length:** 40", 41". **Stock:** Walnut-finished hardwood with Monte Carlo-type comb, checkered grip and forend. **Sights:** Bead front, open adjustable rear. Receiver grooved for scope mounting. **Features:** Thumb-operated rotating safety. Blue finish. Side ejection, bolt hold-open device. Introduced 1990. Made in Canada, from Savage Arms.

Price: **$151.00**
Price: Model 64FSS, stainless **$196.00**
Price: Model 64F, black synthetic stock **$135.00**
Price: Model 64GXP Package Gun includes
4x15 scope and mounts **$156.00**
Price: Model 64FXP (black stock, 4x15 scope) **$144.00**
Price: Model 64F Camo **$166.00**

Savage Model 64FV Auto Rifle
Similar to the Model 64F except has heavy 21" barrel with recessed crown; no sights provided—comes with Weaver-style bases. Introduced 1998. Imported from Canada by Savage Arms, Inc.
Price: **$182.00**
Price: Model 64FVSS, stainless **$235.00**

THOMPSON/CENTER 22 LR CLASSIC RIFLE
Caliber: 22 LR, 8-shot magazine. **Barrel:** 22" match-grade. **Weight:** 5-1/2 pounds. **Length:** 39-1/2" overall. **Stock:** Satin-finished American walnut with Monte Carlo-type comb and pistol grip cap, swivel studs. **Sights:** Ramp-style front and fully adjustable rear, both with fiber optics. **Features:** All-steel receiver drilled and tapped for scope mounting; barrel threaded to receiver; thumb-operated safety; trigger-guard safety lock included. New .22 Classic Benchmark TGT target rifle variant has 18" heavy barrel, brown laminated target stock, blued with matte finish, 10-shot magazine and no sights; drilled and tapped.
Price: T/C 22 LR Classic (blue) **$370.00**
Price: T/C 22 LR Classic Benchmark **$472.00**

TAURUS MODEL 63 RIFLE
Caliber: .22 LR, 10-shot tube-fed magazine. **Barrel:** 23". **Weight:** 72 oz. **Length:** 32-1/2". **Stock:** Hand-fitted walnut-finished hardwood. **Sights:** Adjustable rear, fixed front. **Features:** Manual safety, metal buttplate, can accept Taurus tang sight. Charged and cocked with operating plunger at front of forend. Available in blue or polished stainless steel.
Price: 63 . . . . **$295.00**
Price: 63SS **$311.00**

RIFLES

RIMFIRE RIFLES — LEVER & SLIDE ACTION

Classic and modern models for sport and utility, including training.

Browning BL-22

Henry Lever-Action 22

Henry Golden Boy 22

Henry Pump-Action 22

Marlin Model 39AS

Marlin Model 1897T

BROWNING BL-22 LEVER-ACTION RIFLE
Caliber: 22 S (22), L (17) or LR (15), tubular magazine. **Barrel:** 20" round tapered. **Weight:** 5 lbs. **Length:** 36-3/4" overall. **Stock:** Walnut, two-piece straight grip Western style. **Sights:** Bead post front, folding-leaf rear. **Features:** Short throw lever, half-cock safety, receiver grooved for tip-off scope mounts, gold-colored trigger. Imported from Japan by Browning.
Price: Grade I **$415.00**
Price: Grade II (engraved receiver, checkered grip and forend) . **$471.00**
Price: Classic, Grade I (blued trigger, no checkering) **$415.00**
Price: Classic, Grade II (cut checkering, satin wood finish, polished blueing) **$471.00**

HENRY LEVER-ACTION 22
Caliber: 22 Long Rifle (15-shot). **Barrel:** 18-1/4" round. **Weight:** 5-1/2 lbs. **Length:** 34" overall. **Stock:** Walnut. **Sights:** Hooded blade front, open adjustable rear. **Features:** Polished blue finish; full-length tubular magazine; side ejection; receiver grooved for scope mounting. Introduced 1997. Made in U.S.A. by Henry Repeating Arms Co.
Price: **$239.95**
Price: Youth model (33" overall, 11-rounds 22 LR) **$229.95**

HENRY GOLDEN BOY 22 LEVER-ACTION RIFLE
Caliber: 22 LR, 22 Magnum, 16-shot. **Barrel:** 20" octagonal. **Weight:** 6.25 lbs. **Length:** 38" overall. **Stock:** American walnut. **Sights:** Blade front, open rear. **Features:** Brasslite receiver, brass buttplate, blued barrel and lever. Introduced 1998. Made in U.S.A. from Henry Repeating Arms Co.
Price: **$379.95**
Price: Magnum **$449.95**

HENRY PUMP-ACTION 22 PUMP RIFLE
Caliber: 22 LR, 15-shot. **Barrel:** 18.25". **Weight:** 5.5 lbs. **Length:** NA. **Stock:** American walnut. **Sights:** Bead on ramp front, open adjustable rear. **Features:** Polished blue finish; receiver groved for scope mount; grooved slide handle; two barrel bands. Introduced 1998. Made in U.S.A. from Henry Repeating Arms Co.
Price: **$249.95**

MARLIN MODEL 39A GOLDEN LEVER-ACTION RIFLE
Caliber: 22, S (26), L (21), LR (19), tubular mag. **Barrel:** 24" Micro-Groove®. **Weight:** 6-1/2 lbs. **Length:** 40" overall. **Stock:** Checkered American black walnut; Mar-Shield® finish. Swivel studs; rubber butt pad. **Sights:** Bead ramp front with detachable Wide-Scan™ hood, folding rear semi-buckhorn adjustable for windage and elevation. **Features:** Hammer block safety; rebounding hammer. Takedown action, receiver tapped for scope mount (supplied), offset hammer spur, gold-plated steel trigger. From Marlin Firearms.
Price: **$552.00**

MARLIN MODEL 1897T RIFLE
Caliber: 22, S (21), L (16), LR (14), tubular mag. **Barrel:** 20" tapered octagon. **Weight:** Marble semi-buckhorn rear, Marble front brass beaded. **Features:** Hammer block safety solid top receiver tapped, 2-level base for 3/4", 7/8" scope ring and " detached, blued, safety lock. From Marlin Firearms.
Price: **$748.00**

Remington Model 572 BDL Deluxe Fieldmaster

Ruger Model 96/22

Taurus 62R

Taurus 72C-SS

Winchester 9422 Legacy

REMINGTON 572 BDL DELUXE FIELDMASTER PUMP RIFLE

Caliber: 22 S (20), L (17) or LR (15), tubular mag. **Barrel:** 21" round tapered. **Weight:** 5-1/2 lbs. **Length:** 40" overall. **Stock:** Walnut with checkered pistol grip and slide handle. **Sights:** Big game. **Features:** Cross-bolt safety; removing inner magazine tube converts rifle to single shot; receiver grooved for tip-off scope mount.

Price: **$407.00**

RUGER MODEL 96 LEVER-ACTION RIFLE

Caliber: 22 LR, 10 rounds; 22 WMR, 9 rounds; 44 Magnum, 4 rounds; 17 HMR 9 rounds. **Barrel:** 18-1/2". **Weight:** 5-1/4 lbs. **Length:** 37-1/4" overall. **Stock:** Hardwood. **Sights:** Gold bead front, folding leaf rear. **Features:** Sliding cross button safety, visible cocking indicator; short-throw lever action. Introduced 1996. Made in U.S.A. by Sturm, Ruger & Co.

Price: 96/22 (22 LR) **$349.00**
Price: 96/22M (22 WMR) **$375.00**
Price: 96/22M (44 Mag.) **$525.00**
New! **Price:** 96/17M (17 HMR) **$375.00**

TAURUS MODEL 62 PUMP RIFLE

Caliber: 22 LR, 12- or 13-shot. **Barrel:** 16-1/2" or 23" round. **Weight:** 72 oz-80 oz. **Length:** 39" overall. **Stock:** Premium hardwood. **Sights:** Adjustable rear, bead blade front, optional tang. **Features:** Blue, case hardened or stainless, bolt-mounted safety, pump action, manual firing pin block, integral security lock system. Imported from Brazil by Taurus International.

Price: M62C (blue) **$280.00**
Price: M62C-CH (case hardened-blue) **$280.00**
Price: M62CCH-T (case hardened-blue) **$358.00**
Price: M62C-SS (stainless steel) **$295.00**
Price: M62CSS-T (stainless steel) **$373.00**
Price: M62C-SS-Y (stainless steel) **$327.00**

Price: M62C-T (blue) **$358.00**
Price: M62C-Y (blue) **$311.00**
Price: M62R (blue) **$280.00**
Price: M62R-CH (case hardened-blue) **$280.00**
Price: M62RCH-T (case hardened-blue) **$358.00**
Price: M62R-SS (stainless steel) **$295.00**
Price: M62RSS-T (stainless steel) **$373.00**
Price: M62R-T (blue) **$358.00**

Taurus Model 72 Pump Rifle

Same as Model 62 except chambered in 22 Magnum or .17 HMR; 16-1/2" bbl. holds 10-12 shots, 23" bbl. holds 11-13 shots. Weighs 72 oz.-80 oz. Introduced 2001. Imported from Brazil by Taurus International.

Price: M72C (blue) **$295.00**
Price: M72C-CH (case hardened-blue) **$295.00**
Price: M72CCH-T (case hardened-blue) **$373.00**
Price: M72C-SS (stainless steel) **$311.00**
Price: M72CSS-T (stainless steel) **$389.00**
Price: M72C-T (blue) **$373.00**
Price: M72R (blue) **$295.00**
Price: M72R-CH (case hardened-blue) **$295.00**
Price: M72RCH-T (case hardened-blue) **$373.00**
Price: M72R-SS (stainless steel) **$311.00**
Price: M72RSS-T (stainless steel) **$389.00**
Price: M72R-T (blue) **$373.00**

WINCHESTER MODEL 9422 LEVER-ACTION RIFLES

Caliber: 22 LR, 22 WMR, tubular magazine. **Barrel:** 20-1/2". **Weight:** 6-1/4 lbs. **Length:** 37-1/8" overall. **Stock:** American walnut, two-piece, straight grip (Traditional) or semi-pistol grip (Legacy). **Sights:** Hooded ramp front, adjustable semi-buckhorn rear. **Features:** Side ejection, receiver grooved for scope mounting, takedown action. From U.S. Repeating Arms Co.

Price: Traditional, 22 LR 15-shot **$465.00**
Price: Traditional, 22WMR, 11-shot **$487.00**
Price: Legacy, 22 LR 15-shot **$498.00**
Price: Legacy 22 WMR, 11-shot **$521.00**

RIFLES

Includes models for a variety of sports, utility and competitive shooting.

Anschutz 1518D Luxus

Anschutz 1710D

Charles Daly Field Grade

ANSCHUTZ 1416D/1516D CLASSIC RIFLES

Caliber: 22 LR (1416D), 5-shot clip; 22 WMR (1516D), 4-shot clip. **Barrel:** 22-1/2". **Weight:** 6 lbs. **Length:** 41" overall. **Stock:** European hardwood with walnut finish; classic style with straight comb, checkered pistol grip and forend. **Sights:** Hooded ramp front, folding leaf rear. **Features:** Uses Match 64 action. Adjustable single stage trigger. Receiver grooved for scope mounting. Imported from Germany by AcuSport Corp.

Price: 1416D, 22 LR **$755.95**
Price: 1516D, 22 WMR **$779.95**
Price: 1416D Classic left-hand **$679.95**

Anschutz 1416D/1516D Walnut Luxus Rifles

Similar to the Classic models except have European walnut stocks with Monte Carlo cheekpiece, slim forend with Schnabel tip, cut checkering on grip and forend. Introduced 1997. Imported from Germany by AcuSport Corp.

Price: 1416D (22 LR) **$755.95**
Price: 1516D (22 WMR) **$779.95**

ANSCHUTZ 1518D LUXUS BOLT-ACTION RIFLE

Caliber: 22 WMR, 4-shot magazine. **Barrel:** 19-3/4". **Weight:** 5-1/2 lbs. **Length:** 37-1/2" overall. **Stock:** European walnut. **Sights:** Blade on ramp front, folding leaf rear. **Features:** Receiver grooved for scope mounting; single stage trigger; skip-line checkering; rosewood forend tip; sling swivels. Imported from Germany by AcuSport Corp.

Price: **$1,186.95**

ANSCHUTZ 1710D CUSTOM RIFLE

Caliber: 22 LR, 5-shot clip. **Barrel:** 24-1/4". **Weight:** 7-3/8 lbs. **Length:** 42-1/2" overall. **Stock:** Select European walnut. **Sights:** Hooded ramp front, folding leaf rear; drilled and tapped for scope mounting. **Features:** Match 54 action with adjustable single-stage trigger; roll-over Monte Carlo cheekpiece, slim forend with Schnabel tip, Wundhammer palm swell on pistol grip, rosewood gripcap with white diamond insert; skip-line checkering on grip and forend. Introduced 1988. Imported from Germany by AcuSport Corp.

Price: **$1,289.95**

CABANAS MASTER BOLT-ACTION RIFLE

Caliber: 177, round ball or pellet; single shot. **Barrel:** 19-1/2". **Weight:** 8 lbs. **Length:** 45-1/2" overall. **Stocks:** Walnut target-type with Monte Carlo. **Sights:** Blade front, fully adjustable rear. **Features:** Fires round ball or pellet with 22-cal. blank cartridge. Bolt action. Imported from Mexico by Mandall Shooting Supplies. Introduced 1984.

Price: **$189.95**
Price: Varmint model (has 21-1/2" barrel, 4-1/2 lbs., 41" overall length, varmint-type stock) **$119.95**

Cabanas Leyre Bolt-Action Rifle

Similar to Master model except 44" overall, has sport/target stock.

Price: **$149.95**
Price: Model R83 (17" barrel, hardwood stock, 40" o.a.l.) **$79.95**
Price: Mini 82 Youth (16-1/2" barrel, 33" overall length, 3-1/2 lbs.) **$69.95**
Price: Pony Youth (16" barrel, 34" overall length, 3.2 lbs.). **$69.95**

Cabanas Espronceda IV Bolt-Action Rifle

Similar to the Leyre model except has full sporter stock, 18-3/4" barrel, 40" overall length, weighs 5-1/2 lbs.

Price: **$134.95**

CABANAS LASER RIFLE

Caliber: 177. **Barrel:** 19". **Weight:** 6 lbs., 12 oz. **Length:** 42" overall. **Stock:** Target-type thumbhole. **Sights:** Blade front, open fully adjustable rear. **Features:** Fires round ball or pellets with 22 blank cartridge. Imported from Mexico by Mandall Shooting Supplies.

Price: **$159.95**

CHARLES DALY SUPERIOR BOLT-ACTION RIFLE

Caliber: 22 LR, 10-shot magazine. **Barrel:** 22-5/8". **Weight:** 6.7 lbs. **Length:** 41.25" overall. **Stock:** Walnut-finished mahogany. **Sights:** Bead front, rear adjustable for elevation. **Features:** Receiver grooved for scope mounting. Blued finish. Introduced 1998. Imported by K.B.I., Inc.

Price: **$189.95**

Charles Daly Field Grade Rifle

Similar to the Superior except has short walnut-finished hardwood stock for small shooters. Introduced 1998. Imported by K.B.I., Inc.

Price: **$134.95**
Price: Field Youth (17.5" barrel) **$144.95**

Charles Daly Superior Magnum Grade Rifle

Similar to the Superior except chambered for 22 WMR. Has 22.6" barrel, double lug bolt, checkered stock, weighs 6.5 lbs. Introduced 1987.

Price: About **$204.95**

Charles Daly Empire Magnum Grade Rifle

Similar to the Superior Magnum except has oil-finished American walnut stock with 18 lpi hand checkering; black hardwood gripcap and forend tip; highly polished barreled action; jewelled bolt; recoil pad; swivel studs. Imported from the Philippines by K.B.I., Inc.

Price: **$364.95**

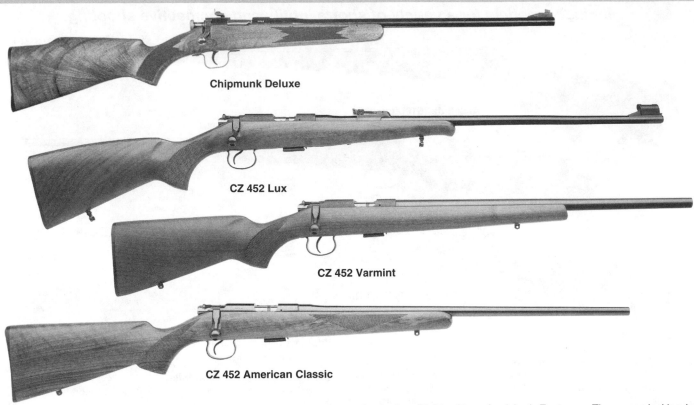

Chipmunk Deluxe

CZ 452 Lux

CZ 452 Varmint

CZ 452 American Classic

Charles Daly Empire Grade Rifle

Similar to the Superior except has oil-finished American walnut stock with 18 lpi hand checkering; black hardwood gripcap and forend tip; highly polished barreled action; jewelled bolt; recoil pad; swivel studs. Imported by K.B.I., Inc.

Price: **$329.00**

CHARLES DALY TRUE YOUTH BOLT-ACTION RIFLE

Caliber: 22 LR, single shot. **Barrel:** 16-1/4". **Weight:** About 3 lbs. **Length:** 32" overall. **Stock:** Walnut-finished hardwood. **Sights:** Blade front, adjustable rear. **Features:** Scaled-down stock for small shooters. Blue finish. Introduced 1998. Imported by K.B.I., Inc.

Price: **$154.95**

CHIPMUNK SINGLE SHOT RIFLE

Caliber: 22 LR, 22 WMR, single shot. **Barrel:** 16-1/8". **Weight:** About 2-1/2 lbs. **Length:** 30" overall. **Stocks:** American walnut. **Sights:** Post on ramp front, peep rear adjustable for windage and elevation. **Features:** Drilled and tapped for scope mounting using special Chipmunk base ($13.95). Engraved model also available. Made in U.S.A. Introduced 1982. From Rogue Rifle Co., Inc.

Price: Standard **$194.25**
Price: Standard 22 WMR **$209.95**
Price: Deluxe (better wood, checkering) **$246.95**
Price: Deluxe 22 WMR **$262.95**
Price: Laminated stock **$209.95**
Price: Laminated stock, 22 WMR **$225.95**
Price: Bull barrel models of above, add **$16.00**

CHIPMUNK TM (TARGET MODEL)

Caliber: 22 S, L, or LR. **Barrel:** 18" blue. **Weight:** 5 lbs. **Length:** 33". **Stocks:** Walnut with accessory rail. **Sights:** 1/4 minute micrometer adjustable. **Features:** Manually cocking single shot bolt action, blue receiver, adjustable butt plate and butt pad.

Price: **$329.95**

COOPER MODEL 57-M BOLT-ACTION RIFLE

Caliber: 22 LR, 22 WMR, 17 HMR. **Barrel:** 23-3/4" stainless steel or 41-40 match grade. **Weight:** 6.6 lbs. **Stock:** Claro walnut, 22 lpi hand checkering. **Sights:** None furnished. **Features:** Three rear locking lug, repeating bolt-action with 5-shot mag. Fully adjustable trigger. Many options. Made 100% in the U.S.A. by Cooper Firearms of Montana, Inc.

Price: Classic **$1,100.00**
Price: LVT **$1,295.00**
Price: Custom Classic **$1,895.00**
Price: Western Classic **$2,495.00**

CZ 452 M 2E LUX BOLT-ACTION RIFLE

Caliber: 22 LR, 22 WMR, 5-shot detachable magazine. **Barrel:** 24.8". **Weight:** 6.6 lbs. **Length:** 42.63" overall. **Stock:** Walnut with checkered pistol grip. **Sights:** Hooded front, fully adjustable tangent rear. **Features:** All-steel construction, adjustable trigger, polished blue finish. Imported from the Czech Republic by CZ-USA.

Price: 22 LR **$351.00**
Price: 22 WMR **$378.00**
Price: Synthetic stock, nickel finish, 22 LR **$344.00**

CZ 452 M 2E Varmint Rifle

Similar to the Lux model except has heavy 20.8" barrel; stock has beavertail forend; weighs 7 lbs.; no sights furnished. Available only in 22 LR. Imported from the Czech Republic by CZ-USA.

Price: **$378.00**

CZ 452 American Classic Bolt-Action Rifle

Similar to the CZ 452 M 2E Lux except has classic-style stock of Circassian walnut; 22.5" free-floating barrel with recessed target crown; receiver dovetail for scope mounting. No open sights furnished. Introduced 1999. Imported from the Czech Republic by CZ-USA.

Price: 22 LR **$351.00**
Price: 22 WMR **$378.00**

HARRINGTON & RICHARDSON ULTRA HEAVY BARREL 22 MAG RIFLE

Caliber: 22 WMR, single shot. **Barrel:** 22" bull. **Stock:** Cinnamon laminated wood with Monte Carlo cheekpiece. **Sights:** None furnished; scope mount rail included. **Features:** Hand-checkered stock and forend; deep-crown rifling; tuned trigger; trigger locking system; hammer extension. Introduced 2001. From H&R 1871 LLC.

Price: **$193.00**

RIFLES

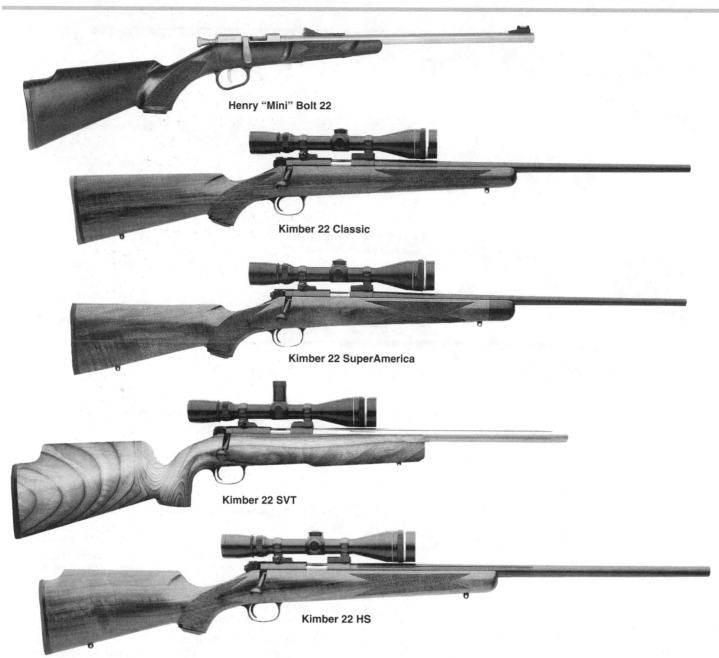

Henry "Mini" Bolt 22

Kimber 22 Classic

Kimber 22 SuperAmerica

Kimber 22 SVT

Kimber 22 HS

HENRY "MINI" BOLT 22 RIFLE

Caliber: 22 LR, single shot. **Barrel:** 16" stainless, 8-groove rifling. **Weight:** 3.25 lbs. **Length:** 30", LOP 11-1/2". **Stock:** Synthetic, pistol grip, wrap-around checkering and beavertail forearm. **Sights:** William Fire sights. **Features:** One piece bolt configuration manually operated safety. Ideal for beginners or ladies.
Price: **$169.95**

KIMBER 22 CLASSIC BOLT-ACTION RIFLE

Caliber: 22 LR, 5-shot magazine. **Barrel:** 18", 22", 24" match grade; 11-degree target crown. **Weight:** 5-8 lbs. **Length:** 35"-43". **Stock:** Classic Claro walnut, hand-cut checkering, steel gripcap, swivel studs. **Sights:** None, drilled and tapped. **Features:** All-new action with Mauser-style full-length claw extractor, two-position wing safety, match trigger, pillar-bedded action with recoil lug. Introduced 1999. Made in U.S.A. by Kimber Mfg., Inc.
Price: New Classic **$1,085.00**
Price: Classic **$949.00**
Price: Hunter **$678.00**
Price: Youth **$746.00**

Kimber 22 SuperAmerica Bolt-Action Rifle

Similar to 22 Classic except has AAA Claro walnut stock with wrap-around 22 l.p.i. hand-cut checkering, ebony forened tip, beaded cheekpiece. Introduced 1999. Made in U.S.A. by Kimber Mfg., Inc.
Price: **$1,764.00**

Kimber 22 SVT Bolt-Action Rilfe

Similar to 22 Classic except has 18" stainless steel, fluted bull barrel, gray laminated, high-comb target-style stock with deep pistol grip, high comb, beavertail forend with bipod stud. Weighs 7.5 lbs., overall length 36.5". Matte finish on action. Introduced 1999. Made in U.S.A. by Kimber Mfg., Inc.
Price: **$949.00**

Kimber 22 HS (Hunter Silhouette) Bolt-Action Rifle

Similar to 22 Classic except 24" medium sporter match-grade barrel with half-fluting; high comb, walnut, Monte Carlo target stock with 18 l.p.i. checkering; matte blue metal finish. Introduced 1999. Made in U.S.A. by Kimber Mfg., Inc.
Price: **$814.00**

Marlin 17V

Marlin Model 15YN "Little Buckaroo"

Marlin Model 880SS

Marlin 880SQ Squirrel

Marlin 25N

Marlin 25MNC

MARLIN MODEL 17V HORNADY MAGNUM

Caliber: 17 Magnum, 7-shot. **Barrel:** 22. **Weight:** 6 lbs., stainless 7 lbs. **Length:** 41". **Stock:** Checkered walnut Monte Carlo SS, laminated black/grey. **Sights:** No sights but receiver grooved. **Features:** Swivel studs, positive thumb safety, red cocking indicator, safety lock, SS 1" brushed aluminum scope rings.

Price:	**$269.00**
Price: Bead blasted SS barrel & receiver	**$402.00**

MARLIN MODEL 15YN "LITTLE BUCKAROO"

Caliber: 22 S, L, LR, single shot. **Barrel:** 16-1/4" Micro-Groove®. **Weight:** 4-1/4 lbs. **Length:** 33-1/4" overall. **Stock:** One-piece walnut-finished, press-checkered Maine birch with Monte Carlo; Mar-Shield® finish. **Sights:** Ramp front, adjustable open rear. **Features:** Beginner's rifle with thumb safety, easy-load feed throat, red cocking indicator. Receiver grooved for scope mounting. Introduced 1989.

Price:	**$209.00**
Price: Stainless steel with fire sights	**$233.00**

MARLIN MODEL 880SS BOLT-ACTION RIFLE

Caliber: 22 LR, 7-shot clip magazine. **Barrel:** 22" Micro-Groove®. **Weight:** 6 lbs. **Length:** 41" overall. **Stock:** Black fiberglass-filled synthetic with nickel-plated swivel studs and moulded-in checkering. **Sights:** Ramp front with orange post and cutaway Wide-Scan™ hood, adjustable semi-buckhorn folding rear. **Features:** Stainless steel barrel, receiver, front breech bolt and striker; receiver grooved for scope mounting. Introduced 1994. Model 880SQ (Squirrel Rifle) is similar but has heavy 22" barrel. Made in U.S.A. by Marlin.

Price: (Model 880SS)	**$316.00**
Price: (Model 880SQ) $330.00	

Marlin Model 81TS Bolt-Action Rifle

Same as Marlin 880SS except blued steel, tubular magazine, holds 17 Long Rifle cartridges. Weighs 6 lbs.

Price:	**$213.00**

Marlin Model 880SQ Squirrel Rifle

Similar to Model 880SS except uses heavy target barrel. Black synthetic stock with moulded-in checkering, double bedding screws, matte blue finish. Without sights, no dovetail or filler screws; receiver grooved for scope mount. Weighs 7 lbs. Introduced 1996. Made in U.S.A. by Marlin.

Price:	**$322.00**

Marlin Model 25N Bolt-Action Repeater

Similar to Marlin 880, except walnut-finished hardwood stock, adjustable open rear sight, ramp front.

Price:	**$212.00**
Price: With 4x scope and mount.	**$220.00**

Marlin Model 25NC Bolt-Action Repeater

Same as Model 25N except Mossy Oak® Break-Up camouflage stock. Made in U.S.A. by Marlin.

Price:	**$248.00**

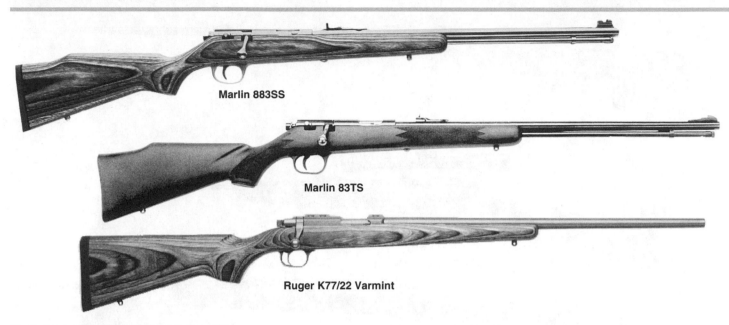

Marlin 883SS

Marlin 83TS

Ruger K77/22 Varmint

Marlin Model 25MN/25MNC Bolt-Action Rifles

Similar to the Model 25N except chambered for 22 WMR. Has 7 shot clip magazine, 22" Micro-Groove® barrel, checkered walnut-finished Maine birch stock. Introduced 1989.

Price: 25MN $241.00
New! Price: 25MNC (Mossy Oak® Break-Up camouflage stock). $278.00

Marlin Model 882 Bolt-Action Rifle

Same as the Marlin 880 except 22 WMR cal. only with 7-shot clip magazine; weight about 6 lbs. Comes with swivel studs.

Price: $324.00
Price: Model 882L (laminated hardwood stock; weighs 6-1/4 lbs.) $342.00

Marlin Model 882SS Bolt-Action Rifle

Same as the Marlin Model 882 except has stainless steel front breech bolt, barrel, receiver and bolt knob. All other parts are either stainless steel or nickel-plated. Has black Monte Carlo stock of fiberglass-filled polycarbonate with moulded-in checkering, nickel-plated swivel studs. Introduced 1995. Made in U.S.A. by Marlin Firearms Co.

Price: $345.00

Marlin Model 882SSV Bolt-Action Rifle

Similar to the Model 882SS except has selected heavy 22" stainless steel barrel with recessed muzzle, and comes without sights; receiver is grooved for scope mount and 1" ring mounts are included. Weighs 7 lbs. Introduced 1997. Made in U.S.A. by Marlin Firearms Co.

Price: $338.00

MARLIN MODEL 883 BOLT-ACTION RIFLE

Caliber: 22 WMR. Barrel: 22"; 1:16" twist. Weight: 6 lbs. Length: 41" overall. Stock: Walnut Monte Carlo with sling swivel studs, rubber butt pad. Sights: Ramp front with brass bead, removable hood; adjustable semi-buckhorn folding rear. Features: Thumb safety, red cocking indicator, receiver grooved for scope mount. Made in U.S.A. by Marlin Firearms Co.

Price: $337.00

Marlin Model 883SS Bolt-Action Rifle

Same as the Model 883 except front breech bolt, striker knob, trigger stud, cartridge lifter stud and outer magazine tube are of stainless steel; other parts are nickel-plated. Has two-tone brown laminated Monte Carlo stock with swivel studs, rubber butt pad. Introduced 1993.

Price: $358.00

Marlin Model 83TS Bolt-Action Rifle

Same as the Model 883 except has a black Monte Carlo fiberglass-filled synthetic stock with sling swivel studs. Weighs 6 lbs., length 41" overall. Introduced 2001. Made in U.S.A. by Marlin Firearms Co.

Price: $259.00

MEACHAM LOW WALL RIFLE

Caliber: 22 RF Match, .17 HMR. Barrel: 28". Weight: 10 lbs. Sights: None. Tang drilled for Win. base, 3/8" dovetail slot, front. Stock: Fancy eastern black walnut with cheekpiece; ebony insert in forend. Features: Available with single trigger, single set trigger, or Schuetzen-style double set triggers. Introduced 2002. From Meacham T&H, Inc.

Price: $2,999.00

NEW ENGLAND FIREARMS SPORTSTER™ SINGLE-SHOT RIFLES

Caliber: 22 LR, 22 WMR, 17 HMR, single-shot. Barrel: 20". Weight: 5-1/2 lbs. Length: 36-1/4" overall. Stock: Black polymer. Sights: None furnished; scope mount included. Features: Break open, side-lever release; automatic ejection; recoil pad; sling swivel studs; trigger locking system. Introduced 2001. Made in U.S.A. by New England Firearms.

Price: $149.00
Price: Youth model (20" bbl., 33" overall, weighs 5-1/3 lbs.) $149.00
Price: Sportster 17 HMR $180.00

NEW ULTRA LIGHT ARMS 20RF BOLT-ACTION RIFLE

Caliber: 22 LR, single shot or repeater. Barrel: Douglas, length to order. Weight: 5-1/4 lbs. Length: Varies. Stock: Kevlar®/graphite composite, variety of finishes. Sights: None furnished; drilled and tapped for scope mount. Features: Timney trigger, hand-lapped action, button-rifled barrel, hand-bedded action, recoil pad, sling-swivel studs, optional Jewell Trigger. Made in U.S.A. by New Ultra Light Arms.

Price: 20 RF single shot $800.00
Price: 20 RF repeater $850.00

ROSSI MATCHED PAIR SINGLE-SHOT RIFLE/SHOTGUN

Caliber: 22 LR or 22 Mag. Barrel: 18-1/2" or 23". Weight: 6 lbs. Stock: Hardwood (brown or black finish). Sights: Fully adjustable front and rear. Features: Break-open breech, transfer-bar manual safety, includes matched 410-, 20- or 12-gauge shotgun barrel with bead front sight. Introduced 2001. Imported by BrazTech/Taurus.

Price: blue $139.95
Price: stainless steel $169.95

RUGER K77/22 VARMINT RIFLE

Caliber: 22 LR, 10-shot, 22 WMR, 9-shot detachable rotary magazine. Barrel: 24", heavy. Weight: 6-7/8 lbs. Length: 43.25" overall. Stock: Laminated hardwood with rubber butt pad, quick-detachable swivel studs. Sights: None furnished. Comes with Ruger 1" scope rings. Features: Stainless steel or blued finish. Three-position safety, dual extractors. Stock has wide, flat forend. Introduced 1993.

Price: K77/22VBZ, 22 LR $645.00
Price: K77/22VMBZ, 22 WMR $645.00

Ruger 77/22R

Sako Finnfire

Savage Mark I-G

Savage Mark I-Y

RUGER 77/22 RIMFIRE BOLT-ACTION RIFLE

Caliber: 22 LR, 10-shot rotary magazine; 22 WMR, 9-shot rotary magazine. **Barrel:** 20". **Weight:** About 5-3/4 lbs. **Length:** 39-3/4" overall. **Stock:** Checkered American walnut, laminated hardwood, or synthetic stocks, stainless sling swivels. **Sights:** Brass bead front, adjustable folding leaf rear or plain barrel with 1" Ruger rings. **Features:** Mauser-type action uses Ruger's rotary magazine. Three-position safety, simplified bolt stop, patented bolt locking system. Uses the dual-screw barrel attachment system of the 10/22 rifle. Integral scope mounting system with 1" Ruger rings. Blued model introduced 1983. Stainless steel and blued with synthetic stock introduced 1989.

Price: 77/22R (no sights, rings, walnut stock) **$580.00**
Price: 77/22RS (open sights, rings, walnut stock) **$605.00**
Price: K77/22RP (stainless, no sights, rings, synthetic stock) . . . **$580.00**
Price: K77/22RSP (stainless, open sights, rings, synthetic stock) **$605.00**
Price: 77/22RM (22 WMR, blue, walnut stock) **$580.00**
Price: K77/22RSMP (22 WMR, stainless, open sights, rings, synthetic stock) **$605.00**
Price: K77/22RMP (22 WMR, stainless, synthetic stock) **$580.00**
Price: 77/22RSM
(22 WMR, blue, open sights, rings, walnut stock) **$585.00**
New!! **Price:** K77/17RM, 17RMP, 17VMBBZ (17 HMR, walnut, synthetic or laminate stocks, no sights, rings, blued or stainless) **$580.00 to $645.00**

SAKO FINNFIRE HUNTER BOLT-ACTION RIFLE

Caliber: 22 LR, 5-shot magazine. **Barrel:** 22". **Weight:** 5.75 lbs. **Length:** 39-1/2" overall. **Stock:** European walnut with checkered grip and forend. **Sights:** Hooded blade front, open adjustable rear. **Features:** Adjustable single-stage trigger; has 50-degree bolt lift. Introduced 1994. Imported from Finland by Beretta USA.

Price: **$854.00**
Price: Varmint (heavy barrel) **$896.00**

SAKO FINNFIRE TARGET RIFLE

Caliber: 22 LR. **Barrel:** 22"; heavy, free-floating. **Stock:** Match style of European walnut; adjustable cheekpiece and buttplate; stippled pistol grip and forend. **Sights:** None furnished; has 11mm integral dovetail scope mount. **Features:** Based on the Sako P94S action with two bolt locking lugs, 50-degree bolt lift and 30mm throw; adjustable trigger. Introduced 1999. Imported from Finland by Beretta USA.

Price: **$951.00**

SAKO 75 FINNLIGHT

Caliber: 243 Rem., 7mm-08 Rem., 308 Win., 25-06 Rem., 270 Win., 280 Rem, 30-06 Spfld, 6.5x55, 7mm Rem. Mag., 300 Win. Mag. **Barrel:** 20", 22". **Weight:** 6-1/2 lbs. **Stock:** Synthetic. **Sights:** None. **Features:** Bolt-action with 3 locking lugs, mechanical ejector, 2 position safety with bolt handle release, single-stage adjustable trigger, detachable magazine with hinged floor plate, stainless steel action and internal parts. Imported from Finland bu Beretta USA.

Price: From . . . . **$1,267.00 to $1,301.00**

SAVAGE MARK I-G BOLT-ACTION RIFLE

Caliber: 22 LR, single shot. **Barrel:** 20-3/4". **Weight:** 5-1/2 lbs. **Length:** 39-1/2" overall. **Stock:** Walnut-finished hardwood with Monte Carlo-type comb, checkered grip and forend. **Sights:** Bead front, open adjustable rear. **Features:** Receiver grooved for scope mounting. **Features:** Thumb-operated rotating safety. Blue finish. Rifled or smooth bore. Introduced 1990. Made in Canada, from Savage Arms Inc.

Price: Mark IG, rifled or smooth bore, right- or left-handed **$144.00**
Price: Mark I-GY (Youth), 19" bbl., 37" overall, 5 lbs.. . . . . **$144.00**
Price: Mark I-LY (Youth), 19" bbl., color laminate **$175.00**
Price: Mark I-Y (Youth), 19" bbl., camo **$174.00**
Price: Mark I-GYXP (Youth), with scope **$162.00**
Price: Mark I-GSB (22 LR shot cartridge). **$144.00**

RIFLES

Savage Mark II-BV

Savage Mark II-FXP

Savage Mark II-FSS

Savage Model 93G

Savage Model 93FSS

SAVAGE MARK II BOLT-ACTION RIFLE

Caliber: 22 LR, 10-shot magazine. **Barrel:** 20-1/2". **Weight:** 5-1/2 lbs. **Length:** 39-1/2" overall. **Stock:** Walnut-finished hardwood with Monte Carlo-type comb, checkered grip and forend. **Sights:** Bead front, open adjustable rear. Receiver grooved for scope mounting. **Features:** Thumb-operated rotating safety. Blue finish. Introduced 1990. Made in Canada, from Savage Arms, Inc.

Price: Mark II-BV **$248.00**
Price: Mark II Camo **$174.00**
Price: Mark II-GY (youth), 19" barrel, 37" overall, 5 lbs. **$156.00**
Price: Mark II-GL, left-hand **$156.00**
Price: Mark II-GLY (youth) left-hand. $156.00
Price: Mark II-GXP Package Gun (comes with 4x15 scope),
right- or left-handed **$164.00**
Price: Mark II-FXP (as above with black synthetic stock). **$151.00**
Price: Mark II-F (as above, no scope) **$144.00**
Price: Mark II-FVXP (as above, with scope and rings) **$252.00**

Savage Mark II-LV Heavy Barrel Rifle

Similar to Mark II-G except heavy 21" barrel with recessed target-style crown, gray, laminated hardwood stock with cut checkering. No sights furnished, has dovetailed receiver for scope mounting. Overall length is 39-3/4", weight is 6-1/2 lbs. Comes with 10-shot clip magazine. Introduced 1997. Imported from Canada by Savage Arms, Inc.

Price: **$235.00**
Price: Mark II-FV, with black graphite/polymer stock **$205.00**

Savage Mark II-FSS Stainless Rifle

Similar to the Mark II-G except has stainless steel barreled action and graphite/polymer filled stock; free-floated barrel. Weighs 5 lbs. Introduced 1997. Imported from Canada by Savage Arms, Inc.

Price: **$205.00**

SAVAGE MODEL 93G MAGNUM BOLT-ACTION RIFLE

Caliber: 22 WMR, 5-shot magazine. **Barrel:** 20-3/4". **Weight:** 5-3/4 lbs. **Length:** 39-1/2" overall. **Stock:** Walnut-finished hardwood with Monte Carlo-type comb, checkered grip and forend. **Sights:** Bead front, adjustable open rear. Receiver grooved for scope mount. **Features:** Thumb-operated rotary safety. Blue finish. Introduced 1994. Made in Canada, from Savage Arms.

Price: **$182.00**
Price: Model 93F (as above with black graphite/fiberglass stock) **$175.00**

Savage Model 93FSS Magnum Rifle

Similar to Model 93G except stainless steel barreled action and black synthetic stock with positive checkering. Weighs 5-1/2 lbs. Introduced 1997. Imported from Canada by Savage Arms, Inc.

Price: **$236.00**

Savage Model 93FVSS Magnum Rifle

Similar to Model 93FSS Magnum except 21" heavy barrel with recessed target-style crown, satin-finished stainless barreled action, black graphite/fiberglass stock. Drilled and tapped for scope mounting; comes with Weaver-style bases. Introduced 1998. Imported from Canada by Savage Arms, Inc.

Price: . . . . **$252.00**, With scope **$287.00**

RIFLES

Savage Model 93FVSS

Savage Model 30G Stevens "Favorite"

Savage Cub G Youth

Winchester Model 52B

Winchester Model 1885 Low Wall

SAVAGE MARK 30G STEVENS "FAVORITE"

Caliber: 22 LR, 22WMR - Model 30GM, 17 HMR - Model 30R17. **Barrel:** 21". **Weight:** 4.25 lbs. **Length:** 36.75". **Stock:** Walnut, straight grip, Schnabel forend. **Sights:** Adjustable rear, bead post front. **Features:** Lever action falling block, inertia firing pin system, Model 30G half octagonal bbl. Model 30GM full octagonal bbl.
Price: Model 30G $221.00
Price: Model 30GM $258.00
Price: Model 30R17 . . . . $284.00

Savage Cub G Youth

NEW! **Caliber:** 22 S, L, LR. **Barrel:** 16.125" **Weight:** 3.3 lbs. **Length:** 33" **Stock:** Walnut finished hardwood. **Sights:** Bead post, front; peep, rear. **Features:** Mini single shot bolt action, free-floating button-rifled barrel, blued finish. From Savage Arms.
Price: $149.00

WINCHESTER MODEL 52B BOLT-ACTION RIFLE

Caliber: 22 Long Rifle, 5-shot magazine. **Barrel:** 24". **Weight:** 7 lbs. **Length:** 41-3/4" overall. **Stock:** Walnut with checkered grip and forend. **Sights:** None furnished; grooved receiver and drilled and tapped for scope mounting. **Features:** Has Micro Motion trigger adjustable for pull and over-travel; match chamber; detachable magazine. Reintroduced 1997. From U.S. Repeating Arms Co.
Price: $662.00

WINCHESTER MODEL 1885 LOW WALL RIMFIRE

Caliber: 22 LR, single-shot. **Barrel:** 24-1/2"; half-octagon. **Weight:** 8 lbs. **Length:** 41" overall. **Stock:** Walnut. **Sights:** Blade front, semi-buckhorn rear. **Features:** Drilled and tapped for scope mount or tang sight; target chamber. Limited production. From U.S. Repeating Arms Co.
Price: Grade I (2,400 made) $936.00

CONSULT

SHOOTER'S MARKETPLACE

Page 233, This Issue

**Includes models for classic American and ISU target competition
and other sporting and competitive shooting.**

Anschutz 1451 Target

Anschutz 2013

RIFLES

ANSCHUTZ 1451R SPORTER TARGET RIFLE

Caliber: 22 LR, 5-shot magazine. **Barrel:** 22" heavy match. **Weight:** 6.4 lbs. **Length:** 39.75" overall. **Stock:** European hardwood with walnut finish. **Sights:** None furnished. Grooved receiver for scope mounting or Anschutz micrometer rear sight. **Features:** Sliding safety, two-stage trigger. Adjustable buttplate; forend slide rail to accept Anschutz accessories. Imported from Germany by AcuSport Corp.
Price: **$549.00**

ANSCHUTZ 1451 TARGET RIFLE

Caliber: 22 LR. **Barrel:** 22". **Weight:** About 6.5 lbs. **Length:** 40". **Sights:** Optional. Receiver grooved for scope mounting. **Features:** Designed for the beginning junior shooter with adjustable length of pull from 13.25" to 14.25" via removable butt spacers. Two-stage trigger factory set at 2.6 lbs. Introduced 1999. Imported from Germany by Gunsmithing, Inc.
Price: **$347.00**
Price: #6834 Match Sight Set **$227.10**

ANSCHUTZ 1808D-RT SUPER RUNNING TARGET RIFLE

Caliber: 22 LR, single shot. **Barrel:** 32-1/2". **Weight:** 9 lbs. **Length:** 50" overall. **Stock:** European walnut. Heavy beavertail forend; adjustable cheekpiece and buttplate. Stippled grip and forend. **Sights:** None furnished. Grooved for scope mounting. **Features:** Designed for Running Target competition. Nine-way adjustable single-stage trigger, slide safety. Introduced 1991. Imported from Germany by Accuracy International, Gunsmithing, Inc.
Price: Right-hand **$1,364.10**

ANSCHUTZ 1903 MATCH RIFLE

Caliber: 22 LR, single shot. **Barrel:** 25.5", .75" diameter. **Weight:** 10.1 lbs. **Length:** 43.75" overall. **Stock:** Walnut-finished hardwood with adjustable cheekpiece; stippled grip and forend. **Sights:** None furnished. **Features:** Uses Anschutz Match 64 action and #5098 two-stage trigger. A medium weight rifle for intermediate and advanced Junior Match competition. Introduced 1987. Imported from Germany by Accuracy International, Gunsmithing, Inc.
Price: Right-hand **$720.40**
Price: Left-hand **$757.90**

ANSCHUTZ 64-MS R SILHOUETTE RIFLE

Caliber: 22 LR, 5-shot magazine. **Barrel:** 21-1/2", medium heavy; 7/8" diameter. **Weight:** 8 lbs. **Length:** 39.5" overall. **Stock:** Walnut-finished hardwood, silhouette-type. **Sights:** None furnished. **Features:** Uses Match 64 action. Designed for metallic silhouette competition. Stock has stippled checkering, contoured thumb groove with Wundhammer swell.

Two-stage #5098 trigger. Slide safety locks sear and bolt. Introduced 1980. Imported from Germany by AcuSport Corp., Accuracy International, Gunsmithing, Inc.
Price: 64-MS R **$704.30**

ANSCHUTZ 2013 BENCHREST RIFLE

Caliber: 22 LR, single shot. **Barrel:** 19.6". **Weight:** About 10.3 lbs. **Length:** 37.75" to 42.5" overall. **Stock:** Benchrest style of European hardwood. Stock length adjustable via spacers and buttplate. **Sights:** None furnished. Receiver grooved for mounts. **Features:** Uses the Anschutz 2013 target action, #5018 two-stage adjustable target trigger factory set at 3.9 oz. Introduced 1994. Imported from Germany by Accuracy International, Gunsmithing, Inc.
Price: **$1,757.20**

Anschutz 2007 Match Rifle

Uses same action as the Model 2013, but has a lighter barrel. European walnut stock in right-hand, true left-hand or extra-short models. Sights optional. Available with 19.6" barrel with extension tube, or 26", both in stainless or blue. Introduced 1998. Imported from Germany by Gunsmithing, Inc., Accuracy International.
Price: Right-hand, blue, no sights **$1,766.60**
Price: Right-hand, blue, no sights, extra-short stock **$1,756.60**
Price: Left-hand, blue, no sights **$1,856.80**

ANSCHUTZ 1827 BIATHLON RIFLE

Caliber: 22 LR, 5-shot magazine. **Barrel:** 21-1/2". **Weight:** 8-1/2 lbs. with sights. **Length:** 42-1/2" overall. **Stock:** European walnut with cheekpiece, stippled pistol grip and forend. **Sights:** Optional globe front specially designed for Biathlon shooting, micrometer rear with hinged snow cap. **Features:** Uses Super Match 54 action and nine-way adjustable trigger; adjustable wooden buttplate, Biathlon butthook, adjustable hand-stop rail. Introduced 1982. Imported from Germany by Accuracy International, Gunsmithing, Inc.
Price: Right-hand, with sights, about . . . . **$1,500.50 to $1,555.00**

Anschutz 1827BT Fortner Biathlon Rifle

Similar to the Anschutz 1827 Biathlon rifle except uses Anschutz/Fortner system straight-pull bolt action, blued or stainless steel barrel. Introduced 1982. Imported from Germany by Accuracy International, Gunsmithing, Inc.
Price: Right-hand, with sights . . . . **$1,908.00 to $2,210.00**
Price: Left-hand, with sights . . . . **$2,099.20 to $2,395.00**
Price: Right-hand, sights, stainless barrel (Gunsmithing, Inc.) . . **$2,045.20**

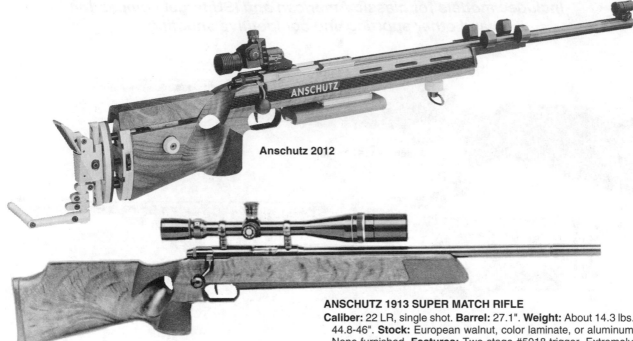

Anschutz 2012

Anschutz 54.18MS REP

ANSCHUTZ SUPER MATCH SPECIAL MODEL 2013 RIFLE

Caliber: 22 LR, single shot. **Barrel:** 25.9". **Weight:** 13 lbs. **Length:** 41.7-42.9". **Stock:** A thumbhole version made of European walnut, both the cheekpiece and buttplate are highly adjustable. **Sights:** None furnished. **Features:** Developed by Anschütz for women to shoot in the sport rifle category. Stainless or blue. This top of the line rifle was introduced in 1997.

Price: Right-hand, blue, no sights, walnut $2,219.30
Price: Right-hand, stainless, no sights, walnut $2,345.30
Price: Left-hand, blue, no sights, walnut $2,319.50

ANSCHUTZ 2012 SPORT RIFLE

Caliber: 22 LR, 5-shot magazine. **Barrel:** 22.4" match; detachable muzzle tube. **Weight:** 7.9 lbs. **Length:** 40.9" overall. **Stock:** European walnut, thumbhole design. **Sights:** None furnished. **Features:** Uses Anschutz 54.18 barreled action with two-stage match trigger. Introduced 1997. Imported from Germany by Accuracy International, AcuSport Corp.

Price: . . . . $1,425.00 to $2,219.95

ANSCHUTZ 1911 PRONE MATCH RIFLE

Caliber: 22 LR, single shot. **Barrel:** 27-1/4". **Weight:** 11 lbs. **Length:** 46" overall. **Stock:** Walnut-finished European hardwood; American prone-style with adjustable cheekpiece, textured pistol grip, forend with swivel rail and adjustable rubber buttplate. **Sights:** None furnished. Receiver grooved for Anschutz sights (extra). **Features:** Two-stage #5018 trigger adjustable from 2.1 to 8.6 oz. Extremely fast lock time. Stainless or blue barrel. Imported from Germany by Accuracy International, Gunsmithing, Inc.

Price: Right-hand, no sights $1,714.20

ANSCHUTZ 1912 SPORT RIFLE

Caliber: 22 LR, single shot. **Barrel:** 25.9". **Weight:** About 11.4 lbs. **Length:** 41.7-42.9". **Stock:** European walnut or aluminum. **Sights:** None furnished. **Features:** Light weight sport rifle version. Still uses the 54 match action like the 1913 but weighs 1.5 pounds less. Stainless or blue barrel. Introduced 1997.

Price: Right-hand, blue, no sights, walnut $1,789.50
Price: Right-hand, blue, no sights, aluminum $2,129.80
Price: Right-hand, stainless, no sights, walnut $1,910.30
Price: Left-hand, blue, no sights, walnut $1,879.00

ANSCHUTZ 1913 SUPER MATCH RIFLE

Caliber: 22 LR, single shot. **Barrel:** 27.1". **Weight:** About 14.3 lbs. **Length:** 44.8-46". **Stock:** European walnut, color laminate, or aluminum. **Sights:** None furnished. **Features:** Two-stage #5018 trigger. Extremely fast lock time. Stainless or blue barrel.

Price: Right-hand, blue, no sights, walnut stock $2,262.90
Price: Right-hand, blue, no sights, color laminate stock $2,275.10
Price: Right-hand, blue, no sights, aluminum stock $2,262.90
Price: Left-hand, blue, no sights, walnut stock $2,382.20

Anschutz 1913 Super Match Rifle

Same as the Model 1911 except European walnut International-type stock with adjustable cheekpiece, or color laminate, both available with straight or lowered forend, adjustable aluminum hook buttplate, adjustable hand stop, weighs 15.5 lbs., 46" overall. Stainless or blue barrel. Imported from Germany by Accuracy International, Gunsmithing, Inc.

Price: Right-hand, blue, no sights, walnut stock. . $2,139.00 to $2,175.00
Price: Right-hand, blue, no sights, color laminate stock. $2,199.40
Price: Right-hand, blue, no sights, walnut, lowered forend $2,181.80
Price: Right-hand, blue, no sights, color laminate,
lowered forend $2,242.20
Price: Left-hand, blue, no sights, walnut stock. . . $2,233.10 to $2,275.00

Anschutz 54.18MS REP Deluxe Silhouette Rifle

Same basic action and trigger specifications as the Anschutz 1913 Super Match but with removable 5-shot clip magazine, 22.4" barrel extendable to 30" using optional extension and weight set. Weight is 8.1 lbs. Receiver drilled and tapped for scope mounting. Stock is thumbhole silhouette version or standard silhouette version, both are European walnut. Introduced 1990. Imported from Germany by Accuracy International, Gunsmithing, Inc.

Price: Thumbhole stock $1,461.40
Price: Standard stock $1,212.10

Anschutz 1907 Standard Match Rifle

Same action as Model 1913 but with 7/8" diameter 26" barrel (stainless or blue). Length is 44.5" overall, weighs 10.5 lbs. Choice of stock configurations. Vented forend. Designed for prone and position shooting ISU requirements; suitable for NRA matches. Also available with walnut flat-forend stock for benchrest shooting. Imported from Germany by Accuracy International, Gunsmithing, Inc.

Price: Right-hand, blue, no sights,
hardwood stock . . . . $1,253.40 to $1,299.00
Price: Right-hand, blue, no sights, colored laminated
stock . . . . $1,316.10 to $1,375.00
Price: Right-hand, blue, no sights, walnut stock. $1,521.10
Price: Left-hand, blue barrel, no sights, walnut stock. $1,584.60

Anschutz 1907

Armalite
AR-10 (T)

Bushmaster XM15

ARMALITE AR-10 (T) RIFLE

Caliber: 308, 10-shot magazine. **Barrel:** 24" target-weight Rock 5R custom. **Weight:** 10.4 lbs. **Length:** 43.5" overall. **Stock:** Green or black compostion; N.M. fiberglass handguard tube. **Sights:** Detachable handle, front sight, or scope mount available. Comes with international-style flattop receiver with Picatinny rail. **Features:** National Match two-stage trigger. Forged upper receiver. Receivers hard-coat anodized. Introduced 1995. Made in U.S.A. by ArmaLite, Inc.
Price: Green **$2,075.00**
Price: Black **$2,090.00**
Price: AR-10 (T) Carbine, lighter 16" barrel, single stage trigger, weighs 8.8 lbs. Green **$1,970.00**
Price: Black **$1,985.00**

ARMALITE M15A4 (T) EAGLE EYE RIFLE

Caliber: 223, 7-shot magazine. **Barrel:** 24" heavy stainless; 1:8" twist. **Weight:** 9.2 lbs. **Length:** 42-3/8" overall. **Stock:** Green or black butt, N.M. fiberglass handguard tube. **Sights:** One-piece international-style flattop receiver with Weaver-type rail, including case deflector. **Features:** Detachable carry handle, front sight and scope mount (30mm or 1") available. Upper and lower receivers have push-type pivot pin, hard coat anodized. Made in U.S.A. by ArmaLite, Inc.
Price: Green **$1,378.00**
Price: Black **$1,393.00**

ARMALITE M15A4 ACTION MASTER RIFLE

Caliber: 223, 7-shot magazine. **Barrel:** 20" heavy stainless; 1:9" twist. **Weight:** 9 lbs. **Length:** 40-1/2" overall. **Stock:** Green or black plastic; N.M. fiberglass handguard tube. **Sights:** One-piece international-style flattop receiver with Weaver-type rail. **Features:** Detachable carry handle, front sight and scope mount available. National Match two-stage trigger group; Picatinny rail; upper and lower receivers have push-type pivot pin; hard coat anodized finish. Made in U.S.A. by ArmaLite, Inc.
Price: **$1,175.00**

BLASER R93 LONG RANGE RIFLE

Caliber: 308 Win., 10-shot detachable box magazine. **Barrel:** 24". **Weight:** 10.4 lbs. **Length:** 44" overall. **Stock:** Aluminum with synthetic lining. **Sights:** None furnished; accepts detachable scope mount. **Features:** Straight-pull bolt action with adjustable trigger; fully adjustable stock; quick takedown; corrosion resistant finish. Introduced 1998. Imported from Germany by Sigarms.
Price: **$2,360.00**

BUSHMASTER XM15 E2S TARGET MODEL RIFLE

Caliber: 223. **Barrel:** 20", 24"; 1:9" twist; heavy. **Weight:** 8.3 lbs. **Length:** 38.25" overall (20" barrel). **Stock:** Black composition; A2 type. **Sights:** Adjustable post front, adjustable aperture rear. **Features:** Patterned after Colt M-16A2. Chrome-lined barrel with manganese phosphate exterior. Forged aluminum receivers with push-pin takedown. Available in stainless barrel and camo stock versions. Made in U.S.A. by Bushmaster Firearms Co.
Price: 20" match heavy barrel (A2 type) **$965.00**
Price: (A3 type) **$1,095.00**

BUSHMASTER DCM COMPETITION RIFLE

Similar to the XM15 E2S Target Model except has 20" extra-heavy (1" diameter) barrel with 1.8" twist for heavier competition bullets. Weighs about 12 lbs. with balance weights. Has special competition rear sight with interchangeable apertures, extra-fine 1/2- or 1/4-MOA windage and elevation adjustments; specially ground front sight post in choice of three widths. Full-length handguards over free-floater barrel tube. Introduced 1998. Made in U.S.A. by Bushmaster Firearms, Inc.
Price: **$1,495.00**

Bushmaster DCM

Bushmaster XM15 E2S V-Match Carbine

Colt Accurized

Colt Match Target HBAR

Colt Match Target HBAR II

BUSHMASTER XM15 E2S V-MATCH RIFLE

Caliber: 223. **Barrel:** 20", 24""; 1:9" twist; heavy. **Weight:** 8.1 lbs. **Length:** 38.25" overall (20" barrel). **Stock:** Black composition. A2 type. **Sights:** None furnished; upper receiver has integral scope mount base. **Features:** Chrome-lined .950" heavy barrel with counter-bored crown, manganese phosphate finish, free-floating aluminum handguard, forged aluminum receivers with push-pin takedown, hard anodized mil-spec finish. Competition trigger optional. Made in U.S.A. by Bushmaster Firearms, Inc.

Price: 20" Match heavy barrel $1,055.00
Price: 24" Match heavy barrel $1,065.00
Price: V-Match Carbine (16" barrel) $1,045.00

COLT MATCH TARGET MODEL RIFLE

Caliber: 223 Rem., 8-shot magazine. **Barrel:** 20". **Weight:** 7.5 lbs. **Length:** 39" overall. **Stock:** Composition stock, grip, forend. **Sights:** Post front, aperture rear adjustable for windage and elevation. **Features:** Five-round detachable box magazine, standard-weight barrel, sling swivels. Has forward bolt assist. Military matte black finish. Model introduced 1991.

Price: $1,144.00
Price: With compensator $1,150.00

Colt Accurized Rifle

Similar to the Colt Match Target Model except has 24" stainless steel heavy barrel with 1.9" rifling, flattop receiver with scope mount and 1"

rings, weighs 9.25 lbs. Introduced 1998. Made in U.S.A. by Colt's Mfg. Co., Inc.

Price: $1,424.00

Colt Match Target HBAR Rifle

Similar to the Target Model except has heavy barrel, 800-meter rear sight adjustable for windage and elevation. Introduced 1991.

Price: $1,194.00

Colt Match Target Competition HBAR Rifle

Similar to the Sporter Target except has flat-top receiver with integral Weaver-type base for scope mounting. Counter-bored muzzle, 1:9" rifling twist. Introduced 1991.

Price: Model R6700 . . . . $1,199.00

Colt Match Target Competition HBAR II Rifle

Similar to the Match Target Competition HBAR except has 16:1" barrel, weighs 7.1 lbs., overall length 34.5"; 1:9" twist barrel. Introduced 1995.

Price: $1,172.00

EAA/IZHMASH URAL 5.1

EAA/IZHMASH Biathlon

EAA/IZHMASH Biathlon Target

Ed Brown Model 702 Light Tactical

Ed Brown Model 702 Tactical

EAA/HW 660 MATCH RIFLE
Caliber: 22 LR. **Barrel:** 26". **Weight:** 10.7 lbs. **Length:** 45.3" overall. **Stock:** Match-type walnut with adjustable cheekpiece and buttplate. **Sights:** Globe front, match aperture rear. **Features:** Adjustable match trigger; stippled pistol grip and forend; forend accessory rail. Introduced 1991. Imported from Germany by European American Armory.
Price: About $999.00
Price: With laminate stock $1,159.00

EAA/IZHMASH URAL 5.1 TARGET RIFLE
Caliber: 22 LR. **Barrel:** 26.5". **Weight:** 11.3 lbs. **Length:** 44.5". **Stock:** Wood, international style. **Sights:** Adjustable click rear, hooded front with inserts. **Features:** Forged barrel with rifling, adjustable trigger, aluminum rail for accessories, hooked adjustable butt plate. Adjustable comb, adjustable large palm rest. Hand stippling on grip area.
Price: .... NA

EAA/Izhmash Biathlon Target Rifle
Similar to URAL with addition of snow covers for barrel and sights, stock holding extra mags, round trigger block. Unique bolt utilizes toggle action.

Designed to compete in 40 meter biathlon event. 22 LR, 19.5" bbl.
Price: $979.00

EAA/Izhmash Biathalon Basic Target Rifle
Same action as Biathlon but designed for plinking or fun. Beech stock, heavy barrel with Weaver rail for scope mount. 22 LR, 19.5" bbl.
Price: $339.00

ED BROWN MODEL 702 LIGHT TACTICAL
Caliber: 223, 308. **Barrel:** 21". **Weight:** 8.75 lbs. **Stock:** Fully glass-bedded fiberglass with recoil pad. Wide varmint-style forend. **Sights:** None furnished. Talley scope mounts utilizing heavy duty 8-40 screws. **Features:** Compact and super accurate, it is ideal for police, military and varmint hunters.
Price: From $2,800.00

ED BROWN MODEL 702 TACTICAL
Caliber: 308, 300 Win. Mag. **Barrel:** 26". **Weight:** 11.25 lbs. **Stock:** Hand bedded McMillan A-3 fiberglass tactical stock with recoil pad. **Sights:** None furnished. Leupold Mark 4 30mm scope mounts utilizing heavy-duty 8-40 screws. **Features:** Custom short or long action, steel trigger guard, hinged floor plate, additional caliber available.
Price: From $2,900.00

Ed Brown 702

Harris Gunworks Long Range

Harris Gunworks M-86

ED BROWN MODEL 702, M40A2 MARINE SNIPER

Caliber: 308 Win., 30-06 Springfield. **Barrel:** Match-grade 24". **Weight:** 9.25 lbs. **Stock:** Hand bedded McMillan GP fiberglass tactical stock with recoil pad in special Woodland Camo molded-in colors. **Sights:** None furnished. Leupold Mark 4 30mm scope mounts with heavy-duty 8-40 screws. **Features:** Steel trigger guard, hinged floor plate, three position safety. Left-hand model available.

Price: From **$2,900.00**

HARRIS GUNWORKS NATIONAL MATCH RIFLE

Caliber: 7mm-08, 308, 5-shot magazine. **Barrel:** 24", stainless steel. **Weight:** About 11 lbs. (std. bbl.). **Length:** 43" overall. **Stock:** Fiberglass with adjustable buttplate. **Sights:** Barrel band and Tompkins front; no rear sight furnished. **Features:** Gunworks repeating action with clip slot, Canjar trigger. Match-grade barrel. Available in right-hand only. Fiberglass stock, sight installation, special machining and triggers optional. Introduced 1989. From Harris Gunworks, Inc.

Price: **$3,500.00**

HARRIS GUNWORKS LONG RANGE RIFLE

Caliber: 300 Win. Mag., 7mm Rem. Mag., 300 Phoenix, 338 Lapua, single shot. **Barrel:** 26", stainless steel, match-grade. **Weight:** 14 lbs. **Length:** 46-1/2" overall. **Stock:** Fiberglass with adjustable buttplate and cheekpiece. Adjustable for length of pull, drop, cant and cast-off. **Sights:** Barrel band and Tompkins front; no rear sight furnished. **Features:** Uses Gunworks solid bottom single shot action and Canjar trigger. Barrel twist 1:12". Introduced 1989. From Harris Gunworks, Inc.

Price: **$3,620.00**

HARRIS GUNWORKS M-86 SNIPER RIFLE

Caliber: 308, 30-06, 4-shot magazine; 300 Win. Mag., 3-shot magazine. **Barrel:** 24", Gunworks match-grade in heavy contour. **Weight:** 11-1/4 lbs. (308), 11-1/2 lbs. (30-06, 300). **Length:** 43-1/2" overall. **Stock:** Specially designed McHale fiberglass stock with textured grip and forend, recoil pad. **Sights:** None furnished. **Features:** Uses Gunworks repeating action. Comes with bipod. Matte black finish. Sling swivels. Introduced 1989. From Harris Gunworks, Inc.

Price: **$2,700.00**

HARRIS GUNWORKS M-89 SNIPER RIFLE

Caliber: 308 Win., 5-shot magazine. **Barrel:** 28" (with suppressor). **Weight:** 15 lbs., 4 oz. **Stock:** Fiberglass; adjustable for length; recoil pad. **Sights:** None furnished. Drilled and tapped for scope mounting. **Features:** Uses Gunworks repeating action. Comes with bipod. Introduced 1990. From Harris Gunworks, Inc.

Price: Standard (non-suppressed) **$3,200.00**

HARRIS GUNWORKS
COMBO M-87 SERIES 50-CALIBER RIFLES

Caliber: 50 BMG, single shot. **Barrel:** 29, with muzzle brake. **Weight:** About 21-1/2 lbs. **Length:** 53" overall. **Stock:** Gunworks fiberglass. **Sights:** None furnished. **Features:** Right-handed Gunworks stainless steel receiver, chrome-moly barrel with 1:15" twist. Introduced 1987. From Harris Gunworks, Inc.

Price: **$3,885.00**
Price: M87R 5-shot repeater **$4,000.00**
Price: M-87 (5-shot repeater) "Combo" **$4,300.00**
Price: M-92 Bullpup (shortened M-87 single shot with bullpup stock) **$4,770.00**
Price: M-93 (10-shot repeater with folding stock, detachable magazine) **$4,150.00**

OLYMPIC ARMS PCR-SERVICEMATCH RIFLE

Caliber: 223, 10-shot magazine. **Barrel:** 20", broach-cut 416 stainless steel. **Weight:** About 10 lbs. **Length:** 39.5" overall. **Stock:** A2 stowaway grip and trapdoor buttstock. **Sights:** Post front, E2-NM fully adjustable aperture rear. **Features:** Based on the AR-15. Conforms to all DCM standards. Free-floating 1:8.5" or 1:10" barrel; crowned barrel; no bayonet lug. Introduced 1996. Made in U.S.A. by Olympic Arms, Inc.

Price: **$1,062.00**

OLYMPIC ARMS PCR-1 RIFLE

Caliber: 223, 10-shot magazine. **Barrel:** 20", 24"; 416 stainless steel. **Weight:** 10 lbs., 3 oz. **Length:** 38.25" overall with 20" barrel. **Stock:** A2 stowaway grip and trapdoor butt. **Sights:** None supplied; flattop upper receiver, cut-down front sight base. **Features:** Based on the AR-15 rifle. Broach-cut, free-floating barrel with 1:8.5" or 1:10" twist. No bayonet lug. Crowned barrel; fluting available. Introduced 1994. Made in U.S.A. by Olympic Arms, Inc.

Price: **$1,038.00**

Remington 40-XB Rangemaster

remington 40-XC KS

Springfield, Inc. M1A Super Match

Springfield, Inc. M1A/M-21

Olympic Arms PCR-2, PCR-3 Rifles

Similar to the PCR-1 except has 16" barrel, weighs 8 lbs., 2 oz.; has post front sight, fully adjustable aperture rear. Model PCR-3 has flattop upper receiver, cut-down front sight base. Introduced 1994. Made in U.S.A. by Olympic Arms, Inc.

Price: **$958.00**

REMINGTON 40-XB RANGEMASTER TARGET CENTERFIRE

Caliber: 15 calibers from 220 Swift to 300 Win. Mag. **Barrel:** 27-1/4". **Weight:** 11-1/4 lbs. **Length:** 47" overall. **Stock:** American walnut, laminated thumbhole or Kevlar with high comb and beavertail forend stop. Rubber non-slip buttplate. **Sights:** None. Scope blocks installed. **Features:** Adjustable trigger. Stainless barrel and action. Receiver drilled and tapped for sights.

Price: Standard single shot. . $1,636.00 (right-hand), $1,761.00 (left-hand)
Price: Repeater. **$1,734.00**

REMINGTON 40-XBBR KS

Caliber: Five calibers from 22 BR to 308 Win. **Barrel:** 20" (light varmint class), 24" (heavy varmint class). **Weight:** 7-1/4 lbs. (light varmint class); 12 lbs. (heavy varmint class). **Length:** 38" (20" bbl.), 42" (24" bbl.). **Stock:** Aramid fiber. **Sights:** None. Supplied with scope blocks. **Features:** Unblued benchrest with stainless steel barrel, trigger adjustable from 1-1/2 lbs. to 3-1/2 lbs. Special 2-oz. trigger extra cost. Scope and mounts extra.

Price: Single shot **$1,876.00**

REMINGTON 40-XC KS TARGET RIFLE

Caliber: 7.62 NATO, 5-shot. **Barrel:** 24", stainless steel. **Weight:** 11 lbs. without sights. **Length:** 43-1/2" overall. **Stock:** Aramid fiber. **Sights:** None furnished. **Features:** Designed to meet the needs of competitive shooters. Stainless steel barrel and action.

Price: **$1,821.00**

REMINGTON 40-XR CUSTOM SPORTER

Caliber: 22 LR, 22 WM. **Features:** Model XR-40 Target rifle action with craftsmanship of Model 700 Custom. Many options available.
Price: Single shot **$3,383.00**

SAKO TRG-22 BOLT-ACTION RIFLE

Caliber: 308 Win., 10-shot magazine. **Barrel:** 26". **Weight:** 10-1/4 lbs. **Length:** 45-1/4" overall. **Stock:** Reinforced polyurethane with fully adjustable cheekpiece and buttplate. **Sights:** None furnished. Optional quick-detachable, one-piece scope mount base, 1" or 30mm rings. **Features:** Resistance-free bolt, free-floating heavy stainless barrel, 60-degree bolt lift. Two-stage trigger is adjustable for length, pull, horizontal or vertical pitch. Introduced 2000. Imported from Finland by Beretta USA.
Price: Green **$2,898.00**
Price: Model TRG-42, as above except in 338 Lapua Mag or 300
Win. Mag. **$2,829.00**
Price: Green (new) **$3,243.00**

SPRINGFIELD, INC. M1A SUPER MATCH

Caliber: 308 Win. **Barrel:** 22", heavy Douglas Premium. **Weight:** About 11 lbs. **Length:** 44.31" overall. **Stock:** Heavy walnut competition stock with longer pistol grip, contoured area behind the rear sight, thicker butt and forend, glass bedded. **Sights:** National Match front and rear. **Features:** Has figure-eight-style operating rod guide. Introduced 1987. From Springfield, Inc.
Price: About **$2,479.00**

Springfield, Inc. M1A/M-21 Tactical Model Rifle

Similar to M1A Super Match except special sniper stock with adjustable cheekpiece and rubber recoil pad. Weighs 11.6 lbs. From Springfield, Inc.
Price: **$2,975.00**

SPRINGFIELD, INC. M-1 GARAND AMERICAN COMBAT RIFLES

Caliber: 30-06, 308 Win., 8-shot. **Barrel:** 24". **Weight:** 9.5 lbs. **Length:** 43.6". **Stock:** American walnut. **Sights:** Military square post front, military aperture, MOA adjustable rear. **Features:** Limited production, certificate of authenticity, all new receiver, barrel and stock wtih remaining parts USGI mil-spec. 2-stage military trigger.
Price: About **$2,479.00**

Stoner SR-15

Stoner SR-25

STONER SR-15 MATCH RIFLE

Caliber: 223. **Barrel:** 20". **Weight:** 7.9 lbs. **Length:** 38" overall. **Stock:** Black synthetic. **Sights:** None furnished; flat-top upper receiver for scope mounting. **Features:** Short Picatinny rail, two-stage match trigger. Introduced 1998. Made in U.S.A. by Knight's Mfg.Co.
Price: **$1,650.00**

STONER SR-25 MATCH RIFLE

Caliber: 7.62 NATO, 10-shot steel magazine, 5-shot optional. **Barrel:** 24" heavy match; 1:11.25" twist. **Weight:** 10.75 lbs. **Length:** 44" overall. **Stock:** Black synthetic AR-15A2 design. Full floating forend of Mil-spec synthetic attaches to upper receiver at a single point. **Sights:** None furnished. Has integral Weaver-style rail. Rings and iron sights optional. **Features:** Improved AR-15 trigger, AR-15-style seven-lug rotating bolt. Gas block rail mounts detachable front sight. Introduced 1993. Made in U.S.A. by Knight's Mfg. Co.
Price: **$3,345.00**
Price: SR-25 Lightweight Match (20" medium match target contour barrel, 9.5 lbs., 40" overall) **$3,345.00**

TANNER 50 METER FREE RIFLE

Caliber: 22 LR, single shot. **Barrel:** 27.7". **Weight:** 13.9 lbs. **Length:** 44.4" overall. **Stock:** Seasoned walnut with palm rest, accessory rail, adjustable hook buttplate. **Sights:** Globe front with interchangeable inserts, Tanner micrometer-diopter rear with adjustable aperture. **Features:** Bolt action with externally adjustable set trigger. Supplied with 50-meter test target. Imported from Switzerland by Mandall Shooting Supplies. Introduced 1984.
Price: About **$3,900.00**

TANNER STANDARD UIT RIFLE

Caliber: 308, 7.5mm Swiss, 10-shot. **Barrel:** 25.9". **Weight:** 10.5 lbs. **Length:** 40.6" overall. **Stock:** Match style of seasoned nutwood with accessory rail; coarsely stippled pistol grip; high cheekpiece; vented forend. **Sights:** Globe front with interchangeable inserts, Tanner micrometer-diopter rear with adjustable aperture. **Features:** Two locking lug revolving bolt encloses case head. Trigger adjustable from 1/2 to 6-1/2 lbs., match trigger optional. Comes with 300-meter test target. Imported from Switzerland by Mandall Shooting Supplies. Introduced 1984.
Price: About **$4,700.00**

TANNER 300 METER FREE RIFLE

Caliber: 308 Win., 7.5 Swiss, single shot. **Barrel:** 27.58". **Weight:** 15 lbs. **Length:** 45.3" overall. **Stock:** Seasoned walnut, thumbhole style, with accessory rail, palm rest, adjustable hook butt. **Sights:** Globe front with interchangeable inserts, Tanner-design micrometer-diopter rear with adjustable aperture. **Features:** Three-lug revolving-lock bolt design, adjustable set trigger; short firing pin travel, supplied with 300-meter test target. Imported from Switzerland by Mandall Shooting Supplies. Introduced 1984.
Price: About **$4,900.00**

TIKKA TARGET RIFLE

Caliber: 223, 22-250, 308, detachable 5-shot magazine. **Barrel:** 23-1/2" heavy. **Weight:** 9 lbs. **Length:** 43-5/8" overall. **Stock:** European walnut with adjustable comb, adjustable buttplate; stippled grip and forend. **Sights:** None furnished; drilled and tapped for scope mounting. **Features:** Buttplate adjustable for distance, angle, height and pitch, adjustable trigger, free-floating barrel. Introduced 1998. Imported from Finland by Beretta USA.
Price: **$950.00**

CONSULT

SHOOTER'S MARKETPLACE

Page 233, This Issue

RIFLES

Includes a wide variety of sporting guns and guns suitable for various competitions.

Benelli Legacy

Benelli M1 Field Camouflage

Benelli Super Black Eagle

BENELLI LEGACY SHOTGUN

Gauge: 12, 20, 2-3/4" and 3" chamber. **Barrel:** 24", 26", 28" (Full, Mod., Imp. Cyl., Imp. Mod., cylinder choke tubes). Mid-bead sight. **Weight:** 5.8 to 7.6 lbs. **Length:** 49-5/8" overall (28" barrel). **Stock:** Select European walnut with satin finish. **Features:** Uses the rotating bolt inertia recoil operating system with a two-piece steel/aluminum etched receiver (bright on lower, blue upper). Drop adjustment kit allows the stock to be custom fitted without modifying the stock. Introduced 1998. Imported from Italy by Benelli USA, Corp.
Price: **$1,400.00**

Benelli Sport II Shotgun

Similar to the Legacy model except has dual tone blue/silver receiver, two carbon fiber interchangeable ventilated ribs, adjustable butt pad, adjustable buttstock, and functions with ultra-light target loads. Walnut stock with satin finish. Introduced 1997. Imported from Italy by Benelli U.S.A.
Price: **$1,400.00**

BENELLI M1 FIELD SHOTGUN

Gauge: 12, 20 ga. **Barrel:** 21", 24", 26", 28". **Weight:** 7 lbs., 4 oz. **Stock:** High impact polymer; wood on 26", 28". **Sights:** Red bar. **Features:** Sporting version of the military & police gun. Uses the rotating Montefeltro bolt system. Ventilated rib; blue finish. Comes with set of five choke tubes. Imported from Italy by Benelli U.S.A.
Price: . . . . (Synthetic) **$985.00**; (Wood) **$1,000.00**; (Timber HD) **$1,085.00**
Price: 24" rifled barrel . . . . . (Synthetic) **$1,060.00**; Timber HD **$1,165.00**
Price: Synthetic stock, left-hand version (24", 26", 28" brls.) . . **$1,005.00**
Price: Timber HD camo left-hand, 21", 24" barrel **$1,105.00**
Price: MI Field Steadygrip **$1,175.00**

Benelli Montefeltro Shotgun

Similar to the M1 Super except has checkered walnut stock with satin finish. Uses the Montefeltro rotating bolt system with a simple inertia recoil design. Full, Imp. Mod, Mod., Imp. Cyl. choke tubes, 12 and 20 ga. Weighs 6.8-7.1 lbs. Finish is blue. Introduced 1987.
Price: 24", 26", 28" **$1,005.00**
Price: Left-hand, 26", 28" **$1,020.00**

BENELLI SUPER BLACK EAGLE SHOTGUN

Gauge: 12, 3-1/2" chamber. **Barrel:** 24", 26", 28" (Cyl. Imp. Cyl., Mod., Imp. Mod., Full choke tubes). **Weight:** 7 lbs., 5 oz. **Length:** 49-5/8" overall (28"

barrel). **Stock:** European walnut with satin finish, or polymer. Adjustable for drop. **Sights:** Red bar front. **Features:** Uses Montefeltro inertia recoil bolt system. Fires all 12 gauge shells from 2-3/4" to 3-1/2" magnums, vent rib. Introduced 1991. Imported from Italy by Benelli U.S.A.
Price: With 26" and 28" barrel, wood stock **$1,300.00**
Price: Timber HD Camo 24", 26", 28" barrel **$1,385.00**
Price: With 24", 26" and 28" barrel, polymer stock. **$1,290.00**
Price: Left-hand, 24", 26", 28", polymer stock **$1,345.00**
Price: Left-hand, 24", 26", 28", camo stock **$1,435.00**
Price: Steadygrip Turkey Gun **$1,465.00**

Benelli Super Black Eagle Slug Gun

Similar to the Benelli Super Black Eagle except has 24" rifled barrel with 2-3/4" and 3" chamber, drilled and tapped for scope. Uses the inertia recoil bolt system. Matte-finish receiver. Weight is 7.5 lbs., overall length 45.5". Wood or polymer stocks available. Introduced 1992. Imported from Italy by Benelli U.S.A.
Price: With wood stock **$1,345.00**
Price: With polymer stock **$1,335.00**
Price: 24" barrel, Timber HD Camo **$1,460.00**

Benelli Executive Series Shotguns

Similar to the Legacy except has grayed steel lower receiver, hand-engraved and gold inlaid (Grade III), and has highest grade of walnut stock with drop adjustment kit. Barrel lengths 26" or 28"; 2-3/4" and 3" chamber. Special order only. Introduced 1995. Imported from Italy by Benelli U.S.A.
Price: Grade I (engraved game scenes) **$5,465.00**
Price: Grade II (game scenes with scroll engraving) **$6,135.00**
Price: Grade III (full coverage, gold inlays) **$7,065.00**

BERETTA AL391 URIKA AUTO SHOTGUNS

Gauge: 12, 20 gauge; 3" chamber. **Barrel:** 22", 24", 26", 28", 30"; five Mobilchoke choke tubes. **Weight:** 5.95 to 7.28 lbs. **Length:** Varies by model. **Stock:** Walnut, black or camo synthetic; shims, spacers and interchangeable recoil pads allow custom fit. **Features:** Self-compensating gas operation handles full range of loads; recoil reducer in receiver; enlarged trigger guard; reduced-weight receiver, barrel and forend; hard-chromed bore. Introduced 2000. Imported from Italy by Beretta USA.
Price: AL391 Urika (12 ga., 26", 28", 30" barrels) **$1,017.00**
Price: AL391 Urika (20 ga., 24", 26", 28" barrels) **$1,017.00**
Price: AL391 Urika Synthetic (12 ga., 24", 26", 28", 30" barrels) **$991.00**
Price: AL391 Urika Camo. (12 ga., Realtree Hardwoods or Advantage Wetlands) **$1,108.00**

Beretta Urika Gold Sporting

Beretta Urika Sporting

Beretta A391 Xtreme

Browning Gold Deer Hunter

Beretta AL391 Urika Gold and Gold Sporting Auto Shotguns
Similar to AL391 Urika except features deluxe wood, jeweled bolt and carrier, gold-inlaid receiver with black or silver finish. Introduced 2000. Imported from Italy by Beretta USA.
Price: AL391 Urika Gold Sporting (12 or 20, black receiver, engraving)
.... **$1,351.00**
Price: AL391 Urika Gold Sporting (12 ga., silver receiver, engraving)
.... **$1,351.00**

Beretta AL391 Urika Sporting Auto Shotguns
Similar to AL391 Urika except has competition sporting stock with rounded rubber recoil pad, wide ventilated rib with white front and mid-rib beads, satin-black receiver with silver markings. Available in 12 and 20 gauge. Introduced 2000. Imported from Italy by Beretta USA.
Price: AL391 Urika Sporting. **$1,070.00**

Beretta AL391 Urika Trap Auto Shotguns
Similar to AL391 Urika except in 12 ga. only, has wide ventilated rib with white front and mid-rib beads, Monte Carlo stock and special trap recoil pad. Gold Trap features highly figured walnut stock and forend, gold-filled Beretta logo and signature on receiver. Optima bore and Optima choke tubes. Introduced 2000. Imported from Italy by Beretta USA.
Price: AL391 Urika Trap **$1,070.00**

Beretta AL391 Urika Parallel Target RL and SL Auto Shotguns
Similar to AL391 Urika except has parallel-comb, Monte Carlo stock with tighter grip radius to reduce trigger reach and stepped ventilated rib. SL model has same features but with 13.5" length of pull stock. Introduced 2000. Imported from Italy by Beretta USA.
Price: AL391 Urika Parallel Target RL **$1,070.00**
Price: AL391 Urika Parallel Target SL **$1,070.00**

Beretta AL391 Urika Youth Shotgun
Similar to AL391 except has a 24" or 26" barrel with 13.5" stock for youth and smaller shooters. Introduced 2000. From Beretta USA.
Price: **$1,017.00**

Beretta ES100 Auto Shotguns
Similar to the ES100 MWTF model except offered with walnut, black synthetic or camouflage stock and fully rifled slug barrel model. Recoil-operated action. Imported from Italy by Beretta U.S.A.
Price: ES100 Pintail (24", 26" or 28" bbl., black synthetic stock) . **$749.00**
Price: ES100 Camouflage (28" bbl., Advantage Wetlands camo stock)
.... **$777.00**
Price: ES100 Rifled Slug (24" rifled bbl.) **$749.00**

BERETTA A391 XTREME 3.5 AUTO SHOTGUNS
Gauge: 12 ga. 3-1/2" chamber. **Barrel:** 24", 26", 28". **Weight:** 7.8 lbs. **Stock:** Synthetic. **Features:** Semi-auto goes with two-lug rotating bolt and self-compensating gas valve, extended tang, cross bolt safety, self-cleaning, with case.
Price: Synthetic **$1,143.00**
Price: Realtree Hardwood HD Camo **$1,260.00**

BROWNING GOLD HUNTER AUTO SHOTGUN
Gauge: 12, 3" or 3-1/2" chamber; 20, 3" chamber. **Barrel:** 12 ga.—26", 28", 30", Invector Plus choke tubes; 20 ga.—26", 30", Invector choke tubes. **Weight:** 7 lbs., 9 oz. (12 ga.), 6 lbs., 12 oz. (20 ga.). **Length:** 46-1/4" overall (20 ga., 26" barrel). **Stock:** 14"x1-1/2"x2-1/3"; select walnut with gloss finish; palm swell grip. **Features:** Self-regulating, self-cleaning gas system shoots all loads; lightweight receiver with special non-glare deep black finish; large reversible safety button; large rounded trigger guard, gold trigger. The 20 gauge has slightly smaller dimensions; 12 gauge have back-bored barrels, Invector Plus tube system. Introduced 1994. Imported by Browning.
Price: 12 or 20 gauge, 3" chamber......................... **$894.00**
Price: 12 ga., 3-1/2" chamber........................... **$1,038.00**
Price: Extra barrels............................ **$336.00 to $415.00**

Browning Gold Sporting Golden Clays

Browning NWTF Mossy Oak Break-Up

Browning Gold Classic Stalker

Browning Gold Fusion

Browning Gold Rifled Deer Hunter Auto Shotgun

Similar to the Gold Hunter except 12 or 20 gauge, 22" rifled barrel with cantilever scope mount, walnut stock with extra-thick recoil pad. Weighs 7 lbs., 12 oz., overall length 42-1/2". Sling swivel studs fitted on the magazine cap and butt. Introduced 1997. Imported by Browning.

Price: 12 gauge **$887.00**
Price: With Mossy Oak Break-up camouflage **$1,046.00**
Price: 20 ga. (satin-finish walnut stock, 3" chamber) **$987.00**

Browning Gold Deer Stalker

Similar to the Gold Deer Hunter except has black composite stock and forend, fully rifled barrel, cantilever scope mount. Introduced 1999. Imported by Browning.

Price: 12 gauge **$967.00**

Browning Gold Sporting Clays Auto

Similar to the Gold Hunter except 12 gauge only with 28" or 30" barrel; front Hi-Viz Pro-Comp and center bead on tapered ventilated rib; ported and back-bored Invector Plus barrel; 2-3/4" chamber; satin-finished stock with solid, radiused recoil pad with hard heel insert; non-glare black alloy receiver has "Sporting Clays" inscribed in gold. Introduced 1996. Imported from Japan by Browning.

Price: **$984.00**

Browning Gold Sporting Golden Clays

Similar to the Sporting Clays except has silvered receiver with gold engraving, high grade wood. Introduced 1999. Imported by Browning.

Price: **$1,457.00**

Browning Gold Ladies/Youth Sporting Clays Auto

Similar to the Gold Sporting Clays except has stock dimensions of 14-1/4"x1-3/4"x2" for women and younger shooters. Introduced 1999. Imported by Browning.

Price: **$920.00**

Browning Gold Micro Auto Shotgun

Similar to the Gold Hunter except has a 26" barrel, 13-7/8" pull length and smaller pistol grip for youths and other small shooters. Weighs 6 lbs., 10 oz. Introduced 2001. From Browning.

Price: **$894.00**

Browning Gold Stalker Auto Shotguns

Similar to the Gold Hunter except has black composite stock and forend. Choice of 3" or 3-1/2" chamber.

Price: 12 ga. with 3" chamber. **$856.00**
Price: With 3-1/2" chamber. **$1,002.00**

Browning Gold Mossy Oak® Shadow Grass Shotguns

Similar to the Gold Hunter except 12 gauge only, completely covered with Mossy Oak® Shadow Grass camouflage. Choice of 3" or 3-1/2" chamber and 26" or 28" barrel. Introduced 1999. Imported by Browning.

Price: 12 ga. 3" chamber **$967.00**
Price: 12 ga., 3-1/2" chamber. **$1,146.00**

Browning Gold Mossy Oak® Break-Up Shotguns

Similar to the Gold Hunter except 12 gauge only, completely covered with Mossy Oak® Break-Up camouflage. Imported by Browning.

Price: 3" chamber. **$1,069.00**
Price: 3-1/2" chamber. **$1,282.00**
Price: NWTF model, 3" chamber, 24" bbl. with Hi-Viz sight **$998.00**
Price: NWTF model, 3-1/2" chamber, 24" bbl. with Hi-Viz sight . **$1,177.00**
Price: Gold Rifled Deer (22" rifled bbl., Cantilever scope mount) **$1,046.00**

Browning Gold Classic Hunter Auto Shotgun

Similar to the Gold Hunter 3" except has semi-hump back receiver, magazine cut-off, adjustable comb, and satin-finish wood. Introduced 1999. Imported by Browning.

Price: 12 or 20 gauge **$912.00**
Price: Classic High Grade (silvered, gold engraved receiver, high-grade wood) **$1,750.00**

Browning Gold Classic Stalker

Similar to the Gold Classic Hunter except has adjustable composite stock and forend. Introduced 1999. Imported by Browning.

Price: **$856.00**

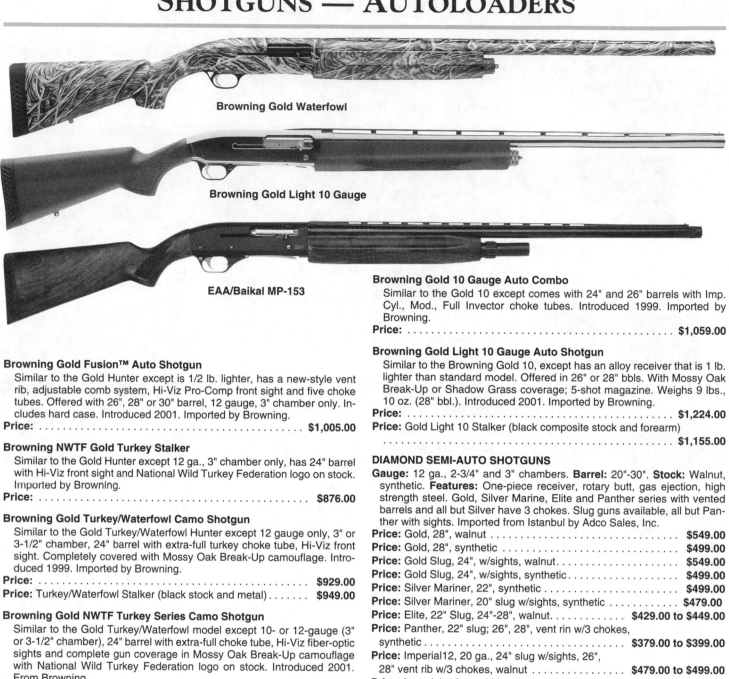

Browning Gold Waterfowl

Browning Gold Light 10 Gauge

EAA/Baikal MP-153

Browning Gold Fusion™ Auto Shotgun

Similar to the Gold Hunter except is 1/2 lb. lighter, has a new-style vent rib, adjustable comb system, Hi-Viz Pro-Comp front sight and five choke tubes. Offered with 26", 28" or 30" barrel, 12 gauge, 3" chamber only. Includes hard case. Introduced 2001. Imported by Browning.

Price: **$1,005.00**

Browning NWTF Gold Turkey Stalker

Similar to the Gold Hunter except 12 ga., 3" chamber only, has 24" barrel with Hi-Viz front sight and National Wild Turkey Federation logo on stock. Imported by Browning.

Price: **$876.00**

Browning Gold Turkey/Waterfowl Camo Shotgun

Similar to the Gold Turkey/Waterfowl Hunter except 12 gauge only, 3" or 3-1/2" chamber, 24" barrel with extra-full turkey choke tube, Hi-Viz front sight. Completely covered with Mossy Oak Break-Up camouflage. Introduced 1999. Imported by Browning.

Price: **$929.00**
Price: Turkey/Waterfowl Stalker (black stock and metal) **$949.00**

Browning Gold NWTF Turkey Series Camo Shotgun

Similar to the Gold Turkey/Waterfowl model except 10- or 12-gauge (3" or 3-1/2" chamber), 24" barrel with extra-full choke tube, Hi-Viz fiber-optic sights and complete gun coverage in Mossy Oak Break-Up camouflage with National Wild Turkey Federation logo on stock. Introduced 2001. From Browning.

Price: 10 gauge **$1,249.00**
Price: 12 gauge, 3-1/2" chamber **$1,177.00**
Price: 12 gauge, 3" chamber **$998.00**

Browning Gold Upland Special Auto Shotgun

Similar to the Gold Classic Hunter except has straight-grip walnut stock, 12 or 20 gauge, 3" chamber. Introduced 2001. From Browning

Price: 12-gauge model (24" bbl., weighs 7 lbs.) **$912.00**
Price: 20-gauge model (26" bbl., weighs 6 lbs., 12 oz.) **$912.00**

BROWNING GOLD 10 AUTO SHOTGUN

Gauge: 10, 3-1/2" chamber, 5-shot magazine. **Barrel:** 26", 28", 30" (Imp. Cyl., Mod., Full standard Invector). **Weight:** 10 lbs. 7 oz. (28" barrel). **Stock:** 14-3/ 8"x1-1/2"x2-3/8". Select walnut with gloss finish, cut checkering, recoil pad. **Features:** Short-stroke, gas-operated action, cross-bolt safety. Forged steel receiver with polished blue finish. Introduced 1993. Imported by Browning.

Price: **$1,007.95**
Price: Extra barrel. **$293.00**

Browning Gold 10 Gauge Auto Combo

Similar to the Gold 10 except comes with 24" and 26" barrels with Imp. Cyl., Mod., Full Invector choke tubes. Introduced 1999. Imported by Browning.

Price: **$1,059.00**

Browning Gold Light 10 Gauge Auto Shotgun

Similar to the Browning Gold 10, except has an alloy receiver that is 1 lb. lighter than standard model. Offered in 26" or 28" bbls. With Mossy Oak Break-Up or Shadow Grass coverage; 5-shot magazine. Weighs 9 lbs., 10 oz. (28" bbl.). Introduced 2001. Imported by Browning.

Price: **$1,224.00**
Price: Gold Light 10 Stalker (black composite stock and forearm)
.... **$1,155.00**

DIAMOND SEMI-AUTO SHOTGUNS

Gauge: 12 ga., 2-3/4" and 3" chambers. **Barrel:** 20"-30". **Stock:** Walnut, synthetic. **Features:** One-piece receiver, rotary butt, gas ejection, high strength steel. Gold, Silver Marine, Elite and Panther series with vented barrels and all but Silver have 3 chokes. Slug guns available, all but Panther with sights. Imported from Istanbul by Adco Sales, Inc.

Price: Gold, 28", walnut **$549.00**
Price: Gold, 28", synthetic **$499.00**
Price: Gold Slug, 24", w/sights, walnut................. **$549.00**
Price: Gold Slug, 24", w/sights, synthetic............. **$499.00**
Price: Silver Mariner, 22", synthetic **$499.00**
Price: Silver Mariner, 20" slug w/sights, synthetic **$479.00**
Price: Elite, 22" Slug, 24"-28", walnut. .... **$429.00 to $449.00**
Price: Panther, 22" slug; 26", 28", vent rin w/3 chokes,
synthetic .... **$379.00 to $399.00**
Price: Imperial12, 20 ga., 24" slug w/sights, 26",
28" vent rib w/3 chokes, walnut .... **$479.00 to $499.00**
Price: Imperial, 12 ga., 28" vent rib w/3 chokes,
3.5" chamber, walnut **$499.00**

EAA/BAIKAL MP-153 AUTO SHOTGUN

Gauge: 12, 3-1/2" chamber. **Barrel:** 18-1/2", 20", 24", 26", 28"; imp., mod. and full choke tubes. **Weight:** 7.8 lbs. **Stock:** Walnut. **Features:** Gas-operated action with automatic gas-adjustment valve allows use of light and heavy loads interchangeably; 4-round magazine; rubber recoil pad. Introduced 2000. Imported by European American Armory.

Price: MP-153 (blued finish, walnut stock and forend) **$509.00**
Price: MP-153 (field grade, synthetic stock)................. **$419.00**

EAA/SAIGA AUTO SHOTGUN

Gauge: 12, 20, 410, 3" chamber. **Barrel:** 19", 21", 22". **Weight:** 6.6-7.6 lbs. **Length:** 40"-45". **Stock:** Synthetic. **Features:** Retains best features of the AK Rifle by Kalashnikov as the semi-auto shotgun. Magazine fed. Imported from Russia by EAA Corp.

Price: 410 ga. **$239.00**
Price: 20 ga. **$389.00**
Price: 12 ga. .... **$429.00 to $469.00**

SHOTGUNS — AUTOLOADERS

Escort Model AS

Fabarm Gold Lion Mark III

Fabarm Sporting Clays Extra

ESCORT AUTO SHOTGUN

Gauge: 12. **Barrel:** 28" (choke tubes, M, IM, F); 3" chambers. **Weight:** 7 lbs. **Stock:** Turkish walnut, checkered pistol grip and forend. **Features:** Aluminum-alloy receiver, blued finish, chrome-plated bolt, adjustment for normal and magnum loads. Gold-plated trigger, trigger-guard safety, magazine cut-off. Tree choke tubes and wrench, two stock-adjustment shims, waterfowl plug, 7-shot magazine extender. Introduced 2002. Camo model introduced 2003. Imported from Turkey by Legacy Sports International.
Price: **$386.00**
Price: Model PS, black polymer stock **$364.00**
Price: Camo with HiViz sights. **$479.00**

FABARM GOLD LION MARK III AUTO SHOTGUN

Gauge: 12, 3" chamber. **Barrel:** 24", 26", 28", choke tubes. **Weight:** 7 lbs. **Length:** 45.5" overall. **Stock:** European walnut with gloss finish; olive wood grip cap. **Features:** TriBore barrel, reversible safety; gold-plated trigger and carrier release button; leather-covered rubber recoil pad. Introduced 1998. Imported from Italy by Heckler & Koch, Inc.
Price: **$939.00**

Fabarm Sporting Clays Extra Auto Shotgun

Similar to Gold Lion except 28" TriBore ported barrel with interchangeable colored front-sight beads, mid-rib bead, 10mm channeled vent rib, carbon-fiber finish, oil-finished walnut stock and forend with olive wood grip-cap. Stock dimensions are 14.58"x1.58"x2.44". Distinctive gold-colored receiver logo. Available in 12 gauge only, 3" chamber. Introduced 1999. Imported from Italy by Heckler & Koch, Inc.
Price: **$1,249.00**

FRANCHI 48AL SHOTGUN

Gauge: 20 or 28, 2-3/4" chamber. **Barrel:** 24", 26", 28" (Full, cyl., mod., choke tubes). **Weight:** 5.5 lbs. (20 gauge). **Length:** 44"-48.". **Stock:** 14-1/4"x1-5/ 8"x2-1/2". Walnut with checkered grip and forend. **Features:** Long recoil-operated action. Chrome-lined bore; cross-bolt safety. Imported from Italy by Benelli U.S.A.
Price: 20 ga. **$715.00**
Price: 28 ga. **$825.00**

Franchi 48AL Deluxe Shotgun

Similar to 48AL but with select walnut stock and forend and high-polish blue finish with gold trigger. Introduced 2000.
Price: (20 gauge, 26" barrel) **$940.00**
Price: (28 gauge, 26" barrel) **$990.00**

Franchi 48AL English

Similar to 48AL Deluxe but with straight grip "English style" stock. 20 ga., 28 ga., 26" bbl, ICMF tubes.
Price: 20 gauge **$940.00**
Price: 28 gauge **$990.00**

Franchi 48AL Short Stock Shotgun

Similar to 48AL but with stock shortened to 12-1/2" length of pull.
Price: (20 gauge, 26" barrel) **$715.00**

FRANCHI 612 AND 620 SHOTGUNS

Gauge: 12, 20, 3" chamber. **Barrel:** 24", 26", 28", IC, MF tubes. **Weight:** 7 lbs. **Stock:** European walnut, synthetic and Timber HD. **Features:** Alloy frame with matte black finish; gas-operated with Vario System, four-lug rotating bolt. Introduced 1996. Imported from Italy by Benelli U.S.A.
Price: Walnut wood **$750.00**
Price: Camo, Timber HD **$875.00**
Price: Synthetic (black synthetic stock, forend) **$710.00**
Price: 20 ga., 24", 26", 28", walnut **$750.00**
Price: Variopress 620 (Timber HD Camo) **$875.00**

Franchi 612 Defense Shotgun

Similar to 612 except has 18-1/2", cylinder-bore barrel with black, synthetic stock. Available in 12 gauge, 3" chamber only. Weighs 6-1/2 lbs. 2-shot magazine extension available. Introduced 2000.
Price: **$635.00**

Franchi 612 Sporting Shotgun

Similar to 612 except has 30" ported barrel to reduce muzzle jump. Available in 12 gauge, 3" chamber only. Introduced 2000.
Price: **$1,275.00**

Franchi 620 Short Stock Shotgun

Similar to 620 but with stock shortened to 12-1/2" length of pull for smaller shooters. Introduced 2000.
Price: (20 gauge, 26" barrel) **$730.00**

FRANCHI MODEL 912

Gauge: 12. **Barrel:** 24", 26", 28", 30". **Weight:** 7.5 to 7.8lbs. **Length:** 46" to 52". **Stock:** Satin walnut; synthetic. **Sights:** White bead, front. **Features:** Chambered for 3-1/2" magnum shells with Dual-Recoil-Reduction-System, multi-lugged rotary bolt. Made in Italy and imported by Benelli USA.
Price: (Walnut) . . . . **$1,000.00**; (Synthetic) **$940.00**
Price: Timber HD Camo **$1,050.00**

Remington Model 11-87 Premier

Remington Model 11-87 Dale Earnhardt Tribute

Remington Model 11-87 Special Purpose Magnum

Remington Model 11-87 SPS Camo

Remington Model 11-87 SPS-T Turkey Camo

REMINGTON MODEL 11-87 PREMIER SHOTGUN

Gauge: 12, 20, 3" chamber. **Barrel:** 26", 28", 30" Rem Choke tubes. Light Contour barrel. **Weight:** About 7-3/4 lbs. **Length:** 46" overall (26" bbl.). **Stock:** Walnut with satin or high-gloss finish; cut checkering; solid brown buttpad; no white spacers. **Sights:** Bradley-type white-faced front, metal bead middle. **Features:** Pressure compensating gas system allows shooting 2-3/4" or 3" loads interchangeably with no adjustments. Stainless magazine tube; redesigned feed latch, barrel support ring on operating bars; pinned forend. Introduced 1987.

Price: Light contour barrel $777.00
Price: Left-hand, 28" barrel. $831.00
Price: Premier cantilever deer barrel, fully-rifled, 21" sling, swivels, Monte Carlo stock $859.00
Price: 3-1/2" Super Magnum, 28" barrel $865.00
Price: Dale Earnhardt Tribute, 12 ga., 28" barrel $972.00

Remington Model 11-87 Special Purpose Magnum

Similar to the 11-87 Premier except has dull stock finish, Parkerized exposed metal surfaces. Bolt and carrier have dull blackened coloring. Comes with 26" or 28" barrel with Rem Chokes, padded Cordura nylon sling and quick detachable swivels. Introduced 1987.
Price: With synthetic stock and forend (SPS). $791.00

Remington Model 11-87 SPS Special Purpose Synthetic Camo

Similar to the 11-87 Special Purpose Magnum except has synthetic stock and all metal (except bolt and trigger guard) and stock covered with Mossy Oak Break-Up camo finish. In 12 gauge only, 26", Rem Choke. Comes with camo sling, swivels. Introduced 1992.
Price: $905.00

Remington Model 11-87 SPS-T Turkey Camo

Similar to the 11-87 Special Purpose Magnum except with synthetic stock, 21" vent. rib barrel with Rem Choke tube. Completely covered with Mossy Oak Break-Up Brown camouflage. Bolt body, trigger guard and recoil pad are non-reflective black.
Price: $905.00
Price: Model 11-87 SPS-T Camo CL cantilever $907.00

Remington Model 11-87 SPS-T Super Magnum Synthetic Camo

Similar to the 11-87 SPS-T Turkey Camo except has 23" vent rib barrel with Turkey Super full choke tube, chambered for 12 ga., 3-1/2", TruGlo rifle sights. Version available without TruGlo sights. Introduced 2001.
Price: $963.00

Remington Model 11-87 SPS-Deer Shotgun

Similar to the 11-87 Special Purpose Camo except has fully-rifled 21" barrel with rifle sights, black non-reflective, synthetic stock and forend, black carrying sling. Introduced 1993.
Price: $824.00
Price: With wood stock (Model 11-87 SP Deer Gun) Rem choke, 21" barrel w/rifle sights $756.00

SHOTGUNS

Remington Model 11-87 SPS-T Synthetic Camo

Remington Model 11-87 SPS-Deer

Remington Model 11-87 SPS Cantilever

Remington Model 11-87 SP

Remington Model 1100 Youth Turkey Camo

Remington Model 11-87 SPS Cantilever Shotgun

Similar to the 11-87 SPS except has fully rifled barrel; synthetic stock with Monte Carlo comb; cantilever scope mount deer barrel. Comes with sling and swivels. Introduced 1994.

Price: **$872.00**

Remington Model 11-87 SP and SPS Super Magnum Shotguns

Similar to Model 11-87 Special Purpose Magnum except has 3-1/2" chamber. Available in flat-finish American walnut or black synthetic stock, 26" or 28" black-matte finished barrel and receiver; imp. cyl., modified and full Rem Choke tubes. Overall length 45-3/4", weighs 8 lbs., 2 oz. Introduced 2000. From Remington Arms Co.

Price: 11-87 SP Super Magnum (walnut stock) **$865.00**
Price: 11-87 SPS Super Magnum (synthetic stock) **$879.00**
Price: 11-87 SPS Super Magnum, 28" (camo) **$963.00**

Remington Model 11-87 Upland Special Shotgun

Similar to 11-87 Premier except has 23" ventilated rib barrel with straight-grip, English-style walnut stock. Available in 12 or 20 gauge. Overall length 43-1/2", weighs 7-1/4 lbs. (6-1/2 lbs. in 20 ga.). Comes with imp. cyl., modified and full choke tubes. Introduced 2000.

Price: 12 or 20 gauge **$777.00**

REMINGTON MODEL 1100 SYNTHETIC LT-20 SHOTGUN

Gauge: 20. **Barrel:** 26" Rem Chokes. **Weight:** 6-3/4 lbs. **Stock:** 14"x1-1/2"x2-1/2". Black synthetic, checkered pistol grip and forend. **Features:** Matted receiver top with scroll work on both sides of receiver.

Price: **$549.00**
Price: Youth Gun LT-20 (21" Rem Choke) **$549.00**
Price: Remington Model 1100 Synthetic, 12 gauge, black synthetic stock; vent. rib 28" barrel, Mod. Rem Choke tube. Weighs about 7-1/2 lbs. Introduced 1996.. .... **$549.00**

Remington Model 1100 Youth Synthetic Turkey Camo

Similar to the Model 1100 LT-20 except has 1" shorter stock, 21" vent rib barrel with Full Rem Choke tube; 3" chamber; synthetic stock and forend are covered with Skyline Excel camo, and barrel and receiver have non-reflective, black matte finish. Introduced 2003.

Price: **$612.00**

Remington Model 1100 LT-20 Synthetic Deer Shotgun

Similar to the Model 1100 LT-20 except has 21" fully rifled barrel with rifle sights, 2-3/4" chamber, and fiberglass-reinforced synthetic stock. Introduced 1997. Made in U.S. by Remington.

Price: **$583.00**

Remington 1100 LT-20 Deer

Remington Model 1100 Sporting 28

Remington Model 1100 Classic Trap

Remington Model 1100 Sporting 12

Remington Model SP-10 121%

Remington Model SP-10 Camo 116%

Remington Model 1100 Sporting 28

Similar to the 1100 LT-20 except in 28 gauge with 25" barrel; comes with Skeet, Imp. Cyl., Light Mod., Mod. Rem Choke tube. Semi-Fancy walnut with gloss finish, Sporting rubber butt pad. Made in U.S. by Remington. Introduced 1996.
Price: **$868.00**

Remington Model 1100 Sporting 20 Shotgun

Similar to Model 1100 LT-20 except tournament-grade American walnut stock with gloss finish and sporting-style recoil pad, 28" Rem choke barrel for Skeet, Imp. Cyl., Light Modified and Modified. Introduced 1998.
Price: **$868.00**

Remington Model 1100 Classic Trap Shotgun

Similar to Standard Model 1100 except 12 gauge with 30", low-profile barrel, semi-fancy American walnut stock, high-polish blued receiver with engraving and gold eagle inlay. Singles, mid handicap and long handicap choke tubes. Overall length 50-1/2", weighs 8 lbs., 4 oz. Introduced 2000. From Remington Arms Co.
Price: **$895.00**

Remington Model 1100 Sporting 12 Shotgun

Similar to Model 1100 Sporting 20 Shotgun except in 12 gauge, 28" ventilated barrel with semi-fancy American walnut stock, gold-plated trigger. Overall length 49", weighs 8 lbs. Introduced 2000. From Remington Arms Co.
Price: **$868.00**

Remington Model 1100 Synthetic Deer Shotgun

Similar to Model 1100 LT-20 except 12 gauge, 21" fully rifled barrel with cantilever scope mount and fiberglass-reinforced synthetic stock with Monte Carlo comb. Introduced 1997. Made in U.S. by Remington.
Price: **$629.00**

REMINGTON MODEL SP-10 MAGNUM SHOTGUN

Gauge: 10, 3-1/2" chamber, 2-shot magazine. **Barrel:** 26", 30" (full and mod. Rem chokes). **Weight:** 10-3/4 to 11 lbs. **Length:** 47-1/2" overall (26" barrel). **Stock:** Walnut with satin finish or black synthetic with 26" barrel. Checkered grip and forend. **Sights:** Twin bead. **Features:** Stainless steel gas system with moving cylinder; 3/8" ventilated rib. Receiver and barrel have matte finish. Brown recoil pad. Comes with padded Cordura nylon sling. Introduced 1989.
Price: **$1,317.00**

SHOTGUNS

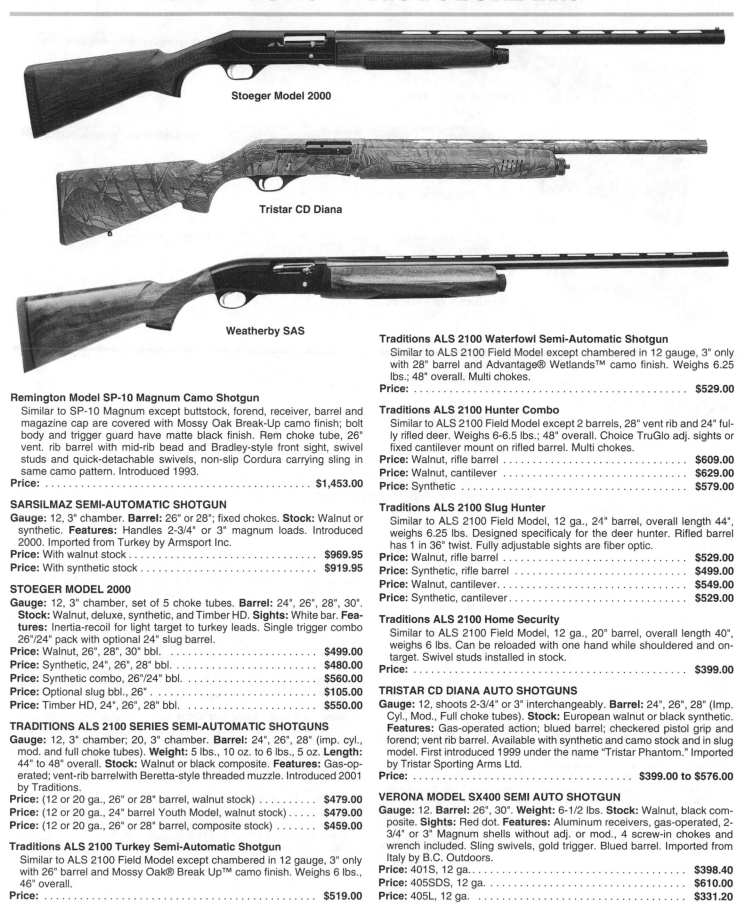

Stoeger Model 2000

Tristar CD Diana

Weatherby SAS

SHOTGUNS

Remington Model SP-10 Magnum Camo Shotgun

Similar to SP-10 Magnum except buttstock, forend, receiver, barrel and magazine cap are covered with Mossy Oak Break-Up camo finish; bolt body and trigger guard have matte black finish. Rem choke tube, 26" vent. rib barrel with mid-rib bead and Bradley-style front sight, swivel studs and quick-detachable swivels, non-slip Cordura carrying sling in same camo pattern. Introduced 1993.

Price: **$1,453.00**

SARSILMAZ SEMI-AUTOMATIC SHOTGUN

Gauge: 12, 3" chamber. **Barrel:** 26" or 28"; fixed chokes. **Stock:** Walnut or synthetic. **Features:** Handles 2-3/4" or 3" magnum loads. Introduced 2000. Imported from Turkey by Armsport Inc.

Price: With walnut stock **$969.95**
Price: With synthetic stock **$919.95**

STOEGER MODEL 2000

Gauge: 12, 3" chamber, set of 5 choke tubes. **Barrel:** 24", 26", 28", 30". **Stock:** Walnut, deluxe, synthetic, and Timber HD. **Sights:** White bar. **Features:** Inertia-recoil for light target to turkey leads. Single trigger combo 26"/24" pack with optional 24" slug barrel.

Price: Walnut, 26", 28", 30" bbl. **$499.00**
Price: Synthetic, 24", 26", 28" bbl. **$480.00**
Price: Synthetic combo, 26"/24" bbl. **$560.00**
Price: Optional slug bbl., 26" **$105.00**
Price: Timber HD, 24", 26", 28" bbl. **$550.00**

TRADITIONS ALS 2100 SERIES SEMI-AUTOMATIC SHOTGUNS

Gauge: 12, 3" chamber; 20, 3" chamber. **Barrel:** 24", 26", 28" (imp. cyl., mod. and full choke tubes). **Weight:** 5 lbs., 10 oz. to 6 lbs., 5 oz. **Length:** 44" to 48" overall. **Stock:** Walnut or black composite. **Features:** Gas-operated; vent-rib barrelwith Beretta-style threaded muzzle. Introduced 2001 by Traditions.

Price: (12 or 20 ga., 26" or 28" barrel, walnut stock) **$479.00**
Price: (12 or 20 ga., 24" barrel Youth Model, walnut stock) **$479.00**
Price: (12 or 20 ga., 26" or 28" barrel, composite stock) **$459.00**

Traditions ALS 2100 Turkey Semi-Automatic Shotgun

Similar to ALS 2100 Field Model except chambered in 12 gauge, 3" only with 26" barrel and Mossy Oak® Break Up™ camo finish. Weighs 6 lbs., 46" overall.

Price: **$519.00**

Traditions ALS 2100 Waterfowl Semi-Automatic Shotgun

Similar to ALS 2100 Field Model except chambered in 12 gauge, 3" only with 28" barrel and Advantage® Wetlands™ camo finish. Weighs 6.25 lbs.; 48" overall. Multi chokes.

Price: **$529.00**

Traditions ALS 2100 Hunter Combo

Similar to ALS 2100 Field Model except 2 barrels, 28" vent rib and 24" fully rifled deer. Weighs 6-6.5 lbs.; 48" overall. Choice TruGlo adj. sights or fixed cantilever mount on rifled barrel. Multi chokes.

Price: Walnut, rifle barrel **$609.00**
Price: Walnut, cantilever **$629.00**
Price: Synthetic **$579.00**

Traditions ALS 2100 Slug Hunter

Similar to ALS 2100 Field Model, 12 ga., 24" barrel, overall length 44", weighs 6.25 lbs. Designed specifically for the deer hunter. Rifled barrel has 1 in 36" twist. Fully adjustable sights are fiber optic.

Price: Walnut, rifle barrel **$529.00**
Price: Synthetic, rifle barrel **$499.00**
Price: Walnut, cantilever. **$549.00**
Price: Synthetic, cantilever **$529.00**

Traditions ALS 2100 Home Security

Similar to ALS 2100 Field Model, 12 ga., 20" barrel, overall length 40", weighs 6 lbs. Can be reloaded with one hand while shouldered and on-target. Swivel studs installed in stock.

Price: **$399.00**

TRISTAR CD DIANA AUTO SHOTGUNS

Gauge: 12, shoots 2-3/4" or 3" interchangeably. **Barrel:** 24", 26", 28" (Imp. Cyl., Mod., Full choke tubes). **Stock:** European walnut or black synthetic. **Features:** Gas-operated action; blued barrel; checkered pistol grip and forend; vent rib barrel. Available with synthetic and camo stock and in slug model. First introduced 1999 under the name "Tristar Phantom." Imported by Tristar Sporting Arms Ltd.

Price: . . . . **$399.00 to $576.00**

VERONA MODEL SX400 SEMI AUTO SHOTGUN

Gauge: 12. **Barrel:** 26", 30". **Weight:** 6-1/2 lbs. **Stock:** Walnut, black composite. **Sights:** Red dot. **Features:** Aluminum receivers, gas-operated, 2-3/4" or 3" Magnum shells without adj. or mod., 4 screw-in chokes and wrench included. Sling swivels, gold trigger. Blued barrel. Imported from Italy by B.C. Outdoors.

Price: 401S, 12 ga. **$398.40**
Price: 405SDS, 12 ga. **$610.00**
Price: 405L, 12 ga. **$331.20**

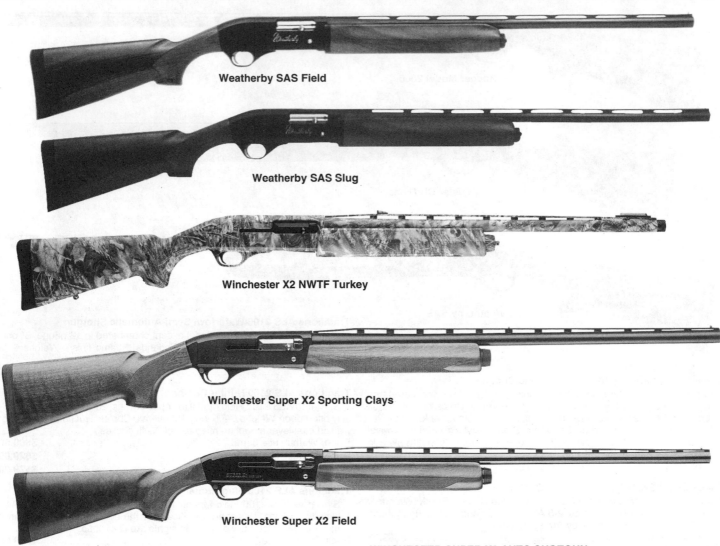

Weatherby SAS Field

Weatherby SAS Slug

Winchester X2 NWTF Turkey

Winchester Super X2 Sporting Clays

Winchester Super X2 Field

WEATHERBY SAS AUTO SHOTGUN

Gauge: 12, 2-3/4" or 3" chamber. **Barrel:** 26", 28" (20 ga.); 26", 28", 30" (12 ga.); Briley Multi-Choke tubes. **Weight:** 6-3/4 to 7-3/4 lbs. **Stock:** 14-1/4"x2-1/ 4"x1-1/2". Claro walnut; black, Shadow Grass or Mossy Oak Break-Up camo synthetic. **Features:** Alloy receiver with matte finish; gold-plated trigger; magazine cut-off. Introduced 1999. Imported by Weatherby.

Price: 12 or 20 ga. (walnut stock) **$945.00**
Price: 12 or 20 ga. (black synthetic stock) **$979.00**
Price: 12 ga. (camo stock) **$1,115.00**

WEATHERBY SAS (SEMI-AUTOMATIC SHOTGUNS)

6 Models: SAS Field, SAS Sporting Clays, SAS Shadow Grass, SAS Break-Up, SAS Synthetic and a Slug Gun.
Gauge: 12 ga. **Barrel:** Vent ribbed, 24"-30". **Stock:** SAS Field and Sporting Clays, walnut. SAS Shadow Grass, Break-Up, Synthetic, composite. **Sights:** SAS Sporting Clays, frass front and mid-point back. SAS Shadow Grass and Break-Up, HiViz front and brass mid. Synthetic has brass front. **Features:** Easy to shoot, load, clean, lightweight, lessened recoil, IMC system includes 3 chrome moly screw-in choke tubes. Slug gun has 22" rifled barrel with matte blue finish and cantilever base for scope mounting.
Price: . . . .**$649.00 to 749.00**

WINCHESTER SUPER X2 AUTO SHOTGUN

Gauge: 12, 3", 3-1/2" chamber. **Barrel:** 24", 26", 28"; Invector Plus choke tubes. **Weight:** 7-1/4 to 7-1/2 lbs. **Stock:** 14-1/4"x1-3/4"x2". Walnut or black synthetic. **Features:** Gas-operated action shoots all loads without adjustment; vent. rib barrels; 4-shot magazine. Introduced 1999. Made in U.S. by U.S. Repeating Arms Co.

Price: Field, walnut or synthetic stock, 3" **$819.00**
Price: Magnum, 3-1/2", synthetic stock, 26" or 28" bbl. **$936.00**
Price: Camo Waterfowl, 3-1/2", Mossy Oak Shadow Grass. . . . **$1,080.00**
Price: NWTF Turkey, 3-1/2", black synthetic stock, 24" bbl. **$997.00**
Price: NWTF Turkey, 3-1/2", Mossy Oak Break-Up camo **$1,080.00**

Winchester Super X2 Sporting Clays Auto Shotgun

Similar to the Super X2 except has two gas pistons (one for target loads, one for heavy 3" loads), adjustable comb system and high-post rib. Back-bored barrel with Invector Plus choke tubes. Offered in 28" and 30" barrels. Introduced 2001. From U.S. Repeating Arms Co.

Price: Super X2 Sporting Clays **$1,206.00**

Winchester Super X2 Field 3" Auto Shotgun

Similar to the Super X2 except has a 3" chamber, walnut stock and forearm and high-profile rib. Back-bored barrel and Invector Plus choke tubes. Introduced 2001. From U.S. Repeating Arms Co.

Price: Super X2 Field 3", 26" or 28" bbl. **$819.00**

SHOTGUNS — SLIDE & LEVER ACTIONS

Includes a wide variety of sporting guns and guns suitable for competitive shooting.

Armscor M-30F Field

Benelli Nova Pump

Benelli Nova Pump Slug

Browning BPS 10 gauge

Browning BPS 10 gauge Mossy Oak® Shadow Grass

ARMSCOR M-30F FIELD PUMP SHOTGUN
Gauge: 12, 3" chamber. **Barrel:** 28" fixed Mod., or with Mod. and Full choke tubes. **Weight:** 7.6 lbs. **Stock:** Walnut-finished hardwood. **Features:** Double action slide bars; blued steel receiver; damascened bolt. Introduced 1996. Imported from the Philippines by K.B.I., Inc.
Price: With fixed choke **$239.00**
Price: With choke tubes **$269.00**

BENELLI NOVA PUMP SHOTGUN
Gauge: 12, 20. **Barrel:** 24", 26", 28". **Stock:** Synthetic, X-tra Brown 12 ga., Timber HD 20 ga. **Sights:** Red bar. **Features:** 2-3/4", 3" chamber (3-2/1" 12 ga. only). Montefeltro rotating bolt design with dual action bars, magazine cut-off, synthetic trigger assembly, 4-shot magazine. Introduced 1999. Imported from Italy by Benelli USA.
Price: Synthetic **$335.00**
Price: Timber HD **$400.00**

Benelli Nova Pump Slug Gun
Similar to the Nova except has 18.5" barrel with adjustable rifle-type or ghost ring sights; weighs 7.2 lbs.; black synthetic stock. Introduced 1999. Imported from Italy by Benelli USA.
Price: With rifle sights **$355.00**
Price: With ghost-ring sights **$395.00**

Benelli Nova Pump Rifled Slug Gun
Similar to Nova Pump Slug Gun except has 24" barrel and rifled bore; open rifle sights; synthetic stock; weighs 8.1 pounds.
Price: . . . . (Synthetic) **$500.00**; Timber HD **$575.00**

BROWNING BPS PUMP SHOTGUN
Gauge: 10, 12, 3-1/2" chamber; 12 or 20, 3" chamber (2-3/4" in target guns), 28, 2-3/4" chamber, 5-shot magazine, 410 ga., 3" chamber. **Barrel:**

10 ga.— 24" Buck Special, 28", 30", 32" Invector; 12, 20 ga.—22", 24", 26", 28", 30", 32" (Imp. Cyl., mod. or full). 410 ga.—26" barrel. (Imp. Cyl., mod. and full choke tubes.) Also available with Invector choke tubes, 12 or 20 ga.; Upland Special has 22" barrel with Invector tubes. BPS 3" and 3-1/2" have back-bored barrel. **Weight:** 7 lbs., 8 oz. (28" barrel). **Length:** 48-3/4" overall (28" barrel). **Stock:** 14-1/4"x1-1/2"x2-1/2". Select walnut, semi-beavertail forend, full pistol grip stock. **Features:** All 12 gauge 3" guns except Buck Special and game guns have back-bored barrels with Invector Plus choke tubes. Bottom feeding and ejection, receiver top safety, high post vent. rib. Double action bars eliminate binding. Vent. rib barrels only. All 12 and 20 gauge guns with 3" chamber available with fully engraved receiver flats at no extra cost. Each gauge has its own unique game scene. Introduced 1977. Imported from Japan by Browning.
Price: 12 ga., 3-1/2" Magnum Hunter, Invector Plus **$548.00**
Price: 12 ga., 3-1/2" Magnum Stalker (black syn. stock) **$548.00**
Price: 12, 20 ga., Hunter, Invector Plus **$464.00**
Price: 12 ga. Deer Hunter (22" rifled bbl., cantilever mount) **$568.00**
Price: 28 ga., Hunter, Invector **$495.00**
Price: 410 ga., Hunter, Invector **$495.00**

Browning BPS 10 Gauge Shotguns
Chambered for the 10 gauge, 3-1/2" load. Offered in 24", 26" and 28" barrels. Offered with walnut, black composite (Stalker models) or camouflage stock and forend. Introduced 1999. Imported by Browning.
Price: Hunter (walnut) **$548.00**
Price: Stalker (composite) **$548.00**
Price: Mossy Oak® Shadow Grass or Break-Up Camo **$652.00**

Browning BPS 10 gauge Camo Pump
Similar to the BPS 10 gauge Hunter except completely covered with Mossy Oak Shadow Grass camouflage. Available with 24", 26", 28" barrel. Introduced 1999. Imported by Browning.
Price: **$652.00**

EAA/Baikal MP-133

Escort AimGuard

Escort FieldHunter

Fabarm Field Pump

Browning BPS Waterfowl Camo Pump Shotgun

Similar to the BPS Hunter except completely covered with Mossy Oak Shadow Grass camouflage. Available in 12 gauge, with 24", 26" or 28" barrel, 3" chamber. Introduced 1999. Imported by Browning.
Price: **$652.00**

Browning BPS Game Gun Deer Hunter

Similar to the standard BPS except has newly designed receiver/magazine tube/barrel mounting system to eliminate play, heavy 20.5" barrel with rifle-type sights with adjustable rear, solid receiver scope mount, "rifle" stock dimensions for scope or open sights, sling swivel studs. Gloss or matte finished wood with checkering, polished blue metal. Introduced 1992.
Price: **$568.00**

Browning BPS Game Gun Turkey Special

Similar to the standard BPS except has satin-finished walnut stock and dull-finished barrel and receiver. Receiver is drilled and tapped for scope mounting. Rifle-style stock dimensions and swivel studs. Has Extra-Full Turkey choke tube. Introduced 1992.
Price: **$500.00**

Browning BPS Stalker Pump Shotgun

Same gun as the standard BPS except all exposed metal parts have a matte blued finish and the stock has a durable black finish with a black recoil pad. Available in 10 ga. (3-1/2") and 12 ga. with 3" or 3-1/2" chamber, 22", 28", 30" barrel with Invector choke system. Introduced 1987.
Price: 12 ga., 3" chamber, Invector Plus **$448.00**
Price: 10, 12 ga., 3-1/2" chamber. **$537.00**

Browning BPS NWTF Turkey Series Pump Shotgun

Similar to the BPS Stalker except has full coverage Mossy Oak® Break-Up camo finish on synthetic stock, forearm and exposed metal parts. Offered in 10 and 12 gauge, 3" or 3-1/2" chamber; 24" bbl. has extra-full choke tube and Hi-Viz fiber optic sights. Introduced 2001. From Browning.
Price: 10 ga., 3-1/2" chamber. **$637.00**
Price: 12 ga., 3-1/2" chamber. **$637.00**
Price: 12 ga., 3" chamber. **$549.00**

Browning BPS Micro Pump Shotgun

Same as BPS Upland Special except 20 ga. only, 22" Invector barrel, stock has pistol grip with recoil pad. Length of pull is 13-1/4"; weighs 6 lbs., 12 oz. Introduced 1986.
Price: **$482.00**

DIAMOND 12 GA. PUMP SHOTGUN

Gauge: 12, 2-3/4" and 3" chambers. **Barrel:** 18"-30". **Weight:** 7 lbs. **Stock:** Walnut, synthetic. **Features:** Aluminum one-piece receiver sculpted for lighter weight. Double locking on fixed bolt. Gold, Elite and Panther series with vented barrels and 3 chokes. All series slug guns available (Gold and Elite with sights). Imported from Istanbul by ADCO Sales.
Price: Gold, 28" vent rib w/3 chokes, walnut **$359.00**
Price: Gold, 28", synthetic **$329.00**
Price: Gold Slug, 24" w/sights, walnut or synthetic . . **$329.00 to $359.00**
Price: Silver Mariner 18.5" Slug, synthetic **$399.00**
Price: Silver Mariner 22" vent rib w/3 chokes **$419.00**
Price: Elite, 22" slug w/sights; 24", 28" ventib w/3 chokes,
walnut . . . . **$329.00 to $349.00**
Price: Panther, 28", 30" ventib w/3 chokes, synthetic **$279.00**
Price: Panther,18.5", 22" Slug, synthetic . . . . **$209.00 to $265.00**
Price: Imperial 12 ga., 28" vent rib w/3 chokes, 3.5" chamber,
walnut **$399.00**

EAA/BAIKAL MP-133 PUMP SHOTGUN

Gauge: 12, 3-1/2" chamber. **Barrel:** 18-1/2", 20", 24", 26", 28"; imp., mod. and full choke tubes. **Weight:** NA. **Stock:** Walnut; checkered grip and grooved forearm. **Features:** Hammer-forged, chrome-lined barrel with ventilated rib; machined steel parts; dual action bars; trigger-block safety; 4-shot magazine tube; handles 2-3/4" through 3-1/2" shells. Introduced 2000. Imported by European American Armory.
Price: MP-133 (blued finish, walnut stock and forend) **$329.00**

ESCORT PUMP SHOTGUN

Gauge: 12, 3" chamber. **Barrel:** 20", fixed (AimGuard model); Multi (M, IC, F) (FieldHunter model). **Weight:** 6.4 to 7 lbs. **Stock:** Polymer. **Features:** AimGuard model has an included pistol grip accessory. FieldHunter has migratory bird magazine plug. Stock drop adjusting spacers included with both models. Mossy Oak camo stock available in FieldHunter. Introduced 2003. From Legacy Sports International.
Price: AimGuard **$189.95**
Price: FieldHunter . . . . **$199.95 to $219.95**

NEW!

SHOTGUNS

SHOTGUNS — SLIDE & LEVER ACTIONS

Ithaca Model 37 Waterfowl

Ithaca Model 37 Deerslayer II

Mossberg Model 835 Mossy Oak Camo

FABARM FIELD PUMP SHOTGUN

Gauge: 12, 3" chamber. **Barrel:** 28" (24" rifled slug barrel available). **Weight:** 76.6 lbs. **Length:** 48.25" overall. **Stock:** Polymer. **Features:** Similar to Fabarm FP6 Pump Shotgun. Alloy receiver; twin action bars; available in black or Mossy Oak Break-Up™ camo finish. Includes cyl., mod. and full choke tubes. Introduced 2001. Imported from Italy by Heckler & Koch Inc.
Price: Matte black finish **$399.00**
Price: Mossy Oak Break-Up™ finish **$469.00**

ITHACA MODEL 37 DELUXE PUMP SHOTGUN

Gauge: 12, 16, 20, 3" chamber. **Barrel:** 26", 28", 30" (12 gauge), 26", 28" (16 and 20 gauge), choke tubes. **Weight:** 7 lbs. **Stock:** Walnut with cut-checkered grip and forend. **Features:** Steel receiver; bottom ejection; brushed blue finish, vent rib barrels. Reintroduced 1996. Made in U.S. by Ithaca Gun Co.
Price: **$633.00**
Price: With straight English-style stock. **$803.00**
Price: Model 37 New Classic (ringtail forend, sunburst recoil pad, hand-finished walnut stock, 26" or 28" barrel) **$803.00**

ITHACA MODEL 37 WATERFOWL

Similar to Model 37 Deluxe except in 12 gauge only with 24", 26", or 30" barrel, special extended steel shot choke tube system. Complete coverage of Advantage Wetlands or Hardwoods camouflage. Introduced 1999. Made in U.S. by Ithaca Gun Co. Storm models have synthetic stock.
Price: . . . . **$499.00 to $549.00**

ITHACA MODEL 37 DEERSLAYER II PUMP SHOTGUN

Gauge: 12, 16, 20; 3" chamber. **Barrel:** 24", 26", fully rifled. **Weight:** 11 lbs. **Stock:** Cut-checkered American walnut with Monte Carlo comb. **Sights:** Rifle-type. **Features:** Integral barrel and receiver. Bottom ejection. Brushed blue finish. Reintroduced 1997. Made in U.S. by Ithaca Gun Co. Storm models have synthetic stock.
Price: **$633.00**
Price: Smooth Bore Deluxe **$582.00**
Price: Rifled Deluxe **$582.00**
Price: Storm **$399.00**

ITHACA MODEL 37 DEERSLAYER III PUMP SHOTGUN

Gauge: 12, 20, 2-3/4" and 3" chambers. **Barrel:** 26" free floated. **Weight:** 9 lbs. **Stock:** Monte Carlo laminate. **Sights:** Rifled. **Features:** Barrel length gives increased velocity. Trigger and sear set hand filed and stoned for creep free operation. Weaver-style scope base. Swivel studs. Matte blue.
Price: **$900.00**

ITHACA MODEL 37 RUFFED GROUSE SPECIAL EDITION

Gauge: 20 ga. **Barrel:** 22", 24", interchangeable choke tubes. **Weight:** 5.25 lbs. **Stock:** American black walnut. **Features:** Laser engraved stock with line art drawing. Bottom eject. Vent rib and English style. Right- or left-hand thru simple safety change. Aluminum receiver. Made in U.S.A. by Ithaca Gun Co.
Price: **$840.00**

ITHACA ELLETT SPECIAL MODEL 37 TURKEYSLAYER

Gauge: 12 ga., 3" chamber. **Barrel:** 22" ported. **Stock:** Composite. **Sights:** Fully adjustable, TruGlo front and rear. **Features:** Recreated from "Golden Age." Complete camo covering. Drilled and tapped. Extended turkey chokes. Matte metal, Realtree Hardwoods 20/200 or Advantage Timber patterns. Storm models are available in 12 or 20 gauge.
Price: **$654.00**
Price: Storm **$459.00**

ITHACA QUAD BORE MODEL 37 TURKEYSLAYER

Gauge: 20 ga. **Barrel:** 22" ported. **Weight:** 6.25 lbs. **Stock:** Black walnut stock and forend. **Sights:** Fully adjustable, TruGlo. **Features:** Sling swivel studs, matte blue, turkey full choke tube, 100% American made.
Price: **$680.00**

ITHACA MODEL 37 ULTRALIGHT DELUXE

Gauge: 16 ga. 2-3/4" chamber. **Barrel:** 24", 26", 28". **Weight:** 5.25 lbs. **Stock:** Standard deluxe. **Sights:** Raybar. **Features:** Vent rib, drilled and tapped, interchangeable barrel. F, M, IC choke tubes.
Price: Deluxe **$649.00**
Price: Classic/English **$824.00**
Price: Classic/Pistol **$824.00**

MOSSBERG MODEL 835 ULTI-MAG PUMP

Gauge: 12, 3-1/2" chamber. **Barrel:** Ported 24" rifled bore, 24", 28", Accu-Mag choke tubes for steel or lead shot. **Weight:** 7-3/4 lbs. **Length:** 48-1/2" overall. **Stock:** 14"x1-1/2"x2-1/2". Dual Comb. Cut-checkered hardwood or camo synthetic; both have recoil pad. **Sights:** White bead front, brass mid-bead; Fiber Optic. **Features:** Shoots 2-3/4", 3" and 3-1/2" shells. Back-bored and ported barrel to reduce recoil, improve patterns. Ambidextrous thumb safety, twin extractors, dual slide bars. Mossberg Cablelock included. Introduced 1988.
Price: 28" vent. rib, hardwood stock. **$370.00**
Price: Combo, 24" rifled bore, rifle sights, 24" vent. rib, Accu-Mag Ulti-Full choke tube, Woodlands camo finish. **$572.00**
Price: RealTree Camo Turkey, 24" vent. rib, Accu-Mag Extra-Full tube, synthetic stock. **$525.00**
Price: Mossy Oak Camo, 28" vent. rib, Accu-Mag tubes, synthetic stock. **$583.00**
Price: OFM Camo, 28" vent. rib, Accu-Mag Mod. tube, synthetic stock. **$407.00**

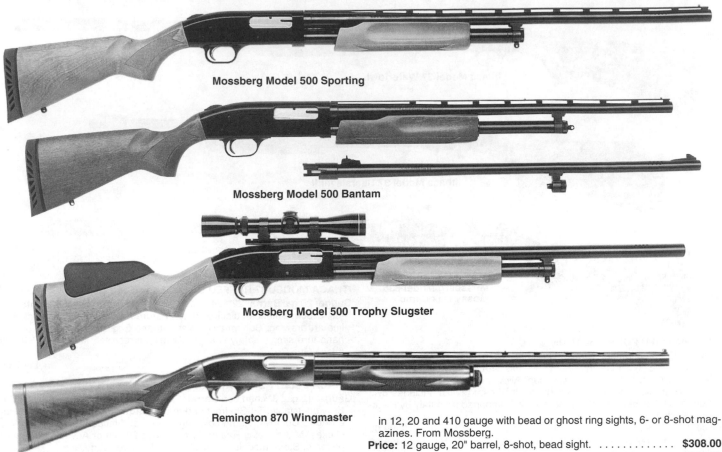

Mossberg Model 500 Sporting

Mossberg Model 500 Bantam

Mossberg Model 500 Trophy Slugster

Remington 870 Wingmaster

Mossberg Model 835 Synthetic Stock
Similar to the Model 835, except with 28" ported barrel with Accu-Mag Mod. choke tube, Parkerized finish, black synthetic stock and forend. Introduced 1998. Made in U.S. by Mossberg.
Price: $370.00

MOSSBERG MODEL 500 SPORTING PUMP
Gauge: 12, 20, 410, 3" chamber. **Barrel:** 18-1/2" to 28" with fixed or Accu-Choke, plain or vent. rib. **Weight:** 6-1/4 lbs. (410), 7-1/4 lbs. (12). **Length:** 48" overall (28" barrel). **Stock:** 14"x1-1/2"x2-1/2". Walnut-stained hardwood. Cut-checkered grip and forend. **Sights:** White bead front, brass mid-bead; Fiber Optic. **Features:** Ambidextrous thumb safety, twin extractors, disconnecting safety, dual action bars. Quiet Carry forend. Many barrels are ported. Mossberg Cablelock included. From Mossberg.
Price: From about...................................... $301.00
Price: Sporting Combos (field barrel and Slugster barrel), from. . $403.00

Mossberg Model 500 Bantam Pump
Same as the Model 500 Sporting Pump except 12 (new for 2001) or 20 gauge, 22" vent. rib Accu-Choke barrel with choke tube set; has 1" shorter stock, reduced length from pistol grip to trigger, reduced forend reach. Introduced 1992.
Price: $301.00
Price: With full Woodlands camouflage finish (20 ga. only) $384.00

Mossberg Model 500 Camo Pump
Same as the Model 500 Sporting Pump except 12 gauge only and entire gun is covered with special camouflage finish. Receiver drilled and tapped for scope mounting. Comes with quick detachable swivel studs, swivels, camouflage sling, Mossberg Cablelock.
Price: From about...................................... $370.00

Mossberg Model 500 Persuader/Cruiser Shotguns
Similar to Mossberg Model 500 except has 18-1/2" or 20" barrel with cylinder bore choke, synthetic stock and blue or parkerized finish. Available in 12, 20 and 410 gauge with bead or ghost ring sights, 6- or 8-shot magazines. From Mossberg.
Price: 12 gauge, 20" barrel, 8-shot, bead sight. $308.00
Price: 20 or 410 gauge, 18-1/2" barrel, 6-shot, bead sight $329.00
Price: 12 gauge, parkerized finish, 6-shot, 18-1/2" barrel, ghost ring sights $437.00
Price: Home Security 410 (410 gauge, 18-1/2" barrel with spreader choke) $335.00

Mossberg Model 590 Special Purpose Shotguns
Similar to Model 500 except has parkerized or Marinecote finish, 9-shot magazine and black synthetic stock (some models feature Speed Feed. Available in 12 gauge only with 20", cylinder bore barrel. Weighs 7-1/4 lbs. From Mossberg.
Price: Bead sight, heat shield over barrel $389.00
Price: Ghost ring sight, Speed Feed stock. $546.00

MOSSBERG MODEL 500 SLUGSTER
Gauge: 12, 20, 3" chamber. **Barrel:** 24", ported rifled bore. Integral scope mount. **Weight:** 7-1/4 lbs. **Length:** 44" overall. **Stock:** 14" pull, 1-3/8" drop at heel. Walnut; Dual Comb design for proper eye positioning with or without scoped barrels. Recoil pad and swivel studs. **Features:** Ambidextrous thumb safety, twin extractors, dual slide bars. Comes with scope mount. Mossberg Cablelock included. Introduced 1988.
Price: Rifled bore, with integral scope mount, Dual-Comb stock, 12 or 20 .... $398.00
Price: Fiber Optic, rifle sights $398.00
Price: Rifled bore, rifle sights $367.00
Price: 20 ga., Standard or Bantam, from $367.00

REMINGTON MODEL 870 WINGMASTER
Gauge: 12ga., 16 ga., 3" chamber. **Barrel:** 26", 28", 30" (Rem chokes). **Weight:** 7-1/4 lbs.. **Length:** 46", 48". **Stock:** Walnut, hardwood, synthetic. **Sights:** Single bead (Twin bead Wingmaster). **Features:** Balistically balanced performance, milder recoil. Light contour barrel. Double action bars, cross-bolt safety, blue finish.
Price: Wingmaster, walnut, blued, 26", 28", 30".............. $584.00
Price: 870 Wingmaster Super Magnum, 3-1/2" chamber, 28" ... $665.00

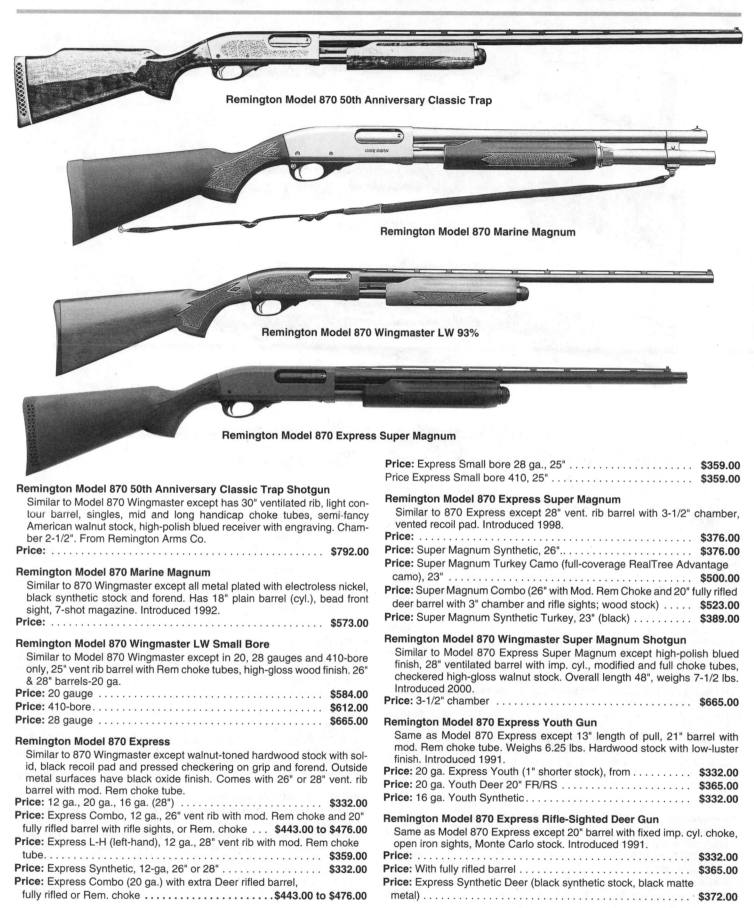

Remington Model 870 50th Anniversary Classic Trap

Remington Model 870 Marine Magnum

Remington Model 870 Wingmaster LW 93%

Remington Model 870 Express Super Magnum

Remington Model 870 50th Anniversary Classic Trap Shotgun
Similar to Model 870 Wingmaster except has 30" ventilated rib, light contour barrel, singles, mid and long handicap choke tubes, semi-fancy American walnut stock, high-polish blued receiver with engraving. Chamber 2-1/2". From Remington Arms Co.
Price: **$792.00**

Remington Model 870 Marine Magnum
Similar to 870 Wingmaster except all metal plated with electroless nickel, black synthetic stock and forend. Has 18" plain barrel (cyl.), bead front sight, 7-shot magazine. Introduced 1992.
Price: **$573.00**

Remington Model 870 Wingmaster LW Small Bore
Similar to Model 870 Wingmaster except in 20, 28 gauges and 410-bore only, 25" vent rib barrel with Rem choke tubes, high-gloss wood finish. 26" & 28" barrels-20 ga.
Price: 20 gauge **$584.00**
Price: 410-bore **$612.00**
Price: 28 gauge **$665.00**

Remington Model 870 Express
Similar to 870 Wingmaster except walnut-toned hardwood stock with solid, black recoil pad and pressed checkering on grip and forend. Outside metal surfaces have black oxide finish. Comes with 26" or 28" vent. rib barrel with mod. Rem choke tube.
Price: 12 ga., 20 ga., 16 ga. (28") **$332.00**
Price: Express Combo, 12 ga., 26" vent rib with mod. Rem choke and 20" fully rifled barrel with rifle sights, or Rem. choke . . . **$443.00 to $476.00**
Price: Express L-H (left-hand), 12 ga., 28" vent rib with mod. Rem choke tube. **$359.00**
Price: Express Synthetic, 12-ga, 26" or 28" **$332.00**
Price: Express Combo (20 ga.) with extra Deer rifled barrel, fully rifled or Rem. choke . . . . **$443.00 to $476.00**

Price: Express Small bore 28 ga., 25" **$359.00**
Price Express Small bore 410, 25" **$359.00**

Remington Model 870 Express Super Magnum
Similar to 870 Express except 28" vent. rib barrel with 3-1/2" chamber, vented recoil pad. Introduced 1998.
Price: **$376.00**
Price: Super Magnum Synthetic, 26" **$376.00**
Price: Super Magnum Turkey Camo (full-coverage RealTree Advantage camo), 23" **$500.00**
Price: Super Magnum Combo (26" with Mod. Rem Choke and 20" fully rifled deer barrel with 3" chamber and rifle sights; wood stock) **$523.00**
Price: Super Magnum Synthetic Turkey, 23" (black) **$389.00**

Remington Model 870 Wingmaster Super Magnum Shotgun
Similar to Model 870 Express Super Magnum except high-polish blued finish, 28" ventilated barrel with imp. cyl., modified and full choke tubes, checkered high-gloss walnut stock. Overall length 48", weighs 7-1/2 lbs. Introduced 2000.
Price: 3-1/2" chamber **$665.00**

Remington Model 870 Express Youth Gun
Same as Model 870 Express except 13" length of pull, 21" barrel with mod. Rem choke tube. Weighs 6.25 lbs. Hardwood stock with low-luster finish. Introduced 1991.
Price: 20 ga. Express Youth (1" shorter stock), from **$332.00**
Price: 20 ga. Youth Deer 20" FR/RS **$365.00**
Price: 16 ga. Youth Synthetic **$332.00**

Remington Model 870 Express Rifle-Sighted Deer Gun
Same as Model 870 Express except 20" barrel with fixed imp. cyl. choke, open iron sights, Monte Carlo stock. Introduced 1991.
Price: **$332.00**
Price: With fully rifled barrel **$365.00**
Price: Express Synthetic Deer (black synthetic stock, black matte metal) **$372.00**

Remington Model 870 Express Deer Gun

Remington Model 870 Express Turkey

Remington Model 870 SPS Super Slug Deer Gun

Remington Model 870 SPS-T Camo

Remington Model 870 Express Turkey
Same as Model 870 Express except 3" chamber, 21" vent rib turkey barrel and extra-full Rem. choke turkey tube; 12 ga. only. Introduced 1991.
Price: $345.00
Price: Express Turkey Camo stock has Skyline Excel camo, matte black metal.............................. $399.00
Price: Express Youth Turkey camo (as above with 1" shorter length of pull), 20 ga., Skyline Excel camo................. $399.00

Remington Model 870 Express Synthetic 18"
Similar to 870 Express with 18" barrel except synthetic stock and forend; 7-shot. Introduced 1994.
Price: $319.00

Remington Model 870 SPS Super Slug Deer Gun
Similar to the Model 870 Express Synthetic except has 23" rifled, modified contour barrel with cantilever scope mount. Comes with black synthetic stock and forend with swivel studs, black Cordura nylon sling. Introduced 1999. Fully rifled centilever barrel.
Price: $580.00

Remington Model 870 SPS-T Synthetic Camo Shotgun
Chambered for 12 ga., 3" shells, has Mossy Oak Break-Up® synthetic stock and metal treatment, TruGlo fiber optic sights. Introduced 2001.
Price: 20" RS, Rem. choke............................ $595.00
Price: Youth version $595.00
Price: Super Magnum Camo, 23", CL Rem. Choke........... $609.00
Price: Super Magnum Camo 23", VT Rem. Choke $591.00

Price: 20 ga., Truglo sights, Rem. Choke, Mossy Oak Break-Up Camo $595.00

Remington Model 870 SPS Super Magnum Camo
Has synthetic stock and all metal (except bolt and trigger guard) and stock covered with Mossy Oak Break-Up camo finish. In 12 gauge 3-1/2", 26", 28" vent rib, Rem choke. Comes with camo sling, swivels.
Price: $591.00

SARSILMAZ PUMP SHOTGUN
Gauge: 12, 3" chamber. **Barrel:** 26" or 28". Stocks: Oil-finished hardwood. **Features:** Includes extra pistol-grip stock. Introduced 2000. Imported from Turkey by Armsport Inc.
Price: With pistol-grip stock $299.95
Price: With metal stock............................... $349.95

TRISTAR MODEL 1887
Gauge: 12. **Barrel:** 22". **Weight:** 8.75 lbs. **Length:** 40-1/2". Stocks: Walnut. **Features:** Imp. cylinder choke, 5 shell, oil finish. Introduced 2002. Made in Australia. Available through AcuSport Corp.
Price: With pistol-grip stock $299.95

WINCHESTER MODEL 1300 WALNUT FIELD PUMP
Gauge: 12, 20, 3" chamber, 5-shot capacity. **Barrel:** 26", 28", vent. rib, with Full, Mod., Imp. Cyl. Winchoke tubes. **Weight:** 6-3/8 lbs. **Length:** 42-5/8" overall. **Stock:** American walnut, with deep cut checkering on pistol grip, traditional ribbed forend; high luster finish. **Sights:** Metal bead front. **Features:** Twin action slide bars; front-locking rotary bolt; roll-engraved receiver; blued, highly polished metal; cross-bolt safety with red indicator. Introduced 1984. From U.S. Repeating Arms Co., Inc.
Price: $405.00

Winchester 1300 Walnut Field Pump

Winchester 1300 Black Shadow Field Gun

Winchester 1300 Deer Black Shadow Gun

Winchester 1300 Ranger Compact

Winchester 9410

Winchester Model 1300 Upland Pump Gun

Similar to Model 1300 Walnut except straight-grip stock, 24" barrel. Introduced 1999. Made in U.S. by U.S. Repeating Arms Co.

Price: **$405.00**

Winchester Model 1300 Black Shadow Field Gun

Similar to Model 1300 Walnut except black composite stock and forend, matte black finish. Has vent rib 26" or 28" barrel, 3" chamber, mod. WinChoke tube. Introduced 1995. From U.S. Repeating Arms Co., Inc.

Price: 12 or 20 gauge **$343.00**

Winchester Model 1300 Deer Black Shadow Gun

Similar to Model 1300 Black Shadow Turkey Gun except ramp-type front sight, fully adjustable rear, drilled and tapped for scope mounting. Black composite stock and forend, matte black metal. Smoothbore 22" barrel with one imp. cyl. WinChoke tube; 12 gauge only, 3" chamber. Weighs 6-3/4 lbs. Introduced 1994. From U.S. Repeating Arms Co., Inc.

Price: **$341.00**
Price: With rifled barrel **$366.00**
Price: With cantilever scope mount **$409.00**
Price: Combo (22" rifled and 28" smoothbore bbls.) **$442.00**
Price: Compact (20 ga., 22" rifled barrel, shorter stock) **$409.00**

WINCHESTER MODEL 1300 RANGER PUMP GUN

Gauge: 12, 20, 3" chamber, 5-shot magazine. **Barrel:** 28" vent. rib with Full, Mod., Imp. Cyl. Winchoke tubes. **Weight:** 7 to 7-1/4 lbs. **Length:** 48-5/8" to 50-5/8" overall. **Stock:** Walnut-finished hardwood with ribbed forend. **Sights:** Metal bead front. **Features:** Cross-bolt safety, black rubber recoil pad, twin action slide bars, front-locking rotating bolt. From U.S. Repeating Arms Co., Inc.

Price: Vent. rib barrel, Winchoke **$357.00**
Price: Model 1300 Compact, 24" vent. rib **$356.00**

Winchester Model 1300 Turkey and Universal Hunter Models

Rotary bolt action. Durable Mossy oak break-up finish on 26" VR barrel extra full turkey improved cylinder, modified and full WinChoke tubes included. 3", 12 gauge chamber.

Price: Universal Hunter **$550.00**
Price: Buck and Tom **$525.00**
Price: Short Turkey **$439.00**

WINCHESTER MODEL 9410 LEVER-ACTION SHOTGUN

Gauge: 410, 2-1/2" chamber. **Barrel:** 24" (Cyl. bore). **Weight:** 6-3/4 lbs. **Length:** 42-1/8" overall. **Stock:** Checkered walnut straight-grip; checkered walnut forearm. **Sights:** Adjustable "V" rear, TruGlo® front. **Features:** Model 94 rifle action (smoothbore) chambered for 410 shotgun. Angle Controlled Eject extractor/ejector; choke tubes; 9-shot tubular magazine; 13-1/2" length of pull. Introduced 2001. From U.S. Repeating Arms Co.

Price: 9410 Lever-Action Shotgun **$553.00**
Price: 9410 Packer Shotgun. **$574.00**

SHOTGUNS

Includes a variety of game guns and guns for competitive shooting.

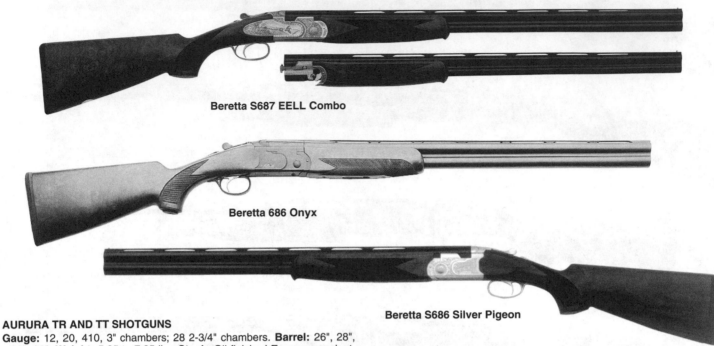

Beretta S687 EELL Combo

Beretta 686 Onyx

Beretta S686 Silver Pigeon

AURURA TR AND TT SHOTGUNS

Gauge: 12, 20, 410, 3" chambers; 28 2-3/4" chambers. **Barrel:** 26", 28", 30", 32". **Weight:** 5.95 to 7.25 lbs. **Stock:** Oil-finished European walnut. **Features:** Boxlock action, hard-chromed bores, automatic ejectors, single selective trigger, choke tubes (12 and 20 ga. only). From Sigarms.

Price: Aurura TR 20 Field **$1,935.00**
Price: Aurura TR 30 Field **$2,301.00**
Price: Aurura TR 40 Silver **$2,704.00**
Price: Aurura TR 40 Gold **$2,767.00**
Price: Aurura TT 25 Competition **$2,073.00**
Price: Aurura TT 45 Competition **$2,905.00**

BERETTA DT10 TRIDENT SHOTGUNS

Gauge: 12, 2-3/4", 3" chambers. **Barrel:** 28", 30", 32", 34"; competition-style vent rib; fixed or Optima Choke tubes. **Weight:** 7.9 to 9 lbs. **Stock:** High-grade walnut stock with oil finish; hand-checkered grip and forend, adjustable stocks available. **Features:** Detachable, adjustable trigger group, raised and thickened receiver, forend iron has replaceable nut to guarantee wood-to-metal fit, Optima Bore to improve shot pattern and reduce felt recoil. Introduced 2000. Imported from Italy by Beretta USA.

Price: DT10 Trident Trap (selective, lockable single trigger, adjustable stock). **$8,500.00**
Price: DT10 Trident Double Trap . . . . **NA**
Price: DT10 Trident X Trap . . . . **NA**
Price: DT10 Trident X Trap Combo (single and o/u barrels) . . **$10,790.00**
Price: DT10 Trident Skeet (skeet stock with rounded recoil pad, tapered rib) **$8,030.00**
Price: DT10 Trident Sporting (sporting clays stock with rounded recoil pad) **$7,850.00**

BERETTA SERIES 682 GOLD E SKEET, TRAP, SPORTING OVER/UNDERS

Gauge: 12, 2-3/4" chambers. **Barrel:** Skeet—28"; trap—30" and 32", imp. mod. & full and Mobilchoke; trap mono shotguns—32" and 34" Mobilchoke; trap top single guns—32" and 34" full and Mobilchoke; trap combo sets—from 30" O/U, to 32" O/U, 34" top single. **Stock:** Close-grained walnut, hand checkered. **Sights:** White Bradley bead front sight and center bead. **Features:** Receiver has Greystone gunmetal gray finish with gold accents. Trap Monte Carlo stock has deluxe trap recoil pad. Various grades available; contact Beretta USA for details. Imported from Italy by Beretta USA.

Price: 682 Gold E Trap with adjustable stock. **$3,905.00**
Price: 682 Gold E X Trap . . . . **NA**
Price: 682 Gold E X Trap Top Combo . . . . **NA**
Price: 682 Gold E Sporting **$3,436.00**
Price: 682 Gold E Skeet, adjustable stock **$3,905.00**
Price: 682 Gold E Double Trap . . . . **NA**
Price: 687 EELL Diamond Pigeon Skeet, adjustable stock **$6,050.00**
Price: 687 EELL Diamond Pigeon Sporting **$6,071.00**

BERETTA MODEL 686 WHITEWING O/U

Gauge: 12, 20. **Barrel:** 26", 28", Mobilchoke tubes (Imp. Cyl., Mod., Full). **Weight:** 6.7 lbs. **Length:** 45.7" overall (28" barrels). **Stock:** 14.5"x2.2"x1.4". American walnut, radiused black buttplate. **Features:** Matte chrome finish on receiver, matte blue barrels, hard-chrome bores; low-profile receiver with dual conical locking lugs, single selective trigger, ejectors. Imported from Italy by Beretta U.S.A.

Price: Whitewing **$1,295.00**

BERETTA 686 ONYX O/U SHOTGUN

Gauge: 12, 3" chambers. **Barrel:** 28", 30" (Mobilchoke tubes). **Weight:** 7.7 lbs. **Stock:** Checkered American walnut. **Features:** Intended for the beginning Sporting Clays shooter. Has wide, vented 12.5mm target rib, radiused recoil pad. Polished black finish on receiver and barrels. Introduced 1993. Imported from Italy by Beretta U.S.A.

Price: **$1,583.00**

BERETTA 686 SILVER PIGEON O/U SHOTGUN

Gauge: 12, 20, 28, 3" chambers (2-3/4" 28 ga.). **Barrel:** 26", 28". **Weight:** 6.8 lbs. **Stock:** Checkered walnut. **Features:** Interchangeable barrels (20 and 28 ga.), single selective gold-plated trigger, boxlock action, auto safety, schnabel forend.

Price: **$1,931.00**
Price: 20 ga. and 28 ga. **$2,676.00**

BERETTA ULTRALIGHT OVER/UNDER

Gauge: 12, 2-3/4" chambers. **Barrel:** 26", 28", Mobilchoke choke tubes. **Weight:** About 5 lbs., 13 oz. **Stock:** Select American walnut with checkered grip and forend. **Features:** Low-profile aluminum alloy receiver with titanium breech face insert. Electroless nickel receiver with game scene engraving. Single selective trigger; automatic safety. Introduced 1992. Imported from Italy by Beretta U.S.A.

Price: **$1,931.00**

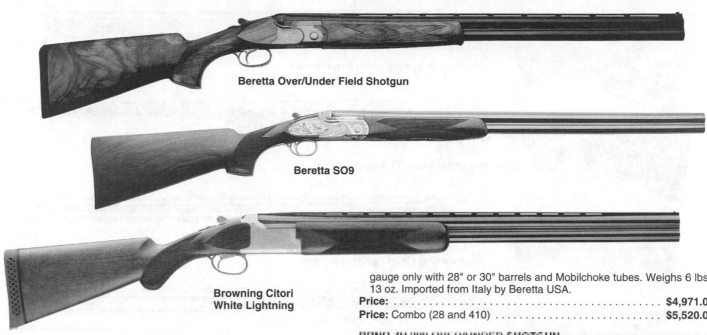

Beretta Over/Under Field Shotgun

Beretta SO9

Browning Citori White Lightning

Beretta Ultralight Deluxe Over/Under Shotgun

Similar to the Ultralight except has matte electroless nickel finish receiver with gold game scene engraving; matte oil-finished, select walnut stock and forend. Imported from Italy by Beretta U.S.A.

Price: **$2,323.00**

BERETTA OVER/UNDER FIELD SHOTGUNS

Gauge: 12, 20, 28, and 410 bore, 2-3/4", 3" and 3-1/2" chambers. **Barrel:** 26" and 28" (Mobilchoke tubes). **Stock:** Close-grained walnut. **Features:** Highly-figured, American walnut stocks and forends, and a unique, weather-resistant finish on barrels. Silver designates standard 686, 687 models with silver receivers; 686 Silver Pigeon has enhanced engraving pattern, Schnabel forend; 686 Silver Essential has matte chrome finish; Gold indicates higher grade 686EL, 687EL models with full sideplates; Diamond is for 687EELL models with highest grade wood, engraving. Case provided with Gold and Diamond grades. Imported from Italy by Beretta U.S.A.

Price: S686 Silver Pigeon two-bbl. set **$2,587.00**
Price: S686 Silver Pigeon. **$1,817.00**
Price: S687 Silver Pigeon II Sporting **$2,196.00**
Price: Combo 29" and 30" **$3,151.00**
Price: S687EL Gold Pigeon (gold inlays, sideplates)........ **$4,099.00**
Price: S687EL Gold Pigeon, 410, 26"; 28 ga., 28" **$4,273.00**
Price: S687 EL Gold Pigeon II (deep relief engraving)....... **$4,513.00**
Price: S687 EL Gold Pigeon II Sporting (d.r. engraving) **$4,554.00**

BERETTA MODEL SO5, SO6, SO9 SHOTGUNS

Gauge: 12, 2-3/4" chambers. **Barrel:** To customer specs. **Stock:** To customer specs. **Features:** SO5—Trap, Skeet and Sporting Clays models SO5; SO6— SO6 and SO6 EELL are field models. SO6 has a case-hardened or silver receiver with contour hand engraving. SO6 EELL has hand-engraved receiver in a fine floral or "fine English" pattern or game scene, with bas-relief chisel work and gold inlays. SO6 and SO6 EELL are available with sidelocks removable by hand. Imported from Italy by Beretta U.S.A.

Price: SO5 Trap, Skeet, Sporting..................... **$13,000.00**
Price: SO6 Trap, Skeet, Sporting..................... **$17,500.00**
Price: SO6 EELL Field, custom specs **$28,000.00**
Price: SO9 (12, 20, 28, 410, 26", 28", 30", any choke) **$31,000.00**

Beretta S687EL Gold Pigeon Sporting O/U

Similar to S687 Silver Pigeon Sporting except sideplates with gold inlay game scene, vent side and top ribs, bright orange front sight. Stock and forend are high grade walnut with fine-line checkering. Available in 12

gauge only with 28" or 30" barrels and Mobilchoke tubes. Weighs 6 lbs., 13 oz. Imported from Italy by Beretta USA.

Price: **$4,971.00**
Price: Combo (28 and 410) **$5,520.00**

BRNO ZH 300 OVER/UNDER SHOTGUN

Gauge: 12, 2-3/4" chambers. **Barrel:** 26", 27-1/2", 29" (Skeet, Imp. Cyl., Mod., Full). **Weight:** 7 lbs. **Length:** 44.4" overall. **Stock:** European walnut. **Features:** Double triggers; automatic safety; polished blue finish engraved receiver. Announced 1998. Imported from the Czech Republic by Euro-Imports.

Price: ZH 301, field.............................. **$594.00**
Price: ZH 302, Skeet **$608.00**
Price: ZH 303, 12 ga. trap **$608.00**
Price: ZH 321, 16 ga. **$595.00**

BRNO 501.2 OVER/UNDER SHOTGUN

Gauge: 12, 2-3/4" chambers. **Barrel:** 27.5" (Full & Mod.). **Weight:** 7 lbs. **Length:** 44" overall. **Stock:** European walnut. **Features:** Boxlock action with double triggers, ejectors; automatic safety; hand-cut checkering. Announced 1998. Imported from The Czech Republic by Euro-Imports.

Price: **$850.00**

BROWNING CITORI O/U SHOTGUNS

Gauge: 12, 20, 28 and 410. **Barrel:** 26", 28" in 28 and 410. Offered with Invector choke tubes. All 12 and 20 gauge models have back-bored barrels and Invector Plus choke system. **Weight:** 6 lbs., 8 oz. (26" 410) to 7 lbs., 13 oz. (30" 12 ga.). **Length:** 43" overall (26" bbl.). **Stock:** Dense walnut, hand checkered, full pistol grip, beavertail forend. Field-type recoil pad on 12 ga. field guns and trap and Skeet models. **Sights:** Medium raised beads, German nickel silver. **Features:** Barrel selector integral with safety, automatic ejectors, three-piece takedown. Imported from Japan by Browning. Contact Browning for complete list of models and prices.

Price: Grade I, Hunter, Invector, 12 and 20 .... **$1,486.00**
Price: Grade I, Lightning, 28 and 410, Invector **$1,594.00**
Price: Grade III, Lightning, 28 and 410, Invector **$2,570.00**
Price: Grade VI, 28 and 410 Lightning, Invector **$3,780.00**
Price: Grade I, Lightning, Invector Plus, 12, 20 .... **$1,534.00**
Price: Grade I, Hunting, 28", 30" only, 3-1/2", Invector Plus ... **$1,489.00**
Price: Grade III, Lightning, Invector, 12, 20 .... **$2,300.00**
Price: Grade VI, Lightning, Invector, 12, 20 .... **$3,510.00**
Price: Gran Lightning, 26", 28", Invector, 12, 20 .... **$2,184.00**
Price: Gran Lightning, 28, 410 .... **$2,302.00**
Price: Micro Lightning, 20 ga., 24" bbl., 6 lbs., 4 oz. **$1,591.00**
Price: White Lightning (silver nitride receiver w/engraving, 12 or 20 ga., 26", 28") **$1,583.00**
Price: White Lightning, 28 or 410 gauge **$1,654.00**
Price: Citori Satin Hunter (12 ga., satin-finished wood, matte-finished barrels and receiver) 3-1/2" chambers **$1,535.00**

SHOTGUNS

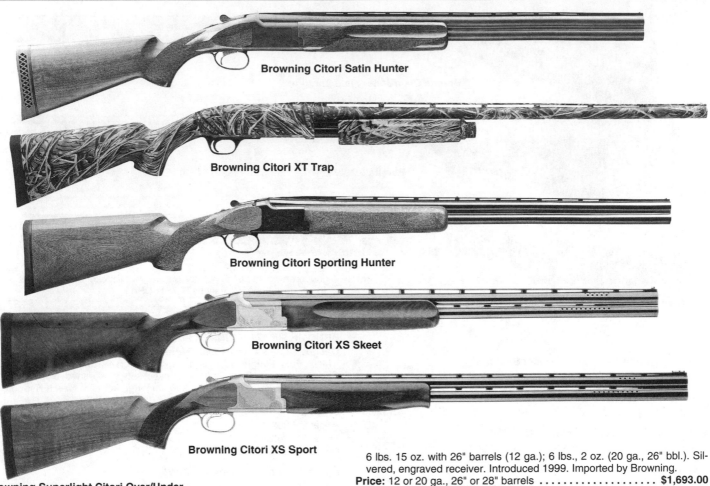

Browning Citori Satin Hunter

Browning Citori XT Trap

Browning Citori Sporting Hunter

Browning Citori XS Skeet

Browning Citori XS Sport

Browning Superlight Citori Over/Under

Similar to the standard Citori except available in 12, 20 with 24", 26" or 28" Invector barrels, 28 or 410 with 26" barrels choked Imp. Cyl. & Mod. or 28" choked Mod. & Full. Has straight grip stock, Schnabel forend tip. Superlight 12 weighs 6 lbs., 9 oz. (26" barrels); Superlight 20, 5 lbs., 12 oz. (26" barrels). Introduced 1982.

Price: Grade I, 28 or 410, Invector **$1,666.00**
Price: Grade III, Invector, 12. . . . . **$2,300.00**
Price: Grade VI, Invector, 12 or 20, gray or blue **$3,510.00**
Price: Grade VI, 28 or 410, Invector, gray or blue **$3,780.00**
Price: Grade I Invector, 12 or 20 . . . . **$1,580.00**
Price: Grade I Invector, White Upland Special (24" bbls.),
12 or 20 . . . . **$1,583.00**
Price: Citori Superlight Feather (12 ga., alloy receiver,
6 lbs. 4 oz.) **$1,756.00**

Browning Citori XT Trap Over/Under

Similar to the Citori Special Trap except has engraved silver nitride receiver with gold highlights, vented side barrel rib. Available in 12 gauge with 30" or 32" barrels, Invector-Plus choke tubes. Introduced 1999. Imported by Browning.

Price: **$1,834.00**
Price: With adjustable-comb stock **$2,054.00**

Browning Micro Citori Lightning

Similar to the standard Citori 20 ga. Lightning except scaled down for smaller shooter. Comes with 24" Invector Plus back-bored barrels, 13-3/4" length of pull. Weighs about 6 lbs., 3 oz. Introduced 1991.

Price: Grade I **$1,486.00**

Browning Citori Lightning Feather O/U

Similar to the 12 gauge Citori Grade I except has 2-3/4" chambers, rounded pistol grip, Lightning-style forend, and lighweight alloy receiver. Weighs

6 lbs. 15 oz. with 26" barrels (12 ga.); 6 lbs., 2 oz. (20 ga., 26" bbl.). Silvered, engraved receiver. Introduced 1999. Imported by Browning.

Price: 12 or 20 ga., 26" or 28" barrels **$1,693.00**
Price: Lightning Feather Combo (20 and 28 ga. bbls., 27" each) **$2,751.00**

Browning Citori Sporting Hunter

Similar to the Citori Hunting I except has Sporting Clays stock dimensions, a Superposed-style forend, and Sporting Clays butt pad. Available in 12 gauge with 3" chambers, back-bored 26", 28" and 30", all with Invector Plus choke tube system. Introduced 1998. Imported from Japan by Browning.

Price: 12 gauge, 3-1/2" **$1,709.00**
Price: 12, 20 gauge, 3" **$1,607.00**

Browning Citori Ultra XS Skeet

Similar to other Citori Ultra models except features a semi-beavertail forearm with deep finger grooves, ported barrels and triple system. Adjustable comb is optional. Introduced 2000.

Price: 12 ga., 28" or 30" barrel **$2,162.00**
Price: 20 ga., 28" or 30" barrel **$2,162.00**
Price: Adjustable comb model, 12 or 20 ga.. . . . . **$2,380.00**

Browning Citori Ultra XS Trap

Similar to other Citori Ultra models except offered in 12 ga. only with 30" or 32" ported barrel, high-post rib, ventilated side ribs, Triple Trigger System™ and silver nitride receiver. Includes full, modified and imp. cyl. choke tubes. From Browning.

Price: 30" or 32" barrel **$2,022.00**
Price: Adjustable-comb model **$2,265.00**

Browning Citori Ultra XS Sporting

Similar to other Citori Ultra XS models except offered in 12, 20, 28 and 410 gauge. Silver nitride receiver, Schnabel forearm, ventilated side rib. Imported by Browning.

Price: 410 or 28 ga. **$2,268.00**
Price: 12 or 20 ga. **$2,196.00**

SHOTGUNS

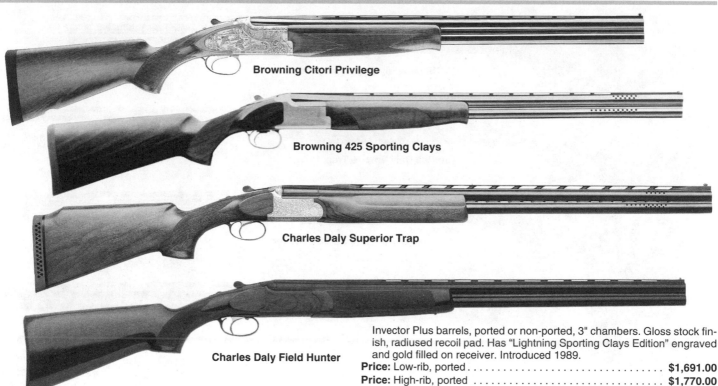

Browning Citori Privilege

Browning 425 Sporting Clays

Charles Daly Superior Trap

Charles Daly Field Hunter

Browning Citori Feather XS Shotguns

Similar to the standard Citori except has lightweight alloy receiver, silver nitrade Nitex receiver, Schnabel forearm, ventilated side rib and Hi-Viz Comp fiber optics sight. Available in 12, 20, 28 and 410 gauges. Introduced 2000.
Price: 28" or 30" barrel . . . . **$2,266.00 to $2,338.00**

Browning Citori High Grade Shotguns

Similar to standard Citori except has full sideplates with engraved hunting scenes and gold inlays, high-grade, hand-oiled walnut stock and forearm. Introduced 2000. From Browning.
Price: Citori Privilege (fully embellished sideplates), 12 or 20 ga.
. . . . **$5,376.00**
Price: Citori BG VI Lightning (gold inlays of ducks and pheasants)
From **$3,340.00**
Price: Citori BG III Superlight (scroll engraving on grayed receiver,
gold inlays) **$2,190.00**
Price: Citori 425 Golden Clays (engraving of game bird-clay bird transition,
gold accents), 12 or 20 ga. **$3,977.00**

Browning Nitra Citori XS Sporting Clays

Similar to the Citori Grade I except has silver nitride receiver with gold accents, stock dimensions of 14-3/4"x1-1/2"x2-1/4" with satin finish, right-hand palm swell, Schnabel forend. Comes with Modified, Imp. Cyl. and Skeet Invector-Plus choke tubes. Back-bored barrels; vented side ribs. Introduced 1999. Imported by Browning.
Price: 12, 20 ga. **$2,011.00**
Price: 28 ga., 410-bore **$2,077.00**

Browning Special Sporting Clays

Similar to the Citori Ultra Sporter except has full pistol grip stock with palm swell, gloss finish, 28", 30" or 32" barrels with back-bored Invector Plus chokes (ported or non-ported); high post tapered rib. Also available as 28" and 30" two-barrel set. Introduced 1989.
Price: With ported barrels **$1,636.00**
Price: As above, adjustable comb **$1,856.00**

Browning Lightning Sporting Clays

Similar to the Citori Lightning with rounded pistol grip and classic forend. Has high post tapered rib or lower hunting-style rib with 30" back-bored Invector Plus barrels, ported or non-ported, 3" chambers. Gloss stock finish, radiused recoil pad. Has "Lightning Sporting Clays Edition" engraved and gold filled on receiver. Introduced 1989.
Price: Low-rib, ported **$1,691.00**
Price: High-rib, ported **$1,770.00**

BROWNING LIGHT SPORTING 802 ES O/U

Gauge: 12, 2-3/4" chambers. **Barrel:** 28", back-bored Invector Plus. Comes with flush-mounted Imp. Cyl. and Skeet; 2" extended Imp. Cyl. and Mod.; and 4" extended Imp. Cyl. and Mod. tubes. **Weight:** 7 lbs., 5 oz. **Length:** 45" overall. **Stock:** 14-3/8" x 1/8" x 1-9/16" x 1-3/4". Select walnut with radiused solid recoil pad, Schnabel-type forend. **Features:** Trigger adjustable for length of pull; narrow 6.2mm ventilated rib; ventilated barrel side rib; blued receiver. Introduced 1996. Imported from Japan from Browning.
Price: **$2,063.00**

BROWNING 425 SPORTING CLAYS

Gauge: 12, 20, 2-3/4" chambers. **Barrel:** 12 ga.—28", 30", 32" (Invector Plus tubes), back-bored; 20 ga.—28", 30" (Invector Plus tubes). **Weight:** 7 lbs., 13 oz. (12 ga., 28"). **Stock:** 14-13/16" (1/8")x1-7/16"x2-3/16" (12 ga.). Select walnut with gloss finish, cut checkering, Schnabel forend. **Features:** Grayed receiver with engraving, blued barrels. Barrels are ported on 12 gauge guns. Has low 10mm wide vent rib. Comes with three interchangeable trigger shoes to adjust length of pull. Introduced in U.S. 1993. Imported by Browning.
Price: Grade I, 12, 20 ga., Invector Plus **$2,006.00**
Price: Golden Clays, 12, 20 ga., Invector Plus **$3,977.00**

CHARLES DALY SUPERIOR TRAP AE MC

Gauge: 12, 2-3/4" chambers. **Barrel:** 30" choke tubes. **Weight:** About 7 lbs. **Stock:** Checkered walnut; pistol grip, semi-beavertail forend. **Features:** Silver engraved receiver, chrome moly steel barrels; gold single selective trigger; automatic safety, automatic ejectors; red bead front sight, metal bead center; recoil pad. Introduced 1997. Imported from Italy by K.B.I., Inc.
Price: **$1,339.00**

CHARLES DALY FIELD HUNTER OVER/UNDER SHOTGUN

Gauge: 12, 20, 28 and 410 bore (3" chambers, 28 ga. has 2-3/4"). **Barrel:** 28" Mod & Full, 26" Imp. Cyl. & Mod (410 is Full & Full). **Weight:** About 7 lbs. **Length:** NA. **Stock:** Checkered walnut pistol grip and forend. **Features:** Blued engraved receiver, chrome moly steel barrels; gold single selective trigger; automatic safety; extractors; gold bead front sight. Introduced 1997. Imported from Italy by K.B.I., Inc.
Price: 12 or 20 ga. **$799.00**
Price: 28 ga. **$879.00**
Price: 410 bore **$919.00**

SHOTGUNS — OVER/UNDERS

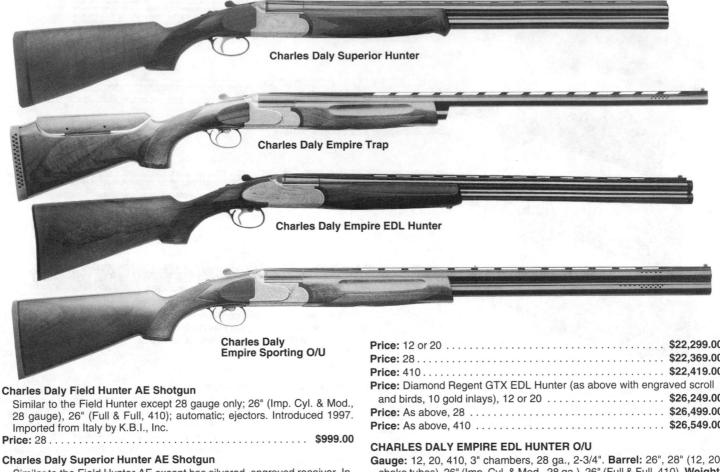

Charles Daly Superior Hunter

Charles Daly Empire Trap

Charles Daly Empire EDL Hunter

Charles Daly Empire Sporting O/U

Charles Daly Field Hunter AE Shotgun
Similar to the Field Hunter except 28 gauge only; 26" (Imp. Cyl. & Mod., 28 gauge), 26" (Full & Full, 410); automatic; ejectors. Introduced 1997. Imported from Italy by K.B.I., Inc.
Price: 28 . . . . **$999.00**

Charles Daly Superior Hunter AE Shotgun
Similar to the Field Hunter AE except has silvered, engraved receiver. Introduced 1997. Imported from Italy by F.B.I., Inc.
Price: 28 ga. **$1,129.00**
Price: 410 bore **$1,129.00**

Charles Daly Field Hunter AE-MC
Similar to the Field Hunter except in 12 or 20 only, 26" or 28" barrels with five multichoke tubes; automatic ejectors. Introduced 1997. Imported from Italy by K.B.I., Inc.
Price: 12 or 20 . . . . **$979.95**

Charles Daly Superior Sporting O/U
Similar to the Field Hunter AE-MC except 28" or 30" barrels; silvered, engraved receiver; five choke tubes; ported barrels; red bead front sight. Introduced 1997. Imported from Italy by K.B.I., Inc.
Price: **$1,259.95**

CHARLES DALY EMPIRE TRAP AE MC
Gauge: 12, 2-3/4" chambers. **Barrel:** 30" choke tubes. **Weight:** About 7 lbs. **Stock:** Checkered walnut; pistol grip, semi-beavertail forend. **Features:** Silvered, engraved, reinforced receiver; chrome moly steel barrels; gold single selective trigger; automatic safety, automatic ejector; red bead front sight, metal bead center; recoil pad. Imported from Italy by K.B.I., Inc.
Price: **$1,539.95**

CHARLES DALY DIAMOND REGENT GTX DL HUNTER O/U
Gauge: 12, 20, 410, 3" chambers, 28, 2-3/4" chambers. **Barrel:** 26", 28", 30" (choke tubes), 26" (Imp. Cyl. & Mod. in 28, 26" (Full & Full) in 410. **Weight:** About 7 lbs. **Stock:** Extra select fancy European walnut with 24" hand checkering, hand rubbed oil finish. **Features:** Boss-type action with internal side lumps. Deep cut hand-engraved scrollwork and game scene set in full sideplates. GTX detachable single selective trigger system with coil springs; chrome moly steel barrels; automatic safety; automatic ejectors, white bead front sight, metal bead center sight. Introduced 1997. Imported from Italy by K.B.I., Inc.

Price: 12 or 20 . . . . $22,299.00
Price: 28 . . . . $22,369.00
Price: 410 . . . . $22,419.00
Price: Diamond Regent GTX EDL Hunter (as above with engraved scroll and birds, 10 gold inlays), 12 or 20 . . . . $26,249.00
Price: As above, 28 . . . . $26,499.00
Price: As above, 410 . . . . $26,549.00

CHARLES DALY EMPIRE EDL HUNTER O/U
Gauge: 12, 20, 410, 3" chambers, 28 ga., 2-3/4". **Barrel:** 26", 28" (12, 20, choke tubes), 26" (Imp. Cyl. & Mod., 28 ga.), 26" (Full & Full, 410). **Weight:** About 7 lbs. **Stocks:** Checkered walnut pistol grip buttstock, semi-beavertail forend; recoil pad. **Features:** Silvered, engraved receiver; chrome moly barrels; gold single selective trigger; automatic safety; automatic ejectors; red bead front sight, metal bead middle sight. Introduced 1997. Imported from Italy by K.B.I., Inc.
Price: Empire EDL (dummy sideplates) 12 or 20 . . . . **$1,559.95**
Price: Empire EDL, 28 . . . . **$1,559.95**
Price: Empire EDL, 410 . . . . **$1,599.95**

Charles Daly Empire Sporting O/U
Similar to the Empire EDL Hunter except 12 or 20 gauge only, 28", 30" barrels with choke tubes; ported barrels; special stock dimensions. Introduced 1997. Imported from Italy by K.B.I., Inc.
Price: **$1,499.95**

CHARLES DALY DIAMOND GTX SPORTING O/U SHOTGUN
Gauge: 12, 20, 3" chambers. **Barrel:** 28", 30" with choke tubes. **Weight:** About 8.5 lbs. **Stock:** Checkered deluxe walnut; Sporting clays dimensions. Pistol grip; semi-beavertail forend; hand rubbed oil finish. **Features:** Chromed, hand-engraved receiver; chrome moly steel barrels; GTX detachable single selective trigger system with coil springs, automatic safety; automatic ejectors; red bead front sight; ported barrels. Introduced 1997. Imported from Italy by K.B.I., Inc.
Price: **$5,804.95**

CHARLES DALY DIAMOND GTX TRAP AE-MC O/U SHOTGUN
Gauge: 12, 2-3/4" chambers. **Barrel:** 30" (Full & Full). **Weight:** About 8.5 lbs. **Stock:** Checkered deluxe walnut; pistol grip; trap dimensions; semi-beavertail forend; hand-rubbed oil finish. **Features:** Silvered, hand-engraved receiver; chrome moly steel barrels; GTX detachable single selective trigger system with coil springs, automatic safety, automatic-ejectors, red bead front sight, metal bead middle; recoil pad. Imported from Italy by K.B.I., Inc.
Price: **$5,804.95**

SHOTGUNS — OVER/UNDERS

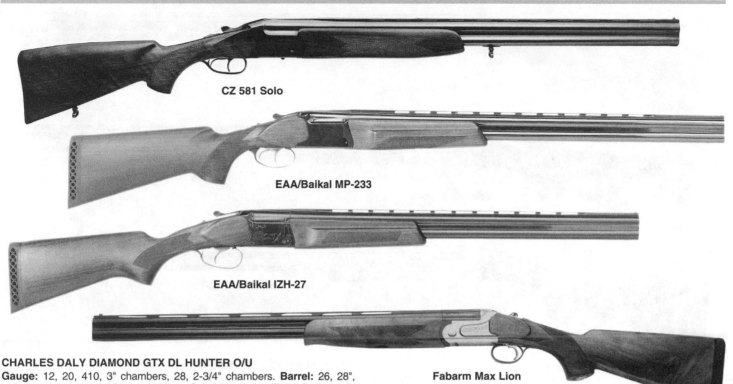

CZ 581 Solo

EAA/Baikal MP-233

EAA/Baikal IZH-27

Fabarm Max Lion

CHARLES DALY DIAMOND GTX DL HUNTER O/U

Gauge: 12, 20, 410, 3" chambers, 28, 2-3/4" chambers. **Barrel:** 26, 28", choke tubes in 12 and 20 ga., 26" (Imp. Cyl. & Mod.), 26" (Full & Full) in 410-bore. **Weight:** About 8.5 lbs. **Stock:** Select fancy European walnut stock, with 24 lpi hand checkering; hand-rubbed oil finish. **Features:** Boss-type action with internal side lugs, hand-engraved scrollwork and game scene. GTX detachable single selective trigger system with coil springs; chrome moly steel barrels, automatic safety, automatic ejectors, red bead front sight, recoil pad. Introduced 1997. Imported from Italy by K.B.I., Inc.

Price: 12 or 20 . . . . **$12,399.00**
Price: 28 . . . . **$12,489.00**
Price: 410 . . . . **$12,529.00**
Price: GTX EDL Hunter (with gold inlays), 12, 20 . . . . **$15,999.00**
Price: As above, 28 . . . . **$16,179.00**
Price: As above, 410 . . . . **$16,219.00**

CZ 581 SOLO OVER/UNDER SHOTGUN

Gauge: 12, 2-3/4" chambers. **Barrel:** 27.6" (Mod. & Full). **Weight:** 7.37 lbs. **Length:** 44.5" overall. **Stock:** Circassian walnut. **Features:** Automatic ejectors; double triggers; Kersten-style double lump locking system. Imported from the Czech Republic by CZ-USA.

Price: **$799.00**

EAA/BAIKAL MP-233 OVER/UNDER SHOTGUN

Gauge: 12, 3" chambers. **Barrel:** 26", 28", 30"; imp., mod. and full choke tubes. **Weight:** 7.28 lbs. **Stock:** Walnut; checkered forearm and grip. **Features:** Hammer-forged barrels; chrome-lined bores; removable trigger assembly (optional single selective trigger or double trigger); ejectors. Introduced 2000. Imported by European American Armory.

Price: MP-233 . . . . **$939.00**

EAA/BAIKAL IZH-27 OVER/UNDER SHOTGUN

Gauge: 12 (3" chambers), 16 (2-3/4" chambers), 20 (3" chambers), 28 (2-3/4" chambers), 410 (3"). **Barrel:** 26-1/2", 28-1/2" (imp., mod. and full choke tubes for 12 and 20 gauges; improved cylinder and modified for 16 and 28 gauges; improved modified and full for 410; 16 also offered in mod. and full). **Weight:** NA. **Stock:** Walnut, checkered forearm and grip. Imported by European American Armory.

Price: IZH-27 (12, 16 and 20 gauge) **$509.00**
Price: IZH-27 (28 and 410 gauge) **$569.00**

EAA IZH-27 Sporting O/U

Basic IZH-27 with barrel porting, wide vent rib with double sight beads, engraved nickel receiver, checkered walnut stock and forend with palm swell and semi beavertail, 3 screw chokes, SS trigger, selectable ejectors, auto tang safety

Price: 12 ga., 29" bbl. **$589.00**

FABARM MAX LION OVER/UNDER SHOTGUNS

Gauge: 12, 3" chambers, 20, 3" chambers. **Barrel:** 26", 28", 30" (12 ga.); 26", 28" (20 ga.), choke tubes. **Weight:** 7.4 lbs. **Length:** 47.5" overall (26" barrel). **Stock:** European walnut; leather-covered recoil pad. **Features:** TriBore barrel, boxlock action with single selective trigger, manual safety, automatic ejectors; chrome-lined barrels; adjustable trigger. Silvered, engraved receiver. Comes with locking, fitted luggage case. Introduced 1998. Imported from Italy by Heckler & Koch, Inc.

Price: 12 or 20 . . . . **$1,799.00**

FABARM ULTRA CAMO MAG LION O/U SHOTGUN

Gauge: 12, 3-1/2" chambers. **Barrel:** 28" (cyl., imp. cyl., mod., imp. mod., full, SS-mod., SS-full choke tubes). **Weight:** 7.9 lbs. **Length:** 50" overall. **Stock:** Camo-colored walnut. **Features:** TriBore barrel, Wetlands Camo finished metal surfaces, single selective trigger, non-auto ejectors, leather-covered recoil pad. Locking hard plastic case. Introduced 1998. Imported from Italy by Heckler & Koch, Inc.

Price: **$1,229.00**

FABARM MAX LION PARADOX

Gauge: 12, 20, 3" chambers. **Barrel:** 24". **Weight:** 7.6 lbs. **Length:** 44.5" overall. **Stock:** Walnut with special enhancing finish. **Features:** TriBore upper barrel, both wood and receiver are enhanced with special finishes, color-case hardened type finish.

Price: 12 or 20 . . . . **$1,129.00**

FABARM SILVER LION OVER/UNDER SHOTGUNS

Gauge: 12, 3" chambers, 20, 3" chambers. **Barrel:** 26", 28", 30" (12 ga.); 26", 28" (20 ga.), choke tubes. **Weight:** 7.2 lbs. **Length:** 47.5" overall (26" barrels). **Stock:** Walnut; leather-covered recoil pad. **Features:** TriBore barrel, boxlock action with single selective trigger; silvered receiver with engraving; automatic ejectors. Comes with locking hard plastic case. Introduced 1998. Imported from Italy by Heckler & Koch, Inc.

Price: 12 or 20 . . . . **$1,229.00**

SHOTGUNS

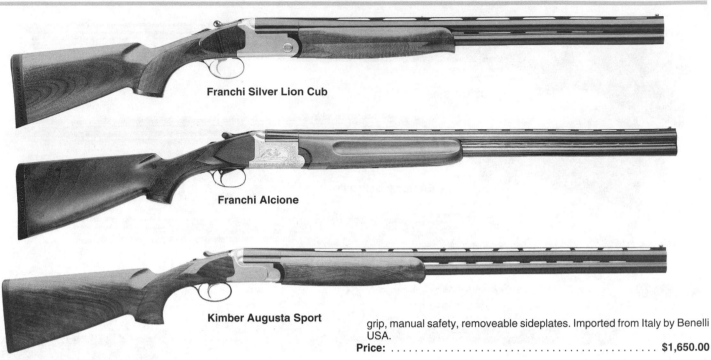

Franchi Silver Lion Cub

Franchi Alcione

Kimber Augusta Sport

Fabarm Silver Lion Cub Model O/U

Similar to the Silver Lion except has 12.5" length of pull, is in 20 gauge only (3-1/2" chambers), and comes with 24" TriBore barrel system. Weight is 6 lbs. Introduced 1999. Imported from Italy by Heckler & Koch, Inc.

Price: **$1,229.00**

FABARM CAMO TURKEY MAG O/U SHOTGUN

Gauge: 12, 3-1/2" chambers. **Barrel:** 20" TriBore (Ultra-Full ported tubes). **Weight:** 7.5 lbs. **Length:** 46" overall. **Stock:** 14.5"x1.5"x2.29". Walnut. **Sights:** Front bar, Picatinny rail scope base. **Features:** Completely covered with Xtra Brown camouflage finish. Unported barrels. Introduced 1999. Imported from Italy by Heckler & Koch, Inc.

Price: **$1,199.00**

FABARM SPORTING CLAYS COMPETITION EXTRA O/U

Gauge: 12, 20, 3" chambers. **Barrel:** 12 ga. has 30", 20 ga. has 28"; ported TriBore barrel system with five tubes. **Weight:** 7 to 7.8 lbs. **Length:** 49.6" overall (20 ga.). **Stock:** 14.50"x1.38"x2.17" (20 ga.); deluxe walnut; leather-covered recoil pad. **Features:** Single selective trigger, auto ejectors; 10mm channeled rib; carbon fiber finish. Introduced 1999. Imported from Italy by Heckler & Koch, Inc.

Price: **$1,749.00**

FRANCHI ALCIONE FIELD OVER/UNDER SHOTGUN

Gauge: 12, 20, 3" chambers. **Barrel:** 26", 28"; IC, M, F tubes. **Weight:** 7.5 lbs. **Length:** 43" overall with 26" barrels. **Stock:** European walnut. **Features:** Boxlock action with ejectors, barrel selector mounted on trigger; silvered, engraved receiver, vent center rib, automatic safety, interchangeable 20 ga. bbls., left-hand available. Imported from Italy by Benelli USA. Hard case included.

Price: **$1,275.00**

Price: (20 gauge barrel set) **$460.00**

Franchi Alcione SX O/U Shotgun

Similar to Alcione Field model with high grade walnut stock and forend. Gold engraved removeable sideplates, interchangeable barrels.

Price: **$1,800.00**

Price: (12 gauge barrel set) . . . . **$450.00 to $500.00**

Price: (20 gauge barrel set) **$450.00**

Franchi Alcione Sport SL O/U Shotgun

Similar to Alcione except 2-3/4" chambers, elongated forcing cones and porting for Sporting Clays shooting. 10mm vent rib, tightly curved pistol grip, manual safety, removeable sideplates. Imported from Italy by Benelli USA.

Price: **$1,650.00**

FRANCHI ALCIONE TITANIUM OVER/UNDER SHOTGUN

Gauge: 12, 20, 3" chambers. **Barrel:** 26", 28"; IC, M, F tubes. **Weight:** 6.8 lbs. **Length:** 43", 45". **Stock:** Select walnut. **Sights:** Front/mid. **Features:** Receiver (titanium inserts) made of aluminum alloy. 7mm vent rib. Fast locking triggers. Left-hand available.

Price: **$1,425.00**

FRANCHI 912 SHOTGUN

Gauge: 12 ga., 2-3/4", 3", 3-1/2"" chambers. **Barrel:** 24"-30". **Weight:** Appx. 7.6 lbs. **Length:** 46"-52". **Stock:** Walnut, synthetic, Timber HD. **Sights:** White bead front. **Features:** Based on 612 design, magazine cut-off, stepped vent rib, dual-recoil-reduction system.

Price: Satin walnut **$1,000.00**

Price: Synthetic **$940.00**

Price: Timber HD Camo **$1,050.00**

FRANCHI VELOCE OVER/UNDER SHOTGUN

Gauge: 20, 28. **Barrel:** 26", 28"; IC, M, F tubes. **Weight:** 5.5-5.8 lbs. **Length:** 43"-45". **Stock:** High grade walnut. **Features:** Aluminum receiver with steel reinforcement scaled to 20 gauge for light weight. Pistol grip stock with slip recoil pad. Imported by Benelli USA. Hard case included.

Price: **$1,425.00**

Price: 28 ga. **$1,500.00**

Franchi Veloce English Over/Under Shotgun

Similar to Veloce standard model with straight grip "English" style stock. Available with 26" barrels in 20 and 28 gauge. Hard case included.

Price: **$1,425.00**

Price: 28 ga. **$1,500.00**

HOENIG ROTARY ROUND ACTION GAME GUN

Gauge: 28. **Barrel:** 26", 28", solid tapered rib. **Weight:** 6 lbs. **Stock:** English walnut. **Features:** Round action opens by rotating barrels, pulling forward. Inertia extractor, rotary safety blocks strikers. Simple takedown without removing forend. Elegance and class of guns of yesteryear. Made in U.S.A. by George Hoenig.

Price: **$19,980.00**

KIMBER AUGUSTA SHOTGUN

Premium over/under, Boss type action. 12 ga. only. Tri-alloy barrel with choke tubes. Backbored 736. Long forcing cones. HiViz sight with center bead on vent ribl. Available with many features. Custom dimensions available. Imported from Italy by Kimber Mfg., Inc.

Price: **$5,000.00**

SHOTGUNS

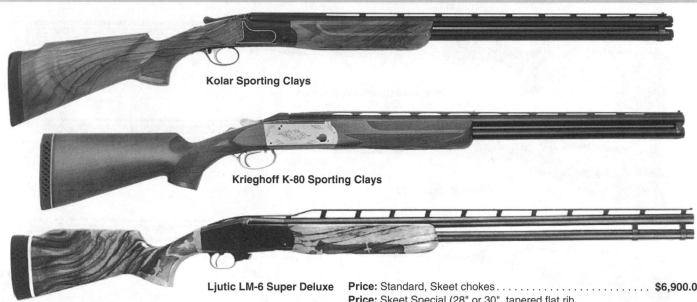

Kolar Sporting Clays

Krieghoff K-80 Sporting Clays

Ljutic LM-6 Super Deluxe

KOLAR SPORTING CLAYS O/U SHOTGUN
Gauge: 12, 2-3/4" chambers. **Barrel:** 30", 32"; extended choke tubes. **Stock:** 14-5/8"x2-1/2"x1-7/8"x1-3/8". French walnut. **Features:** Single selective trigger, detachable, adjustable for length; overbored barrels with long forcing cones; flat tramline rib; matte blue finish. Made in U.S. by Kolar.

Price: Standard	**$7,250.00**
Price: Elite	**$10,245.00**
Price: Elite Gold	**$12,245.00**
Price: Legend	**$13,245.00**
Price: Custom Gold	**$24,750.00**

Kolar AAA Competition Trap Over/Under Shotgun
Similar to the Sporting Clays gun except has 32" O/U /34" Unsingle or 30" O/U /34" Unsingle barrels as an over/under, unsingle, or combination set. Stock dimensions are 14-1/2"x2-1/2"x1-1/2"; American or French walnut; step parallel rib standard. Contact maker for full listings. Made in U.S. by Kolar.

Price: Over/under, choke tubes, Standard	**$7,025.00**
Price: Unsingle, choke tubes, Standard	**$7,775.00**
Price: Combo (30"/34", 32"/34"), Standard	**$10,170.00**

Kolar AAA Competition Skeet Over/Under Shotgun
Similar to the Sporting Clays gun except has 28" or 30" barrels with Kolar-ite AAA sub gauge tubes; stock of American or French walnut with matte finish; flat tramline rib; under barrel adjustable for point of impact. Many options available. Contact maker for complete listing. Made in U.S. by Kolar.

Price: Standard, choke tubes	**$8,645.00**
Price: Standard, choke tubes, two-barrel set	**$10,710.00**

KRIEGHOFF K-80 SPORTING CLAYS O/U
Gauge: 12. **Barrel:** 28", 30" or 32" with choke tubes. **Weight:** About 8 lbs. **Stock:** #3 Sporting stock designed for gun-down shooting. **Features:** Standard receiver with satin nickel finish and classic scroll engraving. Selective mechanical trigger adjustable for position. Choice of tapered flat or 8mm parallel flat barrel rib. Free-floating barrels. Aluminum case. Imported from Germany by Krieghoff International, Inc.

Price: Standard grade with five choke tubes, from	**$8,150.00**

KRIEGHOFF K-80 SKEET SHOTGUN
Gauge: 12, 2-3/4" chambers. **Barrel:** 28", 30", (Skeet & Skeet), optional choke tubes). **Weight:** About 7-3/4 lbs. **Stock:** American Skeet or straight Skeet stocks, with palm-swell grips. Walnut. **Features:** Satin gray receiver finish. Selective mechanical trigger adjustable for position. Choice of ventilated 8mm parallel flat rib or ventilated 8-12mm tapered flat rib. Introduced 1980. Imported from Germany by Krieghoff International, Inc.

Price: Standard, Skeet chokes	**$6,900.00**
Price: Skeet Special (28" or 30", tapered flat rib, Skeet & Skeet choke tubes)	**$7,575.00**

KRIEGHOFF K-80 O/U TRAP SHOTGUN
Gauge: 12, 2-3/4" chambers. **Barrel:** 30", 32" (Imp. Mod. & Full or choke tubes). **Weight:** About 8-1/2 lbs. **Stock:** Four stock dimensions or adjustable stock available; all have palm swell grips. Checkered European walnut. **Features:** Satin nickel receiver. Selective mechanical trigger, adjustable for position. Ventilated step rib. Introduced 1980. Imported from Germany by Krieghoff International, Inc.

Price: K-80 O/U (30", 32", Imp. Mod. & Full), from	**$7,375.00**
Price: K-80 Unsingle (32", 34", Full), Standard, from	**$7,950.00**
Price: K-80 Combo (two-barrel set), Standard, from	**$10,475.00**

Krieghoff K-20 O/U Shotguns
Similar to the K-80 except built on a 20-gauge frame. Designed for skeet, sporting clays and field use. Offered in 20, 28 and 410 gauge, 28" and 30" barrels. Imported from Germany by Krieghoff International Inc.

Price: K-20, 20 gauge, from	**$8,150.00**
Price: K-20, 28 gauge, from	**$8,425.00**
Price: K-20, 410 gauge, from	**$8,425.00**

LEBEAU - COURALLY BOSS-VEREES O/U
Gauge: 12, 20, 2-3/4" chambers. **Barrel:** 25" to 32". **Weight:** To customer specifications. **Stock:** Exhibition-quality French walnut. **Features:** Boss-type sidelock with automatic ejectors; single or double triggers; chopper lump barrels. A custom gun built to customer specifications. Imported from Belgium by Wm. Larkin Moore.

Price: From	**$70,000.00**

LJUTIC LM-6 SUPER DELUXE O/U SHOTGUN
Gauge: 12. **Barrel:** 28" to 34", choked to customer specs for live birds, trap, International Trap. **Weight:** To customer specs. **Stock:** To customer specs. Oil finish, hand checkered. **Features:** Custom-made gun. Hollow-milled rib, pull or release trigger, pushbutton opener in front of trigger guard. From Ljutic Industries.

Price: Super Deluxe LM-6 O/U	**$17,995.00**
Price: Over/Under Combo (interchangeable single barrel, two trigger guards, one for single trigger, one for doubles)	**$24,995.00**
Price: Extra over/under barrel sets, 29"-32"	**$5,995.00**

LUGER CLASSIC O/U SHOTGUNS
Gauge: 12, 3" and 3-1/2" chambers. **Barrel:** 26", 28", 30"; imp. cyl. mod. and full choke tubes. **Weight:** 7-1/2 lbs. **Length:** 45" overall (28" barrel) **Stock:** Select-grade European walnut, hand-checkered grip and forend. **Features:** Gold, single selective trigger; automatic ejectors. Introduced 2000.

Price: Classic (26", 28" or 30" barrel; 3-1/2" chambers)	**$919.00**
Price: Classic Sporting (30" barrel; 3" chambers)	**$964.00**

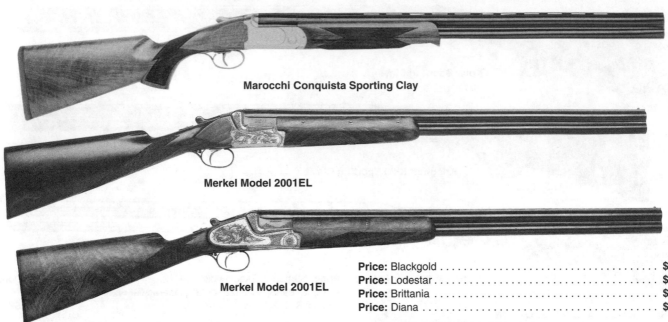

Marocchi Conquista Sporting Clay

Merkel Model 2001EL

Merkel Model 2001EL

MAROCCHI CONQUISTA SPORTING CLAYS O/U SHOTGUNS
Gauge: 12, 2-3/4" chambers. **Barrel:** 28", 30", 32" (ContreChoke tubes); 10mm concave vent rib. **Weight:** About 8 lbs. **Stock:** 14-1/2"-14-7/8"x2-3/16"x1-7/16"; American walnut with checkered grip and forend; Sporting Clays butt pad. **Sights:** 16mm luminescent front. **Features:** Lower monoblock and frame profile. Fast lock time. Ergonomically-shaped trigger adjustable for pull length. Automatic selective ejectors. Coin-finished receiver, blued barrels. Five choke tubes, hard case. Available as true left-hand model—opening lever operates from left to right; stock has left-hand cast. Introduced 1994. Imported from Italy by Precision Sales International.
Price: Grade I, right-hand **$1,490.00**
Price: Grade I, left-hand **$1,615.00**
Price: Grade II, right-hand **$1,828.00**
Price: Grade II, left-hand **$2,180.00**
Price: Grade III, right-hand, from **$3,093.00**
Price: Grade III, left-hand, from **$3,093.00**

Marocchi Conquista Trap Over/Under Shotgun
Similar to Conquista Sporting Clays model except 30" or 32" barrels choked Full & Full, stock dimensions of 14-1/2"-14-7/8"x1-11/16"x1-9/32"; weighs about 8-1/4 lbs. Introduced 1994. Imported from Italy by Precision Sales International.
Price: Grade I, right-hand **$1,490.00**
Price: Grade II, right-hand **$1,828.00**
Price: Grade III, right-hand, from **$3,093.00**

Marocchi Conquista Skeet Over/Under Shotgun
Similar to Conquista Sporting Clays except 28" (Skeet & Skeet) barrels, stock dimensions of 14-3/8"-14-3/4"x2-3/16"x1-1/2". Weighs about 7-3/4 lbs. Introduced 1994. Imported from Italy by Precision Sales International.
Price: Grade I, right-hand **$1,490.00**
Price: Grade II, right-hand **$1,828.00**
Price: Grade III, right-hand, from **$3,093.00**

MAROCCHI MODEL 99 SPORTING TRAP AND SKEET
Gauge: 12, 2-3/4", 3" chambers. **Barrel:** 28", 30", 32". **Stock:** French walnut. **Features:** Boss Locking system, screw-in chokes, low recoil, lightweight monoblock barrels and ribs. Imported from Italy by Precision Sales International.
Price: Grade I **$2,350.00**
Price: Grade II **$2,870.00**
Price: Grade II Gold **$3,025.00**
Price: Grade III **$3,275.00**
Price: Grade III Gold. **$3,450.00**

Price: Blackgold **$4,150.00**
Price: Lodestar **$5,125.00**
Price: Brittania **$5,125.00**
Price: Diana **$6,350.00**

MAROCCHI CONQUISTA USA
MODEL 92 SPORTING CLAYS O/U SHOTGUN
Gauge: 12, 3" chambers. **Barrel:** 30"; back-bored, ported (ContreChoke Plus tubes); 10 mm concave ventilated top rib, ventilated middle rib. **Weight:** 8 lbs. 2 oz. **Stock:** 14-1/4"-14-5/8"x 2-1/8"x1-3/8"; American walnut with checkered grip and forend; Sporting Clays butt pad. **Features:** Low profile frame; fast lock time; automatic selective ejectors; blued receiver and barrels. Comes with three choke tubes. Ergonomically shaped trigger adjustable for pull length without tools. Barrels are back-bored and ported. Introduced 1996. Imported from Italy by Precision Sales International.
Price: **$1,490.00**

MERKEL MODEL 2001EL O/U SHOTGUN
Gauge: 12, 20, 3" chambers, 28, 2-3/4" chambers. **Barrel:** 12—28"; 20, 28 ga.—26-3/4". **Weight:** About 7 lbs. (12 ga.). **Stock:** Oil-finished walnut; English or pistol grip. **Features:** Self-cocking Blitz boxlock action with cocking indicators; Kersten double cross-bolt lock; silver-grayed receiver with engraved hunting scenes; coil spring ejectors; single selective or double triggers. Imported from Germany by GSI, Inc.
Price: 12, 20 . . . . **$7,295.00**
Price: 28 ga. **$7,295.00**
Price: Model 2000EL (scroll engraving, 12, 20 or 28) **$5,795.00**

Merkel Model 303EL O/U Shotgun
Similar to Model 2001 EL except Holland & Holland-style sidelock action with cocking indicators; English-style Arabesque engraving. Available in 12, 20, 28 gauge. Imported from Germany by GSI, Inc.
Price: **$19,995.00**

Merkel Model 2002 EL O/U Shotgun
Similar to Model 2001 EL except dummy sideplates, Arabesque engraving with hunting scenes; 12, 20, 28 gauge. Imported from Germany by GSI, Inc.
Price: **$10,995.00**

PERAZZI MX8 OVER/UNDER SHOTGUNS
Gauge: 12, 2-3/4" chambers. **Barrel:** 28-3/8" (Imp. Mod. & Extra Full), 29-1/2" (choke tubes). **Weight:** 7 lbs., 12 oz. **Stock:** Special specifications. **Features:** Has single selective trigger; flat 7/16"x5/16" vent. rib. Many options available. Imported from Italy by Perazzi U.S.A., Inc.
Price: Sporting **$10,800.00**
Price: Trap Double Trap (removable trigger group) **$9,560.00**
Price: Skeet **$9,560.00**
Price: SC3 grade (variety of engraving patterns) . . . . **Starting at $16,200**
Price: SCO grade (more intricate engraving, gold inlays)
. . . . **Starting at $26,000**

SHOTGUNS

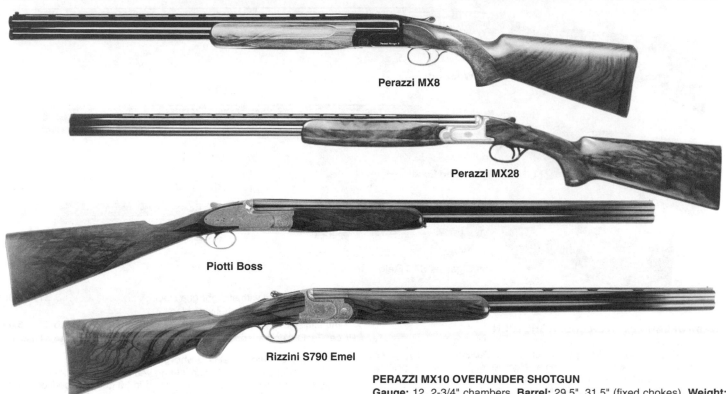

Perazzi MX8

Perazzi MX28

Piotti Boss

Rizzini S790 Emel

PERAZZI MX12 HUNTING OVER/UNDER

Gauge: 12, 2-3/4" chambers. **Barrel:** 26-3/4", 27-1/2", 28-3/8", 29-1/2" (Mod. & Full); choke tubes available in 27-5/8", 29-1/2" only (MX12C). **Weight:** 7 lbs., 4 oz. **Stock:** To customer specs; Interchangeable. **Features:** Single selective trigger; coil springs used in action; Schnabel forend tip. Imported from Italy by Perazzi U.S.A., Inc.
Price: From **$9,560.00**
Price: MX12C (with choke tubes), from **$10,240.00**

Perazzi MX20 Hunting Over/Under

Similar to the MX12 except 20 ga. frame size. Non-removable trigger group. Available in 20, 28, 410 with 2-3/4" or 3" chambers. 26" standard, and choked Mod. & Full. Weight is 6 lbs., 6 oz. Imported from Italy by Perazzi U.S.A., Inc.
Price: From **$9,560.00**
Price: MX20C (as above, 20 ga. only, choke tubes), from **$10,120.00**

PERAZZI MX8/MX8 SPECIAL TRAP, SKEET

Gauge: 12, 2-3/4" chambers. **Barrel:** Trap—29-1/2" (Imp. Mod. & Extra Full), 31-1/2" (Full & Extra Full). Choke tubes optional. Skeet—27-5/8" (Skeet & Skeet). **Weight:** About 8-1/2 lbs. (Trap); 7 lbs., 15 oz. (Skeet). **Stock:** Interchangeable and custom made to customer specs. **Features:** Has detachable and interchangeable trigger group with flat V springs. Flat 7/16" ventilated rib. Many options available. Imported from Italy by Perazzi U.S.A., Inc.
Price: From **$9,560.00**
Price: MX8 Special (adj. four-position trigger), from **$10,120.00**
Price: MX8 Special Combo (o/u and single barrel sets), from . **$13,340.00**

Perazzi MX8 Special Skeet Over/Under

Similar to the MX8 Skeet except has adjustable four-position trigger, Skeet stock dimensions. Imported from Italy by Perazzi U.S.A., Inc.
Price: From **$9,560.00**

Perazzi MX8/20 Over/Under Shotgun

Similar to the MX8 except has smaller frame and has a removable trigger mechanism. Available in trap, Skeet, sporting or game models with fixed chokes or choke tubes. Stock is made to customer specifications. Introduced 1993. Imported from Italy by Perazzi U.S.A., Inc.
Price: From **$9,560.00**

PERAZZI MX10 OVER/UNDER SHOTGUN

Gauge: 12, 2-3/4" chambers. **Barrel:** 29.5", 31.5" (fixed chokes). **Weight:** NA. **Stock:** Walnut; cheekpiece adjustable for elevation and cast. **Features:** Adjustable rib; vent. side rib. Externally selective trigger. Available in single barrel, combo, over/under trap, Skeet, pigeon and sporting models. Introduced 1993. Imported from Italy by Perazzi U.S.A., Inc.
Price: From **$11,500.00**

PERAZZI MX28, MX410 GAME O/U SHOTGUNS

Gauge: 28, 2-3/4" chambers, 410, 3" chambers. **Barrel:** 26" (Imp. Cyl. & Full). **Weight:** NA. **Stock:** To customer specifications. **Features:** Made on scaled-down frames proportioned to the gauge. Introduced 1993. Imported from Italy by Perazzi U.S.A., Inc.
Price: From **$19,120.00**

PIOTTI BOSS OVER/UNDER SHOTGUN

Gauge: 12, 20. **Barrel:** 26" to 32", chokes as specified. **Weight:** 6.5 to 8 lbs. **Stock:** Dimensions to customer specs. Best quality figured walnut. **Features:** Essentially a custom-made gun with many options. Introduced 1993. Imported from Italy by Wm. Larkin Moore.
Price: From **$35,780.00**

REMINGTON MODEL 332 O/U SHOTGUN

Gauge: 12, 3" chambers. **Barrel:** 26", 28", 30". **Weight:** 7.75 lbs. **Length:** 42"-47" **Stock:** Satin-finished American walnut. **Sights:** Twin bead. **Features:** Light-contour, vent rib, Rem chock barrel, blued, traditional M-32 experience with M-300 Ideal performance, standard auto ejectors, set trigger. Proven boxlock action.
Price: **$1,624.00**

RIZZINI S790 EMEL OVER/UNDER SHOTGUN

Gauge: 20, 28, 410. **Barrel:** 26", 27.5" (Imp. Cyl. & Imp. Mod.). **Weight:** About 6 lbs. **Stock:** 14"x1-1/2"x2-1/8". Extra-fancy select walnut. **Features:** Boxlock action with profuse engraving; automatic ejectors; single selective trigger; silvered receiver. Comes with Nizzoli leather case. Introduced 1996. Imported from Italy by Wm. Larkin Moore & Co.
Price: From **$8,200.00**

Rizzini S792 EMEL Over/Under Shotgun

Similar to S790 EMEL except dummy sideplates with extensive engraving coverage. Nizzoli leather case. Introduced 1996. Imported from Italy by Wm. Larkin Moore & Co.
Price: From **$7,900.00**

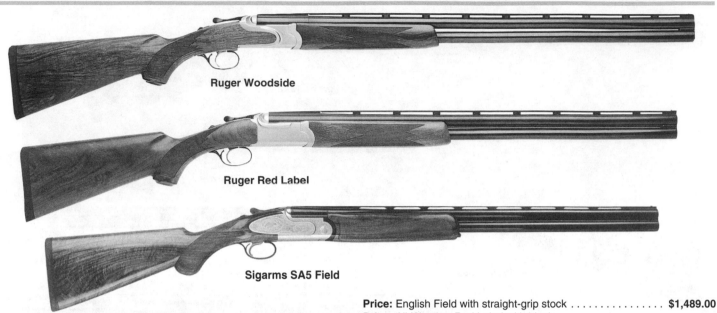

Ruger Woodside

Ruger Red Label

Sigarms SA5 Field

RIZZINI UPLAND EL OVER/UNDER SHOTGUN
Gauge: 12, 16, 20, 28, 410. **Barrel:** 26", 27-1/2", Mod. & Full, Imp. Cyl. & Imp. Mod. choke tubes. **Weight:** About 6.6 lbs. **Stock:** 14-1/2"x1-1/2"x2-1/4". **Features:** Boxlock action; single selective trigger; ejectors; profuse engraving on silvered receiver. Comes with fitted case. Introduced 1996. Imported from Italy by Wm. Larkin Moore & Co.
Price: From **$2,750.00**

Rizzini Artemis Over/Under Shotgun
Same as Upland EL model except dummy sideplates with extensive game scene engraving. Fancy European walnut stock. Fitted case. Introduced 1996. Imported from Italy by Wm. Larkin Moore & Co.
Price: From **$1,800.00**

RIZZINI S782 EMEL OVER/UNDER SHOTGUN
Gauge: 12, 2-3/4" chambers. **Barrel:** 26", 27.5" (Imp. Cyl. & Imp. Mod.). **Weight:** About 6.75 lbs. **Stock:** 14-1/2"x1-1/2"x2-1/4". Extra fancy select walnut. **Features:** Boxlock action with dummy sideplates, extensive engraving with gold inlaid game birds, silvered receiver, automatic ejectors, single selective trigger. Nizzoli leather case. Introduced 1996. Imported from Italy by Wm. Larkin Moore & Co.
Price: From **$9,900.00**

RUGER WOODSIDE OVER/UNDER SHOTGUN
Gauge: 12, 3" chambers. **Barrel:** 26", 28", 30" (Full, Mod., Imp. Cyl. and two Skeet tubes). **Weight:** 7-1/2 to 8 lbs. **Stock:** 14-1/8"x1-1/2"x2-1/2". Select Circassian walnut; pistol grip or straight English grip. **Features:** Newly patented Ruger cocking mechanism for easier, smoother opening. Buttstock extends forward into action as two side panels. Single selective mechanical trigger, selective automatic ejectors; serrated free-floating rib; back-bored barrels with stainless steel choke tubes. Blued barrels, stainless steel receiver. Engraved action available. Introduced 1995. Made in U.S. by Sturm, Ruger & Co.
Price: **$1,889.00**
Price: Woodside Sporting Clays (30" barrels) **$1,889.00**

RUGER RED LABEL O/U SHOTGUN
Gauge: 12, 20, 3" chambers; 28 2-3/4" chambers. **Barrel:** 26", 28" (Skeet [two], Imp. Cyl., Full, Mod. screw-in choke tubes). Proved for steel shot. **Weight:** About 7 lbs. (20 ga.); 7-1/2 lbs. (12 ga.). **Length:** 43" overall (26" barrels). **Stock:** 14"x1-1/2"x2-1/2". Straight grain American walnut or black synthetic. Checkered pistol grip and forend, rubber butt pad. **Features:** Stainless steel receiver. Single selective mechanical trigger, selective automatic ejectors; serrated free-floating vent. rib. Comes with two Skeet, one Imp. Cyl., one Mod., one Full choke tube and wrench. Made in U.S. by Sturm, Ruger & Co.
Price: Red Label with pistol grip stock **$1,489.00**

Price: English Field with straight-grip stock **$1,489.00**
Price: All-Weather Red Label with black
synthetic stock . . . . **$1,489.00 to $1,545.00**
Price: Factory engraved All-Weather models. . . . . **$1,650.00 to $1,725.00**

Ruger Engraved Red Label O/U Shotguns
Similar to Red Label except scroll engraved receiver with 24-carat gold game bird (pheasant in 12 gauge, grouse in 20 gauge, woodcock in 28 gauge, duck on All-Weather 12 gauge). Introduced 2000.
Price: Engraved Red Label (12 gauge, 30" barrel). **$1,725.00**
Price: Engraved Red Label (12, 20 and 28 gauge in 26"
and 28" barrels) **$1,650.00**
Price: Engraved Red Label, All-Weather (synthetic stock, 12 gauge only;
26" and 28" brls.) **$1,650.00**
Price: Engraved Red Label, All-Weather (synthetic stock, 12 gauge only,
30" barrel). **$1,650.00**

Ruger Sporting Clays O/U Shotgun
Similar to Red Label except 30" back-bored barrels, stainless steel choke tubes. Weighs 7.75 lbs., overall length 47". Stock dimensions of 14-1/8"x1-1/2"x2-1/2". Free-floating serrated vent rib with brass front and mid-rib beads. No barrel side spacers. Comes with two Skeet, one imp. cyl., one mod. + full choke tubes. 12 ga. introduced 1992, 20 ga. introduced 1994.
Price: 12 or 20 . . . . **$1,545.00**
Price: All-Weather with black synthetic stock **$1,545.00**

SARSILMAZ OVER/UNDER SHOTGUN
Gauge: 12, 3" chambers. **Barrel:** 26", 28"; fixed chokes or choke tubes. **Weight:** NA. **Length:** NA. **Stock:** Oil-finished hardwood. **Features:** Double or single selective trigger, wide ventilated rib, chrome-plated parts, blued finish. Introduced 2000. Imported from Turkey by Armsport Inc.
Price: Double triggers; mod. and full or imp. cyl. and mod. fixed
chokes **$499.95**
Price: Single selective trigger; imp. cyl. and mod. or mod.
and full fixed chokes **$575.00**
Price: Single selective trigger; five choke tubes and wrench **$695.00**

SIGARMS SA5 OVER/UNDER SHOTGUN
Gauge: 12, 20, 3" chamber. **Barrel:** 26-1/2", 27" (Full, Imp. Mod., Mod., Imp. Cyl., Cyl. choke tubes). **Weight:** 6.9 lbs. (12 gauge), 5.9 lbs. (20 gauge). **Stock:** 14-1/2" x 1-1/2" x 2-1/2". Select grade walnut; checkered 20 l.p.i. at grip and forend. **Features:** Single selective trigger, automatic ejectors; hand-engraved detachable sideplated; matte nickel receiver, rest blued; tapered bolt lock-up. Introduced 1997. Imported by Sigarms, Inc.
Price: Field, 12 gauge **$2,670.00**
Price: Sporting Clays **$2,800.00**
Price: Field 20 gauge **$2,670.00**

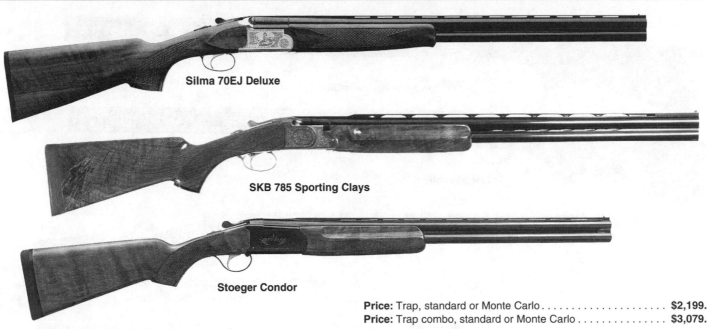

Silma 70EJ Deluxe

SKB 785 Sporting Clays

Stoeger Condor

SILMA MODEL 70EJ DELUXE

Gauge: 12 (3-1/2" chambers), 20, 410 (3" chambers), 28 (2-3/4" chambers). **Barrel:** 28" (12 and 20 gauge, fixed and tubed, 28 and 410 fixed), 26" (12 and 20 fixed). **Weight:** 7.6 lbs 12 gauge, 6.9 lbs, 20, 28 and 410. **Stock:** Checkered select European walnut, pistol grip, solid rubber recoil pad. **Features:** Monobloc construction, chrome-moly blued steel barrels, raised vent rib, automatic safety and ejectors, single mechanical gold-plated trigger, bead front sight. Brushed, engraved receiver. Introduced 2002. Clays models introduced 2003. Imported from Italy by Legacy sports International.

Price: 12, 20 multichokes (IC, M, F) **$823.00**
Price: 28, 410 multichokes (IC, M, F), fixed (M&F) **$961.00**
Price: Clays model, 12, multichokes (IC,M,F) **$1,237.00**

Silma Model 70 EJ Superlight

Similar to Silma 70EJ Deluxe except 12 gauge, 3" chambers, alloy receiver, weighs 5.6 lbs.
Price: 12, 20 multichokes (IC, M, F) **$1,004.00**

Silma Model 70 EJ Standard

Similar to Silma 70EJ Deluxe except 12 and 20 gauge only, standard walnut stock, light engraving, silver-plated trigger.
Price: 12 multichokes (IC, M, F) **$765.00**

SKB MODEL 785 OVER/UNDER SHOTGUN

Gauge: 12, 20, 3"; 28, 2-3/4"; 410, 3". **Barrel:** 26", 28", 30", 32" (Inter-Choke tubes). **Weight:** 6 lbs., 10 oz. to 8 lbs. **Stock:** 14-1/8"x1-1/2"x2-3/16" (Field). Hand-checkered American black walnut with high-gloss finish; semi-beavertail forend. Target stocks available in standard or Monte Carlo styles. **Sights:** Metal bead front (Field), target style on Skeet, trap, Sporting Clays models. **Features:** Boxlock action with Greener-style cross bolt; single selective chrome-plated trigger, chrome-plated selective ejectors; manual safety. Chrome-plated, over-size, back-bored barrels with lengthened forcing cones. Introduced 1995. Imported from Japan by G.U. Inc.

Price: Field, 12 or 20 . . . . $2,119.00
Price: Field, 28 or 410 . . . . $2,199.00
Price: Field set, 12 and 20 . . . . $3,079.00
Price: Field set, 20 and 28 or 28 and 410. . . . . $3,179.00
Price: Sporting Clays, 12 or 20. . . . . $2,269.00
Price: Sporting Clays, 28 . . . . $2,349.00
Price: Sporting Clays set, 12 and 20 . . . . $3,249.00
Price: Skeet, 12 or 20. . . . . $2,199.00
Price: Skeet, 28 or 410. . . . . $2,239.00
Price: Skeet, three-barrel set, 20, 28, 410 . . . . $4,439.00

Price: Trap, standard or Monte Carlo. $2,199.00
Price: Trap combo, standard or Monte Carlo $3,079.00

SKB MODEL 585 OVER/UNDER SHOTGUN

Gauge: 12 or 20, 3"; 28, 2-3/4"; 410, 3". **Barrel:** 12 ga.—26", 28", 30", 32", 34" (Inter-Choke tubes); 20 ga.—26", 28" (Inter-Choke tube); 28—26", 28" (Inter-Choke tubes); 410—26", 28" (Inter-Choke tubes). Ventilated side ribs. **Weight:** 6.6 to 8.5 lbs. **Length:** 43" to 51-3/8" overall. **Stock:** 14-1/8"x1-1/ 2"x2-3/16". Hand checkered walnut with high-gloss finish. Target stocks available in standard and Monte Carlo. **Sights:** Metal bead front (field), target style on Skeet, trap, Sporting Clays. **Features:** Boxlock action; silver nitride finish with Field or Target pattern engraving; manual safety, automatic ejectors, single selective trigger. All 12 gauge barrels are back-bored, have lengthened forcing cones and longer choke tube system. Sporting Clays models in 12 gauge with 28" or 30" barrels available with optional 3/8" step-up target-style rib, matte finish, nickel center bead, white front bead. Introduced 1992. Imported from Japan by G.U., Inc.

Price: Field $1,499.00
Price: Two-barrel Field Set, 12 & 20 . . . . $2,399.00
Price: Two-barrel Field Set, 20 & 28 or 28 & 410. . . . . $2,469.00
Price: Trap, Skeet. $1,619.00
Price: Two-barrel trap combo $2,419.00
Price: Sporting Clays model . . . . $1,679.00 to $1,729.00
Price: Skeet Set (20, 28, 410) $3,779.00

SKB Model 585 Gold Package

Similar to Model 585 Field except gold-plated trigger, two gold-plated game inlays, Schnabel forend. Silver or blue receiver. Introduced 1998. Imported from Japan by G.U. Inc.

Price: 12, 20 ga. $1,689.00
Price: 28, 410 . . . . $1,749.00

SKB Model 505 Shotguns

Similar to Model 585 except blued receiver, standard bore diameter, standard Inter-Choke system on 12, 20, 28, different receiver engraving. Imported from Japan by G.U. Inc.

Price: Field, 12 (26", 28"), 20 (26", 28") $1,189.00
Price: Sporting Clays, 12 (28", 30") $1,299.00

STOEGER CONDOR SPECIAL

Gauge: 12, 20, 2-3/4" 3" chambers. **Barrel:** 26", 28". **Weight:** 7.7 lbs. **Sights:** Brass bead. **Features:** IC and M screw-in choke trubes with each gun. Oil finished hardwood with pistol grip and forend. Auto safety, single trigger, automatic extractors.

Price: $390.00
Price: Condor Special $440.00
Price: Supreme Deluxe w/SS and red bar sights $500.00

Tristar Silver Sporting O/U

Tristar Silver II

Tristar TR-SC "Emilio Rizzini"

Tristar TR Royal Emilio Rizzini

TRADITIONS CLASSIC SERIES O/U SHOTGUNS

Gauge: 12, 3"; 20, 3"; 16, 2-3/4"; 28, 2-3/4"; 410, 3". **Barrel:** 26" and 28". **Weight:** 6 lbs., 5 oz. to 7 lbs., 6 oz. **Length:** 43" to 45" overall. **Stock:** Walnut. **Features:** Single-selective trigger; chrome-lined barrels with screw-in choke tubes; extractors (Field Hunter and Field I models) or automatic ejectors (Field II and Field III models); rubber butt pad; top tang safety. Imported from Fausti of Italy by Traditions.
Price: (Field Hunter — blued receiver; 12 or 20 ga.; 26" bbl. has I.C. and mod. tubes, 28" has mod. and full tubes) $669.00
Price: (Field I — blued receiver; 12, 20, 28 or 410 ga.; fixed chokes [26" has I.C. and mod., 28" has mod. and full]) $619.00
Price: (Field II — coin-finish receiver; 12, 16, 20, 28 or 410 ga.; gold trigger; choke tubes) $789.00
Price: (Field III — coin-finish receiver; gold engraving and trigger; 12 ga.; 26" or 28" bbl.; choke tubes) $999.00
Price: (Upland II — blued receiver; 12 or 20 ga.; English-style straight walnut stock; choke tubes) $839.00
Price: (Upland III — blued receiver, gold engraving; 20 ga.; high-grade pistol grip walnut stock; choke tubes) $1,059.00
Price: (Upland III — blued, gold engraved receiver, 12 ga. Round pistol grip stock, choke tubes) $1,059.00
Price: (Sporting Clay II — silver receiver; 12 ga.; ported barrels with skeet, i.c., mod. and full extended tubes) $959.00
Price: (Sporting Clay III — engraved receivers, 12 and 20 ga., walnut stock, vent rib, extended choke tubes) $1,189.00

TRADITIONS MAG 350 SERIES O/U SHOTGUNS

Gauge: 12, 3-1/2". Barrels: 24", 26" and 28". **Weight:** 7 lbs. to 7 lbs., 4 oz. **Length:** 41" to 45" overall. **Stock:** Walnut or composite with Mossy Oak® Break-Up™ or Advantage® Wetlands ™ camouflage. **Features:** Black matte, engraved receiver; vent rib; automatic ejectors; single-selective trigger; three screw-in choke tubes; rubber recoil pad; top tang safety. Imported from Fausti of Italy by Traditions.
Price: (Mag Hunter II — 28" black matte barrels, walnut stock, includes I.C., Mod. and Full tubes) $799.00

Price: (Turkey II — 24" or 26" camo barrels, Break-Up camo stock, includes Mod., Full and X-Full tubes) $889.00
Price: (Waterfowl II — 28" camo barrels, Advantage Wetlands camo stock, includes I.C., Mod. and Full tubes) $899.00

TRISTAR SILVER SPORTING O/U

Gauge: 12, 2-3/4" chambers, 20 3" chambers. **Barrel:** 28", 30" (Skeet, Imp. Cyl., Mod., Full choke tubes). **Weight:** 7-3/8 lbs. **Length:** 45-1/2" overall. **Stock:** 14-3/8"x1-1/2"x2-3/8". Figured walnut, cut checkering; Sporting Clays quick-mount buttpad. **Sights:** Target bead front. **Features:** Boxlock action with single selective trigger, automatic selective ejectors; special broadway channeled rib; vented barrel rib; chrome bores. Chrome-nickel finish on frame, with engraving. Introduced 1990. Imported from Italy by Tristar Sporting Arms Ltd.
Price: $799.00

Tristar Silver II Shotgun

Similar to the Silver I except 26" barrel (Imp. Cyl., Mod., Full choke tubes, 12 and 20 ga.), 28" (Imp. Cyl., Mod., Full choke tubes, 12 ga. only), 26" (Imp. Cyl. & Mod. fixed chokes, 28 and 410), automatic selective ejectors. Weight is about 6 lbs., 15 oz. (12 ga., 26").
Price: $669.00

TRISTAR TR-SC "EMILIO RIZZINI" OVER/UNDER

Gauge: 12, 20, 3" chambers. **Barrel:** 28", 30" (Imp. Cyl., Mod., Full choke tubes). **Weight:** 7-1/2 lbs. **Length:** 46" overall (28" barrel). **Stock:** 1-1/2"x2-3/ 8"x14-3/8". Semi-fancy walnut; pistol grip with palm swell; semi-beavertail forend; black Sporting Clays recoil pad. **Features:** Silvered boxlock action with Four Locks locking system, auto ejectors, single selective (inertia) trigger, auto safety. Hard chrome bores. Vent. 10mm rib with target-style front and mid-rib beads. Introduced 1998. Imported from Italy by Tristar Sporting Arms, Ltd.
Price: Sporting Clay model $1,047.00
Price: 20 ga. $1,127.00

Tristar TR-Royal "Emilio Rizzini" Over/Under

Similar to the TR-SC except has special parallel stock dimensions (1-1/2"x1-5/8"x14-3/8") to give low felt recoil; Rhino ported, extended choke tubes; solid barrel spacer; has "TR-Royal" gold engraved on the silvered receiver. Available in 12 gauge (28", 30") 20 and 28 gauge (28" only). Introduced 1999. Imported from Italy by Tristar Sporting Arms, Ltd.
Price: 12, 20, 28 ga. $1,319.00

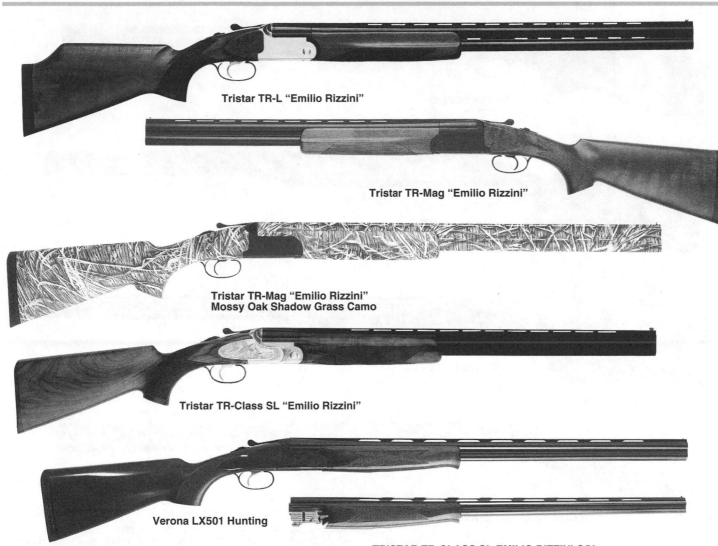

Tristar TR-L "Emilio Rizzini"

Tristar TR-Mag "Emilio Rizzini"

Tristar TR-Mag "Emilio Rizzini"
Mossy Oak Shadow Grass Camo

Tristar TR-Class SL "Emilio Rizzini"

Verona LX501 Hunting

Tristar TR-L "Emilio Rizzini" Over/Under

Similar to the TR-SC except has stock dimensions designed for female shooters (1-1/2" x 3" x 13-1/2"). Standard grade walnut. Introduced 1998. Imported from Italy by Tristar Sporting Arms, Ltd.

Price: **$1,063.00**

TRISTAR TR-I, II "EMILIO RIZZINI" OVER/UNDERS

Gauge: 12, 20, 3" chambers (TR-I); 12, 16, 20, 28, 410 3" chambers. **Barrel:** 12 ga., 26" (Imp. Cyl. & Mod.), 28" (Mod. & Full); 20 ga., 26" (Imp. Cyl. & Mod.), fixed chokes. **Weight:** 7-1/2 lbs. **Stock:** 1-1/2"x2-3/8"x14-3/8". Walnut with palm swell pistol grip, hand checkering, semi-beavertail forend, black recoil pad. **Features:** Boxlock action with blued finish, Four Locks locking system, gold single selective (inertia) trigger system, automatic safety, extractors. Introduced 1998. Imported from Italy by Tristar Sporting Arms, Ltd.

Price: TR-I **$779.00**
Price: TR-II (automatic ejectors, choke tubes) 12, 16 ga. **$919.00**
Price: 20, 28 ga., 410 . . . . **$969.00**

Tristar TR-Mag "Emilio Rizzini" Over/Under

Similar to TR-I, 3-1/2" chambers; choke tubes; 24" or 28" barrels with three choke tubes; extractors; auto safety. Matte blue finish on all metal, non-reflective wood finish. Introduced 1998. Imported from Italy by Tristar Sporting Arms, Ltd.

Price: **$799.00**
Price: Mossy Oak® Break-Up camo. **$969.00**
Price: Mossy Oak® Shadow Grass camo **$969.00**
Price: 10 ga., Mossy Oak® camo patterns. **$1,132.10**

TRISTAR TR-CLASS SL EMILIO RIZZINI O/U

Gauge: 12, 2-3/4" chambers. **Barrel:** 28", 30". **Weight:** 7-3/4 lbs. **Stock:** Fancy walnut, hand checkering, semi-beavertail forend, black recoil pad, gloss finish. **Features:** Boxlock action with silvered, engraved sideplates; Four Lock locking system; automatic ejectors; hard chrome bores; vent tapered 7mm rib with target-style front bead. hand-fitted gun. Introduced 1999. Imported from Italy by Tristar Sporting Arms, Ltd.

Price: **$1,775.00**

TRISTAR WS/OU 12 SHOTGUN

Gauge: 12, 3-1/2" chambers. **Barrel:** 28" or 30" (imp. cyl., mod., full choke tubes). **Weight:** 6 lbs., 15 oz. **Length:** 46" overall. **Stock:** 14-1/8"x1-1/8"x2-3/8". European walnut with cut checkering, black vented recoil pad, matte finish. **Features:** Boxlock action with single selective trigger, automatic selective ejectors; chrome bores. Matte metal finish. Imported by Tristar Sporting Arms Ltd.

Price: **$645.00**

VERONA LX501 HUNTING O/U SHOTGUNS

Gauge: 12, 20, 28, 410 (2-3/4", 3" chambers). **Barrel:** 28"; 12, 20 ga. have Interchoke tubes, 28 ga. and 410 have fixed Full & Mod. **Weight:** 6-7 lbs. **Stock:** Matte-finished walnut with machine-cut checkering. **Features:** Gold-plated single-selective trigger; ejectors; engraved, blued receiver, non-automatic safety; coil spring-operated firing pins. Introduced 1999. Imported from Italy by B.C. Outdoors.

Price: 12 and 20 ga. **$878.08**
Price: 28 ga. and 410 . . . . **$926.72**
Price: 410 . . . . **$907.01**
Price: Combos 20/28, 28/410. . . . . **$1,459.20**

SHOTGUNS — OVER/UNDERS

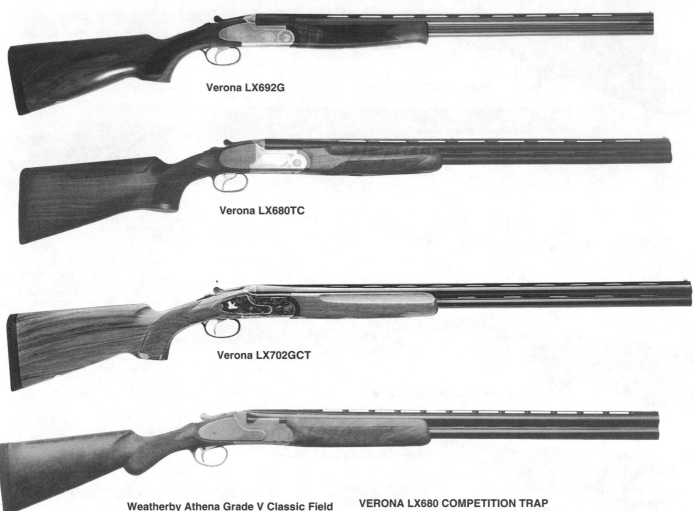

Verona LX692G

Verona LX680TC

Verona LX702GCT

Weatherby Athena Grade V Classic Field

Verona LX692 Gold Hunting Over/Under Shotguns

Similar to Verona LX501 except engraved, silvered receiver with false sideplates showing gold-inlaid bird hunting scenes on three sides; Schnabel forend tip; hand-cut checkering; black rubber butt pad. Available in 12 and 20 gauge only, five InterChoke tubes. Introduced 1999. Imported from Italy by B.C. Outdoors.

Price: **$1,295.00**
Price: LX692G Combo 28/410 . . . . **$2,192.40**

Verona LX680 Sporting Over/Under Shotguns

Similar to Verona LX501 except engraved, silvered receiver; ventilated middle rib; beavertail forend; hand-cut checkering; available in 12 or 20 gauge only with 2-3/4" chambers. Introduced 1999. Imported from Italy by B.C. Outdoors.

Price: **$1,159.68**

Verona LX680 Skeet/Sporting, Trap O/U Shotguns

Similar to Verona LX501 except skeet or trap stock dimensions; beavertail forend, palm swell on pistol grip; ventilated center barrel rib. Introduced 1999. Imported from Italy by B.C. Outdoors.

Price: **$1,736.96**

Verona LX692 Gold Sporting Over/Under Shotguns

Similar to Verona LX680 except false sideplates have gold-inlaid bird hunting scenes on three sides; red high-visibility front sight. Introduced 1999. Imported from Italy by B.C. Outdoors.

Price: Skeet/Sporting **$1,765.12**
Price: trap (32" barrel, 7-7/8 lbs.) **$1,594.80**

VERONA LX680 COMPETITION TRAP

Gauge: 12. **Barrel:** 30" O/U, 32" single bbl. **Weight:** 8-3/8 lbs. combo, 7 lbs. single. **Stock:** Walnut. **Sights:** White front, mid-rib bead. **Features:** Interchangeable barrels switch from O/U to single configurations. 5 Briley chokes in combo, 4 in single bbl. extended forcing cones, parted barrels 32" with raised rib. By B.C. Outdoors.

Price: Trap Single (LX680TGTSB) **$1,736.96**
Price: Trap Combo (LX680TC). **$2,553.60**

VERONA LX702 GOLD TRAP COMBO

Gauge: 20/28, 2-3/4"chamber. **Barrel:** 30". **Weight:** 7 lbs. **Stock:** Turkish walnut with beavertail forearm. **Sights:** White front bead. **Features:** 2-barrel competition gun. Color case-hardened side plates and receiver with gold inlaid pheasant. Ventilated rib between barrels. 5 interchokes. Imported from Italy by B.C. Outdoors.

Price: Combo **$2,467.84**
Price: 20 ga. **$1,829.12**

Verona LX702 Skeet/Trap O/U Shotguns

Similar to Verona LX702. Both are 12 gauge and 2-3/4" chamber. Skeet has 28" barrel and weighs 7-3/4 lbs. Trap has 32" barrel and weighs 7-7/8 lbs. By B.C. Outdoors.

Price: Skeet **$1,829.12**
Price: Trap **$1,829.12**

WEATHERBY ATHENA GRADE V CLASSIC FIELD O/U

Gauge: 12, 20, 3" chambers. **Barrel:** 26", 28", IMC Multi-Choke tubes. **Weight:** 12 ga., 7-1/4-8 lbs.; 20 ga. 6-1/2-7-1/4 lbs. **Stock:** Oil-finished American Claro walnut with fine-line checkering, rounded pistol grip and slender forend. **Features:** Old English recoil pad. Sideplate receiver has rose and scroll engraving.

Price: **$3,037.00**

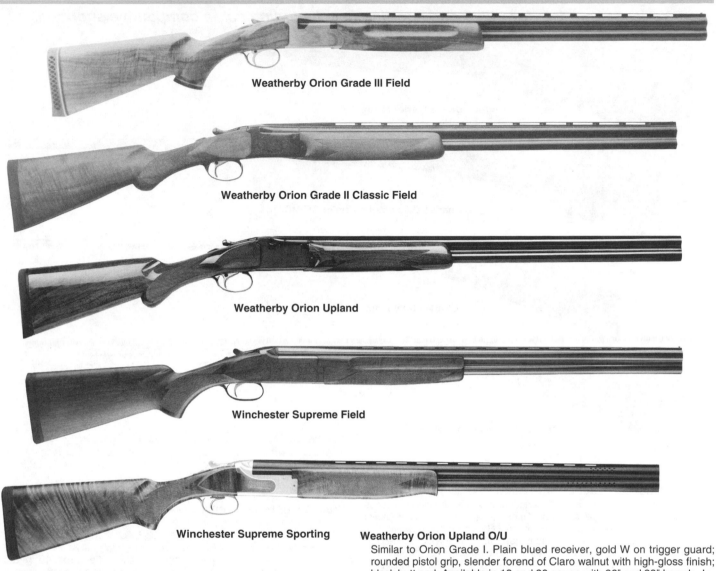

Weatherby Orion Grade III Field

Weatherby Orion Grade II Classic Field

Weatherby Orion Upland

Winchester Supreme Field

Winchester Supreme Sporting

Weatherby Athena Grade III Classic Field O/U

Similar to Athena Grade V, has Grade III Claro walnut with oil finish, rounded pistol grip, slender forend; silver nitride/gray receiver has rose and scroll engraving with gold-overlay upland game scenes. Introduced 1999. Imported from Japan by Weatherby.
Price: 12, 20, 28 ga. **$2,173.00**

WEATHERBY ORION GRADE III FIELD O/U SHOTGUNS

Gauge: 12, 20, 3" chambers. **Barrel:** 26", 28", IMC Multi-Choke tubes. **Weight:** 6-1/2 to 8 lbs. **Stock:** 14-1/4"x1-1/2"x2-1/2". American walnut, checkered grip and forend. Rubber recoil pad. **Features:** Selective automatic ejectors, single selective inertia trigger. Top tang safety, Greener cross bolt. Has silver-gray receiver with engraving and gold duck/pheasant. Imported from Japan by Weatherby.
Price: Orion III, Field, 12, IMC, 26", 28" **$1,955.00**
Price: Orion III, Field, 20, IMC, 26", 28" **$1,955.00**

Weatherby Orion Grade II Classic Field O/U

Similar to Orion III Classic Field except stock has high-gloss finish, and bird on receiver is not gold. Available in 12 gauge, 26", 28", 30" barrels, 20 gauge, 26" 28", both with 3" chambers, 28 gauge, 26", 2-3/4" chambers. All have IMC choke tubes. Imported from Japan by Weatherby.
Price: **$1,622.00**

Weatherby Orion Upland O/U

Similar to Orion Grade I. Plain blued receiver, gold W on trigger guard; rounded pistol grip, slender forend of Claro walnut with high-gloss finish; black butt pad. Available in 12 and 20 gauge with 26" and 28" barrels. Introduced 1999. Imported from Japan by Weatherby.
Price: **$1,299.00**

WEATHERBY ORION SSC OVER/UNDER SHOTGUN

Gauge: 12, 3" chambers. **Barrel:** 28", 30", 32" (Skeet, SC1, Imp. Cyl., SC2, Mod. IMC choke tubes). **Weight:** About 8 lbs. **Stock:** 14-3/4"x2-1/4"x1-1/2". Claro walnut with satin oil finish; Schnabel forend tip; Sporter-style pistol grip; Pachmayr Decelerator recoil pad. **Features:** Designed for Sporting Clays competition. Has lengthened forcing cones and back-boring; ported barrels with 12mm grooved rib with mid-bead sight; mechanical trigger is adjustable for length of pull. Introduced 1998. Imported from Japan by Weatherby.
Price: SSC (Super Sporting Clays) **$2,059.00**

WINCHESTER SUPREME O/U SHOTGUNS

Gauge: 12, 2-3/4", 3" chambers. **Barrel:** 28", 30", Invector Plus choke tubes. **Weight:** 7 lbs. 6 oz. to 7 lbs. 12. oz. **Length:** 45" overall (28" barrel). **Stock:** Checkered walnut stock. **Features:** Chrome-plated chambers; back-bored barrels; tang barrel selector/safety; deep-blued finish. Introduced 2000. From U.S. Repeating Arms. Co.
Price: Supreme Field (26" or 28" barrel, 6mm ventilated rib) . . **$1,383.00**
Price: Supreme Sporting (28" or 30" barrel, 10mm rib,
adj. trigger) **$1,551.00**

Variety of models for utility and sporting use, including some competitive shooting.

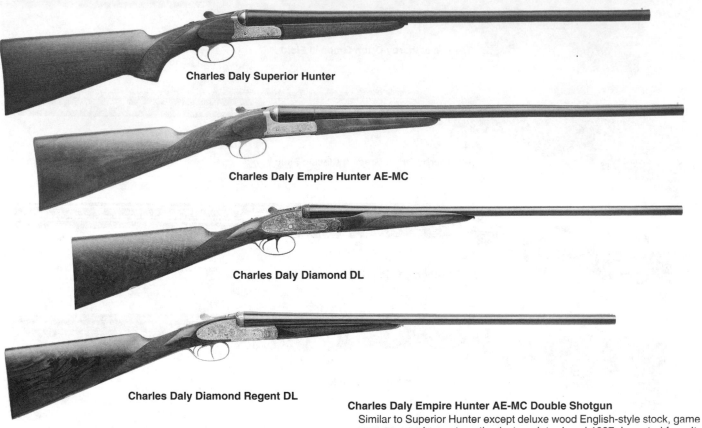

Charles Daly Superior Hunter

Charles Daly Empire Hunter AE-MC

Charles Daly Diamond DL

Charles Daly Diamond Regent DL

ARRIETA SIDELOCK DOUBLE SHOTGUNS

Gauge: 12, 16, 20, 28, 410. **Barrel:** Length and chokes to customer specs. **Weight:** To customer specs. **Stock:** To customer specs. Straight English with checkered butt (standard), or pistol grip. Select European walnut with oil finish. **Features:** Essentially custom gun with myriad options. H&H pattern hand-detachable sidelocks, selective automatic ejectors, double triggers (hinged front) standard. Some have self-opening action. Finish and engraving to customer specs. Imported from Spain by Wingshooting Adventures.

Price: Model 557, auto ejectors, from $3,250.00
Price: Model 570, auto ejectors, from $3,950.00
Price: Model 578, auto ejectors, from $4,350.00
Price: Model 600 Imperial, self-opening, from $6,050.00
Price: Model 601 Imperial Tiro, self-opening, from $6,950.00
Price: Model 801, from $9,135.00
Price: Model 802, from $9,135.00
Price: Model 803, from $6,930.00
Price: Model 871, auto ejectors, from $5,060.00
Price: Model 872, self-opening, from $12,375.00
Price: Model 873, self-opening, from $8,200.00
Price: Model 874, self-opening, from $9,250.00
Price: Model 875, self-opening, from $14,900.00

CHARLES DALY SUPERIOR HUNTER AND SUPERIOR MC DOUBLE SHOTGUN

Gauge: 12, 20, 3" chambers, 28, 2-3/4" chambers. **Barrel:** 28" (Mod. & Full) 26" (Imp. Cyl. & Mod.). **Weight:** About 7 lbs. **Stock:** Checkered walnut pistol grip buttstock, splinter forend. **Features:** Silvered, engraved receiver; chrome-lined barrels; gold single trigger; automatic safety; extractors; gold bead front sight. Introduced 1997. Imported from Italy by K.B.I., Inc.

Price: Superior Hunter, 28 and 410 gauge $1,029.00
Price: Superior Hunter MC 26"-28" $1,059.00

Charles Daly Empire Hunter AE-MC Double Shotgun

Similar to Superior Hunter except deluxe wood English-style stock, game scene engraving, automatic ejectors. Introduced 1997. Imported from Italy by K.B.I., Inc.

Price: 12 or 20 . . . . $1,349.00

CHARLES DALY DIAMOND DL DOUBLE SHOTGUN

Gauge: 12, 20, 410, 3" chambers, 28, 2-3/4" chambers. **Barrel:** 28" (Mod. & Full), 26" (Imp. Cyl. & Mod.), 26" (Full & Full, 410). **Weight:** About 5-7 lbs. **Stock:** Select fancy European walnut, English-style butt, beavertail forend; hand-checkered, hand-rubbed oil finish. **Features:** Drop-forged action with gas escape valves; demiblock barrels with concave rib; selective automatic ejectors; hand-detachable double safety sidelocks with hand-engraved rose and scrollwork. Hinged front trigger. Color case-hardened receiver. Introduced 1997. Imported from Spain by K.B.I., Inc.

Price: $6,999.00

CHARLES DALY DIAMOND REGENT DL DOUBLE SHOTGUN

Gauge: 12, 20, 410, 3" chambers, 28, 2-3/4" chambers. **Barrel:** 28" (Mod. & Full), 26" (Imp. Cyl. & Mod.), 26" (Full & Full, 410). **Weight:** About 5-7 lbs. **Stock:** Special select fancy European walnut, English-style butt, splinter forend; hand-checkered; hand-rubbed oil finish. **Features:** Drop-forged action with gas escape valves; demiblock barrels of chrome-nickel steel with concave rib; selective automatic-ejectors; hand-detachable, double-safety H&H sidelocks with demi-relief hand engraving; H&H pattern easy-opening feature; hinged trigger; coin finished action. Introduced 1997. Imported from Spain by K.B.I., Inc.

Price: Special Custom Order . . . . **NA**

CHARLES DALY FIELD II, AE-MC HUNTER DOUBLE SHOTGUN

Gauge: 12, 20, 28, 410 (3" chambers; 28 has 2-3/4"). **Barrel:** 32" (Mod. & Mod.), 28, 30" (Mod. & Full), 26" (Imp. Cyl. & Mod.) 410 (Full & Full). **Weight:** 6 lbs. to 11.4 lbs. **Stock:** Checkered walnut pistol grip and forend. **Features:** Silvered, engraved receiver; gold single selective trigger in 10-, 12, and 20 ga.; double triggers in 28 and 410; automatic safety; extractors; gold bead front sight. Introduced 1997. Imported from Spain by K.B.I., Inc.

Price: 28 ga., 410-bore $729.00
Price: 12 or 20 AE-MC $799.00

SHOTGUNS — SIDE-BY-SIDES

Charles Daly Field Hunter

EAA/Baikal Bounty Hunter IZH-43K

EAA/Baikal IZH-43 Bounty Hunter

EAA/Baikal MP-213

EAA/Baikal Bounty Hunter MP-213 Coach

DAKOTA PREMIER GRADE SHOTGUNS
Gauge: 12, 16, 20, 28, 410. **Barrel:** 27". **Weight:** NA. **Length:** NA. **Stock:** Exhibition-grade English walnut, hand-rubbed oil finish with straight grip and splinter forend. **Features:** French grey finish; 50 percent coverage engraving; double triggers; selective ejectors. Finished to customer specifications. Made in U.S. by Dakota Arms.
Price: 12, 16, 20 gauge **$13,950.00**
Price: 28 and 410 gauge **$15,345.00**

Dakota The Dakota Legend Shotguns
Similar to Premier Grade except has special selection English walnut, full-coverage scroll engraving, oak and leather case. Made in U.S. by Dakota Arms.
Price: 12, 16, 20 gauge **$18,000.00**
Price: 28 and 410 gauge **$19,800.00**

EAA/BAIKAL BOUNTY HUNTER IZH-43K SHOTGUN
Gauge: 12 (2-3/4", 3" chambers), 20 (3" chambers), 28 (2-3/4" chambers), 410 (3" chambers). **Barrel:** 18-1/2", 20", 24", 26", 28", three choke tubes. **Weight:** 7.28 lbs. **Overall length:** NA. **Stock:** Walnut, checkered forearm and grip. **Features:** Machined receiver; hammer-forged barrels with chrome-line bores; external hammers; double triggers (single, selective trigger available); rifle barrel inserts optional. Imported by European American Armory.
Price: . . . . **$379.00 to $429.00**

EAA/BAIKAL IZH-43 BOUNTY HUNTER SHOTGUNS
Gauge: 12 (2-3/4", 3" chambers), 16 (2-3/4" chambers), 20 (2-3/4" and 3" chambers). **Barrel:** 20", 24", 26", 28"; imp., mod. and full choke tubes.

Stock: Hardwood or walnut; checkered forend and grip. **Features:** Hammer forged barrel; internal hammers; extractors; engraved receiver; automatic tang safety; non-glare rib. Imported by European American Armory.
Price: IZH-43 Bounty Hunter (12 gauge, 2-3/4" chambers, 20" brl., dbl. triggers, hardwood stock) **$299.00**
Price: IZH-43 Bounty Hunter (12 or 20 gauge, 2-3/4" chambers, 20" brl., dbl. triggers, walnut stock) **$359.00**

EAA/BAIKAL MP-213 SHOTGUN
Gauge: 12, 3" chambers. **Barrel:** 24", 26", 28"; imp., mod. and full choke tubes. **Weight:** 7.28 lbs. **Stock:** Walnut, checkered forearm and grip; rubber butt pad. **Features:** Hammer-forged barrels; chrome-lined bores; machined receiver; double trigger (each trigger fires both barrels independently); ejectors. Introduced 2000. Imported by European American Armory.
Price: IZH-213 . . . . **$939.00**

EAA/BAIKAL BOUNTY HUNTER MP-213 COACH GUN
Gauge: 12, 2-3/4" chambers. **Barrel:** 20", imp., mod. and full choke tubes. **Weight:** 7 lbs. **Stock:** Walnut, checkered forend and grip. **Features:** Selective double trigger with removable assembly (single trigger and varied pull weights available); ejectors; engraved receiver. Imported by European American Armory.
Price: MP-213 . . . . **$939.00**

E.M.F. HARTFORD MODEL COWBOY SHOTGUN
Gauge: 12. **Barrel:** 20". **Weight:** NA. **Length:** NA. **Stock:** Checkered walnut. **Sights:** Center bead. **Features:** Exposed hammers; color-case hardened receiver; blued barrel. Introduced 2001. Imported from Spain by E.M.F. Co. Inc.
Price: **$625.00**

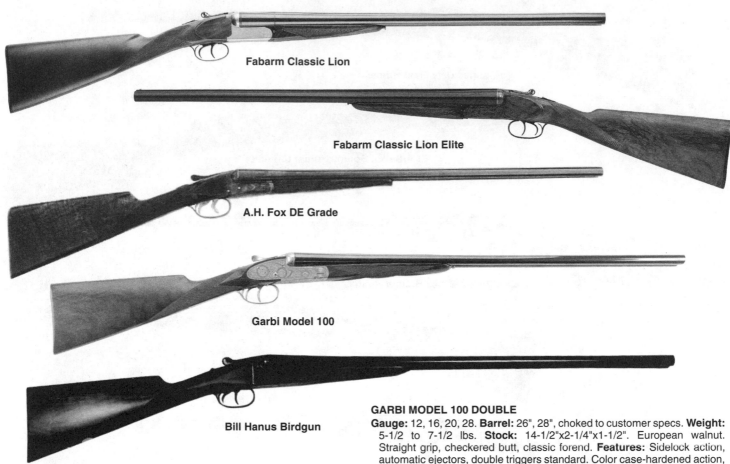

Fabarm Classic Lion

Fabarm Classic Lion Elite

A.H. Fox DE Grade

Garbi Model 100

Bill Hanus Birdgun

FABARM CLASSIC LION DOUBLE SHOTGUN

Gauge: 12, 3" chambers. **Barrel:** 26", 28", 30" (Cyl., Imp. Cyl., Mod., Imp. Mod., Full choke tubes). **Weight:** 7.2 lbs. **Length:** 44.5"-48.5. **Stock:** English-style or pistol grip oil-finished European walnut. **Features:** Boxlock action with double triggers, automatic ejectors, automatic safety. Introduced 1998. Imported from Italy by Heckler & Koch, Inc.

Price: Grade I **$1,499.00**
Price: Grade II **$2,099.00**
Price: Elite (color-case hardened type finish, 44.5") **$1,689.00**

FOX, A.H., SIDE-BY-SIDE SHOTGUNS

Gauge: 16, 20, 28, 410. **Barrel:** Length and chokes to customer specifications. Rust-blued Chromox or Krupp steel. **Weight:** 5-1/2 to 6-3/4 lbs. **Stock:** Dimensions to customer specifications. Hand-checkered Turkish Circassian walnut with hand-rubbed oil finish. Straight, semi or full pistol grip; splinter, Schnabel or beavertail forend; traditional pad, hard rubber buttplate or skeleton butt. **Features:** Boxlock action with automatic ejectors; double or Fox single selective trigger. Scalloped, rebated and color case-hardened receiver; hand finished and hand-engraved. Grades differ in engraving, inlays, grade of wood, amount of hand finishing. Add $1,500 for 28 or 410-bore. Introduced 1993. Made in U.S. by Connecticut Shotgun Mfg.

Price: CE Grade **$11,000.00**
Price: XE Grade **$12,500.00**
Price: DE Grade **$15,000.00**
Price: FE Grade **$20,000.00**
Price: Exhibition Grade **$30,000.00**
Price: 28/410 CE Grade **$12,500.00**
Price: 28/410 XE Grade **$14,000.00**
Price: 28/410 DE Grade **$16,500.00**
Price: 28/410 FE Grade **$21,500.00**
Price: 28/410 Exhibition Grade **$30,000.00**

GARBI MODEL 100 DOUBLE

Gauge: 12, 16, 20, 28. **Barrel:** 26", 28", choked to customer specs. **Weight:** 5-1/2 to 7-1/2 lbs. **Stock:** 14-1/2"x2-1/4"x1-1/2". European walnut. Straight grip, checkered butt, classic forend. **Features:** Sidelock action, automatic ejectors, double triggers standard. Color case-hardened action, coin finish optional. Single trigger; beavertail forend, etc. optional. Five other models are available. Imported from Spain by Wm. Larkin Moore.
Price: From **$4,000.00**

Garbi Model 200 Side-by-Side

Similar to the Garbi Model 100 except has heavy-duty locks, magnum proofed. Very fine Continental-style floral and scroll engraving, well figured walnut stock. Other mechanical features remain the same. Imported from Spain by Wm. Larkin Moore.
Price: **$8,700.00**

Garbi Model 101 Side-by-Side

Similar to the Garbi Model 100 except is hand engraved with scroll engraving, select walnut stock. Better overall quality than the Model 100. Imported from Spain by Wm. Larkin Moore.
Price: From **$5,150.00**

Garbi Model 103A, B Side-by-Side

Similar to the Garbi Model 100 except has Purdey-type fine scroll and rosette engraving. Better overall quality than the Model 101. Model 103B has nickel-chrome steel barrels, H&H-type easy opening mechanism; other mechanical details remain the same. Imported from Spain by Wm. Larkin Moore.
Price: Model 103A, from **$6,600.00**
Price: Model 103B, from **$9,100.00**

HANUS, BILL, BIRDGUN

Gauge: 16, 20, 28. **Barrel:** 27", 20 and 28 ga.; 28", 16 ga. (Skeet 1 & Skeet 2). **Weight:** 5 lbs., 4 oz. to 6 lbs., 4 oz. **Stock:** 14-3/8"x1-1/2"x2-3/8", with 1/4" cast-off. Select walnut. **Features:** Boxlock action with ejectors; splinter forend, straight English grip; checkered butt; English leather-covered handguard and Aya snap caps included. Made by AYA. Introduced 1998. Imported from Spain by Bill Hanus Birdguns.
Price: **$2,295.00**
Price: Single-selective trigger, add **$350.00**

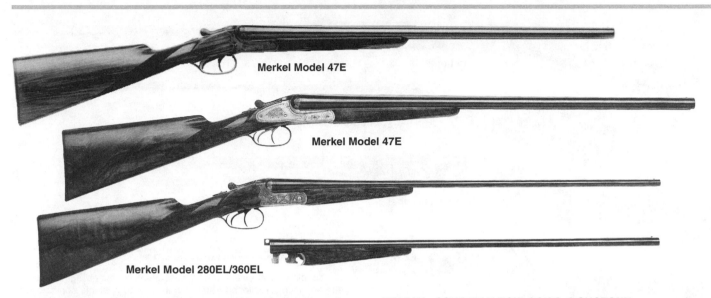

Merkel Model 47E

Merkel Model 47E

Merkel Model 280EL/360EL

ITHACA CLASSIC DOUBLES SKEET GRADE SxS
Gauge: 20, 28, 2-3/4" chambers, 410, 3". **Barrel:** 26", 28", 30", fixed chokes. **Weight:** 5 lbs., 14 oz. (20 gauge). **Stock:** 14-1/2"x2-1/4"x1-3/8". High-grade American black walnut, hand-rubbed oil finish; splinter or beavertail forend, straight or pistol grip. **Features:** Double triggers, ejectors; color case-hardened, engraved action body with matted top surfaces. Introduced 1999. Made in U.S. by Ithaca Classic Doubles.
Price: From **$5,999.00**

Ithaca Classic Doubles Grade 4E Classic SxS Shotgun
Gold-plated triggers, jeweled barrel flats and hand-turned locks. Feather crotch and flame-grained black walnut hand-checkered 28 lpi with fleur de lis pattern. Action body engraved with three game scenes and bank note scroll, color case-hardened. Introduced 1999. Made in U.S. by Ithaca Classic Doubles.
Price: From **$7,500.00**

ITHACA CLASSIC DOUBLES GRADE 7E CLASSIC SxS SHOTGUN
Engraved with bank note scroll and flat 24k gold game scenes: gold setter and gold pointer on opposite action sides, American bald eagle inlaid on bottom plate. Hand-timed, polished, jeweled ejectors and locks. Exhibition grade American black walnut stock and forend with eight-panel fleur de lis borders. Introduced 1999. Made in U.S. by Ithaca Classic Doubles.
Price: From **$11,000.00**

ITHACA CLASSIC DOUBLES GRADE 5E SxS SHOTGUN
NEW! Completely hand-made, it is based on the early Ithaca engraving patterns of master engraver William McGraw. The hand engraving is at 90% coverage in deep chiseled floral scroll with game scenes in 24kt gold inlays. Stocks are of high-grade Turkish and American walnut and are hand-checkered. Available in 12, 16, 20, 28 gauges and .410 bore including two barrel combination sets in 16/20 ga. and 28/410 bore. Introduced 2003. Made in U.S.A. by Ithaca Classic Doubles.
Price: From **$8,500.00**

ITHACA CLASSIC DOUBLES GRADE 6E SxS SHOTGUN
NEW! Features hand engraving of fine English scroll coupled with game scenes and 24kt gold inlays. Stock are hand-made of best quality American, Turkish or English walnut with hand checkering. All metal work is finished in traditional bone and charcoal color case hardening and deep rust blue. Available in 12, 16, 20, 28 gauges and .410 bore. Introduced 2003. Made in U.S.A. by Ithaca Classic Doubles.
Price: From **$9,999.00**

ITHACA CLASSIC DOUBLES SOUSA SPECIAL GRADE SxS SHOTGUN
Presentation grade American black walnut, hand-carved and checkered; hand-engraving with 24-karat gold inlays; tuned action and hand-applied finishes. Made in U.S. by Ithaca Classic Doubles.
Price: From **$18,000.00**

LEBEAU - COURALLY BOXLOCK SxS SHOTGUN
Gauge: 12, 16, 20, 28, 410-bore. **Barrel:** 25" to 32". **Weight:** To customer specifications. **Stock:** French walnut. **Features:** Anson & Deely-type action with automatic ejectors; single or double triggers. Essentially a custom gun built to customer specifications. Imported from Belgium by Wm. Larkin Moore.
Price: From **$21,000.00**

LEBEAU - COURALLY SIDELOCK SxS SHOTGUN
Gauge: 12, 16, 20, 28, 410-bore. **Barrel:** 25" to 32". **Weight:** To customer specifications. **Stock:** Fancy French walnut. **Features:** Holland & Holland-type action with automatic ejectors; single or double triggers. Essentially a custom gun built to customer specifications. Imported from Belgium by Wm. Larkin Moore.
Price: From **$43,000.00**

MERKEL MODEL 47E, 147E SIDE-BY-SIDE SHOTGUNS
Gauge: 12, 3" chambers, 16, 2-3/4" chambers, 20, 3" chambers. **Barrel:** 12, 16 ga.—28"; 20 ga.—26-3/4" (Imp. Cyl. & Mod., Mod. & Full). **Weight:** About 6-3/4 lbs. (12 ga.). **Stock:** Oil-finished walnut; straight English or pistol grip. **Features:** Anson & Deeley-type boxlock action with single selective or double triggers, automatic safety, cocking indicators. Color case-hardened receiver with standard Arabesque engraving. Imported from Germany by GSI.
Price: Model 47E (H&H ejectors) **$3,295.00**
Price: Model 147E (as above with ejectors) **$3,995.00**

Merkel Model 47SL, 147SL Side-by-Sides
Similar to Model 122 except H&H style sidelock action with cocking indicators, ejectors. Silver-grayed receiver and sideplates have Arabesque engraving, engraved border and screws (Model 47S), or fine hunting scene engraving (Model 147S). Imported from Germany by GSI.
Price: Model 47SL **$5,995.00**
Price: Model 147SL **$7,995.00**
Price: Model 247SL (English-style engraving, large scrolls) . . . **$7,995.00**
Price: Model 447SL (English-style engraving, small scrolls) . . . **$9,995.00**

Merkel Model 280EL and 360EL Shotguns
Similar to Model 47E except smaller frame. Greener cross bolt with double under-barrel locking lugs, fine engraved hunting scenes on silver-grayed receiver, luxury-grade wood, Anson and Deely box-lock action. H&H ejectors, single-selective or double triggers. Introduced 2000. From Merkel.
Price: Model 280EL (28 gauge, 28" barrel, imp. cyl. and
  mod. chokes) 4 mod. chokes) **$5,795.00**
Price: Model 360EL (410 gauge, 28" barrel, mod. and
  full chokes). **$5,795.00**
Price: Model 280/360EL two-barrel set (28 and 410 gauge
  as above) **$8,295.00**

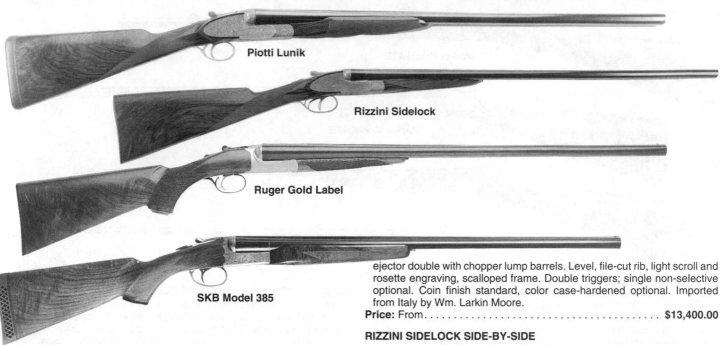

Piotti Lunik

Rizzini Sidelock

Ruger Gold Label

SKB Model 385

Merkel Model 280SL and 360SL Shotguns

Similar to Model 280EL and 360EL except has sidelock action, double triggers, English-style Arabesque engraving. Introduced 2000. From Merkel.
Price: Model 280SL (28 gauge, 28" barrel, imp. cyl. and
mod. chokes) **$8,495.00**
Price: Model 360SL (410 gauge, 28" barrel, mod. and
full chokes) **$8,495.00**
Price: Model 280/360SL two-barrel set **$11,995.00**

PIOTTI KING NO. 1 SIDE-BY-SIDE

Gauge: 12, 16, 20, 28, 410. **Barrel:** 25" to 30" (12 ga.), 25" to 28" (16, 20, 28, 410). To customer specs. Chokes as specified. **Weight:** 6-1/2 lbs. to 8 lbs. (12 ga. to customer specs.). **Stock:** Dimensions to customer specs. Finely figured walnut; straight grip with checkered butt with classic splinter forend and hand-rubbed oil finish standard. Pistol grip, beavertail forend. **Features:** Holland & Holland pattern sidelock action, automatic ejectors. Double trigger; non-selective single trigger optional. Coin finish standard; color case-hardened optional. Top rib; level, file-cut; concave, ventilated optional. Very fine, full coverage scroll engraving with small floral bouquets. Imported from Italy by Wm. Larkin Moore.
Price: From **$20,900.00**

Piotti King Extra Side-by-Side

Similar to the Piotti King No. 1 except with upgraded engraving. Choice of any type of engraving, including bulino game scene engraving and game scene engraving with gold inlays. Engraved and signed by a master engraver. Other mechanical specifications remain the same. Imported from Italy by Wm. Larkin Moore.
Price: From **$25,900.00**

Piotti Lunik Side-by-Side

Similar to the Piotti King No. 1 in overall quality. Has Renaissance-style large scroll engraving in relief. Best quality Holland & Holland-pattern sidelock ejector double with chopper lump (demi-bloc) barrels. Other mechanical specifications remain the same. Imported from Italy by Wm. Larkin Moore.
Price: From **$21,900.00**

PIOTTI PIUMA SIDE-BY-SIDE

Gauge: 12, 16, 20, 28, 410. **Barrel:** 25" to 30" (12 ga.), 25" to 28" (16, 20, 28, 410). **Weight:** 5-1/2 to 6-1/4 lbs. (20 ga.). **Stock:** Dimensions to customer specs. Straight grip stock with walnut checkered butt, classic splinter forend, hand-rubbed oil finish are standard; pistol grip, beavertail forend, satin luster finish optional. **Features:** Anson & Deeley boxlock

ejector double with chopper lump barrels. Level, file-cut rib, light scroll and rosette engraving, scalloped frame. Double triggers; single non-selective optional. Coin finish standard, color case-hardened optional. Imported from Italy by Wm. Larkin Moore.
Price: From **$13,400.00**

RIZZINI SIDELOCK SIDE-BY-SIDE

Gauge: 12, 16, 20, 28, 410. **Barrel:** 25" to 30" (12, 16, 20 ga.), 25" to 28" (28, 410). To customer specs. Chokes as specified. **Weight:** 6-1/2 lbs. to 8 lbs. (12 ga. to customer specs). **Stock:** Dimensions to customer specs. Finely figured walnut; straight grip with checkered butt with classic splinter forend and hand-rubbed oil finish standard. Pistol grip, beavertail forend. **Features:** Sidelock action, auto ejectors. Double triggers or non-selective single trigger standard. Coin finish standard. Imported from Italy by Wm. Larkin Moore.
Price: 12, 20 ga., from **$52,000.00**
Price: 28, 410 bore, from **$60,000.00**

RUGER GOLD LABEL SIDE-BY-SIDE SHOTGUN

Gauge: 12, 3" chambers. **Barrel:** 28" with skeet tubes. **Weight:** 6-1/2 lbs. **Length:** 45". **Stock:** American walnut straight or pistol grip. **Sights:** Gold bead front, full length rib, serrated top. **Features:** Spring-assisted break-open, SS trigger, auto eject. 5 interchangeable screw-in choke tubes, combination safety/barrel selector with auto safety reset.
Price: **$1,950.00**

SKB MODEL 385 SIDE-BY-SIDE

Gauge: 12, 20, 3" chambers; 28, 2-3/4" chambers. **Barrel:** 26" (Imp. Cyl., Mod., Skeet choke tubes). **Weight:** 6-3/4 lbs. **Length:** 42-1/2" overall. **Stock:** 14-1/8"x1-1/2"x2-1/2" American walnut with straight or pistol grip stock, semi-beavertail forend. **Features:** Boxlock action. Silver nitrided receiver with engraving; solid barrel rib; single selective trigger, selective automatic ejectors, automatic safety. Introduced 1996. Imported from Japan by G.U. Inc.
Price: **$2,049.00**
Price: Field Set, 20, 28 ga., 26" or 28", English or pistol grip . . . **$2,929.00**

SKB Model 385 Sporting Clays

Similar to the Field Model 385 except 12 gauge only; 28" barrel with choke tubes; raised ventilated rib with metal middle bead and white front. Stock dimensions 14-1/4"x1-7/16"x1-7/8". Introduced 1998. Imported from Japan by G.U. Inc.
Price: **$2,159.00**
Price: Sporting Clays set, 20, 28 ga. **$3,059.00**

SKB Model 485 Side-by-Side

Similar to the Model 385 except has dummy sideplates, raised ventilated rib with metal middle bead and white front, extensive upland game scene engraving, semi-fancy American walnut English or pistol grip stock. Imported from Japan by G.U. Inc.
Price: **$2,769.00**
Price: Field set, 20, 28 ga., 26" **$2,769.00**

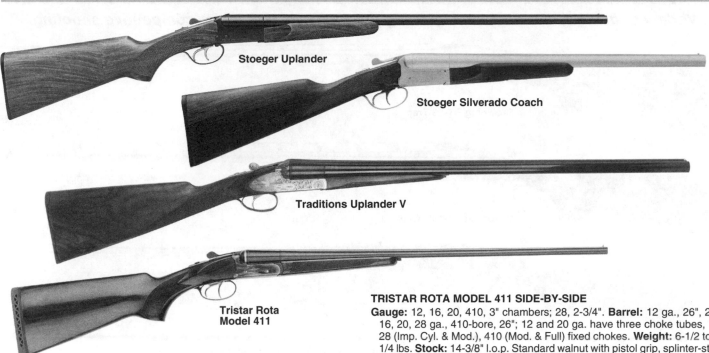

Stoeger Uplander

Stoeger Silverado Coach

Traditions Uplander V

Tristar Rota Model 411

SHOTGUNS

STOEGER UPLANDER SIDE-BY-SIDE SHOTGUN
Gauge: 16, 28, 2-3/4 chambers. 12, 20, 410, 3" chambers. **Barrel:** 26", 28". **Weight:** 7.3 lbs. **Sights:** Brass bead. **Features:** Double trigger, IC, M fixed choke tubes with gun.
Price: . . . . (With fixed chokes) **$335.00**; (With screw-in chokes) **$350.00**
Price: With English stock . . . . **$335.00 to $350.00**
Price: Upland Special **$375.00**
Price: Upland Supreme with SST, red bar sights **$445.00**
Price: Upland Short Stock (Youth) **$335.00**

STOEGER COACH GUN SIDE-BY-SIDE SHOTGUN
Gauge: 12, 20, 410, 2-3/4", 3" chambers. **Barrel:** 20". **Weight:** 6-1/2 lbs. **Stock:** Brown hardwood, classic beavertail forend. **Sights:** Brass bead. **Features:** IC & M fixed chokes, tang auto safety, auto extractors, black plastic butt plate. 12 ga. and 20 ga. also with English style stock.
Price: . . . . **$320.00**; (Nickel) **$375.00**
Price: Silverado . . . . **$375.00**; (With English stock) **$375.00**

TRADITIONS ELITE SERIES SIDE-BY-SIDE SHOTGUNS
Gauge: 12, 3"; 20, 3"; 28, 2-3/4"; 410, 3". **Barrel:** 26". **Weight:** 5 lbs., 12 oz. to 6-1/2 lbs. **Length:** 43" overall. **Stock:** Walnut. **Features:** Chrome-lined barrels; fixed chokes (Elite Field III ST, Field I DT and Field I ST) or choke tubes (Elite Hunter ST); extractors (Hunter ST and Field I models) or automatic ejectors (Field III ST); top tang safety. Imported from Fausti of Italy by Traditions.
Price: (Elite Field I DT — 12, 20, 28 or 410 ga.; I.C. and Mod. fixed chokes [F and F on 410]; double triggers) . . . . **$789.00 to $969.00**
Price: (Elite Field I ST — 12, 20, 28 or 410 ga.; same as DT but with single trigger) . . . . **$969.00 to $1,169.00**
Price: (Elite Field III ST — 28 or 410 ga.; gold-engraved receiver; high-grade walnut stock) **$2,099.00**
Price: (Elite Hunter ST — 12 or 20 ga.; blued receiver; I.C. and Mod. choke tubes) **$999.00**

TRADITIONS UPLANDER SERIES SIDE-BY-SIDE SHOTGUNS
NEW! **Gauge:** 12, 3"; 20, 3". **Barrel:** 26", 28". **Weight:** 6-1/4 lbs. to 6-1/2 lbs. **Length:** 43"-45" overall. **Stock:** Walnut. **Features:** Barrels threaded for choke tubes (Improved Cylinder, Modified and Full); top tang safety, extended trigger guard. Engraved silver receiver with side plates and lavish gold inlays. From Traditions.
Price: Uplander III Silver 12, 20 ga. **$2,699.00**
Price: Uplander V Silver 12, 20 ga. **$3,199.00**

TRISTAR ROTA MODEL 411 SIDE-BY-SIDE
Gauge: 12, 16, 20, 410, 3" chambers; 28, 2-3/4". **Barrel:** 12 ga., 26", 28"; 16, 20, 28 ga., 410-bore, 26"; 12 and 20 ga. have three choke tubes, 16, 28 (Imp. Cyl. & Mod.), 410 (Mod. & Full) fixed chokes. **Weight:** 6-1/2 to 7-1/4 lbs. **Stock:** 14-3/8" l.o.p. Standard walnut with pistol grip, splinter-style forend; hand checkered. **Features:** Engraved, color case-hardened boxlock action; double triggers, extractors; solid barrel rib. Introduced 1998. Imported from Italy by Tristar Sporting Arms, Ltd.
Price: **$849.00**

Tristar Rota Model 411D Side-by-Side
Similar to Model 411 except automatic ejectors, straight English-style stock, single trigger. Solid barrel rib with matted surface; chrome bores; color case-hardened frame; splinter forend. Introduced 1999. Imported from Italy by Tristar Sporting Arms, Ltd.
Price: **$1,110.00**

Tristar Rota Model 411R Coach Gun Side-by-Side
Similar to Model 411 except in 12 or 20 gauge only with 20" barrels and fixed chokes (Cyl. & Cyl.). Double triggers, extractors, choke tubes. Introduced 1999. Imported from Italy by Tristar Sporting Arms, Ltd.
Price: **$745.00**

Tristar Rota Model 411F Side-by-Side
Similar to Model 411 except silver, engraved receiver, ejectors, IC, M and F choke tubes, English-style stock, single gold trigger, cut checkering. Imported from Italy by Tristar Sporting Arms Ltd.
Price: **$1,608.00**

TRISTAR DERBY CLASSIC SIDE-BY-SIDE
Gauge: 12. **Barrel:** 28" Mod. & Full fixed chokes. **Features:** Sidelock action, engraved, double trigger, auto ejectors, English straight stock. Maide in Eruope for Tristar Sporting Arms Ltd.
Price: **$1,059.00**

WEATHERBY ATHENA SIDE-BY-SIDE
Gauge: 12, 20. **Barrel:** 26", 28". **Stock:** Turkish walnut, straight grip. **Sights:** Brass bead front. **Features:** Barrel selector independent of crossbolt safety. Integral multi-choke system, interchangeable screw-in Briley choke tubes (excepting 410 bored IC & Mod.). Receivers engraved with rose and scroll.
Price: **$1,599.00**

WEATHERBY ORION SIDE-BY-SIDE
Gauge: 12, 20, 28, 410. **Barrel:** 26", 28". **Stock:** Turkish walnut, half round pistol grip. **Sights:** Brass bead front. **Features:** Barrel selector independent of crossbolt safety. Integral multi-choke system, interchangeable screw-in Briley choke tubes (excepting 410 bored IC & Mod.). Receivers engraved with rose and scroll.
Price: **$1,149.00**

Variety of designs for utility and sporting purposes, as well as for competitive shooting.

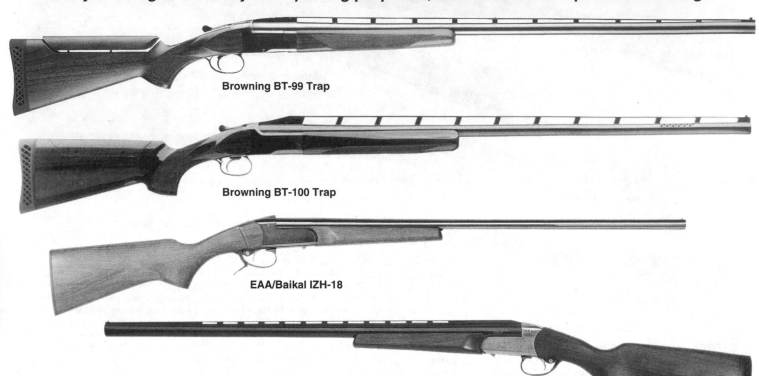

Browning BT-99 Trap

Browning BT-100 Trap

EAA/Baikal IZH-18

EAA/Baikal IZH-18Max

BERETTA DT10 TRIDENT TRAP TOP SINGLE SHOTGUN
Gauge: 12, 3" chamber. **Barrel:** 34"; five Optima Choke tubes (full, full, imp. modified, mod. and imp. cyl.). **Weight:** 8.8 lbs. **Stock:** High-grade walnut; adjustable. **Features:** Detachable, adjustable trigger group; Optima Bore for improved shot pattern and reduced recoil; slim Optima Choke tubes; raised and thickened receiver for long life. Introduced 2000. Imported from Italy by Beretta USA.
Price: **$8,500.00**

BRNO ZBK 100 SINGLE BARREL SHOTGUN
Gauge: 12 or 20. **Barrel:** 27.5". **Weight:** 5.5 lbs. **Length:** 44" overall. **Stock:** Beech. **Features:** Polished blue finish; sling swivels. Announced 1998. Imported from The Czech Republic by Euro-Imports.
Price: **$185.00**

BROWNING BT-99 TRAP SHOTGUN
Gauge: 12, 2-3/4" chamber. **Barrel:** 32" or 34"; Invector choke system (full choke tube only included); High Post Rib; back-bored. **Weight:** 8 lbs., 10 oz. (34" bbl.). **Length:** 50-1/2" overall (34" bbl.). **Stock:** Conventional or adjustable-comb. **Features:** Re-introduction of the BT-99 Trap Shotgun. Full beavertail forearm; checkered walnut stock; ejector; rubber butt pad. Re-introduced 2001. Imported by Browning.
Price: Conventional stock, 32" or 34" barrel **$1,216.00**
Price: Adj.-comb stock, 32" or 34" barrel **$1,449.00**

BROWNING BT-100 TRAP SHOTGUN
Gauge: 12, 2-3/4" chamber. **Barrel:** 32", 34" (Invector Plus); back-bored; also with fixed Full choke. **Weight:** 8 lbs., 10 oz. (34" bbl.). **Length:** 48-1/2" overall (32" barrel). **Stock:** 14-3/8"x1-9/16"x1-7/16x2" (Monte Carlo); 14-3/8"x1-3/4"x1-1/4"x2-1/8" (thumbhole). Walnut with high gloss finish; cut checkering. Wedge-shaped forend with finger groove. **Features:** Available in stainless steel or blue. Has drop-out trigger adjustable for weight of pull from 3-1/2 to 5-1/2 lbs., and for three length positions; Ejector-Selector allows ejection or extraction of shells. Available with adjustable comb stock and thumbhole style. Introduced 1995. Imported from Japan by Browning.
Price: Grade I, blue, Monte Carlo, Invector Plus **$2,222.00**
Price: Grade I, blue, adj. comb, Invector Plus **$2,455.00**
Price: Stainless steel, Monte Carlo, Invector Plus **$2,688.00**
Price: Stainless steel, adj. comb, Invector Plus **$2,923.00**

CHIPMUNK 410 YOUTH SHOTGUN
Gauge: 410. **Barrel:** 18-1/4" tapered, blue. **Weight:** 3.25 lbs. **Length:** 33". **Stock:** Walnut. **Features:** Manually cocking single shot bolt, blued receiver.
Price: **$225.95**

EAA/BAIKAL IZH-18 SINGLE BARREL SHOTGUN
Gauge: 12 (2-3/4" and 3" chambers), 20 (2-3/4" and 3"), 16 (2-3/4"), 410 (3"). **Barrel:** 26-1/2", 28-1/2"; modified or full choke (12 and 20 gauge); full only (16 gauge), improved cylinder (20 gauge) and full or improved modified (410). **Stock:** Walnut-stained hardwood; rubber recoil pad. **Features:** Hammer-forged steel barrel; machined receiver; cross-block safety; cocking lever with external cocking indicator; optional automatic ejector, screw-in chokes and rifle barrel. Imported by European American Armory.
Price: IZH-18 (12, 16, 20 or 410) **$95.00**
Price: IZH-18 (20 gauge with imp. cyl. or 410 with imp. mod.) . . . **$109.00**

EAA/BAIKAL IZH-18MAX SINGLE BARREL SHOTGUN
Gauge: 12, 3"; 20, 3"; 410, 3". **Barrel:** 24" (410), 26" (410 or 20 ga.) or 28" (12 ga.). **Weight:** 6.4 to 6.6 lbs. **Stock:** Walnut. **Features:** Polished nickel receiver; ventilated rib; I.C., Mod. and Full choke tubes; titanium-coated trigger; internal hammer; selectable ejector/extractor; rubber butt pad; decocking system. Imported by European American Armory.
Price: (12 or 20 ga., choke tubes) **$169.00**
Price: (410 ga., full choke only) **$189.00**
Price: Sporting, 12 ga., ported, Monte Carlo stock **$219.00**

FABARM MONOTRAP SHOTGUN
Caliber: 12; 2-3/4" chamber. **Barrel:** 30", 34". **Weight:** 6.7 to 6.9 lbs. **Length:** 48.5" overall (30" bbl.) **Stock:** Walnut; adjustable comb competition-style. **Sights:** Red front sight bar, mid-rib bead. **Features:** Built on 20-gauge receiver for quick handling. Silver receiver with blued barrel; special trap rib (micrometer adjustable); includes three choke tubes (M, IM, F). Introduced 2000.
Price: **$1,799.00**

Fabarm Monotrap

H&R 928 Ultra Slug Hunter Deluxe

H&R Tamer

H&R Topper

H&R Topper Deluxe

HARRINGTON & RICHARDSON NWTF SHOTGUNS
Gauge: 12, 3-1/2" chamber, fixed full choke; 20, 3" chamber, fixed modified choke. **Barrel:** 24" (12 ga.) or 22" (20 ga.) **Weight:** 5 to 6 lbs. **Stock:** Straight-grip camo laminate with recoil pad and sling swivel studs. **Sights:** Bead front. **Features:** Break-open single-shot action with side lever release; hand-checkered stock and forearm; includes trigger lock. Purchase supports National Wild Turkey Federation; NWTF logo on receiver.
Price: 12 ga. **$216.00**
Price: 20 ga. youth gun (12-1/2" length of pull, weighs 5 lbs.) . . . **$207.00**

HARRINGTON & RICHARDSON SB2-980 ULTRA SLUG
Gauge: 12, 20, 3" chamber. **Barrel:** 22" (20 ga. Youth) 24", fully rifled. **Weight:** 9 lbs. **Length:** NA. **Stock:** Walnut-stained hardwood. **Sights:** None furnished; comes with scope mount. **Features:** Uses the H&R 10 gauge action with heavy-wall barrel. Monte Carlo stock has sling swivels; comes with black nylon sling. Introduced 1995. Made in U.S. by H&R 1871, LLC.
Price: **$313.00**

Harrington & Richardson Model 928 Ultra Slug Hunter Deluxe
Similar to the SB2-980 Ultra Slug except uses 12 gauge action and 12 gauge barrel blank bored to 20 gauge, then fully rifled with 1:35" twist. Has hand-checkered camo laminate Monte Carlo stock and forend. Comes with Weaver-style scope base, offset hammer extension, ventilated recoil pad, sling swivels and nylon sling. Introduced 1997. Made in U.S. by H&R 1871 LLC.
Price: **$313.00**

HARRINGTON & RICHARDSON TAMER SHOTGUN
Gauge: 410, 3" chamber. **Barrel:** 20" (Full). **Weight:** 5-6 lbs. **Length:** 33" overall. **Stock:** Thumbhole grip of high density black polymer. **Features:** Uses H&R Topper action with matte electroless nickel finish. Stock holds four spare shotshells. Introduced 1994. From H&R 1871, LLC.
Price: **$161.00**

HARRINGTON & RICHARDSON TOPPER MODEL 098
Gauge: 12, 16, 20, 28 (2-3/4"), 410, 3" chamber. **Barrel:** 12 ga.—28" (Mod., Full); 16 ga.— 28" (Mod.); 20 ga.—26" (Mod.); 28 ga.—26" (Mod.); 410 bore— 26" (Full). **Weight:** 5-6 lbs. **Stock:** Black-finish hardwood with full pistol grip; semi-beavertail forend. **Sights:** Gold bead front. **Features:** Break-open action with side-lever release, automatic ejector. Satin nickel frame, blued barrel. Reintroduced 1992. From H&R 1871, LLC.
Price: **$143.00**
Price: Topper Junior 098 (as above except 22" barrel, 20 ga. (Mod.), 410-bore (Full), 12-1/2" length of pull) **$149.00**

Harrington & Richardson Topper Deluxe Model 098
Similar to the standard Topper 098 except 12 gauge only with 3-1/2" chamber, 28" barrel with choke tube (comes with Mod. tube, others optional). Satin nickel frame, blued barrel, black-finished wood. Introduced 1992. From H&R 1871, LLC.
Price: **$167.00**

Harrington & Richardson Topper Junior Classic Shotgun
Similar to the Topper Junior 098 except available in 20 gauge (3", Mod.), 410-bore (Full) with 3" chamber; 28 gauge, 2-3/4" chamber (Mod.); all have 22" barrel. Stock is American black walnut with cut-checkered pistol grip and forend. Ventilated rubber recoil pad with white line spacers. Blued barrel, blued frame. Introduced 1992. From H&R 1871, LLC.
Price: **$184.00**

SHOTGUNS

H&R Topper Junior

Ljutic Mono Gun

Mossberg 695 Slugster

Mossberg 695

ITHACA CLASSIC DOUBLES KNICKERBOCKER TRAP GUN

A reissue of the famous Ithaca Knickerbocker Trap Gun. Built on a custom basis only. Introduced 2003. Made in U.S.A. by Ithaca Classic Doubles.
Price: From **$9,000.00**

KRIEGHOFF K-80 SINGLE BARREL TRAP GUN

Gauge: 12, 2-3/4" chamber. **Barrel:** 32" or 34" Unsingle. Fixed Full or choke tubes. **Weight:** About 8-3/4 lbs. **Stock:** Four stock dimensions or adjustable stock available. All hand-checkered European walnut. **Features:** Satin nickel finish. Selective mechanical trigger adjustable for finger position. Tapered step vent. rib. Adjustable point of impact.
Price: Standard grade full Unsingle, from **$7,950.00**

KRIEGHOFF KX-5 TRAP GUN

Gauge: 12, 2-3/4" chamber. **Barrel:** 34"; choke tubes. **Weight:** About 8-1/2 lbs. **Stock:** Factory adjustable stock. European walnut. **Features:** Ventilated tapered step rib. Adjustable position trigger, optional release trigger. fully adjustable rib shooter to adjust point of impact from 50%/50% to nearly 90%/10%. Satin gray electroless nickel receiver. Fitted aluminum case. Imported from Germany by Krieghoff International, Inc.
Price: **$4,200.00**

LJUTIC MONO GUN SINGLE BARREL

Gauge: 12 only. **Barrel:** 34", choked to customer specs; hollow-milled rib, 35-1/2" sight plane. **Weight:** Approx. 9 lbs. **Stock:** To customer specs. Oil finish, hand checkered. **Features:** Totally custom made. Pull or release trigger; removable trigger guard contains trigger and hammer mechanism; Ljutic pushbutton opener on front of trigger guard. From Ljutic Industries.
Price: With standard, medium or Olympic rib, custom 32"-34" bbls., and fixed choke. **$5,795.00**

Price: As above with screw-in choke barrel **$6,095.00**
Price: Stainless steel mono gun **$6,795.00**

Ljutic LTX PRO 3 Deluxe Mono Gun

Deluxe light weight version of the Mono Gun with high quality wood, upgrade checkering, special rib height, screw in chokes, ported and cased.
Price: **$8,995.00**
Price: Stainless steel model **$9,995.00**

MOSSBERG MODEL 695 SLUGSTER

Gauge: 12, 3" chamber. **Barrel:** 22"; fully rifled, ported. **Weight:** 7-1/2 lbs. **Stock:** Black synthetic, with swivel studs and rubber recoil pad. **Sights:** Blade front, folding rifle-style leaf rear; Fiber Optic. Comes with Weaver-style scope bases. **Features:** Matte metal finish; rotating thumb safety; detachable 2-shot magazine. Mossberg Cablelock. Made in U.S. by Mossberg. Introduced 1996.
Price: **$345.00**
Price: With Fiber Optic rifle sights **$367.00**
Price: With woodlands camo stock, Fiber Optic sights. **$397.00**

MOSSBERG SSi-ONE 12 GAUGE SLUG SHOTGUN

Gauge: 12, 3" chamber. **Barrel:** 24", fully rifled. **Weight:** 8 pounds. **Length:** 40" overall. **Stock:** Walnut, fluted and cut checkered; sling-swivel studs; drilled and tapped for scope base. **Sights:** None (scope base supplied). **Features:** Frame accepts interchangeable rifle barrels (see Mossberg SSi-One rifle listing); lever-opening, break-action design; ambidextrous, top-tang safety; internal eject/extract selector. Introduced 2000. From Mossberg.
Price: **$480.00**

Mossberg SSi-One Turkey Shotgun

Similar to SSi-One 12 gauge Slug Shotgun, but chambered for 12 ga., 3-1/2" loads. Includes Accu-Mag Turkey Tube. Introduced 2001. From Mossberg.
Price: **$459.00**

New England Firearms Camo Turkey

New England Firearms Tracker II

New England Firearms Special Purpose

New England Firearms Standard Pardner

NEW ENGLAND FIREARMS CAMO TURKEY SHOTGUNS

Gauge: 10, 3-1/2"; 12, 20, 3" chamber. **Barrel:** 24"; extra-full, screw-in choke tube (10 ga.); fixed full choke (12, 20). **Weight:** NA. **Stock:** American hardwood, green and black camouflage finish with sling swivels and ventilated recoil pad. **Sights:** Bead front. **Features:** Matte metal finish; stock counterweight to reduce recoil; patented transfer bar system for hammer-down safety; includes camo sling and trigger lock. Accepts other factory-fitted barrels. Introduced 2000. From New England Firearms.
Price: .... 10 ga. **$279.00**; 12 ga., **$177.00**
Price: 20 ga. youth model (22" bbl.) **$187.00**

NEW ENGLAND FIREARMS TRACKER II SLUG GUN

Gauge: 12, 20, 3" chamber. **Barrel:** 24" (Cyl.), rifle bore. **Weight:** 5-1/4 lbs. **Length:** 40" overall. **Stock:** Walnut-finished hardwood with full pistol grip, recoil pad. **Sights:** Blade front, fully adjustable rifle-type rear. **Features:** Break-open action with side-lever release; blued barrel, color case-hardened frame. Introduced 1992. From New England Firearms.
Price: Tracker II **$183.00**

NEW ENGLAND FIREARMS SPECIAL PURPOSE SHOTGUNS

Gauge: 10, 3-1/2" chamber. **Barrel:** 28" (Full), 32" (Mod.). **Weight:** 9.5 lbs. **Length:** 44" overall (28" barrel). **Stock:** American hardwood with walnut or matte camo finish; ventilated rubber recoil pad. **Sights:** Bead front. **Features:** Break-open action with side-lever release; ejector. Matte finish on metal. Introduced 1992. From New England Firearms.
Price: Walnut-finish wood sling and swivels **$212.00**
Price: Camo finish, sling and swivels **$268.00**
Price: Camo finish, 32", sling and swivels **$268.00**
Price: Black matte finish, 24", Turkey Full choke tube,
sling and swivels **$247.00**

NEW ENGLAND FIREARMS SURVIVOR

Gauge: 12, 20, 410/45 Colt, 3" chamber. **Barrel:** 22" (Mod.); 20" (410/45 Colt, rifled barrel, choke tube). **Weight:** 6 lbs. **Length:** 36 overall. **Stock:** Black polymer with thumbhole/pistol grip, sling swivels; beavertail forend. **Sights:** Bead front. **Features:** Buttplate removes to expose storage for extra ammunition; forend also holds extra ammunition. Black or nickel finish. Introduced 1993. From New England Firearms.

Price: Black **$161.00**
Price: Nickel **$185.00**
Price: 410/45 Colt, black **$203.00**
Price: 410/45 Colt, nickel **$221.00**

NEW ENGLAND FIREARMS STANDARD PARDNER

Gauge: 12, 20, 410, 3" chamber; 16, 28, 2-3/4" chamber. **Barrel:** 12 ga.—28" (Full, Mod.), 32" (Full); 16 ga.—28" (Full), 32" (Full); 20 ga.—26" (Full, Mod.); 28 ga.—26" (Mod.); 410-bore—26" (Full). **Weight:** 5-6 lbs. **Length:** 43" overall (28" barrel). **Stock:** Walnut-finished hardwood with full pistol grip. **Sights:** Bead front. **Features:** Transfer bar ignition; break-open action with side-lever release. Introduced 1987. From New England Firearms.
Price: **$131.00**
Price: Youth model (12, 20, 28 ga., 410, 22" barrel, recoil pad). . **$140.00**
Price: 12 ga., 32" (Full) **$147.00**

ROSSI SINGLE-SHOT SHOTGUN

Gauge: 12, 20, 2-3/4" chamber; 410, 3" chamber. **Barrel:** 28" full, 22"Youth. **Weight:** 5 lbs. **Stock:** Stained hardwood. **Sights:** Bead. **Features:** Break-open, positive ejection, internal transfer bar, trigger block.
Price: **$101.00**

ROSSI MATCHED PAIR SINGLE-SHOT SHOTGUN/RIFLE

Gauge: 410, 20 or 12. **Barrel:** 22" (18.5"Youth), 28" (23"full). **Weight:** 4-6 lbs **Stock:** Hardwood (brown or black finish). **Sights:** Bead front. **Features:** Break-open internal transfer bar manual external safety; blued or stainless steel finish; sling-swivel studs; includes matched 22 LR or 22 Mag. barrel with fully adjustable front and rear sight. Trigger block system. Introduced 2001. Imported by BrazTech/Taurus.
Price: Blue **$139.95**
Price: Stainless steel **$169.95**

RUGER KTS-1234-BRE TRAP MODEL SINGLE-BARREL SHOTGUN

Gauge: 12, 2-3/4" chamber. **Barrel:** 34". **Weight:** 9 lbs. **Length:** 50-1/2" overall. **Stock:** Select walnut checkered; adjustable pull length 13"-15". **Features:** Fully adjustable rib for pattern position; adjustable stock comb cast for right- or left-handed shooters; straight grooves the length of barrel to keep wad from rotating for pattern improvement. Full and modified choke tubes supplied. Gold inlaid eagle and Ruger name on receiver. Introduced 2000. From Sturm Ruger & Co.
Price: **$2,850.00**

Ruger KTS-1234-BRE

Savage 210F Master Shot Slug Gun

Tar-Hunt RSG-20 Mountaineer

Thompson/Center Encore Rifled Slug

Thompson/Center
Encore Turkey

SAVAGE MODEL 210F MASTER SHOT SLUG GUN

Gauge: 12, 3" chamber; 2-shot magazine. **Barrel:** 24" 1:35" rifling twist. **Weight:** 7-1/2 lbs. **Length:** 43.5" overall. **Stock:** Glass-filled polymer with positive checkering. **Features:** Based on the Savage Model 110 action; 60 bolt lift; controlled round feed; comes with scope mount. Introduced 1996. Made in U.S. by Savage Arms.

Price: $440.00
Price: (Camo) $472.00

STOEGER SINGLE-SHOT SHOTGUN

Gauge: 12, 20, 410, 2-3/4", 3" chambers. **Barrel:** 26", 28". **Weight:** 5.4 lbs. **gth:** 40-1/2" to 42-1/2" overall. **Sights:** Brass bead. **Features:** 410 ga. full fixed choke tubes, rest M, screw-in. 410 ga. 12 ga. hardwood pistol-grip stock and forend. 20 ga. 26" bbl., hardwood forend.

Price: Blue; Youth $109.00
Price: Youth with English stock $119.00

TAR-HUNT RSG-12 PROFESSIONAL RIFLED SLUG GUN

Gauge: 12, 16 & 20, 2-3/4" or 3" chamber, 1-shot magazine. **Barrel:** 21-1/2"; 23" fully rifled, with muzzle brake. **Weight:** 7-3/4 lbs. **Length:** 41-1/2" overall. **Stock:** Matte black McMillan fiberglass with Pachmayr Decelerator pad. **Sights:** None furnished; comes with Leupold windage or Weaver bases. **Features:** Uses rifle-style action with two locking lugs; two-position safety; Shaw barrel; single-stage, trigger; muzzle brake. Many options available. Right- and left-hand models at same prices. Introduced 1991. Made in U.S. by Tar-Hunt Custom Rifles, Inc.

Price: Professional model, right- or left-hand, Elite 16 ga. $1,995.00
Price: Millennium/10th Anniversary models (limited to 25 guns):
NP-3 nickel/Teflon metal finish, black McMillan
Fibergrain stock, Jewell adj. trigger $2,300.00

Tar-Hunt RSG-20 Mountaineer Slug Gun

Similar to the RSG-12 Professional except chambered for 20 gauge (2-3/4") shells; 21" Shaw rifled barrel, with muzzle brake; two-lug bolt; one-shot blind magazine; matte black finish; McMillan fiberglass stock with Pachmayr Decelerator pad; receiver drilled and tapped for Rem. 700 bases. Weighs 6-1/2 lbs. Introduced 1997. Made in U.S. by Tar-Hunt Custom Rifles, Inc.

Price: $1,695.00

THOMPSON/CENTER ENCORE RIFLED SLUG GUN

Gauge: 20, 3" chamber. **Barrel:** 26", fully rifled. **Weight:** About 7 pounds. **Length:** 40-1/2" overall. **Stock:** Walnut with walnut forearm. **Sights:** Steel, click-adjustable rear and ramp-style front, both with fiber optics. **Features:** Encore system features a variety of rifle, shotgun and muzzle-loading rifle barrels interchangeable with the same frame. Break-open design operates by pulling up and back on trigger guard spur. Composite stock and forearm available. Introduced 2000.

Price: $665.00

THOMPSON/CENTER ENCORE TURKEY GUN

Gauge: 12 ga. **Barrel:** 24". **Features:** Blued, high definition Realtree Hardwoods HD camo.

Price: $726.00

Designs for utility, suitable for and adaptable to competitions and other sporting purposes.

Benelli M3 Convertible

Benelli M1 Tactical

Benelli M1 Practical

Fabarm FP6

BENELLI M3 CONVERTIBLE SHOTGUN

Gauge: 12, 2-3/4", 3" chambers, 5-shot magazine. **Barrel:** 19-3/4" (Cyl.). **Weight:** 7 lbs., 4oz. **Length:** 41" overall. **Stock:** High-impact polymer with sling loop in side of butt; rubberized pistol grip on stock. **Sights:** Open rifle, fully adjustable. Ghost ring and rifle type. **Features:** Combination pump/auto action. Alloy receiver with inertia recoil rotating locking lug bolt; matte finish; automatic shell release lever. Introduced 1989. Imported by Benelli USA. Price with pistol grip, open rifle sights.
Price: With standard stock, open rifle sights. **$1,135.00**
Price: With ghost ring sight system, standard stock **$1,185.00**
Price: With ghost ring sights, pistol grip stock **$1,200.00**

BENELLI M1 TACTICAL SHOTGUN

Gauge: 12, 2-3/4", 3" chambers, 5-shot magazine. **Barrel:** 18.5" IC, M, F choke tubes. **Weight:** 6.7 lbs. **Length:** 39.75" overall. **Stock:** Black polymer. **Sights:** Rifle type with ghost ring system, tritium night sights optional. **Features:** Semi-auto intertia recoil action. Cross-bolt safety; bolt release button; matte-finish metal. Introduced 1993. Imported from Italy by Benelli USA.
Price: With rifle sights, standard stock **$945.00**
Price: With ghost ring rifle sights, standard stock **$1,015.00**
Price: With ghost ring sights, pistol grip stock **$1,030.00**
Price: With rifle sights, pistol grip stock **$960.00**
Price: MI Entry, 14" barrel (law enforcement only) . **$980.00 to $1,060.00**

Benelli M1 Practical

Similar to M1 Field Shotgun, Picatinny receiver rail for scope mounting, nine-round magazine, 26" compensated barrel and ghost ring sights. Designed for IPSC competition.
Price: **$1,265.00**

BERETTA MODEL 1201FP GHOST RING AUTO SHOTGUN

Gauge: 12, 3" chamber. **Barrel:** 18" (Cyl.). **Weight:** 6.3 lbs. **Stock:** Special strengthened technopolymer, matte black finish. **Stock:** Fixed rifle type. **Features:** Has 5-shot magazine. Adjustable Ghost Ring rear sight, tritium front. Introduced 1988. Imported from Italy by Beretta U.S.A.
Price: **$890.00**

CROSSFIRE SHOTGUN/RIFLE

Gauge/Caliber: 12, 2-3/4" Chamber: 4-shot/223 Rem. (5-shot). **Barrel:** 20" (shotgun), 18" (rifle). **Weight:** About 8.6 lbs. **Length:** 40" overall. **Stock:** Composite. **Sights:** Meprolight night sights. Integral Weaver-style scope rail. **Features:** Combination pump-action shotgun, rifle; single selector, single trigger; dual action bars for both upper and lower actions; ambidextrous selector and safety. Introduced 1997. Made in U.S. From Hesco.
Price: About **$1,895.00**
Price: With camo finish **$1,995.00**

FABARM FP6 PUMP SHOTGUN

Gauge: 12, 3" chamber. **Barrel:** 20" (Cyl.); accepts choke tubes. **Weight:** 6.6 lbs. **Length:** 41.25" overall. **Stock:** Black polymer with textured grip, grooved slide handle. **Sights:** Blade front. **Features:** Twin action bars; anodized finish; free carrier for smooth reloading. Introduced 1998. New features include ghost-ring sighting system, low profile Picatinny rail, and pistol grip stock. Imported from Italy by Heckler & Koch, Inc.
Price: (Carbon fiber finish) **$499.00**
Price: With flip-up front sight, Picatinny rail with rear sight, oversize safety button **$499.00**

FABARM TACTICAL SEMI-AUTOMATIC SHOTGUN

Gauge: 12, 3" chamber. **Barrel:** 20". **Weight:** 6.6 lbs. **Length:** 41.2" overall. **Stock:** Polymer or folding. **Sights:** Ghost ring (tritium night sights optional). **Features:** Gas operated; matte receiver; twin forged action bars; oversized bolt handle and safety button; Picatinny rail; includes cylinder bore choke tube. New features include polymer pistol grip stock. Introduced 2001. Imported from Italy by Heckler & Koch Inc.
Price: **$999.00**

Fabarm Tactical

Mossberg Model 500 Persuader

Mossberg Model 500 Persuader

Mossberg Ghost Ring

Mossberg Model HS410

MOSSBERG MODEL 500 PERSUADER SECURITY SHOTGUNS

Gauge: 12, 20, 410, 3" chamber. **Barrel:** 18-1/2", 20" (Cyl.). **Weight:** 7 lbs. **Stock:** Walnut-finished hardwood or black synthetic. **Sights:** Metal bead front. **Features:** Available in 6- or 8-shot models. Top-mounted safety, double action slide bars, swivel studs, rubber recoil pad. Blue, Parkerized, Marinecote finishes. Mossberg Cablelock included. From Mossberg.

Price: 12 or 20 ga., 18-1/2", blue, wood or synthetic stock,
6-shot **$342.00**
Price: Cruiser, 12 or 20 ga., 18-1/2", blue, pistol grip, heat
shield **$347.00**
Price: As above, 410-bore **$335.00**

Mossberg Model 500, 590 Mariner Pump

Similar to the Model 500 or 590 Security except all metal parts finished with Marinecote metal finish to resist rust and corrosion. Synthetic field stock; pistol grip kit included. Mossberg Cablelock included.
Price: 6-shot, 18-1/2" barrel **$510.00**
Price: 9-shot, 20" barrel **$541.00**

Mossberg Model 500, 590 Ghost-Ring Shotguns

Similar to the Model 500 Security except has adjustable blade front, adjustable Ghost-Ring rear sight with protective "ears." Model 500 has 18.5" (Cyl.) barrel, 6-shot capacity; Model 590 has 20" (Cyl.) barrel,

9-shot capacity. Both have synthetic field stock. Mossberg Cablelock included. Introduced 1990. From Mossberg.
Price: 500 parkerized **$454.00**
Price: 590 parkerized **$463.00**
Price: Parkerized Speedfeed stock .... **$568.00 to $634.00**

Mossberg Model HS410 Shotgun

Similar to the Model 500 Security pump except chambered for 20 gauge or 410 with 3" chamber; has pistol grip forend, thick recoil pad, muzzle brake and has special spreader choke on the 18.5" barrel. Overall length is 37.5", weight is 6.25 lbs. Blue finish; synthetic field stock. Mossberg Cablelock and video included. Introduced 1990.
Price: HS 410 .... **$345.00**

MOSSBERG MODEL 590 SHOTGUN

Gauge: 12, 3" chamber. **Barrel:** 20" (Cyl.). **Weight:** 7-1/4 lbs. **Stock:** Synthetic field or Speedfeed. **Sights:** Metal bead front. **Features:** Top-mounted safety, double slide action bars. Comes with heat shield, bayonet lug, swivel studs, rubber recoil pad. Blue, Parkerized or Marinecote finish. Mossberg Cablelock included. From Mossberg.
Price: Blue, synthetic stock **$406.00**
Price: Parkerized, synthetic stock **$527.00**
Price: Parkerized, Speedfeed stock **$568.00**

Mossberg 590 DA

Tactical Response TR-870

Winchester Model 1300 Defender

Winchester Model 1300 Marine

Winchester Model 1300
Camp Defender®

Mossberg 590DA Double-Action Pump Shotgun

Similar to Model 590 except trigger requires a long stroke for each shot, duplicating the trigger pull of double-action-only pistols and revolvers. Available in 12 gauge only with black synthetic stock and parkerized finish with 14" (law enforcement only), 18-1/2" and 20" barrels. Six-shot magazine tube (nine-shot for 20" barrel). Front bead or ghost ring sights. Weighs 7 pounds (18-1/2" barrel). Introduced 2000. From Mossberg.

Price: Bead sight, 6-shot magazine	$510.00
Price: Ghost ring sights, 6-shot magazine	$558.00
Price: Bead sight, 9-shot magazine	$541.00
Price: Ghost ring sights, 9-shot magazine	$597.00

TACTICAL RESPONSE TR-870 STANDARD MODEL SHOTGUN

Gauge: 12, 3" chamber, 7-shot magazine. **Barrel:** 18" (Cyl.). **Weight:** 9 lbs. **Length:** 38" overall. **Stock:** Fiberglass-filled polypropolene with non-snag recoil absorbing butt pad. Nylon tactical forend houses flashlight. **Sights:** Trak-Lock ghost ring sight system. Front sight has tritium insert. **Features:** Highly modified Remington 870P with Parkerized finish. Comes with nylon three-way adjustable sling, high visibility non-binding follower, high performance magazine spring, Jumbo Head safety, and Side Saddle extended 6-shot shell carrier on left side of receiver. Introduced 1991. From Scattergun Technologies, Inc.

Price: Standard model	$815.00
Price: FBI model	$770.00
Price: Patrol model	$595.00
Price: Border Patrol model	$605.00

Price: K-9 model (Rem. 11-87 action)	$995.00
Price: Urban Sniper, Rem. 11-87 action	$1,290.00
Price: Louis Awerbuck model	$705.00
Price: Practical Turkey model	$725.00
Price: Expert model	$1,350.00
Price: Professional model	$815.00
Price: Entry model	$840.00
Price: Compact model	$635.00
Price: SWAT model	$1,195.00

WINCHESTER MODEL 1300 DEFENDER PUMP GUNS

Gauge: 12, 20, 3" chamber, 5- or 8-shot capacity. **Barrel:** 18" (Cyl.). **Weight:** 6-3/4 lbs. **Length:** 38-5/8" overall. **Stock:** Walnut-finished hardwood stock and ribbed forend, synthetic or pistol grip. **Sights:** Metal bead front or TRUGLO® fiber-optic. **Features:** Cross-bolt safety, front-locking rotary bolt, twin action slide bars. Black rubber butt pad. From U.S. Repeating Arms Co.

Price: 8-Shot (black synthetic stock, TRUGLO® sight)	$326.00
Price: 8-Shot Pistol Grip (pistol grip synthetic stock)	$326.00

Winchester Model 1300 Stainless Marine Pump Gun

Same as the Defender 8-Shot except has bright chrome finish, stainless steel barrel, bead front sight. Phosphate coated receiver for corrosion resistance.

Price:	$518.00

Winchester Model 1300 Camp Defender®

Same as the Defender 8-Shot except has hardwood stock and forearm, fully adjustable open sights and 22" barrel with WinChoke® choke tube system (cylinder choke tube included). Weighs 6-7/8 lbs. Introduced 2001. From U.S. Repeating Arms Co.

Price: Camp Defender®	$373.00

SHOTGUNS

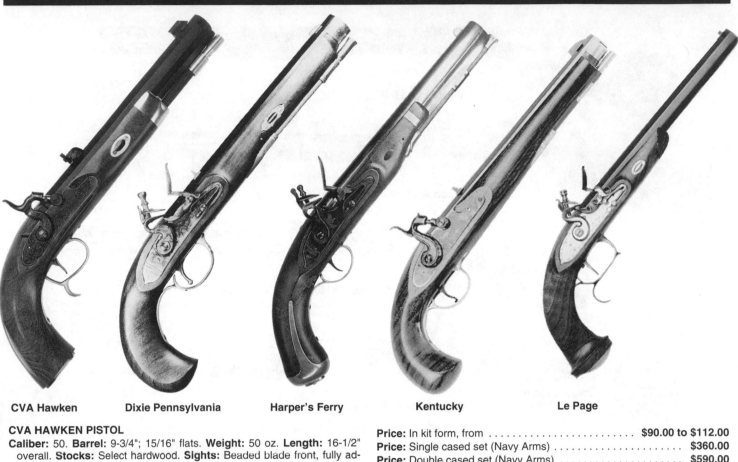

CVA Hawken   Dixie Pennsylvania   Harper's Ferry   Kentucky   Le Page

CVA HAWKEN PISTOL

Caliber: 50. **Barrel:** 9-3/4"; 15/16" flats. **Weight:** 50 oz. **Length:** 16-1/2" overall. **Stocks:** Select hardwood. **Sights:** Beaded blade front, fully adjustable open rear. **Features:** Color case-hardened lock, polished brass wedge plate, instep, ramrod thimble, trigger guard, grip cap. Imported by CVA.

Price: **$167.95**
Price: Kit **$127.95**

DIXIE PENNSYLVANIA PISTOL

Caliber: 44 (.430" round ball). **Barrel:** 10", (7/8" octagon). **Weight:** 2-1/2 labs. **Stocks:** Walnut-stained hardwood. **Sights:** Blade front, open rear drift-adjustable for windage; brass. **Features:** Available in flint only. Brass trigger guard, thimbles, instep, wedge plates; high-luster blue barrel. Imported from Italy by Dixie Gun Works.

Price: Finished **$215.00**
Price: Kit **$195.00**

FRENCH-STYLE DUELING PISTOL

Caliber: 44. **Barrel:** 10". **Weight:** 35 oz. **Length:** 15-3/4" overall. **Stocks:** Carved walnut. **Sights:** Fixed. **Features:** Comes with velvet-lined case and accessories. Imported by Mandall Shooting Supplies.

Price: **$295.00**

HARPER'S FERRY 1806 PISTOL

Caliber: 58 (.570" round ball). **Barrel:** 10". **Weight:** 40 oz. **Length:** 16" overall. **Stocks:** Walnut. **Sights:** Fixed. **Features:** Case-hardened lock, brass-mounted browned barrel. Replica of the first U.S. Gov't.-made flintlock pistol. Imported by Navy Arms, Dixie Gun Works.

Price: . . . . **$275.00 to $405.00**
Price: Kit (Dixie) **$249.00**

KENTUCKY FLINTLOCK PISTOL

Caliber: 44, 45. **Barrel:** 10-1/8". **Weight:** 32 oz. **Length:** 15-1/2" overall. **Stocks:** Walnut. **Sights:** Fixed. **Features:** Specifications, including caliber, weight and length may vary with importer. Case-hardened lock, blued barrel; available also as brass barrel flint Model 1821. Imported by Navy Arms, The Armoury, Dixie Gun Works.

Price: **$300.00**

Price: In kit form, from . . . . **$90.00 to $112.00**
Price: Single cased set (Navy Arms) **$360.00**
Price: Double cased set (Navy Arms) **$590.00**

Kentucky Percussion Pistol

Similar to flint version but percussion lock. Imported by The Armoury, Navy Arms, CVA (50-cal.).

Price: . . . . **$129.95 to $225.00**
Price: Blued steel barrel (CVA) **$167.95**
Price: Kit form (CVA) **$119.95**
Price: Steel barrel (Armoury) **$179.00**
Price: Single cased set (Navy Arms) **$355.00**
Price: Double cased set (Navy Arms) **$600.00**

LE PAGE PERCUSSION DUELING PISTOL

Caliber: 44. **Barrel:** 10", rifled. **Weight:** 40 oz. **Length:** 16" overall. **Stocks:** Walnut, fluted butt. **Sights:** Blade front, notch rear. **Features:** Double-set triggers. Blued barrel; trigger guard and buttcap are polished silver. Imported by Dixie Gun Works.

Price: **$450.00**

LYMAN PLAINS PISTOL

Caliber: 50 or 54. **Barrel:** 8"; 1:30" twist, both calibers. **Weight:** 50 oz. **Length:** 15" overall. **Stocks:** Walnut half-stock. **Sights:** Blade front, square notch rear adjustable for windage. **Features:** Polished brass trigger guard and ramrod tip, color case-hardened coil spring lock, spring-loaded trigger, stainless steel nipple, blackened iron furniture. Hooked patent breech, detachable belt hook. Introduced 1981. From Lyman Products.

Price: Finished **$244.95**
Price: Kit **$189.95**

PEDERSOLI MANG TARGET PISTOL

Caliber: 38. **Barrel:** 10.5", octagonal; 1:15" twist. **Weight:** 2.5 lbs. **Length:** 17.25" overall. **Stocks:** Walnut with fluted grip. **Sights:** Blade front, open rear adjustable for windage. **Features:** Browned barrel, polished breech plug, rest color case-hardened. Imported from Italy by Dixie Gun Works.

Price: **$895.00**

Lyman Plains Pistol   Pedersoli Mang   Queen Anne   Thompson/Center Encore   Traditions Pioneer   Traditions William Parker

QUEEN ANNE FLINTLOCK PISTOL

Caliber: 50 (.490" round ball). **Barrel:** 7-1/2", smoothbore. **Stocks:** Walnut. **Sights:** None. **Features:** Browned steel barrel, fluted brass trigger guard, brass mask on butt. Lockplate left in the white. Made by Pedersoli in Italy. Introduced 1983. Imported by Dixie Gun Works.

Price: **$245.00**
Price: Kit **$195.00**

THOMPSON/CENTER ENCORE 209x50 MAGNUM PISTOL

Caliber: 50. **Barrel:** 15"; 1:20" twist. **Weight:** About 4 lbs. Grips: American walnut grip and forend. **Sights:** Click-adjustable, steel rear, ramp front. **Features:** Uses 209 shotgun primer for closed-breech ignition; accepts charges up to 110 grains of FFg black powder or two, 50-grain Pyrodex pellets. Introduced 2000.

Price: **$611.00**
Price: (barrel only) **$325.00**

TRADITIONS BUCKHUNTER PRO IN-LINE PISTOL

Caliber: 50. **Barrel:** 9-1/2", round. **Weight:** 48 oz. **Length:** 14" overall. **Stocks:** Smooth walnut or black epoxy-coated hardwood grip and forend. **Sights:** Beaded blade front, folding adjustable rear. **Features:** Thumb safety; removable stainless steel breech plug; adjustable trigger; barrel drilled and tapped for scope mounting. From Traditions.

Price: With walnut grip **$229.00**
Price: Nickel with black grip **$239.00**
Price: With walnut grip and 12-1/2" barrel **$239.00**
Price: Nickel with black grip, muzzle brake and 14-3/4" fluted barrel. **$289.00**
Price: 45 cal. nickel w/bl. grip, muzzlebrake and 14-3/4" fluted bbl.
. . . . **$289.00**

TRADITIONS KENTUCKY PISTOL

Caliber: 50. **Barrel:** 10"; octagon with 7/8" flats; 1:20" twist. **Weight:** 40 oz. **Length:** 15" overall. **Stocks:** Stained beech. **Sights:** Blade front, fixed rear. **Features:** Birds-head grip; brass thimbles; color case-hardened lock. Percussion only. Introduced 1995. From Traditions.

Price: Finished **$139.00**
Price: Kit **$109.00**

TRADITIONS PIONEER PISTOL

Caliber: 45. **Barrel:** 9-5/8"; 13/16" flats, 1:16" twist. **Weight:** 31 oz. **Length:** 15" overall. **Stocks:** Beech. **Sights:** Blade front, fixed rear. **Features:**

Traditions Buckhunter Pro

V-type mainspring. Single trigger. German silver furniture, blackened hardware. From Traditions.

Price: **$139.00**
Price: Kit **$119.00**

TRADITIONS TRAPPER PISTOL

Caliber: 50. **Barrel:** 9-3/4"; 7/8" flats; 1:20" twist. **Weight:** 2-3/4 lbs. **Length:** 16" overall. **Stocks:** Beech. **Sights:** Blade front, adjustable rear. **Features:** Double-set triggers; brass buttcap, trigger guard, wedge plate, forend tip, thimble. From Traditions.

Price: Percussion **$189.00**
Price: Flintlock **$209.00**
Price: Kit **$149.00**

TRADITIONS VEST-POCKET DERRINGER

Caliber: 31. **Barrel:** 2-1/4"; brass. **Weight:** 8 oz. **Length:** 4-3/4" overall. **Stocks:** Simulated ivory. **Sights:** Beed front. **Features:** Replica of riverboat gamblers' derringer; authentic spur trigger. From Traditions.

Price: **$109.00**

TRADITIONS WILLIAM PARKER PISTOL

Caliber: 50. **Barrel:** 10-3/8"; 15/16" flats; polished steel. **Weight:** 37 oz. **Length:** 17-1/2" overall. **Stocks:** Walnut with checkered grip. **Sights:** Brass blade front, fixed rear. **Features:** Replica dueling pistol with 1:20" twist, hooked breech. Brass wedge plate, trigger guard, cap guard; separate ramrod. Double-set triggers. Polished steel barrel, lock. Imported by Traditions.

Price: **$269.00**

BLACKPOWDER REVOLVERS

Army 1860

Baby Dragoon 1848

Dixie Wyatt Earp

Le Mat Revolver

Navy Arms 1836 Paterson

ARMY 1860 PERCUSSION REVOLVER

Caliber: 44, 6-shot. **Barrel:** 8". **Weight:** 40 oz. **Length:** 13-5/8" overall. **Stocks:** Walnut. **Sights:** Fixed. **Features:** Engraved Navy scene on cylinder; brass trigger guard; case-hardened frame, loading lever and hammer. Some importers supply pistol cut for detachable shoulder stock, have accessory stock available. Imported by Cabela's (1860 Lawman), E.M.F., Navy Arms, The Armoury, Cimarron, Dixie Gun Works (half-fluted cylinder, not roll engraved), Euroarms of America (brass or steel model), Armsport, Traditions (brass or steel), Uberti U.S.A. Inc., United States Patent Fire-Arms.

Price: About **$190.00**
Price: Hartford model, steel frame, German silver trim,
    cartouches (E.M.F.) **$215.00**
Price: Single cased set (Navy Arms) **$300.00**
Price: Double cased set (Navy Arms). **$490.00**
Price: 1861 Navy: Same as Army except 36-cal., 7-1/2" bbl., weighs 41 oz., cut for shoulder stock; round cylinder (fluted available), from Cabela's, CVA (brass frame, 44-cal.), United States Patent Fire-Arms
    . . . . **$99.95 to $385.00**
Price: Steel frame kit (E.M.F., Euroarms). . . . . **$125.00 to $216.25**
Price: Colt Army Police, fluted cyl., 5-1/2", 36-cal. (Cabela's) . . . **$124.95**
Price: With nickeled frame, barrel and backstrap, gold-tone fluted cylinder, trigger and hammer, simulated ivory grips (Traditions) **$199.00**

BABY DRAGOON 1848, 1849 POCKET, WELLS FARGO

Caliber: 31. **Barrel:** 3", 4", 5", 6"; seven-groove; RH twist. **Weight:** About 21 oz. **Stocks:** Varnished walnut. **Sights:** Brass pin front, hammer notch rear. **Features:** No loading lever on Baby Dragoon or Wells Fargo models. Unfluted cylinder with stagecoach holdup scene; cupped cylinder pin; no grease grooves; one safety pin on cylinder and slot in hammer face; straight (flat) mainspring. From Armsport, Cimarron F.A. Co., Dixie Gun Works, Uberti U.S.A. Inc.

Price: 6" barrel, with loading lever (Dixie Gun Works) **$275.00**
Price: 4" (Uberti USA Inc.) **$335.00**

CABELA'S 1860 ARMY SNUBNOSE REVOLVER

NEW! **Caliber:** .44. **Barrel:** 3". **Weight:** 2 lbs., 3 oz. **Length:** 9" overall. **Grips:** Hardwood. **Sights:** Blade front, hammer notch near. **Features:** Shortened barrels sans loading lever. Separate brass loading tool included.
Price: . . . . **$149.99** (revolver only); **$189.99** (with starter kit).

CABELA'S 1862 POLICE SNUBNOSE REVOLVER

NEW! **Caliber:** .36. **Barrel:** 3". **Weight:** 2 lbs., 3 oz. **Length:** 8.5" overall. **Grips:** Hardwood. **Sights:** Blade front, hammer notch rear. **Features:** Shortened barrel, removed loading lever. Separate brass loading tool included.
Price: . . . . **$169.99** (revolver only); **$209.99** (with starter kit).

DIXIE WYATT EARP REVOLVER

Caliber: 44. **Barrel:** 12", octagon. **Weight:** 46 oz. **Length:** 18" overall. **Stocks:** Two-piece walnut. **Sights:** Fixed. **Features:** Highly polished brass frame, backstrap and trigger guard; blued barrel and cylinder; case-hardened hammer, trigger and loading lever. Navy-size shoulder stock ($45) will fit with minor fitting. From Dixie Gun Works.
Price: **$160.00**

LE MAT REVOLVER

Caliber: 44/65. **Barrel:** 6-3/4" (revolver); 4-7/8" (single shot). **Weight:** 3 lbs., 7 oz. **Stocks:** Hand-checkered walnut. **Sights:** Post front, hammer notch rear. **Features:** Exact reproduction with all-steel construction; 44-cal. 9-shot cylinder, 65-cal. single barrel; color case-hardened hammer with selector; spur trigger guard; ring at butt; lever-type barrel release. From Navy Arms.
Price: Cavalry model (lanyard ring, spur trigger guard) **$595.00**
Price: Army model (round trigger guard, pin-type barrel release) **$595.00**
Price: Naval-style (thumb selector on hammer) **$595.00**

NAVY ARMS NEW MODEL POCKET REVOLVER

Caliber: 31, 5-shot. **Barrel:** 3-1/2", octagon. **Weight:** 15 oz. **Length:** 7-3/4". **Stocks:** Two-piece walnut. **Sights:** Fixed. **Features:** Replica of the Remington New Model Pocket. Available with polisehd brass frame or nickel plated finish. Introduced 2000. Imported by Navy Arms.
Price: **$300.00**

NAVY ARMS 1836 PATERSON REVOLVER

Features: Hidden trigger, 36 cal., blued barrel, replica of 5-shooter, roll-engraved with stagecoach hold-up.
Price: . . . . **$340.00 to $499.00**

BLACKPOWDER REVOLVERS

North American Companion

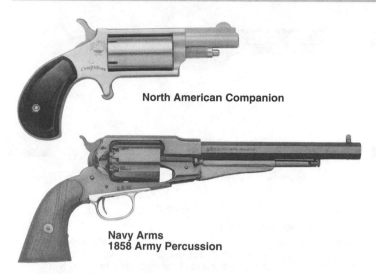

Navy Arms
1858 Army Percussion

Pocket Police 1862

Rogers & Spencer

Ruger Old Army

NAVY MODEL 1851 PERCUSSION REVOLVER

Caliber: 36, 44, 6-shot. **Barrel:** 7-1/2". **Weight:** 44 oz. **Length:** 13" overall. **Stocks:** Walnut finish. **Sights:** Post front, hammer notch rear. **Features:** Brass backstrap and trigger guard; some have 1st Model squareback trigger guard, engraved cylinder with navy battle scene; case hardened frame, hammer, loading lever. Imported by The Armoury, Cabela's, Cimarron F.A. Co., Navy Arms, E.M.F., Dixie Gun Works, Euroarms of America, Armsport, CVA (44-cal. only), Traditions (44 only), Uberti U.S.A. Inc., United States Patent Fire-Arms.

Price: Brass frame	$99.95 to $385.00
Price: Steel frame	$130.00 to $285.00
Price: Kit form	$110.00 to $123.95
Price: Engraved model (Dixie Gun Works)	$182.50
Price: Single cased set, steel frame (Navy Arms)	$280.00
Price: Double cased set, steel frame (Navy Arms)	$455.00
Price: Confederate Navy (Cabela's)	$89.99
Price: Hartford model, steel frame, German silver trim, cartouche (E.M.F.)	$190.00

NEW MODEL 1858 ARMY PERCUSSION REVOLVER

Caliber: 36 or 44, 6-shot. **Barrel:** 6-1/2" or 8". **Weight:** 38 oz. **Length:** 13-1/2" overall. **Stocks:** Walnut. **Sights:** Blade front, groove-in-frame rear. **Features:** Replica of Remington Model 1858. Also available from some importers as Army Model Belt Revolver in 36-cal., a shortened and lightened version of the 44. Target Model (Uberti U.S.A. Inc., Navy Arms) has fully adjustable target rear sight, target front, 36 or 44. Imported by Cabela's, Cimarron F.A. Co., CVA (as 1858 Army, brass frame, 44 only), Dixie Gun Works, Navy Arms, The Armoury, E.M.F., Euroarms of America (engraved, stainless and plain), Armsport, Traditions (44 only), Uberti U.S.A. Inc.

Price: Steel frame, about	$99.95 to $280.00
Price: Steel frame kit (Euroarms, Navy Arms)	$115.95 to $150.00
Price: Single cased set (Navy Arms)	$290.00
Price: Double cased set (Navy Arms)	$480.00
Price: Stainless steel Model 1858 (Euroarms, Uberti U.S.A. Inc., Cabela's, Navy Arms, Armsport, Traditions)	$169.95 to $380.00
Price: Target Model, adjustable rear sight (Cabela's, Euroarms, Uberti U.S.A. Inc., Stone Mountain Arms)	$95.95 to $399.00
Price: Brass frame (CVA, Cabela's, Traditions, Navy Arms)	$79.95 to $159.95
Price: As above, kit (Dixie Gun Works, Navy Arms)	$145.00 to $188.95
Price: Buffalo model, 44-cal. (Cabela's)	$119.99
Price: Hartford model, steel frame, German silver trim, cartouche (E.M.F.)	$215.00

NORTH AMERICAN COMPANION PERCUSSION REVOLVER

Caliber: 22. **Barrel:** 1-1/8". **Weight:** 5.1 oz. **Length:** 4-5/10" overall. **Stocks:** Laminated wood. **Sights:** Blade front, notch fixed rear. **Features:** All stainless steel construction. Uses standard #11 percussion caps. Comes with bullets, powder measure, bullet seater, leather clip holster, gun rug. Long Rifle or Magnum frame size. Introduced 1996. Made in U.S. by North American Arms.

Price: Long Rifle frame	$156.00

North American Magnum Companion Percussion Revolver

Similar to the Companion except has larger frame. Weighs 7.2 oz., has 1-5/8" barrel, measures 5-7/16" overall. Comes with bullets, powder measure, bullet seater, leather clip holster, gun rag. Introduced 1996. Made in U.S. by North American Arms.

Price:	$174.00

POCKET POLICE 1862 PERCUSSION REVOLVER

Caliber: 36, 5-shot. **Barrel:** 4-1/2", 5-1/2", 6-1/2", 7-1/2". **Weight:** 26 oz. **Length:** 12" overall (6-1/2" bbl.). **Stocks:** Walnut. **Sights:** Fixed. **Features:** Round tapered barrel; half-fluted and rebated cylinder; case-hardened frame, loading lever and hammer; silver or brass trigger guard and backstrap. Imported by Dixie Gun Works, Navy Arms (5-1/2" only), Uberti U.S.A. Inc. (5-1/2", 6-1/2" only), United States Patent Fire-Arms and Cimarron F.A. Co.

Price: About	$139.95 to $335.00
Price: Single cased set with accessories (Navy Arms)	$365.00
Price: Hartford model, steel frame, German silver trim, cartouche (E.M.F.)	$215.00

ROGERS & SPENCER PERCUSSION REVOLVER

Caliber: 44. **Barrel:** 7-1/2". **Weight:** 47 oz. **Length:** 13-3/4" overall. **Stocks:** Walnut. **Sights:** Cone front, integral groove in frame for rear. **Features:** Accurate reproduction of a Civil War design. Solid frame; extra large nipple cut-out on rear of cylinder; loading lever and cylinder easily removed for cleaning. From Dixie Gun Works, Euroarms of America (standard blue, engraved, burnished, target models), Navy Arms.

Price:	$160.00 to $299.95
Price: Nickel-plated	$215.00
Price: Engraved (Euroarms)	$287.00
Price: Kit version	$245.00 to $252.00
Price: Target version (Euroarms)	$239.00 to $270.00
Price: Burnished London Gray (Euroarms)	$245.00 to $270.00

BLACKPOWDER REVOLVERS

Spiller & Burr

Texas Paterson

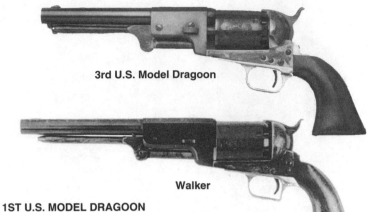

3rd U.S. Model Dragoon

Walker

RUGER OLD ARMY PERCUSSION REVOLVER

Caliber: 45, 6-shot. Uses .457" dia. lead bullets or 454 conical. **Barrel:** 7-1/2" (6-groove; 1:16" twist). **Weight:** 2-7/8 lbs. **Length:** 13-1/2" overall. **Stocks:** Rosewood. **Sights:** Ramp front, rear adjustable for windage and elevation; or fixed (groove). **Features:** Stainless steel; standard size nipples, chrome-moly steel cylinder and frame, same lockwork as original Super Blackhawk. Also stainless steel. Includes hard case and lock. Made in USA. From Sturm, Ruger & Co.

Price: Blued steel, fixed sight (Model BP-5F) $499.00
Price: Stainless steel, fixed sight (Model KBP-5F-I) $576.00
Price: Stainless steel (Model KBP-7) $535.00
Price: Blued steel (Model BP-7) $499.00
Price: Blued steel, fixed sight (BP-7F) $499.00
Price: Stainless steel, fixed sight (KBP-7F) $535.00

SHERIFF MODEL 1851 PERCUSSION REVOLVER

Caliber: 36, 44, 6-shot. **Barrel:** 5". **Weight:** 40 oz. **Length:** 10-1/2" overall. **Stocks:** Walnut. **Sights:** Fixed. **Features:** Brass backstrap and trigger guard; engraved navy scene; case-hardened frame, hammer, loading lever. Imported by E.M.F.

Price: Steel frame $169.95
Price: Brass frame $140.00

SPILLER & BURR REVOLVER

Caliber: 36 (.375" round ball). **Barrel:** 7", octagon. **Weight:** 2-1/2 lbs. **Length:** 12-1/2" overall. **Stocks:** Two-piece walnut. **Sights:** Fixed. **Features:** Reproduction of the C.S.A. revolver. Brass frame and trigger guard. Also available as a kit. From Dixie Gun Works, Navy Arms.

Price: $150.00
Price: Kit form (Dixie) $125.00
Price: Single cased set (Navy Arms) $270.00
Price: Double cased set (Navy Arms) $430.00

TEXAS PATERSON 1836 REVOLVER

Caliber: 36 (.375" round ball). **Barrel:** 7-1/2". **Weight:** 42 oz. **Stocks:** One-piece walnut. **Sights:** Fixed. **Features:** Copy of Sam Colt's first commercially-made revolving pistol. Has no loading lever but comes with loading tool. From Cimarron F.A. Co., Dixie Gun Works, Navy Arms, Uberti U.S.A. Inc.

Price: About $495.00
Price: With loading lever (Uberti U.S.A. Inc.) $450.00
Price: Engraved (Navy Arms) $485.00

UBERTI 1861 NAVY PERCUSSION REVOLVER

Caliber: 36. **Barrel:** 7-1/2", round. **Weight:** 40-1/2 oz. **Stocks:** One-piece oiled American walnut. **Sights:** Brass pin front, hammer notch rear. **Features:** Rounded trigger guard, German silver blade front sight, "creeping" loading lever. Available with fluted or round cylinder. Imported by Uberti U.S.A. Inc.

Price: Steel backstrap, trigger guard, cut for stock $265.00

1ST U.S. MODEL DRAGOON

Caliber: 44. **Barrel:** 7-1/2", part round, part octagon. **Weight:** 64 oz. **Stocks:** One-piece walnut. **Sights:** German silver blade front, hammer notch rear. **Features:** First model has oval bolt cuts in cylinder, square-back flared trigger guard, V-type mainspring, short trigger. Ranger and Indian scene roll-engraved on cylinder. Color case-hardened frame, loading lever, plunger and hammer; blue barrel, cylinder, trigger and wedge. Available with old-time charcoal blue or standard blue-black finish. Polished brass backstrap and trigger guard. From Cimarron F.A. Co., Dixie Gun Works, Uberti U.S.A. Inc., Navy Arms.

Price: . . . . $295.00 to $435.00

2nd U.S. Model Dragoon Revolver

Similar to the 1st Model except distinguished by rectangular bolt cuts in the cylinder. From Cimarron F.A. Co., Uberti U.S.A. Inc., United States Patent Fire-Arms, Navy Arms, Dixie Gunworks.

Price: . . . . $295.00 to $435.00

3rd U.S. Model Dragoon Revolver

Similar to the 2nd Model except for oval trigger guard, long trigger, modifications to the loading lever and latch. Imported by Cimarron F.A. Co., Uberti U.S.A. Inc., United States Patent Fire-Arms, Dixie Gunworks.

Price: Military model (frame cut for shoulder stock,
steel backstrap) . . . . $295.00 to $435.00
Price: Civilian (brass backstrap, trigger guard) . . . . . $295.00 to $325.00

1862 POCKET NAVY PERCUSSION REVOLVER

Caliber: 36, 5-shot. **Barrel:** 5-1/2", 6-1/2", octagonal, 7-groove, LH twist. **Weight:** 27 oz. (5-1/2" barrel). **Length:** 10-1/2" overall (5-1/2" bbl.). **Stocks:** One-piece varnished walnut. **Sights:** Brass pin front, hammer notch rear. **Features:** Rebated cylinder, hinged loading lever, brass or silver-plated backstrap and trigger guard, color-cased frame, hammer, loading lever, plunger and latch, rest blued. Has original-type markings. From Cimarron F.A. Co., Uberti U.S.A. Inc., Dixie Gunworks.

Price: With brass backstrap, trigger guard . . . . $260.00 to $310.00

1861 Navy Percussion Revolver

Similar to Colt 1851 Navy except has round 7-1/2" barrel, rounded trigger guard, German silver blade front sight, "creeping" loading lever. Fluted or round cylinder. Imported by Cimarron F.A. Co., Uberti U.S.A. Inc., Dixie Gunworks.

Price: Steel backstrap, trigger guard, cut for stock. . . $255.00 to $300.00

WALKER 1847 PERCUSSION REVOLVER

Caliber: 44, 6-shot. **Barrel:** 9". **Weight:** 84 oz. **Length:** 15-1/2" overall. **Stocks:** Walnut. **Sights:** Fixed. **Features:** Case-hardened frame, loading lever and hammer; iron backstrap; brass trigger guard; engraved cylinder. Imported by Cabela's, Cimarron F.A. Co., Navy Arms, Dixie Gun Works, Uberti U.S.A. Inc., E.M.F., Cimarron, Traditions, United States Patent Fire-Arms.

Price: About . . . . $225.00 to $445.00
Price: Single cased set (Navy Arms) $405.00
Price: Deluxe Walker with French fitted case (Navy Arms) $540.00
Price: Hartford model, steel frame, German silver trim,
cartouche (E.M.F.) $295.00

Austin & Halleck 420 LR In-Line

Austin & Halleck 320 LR In-Line

Austin & Halleck Mountain

Cabela's Blue Ridge

Cabela's Traditional Hawken

BLACKPOWDER

ARMOURY R140 HAWKEN RIFLE

Caliber: 45, 50 or 54.**Barrel:** 29". **Weight:** 8-3/4 to 9 lbs. **Length:** 45-3/4" overall. **Stock:** Walnut, with cheekpiece. **Sights:** Dovetail front, fully adjustable rear. **Features:** Octagon barrel, removable breech plug; double set triggers; blued barrel, brass stock fittings, color case-hardened percussion lock. From Armsport, The Armoury.
Price: . . . . **$225.00 to $245.00**

AUSTIN & HALLECK MODEL 420 LR IN-LINE RIFLE

Caliber: 50. **Barrel:** 26", 1" octagon to 3/4" round; 1:28" twist. **Weight:** 7-7/8 lbs. **Length:** 47-1/2" overall. **Stock:** Lightly figured maple in Classic or Monte Carlo style. **Sights:** Ramp front, fully adjustable rear. **Features:** Blue or electroless nickel finish; in-line percussion action with removable weather shroud; Timney adjustable target trigger with sear block safety. Introduced 1998. Made in U.S. by Austin & Halleck.
Price: Blue **$459.00**
Price: Stainless steel **$549.00**
Price: Blue, hand-select highly figured stock **$775.00**
Price: Blue, exhibition-grade Monte Carlo stock. **$1,322.00**
Price: Stainless steel, exhibition-grade Monte Carlo stock. **$1,422.00**

Austin & Halleck Model 320 LR In-Line Rifle

Similar to the Model 420 LR except has black resin synthetic stock with checkered grip and forend. Introduced 1998. Made in U.S. by Austin & Halleck.
Price: Blue **$380.00**
Price: Stainless steel **$447.00**

AUSTIN & HALLECK MOUNTAIN RIFLE

Caliber: 50. **Barrel:** 32"; 1:28" or 1:66" twist; 1" flats. **Weight:** 7-1/2 lbs. **Length:** 49" overall. **Stock:** Curly maple. **Sights:** Silver blade front, buckhorn rear. **Features:** Available in percussion or flintlock; double throw adjustable set triggers; rust brown finish. Made in U.S. by Austin & Halleck.
Price: Flintlock **$539.00**
Price: Percussion **$578.00**
Price: Percussion, fancy wood **$592.00**
Price: Percussion, select wood **$660.00**

BOSTONIAN PERCUSSION RIFLE

Caliber: 45. **Barrel:** 30", octagonal. **Weight:** 7-1/4 lbs. **Length:** 46" overall. **Stock:** Walnut. **Sights:** Blade front, fixed notch rear. **Features:** Color case-hardened lock, brass trigger guard, buttplate, patchbox. Imported from Italy by E.M.F.
Price: **$285.00**

CABELA'S BLUE RIDGE RIFLE

Caliber: 32, 36, 45, 50, .54. **Barrel:** 39", octagonal. **Weight:** About 7-3/4 lbs. **Length:** 55" overall. **Stock:** American black walnut. **Sights:** Blade front, rear drift adjustable for windage. **Features:** Color case-hardened lockplate and cock/hammer, brass trigger guard and buttplate, double set, double-phased triggers. From Cabela's.
Price: Percussion **$409.99**
Price: Flintlock **$429.99**

CABELA'S TRADITIONAL HAWKEN

Caliber: 50, 54. **Barrel:** 29". **Weight:** About 9 lbs. **Stock:** Walnut. **Sights:** Blade front, open adjustable rear. **Features:** Flintlock or percussion. Adjustable double-set triggers. Polished brass furniture, color case-hardened lock. Imported by Cabela's.
Price: Percussion, right-hand **$219.99**
Price: Percussion, left-hand **$219.99**
Price: Flintlock, right-hand **$249.99**

BLACKPOWDER MUSKETS & RIFLES

Cook & Brother

Cabela's Sporterized Hawken Hunter Rifle
Similar to the Traditional Hawken except has more modern stock style with rubber recoil pad, blued furniture, sling swivels. Percussion only, in 50- or 54-caliber.
Price: Carbine or rifle, right-hand **$229.99**

CABELA'S KODIAK EXPRESS DOUBLE RIFLE
Caliber: 50, 54, 58, 72. **Barrel:** Length n/a; 1:48" twist. **Weight:** 9.3 lbs. **Length:** 45-1/4" overall. **Stock:** European walnut, oil finish. **Sights:** Fully adjustable double folding-leaf rear, ramp front. **Features:** Percussion. Barrels regulated to point of aim at 75 yards; polished and engraved lock, top tang and trigger guard. From Cabela's.
Price: 50, 54, 58 calibers **$729.99**
Price: 72 caliber **$759.99**

COOK & BROTHER CONFEDERATE CARBINE
Caliber: 58. **Barrel:** 24". **Weight:** 7-1/2 lbs. **Length:** 40-1/2" overall. **Stock:** Select walnut. **Features:** Recreation of the 1861 New Orleans-made artillery carbine. Color case-hardened lock, browned barrel. Buttplate, trigger guard, barrel bands, sling swivels and nosecap of polished brass. From Euroarms of America.
Price: **$447.00**
Price: Cook & Brother rifle (33" barrel) **$480.00**

CVA YOUTH HUNTER RIFLE
Caliber: 50. **Barrel:** 24"; 1:48" twist, octagonal. **Weight:** 5 lbs. **Length:** 38" overall. **Stock:** Stained hardwood. **Sights:** Bead front, Williams adjustable rear. **Features:** Oversize trigger guard; wooden ramrod. From CVA.
Price: **$135.95**

CVA BOBCAT RIFLE
Caliber: 50 or 54. **Barrel:** 26"; 1:48" twist. **Weight:** 6 lbs. **Length:** 42" overall. **Stock:** Dura-Grip synthetic or wood. **Sights:** Blade front, open rear. **Features:** Oversize trigger guard; wood ramrod; matte black finish. From CVA.
Price: (wood stock, 50 cal. only) **$127.95**
Price: (black synthetic stock, 50 or 54 cal.) **$104.95**

CVA ECLIPSE 209 MAGNUM IN-LINE RIFLE
Caliber: 45, 50. **Barrel:** 24" round; 1:28" rifling. **Weight:** 7.3 lbs. **Length:** 42" overall. **Stock:** Black or Mossy Oak® Break-Up™ camo synthetic. **Sights:** Illuminator Fiber Optic Sight System; drilled and tapped for scope mounting. **Features:** In-line action uses modern trigger with automatic safety; stainless percussion bolt; swivel studs. Three-way ignition system (No. 11, musket or No. 209 shotgun primers). From CVA.
Price: Blue, black stock **$149.95**
Price: Blue, Break-Up™ camo stock **$179.95**

CVA Stag Horn 209 Magnum Rifle
Similar to the Eclipse except has light-gathering Solar Sights, manual safety, black synthetic stock and ramrod. From CVA.
Price: 50 cal. **$121.95**

CVA MOUNTAIN RIFLE
Caliber: 50. **Barrel:** 32"; 1:66" rifling. **Weight:** 8-1/2 lbs. **Length:** NA. **Stock:** American hard maple. **Sights:** Blade front, buckhorn rear. **Features:** Browned steel furniture; German silver wedge plates; patchbox. Made in U.S. From CVA.
Price: **$399.95**
Price: Hunter **$259.95**

CVA ST. LOUIS HAWKEN RIFLE
Caliber: 50, 54. **Barrel:** 28", octagon; 15/16" across flats; 1:48" twist. **Weight:** 8 lbs. **Length:** 44" overall. **Stock:** Select hardwood. **Sights:** Beaded blade front, fully adjustable open rear. **Features:** Fully adjustable double-set triggers; synthetic ramrod (kits have wood); brass patchbox, wedge plates, nosecap, thimbles, trigger guard and buttplate; blued barrel; color case-hardened, engraved lockplate. V-type mainspring. Button breech. Introduced 1981. From CVA.
Price: St. Louis Hawken, finished (50- , 54-cal.) **$229.95**
Price: Left-hand, percussion. **$274.95**

CVA Plainsman Rifle
Similar to the St. Louis Hawken except has 26" blued barrel, overall length of 42". Select hardwood stock. Weighs 6-1/2 lbs. From CVA.
Price: **$179.95**

CVA FIREBOLT MUSKETMAG BOLT-ACTION IN-LINE RIFLES
Caliber: 45 or 50. **Barrel:** 26". **Weight:** 7 lbs. **Length:** 44". **Stock:** Rubber-coated black or Mossy Oak® Break-Up™ camo synthetic. **Sights:** CVA Illuminator Fiber Optic Sight System. **Features:** Bolt-action, in-line ignition system handles up to 150 grains blackpowder or Pyrodex; Nickel or matte blue barrel; removable breech plug; trigger-block safety. Three-way ignition system. From CVA.
Price: FiberGrip/nickel, 50 cal. **$259.95**
Price: Breakup/nickel, 50 cal. **$299.95**
Price: FiberGrip/nickel, 45 cal. **$259.95**
Price: Breakup/nickel, 45 cal. **$299.95**
Price: FiberGrip/blue, 50 cal. **$239.95**
Price: Breakup/blue, 50 cal. **$279.95**
Price: FiberGrip/blue, 45 cal. **$239.95**
Price: Breakup/blue, 45 cal. **$279.95**

CVA HunterBolt 209 Magnum Rifle
Similar to the Firebolt except has 24" barrel and black or Mossy Oak® Break-Up™ synthetic stock. Three-way ignition system. Weighs 6 lbs. From CVA.
Price: 45 or 50 cal. . . . . **$189.95 to $239.95**

DIXIE EARLY AMERICAN JAEGER RIFLE
Caliber: 54. **Barrel:** 27-1/2" octagonal; 1:24" twist. **Weight:** 8-1/4 lbs. **Length:** 43-1/2" overall. **Stock:** American walnut; sliding wooden patchbox on on butt. **Sights:** Notch rear, blade front. **Features:** Flintlock or percussion. Browned steel furniture. Imported from Italy by Dixie Gun Works.
Price: Flintlock or percussion **$750.00**

DIXIE DELUXE CUB RIFLE
Caliber: 40. **Barrel:** 28". **Weight:** 6-1/2 lbs. **Stock:** Walnut. **Sights:** Fixed. **Features:** Short rifle for small game and beginning shooters. Brass patchbox and furniture. Flint or percussion. From Dixie Gun Works.
Price: Finished **$450.00**
Price: Kit. **$390.00**
Price: Super Cub (50-caliber) **$435.00**

DIXIE 1863 SPRINGFIELD MUSKET
Caliber: 58 (.570" patched ball or .575" Minie). **Barrel:** 50", rifled. **Stock:** Walnut stained. **Sights:** Blade front, adjustable ladder-type rear. **Features:** Bright-finish lock, barrel, furniture. Reproduction of the last of the regulation muzzleloaders. Imported from Japan by Dixie Gun Works.
Price: Finished **$595.00**
Price: Kit. **$525.00**

BLACKPOWDER MUSKETS & RIFLES

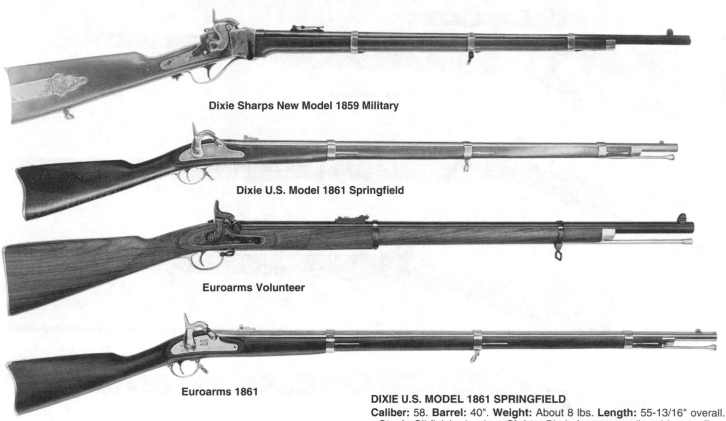

Dixie Sharps New Model 1859 Military

Dixie U.S. Model 1861 Springfield

Euroarms Volunteer

Euroarms 1861

DIXIE INLINE CARBINE

Caliber: 50, 54. **Barrel:** 24"; 1:32" twist. **Weight:** 6.5 lbs. **Length:** 41" overall. **Stock:** Walnut-finished hardwood with Monte Carlo comb. **Sights:** Ramp front with red insert, open fully adjustable rear. **Features:** Sliding "bolt" fully encloses cap and nipple. Fully adjustable trigger, automatic safety. Aluminum ramrod. Imported from Italy by Dixie Gun Works.
Price: **$349.95**

DIXIE PEDERSOLI 1857 MAUSER RIFLE

Caliber: 54. **Barrel:** 39-3/8". **Weight:** N/A. **Length:** 52" overall. **Stock:** European walnut with oil finish, sling swivels. **Sights:** Fully adjustable rear, lug front. **Features:** Percussion (musket caps). Armory bright finish with color case-hardened lock and barrel tang, engraved lockplate, steel ramrod. Introduced 2000. Imported from Italy by Dixie Gun Works.
Price: **$950.00**

DIXIE PEDERSOLI 1766 CHARLEVILLE MUSKET

Caliber: 69. **Barrel:** 44-3/4". **Weight:** 10-1/2 lbs. **Length:** 57-1/2" overall. **Stock:** European walnut with oil finish. **Sights:** Fixed rear, lug front. **Features:** Smoothbore flintlock. Armory bright finish with steel furniture and ramrod. Introduced 2000. Imported from Italy by Dixie Gun Works.
Price: **$865.00**

DIXIE SHARPS NEW MODEL 1859 MILITARY RIFLE

Caliber: 54. **Barrel:** 30", 6-groove; 1:48" twist. **Weight:** 9 lbs. **Length:** 45-1/2" overall. **Stock:** Oiled walnut. **Sights:** Blade front, ladder-style rear. **Features:** Blued barrel, color case-hardened barrel bands, receiver, hammer, nosecap, lever, patchbox cover and buttplate. Introduced 1995. Imported from Italy by Dixie Gun Works.
Price: **$965.00**

DIXIE U.S. MODEL 1816 FLINTLOCK MUSKET

Caliber: 69. **Barrel:** 42", smoothbore. **Weight:** 9.75 lbs. **Length:** 56.5" overall. **Stock:** Walnut with oil finish. **Sights:** Blade front. **Features:** All metal finished "National Armory Bright"; three barrel bands with springs; steel ramrod with button-shaped head. Imported by Dixie Gun Works.
Price: **$825.00**

DIXIE U.S. MODEL 1861 SPRINGFIELD

Caliber: 58. **Barrel:** 40". **Weight:** About 8 lbs. **Length:** 55-13/16" overall. **Stock:** Oil-finished walnut. **Sights:** Blade front, step adjustable rear. **Features:** Exact recreation of original rifle. Sling swivels attached to trigger guard bow and middle barrel band. Lockplate marked "1861" with eagle motif and "U.S. Springfield" in front of hammer; "U.S." stamped on top of buttplate. From Dixie Gun Works.
Price: Kit **$525.00**

E.M.F. 1863 SHARPS MILITARY CARBINE

Caliber: 54. **Barrel:** 22", round. **Weight:** 8 lbs. **Length:** 39" overall. **Stock:** Oiled walnut. **Sights:** Blade front, military ladder-type rear. **Features:** Color case-hardened lock, rest blued. Imported by E.M.F.
Price: **$600.00**

EUROARMS VOLUNTEER TARGET RIFLE

Caliber: .451. **Barrel:** 33" (two-band), 36" (three-band). **Weight:** 11 lbs. (two-band). **Length:** 48.75" overall (two-band). **Stock:** European walnut with checkered wrist and forend. **Sights:** Hooded bead front, adjustable rear with interchangeable leaves. **Features:** Alexander Henry-type rifling with 1:20" twist. Color case-hardened hammer and lockplate, brass trigger guard and nosecap, rest blued. Imported by Euroarms of America, Dixie Gun Works.
Price: Two-band . . . . (Two-band) **$795.00** (Three-band) **$845.00**

EUROARMS 1861 SPRINGFIELD RIFLE

Caliber: 58. **Barrel:** 40". **Weight:** About 10 lbs. **Length:** 55.5" overall. **Stock:** European walnut. **Sights:** Blade front, three-leaf military rear. **Features:** Reproduction of the original three-band rifle. Lockplate marked "1861" with eagle and "U.S. Springfield." Metal left in the white. Imported by Euroarms of America.
Price: **$530.00**

GONIC MODEL 93 M/L RIFLE

Caliber: 45, 50. **Barrel:** 26"; 1:24" twist. **Weight:** 6-1/2 to 7 lbs. **Length:** 43" overall. **Stock:** American hardwood with black finish. **Sights:** Adjustable or aperture rear, hooded post front. **Features:** Adjustable trigger with side safety; unbreakable ram rod; comes with A. Z. scope bases installed. Introduced 1993. Made in U.S. by Gonic Arms, Inc.
Price: Model 93 Standard (blued barrel) **$720.00**
Price: Model 93 Standard (stainless brl., 50 cal. only) **$782.00**

BLACKPOWDER MUSKETS & RIFLES

Gonic Model 93 Thumbhole

Harper's Ferry 1803

J.P. Murray

Kentucky Flintlock

Gonic Model 93 Deluxe M/L Rifle
Similar to the Model 93 except has classic-style walnut or gray laminated wood stock. Introduced 1998. Made in U.S. by Gonic Arms, Inc.
Price: Blue barrel, sights, scope base, choice of stock **$902.00**
Price: Stainless barrel, sights, scope base, choice of stock
(50 cal. only). **$964.00**

Gonic Model 93 Mountain Thumbhole M/L Rifles
Similar to the Model 93 except has high-grade walnut or gray laminate stock with extensive hand-checkered panels, Monte Carlo cheekpiece and beavertail forend; integral muzzle brake. Introduced 1998. Made in U.S. by Gonic Arms, Inc.
Price: Blue or stainless. **$2,700.00**

HARPER'S FERRY 1803 FLINTLOCK RIFLE
Caliber: 54 or 58. **Barrel:** 35". **Weight:** 9 lbs. **Length:** 59-1/2" overall. **Stock:** Walnut with cheekpiece. **Sights:** Brass blade front, fixed steel rear. **Features:** Brass trigger guard, sideplate, buttplate; steel patchbox. Imported by Euroarms of America, Navy Arms (54-cal. only), Cabela's, and Dixie Gun Works.
Price: . . . . **$495.95 to $729.00**
Price: 54-cal. (Navy Arms) **$625.00**
Price: 54-caliber (Cabela's) **$599.99**
Price: 54-caliber (Dixie Gun Works). **$795.00**

HAWKEN RIFLE
Caliber: 45, 50, 54 or 58. **Barrel:** 28", blued, 6-groove rifling. **Weight:** 8-3/4 lbs. **Length:** 44" overall. **Stock:** Walnut with cheekpiece. **Sights:** Blade front, fully adjustable rear. **Features:** Coil mainspring, double-set triggers, polished brass furniture. From Armsport and E.M.F.
Price: . . . . **$220.00 to $345.00**

J.P. MURRAY 1862-1864 CAVALRY CARBINE
Caliber: 58 (.577" Minie). **Barrel:** 23". **Weight:** 7 lbs., 9 oz. **Length:** 39" overall. **Stock:** Walnut. **Sights:** Blade front, rear drift adjustable for windage. **Features:** Browned barrel, color case-hardened lock, blued swivel and band springs, polished brass buttplate, trigger guard, barrel bands. From Euroarms of America.
Price: . . . . **$405.00 to $453.00**

J.P. HENRY TRADE RIFLE
Caliber: 54. **Barrel:** 34"; 1" flats. **Weight:** 8-1/2 lbs. **Length:** 45" overall. **Stock:** Premium curly maple. **Sights:** Silver blade front, fixed buckhorn rear. **Features:** Brass buttplate, side plate, trigger guard and nosecap; browned barrel and lock; L&R Large English percussion lock; single trigger. Made in U.S. by J.P. Gunstocks, Inc.
Price: **$965.50**

KENTUCKIAN RIFLE
Caliber: 44. **Barrel:** 35". **Weight:** 7 lbs. (Rifle), 5-1/2 lbs. (Carbine). **Length:** 51" overall (Rifle), 43" (Carbine). **Stock:** Walnut stain. **Sights:** Brass blade front, steel V-ramp rear. **Features:** Octagon barrel, case-hardened and engraved lockplates. Brass furniture. Imported by Dixie Gun Works.
Price: Flintlock or Percussion **$395.00**

KENTUCKY FLINTLOCK RIFLE
Caliber: 44, 45, or 50. **Barrel:** 35". **Weight:** 7 lbs. **Length:** 50" overall. **Stock:** Walnut stained, brass fittings. **Sights:** Fixed. **Features:** Available in carbine model also, 28" bbl. Some variations in detail, finish. Kits also available from some importers. Imported by The Armoury.
Price: About . . . . **$217.95 to $345.00**

Kentucky Percussion Rifle
Similar to flintlock except percussion lock. Finish and features vary with importer. Imported by The Armoury and CVA.
Price: About **$259.95**
Price: 45- or 50-cal. (Navy Arms). **$425.00**
Price: Kit, 50-cal. (CVA) **$189.95**

BLACKPOWDER MUSKETS & RIFLES

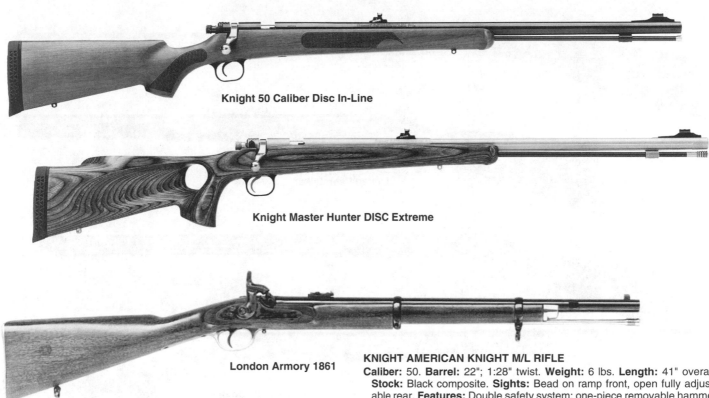

Knight 50 Caliber Disc In-Line

Knight Master Hunter DISC Extreme

London Armory 1861

KNIGHT 50 CALIBER DISC IN-LINE RIFLE

Caliber: 50. **Barrel:** 24", 26". **Weight:** 7 lbs., 14 oz. **Length:** 43" overall (24" barrel). **Stock:** Checkered synthetic with palm swell grip, rubber recoil pad, swivel studs; black, Advantage or Mossy Oak Break-Up camouflage. **Sights:** Bead on ramp front, fully adjustable open rear. **Features:** Bolt-action in-line system uses #209 shotshell primer for ignition; primer is held in plastic drop-in Primer Disc. Available in blued or stainless steel. Made in U.S. by Knight Rifles (Modern Muzzleloading).
Price: .... $439.95 to $632.45

Knight Master Hunter II DISC In-Line Rifle

Similar to Knight 50 caliber DISC rifle except features premier, wood laminated two-tone stock, gold-plated trigger and engraved trigger guard, jeweled bolt and fluted, air-gauged Green Mountain 26" barrel. Length 45" overall, weighs 7 lbs., 7 oz. Includes black composite thumbhole stock. Introduced 2000. Made in U.S. by Knight Rifles (Modern Muzzleloading).
Price: $1,099.95

KNIGHT MUZZLELOADER DISC EXTREME

Caliber: 45 fluted, 50. **Barrel:** 26". **Stock:** Stainless steel laminate, blued walnut, black composite thumbhole with blued or SS. **Sights:** Fully adjustable metallic. **Features:** New full plastic jacket ignition system.
Price: 50 SS laminate................................. $703.95
Price: 45 SS laminate................................. $769.95
Price: 50 blue walnut $626.95
Price: 45 blue walnut $703.95
Price: 50 blue composite $549.95
Price: 45 blue composite $632.45
Price: 50 SS composite $632.45
Price: 45 SS composite $703.95

Knight Master Hunter DISC Extreme

Similar to DISC Extreme except fluted barrel, two-tone laminated thumbhole Monte Carlo-style stock, black composite thumbhole field stock included. Jeweled bolt, adjustable premium trigger.
Price: 50 .... $1,044.95

KNIGHT AMERICAN KNIGHT M/L RIFLE

Caliber: 50. **Barrel:** 22"; 1:28" twist. **Weight:** 6 lbs. **Length:** 41" overall. **Stock:** Black composite. **Sights:** Bead on ramp front, open fully adjustable rear. **Features:** Double safety system; one-piece removable hammer assembly; drilled and tapped for scope mounting. Introduced 1998. Made in U.S. by Knight Rifles.
Price: blued, black comp $197.95
Price: blued, black comp VP $225.45

KNIGHT WOLVERINE 209

Caliber: 50. **Barrel:** 22". **Stock:** HD stock with SS barrel, blued, black composite thumbhole with stainless steel, standard black composite with blued or SS. **Sights:** Metallic with fiber optic. **Features:** Double safety system, adjustable match grade trigger, left-hand model available. Full plastic jacket ignition system.
Price: Starting at $302.45

LONDON ARMORY 2-BAND 1858 ENFIELD

Caliber: .577" Minie, .575" round ball. **Barrel:** 33". **Weight:** 10 lbs. **Length:** 49" overall. **Stock:** Walnut. **Sights:** Folding leaf rear adjustable for elevation. **Features:** Blued barrel, color case-hardened lock and hammer, polished brass buttplate, trigger guard, nosecap. From Navy Arms, Euroarms of America, Dixie Gun Works.
Price: .... $385.00 to $600.00

LONDON ARMORY 1861 ENFIELD MUSKETOON

Caliber: 58, Minie ball. **Barrel:** 24", round. **Weight:** 7 - 7-1/2 lbs. **Length:** 40-1/2" overall. **Stock:** Walnut, with sling swivels. **Sights:** Blade front, graduated military-leaf rear. **Features:** Brass trigger guard, nosecap, buttplate; blued barrel, bands, lockplate, swivels. Imported by Euroarms of America, Navy Arms.
Price: .... $300.00 to $515.00
Price: Kit...................................... $365.00 to $373.00

LONDON ARMORY 3-BAND 1853 ENFIELD

Caliber: 58 (.577" Minie, .575" round ball, .580" maxi ball). **Barrel:** 39". **Weight:** 9-1/2 lbs. **Length:** 54" overall. **Stock:** European walnut. **Sights:** Inverted "V" front, traditional Enfield folding ladder rear. **Features:** Recreation of the famed London Armory Company Pattern 1853 Enfield Musket. One-piece walnut stock, brass buttplate, trigger guard and nosecap. Lockplate marked "London Armoury Co." and with a British crown. Blued Baddeley barrel bands. From Dixie Gun Works, Euroarms of America, Navy Arms.
Price: About .... $350.00 to $645.00
Price: Assembled kit (Dixie, Euroarms of America) $495.00

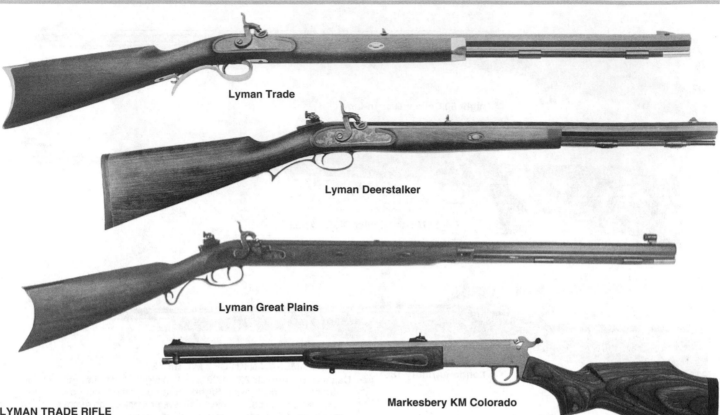

Lyman Trade

Lyman Deerstalker

Lyman Great Plains

Markesbery KM Colorado

LYMAN TRADE RIFLE
Caliber: 50, 54. **Barrel:** 28" octagon;1:48" twist. **Weight:** 8-3/4 lbs. **Length:** 45" overall. **Stock:** European walnut. **Sights:** Blade front, open rear adjustable for windage or optional fixed sights. **Features:** Fast twist rifling for conical bullets. Polished brass furniture with blue steel parts, stainless steel nipple. Hook breech, single trigger, coil spring percussion lock. Steel barrel rib and ramrod ferrules. Introduced 1980. From Lyman.

Price: 50 cal. Percussion **$581.80**
Price: 50 cal. Flintlock. **$652.80**
Price: 54 cal. Percussion **$581.80**
Price: 54 cal. Flintlock. **$652.80**

LYMAN DEERSTALKER RIFLE
Caliber: 50, 54. **Barrel:** 24", octagonal; 1:48" rifling. **Weight:** 7-1/2 lbs. **Stock:** Walnut with black rubber buttpad. **Sights:** Lyman #37MA beaded front, fully adjustable fold-down Lyman #16A rear. **Features:** Stock has less drop for quick sighting. All metal parts are blackened, with color casehardened lock; single trigger. Comes with sling and swivels. Available in flint or percussion. Introduced 1990. From Lyman.

Price: 50 cal. flintlock **$652.80**
Price: 50- or 54-cal., percussion, left-hand, carbine. **$695.40**
Price: 50- or 54-cal., flintlock, left-hand **$645.00**
Price: 54 cal. flintlock **$780.50**
Price: 54 cal. percussion **$821.80**
Price: Stainless steel **$959.80**

LYMAN GREAT PLAINS RIFLE
Caliber: 50- or 54-cal. **Barrel:** 32"; 1:60" twist. **Weight:** 9 lbs. **Stock:** Walnut. **Sights:** Steel blade front, buckhorn rear adjustable for windage and elevation and fixed notch primitive sight included. **Features:** Blued steel furniture. Stainless steel nipple. Coil spring lock, Hawken-style trigger guard and double-set triggers. Round thimbles recessed and sweated into rib. Steel wedge plates and toe plate. Introduced 1979. From Lyman.

Price: Percussion **$469.95**
Price: Flintlock **$494.95**
Price: Percussion kit **$359.95**
Price: Flintlock kit **$384.95**
Price: Left-hand percussion **$474.95**
Price: Left-hand flintlock. **$499.95**

Lyman Great Plains Hunter Rifle
Similar to Great Plains model except 1:32" twist shallow-groove barrel and comes drilled and tapped for Lyman 57GPR peep sight.
Price: **$959.80**

MARKESBERY KM BLACK BEAR M/L RIFLE
Caliber: 36, 45, 50, 54. **Barrel:** 24"; 1:26" twist. **Weight:** 6-1/2 lbs. **Length:** 38-1/2" overall. **Stock:** Two-piece American hardwood, walnut, black laminate, green laminate, black composition, X-Tra or Mossy Oak Break-Up camouflage. **Sights:** Bead front, open fully adjustable rear. **Features:** Interchangeable barrels; exposed hammer; Outer-Line Magnum ignition system uses small rifle primer or standard No. 11 cap and nipple. Blue, black matte, or stainless. Made in U.S. by Markesbery Muzzle Loaders.

Price: American hardwood walnut, blue finish **$536.63**
Price: American hardwood walnut, stainless **$553.09**
Price: Black laminate, blue finish **$539.67**
Price: Black laminate, stainless **$556.27**
Price: Camouflage stock, blue finish **$556.46**
Price: Camouflage stock, stainless **$573.73**
Price: Black composite, blue finish. **$532.65**
Price: Black composite, stainless. **$549.93**
Price: Green laminate, blue finish **$539.00**
Price: Green laminate, stainless **$556.27**

MARKESBERY KM COLORADO ROCKY MOUNTAIN M/L RIFLE
Caliber: 36, 45, 50, 54. **Barrel:** 24"; 1:26" twist. **Weight:** 6-1/2 lbs. **Length:** 38-1/2" overall. **Stock:** American hardwood walnut, green or black laminate. **Sights:** Firesight bead on ramp front, fully adjustable open rear. **Features:** Replicates Reed/Watson rifle of 1851. Straight grip stock with or without two barrel bands, rubber recoil pad, large-spur hammer. Made in U.S. by Markesbery Muzzle Loaders, Inc.

Price: American hardwood walnut, blue finish **$545.92**
Price: Black or green laminate, blue finish **$548.30**
Price: American hardwood walnut, stainless **$563.17**
Price: Black or green laminate, stainless **$566.34**

BLACKPOWDER MUSKETS & RIFLES

Mississippi 1841

Navy Arms Charleville

Navy Arms 1859 Sharps

Markesbery KM Brown Bear M/L Rifle

Similar to KM Black Bear except one-piece thumbhole stock with Monte Carlo comb. Stock in Crotch Walnut composite, green or black laminate, black composite or X-Tra or Mossy Oak Break-Up camouflage. Contact maker for complete price listing. Made in U.S. by Markesbery Muzzle Loaders, Inc.

Price: Black composite, blue finish	$658.83
Price: Crotch Walnut, blue finish	$658.83
Price: Camo composite, blue finish	$682.64
Price: Walnut wood	$662.81
Price: Black wood	$662.81
Price: Black laminated wood	$662.81
Price: Green laminated wood	$662.81
Price: Camo wood	$684.69
Price: Black composite, stainless	$676.11
Price: Crotch Walnut composite, stainless	$676.11
Price: Camo composite, stainless	$697.69
Price: Walnut wood, stainless	$680.07
Price: Black wood, stainless	$680.07
Price: Black laminated wood, stainless	$680.07
Price: Green laminate, stainless	$680.07
Price: Camo wood, stainless	$702.76

Markesbery KM Grizzly Bear M/L Rifle

Similar to KM Black Bear except thumbhole buttstock with Monte Carlo comb. Stock in Crotch Walnut composite, green or black laminate, black composite or X-Tra or Mossy Oak Break-Up camouflage. Contact maker for complete price listing. Made in U.S. by Markesbery Muzzle Loaders, Inc.

Price: Black composite, blue finish	$642.96
Price: Crotch Walnut, blue finish	$642.96
Price: Camo composite, blue finish	$666.67
Price: Walnut wood	$646.93
Price: Black wood	$646.93
Price: Black laminate wood	$646.93
Price: Green laminate wood	$646.93
Price: Camo wood	$670.74
Price: Black composite, stainless	$660.98
Price: Crotch Walnut composite, stainless	$660.98
Price: Black laminate wood, stainless	$664.20
Price: Green laminate, stainless	$664.20
Price: Camo wood, stainless	$685.74
Price: Camo composite, stainless	$684.04
Price: Walnut wood, stainless	$664.20
Price: Black wood, stainless	$664.20

Markesbery KM Polar Bear M/L Rifle

Similar to KM Black Bear except one-piece stock with Monte Carlo comb. Stock in American Hardwood walnut, green or black laminate, black composite, or X-Tra or Mossy Oak Break-Up camouflage. Interchangeable barrel system, Outer-Line ignition system, cross-bolt double safety. Available in 36, 45, 50, 54 caliber. Contact maker for full price listing. Made in U.S. by Markesbery Muzzle Loaders, Inc.

Price: American Hardwood walnut , blue finish	$539.01
Price: Black composite, blue finish	$536.63
Price: Black laminate, blue finish	$541.17
Price: Green laminate, blue finish	$541.17
Price: Camo, blue finish	$560.43
Price: American Hardwood walnut, stainless	$556.27
Price: Black composite, stainless	$556.04
Price: Black laminate, stainless	$570.56
Price: Green laminate, stainless	$570.56
Price: Camo, stainless	$573.94

MDM BUCKWACKA IN-LINE RIFLES

Caliber: 45, 50. **Barrel:** 23", 25". **Weight:** 7 to 7-3/4 lbs. **Stock:** Black, walnut, laminated and camouflage finishes. **Sights:** Williams Fire Sight blade front, Williams fully adjustable rear with ghost-ring peep aperture. **Features:** Break-open action; Incinerating Ignition System incorporates 209 shotshell primer directly into breech plug; 50-caliber models handle up to 150 grains of Pyrodex; synthetic ramrod; transfer bar safety; stainless or blued finish. Made in U.S. by Millennium Designed Muzzleloaders Ltd.

Price: 50 cal., blued finish	$309.95
Price: 50 cal., stainless	$339.95
Price: Camouflage stock	$359.95 to $389.95

MDM M2K In-Line Rifle

Similar to Buckwacka except adjustable trigger and double-safety mechanism designed to prevent misfires. Made in U.S. by Millennium Designed Muzzleloaders Ltd.

Price: ... $529.00 to $549.00

Mississippi 1841 Percussion Rifle

Similar to Zouave rifle but patterned after U.S. Model 1841. **Caliber:** 54, 58. Imported by Dixie Gun Works, Euroarms of America, Navy Arms.

Price: About ... $595.00

NAVY ARMS 1763 CHARLEVILLE

Caliber: 69. **Barrel:** 44-5/8". **Weight:** 8 lbs., 12 oz. **Length:** 59-3/8" overall. **Stock:** Walnut. **Sights:** Brass blade front. **Features:** Replica of French musket used by American troops during the Revolution. Imported by Navy Arms.

Price: ... $1,020.00

NAVY ARMS PARKER-HALE VOLUNTEER RIFLE

Caliber: .451. **Barrel:** 32". **Weight:** 9-1/2 lbs. **Length:** 49" overall. **Stock:** Walnut, checkered wrist and forend. **Sights:** Globe front, adjustable ladder-type rear. **Features:** Recreation of the type of gun issued to volunteer regiments during the 1860s. Rigby-pattern rifling, patent breech, detented lock. Stock is glass bedded for accuracy. Imported by Navy Arms.

Price: ... $905.00

BLACKPOWDER

BLACKPOWDER MUSKETS & RIFLES

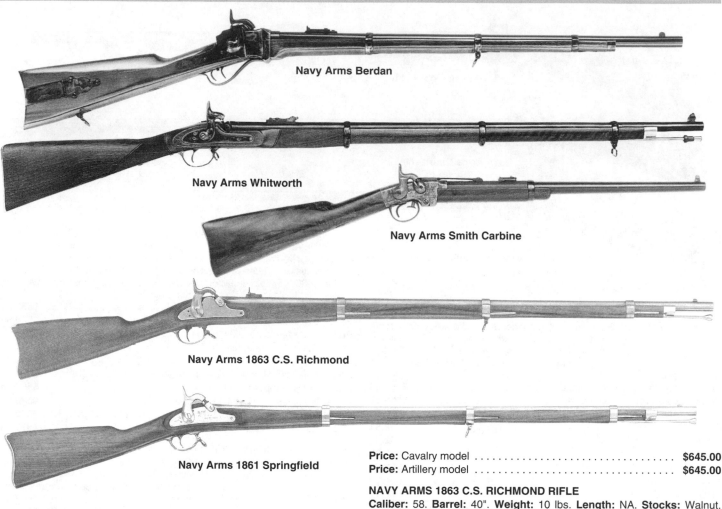

Navy Arms Berdan

Navy Arms Whitworth

Navy Arms Smith Carbine

Navy Arms 1863 C.S. Richmond

Navy Arms 1861 Springfield

NAVY ARMS 1859 SHARPS CAVALRY CARBINE
Caliber: 54. **Barrel:** 22". **Weight:** 7-3/4 lbs. **Length:** 39" overall. **Stock:** Walnut. **Sights:** Blade front, military ladder-type rear. **Features:** Color case-hardened action, blued barrel. Has saddle ring. Introduced 1991. Imported from Navy Arms.
Price: $1,000.00

NAVY ARMS BERDAN 1859 SHARPS RIFLE
Caliber: 54. **Barrel:** 30". **Weight:** 8 lbs., 8 oz. **Length:** 46-3/4" overall. **Stock:** Walnut. **Sights:** Blade front, folding military ladder-type rear. **Features:** Replica of the Union sniper rifle used by Berdan's 1st and 2nd Sharpshooter regiments. Color case-hardened receiver, patchbox, furniture. Double-set triggers. Imported by Navy Arms.
Price: $1,165.00
Price: 1859 Sharps Infantry Rifle (three-band) $1,100.00

NAVY ARMS PARKER-HALE WHITWORTH MILITARY TARGET RIFLE
Caliber: 45. **Barrel:** 36". **Weight:** 9-1/4 lbs. **Length:** 52-1/2" overall. **Stock:** Walnut. Checkered at wrist and forend. **Sights:** Hooded post front, open step-adjustable rear. **Features:** Faithful reproduction of Whitworth rifle, only bored for 45-cal. Trigger has detented lock, capable of being adjusted very finely without risk of the sear nose catching on the half-cock bent and damaging both parts. Introduced 1978. Imported by Navy Arms.
Price: $930.00

NAVY ARMS SMITH CARBINE
Caliber: 50. **Barrel:** 21-1/2". **Weight:** 7-3/4 lbs. **Length:** 39" overall. **Stock:** American walnut. **Sights:** Brass blade front, folding ladder-type rear. **Features:** Replica of breech-loading Civil War carbine. Color case-hardened receiver, rest blued. Cavalry model has saddle ring and bar, Artillery model has sling swivels. Imported by Navy Arms.

Price: Cavalry model $645.00
Price: Artillery model $645.00

NAVY ARMS 1863 C.S. RICHMOND RIFLE
Caliber: 58. **Barrel:** 40". **Weight:** 10 lbs. **Length:** NA. **Stocks:** Walnut. **Sights:** Blade front, adjustable rear. **Features:** Copy of three-band rifle musket made at Richmond Armory for the Confederacy. All steel polished bright. Imported by Navy Arms.
Price: $590.00

NAVY ARMS 1861 SPRINGFIELD RIFLE
Caliber: 58. **Barrel:** 40" **Weight:** 10 lbs., 4 oz. **Length:** 56" overall. **Stock:** Walnut. **Sights:** Blade front, military leaf rear. **Features:** Steel barrel, lock and all furniture have polished bright finish. Has 1855-style hammer. Imported by Navy Arms.
Price: $590.00

NAVY ARMS 1863 SPRINGFIELD
Caliber: 58, uses .575 Minie. **Barrel:** 40", rifled. **Weight:** 9-1/2 lbs. **Length:** 56" overall. **Stock:** Walnut. **Sights:** Open rear adjustable for elevation. **Features:** Full-size, three-band musket. Polished bright metal, including lock. From Navy Arms.
Price: Finished rifle $590.00

CONSULT

SHOOTER'S MARKETPLACE

Page 233, This Issue

New England Firearms Huntsman

Peifer TS-93

Remington Model 700 ML

NEW ENGLAND FIREARMS HUNTSMAN

Caliber: 50. **Barrel:** 24". **Weight:** 6-1/2 lbs. **Length:** 40". **Stock:** Walnut-finished American hardwood with pistol grip. **Sights:** Adjustable fiber optics open sights, tapped for scope base. **Features:** Break-open action, color case-hardened frame, black oxide barrel. Made in U.S.A. by New England Firearms.
Price: **$185.00**

New England Firearms "Stainless" Huntsman

NEW! Similar to Huntsman, but with matte nickel finish receiver. Introduced 2003. From New England Firearms.
Price: **$269.00**

PACIFIC RIFLE MODEL 1837 ZEPHYR

Caliber: 62. **Barrel:** 30", tapered octagon. **Weight:** 7-3/4 lbs. **Length:** NA. **Stock:** Oil-finished fancy walnut. **Sights:** German silver blade front, semi-buckhorn rear. Options available. **Features:** Improved underhammer action. First production rifle to offer Forsyth rifle, with narrow lands and shallow rifling with 1:144" pitch for high-velocity round balls. Metal finish is slow rust brown with nitre blue accents. Optional sights, finishes and integral muzzle brake available. Introduced 1995. Made in U.S. by Pacific Rifle Co.
Price: From **$995.00**

Pacific Rifle Big Bore, African Rifles

Similar to the 1837 Zephyr except in 72-caliber and 8-bore. The 72-caliber is available in standard form with 28" barrel, or as the African with flat buttplate, checkered upgraded wood; weight is 9 lbs. The 8-bore African has dual-cap ignition, 24" barrel, weighs 12 lbs., checkered English walnut, engraving, gold inlays. Introduced 1998. Made in U.S. by Pacific Rifle Co.
Price: 72-caliber, from **$1,150.00**
Price: 8-bore from................................. **$2,500.00**

PEIFER MODEL TS-93 RIFLE

Caliber: 45, 50. **Barrel:** 24" Douglas premium; 1:20" twist in 45; 1:28" in 50. **Weight:** 7 lbs. **Length:** 43-1/4" overall. **Stock:** Bell & Carlson solid composite, with recoil pad, swivel studs. **Sights:** Williams bead front on ramp, fully adjustable open rear. Drilled and tapped for Weaver scope mounts with dovetail for rear peep. **Features:** In-line ignition uses #209 shotshell primer; extremely fast lock time; fully enclosed breech; adjustable trigger; automatic safety; removable primer holder. Blue or stainless. Made in U.S. by Peifer Rifle Co. Introduced 1996.
Price: Blue, black stock **$730.00**
Price: Blue, wood or camouflage composite stock, or stainless with black composite stock............................. **$803.00**
Price: Stainless, wood or camouflage composite stock **$876.00**

PRAIRIE RIVER ARMS PRA BULLPUP RIFLE

Caliber: 50, 54. **Barrel:** 28"; 1:28" twist. **Weight:** 7-1/2 lbs. **Length:** 31-1/2" overall. **Stock:** Hardwood or black all-weather. **Sights:** Blade front, open adjustable rear. **Features:** Bullpup design thumbhole stock. Patented internal percussion ignition system. Left-hand model available. Dovetailed for scope mount. Introduced 1995. Made in U.S. by Prairie River Arms, Ltd.
Price: 4140 alloy barrel, hardwood stock **$199.00**
Price: Stainless barrel, hardwood stock **$225.00**
Price: All Weather stock, alloy barrel **$205.00**
Price: All Weather stock, stainless barrel **$230.00**

REMINGTON MODEL 700 ML, MLS RIFLES

Caliber: 50, new 45 (MLS Magnum).**Barrel:** 24"; 1:28" twist, 26" (Magnum). **Weight:** 7-3/4 lbs. **Length:** 42"-44-1/2" overall. **Stock:** Black fiberglass-reinforced synthetic with checkered grip and forend; magnum-style buttpad. **Sights:** Ramped bead front, open fully adjustable rear. Drilled and tapped for scope mounts. **Features:** Uses the Remington 700 bolt action, stock design, safety and trigger mechanisms; removable stainelss steel breech plug, No. 11 nipple; solid aluminum ramrod. Comes with cleaning tools and accessories; 3-way ignition.
Price: ML, blued, 50-caliber only **$415.00**
Price: MLS, stainless, 45 Magnum, 50-caliber............. **$533.00**
Price: MLS, stainless, Mossy Oak Break-Up camo stock **$569.00**

RICHMOND, C.S., 1863 MUSKET

Caliber: 58. **Barrel:** 40". **Weight:** 11 lbs. **Length:** 56-1/4" overall. **Stock:** European walnut with oil finish. **Sights:** Blade front, adjustable folding leaf rear. **Features:** Reproduction of the three-band Civil War musket. Sling swivels attached to trigger guard and middle barrel band. Lockplate marked "1863" and "C.S. Richmond." All metal left in white. Brass buttplate and forend cap. Imported by Euroarms of America, Navy Arms, and Dixie Gun Works.
Price: Euroarms **$530.00**
Price: Dixie Gun Works **$675.00**

RUGER 77/50 IN-LINE PERCUSSION RIFLE

Caliber: 50. **Barrel:** 22"; 1:28" twist. **Weight:** 6-1/2 lbs. **Length:** 41-1/2" overall. **Stock:** Birch with rubber buttpad and swivel studs. **Sights:** Gold bead front, folding leaf rear. Comes with Ruger scope mounts. **Features:** Shares design features with Ruger 77/22 rifle. Stainless steel bolt and nipple/breech plug; uses #11 caps, three-position safety, blued steel ramrod. Introduced 1997. Made in U.S. by Sturm, Ruger & Co.
Price: 77/50RS **$434.00**
Price: 77/50RSO Officer's (straight-grip checkered walnut stock, blued) **$555.00**
Price: K77/50RSBBZ (stainless steel, black laminated stock) ... **$601.00**
Price: K77/50RSP All-Weather (stainless steel, synthetic stock) . **$580.00**
Price: 77/50 RSP (blued, synthetic stock) **$434.00**

BLACKPOWDER

BLACKPOWDER MUSKETS & RIFLES

C.S. Richmond 1863

Ruger K77/50RSBBZ

Savage 10MLSS-IIXP

Second Model Brown Bess

T/C Firestorm

SAVAGE MODEL 10ML MUZZLELOADER RIFLE SERIES
Caliber: 50. **Barrel:** 24", 1:24 twist, blue or stainless. **Weight:** 7.75 lbs. **Stock:** Black synthetic, Realtree Hardwood JD Camo, brown laminate. **Sights:** Green adjustable rear, Red FiberOptic front. **Features:** XP Models scoped, no sights, smokeless powder, "easy to prime", #209 primer ignition. Removeable breech plut and vent liner.

Price: Model 10ML-II **$496.00**
Price: Model 10ML-II Camo **$533.00**
Price: Model 10MLSS-II Camo **$554.00**
Price: Model 10MLBSS-II **$626.00**
Price: Model 10ML-IIXP **$533.00**
Price: Model 10MLSS-IIXP **$589.00**

SECOND MODEL BROWN BESS MUSKET
Caliber: 75, uses .735" round ball. **Barrel:** 42", smoothbore. **Weight:** 9-1/2 lbs. **Length:** 59" overall. **Stock:** Walnut (Navy); walnut-stained hardwood (Dixie). **Sights:** Fixed. **Features:** Polished barrel and lock with brass trigger guard and buttplate. Bayonet and scabbard available. From Navy Arms, Dixie Gun Works, Cabela's.

Price: Finished . . . . **$475.00 to $850.00**
Price: Kit (Dixie Gun Works, Navy Arms) . . . . **$575.00 to $625.00**

Price: Carbine (Navy Arms) **$835.00**
Price: Dixie Gun Works **$765.00**

THOMPSON/CENTER FIRE STORM RIFLE
Caliber: 50. **Barrel:** 26"; 1:28" twist. **Weight:** 7 lbs. **Length:** 41-3/4" overall. **Stock:** Black synthetic with rubber recoil pad, swivel studs. **Sights:** Click-adjustable steel rear and ramp-style front, both with fiber optic inserts. **Features:** Side hammer lock is the first designed for up to three 50-grain Pyrodex pellets; patented Pyrodex Pyramid breech directs ignition fire 360 degrees around base of pellet. Quick Load Accurizor Muzzle System; aluminum ramrod. Flintlock only. Introduced 2000. Made in U.S. by Thomson/Center Arms.

Price: Blue finish, flintlock model with 1:48" twist for round balls, conicals **$415.00**
Price: SST, flintlock **$465.00**

THOMPSON/CENTER ENCORE 209x50 MAGNUM
Caliber: 50. **Barrel:** 26"; interchangeable with centerfire calibers. **Weight:** 7 lbs. **Length:** 40-1/2" overall. **Stock:** American walnut butt and forend, or black composite. **Sights:** Tru-Glo Fiber Optic front, Tru-Glo Fiber Optic rear. **Features:** Blue or stainless steel. Uses the stock, frame and forend of the Encore centerfire pistol; break-open design using trigger guard spur; stainless steel universal breech plug; uses #209 shotshell primers. Introduced 1998. Made in U.S. by Thompson/Center Arms.

Price: Stainless wtih camo stock **$751.00**
Price: Blue, walnut stock and forend **$640.00**
Price: Blue, composite stock and forend **$613.00**
Price: Stainless, composite stock and forend **$692.00**

BLACKPOWDER MUSKETS & RIFLES

T/C Hawken

Traditions Deerhunter

Traditions Lightning

THOMPSON/CENTER BLACK DIAMOND RIFLE XR

Caliber: 50. **Barrel:** 26" with QLA; 1:28" twist. **Weight:** 6 lbs., 9 oz. **Length:** 41-1/2" overall. **Stock:** Black Rynite with moulded-in checkering and grip cap, or walnut. **Sights:** Tru-Glo Fiber Optic ramp-style front, Tru- Glo Fiber Optic open rear. **Features:** In-line ignition system for musket cap, No. 11 cap, or 209 shotshell primer; removable universal breech plug; stainless steel construction. Selected models available in .45 cal. Made in U.S. by Thompson/Center Arms.

Price: With composite stock, blued **$335.00**
Price: With walnut stock **$405.00**

THOMPSON/CENTER HAWKEN RIFLE

Caliber: 45, 50 or 54. **Barrel:** 28" octagon, hooked breech. **Stock:** American walnut. **Sights:** Blade front, rear adjustable for windage and elevation. **Features:** Solid brass furniture, double-set triggers, button rifled barrel, coil-type mainspring. From Thompson/Center Arms.

Price: Percussion model (45-, 50- or 54-cal.) **$545.00**
Price: Flintlock model (50-cal.) **$570.00**

TRADITIONS BUCKSKINNER CARBINE

Caliber: 50. **Barrel:** 21"; 15/16" flats, half octagon, half round; 1:20" or 1:66" twist. **Weight:** 6 lbs. **Length:** 37" overall. **Stock:** Beech or black laminated. **Sights:** Beaded blade front, fiber optic open rear click adjustable for windage and elevation or fiber optics. **Features:** Uses V-type mainspring, single trigger. Non-glare hardware; sling swivels. From Traditions.

Price: Flintlock **$239.00**
Price: Flintlock, laminated stock **$309.00**

TRADITIONS DEERHUNTER RIFLE SERIES

Caliber: 32, 50 or 54. **Barrel:** 24", octagonal; 15/16" flats; 1:48" or 1:66" twist. **Weight:** 6 lbs. **Length:** 40" overall. **Stock:** Stained hardwood or All-Weather composite with rubber buttpad, sling swivels. **Sights:** Lite Optic blade front, adjustable rear fiber optics. **Features:** Flint or percussion with color case-hardened lock. Hooked breech, oversized trigger guard, blackened furniture, PVC ramrod. All-Weather has composite stock and C-Nickel barrel. Drilled and tapped for scope mounting. Imported by Traditions, Inc.

Price: Percussion, 50; blued barrel; 1:48" twist **$169.00**
Price: Percussion, 54 . . . . **$189.00**
Price: Flintlock, 50 caliber only; 1:48" twist **$199.00**
Price: Flintlock, All-Weather, 50-cal. **$179.00**
Price: Redi-Pak, 50 cal. flintlock **$219.00**
New! **Price:** Flintlock, left-handed hardwood, 50 cal. **$199.00**
Price: Percussion, All-Weather, 50 or 54 cal. **$159.00**
Price: Percussion; 32 cal. **$179.00**

Traditions Panther Sidelock Rifle

Similar to Deerhunter rifle, but has blade front and windage-adjustable-only rear sight, black composite stock.
Price: **$119.00**

TRADITIONS E-BOLT 209 BOLT-ACTION RIFLES

Caliber: 45, 50. **Barrel:** 22" blued or C-Nickel finish, 1:20 and 1:28" twist. **Weight:** 6 lbs., 7 oz. **Length:** 41" overall. **Stock:** Black or Advantage Timber® composite. **Sights:** Lite Optic blade front, adjustable rear. **Features:** Thumb safety; quick-release bolt; covered breech; one-piece breech plug takes 209 shotshell primers; accepts 150 grains of Pyrodex pellets, receiver drilled and tapped for scope, sling swivel studs and rubber butt pad. From Traditions.

Price: Black composite stock with 22" blued barrel **$169.00**
Price: Black composite stock with 22" C-Nickel barrel **$189.00**
Price: Advantage Timber® stock with 22" C-Nickel barrel **$229.00**
Price: Redi-Pak with black stock/blued barrel and powder flask, capper, ball starter, other supplies **$219.00**
Price: Redi-Pak with Advantage Timber® stock/C-Nickel barrel and powder flask, capper, ball starter, other supplies **$279.00**
Price: Blue, Mossy Oak break-up **$219.00**
Price: 4X32 fixed scope **$219.00**
Price: Scoped w/Redi-Pak **$269.00**

TRADITIONS LIGHTNING MAG BOLT-ACTION MUZZLELOADER

Caliber: 50, 54. **Barrel:** 24" round; blued, stainless, C-Nickel or Ultra Coat. **Weight:** 6-1/2 to 7 lbs. 10 oz. **Length:** 43" overall. **Stock:** All-Weather composite, Advantage, or Break-Up camouflage. **Sights:** Fiber Optic blade front, fully adjustable open rear. **Features:** Field-removable stainless steel bolt; silent thumb safety; adjustable trigger; drilled and tapped for scope mounting. Lightning Fire Magnum System allows use of No. 11, musket caps or 209 shotgun primers. Imported by Traditions.

Price: All-Weather composite stock, blue finish **$199.00**
Price: All-Weather composite stock, blue finish, muzzle brake . . **$229.00**
Price: All-Weather composite, stainless steel **$279.00**
Price: Camouflage composite, stainless steel **$309.00**
Price: Camouflage composite **$229.00**
Price: Composite, with muzzle brake, stainless, fluted barrel . . . **$329.00**
Price: Walnut finish, synthetic stock **$239.00**

Traditions Lightning 45 LD Bolt-Action Rifles

Similar to Lightning Mag. but chambered for 45, 50 caliber with 26"fluted blued or C-Nickel barrel, 1:20", 1:28" twist. Black, synthetic break-up or Advantage Timber stock, fiber optic blade front, adjustable rear sights. Accepts 150 grains of Pyrodex. Weighs 7 lbs., 2 oz. Overal length 45". Introduced 2001. From Traditions.

Price: (black stock with blued barrel) **$229.00**
Price: (black stock with C-Nickel barrel) **$239.00**
Price: (Advantage Timber® stock with C-Nickel barrel) **$289.00**

Traditions Lightning Lightweight Magnum Bolt-Action Rifles

Similar to Lightning Mag except features 22" lightweight, fluted barrel and Spider Web-pattern black composite stock. Overall length 41", weighs 6 lb., 5 oz. Introduced 2000. From Traditions.

Price: Blued finish. **$219.00**
Price: C-Nickel finish. **$229.00**
Price: Nickel, camo stock **$259.00**

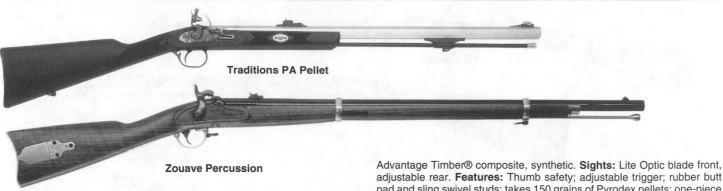

Traditions PA Pellet

Zouave Percussion

BLACKPOWDER (side tab)

TRADITIONS PA PELLET FLINTLOCK
Caliber: 50. **Barrel:** 26", blued, nickel. **Weight:** 7 lbs. **Stock:** Hardwood, synthetic and synthetic break-up. **Sights:** FO. **Features:** Removeable breech plug, left-hand model with hardwood stock. 1:48" twist.
Price: Hardwood, blued **$249.00**
Price: Hardwood left, blued **$269.00**

TRADITIONS HAWKEN WOODSMAN RIFLE
Caliber: 50 and 54. **Barrel:** 28"; 15/16" flats. **Weight:** 7 lbs., 11 oz. **Length:** 44-1/2" overall. **Stock:** Walnut-stained hardwood. **Sights:** Beaded blade front, hunting-style open rear adjustable for windage and elevation. **Features:** Percussion only. Brass patchbox and furniture. Double triggers. From Traditions.
Price: 50 or 54 . . . . **$239.00**
Price: 50-cal., left-hand. **$249.00**
Price: 50-caliber, flintlock **$279.00**

TRADITIONS KENTUCKY RIFLE
Caliber: 50. **Barrel:** 33-1/2"; 7/8" flats; 1:66" twist. **Weight:** 7 lbs. **Length:** 49" overall. **Stock:** Beech; inletted toe plate. **Sights:** Blade front, fixed rear. **Features:** Full-length, two-piece stock; brass furniture; color case-hardened lock. From Traditions.
Price: **$249.00**

TRADITIONS PENNSYLVANIA RIFLE
Caliber: 50. **Barrel:** 40-1/4"; 7/8" flats; 1:66" twist, octagon. **Weight:** 9 lbs. **Length:** 57-1/2" overall. **Stock:** Walnut. **Sights:** Blade front, adjustable rear. **Features:** Brass patchbox and ornamentation. Double-set triggers. From Traditions.
Price: Flintlock **$479.00**
Price: Percussion **$469.00**

TRADITIONS SHENANDOAH RIFLE
Caliber: 36, 50. **Barrel:** 33-1/2" octagon; 1:66" twist. **Weight:** 7 lbs., 3 oz. **Length:** 49-1/2" overall. **Stock:** Walnut. **Sights:** Blade front, buckhorn rear. **Features:** V-type mainspring; double-set trigger; solid brass buttplate, patchbox, nosecap, thimbles, trigger guard. Introduced 1996. From Traditions.
Price: Flintlock **$369.00**
Price: Percussion **$349.00**
Price: 36 cal. Flintlock, 1:48"twist **$399.00**
Price: 36 cal. Percussion, 1:48"twist **$389.00**

TRADITIONS TENNESSEE RIFLE
Caliber: 50. **Barrel:** 24", octagon; 15/16" flats; 1:66" twist. **Weight:** 6 lbs. **Length:** 40-1/2" overall. **Stock:** Stained beech. **Sights:** Blade front, fixed rear. **Features:** One-piece stock has inletted brass furniture, cheekpiece; double-set trigger; V-type mainspring. Flint or percussion. From Traditions.
Price: Flintlock **$299.00**
Price: Percussion **$279.00**

TRADITIONS TRACKER 209 IN-LINE RIFLES
Caliber: 45, 50. **Barrel:** 22" blued or C-Nickel finish; 1:28" twist, 50 cal. 1:20" 45 cal. **Weight:** 6 lbs., 4 oz. **Length:** 41" overall. **Stock:** Black, Advantage Timber® composite, synthetic. **Sights:** Lite Optic blade front, adjustable rear. **Features:** Thumb safety; adjustable trigger; rubber butt pad and sling swivel studs; takes 150 grains of Pyrodex pellets; one-piece breech system takes 209 shotshell primers. Drilled and tapped for scope. From Traditions.
Price: (Black composite or synthetic stock, 22" blued barrel). . . . **$119.00**
Price: (Black composite or synthetic stock, 22" C-Nickel barrel) . **$129.00**
Price: (Advantage Timber® stock, 22" C-Nickel barrel) **$179.00**
Price: (Redi-Pak, black stock and blued barrel, powder flask, capper, ball starter, other accessories) **$169.00**
Price: (Redi-Pak, synthetic stock and blued barrel, with scope) . **$229.00**

WHITE MODEL 97 WHITETAIL HUNTER RIFLE
Caliber: 45, 50. **Barrel:** 22", 1:20 twist (45 cal.); 1:24 twist (50 cal.). **Weight:** 7.7 lbs. **Length:** 40" overall. **Stock:** Black laminated or black composite. **Sights:** Marble TruGlo fully adjustable, steel rear with white diamond, red bead front with high-visibility inserts. **Features:** In-line ignition with FlashFire one-piece nipple and breech plug that uses standard or magnum No. 11 caps, fully adjustable trigger, double safety system, aluminum ramrod; drilled and tapped for scope. Hard gun case. Made in U.S.A. by Split Fire Sporting Goods.
Price: Whitetail w/laminated or composite stock **$449.95**
Price: Adventurer w/26" stainless barrel & thumbhole stock) . . . **$799.95**
Price: Odyssey w/24" carbon fiber wrapped barrel & thumbhole stock **$1,199.95**

WHITE MODEL 98 ELITE HUNTER Rifle
Caliber: 45, 50. **Barrel:** 24", 1:24" twist (50 cal). **Weight:** 8.6 lbs. **Length:** 43-1/2" overall. **Stock:** Black laminate wtih swivel studs. **Sights:** TruGlo fully adjustable, steel rear with white diamond, red bead front with high-visibility inserts. **Features:** In-line ignition with FlashFire one-piece nipple and breech plug that uses standard or magnum No. 11 caps, fully adjustable trigger, double safety system, aluminum ramrod, drilled and taped for scope, hard gun case. Made in U.S.A. by Split Fire Sporting Goods.
Price: Composite or laminate wood stock **$599.95**

White Model Thunderbolt Rifle
Similar to the Elite Hunter but is designed to handle 209 shotgun primers only. Has 26" stainless steel barrel, weighs 9.3 lbs. and is 45-1/2" long. Composite or laminate stock.
Price: **$699.95**

WHITE MODEL 2000 BLACKTAIL HUNTER RIFLE
Caliber: 50. **Barrel:** 22", 1:24" twist (50 cal.). **Weight:** 7.6 lbs. **Length:** 39-7/8" overall. **Stock:** Black laminated with swivel studs with laser engraved deer or elk scene. **Sights:** TruGlo fully adjustable, steel rear with white diamond, red bead front with high-visibility inserts. **Features:** Teflon finished barrel, in-line ignition with FlashFire one-piece nipple and breech plug that uses standard or magnum No. 11 caps, fully adjustable trigger, double safety system, aluminum ramrod, drilled and tapped for scope. Hard gun case. Made in U.S.A. by Split Fire Sporting Goods.
Price: Laminate wood stock, w/laser engraved game scene . . . **$599.95**

ZOUAVE PERCUSSION RIFLE
Caliber: 58, 59. **Barrel:** 32-1/2". **Weight:** 9-1/2 lbs. **Length:** 48-1/2" overall. **Stock:** Walnut finish, brass patchbox and buttplate. **Sights:** Fixed front, rear adjustable for elevation. **Features:** Color case-hardened lockplate, blued barrel. From Navy Arms, Dixie Gun Works, E.M.F., Cabela's, Euroarms of America.
Price: About . . . . **$415.00 to $515.00**

Knight TK2000

Traditions Buckhunters Pro

CABELA'S BLACKPOWDER SHOTGUNS

Gauge: 10, 12, 20. **Barrel:** 10-ga., 30"; 12-ga., 28-1/2" (Extra-Full, Mod., Imp. Cyl. choke tubes); 20-ga., 27-1/2" (Imp. Cyl. & Mod. fixed chokes). **Weight:** 6-1/2 to 7 lbs. **Length:** 45" overall (28-1/2" barrel). **Stock:** American walnut with checkered grip; 12- and 20-gauge have straight stock, 10-gauge has pistol grip. **Features:** Blued barrels, engraved, color case-hardened locks and hammers, brass ramrod tip. From Cabela's.
Price: 10-gauge **$599.99**
Price: 12-gauge **$559.99**
Price: 20-gauge **$539.99**

CVA TRAPPER PERCUSSION SHOTGUN

Gauge: 12. **Barrel:** 28". **Weight:** 6 lbs. **Length:** 46" overall. **Stock:** English-style checkered straight grip of walnut-finished hardwood. **Sights:** Brass bead front. **Features:** Single-blued barrel; color case-hardened lockplate and hammer; screw adjustable sear engagements, V-type mainspring; brass wedge plates; color case-hardened and engraved trigger guard and tang. From CVA.
Price: Finished **$287.95**

DIXIE MAGNUM PERCUSSION SHOTGUN

Gauge: 10, 12, 20. **Barrel:** 30" (Imp. Cyl. & Mod.) in 10-gauge; 28" in 12-gauge. **Weight:** 6-1/4 lbs. **Length:** 45" overall. **Stock:** Hand-checkered walnut, 14" pull. **Features:** Double triggers; light hand engraving; case-hardened locks in 12-gauge; polished steel in 10-gauge; sling swivels. From Dixie Gun Works.
Price: Upland **$449.00**
Price: 12-ga. kit. **$445.00**
Price: 20-ga. **$525.00**
Price: 10-ga. **$525.00**
Price: 10-ga. kit. **$445.00**

KNIGHT TK2000 MUZZLELOADING SHOTGUN (209)

Gauge: 12. **Barrel:** 26", extra-full choke tube. **Weight:** 7 lbs., 9 oz. **Length:** 45" overall. **Stock:** Synthetic black or Advantage Timber HD; recoil pad; swivel studs. **Sights:** Fully adjustable rear, blade front with fiber optics. **Features:** Receiver drilled and tapped for scope mount; in-line ignition; adjustable trigger; removable breech plug; double safety system; imp. cyl. choke tube available. Made in U.S. by Knight Rifles.
Price: . . . . **$349.95 to $399.95**

KNIGHT VERSATILE TK2002

Gauge: 12. **Stock:** Black composite, blued, Advantage Timber HD finish. Both with sling swivel studs installed. **Sights:** Adjustable metallic TruGol fiber optic. **Features:** Full plastic jacket ignition system, screw-on choke tubes, load without removing choke tubes, incredible shot density with jug-chocked barrel design. Improved cylinder and modified choke tubes available.
Price: . . . . **$349.95 to $399.95**

NAVY ARMS STEEL SHOT MAGNUM SHOTGUN

Gauge: 10. **Barrel:** 28" (Cyl. & Cyl.). **Weight:** 7 lbs., 9 oz. **Length:** 45-1/2" overall. **Stock:** Walnut, with cheekpiece. **Features:** Designed specifically for steel shot. Engraved, polished locks; sling swivels; blued barrels. Imported by Navy Arms.
Price: **$605.00**

NAVY ARMS T&T SHOTGUN

Gauge: 12. **Barrel:** 28" (Full & Full). **Weight:** 7-1/2 lbs. **Stock:** Walnut. **Sights:** Bead front. **Features:** Color case-hardened locks, double triggers, blued steel furniture. From Navy Arms.
Price: **$580.00**

TRADITIONS BUCKHUNTER PRO SHOTGUN

Gauge: 12. **Barrel:** 24", choke tube. **Weight:** 6 lbs., 4 oz. **Length:** 43" overall. **Stock:** Composite matte black, Break-Up or Advantage camouflage. **Features:** In-line action with removable stainless steel breech plug; thumb safety; adjustable trigger; rubber buttpad. Introduced 1996. From Traditions.
Price: **$248.00**
Price: With Advantage, Shadow Branch, or Break-Up camouflage stock **$292.00**

WHITE TOMINATOR SHOTGUN

Caliber: 12. **Barrel:** 25" blue, straight, tapered stainless steel. **Weight:** NA. **Length:** NA. **Stock:** Black laminated or black wood. **Sights:** Drilled and tapped for easy scope mounting. **Features:** Internchangeable choke tubes. Custom vent-rib with high visibility front bead. Double safeties. Fully adjustable custom trigger. Recoil pad and sling swivel studs.
Price: **$349.95**

BLACKPOWDER

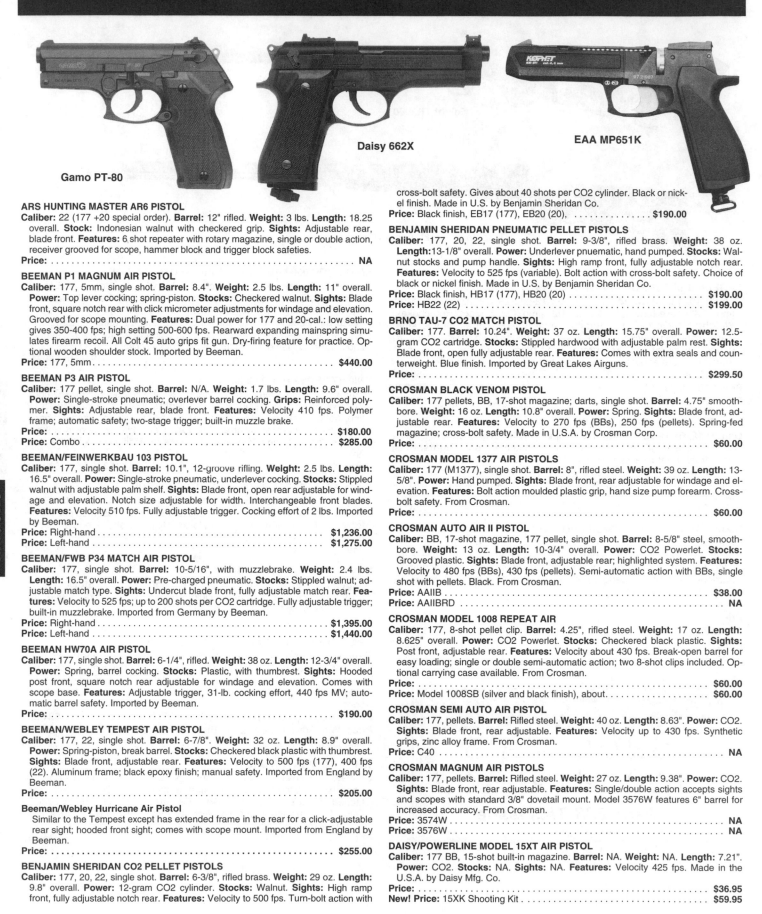

Gamo PT-80

Daisy 662X

EAA MP651K

ARS HUNTING MASTER AR6 PISTOL
Caliber: 22 (177 +20 special order). **Barrel:** 12" rifled. **Weight:** 3 lbs. **Length:** 18.25 overall. **Stock:** Indonesian walnut with checkered grip. **Sights:** Adjustable rear, blade front. **Features:** 6 shot repeater with rotary magazine, single or double action, receiver grooved for scope, hammer block and trigger block safeties.
Price: .... NA

BEEMAN P1 MAGNUM AIR PISTOL
Caliber: 177, 5mm, single shot. **Barrel:** 8.4". **Weight:** 2.5 lbs. **Length:** 11" overall. **Power:** Top lever cocking; spring-piston. **Stocks:** Checkered walnut. **Sights:** Blade front, square notch rear with click micrometer adjustments for windage and elevation. Grooved for scope mounting. **Features:** Dual power for 177 and 20-cal.: low setting gives 350-400 fps; high setting 500-600 fps. Rearward expanding mainspring simulates firearm recoil. All Colt 45 auto grips fit gun. Dry-firing feature for practice. Optional wooden shoulder stock. Imported by Beeman.
Price: 177, 5mm. $440.00

BEEMAN P3 AIR PISTOL
Caliber: 177 pellet, single shot. **Barrel:** N/A. **Weight:** 1.7 lbs. **Length:** 9.6" overall. **Power:** Single-stroke pneumatic; overlever barrel cocking. **Grips:** Reinforced polymer. **Sights:** Adjustable rear, blade front. **Features:** Velocity 410 fps. Polymer frame; automatic safety; two-stage trigger; built-in muzzle brake.
Price: $180.00
Price: Combo $285.00

BEEMAN/FEINWERKBAU 103 PISTOL
Caliber: 177, single shot. **Barrel:** 10.1", 12-groove rifling. **Weight:** 2.5 lbs. **Length:** 16.5" overall. **Power:** Single-stroke pneumatic, underlever cocking. **Stocks:** Stippled walnut with adjustable palm shelf. **Sights:** Blade front, open rear adjustable for windage and elevation. Notch size adjustable for width. Interchangeable front blades. **Features:** Velocity 510 fps. Fully adjustable trigger. Cocking effort of 2 lbs. Imported by Beeman.
Price: Right-hand $1,236.00
Price: Left-hand $1,275.00

BEEMAN/FWB P34 MATCH AIR PISTOL
Caliber: 177, single shot. **Barrel:** 10-5/16", with muzzlebrake. **Weight:** 2.4 lbs. **Length:** 16.5" overall. **Power:** Pre-charged pneumatic. **Stocks:** Stippled walnut; adjustable match type. **Sights:** Undercut blade front, fully adjustable match rear. **Features:** Velocity to 525 fps; up to 200 shots per CO2 cartridge. Fully adjustable trigger; built-in muzzlebrake. Imported from Germany by Beeman.
Price: Right-hand $1,395.00
Price: Left-hand $1,440.00

BEEMAN HW70A AIR PISTOL
Caliber: 177, single shot. **Barrel:** 6-1/4", rifled. **Weight:** 38 oz. **Length:** 12-3/4" overall. **Power:** Spring, barrel cocking. **Stocks:** Plastic, with thumbrest. **Sights:** Hooded post front, square notch rear adjustable for windage and elevation. Comes with scope base. **Features:** Adjustable trigger, 31-lb. cocking effort, 440 fps MV; automatic barrel safety. Imported by Beeman.
Price: $190.00

BEEMAN/WEBLEY TEMPEST AIR PISTOL
Caliber: 177, 22, single shot. **Barrel:** 6-7/8". **Weight:** 32 oz. **Length:** 8.9" overall. **Power:** Spring-piston, break barrel. **Stocks:** Checkered black plastic with thumbrest. **Sights:** Blade front, adjustable rear. **Features:** Velocity to 500 fps (177), 400 fps (22). Aluminum frame; black epoxy finish; manual safety. Imported from England by Beeman.
Price: $205.00

Beeman/Webley Hurricane Air Pistol
Similar to the Tempest except has extended frame in the rear for a click-adjustable rear sight; hooded front sight; comes with scope mount. Imported from England by Beeman.
Price: $255.00

BENJAMIN SHERIDAN CO2 PELLET PISTOLS
Caliber: 177, 20, 22, single shot. **Barrel:** 6-3/8", rifled brass. **Weight:** 29 oz. **Length:** 9.8" overall. **Power:** 12-gram CO2 cylinder. **Stocks:** Walnut. **Sights:** High ramp front, fully adjustable notch rear. **Features:** Velocity to 500 fps. Turn-bolt action with

cross-bolt safety. Gives about 40 shots per CO2 cylinder. Black or nickel finish. Made in U.S. by Benjamin Sheridan Co.
Price: Black finish, EB17 (177), EB20 (20), ... $190.00

BENJAMIN SHERIDAN PNEUMATIC PELLET PISTOLS
Caliber: 177, 20, 22, single shot. **Barrel:** 9-3/8", rifled brass. **Weight:** 38 oz. **Length:** 13-1/8" overall. **Power:** Underlever pnuematic, hand pumped. **Stocks:** Walnut stocks and pump handle. **Sights:** High ramp front, fully adjustable notch rear. **Features:** Velocity to 525 fps (variable). Bolt action with cross-bolt safety. Choice of black or nickel finish. Made in U.S. by Benjamin Sheridan Co.
Price: Black finish, HB17 (177), HB20 (20) $190.00
Price: HB22 (22) $199.00

BRNO TAU-7 CO2 MATCH PISTOL
Caliber: 177. **Barrel:** 10.24". **Weight:** 37 oz. **Length:** 15.75" overall. **Power:** 12.5-gram CO2 cartridge. **Stocks:** Stippled hardwood with adjustable palm rest. **Sights:** Blade front, open fully adjustable rear. **Features:** Comes with extra seals and counterweight. Blue finish. Imported by Great Lakes Airguns.
Price: $299.50

CROSMAN BLACK VENOM PISTOL
Caliber: 177 pellets, BB, 17-shot magazine; darts, single shot. **Barrel:** 4.75" smoothbore. **Weight:** 16 oz. **Length:** 10.8" overall. **Power:** Spring. **Sights:** Blade front, adjustable rear. **Features:** Velocity to 270 fps (BBs), 250 fps (pellets). Spring-fed magazine; cross-bolt safety. Made in U.S.A. by Crosman Corp.
Price: $60.00

CROSMAN MODEL 1377 AIR PISTOLS
Caliber: 177 (M1377), single shot. **Barrel:** 8", rifled steel. **Weight:** 39 oz. **Length:** 13-5/8". **Power:** Hand pumped. **Sights:** Blade front, rear adjustable for windage and elevation. **Features:** Bolt action moulded plastic grip, hand size pump forearm. Cross-bolt safety. From Crosman.
Price: $60.00

CROSMAN AUTO AIR II PISTOL
Caliber: BB, 17-shot magazine, 177 pellet, single shot. **Barrel:** 8-5/8" steel, smoothbore. **Weight:** 13 oz. **Length:** 10-3/4" overall. **Power:** CO2 Powerlet. **Stocks:** Grooved plastic. **Sights:** Blade front, adjustable rear; highlighted system. **Features:** Velocity to 480 fps (BBs), 430 fps (pellets). Semi-automatic action with BBs, single shot with pellets. Black. From Crosman.
Price: AAIIB $38.00
Price: AAIIBRD .... NA

CROSMAN MODEL 1008 REPEAT AIR
Caliber: 177, 8-shot pellet clip. **Barrel:** 4.25", rifled steel. **Weight:** 17 oz. **Length:** 8.625" overall. **Power:** CO2 Powerlet. **Stocks:** Checkered black plastic. **Sights:** Post front, adjustable rear. **Features:** Velocity about 430 fps. Break-open barrel for easy loading; single or double semi-automatic action; two 8-shot clips included. Optional carrying case available. From Crosman.
Price: $60.00
Price: Model 1008SB (silver and black finish), about. $60.00

CROSMAN SEMI AUTO AIR PISTOL
Caliber: 177, pellets. **Barrel:** Rifled steel. **Weight:** 40 oz. **Length:** 8.63". **Power:** CO2. **Sights:** Blade front, rear adjustable. **Features:** Velocity up to 430 fps. Synthetic grips, zinc alloy frame. From Crosman.
Price: C40 .... NA

CROSMAN MAGNUM AIR PISTOLS
Caliber: 177, pellets. **Barrel:** Rifled steel. **Weight:** 27 oz. **Length:** 9.38". **Power:** CO2. **Sights:** Blade front, rear adjustable. **Features:** Single/double action accepts sights and scopes with standard 3/8" dovetail mount. Model 3576W features 6" barrel for increased accuracy. From Crosman.
Price: 3574W .... NA
Price: 3576W .... NA

DAISY/POWERLINE MODEL 15XT AIR PISTOL
Caliber: 177 BB, 15-shot built-in magazine. **Barrel:** NA. **Weight:** NA. **Length:** 7.21". **Power:** CO2. **Stocks:** NA. **Sights:** NA. **Features:** Velocity 425 fps. Made in the U.S.A. by Daisy Mfg. Co.
Price: $36.95
New! Price: 15XK Shooting Kit $59.95

AIRGUNS—HANDGUNS

DAISY/POWERLINE 717 PELLET PISTOL
Caliber: 177, single shot. **Barrel:** 9.61". **Weight:** 2.25 lbs. **Length:** 13-1/2" overall. **Stocks:** Moulded wood-grain plastic, with thumbrest. **Sights:** Blade and ramp front, micro-adjustable notch rear. **Features:** Single pump pneumatic pistol. Rifled steel barrel. Cross-bolt trigger block. Muzzle velocity 385 fps. From Daisy Mfg. Co.
Price: $71.95

DAISY/POWERLINE 1270 CO2 AIR PISTOL
Caliber: BB, 60-shot magazine. **Barrel:** Smoothbore steel. **Weight:** 17 oz. **Length:** 11.1" overall. **Power:** CO2 pump action. **Stocks:** Moulded black polymer. **Sights:** Blade on ramp front, adjustable rear. **Features:** Velocity to 420 fps. Crossbolt trigger block safety; plated finish. Made in U.S. by Daisy Mfg. Co.
Price: $39.95

DAISY/POWERLINE 93 AIR PISTOL
Caliber: BB, 15-shot magazine. **Barrel:** Smoothbore steel. **Weight:** 1.1 lbs. **Length:** 7.9" overall. **Power:** CO2 powered semi-auto. **Stocks:** Moulded brown checkered. **Sights:** Blade on ramp front, fixed open rear. **Features:** Velocity to 400 fps. Manual trigger block. Made in U.S.A. by Daisy Mfg. Co.
Price: $48.95

Daisy/Powerline 693 Air Pistol
   Similar to Model 93 except has velocity to 235 fps.
Price: $52.95

DAISY/POWERLINE 622X PELLETPISTOL
Caliber: 22 (5.5mm), 6-shot. **Barrel:** Rifled steel. **Weight:** 1.3 lbs. **Length:** 8.5". **Power:** CO2. **Grips:** Molded black checkered. **Sights:** Fiber optic front, fixed open rear. **Features:** Velocity 225 fps. Rotary hammer block. Made by Daisy Mfg. Co.
Price: $69.95

DAISY/POWERLINE 45 AIR PISTOL
Caliber: BB, 13-shot magazine. **Barrel:** Rifled steel. **Weight:** 1.25 lbs. **Length:** 8.5" overall. **Power:** CO2 powered semi-auto. **Stocks:** Moulded black checkered. **Sights:** TRUGLO® fiber optic front, fixed open rear. **Features:** Velocity to 224 fps. Manual trigger block. Made in U.S.A. by Daisy Mfg. Co.
Price: $54.95

Daisy/Powerline 645 Air Pistol
   Similar to Model 93 except has distinctive black and nickel-finish.
Price: $59.95

EAA/BAIKAL IZH-M46 TARGET AIR PISTOL
Caliber: 177, single shot. **Barrel:** 10". **Weight:** 2.4 lbs. **Length:** 16.8" overall. **Power:** Underlever single-stroke pneumatic. **Grips:** Adjustable wooden target. **Sights:** Micrometer fully adjustable rear, blade front. **Features:** Velocity about 420 fps. Hammer-forged, rifled barrel. Imported from Russia by European American Armory.
Price $319.00

EAA/BAIKAL MP-651K AIR PISTOL/RIFLE
Caliber: 177 pellet (8-shot magazine); 177 BB (23-shot). **Barrel:** 5.9" (17.25" with rifle attachment). **Weight:** 1.54 lbs. (3.3 lbs. with rifle attachment). **Length:** 9.4" (31.3" with rifle attachment) **Power:** CO2 cartridge, semi-automatic. **Stock:** Plastic. **Sights:** Notch rear/blade front (pistol); periscopic sighting system (rifle). **Features:** Velocity 328 fps. Unique pistol/rifle combination allows the pistol to be inserted into the rifle shell. Imported from Russia by European American Armory.
Price: $99.00

GAMO AUTO 45
Caliber: .177 (12-shot). **Barrel:** 4.25". **Weight:** 1.10 lbs. **Length:** 7.50". **Power:** CO2 cartridge, semi-automatic, 410 fps. **Stock:** Plastic. **Sights:** Rear sights adjusts for windage. **Features:** Looking very much like a Glock cartridge pistol, it fires in the double-action mode and has a manual safety. Imported from Spain by Gamo.
Price: $99.95

GAMO COMPACT TARGET PISTOL
Caliber: .177, single shot. **Barrel:** 8.26". **Weight:** 1.95 lbs. **Length:** 12.60. **Power:** Spring-piston, 400 fps. **Stock:** Walnut. **Sights:** Micro-adjustable. **Features:** Rifle steel barrel, adjustable match trigger, recoil and vibration-free. Imported from Spain by Gamo.
Price: $229.95

GAMO P-23, P-23 LASER PISTOL
Caliber: .177 (12-shot). **Barrel:** 4.25". **Weight:** 1 lb. **Length:** 7.5". **Power:** CO2 cartridge, semi-automatic, 410 fps. **Stock:** Plastic. **Sights:** NA. **Features:** Style somewhat like a Walther PPK cartridge pistol, an optional laser allows fast sight acquisition. Imported from Spain by Gamo.
Price: .... $89.95, (with laser) $129.95

GAMO PT-80, PT-80 LASER PISTOL
Caliber: .177 (8-shot). **Barrel:** 4.25". **Weight:** 1.2 lbs. **Length:** 7.2". **Power:** CO2 cartridge, semi-automatic, 410 fps. **Stock:** Plastic. **Sights:** 3-dot. **Features:** Available with optional laser sight and wit optional walnut grips. Imported from Spain by Gamo.
Price: .... $108.95, (with laser) $129.95, (with walnut grip) $119.95

"GAT" AIR PISTOL
Caliber: 177, single shot. **Barrel:** 7-1/2" cocked, 9-1/2" extended. **Weight:** 22 oz. **Power:** Spring-piston. **Stocks:** Cast checkered metal. **Sights:** Fixed. **Features:** Shoots pellets, corks or darts. Matte black finish. Imported from England by Stone Enterprises, Inc.
Price: $24.95

HAMMERLI AP40 AIR PISTOL
Caliber: 177. **Barrel:** 10". **Stocks:** Adjustable orthopaedic. **Sights:** Fully adjustable micrometer. **Features:** Sleek, light, well balanced and accurate. Imported from Switzerland by Nygord Precision Products.
Price: $1,195.00

MARKSMAN 2000 REPEATER PISTOL
Caliber: 177, 18-shot BB repeater. **Barrel:** 2-1/2", smoothbore. **Weight:** 24 oz. **Length:** 8-1/4" overall. **Power:** Spring. **Features:** Velocity to 200 fps. Thumb safety. Uses BBs, darts, bolts or pellets. Repeats with BBs only. From Marksman Products.
Price: $27.00

MARKSMAN 2005 LASERHAWK SPECIAL EDITION AIR PISTOL
Caliber: 177, 24-shot magazine. **Barrel:** 3.8", smoothbore. **Weight:** 22 oz. **Length:** 10.3" overall. **Power:** Spring-air. **Stocks:** Checkered. **Sights:** Fixed fiber optic front sight. **Features:** Velocity to 300 fps with Hyper-Velocity pellets. Square trigger guard with skeletonized trigger; extended barrel for greater velocity and accuracy. Shoots BBs, pellets, darts or bolts. Made in the U.S. From Marksman Products.
Price: $32.00

MORINI 162E MATCH AIR PISTOL
Caliber: 177, single shot. **Barrel:** 9.4". **Weight:** 32 oz. **Length:** 16.1" overall. **Power:** Scuba air. **Stocks:** Adjustable match type. **Sights:** Interchangeable blade front, fully adjustable match-type rear. **Features:** Power mechanism shuts down when pressure drops to a pre-set level. Adjustable electronic trigger. Imported from Switzerland by Nygord Precision Products.
Price: $825.00
Price: 162 EI $1,075.00

MORINI SAM K-11 AIR PISTOL
Caliber: 177. **Barrel:** 10". **Weight:** 38 oz. **Stocks:** Fully adjustable. **Sights:** Fully adjustable. **Features:** Improved trigger, more angle adjustment on grip. Sophisticated counter balance system. Deluxe aluminum case, two cylinders and manometer. Imported from Switzerland by Nygord Precision Products.
Price: $975.00

PARDINI K58 MATCH AIR PISTOL
Caliber: 177, single shot. **Barrel:** 9". **Weight:** 37.7 oz. **Length:** 15.5" overall. **Power:** Pre-charged compressed air; single-stroke cocking. **Stocks:** Adjustable match type; stippled walnut. **Sights:** Interchangeable post front, fully adjustable match rear. **Features:** Fully adjustable trigger. Short version K-2 available. Imported from Italy by Nygord Precision Products.
Price: $795.00
Price: K2S model, precharged air pistol, introduced in 1998 .... $945.00

RWS 9B/9N AIR PISTOLS
Caliber: 177, single shot. **Grips:** Plastic with thumbrest. **Sights:** Adjustable. **Features:** Spring-piston powered; 550 fps. Black or nickel finish. Imported from Spain by Dynamit Nobel-RWS.
Price: 9B $169.00
Price: 9N $185.00

STEYR LP 5CP MATCH AIR PISTOL
Caliber: 177, 5-shot magazine. **Weight:** 40.7 oz. **Length:** 15.2" overall. **Power:** Precharged air cylinder. **Stocks:** Adjustable match type. **Sights:** Interchangeable blade front, fully adjustable match rear. **Features:** Adjustable sight radius; fully adjustable trigger. Barrel compensator. One-shot magazine available. Imported from Austria by Nygord Precision Products.
Price: $1,100.00

STEYR LP10P MATCH PISTOL
Caliber: 177, single shot. **Barrel:** 9". **Weight:** 38.7 oz. **Length:** 15.3" overall. **Power:** Scuba air. **Stocks:** Fully adjustable Morini match, palm shelf, stippled walnut. **Sights:** Interchangeable blade in 4mm, 4.5mm or 5mm widths, fully adjustable open rear, interchangeable 3.5mm or 4mm leaves. **Features:** Velocity about 500 fps. Adjustable trigger, adjustable sight radius from 12.4" to 13.2". With compensator. New "aborber" eliminates recoil. Imported from Austria by Nygord Precision Products.
Price: $1,175.00

TECH FORCE SS2 OLYMPIC COMPETITION AIR PISTOL
Caliber: 177 pellet, single shot. **Barrel:** 7.4". **Weight:** 2.8 lbs. **Length:** 16.5" overall. **Power:** Spring piston, sidelever. **Grips:** Hardwood. **Sights:** Extended adjustable rear, blade front accepts inserts. **Features:** Velocity 520 fps. Recoilless design; adjustments allow duplication of a firearm's feel. Match-grade, adjustable trigger; includes carrying case. Imported from China by Compasseco Inc.
Price: $295.00

TECH FORCE 35 AIR PISTOL
Caliber: 177 pellet, single shot. **Weight:** 2.86 lbs. **Length:** 14.9" overall. **Power:** Spring piston, underlever. **Grips:** Hardwood. **Sights:** Micrometer adjustable rear, blade front. **Features:** Velocity 400 fps. Grooved for scope mount; trigger safety. Imported from China by Compasseco Inc.
Price: $39.95

Tech Force 8 Air Pistol
   Similar to Tech Force 35, but with break-barrel action, ambidextrous polymer grips.
Price: $59.95

Tech Force S2-1 Air Pistol
   Similar to Tech Force 8, more basic grips and sights for plinking.
Price: $29.95

AIRGUNS

Crosman 2289G

Daisy 7840 Buckmaster

WALTHER LP300 MATCH PISTOL
Caliber: 177. **Barrel:** 236mm. **Weight:** 1.018g. **Length:** NA. **Power:** NA. **Stocks:** NA. **Sights:** Integrated front with three different widths, adjustable rear. **Features:** Adjustable grip and trigger. Imported from Germany by Nygord Precision Products.
Price: **$1,095.00**

AIRFORCE TALON AIR RIFLE
Caliber: .177, .22, single-shot. **Barrel:** 18". **Weight:** 5.5 lbs. **Length:** 32.6". **Power:** Precharged pneumatic. **Sights:** Intended for scope use, fiber optic open sights optional. **Features:** Lothar Walther match barrel, adjustable power levels from 400-1000 FPS, operates on high pressure air from scuba tank or hand pump. Wide variety of accessories easily attach to multiple dovetail mounting rails. Manufactured in the U.S.A. by AirForce Airguns.
Price: **$439.95**

AIRFORCE TALON SS AIR RIFLE
Caliber: 177, 22, single-shot. **Barrel:** 12". **Weight:** 5.25 lbs. **Length:** 32.75". **Power:** Precharged pneumatic. **Sights:** Intended for scope use, fiber optic open sights optional. **Features:** Lothar Walther match barrel, adjustable power levels from 400-1000 FPS. Chamber in front of barrel strips away air turbulence, protects muzzle and reduces firing report. Operates on high pressure air from scuba tank or hand pump. Wide variety of accessories easily attach to multiple dovetail mounting rails. Manufactured in the U.S.A. by AirForce Airguns.
Price: **$439.95**

AIRROW MODEL A-8SRB STEALTH AIR GUN
Caliber: 177, 22, 25, 9-shot. **Barrel:** 20"; rifled. **Weight:** 6 lbs. **Length:** 34" overall. **Power:** CO2 or compressed air; variable power. **Stock:** Telescoping CAR-15-type. **Sights:** Variable 3.5-10x scope. **Features:** Velocity 1100 fps in all calibers. Pneumatic air trigger. All aircraft aluminum and stainless steel construction. Mil-spec materials and finishes. From Swivel Machine Works, Inc.
Price: About **$2,299.00**

AIRROW MODEL A-8S1P STEALTH AIR GUN
Caliber: #2512 16" arrow. **Barrel:** 16". **Weight:** 4.4 lbs. **Length:** 30.1" overall. **Power:** CO2 or compressed air; variable power. **Stock:** Telescoping CAR-15-type. **Sights:** Scope rings only. 7 oz. rechargeable cylinder and valve. **Features:** Velocity to 650 fps with 260-grain arrow. Broadhead guard. All aircraft aluminum and stainless steel construction. Mil-spec materials and finishes. A-8S Models perform to 2,000 PSIG above or below water levels. Waterproof case. From Swivel Machine Works, Inc.
Price: **$1,699.00**

ARS HUNTING MASTER AR6 AIR RIFLE
Caliber: 22, 6-shot repeater. **Barrel:** 25-1/2". **Weight:** 7 lbs. **Length:** 41-1/4" overall. **Power:** Pre-compressed air from 3000 psi diving tank. **Stock:** Indonesian walnut with checkered grip; rubber buttpad. **Sights:** Blade front, adjustable peep rear. **Features:** Velocity over 1000 fps with 32-grain pellet. Receiver grooved for scope mounting. Has 6-shot rotary magazine. Imported by Air Rifle Specialists.
Price: **$580.00**

ARS/CAREER 707 AIR RIFLE
Caliber: 22, 6-shot repeater. **Barrel:** 23". **Weight:** 7.75 lbs. **Length:** 40.5" overall. **Power:** Pre-compressed air; variable power. **Stock:** Indonesian walnut with checkered grip, gloss finish. **Sights:** Hooded post front with interchangeable inserts, fully adjustable diopter rear. **Features:** Velocity to 1000 fps. Lever-action with straight feed magazine; pressure gauge in lower front air reservoir; scope mounting rail included. Imported from the Philippines by Air Rifle Specialists.
Price: **$580.00**

ANSCHUTZ 2002 MATCH AIR RIFLE
Caliber: 177, single shot. **Barrel:** 25.2". **Weight:** 10.4 lbs. **Length:** 44.5" overall. **Stock:** European walnut, blonde hardwood or colored laminated hardwood; stippled grip and forend. Also available with flat-forend walnut stock for benchrest shooting and aluminum. **Sights:** Optional sight set #6834. **Features:** Muzzle velocity 575 fps. Balance, weight match the 1907 ISU smallbore rifle. Uses #5021 match trigger. Recoil and vibration free. Fully adjustable cheekpiece and buttplate; accessory rail under forend. Available in Pneumatic and Compressed Air versions. Imported from Germany by Gunsmithing, Inc., Accuracy International, Champion's Choice.
Price: Right-hand, blonde hardwood stock, with sights **$1,275.00**
Price: Right-hand, walnut stock **$1,275.00**
Price: Right-hand, color laminate stock **$1,300.00**
Price: Right-hand, aluminum stock, butt plate **$1,495.00**
Price: Left-hand, color laminate stock **$1,595.00**
Price: Model 2002D-RT Running Target, right-hand, no sights **$1,248.90**
Price: #6834 Sight Set **$227.10**

BEEMAN CROW MAGNUM AIR RIFLE
Caliber: 20, 22, 25, single shot. **Barrel:** 16"; 10-groove rifling. **Weight:** 8.5 lbs. **Length:** 46" overall. **Power:** Gas-spring; adjustable power to 32 foot pounds muzzle energy. Barrel-cocking. **Stock:** Classic-style hardwood; hand checkered. **Sights:** For scope use only; built-in base and 1" rings included. **Features:** Adjustable two-stage trigger. Automatic safety. Available in 22-caliber on special order. Imported by Beeman.
Price: **$1,290.00**

BEEMAN KODIAK AIR RIFLE
Caliber: 25, single shot. **Barrel:** 17.6". **Weight:** 9 lbs. **Length:** 45.6" overall. **Power:** Spring-piston, barrel cocking. **Stock:** Stained hardwood. **Sights:** Blade front, open fully adjustable rear. **Features:** Velocity to 820 fps. Up to 30 foot pounds muzzle energy. Imported by Beeman.
Price: **$670.00**

BEEMAN MAKO MKII AIR RIFLE
Caliber: 177, 22 single shot. **Barrel:** 20", with compensator. **Weight:** 5.5 to 7.8 lbs. **Length:** 39" overall. **Power:** Pre-charged pneumatic. **Stock:** Stained beech; Monte Carlo cheekpiece; checkered grip. **Sights:** None furnished. **Features:** Velocity to 930 fps. Gives over 50 shots per charge. Manual safety; brass trigger blade; vented rubber butt pad. Requires scuba tank for air. Imported from England by Beeman.
Price: **$999.00**

BEEMAN R1 AIR RIFLE
Caliber: 177, 20 or 22, single shot. **Barrel:** 19.6", 12-groove rifling. **Weight:** 8.5 lbs. **Length:** 45.2" overall. **Power:** Spring-piston, barrel cocking. **Stock:** Walnut-stained beech; cut-checkered pistol grip; Monte Carlo comb and cheekpiece; rubber buttpad. **Sights:** Tunnel front with interchangeable inserts, open rear click-adjustable for windage and elevation. Grooved for scope mounting. **Features:** Velocity of 940-1000 fps (177), 860 fps (20), 800 fps (22). Non-drying nylon piston and breech seals. Adjustable metal trigger. Milled steel safety. Right- or left-hand stock. Adjustable cheekpiece and buttplate at extra cost. Custom and Super Laser versions available. Imported by Beeman.
Price: Right-hand, 177, 20, 22 .... **$605.00**
Price: Left-hand, 177, 20, 22 .... **$680.00**

BEEMAN R7 AIR RIFLE
Caliber: 177, 20, single shot. **Barrel:** 17". **Weight:** 6.1 lbs. **Length:** 40.2" overall. **Power:** Spring piston. **Stock:** Stained beech. **Sights:** Hooded front, fully adjustable micrometer click open rear. **Features:** Velocity to 700 fps (177), 620 fps (20). Receiver grooved for scope mounting; double-jointed cocking lever; fully adjustable trigger; checkered grip. Imported by Beeman.
Price: **$330.00**

BEEMAN R9 AIR RIFLE
Caliber: 177, 20, single shot. **Barrel:** NA. **Weight:** 7.3 lbs. **Length:** 43" overall. **Power:** Spring-piston, barrel cocking. **Stock:** Stained hardwood. **Sights:** Tunnel post front, fully adjustable open rear. **Features:** Velocity to 1000 fps (177), 800 fps (20). Adjustable Rekord trigger; automatic safety; receiver dovetailed for scope mounting. Imported from Germany by Beeman Precision Airguns.
Price: **$360.00**

Beeman R9 Deluxe Air Rifle
Same as R9 except has extended forend stock, checkered pistol grip, grip cap, carved Monte Carlo cheekpiece. Globe front sight with inserts. Imported by Beeman.
Price: **$440.00**

BEEMAN R11 MKII AIR RIFLE
Caliber: 177, single shot. **Barrel:** 19.6". **Weight:** 8.6 lbs. **Length:** 43.5" overall. **Power:** Spring-piston, barrel cocking. **Stock:** Walnut-stained beech; adjustable buttplate and cheekpiece. **Sights:** None furnished. Has dovetail for scope mounting. **Features:** Velocity 910-940 fps. All-steel barrel sleeve. Imported by Beeman.
Price: **$620.00**

BEEMAN SUPER 12 AIR RIFLE
Caliber: 22, 25, 12-shot magazine. **Barrel:** 19", 12-groove rifling. **Weight:** 7.8 lbs. **Length:** 41.7" overall. **Power:** Pre-charged pneumatic; external air reservoir. **Stock:** European walnut. **Sights:** None furnished; drilled and tapped for scope mounting; scope mount included. **Features:** Velocity to 850 fps (25-caliber). Adjustable power setting gives 30-70 shots per 400 cc air bottle. Requires scuba tank for air. Imported by Beeman.
Price: **$1,940.00**

AIRGUNS

BEEMAN RX-2 GAS-SPRING MAGNUM AIR RIFLE

Caliber: 177, 20, 22, 25, single shot. **Barrel:** 19.6", 12-groove rifling. **Weight:** 8.8 lbs. **Power:** Gas-spring piston air; single stroke barrel cocking. **Stock:** Walnut-finished hardwood, hand checkered, with cheekpiece. Adjustable cheekpiece and buttplate. **Sights:** Tunnel front, click-adjustable rear. **Features:** Velocity adjustable to about 1200 fps. Uses special sealed chamber of air as a mainspring. Gas-spring cannot take a set. Imported by Beeman.

Price: 177, 20, 22 or 25 regular, right-hand **$670.00**
Price: 177, 20, 22, 25, left-hand **$670.00**

BEEMAN R1 CARBINE

Caliber: 177, 20, 22, 25, single shot. **Barrel:** 16.1". **Weight:** 8.6 lbs. **Length:** 41.7" overall. **Power:** Spring-piston, barrel cocking. **Stock:** Stained beech; Monte Carlo comb and checkpiece; cut checkered pistol grip; rubber buttpad. **Sights:** Tunnel front with interchangeable inserts, open adjustable rear; receiver grooved for scope mounting. **Features:** Velocity up to 1000 fps (177). Non-drying nylon piston and breech seals. Adjustable metal trigger. Machined steel receiver end cap and safety. Right- or left-hand stock. Imported by Beeman.

Price: 177, 20, 22, 25, right-hand **$605.00**
Price: As above, left-hand **$680.00**

BEEMAN/FEINWERKBAU 603 AIR RIFLE

Caliber: 177, single shot. **Barrel:** 16.6". **Weight:** 10.8 lbs. **Length:** 43" overall. **Power:** Single stroke pneumatic. **Stock:** Special laminated hardwoods and hard rubber for stability. Multi-colored stock also available. **Sights:** Tunnel front with interchangeable inserts, click micrometer match aperture rear. **Features:** Velocity to 570 fps. Recoilless action; double supported barrel; special, short rifled area frees pellet form barrel faster so shooter's motion has minimum effect on accuracy. Fully adjustable match trigger with separately adjustable trigger and trigger slack weight. Trigger and sights blocked when loading latch is open. Imported by Beeman.

Price: Right-hand **$1,625.00**
Price: Left-hand **$1,775.00**
Price: Junior **$1,500.00**

BEEMAN/FEINWERKBAU 300-S AND 300 JUNIOR MINI-MATCH

Caliber: 177, single shot. **Barrel:** 17-1/8". **Weight:** 8.8 lbs. **Length:** 40" overall. **Power:** Spring-piston, single stroke sidelever cocking. **Stock:** Walnut. Stippled grip, adjustable buttplate. Scaled-down for youthful or slightly built shooters. **Sights:** Globe front with interchangeable inserts, micro. adjustable rear. Front and rear sights move as a single unit. **Features:** Recoilless, vibration free. Grooved for scope mounts. Steel piston ring. Cocking effort about 9-1/2 lbs. Barrel sleeve optional. Left-hand model available. Imported by Beeman.

Price: Right-hand **$1,680.00**
Price: Left-hand **$1,825.00**

BEEMAN/FEINWERKBAU P70 AND P70 JUNIOR AIR RIFLE

Caliber: 177, single shot. **Barrel:** 16.6". **Weight:** 10.6 lbs. **Length:** 42.6" overall. **Power:** Precharged pneumatic. **Stock:** Laminated hardwoods and hard rubber for stability. Multi-colored stock also available. **Sights:** Tunnel front with interchangeable inserts, click micormeter match aperture rear. **Features:** Velocity to 570 fps. Recoilless action; double supported barrel; special short rifled area frees pellet from barrel faster so shooter's motion has minimum effect on accuracy. Fully adjustable match trigger with separately adjustable trigger and trigger slack weight. Trigger and sights blocked when loading latch is open. Imported by Beeman.

Price: P70, pre-charged, right-hand **$1,600.00**
Price: P70, pre-charged, left-hand **$1,690.00**
Price: P70, pre-charged, Junior **$1,600.00**
Price: P70, pre-charged, right-hand, multi **$1,465.00**

BEEMAN/HW 97 AIR RIFLE

Caliber: 177, 20, single shot. **Barrel:** 17.75". **Weight:** 9.2 lbs. **Length:** 44.1" overall. **Power:** Spring-piston, underlever cocking. **Stock:** Walnut-stained beech; rubber buttpad. **Sights:** None. Receiver grooved for scope mounting. **Features:** Velocity 830 fps (177). Fixed barrel with fully opening, direct loading breech. Adjustable trigger. Imported by Beeman Precision Airguns.

Price: Right-hand only **$605.00**

BENJAMIN SHERIDAN PNEUMATIC (PUMP-UP) AIR RIFLES

Caliber: 177 or 22, single shot. **Barrel:** 19-3/8", rifled brass. **Weight:** 5-1/2 lbs. **Length:** 36-1/4" overall. **Power:** Underlever pneumatic, hand pumped. **Stock:** American walnut stock and forend. **Sights:** High ramp front, fully adjustable notch rear. **Features:** Variable velocity to 800 fps. Bolt action with ambidextrous push-pull safety. Black or nickel finish. Made in the U.S. by Benjamin Sheridan Co.

Price: Black finish, Model 397 (177), Model 392 (22) **$224.00**
Price: Nickel finish, Model S397 (177), Model S392 (22) **$245.00**

BENJAMIN SHERIDAN AIR RIFLE

Caliber: 177 single-shot. **Barrel:** 19-3/8", rifled brass. **Weight:** 5 lbs. **Length:** 36-1/2" overall. Power 12-gram CO2 cylinder. **Stocks:** American walnut with buttplate. **Sights:** High ramp front, fully adjustable notch rear. **Features:** Velocity to 680 fps (177). Bolt action with ambidextrous push-pull safety. Gives about 40 shots per cylinder. Black finish. Made in the U.S. by Benjamin Sheridan Co.

Price: Black finish, Model G397 (177) **$140.00**

BRNO TAU-200 AIR RIFLE

Caliber: 177, single shot. **Barrel:** 19", rifled. **Weight:** 7-1/2 lbs. **Length:** 42" overall. **Power:** 6-oz. CO2 cartridge. **Stock:** Wood match style with adjustable comb and buttplate. **Sights:** Globe front with interchangeable inserts, fully adjustable open rear. **Features:** Adjustable trigger. Comes with extra seals, large CO2 bottle, counterweight. Imported by Great Lakes Airguns. Available in Standard Universal, Deluxe Universal, International and Target Sporter versions.

Price: Standard Universal (ambidex. stock with buttstock extender, adj. cheekpiece).. . . . . **$349.50**
Price: Deluxe Universal (as above but with micro-adj. aperture sight) **$449.50**
Price: International (like Deluxe Universal but with right- or left-hand stock) **$454.50**
Price: Target Sporter (like Std. Universal but with 4X scope, no sights) **$412.50**

BSA MAGNUM SUPERSTAR™ MK2 MAGNUM AIR RIFLE, CARBINE

Caliber: 177, 22, 25, single shot. **Barrel:** 18-1/2". **Weight:** 8 lbs., 8 oz. **Length:** 43" overall. **Power:** Spring-air, underlever cocking. **Stock:** Oil-finished hardwood; Monte Carlo with cheekpiece, checkered at grip; recoil pad. **Sights:** Ramp front, micrometer adjustable rear. Maxi-Grip scope rail. **Features:** Velocity 950 fps (177), 750 fps (22), 600 fps (25). Patented rotating breech design. Maxi-Grip scope rail protects optics from recoil; automatic anti-beartrap plus manual safety. Imported from U.K. by Precision Sales International, Inc.

Price: **$349.95**
Price: MKII Carbine (14" barrel, 39-1/2" overall) **$349.95**

BSA MAGNUM SUPERSPORT™ AIR RIFLE

Caliber: 177, 22, 25, single shot. **Barrel:** 18-1/2". **Weight:** 6 lbs., 8 oz. **Length:** 41" overall. **Power:** Spring-air, barrel cocking. **Stock:** Oil-finished hardwood; Monte Carlo with cheekpiece, recoil pad. **Sights:** Ramp front, micrometer adjustable rear. Maxi-Grip scope rail. **Features:** Velocity 950 fps (177), 750 fps (22), 600 fps (25). Patented Maxi-Grip scope rail protects optics from recoil; automatic anti-beartrap plus manual tang safety. Muzzle brake standard. Imported for U.K. by Precision Sales International, Inc.

Price: **$194.95**
Price: Carbine, 14" barrel, muzzle brake **$214.95**

BSA MAGNUM GOLDSTAR MAGNUM AIR RIFLE

Caliber: 177, 22, 10-shot repeater. **Barrel:** 17-1/2". **Weight:** 8 lbs., 8 oz. **Length:** 42.5" overall. **Power:** Spring-air, underlever cocking. **Stock:** Oil-finished hardwood; Monte Carlo with cheekpiece, checkered at grip; recoil pad. **Sights:** Ramp front, micrometer adjustable rear; comes with Maxi-Grip scope rail. **Features:** Velocity 950 fps (177), 750 fps (22). Patented 10-shot indexing magazine; Maxi-Grip scope rail protects optics from recoil; automatic anti-beartrap plus manual safety; muzzlebrake standard. Imported from U.K. by Precision Sales International, Inc.

Price: **$499.95**

BSA MAGNUM SUPERTEN AIR RIFLE

Caliber: 177, 22 10-shot repeater. **Barrel:** 17-1/2". **Weight:** 7 lbs., 8 oz. **Length:** 37" overall. **Power:** Precharged pneumatic via buddy bottle. **Stock:** Oil-finished hardwood; Monte Carlo with cheekpiece, cut checkering at grip; adjustable recoil pad. **Sights:** No sights; intended for scope use. **Features:** Velocity 1000+ fps (177), 1000+ fps (22). Patented 10-shot indexing magazine, bolt-action loading. Left-hand version also available. Imported from U.K. by Precision Sales International, Inc.

Price: **$599.95**

BSA METEOR MK6 AIR RIFLE

Caliber: 177, 22, single shot. **Barrel:** 18-1/2". **Weight:** 6 lbs. **Length:** 41" overall. **Power:** Spring-air, barrel cocking. **Stock:** Oil-finished hardwood. **Sights:** Ramp front, micrometer adjustable rear. **Features:** Velocity 650 fps (177), 500 fps (22). Automatic anti-beartrap; manual tang safety. Receiver grooved for scope mounting. Imported from U.K. by Precision Sales International, Inc.

Price: Rifle **$144.95**
Price: Carbine **$164.95**

CROSMAN MODEL 66 POWERMASTER

Caliber: 177 (single shot pellet) or BB, 200-shot reservoir. **Barrel:** 20", rifled steel. **Weight:** 3 lbs. **Length:** 38-1/2" overall. **Power:** Pneumatic; hand pumped. **Stock:** Wood-grained ABS plastic; checkered pistol grip and forend. **Sights:** Ramp front, fully adjustable open rear. **Features:** Velocity about 645 fps. Bolt action, cross-bolt safety. From Crosman.

Price: Model 66BX **$60.00**
Price: Model 664X (as above, with 4x scope) **$70.00**
Price: Model 664SB (as above with silver and black finish), about **$75.00**
Price: Model 664GT (black and gold finish, 4x scope) about. **$73.00**

CROSMAN MODEL 760 PUMPMASTER

Caliber: 177 pellets (single shot) or BB (200-shot reservoir). **Barrel:** 19-1/2", rifled steel. **Weight:** 2 lbs., 12 oz. **Length:** 33.5" overall. **Power:** Pneumatic, hand pumped. **Stock:** Walnut-finished ABS plastic stock and forend. **Features:** Velocity to 590 fps (BBs, 10 pumps). Short stroke, power determined by number of strokes. Post front sight and adjustable rear sight. Cross-bolt safety. From Crosman.

Price: Model 760B **$40.00**
Price: Model 764SB (silver and black finish), about. **$55.00**
Price: Model 760SK. . . . . **NA**
Price: Model 760BRO . . . . **NA**

CROSMAN MODEL 1077 REPEATAIR RIFLE
Caliber: 177 pellets, 12-shot clip. **Barrel:** 20.3", rifled steel. **Weight:** 3 lbs., 11 oz. **Length:** 38.8" overall. **Power:** CO2 Powerlet. **Stock:** Textured synthetic or American walnut. **Sights:** Blade front, fully adjustable rear. **Features:** Velocity 590 fps. Removable 12-shot clip. True semi-automatic action. From Crosman.
Price: $75.00
Price: 1077W (walnut stock) $110.00

CROSMAN 2260 AIR RIFLE
Caliber: 22, single shot. **Barrel:** 24". **Weight:** 4 lbs., 12 oz. **Length:** 39.75" overall. **Power:** CO2 Powerlet. **Stock:** Hardwood. **Sights:** Blade front, adjustable rear open or peep. **Features:** About 600 fps. Made in U.S. by Crosman Corp.
Price: .... NA

CROSMAN MODEL 2289 RIFLE
Caliber: .22, single shot. **Barrel:** 14.625", rifled steel. **Weight:** 2 lbs. 15 oz. **Length:** 30.25" overall. **Power:** Hand pumped, pneumatic. **Stock:** Composition, skeletal type. **Sights:** Fixed front, rear peep or open, fully adjustable. **Features:** Velocity to 495 fps. Synthetic stock. From Crosman.
Price: $73.00

CROSMAN MODEL 2100 CLASSIC AIR RIFLE
Caliber: 177 pellets (single shot), or BB (200-shot BB reservoir). **Barrel:** 21", rifled. **Weight:** 4 lbs., 13 oz. **Length:** 39-3/4" overall. **Power:** Pump-up, pneumatic. **Stock:** Wood-grained checkered ABS plastic. **Features:** Three pumps give about 450 fps, 10 pumps about 755 fps (BBs). Cross-bolt safety; concealed reservoir holds over 200 BBs. From Crosman.
Price: Model 2100B $75.00
Price: Model 2104GT (black and gold finish, 4x scope), about $95.00

CROSMAN MODEL 2200 MAGNUM AIR RIFLE
Caliber: 22, single shot. **Barrel:** 19", rifled steel. **Weight:** 4 lbs., 12 oz. **Length:** 39" overall. **Stock:** Full-size, wood-grained ABS plastic with checkered grip and forend or American walnut. **Sights:** Ramp front, open step-adjustable rear. **Features:** Variable pump power—three pumps give 395 fps, six pumps 530 fps, 10 pumps 595 fps (average). Full-size adult air rifle. Has white line spacers at pistol grip and buttplate. From Crosman.
Price: $75.00

DAISY 1938 RED RYDER 60th ANNIVERSARY CLASSIC
Caliber: BB, 650-shot repeating action. **Barrel:** Smoothbore steel with shroud. **Weight:** 2.2 lbs. **Length:** 35.4" overall. **Stock:** Walnut stock burned with Red Ryder lariat signature. **Sights:** Post front, adjustable V-slot rear. **Features:** Walnut forend. Saddle ring with leather thong. Lever cocking. Gravity feed. Controlled velocity. One of Daisy's most popular guns. From Daisy Mfg. Co.
Price: $39.95

DAISY MODEL 840 GRIZZLY
Caliber: 177 pellet single shot; or BB 350-shot. **Barrel:** 19", smoothbore, steel. **Weight:** 2.25 lbs. **Length:** 36.8" overall. **Power:** Pneumatic, single pump. **Stock:** Moulded wood-grain stock and forend. **Sights:** Ramp front, open, adjustable rear. **Features:** Muzzle velocity 320 fps (BB), 300 fps (pellet). Steel buttplate; straight pull bolt action; cross-bolt safety. Forend forms pump lever. From Daisy Mfg. Co.
Price: $32.95
Price: 840C Mossy Oak® Break Up™ camo $49.95

DAISY MODEL 7840 BUCKMASTER
Caliber: 177 pellets, or BB. **Barrel:** Smoothbore steel. **Weight:** 2.25 lbs. **Length:** 36.8" overall. **Power:** Single-pump pneumatic. **Stock:** Moulded with checkering and woodgrain. **Sights:** Ramp and blade front, adjustable open rear plus Electronic Point Sight. **Features:** Velocity to 320 fps (BB), 300fps (pellet). Cross-bolt trigger block safety. From Daisy Mfg. Co.
Price: $54.95

DAISY MODEL 105 BUCK
Caliber: 177 or BB. **Barrel:** Smoothbore steel. **Weight:** 1.6 lbs. **Length:** 29.8" overall. **Power:** Lever cocking, spring air. **Stock:** Stained solid wood. **Sights:** TRUGLO® Fiber Optic, open fixed rear. **Features:** Velocity to 275. Cross-bolt trigger block safety. From Daisy Mfg. Co.
Price: .... NA

Daisy Model 95 Timberwolf
Similar to the 105 Buck except velocity to 325 fps. Weighs 2.4 lbs, overall length 35.2".
Price: $38.95

DAISY/POWERLINE 853
Caliber: 177 pellets, single shot. **Barrel:** 20.9"; 12-groove rifling, high-grade solid steel by Lothar Walther®, precision crowned; bore size for precision match pellets. **Weight:** 5.08 lbs. **Length:** 38.9" overall. **Power:** Single-pump pneumatic. **Stock:** Full-length select American hardwood, stained and finished; black buttplate with white spacers. **Sights:** Globe front with four aperture inserts; precision micrometer adjustable rear peep sight mounted on a standard 3/8" dovetail receiver mount.
Price: $225.00

DAISY/POWERLINE 856 PUMP-UP AIRGUN
Caliber: 177 pellets (single shot) or BB (100-shot reservoir). **Barrel:** Rifled steel with shroud. **Weight:** 2.7 lbs. **Length:** 37.4" overall. **Power:** Pneumatic pump-up. **Stock:** Moulded wood-grain with Monte Carlo cheekpiece. **Sights:** Ramp and blade front, open rear adjustable for elevation. **Features:** Velocity from 315 fps (two pumps) to 650 fps (10 pumps). Shoots BBs or pellets. Heavy die-cast metal receiver. Cross-bolt trigger-block safety. From Daisy Mfg. Co.
Price: $39.95
Price: 856C $59.95

DAISY/POWERLINE 1170 PELLET RIFLE
Caliber: 177, single shot. **Barrel:** Rifled steel. **Weight:** 5.5 lbs. **Length:** 42.5" overall. **Power:** Spring-air, barrel cocking. **Stock:** Hardwood. **Sights:** Hooded post front, micrometer adjustable open rear. **Features:** Velocity to 800 fps. Monte Carlo comb. From Daisy Mfg. Co.
Price: $129.95
Price: Model 131 (velocity to 600 fps) $117.95
Price: Model 1150 (black copolymer stock, velocity to 600 fps) $77.95

DAISY/POWERLINE EAGLE 7856 PUMP-UP AIRGUN
Caliber: 177 (pellets), BB, 100-shot BB magazine. **Barrel:** Rifled steel with shroud. **Weight:** 3.3 lbs. **Length:** 37.4" overall. **Power:** Pneumatic pump-up. **Stock:** Moulded wood-grain plastic. **Sights:** Ramp and blade front, open rear adjustable for elevation. **Features:** Velocity from 315 fps (two pumps) to 650 fps (10 pumps). Finger grooved forend. Cross-bolt trigger-block safety. From Daisy Mfg. Co.
Price: With 4x scope, about $49.95

DAISY/POWERLINE 880
Caliber: 177 pellet or BB, 50-shot BB magazine, single shot for pellets. **Barrel:** Rifled steel. **Weight:** 3.7 lbs. **Length:** 37.6" overall. **Power:** Multi-pump pneumatic. **Stock:** Moulded wood grain; Monte Carlo comb. **Sights:** Hooded front, adjustable rear. **Features:** Velocity to 685 fps. (BB). Variable power (velocity, range) increase with pump strokes; resin receiver with dovetail scope mount. Made in U.S.A. by Daisy Mfg. Co.
Price: $50.95

DAISY/POWERLINE 1000 AIR RIFLE
Caliber: 177, single shot. **Barrel:** NA. **Weight:** 6.15 lbs. **Length:** 43" overall. **Power:** Spring-air, barrel cocking. **Stock:** Stained hardwood. **Sights:** Hooded blade front on ramp, fully adjustable micrometer rear. **Features:** Velocity to 1000 fps. Blued finish; trigger block safety. From Daisy Mfg. Co.
Price: $208.95

DAISY/YOUTHLINE MODEL 105 AIR RIFLE
Caliber: BB, 400-shot magazine. **Barrel:** 13-1/2". **Weight:** 1.6 lbs. **Length:** 29.8" overall. **Power:** Spring. **Stock:** Moulded woodgrain. **Sights:** Blade on ramp front, fixed rear. **Features:** Velocity to 275 fps. Blue finish. Cross-bolt trigger block safety. Made in U.S. by Daisy Mfg. Co.
Price: $28.95

DAISY/YOUTHLINE MODEL 95 AIR RIFLE
Caliber: BB, 700-shot magazine. **Barrel:** 18". **Weight:** 2.4 lbs. **Length:** 35.2" overall. **Power:** Spring. **Stock:** Stained hardwood. **Sights:** Blade on ramp front, open adjustable rear. **Features:** Velocity to 325 fps. Cross-bolt trigger block safety. Made in U.S. by Daisy Mfg. Co.
Price: $38.95

EAA/BAIKAL MP-512 AIR RIFLE
Caliber: 177, single shot. **Barrel:** 17.7". **Weight:** 6.2 lbs. **Length:** 41.3" overall. **Power:** Spring-piston, single stroke. **Stock:** Black synthetic. **Sights:** Adjustable rear, hooded front. **Features:** Velocity 490 fps. Hammer-forged, rifled barrel; automatic safety; scope mount rail. Imported from Russia by European American Armory.
Price: 177 caliber $50.00
Price: 512M (590 fps) .... $NA

EAA/BAIKAL IZH-61 AIR RIFLE
Caliber: 177 pellet, 5-shot magazine. **Barrel:** 17.8". **Weight:** 6.4 lbs. **Length:** 31" overall. **Power:** Spring piston, side-cocking lever. **Stock:** Black plastic. **Sights:** Adjustable rear, fully hooded front. **Features:** Velocity 490 fps. Futuristic design with adjustable stock. Imported from Russia by European American Armory.
Price: $99.00

EAA/BAIKAL IZHMP-532 AIR RIFLE
Caliber: 177 pellet, single shot. **Barrel:** 15.8". **Weight:** 9.3 lbs. **Length:** 46.1" overall. **Power:** Single-stroke pneumatic. **Stock:** One- or two-piece competition-style stock with adjustable butt pad, pistol grip. **Sights:** Fully adjustable rear, hooded front. **Features:** Velocity 460 fps. Five-way adjustable trigger. Imported from Russia by European American Armory.
Price: $599.00

GAMO DELTA AIR RIFLE
Caliber: 177. **Barrel:** 15.7". **Weight:** 4.2 lbs. **Length:** 37.8". **Power:** Single-stroke pneumatic, 525 fps. **Stock:** Synthetic. **Sights:** Truglo fiber optic.
Price: $89.95

GAMO YOUNG HUNTER AIR RIFLE
Caliber: 177. **Barrel:** 17.7". **Weight:** 5.5 lbs. **Length:** 41". **Power:** Single-stroke pneumatic, 640 fps. **Stock:** Wood. **Sights:** Truglo fiber optic adjustable. **Features:** Excellent for young adults, it has a rifled steel barrel, hooded front sight, grooved receiver for scope. Imported from Spain by Gamo.
Price: $129.95
Price: Combo packed with BSA 4x32 scope and rings $169.95

AIRGUNS

AIRGUNS—LONG GUNS

GAMO SPORTER AIR RIFLE
Caliber: 177. **Barrel:** NA **Weight:** 5.5 lbs. **Length:** 42.5". **Power:** Single-stroke pneumatic, 760 fps. **Stock:** Wood. **Sights:** Adjustable Truglo fiber optic. **Features:** Intended to bridge the gap between Gamo's Young Hunter model and the adult-sized Hunter 440. Imported from Spain by Gamo.
Price: **$159.95**

GAMO HUNTER 440 AIR RIFLE
Caliber: 177, 22. **Barrel:** NA. **Weight:** 6.6 lbs. **Length:** 43.3". **Power:** Single-stroke pneumatifc, 1,000 fps (177), 750 fps (22). **Stock:** Wood. **Sights:** Adjustable Truglo fiber optic. **Features:** Adjustable two-stage trigger, rifled barrel, raised scope ramp on receiver. Realtree camo model available.
Price: **$229.95**
Price: Hunter 440 Combo with BSA 4x32mm scope **$259.95**

HAMMERLI AR 50 AIR RIFLE
Caliber: 177. **Barrel:** 19.8". **Weight:** 10 lbs. **Length:** 43.2" overall. **Power:** Compressed air. **Stock:** Anatomically-shaped universal and right-hand; match style; multi-colored laminated wood. **Sights:** Interchangeable element tunnel front, fully adjustable Hammerli peep rear. **Features:** Vibration-free firing release; fully adjustable match trigger and trigger stop; stainless air tank, built-in pressure gauge. Gives 270 shots per filling. Imported from Switzerland by Sigarms, Inc.
Price: **$1,653.00**

HAMMERLI MODEL 450 MATCH AIR RIFLE
Caliber: 177, single shot. **Barrel:** 19.5". **Weight:** 9.8 lbs. **Length:** 43.3" overall. **Power:** Pneumatic. **Stock:** Match style with stippled grip, rubber buttpad. Beach or walnut. **Sights:** Match tunnel front, Hammerli diopter rear. **Features:** Velocity about 560 fps. Removable sights; forend sling rail; adjustable trigger; adjustable comb. Imported from Switzerland by Sigarms, Inc.
Price: Beech stock **$1,355.00**
Price: Walnut stock **$1,395.00**

MARKSMAN BB BUDDY AIR RIFLE
Caliber: 177, 20-shot magazine. **Barrel:** 10.5" smoothbore. **Weight:** 1.6 lbs. **Length:** 33" overall. **Power:** Spring-air. **Stock:** Moulded composition. **Sights:** Blade on ramp front, adjustable V-slot rear. **Features:** Velocity 275 fps. Positive feed; automatic safety. Youth-sized lightweight design. Made in U.S. From Marksman Products.
Price: **$27.95**

MARKSMAN 2015 LASERHAWK™ BB REPEATER AIR RIFLE
Caliber: 177 BB, 20-shot magazine. **Barrel:** 10.5" smoothbore. **Weight:** 1.6 lbs. **Length:** Adjustable to 33", 34" or 35" overall. **Power:** Spring-air. **Stock:** Moulded composition. **Sights:** Fixed fiber optic front sight, adjustable elevation V-slot rear. **Features:** Velocity about 275 fps. Positive feed; automatic safety. Adjustable stock. Made in the U.S. From Marksman Products.
Price: **$33.00**

RWS/DIANA MODEL 24 AIR RIFLE
Caliber: 177, 22, single shot. **Barrel:** 17", rifled. **Weight:** 6 lbs. **Length:** 42" overall. **Power:** Spring-air, barrel cocking. **Stock:** Beech. **Sights:** Hooded front, adjustable rear. **Features:** Velocity of 700 fps (177). Easy cocking effort; blue finish. Imported from Germany by Dynamit Nobel-RWS, Inc.
Price: 24, 24C **$215.00**

RWS/Diana Model 34 Air Rifle
Similar to the Model 24 except has 19" barrel, weighs 7.5 lbs. Gives velocity of 1000 fps (177), 800 fps (22). Adjustable trigger, synthetic seals. Comes with scope rail.
Price: 177 or 22 .... **$290.00**
Price: Model 34N (nickel-plated metal, black epoxy-coated wood stock) ... **$350.00**
Price: Model 34BC (matte black metal, black stock, 4x32 scope, mounts) .. **$510.00**

RWS/DIANA MODEL 36 AIR RIFLE
Caliber: 177, 22, single shot. **Barrel:** 19", rifled. **Weight:** 8 lbs. **Length:** 45" overall. **Power:** Spring-air, barrel cocking. **Stock:** Beech. **Sights:** Hooded front (interchangeable inserts available), adjustable rear. **Features:** Velocity of 1000 fps (177-cal.). Comes with scope mount; two-stage adjustable trigger. Imported from Germany by Dynamit Nobel-RWS, Inc.
Price: 36, 36C **$435.00**

RWS/DIANA MODEL 52 AIR RIFLE
Caliber: 177, 22, 25, single shot. **Barrel:** 17", rifled. **Weight:** 8-1/2 lbs. **Length:** 43" overall. **Power:** Spring-air, sidelever cocking. **Stock:** Beech, with Monte Carlo, cheekpiece, checkered grip and forend. **Sights:** Ramp front, adjustable rear. **Features:** Velocity of 1100 fps (177). Blue finish. Solid rubber buttpad. Imported from Germany by Dynamit Nobel-RWS, Inc.
Price: 177, 22 .... **$565.00**
Price: 25 .... **$605.00**
Price: Model 52 Deluxe (177). **$810.00**
Price: Model 48B (as above except matte black metal, black stock) **$535.00**
Price: Model 48 (same as Model 52 except no Monte Carlo, cheekpiece or checkering). **$520.00**

RWS/DIANA MODEL 45 AIR RIFLE
Caliber: 177, single shot. **Weight:** 8 lbs. **Length:** 45" overall. **Power:** Spring-air, barrel cocking. **Stock:** Walnut-finished hardwood with rubber recoil pad. **Sights:** Globe front with interchangeable inserts, micro, click open rear with four-way blade. **Features:** Velocity of 820 fps. Dovetail base for either micrometer peep sight or

scope mounting. Automatic safety. Imported from Germany by Dynamit Nobel-RWS, Inc,
Price: **$350.00**

RWS/DIANA MODEL 46 AIR RIFLE
Caliber: 177, 22, single shot. **Barrel:** 18". **Weight:** 8.2 lbs. **Length:** 45" overall. **Stock:** Hardwood Monte Carlo. **Sights:** Blade front, adjustable rear. **Features:** Underlever cocking spring-air (950 fps in 177, 780 fps in 22); extended scope rail, automatic safety, rubber buttpad, adjustable trigger. Imported from Germany by Dynamit Nobel-RWS Inc.
Price: **$470.00**
Price: Model 46E (as above except matte black metal, black stock) **$430.00**

RWS/DIANA MODEL 54 AIR RIFLE
Caliber: 177, 22, single shot. **Barrel:** 17". **Weight:** 9 lbs. **Length:** 43" overall. **Power:** Spring-air, single shot. **Stock:** Walnut with Monte Carlo cheekpiece, checkered grip and forend. **Sights:** Ramp front, fully adjustable rear. **Features:** Velocity to 1000 fps (177), 900 fps (22). Totally recoilless system; floating action absorbs recoil. Imported from Germany by Dynamit Nobel-RWS, Inc.
Price: **$785.00**

RWS/DIANA MODEL 92/93/94 AIR RIFLES
Caliber: 177, 22, single shot. **Barrel:** N/A. **Weight:** N/A. **Length:** N/A. **Stock:** Beechwood; Monte Carlo. **Sights:** Hooded front, fully adjustable rear. **Features:** Break-barrel, spring-air; receiver grooved for scope; adjustable trigger; lifetime warranty. Imported from Spain by Dynamit Nobel-RWS Inc.
Price: Model 92 (auto safety, 700 fps in 177) .... **NA**
Price: Model 93 (manual safety, 850 fps in 177) .... **NA**
Price: Model 94 (auto safety, 1,000 fps in 177) .... **NA**

RWS/DIANA MODEL 350 MAGNUM AIR RIFLE
Caliber: 177, 22, single shot. **Barrel:** 19-1/2". **Weight:** 8 lbs. **Length:** 48". **Stock:** Beechwood; Monte Carlo. **Sights:** Hooded front, fully adjustable rear. **Features:** Break-barrel, spring-air; 1,250 fps. Imported from Germany by Dynamit Nobel-RWS Inc.
Price: Model 350 .... **NA**

TECH FORCE BS4 OLYMPIC COMPETITION AIR RIFLE
Caliber: 177 pellet, single shot. **Barrel:** N/A. **Weight:** 10.8 lbs. **Length:** 43.3" overall. **Power:** Spring piston, sidelever action. **Stock:** Wood with semi-pistol grip, adjustable butt plate. **Sights:** Micro-adjustable competition rear, hooded front. **Features:** Velocity 640 fps. Recoilless action; adjustable trigger. Includes carrying case. Imported from China by Compasseco Inc.
Price: **$595.00**
Price: Optional diopter rear sight **$79.95**

TECH FORCE 6 AIR RIFLE
Caliber: 177 pellet, single shot. **Barrel:** 14". **Weight:** 6 lbs. **Length:** 35.5" overall. **Power:** Spring piston, sidelever action. **Stock:** Paratrooper-style folding, full pistol grip. **Sights:** Adjustable rear, hooded front. **Features:** Velocity 800 fps. All-metal construction; grooved for scope mounting. Imported from China by Compasseco Inc.
Price: **$69.95**

Tech Force 51 Air Rifle
Similar to Tech Force 6, but with break-barrel cocking mechanism and folding stock fitted with recoil pad. Overall length, 36". Weighs 6 lbs. From Compasseco Inc.
Price: **$69.95**

TECH FORCE 25 AIR RIFLE
Caliber: 177, 22 pellet; single shot. **Barrel:** N/A. **Weight:** 7.5 lbs. **Length:** 46.2" overall. **Power:** Spring piston, break-action barrel. **Stock:** Oil-finished wood; Monte Carlo stock with recoil pad. **Sights:** Adjustable rear, hooded front with insert. **Features:** Velocity 1,000 fps (177); grooved receiver and scope stop for scope mounting; adjustable trigger; trigger safety. Imported from China by Compasseco Inc.
Price: 177 or 22 caliber **$125.00**
Price: Includes rifle and Tech Force 96 red dot point sight **$164.95**

TECH FORCE 36 AIR RIFLE
Caliber: 177 pellet, single shot. **Barrel:** N/A. **Weight:** 7.4 lbs. **Length:** 43" overall. **Power:** Spring piston, underlever cocking. **Stock:** Monte Carlo hardwood stock; recoil pad. **Sights:** Adjustable rear, hooded front. **Features:** Velocity 900 fps; grooved receiver and scope stop for scope mounting; auto-reset safety. Imported from China by Compasseco Inc.
Price: **$89.95**

WHISCOMBE JW SERIES AIR RIFLES
Caliber: 177, 20, 22, 25, single shot. **Barrel:** 15", Lothar Walther. Polygonal rifling. **Weight:** 9 lbs., 8 oz. **Length:** 39" overall. **Power:** Dual spring-piston, multi-stroke; underlever cocking. **Stock:** Walnut with adjustable buttplate and cheekpiece. **Sights:** None furnished; grooved scope rail. **Features:** Velocity 660-1000 (JW80) fps (22-caliber, fixed barrel) depending upon model. Interchangeable barrels; automatic safety; muzzle weight; semi-floating action; twin opposed pistons with counterwound springs; adjustable trigger. All models include H.O.T. System (Harmonic Optimization Tunable System). Imported from England by Pelaire Products.
Price: JW50, MKII fixed barrel only **$2,085.00**
Price: JW65, MKII **$2,085.00**
Price: JW80, MKII **$2,195.00**

AIRGUNS

CH4D Heavyduty Champion

Frame: Cast iron
Frame Type: O-frame
Die Thread: 7/8-14 or 1-14
Avg. Rounds Per Hour: NA
Ram Stroke: 3-1/4"
Weight: 26 lbs.
Features: 1.185" diameter ram with 16 square inches of bearing surface; ram drilled to allow passage of spent primers; solid steel handle; toggle that slightly breaks over the top dead center. Includes universal primer arm with large and small punches. From CH Tool & Die/4D Custom Die.
Price: **$220.00**

CH4D No. 444 4-Station "H" Press

Frame: Aluminum alloy
Frame Type: H-frame
Die Thread: 7/8-14
Avg. Rounds Per Hour: 200
Ram Stroke: 3-3/4"
Weight: 12 lbs.
Features: Two 7/8" solid steel shaft "H" supports; platen rides on permanently lubed bronze bushings; loads smallest pistol to largest magnum rifle cases and has strength to full-length resize. Includes four rams, large and small primer arm and primer catcher. From CH Tool & Die/4D Custom Die, Co.
Price: **$195.00**

CH4D No. 444-X Pistol Champ

Frame: Aluminum alloy
Frame Type: H-frame
Die Thread: 7/8-14
Avg. Rounds Per Hour: 200
Ram Stroke: 3-3/4"
Weight: 12 lbs.
Features: Tungsten carbide sizing die; Speed Seater seating die with tapered entrance to automatically align bullet on case mouth; automatic primer feed for large or small primers; push-button powder measure with easily changed bushings for 215 powder/load combinations; taper crimp die. Conversion kit for caliber changeover available. From CH Tool & Die/4D Custom Die, Co.
Price: . . . . **$292.00-$316.50**

New CORBIN CSP-2 MEGA MITE

Frame: N/A
Frame Type: N/A
Die Thread: 1-1/2 x 12
Avg. Rounds Per Hour: N/A
Ram Stroke: 6"
Weight: 70 lbs.
Features: Roller bearing linkage, hardened tool steel pivots, precision bush bushings glide on polished steel guide rods. Made for use with –H type (hydraulic) swage dies, it is capable of swaging rifle calibers up to .600 Nitro, lead shotgun slugs up to 12 gauge and the reloading of .50 BMG ammo. From Corbin Manufacturing.
Price: **$750.00**

FORSTER Co-Ax Press B-2

Frame: Cast iron
Frame Type: Modified O-frame
Die Thread: 7/8-14
Avg. Rounds Per Hour: 120
Ram Stroke: 4"
Weight: 18 lbs.
Features: Snap in/snap out die change; spent primer catcher with drop tube threaded into carrier below shellholder; automatic, handle-activated, cammed shellholder with opposing spring-loaded jaws to contact extractor groove; floating guide rods for alignment and reduced friction; no torque on the head due to design of linkage and pivots; shellholder jaws that float with die permitting case to center in the die; right- or left-hand operation; priming device for seating to factory specifications. "S" shellholder jaws included. From Forster Products.
Price: **$298.00**
Price: Extra shellholder jaws. **$26.00**

HOLLYWOOD Senior Press

Frame: Ductile iron
Frame Type: O-frame
Die Thread: 7/8-14
Avg. Rounds Per Hour: 50-100
Ram Stroke: 6-1/2"
Weight: 50 lbs.
Features: Leverage and bearing surfaces ample for reloading cartridges or swaging bullets. Precision ground one-piece 2-1/2" pillar with base; operating handle of 3/4" steel and 15" long; 5/8" steel tie-down rod fro added strength when swaging; heavy steel toggle and camming arms held by 1/2" steel pins in reamed holes. The 1-1/2" steel die bushing takes standard threaded dies; removed, it allows use of Hollywood shotshell dies. From Hollywood Engineering.
Price: **$500.00**

HOLLYWOOD Senior Turret Press

Frame: Ductile iron
Frame Type: H-frame
Die Thread: 7/8-14
Avg. Rounds Per Hour: 50-100
Ram Stroke: 6-1/2"
Weight: 50 lbs.
Features: Same features as Senior press except has three-position turret head; holes in turret may be tapped 1-1/2" or 7/8" or four of each. Height, 15". Comes complete with one turret indexing handle; one 1-1/2" to 7/8" die hole bushing; one 5/8" tie down bar for swaging. From Hollywood Engineering.
Price: **$600.00**

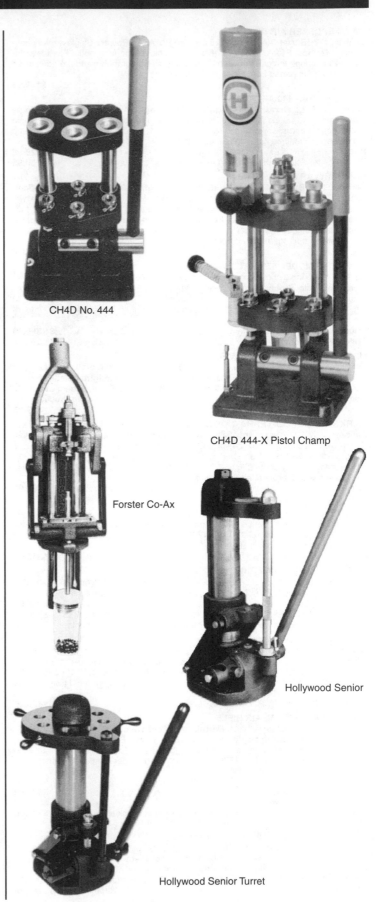

CH4D No. 444

CH4D 444-X Pistol Champ

Forster Co-Ax

Hollywood Senior

Hollywood Senior Turret

ACCESSORIES

METALLIC CARTRIDGE PRESSES

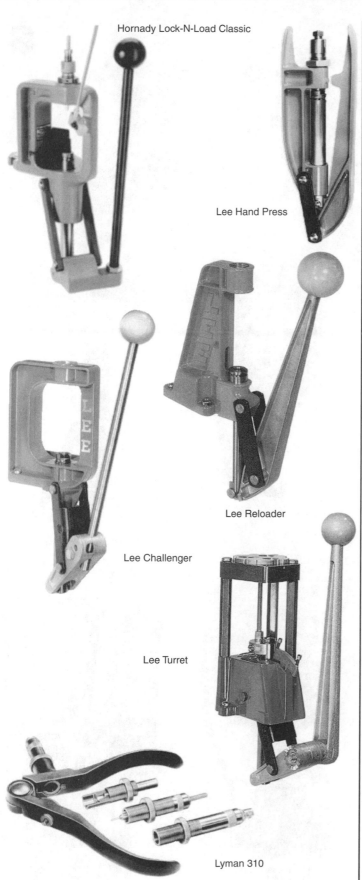

Hornady Lock-N-Load Classic

Lee Hand Press

Lee Reloader

Lee Challenger

Lee Turret

Lyman 310

HORNADY Lock-N-Load Classic

Frame: Die cast heat-treated aluminum alloy
Frame Type: O-frame
Die Thread: 7/8-14
Avg. Rounds Per Hour: NA
Ram Stroke: 3-5/8"
Weight: 14 lbs.

Features: Features Lock-N-Load bushing system that allows instant die changeovers. Solid steel linkage arms that rotate on steel pins; 30° angled frame design for improved visibility and accessibility; primer arm automatically moves in and out of ram for primer pickup and solid seating; two primer arms for large and small primers; long offset handle for increased leverage and unobstructed reloading; lifetime warranty. Comes as a package with primer catcher, PPS automatic primer feed and three Lock-N-Load die bushings. Dies and shellholder available separately or as a kit with primer catcher, positive priming system, automatic primer feed, three die bushings and reloading accessories. From Hornady Mfg. Co.
Price: Press and Three Die Bushings $99.95
Price: Classic Reloading Kit..................................$259.95

LEE Hand Press

Frame: ASTM 380 aluminum
Frame Type: NA
Die Thread: 7/8-14
Avg. Rounds Per Hour: 100
Ram Stroke: 3-1/4"
Weight: 1 lb., 8 oz.

Features: Small and lightweight for portability; compound linkage for handling up to 375 H&H and case forming. Dies and shellholder not included. From Lee Precision, Inc.
Price: $26.98

LEE Challenger Press

Frame: ASTM 380 aluminum
Frame Type: O-frame
Die Thread: 7/8-14
Avg. Rounds Per Hour: 100
Ram Stroke: 3-1/2"
Weight: 4 lbs., 1 oz.

Features: Larger than average opening with 30° offset for maximum hand clearance; steel connecting pins; spent primer catcher; handle adjustable for start and stop positions; handle repositions for left- or right-hand use; shortened handle travel to prevent springing the frame from alignment. Dies and shellholders not included. From Lee Precision, Inc.
Price: $45.00

LEE Loader

Kit consists of reloading dies to be used with mallet or soft hammer. Neck sizes only. Comes with powder charge cup. From Lee Precision, Inc.
Price: $19.98

LEE Reloader Press

Frame: ASTM 380 aluminum
Frame Type: C-frame
Die Thread: 7/8-14
Avg. Rounds Per Hour: 100
Ram Stroke: 3"
Weight: 1 lb., 12 oz.

Features: Balanced lever to prevent pinching fingers; unlimited hand clearance; left- or right-hand use. Dies and shellholders not included. From Lee Precision, Inc.
Price: $26.98

LEE Turret Press

Frame: ASTM 380 aluminum
Frame Type: O-frame
Die Thread: 7/8-14
Avg. Rounds Per Hour: 300
Ram Stroke: 3"
Weight: 7 lbs., 2 oz.

Features: Replaceable turret lifts out by rotating 30°; T-primer arm reverses for large or small primers; built-in primer catcher; adjustable handle for right- or left-hand use or changing angle of down stroke; accessory mounting hole for Lee Auto-Disk powder measure. Optional Auto-Index rotates die turret to next station for semi-progressive use. Safety override prevents overstressing should turret not turn. From Lee Precision, Inc.
Price: $69.98
Price: With Auto-Index $83.98
Price: Four-Hole Turret with Auto-Index $85.98

LYMAN 310 Tool

Frame: Stainless steel
Frame Type: NA
Die Thread: 7/8-14
Avg. Rounds Per Hour: NA
Ram Stroke: NA
Weight: 10 oz.

Features: Compact, portable reloading tool for pistol or rifle cartridges. Adapter allows loading rimmed or rimless cases. Die set includes neck resizing/decapping die, primer seating chamber; neck expanding die; bullet seating die; and case head adapter. From Lyman Products Corp.
Price: Dies $45.00
Price: Handles $47.50
Price: Carrying pouch..$9.95

ACCESSORIES

LYMAN AccuPress

Frame: Die cast
Frame Type: C-frame
Die Thread: 7/8-14
Avg. Rounds Per Hour: 75
Ram Stroke: 3.4"
Weight: 4 lbs.
Features: Reversible, contoured handle for bench mount or hand-held use; for rifle or pistol; compound leverage; Delta frame design. Accepts all standard powder measures. From Lyman Products Corp.
Price: $34.95

LYMAN Crusher II

Frame: Cast iron
Frame Type: O-frame
Die Thread: 7/8-14
Avg. Rounds Per Hour: 75
Ram Stroke: 3-7/8"
Weight: 19 lbs.
Features: Reloads both pistol and rifle cartridges; 1" diameter ram; 4-1/2" press opening for loading magnum cartridges; direct torque design; right- or left-hand use. New base design with 14 square inches of flat mounting surface with three bolt holes. Comes with priming arm and primer catcher. Dies and shellholders not included. From Lyman Products Corp.
Price: $116.50

LYMAN T-Mag II

Frame: Cast iron with silver metalflake powder finish
Frame Type: Turret
Die Thread: 7/8-14
Avg. Rounds Per Hour: 125
Ram Stroke: 3-13/16"
Weight: 18 lbs.
Features: Reengineered and upgraded with new turret system for ease of indexing and tool-free turret removal for caliber changeover; new flat machined base for bench mounting; new nickel-plated non-rust handle and links; and new silver hammertone powder coat finish for durability. Right- or left-hand operation; handles all rifle or pistol dies. Comes with priming arm and primer catcher. Dies and shellholders not included. From Lyman Products Corp.
Price: $164.95
Price: Extra turret $37.50

New MEACHAM ANYWHERE PORTABLE RELOADING PRESS

Frame: Anodized 6061 T6 aircraft aluminum
Frame Type: Cylindrical
Die Thread: 7/8-14
Avg. Rounds Per Hour: N/A
Ram Stroke: 2.7"
Weight: 2 lbs. (hand held); 5 lbs. (with docking kit)
Features: A light weight, portable press that can be used hand-held (or with a docking kit) can be clamped to a table top up to 9.75" thick. Docking kit includes a threaded powder measure mount and holder for the other die. Designed for neck sizing abd bullet seating of short action cartridges, it can be used for long action cartridges with the addition of an Easy Seater straight line seating die. Dies not included.
Price: $99.95
Price: (with docking kit) $144.95
Price: Easy Seater $114.95
Price: Re-De-Capper .... **N/A**

PONSNESS/WARREN Metal-Matic P-200

Frame: Die cast aluminum
Frame Type: Unconventional
Die Thread: 7/8-14
Avg. Rounds Per Hour: 200+
Weight: 18 lbs.
Features: Designed for straight-wall cartridges; die head with 10 tapped holes for holding dies and accessories for two calibers at one time; removable spent primer box; pivoting arm moves case from station to station. Comes with large and small primer tool. Optional accessories include primer feed, extra die head, primer speed feeder, powder measure extension and dust cover. Dies, powder measure and shellholder not included. From Ponsness/Warren.
Price: $215.00
Price: Extra die head $44.95
Price: Powder measure extension $29.95
Price: Primer feed $44.95
Price: Primer speed feed $14.50
Price: Dust cover $21.95

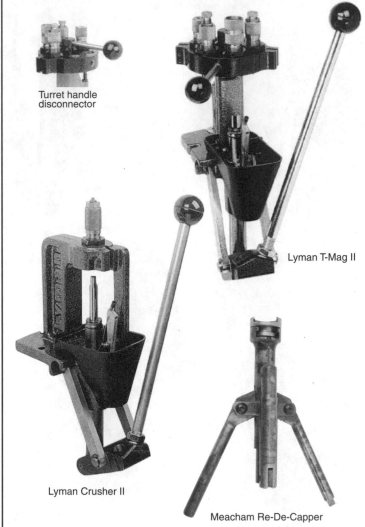

Turret handle disconnector

Lyman T-Mag II

Lyman Crusher II

Meacham Re-De-Capper

Ponsness/Warren Metal-Matic P-200

RCBS AmmoMaster Single

ACCESSORIES

METALLIC CARTRIDGE PRESSES

RCBS Partner

RCBS Reloader Special-5

RCBS Rock Chucker

Redding Turret Press

Redding Boss

RCBS Partner

Frame: Aluminum
Frame Type: O-frame
Die Thread: 7/8-14
Avg. Rounds Per Hour: 50-60
Ram Stroke: 3-5/8"
Weight: 5 lbs.
Features: Designed for the beginning reloader. Comes with primer arm equipped with interchangeable primer plugs and sleeves for seating large and small primers. Shellholder and dies not included. Available in kit form (see Metallic Presses—Accessories). From RCBS.
Price:.. **$66.95**

RCBS AmmoMaster Single

Frame: Aluminum base; cast iron top plate connected by three steel posts.
Frame Type: NA
Die Thread: 1-1/4"-12 bushing;
7/8-14 threads
Avg. Rounds Per Hour: 50-60
Ram Stroke: 5-1/4"
Weight: 19 lbs.
Features: Single-stage press convertible to progressive. Will form cases or swage bullets. Case detection system to disengage powder measure when no case is present in powder charging station; five-station shellplate; Uniflow Powder measure with clear powder measure adaptor to make bridged powders visible and correctable. 50-cal. conversion kit allows reloading 50 BMG. Kit includes top plate to accommodate either 1-3/8" x 12 or 1-1/2" x 12 reloading dies. Piggyback die plate for quick caliber change-overs available. Reloading dies not included. From RCBS.
Price:.. **$219.95**
Price: 50 conversion kit.. **$96.95**
Price: Piggyback/AmmoMaster die plate......................... **$25.95**
Price: Piggyback/AmmoMaster shellplate....................... **$25.95**
Price: Press cover...................................... **$10.95**

RCBS Reloader Special-5

Frame: Aluminum
Frame Type: 30° offset O-frame
Die Thread: 1-1/4"-12 bushing;
7/8-14 threads
Avg. Rounds Per Hour: 50-60
Ram Stroke: 3-1/16"
Weight: 7.5 lbs.
Features: Single-stage press convertible to progressive with RCBS Piggyback II. Primes cases during resizing operation. Will accept RCBS shotshell dies. From RCBS.
Price:... **$119.95**

RCBS Rock Chucker Supreme

Frame: Cast iron
Frame Type: O-frame
Die Thread: 1-1/4"-12 bushing;
7/8-14 threads
Avg. Rounds Per Hour: 50-60
Ram Stroke: 3-1/16"
Weight: 17 lbs.
Features: Redesigned to allow loading of longer cartridge cases. Made for heavy-duty reloading, case forming and bullet swaging. Provides 4" of ram-bearing surface to support 1" ram and ensure alignment; ductile iron toggle blocks; hardened steel pins. Comes standard with Universal Primer Arm and primer catcher. Can be converted from single-stage to progressive with Piggyback II conversion unit. From RCBS.
Price:... **$150.95**

REDDING Turret Press

Frame: Cast iron
Frame Type: Turret
Die Thread: 7/8-14
Avg. Rounds Per Hour: NA
Ram Stroke: 3.4"
Weight: 23 lbs., 2 oz.
Features: Strength to reload pistol and magnum rifle, case form and bullet swage; linkage pins heat-treated, precision ground and in double shear; hollow ram to collect spent primers; removable turret head for caliber changes; progressive linkage for increased power as ram nears die; slight frame tilt for comfortable operation; rear turret support for stability and precise alignment; six-station turret head; priming arm for both large and small primers. Also available in kit form with shellholder, primer catcher and one die set. From Redding Reloading Equipment.
Price:... **$298.50**
Price: Kit.. **$336.00**

REDDING Boss

Frame: Cast iron
Frame Type: O-frame
Die Thread: 7/8-14
Avg. Rounds Per Hour: NA
Ram Stroke: 3.4"
Weight: 11 lbs., 8 oz.
Features: 36° frame offset for visibility and accessibility; primer arm positioned at bottom ram travel; positive ram travel stop machined to hit exactly top-dead-center. Also available in kit form with shellholder and set of Redding A dies. From Redding Reloading Equipment.
Price:... **$135.00**
Price: Kit.. **$172.00**

ACCESSORIES

METALLIC CARTRIDGE PRESSES

REDDING Ultramag

Frame: Cast iron
Frame Type: Non-conventional
Die Thread: 7/8-14
Avg. Rounds Per Hour: NA
Ram Stroke: 4-1/8"
Weight: 23 lbs., 6 oz.
Features: Unique compound leverage system connected to top of press for tons of ram pressure; large 4-3/4" frame opening for loading outsized cartridges; hollow ram for spent primers. Kit available with shellholder and one set Redding A dies. From Redding Reloading Equipment.
Price: $298.50
Price: Kit $336.00

ROCK CRUSHER Press

Frame: Cast iron
Frame Type: O-frame
Die Thread: 2-3/4"-12 with bushing reduced to 1-1/2"-12
Avg. Rounds Per Hour: 50
Ram Stroke: 6"
Weight: 67 lbs.
Features: Designed to load and form ammunition from 50 BMG up to 23x115 Soviet. Frame opening of 8-1/2"x3-1/2"; 1-1/2"x12"; bushing can be removed and bushings of any size substituted; ram pressure can exceed 10,000 lbs. with normal body weight; 40mm diameter ram. Angle block for bench mounting and reduction bushing for RCBS dies available. Accessories for Rock Crusher include powder measure, dies, shellholder, bullet puller, priming tool, case gauge and other accessories found elsewhere in this catalog. From The Old Western Scrounger.
Price: $795.00
Price: Angle block $57.95
Price: Reduction bushing $21.00
Price: Shellholder $47.25
Price: Priming tool, 50 BMG, 20 Lahti $65.10

PROGRESSIVE PRESSES

CORBIN BENCHREST S-PRESS

Frame: All steel
Frame Type: O-Frame
Die Thread: 7/8-14 and T-slot adapter
Avg. Rounds Per Hour: NA
Ram Stroke: 4"
Weight: 22 lbs.
Features: Roller bearing linkage, removeable head, right- or left-hand mount.
Price: $298.00

DILLON AT 500

Frame: Aluminum alloy
Frame Type: NA
Die Thread: 7/8-14
Avg. Rounds Per Hour: 200-300
Ram Stroke: 3-7/8"
Weight: NA
Features: Four stations; removable tool head to hold dies in alignment and allow caliber changes without die adjustment; manual indexing; capacity to be upgraded to progressive RL 550B. Comes with universal shellplate to accept 223, 22-250, 243, 30-06, 9mm, 38/357, 40 S&W, 45 ACP. Dies not included. From Dillon Precision Products.
Price: $193.95

DILLON RL 550B

Frame: Aluminum alloy
Frame Type: NA
Die Thread: 7/8-14
Avg. Rounds Per Hour: 500-600
Ram Stroke: 3-7/8"
Weight: 25 lbs.
Features: Four stations; removable tool head to hold dies in alignment and allow caliber changes without die adjustment; auto priming system that emits audible warning when primer tube is low; a 100-primer capacity magazine contained in DOM steel tube for protection; new auto powder measure system with simple mechanical connection between measure and loading platform for positive powder bar return; a separate station for crimping with star-indexing system; 220 ejected-round capacity bin; 3/4-lb. capacity powder measure. Height above bench, 35"; requires 3/4" bench overhang. Will reload 120 different rifle and pistol calibers. Comes with one caliber conversion kit. Dies not included. From Dillon Precision Products, Inc.
Price: $325.95

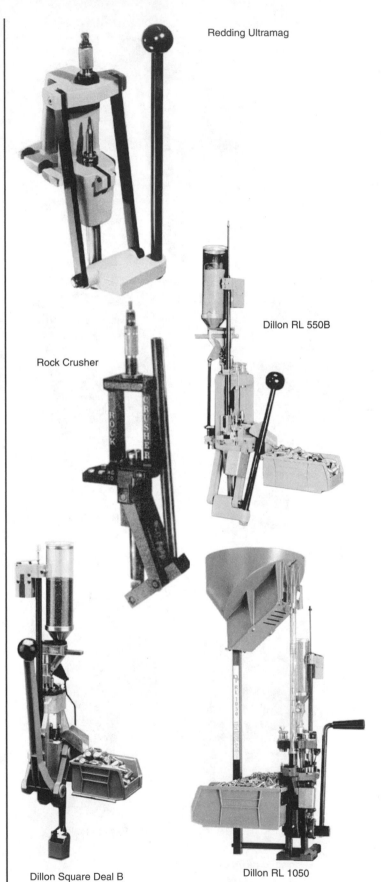

Redding Ultramag

Dillon RL 550B

Rock Crusher

Dillon Square Deal B

Dillon RL 1050

METALLIC CARTRIDGE PRESSES

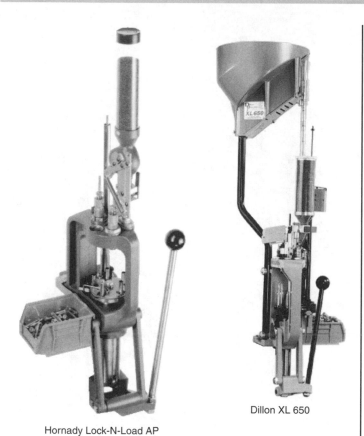

Hornady Lock-N-Load AP

Dillon XL 650

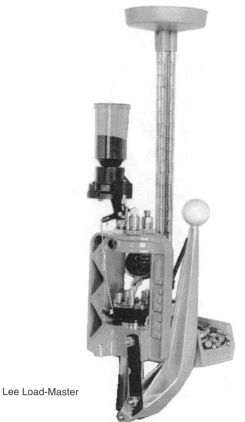

Lee Load-Master

DILLON RL 1050

Frame: Ductile iron
Frame Type: Platform type
Die Thread: 7/8-14
Avg. Rounds Per Hour: 1000-1200
Ram Stroke: 2-5/16"
Weight: 62 lbs.
Features: Eight stations; auto case feed; primer pocket swager for military cartridge cases; auto indexing; removable tool head; auto prime system with 100-primer capacity; low primer supply alarm; positive powder bar return; auto powder measure; 515 ejected round bin capacity; 500-600 case feed capacity; 3/4-lb. capacity powder measure. Loads all pistol rounds as well as 30 M1 Carbine, 223, and 7.62x39 rifle rounds. Height above the bench, 43". Dies not included. From Dillon Precision Products, Inc.
Price: $1,199.95

DILLON Super 1050

Similar to RL1050, but has lengthened frame and short-stroke crank to accommodate long calibers.
Price: $1,299.95

DILLON Square Deal B

Frame: Zinc alloy
Frame Type: NA
Die Thread: None
(unique Dillon design)
Avg. Rounds Per Hour: 400-500
Ram Stroke: 2-5/16"
Weight: 17 lbs.
Features: Four stations; auto indexing; removable tool head; auto prime system with 100-primer capacity; low primer supply alarm; auto powder measure; positive powder bar return; 170 ejected round capacity bin; 3/4-lb. capacity powder measure. Height above the bench, 34". Comes complete with factory adjusted carbide die set. From Dillon Precision Products, Inc.
Price: $252.95

DILLON XL 650

Frame: Aluminum alloy
Frame Type: NA
Die Thread: 7/8-14
Avg. Rounds Per Hour: 800-1000
Ram Stroke: 4-9/16"
Weight: 46 lbs.
Features: Five stations; auto case feed; removable tool head; auto prime system with 100-primer capacity; low primer supply alarm; auto powder measure; positive powder bar return; 220 ejected round capacity bin; 3/4-lb. capacity powder measure. 500-600 case feed capacity with optional auto case feed. Loads all pistol/rifle calibers less than 3-1/2" in length. Height above the bench, 44"; 3/4" bench overhang required. From Dillon Precision Products, Inc.
Price: Less dies... $443.95

HORNADY Lock-N-Load AP

Frame: Die cast heat-treated aluminum alloy
Frame Type: O-frame
Die Thread: 7/8-14
Avg. Rounds Per Hour: NA
Ram Stroke: 3-3/4"
Weight: 26 lbs.
Features: Features Lock-N-Load bushing system that allows instant die changeovers; five-station die platform with option of seating and crimping separately or adding taper-crimp die; auto prime with large and small primer tubes with 100-primer capacity and protective housing; brass kicker to eject loaded rounds into 80-round capacity cartridge catcher; offset operating handle for leverage and unobstructed operation; 2" diameter ram driven by heavy-duty cast linkage arms rotating on steel pins. Comes with five Lock-N-Load die bushings, shellplate, deluxe powder measure, auto powder drop, and auto primer feed and shut-off, brass kicker and primer catcher. Lifetime warranty. From Hornady Mfg. Co.
Price: $367.65

LEE Load-Master

Frame: ASTM 380 aluminum
Frame Type: O-frame
Die Thread: 7/8-14
Avg. Rounds Per Hour: 600
Ram Stroke: 3-1/4"
Weight: 8 lbs., 4 oz.
Features: Available in kit form only. A 1-3/4" diameter hard chrome ram for handling largest magnum cases; loads rifle or pistol rounds; five station press to factory crimp and post size; auto indexing with wedge lock mechanism to hold one ton; auto priming; removable turrets; four- tube case feeder with optional case collator and bullet feeder (late 1995); loaded round ejector with chute to optional loaded round catcher; quick change shellplate; primer catcher. Dies and shellholder for one caliber included. From Lee Precision, Inc.
Price: Rifle $320.00
Price: Pistol $330.00
Price: Extra turret $14.98
Price: Adjustable charge bar $9.98

LEE Pro 1000

Frame: ASTM 380 aluminum and steel
Frame Type: O-frame
Die Thread: 7/8-14
Avg. Rounds Per Hour: 600
Ram Stroke: 3-1/4"
Weight: 8 lbs., 7 oz.
Features: Optional transparent large/small or rifle case feeder; deluxe auto-disk case-activated powder measure; case sensor for primer feed. Comes complete with carbide die set (steel dies for rifle) for one caliber. Optional accessories include: case feeder for large/small pistol cases or rifle cases; shell plate carrier with auto prime, case ejector, auto-index and spare parts; case collator for case feeder. From Lee Precision, Inc.
Price: $199.98

PONSNESS/WARREN Metallic II

Frame: Die cast aluminum
Frame Type: H-frame
Die Thread: 7/8-14
Avg. Rounds Per Hour: 150+
Ram Stroke: NA
Weight: 32 lbs.
Features: Die head with five tapped 7/8-14 holes for dies, powder measure or other accessories; pivoting die arm moves case from station to station; depriming tube for removal of spent primers; auto primer feed; interchangeable die head. Optional accessories include additional die heads, powder measure extension tube to accommodate any standard powder measure, primer speed feeder to feed press primer tube without disassembly. Comes with small and large primer seating tools. Dies, powder measure and shellholder not included. From Ponsness/ Warren.
Price: $375.00
Price: Extra die head $56.95
Price: Primer speed feeder $14.50
Price: Powder measure extension $29.95
Price: Dust cover $27.95

RCBS Pro 2000™

Frame: Cast iron
Frame Type: H-Frame
Die Thread: 7/8 x 14
Avg. Rounds Per Hour: NA
Ram Stroke: NA
Weight: NA
Features: Five-station manual indexing; full-length sizing; removable die plate; fast caliber conversion. Uses APS Priming System. From RCBS.
Price: $516.95

RCBS Turret Press

Frame: Cast iron
Frame Type: NA
Die Thread: 7/8x14
Avg. Rounds Per Hour: 50 to 200
Ram Stroke: NA
Weight: NA
Features: Six-station turret head; positive alignment; on-press priming.
Price: $207.95

STAR Universal Pistol Press

Frame: Cast iron with aluminum base
Frame Type: Unconventional
Die Thread: 11/16-24 or 7/8-14
Avg. Rounds Per Hour: 300
Ram Stroke: NA
Weight: 27 lbs.
Features: Four or five-station press depending on need to taper crimp; handles all popular handgun calibers from 32 Long to 45 Colt. Comes completely assembled and adjusted with carbide dies (except 30 Carbine) and shellholder to load one caliber. Prices slightly higher for 9mm and 30 Carbine. From Star Machine Works.
Price: With taper crimp $1,055.00
Price: Without taper crimp $1,025.00
Price: Extra tool head, taper crimp $425.00
Price: Extra tool head, w/o taper crimp........................ $395.00

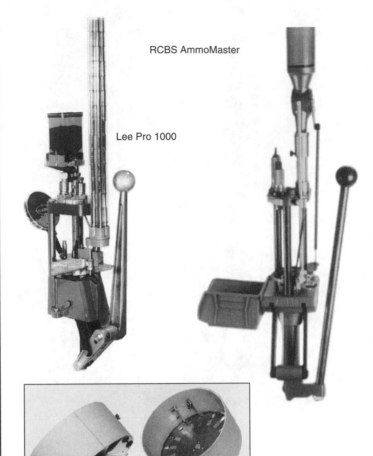

RCBS AmmoMaster

Lee Pro 1000

Fully-automated Star Universal

ACCESSORIES

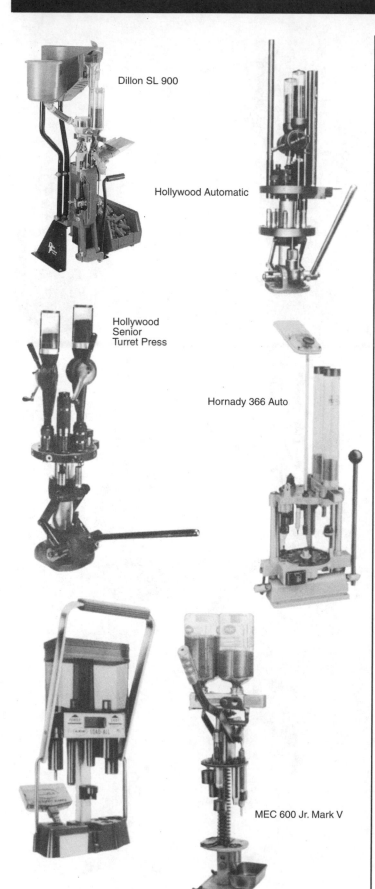

Dillon SL 900

Hollywood Automatic

Hollywood Senior Turret Press

Hornady 366 Auto

MEC 600 Jr. Mark V

DILLON SL 900

Press Type: Progressive
Avg. Rounds Per Hour: 700-900
Weight: 51 lbs.
Features: 12-ga. only; factory adjusted to load AA hulls; extra large 25-pound capacity shot hopper; fully-adjustable case-activated shot system; hardened steel starter crimp die; dual-action final crimp and taper die; tilt-out wad guide; auto prime; auto index; strong mount machine stand. From Dillon Precision Products.
Price: **$819.95**

HOLLYWOOD Automatic Shotshell Press

Press Type: Progressive
Avg. Rounds Per Hour: 1,800
Weight: 100 lbs.
Features: Ductile iron frame; fully automated press with shell pickup and ejector; comes completely set up for one gauge; one starter crimp; one finish crimp; wad guide for plastic wads; decap and powder dispenser unit; one wrench for inside die lock screw; one medium and one large spanner wrench for spanner nuts; one shellholder; powder and shot measures. Available for 10, 12, 20, 28 or 410. From Hollywood Engineering.
Price: **$3,600.00**

HOLLYWOOD Senior Turret Press

Press Type: Turret
Avg. Rounds Per Hour: 200
Weight: 50 lbs.
Features: Multi-stage press constructed of ductile iron comes completely equipped to reload one gauge; one starter crimp; one finish crimp; wad guide for plastic wads; decap and powder dispenser unit; one wrench for inside die lock screw; one medium and one large spanner wrench for spanner nuts; one shellholder; powder and shot measures. Available for 10, 12, 16, 20, 28 or 410. From Hollywood Engineering.
Price: Press only **$700.00**
Price: Dies **$195.00**

HORNADY 366 Auto

Press Type: Progressive
Avg. Rounds Per Hour: NA
Weight: 25 lbs.
Features: Heavy-duty die cast and machined steel body and components; auto primer feed system; large capacity shot and powder tubes; adjustable for right- or left-hand use; automatic charge bar with shutoff; swing-out wad guide; primer catcher at base of press; interchangeable shot and powder bushings; life-time warranty. Available for 12, 20, 28 2-3/4" and 410 2-1/2. From Hornady Mfg. Co.
Price: **$434.95**
Price: Die set, 12, 20, 28 . . . . **$196.86**
Price: Magnum conversion dies, 12, 20 . . . . **$43.25**

LEE Load-All II

Press Type: Single stage
Avg. Rounds Per Hour: 100
Weight: 3 lbs., 3 oz.
Features: Loads steel or lead shot; built-in primer catcher at base with door in front for emptying; recesses at each station for shell positioning; optional primer feed. Comes with safety charge bar with 24 shot and powder bushings. Available for 12-, 16- or 20-gauge. From Lee Precision, Inc.
Price: **$49.98**

MEC 600 Jr. Mark V

Press Type: Single stage
Avg. Rounds Per Hour: 200
Weight: 10 lbs.
Features: Spindex crimp starter for shell alignment during crimping; a cam-action crimp die; Pro-Check to keep charge bar properly positioned; adjustable for three shells. Available in 10, 12, 16, 20, 28 gauges and 410 bore. Die set not included. From Mayville Engineering Company, Inc.
Price: **$112.35**
Price: Die set **$59.97**

ACCESSORIES

SHOTSHELL RELOADING PRESSES

MEC 650

Press Type: Progressive
Avg. Rounds Per Hour: 400
Weight: 19 lbs.
Features: Six-station press; does not resize except as separate operation; auto primer feed standard; three crimping stations for starting, closing and tapering crimp. Die sets not available. Available in 12, 16, 20, 28 and 410. From Mayville Engineering Company, Inc.
Price: $213.10

MEC 8567 Grabber

Press Type: Progressive
Avg. Rounds Per Hour: 400
Weight: 22 lbs.
Features: Six-station press; auto primer feed; auto-cycle charging; three-stage crimp; power ring resizer returns base to factory specs; resizes high and low base shells; optional kits to reload three shells and steel shot. Available in 12, 16, 20, 28 gauge and 410 bore. From Mayville Engineering Company, Inc.
Price: $306.05
Price: 3" kit, 12-ga. $70.70
Price: 3" kit, 20-ga. $40.40
Price: Steel shot kit $35.35

MEC 9000 Grabber

Press Type: Progressive
Avg. Rounds Per Hour: 400
Weight: 26 lbs.
Features: All same features as the MEC Grabber, but with auto-indexing and auto-eject. Finished shells automatically ejected from shell carrier to drop chute for boxing. Available in 12, 16, 20, 28 and 410. From Mayville Engineering Company, Inc.
Price: $371.70
Price: 3" kit, 12-ga. $70.70
Price: 3" kit, 20-ga. $40.40
Price: Steel shot kit $35.35

MEC 9000 Hustler

Press Type: Progressive
Avg. Rounds Per Hour: 400
Weight: 30 lbs.
Features: Same features as 9000G with addition of foot pedal-operated hydraulic system for complete automation. Operates on standard 110V household current. Comes with bushing-type charge bar and three bushings. Available in 12, 16, 20, 28 gauge and 410 bore. From Mayville Engineering Company, Inc.
Price: $896.90
Price: Steel shot kit $35.35

MEC Sizemaster

Press Type: Single stage
Avg. Rounds Per Hour: 150
Weight: 20 lbs.
Features: Power ring eight-fingered collet resizer returns base to factory specs; handles brass or steel, high or low base heads; auto primer feed; adjustable for three shells. Available in 10, 12, 16, 20, 28 gauges and 410 bore. From Mayville Engineering Company, Inc.
Price: $170.10
Price: Die set, 12, 16, 20, 28, 410 .... $89.56
Price: Die set, 10-ga. $105.10
Price: Steel shot kit $20.20
Price: Steel shot kit, 12-ga. 3-1/2" $70.97

MEC Steelmaster

Press Type: Single stage
Avg. Rounds Per Hour: 150
Weight: 20 lbs.
Features: Same features as Sizemaster except can load steel shot. Press is available for 3-1/2" 10-ga. and 12-ga. 2-3/4", 3" or 3-1/2". For loading lead shot, die sets available in 10, 12, 16, 20, 28 and 410. From Mayville Engineering Company, Inc.
Price: $183.75
Price: 12 ga. 3-1/2" $205.80

MEC 650

MEC 9000 Grabber

MEC 9000 Hustler

MEC 8567 Grabber

MEC Steelmaster

MEC Sizemaster

SHOTSHELL RELOADING PRESSES

Ponsness/Warren
Du-O-Matic 375C

Ponsness/Warren
Hydro-Multispeed

Ponsness/Warren
Size-O-Matic
900 Elite

Ponsness/Warren
Platinum 2000

RCBS The Grand

PONSNESS/WARREN Du-O-Matic 375C
Press Type: Progressive
Avg. Rounds Per Hour: NA
Weight: 31 lbs.
Features: Steel or lead shot reloader; large shot and powder reservoirs; bushing access plug for dropping in shot buffer or buckshot; positive lock charging ring to prevent accidental flow of powder; double-post construction for greater leverage; removable spent primer box; spring-loaded ball check for centering size die at each station; tip-out wad guide; two-gauge capacity tool head. Available in 10 (extra charge), 12, 16, 20, 28 and 410 with case lengths of 2-1/2, 2-3/4, 3 and 3-1/2 inches. From Ponsness/ Warren.
Price: 12-, 20-, and 28-ga., 2-3/4" and 410, 2-1/2" $289.00
Price: 12-ga. 3-1/2"; 3" 12, 20, 410 . . . . $305.00
Price: 12, 20 2-3/4" $383.95
Price: 10-ga. press $315.00

PONSNESS/WARREN Hydro-Multispeed
Hydraulic system developed for Ponsness/Warren L/S-1000. Usable for the 950, 900 and 800 series presses. Three reloading speed settings operated with variable foot pedal control. Features stop/reverse at any station; automatic shutdown with pedal control release; fully adjustable hydraulic cylinder rod to prevent racking or bending of machine; quick disconnect hoses for ease of installation. Preassembled with step-by-step instructions. From Ponsness/Warren.
Price: $879.00
Price: Cylinder kit $399.95

PONSNESS/WARREN L/S-1000
Frame: Die cast aluminum
Avg. Rounds Per Hour: NA
Weight: 55 lbs.
Features: Fully progressive press to reload steel, bismuth or lead shot. Equipped with new Uni-Drop shot measuring and dispensing system which allows the use of all makes of shot in any size. Shells automatically resized and deprimed with new Auto-Size and De-Primer system. Loaded rounds drop out of shellholders when completed. Each shell pre-crimped and final crimped with Tru-Crimp system. Available in 10-gauge 3-1/2" or 12-gauge 2-3/4" and 3". 12-gauge 3-1/2" conversion kit also available. 20-gauge 2-3/4" and 3" special order only. From Ponsness/Warren.
Price: 12 ga. $849.00
Price: 10 ga. $895.00
Price: Conversion kit $199.00

PONSNESS/WARREN Size-O-Matic 900 Elite
Press Type: Progressive
Avg. Rounds Per Hour: 500-800
Weight: 49 lbs.
Features: Progressive eight-station press; frame of die cast aluminum; center post design index system ensures positive indexing; timing factory set, drilled and pinned. Automatic features include index, deprime, reprime, powder and shot drop, crimp start, tapered final crimp, finished shell ejection. Available in 12, 20, 28 and 410. 16-ga. special order. Kit includes new shellholders, seating port, resize/primer knockout assembly, new crimp assembly. From Ponsness/Warren.
Price: $749.00
Price: Conversion tooling, 12, 20, 28, 410 . . . . $189.00

PONSNESS/WARREN Platinum 2000
Press Type: Progressive
Avg. Rounds Per Hour: 500-800
Weight: 52 lbs.
Features: Progressive eight-station press, similar to 900 and 950 except has die removal system that allows removal of any die component during reloading cycle. Comes standard with 25-lb. shot tube, 19" powder tube, brass adjustable priming feed allows adjustment of primer seating depth. From Ponsness/Warren.
Price $889.00

RCBS The Grand
Press Type: Progressive
Avg. Rounds Per Hour: NA
Weight: NA
Features: Constructed from a high-grade aluminum casting, allows complete resizing of high and low base hulls. Available for 12 and 20 gauge.
Price: $688.95

ACCESSORIES

Maker and Model	Magn.	Field at 100 Yds. (feet)	Eye Relief (in.)	Length (in.)	Tube Dia. (in.)	W & E Adjustments	Weight (ozs.)	Price	Other Data
ADCO									
Magnum 50 mm[5]	0			4.1	45 mm	Int.	6.8	$269.00	[1]Multi-Color Dot system changes from red to green. [2]For airguns, paint ball, rimfires. Uses common lithium water battery. [3]Comes with standard dovetail mount. [4].75" dovetail mount; poly body; adj. intensity diode. [5]10 MOA dot; black or nickel. [6]Square format; with mount battery. From ADCO Sales.
MIRAGE Ranger 1"	0			5.2	1	Int.	3.9	159.00	
MIRAGE Ranger 30mm	0			5.5	30mm	Int.	5	159.00	
MIRAGE Competitor	0			5.5	30mm	Int.	5.5	229.00	
IMP Sight[2]	0			4.5		Int.	1.3	17.95	
Square Shooter 2[3]	0			5		Int.	5	99.00	
MIRAGE Eclipse[1]	0			5.5	30mm	Int.	5.5	229.00	
Champ Red Dot	0			4.5		Int.	2	33.95	
Vantage 1"	0			3.9	1	Int.	3.9	129.00	
Vantage 30mm	0			4.2	30mm	Int.	4.9	159.00	
Vision 2000[6]	0	60		4.7		Int.	6.2	79.00	
e-dot ESB[1]	0			4.12	1	Int.	3.7	139.00	
e-dot E1B	0			4.12	1	Int.	3.7	99.00	
e-dot ECB	0			3.8	30mm	Int.	6.4	99.00	
e-dot E30B	0			4.3	30mm	Int.	4.6	99.00	
AIMPOINT									
Comp	0			4.6	30mm	Int.	4.3	331.00	Illuminates red dot in field of view. Noparallax (dot does not need to be centered). Unlimited field of view and eye relief. On/off, adj. intensity. Dot covers 3" @100 yds. [1]Comes with 30mm rings, battery, lense cloth. [2]Requires 1" rings. Black fin ish. AP Comp avail. in black, blue, SS, camo. [3]Black finish (AP 5000-B) ; avail. with regular 3-min. or 10-min. Mag Dot as B2 or S2. [4]Band pass reflection coating for compatibility with night vision equipment; U.S. Army contract model; with anti-reflex coated lenses (Comp ML), **$359.00**. From Aimpoint U.S.A.
Comp M[4]	0			5	30mm	Int.	6.1	409.00	
Series 5000[3]	0			6	30mm	Int.	6	297.00	
Series 3000 Universal[2]	0			6.25	1	Int.	6	232.00	
Series 5000/2x[1]	2			7	30mm	Int.	9	388.00	
ARMSON O.E.G.									
Standard	0			5.125	1	Int.	4.3	202.00	Shown red dot aiming point. No batteries needed. Standard model fits 1" ring mounts (not incl.). Other O.E.G. models for shotguns and rifles can be special ordered. [1]Daylight Only Sight with .375 dovetail mount for 22s. Does not contain tritium. From Trijicon, Inc.
22 DOS[1]	0			3.75		Int.	3	127.00	
22 Day/Night	0			3.75		Int.	3	169.00	
M16/AR-15	0			5.125		Int.	5.5	226.00	
ARTEMIS 2000									
4x32	4	34.4	3.15	10.7	1	Int.	17.5	215.00	Click-stop windage and elevation adjustments; constantly centered reticle; rubber eyepiece ring; nitrogen filled. Imported from the Czech Republic by CZ-USA.
6x42	6	23	3.15	13.7	1	Int.	17.5	317.00	
7x50	7	18.7	3.15	13.9	1	Int.	17.5	329.00	
1.5-6x42	1.5-6	40-12.8	2.95	12.4	30mm	Int.	19.4	522.00	
2-8x42	2-8	31-9.5	2.95	13.1	30mm	Int.	21.1	525.00	
3-9x42	3-9	24.6-8.5	2.95	12.4	30mm	Int.	19.4	466.00	
3-12x50	3-12	20.6-6.2	2.95	14	30mm	Int.	22.9	574.00	
BEC									
EuroLux									
EL2510x56	2.5-10	39.4-11.5	3.25-2	15.1	30mm	Int.	25.4	249.90	Black matte finish. Multi-coated lenses; 1/4-MOA click adjustments (1/2-MOA on EL4x25, AR4x22WA); fog and water-proof. [1]For AR-15;bullet drop compensator; q.d. mount. [2]Rubber armored. Imported by BEC Inc. Partial listing shown. Contact BEC for complete details. [3]All Goldlabel scopes feature lighted reticles and finger-adjustable windage and elevation adjustments. [4]Bullet-drop compensator system for Mini-14 and AR-15 rifles.
EL39x42	3-9	34.1-13.2	3.5-3	12.3	30mm	Int.	17.7	99.80	
EL28x36	2-8	44.9-11.5	3.8-3	12.2	30mm	Int.	15.9	149.50	
ELA39x40RB[2]	3-9	39-13	3	12.7	30mm	Int.	14.3	95.95	
EL6x42	6	21	3	12.6	30mm	Int.	14.8	69.00	
EL4x42	4	29	3	12.6	30mm	Int.	14.8	59.60	
EL4x36	4	29	3	12	30mm	Int.	14	49.90	
EL4x25	4	26	3	7	30mm	Int.	7.6	37.00	
AR4x22WA[1]	4	24	3	7	34mm	Int.	13.6	109.97	
Goldlabel[3]									
GLI 624x50	6-24	16-4	3.5-3	15.3	1	Int.	22.5	139.00	
GLI 416x50	4-16	25-6	3.5-3	13.5	1	Int.	21.8	135.00	
GLI 39x40R[2]	3-9	39-13	3.5-3	12.7	28mm	Int.	18.5	99.00	
GLC 5x42BD[4]	5	24	3.5	8.7	1	Int.	16.5	79.00	
BEEMAN									
Rifle Scopes									
5045[1]	4-12	26.9-9	3	13.2	1	Int.	15	275.00	All scopes have 5 point reticle, all glass fully coated lenses. [1]Parallel adjustable. [2]Reticle lighted by ambient light. [3]Available with lighted Electro-Dot reticle. Imported by Beeman.
5046[1]	6-24	18-4.5	3	16.9	1	Int.	20.2	395.00	
5050[1]	4	26	3.5	11.7	1	Int.	11	80.00	
5055[1]	3-9	38-13	3.5	10.75	1	Int.	11.2	90.00	
5060[1]	4-12	30-10	3	12.5	1	Int.	16.2	210.00	
5065[1]	6-18	17-6	3	14.7	1	Int.	17.3	265.00	
5066RL[2]	2-7	58-15	3	11.4	1	Int.	17	380.00	
5047L[2]	4	25	3.5	7	1	Int.	13.7	NA	
Pistol Scopes									
5021	2	19	10-24	9.1	1	Int.	7.4	85.50	
5020	1.5	14	11-16	8.3	.75	Int.	3.6	NA	
BSA									
Catseye[1]									
CE1545x32	1.5-4.5	78-23	4	11.25	1	Int.	12	91.95	[1]Waterproof, fogproof; multi-coated lenses; finger-adjustable knobs. [2]Waterproof, fogproof; matte black finish. [3]With 4" sunshade; target knobs; 1/8-MOA click adjustments. [4]Adjustable for parallax; with sun shades; target knobs, 1/8-MOA adjustments. Imported by BSA. [5]Illuminated reticle model; also available in 3-10x, 3.5-10x, and 3-9x. [6]Red dot sights also available in 42mm and 50mm versions. [7]Includes Universal Bow Mount. [8]Five other models offered. From BSA.
CE310x44	3-10	39-12	3.25	12.75	1	Int.	16	151.95	
CE3510x50	3.5-10	30-10.5	3.25	13.25	1	Int.	17.25	171.95	
CE416x50	4-16	25-6	3	15.25	1	Int.	22	191.95	
CE624x50	6-24	16-3	3	16	1	Int.	23	222.95	
CE1545x32IR	1.5-4.5	78-23	5	11.25	1	Int.	12	121.95	
Deer Hunter[2]									
DH25x20	2.5	72	6	7.5	1	Int.	7.5	59.95	
DH4x32	4	32	3	12	1	Int.	12.5	49.95	
DH39x32	3-9	39-13	3	12	1	Int.	11	69.95	

SCOPES / HUNTING, TARGET & VARMINT

Maker and Model	Magn.	Field at 100 Yds. (feet)	Eye Relief (in.)	Length (in.)	Tube Dia. (in.)	W & E Adjustments	Weight (ozs.)	Price	Other Data
DH39x40	3-9	39-13	3	13	1	Int.	12.1	89.95	
DH39x50	3-9	41-15	3	12.75	1	Int.	13	109.95	
DH2510x44	2.5-10	42-12	3	13	1	Int.	12.5	99.95	
DH1545x32	1.5-4.5	78-23	5	11.25	1	Int.	12	79.95	
Contender[3]									
CT24x40TS	24	6	3	15	1	Int.	18	129.95	
CT36x40TS	36	3	3	15.25	1	Int.	19	139.95	
CT312x40TS	3-12	28-7	3	13	1	Int.	17.5	129.95	
CT416x40TS	4-16	21-5	3	13.5	1	Int.	18	131.95	
CT624x40TS	6-24	16-4	3	15.5	1	Int.	20	149.95	
CT832x40TS	8-32	11-3	3	15.5	1	Int.	20	171.95	
CT312x50TS	3-12	28-7	3	13.75	1	Int.	21	131.95	
CT416x50TS	4-16	21-5	3	15.25	1	Int.	22	151.95	
CT624x50TS	6-24	16-4	3	16	1	Int.	23	171.95	
CT832x50TS	8-32	11-3	3	16.5	1	Int.	24	191.95	
Pistol									
P52x20	2	N/A	N/A	N/A	N/A	Int.	N/A	89.95	
Platinum[4]									
PT24x44TS	24	4.5	3	16.25	1	Int.	17.9	189.55	
PT36x44TS	36	3	3	14.9	1	Int.	17.9	199.95	
PT624x44TS	6-24	15-4.5	3	15.25	1	Int.	18.5	221.95	
PT832x44TS	8-32	11-3.5	3	17.25	1	Int.	19.5	229.95	
.22 Special									
S39x32WR	3-9	37.7-14.1	3	12	1	Int.	12.3	89.95	
S4x32WR	4	26	3	10.75	1	Int.	9	39.95-44.95	
Air Rifle									
AR4x32	4	33	3	13	1	Int.	14	69.95	
AR27x32	2-7	48	3	12.25	1	Int.	14	79.95	
AR312x44	3-12	36	3	12.25	1	Int.	15	109.95	
Red Dot									
RD30[6]	0			3.8	30mm	Int.	5	59.95	
PB30[6]	0			3.8	30mm	Int.	4.5	79.95	
Bow30[7]	0			N/A	30mm	Int.	5	89.95	
Big Cat									
BigCat[8]	3.5-10	30-11	5	9.7	1	Int.	16.8	219.95	

BURRIS

Maker and Model	Magn.	Field at 100 Yds. (feet)	Eye Relief (in.)	Length (in.)	Tube Dia. (in.)	W & E Adjustments	Weight (ozs.)	Price
Mr. T Black Diamond Titanium								
2.5-10x50A	2.5-10	4.25-4.75	3.3-3.8	13.6	30mm	Int.	29	1,786.00
4-16x50	4-16	27-7.5		13.6	30mm	Int.	27	1,875.00
Black Diamond								
3-12x50[3,4,6]	3.2-11.9	34-12	3.5-4	13.8	30mm	Int.	25	974.00
6-24x50	6-24	18-6	3.5-4	16.2	30mm	Int.	25	1,076.00
Fullfield II								
2.5x9	2.5	55	3.5-3.75	10.25	1	Int.	9	308.00
4x[1,2,3]	3.75	36	3.5-3.75	11.25	1	Int.	11.5	314.00
6x[1,3]	5.8	23	3.5-3.75	13	1	Int.	12	343.00
1.75-5x[1,2,9,10]	1.7-4.6	66-25	3.5-3.75	10.875	1	Int.	13	400.00
2-7x[1,2,3]	2.5-6.8	47-18	3.5-3.75	12	1	Int.	14	399.00
3-9x40[1,2,3,10]	3.3-8.7	38-15	3.5-3.75	12.625	1	Int.	15	336.00
3-9x50	3-9	35-15	3.5-3.75	13	1	Int.	18	481.00
3.5-10x50mm[3,5,10]	3.7-9.7	29.5-11	3.5-3.75	14	1	Int.	19	542.00
4-12x[1,4,8,11]	4.4-11.8	27-10	3.5-3.75	15	1	Int.	18	500.00
6-18x[1,3,4,6,7,8]	6.5-17.6	16.7	3.5-3.75	15.8	1	Int.	18.5	527.00
Compact Scopes								
1x XER[3]	1	51	4.5-20	8.8	1	Int.	7.9	320.00
4x[4,5]	3.6	24	3.75-5	8.25	1	Int.	7.8	270.00
6x[1,4]	5.5	17	3.75-5	9	1	Int.	8.2	287.00
6x HBR[1,5,8]	6	13	4.5	11.25	1	Int.	13	538.00
1-4x XER[3]	1-3.8	53-15	4.25-30	8.8	1	Int.	10.3	397.00
3-9x[4,5]	3.6-8.8	25-11	3.75-5	12.625	1	Int.	11.5	442.00
4-12x[1,4,6]	4.5-11.6	19-8	3.75-4	15	1	Int.	15	527.00
Signature Series								
1.5-6x[2,3,5,9,10]	1.7-5.8	70-20	3.5-4	10.8	1	Int.	13	518.00
6x[3]	6	20	3.5-4	12.125	1	Int.	14	413.00
2-8x[3,5,11]	2.1-7.7	53-17	3.5-4	11.75	1	Int.	14	558.00
3-9x[3,5,10,13]	3.3-8.8	36-14	3.5-4	12.875	1	Int.	15.5	611.00
2.50-10x[3,5,10]	2.7-9.5	37-10.5	3.5-4	14	1	Int.	19	647.00
3-12x[3,10]	3.3-11.7	34-9	3.5-4	14.25	1	Int.	21	691.00
4-16x[1,3,5,6,8,10]	4.3-15.7	33-9	3.5-4	15.4	1	Int.	23.7	738.00
6-24x[1,3,5,6,8,10,13]	6.6-23.8	17-6	3.5-4	16	1	Int.	22.7	776.00
8-32x[8,10,12]	8.6-31.4	13-3.8	3.5-4	17	1	Int.	24	813.00
Speeddot 135[14]								
Red Dot	1			4.85	35mm	Int.	5	291.00
Handgun								
1.50-4x LER[1,5,10]	1.6-3.	16-11	11-25	10.25	1	Int.	11	411.00
2-7x LER[3,4,5,10]	2-6.5	21-7	7-27	9.5	1	Int.	12.6	458.00
3-9x LER[4,5,10]	3.4-8.4	12-5	22-14	11	1	Int.	14	453.00
2x LER[4,5,6]	1.7	21	10-24	8.75	1	Int.	6.8	286.00
4x LER[1,4,5,6,10]	3.7	11	10-22	9.625	1	Int.	9	338.00
10x LER[1,4,6]	9.5	4	8-12	13.5	1	Int.	14	460.00
Scout Scope								
1xXER[3,9]	1.5	32	4-24	9	1	Int.	7.0	320.00
2.75x[3,9]	2.7	15	7-14	9.375	1	Int.	7.0	349.00

Available in Carbon Black, Titanium Gray and Autumn Gold finishes.

Black Diamond & Fullfield: All scopes avail. with Plex reticle. Steel-on-steel click adjustments. [1]Dot reticle on some models. [2]Post crosshair reticle extra. [3]Matte satin finish. [4]Available with parallax adjustment (standard on 10x, 12x, 4- 12x, 6-12x, 6-18x, 6x HBR and 3-12x Signature). [5]Silver matte finish extra. [6]Target knobs extra, standard on silhouette models. LER and XER with P.A., 6x HBR. [7]Sunshade avail. [8]Avail. with Fine Plex reticle. [9]Available with Heavy Plex reticle. [10]Available with Posi-Lock. [11]Available with Peep Plex reticle. [12]Also avail. for rimfires, airguns. [13]Selected models available with camo finish.

Signature Series: LER=Long Eye Relief; IER=Intermediate Eye Relief; XER=Extra Eye Relief.

Speeddot 135: [14]Waterproof, fogproof, coated lenses, 11 bright ness set tings; 3-MOA or 11-MOA dot size; includes Weaver-style rings and battery.

Partial listing shown. Contact Burris for com plete details.

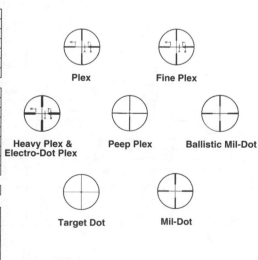

Plex Fine Plex

Heavy Plex & Electro-Dot Plex Peep Plex Ballistic Mil-Dot

Target Dot Mil-Dot

Maker and Model	Magn.	Field at 100 Yds. (feet)	Eye Relief (in.)	Length (in.)	Tube Dia. (in.)	W & E Adjustments	Weight (ozs.)	Price	Other Data
BUSHNELL (Bausch & Lomb Elite rifle scopes now sold under Bushnell brand)									
Elite 4200 RainGuard									(Bushnell Elite)
42-6244M[1]	6-24	18-6	3	16.9	1	Int.	20.2	729.95	[1]Adj. objective, sunshade; with 1/4-MOA dot or Mil Dot reticle. [2]Also in
42-2104G[2]	2.5-10	41.5-10.8	3	13.5	1	Int.	16	642.95	matte and silver finish. [3]Only in matte finish. [4]Also in matte and silver
42-2151M[6, 9]	2.5-10	40.3-10.8	3.3	14.3	1	Int.	18	798.95	finish. [5]Adjustable objective. [6]50mm objective; also in matte finish. [7]Also
42-1636M[3]	1.5-6	61.8-16.1	3	12.8	1	Int.	15.4	608.95	in silver finish. [8]40mm. [9]Ill. dot reticle. **Partial listings shown. Contact**
42-4164M[5, 6]	4-16	26-7	3.5	18.6	1	Int.	18.6	645.95	**Bushnell Performance Optics for details.**
42-4165M[5]	4-16	26-7	3	15.6	1	Int.	22	834.95	
42-8324M	8-32	14-3.75	3.3	18	1	Int.	22	802.95	
Elite 3200 RainGuard									
32-5155M	5-15	21-7	3	15.9	1	Int.	19	528.95	
32-4124M[1]	4-12	26.9-9	3	13.2	1	Int.	15	469.95	
32-1040M	10	11	3.5	11.7	1	Int.	15.5	319.95	
32-3940G[4]	3-9	33.8-11.5	3	12.6	1	Int.	13	319.95	
32-2732M	2-7	44.6-12.7	3	11.6	1	Int.	12	303.95	
32-3950G[6]	3-9	31.5-10.5	3	15.7	1	Int.	19	382.95	
32-3955E	3-9	31.5-10.5	3	15.6	30mm	Int.	22	640.95	
Elite 3200 Handgun RainGuard									(Bushnell)
32-2632M[7]	2-6	10-4	20	9	1	Int.	10	444.95	
32-2632G	2-6	10-4	20	9	1	Int.	10	444.95	
Trophy									[1]Wide Angle. [2]Also silver finish. [3]Also silver finish. [4]Matte finish. [5]Also
73-0134	1	68	Unlim ited	5.5	1	Int.	6	136.95	silver finish. [7]Adj. obj. [8]Variable intensity; fits Weaver-style base.
73-1500[1]	1.75-5	68-23	3.5	10.8	1	Int.	12.3	177.95	[9]Blackpowder scope; extended eye relief, Circle-X reticle. [10]50mm objec-
73-4124[1]	4-12	32-11	3	12.5	1	Int.	16.1	300.95	tive. [11]With Circle-X reticle, matte finish. [12]Matte finish, adjustable objec-
73-3940[2]	3-9	42-14	3	11.7	1	Int.	13.2	159.95	tive.
73-6184[7]	6-18	17.3-6	3	14.8	1	Int.	17.9	378.95	
Turkey & Brush									
73-1421[11]	1.75-4	73-30	3.5	10.8	32mm	Int.	10.9	171.95	
HOLOsight Model[8]	1			6		Int.	8.7	444.95	
Trophy Handgun									
73-0232[2]	2	20	9-26	8.7	1	Int.	7.7	218.95	
73-2632[3]	2-6	21-7	9-26	9.1	1	Int.	10.9	287.95	
Banner									
71-1545	1.5-4.5	67-23	3.5	10.5	1	Int.	10.5	116.95	
71-3944[9]	3-9	36-13	4	11.5	1	Int.	12.5	125.95	
71-3950[10]	3-9	26-10	3	16	1	Int.	19	186.95	
71-4124[7]	4-12	29-11	3	12	1	Int.	15	157.95	
71-4228	4	26.5	3	11.75	1	Int.	10	81.95	
71-6185[10]	6-18	17-6	3	16	1	Int.	18	209.95	
Sportsman									
72-0004	4	31	4	11.7	1	Int.	11.2	98.95	
72-0038	3-9	37-14	3.5	12	1	Int.	6	79.95	
72-0039	3-9	38-13	3.5	10.75	1	Int.	11.2	116.95	
72-0412[7]	4-12	27-9	3.2	13.1	1	Int.	14.6	141.95	
72-1393[6]	3-9	35-12	3.5	11.75	1	Int.	10	68.95	
72-1545	1.5-4.5	69-24	3	10.7	1	Int.	8.6	86.95	
72-1548[11]	1.5-4.5	71-25	3.5	10.4	1	Int.	11.8	104.95	
72-1403	4	29	4	11.75	1	Int.	9.2	57.95	
72-3940M	3-9	42-14	3	12.7	1	Int.	12.5	95.95	
22 Rimfire									
76-2239	3-9	40-13	3	11.75	1	Int.	11.2	61.95	
76-2243	4	30	3	11.5	1	Int.	10	52.95	
EUROPTIK SUPREME									
4x36K	4	39	3.5	11.6	26mm	Int.	14	795.00	[1]Military scope with adjustable parallax. Fixed powers have 26mm tubes,
6x42K	6	21	3.5	13	26mm	Int.	15	875.00	variables have 30mm tubes. Some models avail. with steel tubes. All
8x56K	8	18	3.5	14.4	26mm	Int.	20	925.00	lenses multi-coated. Dust and water tight. From Europtik.
1.5-6x42K	1.5-6	61.7-23	3.5	12.6	30mm	Int.	17	1,095.00	
2-8x42K	2-8	52-17	3.5	13.3	30mm	Int.	17	1,150.00	
2.5-10x56K	2.5-10	40-13.6	3.5	15	30mm	Int.	21	1,295.00	
3-12x56 Super	3-12	10.8-34.7	3.5-2.5	15.2	30mm	Int.	24	1,495.00	
4-16x56 Super	4-16	9.8-3.9	3.1	18	30mm	Int.	26	1,575.00	
3-9x40 Micro	3-9	3.2-12.1	2.7	13	1	Int.	14	1,450.00	
2.5-10x46 Micro	2.5-10	13.7-33.4	2.7	14	30mm	Int.	20	1,395.00	
4-16x56 EDP[1]	4-16	22.3-7.5	3.1	18	30mm	Int.	29	1,995.00	
7-12x50 Target	7-12	8.8-5.5	3.5	15	30mm	Int.	21	1,495.00	
KAHLES									
4x36	4	34.5	3.15	11.2	1	Int.	12.7	555.00	Aluminum tube. Multi-coated, waterproof. [1]Also available with illuminated
6x42	6	23	3.15	12.4	1	Int.	14.4	694.00	reticle. Imported from Austria by Swarovski Optik.
8x50[1]	8	17.3	3.15	13	1	Int.	16.5	749.00	
1.1-4x24	1.1-4	108-31.8	3.5	10.8	30mm	Int.	12.7	722.00	
1.5-6x42[1]	1.5-6	72-21.3	3.5	12.0	30mm	Int.	15.8	832.00	
2.5-10x50[1]	2.5-10	43.5-12.9	3.5	12.8	30mm	Int.	15.8	1,353.00	
3-9x42	3-9	43-16	3.5	12	1	Int.	13	621.06	
3-9x42AH	3-9	43-15	3.5	12.36	1	Int.	12.7	665.00	
3-12x56[1]	3-12	30-11	3.5	15.4	30mm	Int.	18	1,377.72	

Multi   Euro   Circle-X

German #1   German #2   Turkey Reticle

3/4-Mil. Dot   Crosshair

No. 4A   No. 7A   Plex   Illuminated No. 4N   Illuminated Plex N   TD Smith

Maker and Model	Magn.	Field at 100 Yds. (feet)	Eye Relief (in.)	Length (in.)	Tube Dia. (in.)	W & E Adjustments	Weight (ozs.)	Price	Other Data
LEICA									
Ultravid 1.75-6x32	1.75-6	47-18	4.8-3.7	11.25	30mm	Int.	14	749.00	Aluminum tube with hard anodized matte black finish with titanium
Ultravid 3.5-10x42	3.5-10	29.5-10.7	4.6-3.6	12.62	30mm	Int.	16	849.00	accents; finger-adjustable windage and elevation with 1/4-MOA clicks.
Ultravid 4.5-14x42	4.5-14	20.5-7.4	5-3.7	12.28	30mm	Int.	18	949.00	Made in U.S. From Leica.

Leicaplex Standard   Leica Dot   Standard Dot   Crosshair   Euro   Post & Plex

Maker and Model	Magn.	Field at 100 Yds. (feet)	Eye Relief (in.)	Length (in.)	Tube Dia. (in.)	W & E Adjustments	Weight (ozs.)	Price	Other Data
LEUPOLD									
Vari-X III 3.5x10 Tactical	3.5-10	29.5-10.7	3.6-4.6	12.5	1	Int.	13.5	801.80	Constantly centered reticles, choice of Duplex, tapered CPC, Leupold Dot, Crosshair and Dot. CPC and Dot reticles extra. [1]2x and 4x scopes
M8-2X EER[1]	1.7	21.2	12-24	7.9	1	Int.	6	312.50	have from 12"-24" of eye relief and are suitable for handguns, top ejection
M8-2X EER Silver[1]	1.7	21.2	12-24	7.9	1	Int.	6	337.50	arms and muzzleloaders. [2]3x9 Compact, 6x Compact, 12x, 3x9, and
M8-2.5x28 IER Scout	2.3	22	9.3	10.1	1	Int.	7.5	408.90	6.5x20 come with adjustable objective. Sunshade available for all adjust
M8-4X EER[1]	3.7	9	12-24	8.4	1	Int.	7	425.00	able objective scopes, **$23.20-$41.10**. [3]Long Range scopes have side
M8-4X EER Silver[1]	3.7	9	12-24	8.4	1	Int.	7	425.00	focus parallax adjustment, additional windage and elevation travel. Partial
Vari-X 2.5-8 EER	2.5-8	13-4.3	11.7-12	9.7	1	Int.	10.9	608.90	listing shown. **Contact Leupold for complete details.**
M8-4X Compact	3.6	25.5	4.5	9.2	1	Int.	7.5	382.10	*Models available with illuminated reticle for additional cost.
Vari-X 2-7x Compact	2.5-6.6	41.7-16.5	5-3.7	9.9	1	Int.	8.5	478.60	
Vari-X 3-9x Compact	3.2-8.6	34-13.5	4-3	11-11.3	1	Int.	11	519.60	
M8-4X	4	24	4	10.7	1	Int.	9.3	385.70	
M8-6X36mm	5.9	17.7	4.3	11.4	1	Int.	10	410.70	
M8-6x 42mm	6	17	4.5	12	1	Int.	11.3	510.70	
*M8-6x42 A.O. Tactical	6	17	4.2	12.1	1	Int.	11.3	628.60	
M8-12x A.O. Varmint	11.6	9.1	4.2	13	1	Int.	13.5	571.40	
Vari-X 3-9x Compact EFR A.O.	3.8-8.6	34-13.5	4-3	11	1	Int.	11	550.00	
*Vari-X-III 1.5-5x20	1.5-4.5	66-23	5.3-3.7	9.4	1	Int.	9.5	635.70	
Vari-X-III 1.75-6x32	1.9-5.6	47-18	4.8-3.7	9.8	1	Int.	11	683.90	
Vari-X-III 2.5x8	2.6-7.8	37-13.5	4.7-3.7	11.3	1	Int.	11.5	678.60	
Vari-X-III 3.5-10x40 Long Range M34	3.9-9.7	29.8-11	4-3.5	13.5	30mm	Int.	19.5	1,157.10	
Vari-X-III 3.5-10x50	3.3-9.7	29.5-10.7	4.6-3.6	12.4	1	Int.	13	796.40	
Vari-X-III 4.5-14x40 A.O.	4.7-13.7	20.8-7.4	5-3.7	12.4	1	Int.	14.5	780.40	
*Vari-X-III 4.5-14x50 A.O.	4.7-13.7	20.8-7.4	5-3.7	12.4	1	Int.	14.5	903.60	
Vari-X III 4.5-14x 50 Long Range Tactical4	4.9-14.3	19-6	5-3.7	12.1	30mm	Int.	17.5	1,082.10	
Vari-X-III 6.5-20x A.O.	6.5-19.2	14.2-5.5	5.3-3.6	14.2	1	Int.	17.5	823.20	
Vari-X-III 6.5x20x Target EFR A.O.	6.5-19.2		5.3-3.6	14.2	1	Int.	16.5	919.60	
Vari-X III 6.5-20x 50 Long Range Target4	6.8-19.2	14.7-5.4	4.9-3.7	14.3	30mm	Int.	19	1,166.10	
Vari-X III 8.5-25x40 A.O. Target	8.5-25	10.86-4.2	5.3	14.3	1	Int.	17.5	900.00	
Vari-X III 8.5-25x 50 Long Range Target4	8.3-24.2	11.4-4.3	4.4-3.6	14.3	30mm	Int.	19	1,260.70	
Mark 4 M1-10x40	10	11.1	3.6	13.125	30mm	Int.	21	1,807.10	
Mark 4 M1-16x40	16	6.6	4.1	12.875	30mm	Int.	22	1,807.10	
Mark 4 M3-10x40	10	11.1	3.6	13.125	30mm	Int.	21	1,807.10	
Vari-X-III 6.5x20[2] A.O.	6.5-19.2	14.2-5.5	5.3-3.6	14.2	1	Int.	16	823.20	
LPS 1.5-6x42	1.5-6	58.7-15.7	4	11.2	30mm	Int.	16	1,476.80	
LPS 2.5-10x45	2.6-9.8	37.2	4.5-3.8		1	Int.	17.2	1,480.00	
LPS 3.5-14x52 A.O.	3.5-14	28-7.2	4	13.1	30mm	Int.	22	1,569.60	
Rimfire									
Vari-X 2-7x RF Special	3.6	25.5	4.5	9.2	1	Int.	7.5	478.60	
Shotgun									
M8 4x33	3.7	9	12-24	8.4	1	Int.	6	410.70	
LYMAN									
Super TargetSpot[1]	10, 12, 15, 20, 25, 30	5.5	2	24.3	.75	Int.	27.5	685.00	Made under license from Lyman to Lyman's orig. specs. Blue steel. Three-point suspension rear mount with .25-min. click adj. Data listed for 20x model. [1]Price appx. Made in U.S. by Parsons Optical Mfg. Co.
McMILLAN									
Vision Master 2.5-10x	2.5-10	14.2-4.4	4.3-3.3	13.3	30mm	Int.	17	1,250.00	42mm obj. lens; .25-MOA clicks; nitrogen filled, fogproof, waterproof;
Vision Master Model 1[1]	2.5-10	14.2-4.4	4.3-3.3	13.3	30mm	Int.	17	1,250.00	etched duplex-type reticle. [1]Tactical Scope with external adj. knobs, military reticle; 60+ min. adj.
MEOPTA									
Artemis									
4x32A[1]	4	34	3.15	11	1	Int.	14.7	194.00	Steel tubes are waterproof, dustproof, and shockproof; nitrogen filled. Anti-reflective coatings, protective rubber eye piece, clear caps. Made in Czech
6x42A[1]	6	23	3.15	13.6	1	Int.	18.2	267.00	Republic by Meopta. [1]Range finder reticles available. Partial listing
7x50A[1]	7	18	3.15	14.1	1	Int.	19	278.00	shown.
MEPROLIGHT									
Meprolight Reflex Sights 14-21 5.5 MOA 1x30[1]	1			4.4	30mm	Int.	5.2	335.00	[1]Also available with 4.2 MOA dot. Uses tritium and fiber optics-no batteries required. From Hesco, Inc.

Duplex   CPC   Post & Duplex

Leupold Dot   Dot

Maker and Model	Magn.	Field at 100 Yds. (feet)	Eye Relief (in.)	Length (in.)	Tube Dia. (in.)	W & E Adjustments	Weight (ozs.)	Price	Other Data
MILLETT									
Buck 3-9x44	3-9	38-14	3.25-4	13	1	Int.	16.2	238.00	[1]3-MOA dot. 25-MOA dot. 33-, 5-, 8-, 10-MOA dots. 410-MOA dot. All
Buck 3.5-10x50	3.5-10	NA	NA	NA	1	NA	NA	258.00	have click adjustments; waterproof, shockproof; 11 dot intensity settings.
Buck 3-12x44 A/O	3-12	NA	NA	NA	1	NA	NA	258.00	All avail. in matte/black or silver finish. From Millett Sights.
Buck 4-16x44 A/O	4-16	NA	NA	NA	1	NA	NA	270.00	
Buck Varmint 4-16x56	4-16	NA	NA	NA	30mm	NA	NA	318.00	
Buck Varmint 6-25x56	6-25	NA	NA	NA	30mm	NA	NA	338.00	
Buck Varmint 6-25x56	6-25	NA	NA	NA	30mm	NA	NA	370.00	
Buck Lightning 1.5-6x44	1.5-6	NA	NA	NA	1	NA	NA	270.00	
Buck Lightning 3-9x44	3-9	NA	NA	NA	1	NA	NA	270.00	
Buck Silver 3-9x40	3-9	NA	NA	NA	1	NA	NA	129.95	
Buck Silver 4-12x40 A/O	4-12	NA	NA	NA	1	NA	NA	172.00	
Buck Silver 6-18x40 A/O	6-18	NA	NA	NA	1	NA	NA	172.00	
Buck Silver Compact 2x20	2	NA	NA	NA	1	NA	NA	99.50	
Buck Silver Compact 4x32	4	NA	NA	NA	1	NA	NA	105.00	
Buck Silver Compact 1.5-4x32	1.5-4	NA	NA	NA	1	NA	NA	136.00	
SP-1 Compact[1] Red Dot	1	36.65		4.1	1	Int.	3.2	147.45	
SP-2 Compact[2] Red Dot	1	58		4.5	30mm	Int.	4.3	147.45	
MultiDot SP[3]	1	50		4.8	30mm	Int.	5.3	179.45	
30mm Wide View[4]	1	60		5.5	30mm	Int.	5	179.45	
MIRADOR									
RXW 4x40[1]	4	37	3.8	12.4	1	Int.	12	179.95	[1]Wide angle scope. Multi-coated objective lens. Nitrogen filled; water-
RXW 1.5-5x20[1]	1.5-5	46-17.4	4.3	11.1	1	Int.	10	188.95	proof; shockproof. From Mirador Optical Corp.
RXW 3-9x40	3-9	43-14.5	3.1	12.9	1	Int.	13.4	251.95	
NIGHTFORCE									
2.5-10x50	2.5-10	31.4-9.4	3.3	13.9	30mm	Int.	28	847.87	Lighted reticles with eleven intensity levels. Most scopes have choice of
3.5-15x56	3.5-15	24.5-6.9	3	15.8	30mm	Int.	32	507.78	reticles. From Lightforce U.S.A.
5.5-22x56	5.5-22	15.7-4.4	3	19.4	30mm	Int.	38.5	965.53	
8-32x56	8-32	9.4-3.1	3	16.6	30mm	Int.	36	997.90	
12-42x56	12-42	6.7-2.3	3	17	30mm	Int.	36	1,053.64	
NIKON									
Monarch UCC									
4x40[2]	4	26.7	3.5	11.7	1	Int.	11.7	229.99	Super multi-coated lenses and blackening of all internal metal parts for
1.5-4.5x20[3]	1.5-4.5	67.8-22.5	3.7-3.2	10.1	1	Int.	9.5	239.99	maximum light gathering capability; positive .25-MOA; fogproof; water-
2-7x32	2-7	46.7-13.7	3.9-3.3	11.3	1	Int.	11.3	259.99	proof; shockproof; luster and matte finish. [1]Also available in matte silver
3-9x40[1]	3-9	33.8-11.3	3.6-3.2	12.5	1	Int.	12.5	299.99	finish. [2]Available in silver matte finish. [3]Available with TurkeyPro or Niko-
3.5-10x50	3.5-10	25.5-8.9	3.9-3.8	13.7	1	Int.	15.5	429.99	plex reticle. [4]Silver Shadow finish; black matte **$296.95**. Partial listing
4-12x40 A.O.	4-12	25.7-8.6	3.6-3.2	14	1	Int.	16.6	369.99	shown. From Nikon, Inc.
6.5-20x44	6.5-19.4	16.2-5.4	3.5-3.1	14.8	1	Int.	19.6	459.99	
2x20 EER	2	22	26.4	8.1	1	Int.	6.3	169.99	
Buckmasters									
4x40	4	30.4	3.3	12.7	1	Int.	11.8	159.99	
3-9x40[4]	3.3-8.6	33.8-11.3	3.5-3.4	12.7	1	Int.	13.4	209.99	
3-9x50	3.3-8.6	33.8-11.3	3.5-3.4	12.9	1	Int.	18.2	299.99	
NORINCO									
N2520	2.5	44.1	4		1	Int.		52.28	Partial listing shown. Some with Ruby Lens coating, blue/black and matte
N420	4	29.3	3.7		1	Int.		52.70	finish. Imported by Nic Max, Inc.
N640	6	20	3.1		1	Int.		67.88	
N154520	1.5-4.5	63.9-23.6	4.1-3.2			Int.		80.14	
N251042	2.5-10	27-11	3.5-2.8		1	Int.		206.60	
N3956	3-9	35.1-6.3	3.7-2.6		1	Int.		231.88	
N31256	3-12	26-10	3.5-2.8		1	Int.		290.92	
NC2836M	2-8	50.8-14.8	3.6-2.7		1	Int.		255.60	
PARSONS									
Parsons Long Scope	6	10	2	28-34+	.75	Ext.	13	475.00-525.00	Adj. for parallax, focus. Micrometer rear mount with .25-min. click adjust-ments. Price is approximate. Made in U.S. by Parsons Optical Mfg. Co.
PENTAX									
Lightseeker 1.75-6x[1]	1.75-6	71-20	3.5-4	10.8	1	Int.	13	546.00	[1]Glossy finish; Matte finish, Heavy Plex or Penta-Plex, **$546.00**. [2]Glossy
Lightseeker 2-8x[2]	2-8	53-17	3.5-4	11.7	1	Int.	14	594.00	finish; Matte finish, **$594.00**. [3]Glossy finish; Matte finish, **$628.00**; Heavy
Lightseeker 3-9x[3, 4, 10, 11]	3-9	36-14	3.5-4	12.7	1	Int.	15	594.00	Plex, add **$20.00**. [4]Matte finish; Mil-Dot, **$798.00**. [5]Glossy finish; Matte
Lightseeker 3.5-10x[5]	3.5-10	29.5-11	3.5-4	14	1	Int.	19.5	630.00	finish, **$652.00**; Heavy Plex, add **$10.00**. [6]Glossy finish; Matte finish, **$816.00**; with Heavy Plex, **$830.00**; with Mil-Dot, **$978.00**. [7]Matte finish;
Lightseeker 4-16x[6, 9]	4-16	33-9	3.5-4	15.4	1	Int.	22.7	888.00	with Mil-Dot, **$1,018.00**. [8]Matte finish, with Mil-Dot, **$1098.00**.
Lightseeker 6-24x[7, 12]	6-24	18-5.5	3.5-4	16	1	Int.	23.7	1,028.0 0	[9]Lightseeker II, Matte finish, **$844.00**. [10]Lightseeker II, Glossy finish,
Lightseeker 8.5-32x[8]	8.5-32	13-3.8	3.5-4	17.2	1	Int.	24	968.00	**$636.00**. [11]Lightseeker II, Matte finish, **$660.00**. [12]Lightseeker II, Matte
Shotgun									finish, **$878.00**. [13]Matte finish; Advantage finish, Break-up Mossy Oak
Lightseeker 2.5x1[13]	2.5	55	3.5-4	10	1	Int.	9	398.00	finish, Treestand Mossy Oak finish, **$364.00**. From Pentax Corp.
Lightseeker Zero-X SG Plus	0	51	4.5-15	8.9	1	Int.	7.9	372.00	
Lightseeker Zero-X/ V Still-Target	0-4	53.8-15	3.5-7	8.9	1	Int.	10.3	476.00	
Lightseeker Zero X/ V	0-4	53.8-15	3.5-7	8.9	1	Int.	10.3	454.00	

Pentax Reticles

Heavy Plex	Fine Plex	Penta-Plex	Deepwoods Plex	Comp-Plex	Mil-dot

Maker and Model	Magn.	Field at 100 Yds. (feet)	Eye Relief (in.)	Length (in.)	Tube Dia. (in.)	W & E Adjustments	Weight (ozs.)	Price	Other Data
RWS									
300	4	36	3.5	11.75	1	Int.	13.2	**170.00**	
450	3-9	43-14	3.5	12	1	Int.	14.3	**215.00**	
SCHMIDT & BENDER									
Fixed									
4x36	4	30	3.25	11	1	Int.	14	**760.00**	All scopes have 30-yr. warranty, click adjustments, centered reticles, rota-tion indicators. [1]Glass reticle; aluminum. Available in aluminum with mounting rail. [2]Aluminum only. [3]Aluminum tube. Choice of two bullet drop compensators, choice of two sunshades, two range find ing reticles. From Schmidt & Bender, Inc. [4]Parallax adjustment in third turret; extremely fine crosshairs. [5]Available with illuminated ret icle that glows red; third turret houses on/off switch, dimmer and bat tery. [6]4-16x50/Long Range. [7]Also with Long Eye Relief. From Schmidt & Bender, Inc. Available with illumi-nated crosshairs and parallax adjustment.
6x42	6	21	3.25	13	1	Int.	17	**835.00**	
8x56	8	16.5	3.25	14	1	Int.	22	**960.00**	
10x42	10	10.5	3.25	13	1	Int.	18	**955.00**	
Variables									
1.25-4x20[5]	1.25-4	96-16	3.75	10	30mm	Int.	15.5	**995.00**	
1.5-6x42[1, 5]	1.5-6	60-19.5	3.70	12	30mm	Int.	19.7	**1,125.00**	
2.5-10x56[1, 5]	2.5-10	37.5-12	3.90	14	30mm	Int.	24.6	**1,290.00**	
3-12x42[2]	3-12	34.5-11.5	3.90	13.5	30mm	Int.	19	**1,360.00**	
3-12x50[1, 5]	3-12	33.3-12.6	3.90	13.5	30mm	Int.	22.9	**1,390.00**	
4-16x50 Varmint[4, 6]	4-16	22.5-7.5	3.90	14	30mm	Int.	26	**1,595.00**	
Police/Marksman II									
3-12x50[7]	3-12	33.3-12.6	3.74	13.9	34mm	Int.	18.5	**1,430.00**	
***New* SCHMIDT & BENDER ZENITH SERIES**									
3-12x50	3-12	33.3-11.4	3.70	13.71	NA	NA	23.4	**1,490.00 to1,795**	
2.5-10x56	2.5-10	39.6-12	3.70	14.81	NA	NA	24	**1,490.00 to 1,795**	

No 1 (fixed)	No. 1 variable	No. 2	No. 3	No. 4	No. 6	No. 7	No. 8	No. 8 Dot	No. 9

Maker and Model	Magn.	Field at 100 Yds. (feet)	Eye Relief (in.)	Length (in.)	Tube Dia. (in.)	W & E Adjustments	Weight (ozs.)	Price	Other Data
SIGHTRON									
Variables									
SII 1.56x42	1.5-6	50-15	3.8-4	11.69	1	Int.	15.35	**287.95**	[1]Adjustable objective. [2]3MOA dot; also with 5 or 10 MOA dot. [3]Variable 3, 5, 10 MOA dot; black finish; also stainless. [4]Satin black; also stainless. Electronic Red Dot scopes come with ring mount, front and rear extension tubes, polarizing fil ter, battery, haze filter caps, wrench. Rifle, pistol, shot-gun scopes have aluminum tubes, Exac Trak adjustments. Lifetime war-ranty. From Sightron, Inc. 53" sun shade. [6]Mil Dot or Plex reticle. [7]Dot or Plex reticle. [8]Double Diamond reticle.
SII 2.58x42	2.5-8	36-12	3.6-4.2	11.89	1	Int.	12.82	**261.95**	
SII 39x42[4, 6, 7]	3-9	34-12	3.6-4.2	12.00	1	Int.	13.22	**274.95**	
SII 312x42[6]	3-12	32-9	3.6-4.2	11.89	1	Int.	12.99	**311.95**	
SII 3.510x42	3.5-10	32-11	3.6	11.89	1	Int.	13.16	**324.95**	
SII 4.514x42[1]	4.5-14	22-7.9	3.6	13.88	1	Int.	16.07	**371.95**	
Target									
SII 24x44	24	4.1	4.33	13.30	1	Int.	15.87	**341.95**	
SII 416x42[1, 4, 5,6, 7]	4-16	26-7	3.6	13.62	1	Int.	16	**371.95**	
SII 624-42[1, 4, 5, 7]	6-24	16-5	3.6	14.6	1	Int.	18.7	**393.95**	
SII1040x42	10-40	8.9-4	3.6	16.1	1	Int.	19	**563.95**	
Compact									
SII 4x32	4	25	4.5	9.69	1	Int.	9.34	**205.95**	
SII2.5-10x32	2.5-10	41-10.5	3.75-3.5	10.9	1	Int.	10.39	**260.95**	
Shotgun									
SII 2.5x20SG	2.5	41	4.3	10.28	1	Int.	8.46	**194.95**	
Pistol									
SII 1x28P[4]	1	30	9-24	9.49	1	Int.	8.46	**212.95**	
SII 2x28P[4]	2	16-10	9-24	9.49	1	Int.	8.28	**212.95**	
SIMMONS									
22 Mag.									
80102[2]	4	29.5	3	11.75			11	**49.99**	[1]Matte; also polished finish. [2]Silver; also black matte or polished. [3]Black matte finish. [4]Granite finish. [5]Camouflage. [6]Black polish. [7]With ring mounts. [8]Silver; black polish avail. [10]50mm obj.; black matte. [11]Black or silver matte. [12]75-yd. par allax; black or silver matte. [13]TV view. [14]Adj. obj. [15]Silver matte. [16]Adj. objective; 4" sunshade; black matte. [17]Octagon body; rings included; black matte or silver finish. [18]Black matte finish; also available in silver. [19]Smart reticle. [20]Target turrets. [21]With dovetail rings. [23]With 3V lithium battery, extension tube, polarizing filter, Weaver rings. **Only selected models shown.** Contact Simmons Outdoor Corp. for com-plete details.
80103[1]	4	23.5	3	7.25			8.25	**49.99**	
80103[7]	3-9	29.5	3.3	11.5			10	**59.99**	
AETEC									
2100[8]	2.8-10	44-14	5	11.9	1	Int.	15.5	**189.99**	
21041[6]	3.8-12	33-11	4	13.5	1	Int.	20	**199.99**	
44Mag									
M-1044[3]	3-10	34-10.5	3	12.75	1	Int.	15.5	**149.99**	
M-1045[3]	4-12	29.5-9.5	3	13.2	1	Int.	18.25	**169.99**	
M-1047[3]	6.5-20	14-.5	2.6-3.4	12.8	1	Int.	19.5	**199.99**	
1048[3,20] (3)	6.5-20	16-5.5	2.6-3.4	14.5	1	Int.	20	**219.99**	
M-1050DM[3,19]	3.8-12	26-9	3	13.08	1	Int.	16.75	**189.99**	
8-Point									
4-12x40mmAO[3]	4-12	29-10	3-2 7/8	13.5	1	Int.	15.75	**99.99**	
4x32mm[3]	4	28.75	3	11.625	1	Int.	14.25	**34.99**	
3-9x32mm[3]	3-9	37.5-13	3-2 7/8	11.875	1	Int.	11.5	**39.99**	
3-9x40mm[18]	3-9	37-13	3-2 7/8	12.25	1	Int.	12.25	**49.99-79.99**	
3-9x50mm[3]	3-9	32-11.75	3-2 7/8	13	1	Int.	15.25	**79.99**	

Truplex™	Smart	ProDiamond®	Crossbow

Maker and Model	Magn.	Field at 100 Yds. (feet)	Eye Relief (in.)	Length (in.)	Tube Dia. (in.)	W & E Adjustments	Weight (ozs.)	Price	Other Data
Prohunter									
7700	2-7	53-16.25	3	11.5	1	Int.	12.5	79.99	
7710[2]	3-9	36-13	3	12.6	1	Int.	13.5	89.99	
7716	4-12	26-9	3	12.6	1	Int.	16.75	129.99	
7721	6-18	18.5-6	3	13.75	1	Int.	16	144.99	
7740[3]	6	21.75	3	12.5	1	Int.	12	99.99	
Prohunter Handgun									
7732[18]	2	22	9-17	8.75	1	Int.	7	109.99	
7738[18]	4	15	11.8-17.6	8.5	1	Int.	8	129.99	
82200[9]	2-6							159.99	
Whitetail Classic									
WTC 11[4]	1.5-5	75-23	3.4-3.2	9.3	1	Int.	9.7	184.99	
WTC 12[4]	2.5-8	45-14	3.2-3	11.3	1	Int.	13	199.99	
WTC 13[4]	3.5-10	30-10.5	3.2	12.4	1	Int.	13.5	209.99	
WTC 15[4]	3.5-10	29.5-11.5	3.2	12.75	1	Int.	13.5	289.99	
WTC 45[4]	4.5-14	22.5-8.6	3.2	13.2	1	Int.	14	265.99	
Whitetail Expedition									
1.5-6x32mm[3]	1.5-6	72-19	3	11.16	1	Int.	15	259.99	
3-9x42mm[3]	3-9	40-13.5	3	13.2	1	Int.	17.5	269.99	
4-12x42mm[3]	4-12	29-9.6	3	13.46	1	Int.	21.25	299.99	
6-18x42mm[3]	6-18	18.3-6.5	3	15.35	1	Int.	22.5	319.99	
Pro50									
8800[10]	4-12	27-9	3.5	13.2	1	Int.	18.25	179.99	
8810[10]	6-18	17-5.8	3.6	13.2	1	Int.	18.25	174.99	
808825	3.5-10	32-8.75	3.5	3.25			14.5	179.99	
808830	2.5-10	39-12.2	2.75	12.75			15.9	179.99	
Shotgun									
2100[4]	4	16	5.5	8.8	1	Int.	9.1	84.99	
2100[5]	2.5	24	6	7.4	1	Int.	7	59.99	
7789D	2	31	5.5	8.8	1	Int.	8.75	99.99	
7790D	4	17	5.5	8.5	1	Int.	8.75	114.99	
7791D	1.5-5	76-23.5	3.4	9.5	1	Int.	10.75	138.99	
Blackpowder									
BP0420M17	4	19.5	4	7.5	1	Int.	8.3	59.99	
BP2732M12	2-7	57.7-16.6	3	11.6	1	Int.	12.4	129.99	
Red Dot									
5100421	1			4.8	30mm	Int.	4.7	44.99	
5111222	1			5.25	42mm	Int.	6	49.99	
Pro Air Gun									
21608 A.O.	4	25	3.5	12	1	Int.	11.3	99.99	
21613 A.O.	4-12	25-9	3.1-2.9	13.1	1	Int.	15.8	179.99	
21619 A.O.	6-18	18-7	2.9-2.7	13.8	1	Int.	18.2	189.99	

SPRINGFIELD ARMORY

	6		3.5	13	1	Int.	14.7	379.00	
4-14x70 Tactical Government Model[2]	4-14		3.5	14.25	1	Int.	15.8	395.00	
4-14x56 1st Gen. Government Model[3]	4-14		3.5	14.75	30mm	Int.	23	480.00	
10x56 Mil Dot Government Model[4]	10		3.5	14.75	30mm	Int.	28	672.00	
6-20x56 Mil Dot Government Model	6-20		3.5	18.25	30mm	Int.	33	899.00	

[1]Range finding reticle with automatic bullet drop compensator for 308 match ammo to 700 yds. [2]Range finding reticle with automatic bullet drop compensator for 223 match ammo to 700 yds. [3]Also avail. as 2nd Gen. with target knobs and adj. obj., $549.00; as 3rd Gen. with illuminated reticle, $749.00; as Mil Dot model with illuminated Target Tracking reticle, target knobs, adj. obj., $698.00. [4]Unlimited range finding, target knobs, adj. obj., illuminated Target Tracking green reticle. All scopes have matte black finish, internal bubble level, 1/4-MOA clicks. From Springfield, Inc.

SWAROVSKI OPTIK

PF Series									
8x50[1, 3]	8	17	3.15	13.9	30mm	Int.	21.5	987.78	
8x56[1, 3]	8	17	3.15	14.29	30mm	Int.	24	1,054.44	
PH Series									
1.25-4x24[1]	1.25-4	98.4-31.2	3.15	10.63	30mm	Int.	16.2	1,087.78	
1.5-6x42[1]	1.5-6	65.4-21	3.15	12.99	30mm	Int.	20.8	1,221.11	
2.5-10x42[1, 2]	2.5-10	39.6-12.6	3.15	13.23	30mm	Int.	19.8	1,376.67	
3-12x50[1]	3-12	33-10.5	3.15	14.33	30mm	Int.	22.4	1,421.11	
4-16x50	4-16	30-8.5	3.15	14.22	30mm	Int.	22.3	1,476.67	
6-24x50	6-24	18.6-5.4	3.15	15.4	30mm	Int.	23.6	1,687.78	

[1]Aluminum tubes; special order for steel. [2]Also with 56mm obj., $1,398.89. [3]Also available with illuminated reticle. [4]Aluminum only. Partial listing shown. Imported from Austria by Swarovski Optik.

No. 1	No. 1A	No. 2	No. 4	No. 4A	No. 7A	Plex	No. 24

A-Line Series									
3-9x36AV[4]	3-9	39-13.5	3.35	11.8	1	Int.	11.7	743.33	
3-10x42AV[4]	3-10	33-11.7	3.35	12.44	1	Int.	12.7	821.11	
4-12x50AV[4]	4-12	29.1-9.9	3.35	13.5	1	Int.	13.9	843.33	

SWIFT

600 4x15	4	17	2.8	10.6	.75	Int.	3.5	15.00	
601 3-7x20	3-7	25-12	3-2.9	11	.75	Int.	5.6	35.00	
650 4x32	4	26	4	12	1	Int.	9.1	75.00	
653 4x40WA[1]	4	35	4	12.2	1	Int.	12.6	125.00	
654 3-9x32	3-9	35-12	3.4-2.9	12	1	Int.	9.8	125.00	
656 3-9x40WA[1]	3-9	40-14	3.4-2.8	12.6	1	Int.	12.3	140.00	
657 6x40	6	28	4	12.6	1	Int.	10.4	125.00	
658 2-7x40WA[3]	2-7	55-18	3.3-3	11.6	1	Int.	12.5	160.00	
659 3.5-10x44WA	3.5-10	34-12	3-2.8	12.8	1	Int.	13.5	230.00	

All Swift scopes, with the exception of the 4x15, have Quadraplex reticles and are fogproof and waterproof. The 4x15 has crosshair reticle and is non-waterproof. [1]Available in regular matte black or silver finish. [2]Comes with ring mounts, wrench, lens caps, extension tubes, filter, battery. [3]Regular and matte black finish. [4]Speed Focus scopes. Partial listing shown. From Swift Instruments.

Maker and Model	Magn.	Field at 100 Yds. (feet)	Eye Relief (in.)	Length (in.)	Tube Dia. (in.)	W & E Adjustments	Weight (ozs.)	Price	Other Data
665 1.5-4.5x21	1.5-4.5	69-24.5	3.5-3	10.9	1	Int.	9.6	125.00	
665M 1.5-4.5x21	1.5-4.5	69-24.5	3.5-3	10.9	1	Int.	9.6	125.00	
666M Shotgun 1x20	1	113	3.2	7.5	1	Int.	9.6	130.00	
667 Fire-Fly[2]	1	40		5.4	30mm	Int.	5	220.00	
668M 4x32	4	25	4	10	1	Int.	8.9	120.00	
669M 6-18x44	6-18	18-6.5	2.8	14.5	1	Int.	17.6	220.00	
680M	3.9	43-14	4	18	40mm	Int.	17.5	399.95	
681M	1.5-6	56-13	4	11.8	40mm	Int.	17.5	399.95	
682M	4-12	33-11	4	15.4	50mm	Int.	21.7	499.95	
683M	2-7	55-17	3.3	11.6	32mm	Int.	10.6	499.95	
Premier[4]									
649R 4-12x50WA[3]	4-12	29.5-9.5	3.2-3	13.8	1	Int.	17.8	245.00	
671M 3-9x50WA	3-9	35-12	3.24- 3.12	15.5	1	Int.	18.2	250.00	
672M 6-18x50WA	6-18	19.4-6.7	3.25-3	15.8	1	Int.	20.9	260.00	
673M 2.5-10x50WA	2.5-10	33-9	4-3.5	11.8	30mm	Int.	18.9	295.00	
674M 3-5x40WA	3-9	40-14.2	3.6-2.9	12	1	Int.	13.1	170.00	
676 4-12x40WA[1]	4-12	29.3-10.5	3.15-2.9	12.4	1	Int.	15.4	180.00	
Pistol									
679M 1.25-4x28	1.25-4	23-9	23-15	9.3	1	Int.	8.2	250.00	
Pistol Scopes									
661 4x32	4	90	10-22	9.2	1	Int.	9.5	130.00	
663 2x20[1]	2	18.3	9-21	7.2	1	Int.	8.4	130.00	

THOMPSON/CENTER RECOIL PROOF SERIES

Maker and Model	Magn.	Field at 100 Yds. (feet)	Eye Relief (in.)	Length (in.)	Tube Dia. (in.)	W & E Adjustments	Weight (ozs.)	Price	Other Data
Pistol Scopes									
8315[2]	2.5-7	15-5	8-21, 8- 11	9.25	1	Int.	9.2	349.00	[1]Black finish; silver optional. [2]Black; lighted reticle. From Thompson/Center Arms.
8326[4]	2.5-7	15-5	8-21, 8- 11	9.25	1	Int.	10.5	416.00	
Muzzleloader Scopes									
8658	1	60	3.8	9.125	1	Int.	10.2	149.00	
8662	4	16	3	8.8	1	Int.	9.1	141.00	

TRIJICON

Maker and Model	Magn.	Field at 100 Yds. (feet)	Eye Relief (in.)	Length (in.)	Tube Dia. (in.)	W & E Adjustments	Weight (ozs.)	Price	Other Data
ReflexII 1x24	1			4.25		Int.	4.2	425.00	[1]Advanced Combat Optical Gunsight for AR-15, M16, with integral mount. Other mounts available. All models feature tritium and fiber optics dual-lighting system that requires no batteries. From Trijicon, Inc.
TA44 1.5x16[1]	1.5	43.8	2.4	5.34		Int.	5.31	895.00	
TA45 1.5x24[1]	1.5	28.9	3.6	5.76		Int.	5.92	895.00	
TA47 2x20[1]	2	33.1	2.1	5.3		Int.	5.82	895.00	
TA50 3x24[1]	3	28.9	1.4	5		Int.	5.89	895.00	
TA11 3.5x35[1]	3.5	28.9	2.4	8		Int.	14	1,295.00	
TA01 4x32[1]	4	36.8	1.5	5.8		Int.	9.9	950.00	
Variable AccuPoint									
3-9x40	3-9	33.8-11.3	3.6-3.2	12.2	1	Int.	12.8	720.00	
1.25-4x24	1.25-4	61.6-20.5	4.8-3.4	10.2	1	Int.	11.4	700.00	

ULTRA DOT

Maker and Model	Magn.	Field at 100 Yds. (feet)	Eye Relief (in.)	Length (in.)	Tube Dia. (in.)	W & E Adjustments	Weight (ozs.)	Price	Other Data
Micro-Dot Scopes[1]									
1.5-4.5x20 Rifle	1.5-4.5	80-26	3	9.8	1	Int.	10.5	297.00	[1]Brightness-adjustable fiber optic red dot reticle. Waterproof, nitrogen-filled one-piece tube. Tinted see-through lens covers and battery included. [2]Parallax adjustable. [3]Ultra Dot sights include rings, battery, polarized filter, and 5-year warranty. All models available in black or satin finish. [4]Illuminated red dot has eleven brightness settings. Shock-proof aluminum tube. From Ultra Dot Distribution.
2-7x32	2-7	54-18	3	11	1	Int.	12.1	308.00	
3-9x40	3-9	40-14	3	12.2	1	Int.	13.3	327.00	
4x-12x56[2]	4-12	30-10	3	14.3	1	Int.	18.3	417.00	
Ultra-Dot Sights[3]									
Ultra-Dot 25[4]	1			5.1	1	Int.	3.9	159.00	
Ultra-Dot 30[4]	1			5.1	30mm	Int.	4	179.00	

UNERTL

Maker and Model	Magn.	Field at 100 Yds. (feet)	Eye Relief (in.)	Length (in.)	Tube Dia. (in.)	W & E Adjustments	Weight (ozs.)	Price	Other Data
1" Target	6, 8, 10	16-10	2	21.5	.75	Ext.	21	675.00	[1]Dural .25-MOA click mounts. Hard coated lenses. Non-rotating objective lens focusing. [2].25-MOA click mounts. [3]With target mounts. [4]With calibrated head. [5]Same as 1" Target but without objective lens focusing. [6]With new Posa mounts. [7]Range focus unit near rear of tube. Price is with Posa or standard mounts. Magnum clamp. From Unertl.
10X	10	10.3	3	12.5	1	Ext.	35	2,500.00	
1.25: Target[1]	8, 10, 12, 14	12-16	2	25	.75	Ext.	21	715.00	
1.5" Target	10, 12, 14, 16, 18, 20	11.5-3.2	2.25	25.5	.75	Ext.	31	753.50	
2" Target[2]	10, 12, 14, 16, 18, 24, 30, 32, 36,	8	2.25	26.25	1	Ext.	44	918.50	
Varmint, 1.25"[3]3" Ultra Varmint, 2"[4]	15	12.6-7	2.25	24	1	Ext.	34	918.50	
Small Game[5]	3, 4, 6	25-17	2.25	18	.75	Ext.	16	550.00	
Programmer 200[7]	10, 12, 14, 16, 18, 20, 24, 30, 36	11.3-4		26.5	1	Ext.	45	1,290.00	
B8									
Tube Sight				17		Ext.		420.00	

U.S. OPTICS

Maker and Model	Magn.	Field at 100 Yds. (feet)	Eye Relief (in.)	Length (in.)	Tube Dia. (in.)	W & E Adjustments	Weight (ozs.)	Price	Other Data
SN-1/TAR Fixed Power System									
16.2x	15	8.6	4.3	16.5	30mm	Int.	27	1,700.00	Prices shown are estimates; scopes built to order; choice of reticles; choice of front or rear focal plane; extra-heavy MIL-SPEC construction; extra-long turrets; individual w&e rebound springs; up to 100mm dia. objectives; up to 50mm tubes; all lenses multi-coated. Other magnifications available. [1]Modular components allow a variety of fixed or variable magnifications, night vision, etc. Made in U.S. by U.S. Optics.
22.4x	20	5.8	3.8	18	30mm	Int.	29	1,800.00	
26x	24	5	3.4	18	30mm	Int.	31	1,900.00	
31x	30	4.6	3.5	18	30mm	Int.	32	2,100.00	
37x	36	4	3.6	18	30mm	Int.	32	2,300.00	
48x	50	3	3.8	18	30mm	Int.	32	2,500.00	
Variables									
SN-2	4-22	26.8-5.8	5.4-3.8	18	30mm	Int.	24	1,762.00	
SN-3	1.6-8		4.4-4.8	18.4	30mm	Int.	36	1,435.00	
SN-4	1-4	116-31.2	4.6-4.9	18	30mm	Int.	35	1,065.00	

ACCESSORIES

Maker and Model	Magn.	Field at 100 Yds. (feet)	Eye Relief (in.)	Length (in.)	Tube Dia. (in.)	W & E Adjustments	Weight (ozs.)	Price	Other Data
Fixed Power									
SN-6	8, 10, 17, 22	14-8.5	3.8-4.8	9.2	30mm	Int.	18	1,195.00	
SN-8 Modular[1]	4, 10, 20, 40	32	3.3	7.5	30mm	Int.	11.1	890.00-4,000.00	

WEAVER

Maker and Model	Magn.	Field at 100 Yds. (feet)	Eye Relief (in.)	Length (in.)	Tube Dia. (in.)	W & E Adjustments	Weight (ozs.)	Price	Other Data
Riflescopes									
K2.5[1]	2.5	35	3.7	9.5	1	Int.	7.3	132.86	[1]Gloss black. [2]Matte black. [3]Silver. [4]Satin. [5]Silver and black (slightly
K4[1-2]	3.7	26.5	3.3	11.3	1	Int.	10	149.99	higher in price). [6]Field of view measured at 18" eye relief. .25 MOA click
K6[1]	5.7	18.5	3.3	11.4	1	Int.	10	154.99	adjustments, except T-Series which vary from .125 to .25 clicks. One-
KT15[1]	14.6	7.5	3.2	12.9	1	Int.	14.7	281.43	piece tubes with multi-coated lenses. All scopes are shock-proof, water-
V3[1-2]	1.1-2.8	88-32	3.9-3.7	9.2	1	Int.	8.5	189.99	proof, and fogproof. Dual-X reticle available in all except V24 which has
V9[1-2]	2.8-8.7	33-11	3.5-3.4	12.1	1	Int.	11.1	249.99-299.99	a fine X-hair and ot; T-Series in which certain models are available in fine
V9x50[1-2]	3-9	29.4-9.9	3.6-3	13.1	1	Int.	14.5	239.99	X-hair and dots; Qwik-Point red dot scopes which are available in fixed 4
V10[1-2-3]	2.2-9.6	38.5-9.5	3.4-3.3	12.2	1	Int.	11.2	259.99-269.99	or 12 MOA, or variable 4-8-12 MOA. V16 also avail able with fine X-hair,
V10-50[1-2-3]	2.3-9.7	40.2-9.2	2.9-2.8	13.75	1	Int.	15.2	279.99	dot or Dual-X reticle. T-Series scopes have Micro-Trac® adjustments.
V16 MDX[2-3]	3.8-15.5	26.8-6.8	3.1	13.9	1	Int.	16.5	329.99	From Weaver Products.
V16 MFC[2-3]	3.8-15.5	26.8-6.8	3.1	13.9	1	Int.	16.5	329.99	
V16 MDT[2-3]	3.8-15.5	26.8-6.8	3.1	13.9	1	Int.	16.5	329.99	
V24 Varmint[2]	6-24	15.3-4	3.15	14.3	1	Int.	17.5	379.99 to 399.99	
Handgun									
H2[1-3]	2	21	4-29	8.5	1	Int.	6.7	161.43	
H4[1-3]	4	18	11.5-18	8.5	1	Int.	6.7	175.00	
VH4[1-3]	1.5-4	13.6-5.8	11-17	8.6	1	Int.	8.1	215.71	
VH8[1-2-3]	2.5-8	8.5-3.7	12.16	9.3	1	Int.	8.3	228.57	
Rimfire									
RV7[2]	2.5-7	37-13	3.7-3.3	10.75	1	Int.	10.7	148.57	
Grand Slam									
6-20x40mm Varminter Reticle[2]	6-20X	16.5-5.25	2.75-3	14.48	1	Int.	17.75	419.99	
6-20x40mm Fine Crosshairs with a Dot[2]	6-20X	16.5-5.25	2.75-3	14.48	1	Int.	17.75	419.99	
1.5-5x32mm[2]	1.5-5X	71-21	3.25	10.5	1	Int.	10.5	349.99	
4.75x40mm[2]	4.75X	14.75	3.25	11	1	Int.	10.75	299.99	
3-10x40mm[2]	3-10X	35-11.33	3.5-3	12.08	1	Int.	12.08	329.99	
3.5-10x50mm[2]	3.5-10X	30.5-10.8	3.5-3	12.96	1	Int.	16.25	389.99	
4.5-14x40mm	4.5-14X	22.5-10.5	3.5-3	14.48	1	Int.	17.5	399.99	
T-Series									
T-64	614	14	3.58	12.75	1	Int.	14.9	424.95	
T-36[3-4]	36	3	3	15.1	1	Int.	16.7	489.99	

ZEISS

Maker and Model	Magn.	Field at 100 Yds. (feet)	Eye Relief (in.)	Length (in.)	Tube Dia. (in.)	W & E Adjustments	Weight (ozs.)	Price	Other Data
ZM/Z									
6x42MC	6	22.9	3.2	12.7	1	Int.	13.4	749.00	[1]Also avail. with illuminated reticle. [2]Illuminated Vari-point reticle. Black
8x56MC	8	18	3.2	13.8	1	Int.	17.6	829.00	matte finish. All scopes have .25-min. click-stop adjustments. Choice of
1.25-4x24MC	1.25-4	105-33	3.2	11.46	30mm	Int.	17.3	779.00	Z-Plex or fine crosshair reticles. Rubber armored objective bell, rubber
1.5-6x42MC	1.5-6	65.5-22.9	3.2	12.4	30mm	Int.	18.5	899.00	eyepiece ring. Lenses have T-Star coating for highest light transmission.
2.5-10x48MC[1]	2.5-10	33-11.7	3.2	14.5	30mm	Int.	24	1,029.00	VM/V scopes avail. with rail mount. Partial listing shown. From Carl Zeiss
3-12x56MC[1]	3-12	27.6-9.9	3.2	15.3	30mm	Int.	25.8	1,099.00	Optical, Inc.
Conquest									
3-9x36MC	3-9	34-11	4	13.15	1	Int.	15	499.00	
VM/V									
1.1-4x24 VariPoint T[2]	1.1-4	120-34	3.5	11.8	30mm	Int.	15.8	1,799.00	
1.5-6x42T*	1.5-6	65.5-22.9	3.2	12.4	30mm	Int.	18.5	1,349.00	
2.5-10x50T*[1]	2.5-10	47.1-13	3.5	12.5	30mm	Int.	16.25	1,549.00	
3-12x56T*	3-12	37.5-10.5	3.5	13.5	30mm	Int.	19.5	1,599.00	
3-9x42T*	3-9	42-15	3.74	13.3	1	Int.	15.3	1,249.00	
5-15x42T*	5-15	25.7-8.5	3.74	13.3	1	Int.	15.4	1,499.00	

Hunting scopes in general are furnished with a choice of reticlecrosshairs, post with crosshairs, tapered or blunt post, or dot crosshairs, etc. The great majority of target and varmint scopes have medium or fine crosshairs but post or dot reticles may be ordered. Wwindage EElevation MOAMinute of Angle or 1" (approx.) at 100 yards.

LASER SIGHTS

Lasergrips LG-206

Alpec Mini Shot

Laser Devices ULS 2001 with TLS 8R light

Maker and Model	Wave length (nm)	Beam Color	Lens	Operating Temp. (degrees F.)	Weight (ozs.)	Price	Other Data
ALPEC							1Range 1000 yards. 2Range 300 yards. Mini Shot II range 500 yards, output 650mm, **$129.95**. 3Range 300 yards; Laser Shot II 500 yards; Super Laser Shot 1000 yards. Black or stainless fin ish aluminum; removable pressure or push-button switch. Mounts for most handguns, many rifles and shotguns. From Alpec Team, Inc.
Power Shot1	635	Red	Glass	NA	2.5	$199.95	
Mini Shot2	670	Red	Glass	NA	2.5	99.95	
Laser Shot3	670	Red	Glass	NA	3.0	99.95	
BEAMSHOT							1Black or silver finish; adj. for windage and elevation; 300-yd. range; also M1000/S (500- yd. range), M1000/u (800-yd.). 2Black finish; 300-, 500-, 800-yd. models. All come with removable touch pad switch, 5" cable. Mounts to fit virtually any firearm. From Quarton USA Co.
10001	670	Red	Glass		3.8	NA	
30002	635/670	Red	Glass		2	NA	
1001/u	635	Red	Glass		3.8	NA	
780	780	Red	Glass		3.8	NA	
BSA							1Comes with mounts for 22/air rifle and Weaver-style bases.
LS6501	N/A	Red	N/A	N/A	N/A	49.95	
LASERAIM							1Red dot/laser combo; 300-yd. range: LA3xHD Hotdot has 500-yd. range **$249.00**; 4 MOA dot size, laser gives 2" dot size at 100 yds. 230mm obj. lens: 4 MOA dot at 100 yds: fits Weaver base. 3300-yd range; 2" dot at 100 yds.; rechargeable Nicad battery 41.5-mile range; 1" dot at 100 yds.; 20+ hrs. batt. life. 51.5-mile range; 1" dot at 100 yds; rechargeable Nicad battery (comes with in-field charger); 6Black or satin finish. With mount, **$169.00**. 7Laser projects 2" dot at 100 yds.: with rotary switch; with Hotdot **$237.00**; with Hotdot touch switch **$357.00**. 8For Glock 17-27; G1 Hotdot **$299.00**. 9For Glock 17-27; G1 Hotdot **$299.00**; price installed. 10Fits std. Weaver base, no rings required; 6- MOA dot; seven brightness settings. All have w&e adj.; black or satin silver finish. From Laser aim Technologies, Inc.
LA10 Hotdot4					NA	199.00	
Lasers							
MA-35RB Mini Aimer7					1.0	129.00	
G1 Laser8					2.0	229.00	
LASER DEVICES							1For S&W P99 semi-auto pistols; also BA-2, 5 oz., **$339.00**. 2For revolvers. 3For HK, Walther P99. 4For semi-autos. 5For rifles; also FA-4/ULS, 2.5 oz., **$325.00**. 6For HK sub guns. 7For mil itary rifles. 8For shotguns. 9For SIG-Pro pistol. 10Universal, semi-autos. 11For AR-15 variants. All avail. with Magnum Power Point (650nM) or daytime-visible Super Power Point (632nM) diode. Infrared diodes avail. for law enforcement. From Laser Devices, Inc.
BA-11	632	Red	Glass		2.4	372.00	
BA-32	632	Red	Glass		3.3	332.50	
BA-53	632	Red	Glass		3.2	372.00	
Duty-Grade4	632	Red	Glass		3.5	372.00	
FA-45	632	Red	Glass		2.6	358.00	
LasTac1	632	Red	Glass		5.5	298.00 to 477.00	
MP-5 6	632	Red	Glass		2.2	495.00	
MR-27	632	Red	Glass		6.3	485.00	
SA-28	632	Red	Glass		3.0	360.00	
SIG-Pro9	632	Red	Glass		2.6	372.00	
ULS-200110	632	Red	Glass		4.5	210.95	
Universal AR-2A	632	Red	Glass		4.5	445.00	
LASERGRIPS							Replaces existing grips with built-in laser high in the right grip panel. Integrated pressure sensi tive pad in grip activates the laser. Also has master on/off switch. 1For Colt 1911/Commander. 2For all Glock models. Option on/off switch. Requires factory installation. 3For S&W K, L, N frames, round or square butt (LG-207); 4For Taurus small-frame revolvers. 5For Ruger SP-101. 6For SIG Sauer P226. From Crimson Trace Corp. 7For Beretta 92/96. 8For Ruger MK II. 9For S&W J-frame. 10For Sig Sauer P228/229. 11For Colt 1911 full size, wraparound. 12For Beretta 92/96, wraparound. 13For Colt 1911 compact, wraparound. 14For S&W J-frame, rubber.
LG-2011	633	Red- Orange	Glass	NA		299.00	
LG-2063	633	Red- Orange	Glass	NA		229.00	
LG-0854	633	Red- Orange	Glass	NA		229.00	
LG-1015	633	Red- Orange	Glass	NA		229.00	
LG-2266	633	Red- Orange	Glass	NA		229.00	
GLS-6302	633	Red- Orange	Glass	NA		595.00	
LG2027	633	Red- Orange	Glass	NA		299.00	
LG2038	633	Red- Orange	Glass	NA		299.00	
LG2059	633	Red- Orange	Glass	NA		299.00	
LG22910	633	Red- Orange	Glass	NA		299.00	
LG30111	633	Red- Orange	Glass	NA		329.00	
LG30212	633	Red- Orange	Glass	NA		329.00	
LG30413	633	Red- Orange	Glass	NA		329.00	
LG30514	633	Red- Orange	Glass	NA		299.00	
LASERLYTE							1Dot/circle or dot/crosshair projection; black or stainless. 2Also 635/645mm model. From Tac Star Laserlyte. in grip activates the laser. Also has master on/off switch. 1For Colt 1911/Comma
LLX-0006-140/0901	635/645	Red			1.4	159.95	
WPL-0004-140/0902	670	Red			1.2	109.95	
TPL-0004-140/0902	670	Red			1.2	109.95	
T7S-0004-1402	670	Red			0.8	109.95	
LASERMAX							Replaces the recoil spring guide rod; includes a customized takedown lever that serves as the laser's insta in grip activates the laser. Also has master on/off switch. 1For Colt 1911/Commant on/off switch. For Glock, Smith & Wesson, Sigarms, Beretta, Colt, Kimber, Springfield Gov't. Model 1911, Heckler & Koch and select Taurus models. Installs in most pistols without gunsmithing. Battery life 1/2 hour to 2 hours in continuous use. From Laser Max.
LMS-1000 Internal Guide Rod	635	Red- Orange	Glass	40-120	.25	389.00	
NIGHT STALKER							Waterproof; LCD panel displays power remaining; programmable blink rate; con stant or memory on. From Wilcox Industri in grip activates the laser. Also has master on/off switch. 1For Colt 1911/Commaes Corp.
S0 Smart	635	Red	NA	NA	2.46	515.00	

Maker, Model, Type	Adjust.	Scopes	Price
ADCO			
Std. Black or nickel		1"	$13.95
Std. Black or nickel		30mm	13.95
Rings Black or nickel		30mm w/ 3/8" grv.	13.95
Rings Black or nickel		1" raised 3/8" grv.	13.95
AIMTECH			
AMT Auto Mag II .22 Mag.	No	Weaver rail	$56.99
Astra .44 Mag Revolver	No	Weaver rail	63.25
Beretta/Taurus 92/99	No	Weaver rail	63.25
Browning Buckmark/Challenger II	No	Weaver rail	56.99
Browning Hi-Power	No	Weaver rail	63.25
Glock 17, 17L, 19, 23, 24 etc. no rail	No	Weaver rail	63.25
Glock 20, 21 no rail	No	Weaver rail	63.25
Glock 9mm and .40 with access. rail	No	Weaver rail	74.95
Govt. 45 Auto/.38 Super	No	Weaver rail	63.25
Hi-Standard (Mitchell version) 107	No	Weaver rail	63.25
H&K USP 9mm/40 rail mount	No	Weaver rail	74.95
Rossi 85/851/951 Revolvers	No	Weaver rail	63.25
Ruger Mk I, Mk II	No	Weaver rail	49.95
Ruger P85/P89	No	Weaver rail	63.25
S&W K, L, N frames	No	Weaver rail	63.25
S&W K, L, N with tapped top strap*	No	Weaver rail	69.95
S&W Model 41 Target 22	No	Weaver rail	63.25
S&W Model 52 Target 38	No	Weaver rail	63.25
S&W Model 99 Walther frame rail mount	No	Weaver rail	74.95
S&W 2nd Gen. 59/459/659 etc.	No	Weaver rail	56.99
S&W 3rd Gen. full size 5906 etc.	No	Weaver rail	69.95
S&W 422, 622, 2206	No	Weaver rail	56.99
S&W 645/745	No	Weaver rail	56.99
S&W Sigma	No	Weaver rail	64.95
Taurus PT908	No	Weaver rail	63.25
Taurus 44 6.5" bbl.	No	Weaver rail	69.95
Walther 99	No	Weaver rail	74.95
Shotguns			
Benelli M-1 Super 90	No	Weaver rail	44.95
Benelli Montefeltro	No	Weaver rail	44.95
Benelli Nova	No	Weaver rail	69.95
Benelli Super Black Eagle	No	Weaver rail	49.95
Browning A-5 12-ga.	No	Weaver rail	40.95
Browning BPS 12-ga.	No	Weaver rail	40.95
Browning Gold Hunter 12-ga.	No	Weaver rail	44.95
Browning Gold Hunter 20-ga.	No	Weaver rail	49.95
Browning Gold Hunter 10-ga.	No	Weaver rail	49.95
Berotta 303 12-ga.	No	Weaver rail	44.95
Beretta 390 12-ga.	No	Weaver rail	44.95
Beretta Pintail	No	Weaver rail	44.95
H&K Fabarms Gold/SilverLion	no	Weaver rail	49.95
Ithaca 37/87 12-ga.	No	Weaver rail	40.95
Ithaca 37/87 20-ga.	No	Weaver rail	40.95
Mossberg 500/Maverick 12-ga.	No	Weaver rail	40.95
Mossberg 500/Maverick 20-ga.	No	Weaver rail	40.95
Mossberg 835 3.5" Ulti-Mag	No	Weaver rail	40.95
Mossberg 5500/9200	No	Weaver rail	40.95
Remington 1100/1187 12-ga.	No	Weaver rail	40.95
Remington 1100/1187 12-ga. LH	No	Weaver rail	40.95
Remington 1100/1187 20-ga.	No	Weaver rail	40.95
Remington 1100/1187 20-ga. LH	No	Weaver rail	40.95
Remington 870 12-ga.	No	Weaver rail	40.95
Remington 870 12-ga. LH	No	Weaver rail	40.95
Remington 870 20-ga.	No	Weaver rail	40.95
Remington 870 20-ga. LH	No	Weaver rail	40.95
Remington 870 Express Magnum	No	Weaver rail	40.95
Remington SP-10 10-ga.	No	Weaver rail	49.95
Winchester 1300 12-ga.	No	Weaver rail	40.95
Winchester 1400 12-ga.	No	Weaver rail	40.95
Winchester Super X2	No	Weaver rail	44.95
"Rib Rider" Ultra Low Profile Mounts			
Non See Through 2-piece rib attached			
Mossberg 500/835/9200	No	Weaver rail	29.95
Remington 1100/1187/870	No	Weaver rail	29.95
Winchester 1300	No	Weaver rail	29.95
1-Piece Rib Rider Low Rider Mounts			
Mossberg 500/835/9200	No	Weaver rail	29.95
Remington 1100/1187/870	No	Weaver rail	29.95
Winchester 1300	No	Weaver rail	29.95
2-Piece Rib Rider See-Through			
Mossberg 500/835/9200	No	Weaver rail	29.95
Remington 1100/1187/87	No	Weaver rail	29.95
Winchester 1300	No	Weaver rail	29.95
1-Piece Rib Rider See-Through			
Mossberg 500/835/9200	No	Weaver rail	29.95
Remington 1100/1187/870	No	Weaver rail	29.95
Winchester 1300	No	Weaver rail	29.95
Rifles			
AR-15/M16	No	Weaver rail	21.95
Browning A-Bolt	No	Weaver rail	21.95
Browning BAR	No	Weaver rail	21.95
Browning BLR	No	Weaver rail	21.95
CVA Apollo	No	Weaver rail	21.95
Marlin 336	No	Weaver rail	21.95

Maker, Model, Type	Adjust.	Scopes	Price
AIMTECH (cont.)			
Mauser Mark X	No	Weaver rail	21.95
Modern Muzzleloading	No	Weaver rail	21.95
Remington 700 Short Action	No	Weaver rail	21.95
Remington 700 Long Action	No	Weaver rail	21.95
Remington 7400/7600	No	Weaver rail	21.95
Ruger 10/22	No	Weaver rail	21.95
Ruger Mini 14 Scout Rail**	No	Weaver rail	89.50
Savage 110, 111, 113, 114, 115, 116	No	Weaver rail	21.95
Thompson Center Thunderhawk	No	Weaver rail	21.95
Traditions Buckhunter	No	Weaver rail	21.95
White W Series	No	Weaver rail	21.95
White G Series	No	Weaver rail	21.95
White WG Series	No	Weaver rail	21.95
Winchester Model 70	No	Weaver rail	21.95
Winchester 94 AE	No	Weaver rail	21.95

All mounts no-gunsmithing, iron sight usable. Rifle mounts are solid see-through bases. All mounts accommodate standard Weaver-style rings of all makers. From Aimtech division, L&S Technologies, Inc. *3-blade sight mount combination. **Replacement handguard and mounting rail.

Maker, Model, Type	Adjust.	Scopes	Price
A.R.M.S.			
M16A1,A2,AR-15	No	Weaver rail	$59.95
Multibase	No	Weaver rail	59.95
#19 ACOG Throw Lever Mt.	No	Weaver rail	150.00
#19 Weaver/STANAG Throw Lever Rail	No	Weaver rail	140.00
STANAG Rings	No	30mm	75.00
Throw Lever Rings	No	Weaver rail	99.00
Ring Inserts	No	1", 30mm	29.00
#22M68 Aimpoint Comp Ring Throw Lever	No	Weaver rail	99.00
#38 Std. Swan Sleeve[1]	No		180.00
#39 A2 Plus Mod. Mt.	No	#39T rail	125.00

[1]Avail. in three lengths. From A.R.M.S., Inc.

Maker, Model, Type	Adjust.	Scopes	Price
ARMSON			
AR-15[1]	No	1"	45.00
Mini-14[2]	No	1"	66.00
H&K3	No	1"	82.00

[1]Fastens with one nut. [2]Models 181, 182, 183, 184, etc. 3Claw mount. From Trijicon, Inc.

Maker, Model, Type	Adjust.	Scopes	Price
ARMSPORT			
100 Series [1]	No	1" rings, Low, med., high	10.75
104 22-cal.	No	1"	10.75
201 See-Thru	No	1"	13.00
1-Piece Base[2]	No		5.50
2-Piece Base[2]	No		2.75

[1]Weaver-type ring. [2]Weaver-type base; most popular rifles. Made in U.S. From Arm Sport.

Maker, Model, Type	Adjust.	Scopes	Price
AO			
AO/Lever Scout Scope	No	Weaver rail	50.00

No gunsmithing required for lever-action rifles with 8" Weaver-style rails; surrounds barrel shank; 6" long; low profile. AO Sight Systems Inc.

Maker, Model, Type	Adjust.	Scopes	Price
B-SQUARE			
Pistols (centerfire)			
Beretta 92, 96/Taurus 99	No	Weaver rail	69.95
Colt M1911	E only	Weaver rail	69.95
Desert Eagle	No	Weaver rail	69.95
Glock	No	Weaver rail	69.95
H&K USP, 9mm and 40 S&W	No	Weaver rail	69.95
Ruger P85/89	E only	Weaver rail	69.95
SIG Sauer P226	E only	Weaver rail	69.95
Pistols (rimfire)			
Browning Buck Mark	No	Weaver rail	32.95
Colt 22	No	Weaver rail	49.95
Ruger Mk I/II, bull or taper	No	Weaver rail	32.95-49.95
Smith & Wesson 41, 2206	No	Weaver rail	36.95-49.95
Revolvers			
Colt Anaconda/Python	No	Weaver rail	35.95-74.95
Ruger Single-Six	No	Weaver rail	64.95
Ruger GP-100	No	Weaver rail	64.95
Ruger Blackhawk, Super	No	Weaver rail	64.95
Ruger Redhawk, Super	No	Weaver rail	64.95
Smith & Wesson K, L, N	No	Weaver rail	36.95-74.95
Taurus 66, 669, 607, 608	No	Weaver rail	64.95
Rifles (sporting)			
Browning BAR, A-Bolt	No	Weaver rail	45.90
Marlin MR7	No	Weaver rail	45.90
Mauser 98 Large Ring	No	Weaver rail	45.90
Mauser 91/93/95/96 Small Ring	No	Weaver rail	45.90
Remington 700, 740, 742, 760	No	Weaver rail	45.90
Remington 7400, 7600	No	Weaver rail	45.90
Remington Seven	No	Weaver rail	45.90
Rossi 62, 59 and 92	No	Weaver rail	44.95
Ruger Mini-14	W&E	Weaver rail	66.95
Ruger 96/22	No	Weaver rail	45.90

SCOPE RINGS & BASES

Maker, Model, Type	Adjust.	Scopes	Price
B-SQUARE (cont.)			
Ruger M77 (short and long)	No	Weaver rail	62.95
Ruger 10/22 (reg. and See-Thru)	No	Weaver rail	45.90
Savage 110-116, 10-16	No	Weaver rail	45.90
Modern Military (rings incl.)			
AK-47/MAC 90	No	Weaver rail	49.95
Colt AR-15	No	Weaver rail	66.95-81.95
FN/FAL/LAR (See-Thru rings)	No	Weaver rail	81.95
Classic Military (rings incl.)			
FN 49	No	Weaver rail	72.95
Hakim	No	Weaver rail	72.95
Mauser 38, 94, 96, 98	E only	Weaver rail	72.95
Mosin-Nagant (all)	E only	Weaver rail	72.95
Air Rifles			
RWS, Diana, BSA, Gamo	W&E	11mm rail	49.95-59.95
Weihrauch, Anschutz, Beeman, Webley	W&E	11mm rail	59.95-69.95
Shotguns/Slug Guns			
Benelli Super 90 (See-Thru)	No	Weaver rail	53.95
Browning BPS, A-5 9 (See-Thru)	No	Weaver rail	53.95
Browning Gold 10/12/20-ga. (See- Thru)	No	Weaver rail	53.95
Ithaca 37, 87	No	Weaver rail	53.95
Mossberg 500/Mav. 88	No	Weaver rail	53.95
Mossberg 835/Mav. 91	No	Weaver rail	53.95
Remington 870/1100/11-87	No	Weaver rail	53.95
Remington SP10	No	Weaver rail	53.95
Winchester 1200-1500	No	Weaver rail	53.95

Prices shown for anodized black finish; add $10 for stainless finish. Par tial listing of mounts shown here. Contact B-Square for complete list ing and details.

Maker, Model, Type	Adjust.	Scopes	Price
BEEMAN			
Two-Piece, Med.	No	1"	31.50
Deluxe Two-Piece, High	No	1"	33.00
Deluxe Two-Piece	No	30mm	41.00
Deluxe One-Piece	No	1"	50.00
Dampa Mount	No	1"	120.00

All grooved receivers and scope bases on all known air rifles and 22-cal. rimfire rifles (1/2" to 5/8"6mm to 15mm).

Maker, Model, Type	Adjust.	Scopes	Price
BOCK			
Swing ALK[1]	W&E	1", 26mm, 30mm	349.00
Safari KEMEL[2]	W&E	1", 26mm, 30mm	149.00
Claw KEMKA[3]	W&E	1", 26mm, 30mm	224.00
ProHunter Fixed[4]	No	1", 26mm, 30mm	95.00

[1]Q.D.: pivots right for removal. For Steyr-Mannlicher, Win. 70, Rem. 700, Mauser 98, Dakota, Sako, Sauer 80, 90. Magnum has extra-wide rings, same price. [2]Heavy-duty claw-type reversible for front or rear removal. For Steyr-Mannlicher rifles. [3]True claw mount for bolt-action rifles. Also in extended model. For Steyr-Mannlicher, Win. 70, Rem. 700. Also avail. as Gunsmith Basesbases not drilled or contoured same price. [4]Extra-wide rings. Imported from Germany by GSI, Inc.

Maker, Model, Type	Adjust.	Scopes	Price
BSA			
AA Airguns	Yes	Super Ten, 240 Magnum, Maxi gripped scope rail equipped air rifles	59.99 (adj). 29.99 (fixed)

Maker, Model, Type	Adjust.	Scopes	Price
BURRIS			
Supreme (SU) One-Piece (T)[1]	W only	1" split rings, 3 heights	1-piece base - 23.00-27.00
Trumount (TU) Two-Piece (T)	W only	1" split rings, 3 heights	2-piece base - 21.00-30.00
Trumount (TU) Two-Piece Ext.	W only	1" split rings	26.00
Browning 22-cal. Auto Mount[2]	No	1" split rings	20.00
1" 22-cal. Ring Mounts[3]	No	1" split rings	1"rings - 24.00-41.00
L.E.R. (LU) Mount Bases[4]	W only	1" split rings	24.00-52.00
L.E.R. No Drill-No Tap Bases[4,7,8]	W only	1" split rings	48.00-52.00
Extension Rings[5]	No	1" scopes	28.00-46.00
Ruger Ring Mount[6,9]	W only	1" split rings	50.00-68.00
Std. 1" Rings[9]		Low, medium, high heights	29.00-43.00
Zee Rings[9]		Fit Weaver bases; medium and high heights	29.00-44.00
Signature Rings	No	30mm split rings	68.00
Rimfire/Airgun Rings	W only	1" split rings, med. & high	24.00-41.00
Double Dovetail (DD) Bases	No	30mm Signature	23.00-26.00

[1]Most popular rifles. Universal rings, mounts fit Burris, Universal, Redfield, Leupold and Browning bases. Comparable prices. [2]Browning Standard 22 Auto rifle. [3]Grooved receivers. [4]Universal dovetail; accepts Burris, Universal, Redfield, Leupold rings. For Dan Wesson, S&W, Virginian, Ruger Blackhawk, Win. 94. [5]Medium standard front, extension rear, per pair. Low standard front, extension rear per pair. [6]Compact scopes, scopes with 2" bell for M77R. [7]Selected rings and bases available with matte Safari or silver finish. [8]For S&W K, L, N frames, Colt Python, Dan Wesson with 6" or longer barrels. [9]Also in 30mm.

Maker, Model, Type	Adjust.	Scopes	Price
CATCO			
Enfield Drop-In	No	1"	39.95

Uses Weaver-style rings (not incl.). No gunsmithing required. See-Thru design. From CATCO.

Maker, Model, Type	Adjust.	Scopes	Price
CLEAR VIEW			
Universal Rings, Mod. 101[1]	No	1" split rings	21.95
Standard Model[2]	No	1" split rings	21.95
Broad View[3]	No	1"	21.95
22 Model[4]	No	3/4", 7/8", 1"	13.95
SM-94 Winchester[5]	No	1" split rings	23.95
94 EJ[6]	No	1" split rings	21.95

[1]Most rifles by using Weaver-type base; allows use of iron sights. [2]Most popular rifles; allows use of iron sights. [3]Most popular rifles; low profile, wide field of view. [4]22 rifles with grooved receiver. [5]Side mount. [6]For Win. A.E. From Clear View Mfg.

Maker, Model, Type	Adjust.	Scopes	Price
CONETROL			
Huntur[1] (base & rings)	W only	1", split rings, 3 heights	99.96
Gunnur[2] (base & rings)	W only	1", split rings, 3 heights	119.88
Custum[3] (base & rings)	W only	1", split rings, 3 heights	149.88
One-Piece Side Mount Base[4]	W only	1" rings, 3 heights	$99.96
DapTar Bases[5]	W only	1", rings, 3 heights	$119.88
Pistol Bases, 2-or 3-ring[6]	W only		$149.88
Fluted Bases[7]	W only		149.88
Metric Rings[8]	W only	26mm, 26.5mm, 30mm	99.96-149.88

[1]All popular rifles, including metric-drilled foreign guns. Price shown for base, two rings. Matte finish. [2]Gunnur grade has mirror-finished rings to match scopes. Satin-finish base to match guns. Price shown for base, two rings. [3]Custom grade has mirror-finished rings and mirror-finished, streamlined base. Price shown for base, two rings. [4]Win. 94, Krag, older split-bridge Mannlicher-Schoenauer, Mini-14, etc. Prices same as above. [5]For all popular guns with integral mounting provision, including Sako. BSA Ithacagun, Ruger, Tikka, H&K, BRNO $39.96-$59.94 and many others. Also for grooved-receiver rimfires and air rifles. Prices same as above. [6]For XP-100, T/C Contender, Colt SAA, Ruger Blackhawk, S&W and others. [7]Sculptured two-piece bases as found on fine custom rifles. Price shown is for base alone. Also available unfinished $99.96, or finished but unblued $119.88. [8]26mm, 26.5mm, and 30mm rings made in projectionless style, in three heights. Three-ring mount for T/C Contender and other pistols in Conetrol's three grades. Any Conetrol mount available in stainless or Teflon for double regular cost of grade. Adjust-Quik-Detach (AQD) mounting is now available from Conetrol. Jam screws return the horizontal-split rings to zero. Adjustable for windage. AQD bases: $99.96. AQD rings: $99.96. (Total cost of complete setup, rings and 2-piece base, is $199.92).

Maker, Model, Type	Adjust.	Scopes	Price
CUSTOM QUALITY			
Custom See-Thru	No	Up to 44mm	29.95
Dovetail 101-1 See-Thru	No	1"	29.95
Removable Rings	No	1"	29.95
Solid Dovetail	No	1", 30mm verti cally split	29.95
Dovetail 22 See-Thru	No	1"	29.95

Mounts for many popular rifles. From Custom Quality Products, Inc.

Maker, Model, Type	Adjust.	Scopes	Price
EAW			
Quick-Loc Mount	W&E	1", 26mm	253.00
	W&E	30mm	271.00
Magnum Fixed Mount	W&E	1", 26mm	198.00
	W&E	30mm	215.00

Fit most popular rifles. Avail. in 4 heights, 4 extensions. Reliable return to zero. Stress-free mounting. Imported by New England Custom Gun Svc.

Maker, Model, Type	Adjust.	Scopes	Price
EXCEL INDUSTRIES, INC.			
Titanium Weaver-Style Rings	No	1" and 30mm, low and high	179.00
Steel Weaver-Style Rings	No	1" and 30mm, low and high	149.00
Flashlight Mounts - Titanium and Steel	No	1" and 30mm, low and high	89.50/75.00

Maker, Model, Type	Adjust.	Scopes	Price
GENTRY			
Feather-Light Rings and Bases	No	1", 30mm	90.00-125.00

Bases for Rem. Seven, 700, Mauser 98, Browning A-Bolt, Weatherby Mk. V, Win. 70, HVA, Dakota. Two-piece base for Rem. Seven, chrome moly or stainless. Rings in matte or regular blue, or stainless gray; four heights. From David Gentry.

Maker, Model, Type	Adjust.	Scopes	Price
GRIFFIN & HOWE			
Topmount[1]	No	1", 30mm	625.00
Sidemount[2]	No	1", 30mm	255.00
Garand Mount[3]	No	1"	255.00

[1]Quick-detachable, double-lever mount with 1" rings, installed; with 30mm rings $875.00. [2]Quick-detachable, double-lever mount with 1" rings; with 30mm rings $375.00; installed, 1" rings $405.00; installed, 30mm rings $525.00. [3]Price installed, with 1" rings $405.00. From Griffin & Howe.

Maker, Model, Type	Adjust.	Scopes	Price
G. G. & G.			
Remington 700 Rail	No	Weaver base	135.00
Sniper Grade Rings	No	30mm	159.95
M16/AR15 F.I.R.E. Std.[1]	No	Weaver rail	75.00
M16/AR15 F.I.R.E. Scout	No	Weaver rail	82.95
Aimpoint Standard Ring	No		164.95
Aimpoint Cantilever Ring	No	Weaver rail	212.00

[1]For M16/A3, AR15 flat top receivers; also in extended length. [2]For Aimpoint 5000 and Comp; quick detachable; spare battery compartment. [3]Low profile; quick release. From G. G. & G.

Maker, Model, Type	Adjust.	Scopes	Price
IRONSIGHTER			
Ironsighter See-Through Mounts[1]	No	1" split rings	29.40-64.20
Ironsighter S-9[4]	No	1" split rings	45.28

Maker, Model, Type	Adjust.	Scopes	Price
IRONSIGHTER (cont.)			
Ironsighter AR-15/M-16[8]	No	1", 30mm	70.10
Ironsighter 22-Cal.Rimfire[2]	No	1"	18.45
Model #570[9]	No	1" split rings	29.40
Model #573[9]	No	30mm split rings	45.28
Model #727[3]	No	.875" split rings	18.45
Blackpowder Mount[7]	No	1"	34.20-78.25

[1]Most popular rifles. Rings have oval holes to permit use of iron sights. [2]For 1" dia. scopes. [3]For .875" dia. scopes. [4]For 1" dia. extended eye relief scopes. [7]Fits most popular blackpowder rifles; two-piece (CVA, Knight, Marlin and Austin & Halleck) and one-piece integral (T/C). [8]Model 716 with 1" #540 rings; Fits Weaver-style bases. Some models in stainless finish. [9]New detachable Weaver style rings fit all Weaver style bases. **Price:** **$26.95** From Ironsighter Co.

K MOUNT By KENPATABLE			
Shotgun Mount	No	1", laser or red dot device	49.95
SKS1	No	1"	39.95

Wrap-around design; no gunsmithing required. Models for Browning BPS, A-5 12-ga., Sweet 16, 20, Rem. 870/1100 (LTW, and L.H.), S&W 916, Mossberg 500, Ithaca 37 & 51 12- ga., S&W 1000/3000, Win. 1400. [1]Requires simple modification to gun. From KenPatable Ent.

KRIS MOUNTS			
Side-Saddle[1]	No	1",26mm split rings	12.98
Two-Piece (T)[2]	No	1", 26mm split rings	8.98
One Piece (T)[3]	No	1", 26mm split rings	12.98

[1]One-piece mount for Win. 94. [2]Most popular rifles and Ruger. [3]Blackhawk revolver. Mounts have oval hole to permit use of iron sights.

KWIK-SITE			
Adapter	No	1"	27.95-57.95
KS-W2[2]	No	1"	21.95
KS-W94[3]	No	1"	42.95
KS-WEV (Weaver-style rings)	No	1"	19.95
KS-WEV-HIGH	No	1"	19.95
KS-T22 1"[4]	No	1"	17.95
KS-FL Flashlite[5]	No	Mini or C cell flash light	37.95
KS-T88[6]	No	1"	21.95
KS-T89	No	30mm	21.95
KSN 22 See-Thru	No	1", 7/8"	17.95
KSN-T22	No	1", 7/8"	17.95
KSN-M-16 See-Thru (for M16 + AR- 15)	No	1"	49.95
KS-202[1]	No	1"	27.97
KS-203	No	30mm	42.95
KSBP[7]	No	Integral	76.95
KSB Base Set			5.95
Combo Bases & Rings	No	1"	21.95

Bases interchangeable with Weaver bases. [1]Most rifles. Allows use of iron sights. [2]22-cal. rifles with grooved receivers. Allows use of iron sights. [3]Model 94, 94 Big Bore. No drilling or tapping. Also in adjustable model **$57.95**. [4]Non-See-Thru model for grooved receivers. [5]Allows C-cell or, Mini Mag Lites to be mounted atop See-Thru mounts. [6]Fits any Redfield, Tasco, Weaver or Universal-style Kwik-Site dovetail base. [7]Blackpowder mount with integral rings and sights. [8]Shotgun side mount. Bright blue, black matte or satin finish. Standard, high heights.

LASER AIM	No	Laser Aim	19.99-69.00

Mounts Laser Aim above or below barrel. Avail. for most popular hand guns, rifles, shotguns, including militaries. From Laser Aim Technolo gies, Inc.

LEUPOLD			
STD Bases[1]	W only	One- or two-piece bases	24.60
STD Rings[2]		1" super low, low, medium, high	32.40
DD RBH Handgun Mounts[2]	No		59.40
Dual Dovetail Bases[3]	No		24.60
Dual Dovetail Rings[8]		1", low, med, high	32.40
Ring Mounts[4,5,6]	No	7/8", 1"	81.00
22 Rimfire[8]	No	7/8", 1"	60.00
Gunmaker Base[7]	W only		16.50
Quick Release Rings		1", low, med., high	33.00-71.00
Quick Release Bases[9]	No	1", one- or two- piece	71.40

[1]Base and two rings; Casull, Ruger, S&W, T/C; add $5.00 for silver finish. [2]Rem. 700, Win. 70-type actions. For Ruger No. 1, 77, 77/22; interchangeable with Ruger units. For dovetailed rimfire rifles. Sako; high, medium, low. [7]Must be drilled, tapped for each action. [8]13mm dovetail receiver. [9]BSA Monarch, Rem. 40x, 700, 721, 725, Ruger M77, S&W 1500, Weatherby Mark V, Vanguard, Win. M70.

MARLIN			
One-Piece QD (T)	No	1" split rings	10.10
Most Marlin lever actions.			

MILLETT			
Black Onyx Smooth		1", low, medium, high	32.71
Chaparral Engraved		engraved	50.87
One-Piece Bases[6]	Yes	1"	26.41
Universal Two-Piece Bases			
700 Series	W only	Two-piece bases	26.41
FN Series	W only	Two-piece bases	26.41
70 Series[1]	W only	1", two-piece bases	26.41

Maker, Model, Type	Adjust.	Scopes	Price
MILLETT (cont.)			
Angle-Loc Rings[2]	W only	1", low, medium, high	35.49
Ruger 77 Rings[3]		1"	38.14
Shotgun Rings[4]		1"	32.55
Handgun Bases, Rings[5]		1"	36.07-80.38
30mm Rings[7]		30mm	20.95-41.63
Extension Rings[8]		1"	40.43-56.44
See-Thru Mounts[9]	No	1"	29.35-31.45
Shotgun Mounts[10]	No	1"	52.45
Timber Mount	No	1"	81.90

BRNO, Rem. 40x, 700, 722, 725, 7400 Ruger 77 (round top), Marlin, Weatherby, FN Mauser, FN Brownings, Colt 57, Interarms Mark X, Parker-Hale, Savage 110, Sako (round receiver), many others. [1]Fits Win. M70 70XTR, 670, Browning BBR, BAR, BLR, A-Bolt, Rem. 7400/7600, Four, Six, Marlin 336, Win. 94 A. E., Sav. 110. [2]To fit Weaver-type bases. [3]Engraved. Smooth **$34.60**. [4]For Rem. 870, 1100; smooth. [5]Two- and three-ring sets for Colt Python, Trooper, Diamondback, Peacekeeper, Dan Wesson, Ruger Redhawk, Super Redhawk. [6]Turn-in bases and Weaver-style for most popular rifles and T/C Contender, XP-100 pistols. [7]Both Weaver and turn-in styles; three heights. [8]Med. or high; ext. frontstd. rear, ext. rearstd. front, ext. frontext. rear; **$40.90** for double extension. [9]Many popular rifles, Knight MK-85, T/C Hawken, Renegade, Mossberg 500 Slugster, 835 slug. [10]For Rem. 879/1100, Win. 1200, 1300/1400, 1500, Mossberg 500. Some models available in nickel at extra cost. [11]For T/C Hawken and Renegade; See-Thru with adj. open sight inside.
New Angle-Loc two-piece bases fit all Weaver-style rings. In smooth, matte and nickel finishes, they are available for: Browning A-Bolt, Browning BAR/BLR, Interarms MK X, FN, Mauser 98, CVA rifles with octagon barrels, CVA rifles with round receiver, Knight MK-85, Knight Wolverine, Remington 700, Sauer SHR 970, Savage 110, Winchester 70. **$24.95 to $28.95.** From Millett Sights.

MMC			
AK[1]	No		39.95
FN FAL/LAR[2]	No		59.95

[1]Fits all AK derivative receivers; Weaver-style base; low-profile scope position. [2]Fits all FAL versions; Weaver-style base. From MMC.

RAM-LINE			
Mini-14 Mount	Yes	1"	24.97

No drilling or tapping. Uses std. dovetail rings. Has built-in shell deflector. Made of solid black polymer. From Ram-Line, Inc.

REDFIELD			
JR-SR (T)1. One/two-piece bases.	W only	3/4", 1", 26mm, 30mm	JR-15.99-46.99 SR-15.99-33.49
Ring (T)[2]	No	3/4" and 1"	27.95-29.95
Widefield See-Thru Mounts	No	1"	15.95
Ruger Rings[4]	No	1", med., high	30.49-36.49
Ruger 30mm[5]	No	1"	37.99-40.99
Midline Ext. Rings	No	1"	24.95

[1]Low, med. & high, split rings. Reversible extension front rings for 1". 2-piece bases for Sako. Colt Sauer bases **$39.95**. Med. Top Access JR rings nickel-plated, **$28.95**. SR two-piece nickel-plated **$22.95**. [2]Split rings for grooved 22s; 30mm, black matte **$42.95**. [3]Used with MP scopes for; S&W K, L or N frame, XP-100, T/C Contender, Ruger receivers. [4]For Ruger Model 77 rifles. Standard and high; medium only for M77/22. [5]For Model 77. Also in matte finish **$45.95**. [6]Aluminun 22 groove mount **$14.95**; base and medium rings **$18.95**. [7]Fits American or Weaver-style base. Non-Gunsmithing mount system. For many popular shotguns, rifles, handguns and blackpowder rifles. Uses existing screw holes.

S&K			
Insta-Mount (T) Bases and Rings[1]	W only	Uses S&K rings only	47.00-117.00
Conventional Rings and Bases[2]	W only	1" split rings	From 65.00
Sculptured Bases, Rings[2]	W only	1", 26mm, 30mm	From 65.00
Smooth Contoured Rings[3]	Yes	1", 26mm, 30mm	90.00-120.00

[1]1903, A3, M1 Carbine, Lee Enfield #1. Mk.III, #4, #5, M1917, M98 Mauser, AR-15, AR-180, M-14, M-1, Ger. K-43, Mini-14, M1-A, Krag, AKM, Win. 94, SKS Type 56, Daewoo, H&K. [2]Most popular rifles already drilled and tapped and Sako, Tikka dovetails. [3]No projections; weigh 1/2-oz. each; matte or gloss finish. Horizontally and vertically split rings, matte or high gloss.

SAKO			
QD Dovetail	W only	1"	70.00-155.00

Sako, or any rifle using Sako action, 3 heights available. Stoeger, importer.

SPRINGFIELD, INC.			
M1A Third Generation	No	1" or 30mm	123.00
M1A Standard	N0	1" or 30mm	77.00
M6 Scout Mount	No		29.00

Weaver-style bases. From Springfield, Inc.

TALBOT			
QD Bases	No		180.00-190.00
Rings	No	1", 30mm	50.00-70.00

Blue or stainless steel; standard or extended bases; rings in three heights. For most popular rifles. From Talbot QD Mounts.

TASCO			
World Class			
Aluminum Ringsets	Yes	1", 30mm	12.00-17.00
See-Thru	No	1"	19.00
Shotgun Bases	Yes		34.00

From Tasco.

ACCESSORIES

SCOPE RINGS & BASES

Maker, Model, Type	Adjust.	Scopes	Price
THOMPSON/CENTER			
Duo-Ring Mount[1]	No	1"	73.80
Weaver-Style Bases	No		13.00–42.50
Weaver-Style Rings[2]	No	1"	36.00
Weaver-Style See-Thru Rings[3]	No	1"	36.00

[1]Attaches directly to T/C Contender bbl., no drilling/tapping; also for T/C M/L rifles, needs base adapter; blue or stainless. [2]Medium and high; blue or silver finish. [3]For T.C FireHawk, ThunderHawk; blue; silver **$29.80**. From Thompson/Center.

Maker, Model, Type	Adjust.	Scopes	Price
UNERTL			
1/4 Click[1]	Yes	3/4", 1" target scopes	Per set 285.00

[1]Unertl target or varmint scopes. Posa or standard mounts, less bases. From Unertl.

Maker, Model, Type	Adjust.	Scopes	Price
WARNE			
Premier Series (all steel)			
T.P.A. (Permanently Attached)	No	1", 4 heights 30mm, 2 heights	87.75 98.55
Premier Series Rings fit Premier Series Bases			
Premier Series (all-steel Q.D. rings)			
Premier Series (all steel) Quick detachable lever	No	1", 4 heights 26mm, 2 heights 30mm, 3 heights	131.25 129.95 142.00
BRNO 19mm	No	1", 3 heights 30mm, 2 heights	125.00 136.70
BRNO 16mm		1", 2 heights	125.00
Ruger	No	1", 4 heights 30mm, 3 heights	125.00 136.70
Ruger M77	No	1", 3 heights 30mm, 2 heights	125.00 136.70
Sako Medium & Long Action	No	1", 4 heights 30mm, 3 heights	125.00 136.70
Sako Short Action	No	1", 3 heights	125.00
All-Steel One-Piece Base, ea.			38.50
All-Steel Two-Piece Base, ea.			14.00
Maxima Series (fits all Weaver-style bases)			
Permanently Attached1	No	1", 3 heights 30mm, 3 heights	25.50 36.00
Adjustable Double Lever2	No	1", 3 heights 30mm, 3 heights	72.60 80.75
Thumb Knob	No	1", 3 heights 30mm, 3 heights	59.95 68.25
Stainless-Steel Two-Piece Base, ea.			15.25

Vertically split rings with dovetail clamp, precise return to zero. Fit most popular rifles, handguns. Regular blue, matte blue, silver finish. 1All-Steel, non-Q.D. rings. 2All-steel, Q.D. rings. From Warne Mfg. Co.

Maker, Model, Type	Adjust.	Scopes	Price
WEAVER			
Detachable Mounts			
Top Mount	No	7/8", 1", 30mm, 33mm	24.95-38.95
Side Mount	No	1", 1" long	14.95-34.95
Tip-Off Rings	No	7/8", 1"	24.95-32.95
Pivot Mounts	No	1"	38.95
Complete Mount Systems			
Pistol	No	1"	75.00-105.00
Rifle	No	1"	32.95
SKS Mount System	No	1"	49.95
Pro-View (no base required)	No	1"	13.95-15.95
Converta-Mount, 12-ga. (Rem. 870, Moss. 500)	No	1", 30mm	74.95
See-Thru Mounts			
Detachable	No	1"	27.00-32.00
System (no base required)	No	1"	15.00-35.00
Tip-Off	No	1"	15.00

Nearly all modern rifles, pistols, and shotguns. Detachable rings in standard, See-Thru, and extension styles, in Low, Medium, High or X- High heights; gloss (blued), silver and matte finishes to match scopes. Extension rings are only available in 1" High style and See- Thru X-tensions only in gloss finish. Tip-Off rings only for 3/8" grooved receivers or 3/8"grooved adaptor bases; no base required. See-Thru & Pro-View mounts for most modern big bore rifles, some in silver. No Drill & Tap Pistol systems in gloss or silver for: Colt Python, Trooper, 357, Officer's Model; Ruger Single-Six, Security- Six (gloss finish only), Blackhawk, Super Blackhawk, Blackhawk SRM 357, Redhawk, Mini-14 Series (not Ranch), Ruger 22 Auto Pistols, Mark II; Smith & Wesson I- and current K-frames with adj. rear sights. Converta-Mount Systems in Standard and See-Under for: Mossberg 500 (12- and 20-ga.); Remington 870, 11-87 (12- and 20- ga. lightweight); Winchester 1200, 1300, 1400, 1500. Converta Brackets, Bases, Rings also avail. for Beretta A303 and A390; Browning A-5, BPS Pump; Ithaca 37, 87. From Weaver.

Maker, Model, Type	Adjust.	Scopes	Price
WEIGAND			
Browning Buck Mark[1]	No		29.95
Integra Mounts[2]	No		39.95-69.00
S&W Revolver[3]	No		29.95
Ruger 10/22[4]	No		14.95-39.95
Ruger Revolver[5]	No		29.95
Taurus Revolver[4]	No		29.95-65.00
Lightweight Rings	No	1", 30mm	29.95-39.95
1911			
SM36	No	Weaver rail	99.95
APCMNT[7]	No		69.95

[1]No gunsmithing. [2]S&W K, L, N frames; Taurus vent rib models; Colt Anaconda/ Python; Ruger Redhawk; Ruger 10/22. [3]K, L, N frames. [4]Three models. [5]Redhawk, Blackhawk, GP-100. [6]3rd Gen.; drill and tap; without slots **$59.95**. [7]For Aimpoint Comp. Red Dot scope, silver only. From Weigand Combat Handguns, Inc.

Maker, Model, Type	Adjust.	Scopes	Price
WIDEVIEW			
Premium 94 Angle Eject and side mount	No	1"	18.70
Premium See-Thru	No	1"	18.70
22 Premium See-Thru	No	3/4", 1"	13.60
Universal Ring Angle Cut	No	1"	18.70
Universal Ring Straight Cut	No	1"	18.70
Solid Mounts			
Lo Ring Solid[1]	No	1"	13.60
Hi Ring Solid[1]	No	1"	13.60
SR Rings		1", 30mm	13.60
22 Grooved Receiver	No	1"	13.60
Blackpowder Mounts[2]	No	1"	18.70-37.40
High, extra-high ring mounts with base	No	up to 60mm	18.70
Desert Eagle Pistol Mount	No	1", 30mm	34.95-44.95

[1]For Weaver-type base. Models for many popular rifles. Low ring, high ring and grooved receiver types. [2]No drilling, tapping, for T/C Renegade, Hawken, CVA, Knight Traditions guns. From Wideview Scope Mount Corp.

Maker, Model, Type	Adjust.	Scopes	Price
WILLIAMS			
Side Mount with HCO Rings[1]	No	1", split or extension rings	74.35
Side Mount, Offset Rings[2]	No	Same	61.45
Sight-Thru Mounts[3]	No	1", 7/8" sleeves	19.50
Streamline Mounts	No	1" (bases form rings)	26.50

[1]Most rifles, Br. S.M.L.E. (round rec.) **$14.41** extra. [2]Most rifles including Win. 94 Big Bore. [3]Many modern rifles, including CVA Apollo, others with 1" octagon barrels.

Maker, Model, Type	Adjust.	Scopes	Price
YORK			
M-1 Garand	Yes	1"	39.95

Centers scope over the action. No drilling, tapping or gunsmithing. Uses standard dovetail rings. From York M-1 Conversions.

NOTES

(S)Side Mount; (T)Top Mount; 22mm=.866"; 25.4mm=1.024"; 26.5mm=1.045"; 30mm−1.81".

ACCESSORIES

Sporting Leaf and Open Sights

AUTOMATIC DRILLING REAR SIGHT Most German and Austrian drillings have this kind of rear sight. When rifle barrel is selected, the rear sight automatically comes to the upright position. Base length 2.165", width .472", folding leaf height .315". From New England Custom Gun Service.
Price:.......... **$48.50**

CLASSIC MARBLE/WILLIAMS STYLE FULLY ADJUSTABLE REAR SPORTING SIGHTS Screw-on attachment. Dovetailed graduated windage and elevation adjustment. Elevation and windage lock with set screws. Available in steel or lightweight alloy construction. From Sarco, Inc.
Price:.......... **$13.50**

ERA MASTERPIECE ADJUSTABLE REAR SIGHTS Precision-machined, all-steel, polished and blued. Attaches with 8-36 socket head screw. Use small screwdriver to adjust windage and elevation. Available for various barrel widths. From New England Custom Gun Service.
Price:.......... **$82.00**

ERA CLASSIC ADJUSTABLE REAR SIGHT Similar to the Masterpiece unit except windage is adjusted by pushing sight sideways, then locking it with a reliable clamp. Precision machined all steel construction, polished, with 6-48 fastening screw and Allen wrench. Shallow "V" and "U" notch. Length 2.170", width .550". From New England Custom Gun Service.
Price: **$55.00**

ERA EXPRESS SIGHTS A wide variety of open sights and bases for custom installation. Partial listing shown. From New England Custom Gun Service.
Price: One-leaf express.......... **$66.00**
Price: Two-leaf express.......... **$71.50**
Price: Three-leaf express.......... **$77.00**
Price: Bases for above **$27.50**
Price: Standing rear sight, straight.......... **$13.25**
Price: Base for above.......... **$16.50**

ERA CLASSIC EXPRESS SIGHTS Standing or folding leaf sights are securely locked to the base with the ERA Magnum Clamp, but can be loosened for sighting in. Base can be attached with two socket-head cap screws or soldered. Finished and blued. Barrel diameters from .600" to .930". From New England Custom Gun Service.
Price: Standing leaf.......... **$54.00**
Price: One-leaf express.......... **$96.00**
Price: Two-leaf express.......... **$101.00**
Price: Three-leaf express.......... **$120.00**

ERA MASTERPIECE REAR SIGHT Adjustable for windage and elevation, and adjusted and locked with a small screwdriver. Comes with 8-36 socket-head cap screw and wrench. Barrel diameters from .600" to .930".
Price:.......... **$75.00**

G.G. & G. SAME PLANE APERTURE M-16/AR-15 A2-style dual aperture rear sight with both large and small apertures centered on the same plane.
Price:.......... **$45.00**

LYMAN No.16 Middle sight for barrel dovetail slot mounting. Folds flat when scope or peep sight is used. Sight notch plate adjustable for elevation. White triangle for quick aiming. Designed to fit 3/8" dovetail slots. Three heights: A-.400" to.500", B-.345" to .445", C-.500" to .600". A slot blank designed to fill dovetail notch when sight is removed is available
Price: **$5.00**
Price:.......... **$13.25**

MARBLE FALSE BASE #76, #77, #78 New screw-on base for most rifles replaces factory base. 3/8" dovetail slot permits installation of any folding rear sight. Can be had in sweat-on models also.
Price:.......... **$8.00**

MARBLE FOLDING LEAF Flattop or semi-buckhorn style. Folds down when scope or peep sights are used. Reversible plate gives choice of "U" or "V" notch. Adjustable for elevation.
Price:.......... **$16.00**
Price: Also available with both windage and elevation adjustment.......... **$18.00**

MARBLE SPORTING REAR With white enamel diamond, gives choice of two "U" and two "V" notches or different sizes. Adjustment in height by means of double step elevator and sliding notch piece. For all rifles; screw or dovetail installation.
Price:.......... **$16.00 to $17.00**

MARBLE #20 UNIVERSAL New screw or sweat-on base. Both have .100" elevation adjustment. In five base sizes. Three styles of U-notch, square notch, peep. Adjustable for windage and elevation.
Price: Screw-on.......... **$23.00**
Price: Sweat-on.......... **$21.00**

MILLETT SPORTING & BLACKPOWDER RIFLE Open click adjustable rear fits 3/8" dovetail cut in barrel. Choice of white outline, target black or open express V rear blades. Also available is a replacement screw-on sight with express V, .562" hole centers. Dovetail fronts in white or blaze orange in seven heights (.157"-.540").
Price: Dovetail or screw-on rear.......... **$58.38**
Price: Front sight.......... **$12.96**

MILLETT SCOPE-SITE Open, adjustable or fixed rear sights dovetail into a base integral with the top scope-mounting ring. Blaze orange front ramp sight is integral with the front ring half. Rear sights have white outline aperture. Provides fast, short-radius, Patridge-type open sights on the top of the scope. Can be used with all Millett rings, Weaver-style bases, Ruger 77 (also fits Redhawk), Ruger Ranch Rifle, No. 1, No. 3, Rem. 870, 1100; Burris, Leupold and Redfield bases.
Price: Scope-Site top only, windage only.......... **$31.15**
Price: As above, fully adjustable.......... **$66.10**
Price: Scope-Site Hi-Turret, fully adjustable, low, medium, high.......... **$66.10**

RUGER WINDAGE ADJUSTABLE FOLDING REAR SIGHT Fits all Ruger rifles produced with standard folding rear sights. Available in low (.480"), medium (.503") and high (.638") heights. From Sturm, Ruger & Co., Inc.
Price:.......... **$19.80**

TRIJICON 3-DOT NIGHT SIGHTS Self-luminous and machined from steel. Available for the M16/AR-15, H&K rifles. Front and rear sets and front only.
Price:.......... **$52.00-$84.00**

WHITWORTH STYLE ENGLISH 3 LEAF EXPRESS SIGHTS Folding leafs marked in 100, 200 and 300 yard increments. Slide assembly is dovetailed in base. Available in four different styles: 3 folding leaves, flat bottom; 1 fixed, 2 folding leaves, flat bottom; 3 folding leaves, round bottom; 1 fixed, 2 folding leaves, round bottom. Available from Sarco, Inc.
Price: **$49.95**

WICHITA MULTI RANGE SIGHT SYSTEM Designed for silhouette shooting. System allows you to adjust the rear sight to four repeatable range settings, once it is pre-set. Sight clicks to any of the settings by turning a serrated wheel. Front sight is adjustable for weather and light conditions with one adjustment. Specify gun when ordering.
Price: Rear sight.......... **$125.00**
Price: Front sight.......... **$95.00**

WILLIAMS DOVETAIL OPEN SIGHT (WDOS) Open rear sight with windage and elevation adjustment. Furnished "U" notch or choice of blades. Slips into dovetail and locks with gib lock. Heights from .281" to .531".
Price:With blade.......... **$17.95**
Price:Less blade.......... **$11.05**
Price:Rear sight blades, each.......... **$6.29**

WILLIAMS GUIDE OPEN SIGHT (WGOS) Open rear sight with windage and elevation adjustment. Bases to fit most military and commercial barrels. Choice of square "U" or "V" notch blade, 3/16", 1/4", 5/16", or 3/8" high.
Price: Less blade.......... **$17.95 to $19.50**
Price: Extra blades, each.......... **$6.90**

WILLIAMS WGOS OCTAGON Open rear sight for 1" octagonal barrels. Installs with two 6-48 screws and uses same hole spacing as most T/C muzzleloading rifles. Four heights, choice of square, U, V, or B blade.
Price:.......... **$21.99**

WILLIAMS WSKS,WAK47 Replaces original military-type rear sight. Adjustable for windage and elevation. No drilling or tapping. Peep aperture or open. For SKS carbines, AK-47-style rifles.
Price: Aperture.......... **$25.95**
Price: Open.......... **$24.00**

WILLIAMS WM–96 Fits Mauser 96-type military rifles. Replaces original rear sight with open blade or aperture. Fully adjustable for windage and elevation. No drilling or tapping.
Price: Aperture.......... **$25.95**
Price: Open.......... **$24.00**

WILLIAMS FIRE RIFLE SETS Replacement front and rear fiber optic sights. Red bead front, two green elements in the fully-adjustable rear. Made of CNC-machined metal.
Price: For Ruger 10/22.......... **$35.95**
Price: For most Marlin and Win. (3/8" dovetail).......... **$29.95**
Price: For Remington (newer style sight base).......... **$24.95**

Aperture and Micrometer Receiver Sights

A2 REAR SIGHT KIT Featuring an exclusive numbered windage knob. For .223 AR-style rifles. From ArmaLite, Inc.
Price: **$55.00**

AO GHOST RING HUNTING SIGHT Fully adjustable for windage and elevation. Available for most rifles, including blackpowder guns. Minimum gunsmithing required for most installations; matches most mounting holes. From AO Sight Systems, Inc.
Price:.......... **$90.00**

AO AR-15/M-16 APERTURE Drop-in replacement of factory sights. Both apertures are on the same plane. Large ghost ring has .230" inside diameter; small ghost ring has .100" inside diameter. From AO Sight Systems, Inc.
Price:.......... **$30.00**

AO Ghost Ring

AO BACKUP GHOST RING SIGHTS Mounts to scope base and retains zero when reinstalled in the field. Affords same elevation/windage adjustability as AO Hunting Ghost Rings. Included are both .191" and .230" apertures and test posts. Available for Ruger, Sako, Remington 700 and other rifles. From AO Sight Systems, Inc.
Price:.......... **$65.00**

AO TACTICAL SIGHTS For HK UMP/USC/G36/SL8/MP5. The Big Dot Tritium or standard dot tritium is mated with a large .300" diameter rear ghost ring. The "same plane" rear aperture flips from the .300" to a .230" diameter ghost ring. From AO Sight Systems, Inc.
Price: .... **$90 to $120.00**

BEEMAN/FEINWERKBAU 5454 MATCH APERTURE SIGHT Small size, new-design sight uses constant-pressure flat springs to eliminate point of impact shifts.
Price: **$350.00**

BEEMAN SPORT APERTURE SIGHT Positive click micrometer adjustments. Standard units with flush surface screwdriver adjustments. Deluxe version has target knobs. For air rifles with grooved receivers.
Price: Standard.......... **$40.00**
Price: Deluxe.......... **$50.00**

ACCESSORIES

METALLIC SIGHTS

BUSHMASTER COMPETITION A2 REAR SIGHT ASSEMBLY Elevation and windage mechanism feature either 1/2 or 1/4 minute of adjustment. Long distance aperture allows screw-in installation of any of four interchangeable micro-apertures.
Price: 1/2 M.O.A. **$109.95**
Price: 1/4 M.O.A. **$114.95**

DPMS NATIONAL MATCH Replaces the standard A2 rear sight on M16/AR-15 rifles. Has 1/4-minute windage and 1/2-minute elevation adjustments. Includes both a .052" and .200" diameter aperture.
Price: **$92.99**

ENFIELD No. 4 TARGET/MATCH SIGHT Originally manufactured by Parker-Hale, has adjustments up to 1,300 meters. Micrometer click adjustments for windage. Adjustable aperture disc has six different openings from .030" to .053". From Sarco, Inc.
Price: **$49.95**

EAW RECEIVER SIGHT A fully adjustable aperture sight that locks securely into the EAW quick-detachable scope mount rear base. Made by New England Custom Gun Service.
Price:. **$80.00**

ERA SEE-THRU Contains fiber optic center dot. Fits standard 3/8" American dovetails. Locks in place with set screw. Ideal for use on moving targets. Width 19.5mm. Available in low (.346", medium .425" and high .504" models. From New England Custom Gun Service.
Price:. **$27.50**

G. G.& G. MAD IRIS Multiple Aperture Device is a four sight, rotating aperture disk with small and large apertures on the same plane. Mounts on M-16/AR-15 flattop receiver. Fully adjustable.
Price:. **$141.95**
Price: A2 IRIS, two apertures, full windage adjustments. **$124.95**

KNIGHT'S ARMAMENT 600 METER FOLDING REAR SIGHT Click adjustable from 200 to 600 meters with clearly visible range markings. Intermediate clicks allows for precise zero at known ranges. Allows use of optical scopes by folding don. Mounts on rear of upper receiver rail on SR-25 and similar rifles. From Knight's Armament Co.
Price:. **$181.00**

KNIGHT'S ARMAMENT FOLDING 300M SIGHT Mounts on flat-top upper receivers on SR-25 and similar rifles. May be used as a back-up iron sight for a scoped rifle/carbine or a primary sight. Peep insert may be removed to expose the 5mm diameter ghost ring aperture. From Knight's Armament Co.
Price:. **$144.00**

LYMAN NO. 2 TANG SIGHT Designed for the Winchester Model 94. Has high index marks on aperture post; comes with both .093" quick sighting aperture, .040" large disk aperture, and replacement mounting screws.
Price:. **$76.00**
Price: For Marlin lever actions. **$76.00**

LYMAN No. 57 1/4-minute clicks. Stayset knobs. Quick-release slide, adjustable zero scales. Made for almost all modern rifles.
Price:. **$67.50**
Price: No. 57SME, 57SMET (for White Systems Model 91 and Whitetail rifles). **$62.50**

LYMAN 57GPR Designed especially for the Lyman Great Plains Rifle. Mounts directly onto the tang of the rifle and has 1/4-minute micrometer click adjustments.
Price:. **$62.50**

LYMAN No. 66 Fits close to the rear of flat-sided receivers, furnished with Stayset knobs. Quick-release slide, 1/4-min. adjustments. For most lever or slide action or flat-sided automatic rifles.
Price:. **$67.50**
Price: No. 66MK (for all current versions of the Knight MK-85 in-line rifle with flat-sided receiver). **$67.50**
Price: No. 66 SKS fits Russian and Chinese SKS rifles; large and small apertures. **$67.50**
Price: No. 66 WB for Model 1886 Winchester lever actions. **$67.50**

Lyman No. 57

LYMAN No. 66U Light weight, designed for most modern shotguns with a flat-sided, round-top receiver. 1/4-minute clicks. Requires drilling, tapping. Not for Browning A-5, Rem. M11.
Price: **$71.50**

LYMAN 90MJT RECEIVER SIGHT Mounts on standard Lyman and Williams FP bases. Has 1/4-minute audible micrometer click adjustments, target knobs with direction indicators. Adjustable zero scales, quick-release slide. Large 7/8" diameter aperture disk.
Price: Right- or left-hand. **$74.95**

LYMAN RECEIVER SIGHT Audible-click adjustments for windage and elevation, coin-slotted "stayset" knobs and two interchangeable apertures. For Mauser, Springfield, Sako, T/C Hawken, Rem. 700, Win. 70, Savage 110, SKS, Win. 94, Marlin 336 and 1894.
Price:. **$53.99**

LYMAN 1886 #2 TANG SIGHT Fits the Winchester 1886 lever action rifle and replicas thereof not containing a tang safety. Has height index marks on the aperture post and an .800" maximum elevation adjustment. Included is a .093" x 1/2" quick-sighting aperture and .040 x 5/8" target disk.
Price:. **$76.00**

MARBLE PEEP TANG SIGHT All-steel construction. Micrometer-like click adjustments for windage and elevation. For most popular old and new lever-action rifles.
Price:. **$125.00**

MILLETT PEEP RIFLE SIGHTS Fully adjustable, heat-treated nickel steel peep aperture receiver sight for the Mini-14. Has fine windage and elevation adjustments; replaces original.
Price: Rear sight, Mini-14. . . . . **$51.45**
Price: Front sight, Mini-14. . . . . **$19.69**
Price: Front and rear combo with hood. **$67.20**

NATIONAL MATCH REAR SIGHT KIT For AR-15 style rifles. From Armalite, Inc.
Price: 1/2 W, 1/2E. **$80.00**
Price: 1/4 W, 1/2 E **$80.00**

NECG PEEP SIGHT FOR WEAVER SCOPE MOUNT BASES Attaches to Weaver scope mount base. Windage adjusts with included Allen wrenches, elevation with a small screwdriver. Furnished with two apertures (.093" and .125" diameter hole) and two interchangeable elevation slides for high or low sight line. From New England Custom Gun Service.
Price:. **$80.00**

NECG RUGER PEEP SIGHT Made for Ruger M-77 and No. 1 rifles, it is furnished with .093" and .125" opening apertures. Can be installed on a standard Ruger rear mount base or quarter rib. Tightening the aperture disk will lock the elevation setting in place. From New England Custom Gun Service.
Price:. **$80.00**

T/C HUNTING STYLE TANG PEEP SIGHT Compact, all steel construction, with locking windage and elevation adjustments. For use with "bead style" and fiber optic front sights. Models available to fit all traditional T/C muzzleloading rifles. From Thompson/Center Arms.
Price:. **$58.00**

T/C CONTENDER CARBINE PEEP SIGHT All-steel, low profile, click-adjustable unit mounting on the pre-drilled tapped scope mount holes on the T/C Contender Carbine. From Thompson/Center Arms.
Price:. **$56.00**

WILLIAMS APERTURE SIGHT Made to fit SKS rifles.
Price:. **$23.49**

WILLIAMS FIRE SIGHT PEEP SETS Combines the Fire Sight front bead with Williams fully adjustable metallic peep rear.
Price: For SKS. **$39.95**
Price: For Ruger 10/22. . . . . **$39.95**
Price: For Marlin or Winchester lever actions. **$73.95**

WILLIAMS FP Internal click adjustments. Positive locks. For virtually all rifles, T/C Contender, Heckler & Koch HK-91, Ruger Mini-14, plus Win., Rem., and Ithaca shotguns.
Price: From. **$57.99**
Price: With Target Knobs. **$71.20**
Price: With Square Notched Blade. **$63.03**
Price: With Target Knobs & Square Notched Blade. **$74.45**
Price: FP-GR (for dovetail-grooved receivers, .22s and air guns). **$59.95**
Price: FP-94BBSE (for Win. 94 Big Bore A.E.; uses top rear scope mount holes). **$59.95**

WILLIAMS TARGET FP Similar to the FP series but developed for most bolt-action rimfire rifles. Target FP High adjustable from 1.250" to 1.750" above centerline of bore; Target FP Low adjustable from .750" to 1.250". Attaching bases for Rem. 540X, 541-S, 580, 581, 582 (#540); Rem. 510, 511, 512, 513-T, 521-T (#510); Win. 75 (#75); Savage/ Anschutz 64 and Mark 12 (#64). Some rifles require drilling, tapping.
Price: High or Low. . . . . **$73.90 to $77.15**
Price: Base only. **$13.30**
Price: FP-T/C Scout rifle, from. **$59.95**
Price: FP-94BBSE (for Win. 94 Big Bore A.E.; uses top rear scope mount holes). **$59.95**

WILLIAMS 5-D SIGHT Low cost sight for shotguns, 22s and the more popular big game rifles. Adjustment for windage and elevation. Fits most guns without drilling and tapping. Also for British SMLE, Winchester M94 Side Eject.
Price: From. **$34.50**
Price: With Shotgun Aperture **$34.50**

WILLIAMS 5D RECEIVER SIGHT Alloy construction and similar design to the FP model except designed to fit Win. 94, Marlin 336, Marlin 1895, Mauser 98.
Price: **$34.50**

WILLIAMS GUIDE (WGRS) Receiver sight for 30 M1 Carbine, M1903A3 Springfield, Savage 24s, Savage-Anschutz and Weatherby XXII. Utilizes military dovetail; no drilling. Double-dovetail windage adjustment, sliding dovetail adjustment for elevation.
Price:. . . . . **$32.80 to $45.95**

Vernier Tang Sights

BALLARD TANG SIGHTS Available in variety of models including short & long staff hunter, Pacific & Montana, custom units allowing windage & elevation adjustments. Uses 8x40 base screws with screw spacing of 1.120". From Axtell Rifle Co.
Price: . . . . **$175.00 to $325.00**

LYMAN TANG SIGHT Made for Win. 94, 1886, Marlin 30, 336 and 1895.
Price:. . . . . **$59.99-$64.99**

MARLIN TANG SIGHTS Available in short and long staff hunter models using 8x40 base screws and screw spacing of 1.120". From Axtell Rifle Co.
Price:. . . . . **$170.00 to $180.00**

METALLIC SIGHTS

PEDERSOLI CREEDMORE Adjustable for windage and elevation, fits Traditions by Pedersoli rifles and other brands. From Dixie Gun Works.
Price:.. **$110.00**
REMINGTON TANG SIGHTS Available in short-range hunter and vernier, mid- and long-range vernier and custom models with windage and elevation adjustments. Uses 10x28 base screws, with screw spacing of 1.940". Eye disk has .052" hole with 10x40 thread. From Axtell Rifle Co.
Price:.. **$175.00 to $325.00**
SHARPS TANG SIGHTS Reproduction tang sights as manufactured for various Sharps rifles through the years 1859 –1878. Wide variety of models available including Standard Issue Sporting Peep, Hartford Transition Mid and Long Range, and Custom Express Sights. From Axtell Rifle Co.
Price:.. **$150.00 to $340.00**
STEVENS CUSTOM Available in thin base short and long staff hunter, mid and long range sporting vernier, custom mid and long range (custom models allow windage and elevation adjustments) models. Uses 5x40 base screws with screw spacing of 1.485". From Axtell Rifle Co.
Price:.. **$170.00 to $325.00**
TAURUS TANG SIGHT Made of blue steel, available for Taurus Models 62, 72, 172, 63, 73 and 173. Folds down, aperture disk sight, height index marks on aperture post.
Price:... **$77.00**
WINCHESTER & BROWNING TANG SIGHTS Available in variety of models, including thin & thick base short & long staff hunter, mid & long range sporting vernier and custom units. Screw spacing of 2.180" on all models. From Axtell Rifle Co.
Price:.. **$170.00 to $325.00**

Globe Target Front Sights

AXTELL CUSTOM GLOBE Designed similar to the original Winchester #35 sight, it contains five inserts. Also available with spirit level. From Axtell Rifle Co.
Price:.. **$125.00 to $175.00**
BALLARD FRONT SIGHTS Available in windgauge with spirit level, globe with clip, and globe with spirit level (all with five inserts) and beach combination with gold plated rocker models. Dovetail of .375" for all. From Axtell Rifle Co.
Price:.. **$125.00 to $240.00**
LYMAN 20 MJT TARGET FRONT Has 7/8" diameter, one-piece steel globe with 3/8" dovetail base. Height is .700" from bottom of dovetail to center of aperture; height on 20 LJT is .750". Comes with seven Anschutz-size steel inserts—two posts and five apertures .126" through .177".
Price: 20 MJT or 20 LJT..................................... **$33.75**

Lyman No. 17A Target

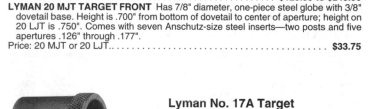

LYMAN No. 17A TARGET Includes seven interchangeable inserts: four apertures, one transparent amber and two posts .50" and .100" in width.
Price:... **$28.25**
Price: Insert set... **$13.25**
LYMAN 17AEU Similar to the Lyman 17A except has a special dovetail design to mount easily onto European muzzleloaders such as CVA, Traditions and Investarm. All steel, comes with eight inserts.
Price:... **$26.00**
LYMAN No. 93 MATCH Has 7/8" diameter, fits any rifle with a standard dovetail mounting block. Comes with seven target inserts and accepts most Anschutz accessories. Hooked locking bolt and nut allows quick removal, installation. Base available in .860" (European) and .562" (American) hole spacing.
Price:... **$45.00**
MAYNARD FRONT SIGHTS Custom globe with five inserts and clip. Also available with spirit level bracket and windgauge styles. From Axtell Rifle Co.
Price:.. **$125.00 to $240.00**
PEDERSOLI GLOBE A tunnel front sight with 12 interchangeable inserts for high precision target shooting. Fits Traditions by Pedersoli and other rifles.
Price:... **$69.95**
REMINGTON FRONT SIGHTS Available in windgauge with spirit level, custom globe with clip and custom globe with spirit level (all with five inserts) and beach combination with gold plated rocker models. Dovetail .460". From Axtell Rifle Co.
Price:.. **$125.00 to $250.00**
SHARPS FRONT SIGHTS Original-style globe with non-moveable post and pinhead. Also available with windgauge and spirit level. From Axtell Rifle Co.
Price:.. **$100.00 to $265.00**
WILLIAMS TARGET GLOBE FRONT Adapts to many rifles. Mounts to the base with a knurled locking screw. Height is .545" from center, not including base. Comes with inserts.
Price:... **$42.00**
Price: Dovetail base (low) .220".............................. **$17.50**
Price: Dovetail base (high) .465"............................. **$17.50**
Price: Screw-on base, .300" height, .300" radius.............. **$15.90**
Price: Screw-on base, .450" height, .350" radius.............. **$15.90**
Price: Screw-on base, .215" height, .400" radius.............. **$15.90**

WINCHESTER & BROWNING FRONT SIGHTS Available in windgauge with spirit level, globe with clip, globe with spirit level (all with five inserts) and beach combination with gold plated rocker models. From Axtell Rifle Co.
Price:.. **$125.00 to $240.00**

Front Sights

AO TACTICAL SIGHTS Three types of drop-in replacement front posts – round top or square top night sight posts in standard and Big Dot sizes, or white stripe posts in .080 and .100 widths. For AR15 and M16 rifles. From AO Sight Systems, Inc.
Price:... **$30.00 to $90.00**
AO RIFLE TEST POSTS Allows easy establishment of correct front post height. Provides dovetail post with .050" segments to allow shooter to "shoot-n-snip", watching point- of-impact walk into point of aim. Available for 3/8" standard dovetail, Ruger-style or Mauser. From AO Sight Systems, Inc.
Price:.. **$5.00**
AR-10 DETACHABLE FRONT SIGHT Allows use of the iron rear sight, but are removable for use of telescopic sights with no obstruction to the sight line, For AR-style rifles. From ArmaLite, Inc.
Price:... **$50.00 to $70.00**
ASHLEY AR-15/M-16 FRONT SIGHTS Drop-in replacement sight post. Double faced so it can be rotated 180 degrees for 2.5 MOA elevation adjustment. Available in .080" width with .030" white stripe, or .100" with .040" stripe. From Ashley Outdoors, Inc.
Price:... **$30.00**
Price: Tritium Dot Express.................................... **$60.00**
BUSHMASTER FLIP-UP FRONT SIGHT Made for V Match AR-style rifles. This sight unit slips over milled front sight bases and clamps around barrel. Locks with the push of a button. For use with flip-up style rear sights or the A3 removable carry handle. From Bushmaster Firearms.
Price:... **$99.95**
BUSHMASTER A2 COMPETITION FRONT SIGHT POST Surface ground on three sides for optimum visual clarity. Available in two widths: .052"; and .062". From Bushmaster Firearms.
Price:... **$12.95**
CLASSIC STREAMLINED FRONT SPORTER RAMP SIGHT Comes with blade and sight cover. Serrated and contoured ramp. Screw-on attachment. Slide-on sight cover is easily detachable. Gold bead. From Sarco, inc.
Price:... **$13.50**
ERA BEADS FOR RUGER RIFLES White bead and fiber optic front sights that replace the standard sights on M-77 and No. 1 Ruger rifles. Using 3/32" beads, they are available in heights of .330", .350", .375", .415" and .435". From New England Custom Gun Service.
Price:... **$16.00 to $24.00**
ERA FRONT SIGHTS European-type front sights inserted from the front. Various heights available. From New England Custom Gun Service.
Price: 1/16" silver bead...................................... **$11.50**
Price: 3/32" silver bead...................................... **$16.00**
Price: Sourdough bead.. **$14.50**
Price: Fiber optic... **$24.00**
Price: Folding night sight with ivory bead..................... **$39.50**

Knight's Armament

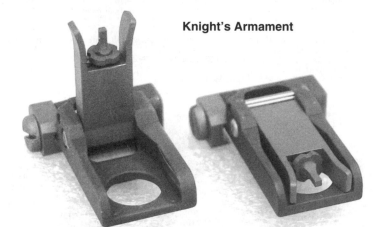

KNIGHT'S ARMAMENT FRONT STANDING/FOLDING SIGHT Mounts to the SR-25 rifle barrel gas block's MilStd top rail. Available in folding sight model. From Knight's Armament Co.
Price:.. **$145.00 to $175.00**
KNIGHT'S ARMAMENT CARRYING HANDLE SIGHT Rear sight and carry handle for the SR-25 rifle. Has fixed range and adjustable windage. From Knight's Armament Co.
Price:.. **$181.15**
KNIGHT'S ARMAMENT Mk II FOLDING FRONT SIGHT For the SR-25 rifle. Requires modified handguard. From Knight's Armament Co.
Price:.. **$175.00**

METALLIC SIGHTS

KNIGHT'S ARMAMENT FOR FREE-FLOATING RAS Mounts to free-floating SR-25 and SR-15 RAS (rail adapter system) rifle forends. Adjustable for elevation. Made of aluminum. From Knight's Armament Co.
Price: **$155.25**

KNS PRECISION SYSTEMS SIGHT Screws into front base. Hooded for light consistency; precision machined with fine wire crosshairs measuring .010-inches thick. Aperture measures .240-inches diameter. Standard and duplex reticles. Available for AK-47, MAK-90, AR-15, M16, FN-FAL, H&K 91, 93, 94, MP5, SP89, L1A1, M1 Garand.
Price: **$25.99**

LYMAN HUNTING SIGHTS Made with gold or white beads 1/16" to 3/32" wide and in varying heights for most military and commercial rifles. Dovetail bases.
Price: **$8.95**

MARBLE STANDARD Ivory, red, or gold bead. For all American-made rifles, 1/16" wide bead with semi-flat face that does not reflect light. Specify type of rifle when ordering.
Price: **$10.00**

MARBLE CONTOURED Has 3/8" dovetail base, .090" deep, is 5/8" long. Uses standard 1/16" or 3/32" bead, ivory, red, or gold. Specify rifle type.
Price: **$11.50**

NATIONAL MATCH FRONT SIGHT POST Has .050" blade. For AR-style rifle. From ArmaLite, Inc.
Price: **$12.00**

T/C FIBER OPTIC FRONT MUZZLELOADER SIGHT Ramp-style steel with fiber optic bead for all tradition cap locks, both octagonal and round barrels with dovetail, and most T/C rifles. From Thompson/Center Arms.
Price: . . . . **$16.95 to $36.00**

TRIJICON NIGHT SIGHT Self-luminous tritium gas-filled front sight for the M16/AR-15 series.
Price: **$52.00**

WILLIAMS STREAMLINED HOODLESS RAMP Available in 3/16", 5/16", 3/8", and 7/16" models.
Price: Less blade. **$15.49**

WILLIAMS SHORTY RAMPS Available in 1/8", 3/16", 9/32" and 3/8" models.
Price: Less blade. **$15.49**

WILLIAMS GOLD BEAD Available in .312", .343", and .406" high models all with 3/32" bead.
Price: **$8.49**

WILLIAMS RISER BLOCKS For adding .250" height to front sights when using a receiver sight. Two widths available: .250" for Williams Streamlined Ramp or .340" on all standard ramps having this base width. Uses standard 3/8" dovetail.
Price: **$5.46**

WILLIAMS AR-15 FIRESIGHT Fiber optic unit attaches to any standard AR-15-style front sight assembly. Machined from aircraft-strength aluminum. Adjustable for elevation. Green-colored light-gathering fiber optics. From Williams Gun Sight Co.
Price: . . . . **NA**

Ramp Sights

ERA MASTERPIECE Banded ramps; 21 sizes; hand-detachable beads and hood; beads inserted from the front. Various heights available. From New England Custom Gun Service.
Price: Banded ramp. **$54.00**
Price: Hood. **$10.50**
Price: 1/16" silver bead. **$11.50**
Price: 3/32" silver bead. **$16.00**
Price: Sourdough bead. **$14.50**
Price: Fiber optic. **$22.00**
Price: Folding night sight with ivory bead. **$39.50**

HOLLAND & HOLLAND STYLE FRONT SIGHT RAMPS Banded and screw-on models in the Holland & Holland-style night sight. Flips forward to expose a .0781" silver bead. Flip back for use of the .150" diameter ivory bead for poor light or close-up hunting. Band thickness .040", overall length 3.350", band length 1.180". From New England Custom Gun Service.
Price: . . . . **$90.00 to $115.00**

LYMAN NO. 18 SCREW-ON RAMP Used with 8-40 screws but may also be brazed on. Heights from .10" to .350". Ramp without sight.
Price: **$13.75**

MARBLE FRONT RAMPS Available in polished or dull matte finish or serrated style. Standard 3/8x.090" dovetail slot. Made for MR-width (.340") front sights. Can be used as screw-on or sweat-on. Heights: .100", .150", .300".
Price: Polished or matte. **$14.00**
Price: Serrated **$10.00**

NECG UNIVERSAL FRONT SIGHTS Available in five ramp heights and three front sight heights. Sights can be adjusted up or down .030" with an Allen wrench. Slips into place and then locks into position with a set screw. Six different front sight shapes are offered, including extra large and fiber optic. All hoods except the extra low ramp slide on from the rear and click in place. Extra low ramp has spring-loaded balls to lock hood. Choose from three hood sizes. From New England Custom Gun Service.
Price: **$25.50**

T/C TARGET SIGHT FOR OCTAGON BARREL MUZZLELOADERS A precision rear sight with click adjustments (via knurled knobs) for windage and elevation. Available for 15/16-inch and 1-inch octagon barrels with a screw hole spacing of .836-inch between centers. From Thompson/Center Arms.
Price: **$56.00**

T/C FIBER OPTIC MUZZLELOADER SIGHT Click adjustable for windage and elevation. Steel construction fitted with Tru-Glo™ fiber optics. Models available for most T/C muzzleloading rifles. Fits others with 1-inch and 15/16-inch octagon barrels with a hole spacing of .836-inch between screws. From Thompson/Center Arms.
Price: **$36.00**

WILLIAMS SHORTY RAMP Companion to "Streamlined" ramp, about 1/2" shorter. Screw-on or sweat-on. It is furnished in 1/8", 3/16", 9/32", and 3/8" heights without hood only. Also for shotguns.
Price: **$15.90**
Price: With dovetail lock. **$18.55**

WILLIAMS STREAMLINED RAMP Available in screw-on or sweat-on models. Furnished in 9/16", 7/16", 3/8", 5/16", 3/16" heights.
Price: **$17.35**
Price: Sight hood. **$3.95**

WILLIAMS STREAMLINED FRONT SIGHTS Narrow (.250" width) for Williams Streamlined ramps and others with 1/4" top width; medium (.340" width) for all standard factory ramps. Available with white, gold or fluorescent beads, 1/16" or 3/32".
Price: . . . . **$8.93 to $9.25**

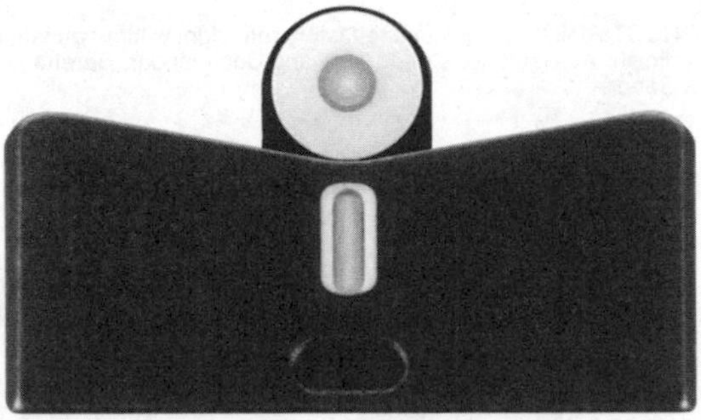

AO Express

Handgun Sights

AO EXPRESS SIGHTS Low-profile, snag-free express-type sights. Shallow V rear with white vertical line, white dot front. All-steel, matte black finish. Rear is available in different heights. Made for most pistols, many with double set-screws. From AO Sight Systems, Inc.
Price: Standard Set, front and rear. **$60.00**
Price: Big Dot Set, front and rear. **$60.00**
Price: Tritium Set, Standard or Big Dot. **$90.00**
Price: 24/7 Pro Express, Std. or Big Dot Tritium **$120.00**

BO-MAR DELUXE BMCS Gives 3/8" windage and elevation adjustment at 50 yards on Colt Gov't 45; sight radius under 7". For GM and Commander models only. Uses existing dovetail slot. Has shield-type rear blade.
Price: **$65.95**
Price: BMCS-2 (for GM and 9mm). **$68.95**
Price: Flat bottom. **$65.95**
Price: BMGC (for Colt Gold Cup), angled serrated blade, rear. **$68.95**
Price: BMGC front sight. **$12.95**
Price: BMCZ-75 (for CZ-75,TZ-75, P-9 and most clones).
Works with factory front. **$68.95**

BO-MAR FRONT SIGHTS Dovetail style for S&W 4506, 4516, 1076; undercut style (.250", .280", 5/16" high); Fast Draw style (.210", .250", .230" high).
Price: **$12.95**

BO-MAR BMU XP-100/T/C CONTENDER No gunsmithing required; has .080" notch.
Price: **$77.00**

BO-MAR BMML For muzzleloaders; has .062" notch, flat bottom.
Price: **$65.95**
Price: With 3/8" dovetail. **$65.95**

BO-MAR RUGER "P" ADJUSTABLE SIGHT Replaces factory front and rear sights.
Price: Rear sight. **$65.95**
Price: Front sight. **$12.00**

BO-MAR BMR Fully adjustable rear sight for Ruger MKI, MKII Bull barrel autos.
Price: Rear. **$65.95**
Price: Undercut front sight. **$12.00**

BO-MAR GLOCK Fully adjustable, all-steel replacement sights. Sight fits factory dovetail. Longer sight radius. Uses Novak Glock .275" high, .135" wide front, or similar.
Price: Rear sight. **$68.95**
Price: Front sight. **$20.95**

BO-MAR LOW PROFILE RIB & ACCURACY TUNER Streamlined rib with front and rear sights; 7 1/8" sight radius. Brings sight line closer to the bore than standard or extended sight and ramp. Weight 5 oz. Made for Colt Gov't 45, Super 38, and Gold Cup 45 and 38.
Price: **$140.00**

BO-MAR COMBAT RIB For S&W Model 19 revolver with 4" barrel. Sight radius 5 3/4", weight 5 1/2 oz.
Price: **$127.00**

BO-MAR WINGED RIB For S&W 4" and 6" length barrels—K-38, M10, HB 14 and 19. Weight for the 6" model is about 7 1/4 oz.
Price: **$140.00**

BO-MAR COVER-UP RIB Adjustable rear sight, winged front guards. Fits right over revolver's original front sight. For S&W 4" M-10HB, M-13, M-58, M-64 & 65, Ruger 4" models SDA-34, SDA-84, SS-34, SS-84, GF-34, GF-84.
Price: **$130.00**

ACCESSORIES

METALLIC SIGHTS

CHIP MCCORMICK "DROP-IN" A low mount sight that fits any 1911-style slide with a standard military-type dovetail sight cut (60x.290"). Dovetail front sights also available. From Chip McCormick Corp.
Price: **$47.95**

CHIP MCCORMICK FIXED SIGHTS Same sight picture (.110" rear - .110" front) that's become the standard for pro combat shooters. Low mount design with rounded edges. For 1911-style pistols. May require slide machining for installation. From Chip McCormick Corp.
Price: **$24.95**

C-MORE SIGHTS Replacement front sight blades offered in two types and five styles. Made of Du Pont Acetal, they come in a set of five high-contrast colors: blue, green, pink, red and yellow. Easy to install. Patridge style for Colt Python (all barrels), Ruger Super Blackhawk (7 1/2"), Ruger Blackhawk (4 5/8"); ramp style for Python (all barrels), Blackhawk (4 5/8"), Super Blackhawk (7 1/2" and 10 1/2"). From C-More Systems.
Price: Per set. **$19.95**

G.G. & G. GHOST RINGS Replaces the factory rear sight without gunsmithing. Black phosphate finish. Available for Colt M1911 and Commander, Beretta M92F, Glock, S&W, SIG Sauer.
Price:. **$65.00**

Heinie Slant Pro

HEINIE SLANT PRO Made with a slight forward slant, the unique design of these rear sights is snag free for unimpeded draw from concealment. The combination of the slant and the rear serrations virtually eliminates glare. Made for most popular handguns. From Heinie Specialty Products.
Price: . . . . **$50.35 to $122.80**

HEINIE STRAIGHT EIGHT SIGHTS Consists of one tritium dot in the front sight and a slightly smaller Tritium dot in the rear sight. When aligned correctly, an elongated 'eight' is created. The Tritium dots are green in color. Designed with the belief that the human eye can correct vertical alignment faster than horizontal. Available for most popular handguns. From Heinie Specialty Products.
Price: . . . . **$104.95 to $122.80**

HEINIE CROSS DOVETAIL FRONT SIGHTS Made in a variety of heights, the standard dovetail is 60 degrees x .305" x .062" with a .002 taper. From Heinie Specialty Products.
Price: . . . . **$20.95 to $47.20**

JP GHOST RING Replacement bead front, ghost ring rear for Glock and M1911 pistols. From JP Enterprises.
Price:. **$79.95**
Price: Bo-Mar replacement leaf with JP dovetail front bead. **$99.95**

LES BAER CUSTOM ADJUSTABLE LOW MOUNT REAR SIGHT Considered one of the top adjustable sights in the world for target shooting with 1911-style pistols. Available with Tritium inserts. From Les Baer Custom.
Price:. . . . . **$49.00** (standard); **$99.00** (tritium)

LES BAER DELUXE FIXED COMBAT SIGHT A tactical-style sight with a very low profile. Incorporates a no-snag design and has serrations on sides. For 1911-style pistols. Available with Tritium inserts for night shooting. From Les Baer Custom.
Price:. . . . . **$26.00** (standard); **$67.00** (with Tritium)

LES BAER DOVETAIL FRONT SIGHT Blank dovetail sight machined from bar stock. Can be contoured to many different configurations to meet user's needs. Available with Tritium insert. From Les Baer Custom.
Price:. **$17.00** (standard); **$47.00** (with Tritium insert)

LES BAER FIBER OPTIC FRONT SIGHT Dovetail .330x65 degrees, .125" wide post, .185" high, .060" diameter. Red and green fiber optic. From Les Baer Custom.
Price: **$24.00**

LES BAER PPC-STYLE ADJUSTABLE REAR SIGHT Made for use with custom built 1911-style pistols, allows the user to preset three elevation adjustments for PPC-style shooting. Milling required for installation. Made from 4140 steel. From Les Baer Custom.
Price: **$120.00**

LES BAER DOVETAIL FRONT SIGHT WITH TRITIUM INSERT This fully contoured and finished front sight comes ready for gunsmith installation. From Les Baer Custom.
Price: **$47.00**

MMC TACTICAL ADJUSTABLE SIGHTS Low-profile, snag free design. Twenty-two click positions for elevation, drift adjustable for windage. Machined from 4140 steel and heat treated to 40 RC. Tritium and non-tritium. Ten different configurations and colors. Three different finishes. For 1911s, all Glock, HK USP, S&W, Browning Hi-Power.
Price: Sight set, tritium. **$144.92**
Price: Sight set, white outline or white dot. **$99.90**
Price: Sight set, black. **$93.90**

MEPROLIGHT TRITIUM NIGHT SIGHTS Replacement sight assemblies for use in low-light conditions. Available for rifles, shotguns, handguns and bows. TRU-DOT models carry a 12-year warranty on the useable illumination, while non-TRU-DOT have a 5-year warranty. Contact Hesco, Inc. for complete list of available models.
Price: Kahr K9, K40, fixed, TRU-DOT. **$100.00**
Price: Ruger P85, P89, P94, adjustable, TRU-DOT. **$156.00**
Price: Ruger Mini-14R sights. **$140.00**
Price: SIG Sauer P220, P225, P226, P228, adjustable, TRU-DOT. **$156.00**
Price: Smith&Wesson autos, fixed or adjustable, TRU-DOT. **$100.00**
Price: Taurus PT92, PT100, adjustable, TRU-DOT. **$156.00**
Price: Walther P-99, fixed, TRU-DOT. **$100.00**
Price: Shotgun bead. **$32.00**
Price: Beretta M92, Cougar, Brigadier, fixed, TRU-DOT. **$100.00**
Price: Browning Hi-Power, adjustable, TRU-DOT. **$156.00**
Price: Colt M1911 Govt., adjustable, TRU-DOT. **$156.00**

MILLETT SERIES 100 REAR SIGHTS All-steel highly visible, click adjustable. Blades in white outline, target black, silhouette, 3-dot. Fit most popular revolvers and autos.
Price:. . . . . **$51.77 to $84.00**

MILLETT BAR-DOT-BAR TRITIUM NIGHT SIGHTS Replacement front and rear combos fit most automatics. Horizontal tritium bars on rear, dot front sight.
Price:. **$152.25**

MILLETT BAR/DOT Made with orange or white bar or dot for increased visibility. Available for Beretta 84, 85, 92S, 92SB, Browning, Colt Python & Trooper, Ruger GP 100, P85, Redhawk, Security Six.
Price:. . . . . **$14.99 to $24.99**

MILLETT 3-DOT SYSTEM SIGHTS The 3-Dot System sights use a single white dot on the front blade and two dots flanking the rear notch. Fronts available in Dual-Crimp and Wide Stake-On styles, as well as special applications. Adjustable rear sight available for most popular auto pistols and revolvers including Browning Hi-Power, Colt 1911 Government and Ruger P85.
Price: Front, from. **$16.80**
Price: Adjustable rear. **$55.60**

MILLETT REVOLVER FRONT SIGHTS All-steel replacement front sights with either white or orange bar. Easy to install. For Ruger GP-100, Redhawk, Security-Six, Police- Six, Speed-Six, Colt Trooper, Diamondback, King Cobra, Peacemaker, Python, Dan Wesson 22 and 15-2.
Price: . . . . **$13.60 to $16.00**

MILLETT DUAL-CRIMP FRONT SIGHT Replacement front sight for automatic pistols. Dual-Crimp uses an all-steel two-point hollow rivet system. Available in eight heights and four styles. Has a skirted base that covers the front sight pad. Easily installed with the Millett Installation Tool Set. Available in Blaze Orange Bar, White Bar, Serrated Ramp, Plain Post. Available in heights of .185", .200", .225", .275", .312", .340" and .410".
Price:. **$16.80**

MILLETT STAKE-ON FRONT SIGHT Replacement front sight for automatic pistols. Stake-On sights have skirted base that covers the front sight pad. Easily installed with the Millet Installation Tool Set. Available in seven heights and four styles—Blaze Orange Bar, White Bar, Serrated Ramp, Plain Post. Available for Glock 17L and 24, others.
Price:. **$16.80**

MILLETT ADJUSTABLE TARGET Positive light-deflection serration and slant to eliminate glare and sharp edge sight notch. Audible "click" adjustments. For AMT Hardballer, Beretta 84, 85, 92S, 92SB, Browning Hi-Power, Colt 1911 Government and Gold Cup, Colt revolvers, Dan Wesson 15, 41, 44, Ruger revolvers, Glock 17, 17L, 19, 20, 21, 22, 23.
Price:. **$44.99**

MILLETT ADJUSTABLE WHITE OUTLINE Similar to the Target sight, except has a white outline on the blade to increase visibility. Available for the same handguns as the Target model, plus BRNO CZ-75/TZ-75/TA-90 without pin on front sight, and Ruger P85.
Price:. . . . . **$44.99 to $49.99**

OMEGA OUTLINE SIGHT BLADES Replacement rear sight blades for Colt and Ruger single action guns and the Interarms Virginian Dragoon. Standard Outline available in gold or white notch outline on blue metal. From Omega Sales, Inc.
Price:. **$10.00**

OMEGA MAVERICK SIGHT BLADES Replacement "peep-sight" blades for Colt, Ruger SAs, Virginian Dragoon. Three models available—No. 1, Plain; No. 2, Single Bar; No. 3, Double Bar Rangefinder. From Omega Sales, Inc.
Price: Each. **$10.00**

ONE RAGGED HOLE Replacement rear sight ghost ring sight for Ruger handguns. Fits Blackhawks, Redhawks, Super Blackhawks, GP series and Mk. II target pistols with adjustable sights. From One Ragged Hole, Tallahassee, Florida.
Price:. . . . . **NA**

PACHMAYR ACCU-SET Low-profile, fully adjustable rear sight to be used with existing front sight. Available with target, white outline or 3-dot blade. Blue finish. Uses factory dovetail and locking screw. For Browning, Colt, Glock, SIG Sauer, S&W and Ruger autos. From Pachmayr.
Price:. **$59.98**

P-T TRITIUM NIGHT SIGHTS Self-luminous tritium sights for most popular handguns, Colt AR-15, H&K rifles and shotguns. Replacement handgun sight sets available in 3- Dot style (green/green, green/yellow, green/orange) with bold outlines around inserts; Bar-Dot available in green/green with or without white outline rear sight. Functional life exceeds 15 years. From Innovative Weaponry, Inc.
Price: Handgun sight sets. **$99.95**
Price: Rifle sight sets. **$99.95**
Price: Rifle, front only. **$49.95**
Price: Shotgun, front only. **$49.95**

T/C ENCORE FIBER OPTIC SIGHT SETS Click adjustable, steel rear sight and ramp-style front sight, both fitted with Tru-Glo™ fiber optics. Specifically-designed for the T/C Encore pistol series. From Thompson/Center arms.
Price **$49.35**

T/C ENCORE TARGET REAR SIGHT Precision, steel construction with click adjustments (via knurled knobs) for windage and elevation. Models available with low, medium and high blades. From Thompson/Center Arms.
Price:' **$54.00**

METALLIC SIGHTS

TRIJICON NIGHT SIGHTS Three-dot night sight system uses tritium lamps in the front and rear sights. Tritium "lamps" are mounted in silicone rubber inside a metal cylinder. A polished crystal sapphire provides protection and clarity. Inlaid white outlines provide 3-dot aiming in daylight also. Available for most popular handguns including Glock 17, 19, 20, 21, 23, 24, 25, 26, 29, 30, H&K USP, Ruger P94, SIG P220, P225, 226, Colt 1911. Front and rear sets available. From Trijicon, Inc.
Price: **$80.00** to **$299.00**

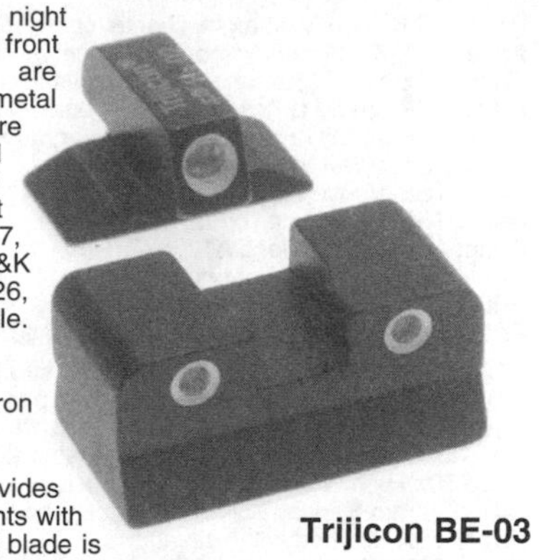

Trijicon BE-03

TRIJICON 3-DOT Self-luminous front iron night sight for the Ruger SP101.
Price: **$39.99**

WICHITA SERIES 70/80 SIGHT Provides click windage and elevation adjustments with precise repeatability of settings. Sight blade is grooved and angled back at the top to reduce glare. Available in Low Mount Combat or Low Mount Target styles for Colt 45s and their copies, S&W 645, Hi-Power, CZ 75 and others.
Price: Rear sight, target or combat. **$75.00**
Price: Front sight, Patridge or ramp. **$18.00**

WICHITA GRAND MASTER DELUXE RIBS Ventilated rib has wings machined into it for better sight acquisition and is relieved for Mag-Na-Porting. Milled to accept Weaver see-thru-style rings. Made of stainless; front and rear sights blued. Has Wichita Multi-Range rear sight system, adjustable front sight. Made for revolvers with 6" barrel.
Price: Model 301S, 301B (adj. sight K frames with custom bbl. of 1" to 1.032" dia. L and N frame with 1.062" to 1.100" dia. bbl.). **$225.00**
Price: Model 303S, 303B (adj. sight K, L, N frames with factory barrel). **$225.00**

WICHITA MULTI-RANGE QUICK CHANGE SIGHTING SYSTEM Multi-range rear sight can be pre-set to four positive repeatable range settings. Adjustable front sight allows compensation for changing lighting and weather conditions with just one front sight adjustment. Front sight comes with Lyman 17A Globe and set of apertures.
Price: Rear sight **$125.00**
Price: Front, sight **$95.00**

WILLIAMS FIRE SIGHT SETS Red fiber optic metallic sight replaces the original. Rear sight has two green fiber optic elements. Made of CNC-machined aluminum. Fits all Glocks, Ruger P-Series (except P-85), S&W 910, Colt Gov't. Model Series 80, Ruger GP 100 and Redhawk, and SIG Sauer (front only).
Price: Front and rear set **$39.95**
Price: SIG Sauer front. **$19.95**

WILSON ADJUSTABLE REAR SIGHTS Machined from steel, the click adjustment design requires simple cuts and no dovetails for installation. Available in several configurations: matte black standard blade with .128" notch; with .110" notch; with Tritium dots and .128" square or "U" shaped notch; and Combat Pyramid. From Wilson Combat.
Price:. . . . . **$24.95 to $69.95**

WILSON NITE-EYES SIGHTS Low-profile, snag free design with green and yellow Tritium inserts. For 1911-style pistols. From Wilson Combat.
Price: **$119.95**

WILSON TACTICAL COMBAT SIGHTS Low-profile and snag-free in design, the sight employs the Combat Pyramid shape. For many 1911-style pistols and some Glock models. From Wilson Combat.
Price: **$139.95**

Shotgun Sights

AO SHOTGUN SIGHTS 24/7 Pro Express sights fit Remington rifle sighted barrels. Front sight divetails into existing ramp, rear installs on Remington rear ramp. Available in Big Dot Tritium or Standard Dot Tritium. Three other styles (for pedestal base, beaded, and ribbed barrels) provide a Big Dot Tritium front that epoxies over the existing bead front sight. From AO Sight Systems, Inc.
Price: 24/7 Tritium Sets. . . . . **$90.00 to $120.00**
Price: Big Dot Tritium (front only). **$60.00**

ACCURA-SITE For shooting shotgun slugs. Three models to fit most shotguns—"A" for vent. rib barrels, "B" for solid ribs, "C" for plain barrels. Rear sight has windage and elevation provisions. Easily removed and replaced. Includes front and rear sights. From All's, The Jim Tembeils Co.
Price:. . . . . **$27.95 to $34.95**

BRADLEY SHOTGUN SIGHTS Front beads available in sizes of 1/8" and 5/32" in thread sizes of #3-56, #6-48, and #8-40. From 100 Straight Products.
Price:. **$5.00**

BRADLEY CENTER SIGHTS Available in 1/16" bead size and #3-56 thread or taper. Plain brass, bright silver and white finishes. From 100 Straight Products.
Price: . . . . . **$2.50 to $6.00 each**

BRADLEY SHOTGUN SIGHT ASSORTMENT An assortment of the most frequently used sights including six each of 18-3, 18-6,532-3, 532-7, 532-9, MB-01 and MB-11. From 100 Straight Products.
Price:. **$119.95**

CARLSON SHOTGUN SIGHT A brilliant orange bead securely held by two bands. Used for low light conditions. Bead size .150", thread size 6-48. From Carlson's and 100 Straight Products.
Price:. **$7.50**

FIRE FLY EM-109 SL SHOTGUN SIGHT Made of aircraft-grade aluminum, this 1/4-oz. "channel" sight has a thick, sturdy hollowed post between the side rails to give a Patridge sight picture. All shooting is done with both eyes open, allowing the shooter to concentrate on the target, not the sights. The hole in the sight post gives reduced-light shooting capability and allows for fast, precise aiming. For sport or combat shooting. Model EM-109 fits all vent. rib and double barrel shotguns and muzzleloaders with octagon barrel. Model MOC-110 fits all plain barrel shotguns without screw-in chokes. From JAS, Inc.
Price:. **$35.00**

LYMAN Three sights of over-sized ivory beads. No. 10 Front (press fit) for double barrel or ribbed single barrel guns **$4.50**; No. 10D Front (screw fit) for non-ribbed single barrel guns (comes with wrench) **$5.50**; No. 11 Middle (press fit) for double and ribbed single barrel guns**$4.75**

MMC M&P COMBAT SHOTGUN SIGHT SET A durable, protected ghost ring aperture, combat sight made of steel. Fully adjustable for windage and elevation.
Price: M&P Sight Set (front and rear). **$73.45**
Price: As above, installed. **$83.95**

MMC TACTICAL GHOST RING SIGHT Click adjustable for elevation with 30 MOA total adjustment in 3 MOA increments. Click windage adjustment. Machined from 4140 steel, heat-treated to 40 RC. Front sight available in banded tactical or serrated ramp. Front and rear sights available with or without tritium. Available in three different finishes.
Price: Rear Ghost Ring with tritium. **$119.95**
Price: Rear Ghost Ring without tritium. **$99.95**
Price: Front Banded Tactical with tritium. **$59.95**
Price: Front Banded Tactical without tritium. **$39.95**
Price: Front serrated ramp. **$24.95**

MARBLE SHOTGUN BEAD SIGHTS No. 214—Ivory front bead, 11/64", tapered shank **$4.40**; No. 223—Ivory rear bead, .080", tapered shank **$4.40**; No. 217— Ivory front bead, 11/64", threaded shank **$4.75**; No. 223-T—Ivory rear bead, .080, threaded shank **$5.95.** Reamers, taps and wrenches available from Marble Arms.

MEPROLIGHT Ghost ring sight set for Benelli tactical shotguns. From MEPROLIGHT, Inc.
Price: **$100.00**

MILLETT SHURSHOT SHOTGUN SIGHT A sight system for shotguns with ventilated rib. Rear sight attaches to the rib, front sight replaces the front bead. Front has an orange face, rear has two orange bars. For 870, 1100 or other models.
Price: Rear, fixed. **$13.81**
Price: Adjustable front and rear set. **$32.55**
Price: Front. **$13.60**

NECG IVORY SHOTGUN BEAD Genuine ivory shotgun beads with 6-48 thread. Available in heights of .157" and .197". From New England Custom Gun Service.
Price:. **$9.00**

POLY-CHOKE Replacement front shotgun sights in four styles—Xpert, Poly Bead, Xpert Mid Rib sights, and Bev-L-Block. Xpert Front available in 3x56, 6x48 thread, 3/32" or 5/32" shank length, gold, ivory **$4.70;** or Sun Spot orange bead **$5.95**; Poly Bead is standard replacement 1/8" bead, 6x48 **$2.95;** Xpert Mid Rib in tapered carrier (ivory only) **$5.95,** or 3x56 threaded shank (gold only) **$2.95;** Hi and Lo Blok sights with 6x48 thread, gold or ivory **$5.25**. From Marble Arms.

SLUG SIGHTS Made of non-marring black nylon, front and rear sights stretch over and lock onto barrel. Sights are low profile with blaze orange front blade. Adjustable for windage and elevation. For plain-barrel (non-ribbed) guns in 12-, 16- and 20-gauge, and for shotguns with 5/16" and 3/8" ventilated ribs. From Innovision Ent.
Price:. **$11.95**

TRIJICON 3-DOT NIGHT SIGHTS Self-luminous and machined from steel. Available for Remington 870, 1100, 1187.
Price:. . . . . **$75.00 to $175.00**

WILLIAMS GUIDE BEAD SIGHT Fits all shotguns, 1/8" ivory, red or gold bead. Screws into existing sight hole. Various thread sizes and shank lengths.
Price:. **$4.77**

WILLIAMS SLUGGER SIGHTS Removable aluminum sights attach to the shotgun rib. High profile front, fully adjustable rear. Fits 1/4", 5/16" or 3/8" (special) ribs.
Price:. **$34.95**

WILLIAMS FIRE SIGHTS Fiber optic light gathering front sights in red or yellow, glow with natural light. Fit 1/4", 5/16" or 3/8" vent. ribs, most popular shotguns.
Price:. **$13.95**

WILLIAMS SIGHT KITS Contains over 36 beads to fit any shotgun (with drills and taps).
Price:. **$102.99**

Sight Attachments

MERIT ADJUSTABLE APERTURES Eleven clicks give 12 different apertures. No. 3 Disc and Master, primarily target types, 0.22" to .125"; No. 4, 1/2" dia. hunting type, .025" to .155". Available for all popular sights. The Master, with flexible rubber light shield, is particularly adapted to extension, scope height, and tang sights. All models have internal click springs; are hand fitted to minimum tolerance.
Price: No. 3 Master Disk. **$66.00**
Price: No. 3 Target Disc (Plain Face). **$56.00**
Price: No. 4 Hunting Disc. **$48.00**

MERIT LENS DISC Similar to Merit Iris Shutter (Model 3 or Master) but incorporates provision for mounting prescription lens integrally. Lens may be obtained locally from your optician. Sight disc is 7/16" wide (Model 3), or 3/4" wide (Master).
Price: No. 3 Target Lens Disk. **$68.00**
Price: No. 3 Master Lens Disk. **$78.00**

MERIT OPTICAL ATTACHMENT For iron sight shooting with handgun or rifle. Instantly attached by rubber suction cup to prescription or shooting glasses. Swings aside. Aperture adjustable from .020" to .156".
Price:. **$65.00**

WILLIAMS APERTURES Standard thread, fits most sights. Regular series 3/8" to 1/2" O.D., .050" to .125" hole. "Twilight" series has white reflector ring.
Price: Regular series. **$4.97**
Price: Twilight series. **$6.79**
Price: Wide open 5/16" aperture for shotguns fits 5-D or Foolproof sights (specify model). **$8.77**

ACCESSORIES

SPOTTING SCOPES

Bushnell Sentry

BAUSCH & LOMB DISCOVERER 15x to 60x zoom, 60mm objective. Constant focus throughout range. Field at 1000 yds. 38 ft (60x), 150 ft. (15x). Comes with lens caps. Length 17 1/2"; weight 48.5 oz.
Price: **$391.95**

BAUSCH & LOMB ELITE 15x to 45x zoom, 60mm objective. Field at 1000 yds., 125-65 ft. Length is 12.2"; weight, 26.5 oz. Waterproof, armored. Tripod mount. Comes with black case.
Price: **$766.95**

BAUSCH & LOMB ELITE ZOOM 20x-60x, 70mm objective. Roof prism. Field at 1000 yds. 90-50 ft. Length is 16"; weight 40 oz. Waterproof, armored. Tripod mount. Comes with black case.
Price: **$921.95**

BAUSCH & LOMB 80MM ELITE 20x-60x zoom, 80mm objective. Field of view at 1000 yds. 98-50 ft. (zoom). Weight 51 oz. (20x, 30x), 54 oz. (zoom); length 17". Interchangeable bayonet-style eyepieces. Built-in peep sight.
Price: With EDPrime Glass **$1,276.95**

BUSHNELL TROPHY 63mm objective, 20x-60x zoom. Field at 1000 yds. 90ft. (20x), 45 ft. (60x). Length 12.7"; weight 20 oz. Black rubber armored, waterproof. Case included.
Price: **$421.95**

BUSHNELL COMPACT TROPHY 50mm objective, 20x-50x zoom. Field at 1000 yds. 92 ft. (20x), 52 ft. (50X). Length 12.2"; weight 17 oz. Black rubber armored, waterproof. Case included.
Price: **$337.95**

BUSHNELL SENTRY 16-32 zoom, 50mm objective. Field at 1000 yds. 140-65 ft. Length 8.7", weight 21.5 oz. Black rubber armored. Built-in peep sight. Comes with tripod and hardcase.
Price: **$205.95**

BUSHNELL SPACEMASTER 20x-45x zoom. Long eye relief. Rubber armored, prismatic. 60mm objective. Field at 1000 yds. 90-58 ft. Minimum focus 20 ft. Length 12.7"; weight 43 oz.
Price: With tripod, carrying case and 20x-45x LER eyepiece. **$560.95**

BUSHNELL SPORTVIEW 12x-36x zoom, 50mm objective. Field at 100 yds. 160 ft. (12x), 90 ft. (36x). Length 14.6"; weight 25 oz.
Price: With tripod and carrying case **$159.95**

BUSHNELL XTRA-WIDE® 15-45x zoom, 60mm objective. Field at 1000 yds. 160-87 ft. Length 13"; weight 35 oz.
Price: **$640.95**

HERMES 1 70mm objective, 16x, 25x, 40x. Field at 1000 meters 160 ft. (16x), 75ft. (40x). Length 12.2"; weight 33 oz. From CZ-USA.
Price: Body **$359.00**
Price: 25x eyepiece **$86.00**
Price: 40x eyepiece **$128.00**

KOWA TS-500 SERIES Offset 45° or straight body. Comes with 20-40x zoom eyepiece or 20x fixed eyepiece. 50mm obj. Field of view at 1000 yds.: 171 ft. (20x fixed), 132-74 ft. (20-40x zoom). Length 8.9-10.4", weight 13.4-14.8 oz.
Price: TS-501 (offset 45° body w/20x fixed eyepiece) **$258.00**
Price: TS-502 (straight body w/20x fixed eyepiece) **$231.00**
Price: TS-501Z (offset 45° body w/20-40x zoom eyepiece) **$321.00**
Price: TS-502Z (straight body w/20-40x zoom eyepiece). **$290.00**

KOWA TS-610 SERIES Offset 45° or straight body. Available with fluroite lens. Sunshade. 60mm obj. Field of view at 1000 yds.: 177 ft. (20xW), 154 ft. (22xW), 102 ft. (25x), 92 ft. (25xLER), 62 ft. (40x), 102-56 ft. (20-60x zoom). Length 11.2"; weight 27 oz. Note: Eyepieces for TSN 7mm series, TSN-660 series, and TS-610 series are interchangeable.
Price: TS-611 body (45° offset) **$530.00**
Price: TS-612 body (straight). **$489.00**

Price: TS-614 body (straight, fluorite lens) **$1,010.00**
Price: TSE-Z2M (20-60x zoom eyepiece) **$231.00**
Price: TSE-17HB (25x long eye relief eyepiece) **$240.00**
Price: TSE-15WM (27x wide angle eyepiece) **$182.00**
Price: TSE-21WB (20x wide angle high-grade eyepiece) **$230.00**
Price: TSE-10PM (40x eyepiece) **$108.00**
Price: TSE-16PM (25x eyepiece) **$108.00**
Price: TSN-DA1 (digital photo adapter) **$105.00**
Price: Adapter rings for DA1. .... **$43.00**
Price: TSN-PA2 (800mm photo adapter) **$269.00**
Price: TSN-PA4 (1200mm photo adapter) **$330.00**
Price: Camera mounts (for use with photo adapter) **$30.00**

KOWA TSN-660 SERIES Offset 45° or straight body. Fully waterproof. Available with fluorite lens. Sunshade and rotating tripod mount. 66mm obj., field of view at 1000 yds.: 177 ft. (20x@), 154 ft. (27xW), 131 ft. (30xW), 102 ft. (25x), 92 ft. (25xLER), 62 ft. (40x), 108-79 ft. (20-40x Multi-Coated Zoom), 102-56 ft. (20-60x Zoom), 98-62 ft. (20-60x High Grade Zoom). Length 12.3"; weight 34.9-36.7 oz. Note: Eyepieces for TSN 77mm Series, TSN-660 Series, and TSN610 Series are interchangeable.
Price: TSN-661 body (45° offset) **$660.00**
Price: TSN-662 body (straight). **$610.00**
Price: TSN-663 body (45° offset, fluorite lens). **$1,070.00**
Price: TSN-664 body (straight, fluorite lens) **$1,010.00**
Price: TSE-Z2M (20-60x zoom eyepiece) **$231.00**
Price: TSE-Z4 (20-60x high-grade zoom eyepiece) **$378.00**
Price: TSE-Z6 (20-40x multi-coated zoom eyepiece) **$250.00**
Price: TSE-17HB (25x long eye relief eyepiece) **$240.00**
Price: TSE-14W (30x wide angle eyepiece) **$288.00**
Price: TSE-21WB (20x wide angle eyepiece) **$230.00**
Price: TSE-15PM (27x wide angle eyepiece) **$182.00**
Price: TSE-10PM (40x eyepiece) **$108.00**
Price: TSE-16PM (25x eyepiece) **$108.00**
Price: TSNE5B (77x eyepiece). **$235.00**
Price: TSNE7B (60x eyepiece). **$230.00**
Price: TSN-DA1 (digital photo adapter) **$105.00**
Price: Adapter rings for DA1. .... **$43.00**
Price: TSN-PA2 (800mm photo adapter). **$269.00**
Price: TSN-PA4 (1200mm photo adapter) **$330.00**
Price: Camera mounts (for use with photo adapter) **$30.00**

KOWA TSN-820 SERIES Offset 45° or straight body. Fully waterproof. Available with fluorite lens. Sunshade and rotating tripod mount. 82mm obj., field of view at 1000 yds.: 75 ft (27xLER, 50xW), 126 ft. (32xW), 115-58 ft. (20-60xZoom). Length 15"; weight 49.4-52.2 oz.
Price: TSN-821M body (45° offset) **$850.00**
Price: TSN-822M body (straight) **$770.00**
Price: TSN-823M body (45° offset, fluorite lens) **$1,850.00**
Price: TSN-824M body (straight, fluorite lens) **$1,730.00**
Price: TSE-Z7 (20-60x zoom eyepiece). **$433.00**
Price: TSE-9W (50x wide angle eyepiece) **$345.00**
Price: TSE-14WB (32x wide angle eyepiece) **$366.00**
Price: TSE-17HC (27x long eye relief eyepiece) **$248.00**
Price: TSN-Da1 (digital photo adapter) **$105.00**
Price: Adapter rings for DA1. .... **$43.00**
Price: TSN-PA2C (850mm photo adapter) **$300.00**
Price: Camera mounts (for use with photo adapter) **$30.00**

LEUPOLD 12-40x60 VARIABLE 60mm objective, 12-40x. Field at 100 yds. 17.5-5.3 ft.; eye relief 1.2" (20x). Overall length 11.5", weight 32 oz. Rubber armored.
Price: **$1,217.90**

LEUPOLD 25x50 COMPACT 50mm objective, 25x. Field at 100 yds. 8.3 ft.; eye relief 1"; length overall 9.4"; weight 20.5 oz.
Price: Armored model. **$848.20**
Price: Packer Tripod **$96.40**

MIRADOR TTB SERIES Draw tube armored spotting scopes. Available with 75mm or 80mm objective. Zoom model (28x-62x, 80mm) is 11 7/8" (closed), weighs 50 oz. Field at 1000 yds. 70-42 ft. Comes with lens covers.
Price: 28-62x80mm. **$1,133.95**
Price: 32x80mm **$971.95**
Price: 26-58x75mm. **$989.95**
Price: 30x75mm **$827.95**

MIRADOR SSD SPOTTING SCOPES 60mm objective, 15x, 20x, 22x, 25x, 40x, 60x, 20-60x; field at 1000 yds. 37 ft.; length 10 1/4"; weight 33 oz.
Price: 25x **$575.95**
Price: 22x Wide Angle **$593.95**
Price: 20-60x Zoom. **$746.95**
Price: As above, with tripod, case **$944.95**

MIRADOR SIA SPOTTING SCOPES Similar to the SSD scopes except with 45° eyepiece. Length 12 1/4"; weight 39 oz.
Price: 25x **$809.95**
Price: 22x Wide Angle **$827.95**
Price: 20-60x Zoom. **$980.95**

MIRADOR SSR SPOTTING SCOPES 50mm or 60mm objective. Similar to SSD except rubber armored in black or camouflage. Length 11 1/8"; weight 31 oz.
Price: Black, 20x **$521.95**
Price: Black, 18x Wide Angle **$539.95**
Price: Black, 16-48x Zoom **$692.95**
Price: Black, 20x, 60mm, EER. **$692.95**
Price: Black, 22x Wide Angle, 60mm. **$701.95**
Price: Black, 20-60x Zoom **$854.95**

SPOTTING SCOPES

MIRADOR SSF FIELD SCOPES Fixed or variable power, choice of 50mm, 60mm, 75mm objective lens. Length 9 3/4"; weight 20 oz. (15-32x50).
Price: 20x50mm **$359.95**
Price: 25x60mm **$440.95**
Price: 30x75mm **$584.95**
Price: 15-32x50mm Zoom **$548.95**
Price: 18-40x60mm Zoom **$629.95**
Price: 22-47x75mm Zoom **$773.95**

MIRADOR SRA MULTI ANGLE SCOPES Similar to SSF Series except eyepiece head rotates for viewing from any angle.
Price: 20x50mm **$503.95**
Price: 25x60mm **$647.95**
Price: 30x75mm **$764.95**
Price: 15-32x50mm Zoom **$692.95**
Price: 18-40x60mm Zoom **$836.95**
Price: 22-47x75mm Zoom **$953.95**

MIRADOR SIB FIELD SCOPES Short-tube, 45° scopes with porro prism design. 50mm and 60mm objective. Length 10 1/4"; weight 18.5 oz. (15-32x50mm); field at 1000 yds. 129-81 ft.
Price: 20x50mm **$386.95**
Price: 25x60mm **$449.95**
Price: 15-32x50mm Zoom **$575.95**
Price: 18-40x60mm Zoom **$638.95**

NIKON FIELDSCOPES 60mm and 78mm lens. Field at 1000 yds. 105 ft. (60mm, 20x), 126 ft. (78mm, 25x). Length 12.8" (straight 60mm), 12.6" (straight 78mm); weight 34.5- 47.5 oz. Eyepieces available separately.
Price: 60mm straight body **$499.99**
Price: 60mm angled body **$519.99**
Price: 60mm straight ED body **$779.99**
Price: 60mm angled ED body **$849.99**
Price: 78mm straight ED body **$899.99**
Price: 78mm angled ED body **$999.99**
Price: Eyepieces (15x to 60x) . . . . . **$146.95** to **$324.95**
Price: 20-45x eyepiece (25-56x for 78mm) **$320.55**

NIKON SPOTTING SCOPE 60mm objective, 20x fixed power or 15-45x zoom. Field at 1000 yds. 145 ft. (20x). Gray rubber armored. Straight or angled eyepiece. Weighs 44.2 oz., length 12.1" (20x).
Price: 20x60 fixed (with eyepiece) **$290.95**
Price: 15-45x zoom (with case, tripod, eyepiece) **$578.95**

PENTAX PF-80ED spotting scope 80mm objective lens available in 18x, 24x, 36x, 48x, 72x and 20-60x. Length 15.6", weight 11.9 to 19.2 oz.
Price: **$1,320.00**

SIGHTRON SII 2050X63 63mm objective lens, 20x-50x zoom. Field at 1000 yds 91.9 ft. (20x), 52.5 ft. (50x). Length 14"; weight 30.8 oz. Black rubber finish. Also available with 80mm objective lens.
Price: 63mm or 80mm **$339.95**

SIMMONS 1280 50mm objective, 15-45x zoom. Black matte finish. Ocular focus. Peep finder sight. Waterproof. FOV 95-51 ft. @ 1000 yards. Wgt. 33.5 oz., length 12".
Price: With tripod **$189.99**

SIMMONS 1281 60mm objective, 20-60x zoom. Black matte finish. Ocular focus. Peep finder sight. Waterproof. FOV 78-43 ft. @ 1000 yards. Wgt. 34.5 oz. Length 12".
Price: With tripod **$209.99**

SIMMONS 77206 PROHUNTER 50mm objectives, 25x fixed power. Field at 1000 yds. 113 ft.; length 10.25"; weighs 33.25 oz. Black rubber armored.
Price: With tripod case **$160.60**

SIMMONS 41200 REDLINE 50mm objective, 15x-45x zoom. Field at 1000 yds. 104-41 ft.; length 16.75"; weighs 32.75 oz.
Price: With hard case and tripod **$74.99**
Price: 20-60x, 60mm objective **$99.99**

SWAROVSKI CT EXTENDIBLE SCOPES 75mm or 85mm objective, 20-60x zoom, or fixed 15x, 22x, 30x, 32x eyepieces. Field at 1000 yds. 135 ft. (15x), 99 ft. (32x); 99 ft. (20x), 5.2 ft. (60x) for zoom. Length 12.4" (closed), 17.2" (open) for the CT75; 9.7"/17.2" for CT85. Weight 40.6 oz. (CT75), 49.4 oz. (CT85). Green rubber armored.
Price: CT75 body **$765.56**
Price: CT85 body **$1,094.44**
Price: 20-60x eyepiece **$343.33**
Price: 15x, 22x eyepiece **$232.22**
Price: 30x eyepiece **$265.55**

SWAROVSKI AT-80/ST-80 SPOTTING SCOPES 80mm objective, 20-60x zoom, or fixed 15x, 22x, 30x, 32x eyepieces. Field at 1000 yds. 135 ft. (15x), 99 ft. (32x); 99 ft. (20x), 52.5 ft. (60x) for zoom. Length 16" (AT-80), 15.6" (ST-80); weight 51.8 oz. Available with HD (high density) glass.
Price: AT-80 (angled) body **$1,094.44**
Price: ST-80 (straight) body **$1,094.44**
Price: With HD glass **$1,555.00**
Price: 20-60x eyepiece **$343.33**
Price: 15x, 22x eyepiece **$232.22**
Price: 30x eyepiece **$265.55**

SWIFT LYNX M836 15x-45x zoom, 60mm objective. Weight 7 lbs., length 14". Has 45° eyepiece, sunshade.
Price: **$315.00**

SWIFT NIGHTHAWK M849U 80mm objective, 20x-60x zoom, or fixed 19, 25x, 31x, 50x, 75x eyepieces. Has rubber armored body, 1.8x optical finder, retractable lens hood, 45° eyepiece. Field at 1000 yds. 60 ft. (28x), 41 ft. (75x). Length 13.4 oz.; weight 39 oz.
Price: Body only **$870.00**
Price: 20-68x eyepiece **$370.00**
Price: Fixed eyepieces . . . . . **$130.00** to **$240.00**
Price: Model 849 (straight) body **$795.00**

SWIFT NIGHTHAWK M850U 65mm objective, 16x-48x zoom, or fixed 19x, 20x, 25x, 40x, 60x eyepieces. Rubber armored with a 1.8x optical finder, retractable lens hood. Field at 1000 yds. 83 ft. (22x), 52 ft. (60x). Length 12.3"; weight 30 oz. Has 45° eyepiece.
Price: Body only **$650.00**
Price: 16x-48x eyepiece **$370.00**
Price: Fixed eyepieces . . . . . **$130.00** to **$240.00**
Price: Model 850 (straight) body **$575.00**

SWIFT LEOPARD M837 50mm objective, 25x. Length 9 11/16" to 10 1/2". Weight with tripod 28 oz. Rubber armored. Comes with tripod.
Price: **$160.00**

SWIFT TELEMASTER M841 60mm objective. 15x to 60x variable power. Field at 1000 yds. 160 feet (15x) to 40 feet (60x). Weight 3.25 lbs.; length 18" overall.
Price: **$399.50**

SWIFT PANTHER M844 15x-45x zoom or 22x WA, 15x, 20x, 40x. 60mm objective. Field at 1000 yds. 141 ft. (15x), 68 ft. (40x), 95-58 ft. (20x-45x).
Price: Body only **$380.00**
Price: 15x-45x zoom eyepiece **$120.00**
Price: 20x-45x zoom (long eye relief) eyepiece **$140.00**
Price: 15x, 20x, 40x eyepiece **$65.00**
Price: 22x WA eyepiece **$80.00**

SWIFT M700T 12x-36x, 50mm objective. Field of view at 100 yds. 16 ft. (12x), 9 ft. (36x). Length 14"; weight with tripod 3.22 lbs.
Price: **$225.00**

SWIFT SEARCHER M839 60mm objective, 20x, 40x. Field at 1000 yds. 118 ft. (30x), 59 ft. (40x). Length 12.6"; weight 3 lbs. Rotating eyepiece head for straight or 45° viewing.
Price: **$580.00**
Price: 30x, 50x eyepieces, each **$67.00**

TASCO 29TZBWP WATERPROOF SPOTTER 60mm objective lens, 20x-60x zoom. Field at 100 yds. 7 ft., 4 in. to 3 ft., 8 in. Black rubber armored. Comes with tripod, hard case.
Price: **$356.50**

TASCO WC28TZ WORLD CLASS SPOTTING SCOPE 50mm objective, 12-36x zoom. Field at 100 yds. World Class. 13-3.8 ft. Comes with tripod and case.
Price: **$220.00**

TASCO CW5001 COMPACT ZOOM 50mm objective, 12x-36x zoom. Field at 100 yds. 16 ft., 9 in. Includes photo adapter tube, tripod with panhead lever, case.
Price: **$280.00**

TASCO 3700WP WATERPROOF SPOTTER 50mm objective, 18x-36x zoom. Field at 100 yds. 12ft., 6 in. to 7 ft., 9 in. Black rubber armored. Comes with tripod, hard case.
Price: **$288.60**

TASCO 3700, 3701 SPOTTING SCOPE 50mm objective. 18x-36x zoom. Field at 100 yds. 12 ft., 6 in. to 7 ft., 9 in. Black rubber armored.
Price: Model 3700 (black, with tripod, case) **$237.00**
Price: Model 3701 (as above, brown camo) **$237.00**

TASCO 21EB ZOOM 50mm objective lens, 15x-45x zoom. Field at 100 yds. 11 ft. (15x). Weight 22 oz.; length 18.3" overall. Comes with panhead lever tripod.
Price: **$119.00**

TASCO 22EB ZOOM 60mm objective lens, 20x-60x zoom. Field at 100 yds. 7 ft., 2 in. (20x). Weight 28 oz.; length 21.5" overall. Comes with micro-adjustable tripod.
Price: **$183.00**

UNERTL "FORTY-FIVE" 54mm objective. 20x (single fixed power). Field at 100 yds. 10',10"; eye relief 1"; focusing range infinity to 33 ft. Weight about 32 oz.; overall length 15 3/4". With lens covers.
Price: With mono-layer magnesium coating **$810.00**

UNERTL STRAIGHT PRISMATIC 63.5mm objective, 24x. Field at 100 yds., 7 ft. Relative brightness, 6.96. Eye relief 1/2". Weight 40 oz.; length closed 19". Push-pull and screw-focus eyepiece. 16x and 32x eyepieces **$125.00** each.
Price: **$786.00**

UNERTL 20x STRAIGHT PRISMATIC 54mm objective, 20x. Field at 100 yds. 8.5 ft. Relative brightness 6.1. Eye relief 1/2". Weight 36 oz.; length closed 13 1/2". Complete with lens covers.
Price: **$695.00**

UNERTL TEAM SCOPE 100mm objective. 15x, 24x, 32x eyepieces. Field at 100 yds. 13 to 7.5 ft. Relative brightness, 39.06 to 9.79. Eye relief 2" to 1 1/2". Weight 13 lbs.; length 29 7/8" overall. Metal tripod, yoke and wood carrying case furnished (total weight 80 lbs.).
Price: **$3,624.50**

WEAVER 20x50 50mm objective. Field of view 124 ft. at 100 yds. Eye relief .85"; weighs 21 oz.; overall length 10". Waterproof, armored.
Price: **$249.99**

WEAVER 15-40x60 ZOOM 60mm objective. 15x-40x zoom. Field at 100 yds. 119 ft. (15x), 66 ft. (60x). Overall length 12.5", weighs 26 oz. Waterproof, armored.
Price: **$399.99**

CHOKES & BRAKES

Briley Screw-In Chokes

Installation of these choke tubes requires that all traces of the original choking be removed, the barrel threaded internally with square threads and then the tubes are custom fitted to the specific barrel diameter. The tubes are thin and, therefore, made of stainless steel. Cost of installation for single-barrel guns (pumps, autos), lead shot, 12-gauge, **$149.00**, 20-gauge **$159.00**; steel shot **$179.00** and **$189.00**, all with three chokes; un-single target guns run **$219.00**; over/unders and side-by-sides, lead shot, 12-gauge, **$369.00**, 20-gauge **$389.00**; steel shot **$469.00** and **$489.00**, all with five chokes. For 10-gauge auto or pump with two steel shot chokes, **$189.00**; over/unders, side-by-sides with three steel shot chokes, **$349.00**. For 16-gauge auto or pump, three lead shot chokes, **$179.00**; over/unders, side-by-sides with five lead shot chokes, **$449.00**. The 28 and 410-bore run **$179.00** for autos and pumps with three lead shot chokes, **$449.00** for over/unders and side-by-sides with five lead shot chokes.

Cutts Compensator

The Cutts Compensator is one of the oldest variable choke devices available. Manufactured by Lyman Gunsight Corporation, it is available with a steel body. A series of vents allows gas to escape upward and downward. For the 12-ga. Comp body, six fixed-choke tubes are available: the Spreader—popular with Skeet shooters; Improved Cylinder; Modified; Full; Superfull, and Magnum Full. Full, Modified and Spreader tubes are available for 12 or 20. Cutts Compensator, complete with wrench, adaptor and any single tube **$87.50**. All single choke tubes **$26.00** each. No factory installation available.

Dayson Automatic Brake System

This system fits most single barrel shotguns threaded for choke tubes, and cuts away 30 grooves on the exterior of a standard one-piece wad as it exits the muzzle. This slows the wad, allowing shot and wad to separate faster, reducing shot distortion and tightening patterns. The A.B.S. Choke Tube is claimed to reduce recoil by about 25 percent, and with the Muzzle Brake up to 60 percent. Ventilated Choke Tubes available from .685" to .725", in .005" increments. Model I Ventilated Choke Tube for use with A.B.S. Muzzle Brake, **$49.95**; for use without Muzzle Brake, **$52.95**; A.B.S. Muzzle Brake, from **$69.95**. Contact Dayson Arms for more data.

Gentry Quiet Muzzle Brake

Developed by gunmaker David Gentry, the "Quiet Muzzle Brake" is said to reduce recoil by up to 85 percent with no loss of accuracy or velocity. There is no increase in noise level because the noise and gases are directed away from the shooter. The barrel is threaded for installation and the unit is blued to match the barrel finish. Price, installed, is **$150.00**. Add **$15.00** for stainless steel, **$45.00** for knurled cap to protect threads. Shipping extra.

JP Muzzle Brake

JP Muzzle Brake

Designed for single shot handguns, AR-15, Ruger Mini-14, Ruger Mini Thirty and other sporting rifles, the JP Muzzle Brake redirects high pressure gases against a large frontal surface which applies forward thrust to the gun. All gases are directed up, rearward and to the sides. Priced at **$79.95** (AR-15 or sporting rifles), **$89.95** (bull barrel and SKS, AK models), **$89.95** (Ruger Minis), Dual Chamber model **$79.95**. From JP Enterprises, Inc.

KDF Slim Line Muzzle Brake

This threaded muzzle brake has 30 pressure ports that direct combustion gases in all directions to reduce felt recoil up to a claimed 80 percent without affecting accuracy or ballistics. It is said to reduce felt recoil of a 30-06 to that of a 243. Price, installed, is **$179.00**. From KDF, Inc.

Laseraim

Simple, no-gunsmithing compensator reduces felt recoil and muzzle flip by up to 30 percent. Machined from single piece of Stainless Steel (Beretta/Taurus model made of aircraft aluminum). In black and polished finish. For Colt Government/Commander and Beretta/Taurus full-size pistols. Weighs 1 ounce. **$49.00**. From Laseraim Arms Inc.

Mag-Na-Port

Electrical Discharge Machining works on any firearm except those having non-conductive shrouded barrels. EDM is a metal erosion technique using carbon electrodes that control the area to be processed. The Mag-Na-Port venting process utilizes small trapezoidal openings to direct powder gases upward and outward to reduce recoil. No effect is had on bluing or nickeling outside the Mag-Na-Port area so no refinishing is needed. Rifle-style porting on single shot or large caliber handguns with barrels 7 1/2" or longer is **$115.00**; Dual Trapezoidal porting on most handguns with minimum barrel length of 3", **$115.00**; standard revolver porting, **$88.50**; porting through the slide and barrel for semi-autos, **$129.50**; traditional rifle porting, **$135.00**. Prices do not include shipping, handling and insurance. From Mag-Na-Port International.

Mag-Na-Brake

A screw-on brake under 2" long with progressive integrated exhaust chambers to neutralize expanding gases. Gases dissipate with an opposite twist to prevent the brake from unscrewing, and with a 5-degree forward angle to minimize sound pressure level. Available in blue, satin blue, bright or satin stainless. Standard and Light Contour installation cost **$195.00** for bolt-action rifles, many single action and single shot handguns. A knurled thread protector supplied at extra cost. Also available in Varmint style with exhaust chambers covering 220 degrees for prone-position shooters. From Mag-Na-Port International.

Poly-Choke

Marble Arms Corp., manufacturer of the Poly-Choke adjustable shotgun choke, now offers two models in 12-, 16-, 20-, and 28-gauge—the Ventilated and Standard style chokes. Each provides nine choke settings including Xtra-Full and Slug. The Ventilated model reduces 20 percent of a shotgun's recoil, the company claims, and is priced at **$135.00**. The Standard Model is **$125.00**. Postage not included. Contact Marble Arms for more data.

Pro-port

A compound ellipsoid muzzle venting process similar to Mag-Na-Porting, only exclusively applied to shotguns. Like Mag-Na-Porting, this system reduces felt recoil, muzzle jump, and shooter fatigue. Very helpful for trap doubles shooters. Pro-Port is a patented process and installation is available in both the U.S. and Canada. Cost for the Pro-Port process is **$139.00** for over/unders (both barrels); **$110.00** for only the top or bottom barrel; and **$88.50** for single-barrel shotguns. Optional pigeon porting costs **$25.00** extra per barrel. Prices do not include shipping and handling. From Pro-port Ltd.

Que Industries Adjustable Muzzle Brake

The Que Brake allows for fine-tuning of a rifle's accuracy by rotating the brake to one of 100 indexed stops. Mounts in minutes without barrel modification with heat-activated tensioning ring. The slotted exhaust ports reduce recoil by venting gases sideways, away from rifle. **$189.50**. From Que Industries.

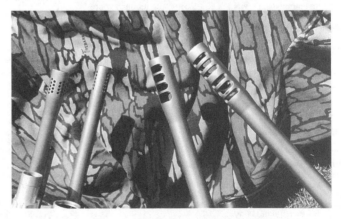

SSK Arrestor muzzle brakes

SSK Arrestor Brake

This is a true muzzle brake with an expansion chamber. It takes up about 1" of barrel and reduces velocity accordingly. Some Arrestors are added to a barrel, increasing its length. Said to reduce the felt recoil of a 458 to that approaching a 30-06. Can be set up to give zero muzzle rise in any caliber, and can be added to most guns. For handgun or rifle. Prices start at **$95.00**. Contact SSK Industries for full data.

PERIODICAL PUBLICATIONS

AAFTA News (M)
5911 Cherokee Ave., Tampa, FL 33604. Official newsletter of the American Airgun Field Target Assn.

Action Pursuit Games Magazine (M)
CFW Enterprises, Inc., 4201 W. Vanowen Pl., Burbank, CA 91505 818-845-2656. $4.99 single copy U.S., $5.50 Canada. Editor: Dan Reeves. World's leading magazine of paintball sports.

Air Gunner Magazine
4 The Courtyard, Denmark St., Wokingham, Berkshire RG11 2AZ, England/011-44-734-771677. $U.S. $44 for 1 yr. Leading monthly airgun magazine in U.K.

Airgun Ads
Box 33, Hamilton, MT 59840/406-363-3805; Fax: 406-363-4117. $35 1 yr. (for first mailing; $20 for second mailing; $35 for Canada and foreign orders.) Monthly tabloid with extensive For Sale and Wanted airgun listings.

The Airgun Letter
Gapp, Inc., 4614 Woodland Rd., Ellicott City, MD 21042-6329/410-730-5496; Fax: 410-730-9544; e-mail: staff@airgnltr.net; http://www.airgunletter.com. $21 U.S., $24 Canada, $27 Mexico and $33 other foreign orders, 1 yr. Monthly newsletter for airgun users and collectors.

Airgun World
4 The Courtyard, Denmark St., Wokingham, Berkshire RG40 2AZ, England/011-44-734-771677. Call for subscription rates. Oldest monthly airgun magazine in the U.K., now a sister publication to Air Gunner.

Alaska Magazine
Morris Communications, 735 Broad Street, Augusta, GA 30901/706-722-6060. Hunting, Fishing and Life on the Last Frontier articles of Alaska and western Canada.

American Firearms Industry
Nat'l. Assn. of Federally Licensed Firearms Dealers, 2455 E. Sunrise Blvd., Suite 916, Ft. Lauderdale, FL 33304. $35.00 yr. For firearms retailers, distributors and manufacturers.

American Guardian
NRA, 11250 Waples Mill Rd., Fairfax, VA 22030. Publications division. $15.00 1 yr. Magazine features personal protection; home-self-defense; family recreation shooting; women's issues; etc.

American Gunsmith
Belvoir Publications, Inc., 75 Holly Hill Lane, Greenwich, CT 06836-2626/203-661-6111. $49.00 (12 issues). Technical journal of firearms repair and maintenance.

American Handgunner*
Publisher's Development Corp., 591 Camino de la Reina, Suite 200, San Diego, CA 92108/800-537-3006 $16.95 yr. Articles for handgun enthusiasts, competitors, police and hunters.

American Hunter (M)
National Rifle Assn., 11250 Waples Mill Rd., Fairfax, VA 22030 (Same address for both.) Publications Div. $35.00 yr. Wide scope of hunting articles.

American Rifleman (M)
National Rifle Assn., 11250 Waples Mill Rd., Fairfax, VA 22030 (Same address for both.) Publications Div. $35.00 yr. Firearms articles of all kinds.

American Survival Guide
McMullen Angus Publishing, Inc., 774 S. Placentia Ave., Placentia, CA 92670-6846. 12 issues $19.95/714-572-2255; FAX: 714-572-1864.

Armes & Tir*
c/o FABECO, 38, rue de Trévise 75009 Paris, France. Articles for hunters, collectors, and shooters. French text.

Arms Collecting (Q)
Museum Restoration Service, P.O. Box 70, Alexandria Bay, NY 13607-0070. $22.00 yr.; $62.00 3 yrs.; $112.00 5 yrs.

Australian Shooter (formerly Australian Shooters Journal)
Sporting Shooters' Assn. of Australia, Inc., P.O. Box 2066, Kent Town SA 5071, Australia. $60.00 yr. locally; $65.00 yr. overseas surface mail. Hunting and shooting articles.

The Backwoodsman Magazine
P.O. Box 627, Westcliffe, CO 81252. $16.00 for 6 issues per yr.; $30.00 for 2 yrs.; sample copy $2.75. Subjects include muzzle-loading, woodslore, primitive survival, trapping, homesteading, blackpowder cartridge guns, 19th century how-to.

Black Powder Cartridge News (Q)
SPG, Inc., P.O. Box 761, Livingston, MT 59047/Phone/Fax: 406-222-8416. $17 yr. (4 issues) ($6 extra 1st class mailing). For the blackpowder cartridge enthusiast.

Blackpowder Hunting (M)
Intl. Blackpowder Hunting Assn., P.O. Box 1180Z, Glenrock, WY 82637/307-436-9817. $20.00 1 yr., $36.00 2 yrs. How-to and where-to features by experts on hunting; shooting; ballistics; traditional and modern blackpowder rifles, shotguns, pistols and cartridges.

Black Powder Times
P.O. Box 234, Lake Stevens, WA 98258. $20.00 yr.; add $5 per year for Canada, $10 per year other foreign. Tabloid newspaper for blackpowder activities; test reports.

Blade Magazine
Krause Publications, 700 East State St., Iola, WI 54990-0001. $25.98 for 12 issues. Foreign price (including Canada-Mexico) $50.00. A magazine for all enthusiasts of handmade, factory and antique knives.

Caliber
GFI-Verlag, Theodor-Heuss Ring 62, 50668 K"ln, Germany. For hunters, target shooters and reloaders.

The Caller (Q) (M)
National Wild Turkey Federation, P.O. Box 530, Edgefield, SC 29824. Tabloid newspaper for members; 4 issues per yr. (membership fee $25.00)

Cartridge Journal (M)
Robert Mellichamp, 907 Shirkmere, Houston, TX 77008/713-869-0558. Dues $12 for U.S. and Canadian members (includes the newsletter); 6 issues.

The Cast Bullet*(M)**
Official journal of The Cast Bullet Assn. Director of Membership, 203 E. 2nd St., Muscatine, IA 52761. Annual membership dues $14, includes 6 issues.

COLTELLI, che Passione (Q)
Casella postale N.519, 20101 Milano, Italy/Fax:02-48402857. $15 1 yr.; $27 2 yrs. Covers all types of knives—collecting, combat, historical. Italian text.

Combat Handguns*
Harris Publications, Inc., 1115 Broadway, New York, NY 10010.

Deer & Deer Hunting Magazine
Krause Publications, 700 E. State St., Iola, WI 54990-0001. $19.95 yr. (9 issues). For the serious deer hunter. Website: www.krause.com

The Derringer Peanut (M)
The National Association of Derringer Collectors, P.O. Box 20572, San Jose, CA 95160. A newsletter dedicated to developing the best derringer information. Write for details.

Deutsches Waffen Journal
Journal-Verlag Schwend GmbH, Postfach 100340, D-74503 Schwäbisch Hall, Germany/0791-404-500; FAX:0791-404-505 and 404-424. DM102 p. yr. (interior); DM125.30 (abroad), postage included. Antique and modern arms and equipment. German text.

Double Gun Journal
P.O. Box 550, East Jordan, MI 49727/800-447-1658. $35 for 4 issues.

Ducks Unlimited, Inc. (M)
1 Waterfowl Way, Memphis, TN 38120

The Engraver (M) (Q)
P.O. Box 4365, Estes Park, CO 80517/970-586-2388; Fax: 970-586-0394. Mike Dubber, editor. The journal of firearms engraving.

The Field
King's Reach Tower, Stamford St., London SE1 9LS England. £36.40 U.K. 1 yr.; 49.90 (overseas, surface mail) yr.; £82.00 (overseas, air mail) yr. Hunting and shooting articles, and all country sports.

Field & Stream
Time4 Media, Two Park Ave., New York, NY 10016/212-779-5000. Monthly shooting column. Articles on hunting and fishing.

Field Tests
Belvoir Publications, Inc., 75 Holly Hill Lane; P.O. Box 2626, Greenwich, CT 06836-2626/203-661-6111; 800-829-3361 (subscription line). U.S. & Canada $29 1 yr., $58 2 yrs.; all other countries $45 1 yr., $90 2 yrs. (air).

Fur-Fish-Game
A.R. Harding Pub. Co., 2878 E. Main St., Columbus, OH 43209. $15.95 yr. Practical guidance regarding trapping, fishing and hunting.

The Gottlieb-Tartaro Report
Second Amendment Foundation, James Madison Bldg., 12500 NE 10th Pl., Bellevue, WA 98005/206-454-7012;Fax:206-451-3959. $30 for 12 issues. An insiders guide for gun owners.

Gray's Sporting Journal
Gray's Sporting Journal, P.O. Box 1207, Augusta, GA 30903. $36.95 per yr. for 6 issues. Hunting and fishing journals. Expeditions and Guides Book (Annual Travel Guide).

Gun List†
700 E. State St., Iola, WI 54990. $36.98 yr. (26 issues); $65.98 2 yrs. (52 issues). Indexed market publication for firearms collectors and active shooters; guns, supplies and services. Website: www.krause.com

Gun News Digest (Q)
Second Amendment Fdn., P.O. Box 488, Station C, Buffalo, NY 14209/716-885-6408;Fax:716-884-4471. $10 U.S.; $20 foreign.

The Gun Report
World Wide Gun Report, Inc., Box 38, Aledo, IL 61231-0038. $33.00 yr. For the antique and collectable gun dealer and collector.

Gunmaker (M) (Q)
ACGG, P.O. Box 812, Burlington, IA 52601-0812. The journal of custom gunmaking.

The Gunrunner
Div. of Kexco Publ. Co. Ltd., Box 565G, Lethbridge, Alb., Canada T1J 3Z4. $23.00 yr., sample $2.00. Monthly newspaper, listing everything from antiques to artillery.

Gun Show Calendar (Q)
700 E. State St., Iola, WI 54990. $14.95 yr. (4 issues). Gun shows listed; chronologically and by state. Website: www.krause.com

Gun Tests
11 Commerce Blvd., Palm Coast, FL 32142. The consumer resource for the serious shooter. Write for information.

Gun Trade News
Bruce Publishing Ltd., P.O. Box 82, Wantage, Ozon OX12 7A8, England/44-1-235-771770; Fax: 44-1-235-771848. Britain's only "trade only" magazine exclusive to the gun trade.

Gun Week†
Second Amendment Foundation, P.O. Box 488, Station C, Buffalo, NY 14209. $35.00 yr. U.S. and possessions; $45.00 yr. other countries. Tabloid paper on guns, hunting, shooting and collecting (36 issues).

Gun World
Y-Visionary Publishing, LP 265 South Anita Drive, Ste. 120, Orange, CA 92868. $21.97 yr.; $34.97 2 yrs. For the hunting, reloading and shooting enthusiast.

Guns & Ammo
Primedia, 6420 Wilshire Blvd., Los Angeles, CA 90048/213-782-2780. $23.94 yr. Guns, shooting, and technical articles.

Guns
Publishers Development Corporation, P.O. Box 85201, San Diego, CA 92138/800-537-3006. $19.95 yr. In-depth articles on a wide range of guns, shooting equipment and related accessories for gun collectors, hunters and shooters.

Guns Review
Ravenhill Publishing Co. Ltd., Box 35, Standard House, Bonhill St., London EC 2A 4DA, England. £20.00 sterling (approx. U.S. $38 USA & Canada) yr. For collectors and shooters.

H.A.C.S. Newsletter (M)
Harry Moon, Pres., P.O. Box 50117, South Slope RPO, Burnaby BC, V5J 5G3, Canada/604-438-0950; Fax:604-277-3646. $25 p. yr. U.S. and Canada. Official newsletter of The Historical Arms Collectors of B.C. (Canada).

Handgunner*
Richard A.J. Munday, Seychelles house, Brightlingsen, Essex CO7 ONN, England/012063-305201. £18.00 (sterling).

Handguns
Primedia, 6420 Wilshire Blvd., Los Angeles, CA 90048/323-782-2868. $23/94 yr. For the handgunning and shooting enthusiast.

Handloader*
Wolfe Publishing Co., 2626 Stearman Road, Ste. A, Prescott, AZ 86301/520-445-7810;Fax:520-778-5124. $22.00 yr. The journal of ammunition reloading.

INSIGHTS*
NRA, 11250 Waples Mill Rd., Fairfax, VA 22030. Editor, John E. Robbins. $15.00 yr., which includes NRA junior membership; $10.00 for adult subscriptions (12 issues). Plenty of details for the young hunter and target shooter; emphasizes gun safety, marksmanship training, hunting skills.

International Arms & Militaria Collector (Q)
Arms & Militaria Press, P.O. Box 80, Labrador, Qld. 4215, Australia. A$39.50 yr. (U.S. & Canada), 2 yrs. A$77.50; A$37.50 (others), 1 yr., 2 yrs. $73.50 all air express mail; surface mail is less. Editor: Ian D. Skennerton.

International Shooting Sport*/UIT Journal
International Shooting Union (UIT), Bavariaring 21, D-80336 Munich, Germany. Europe: (Deutsche Mark) DM44.00 yr., 2 yrs. DM83.00; outside Europe: DM50.00 yr., 2 yrs. DM95.00 (air mail postage included.) For international sport shooting.

Internationales Waffen-Magazin
Habegger-Verlag Zürich, Postfach 9230, CH-8036 Zürich, Switzerland. SF 105.00 (approx. U.S. $73.00) surface mail for 10 issues. Modern and antique arms, self-defense. German text; English summary of contents.

The Journal of the Arms & Armour Society (M)
A. Dove, P.O. Box 10232, London, SW19 2ZD England. £15.00 surface mail; £20.00 airmail sterling only yr. Articles for the historian and collector.

Journal of the Historical Breechloading Smallarms Assn.
Published annually. P.O. Box 12778, London, SE1 6XB, England. £21.00 yr. Articles for the collector plus mailings of short articles on specific arms, reprints, newsletters, etc.

Knife World
Knife World Publications, P.O. Box 3395, Knoxville, TN 37927. $15.00 yr.; $25.00 2 yrs. Published monthly for knife enthusiasts and collectors. Articles on custom and factory knives; other knife-related interests, monthly column on knife identification, military knives.

Man At Arms*
P.O. Box 460, Lincoln, RI 02865. $27.00 yr., $52.00 2 yrs. plus $8.00 for foreign subscribers. The N.R.A. magazine of arms collecting-investing, with excellent articles for the collector of antique arms and militaria.

The Mannlicher Collector (Q)(M)
Mannlicher Collectors Assn., Inc., P.O. Box 7144, Salem Oregon 97303. $20/ yr. subscription included in membership.

---

*Published bi-monthly
† Published weekly
‡Published three times per month. All others are published monthly.

M=Membership requirements; write for details.
Q=Published Quarterly.

REFERENCE

Periodical Publications

MAN/MAGNUM
S.A. Man (Pty) Ltd., P.O. Box 35204, Northway, Durban 4065, Republic of South Africa. SA Rand 200.00 for 12 issues. Africa's only publication on hunting, shooting, firearms, bushcraft, knives, etc.

The Marlin Collector (M)
R.W. Paterson, 407 Lincoln Bldg., 44 Main St., Champaign, IL 61820.

Muzzle Blasts (M)
National Muzzle Loading Rifle Assn., P.O. Box 67, Friendship, IN 47021/812-667-5131. $35.00 yr. annual membership. For the blackpowder shooter.

Muzzleloader Magazine*
Scurlock Publishing Co., Inc., Dept. Gun, Route 5, Box 347-M, Texarkana, TX 75501. $18.00 U.S.; $22.50 U.S./yr. for foreign subscribers. The publication for blackpowder shooters.

National Defense (M)*
American Defense Preparedness Assn., Two Colonial Place, Suite 400, 2101 Wilson Blvd., Arlington, VA 22201-3061/703-522-1820; FAX: 703-522-1885. $35.00 yr. Articles on both military and civil defense field, including weapons, materials technology, management.

National Knife Magazine (M)
Natl. Knife Coll. Assn., 7201 Shallowford Rd., P.O. Box 21070, Chattanooga, TN 37424-0070. Membership $35 yr.; $65.00 International yr.

National Rifle Assn. Journal (British) (Q)
Natl. Rifle Assn. (BR.), Bisley Camp, Brookwood, Woking, Surrey, England. GU24, OPB. £24.00 Sterling including postage.

National Wildlife*
Natl. Wildlife Fed., 1400 16th St. NW, Washington, DC 20036, $16.00 yr. (6 issues); International Wildlife, 6 issues, $16.00 yr. Both, $22.00 yr., includes all membership benefits. Write attn.: Membership Services Dept., for more information.

New Zealand GUNS*
Waitekauri Publishing, P.O. 45, Waikino 3060, New Zealand. $NZ90.00 (6 issues) yr. Covers the hunting and firearms scene in New Zealand.

New Zealand Wildlife (Q)
New Zealand Deerstalkers Assoc., Inc., P.O. Box 6514, Wellington, N.Z. $30.00 (N.Z.). Hunting, shooting and firearms/game research articles.

North American Hunter* (M)
P.O. Box 3401, Minnetonka, MN 55343/612-936-9333; e-mail: huntingclub@pclink.com. $18.00 yr. (7 issues). Articles on all types of North American hunting.

Outdoor Life
Time4 Media, Two Park Ave., New York, NY 10016. $16.95/yr. Extensive coverage of hunting and shooting. Shooting column by Jim Carmichel.

La Passion des Courteaux (Q)
Phenix Editions, 25 rue Mademoiselle, 75015 Paris, France. French text.

Paintball Games International Magazine
Aceville Publications, Castle House, 97 High St., Colchester, Essex, England CO1 1TH/011-44-206-564840. Write for subscription rates. Leading magazine in the U.K. covering competitive paintball activities.

Paintball News
PBN Publishing, P.O. Box 1608, 24 Henniker St., Hillsboro, NH 03244/603-464-6080. $35 U.S. 1 yr. Bi-weekly. Newspaper covering the sport of paintball, new product reviews and industry features.

Paintball Sports (Q)
Paintball Publications, Inc., 540 Main St., Mount Kisco, NY 10549/941-241-7400. $24.75 U.S. 1 yr.; $32.75 foreign. Covering the competitive paintball scene.

Performance Shooter
Belvoir Publications, Inc., 75 Holly Hill Lane, Greenwich, CT 06836-2626/203-661-6111. $45.00 yr. (12 issues). Techniques and technology for improved rifle and pistol accuracy.

Petersen's HUNTING Magazine
Primedia, 6420 Wilshire Blvd., Los Angeles, CA 90048. $19.94 yr.; Canada $29.34 yr.; foreign countries $29.94 yr. Hunting articles for all game; test reports.

P.I. Magazine
America's Private Investigation Journal, 755 Bronx Dr., Toledo, OH 43609. Chuck Klein, firearms editor with column about handguns.

Pirsch
BLV Verlagsgesellschaft mbH, Postfach 400320, 80703 Munich, Germany/089-12704-0;Fax:089-12705-354. German text.

Point Blank
Citizens Committee for the Right to Keep and Bear Arms (sent to contributors), Liberty Park, 12500 NE 10th Pl., Bellevue, WA 98005

POINTBLANK (M)
Natl. Firearms Assn., Box 4384 Stn. C, Calgary, AB T2T 5N2, Canada. Official publication of the NFA.

The Police Marksman*
6000 E. Shirley Lane, Montgomery, AL 36117. $17.95 yr. For law enforcement personnel.

Police Times (M)
3801 Biscayne Blvd., Miami, FL 33137/305-573-0070.

Popular Mechanics
Hearst Corp., 224 W. 57th St., New York, NY 10019. Firearms, camping, outdoor oriented articles.

Precision Shooting
Precision Shooting, Inc., 222 McKee St., Manchester, CT 06040. $37.00 yr. U.S. Journal of the International Benchrest Shooters, and target shooting in general. Also considerable coverage of varmint shooting, as well as big bore, small bore, schuetzen, lead bullet, wildcats and precision reloading.

Rifle*
Wolfe Publishing Co., 2626 Stearman Road, Ste. A, Prescott, AZ 86301/520-445-7810; Fax: 520-778-5124. $19.00 yr. The sporting firearms journal.

Rifle's Hunting Annual
Wolfe Publishing Co., 2626 Stearman Road, Ste. A, Prescott, AZ 86301/520-445-7810; Fax: 520-778-5124. $4.99 Annual. Dedicated to the finest pursuit of the hunt.

Rod & Rifle Magazine
Lithographic Serv. Ltd., P.O. Box 38-138, Wellington, New Zealand. $50.00 yr. (6 issues). Hunting, shooting and fishing articles.

Safari* (M)
Safari Magazine, 4800 W. Gates Pass Rd., Tucson, AZ 85745/602-620-1220. $55.00 (6 times). The journal of big game hunting, published by Safari Club International. Also publish Safari Times, a monthly newspaper, included in price of $55.00 national membership.

Second Amendment Reporter
Second Amendment Foundation, James Madison Bldg., 12500 NE 10th Pl., Bellevue, WA 98005. $15.00 yr. (non-contributors).

Shoot! Magazine*
Shoot! Magazine Corp., 1770 West State Stret PMB 340, Boise ID 83702/208-368-9920; Fax: 208-338-8428. Website: www.shootmagazine.com $32.95 (6 times/yr.). Articles of interest to the cowboy action shooter, or others interested the Western-era firearms and ammunition.

Shooter's News
23146 Lorain Rd., Box 349, North Olmsted, OH 44070/216-979-5258;Fax:216-979-5259. $29 U.S. 1 yr., $54 2 yrs.; $52 foreign surface. A journal dedicated to precision riflery.

Shooting Industry
Publisher's Dev. Corp., 591 Camino de la Reina, Suite 200, San Diego, CA 92108. $50.00 yr. To the trade. $25.00.

Shooting Sports USA
National Rifle Assn. of America, 11250 Waples Mill Road, Fairfax, VA 22030. Annual subscriptions for NRA members are $5 for classified shooters and $10 for non-classified shooters. Non-NRA member subscriptions are $15. Covering events, techniques and personalities in competitive shooting.

Shooting Sportsman*
P.O. Box 11282, Des Moines, IA 50340/800-666-4955 (for subscriptions). Editorial: P.O. Box 1357, Camden, ME 04843. $19.95 for six issues. The magazine of wingshooting and fine guns.

The Shooting Times & Country Magazine (England)†
IPC Magazines Ltd., King's Reach Tower, Stamford St, 1 London SE1 9LS, England/0171-261-6180;Fax:0171-261-7179. £65 (approx. $98.00) yr.; £79 yr. overseas (52 issues). Game shooting, wild fowling, hunting, game fishing and firearms articles. Britain's best selling field sports magazine.

Shooting Times
Primedia, 2 News Plaza, P.O. Box 1790, Peoria, IL 61656/309-682-6626. $16.97 yr. Guns, shooting, reloading; articles on every gun activity.

The Shotgun News‡
Primedia, 2 News Plaza, P.O. Box 1790, Peoria, IL 61656/800-495-8362. $28.95 yr.; foreign subscription call for rates. Sample copy $4.00. Gun ads of all kinds.

SHOT Business
National Shooting Sports Foundation, Flintlock Ridge Office Center, 11 Mile Hill Rd., Newtown, CT 06470-2359/203-426-1320; FAX: 203-426-1087. For the shooting, hunting and outdoor trade retailer.

Shotgun Sports
P.O. Box 6810, Auburn, CA 95604/916-889-2220; FAX:916-889-9106. $31.00 yr. Trapshooting how-to's, shotshell reloading, shotgun patterning, shotgun tests and evaluations, Sporting Clays action, waterfowl/upland hunting. Call 1-800-676-8920 for a free sample copy.

The Single Shot Exchange Magazine
PO Box 1055, York SC 29745/803-628-5326 phone/fax. $31.50/yr., monthly. Articles of interest to the blackpowder cartridge shooter and antique arms collector.

Single Shot Rifle Journal* (M)
Editor John Campbell, PO Box 595, Bloomfield Hills, MI 48303/248-458-8415. Email: jcampbell@chemistri.com Annual dues $35 for 6 issues. Journal of the American Single Shot Rifle Assn.

The Sixgunner (M)
Handgun Hunters International, P.O. Box 357, MAG, Bloomingdale, OH 43910

The Skeet Shooting Review
National Skeet Shooting Assn., 5931 Roft Rd., San Antonio, TX 78253. $20.00 yr. (Assn. membership includes mag.) Competition results, personality profiles of top Skeet shooters, how-to articles, technical, reloading information.

Soldier of Fortune
Subscription Dept., P.O. Box 348, Mt. Morris, IL 61054. $29.95 yr.; $39.95 Canada; $50.95 foreign.

Sporting Clays Magazine
Patch Communications, 5211 South Washington Ave., Titusville, FL 32780/407-268-5010; FAX: 407-267-7216. $29.95 yr. (12 issues). Official publication of the National Sporting Clays Association.

Sporting Goods Business
Miller Freeman, Inc., One Penn Plaza, 10th Fl., New York, NY 10119-0004. Trade journal.

Sporting Goods Dealer
Two Park Ave., New York, NY 10016. $100.00 yr. Sporting goods trade journal.

Sporting Gun
Bretton Court, Bretton, Peterborough PE3 8DZ, England. £27.00 (approx. U.S. $36.00), airmail £35.50 yr. For the game and clay enthusiasts.

The Squirrel Hunter
P.O. Box 368, Chireno, TX 75937. $14.00 yr. Articles about squirrel hunting.

Stott's Creek Calendar
Stott's Creek Printers, 2526 S 475 W, Morgantown, IN 46160/317-878-5489. 1 yr (3 issues) $11.50; 2 yrs. (6 issues) $20.00. Lists all gun shows everywhere in convenient calendar form; call for information.

Super Outdoors
2695 Aiken Road, Shelbyville, KY 40065/502-722-9463; 800-404-6064; Fax: 502-722-8093. Mark Edwards, publisher. Contact for details.

TACARMI
Via E. De Amicis, 25; 20123 Milano, Italy. $100.00 yr. approx. Antique and modern guns. (Italian text.)

Territorial Dispatch—1800s Historical Publication (M)
National Assn. of Buckskinners, 4701 Marion St., Suite 324, Livestock Exchange Bldg., Denver, CO 80216. Michael A. Nester & Barbara Wyckoff, editors. 303-297-9671.

Trap & Field
1000 Waterway Blvd., Indianapolis, IN 46202. $25.00 yr. Official publ. Amateur Trapshooting Assn. Scores, averages, trapshooting articles.

Turkey Call* (M)
Natl. Wild Turkey Federation, Inc., P.O. Box 530, Edgefield, SC 29824. $25.00 with membership (6 issues per yr.)

Turkey & Turkey Hunting*
Krause Publications, 700 E. State St., Iola, WI 54990-0001. $13.95 (6 issue p. yr.). Magazine with leading-edge articles on all aspects of wild turkey behavior, biology and the successful ways to hunt better with that info. Learn the proper techniques to calling, the right equipment, and more.

The Accurate Rifle
Precisions Shooting, Inc., 222 Mckee Street, Manchester CT 06040. $37 yr. Dedicated to the rifle accuracy enthusiast.

The U.S. Handgunner* (M)
U.S. Revolver Assn., 40 Larchmont Ave., Taunton, MA 02780. $10.00 yr. General handgun and competition articles. Bi-monthly sent to members.

U.S. Airgun Magazine
P.O. Box 2021, Benton, AR 72018/800-247-4867; Fax: 501-316-8549. 10 issues a yr. Cover the sport from hunting, 10-meter, field target and collecting. Write for details.

The Varmint Hunter Magazine (Q)
The Varmint Hunters Assn., Box 759, Pierre, SD 57501/800-528-4868. $24.00 yr.

Waffenmarkt-Intern
GFI-Verlag, Theodor-Heuss Ring 62, 50668 K"ln, Germany. Only for gunsmiths, licensed firearms dealers and their suppliers in Germany, Austria and Switzerland.

Wild Sheep (M) (Q)
Foundation for North American Wild Sheep, 720 Allen Ave., Cody, WY 82414. Website: http://iigi.com/os/non/fnaws/fnaws.htm; e-mail: fnaws@wyoming.com. Official journal of the foundation.

Wisconsin Outdoor Journal
Krause Publications, 700 E. State St., Iola, WI 54990-0001. $17.97 yr. (8 issues). For Wisconsin's avid hunters and fishermen, with features from all over that state with regional reports, legislative updates, etc. Website: www.krause.com

Women & Guns
P.O. Box 488, Sta. C, Buffalo, NY 14209. $24.00 yr. U.S.; $72.00 foreign (12 issues). Only magazine edited by and for women gun owners.

World War II*
Cowles History Group, 741 Miller Dr. SE, Suite D-2, Leesburg, VA 20175-8920. Annual subscriptions $19.95 U.S.; $25.95 Canada; 43.95 foreign. The title says it—WWII; good articles, ads, etc.

*Published bi-monthly
† Published weekly
‡Published three times per month. All others are published monthly.

M=Membership requirements; write for details.
Q=Published Quarterly.

REFERENCE

THE ARMS LIBRARY

FOR COLLECTOR ◆ HUNTER ◆ SHOOTER ◆ OUTDOORSMAN

IMPORTANT NOTICE TO BOOK BUYERS

Books listed here may be bought from Ray Riling Arms Books Co., 6844 Gorsten St., P.O. Box 18925, Philadelphia, PA 19119, Phone 215/438-2456; FAX: 215-438-5395. E-Mail: sales@rayrilingarms-books.com. Larry Riling is the researcher and compiler of "The Arms Library" and a seller of gun books for over 32 years. The Riling stock includes books classic and modern, many hard-to-find items, and many not obtainable elsewhere. These pages list a portion of the current stock. They offer prompt, complete service, with delayed shipments occurring only on out-of-print or out-of-stock books.

Visit our web site at **www.rayrilingarmsbooks.com** and order all of your favorite titles on line from our secure site.

NOTICE FOR ALL CUSTOMERS: Remittance in U.S. funds must accompany all orders. For your convenience we now accept VISA, Master-Card & American Express. For shipments in the U.S. add $7.00 for the 1st book and $2.00 for each additional book for postage and insurance. Mini-

mum order $10.00. International Orders add $13.00 for the 1st book and $5.00 for each additional book. All International orders are shipped at the buyer's risk unless an additional $5 for insurance is included. USPS does not offer insurance to all countries unless shipped Air-Mail please e-mail or call for pricing.

Payments in excess of order or for "Backorders" are credited or fully refunded at request. Books "As-Ordered" are not returnable except by permission and a handling charge on these of 10% or $2.00 per book which ever is greater is deducted from refund or credit. Only Pennsylvania customers must include current sales tax.

A full variety of arms books also available from Rutgers Book Center, 127 Raritan Ave., Highland Park, NJ 08904/908-545-4344; FAX: 908-545-6686 or I.D.S.A. Books, 1324 Stratford Drive, Piqua, OH 45356/937-773-4203; FAX: 937-778-1922.

BALLISTICS AND HANDLOADING

ABC's of Reloading, 6th Edition, by C. Rodney James and the editors of Handloader's Digest, DBI Books, a division of Krause Publications, Iola, WI, 1997. 288 pp., illus. Paper covers. $21.95
The definitive guide to every facet of cartridge and shotshell reloading.

Accurate Arms Loading Guide Number 2, by Accurate Arms. McEwen, TN: Accurate Arms Company, Inc., 2000. Paper Covers. $18.95
Includes new data on smokeless powders XMR4064 and XMP5744 as well as a special section on Cowboy Action Shooting. The new manual includes 50 new pages of data. An appendix includes nominal rotor charge weights, bullet diameters.

American Cartridge, The, by Charles Suydam, Borden Publishing Co. Alhambra, CA, 1986. 184 pp., illus. Softcover $24.95
An illustrated study of the rimfire cartridge in the United States.

Ammo and Ballistics, by Robert W. Forker, Safari Press, Inc., Huntington Beach, CA., 1999. 252 pp., illustrated. Paper covers. $18.95
Ballistic data on 125 calibers and 1,400 loads out to 500 yards.

Ammunition: Grenades and Projectile Munitions, by Ian V. Hogg, Stackpole Books, Mechanicsburg, PA, 1998. 144 pp., illus. $22.95
Concise guide to modern ammunition. International coverage with detailed specifications and illustrations.

Barnes Reloading Manual #2, Barnes Bullets, American Fork, UT, 1999. 668 pp., illus. $24.95
Features data and trajectories on the new weight X, XBT and Solids in calibers from .22 to .50 BMG.

Black Powder Guide, 2nd Edition, by George C. Nonte, Jr., Stoeger Publishing Co., So. Hackensack, NJ, 1991. 288 pp., illus. Paper covers. $14.95
How-to instructions for selection, repair and maintenance of muzzleloaders, making your own bullets, restoring and refinishing, shooting techniques.

Blackpowder Loading Manual, 3rd Edition, by Sam Fadala, DBI Books, a division of Krause Publications, Iola, WI, 1995. 368 pp., illus. Paper covers. $20.95
Revised and expanded edition of this landmark blackpowder loading book. Covers hundreds of loads for most of the popular blackpowder rifles, handguns and shotguns.

Cartridges of the World, 9th Edition, by Frank Barnes, Krause Publications, Iola, WI, 2000. 512 pp., illus. Paper covers. $27.95
Completely revised edition of the general purpose reference work for which collectors, police, scientists and laymen reach first for answers to cartridge identification questions.

Cartridge Reloading Tools of the Past, by R.H. Chamberlain and Tom Quigley, Tom Quigley, Castle Rock, WA, 1998. 167 pp., illustrated. Paper covers. $25.00
A detailed treatment of the extensive Winchester and Ideal line of handloading tools and bullet molds, plus Remington, Marlin, Ballard, Browning, Maynard, and many others.

Cast Bullets for the Black Powder Rifle, by Paul A. Matthews, Wolfe Publishing Co., Prescott, AZ, 1996. 133 pp., illus. Paper covers. $22.50
The tools and techniques used to make your cast bullet shooting a success.

Complete Blackpowder Handbook, 4th Edition, by Sam Fadala, DBI Books, a division of Krause Publications, Iola, WI, 2001. 400 pp., illus. Paper covers. $22.95
Expanded and completely rewritten edition of the definitive book on the subject of blackpowder.

Complete Reloading Manual, One Book / One Caliber. California: Load Books USA, 2000. $7.95 each
Containing unabridged information from U. S. Bullet and Powder Makers. With thousands of proven and tested loads, plus dozens of various bullet designs and different powders. Spiral bound. Available in all Calibers.

Designing and Forming Custom Cartridges for Rifles and Handguns, by Ken Howell. Precision Shooting, Manchester, CT. 2002. 600 pages, illus. $59.95
The classic work in its field, out of print for the last few years, and virtually unobtainable on the used book market, now returns in an exact reprint of the original. Some 600 pages, full size (8 1/2" x 11"), hard covers. Dozens of cartridge drawings never published anywhere before-dozens you've never heard of (guaranteed!). Precisely drawn to the dimensions specified by men who designed them, the factories that made them, and the authorities that set the standards. All

drawn to the same format and scale (1.5x)-for most, how to form them from brass. Some 450 pages of them, two to a page. Plus other practical information.

Early Loading Tools & Bullet Molds, Pioneer Press, 1988. 88 pages, illustrated. Softcover. $7.50

Handbook for Shooters and Reloaders, by P.O. Ackley, Salt Lake City, UT, 1998, (Vol. I), 567 pp., illus. Includes a separate exterior ballistics chart. $21.95 (Vol. II), a new printing with specific new material. 495 pp., illus. $20.95

Handgun Stopping Power; The Definitive Study, by Marshall & Sandow. Boulder, CO: Paladin Press, 1992. 240 pages. $45.00
Offers accurate predictions of the stopping power of specific loads in calibers from .380 Auto to .45 ACP, as well as such specialty rounds as the Glaser Safety Slug, Federal Hydra-Shok, MagSafe, etc. This is the definitive methodology for predicting the stopping power of handgun loads, the first to take into account what really happens when a bullet meets a man.

Handloader's Manual of Cartridge Conversions, 2nd Revised Edition by John J. Donnelly, Stoeger Publishing Co., So. Hackensack, NJ, 2002. Unpaginated. $39.95
From 14 Jones to 70-150 Winchester in English and American cartridges, and from 4.85 U.K. to 15.2x28R Gevelot in metric cartridges. Over 900 cartridges described in detail.

Hatcher's Notebook, by S. Julian Hatcher, Stackpole Books, Harrisburg, PA, 1992. 488 pp., illus. $39.95
A reference work for shooters, gunsmiths, ballisticians, historians, hunters and collectors.

History and Development of Small Arms Ammunition; Volume 2 Centerfire: Primitive, and Martial Long Arms. by George A. Hoyem. Oceanside, CA: Armory Publications, 1991. 303 pages, illustrated. $60.00
Covers the blackpowder military centerfire rifle, carbine, machine gun and volley gun ammunition used in 28 nations and dominions, together with the firearms that chambered them.

History and Development of Small Arms Ammunition; Volume 4, American Military Rifle Cartridges. Oceanside, CA: Armory Publications, 1998. 244pp., illus. $60.00
Carries on what Vol. 2 began with American military rifle cartridges. Now the sporting rifle cartridges are at last organized by their originators-235 individual case types designed by eight makers of single shot rifles and four of magazine rifles from .50-140 Winchester Express to .22-15-60 Stevens. plus experimentals from .70-150 to .32-80. American Civil War enthusiasts and European collectors will find over 150 primitives in Appendix A to add to those in Volumes One and Two. There are 16 pages in full color of 54 box labels for Sharps, Remington and Ballard cartridges. There are large photographs with descriptions of 15 Maynard, Sharps, Winchester, Browning, Freund, Remington-Hepburn, Farrow and other single shot rifles, some of them rare one of a kind specimens.

Hodgdon Powder Data Manual #27, Hodgdon Powder Co., Shawnee Mission, KS, 1999. 800 pp. $27.95
Reloading data for rifle and pistol loads.

Hodgdon Shotshell Data Manual, Hodgdon Powder Co., Shawnee Mission, KS, 1999. 208 pp. $19.95
Contains hundreds of loads for lead shot, buck shot, slugs, bismuth shot and steel shot plus articles on ballistics, patterning, special reloads and much more.

Home Guide to Cartridge Conversions, by Maj. George C. Nonte Jr., The Gun Room Press, Highland Park, NJ, 1976. 404 pp., illus. $24.95
Revised and updated version of Nonte's definitive work on the alteration of cartridge cases for use in guns for which they were not intended.

Hornady Handbook of Cartridge Reloading, 5th Edition, Vol. I and II, Edited by Larry Steadman, Hornady Mfg. Co., Grand Island, NE, 2000., illus. $49.95
2 Volumes; Volume 1, 773 pp.; Volume 2, 717 pp. New edition of this famous reloading handbook covers rifle and handgun reloading data and ballistic tables.
Latest loads, ballistic information, etc.

How-To's for the Black Powder Cartridge Rifle Shooter, by Paul A. Matthews, Wolfe Publishing Co., Prescott, AZ, 1995. 45 pp. Paper covers. $22.50
Covers lube recipes, good bore cleaners and over-powder wads. Tips include compressing powder charges, combating wind resistance, improving ignition and much more.

THE ARMS LIBRARY

Illustrated Reference of Cartridge Dimensions, The, edited by Dave Scovill, Wolfe Publishing Co., Prescott, AZ, 1994. 343 pp., illus. Paper covers. $19.00

A comprehensive volume with over 300 cartridges. Standard and metric dimensions have been taken from SAAMI drawings and/or fired cartridges.

Lee Modern Reloading, by Richard Lee, 350 pp. of charts and data and 85 illustrations. 512 pp. $24.95

Bullet casting, lubricating and author's formula for calculating proper charges for cast bullets. Includes virtually all current load data published by the powder suppliers. Exclusive source of volume measured loads.

Loading the Black Powder Rifle Cartridge, by Paul A Matthews, Wolfe Publishing Co., Prescott, AZ, 1993. 121 pp., illus. Paper covers. $22.50

Author Matthews brings the blackpowder cartridge shooter valuable information on the basics, including cartridge care, lubes and moulds, powder charges and developing and testing loads in his usual authoritative style.

Loading the Peacemaker—Colt's Model P, by Dave Scovill, Wolfe Publishing Co., Prescott, AZ, 1996. 227 pp., illus. $24.95

A comprehensive work about the history, maintenance and repair of the most famous revolver ever made, including the most extensive load data ever published.

Lyman Cast Bullet Handbook, 3rd Edition, edited by C. Kenneth Ramage, Lyman Publications, Middlefield, CT, 1980. 416 pp., illus. Paper covers. $19.95

Information on more than 5000 tested cast bullet loads and 19 pages of trajectory and wind drift tables for cast bullets.

Lyman Black Powder Handbook, 2nd Edition, edited by C. Kenneth Ramage, Lyman Products for Shooters, Middlefield, CT, 2000. 239 pp., illus. Paper covers. $19.95

Comprehensive load information for the modern blackpowder shooter.

Lyman Pistol & Revolver Handbook, 2nd Edition, edited by Thomas J. Griffin, Lyman Products Co., Middlefield, CT, 1996. 287 pp., illus. Paper covers. $18.95

The most up-to-date loading data available including the hottest new calibers, like 40 S&W, 9x21, 9mm Makarov, 9x25 Dillon and 454 Casull.

Lyman Reloading Handbook No. 48, edited by Edward A. Matunas, Lyman Publications, Middlefield, CT, 2003. 480 pp., illus. Paper covers. $24.95

A comprehensive reloading manual complete with "How to Reload" information. Expanded data section with all the newest rifle and pistol calibers.

Lyman Shotshell Handbook, 4th Edition, edited by Edward A. Matunas, Lyman Products Co., Middlefield, CT, 1996. 330 pp., illus. Paper covers. $24.95

Has 9000 loads, including slugs and buckshot, plus feature articles and a full color I.D. section.

Lyman's Guide to Big Game Cartridges & Rifles, by Edward Matunas, Lyman Publishing Corporation, Middlefield, CT, 1994. 287 pp., illus. Paper covers. $17.95

A selection guide to cartridges and rifles for big game—antelope to elephant.

Military Rifle and Machine Gun Cartridges, by Jean Huon, Alexandria, VA: Ironside International, 1995. 1st edition. 378 pages, over 1,000 photos. $34.95

Superb reference text.

Modern Combat Ammunition, by Duncan Long, Paladin Press, Boulder, CO, 1997, soft cover, photos, illus., 216 pp. $34.00

Now, Paladin's leading weapons author presents his exhaustive evaluation of the stopping power of modern rifle, pistol, shotgun and machine gun rounds based on actual case studies of shooting incidents. He looks at the hot new cartridges that promise to dominate well into the next century .40 S&W, 10mm auto, sub-sonic 9mm's - as well as the trusted standbys. Find out how to make your own exotic tracers, fléchette and sabot rounds, caseless ammo and fragmenting bullets.

Modern Exterior Ballistics, by Robert L. McCoy, Schiffer Publishing Co., Atglen, PA, 1999. 128 pp. $95.00

Advanced students of exterior ballistics and flight dynamics will find this comprehensive textbook on the subject a useful addition to their libraries.

Modern Reloading, by Richard Lee, Inland Press, 1996. 510 pp., illus. $24.98

The how-to's of rifle, pistol and shotgun reloading plus load data for rifle and pistol calibers.

Modern Reloading 2nd Edition, by Richard Lee, Inland Press, 2003. 623 pp., illus. $29.95

The how-to's of rifle, pistol and shotgun reloading plus load data for rifle and pistol calibers.

Modern Sporting Rifle Cartridges, by Wayne van Zwoll, Stoeger Publishing Co., Wayne, NJ, 1998. 310 pp., illustrated. Paper covers. $21.95

Illustrated with hundreds of photos and backed up by dozens of tables and schematic drawings, this four-part book tells the story of how rifle bullets and cartridges were developed and, in some cases, discarded.

Mr. Single Shot's Cartridge Handbook, by Frank de Haas, Mark de Haas, Orange City, IA, 1996. 116 pp., illus. Paper covers. $21.50

This book covers most of the cartridges, both commercial and wildcat, that the author has known and used.

Nosler Reloading Manual #5, edited by Gail Root, Nosler Bullets, Inc., Bend, OR, 2002. 516 pp., illus. $29.99

Combines information on their Ballistic Tip, Partition and Handgun bullets with traditional powders and new powders never before used, plus trajectory information from 100 to 500 yards.

Paper Jacket, The, by Paul Matthews, Wolfe Publishing Co., Prescott, AZ, 1991. Paper covers. $14.50

Up-to-date and accurate information about paper-patched bullets.

Reloading Tools, Sights and Telescopes for S/S Rifles, by Gerald O. Kelver, Brighton, CO, 1982. 163 pp., illus. Softcover. $15.00

A listing of most of the famous makers of reloading tools, sights and telescopes with a brief description of the products they manufactured.

Reloading for Shotgunners, 4th Edition, by Kurt D. Fackler and M.L. McPherson, DBI Books, a division of Krause Publications, Iola, WI, 1997. 320 pp., illus. Paper covers. $19.95

Expanded reloading tables with over 11,000 loads. Bushing charts for every major press and component maker. All new presentation on all aspects of shotshell reloading by two of the top experts in the field.

Rimfire Cartridge in the United States and Canada, The, Illustrated history of rimfire cartridges, manufacturers, and the products made from 1857-1984. by John L. Barber, Thomas Publications, Gettysburg, PA 2000. 1st edition. Profusely illustrated. 221 pages. $50.00

The author has written an encyclopedia of rimfire cartridges from the .22 to the massive 1.00 in. Gatling. Fourteen chapters, six appendices and an excellent bibliography make up a reference volume that all cartridge collectors should aquire.

Shotshells & Ballistics. Long Beach, CA: Safari Press, 2002. 275pp, photos. Softcover. $19.95

There is a bewildering array of commercially loaded shotgun shells for sale, from the .410 to the 10-gauge. In fact, there are more types of shells and shot sizes on the market now than ever before. With this overwhelming selection of shells available, here, finally, is a practical, reasonably priced book that makes sense of it all. It lists commercially available shotshell loads from the .410-bore to the 10-gauge, in all shot sizes available, different shot types (lead, steel, bismuth, tungsten, and others) so that the shooter or hunter can quickly find what will be best for the gun he has and the game or targets he wants to shoot. Each shotgun shell with each loading has its own table--over 1,600 tables!!--showing shot size; weight of shot; recoil; average number of pellets in the shell; manufacturer's order number; shell length and type of hull; type of wad; and whether the shot is buffered or not. In addition, each table contains data that details velocity (in 10-yard intervals from 0 to 70 yards); average pellet energy; and time of flight in seconds. This book includes complete listings and tables of every load made from the following manufacturers: Aguilla, Armscorp, ARMUSA, Baschieri & Pellagri, Bismuth Cartridge Company, Clever, Dionisi, Dynamit Nobel, Eley Hawk, Federal, Fiocchi, Hevi-Shot (now loaded exclusively by Remington), Kent, Lightfield, Nobel Sport, PMC, RIO, Remington, Rotweil, Sellier & Bellot, RST, RWS, and Winchester. In addition, this informative reference contains authoritative articles on the history and development of shotshells, the components and technical data that govern production of shotshells, what load and shot size to use for what type of game or target, and much more. Never before has so much information on shotshells and ballistics been placed in a single book. Accentuated with photos from the field and the range, this is a reference book unlike any other.

Sierra Reloading Manual, 5th Edition: Rifle and Handgun Manual of Reloading Data. Sedalia, MO: Sierra Bullets, 2003. 5th edition. Hardcover. $39.95

This 1152 page manual retains the popular three-ring binder format and has been modernized with new cartridge information, histories and reloading recommendations. New bullets, new cartridges and new powders make this manual a necessity in every reloader's library.

Sixgun Cartridges and Loads, by Elmer Keith, The Gun Room Press, Highland Park, NJ, 1986. 151 pp., illus. $24.95

A manual covering the selection, uses and loading of the most suitable and popular revolver cartridges. Originally published in 1936. Reprint.

Speer Reloading Manual No. 13, edited by members of the Speer research staff, Omark Industries, Lewiston, ID, 1999. 621 pp., illustrated. $24.95

With thirteen new sections containing the latest technical information and reloading trends for both novice and expert in this latest edition. More than 9,300 loads are listed, including new propellant powders from Accurate Arms, Alliant, Hodgdon and Vihtavuori.

Stopping Power: A Practical Analysis of the Latest Handgun Ammunition, by Marshall & Sanow. Boulder, CO: Paladin Press, 2002. 1st edition. 600+ photos, 360 pp. Softcover. $49.95

If you want to know how handgun ammunition will work against human targets in the future, you must look at how similar ammo has worked against human targets in the past. Stopping Power bases its conclusions on real-world facts from real-world gunfights. It provides the latest street results of actual police and civilian shootings in all of the major handgun calibers, from .22 LR to .45 ACP, plus more than 30 chapters of vital interest to all gun owners. The only thing worse than being involved in a gunfight is losing one. The info. in this book will help you choose the right bullets for your gun so you don't lose.

Street Stoppers, The Latest Handgun Stopping Power Street Results, by Marshall & Lanow**.** Boulder, CO, Paladin Press, 1996. 374 pages, illus. Softcover. $42.95

Street Stoppers is the long-awaited sequel to Handgun Stopping Power. It provides the latest results of real-life shootings in all of the major handgun calibers, plus more than 25 thought-provoking chapters that are vital to anyone interested in firearms, would ballistics, and combat shooting. This book also covers the street results of the hottest new caliber to hit the shooting world in years, the .40 Smith & Wesson. Updated street results of the latest exotic ammunition including Remington Golden Saber and CCI-Speer Gold Dot, plus the venerable offerings from MagSafe, Glaser, Cor-Bon and others. A fascinating look at the development of Hydra-Shok ammunition is included.

Understanding Ballistics, Revised 2nd Edition by Robert A. Rinker, Mulberry House Publishing Co., Corydon, IN, 2000. 430 pp., illus Paper covers. New, Revised and Expanded. 2nd Edition. $24.95

Explains basic to advanced firearm ballistics in understandable terms.

Why Not Load Your Own?, by Col. T. Whelen, Gun Room Press, Highland Park, NJ 1996, 4th ed., rev. 237 pp., illus. $20.00

A basic reference on handloading, describing each step, materials and equipment. Includes loads for popular cartridges.

Wildcat Cartridges Volumes 1 & 2 Combination, by the editors of Handloaders magazine, Wolfe Publishing Co., Prescott, AZ, 1997. 350 pp., illus. Paper covers. $39.95

A profile of the most popular information on wildcat cartridges that appeared in the Handloader magazine.

COLLECTORS

18th Century Weapons of the Royal Welsh Fuziliers from Flixton Hall, by Goldstein, Erik. Thomas Publications, Gettysburg, PA: 2002. 1st edition. 126 pages, illustrated with B & W photos. Softcover. $19.95

Ackermann Military Prints: Uniforms of the British and Indian Armies 1840-1855, The, by Carman, William Y. with Robert W. Kenny Jr. Schiffer Publications, Atglen, PA: 2002. 1st edition. 176 pages, with over 160 color images. $69.95

Accoutrements of the United States Infantry, Riflemen, and Dragoons 1834-1839. by R.T. Huntington, Historical Arms Series No. 20. Canada: Museum Restoration. 58 pp. illus. Softcover. $8.95

Although the 1841 edition of the U.S. Ordnance Manual provides ample information on the equipment that was in use during the 1840s, it is evident that the patterns of equipment that it describes were not introduced until 1838 or 1839. This guide is intended to fill this gap in our

REFERENCE

knowledge by providing an overview of what we now know about the accoutrements that were issued to the regular infantryman, rifleman, and dragoon, in the 1830's with excursions into earlier and later years.

Age of the Gunfighter; Men and Weapons on the Frontier 1840-1900, by Joseph G. Rosa, University of Oklahoma Press, Norman, OK, 1999. 192 pp., illustrated. Paper covers. $21.95

Stories of gunfighters and their encounters and detailed descriptions of virtually every firearm used in the old West.

Air Guns, by Eldon G. Wolff, Duckett's Publishing Co., Tempe, AZ, 1997. 204 pp., illus Paper covers. $35.00

Historical reference covering many makers, European and American guns, canes and more.

Allied and Enemy Aircraft: May 1918; Not to be Taken from the Front Lines, Historical Arms Series No. 27. Canada: Museum Restoration. Softcover. $8.95

The basis for this title is a very rare identification manual published by the French government in 1918 that illustrated 60 aircraft with three or more views: French, English American, German, Italian, and Belgian, which might have been seen over the trenches ofFrance. Each is describe in a text translated from the original French. This is probably the most complete collection of illustrations of WW1 aircraft which has survived.

American Military and Naval Belts, 1812-1902, by Dorsey, R. Stephen. Eugene, OR: Collectors Library, 2002. 1st edition. Hardcover. $80.00

With introduction by Norm Flayderman, this massive work is the NEW key reference on Sword Belts, Waist Belts, Sabre Belts, Shoulder Belts and Cartridge Belts (looped and non-looped). At over 460 pages, this 8.5x 11 inch book offers over 840 photos (primarily in colour) and original period drawings. In addition, this work offers the first, comprehensive research on the Anson Mills Woven Cartridge Belts: the man, the company and its personalities, the belt-related patents and the government contracts from 1880 through 1902. This book is a "must" for all accoutrements collectors, military historians and museums.

American Military Belt Plates, by O'Donnell, Michael J. and J. Duncan Campbell. Alexandria, VA: O'Donnell Publishing, 2000. 2nd edition. 614 pages, illus. Hardcover $49.00

At last available and well worth the wait! This massive study encompasses all the known plates from the Revolutionary War through the Spanish-American conflict. A sweeping, handsomely presented study that covers 1776 through 1910. Over 1,025 specimens are illustrated front and back along with many images of soldiers wearing various plates.

American Military Saddle, 1776-1945, The, by R. Stephen Dorsey & Kenneth L. McPheeters, Collector's Library, Eugene, OR, 1999. 400 pp., illustrated. $59.95

The most complete coverage of the subject ever writeen on the American Military Saddle. Nearly 1000 actual photos and official drawings, from the major public and private collections in the U.S. and Great Britain.

American Police Collectibles; Dark Lanterns and Other Curious Devices, by Matthew G. Forte, Turn of the Century Publishers, Upper Montclair, NJ, 1999. 248 pp., illustrated. $24.95

For collectors of police memorabilia (handcuffs, police dark lanterns, mechanical and chain nippers, rattles, billy clubs and nightsticks) and police historians.

Ammunition; Small Arms, Grenades, and Projected Munitions, by Greenhill Publishing. 144 pp., Illustrated. $22.95

The best concise guide to modern ammunition available today. Covers ammo for small arms, grenades, and projected munitions. 144 pp., Illustrated. As New – Hardcover.

Antique Guns, the Collector's Guide, 2nd Edition, edited by John Traister, Stoeger Publishing Co., So. Hackensack, NJ, 1994. 320 pp., illus. Paper covers. $19.95

Covers a vast spectrum of pre-1900 firearms: those manufactured by U.S. gunmakers as well as Canadian, French, German, Belgian, Spanish and other foreign firms.

Arming the Glorious Cause; Weapons of the Second War for Independence, by James B. Whisker, Daniel D. Hartzler and Larry W. Tantz, Old Bedford Village Press, Bedford, PA., 1998. 175 pp., illustrated. $45.00

A photographic study of Confederate weapons.

Arms & Accoutrements of the Mounted Police 1873-1973, by Roger F. Phillips and Donald J. Klancher, Museum Restoration Service, Ont., Canada, 1982. 224 pp., illus. $49.95

A definitive history of the revolvers, rifles, machine guns, cannons, ammunition, swords, etc. used by the NWMP, the RNWMP and the RCMP during the first 100 years of the Force.

Arms and Armor in the Art Institute of Chicago. By Waltler J. Karcheski, Bulfinch, New York 1999. 128 pp., 103 color photos, 12 black & white illustrations. $50.00

The George F. Harding Collection of arms and armor is the most visited installation at the Art Institute of Chicago - a testament to the enduring appeal of swords, muskets and the other paraphernalia of medieval and early modern war. Organized both chronologically and by type of weapon, this book captures the best of this astonishing collection in 115 striking photographs - most in color - accompanied by illuminating text. Here are intricately filigreed breastplates and ivory-handled crossbows, samurai katana and Toledo-steel scimitars, elaborately decorated maces and beautifully carved flintlocks - a treat for anyone who has ever been beguiled by arms, armor and the age of chivalry.

Arms and Armor in Colonial America 1526-1783. by Harold Peterson, Dover Publishing, New York, 2000. 350 pages with over 300 illustrations, index, bibliography & appendix. Softcover. $34.95

Over 200 years of firearms, ammunition, equipment & edged weapons.

Arms and Armor: The Cleveland Museum of Art. By Stephen N. Fliegel, Abrams, New York, 1998. 172 color photos, 17 halftones. 181 pages. $49.50

Intense look at the culture of the warrior and hunter, with an intriguing discussion of the decorative arts found on weapons and armor, set against the background of political and social history. Also provides information on the evolution of armor, together with manufacture and decoration, and weapons as technology and art.

Arms Makers of Maryland, by Daniel D. Hartzler, George Shumway, York, PA, 1975. 200 pp., illus. $50.00

A thorough study of the gunsmiths of Maryland who worked during the late 18th and early 19th centuries.

Arms Makers of Pennsylvania, by James B. Whisker, Selinsgrove, PA, Susquehanna Univ. Press, 1990. 1st edition. 218 pages, illustrated in black and white and color. $50.00

Concentrates primarily on the cottage industry gunsmiths & gun makers who worked in the Keystone State from it's early years through 1900.

Arms Makers of Western Pennsylvania, by James B. Whisker, Old Bedford Village Press. 1st edition. This deluxe hard bound edition has 176 pages, $50.00

Printed on fine coated paper, with many large photographs, and detailed text describing the period, lives, tools, and artistry of the Arms Makers of Western Pennsylvania.

Arsenal Of Freedom: The Springfield Armory 1890-1948, by Lt. Col. William Brophy, Andrew Mowbray, Inc., Lincoln, RI,1997. 20 pgs. of photos. 400 pages. As new — Softcover. $29.95

A year by year account drawn from offical records. Packed with reports, charts, tables, line drawings, and 20 page photo section.

Artistic Ingredients of the Longrifle, by George Shumway Publisher, 1989 102 pp., with 94 illus. $20.00

After a brief review of Pennsylvania-German folk art and architecture, to establish the artistic enviroment in which the longrifle was made, the author demonstrates that the sophisticated rococo decoration on the many of the finer longrifles is comparable to the best rococo work of Philadelphia cabinet makers and silversmiths.

Art of Miniature Firearms: Centuries of Craftsmanship, The, by Miniature Arms Society. Plainfield, IL: MAS Publications, 1999. 1st edition. Hardcover. $100.00

This volume of miniature arms includes some of the finest collector's items in existence, from antique replicas to contemporary pieces made by premium craftsmen working today, many of whom are members of the Miniature Arms Society. Beautiful color photographs highlight details of miniature firearms, including handguns, shoulder guns, and machine guns; cannon weaponry; weapons systems such as suits of armor, crossbows, and Gatling guns; and hand weapons, which include bows and arrows, daggers, knives, swords, maces, and spears. Also featured are exquisite replicas of accessories, from gun cases to cavalry saddles. 335 pages, full color photos.

Art of Gun Engraving, The, by Claude Gaier and Pietro Sabatti, Knickerbocker Press, N.Y., 1999. 160 pp., illustrated. $34.95

The richness and detail lavished on early firearms represents a craftmanship nearly vanished. Beginning with crossbows in the 100's, hunting scenes, portraits, or mythological themes are intricately depicted within a few square inches of etched metal. The full-color photos contained herein recaptures this lost art with exquisite detail.

Artillery Fuses of the Civil War, by Jones, Charles H., O'Donnell Publishing, Alexandria, VA: 2001. 1st edition. Hardcover. $34.00

Chuck Jones has been recognized as the leading authority on Civil War fuses for decades. Over the course of "Artillery Fuses" 167 pages Mr. Jones imparts the reader with the culmination of his life-long study of the subject with well-researched text and hundreds of photographs of every type of Civil War fuse known. The book is hardbound, color cover format, printed on lustrous glossy paper. A valuable reference for every serious Civil War collector.

Astra Automatic Pistols, by Leonardo M. Antaris, FIRAC Publishing Co., Sterling, CO, 1989. 248 pp., illus. $55.00

Charts, tables, serial ranges, etc. The definitive work on Astra pistols.

Ballard: The Great American Single Shot Rifle, by John T. Dutcher. Denver, CO: Privately Printed, 2002. 1st edition. 380 pages, illustrated with black & white photos, with 8-page color insert. Hardcover. New in New Dust Jacket. $79.95

Basic Documents on U.S. Martial Arms, commentary by Col. B. R. Lewis, reissue by Ray Riling, Phila., PA, 1956 and 1960. *Rifle Musket Model 1855.*

The first issue rifle of musket caliber, a muzzle loader equipped with the Maynard Primer, 32 pp. *Rifle Musket Model 1863.* The typical Union muzzle-loader of the Civil War, 26 pp. *Breech-Loading Rifle Musket Model 1866.* The first of our 50-caliber breechloading rifles, 12 pp. *Remington Navy Rifle Model 1870.* A commercial type breech-loader made at Springfield, 16 pp. *Lee Straight Pull Navy Rifle Model 1895.* A magazine cartridge arm of 6mm caliber. 23 pp. *Breech-Loading Arms* (five models) 27 pp. *Ward-Burton Rifle Musket 1871*-16 pp. Each $10.00

Battle Weapons of the American Revolution, by George C. Neuman, Scurlock Publishing Co., Texarkana, TX, 2001. 400 pp. Illus. Softcovers. $34.95

The most extensive photographic collection of Revolutionary War weapons ever in one volume. More than 1,600 photos of over 500 muskets, rifles, swords, bayonets, knives and other arms used by both sides in America's War for Independence.

Bedford County Rifle and Its Makers, The, by George Shumway. 40pp. illustrated, Softcover. $10.00

The authors study of the graceful and distinctive muzzle-loading rifles made in Bedford County, Pennsylvania. Stands as a milestone on the long path to the understanding of America's longrifles.

Belgian Rattlesnake; The Lewis Automatic Machine Gun, The, by William M. Easterly, Collector Grade Publications, Cobourg, Ontario, Canada, 1998. 584 pp., illustrated. $79.95

The most complete account ever published on the life and times of Colonel Isaac Newton Lewis and his crowning invention, the Lewis Automatic machine gun.

Beretta Automatic Pistols, by J.B. Wood, Stackpole Books, Harrisburg, PA, 1985. 192 pp., illus. $24.95

Only English-language book devoted to the Beretta line. Includes all important models.

Best of Holland & Holland, England's Premier Gunmaker, The, by McIntosh, Michael & Roosenburg, Jan G. Safari Press, Inc., Long Beach, CA: 2002. 1st edition. 298 pages. Profuse color illustrations. $69.95

Holland & Holland has had a long history of not only building London's "best" guns but also providing superior guns--the ultimate gun in finish, engraving, and embellishment. From the days of old in which a maharaja would order 100 fancifully engraved H&H shotguns for his guests to use at his duck shoot to the recent elaborately decorated sets depicting the Apollo 11 moon landing or the history of the British Empire, all of these guns represent the zenith in the art and craft of gunmaking and engraving. These and other H&H guns in the series named "Products of Excellence" are a cut above the ordinary H&H gun and hark back to a time when the British Empire ruled over one-third of the globe--a time when rulers, royalty, and the rich worldwide came to H&H for a gun that would elevate them above the crowd. In this book master gunwriter and acknowledged English gun expert Michael McIntosh and former H&H director Jan Roosenburg show us in words and pictures the finest products ever produced by H&H and, many would argue, by any gun company on earth. From a dainty and elegant .410 shotgun with gold relief engraving of scenes from Greek and Roman antiquity to the massive .700 Nitro Express double rifle, some of the most expensive and opulent guns ever produced on earth parade through these pages. An overview of the Products of Excellence series is given as well as a description and history of these special H&H guns. Never before have so many superlative guns from H&H--or any other maker for that manner--been displayed in one book. Many photos

58TH EDITION, 2004 • 489

shown are firearms from private collections, which cannot be seen publicly anywhere except in this book. In addition, many interesting details and a general history of H&H are provided.

Big Guns, Civil War Siege, Seacoast, and Naval Cannon, The, by Edwin Olmstead, Wayne E. Stark, and Spencer C. Tucker, Museum Restoration Service, Bloomfield, Ontario, Canada, 1997. 360 pp., illustrated. $80.00

This book is designed to identify and record the heavy guns available to both sides by the end of the Civil War.

Blue Book of Air Guns, 2nd Edition, edited by S.P. Fjestad, Blue Book Publications, Inc. Minneapolis, MN 2002. $14.95

This new 2nd edition simply contains more airgun values and information than any other single publication.

Blue Book of Gun Values, 23rd Edition, edited by S.P. Fjestad, Blue Book Publications, Inc. Minneapolis, MN 2003. $39.95

This new 23rd edition simply contains more firearms values and information than any other single publication. Expanded to over 1,600 pages featuring over 100,000 firearms prices, the new Blue Book of Gun Values also contains over Ω million words of text – no other book is even close! Most of the information contained in this publication is simply not available anywhere else, for any price!

Blue Book of Modern Black Powder Values, 2nd Edtion by Dennis Adler, Blue Book Publications, Inc. Minneapolis, MN 2002. 200 pp., illustrated. 41 color photos. Softcover. $17.95

This new title contains more up-to-date black powder values and related information than any other single publication. With 163 pages, this new book will keep you up to date on modern black powder models and prices, including most makes & models introduced this year! .

Blunderbuss 1500-1900, The, by James D. Forman, Historical Arms Series No. 32. Canada: Museum Restoration, 1994. An excellent and authoritative booklet giving tons of information on the Blunderbuss, a very neglected subject. 40 pages, illustrated. Softcover. $8.95

Boarders Away I: With Steel-Edged Weapons & Polearms, by William Gilkerson, Andrew Mowbray, Inc. Publishers, Lincoln, RI, 1993. 331 pages. $48.00

Contains the essential 24 page chapter 'War at Sea' which sets the historical and practical context for the arms discussed. Includeds chapters on, Early Naval Weapons, Boarding Axes, Cutlasses, Officers Fighting Swords and Dirks, and weapons at hand of Random Mayhem.

Boarders Away, Volume II: Firearms of the Age of Fighting Sail, by William Gilkerson, Andrew Mowbray, Inc. Publishers, Lincoln, RI, 1993. 331 pp., illus. $65.00

Covers the pistols, muskets, combustibles and small cannon used aboard American and European fighting ships, 1626-1826.

Boston's Gun Bible, by Boston T. Party, Ignacio, CO: Javelin Press, August 2000. Expanded Edition. Softcover. $28.00

This mammoth guide for gun owners everywhere is a completely updated and expanded edition (more than 500 new pages!) of Boston T. Party's classic Boston on Guns and Courage. Pulling no punches, Boston gives new advice on which shoulder weapons and handguns to buy and why before exploring such topics as why you should consider not getting a concealed carry permit, what guns and gear will likely be outlawed next, how to spend within your budget, why you should go to a quality defensive shooting academy now, which guns and gadgets are inferior and why, how to stay off illegal government gun registration lists, how to spot an undercover agent trying to entrap law-abiding gun owners and much more.

Breech-Loading Carbines of the United States Civil War Period, by Brig. Gen. John Pitman, Armory Publications, Tacoma, WA, 1987. 94 pp., illus. $29.95

The first in a series of previously unpublished manuscripts originated by the late Brigadier General John Putnam. Exploded drawings showing parts actual size follow each sectioned illustration.

Breech-Loading Single-Shot Rifle, The, by Major Ned H. Roberts and Kenneth L. Waters, Wolfe Publishing Co., Prescott, AZ, 1995. 333 pp., illus. $28.50

A comprehensive and complete history of the evolution of the Schutzen and single-shot rifle.

Bren Gun Saga, The, by Thomas B. Dugelby, Collector Grade Publications, Cobourg, Ontario, Canada, 1999, revised and expanded edition. 406 pp., illustrated. $65.95

A modern, definitive book on the Bren in this revised expanded edition, which in terms of numbers of pages and illustrations is nearly twice the size of the original.

British Board of Ordnance Small Arms Contractors 1689-1840, by De Witt Bailey, Rhyl, England: W. S. Curtis, 2000. 150 pp. $18.00

Thirty years of research in the Archives of the Ordnance Board in London has identified more than 600 of these suppliers. The names of many can be found marking the regulation firearms of the period. In the study, the contractors are identified both alphabetically and under a combination of their date period together with their specialist trade.

British Enfield Rifles, The, Volume 1, The SMLE Mk I and Mk III Rifles, by Charles R. Stratton, North Cape Pub. Tustin, CA, 1997. 150 pp., illus. Paper covers. $16.95

A systematic and thorough examination on a part-by-part basis of the famous British battle rifle that endured for nearly 70 years as the British Army's number one battle rifle.

British Enfield Rifles, Volume 2, No.4 and No.5 Rifles, by Charles R. Stratton, North Cape Publications, Tustin, CA, 1999. 150 pp., illustrated. Paper covers. $16.95

The historical background for the development of both rifles describing each variation and an explanation of all the "marks", "numbers" and codes found on most parts.

British Enfield Rifles, Volume 4, The Pattern 1914 and U. S. Model 1917 Rifles, by Charles R. Stratton, North Cape Publications, Tustin, CA, 2000. Paper covers. $16.95

One of the lease know American and British collectible military rifles is analyzed on a part by part basis. All markings and codes, refurbishment procedures and WW 2 upgrade are included as are the varios sniper rifle versions.

British Falling Block Breechloading Rifle from 1865, The, by Jonathan Kirton, Tom Rowe Books, Maynardsville, TN, 2nd edition, 1997. 380 pp., illus. $70.00

Expanded 2nd edition of a comprehensive work on the British falling block rifle.

British Gun Engraving, by Douglas Tate, Safari Press, Inc., Huntington Beach, CA, 1999. 240 pp., illustrated. Limited, signed and numbered edition, in a slipcase. $80.00

A historic and photographic record of the last two centuries.

British Military Flintlock Rifles 1740-1840. 264 pages with over 320 photographs. Hardcover. $47.95

With a remarkable weath of data about the Rifleman and Regiments that carried these weapons, by Bailey, De Witt. Andrew Mowbray, Inc. Lincoln, RI:, 2002. 1st edition. Pattern 1776 Rifles, The Ferguson Breechloader, The Famous Baker Rifle, Rifles of the Hessians and other German Mercenaries, American Loylist Rifles, Rifles given to indians, Cavalry Rifles and Rifled Carbines, Bayonets, Accoutrements, Ammunition and more.

British Service Rifles and Carbines 1888-1900, by Alan M. Petrillo, Excaliber Publications, Latham, NY, 1994. 72 pp., illus, Paper covers. $11.95

A complete review of the Lee-Metford and Lee-Enfield rifles and carbines.

British Single Shot Rifles, Volume 1, Alexander Henry, by Wal Winfer, Tom Rowe, Maynardsville, TN, 1998, 200 pp., illus. $50.00

Detailed Study of the single shot rifles made by Henry. Illustrated with hundreds of photographs and drawings.

British Single Shot Rifles Volume 2, George Gibbs, by Wal Winfer, Tom Rowe, Maynardsville, TN, 1998. 177 pp., illus. $50.00

Detailed study of the Farquharson as made by Gibbs. Hundreds of photos.

British Single Shot Rifles, Volume 3, Jeffery, by Wal Winfer, Rowe Publications, Rochester, N.Y., 1999. 260 pp., illustrated. $60.00

The Farquharsen as made by Jeffery and his competitors, Holland & Holland, Bland, Westley, Manton, etc. Large section on the development of nitro cartridges including the .600.

British Single Shot Rifles, Vol. 4; Westley Richards, by Wal Winfer, Rowe Publications, Rochester, N.Y., 2000. 265 pages, illustrated, photos. $60.00

In his 4th volume Winfer covers a detailed study of the Westley Richards single shot rifles, including Monkey Tails, Improved Martini, 1872,1873, 1878,1881, 1897 Falling Blocks. He also covers Westley Richards Cartridges, History and Reloading information.

British Small Arms Ammunition, 1864-1938 (Other than .303 inch), by Peter Labbett, Armory Publications, Seattle, WA. 1993, 358 pages, illus. Four-color dust jacket. $79.00

A study of British military rifle, handgun, machine gun, and aiming tube ammunition through 1 inch from 1864 to 1938. Photo-illustrated including the firearms that chambered the cartridges.

British Soldier's Firearms from Smoothbore to Rifled Arms, The, 1850-1864, by Dr. C.H. Roads, R&R Books, Livonia, NY, 1994. 332 pp., illus. $49.00

A reprint of the classic text covering the development of British military hand and shoulder firearms in the crucial years between 1850 and 1864.

British Sporting Guns & Rifles, compiled by George Hoyem, Armory Publications, Coeur d'Alene, ID, 1997. 1024 pp., illus. In two volumes. $250.00

Eighteen old sporting firearms trade catalogs and a rare book reproduced with their color covers in a limited, signed and numbered edition.

Browning Dates of Manufacture, compiled by George Madis, Art and Reference House, Brownsboro, TX, 1989. 48 pp. $10.00

Gives the date codes and product codes for all models from 1824 to the present.

Buffalo Bill's Wild West: An American Legend, by R.L. Wilson and Greg Martine, Random House, N.Y., 1999. 3,167 pp., illustrated. $60.00

Over 225 color plates and 160 black-and-white illustrations, with in-depth text and captions, the colorful arms, posters, photos, costumes, saddles, accoutrement are brought to life.

Bullard Firearms, by Jamieson, G. Scott, Schiffer Publications, Atglen, PA 2002. 1st edition. 400 pages, with over 1100 color and b/w photographs, charts, diagrams. Hardcover. $100.00

Bullard Firearms is the story of a mechanical genius whose rifles and cartridges were the equal of any made in America in the 1880s, yet little of substance had been written about James H. Bullard or his arms prior to 1988 when the first edition called Bullard Arms was published. This greatly expanded volume with over 1,000 black and white and 150 color plates, most not previously published answers many of the questions posed in the first edition. The book is divided into eleven chapters each covering a different aspect of the Bullard story. For example, chapter two discusses Bullard's pioneering automotive work for the Overman Automobile Company (he was probably first to use a metal body on a production automobile (1899). Chapters four through eight outline in detail the large-frame repeaters, the small-frame repeaters, the solid-frame single-shot rifles, the detachable-interchangeable barrel model single-shots and lastly the very rare military and experimental models. Each model is covered in depth with many detailed photographs of the interior parts and workings of the repeaters. Chapter nine covers the fascinating and equally unknown world of Bullard cartridges and reloading tools. The final chapter outlines in chart form almost 500 Bullard rifles by serial number, caliber and type. Quick and easy to use, this book is a real benefit for collectors and dealers alike.

Burning Powder, compiled by Major D.B. Wesson, Wolfe Publishing Company, Prescott, AZ, 1992. 110 pp. Soft cover. $10.95

A rare booklet from 1932 for Smith & Wesson collectors.

Burnside Breech Loading Carbines, The, by Edward A. Hull, Andrew Mowbray, Inc., Lincoln, RI, 1986. 95 pp., illus. $16.00

No. 1 in the "Man at Arms Monograph Series." A model-by-model historical/technical examination of one of the most widely used cavalry weapons of the American Civil War based upon important and previously unpublished research.

Camouflage Uniforms of European and NATO Armies; 1945 to the Present, by J. F. Borsarello, Atglen, PA: Schiffer Publications. Over 290 color and b/w photographs, 120 pages. Softcover. $29.95

This full-color book covers nearly all of the NATO, and other European armies' camouflaged uniforms, and not only shows and explains the many patterns, but also their efficacy of design. Described and illustrated are the variety of materials tested in over forty different armies, and includes the history of obsolete trial tests from 1945 to the present time. More than two hundred patterns have been manufactured since World War II using various landscapes and seasonal colors for their look. The Vietnam and Gulf Wars, African or South American events, as well as recent Yugoslavian independence wars have been used as experimental terrains to test a variety of patterns. This book provides a superb reference for the historian, reenactor, designer, and modeler.

Camouflage Uniforms of the Waffen-SS A Photographic Reference, by Michael Beaver, Schiffer Publishing, Atglen, PA. Over 1,000 color and b/w photographs and illustrations, 296 pages. $69.95

Finally a book that unveils the shroud of mystery surrounding Waffen-SS camouflage clothing. Illustrated here, both in full color and in contemporary black and white photographs, this unparalleled look at Waffen-SS combat troops and their camouflage clothing will benefit both the historian and collector.

Canadian Gunsmiths from 1608: A Checklist of Tradesmen, by John Belton, Historical Arms Series No. 29. Canada: Museum Restoration, 1992. 40 pp., 17 illustrations. Softcover. $8.95

This Checklist is a greatly expanded version of HAS No. 14, listing the names, occupation, location, and dates of more than 1,500 men and women who worked as gunmakers, gunsmiths, armorers, gun merchants, gun patent holders, and a few other gun related trades. A collection of contemporary gunsmiths' letterhead have been provided to add color and depth to the study.

Cap Guns, by James Dundas, Schiffer Publishing, Atglen, PA, 1996. 160 pp., illus. Paper covers. $29.95

Over 600 full-color photos of cap guns and gun accessories with a current value guide.

Carbines of the Civil War, by John D. McAulay, Pioneer Press, Union City, TN, 1981. 123 pp., illus. Paper covers. $12.95

A guide for the student and collector of the colorful arms used by the Federal cavalry.

Carbines of the U.S. Cavalry 1861-1905, by John D. McAulay, Andrew Mowbray Publishers, Lincoln, RI, 1996. $35.00

Covers the crucial use of carbines from the beginning of the Civil War to the end of the cavalry carbine era in 1905.

Cartridge Carbines of the British Army, by Alan M. Petrillo, Excalibur Publications, Latham, NY, 1998. 72 pp., illustrated. Paper covers. $11.95

Begins with the Snider-Enfield which was the first regulation cartridge carbine introduced in 1866 and ends with the .303 caliber No.5, Mark 1 Enfield.

Cartridge Catalogues, compiled by George Hoyem, Armory Publications, Coeur d'Alene, ID., 1997. 504 pp., illus. $125.00

Fourteen old ammunition makers' and designers' catalogs reproduced with their color covers in a limited, signed and numbered edition. Completely revised edition of the general purpose reference work for which collectors, police, scientists and laymen reach first for answers to cartridge identification questions.

Cartridge Reloading Tools of the Past, by R.H. Chamberlain and Tom Quigley, Tom Quigley, Castle Rock, WA, 1998. 167 pp., illustrated. Paper covers. $25.00

A detailed treatment of the extensive Winchester and Ideal lines of handloading tools and bulletmolds plus Remington, Marlin, Ballard, Browning and many others.

Cartridges for Collectors, by Fred Datig, Pioneer Press, Union City, TN, 1999. In three volumes of 176 pp. each. Vol.1 (Centerfire); Vol.2 (Rimfire and Misc.) types; Vol.3 (Additional Rimfire, Centerfire, and Plastic.). All illustrations are shown in full-scale drawings. Volume 1, softcover only, $19.95. Volumes 2 & 3, Hardcover $19.95

Civil War Arms Makers and Their Contracts, edited by Stuart C. Mowbray and Jennifer Heroux, Andrew Mowbray Publishing, Lincoln, RI, 1998. 595 pp. $39.50

A facsimile reprint of the Report by the Commissioner of Ordnance and Ordnance Stores, 1862.

Civil War Arms Purchases and Deliveries, edited by Stuart C. Mowbray, Andrew Mowbray Publishing, Lincoln, RI, 1998. 300pp., illus. $39.50

A facsimile reprint of the master list of Civil War weapons purchases and deliveries including Small Arms, Cannon, Ordnance and Projectiles.

Civil War Breech Loading Rifles, by John D. McAulay, Andrew Mowbray, Inc., Lincoln, RI, 1991. 144 pp., illus. Paper covers. $15.00

All the major breech-loading rifles of the Civil War and most, if not all, of the obscure types are detailed, illustrated and set in their historical context.

Civil War Cartridge Boxes of the Union Infantryman, by Paul Johnson, Andrew Mowbray, Inc., Lincoln, RI, 1998. 352 pp., illustrated. $45.00

There were four patterns of infantry cartridge boxes used by Union forces during the Civil War. The author describes the development and subsequent pattern changes to these cartridge boxes.

Civil War Collector's Price Guide; Expanded Millennium Edition, by North South Trader. Orange, VA: Publisher's Press, 2000. 9th edition. 260 pps., illus. Softcover. $29.95

All updated prices, scores of new listings, and hundreds of new pictures! It's the one reference work no collector should be without. An absolute must.

Civil War Commanders, by Dean Thomas, Thomas Publications, Gettysburg, PA. 1998. 72 pages, illustrated, photos. Paper Covers. $9.95

138 photographs and capsule biographies of Union and Confederate officers. A convenient personalities reference guide.

Civil War Guns, by William B. Edwards, Thomas Publications, Gettysburg, PA, 1997. 444 pp., illus. $40.00

The complete story of Federal and Confederate small arms; design, manufacture, identifications, procurement issue, employment, effectiveness, and postwar disposal by the recognized expert.

Civil War Infantryman: In Camp, On the March, And in Battle, by Dean Thomas, Thomas Publications, Gettysburg, PA. 1998. 72 pages, illustrated, Softcovers. $12.95

Uses first-hand accounts to shed some light on the "common soldier" of the Civil War from enlistment to muster-out, including camp, marching, rations, equipment, fighting, and more.

Civil War Pistols, by John D. McAulay, Andrew Mowbray Inc., Lincoln, RI, 1992. 166 pp., illus. $38.50

A survey of the handguns used during the American Civil War.

Civil War Projectiles II; Small Arms & Field Artillery, With Supplement, by McKee, W. Reid, and M. E. Mason, Jr. Orange, VA: Publisher's Press, 2001. 202 pages, illus. Hardcover. $40.00

The standard reference work is now available. Essential for every Civil War bullet collector.

Civil War Sharps Carbines and Rifles, by Earl J. Coates and John D. McAulay, Thomas Publications, Gettysburg, PA, 1996. 108 pp., illus. Paper covers. $12.95

Traces the history and development of the firearms including short histories of specific serial numbers and the soldiers who received them.

Civil War Small Arms of the U.S. Navy and Marine Corps, by John D. McAulay, Mowbray Publishing, Lincoln, RI, 1999. 186 pp., illustrated. $39.00

The first reliable and comprehensive guide to the firearms and edged weapons of the Civil War Navy and Marine Corps.

Cody Buffalo Bill Collector's Guide with Values, The W.F., by James W. Wojtowicz, Collector Books, Paducah, KY, 1998. 271 pp., illustrated. $24.95

A profusion of colorful collectibles including lithographs, programs, photographs, books, medals, sheet music, guns, etc. and today's values.

Col. Burton's Spiller & Burr Revolver, by Matthew W. Norman, Mercer University Press, Macon, GA, 1997. 152 pp., illus. $22.95

A remarkable archival research project on the arm together with a comprehensive story of the establishment and running of the factory.

Collector's Guide to United States Combat Shotguns, A, by Bruce N. Canfield, Andrew Mowbray Inc., Lincoln, RI, 1992. 184 pp., illus. Paper covers. $24.00

This book provides full coverage of combat shotguns, from the earliest examples right up to the Gulf War and beyond.

Collector's Guide to Winchester in the Service, A, by Bruce N. Canfield, Andrew Mowbray, Inc., Lincoln, RI, 1991. 192 pp., illus. Paper covers. $22.00

The firearms produced by Winchester for the national defense. From Hotchkiss to the M14, each firearm is examined and illustrated.

Collector's Guide to the '03 Springfield, A, by Bruce N. Canfield, Andrew Mowbray Inc., Lincoln, RI, 1989. 160 pp., illus. Paper covers. $22.00

A comprehensive guide follows the '03 through its unparalleled tenure of service. Covers all of the interesting variations, modifications and accessories of this highly collectible military rifle.

Collector's Illustrated Encyclopedia of the American Revolution, by George C. Neumann and Frank J. Kravic, Rebel Publishing Co., Inc., Texarkana, TX, 1989. 286 pp., illus. $36.95

A showcase of more than 2,300 artifacts made, worn, and used by those who fought in the War for Independence.

Colonial Frontier Guns, by T.M. Hamilton, Pioneer Press, Union City, TN, 1988. 176 pp., illus. Paper covers. $17.50

A complete study of early flint muskets of this country.

Colt: An American Legend, by R.L. Wilson, Artabras, New York, 1997. 406 pages, fully illustrated, most in color. $35.00

A reprint of the commemorative album celebrates 150 years of the guns of Samuel Colt and the manufacturing empire he built, with expert discussion of every model ever produced, the innovations of each model and variants, updated model and serial number charts and magnificent photographic showcases of the weapons.

Colt Engraving Book, The, Volumes I & II, by R. L. Wilson. Privately printed, 2001. Each volume is approximately 500 pages, with 650 illustrations, most in color. $390.00

This third edition from the original texts of 1974 and 1982 has been fine-tuned and dramatically expanded, and is by far the most illuminating and complete. With over 1,200 illustrations, more than 2/3 of which are in color, this book joins the author's The Book of Colt Firearms, and Fine Colts as companion volumes. Approximately 1,000 pages in two volumes, each signed by the author, serial numbered, and strictly limited to 3000 copies. Volume I covers from the Paterson and pre-Paterson period through c.1921 (end of the Helfricht period). Volume II commences with Kornbrath, and Glahn, and covers Colt embellished arms from c.1919 through 2000.

Colt Model 1905 Automatic Pistol, The, by John Potocki, Andrew Mowbray Publishing, Lincoln, RI, 1998. 191 pp., illus. $28.00

Covers all aspects of the Colt Model 1905 Automatic Pistol, from its invention by the legendary John Browning to its numerous production variations.

Colt Peacemaker British Model, by Keith Cochran, Cochran Publishing Co., Rapid City, SD, 1989. 160 pp., illus. $35.00

Covers those revolvers Colt squeezed in while completing a large order of revolvers for the U.S. Cavalry in early 1874, to those magnificent cased target revolvers used in the pistol competitions at Bisley Commons in the 1890s.

Colt Peacemaker Encyclopedia, by Keith Cochran, Keith Cochran, Rapid City, SD, 1986. 434 pp., illus. $60.00

A must book for the Peacemaker collector.

Colt Peacemaker Encyclopedia, Volume 2, by Keith Cochran, Cochran Publishing Co., SD, 1992. 416 pp., illus. $60.00

Included in this volume are extensive notes on engraved, inscribed, historical and noted revolvers, as well as those revolvers used by outlaws, lawmen, movie and television stars.

Colt Presentations: From The Factory Ledgers 1856-1869, by Herbert G. Houze. Lincoln, RI: Andrew Mowbray, Inc., 2003. 112 pages, 45 b&w photos. Softcover. $21.95

Samuel Colt was a generous man. He also used gifts to influence government decision makers. But after Congress investigated him in 1854, Colt needed to hide the gifts from prying eyes, which makes it very difficult for today's collectors to document the many revolvers presented by Colt and the factory. Using the original account journals of the Colt's Patent Fire Arms Manufacturing Co., renowned arms authority Herbert G. Houze finally gives us the full details behind hundreds of the most exciting Colts ever made.

Colt Revolvers and the Tower of London, by Joseph G. Rosa, Royal Armouries of the Tower of London, London, England, 1988. 72 pp., illus. Soft covers. $15.00

Details the story of Colt in London through the early cartridge period.

Colt's SAA Post War Models, by George Garton, The Gun Room Press, Highland Park, NJ, 1995. 166 pp., illus. $39.95

Complete facts on the post-war Single Action Army revolvers. Information on calibers, production numbers and variations taken from factory records.

Colt Single Action Army Revolvers: The Legend, the Romance and the Rivals, by "Doc" O'Meara, Krause Publications, Iola, WI, 2000. 160 pp., illustrated with 250 photos in b&w and a 16 page color section. $34.95

Production figures, serial numbers by year, and rarities.

Colt Single Action Army Revolvers and Alterations, by C. Kenneth Moore, Mowbray Publishers, Lincoln, RI, 1999. 112 pp., illustrated. $35.00

A comprehensive history of the revolvers that collectors call "Artillery Models." These are the most historical of all S.A.A. Colts, and this new book covers all the details.

Colt Single Action Army Revolvers and the London Agency, by C. Kenneth Moore, Andrew Mowbray Publishers, Lincoln, RI, 1990. 144 pp., illus. $35.00

Drawing on vast documentary sources, this work chronicles the relationship between the London Agency and the Hartford home office.

58TH EDITION, 2004 • 491

THE ARMS LIBRARY

Colt U.S. General Officers' Pistols, The, by Horace Greeley IV, Andrew Mowbray Inc., Lincoln, RI, 1990. 199 pp., illus. $38.00

These unique weapons, issued as a badge of rank to General Officers in the U.S. Army from WWII onward, remain highly personal artifacts of the military leaders who carried them. Includes serial numbers and dates of issue.

Colts from the William M. Locke Collection, by Frank Sellers, Andrew Mowbray Publishers, Lincoln, RI, 1996. 192 pp., illus. $55.00

This important book illustrates all of the famous Locke Colts, with captions by arms authority Frank Sellers.

Colt's Dates of Manufacture 1837-1978, by R.L. Wilson, published by Maurie Albert, Coburg, Australia; N.A. distributor Madis Books, TX, 1997. 61 pp. $7.50

An invaluable pocket guide to the dates of manufacture of Colt firearms up to 1978.

Colt's Pocket '49: Its Evolution Including the Baby Dragoon and Wells Fargo, by Robert Jordan and Darrow Watt, privately printed, Loma Mar, CA 2000. 304 pages, with 984 color photos, illus. Beautifully bound in a deep blue leather like case. $125.00

Detailed information on all models and covers engaving, cases, accoutrements, holsters, fakes, and much more. Included is a summary booklet containing information such as serial numbers, production ranges & identifing photos. This book is a masterpiece on its subject.

Complete Guide to all United States Military Medals 1939 to Present, by Colonel Frank C. Foster, Medals of America Press, Fountain Inn, SC, 2000. 121 pp,.illustrated, photos. $29.95

Complete criteria for every Army, Navy, Marines, Air Force, Coast Guard, and Merchant Marine awards since 1939. All decorations, service medals, and ribbons shown in full-color and accompanied by dates and campaigns as well as detailed descriptions on proper wear and display.

Complete Guide to the M1 Garand and the M1 Carbine, by Bruce N. Canfield, 2nd printing, Andrew Mowbray Inc., Lincoln, RI, 1999. 296 pp., illus. $39.50

Expanded and updated coverage of both the M1 Garand and the M1 Carbine, with more than twice as much information as the author's previous book on this topic.

Complete Guide to U.S. Infantry Weapons of the First War, The, by Bruce Canfield, Andrew Mowbray, Publisher, Lincoln, RI, 2000. 304 pp., illus. $39.95

The definitive study of the U.S. Infantry weapons used in WWI.

Complete Guide to U.S. Infantry Weapons of World War Two, The, by Bruce Canfield, Andrew Mowbray, Publisher, Lincoln, RI, 1995. 303 pp., illus. $39.95

A definitive work on the weapons used by the United States Armed Forces in WWII.

Confederate Belt Buckles & Plates, by Mullinax, Steve E. O'Donnell Publishing, Alexandria, VA: 1999. Expanded edition. Hardbound, 247 pages, illus. Hardcover. $34.00

Hundreds of crisp photographs augment this classic study of Confederate accoutrement plates.

Confederate Carbines & Musketoons Cavalry Small Arms manufactured in and for the Southern Confederacy 1861-1865, by Murphy, John M. Santa Ana, CA: Privately Printed, 2002. Reprint. 320 pages, illustrated with B & W drawings and photos. Color Frontis by Don Troiani. Hardcover. $79.95

This is Dr. Murphy's first work on Confederate arms. See also "Confederate Rifles & Muskets". Exceptional photography compliments the text. John Murphy has one of the finest collections of Confederate arms known.

Confederate Rifles & Muskets Infantry Small Arms Manufactured in the Southern Confederacy 1861-1865, by Murphy, John M. Santa Ana, CA: Privately Printed, 1996. Reprint. 768pp, 8pp color plates, profusely illustrated. Hardcover. $119.95

The first in-depth and academic analysis and discussion of the "long" longarms produced in the South by and for the Confederacy during the American Civil War. The collection of Dr. Murphy is doubtless the largest and finest grouping of Confederate longarms in private hands today.

Confederate Saddles & Horse Equipment, by Knopp, Ken R. Orange, VA: Publisher's Press, 2002. 194 pps., illus. Hardcover. $39.95

Confederate Saddles & Horse Equipment is a pioneer work on the subject. After ten years of research Ken Knopp has compiled a thorough and fascinating study of the little-known field of Confederate saddlery and equipment. His analysis of ordnance operations coupled with his visual presentation of surviving examples offers an indispensable source for collectors and historians.

Concise Guide to the Artillery at Gettysburg, A, by Gregory Coco, Thomas Publications, Gettysburg, PA, 1998. 96 pp., illus. Paper Covers. $10.00

Coco's tenth book on Gettysburg is a beginner's guide to artillery and its use at the battle. It covers the artillery batteries describing the types of cannons, shells, fuses, etc.using interesting narrative and human interest stories.

Cooey Firearms, Made in Canada 1919-1979, by John A. Belton, Museum Restoration, Canada, 1998. 36pp., with 46 illus. Paper Covers. $8.95

More than 6 million rifles and at least 67 models, were made by this small Canadian riflemaker. They have been identified from the first 'Cooey Canuck' through the last variations made by the 'Winchester-Cooey'. Each is descibed and most are illustrated in this first book on The Cooey.

Cowboy Collectibles and Western Memorabilia, by Bob Bell and Edward Vebell, Schiffer Publishing, Atglen, PA, 1992. 160 pp., illus. Paper covers. $29.95

The exciting era of the cowboy and the wild west collectibles including rifles, pistols, gun rigs, etc.

Cowboy Culture: The Last Frontier of American Antiques, by Michael Friedman, Schiffer Publishing, Ltd., West Chester, PA, 1992. 300 pp., illustrated.

Covers the artful aspects of the old west, the antiques and collectibles. Illustrated with clear color plates of over 1,000 items such as spurs, boots, guns, saddles etc.

Cowboy and Gunfighter Collectible, by Bill Mackin, Mountain Press Publishing Co., Missoula, MT, 1995. 178 pp., illus. Paper covers. $25.00

A photographic encyclopedia with price guide and makers' index.

Cowboys and the Trappings of the Old West, by William Manns and Elizabeth Clair Flood, Zon International Publishing Co., Santa Fe, NM, 1997, 1st edition. 224 pp., illustrated. $45.00

A pictorial celebration of the cowboys dress and trappings.

Cowboy Hero Cap Pistols, by Rudy D'Angelo, Antique Trader Books, Dubuque, IA, 1998. 196 pp., illus. Paper covers. $34.95

Aimed at collectors of cap pistols created and named for famous film and television cowboy heros, this in-depth guide hits all the marks. Current values are given.

Custom Firearms Engraving, by Tom Turpin, Krause Publications, Iola, WI, 1999. 208 pp., illustrated. $49.95

Over 200 four-color photos with more than 75 master engravers profiled. Engravers Directory with addresses in the U.S. and abroad.

Daisy Air Rifles & BB Guns: The First 100 Years, by Punchard, Neal. St. Paul, MN: Motorbooks, 2002. 1st edition. Hardcover, 10 x 10, 156 pp, 300 color. Hardcover. $29.95

Flash back to the days of your youth and recall fond memories of your Daisy. Daisy Air Rifles and BB Guns looks back fondly on the first 100 years of Daisy BB rifles and pistols, toy and cork guns, accessories, packaging, period advertising and literature. Wacky ads and catalogs conjure grins of pure nostalgia as chapters reveal how Daisy used a combination of savvy business sense and quality products to dominate the market.

Decorations, Medals, Ribbons, Badges and Insignia of the United States Army; World War 2 to Present, The, by Col. Frank C. Foster, Medals of America Press, Fountain Inn, SC. 2001. 145 pages, illustrated. $29.95

The most complete guide to United States Army medals, ribbons, rank, insignia nad patches from WWII to the present day. Each medal and insignia shown in full color. Includes listing of respective criteria and campaigns.

Decorations, Medals, Ribbons, Badges and Insignia of the United States Navy; World War 2 to Present, The, by James G. Thompson, Medals of America Press, Fountain Inn, SC. 2000. 123 pages, illustrated. $29.95

The most complete guide to United States Army medals, ribbons, rank, insignia nad patches from WWII to the present day. Each medal and insignia shown in full color. Includes listing of respective criteria and campaigns.

Derringer in America, The, Volume 1, The Percussion Period, by R.L. Wilson and L.D. Eberhart, Andrew Mowbray Inc., Lincoln, RI, 1985. 271 pp., illus. $48.00

A long awaited book on the American percussion deringer.

Derringer in America, The, Volume 2, The Cartridge Period, by L.D. Eberhart and R.L. Wilson, Andrew Mowbray Inc., Publishers, Lincoln, RI, 1993. 284 pp., illus. $65.00

Comprehensive coverage of cartridge deringers organized alphabetically by maker. Includes all types of deringers known by the authors to have been offered to the American market.

Devil's Paintbrush: Sir Hiram Maxim's Gun, The, by Dolf Goldsmith, 3rd Edition, expanded and revised, Collector Grade Publications, Toronto, Canada, 2002. 384 pp., illus. $79.95

The classic work on the world's first true automatic machine gun.

Dr. Josephus Requa Civil War Dentist and the Billinghurst-Requa Volley Gun, by John M. Hyson, Jr., & Margaret Requa DeFrancisco, Museum Restoration Service, Bloomfield, Ont., Canada, 1999. 36 pp., illus. Paper covers. $8.95

The story of the inventor of the first practical rapid-fire gun to be used during the American Civil War.

Dutch Luger (Parabellum) A Complete History, The, by Bas J. Martens and Guus de Vries, Ironside International Publishers, Inc., Alexandria, VA, 1995. 268 pp., illus. $49.95

The history of the Luger in the Netherlands. An extensive description of the Dutch pistol and trials and the different models of the Luger in the Dutch service.

Eagle on U.S. Firearms, The, by John W. Jordan, Pioneer Press, Union City, TN, 1992. 140 pp., illus. Paper covers. $17.50

Stylized eagles have been stamped on government owned or manufactured firearms in the U.S. since the beginning of our country. This book lists and illustrates these various eagles in an informative and refreshing manner.

Encyclopedia of Rifles & Handguns; A Comprehensive Guide to Firearms, edited by Sean Connolly, Chartwell Books, Inc., Edison, NJ., 1996. 160 pp., illustrated. $26.00

A lavishly illustrated book providing a comprehensive history of military and civilian personal firepower.

Eprouvettes: A Comprehensive Study of Early Devices for the Testing of Gunpowder, by R.T.W. Kempers, Royal Armouries Museum, Leeds, England, 1999. 352 pp., illustrated with 240 black & white and 28 color plates. $125.00

The first comprehensive study of eprouvettes ever attempted in a single volume.

European Firearms in Swedish Castles, by Kaa Wennberg, Bohuslaningens Boktryckeri AB, Uddevalla, Sweden, 1986. 156 pp., illus. $50.00

The famous collection of Count Keller, the Ettersburg Castle collection, and others. English text.

Fifteen Years in the Hawken Lode, by John D. Baird, The Gun Room Press, Highland Park, NJ, 1976. 120 pp., illus. $24.95

A collection of thoughts and observations gained from many years of intensive study of the guns from the shop of the Hawken brothers.

'51 Colt Navies, by Nathan L. Swayze, The Gun Room Press, Highland Park, NJ, 1993. 243 pp., illus. $59.95

The Model 1851 Colt Navy, its variations and markings.

Fighting Iron, by Art Gogan, Andrew Mowbray, Inc., Lincoln, R.I., 2002. 176 pp., illustrated. $28.00

It doesn't matter whether you collect guns, swords, bayonets or accountrement— sooner or later you realize that it all comes down to the metal. If you don't understand the metal you don't understand your collection.

Fine Colts, The Dr. Joseph A. Murphy Collection, by R.L. Wilson, Sheffield Marketing Associates, Inc., Doylestown, PA, 1999. 258 pp., illustrated. Limited edition signed and numbered. $99.00

This lavish new work covers exquisite, deluxe and rare Colt arms from Paterson and other percussion revolvers to the cartridge period and up through modern times.

Firearms, by Derek Avery, Desert Publications, El Dorado, AR, 1999. 95 pp., illustrated. $9.95

The firearms included in this book are by necessity only a selection, but nevertheless one that represents the best and most famous weapons seen since the Second World War.

THE ARMS LIBRARY

Firearms and Tackle Memorabilia, by John Delph, Schiffer Publishing, Ltd., West Chester, PA, 1991. 124 pp., illus. $39.95
A collector's guide to signs and posters, calendars, trade cards, boxes, envelopes, and other highly sought after memorabilia. With a value guide.

Firearms of the American West 1803-1865, Volume 1, by Louis A. Garavaglia and Charles Worman, University of Colorado Press, Niwot, CO, 1998. 402 pp., illustrated. $59.95
Traces the development and uses of firearms on the frontier during this period.

Firearms of the American West 1866-1894, by Louis A. Garavaglia and Charles G. Worman, University of Colorado Press, Niwot, CO, 1998. 416 pp., illus. $59.95
A monumental work that offers both technical information on all of the important firearms used in the West during this period and a highly entertaining history of how they were used, who used them, and why.

Firearms from Europe, 2nd Edition, by David Noe, Larry W. Yantz, Dr. James B. Whisker, Rowe Publications, Rochester, N.Y., 2002. 192 pp., illustrated. $45.00
A history and description of firearms imported during the American Civil War by the United States of America and the Confederate States of America.

Firepower from Abroad, by Wiley Sword, Andrew Mowbray Publishing, Lincoln, R.I., 2000. 120 pp., illustrated. $23.00
The Confederate Enfield and the LeMat revolver and how they reached the Confederate market.

Flayderman's Guide to Antique American Firearms and Their Values, 8th Edition, edited by Norm Flayderman, Krause Publications, Iola, WI, 2001. 692 pp., illus. Paper covers. $34.95
A completely updated and new edition with more than 3,600 models and variants extensively described with all marks and specifications necessary for quick identification.

FN-FAL Rifle, et al, The, by Duncan Long, Paladin Press, Boulder, CO, 1999. 144 pp., illustrated. Paper covers. $18.95
Detailed descriptions of the basic models produced by Fabrique Nationale and the myriad variants that evolved as a result of the firearms universal acceptance.

.45-70 Springfield; Book 1, The, by Frasca, Albert and Robert Hill. Frasca, Albert and Robert Hill. Frasca Publishing, 2000. Memorial edition. Hardback with gold embossed cover and spine. $95.00
The Memorial Edition reprint of The .45-70 Springfield was done to honor Robert H. Hill who was an outstanding Springfield collector, historian, researcher, and gunsmith. Only 1000 of these highly regarded books were printed using the same binding and cover material as the original 1980 edition. The book is considered The Bible for .45-70 Springfield Trapdoor collectors.

.45-70 Springfield Book II 1865-1893, The, by Frasca, Albert. Frasca Publishing, Springfield, Ohio 1997 Hardback with gold embossed cover and spine. The book has 400+ pages and 400+ photographs which cover ALL the trapdoor Springfield models. A MUST for the trapdoor collector! Hardback with gold embossed cover and spine. $85.00

.45-70 Springfield, The, by Joe Poyer and Craig Riesch, North Cape Publications, Tustin, CA, 1996. 150 pp., illus. Paper covers. $16.95
A revised and expanded second edition of a best-selling reference work organized by serial number and date of production to aid the collector in identifying popular "Trapdoor" rifles and carbines.

The French 1935 Pistols, by Eugene Medlin and Colin Doane, Eugene Medlin, El Paso, TX, 1995. 172 pp., illus. Paper covers. $25.95
The development and identification of successive models, fakes and variants, holsters and accessories, and serial numbers by dates of production.

Freund & Bro. Pioneer Gunmakers to the West, by F.J. Pablo Balentine, Graphic Publishers, Newport Beach, CA, 1997. 380 pp., illustrated $69.95
The story of Frank W. and George Freund, skilled German gunsmiths who plied their trade on the Western American frontier during the final three decades of the nineteenth century.

Fusil de Tulole in New France, 1691-1741, The, by Russel Bouchard, Museum Restorations Service, Bloomfield, Ontario, Canada, 1997. 36 pp., illus. Paper covers. $8.95
The development of the company and the identification of their arms.

Game Guns & Rifles: Percussion to Hammerless Ejector in Britain, by Richard Akehurst, Trafalgar Square, N. Pomfret, VT, 1993. 192 pp., illus. $39.95
Long considered a classic this important reprint covers the period of British gunmaking between 1830-1900.

Gas Trap Garand, The, by Billy Pyle, Collector Grade Publications, Cobourg, Ontario, Canada, 1999 316 pp., illustrated. $59.95
The in-depth story of the rarest Garands of them all, the initial 80 Model Shop rifles made under the personal supervision of John Garand himself in 1934 and 1935, and the first 50,000 plus production "gas trap" M1's manufactured at Springfield Armory between August, 1937 and August, 1940.

George Schreyer, Sr. and Jr., Gunmakers of Hanover, Pennsylvania, by George Shumway, George Shumway Publishers, York, PA, 1990. 160pp., illus. $50.00
This monograph is a detailed photographic study of almost all known surviving long rifles and smoothbore guns made by highly regarded gunsmiths George Schreyer, Sr. and Jr.

German Assault Rifle 1935-1945, The, by Peter R. Senich, Paladin Press, Boulder, CO, 1987. 328 pp., illus. $60.00
A complete review of machine carbines, machine pistols and assault rifles employed by Hitler's Wehrmacht during WWII.

German K98k Rifle, 1934-1945, The: The Backbone of the Wehrmacht, by Richard D. Law, Collector Grade Publications, Toronto, Canada, 1993. 336 pp., illus. $69.95
The most comprehensive study ever published on the 14,000,000 bolt-action K98k rifles produced in Germany between 1934 and 1945.

German Machine Guns, by Daniel D. Musgrave, revised edition, Ironside International Publishers, Inc. Alexandria, VA, 1992. 586 pp., 650 illus. $49.95
The most definitive book ever written on German machineguns. Covers the introduction and development of machineguns in Germany from 1899 to the rearmament period after WWII.

German Military Rifles and Machine Pistols, 1871-1945, by Hans Dieter Gotz, Schiffer Publishing Co., West Chester, PA, 1990. 245 pp., illus. $35.00
This book portrays in words and pictures the development of the modern German weapons and their ammunition including the scarcely known experimental types.

Glossary of the Construction, Decoration and Use of Arms and Armor in All Countries and in All Times, A, by George Cameron Stone., Dover Publishing, New York 1999. Softcover. $39.95
An exhaustive study of arms and armor in all countries through recorded history - from the stone age up to the second world war. With over 4500 Black & White Illustrations. This Dover edition is an unabridged republication of the work originally published in 1934 by the Southworth Press, Portland MA. A new Introduction has been specially prepared for this edition.

Government Models, The, by William H.D. Goddard, Andrew Mowbray Publishing, Lincoln, RI, 1998. 296 pp., illustrated. $58.50
The most authoritative source on the development of the Colt model of 1911.

Grasshoppers and Butterflies, by Adrian B. Caruana, Museum Restoration Service, Alexandria, Bay, N.Y., 1999. 32 pp., illustrated. Paper covers. $8.95
No.39 in the Historical Arms Series. The light 3 pounders of Pattison and Townsend.

Greener Story, The, by Graham Greener, Quiller Press, London, England, 2000. 256 pp., illustrated with 32 pages of color photos. $64.50
W.W. Greener, his family history, inventions, guns, patents, and more.

Greenhill Dictionary of Guns And Gunmakers: From Colt's First Patent to the Present Day, 1836-2001, The, by John Walter, Greenhill Publishing, 2001, 1st edition, 576 pages, illustrated with 200 photos, 190 trademarks and 40 line drawings, Hardcover: $59.95
Covers military small arms, sporting guns and rifles, air and gas guns, designers, inventors, patentees, trademarks, brand names and monograms.

Guide to American Trade Catalogs 1744-1900, A, by Lawrence B. Romaine, Dover Publications, New York, NY. 422 pp., illus. Paper covers. $12.95

Guide to Ballard Breechloaders, A, by George J. Layman, Pioneer Press, Union City, TN, 1997. 261 pp., illus. Paper covers. $19.95
Documents the saga of this fine rifle from the first models made by Ball & Williams of Worchester, to its production by the Marlin Firearms Co, to the cessation of 19th century manufacture in 1891, and finally to the modern reproductions made in the 1990's.

Guide to Civil War Artillery Projectiles, A, by Jack W. Melton, and Lawrence E. Pawl . Kennesaw, GA: Kennesaw Mounton Press, 1996
The concise pictorial study belongs on the shelf of every enthusiast. Hundreds of crisp photographs and a wealth of rich, well-researched information. 96 pps., illus. Softcover. $9.95

Guide to the Maynard Breechloader, A, by George J. Layman, George J. Layman, Ayer, MA, 1993. 125 pp., illus. Paper covers. $11.95
The first book dedicated entirely to the Maynard family of breech-loading firearms. Coverage of the arms is given from the 1850s through the 1880s.

Guide to U. S. Army Dress Helmets 1872-1904, A, by Kasal and Moore, North Cape Publications, 2000. 88 pp., illus. Paper covers. $15.95
This thorough study provides a complete description of the Model 1872 & 1881 dress helmets worn by the U.S. Army. Including all componets from bodies to plates to plumes & shoulder cords and tells how to differentiate the originals from reproductions. Extensively illustrated with photographs, '8 pages in full color' of complete helmets and their components.

The Gun and Its Development, by W.W. Greener, New York: Lyons Press, 2002. 9th edition. Rewritten, and with many additional illustrations. 804 pages plus advertising section. Contains over 700 illustrations plus many tables. Softcover. $19.95
A famed book of great value, truly encyclopedic in scope and sought after by firearms collectors.

Gun Collecting, by Geoffrey Boothroyd, Sportsman's Press, London, 1989. 208 pp., illus. $29.95
The most comprehensive list of 19th century British gunmakers and gunsmiths ever published.

Gunmakers of London 1350-1850 with Supplement, by Howard L. Blackmore, Museum Restoration Service, Alexandria Bay, NY, 1999. 222 pp., illus. $135.00
A listing of all the known workmen of gun making in the first 500 years, plus a history of the guilds, cutlers, armourers, founders, blacksmiths, etc. 260 gunmarks are illustrated. Supplement is 156 pages, and Begins with an introductory chapter on "foreighn" gunmakers followed by records of all the new information found about previously unidentified armourers, gunmakers and gunsmiths. 2 Volumes Slipcased

Guns that Won the West: Firearms of the American Frontier, 1865-1898, The, by John Walter, Stackpole Books, Inc., Mechanicsburg, PA.,1999. 256 pp., illustrated. $34.95
Here is the story of the wide range of firearms from pistols to rifles used by plainsmen and settlers, gamblers, native Americans and the U.S. Army.

Gunsmiths of Illinois, by Curtis L. Johnson, George Shumway Publishers, York, PA, 1995. 160 pp., illus. $50.00
Genealogical information is provided for nearly one thousand gunsmiths. Contains hundreds of illustrations of rifles and other guns, of handmade origin, from Illinois.

Gunsmiths of Manhattan, 1625-1900: A Checklist of Tradesmen, The, by Michael H. Lewis, Museum Restoration Service, Bloomfield, Ont., Canada, 1991. 40 pp., illus. Paper covers. $8.95
This listing of more than 700 men in the arms trade in New York City prior to about the end of the 19th century will provide a guide for identification and further research.

Guns of Dagenham: Lanchester, Patchett, Sterling, The, by Peter Laidler and David Howroyd, Collector Grade Publications, Inc., Cobourg, Ont., Canada, 1995. 310 pp., illus. $39.95
An in-depth history of the small arms made by the Sterling Company of Dagenham, Essex, England, from 1940 until Sterling was purchased by British Aerospace in 1989 and closed.

Guns of the Western Indian War, by R. Stephen Dorsey, Collector's Library, Eugene, OR, 1997. 220 pp., illus. Paper covers. $30.00
The full story of the guns and ammunition that made western history in the turbulent period of 1865-1890.

Gun Powder Cans & Kegs, by Ted & David Bacyk and Tom Rowe, Rowe Publications, Rochester, NY, 1999. 150 pp., illus. $65.00
The first book devoted to powder tins and kegs. All cans and kegs in full color. With a price guide and rarity scale.

Gun Tools, Their History and Identification by James B. Shaffer, Lee A. Rutledge and R. Stephen Dorsey, Collector's Library, Eugene, OR, 1992. 375 pp., illus. $30.00

Written history of foreign and domestic gun tools from the flintlock period to WWII.

Gun Tools, Their History and Identifications, Volume 2, by Stephen Dorsey and James B. Shaffer, Collectors' Library, Eugene, OR, 1997. 396 pp., illus. Paper covers. $30.00

Gun tools from the Royal Armouries Museum in England, Pattern Room, Royal Ordnance Reference Collection in Nottingham and from major private collections.

Gunsmiths of Maryland, by Daniel D. Hartzler and James B. Whisker, Old Bedford Village Press, Bedford, PA, 1998. 208 pp., illustrated. $40.00

Covers firelock Colonial period through the breech-loading patent models. Featuring longrifles.

Gunsmiths of Virginia, by Daniel D. Hartzler and James B. Whisker, Old Bedford Village Press, Bedford, PA, 1992. 206 pp., illustrated. $40.00

A photographic study of American longrifles.

Gunsmiths of West Virginia, by Daniel D. Hartzler and James B. Whisker, Old Bedford Village Press, Bedford, PA, 1998. 176 pp., illustrated. $40.00

A photographic study of American longrifles.

Hall's Military Breechloaders, by Peter A. Schmidt, Andrew Mowbray Publishers, Lincoln, RI, 1996. 232 pp., illus. $55.00

The whole story behind these bold and innovative firearms.

Handgun, The, by Geoffrey Boothroyd, David and Charles, North Pomfret, VT, 1989. 566 pp., illus. $50.00

Every chapter deals with an important period in handgun history from the 14th century to the present.

Handguns & Rifles: The Finest Weapons from Around the World, by Ian Hogg, Random House Value Publishing, Inc., N.Y., 1999. 128 pp., illustrated. $18.98

The serious gun collector will welcome this fully illustrated examination of international handguns and rifles. Each entry covers the history of the weapon, what purpose it serves, and its advantages and disadvantages.

Hawken Rifle: Its Place in History, The, by Charles E. Hanson, Jr., The Fur Press, Chadron, NE, 1979. 104 pp., illus. Paper covers. $15.00

A definitive work on this famous rifle.

Hawken Rifles, The Mountain Man's Choice, by John D. Baird, The Gun Room Press, Highland Park, NJ, 1976. 95 pp., illus. $29.95

Covers the rifles developed for the Western fur trade. Numerous specimens are described and shown in photographs.

High Standard: A Collector's Guide to the Hamden & Hartford Target Pistols, by Tom Dance, Andrew Mowbray, Inc., Lincoln, RI, 1991. 192 pp., illus. Paper covers. $24.00

From Citation to Supermatic, all of the production models and specials made from 1951 to 1984 are covered according to model number or series.

Historical Hartford Hardware, by William W. Dalrymple, Colt Collector Press, Rapid City, SD, 1976. 42 pp., illus. Paper covers. $10.00

Historically associated Colt revolvers.

History and Development of Small Arms Ammunition, The, Volume 2, by George A. Hoyem, Armory Publications, Oceanside, CA, 1991. 303 pp., illus. $65.00

Covers the blackpowder military centerfire rifle, carbine, machine gun and volley gun ammunition used in 28 nations and dominions, together with the firearms that chambered them.

History and Development of Small Arms Ammunition, The, Volume 4, by George A. Hoyem, Armory Publications, Seattle, WA, 1998. 200 pp., illustrated $65.00

A comprehensive book on American black powder and early smokeless rifle cartridges.

History of Colt Firearms, The, by Dean Boorman, Lyons Press, New York, NY, 2001. 144 pp., illus. $29.95

Discover the fascinating story of the world's most famous revolver, complete with more than 150 stunning full-color photographs.

History of the German Steel Helmet: 1916-1945, by Ludwig Baer. Bender Publishing, San Jose, CA, 2001. 448 pages, nearly 1,000 photos & illustrations. $54.95

This publication is the most complete and detailed German steel helmet book ever produced, with in-depth documented text and nearly 1,000 photographs and illustrations encompassing all German steel helmets from 1916 through 1945. The regulations, modifications and use of camouflage are carefully clarified for the Imperial Army, Reichswehr and the numerous 3rd Reich organizations.

History of Modern U.S. Military Small Arms Ammunition. Volume 1, 1880-1939, revised by F.W. Hackley, W.H. Woodin and E.L. Scranton, Thomas Publications, Gettysburg, PA, 1998. 328 pp., illus. $49.95

This revised edition incorporates all publicly available information concerning military small arms ammunition for the period 1880 through 1939 in a single volume.

History of Modern U.S. Military Small Arms Ammunition. Volume 2, 1940-1945 by F.W. Hackley, W.H. Woodin and E.L. Scranton. Gun Room Press, Highland Park, NJ. 300 + pages, illustrated. $39.95

Based on decades of original research conducted at the National Archives, numerous military, public and private museums and libraries, as well as individual collections, this edition incorporates all publicly available information concerning military small arms ammunition for the period 1940 through 1945.

The History of Smith & Wesson Firearms, by Dean Boorman, Lyons Press, New York, NY, 2002. 144 pp., illustrated in full color. Hardcover. New dust jacket. $29.95

The definitive guide to one of the world's best-known firearms makers. Takes the story through the years of the Military & Police .38 & of the Magnum cartridge, to today's wide range of products for law-enforcement customers.

The History of Winchester Rifles, by Dean Boorman, Lyons Press, New York, NY, 2001. 144 pp., illus. $29.95

A captivating and wonderfully photographed history of one of the most legendary names in gun lore. 150 full-color photos.

History of Winchester Firearms 1866-1992, The, sixth edition, updated, expanded, and revised by Thomas Henshaw, New Win Publishing, Clinton, NJ, 1993. 280 pp., illus. $27.95

This classic is the standard reference for all collectors and others seeking the facts about any Winchester firearm, old or new.

Honour Bound: The Chauchat Machine Rifle, by Gerard Demaison and Yves Buffetaut, Collector Grade Publications, Inc., Cobourg, Ont., Canada, 1995. $39.95.

The story of the CSRG (Chauchat) machine rifle, the most manufactured automatic weapon of World War One.

Hunting Weapons From the Middle Ages to the Twentieth Century, by Howard L. Blackmore, Dover Publications, Meneola, NY, 2000. 480 pp., illustrated. Paper covers. $16.95

Dealing mainly with the different classes of weapons used in sport—swords, spears, crossbows, guns, and rifles—from the Middle Ages until the present day.

Identification Manual on the .303 British Service Cartridge, No. 1-Ball Ammunition, by B.A. Temple, I.D.S.A. Books, Piqua, OH, 1986. 84 pp., 57 illus. $12.50

Identification Manual on the .303 British Service Cartridge, No. 2-Blank Ammunition, by B.A. Temple, I.D.S.A. Books, Piqua, OH, 1986. 95 pp., 59 illus. $12.50

Identification Manual on the .303 British Service Cartridge, No. 3-Special Purpose Ammunition, by B.A. Temple, I.D.S.A. Books, Piqua, OH, 1987. 82 pp., 49 illus. $12.50

Identification Manual on the .303 British Service Cartridge, No. 4-Dummy Cartridges Henry 1869-c.1900, by B.A. Temple, I.D.S.A. Books, Piqua, OH, 1988. 84 pp., 70 illus. $12.50

Identification Manual on the .303 British Service Cartridge, No. 5-Dummy Cartridges (2), by B.A. Temple, I.D.S.A. Books, Piqua, OH, 1994. 78 pp. $12.50

Illustrated Book of Guns, The, by David Miller, Salamander Books, N.Y., N.Y., 2000. 304 pp., illustrated in color. $34.95

An illustrated directory of over 1,000 military and sporting firearms.

Illustrated Encyclopedia of Civil War Collectibles, The, by Chuck Lawliss, Henry Holt and Co., New York, NY, 1997. 316 pp., illus. Paper covers. $22.95

A comprehensive guide to Union and Confederate arms, equipment, uniforms, and other memorabilia.

Illustrations of United States Military Arms 1776-1903 and Their Inspector's Marks, compiled by Turner Kirkland, Pioneer Press, Union City, TN, 1988. 37 pp., illus. Paper covers. $7.00

Reprinted from the 1949 Bannerman catalog. Valuable information for both the advanced and beginning collector.

Indian War Cartridge Pouches, Boxes and Carbine Boots, by R. Stephen Dorsey, Collector's Library, Eugene, OR, 1993. 156 pp., illus. Paper Covers. $20.00

The key reference work to the cartridge pouches, boxes, carbine sockets and boots of the Indian War period 1865-1890.

International Armament, with History, Data, Technical Information and Photographs of Over 800 Weapons, by George Johnson. Alexandria, VA: Ironside International, 2002. 2nd edition, new printing. Over 947 pages, illustrated with over 800 photos. Hardcover. $59.95

The development and progression of modern military small arms. All significant weapons have been included and examined in depth. Over 800 photographs and illustrations with both historical and technical data. Two volumes are now bound into one book.

Introduction to the Civil War Small Arms, An, by Earl J. Coates and Dean S. Thomas, Thomas Publishing Co., Gettysburg, PA, 1990. 96 pp., illus. Paper covers. $10.00

The small arms carried by the individual soldier during the Civil War.

Japanese Rifles of World War Two, by Duncan O. McCollum, Excalibur Publications, Latham, NY, 1996. 64 pp., illus. Paper covers. $18.95

A sweeping view of the rifles and carbines that made up Japan's arsenal during the conflict.

Kalashnikov "Machine Pistols, Assault Rifles, and Machine Guns, 1945 to the Present", by John Walter, Paladin Press, Boulder, CO, 1999, hardcover, photos, illus., 146 pp. $22.95

This exhaustive work published by Greenhill Military Manuals features a gun-by-gun directory of Kalashnikov variants. Technical specifications and illustrations are provided throughout, along with details of sights, bayonets, markings and ammunition. A must for the serious collector and historian.

Kentucky Pistol, The, by Roy Chandler and James Whisker, Old Bedford Village Press, Bedford, PA, 1997. 225 pp., illus. $60.00

A photographic study of Kentucky pistols from famous collections.

Kentucky Rifle, The, by Captain John G.W. Dillin, George Shumway Publisher, York, PA, 1993. 221 pp., illus. $50.00

This well-known book was the first attempt to tell the story of the American longrifle. This edition retains the original text and illustrations with supplemental footnotes provided by Dr. George Shumway.

Know Your Broomhandle Mausers, by R.J. Berger, Blacksmith Corp., Southport, CT, 1996. 96 pp., illus. Paper covers. $14.95

An interesting story on the big Mauser pistol and its variations.

Law Enforcement Memorabilia Price and Identification Guide, by Monty McCord, DBI Books a division of Krause Publications, Inc. Iola, WI, 1999. 208 pp., illustrated. Paper covers. $19.95

An invaluable reference to the growing wave of law enforcement collectors. Hundreds of items are covered from miniature vehicles to clothes, patches, and restraints.

Legendary Sporting Guns, by Eric Joly, Abbeville Press, New York, N.Y., 1999. 228 pp., illustrated. $65.00

A survey of hunting through the ages and relates how many different types of firearms were created and refined for use afield.

Legends and Reality of the AK, by Val Shilin and Charlie Cutshaw, Paladen Press, Boulder, CO, 2000. 192 pp., illustrated. Paper covers. $35.00

A behind-the-scenes look at history, design and impact of the Kalashnikov family of weapons.

LeMat, the Man, the Gun, by Valmore J. Forgett and Alain F. and Marie-Antoinette Serpette, Navy Arms Co., Ridgefield, NJ, 1996. 218 pp., illus. $49.95

The first definitive study of the Confederate revolvers invention, development and delivery by Francois Alexandre LeMat.

THE ARMS LIBRARY

Light 6-Pounder Battalion Gun of 1776, The, by Adrian Caruana, Museum Restoration Service, Bloomfield, Ontario, Canada, 2001. 76 pp., illus. Paper covers. $8.95

London Gun Trade, 1850-1920, The, by Joyce E. Gooding, Museum Restoration Service, Bloomfield, Ontario, Canada, 2001. 48 pp., illus. Paper covers. $8.95

Names, dates and locations of London gunmakers working between 1850 and 1920 are listed. Compiled from the original Kelly's Post Office Directories of the City of London.

London Gunmakers and the English Duelling Pistol, 1770-1830, The, by Keith R. Dill, Museum Restoration Service, Bloomfield, Ontario, Canada, 1997. 36 pp., illus. Paper covers. $8.95

Ten gunmakers made London one of the major gunmaking centers of the world. This book examines how the design and construction of their pistols contributed to that reputation and how these characteristics may be used to date flintlock arms.

Longrifles of Pennsylvania, Volume 1, Jefferson, Clarion & Elk Counties, by Russel H. Harringer, George Shumway Publisher, York, PA, 1984. 200 pp., illus. $50.00

First in series that will treat in great detail the longrifles and gunsmiths of Pennsylvania.

Luger Handbook, The, by Aarron Davis, Krause Publications, Iola, WI, 1997. 112 pp., illus. Paper covers. $9.95

Quick reference to classify Luger models and variations with complete details including proofmarks.

Lugers at Random, by Charles Kenyon, Jr., Handgun Press, Glenview, IL, 1990. 420 pp., illus. $59.95

A new printing of this classic, comprehensive reference for all Luger collectors.

Luger Story, The, by John Walter, Stackpole Books, Mechanicsburg, PA, 2001. 256 pp., illus. Paper Covers $19.95

The standard history of the world's most famous handgun.

M1 Carbine, by Larry Ruth, Gun room Press, Highland Park, NJ, 1987. 291 pp., illus. Paper $19.95

The origin, development, manufacture and use of this famous carbine of World War II.

M-1 Carbine—A Revolution in Gun-Stocking, The, by Grafton H. Cook II and Barbara W. Cook. Lincoln, RI: Andrew Mowbray, Inc., 2002. 1st edition. 208 pages, heavily illustrated with 157 rare photographs of the guns and the men and women who made them. Softcover. $29.95

Shows you, step by step, how M1 Carbine stocks were made, right through to assembly with the hardware. Learn about M1 Carbine development, and how the contracting and production process actually worked. Also contains lots of detailed information about other military weapons, like the M1A1, the M1 Garand, the M14 and much, much more. Includes more than 200 short biographies of the people who made M1 Carbines. The depth of this information will amaze you. Shows and explains the machinery used to make military rifle stocks during World War II, with photos of these remarkable machines and data about when they were invented and shipped. Explains why walnut gunstocks are so very difficult to make, and why even large gun manufacturers are usually unable to do this specialized work.

M1 Carbine: Owner's Guide, The by Scott A. Duff, Scott A. Duff, Export, PA, 1997. 126 pp., illus. Paper covers. $21.95

This book answers the questions M1 owners most often ask concerning maintenance activities not encounted by military users.

M1 Garand: Owner's Guide, The by Scott A. Duff, Scott A. Duff, Export, PA, 1998. 132 pp., illus. Paper covers. $21.95

This book answers the questions M1 owners most often ask concerning maintenance activities not encounted by military users.

M1 Garand Serial Numbers and Data Sheets, The by Scott A. Duff, Export, PA, 1995. 101 pp., illus. Paper covers. $11.95

Provides the reader with serial numbers related to dates of manufacture and a large sampling of data sheets to aid in identification or restoration.

M1 Garand 1936 to 1957, The by Joe Poyer and Craig Riesch, North Cape Publications, Tustin, CA, 1996. 216 pp., illus. Paper covers. $19.95

Describes the entire range of M1 Garand production in text and quick-scan charts.

M1 Garand: Post World War, The by Scott A. Duff, Scott A. Duff, Export, PA, 1990. 139 pp., illus. Soft covers. $21.95

A detailed account of the activities at Springfield Armory through this period. International Harvester, H&R, Korean War production and quantities delivered. Serial numbers.

M1 Garand: World War 2, The by Scott A. Duff, Scott A. Duff, Export, PA, 2001. 210 pp., illus. Paper covers. $34.95

The most comprehensive study available to the collector and historian on the M1 Garand of World War II.

Machine Guns, by Ian V. Hogg. Iola, WI: Krause Publications, 2002. 1st edition. 336 pages, illustrated with b & w photos with a 16 page color section. Softcover. $29.95

A detailed history of the rapid-fire gun, 14th century to present. Covers the development, history and specifications.

Maine Made Guns and Their Makers, by Dwight B. Demeritt Jr., Maine State Museum, Augusta, ME, 1998. 209 pp., illustrated. $55.00

An authoritative, biographical study of Maine gunsmiths.

Marlin Firearms: A History of the Guns and the Company That Made Them, by Lt. Col. William S. Brophy, USAR, Ret., Stackpole Books, Harrisburg, PA, 1989. 672 pp., illus. $80.00

The definitive book on the Marlin Firearms Co. and their products.

Martini-Henry .450 Rifles & Carbines, by Dennis Lewis, Excalibur Publications, Latham, NY, 1996. 72 pp., illus. Paper covers. $11.95

The stories of the rifles and carbines that were the mainstay of the British soldier through the Victorian wars.

Mauser Bolt Rifles, by Ludwig Olson, F. Brownell & Son, Inc., Montezuma, IA, 1999. 364 pp., illus. $59.95

The most complete, detailed, authoritative and comprehensive work ever done on Mauser bolt rifles. Completely revised deluxe 3rd edition.

Mauser Military Rifles of the World, 2nd Edition, by Robert Ball, Krause Publications, Iola, WI, 2000. 304 pp., illustrated with 1,000 b&w photos and a 48 page color section. $44.95

This 2nd edition brings more than 100 new photos of these historic rifles and the wars in which they were carried.

Mauser Military Rifle Markings, by Terence W. Lapin, Arlington, VA: Hyrax Publishers, LLC, 2001. 167 pages, illustrated. 2nd edition. Revised and expanded. Softcover. $22.95

A general guide to reading and understanding the often mystifying markings found on military Mauser Rifles. Includes German Regimental markings as well as German police markings and W.W. 2 German Mauser subcontractor codes. A handy reference to take to gun shows.

Mauser Smallbores Sporting, Target and Training Rifles, by Jon Speed, Collector Grade Publications, Cobourg, Ontario, Canada 1998. 349 pp., illustrated. $67.50

A history of all the smallbore sporting, target and training rifles produced by the legendary Mauser-Werke of Obendorf Am Neckar.

Military Holsters of World War 2, by Eugene J. Bender, Rowe Publications, Rochester, NY, 1998. 200 pp., illustrated. $45.00

A revised edition with a new price guide of the most definitive book on this subject.

Military Pistols of Japan, by Fred L. Honeycutt, Jr., Julin Books, Palm Beach Gardens, FL, 1997. 168 pp., illus. $42.00

Covers every aspect of military pistol production in Japan through WWII.

Military Remington Rolling Block Rifle, The, by George Layman, Pioneer Press, TN, 1998. 146 pp., illus. Paper covers. $24.95

A standard reference for those with an interest in the Remington rolling block family of firearms.

Military Rifles of Japan, 5th Edition, by F.L. Honeycutt, Julin Books, Lake Park, FL, 1999. 208 pp., illus. $42.00

A new revised and updated edition. Includes the early Murata-period markings, etc.

Military Small Arms Data Book, by Ian V. Hogg, Stackpole Books, Mechanicsburg, PA, 1999. $44.95. 336 pp., illustrated.

Data on more than 1,500 weapons. Covers a vast range of weapons from pistols to anti-tank rifles. Essential data, 1870-2000, in one volume.

MP38, 40, 40/1 & 41 Submachine Gun, The, by de Vries & Martens. Propaganda Photo Series, Volume II. Alexandria, VA: Ironside International, 2001. 1st edition. 150 pages, illustrated with 200 high quality black & white photos. Hardcover. $34.95

Covers all essential information on history and development, ammunition and accessories, codes and markings, and contains photos of nearly every model and accessory. Includes a unique selection of original German WWII propoganda photos, most never published before.

Modern Beretta Firearms, by Gene Gangarosa, Jr., Stoeger Publishing Co., So. Hackensack, NJ, 1994. 288 pp., illus. Paper covers. $16.95

Traces all models of modern Beretta pistols, rifles, machine guns and combat shotguns.

Modern Gun Values, The Gun Digest Book of, 11th Edition, by the Editors of Gun Digest. Krause Publications, Iola, WI., 2002. 560 pp. illus. Paper covers. $21.95

Greatly updated and expanded edition describing and valuing over 7,000 firearms manufactured from 1900 to 1996. The standard for valuing modern firearms.

Modern Gun Identification & Value Guide, 13th Edition, by Russell and Steve Quertermous, Collector Books, Paducah, KY, 1998. 504 pp., illus. Paper covers. $14.95

Features current values for over 2,500 models of rifles, shotguns and handguns, with over 1,800 illustrations.

More Single Shot Rifles, by James C. Grant, The Gun Room Press, Highland Park, NJ, 1976. 324 pp., illus. $35.00

Details the guns made by Frank Wesson, Milt Farrow, Holden, Borchardt, Stevens, Remington, Winchester, Ballard and Peabody-Martini.

Mortimer, the Gunmakers, 1753-1923, by H. Lee Munson, Andrew Mowbray Inc., Lincoln, RI, 1992. 320 pp., illus. $65.00

Seen through a single, dominant, English gunmaking dynasty this fascinating study provides a window into the classical era of firearms artistry.

Mosin-Nagant Rifle, The, by Terence W. Lapin, North Cape Publications, Tustin, CA, 1998. 30 pp., illustrated. Paper covers. $19.95

The first ever complete book on the Mosin-Nagant rifle written in English. Covers every variation.

Navy Luger, The, by Joachim Gortz and John Walter, Handgun Press, Glenview, IL, 1988. 128 pp., illus. $24.95

The 9mm Pistole 1904 and the Imperial German Navy. A concise illustrated history.

New World of Russian Small Arms and Ammunition, The, by Charlie Cutshaw, Paladin Press, Boulder, CO, 1998. 160 pp., illustrated. $42.95

Detailed descriptions, specifications and first-class illustrations of the AN-94, PSS silent pistol, Bizon SMG, Saifa-12 tactical shotgun, the GP-25 grenade launcher and more cutting edge Russian weapons.

Number 5 Jungle Carbine, The, by Alan M. Petrillo, Excalibur Publications, Latham, NY, 1994. 32 pp., illus. Paper covers. $7.95

A comprehensive treatment of the rifle that collectors have come to call the "Jungle Carbine"—the Lee-Enfield Number 5, Mark 1.

Observations on Colt's Second Contract, November 2, 1847, by G. Maxwell Longfield and David T. Basnett, Museum Restoration Service, Bloomfield, Ontario, Canada, 1997. 36 pp., illus. Paper covers. $6.95

This study traces the history and the construction of the Second Model Colt Dragoon supplied in 1848 to the U.S. Cavalry.

Official Price Guide to Gun Collecting, by R.L. Wilson, Ballantine/House of Collectibles, New York, NY, 1998. 450 pp., illus. Paper covers. $21.50

Covers more than 30,000 prices from Colt revolvers to Winchester rifles and shotguns to German Lugers and British sporting rifles and game guns.

Official Price Guide to Military Collectibles, 6th edition, by Richard J. Austin, Random House, Inc., New York, NY, 1998. 200 pp., illus. Paper cover. $20.00

Covers weapons and other collectibles from wars of the distant and recent past. More than 4,000 prices are listed. Illustrated with 400 black & white photos plus a full-color insert.

Official Soviet SVD Manual, The, by Major James F. Gebhardt (Ret.) Paladin Press, Boulder, CO, 1999. 112 pp., illustrated. Paper covers. $15.00

Operating instructions for the 7.62mm Dragunov, the first Russian rifle developed from scratch specifically for sniping.

Old Gunsights: A Collector's Guide, 1850 to 2000, by Nicholas Stroebel, Krause Publications, Iola, WI, 1998. 320 pp., illus. Paper covers. $29.95

An in-depth and comprehensive examination of old gunsights and the rifles on which they were used to get accurate feel for prices in this expanding market.

THE ARMS LIBRARY

Old Rifle Scopes, by Nicholas Stroebel, Krause Publications, Iola, WI, 2000. 400 pp., illustrated. Paper covers. $31.95
This comprehensive collector's guide takes aim at more than 120 scope makers and 60 mount makers and features photos and current market values for 300 scopes and mounts manufactured from 1950-1985.

Ordnance Tools, Accessories & Appendages of the M1 Rifle, by Billy Pyle. Houston, TX: Privately Printed, 2002. 2nd edition. 206 pages, illustrated with b & w photos. Softcover $40.00
This is the new updated second edition with over 350 pictures and drawings - 30 of which are new. Part I contains accessories, appendages, and equipment including such items as bayonets, blank firing attachments, cheek pads, cleaning equipment, clips, flash hiders, grenade launchers, scabbards, slings, telescopes and mounts, winter triggers, and much more. Part II covers ammunition, grenades, and pyrotechnics. Part III shows the inspection gages. Part IV presents the ordnance tools, fixtures, and assemblies. Part V contains miscellaneous items related to the M1 Rifle such as arms racks, rifle racks, clip loading machine, and other devices.

Orders, Decorations and Badges of the Socialist Republic of Vietnam and the National Front for the Liberation of South Vietnam, by Edward J. Emering. Schiffer Publications, Atglen, PA. 2000. 96 pages, 190 color and b/w photographs, line drawings. $24.95
The Orders and Decorations of the "enemy" during the Vietnam War have remained shrouded in mystery for many years. References to them are scarce and interrogations of captives during the war often led to the proliferation of misinformation concerning them. Includes value guide.

Packing Iron, by Richard C. Rattenbury, Zon International Publishing, Millwood, NY, 1993. 216 pp., illus. $45.00
The best book yet produced on pistol holsters and rifle scabbards. Over 300 variations of holster and scabbards are illustrated in large, clear plates.

Painted Steel, Steel Pots Volume 2, by Chris Armold. Bender Publishing, San Jose, CA, 2001. 384 pages - 1,053 photos (hundreds in color) $57.95
From the author of "Steel Pots: The History of America's Steel Combat Helmets" comes "Painted Steel: Steel Pots, Vol. II." This companion volume features detailed chapters on painted and unit marked helments of WWI and WWII, plus a variety of divisional, regimental and subordinate markings. Special full-color plates detail subordinate unit markings such as the tactical markings used by the U.S. 2nd Division in WWI. In addition, insignia and specialty markings such as USN beach battalion, Army engineers, medics, MP and airborne division tactical markings are examined. For those interested in American armored forces, a complete chapter is devoted to the history of the U.S. tank and combat vehicle crewman's helmet from WWI to present. Other chapters provide tips on reproductions and fake representations of U.S. helmets and accessories. With over 1,000 photos and images (many in color), "Painted Steel" will be a prized addition to any collector's reference bookshelf.

Parabellum: A Technical History of Swiss Lugers, by Vittorio Bobba, Priuli & Verlucca, Editori, Torino, Italy, 1996. Italian and English text. Illustrated. $100.00

Patents for Inventions, Class 119 (Small Arms), 1855-1930. British Patent Office, Armory Publications, Oceanside, CA, 1993. 7 volume set. $375.00
Contains 7980 abridged patent descriptions and their sectioned line drawings, plus a 37-page alphabetical index of the patentees.

Pattern Dates for British Ordnance Small Arms, 1718-1783, by DeWitt Bailey, Thomas Publications, Gettysburg, PA, 1997. 116 pp., illus. Paper covers. $20.00
The weapons discussed in this work are those carried by troops sent to North America between 1737 and 1783, or shipped to them as replacement arms while in America.

Peters & King, by Thomas D. Schiffer. Krause Publications, Iola, WI 2002. 1st edition. 256 pages, 200+ black & white photos with a 32 page color section. Hardcover. $44.95
Discover the history behind Peters Cartridge and King Powder and see how they shaped the arms industry into what it is today and why their products fetch hundreds and even thousands of dollars at auctions. Current values are provided for their highly collectible product packaging and promotional advertising premiums such as powder kegs, tins, cartridge boxes, and calendars.

Pitman Notes on U.S. Martial Small Arms and Ammunition, 1776-1933, Volume 2, Revolvers and Automatic Pistols, The, by Brig. Gen. John Pitman, Thomas Publications, Gettysburg, PA, 1990. 192 pp., illus. $29.95
A most important primary source of information on United States military small arms and ammunition.

Plates and Buckles of the American Military 1795-1874, by Sydney C. Kerksis, Orange, VA: Publisher's Press, 1998. 5th edition. 568 pages, illustrated with 100's of black and white photos. Hardcover. $39.00
The single most comprehensive reference for U.S. and Confederate plates.

Plains Rifle, The, by Charles Hanson, Gun Room Press, Highland Park, NJ, 1989. 169 pp., illus. $35.00
All rifles that were made with the plainsman in mind, including pistols.

Powder and Ball Small Arms, by Martin Pegler, Windrow & Green, London, 1998. 128 pp., illus. $39.95
Part of the new "Live Firing Classic Weapons" series featuring full color photos of experienced shooters dressed in authentic costumes handling, loading and firing historic weapons.

Powder Flask Book, The, by Ray Riling, R&R Books, Livonia, NY, 1993. 514 pp., illus. $69.95
The complete book on flasks of the 19th century. Exactly scaled pictures of 1,600 flasks are illustrated.

Proud Promise: French Autoloading Rifles, 1898-1979,by Jean Huon, Collector Grade Publications, Inc., Cobourg, Ont., Canada, 1995. 216 pp., illus. $39.95
The author has finally set the record straight about the importance of French contributions to modern arms design.

E. C. Prudhomme's Gun Engraving Review, by E. C. Prudhomme, R&R Books, Livonia, NY, 1994. 164 pp., illus. $60.00
As a source for engravers and collectors, this book is an indispensable guide to styles and techniques of the world's foremost engravers.

Purdey Gun and Rifle Makers: The Definitive History, by Donald Dallas, Quiller Press, London, 2000. 245 pp., illus. Color throughout. $100.00
A limited edition of 3,000 copies. Signed and numbered. With a PURDEY book plate.

Queen Anne Pistol, 1660-1780: A History of the Turn-Off Pistol, The, by John W. Burgoyne, Bloomfield, Ont. CANADA: Museum Restoration Service, 2002. 1st edition — Historical Arms New Series No. 1. ISBN: 0-88855-0154. 120 pages. Pictorial Hardcover. $35.00
A detailed, fast moving, thoroughly researched text and almost 200 cross-referenced illustrations. This distinctive breech-loading arm was developed in the middle years of the 17th century but found popularity during the reign of the monarch (1702-1714), by whose name it is known.

Red Shines the Sun: A Pictorial History of the Fallschirm-Infantrie, by Eric Queen. San Jose, CA: R. James Bender Publishing, 2003. 1st edition. Hardcover. $69.95
A culmination of 12 years of research, this reference work traces the history of the Army paratroopers of the Fallschirm-Infanterie from their origins in 1937, to the expansion to battalion strength in 1938, then on through operations at Wola Gulowska (Poland), and Moerdijk (Holland). This 240 page comprehensive look at their history is supported by 600 images, many of which are in full color, and nearly 90% are previously unpublished. This work also features original examples of nearly all documents awarded to the Army paratroopers, as well as the most comprehensive study to date of the Army paratrooper badge or Fallschirmschützenabzeichen (Heer). Original examples of all known variations (silver, aluminum, cloth, feinzink) are pictured in full color. If you are interested in owning one of these badges, this book can literally save you from making a $2,000.00 mistake.

Reloading Tools, Sights and Telescopes for Single Shot Rifles, by Gerald O. Kelver, Brighton, CO, 1982. 163 pp., illus. Paper covers. $13.95
A listing of most of the famous makers of reloading tools, sights and telescopes with a brief description of the products they manufactured.

The Remington-Lee Rifle, by Eugene F. Myszkowski, Excalibur Publications, Latham, NY, 1995. 100 pp., illus. Paper covers. $22.50
Features detailed descriptions, including serial number ranges, of each model from the first Lee Magazine Rifle produced for the U.S. Navy to the last Remington-Lee Small Bores shipped to the Cuban Rural Guard.

Remington 'America's Oldest Gunmaker' The Official Authorized History Of The Remington Arms Company, by Roy Marcot. Madison, NC: Remington Arms Company, 1999. 1st edition. 312 pages, with 167 black & white illustrations, plus 291 color plates. $79.95
This is without a doubt the finest history of that firm ever to have been compiled. Based on firsthand research in the Remington companies archives, it is extremely well written.

Remington's Vest Pocket Pistols, by Hatfield, Robert E. Lincoln, RI: Andrew Mowbray, Inc., 2002. 117 pages. Hardcover. $29.95
While Remington Vest Pocket Pistols have always been popular with collectors, very little solid information has been available about them. Such simple questions such as "When were they made?"..."How many were produced?"...and "What calibers were they available in?" have all remained unanswered. This new book, based upon years of study and a major survey of surviving examples, attempts to answer these critical questions. Specifications, markings, mechanical design and patents are also presented here. Inside you will find 100+ photographs, serial number data, exploded views of all four Remington Vest Pocket Pistol sizes, component parts lists and a guide to disassembly and reassembly. Also includes a discussion of Vest Pocket Wire-Stocked Buggy/Bicycle rifles, plus the documented serial number story.

Revolvers of the British Services 1854-1954, by W.H.J. Chamberlain and A.W.F. Taylerson, Museum Restoration Service, Ottawa, Canada, 1989. 80 pp., illus. $27.50
Covers the types issued among many of the United Kingdom's naval, land or air services.

Rifles of the World, by Oliver Achard, Chartwell Books, Inc., Edison, NJ, 141 pp., illus. $24.95
A unique insight into the world of long guns, not just rifles, but also shotguns, carbines and all the usual multi-barreled guns that once were so popular with European hunters, especially in Germany and Austria.

Round Ball to Rimfire, Vol. 1, by Dean Thomas, Thomas Publications, Gettysburg, PA, 1997. 144 pp., illus. $49.95
The first of a two-volume set of the most complete history and guide for all small arms ammunition used in the Civil War. The information includes data from research and development to the arsenals that created it.

Round Ball to Rimfire: A History of Civil War Small Arms Ammunition, Vol. 2. by Dean Thomas, Thomas Publications, Gettysburg, PA 2002. 528 pages. Hardcover. $49.95
Completely discusses the ammunition for Federal Breechloading Carbines and Rifles. The seven chapters with eighteen appendices detailing the story of the twenty-seven or so different kinds of breechloaders actually purchased or ordered by the Ordnance Department during the Civil War. The book is conveniently divided by the type of priming — external or internal — and then alphabetically by maker or supplier. A wealth of new information and research has proven that these weapons either functioned properly or were inadequate relative to the design and ingenuity of the proprietary cartridges.

Russell M. Catron and His Pistols, by Warren H. Buxton, Ucross Books, Los Alamos, NM, 1998. 224 pp., illustrated. Paper covers. $49.50
An unknown American firearms inventor and manufacturer of the mid twentieth century. Military, commerical, ammunition.

SAFN-49 and The FAL, The, by Joe Poyer and Dr. Richard Feirman, North Cape Publications, Tustin, CA, 1998. 160 pp., illus. Paper covers. $14.95
The first complete overview of the SAFN-49 battle rifle, from its pre-World War 2 beginnings to its military service in countries as diverse as the Belgian Congo and Argentina. The FAL was "light" version of the SAFN-49 and it became the Free World's most adopted battle rifle.

Sauer & Sohn, Sauer "Dein Waffenkamerad" Volume 2, J. P., by Cate & Krause, Walsworth Publishing, Chattanooga, TN, 2000. 440 pp., illus. $69.95
A historical study of Sauer automatic pistols. This new volume includes a great deal of new knowledge that has surfaced about the firm J.P. Sauer. You will find new photos, documentation, serial number ranges and historial facts which will expand the knowledge and interest in the oldest and best of the German firearms companies.

Scottish Firearms, by Claude Blair and Robert Woosnam-Savage, Museum Restoration Service, Bloomfield, Ont., Canada, 1995. 52 pp., illus. Paper covers. $8.95
This revision of the first book devoted entirely to Scottish firearms is supplemented by a register of surviving Scottish long guns.

Scottish Pistol, The, by Martin Kelvin. Fairleigh Dickinson University Press, Dist. By Associated University Presses, Cranbury, NJ, 1997. 256 pp., illus. $49.50
The Scottish pistol, its history, manufacture and design.

The Arms Library

Sharps Firearms, by Frank Seller, Frank M. Seller, Denver, CO, 1998. 358 pp., illus. $59.95

Traces the development of Sharps firearms with full range of guns made including all martial variations.

Simeon North: First Official Pistol Maker of the United States, by S. North and R. North, The Gun Room Press, Highland Park, NJ, 1972. 207 pp., illus. $15.95

Reprint of the rare first edition.

SKS Carbine, The, by Steve Kehaya and Joe Poyer, North Cape Publications, Tustin, CA, 1997. 150 pp., illus. Paper covers. $16.95

The first comprehensive examination of a major historical firearm used through the Vietnam conflict to the diamond fields of Angola.

SKS Type 45 Carbines, The, by Duncan Long, Desert Publications, El Dorado, AZ, 1992. 110 pp., illus. Paper covers. $19.95

Covers the history and practical aspects of operating, maintaining and modifying this abundantly available rifle.

Smith & Wesson 1857-1945, by Robert J. Neal and Roy G. Jinks, R&R Books, Livonia, NY, 1996. 434 pp., illus. $50.00

The bible for all existing and aspiring Smith & Wesson collectors.

Sniper Variations of the German K98k Rifle, by Richard D. Law, Collector Grade Publications, Ontario, Canada, 1997. 240 pp., illus. $47.50

Volume 2 of "Backbone of the Wehrmacht" the author's in-depth study of the German K98k rifle. This volume concentrates on the telescopic-sighted rifle of choice for most German snipers during World War 2.

Southern Derringers of the Mississippi Valley, by Turner Kirkland, Pioneer Press, Tenn., 1971. 80 pp., illus., paper covers. $4.00

A guide for the collector, and a much-needed study.

Soviet Russian Postwar Military Pistols and Cartridges, by Fred A. Datig, Handgun Press, Glenview, IL, 1988. 152 pp., illus. $29.95

Thoroughly researched, this definitive sourcebook covers the development and adoption of the Makarov, Stechkin and the new PSM pistols. Also included in this source book is coverage on Russian clandestine weapons and pistol cartridges.

Soviet Russian Tokarev "TT" Pistols and Cartridges 1929-1953, by Fred Datig, Graphic Publishers, Santa Ana, CA, 1993. 168 pp., illus. $39.95

Details of rare arms and their accessories are shown in hundreds of photos. It also contains a complete bibliography and index.

Spencer Repeating Firearms, by Roy M. Marcot. New York: Rowe Publications, 2002. 316 pages; numerous B&W photos & illustrations. Hardcover. $65.00

Sporting Collectibles, by Jim and Vivian Karsnitz, Schiffer Publishing Ltd., West Chester, PA, 1992. 160 pp., illus. Paper covers. $29.95.

The fascinating world of hunting related collectibles presented in an informative text.

Springfield 1903 Rifles, The, by Lt. Col. William S. Brophy, USAR, Ret., Stackpole Books Inc., Harrisburg, PA, 1985. 608 pp., illus. $75.00

The illustrated, documented story of the design, development, and production of all the models, appendages, and accessories.

Springfield Armory Shoulder Weapons 1795-1968, by Robert W.D. Ball, Antique Trader Books, Dubuque, IA, 1998. 264 pp., illus. $34.95

This book documents the 255 basic models of rifles, including test and trial rifles, produced by the Springfield Armory. It features the entire history of rifles and carbines manufactured at the Armory, the development of each weapon with specific operating characteristics and procedures.

Springfield Model 1903 Service Rifle Production and Alteration, 1905-1910, by C.S. Ferris and John Beard, Arvada, CO, 1995. 66 pp., illus. Paper covers. $12.50

A highly recommended work for any serious student of the Springfield Model 1903 rifle.

Springfield Shoulder Arms 1795-1865, by Claud E. Fuller, S. & S. Firearms, Glendale, NY, 1996. 76 pp., illus. Paper covers. $14.95

Exact reprint of the scarce 1930 edition of one of the most definitive works on Springfield flintlock and percussion muskets ever published.

SS Headgear, by Kit Wilson. Johnson Reference Books, Fredericksburg, VA. 72 pages, 15 full-color plates and over 70 black and white photos. $16.50

An excellent source of information concerning all types of SS headgear, to include Allgemeine-SS, Waffen-SS, visor caps, helmets, overseas caps, M-43's and miscellaneous headgear. Also included is a guide on the availability and current values of SS headgear. This guide was compiled from auction catalogs, dealer price lists, and input from advanced collectors in the field.

SS Helmets: A Collector's Guide, Vol 1, by Kelly Hicks. Johnson Reference Books, Fredericksburg, VA. 96 pages, illustrated. $17.50

Deals only with SS helmets and features some very nice color close-up shots of the different SS decals used. Also, has some nice color shots of entire helmets. Over 85 photographs, 27 in color. The author has documented most of the known types of SS helmets, and describes in detail all of the vital things to look for in determining the originality, style type, and finish. Complete descriptions of each helmet are provided along with detailed close-ups of interior and exterior views of the markings and insignia. Also featured are several period photos of helmets in wear.

SS Helmets: A Collector's Guide, Vol 2, by Kelly Hicks. Johnson Reference Books, Fredericksburg, VA. 2000. 128 pages. 107 full-color photos, 14 period photos. $25.00

Volume II contains dozen of highly detailed, full-color photos of rare and original SS and Field Police helmets, featuring both sides as well as interior view. The very best graphics techniques ensure that these helmets are presented in such a way that the reader can 'almost feel' the different paint textures of the camo and factory finishes. The outstanding decal section offers detailed close-ups of original SS and Police decals, and in conjunction with Volume I, completes the documentation of virtually all types of original decal variations used between 1934 and 1945.

SS Uniforms, Insignia and Accoutrements, by A. Hayes. Schiffer Publications, Atglen, PA. 1996. 248 pages, with over 800 color and b/w photographs. $69.95

This new work explores in detailed color the complex subject of Allgemeine and Waffen-SS uniforms, insignia, and accoutrements. Hundreds of authentic items are extensively photographed in close-up to enable the reader to examine and study.

Steel Pots: The History of America's Steel Combat Helmets, by Chris Armold. Bender Publishing, San Jose, CA, 2000. $47.95

Packed with hundreds of color photographs, detailed specification diagrams and supported with meticulously researched data, this book takes the reader on a fascinating visual journey covering 80 years of American helmet design and development. From the classic Model 1917 "Doughboy" helmet to the distinctive ballistic "Kelvar" helmet, Steel Pots will introduce you to over 50 American helmet variations. Also, rare WWI experimental helmets to specialized WWII aircrew anti-flak helmets, plus liners, suspensions, chinstraps, camouflage covers, nets and even helmet radios!

Standard Catalog of Firearms, 13th Edition, by Ned Schwing, Krause Publications, Iola, WI, 2003.1382 Pages, illustrated. 6,000+ b&w photos plus a 16-page color section. Paper covers. $34.95

This is the largest, most comprehensive and best-selling firearm book of all time! And this year's edition is a blockbuster for both shooters and firearm collectors. More than 14,000 firearms are listed and priced in up to six grades of condition. That's almost 100,000 prices! Gun enthusiasts will love the new full-color section of photos highlighting the finest firearms sold at auction this past year.

Steel Canvas: The Art of American Arms, by R.L. Wilson, Random House, NY, 1995, 384 pp., illus. $65.00

Presented here for the first time is the breathtaking panorama of America's extraordinary engravers and embellishers of arms, from the 1700s to modern times.

Stevens Pistols & Pocket Rifles, by K.L. Cope, Museum Restoration Service, Alexandria Bay, NY, 1992. 114 pp., illus. $24.50

This is the story of the guns and the man who designed them and the company which he founded to make them.

Sumptuous Flaske, The, by Herbert G. Houze, Andrew Mowbray, Inc., Lincoln, RI, 1989. 158 pp., illus. Soft covers. $35.00

Catalog of a recent show at the Buffalo Bill Historical Center bringing together some of the finest European and American powder flasks of the 16th to 19th centuries.

Swedish Mauser Rifles, The, by Steve Kehaya and Joe Poyer, North Cape Publications, Tustin, CA, 1999. 267 pp., illustrated. Paper covers. $19.95

Every known variation of the Swedish Mauser carbine and rifle is described including all match and target rifles and all sniper fersions. Includes serial number and production data.

System Lefaucheaux, by Chris C. Curtis, with a Foreword by Norm Flayderman. Armslore Press, 2002. 312 pages, heavily illustrated with b & w photos. Hardcover. $44.95

The study of pinfire cartridge arms including their role in the American Civil War.

Televisions Cowboys, Gunfighters & Cap Pistols, by Rudy A. D'Angelo, Antique Trader Books, Norfolk, VA, 1999. 287 pp., illustrated in color and black and white. Paper covers. $31.95

Over 850 beautifully photographed color and black and white images of cap guns, actors, and the characters they portrayed in the "Golden Age of TV Westerns. With accurate descriptions and current values.

Thompson: The American Legend, by Tracie L. Hill, Collector Grade Publications, Ontario, Canada, 1996. 584 pp., illus. $85.00

The story of the first American submachine gun. All models are featured and discussed.

Thoughts on the Kentucky Rifle in its Golden Age by Kindig, Joe K. III. York, PA: George Shumway Publisher, 2002. Annotated Second Edition. 561pp; Illustrated. Hardcover. $85.00

The definitive book on the Kentucky Rifle, illustrating 266 of these guns in 856 detailed photographs. This scarce title, long out of print, is once again available.

Toys that Shoot and other Neat Stuff, by James Dundas, Schiffer Books, Atglen, PA, 1999. 112 pp., illustrated. Paper covers. $24.95

Shooting toys from the twentieth century, especially 1920's to 1960's, in over 420 color photographs of BB guns, cap shooters, marble shooters, squirt guns and more. Complete with a price guide.

Trapdoor Springfield, The, by M.D. Waite and B.D. Ernst, The Gun Room Press, Highland Park, NJ, 1983. 250 pp., illus. $39.95

The first comprehensive book on the famous standard military rifle of the 1873-92 period.

Treasures of the Moscow Kremlin: Arsenal of the Russian Tsars, A Royal Armories and the Moscow Kremlin exhibition. HM Tower of London 13, June 1998 to 11 September, 1998. BAS Printers, Over Wallop, Hampshire, England. XXII plus 192 pp. over 180 color illustrations. Text in English and Russian. $65.00

For this exchibition catalog each of the 94 objects on display are photographed and described in detail to provide a most informative record of this important exhibition.

U.S. Army Headgear 1812-1872, by Langellier, John P. and C. Paul Loane. Atglen, PA: Schiffer Publications, 2002. 167 pages, with over 350 color and b/w photos. $69.95

This profusely illustrated volume represents more than three decades of research in public and private collections by military historian John P. Langellier and Civil War authority C. Paul Loane. Hardcover.

U.S. Army Rangers & Special Forces of World War II Their War in Photographs, by Robert Todd Ross. Atglen, PA: Schiffer Publications, 2002. 216 pages, over 250 b/w & color photographs. Hardcover. $59.95

Never before has such an expansive view of World War II elite forces been offered in one volume. An extensive search of public and private archives unearthed an astonishing number of rare and never before seen images, including color. Most notable are the nearly twenty exemplary photographs of Lieutenant Colonel William O. Darby's Ranger Force in Italy, taken by Robert Capa, considered by many to be the greatest combat photographer of all time. Complementing the period photographs are numerous color plates detailing the rare and often unique items of insignia, weapons, and equipment that marked the soldiers whose heavy task it was to Lead the Way. Includes rare, previously unpublished photographs by legendary combat photographer Robert Capa.

U.S. Breech-Loading Rifles and Carbines, Cal. 45, by Gen. John Pitman, Thomas Publications, Gettysburg, PA, 1992. 192 pp., illus. $29.95

The third volume in the Pitman Notes on U.S. Martial Small Arms and Ammunition, 1776-1933. This book centers on the "Trapdoor Springfield" models.

U.S. Handguns of World War 2: The Secondary Pistols and Revolvers, by Charles W. Pate, Andrew Mowbray, Inc., Lincoln, RI, 1998. 515 pp., illus. $39.00

This indispensable new book covers all of the American military handguns of World War 2 except for the M1911A1 Colt automatic.

THE ARMS LIBRARY

United States Martial Flintlocks, by Robert M. Reilly, Mowbray Publishing Co., Lincoln, RI, 1997. 264 pp., illus. $40.00

A comprehensive history of American flintlock longarms and handguns (mostly military) c. 1775 to c. 1840.

U.S. Martial Single Shot Pistols, by Daniel D. Hartzler and James B. Whisker, Old Bedford Village Pess, Bedford, PA, 1998. 128 pp., illus. $45.00

A photographic chronicle of military and semi-martial pistols supplied to the U.S. Government and the several States.

U.S. Military Arms Dates of Manufacture from 1795, by George Madis, David Madis, Dallas, TX, 1995. 64 pp. Soft covers. $9.95

Lists all U.S. military arms of collector interest alphabetically, covering about 250 models.

U.S. Military Small Arms 1816-1865, by Robert M. Reilly, The Gun Room Press, Highland Park, NJ, 1983. 270 pp., illus. $39.95

Covers every known type of primary and secondary martial firearms used by Federal forces.

U.S. M1 Carbines: Wartime Production, by Craig Riesch, North Cape Publications, Tustin, CA, 1994. 72 pp., illus. Paper covers. $16.95

Presents only verifiable and accurate information. Each part of the M1 Carbine is discussed fully in its own section; including markings and finishes.

U.S. Naval Handguns, 1808-1911, by Fredrick R. Winter, Andrew Mowbray Publishers, Lincoln, RI, 1990. 128 pp., illus. $26.00

The story of U.S. Naval Handguns spans an entire century—included are sections on each of the important naval handguns within the period.

Uniform and Dress Army and Navy of the Confederate States of America. (Official Regulations), by Confederate States of America. Ray Riling Arms Books, Philadelphia, PA. 1960. $20.00

A portfolio containing a complete set of nine color plates expecially prepared for framing Reproduced in exactly 200 sets from the very rare Richmond, VA., 1861 regulations.

Uniform Buttons of the United States 1776-1865, by Warren K. Tice. Thomas Publications, Gettysburg, PA. 1997. 520 pages over 3000 illustrations. $60.00

A timely work on US uniform buttons for a growing area of collecting. This work interrelates diverse topics such as manufacturing proceses, history of manufacturing companies, known & recently discovered button patterns and the unist that wore them.

Uniforms & Equipment of the Imperial German Army 1900-1918: A Study in Period Photographs, by Charles Woolley. Schiffer Publications, Atglen, PA. 2000. 375 pages, over 500 b/w photographs and 50 color drawings. $69.95

Features formal studio portraits of pre-war dress and wartime uniforms of all arms. Also contains photo postal cards taken in the field of Infantry, Pionier, Telegraph-Signal, Landsturm, and Mountain Troops, vehicles, artillery, musicians, the Bavarian Leib Regiment, specialized uniforms and insignia, small arms close-ups, unmotorized transport, group shots and Balloon troops and includes a 60 page full-color uniform section reproduced from rare 1914 plates. Fully illustrated.

Uniforms & Equipment of the Imperial German Army 1900-1918: A Study in Period Photographs, Volume 2. by Charles Woolley. Schiffer Publications, Atglen, PA. 2000. 320 pages, over 500 b/w photographs and 50 color drawings. $69.95

Contains over 500 never before published photographic images of Imperial German military subjects. This initial volume, of a continuing study, features formal studio portraits of pre-war dress and wartime uniforms of all arms. It also contains photo postal cards taken in the field of Infantry, Pionier, Telegraph-Signal, Landsturm and Mountain Troops, Vehicles, Artillery, Musicians, the Bavarian Leib Regiment, specialized uniforms and insignia, small arms close-ups, unmotorized transport, group shots and Balloon troops.

Uniforms of the Third Reich: A Study in Photographs, by Maguire Hayes. Schiffer Publications, Atglen, PA. 1997. 200 pages, with over 400 color photographs. $69.95

This new book takes a close look at a variety of authentic World War II era German uniforms including examples from the Army, Luftwaffe, Kriegsmarine, Waffen-SS, Allgemeine-SS, Hitler Youth and Political Leaders. The pieces are shown in large full frame front and rear shots, and in painstaking detail to show tailors tags, buttons, insignia detail etc. and allow the reader to see what the genuine article looks like. Various accoutrements worn with the uniforms are also included to aid the collector.

Uniforms of The United States Army, 1774-1889, by Henry Alexander Ogden. Dover Publishing, Mineola, NY. 1998. 48 pages of text plus 44 color plates. Softcover. $9.95

A republication of the work published by the quarter-master general, United States army in 1890. A striking collection of lithographs and a marvelous archive of military, social, and costume history portraying the gamut of U.S. Army uniforms from fatigues to full dress, between 1774 and 1889.

Uniforms, Organization, and History of the NSKK/NSFK, by John R. Angolia & David Littlejohn. Bender Publishing, San Jose, CA, 2000. $44.95

This work is part of the on-going study of political organizations that formed the structure of the Hitler hierarchy, and is authored by two of the most prominent authorities on the subject of uniforms and insignia of the Third Reich. This comprehensive book covers details on the NSKK and NSFK such as history, organization, uniforms, insignia, special insignia, flags and standards, gorgets, daggers, awards, "day badges," and much more!

Uniforms of the Waffen-SS; Black Service Uniform —LAH Guard Uniform—SS Earth-Grey Service Uniform—Model 1936 Field Service Uniform—1939-1940 — 1941 Volume 1, by Michael D. Beaver. Schiffer Publications, Atglen, PA. 2002. 272 pages, with 500 color, and black and white photos. $79.95

This spectacular work is a heavily documented record of all major clothing articles of the Waffen-SS. Hundreds of unpublished photographs were used in production. Original and extremely rare SS uniforms of various types are carefully photographed and presented here. Among the subjects covered in this multi volume series are field-service uniforms, sports, drill, dress, armored personnel, tropical, and much more. A large updated chapter on SS camouflage clothing is also provided. Special chapters on the SD and concentration camp personnel assist the reader in differentiating these elements from combat units of the Waffen-SS. Difficult areas such as mountain and ski troops, plus ultra-rare pre-war uniforms are covered. Included are many striking and exquisite uniforms worn by such men as Himmler, Dietrich, Ribbentrop (father and son), Wolff, Demelhuber, and many others. From the enlisted man to the top of the SS empire, this book covers it all. This book is indispensable and an absolute must-have for any serious historian of World War II German uniforms.

Uniforms of the Waffen-SS; 1942-1943 — 1944-1945 — Ski Uniforms — Overcoats — White Service Uniforms — Tropical Clothing, Volume 2, by Michael D. Beaver. Schiffer Publications, Atglen, PA. 2002. 272 pages, with 500 color, and black and white photos. $79.95

Uniforms of the Waffen-SS; Sports and Drill Uniforms — Black Panzer Uniform — Camouflage — Concentration Camp Personnel-SD-SS Female Auxiliaries, Volume 3, by Michael D. Beaver. Schiffer Publications, Atglen, PA. 2002. 272 pages, with 500 color, and black and white photos. $79.95

U.S. Silent Service - Dolphins & Combat Insignia 1924-1945, by David Jones. Bender Publishing, San Jose, CA, 2001. 224 pages, 532 photos. (most in full color) $39.95

After eight years of extensive research, the publication of this book is a submarine buff and collector∂s dream come true. This beautiful full-color book chronicles, with period letters and sketches, the developmental history of US submarine insignia prior to 1945. It also contains many rare and never before published photographs, plus interviews with WWII submarine veterans, from enlisted men to famous skippers. Each insignia is photographed (obverse and reverse) and magnified in color. All known contractors are covered plus embroidered versions, mess dress variations, the Roll of Honor, submarine combat insignia, battleflags, launch memorabilia and related submarine collectibles (postal covers, match book covers, jewelry, posters, advertising art, postcards, etc.)

Variations of Colt's New Model Police and Pocket Breech Loading Pistols, by Breslin, John D., Pirie, William Q., & Price, David E.: Lincoln, RI: Andrew Mowbray Publishers, 2002. 1st edition. 158 pages, heavily illustrated with over 160 photographs and superb technical detailed drawings and diagrams. Pictorial Hardcover. $37.95

A type-by-type guide to what collectors call small frame conversions.

Walther: A German Legend, by Manfred Kersten, Safari Press, Inc., Huntington Beach, CA, 2000. 400 pp., illustrated. $85.00

This comprehensive book covers, in rich detail, all aspects of the company and its guns, including an illustrious and rich history, the WW2 years, all the pistols (models 1 through 9), the P-38, P-88, the long guns, .22 rifles, centerfires, Wehrmacht guns, and even a gun that could shoot around a corner.

Walther Pistols: Models 1 Through P99, Factory Variations and Copies, by Dieter H. Marschall, Ucross Books, Los Alamos, NM. 2000. 140 pages, with 140 b & w illustrations, index. Paper Covers. $19.95

This is the English translation, revised and updated, of the highly successful and widely acclaimed German language edition. This book provides the collector with a reference guide and overview of the entire line of the Walther military, police, and self-defense pistols from the very first to the very latest. Models 1-9, PP, PPK, MP, AP, HP, P.38, P1, P4, P38K, P5, P88, P99 and the Manurhin models. Variations, where issued, serial ranges, calibers, marks, proofs, logos, and design aspects in an astonishing quantity and variety are crammed into this very well researched and highly regarded work.

Walther Handgun Story: A Collector's and Shooter's Guide, The, by Gene Gangarosa, Steiger Publications, 1999. 300., illustrated. Paper covers. $21.95

Covers the entire history of the Walther empire. Illustrated with over 250 photos.

Walther P-38 Pistol, by Maj. George Nonte, Desert Publications, Cornville, AZ, 1982. 100 pp., illus. Paper covers. $12.95

Complete volume on one of the most famous handguns to come out of WWII. All models covered.

Walther Models PP & PPK, 1929-1945 – Volume 1, by James L. Rankin, Coral Gables, FL, 1974. 142 pp., illus. $40.00

Complete coverage on the subject as to finish, proofmarks and Nazi Party inscriptions.

Walther Volume II, Engraved, Presentation and Standard Models, by James L. Rankin, J.L. Rankin, Coral Gables, FL, 1977. 112 pp., illus. $40.00

The new Walther book on embellished versions and standard models. Has 88 photographs, including many color plates.

Walther, Volume III, 1908-1980, by James L. Rankin, Coral Gables, FL, 1981. 226 pp., illus. $40.00

Covers all models of Walther handguns from 1908 to date, includes holsters, grips and magazines.

Winchester Bolt Action Military & Sporting Rifles 1877 to 1937, by Herbert G. Houze, Andrew Mowbray Publishing, Lincoln, RI, 1998. 295 pp., illus. $45.00

Winchester was the first American arms maker to commercially manufacture a bolt action repeating rifle, and this book tells the exciting story of these Winchester bolt actions.

Winchester Book, The, by George Madis, David Madis Gun Book Distributor, Dallas, TX, 2000. 650 pp., illus. $54.50

A new, revised 25th anniversary edition of this classic book on Winchester firearms. Complete serial ranges have been added.

Winchester Dates of Manufacture 1849-1984, by George Madis, Art & Reference House, Brownsboro, TX, 1984. 59 pp. $7.50

A most useful work, compiled from records of the Winchester factory.

Winchester Model 1876 "Centennial" Rifle, The, by Houze, Herbert G. Lincoln, RI: Andrew Mowbray, Inc., 2001. Illustrated with over 180 black and white photographs. 192 Pages. Hardcover. $45.00

The first authoritative study of the Winchester Model 1876 written using the company's own records. This book dispels the myth that the Model 1876 was merely a larger version of the Winchester company's famous Model 1873 and instead traces its true origins to designs developed immediately after the American Civil War. The specifics of the model-such as the numbers made in its standard calibers, barrel lengths, finishes and special order features-are fully listed here for the first time. In addition, the actual processes and production costs involved in its manufacture are also completely documented. For Winchester collectors, and those interested in the mechanics of the 19th-century arms industry, this book provides a wealth of previously unpublished information.

Winchester Engraving, by R.L. Wilson, Beinfeld Books, Springs, CA, 1989. 500 pp., illus. $135.00

A classic reference work of value to all arms collectors.

Winchester Handbook, The, by George Madis, Art & Reference House, Lancaster, TX, 1982. 287 pp., illus. $26.95

The complete line of Winchester guns, with dates of manufacture, serial numbers, etc.

Winchester-Lee Rifle, The, by Eugene Myszkowski, Excalibur Publications, Tucson, AZ 2000. 96 pp., illustrated. Paper Covers. $22.95

The development of the Lee Straight Pull, the cartridge and the approval for military use. Covers details of the inventor and memorabilia of Winchester-Lee related material.

Winchester Lever Action Repeating Firearms, Vol. 1, The Models of 1866, 1873 and 1876, by Arthur Pirkle, North Cape Publications, Tustin, CA, 1995. 112 pp., illus. Paper covers. $19.95
Complete, part-by-part description, including dimensions, finishes, markings and variations throughout the production run of these fine, collectible guns.

Winchester Lever Action Repeating Rifles, Vol. 2, The Models of 1886 and 1892, by Arthur Pirkle, North Cape Publications, Tustin, CA, 1996. 150 pp., illus. Paper covers. $19.95
Describes each model on a part-by-part basis by serial number range complete with finishes, markings and changes.

Winchester Lever Action Repeating Rifles, Volume 3, The Model of 1894, by Arthur Pirkle, North Cape Publications, Tustin, CA, 1998. 150 pp., illus. Paper covers. $19.95
The first book ever to provide a detailed description of the Model 1894 rifle and carbine.

Winchester Lever Legacy, The, by Clyde "Snooky" Williamson, Buffalo Press, Zachary, LA, 1988. 664 pp., illustrated. $75.00
A book on reloading for the different calibers of the Winchester lever action rifle.

Winchester Model 94: The First 100 Years, The, by Robert C. Renneberg, Krause Publications, Iola, WI, 1991. 208 pp., illus. $34.95
Covers the design and evolution from the early years up to the many different editions that exist today.

Winchester Rarities, by Webster, Krause Publications, Iola, WI, 2000. 208 pp., with over 800 color photos, illus. $49.95
This book details the rarest of the rare; the one-of-a-kind items and the advertising pieces from years gone by. With nearly 800 full color photos and detailed pricing provided by experts in the field, this book gives collectors and enthusiasts everything they need.

Winchester Shotguns and Shotshells, by Ronald W. Stadt, Krause Publications, Iola, WI, 1995. 256 pp., illus. $34.95
The definitive book on collectible Winchester shotguns and shotshells manufactured through 1961.

Winchester Single-Shot—Volume 1; A History and Analysis, The, by John Campbell, Andrew Mowbray, Inc., Lincoln RI, 1995. 272 pp., illus. $55.00
Covers every important aspect of this highly-collectible firearm.

Winchester Single-Shot—Volume 2; Old Secrets and New Discoveries, The, by John Campbell, Andrew Mowbray, Inc., Lincoln RI, 2000. 280 pp., illus. $55.00
An exciting follow-up to the classic first volume.

Winchester Slide-Action Rifles, Volume 1: Model 1890 & 1906, by Ned Schwing, Krause Publications, Iola, WI, 1992. 352 pp., illus. $39.95
First book length treatment of models 1890 & 1906 with over 50 charts and tables showing significant new information about caliber style and rarity.

Worldwide Webley and the Harrington and Richardson Connection, by Stephen Cuthbertson, Ballista Publishing and Distributing Ltd., Gabriola Island, Canada, 1999. 259 pp., illus. $50.00
A masterpiece of scholarship. Over 350 photographs plus 75 original documents, patent drawings, and advertisements accompany the text.

EDGED WEAPONS

Advertising Cutlery; With Values, by Richard White, Schiffer Publishing, Ltd., Atglen, PA. 176 pages, with over 400 color photos. Softcover. $29.95
Advertising Cutlery is the first-ever publication to deal exclusively with the subject of promotional knives. Containing over 400 detailed color photographs, this book explores over one hundred years of advertisements stamped into the sides of knives. In addition to the book's elegant photographic presentation, extensive captions and text give the reader the background information necessary for evaluating collectible advertising knives. Significant examples of advertising specimens are described in detailed stories. Evaluative schemes are included, and all captions contain accurate pricing information. Future trends are also discussed.

Allied Military Fighting Knives; And The Men Who Made Them Famous, by Robert A. Buerlein, Paladin Press, Boulder, CO: 2001. 185 pages, illustrated with black & white photos. Softcover. $35.00

American Eagle Pommel Sword: The Early Years 1794-1830, The, by Andrew Mowbray, Manrat Arms Publications, Lincoln, RI, 1997. 244 pp., illus. $65.00
The standard guide to the most popular style of American sword.

American Knives; The First History and Collector's Guide, by Harold L. Peterson, The Gun Room Press, Highland Park, NJ, 1980. 178 pp., illus. $24.95
A reprint of this 1958 classic. Covers all types of American knives.

American Military Bayonets of the 20th Century, by Gary M. Cunningham, Scott A. Duff Publications, Export, PA, 1997. 116 pp., illus. Paper covers. $21.95
A guide for collectors, including notes on makers, markings, finishes, variations, scabbards, and production data.

American Primitive Knives 1770-1870, by G.B. Minnes, Museum Restoration Service, Ottawa, Canada, 1983. 112 pp., illus. $24.95
Origins of the knives, outstanding specimens, structural details, etc.

American Socket Bayonets and Scabbards, by Robert M. Reilly, 2nd printing, Andrew Mowbray, Inc., Lincoln, RI, 1998. 208 pp., illustrated. $45.00
Full coverage of the socket bayonet in America, from Colonial times through the post-Civil War.

American Sword, The, 1775-1945, by Harold L. Peterson, Ray Riling Arms Books, Co., Phila., PA, 2001. 286 pp. plus 60 pp. of illus. $49.95
1977 reprint of a survey of swords worn by U.S. uniformed forces, plus the rare "American Silver Mounted Swords, (1700-1815)."

American Swords and Makers Marks; A Photographic Guide for Collectors, by Donald Furr, Paragon Agency, Orange, CA, 1999. 253 pp., illus. $64.95
An indepth guide for collectors and dealers of American swords. This new reference book contains over 525 photos of Silverhilts, Cavalry sabres, Eaglehead, Presentation swords, Regalia, Militia, Enlisted & Officers swords of both the U.S. & Confederacy. 8 page color section. Profusely illus & price guide.

American Swords and Sword Makers, by Richard H. Bezdek, Paladin Press, Boulder, CO, 1994. 648 pp., illus. $79.95
The long-awaited definitive reference volume to American swords, sword makers and sword dealers from Colonial times to the present.

American Swords & Sword Makers Volume 2, by Richard H. Bezdek, Paladin Press, Boulder, CO, 1999. 376 pp., illus. $69.95
More than 400 stunning photographs of rare, unusual and one-of-a-kind swords from the top collections in the country

American Swords from the Philip Medicus Collection, edited by Stuart C. Mowbray, with photographs and an introduction by Norm Flayderman, Andrew Mowbray Publishers, Lincoln, RI, 1998. 272 pp., with 604 swords illustrated. $55.00
Covers all areas of American sword collecting.

Ames Sword Company Catalog: An Exact Reprint of the Original 19th Century Military and Fraternal Sword Catalog, The, by Mowbray, Stuart C. (Intro. by). Lincoln, RI: Andrew Mowbray, Inc., 2003. 1st edition. 200 pp, 541 swords illustrated with original prices and descriptions. Pictorial Hardcover. $37.50
The level of detail in these original catalog images will surprise you. Dealers who sold Ames swords used this catalog in their stores, and every feature is clearly shown. Reproduced directly from the incredibly rare originals, Military, Fraternal and more! The key to identifying hundreds of Ames Swords! Shows the whole Ames line, including swords from the Civil War and even earlier. Lots of related military items like belts, bayonets, etc.

Ames Sword Company, 1829-1935, The, by John D. Hamilton, Andrew Mowbray Publisher, Lincoln, RI, 1995. 255 pp., illus. $45.00
An exhaustively researched and comprehensive history of America's foremost sword manufacturer and arms supplier during the Civil War.

Antlers & Iron II, by Krause Publications, Iola, WI, 1999. 40 Pages, illustrated with a 100 photos. Paper covers. $12.00
Lays out actual plans so you can build your mountain man folding knife using ordinary hand tools. Step-by-step instructions, with photos, for layout, design, antler slotting and springs.

Art of Throwing Weapons, The, by James W. Madden, Paladin Press, Boulder, CO, 1993. 102 pp., illus. $14.00
This comprehensive manual covers everything from the history and development of the five most common throwing weapons--spears, knives, tomahawks, shurikens and boomerangs--to their selection or manufacture, grip, distances, throwing motions and advanced combat methods.

Arte of Defence An Introduction to the Use of the Rapier. By Wilson, William E. Union City, CA: Chivalry Bookshelf, 2002. 1st edition. 167 pages, illustrated with over 300 photographs. Softcover $24.95

Battle Blades: A Professional's Guide to Combat Fighting Knives, by Greg Walker; Foreword by Al Mar, Paladin Press, Boulder, CO, 1993. 168 pp., illus. $40.95
The author evaluates daggers, Bowies, switchblades and utility blades according to their design, performance, reliability and cost.

The Bayonet in New France, 1665-1760, by Erik Goldstein, Museum Restoration Service, Bloomfield, Ontario, Canada, 1997. 36 pp., illus. Paper covers. $8.95
Traces bayonets from the recently developed plug bayonet, through the regulation socket bayonets which saw service in North America.

Bayonets from Janzen's Notebook, by Jerry Jansen. Cedar Ridge Publications, Tulsa, Ok 2000. 6th printing. 258 pages, illus. Hardcover. $45.00
This collection of over 1000 pieces is one of the largest in the U.S.

Bayonets, Knives & Scabbards; United States Army Weapons Report 1917 Thru 1945, edited by Frank Trzaska, Knife Books, Deptford, NJ, 1999. 80 pp., illustrated. Paper covers. $15.95
Follows the United States edged weapons from the close of World War 1 through the end of World War 2. Manufacturers involved, dates, numbers produced, problems encountered, and production data.

Best of U. S. Military Knives, Bayonets & Machetes, The, by Cole, M. H. (edited by) Michael W. Silvey. IDSA Books, 2002. 335 pages, illustrated. Hardcover. $59.95
This book consolidates Cole's four books into one usable text that includes drawings and information about all the significant U.S. issue and private purchase knives, bayonets, and machetes.

Book of the Sword, The, by Richard F. Burton, Dover Publications, New York, NY, 1987. 199 pp., illus. Paper covers. $12.95
Traces the swords origin from its birth as a charged and sharpened stick through diverse stages of development.

Borders Away, Volume 1: With Steel, by William Gilkerson, Andrew Mowbray, Inc., Lincoln, RI, 1991. 184 pp., illus. $48.00
A comprehensive study of naval armament under fighting sail. This first voume covers axes, pikes and fighting blades in use between 1626-1826.

Borders Away, Volume 2: Firearms of the Age of Fighting Sail, by William Gilkerson, Andrew Mowbray, Inc., Lincoln, RI, 1999. 331 pp., illus. $65.00
Completing a two volume set, this impressive work covers the pistols, muskets, combustibles, and small cannon once employed aboard American and European fightng ships. 200 photos, 16 color plates.

Bowie Knives and Bayonets of the Ben Palmer Collection, 2nd Edition, by Palmer, Ben, Bill Moran and Jim Phillips. Williamstown, NJ: Phillips Publications, 2002. Hardcover. $49.95
Vastly expanded with more than 300 makers, distributors & dealers added to the makers list; chapter on Bowie knife photograph with 50 image photo gallery of knife holders from the Mexican War, Civil War, & the West; contains a chapter on Bowie Law; includes several unpublished Bowie documents, including the first account of the Alamo. 224 pages, illustrated with photos. As things stand, it is a 'must' read for collectors, particularly if you're looking for photos of some knives not often seen, or curious about what Bill Moran might have to say about some of the old bowie designs.

Bowies, Big Knives, and the Best of Battle Blades, by Bill Bagwell, Paladin Press, Boulder, CO. 2001. 184 pp., illus. Paper covers. $30.00
This book binds the timeless observations and invaluable advice of master bladesmith and blade combat expert Bill Bagwell under one cover for the first time. As the outspoken author of Soldier of Fortune's "Battle Blades" column from 1984 to 1988, Bagwell was considered both outrageous and revolutionary in his advocacy of carrying fighting knives as long as 10 inches and his firm belief that the Bowie was the most effective and efficient fighting knife ever developed. Here, you'llfind all of Bagwell's classic SOF columns, plus all-new material linking his early insights with his latest conclusions. Must reading for serious knife fans.

British & Commonwealth Bayonets, by Ian D. Skennerton and Robert Richardson, I.D.S.A. Books, Piqua, OH, 1986. 404 pp., 1300 illus. $40.00

THE ARMS LIBRARY

British and Commonwealth Military Knives, by Ron Flook, Airlife, Shrewsbury, 1999. 256 pp., illus. 49.95

First major reference on Knives issued to British & Commonwealth Forces from 1850 to the present. Over 500 Knives illustrated and described .

Broad Arrow: British & Empire Factory Production, Proof, Inspection, Armourers, Unit & Issue Markings, The, Skennerton, Ian. Australia: Arms & Militaria Press, 2001. 140 pp, circa 80 illus. Stiff Paper Covers. $29.95

Thousands of service markings are illustrated and their applications described. Invaluable reference on units, also ideal for medal collectors.

Civil War Cavalry & Artillery Sabers, 1833-1865, by Thillmann, John H., Andrew Mowbray, Inc. Lincoln, RI: 2002. 1st edition. 500+ pages, over 50 color photographs, 1,373 B&W illustrations, coated paper, dust jacket, premium hardcover binding. Hardcover $79.95

Collecting the Edged Weapons of Imperial Germany, by Thomas M. Johnson and Thomas T. Wittmann, Johnson Reference Books, Fredericksburg, VA, 1989. 363 pp., illus. $39.50

An in-depth study of the many ornate military, civilian, and government daggers and swords of the Imperial era.

Clandestine Edged Weapons, by Windrum, William. Phillips Publications, Williamstown, NJ 2001. 74 pages, illustrated with black and white photographs. Pictorial Softcover $9.95

Collecting Indian Knives, 2nd Edition, by Lar Hothem, Krause Publications, Iola, WI, 2000. 176 pp., illustrated. Paper covers. $19.95

Expanded and updated with new photos and information, this 2nd edition will be a must have for anyone who collects or wants to learn about chipped Indian artifacts in the knife family. With an emphasis on prehistoric times, the book is loaded with photos, values and identification guidelines to help identify blades as to general time-period and, in many cases, help date sites where such artifacts are found. Includes information about different regional materials and basic styles, how knives were made and for what they were probably used.

Collector's Guide to Ames U.S. Contract Military Edged Weapons: 1832-1906, by Ron G. Hickox, Pioneer Press, Union City, IN, 1993. 70 pp., illus. Paper covers. $17.50

While this book deals primarily with edged weapons made by the Ames Manufacturing Company, this guide refers to other manufactureres of United States swords.

Collectors Guide to Switchblade Knives, An Illustrated Historical and Price Reference, by Richard V. Langston. Paladin Press, Boulder, CO. 2001. 224 pp., illus. $49.95

It has been more than 20 years since a major work on switchblades has been published, and never has one showcased as many different types as Rich Langston's welcome new book. The Collector's Guide to Switchblade Knives contains a history of the early cutlery industry in America; a detailed examination of the evolution of switchblades; and a user-friendly, up-to-the-minute, illustrated reference section that helps collectors and novices alike identify all kinds of knives, from museum-quality antiques to Granddad's old folder that's been hidden in the attic for decades. Langston, a life-long knife lover and collector, provides an honest appraisal of more than 160 autos based on maker, condition, markings, materials, functioning and availability.

Collector's Guide to Swords, Daggers & Cutlasses, A, by Gerald Weland, Chartwell Press, London, 1999. 128 pp., illustrated in color. $24.95

An informative overview of edged weapons from medieval through 19th century. Explains the military and technological background and distinguishing features of the most sought-after pieces. Includes lists of leading museums and weapons collections plus a comprehensive bibliography and index.

Collector's Handbook of World War 2 German Daggers, by LtC. Thomas M. Johnson, Johnson Reference Books, Fredericksburg, VA, 2nd edition, 1991. 252 pp., illus. Paper covers. $25.00

Concise pocket reference guide to Third Reich daggers and accoutrements in a convenient format. With value guide.

Collins Machetes and Bowies 1845-1965, by Daniel E. Henry, Krause Publications, Iola, WI, 1996. 232 pp., illus. Paper covers. $19.95

A comprehensive history of Collins machetes and bowies including more than 1200 blade instruments and accessories.

Complete Bladesmith: Forging Your Way to Perfection, The, by Jim Hrisoulas, Paladin Press, Boulder, CO, 1987. 192 pp., illus. $42.95

Novice as well as experienced bladesmith will benefit from this definitive guide to smithing world-class blades.

Complete Book of Pocketknife Repair, The, by Ben Kelly, Jr., Krause Publications, Iola, WI, 1995. 130 pp., illus. Paper covers. $10.95

Everything you need to know about repairing knives can be found in this step-by-step guide to knife repair.

Confederate Edged Weapons, by W.A. Albaugh, R&R Books, Lavonia, NY, 1994. 198 pp., illus. $40.00

The master reference to edged weapons of the Confederate forces. Features precise line drawings and an extensive text.

Connoisseur's Book of Japanese Swords, The, by Nagayama, Kodauska International, Tokyo, Japan, 1997. 348pp., illustrated. $69.95

Translated by Kenji Mishina. A comprehensive guide to the appreciation and appraisal of the blades of Japanese swords. The most informative guide to the blades of Japanese swords ever to appear in English.

Counterfeiting Antique Cutlery, by Gerald Witcher. National Brokerage And Sales, Inc., Brentwood, TN. 1997. $24.95

512 pages, illustrated with 1500-2000 black and white photographs.

Daggers and Bayonets a History, by Logan Thompson, Paladin Press, Boulder, CO, 1999. 128 pp., illustrated. $40.00

This authoritative history of military daggers and bayonets examines all patterns of daggers in detail, from the utilitarian Saxon scamasax used at Hastings to lavishly decorated Cinquedas, Landsknecht and Holbein daggers of the late high Renaissance.

Daggers and Fighting Knives of the Western World: From the Stone Age till 1900, by Harold Peterson, Dover Publishing, Mineola, NY, 2001. 96 pages, plus 32 pages of matte stock. Over 100 illustrations. Softcover. $9.95

The only full-scale reference book devoted entirely to the subject of fighting knives: flint knives, daggers of all sorts, scramasaxes, hauswehren, dirks and more. 108 plates, bibliography and Index.

Earliest Commando Knives, The, by William Windrum. Phillips Publications, Williamstown, NJ. 2001. 74 pages, illustrated. Softcover. $9.95

Edged Weapon Accouterments of Germany 1800-1945, by Kreutz, Hofmann, Johnson, Reddick. Pottsboro, TX: Reddick Enterprises, 2002. 1st edition. Profusely illustrated, with 160 pages. 54 full color plates of illustrations, 26 pages of full color photographs and over 125 black & white photos, including over 90 period in wear photos. Hardcover $49.90

Eickhorn Edged Weapons Exports, Vol. 1: Latin America, by A.M. de Quesada, Jr. and Ron G. Hicock, Pioneer Press, Union City, TN, 1996. 120 pp., illus. Paper covers. $15.00

This research studies the various Eickhorn edged weapons and accessories manufactured for various countries outside of Germany.

Exploring the Dress Daggers of the German Army, by Thomas T. Wittmann, Johnson Reference Books, Fredericksburg, VA, 1995. 350 pp., illus. $59.95

The first in-depth analysis of the dress daggers worn by the German Army.

Exploring the Dress Daggers of the German Luftwaffe, by Thomas T. Wittmann, Johnson Reference Books, Fredericksburg, VA, 1998. 350 pp., illus. $59.95

Examines the dress daggers and swords of the German Luftwaffe. The designs covered include the long DLV patterns, the Glider Pilot designs of the NSFK and DLV, 1st and 2nd model Luftwaffe patterns, the Luftwaffe sword and the General OFficer Dengen. Many are pictured for the first time in color.

Exploring The Dress Daggers Of The German Navy, by Thomas T. Wittmann, Johnson Reference Books, Fredericksburg, VA, 2000. 560 pp., illus. $79.95

Explores the dress daggers and swords of the Imperial, Weimar, and Third Reich eras, from 1844-1945. Provides detailed information, as well as many superb black and white and color photographs of individual edged weapons. Many are pictured for the first time in full color.

Exploring the Dress Daggers and Swords of the SS, by Thomas T. Wittmann, Johnson Reference Books, Fredericksburg, VA, 2003. 1st edition. 750 pages, illustrated with nearly 1000 photographs, many in color. $124.95

Covers all model SS Service Daggers, Chained SS Officer Daggers, Himmler & Rohm Inscriptions, Damascus presentations, SS Officer Degen, Himmler Birthday Degen, Silver Lionhead Swords, Blade etch study & much more. Profusely illustrated with historically important period in-wear photographs. Most artifacts appearing for the first time in reference.

First Commando Knives, The, by Prof. Kelly Yeaton and Col. Rex Applegate, Phillips Publications, Williamstown, NJ, 1996. 115 pp., illus. Paper covers. $12.95

Here is the full story of the Shanghai origins of the world's best known dagger.

German Clamshells and Other Bayonets, by G. Walker and R.J. Weinard, Johnson Reference Books, Fredericksburg, VA, 1994. 157 pp., illus. $22.95

Includes unusual bayonets, many of which are shown for the first time. Current market values are listed.

German Etched Dress Bayonets (Extra-Seitengewehr) 1933-1945, by Wayne H. Techet. Printed by the Author, Las Vegas, NV. 2002. 262 pages. A limited edition of 1,300 copies. Signed and Numbered. $55.00

Photographs of over 200 Obverse and Reverse motifs. Rare SS and Panzer patterns pictured for the first time, with an extensive chapter on Reproductions and Red Flags. Close-up photography revealing design details within patterns, plus many more details, insights, and observations relating to collecting the etched dress bayonets of the Third Reich. Color section, and value guide.

German Military Fighting Knives 1914-1945, by Gordon A. Hughes, Johnson Reference Books, Fredericksburg, VA, 1994. 64 pp., illus. Paper covers. $24.50

Documents the different types of German military fighting knives used during WWI and WWII. Makers' proofmarks are shown as well as details of blade inscriptions, etc.

German Swords and Sword Makers: Edged Weapons Makers from the 14th to the 20th Centuries, by Richard H. Bezdek, Paladin Press, Boulder, CO, 2000. 248 pp., illustrated. $59.95

This book contains the most informations ever published on German swords and edged weapons makers from the Middle Ages to the present.

Guide to Military Dress Daggers, Volume 1, A, by Kurt Glemser, Johnson Reference Books, Fredericksburg, VA, 1991. 160 pp., illus. Softcover. $26.50

Very informative guide to dress daggers of foreign countries, to include an excellent chapter on DDR daggers. There is also a section on reproduction Third Reich period daggers. Provides, for the first time, identification of many of the war-time foreign dress daggers. There is also a section on Damascus blades. Good photographic work. Mr. Glemser is certainly to be congratulated on this book on such a neglected area of militaria.

Guide to Military Dress Daggers, Volume 2, A, by Kurt Glemser, Johnson Reference Books, Fredericksburg, VA, 1993. 160 pp., illus. $32.50

As in the first volume, reproduction daggers are covered in depth (Third Reich, East German, Italian, Polish and Hungarian). American Navy dirks are featured for the first time. Bulgarian Youth daggers, Croatioan daggers and Imperial German Navy dagger scabbards all have chapters devoted to them. Continues research initiated in Volume I on such subjects as dress daggers, Solingen export daggers, East German daggers and Damascus Smith Max Dinger.

Guide to Military Dress Daggers, Volume 3, A, by Kurt Glemser, Johnson Reference Books, Fredericksburg, VA, 1996. 260 pp., illus. $39.50

Includes studies of Swedish daggers, Italian Cadet daggers, Rumanian daggers, Austrian daggers, Dress daggers of the Kingdom of Yugoslavia, Czechoslovakian daggers, Paul Dinger Damastschmied, Swiss Army daggers, Polish daggers (1952-1994), and Hungarian Presentation daggers.

Guide to Military Dress Daggers, Volume 4, A, by Kurt Glemser, Johnson Reference Books, Fredericksburg, VA, 2001. 252 pp., illus. $49.50

Several chapters dealing with presentation daggers to include a previously unknown series of East German daggers. Other chapters cover: Daggers in wear; Czech & Slovak daggers; Turkish daggers; swiss Army daggers; Solingen Export daggers; Miniature daggers, Youth knives.

THE ARMS LIBRARY

Halberd and Other European Polearms 1300-1650, The, by George Snook, Museum Restoration Service, Bloomfield, Ontario, Canada, 1998. 40 pp., illus. Paper covers. $8.95

A comprehensive introduction to the history, use, and identification of the staff weapons of Europe.

Highland Swordsmanship: Techniques of the Scottish Swordmasters, edited by Mark Rector. Chivalry Bookshelf, Union City, CA 2001. 208 pages, Includes more than 100 illustrative photographs. Softcover $29.95

Rector has done a superb job at bringing together two influential yet completely different 18th century fencing manuals from Scotland. Adding new interpretative plates, Mark offers new insights and clear presentations of many useful techniques. With contributions by Paul MacDonald and Paul Wagner, this book promises to be a treat for students of historical fencing, Scottish history and reenactors.

How to Make Folding Knives, by Ron Lake, Frank Centofante and Wayne Clay, Krause Publications, Iola, WI, 1995. 193 pp., illus. Paper covers. $13.95

With step-by-step instructions, learn how to make your own folding knife from three top custom makers.

How to Make Knives, by Richard W. Barney and Robert W. Loveless, Krause Publications, Iola, WI, 1995. 182 pp., illus. Paper covers. $13.95

Complete instructions from two premier knife makers on making high-quality, handmade knives.

How to Make Multi-Blade Folding Knives, by Eugene Shadley & Terry Davis, Krause Publications, Iola, WI, 1997. 192 pp., illus. Paper covers. $19.95

This step-by-step instructional guide teaches knifemakers how to craft these complex folding knives.

How to Make a Tactical Folder, by Bob Tetzuola, Krause Publications, Iola, WI, 2000. 160 pp., illustrated. Paper covers. $16.95

Step-by-step instructions and outstanding photography guide the knifemaker from start to finish.

Modern Swordsman, The, by Fred Hutchinson, Paladin Press, Boulder, CO, 1999. 80 pp., illustrated. Paper covers. $22.00

Realistic training for serious self-defense.

KA-BAR: The Next Generation of the Ultimate Fighting Knife, by Greg Walker, Paladin Press, Boulder, CO, 2001. 88 pp., illus. Soft covers. $16.00

The KA-BAR Fighting/Utility Knife is the most widely recognized and popular combat knife ever to be produced in the United States. Since its introduction on 23 November 1942, the KA-BAR has performed brilliantly on the battlefields of Europe, the South Pacific, Korea, Southeast Asia, Central America and the Middle East, earning its moniker as the "ultimate fighting knife." In this book, Greg Walker gives readers an inside view of the exacting design criteria, cutting-edge materials, extensivefactory tests and exhaustive real-life field tests that went into the historic redesign of the blade, handguard, handle, pommel, and sheath of the ultimate fighting knife of the future. The new knife excelled at these rigorous tests, earning the right tobe called a KA-BAR.

Kalashnikov Bayonets: The Collector's Guide to Bayonets for the AK and its Variations, by Martin D. Ivie, Texas: Diamond Eye Publications, 2002. 1st edition. 220 pages, with over 250 color photos and illustrations. Hardcover. $59.95

Knife and Tomahawk Throwing: The Art of the Experts, by Harry K. McEvoy, Charles E. Tuttle, Rutland, VT, 1989. 150 pp., illus. Soft covers. $8.95

The first book to employ side-by-side the fascinating art and science of knives and tomahawks.

Knife in Homespun America and Related Items: Its Construction and Material, as Used by Woodsmen, Farmers, Soldiers, Indians and General Population, The, by Madison Grant,. York, PA: Privately Printed, 1984. 1st edition. 187 pages, profusely illustrated. $45.00

Shows over 300 examples of knives and related items made and used by woodsman, farmers, soldiers, indians and the general frontier population.

Knife Talk, The Art and Science of Knifemaking, by Ed. Fowler, Krause Publications, Iola, WI, 1998. 158 pp., illus. Paper covers. $14.95

Valuable how-to advice on knife design and construction plus 20 years of memorable articles from the pages of "Blade" Magazine.

Knifemakers of Old San Francisco, by Bernard Levine, 2nd edition, Paladin Press, Boulder, CO, 1998. 150 pp., illus. $39.95

The definitive history of the knives and knife-makers of 19th century San Francisco.

Knives, 5th Edition, The Gun Digest Book of, edited by Jack Lewis and Roger Combs, DBI Books, a division of Krause Publications, Iola, WI, 1997. 256 pp., illus. Paper covers. $19.95

Covers practically every aspect of the knife world.

Knives of the United States Military — World War II, by Michael W. Silvey. Privately Printed, Sacramento, CA 1999. 250 pages, illustrated with full color photos. Hardcover $60.00

There are 240 full page color plates depicting the knives of World War II displayed against a background of wartime accoutrements and memorabilia. The book focuses on knives and their background.

Knives of the United States Military In Vietnam: 1961-1975, by Michael W. Silvey. Privately Printed, Sacramento, CA., 139 pp. Hardcover. $45.00

A beautiful color celebration of the most interesting and rarest knives of the Vietnam War, emphasizing SOG knives, Randalls, Gerbers, Eks, and other knives of this era. Shown with these knives are the patches and berets of the elite units who used them.

Knives 2003, 23rd Annual Edition, edited by Joe Kertzman, Krause Publications, Iola, WI, 2002. 320 pp., illustrated. Paper covers. $22.95

More than 1,200 photos and listings of new knives plus articles from top writers in the field.

Les Baionnettes Reglementaires Francises de 1840 a 1918 'The Bayonets; Military Issue 1840-1918, by French Assoc.of Bayonet Collectors, 2000. 77 pp. illus. $24.95

Profusely illustrated. By far the most comprehenive guide to French military bayonets done for this period. Includes hundreds of illustrations. 77 large 8 1/4 x ll 1/2 inch pages. French Text. Color photos are magnificant!

Master Bladesmith: Advanced Studies in Steel, The, by Jim Hrisoulas, Paladin Press, Boulder, CO, 1990. 296 pp., illus. $49.95

The author reveals the forging secrets that for centuries have been protected by guilds.

Medieval Swordsmanship, Illustrated Methods and Techniques, by John Clements, Paladin Press, Boulder, CO, 1998. 344 pp., illustrated. $40.00

The most comprehensive and historically accurate view ever written of the lost fighting arts of Medieval knights.

Military Knife & Bayonet Book, The, by Homer Brett. World Photo Press, Japan. 2001. 392 pages, illus. $69.95

Professional studio color photographs, with more than 1,000 military knives and knife-bayonets illustrated. Both the U.S. and foreign sections are extensive, and includes standard models, prototypes and experimental models. Many of the knives and bayonets photographed have never been previously illustrated in any other book. The U.S. section also includes the latest developments in military Special Operations designs. Written in Japanese and English. This book is a must for any collector.

Military Knives: A Reference Book, by Frank Trzaska (editor), Knife Books, Deptford, NJ, 2001. 255 pp., illustrated. Softcover. $17.95

A collection of your favorite Military Knive articles fron the pages of Knife World Magazine. 67 articles ranging from the Indian Wars to the present day modern military knives.

Modern Combat Blades, by Duncan Long, Paladin Press, Boulder, CO, 1993. 128 pp., illus. $30.00

Long discusses the pros and cons of bowies, bayonets, commando daggers, kukris, switchblades, butterfly knives, belt-buckle blades and many more.

Officer Swords of the German Navy 1806-1945, Claus P. Stefanski & Dirk. Schiffer Publications, Atglen, PA, 2002. 1st edition. 176 pages, with over 250 b/w and color photos. Hardcover. $59.95

On Damascus Steel, by Dr. Leo S. Figiel, Atlantis Arts Press, Atlantis, FL, 1991. 145 pp., illus. $65.00

The historic, technical and artistic aspects of Oriental and mechanical Damascus. Persian and Indian sword blades, from 1600-1800, which have never been published, are illustrated.

Pattern-Welded Blade: Artistry in Iron, The, by Jim Hrisoulas, Paladin Press, Boulder, CO, 1994. 120 pp., illus. $44.95

Reveals the secrets of this craft—from the welding of the starting billet to the final assembly of the complete blade.

Photographic Supplement of Confederate Swords, with addendum, A, by William A. Albaugh III. Broadfoot Publishing, Wilmington, NC. 1999. 205 plus 54 pages of the addendum, illustrated with black and white photos. $45.00

Plug Bayonet: An Identification Guide for Collector, The, by R.D.C. Evans. West Yorkshire, UK: Privately Printed, 2002. 1st edition. 263 pages, illustrated. 507 Plug Bayonets are covered. Hardcover. $67.95

This volume is intended to allow the collector to place a particular plug bayonet in its correct time period & country of origin. Separate countries covered British Isles, France, Germanic countries, Italian states, Low countries, Russia, E. Europe, America, India, Spain & Portugal. Cutler's marks found on bayonets are covered in detail.

Pocket Knife Trader's Price Guide — Volume 6, by Jim Parker. Chatanooga, TN: James F. Parker Trust, 2003. 6th Edition. 384 pages, illustrated with black and white photographs and detailed line drawings. Softcover. $14.95

Pocket Knives of the United States Military, by Michael W. Silvey. Sacramento, CA: Privately printed, 2002. 135 pages. Hardcover. $34.95

This beautiful new full color book is the definitive reference on U.S. Military folders. Pocket Knives of the United States Military is organized into the following sections: Introduction, The First Folders, World War I, World War II, and Postwar (which covers knives up through the late 1980s). Coverage ranges from the expected pages of TL-29s and 4-blade utility knives to rare switchblades, demolition knives, OSS and CIA folders, and far, far more U.S. Navy rope knives than I ever knew existed. The photos are as beautiful as expected, and the knives pictured the finest that could be procured. A bibliography is included as an added bonus. Essential reading for pocketknife and military knife collectors alike!

Randall Chronicles, The, by Hamilton, Pete. Privately Printed, 2002. 160 pages, profusely illustrated in color. Hardcover in Dust Jacket. $79.95

Randall Fighting Knives In Wartime: WWII, Korea, and Vietnam, by Hunt, Robert E. Sacramento, CA: Privately Printed, 2002. 1st edition. 192 pages. Hardcover. $44.95

While other books on Randall knives have been published, this new title is the first to focus specifically on Randalls with military ties. There are three main sections, containing more than 80 knives from the WWII, Korea, and Vietnam War periods. Each knife is featured in a high quality, full page, full color photograph, with the opposing page carrying a detailed description of the knife and its history or other related information. Some interesting military accessories can be found in the photos as well. One of the most useful parts of the book is the section in the back devoted to explaining such complexities as wrist thong attachments for model #1 and #2 knives, sheath snaps, Springfield fighters, small stamps, Johnson split-back sheaths with small rivets, and "fighter sets." All of this is important information for the Randall devotee. A price guide is also included, which I thought a nice touch. My complaints about the book are minor: the abbreviations used should have been better explained, and some additional photos would have been very useful in helping the reader understand the plethora of variations described in the text. Page after page of classic Randall fighting knives from WWII, Korea, and Vietnam, all in beautiful full color.

Randall Made Knives, by Robert L. Gaddis, Paladin Press, Boulder, CO, 2000. 292 pp., illus. $59.95

Plots the designs of all 24 of Randall's unique knives. This step-by-step book, seven years in the making, is worth every penny and moment of your time.

Razor Anthology, The, by Krause Publications, Iola, WI. 1998. 246 pp., illustrated. Paper covers. $14.95

Razor Anthology is a cut above the rest. Razor aficionados will find this collection of articles about razors both informative and interesting.

Razor Edge, by John Juranitch, Krause Publications, Iola, WI. 1998. 132 pp., illustrated. Paper covers. $15.00

Reveals step-by-step instructions for sharpening everything from arrowheads, to blades, to fish hooks.

Renaissance Swordsmanship, by John Clements, Paladin Press, Boulder, CO, 1997. 152 pp., illus. Paper covers. $25.00

The illustrated use of rapiers and cut-and-thrust swords.

THE ARMS LIBRARY

Rice's Trowel Bayonet, reprinted by Ray Riling Arms Books, Co., Phila., PA, 1968. 8 pp., illus. Paper covers. $3.00

A facsimile reprint of a rare circular originally published by the U.S. government in 1875 for the information of U.S. troops.

Scottish Dirk, The, by James D. Forman, Museum Restoration Service, Bloomfield, Ont., Canada, 1991. 60 pp., illus. Paper covers. $8.95

More than 100 dirks are illustrated with a text that sets the dirk and Sgian Dubh in their socio-historic content following design changes through more than 300 years of evolution.

Scottish Swords from the Battlefield at Culloden, by Lord Archibald Campbell, The Mowbray Co., Providence, RI, 1973. 63 pp., illus. $15.00

A modern reprint of an exceedingly rare 1894 privately printed edition.

Seitengewehr: History of the German Bayonet, 1919-1945, by George T. Wheeler, Johnson Reference Books, Fredericksburg, VA, 2000. 320 pp., illus. $44.95

Provides complete information on Weimar and Third Reich bayonets, as well astheir accompanying knots and frogs. Illustrates re-issued German and foreign bayonets utilized by both the Reichswehr and the Wehrmacht, and details the progression ofnewly manufactured bayonets produced after Hitler's rise to power. Photos illustrate rarely seen bayonets worn by the Polizei, Reichsbahn, Postschutz, Hitler Jugend, and other civil and political organiztions. German modified bayonets from other countries are pictured and described. Book contains an up-to-date price guide including current valuations of various Imperial, Weimar, and Third Reich bayonets.

Silver Mounted Swords: The Lattimer Family Collection; Featuring Silver Hilts Through the Golden Age, by Daniel Hartzler, Rowe Publications, New York, 2000. 300 pages, with over 1000 illustrations and 1350 photo's. Oversize 9x12. $75.00

The world's largest silver hilt collection.

Small Arms Identification Series, No. 6-British Service Sword & Lance Patterns, by Ian Skennerton, I.D.S.A. Books, Piqua, OH, 1994. 48 pp. $9.50

Small Arms Series, No. 2. The British Spike Bayonet, by Ian Skennerton, I.D.S.A. Books, Piqua, OH, 1982. 32 pp., 30 illus. $9.00

Socket in the British Army 1667-1783, The, by Erik Goldstein, Andrew Mowbray, Inc., Lincoln, RI, 2001. 136 pp., illus. $23.00

The spectacle of English "redcoats" on the attack, relentlessly descending upon enemy lines with fixed bayonets, is one of the most chilling images from European history and the American Revolution. The bayonets covered in this book stood side by side with the famous "Brown Bess" as symbols of English military power throughout the world. Drawing upon new information from archaeological digs and archival records, the author explains how to identify each type of bayonet and shows which bayonets were used where and with which guns. No student of military history or weapons development can afford to do without this useful new book.

Socket Bayonets of the Great Powers, by Robert W. Shuey, Excalibur Publications, Tucson, AZ, 2000 96 pp., illus. Paper covers $22.95

With 175 illustrations the author brings together in one place, many of the standard socket arrnagements used by some of the " Great Powers". With an illustrated glossary of blade shape and socket design.

Spyderco Story: The New Shape of Sharp, by Kenneth T. Delavigne, Paladin Press, Boulder, CO, 1998. 312 pp., illus. $69.95

Discover the history and inner workings of the company whose design innovations have redefined the shape of the modern folding knife and taken high-performance cutting to a new level.

Swords and Sword Makers of the War of 1812, by Richard Bezdek, Paladin Press, Boulder, CO, 1997. 104 pp., illus. $49.95

The complete history of the men and companies that made swords during and before the war. Includes examples of cavalry and artillery sabers.

Swords from Public Collections in the Commonwealth of Pennsylvania, edited by Bruce S. Bazelon, Andrew Mowbray Inc., Lincoln, RI, 1987. 127 pp., illus. Paper covers. $12.00

Contains new information regarding swordmakers of the Philadelphia area.

Swords and Sabers of the Armory at Springfield, by Burton A. Kellerstedt, Burton A. Kellerstedt, New Britain, CT, 1998. 121 pp, illus. Softcover. $29.95

The basic and most important reference for it's subject, and one that is unlikely to be surpassed for comprehensiveness and accuracy.

Swords and Blades of the American Revolution, by George C. Neumann, Rebel Publishing Co., Inc., Texarkana, TX, 1991. 288 pp., illus. $36.95

The encyclopedia of bladed weapons—swords, bayonets, spontoons, halberds, pikes, knives, daggers, axes—used by both sides, on land and sea, in America's struggle for independence.

Swords of Imperial Japan, 1868-1945, by Jim Dawson, Published by the Author. 160 Pages, illustrated with 263 b&w photos. Paper covers. $29.95

Details the military, civilian, diplomatic and civil, police and colonial swords and the post-Samurai era as well as the swords of Manchukuo, the Japanese independent territory.

Tactical Folding Knife; A Study of the Anatomy and Construction of the Liner-Locked Folder, by Terzuola, Krause Publications, Iola, WI. 2000. 160 Pages, 200 b&w photos, illustrated. Paper covers. $16.00

Step-by-step instructions and outstanding photography guide the knifemaker from start to finish. Knifemaker Bob Terzuola has been called the father of the tactical folding knife. This book details everything from the basic definition of a tactical folder to the final polishing as the knife is finished.

U.S. M3 Trench Knife of World War II, The, by Coniglio and Laden. Privately printed, 2003. Reprint. 41 pages, illustrated. Softcover. $18.00

A superb reference book on that hot WWII collectable, filled with information for collectors and researchers.

U.S. Military Knives, Bayonets and Machetes Price Guide, 4th ed. by Frank Trzaska (editor), Knife Books, Deptford, NJ, 2001. 80 pp., illustrated. Softcover. $7.95

This volume follows in the tradition of the previous three versions of using major works on the subject as a reference to keep the price low to you.

Wayne Goddard's $50 Knife Shop, by Wayne Goddard, Krause Publications, Iola, WI. 2000. 160 Pages, illus. Soft covers. $19.95

This new book expands on information from Goddard's popular column in Blade magazine to show knifemakers of all skill levels how to create helpful gadgets and supply their shop on a shoestring.

Wonder of Knifemaking, The, by Wayne Goddard, Krause Publications, Iola, WI. 2000. 160 Pages, illus. Soft covers. $19.95

Master bladesmith Wayne Goddard draws on his decades of experience to answer questions of knifemakers at all levels. As a columnist for *Blade* magazine, Goddard has been answering real questions from real knifemakers for the past eight years. Now, all the details are compiled in one place as a handy reference for every knifemaker, amateur or professional.

Working Folding Knife, The, by Steven Dick, Stoeger Publishing Co., Wayne, NJ, 1998. 280 pp., illus. Paper covers. $21.95

From the classic American Barlow to exotic folders like the spanish Navaja this book has it all

GENERAL

Action Shooting: Cowboy Style, by John Taffin, Krause Publications, Iola, WI, 1999. 320 pp., illustrated. $39.95

Details on the guns and ammunition. Explanations of the rules used for many events. The essential cowboy wardrobe.

Advanced Muzzleloader's Guide, by Toby Bridges, Stoeger Publishing Co., So. Hackensack, NJ, 1985. 256 pp., illus. Paper covers. $14.95

The complete guide to muzzle-loading rifles, pistols and shotguns—flintlock and percussion.

Aids to Musketry for Officers & NCOs, by Capt. B.J. Friend, Excalibur Publications, Latham, NY, 1996. 40 pp., illus. Paper covers. $7.95

A facsimile edition of a pre-WWI British manual filled with useful information for training the common soldier.

Air Gun Digest, 3rd Edition, by J.I. Galan, DBI Books, a division of Krause Publications, Iola, WI, 1995. 258 pp., illus. Paper covers. $19.95

Everything from A to Z on air gun history, trends and technology.

American Air Rifles, by House, James E. Krause Publications, Iola, WI. 2002. 1st edition. 208 pages, with 198 b&w photos. Softcover. $22.95

Air rifle ballistics, sights, pellets, games, and hunting caliber recommendations are thoroughly explained to help shooters get the most out of their American air rifles. Evaluation of more than a dozen American-made and American-imported air rifle models.

American B.B. Gun: A Collector's Guide, The, by Dunathan, Arni T. A.S. Barnes And Co., Inc., South Brunswick. 2001. 154 pages, illustrated with nearly 200 photographs, drawings and detailed diagrams. Hardcover. $35.00

American and Imported Arms, Ammunition and Shooting Accessories, Catalog No. 18 of the Shooter's Bible, Stoeger, Inc., reprinted by Fayette Arsenal, Fayetteville, NC, 1988. 142 pp., illus. Paper covers. $10.95

A facsimile reprint of the 1932 Stoeger's Shooter's Bible.

America's Great Gunmakers, by Wayne van Zwoll, Stoeger Publishing Co., So. Hackensack, NJ, 1992. 288 pp., illus. Paper covers. $16.95

This book traces in great detail the evolution of guns and ammunition in America and the men who formed the companies that produced them.

Armed and Female, by Paxton Quigley, E.P. Dutton, New York, NY, 1989. 237 pp., illus. $16.95

The first complete book on one of the hottest subjects in the media today, the arming of the American woman.

Arming the Glorious Cause: Weapons of the Second War for Independence, by James B. Whisker, Daniel D. Hartzler and Larry W. Yantz, R & R Books, Livonia, NY, 1998. 175 pp., illustrated. $45.00.

A photographic study of Confederate weapons.

Arms and Armour in Antiquity and the Middle Ages, by Charles Boutell, Stackpole Books, Mechanicsburg, PA, 1996. 352 pp., illus. $22.95

Detailed descriptions of arms and armor, the development of tactics and the outcome of specific battles.

Arms & Armor in the Art Institute of Chicago, by Walter J. Karcheski, Jr., Bulfinch Press, Boston, MA, 1995. 128 pp., illus. $35.00

Now, for the first time, the Art Institute of Chicago's arms and armor collection is presented in the visual delight of 103 color illustrations.

Arms for the Nation: Springfield Longarms, edited by David C. Clark, Scott A. Duff, Export, PA, 1994. 73 pp., illus. Paper covers. $9.95

A brief history of the Springfield Armory and the arms made there.

Arsenal of Freedom, The Springfield Armory, 1890-1948: A Year-by-Year Account Drawn from Official Records, compiled and edited by Lt. Col. William S. Brophy, USAR Ret., Andrew Mowbray, Inc., Lincoln, RI, 1991. 400 pp., illus. Soft covers. $29.95

A "must buy" for all students of American military weapons, equipment and accoutrements.

Assault Pistols, Rifles and Submachine Guns, by Duncan Long, Paladin Press, Boulder, CO, 1997, 8 1/2 x 11, soft cover, photos, illus. 152 pp. $21.95

This book offers up-to-date, practical information on how to operate and field-strip modern military, police and civilian combat weapons. Covers new developments and trends such as the use of fiber optics, liquid-recoil systems and lessening of barrel length are covered. Troubleshooting procedures, ballistic tables and a list of manufacturers and distributors are also included.

Assault Weapons, 5th Edition, The Gun Digest Book of, edited by Jack Lewis and David E. Steele, DBI Books, a division of Krause Publications, Iola, WI, 2000. 256 pp., illustrated. Paper covers. $21.95

This is the latest word on true assault weaponry in use today by international military and law enforcement organizations.

Benchrest Shooting Primer, The, by Brennan, Dave (Editor). Precision Shooting, Inc., Manchester, CT 2000. 2nd edition. 420 pages, illustrated with black and white photographs, drawings and detailed diagrams. Pictorial softcover. $24.95

The very best articles on shooting and reloading for the most challenging of all the rifle accuracy disciplines...benchrest shooting.

Black Powder, Pig Lead and Steel Silhouettes, by Matthews, Paul A. Wolfe Publishing, Prescott, AZ, 2002. 132 pages, illustrated with black and white photographs and detailed drawings and diagrams. Softcover. $16.95

Book of the Crossbow The, by Sir Ralph Payne-Gallwey, Dover Publications, Mineola, NY, 1996. 416 pp., illus. Paper covers. $14.95

Unabridged republication of the scarce 1907 London edition of the book on one of the most devastating hand weapons of the Middle Ages.

THE ARMS LIBRARY

British Small Arms of World War 2, by Ian D. Skennerton, I.D.S.A. Books, Piqua, OH, 1988. 110 pp., 37 illus. $25.00

Carbine And Shotgun Speed Shooting: How To Hit Hard And Fast In Combat, by Moses, Steve. Paladin Press, Boulder, CO. 2002. 96 pages, illus. Softcover $18.00

In this groundbreaking book, he breaks down the mechanics of speed shooting these weapons, from stance and grip to sighting, trigger control and more, presenting them in a concise and easily understood manner. Whether you wish to further your defensive, competitive or recreational shooting skills, you will find this book a welcome resource for learning to shoot carbines and shotguns with the speed and accuracy that are so critical at short distances.

Combat Handgunnery, 5th Edition, The Gun Digest Book of, by Chuck Taylor, DBI Books, a division of Krause Publications, Iola, WI, 2002. 256 pp., illus. Paper covers. $21.95

This edition looks at real world combat handgunnery from three different perspectives—military, police and civilian.

Complete Blackpowder Handbook, 4th Edition, The, by Sam Fadala, DBI Books, a division of Krause Publications, Iola, WI, 2002. 400 pp., illus. Paper covers. $21.95

Expanded and completely rewritten edition of the definitive book on the subject of blackpowder.

Complete .50-caliber Sniper Course, The, by Dean Michaelis, Paladin Press, Boulder, CO, 2000. 576 pp, illustrated, $60.00

The history from German Mauser T-Gewehr of World War 1 to the Soviet PTRD and beyond. Includes the author's Program of Instruction for Special Operations Hard-Target Interdiction Course.

cowboy Action Shooting, by Charly Gullett, Wolfe Publishing Co., Prescott, AZ, 1995. 400 pp., illus. Paper covers. $24.50

The fast growing of the shooting sports is comprehensively covered in this text— the guns, loads, tactics and the fun and flavor of this Old West era competition.

Custom Firearms Engraving, by Tom Turpin, Krause Publications, Iola, WI, 1999. 208 pp., illustrated. $49.95

Provides a broad and comprehensive look at the world of firearms engraving. The exquisite styles of more than 75 master engravers are shown on beautiful examples of handguns, rifles, shotguns, and other firearms, as well as knives.

Dead On, by Tony Noblitt and Warren Gabrilska, Paladin Press, Boulder, CO, 1998. 176 pp., illustrated. Paper covers. $22.00

The long-range marksman's guide to extreme accuracy.

Elmer Keith: The Other Side of A Western Legend, by Gene Brown., Precision Shooting, Inc., Manchester, CT 2002. 1st edition. 168 pages, illustrated with black and white photographs. Softcover. $19.95

An updated and expanded edition of his original work, incorporating new tales and information that has come to light in the past six years. Additional photos have been added, and the expanded work has been professionally edited and formatted. Gene Brown was a long time friend of Keith, and today is unquestionably the leading authority on Keith's books. The chapter on the topic is worth the price of admission by itself.

Encyclopedia of Native American Bows, Arrows and Quivers, by Steve Allely and Jim Hamm, The Lyons Press, N.Y., 1999. 160 pp., illustrated. $29.95

A landmark book for anyone interested in archery history, or Native Americans.

Exercise of Armes, The, by Jacob de Gheyn, edited and with an introduction by Bas Kist, Dover Publications, Inc., Mineola, NY, 1999. 144 pp., illustrated. Paper covers. $14.95

Republications of all 117 engravings from the 1607 classic military manual. A meticulously accurate portrait of uniforms and weapons of the 17th century Netherlands.

Federal Civil War Shelter Tent, The, by Gaede, Frederick C., Alexandria, VA: O'Donnell Publishing, 2001. 1st edition. 134 pages, and illustrated. Softcover $20.00

This is a great monograph for all Civil War collectors. The text covers everything from government patents, records, and contract data to colorful soldier's descriptions. In addition, it is extensively illustrated with drawings and photos of over 30 known examples with close-ups of stitching, fastening buttons, and some that were decorated with soldier's art. This book is a well-presented study by a leading researcher, collector, and historian.

Fighting Iron; A Metals Handbook for Arms Collectors, by Art Gogan, Mowbray Publishers, Inc., Lincoln, RI, 2002. 176 pp., illustrated. $28.00

A guide that is easy to use, explains things in simple English and covers all of the different historical periods that we are interested in.

Fighting Submachine Gun, Machine Pistol, and Shotgun, a Hands-On Evaluation, The, by Timothy J. Mullin, Paladin Press, Boulder, CO, 1999. 224 pp., illustrated. Paper covers. $35.00

An invaluable reference for military, police and civilian shooters who may someday need to know how a specific weapon actually performs when the targets are shooting back and the margin of errors is measured in lives lost.

Fireworks: A Gunsight Anthology, by Jeff Cooper, Paladin Press, Boulder, CO, 1998. 192 pp., illus. Paper cover. $27.00

A collection of wild, hilarious, shocking and always meaningful tales from the remarkable life of an American firearms legend.

Frank Pachmayr: The Story of America's Master Gunsmith and his Guns, by John Lachuk, Safari Press, Huntington Beach, CA, 1996. 254 pp., illus. First edition, limited, signed and slipcased. $85.00; Second printing trade edition. $50.00

The colorful and historically significant biography of Frank A. Pachmayr, America's own gunsmith emeritus.

From a Stranger's Doorstep to the Kremlin Gate, by Mikhail Kalashnikov, Ironside International Publishers, Inc., Alexandria, VA, 1999. 460 pp., illustrated. $34.95

A biography of the most influential rifle designer of the 20th century. His AK-47 assault rifle has become the most widely used (and copied) assault rifle of this century.

Frontier Rifleman, The, by H.B. LaCrosse Jr., Pioneer Press, Union City, TN, 1989. 183 pp., illus. Soft covers. $17.50

The Frontier rifleman's clothing and equipment during the era of the American Revolution, 1760-1800.

Gatling Gun: 19th Century Machine Gun to 21st Century Vulcan, The, by Joseph Berk, Paladin Press, Boulder, CO, 1991. 136 pp., illus. $34.95

Here is the fascinating on-going story of a truly timeless weapon, from its beginnings during the Civil War to its current role as a state-of-the-art modern combat system.

German Artillery of World War Two, by Ian V. Hogg, Stackpole Books, Mechanicsburg, PA, 1997. 304 pp., illus. $44.95

Complete details of German artillery use in WWII.

Gone Diggin: Memoirs of A Civil War Relic Hunter, by Toby Law. Orange, VA: Publisher's Press, 2002. 1st edition signed. ISBN: 0942365138. 151 pages, illustrated with black & white photos. $24.95

The true story of one relic hunter's life - the author kept exacting records of every relic hunt and every relic hunter he was with working with.

Grand Old Lady of No Man's Land: The Vickers Machine Gun, by Dolf L. Goldsmith, Collector Grade Publications, Cobourg, Canada, 1994. 600 pp., illus. $79.95

Goldsmith brings his years of experience as a U.S. Army armourer, machine gun collector and shooter to bear on the Vickers, in a book sure to become a classic in its field.

Grenade Recognition Manual, Volume 1, U.S. Grenades & Accessories, The, by Darryl W. Lynn, Service Publications, Ottawa, Canada, 1998. 112 pp., illus. Paper covers. $29.95

This new book examines the hand grenades of the United States beginning with the hand grenades of the U.S. Civil War and continues through to the present.

Grenade Recognition Manual, Vol. 2, British and Commonwealth Grenades and Accessories, The, by Darryl W. Lynn, Printed by the Author, Ottawa, Canada, 2001. 201 pp., illustrated with over 200 photos and drawings. Paper covers. $40.00

Covers British, Australian, and Canadian Grenades. It has the complete British Numbered series, most of the L series as well as the Australian and Canadian grenades in use. Also covers Launchers, fuzes and lighters, launching cartridges, fillings, and markings.

Gun Digest 2003, 57th Edition, edited by Ken Ramage, DBI Books a division of Krause Publications, Iola, WI, 2002. 544 pp., illustrated. Paper covers. $27.95

This all new 56th edition continues the editorial excellence, quality, content and comprehensive cataloguing that firearms enthusiasts have come to know and expect. The most read gun book in the world for the last half century.

Gun Engraving, by C. Austyn, Safari Press Publication, Huntington Beach, CA, 1998. 128 pp., plus 24 pages of color photos. $50.00

A well-illustrated book on fine English and European gun engravers. Includes a fantastic pictorial section that lists types of engravings and prices.

Gun Notes, Volume 1, by Elmer Keith, Safari Press, Huntington Beach, CA, 2002. 219 pp., illustrated Softcover. $24.95

A collection of Elmer Keith's most interesting columns and feature stories that appeared in "Guns & Ammo" magazine from 1961 to the late 1970's.

Gun Notes, Volume 2, by Elmer Keith, Safari Press, Huntington Beach, CA, 2002. 292 pp., illustrated. Softcover. $24.95

Covers articles from Keith's monthly column in "Guns & Ammo" magazine during the period from 1971 through Keith's passing in 1982.

Gun Talk, edited by Dave Moreton, Winchester Press, Piscataway, NJ, 1973. 256 pp., illus. $9.95

A treasury of original writing by the top gun writers and editors in America. Practical advice about every aspect of the shooting sports.

Gun That Made the Twenties Roar, The, by Wm. J. Helmer, rev. and enlarged by George C. Nonte, Jr., The Gun Room Press, Highland Park, NJ, 1977. Over 300 pp., illus. $24.95

Historical account of John T. Thompson and his invention, the infamous "Tommy Gun."

Gun Trader's Guide, 24th Edition, published by Stoeger Publishing Co., Wayne, NJ, 2002. 592 pp., illus. Paper covers. $23.95

Complete specifications and current prices for used guns. Prices of over 5,000 handguns, rifles and shotguns both foreign and domestic.

Gunfighter, Man or Myth?, The, by Joseph G. Rosa, Oklahoma Press, Norman, OK, 1969. 229 pp., illus. (including weapons). Paper covers. $14.95

A well-documented work on gunfights and gunfighters of the West and elsewhere. Great treat for all gunfighter buffs.

Guns Illustrated 2003, 23rd Edition, edited by Ken Ramage, DBI Books a division of Krause Publications, Iola, WI, 2003. 352 pp., illustrated. Softcovers. $22.95

Highly informative, technical articles on a wide range of shooting topics by some of the top writers in the industry. A catalog section lists more than 3,000 firearms currently manufactured in or imported to the U.S.

Guns Of The Old West, by Dean K. Boorman, New York: Lyons Press, 2002. Color & b&w illus, 144 pgs. Hardcover. $29.95

An illustrated history of the firearms used by pioneers, hunters, soldiers, lawmen, & the lawless.

Guns & Shooting: A Selected Bibliography, by Ray Riling, Ray Riling Arms Books Co., Phila., PA, 1982. 434 pp., illus. Limited, numbered edition. $75.00

A limited edition of this superb bibliographical work, the only modern listing of books devoted to guns and shooting.

Guns, Bullets, and Gunfighters, by Jim Cirillo, Paladin Press, Boulder, CO, 1996. 119 pp., illus. Paper covers. $16.00

Lessons and tales from a modern-day gunfighter.

Hidden in Plain Sight, "A Practical Guide to Concealed Handgun Carry" (Revised 2nd Edition), by Trey Bloodworth and Mike Raley, Paladin Press, Boulder, CO, 1997, 5 1/2 x 8 1/2, softcover, photos, 176 pp. $20.00

Concerned with how to comfortably, discreetly and safely exercise the privileges granted by a CCW permit? This invaluable guide offers the latest advice on what to look for when choosing a CCW, how to dress for comfortable, effective concealed carry, traditional and more unconventional carry modes, accessory holsters, customized clothing and accessories, accessibility data based on draw-time comparisons and new holsters on the market. Includes 40 new manufacturer listings.

HK Assault Rifle Systems, by Duncan Long, Paladin Press, Boulder, CO, 1995. 110 pp., illus. Paper covers. $27.95

The little known history behind this fascinating family of weapons tracing its beginnings from the ashes of World War Two to the present time.

THE ARMS LIBRARY

Hunting Time: Adventures In Pursuit Of North American Big Game: A Forty Year Chronicle, The, by John E. Howard, Deforest, WI: Saint Huberts Press, 2002. 1st edition. ISBN: 0963309447. 537 pages, illustrated with drawings. Hardcover. $29.95

From a novice's first hunt for whitetailed deer in his native Wisconsin, to a seasoned hunter's pursuit of a Boone and Crockett Club record book caribou in the northwest territories, the author carries the reader along on his forty year journey through the big game fields of North America.

I Remember Skeeter, compiled by Sally Jim Skelton, Wolfe Publishing Co., Prescott, AZ, 1998. 401 pp., illus. Paper covers. $19.95

A collection of some of the beloved storyteller's famous works interspersed with anecdotes and tales from the people who knew best.

Indian Tomahawks and Frontiersmen Belt Axes, by Daniel Hartzler & James Knowles. New Windsor, MD: Privately Printed, 2002. 4th revised edition. 279 pages, illustrated with photos and drawings. Hardcover. $65.00

This fourth revised edition has over 160 new tomahawks and trade axes added since the first edition, also a list of 205 makers names. There are 15 chapters from the earliest known tomahawks to the present day. Some of the finest tomahawks in the country are shown in this book with 31 color plates. This comprehensive study is invaluable to any collector.

Jack O'Connor Catalogue of Letters, by Enzler-Herring, E. Cataloguer. Agoura CA: Trophy Room Books, 2002. 262 pages, 18 illustrations. Hardcover. $55.00

During a sixteen year period beginning in 1960, O'Connor exchanged many letters with his pal, John Jobson. Material from nearly three hundred of these has been assembled and edited by Ellen Enzler Herring and published in chronological order. A number of the letters have been reproduced in full or part. They offer considerable insight into the beloved gun editor and "Dean of Outdoor Writers" over and beyond what we know about him from his books.

Jack O'Connor — The Legendary Life of America's Greatest Gunwriter, by R. Anderson. Long Beach, CA: Safari Press, 2002. 1st edition. 240pp, profuse photos. Hardcover. $29.95

This is the book all hunters in North America have been waiting for—the long-awaited biography on Jack O'Connor! Jack O'Connor was the preeminent North American big-game hunter and gunwriter of the twentieth century, and Robert Anderson's masterfully written new work is a blockbuster filled with fascinating facts and stories about this controversial character. With the full cooperation of the O'Connor children, Anderson spent three years interviewing O'Connor's family and friends as well as delving into JOC's papers, photos, and letters, including the extensive correspondence between O'Connor and Bob Householder, and the O'Connor papers from Washington State University. O'Connor's lifelong friend Buck Buckner has contributed two chapters on his experiences with the master of North American hunting.

Kill or Get Killed, by Col. Rex Applegate, Paladin Press, Boulder, CO, 1996. 400 pp., illus. $49.95

The best and longest-selling book on close combat in history.

Long-Range War: Sniping in Vietnam, The, by Peter R. Senich, Paladin Press, Boulder, CO, 1999. 280 pp., illus. Softcover $59.95

The most complete report on Vietnam-era sniping ever documented.

Manual for H&R Reising Submachine Gun and Semi-Auto Rifle, edited by George P. Dillman, Desert Publications, El Dorado, AZ, 1994. 81 pp., illus. Paper covers. $12.95

A reprint of the Harrington & Richardson 1943 factory manual and the rare military manual on the H&R submachine gun and semi-auto rifle.

Manufacture of Gunflints, The, by Sydney B.J. Skertchly, facsimile reprint with new introduction by Seymour de Lotbiniere, Museum Restoration Service, Ontario, Canada, 1984. 90 pp., illus. $24.50

Limited edition reprinting of the very scarce London edition of 1879.

Master Tips, by J. Winokur, Potshot Press, Pacific Palisades, CA, 1985. 96 pp., illus. Paper covers. $11.95

Basics of practical shooting.

Military and Police Sniper, The, by Mike R. Lau, Precision Shooting, Inc., Manchester, CT, 1998. 352 pp., illustrated. Paper covers. $44.95

Advanced precision shooting for combat and law enforcement.

Military Rifle & Machine Gun Cartridges, by Jean Huon, Paladin Press, Boulder, CO, 1990. 392 pp., illus. $34.95

Describes the primary types of military cartridges and their principal loadings, as well as their characteristics, origin and use.

Military Small Arms of the 20th Century, 7th Edition, by Ian V. Hogg and John Weeks, DBI Books, a division of Krause Publications, Iola, WI, 2000. 416 pp., illustrated. Paper covers. $24.95

Cover small arms of 46 countries. Over 800 photographs and illustrations.

Modern Custom Guns, Walnut, Steel, and Uncommon Artistry, by Tom Turpin, Krause Publications, Iola, WI, 1997. 206 pp., illus. $49.95

From exquisite engraving to breathtaking exotic woods, the mystique of today's custom guns is expertly detailed in word and awe-inspiring color photos of rifles, shotguns and handguns.

Modern Law Enforcement Weapons & Tactics, 2nd Edition, by Tom Ferguson, DBI Books, a division of Krause Publications, Iola, WI, 1991. 256 pp., illus. Paper covers. $18.95

An in-depth look at the weapons and equipment used by law enforcement agencies of today.

Modern Machine Guns, by John Walter, Stackpole Books, Inc. Mechanicsburg, PA, 2000. 144 pp., with 146 illustrations. $22.95

A compact and authoritative guide to post-war machine-guns. A gun-by-gun directory identifying individual variants and types including detailed evaluations and technical data.

Modern Sporting Guns, by Christopher Austyn, Safari Press, Huntington Beach, CA, 1994. 128 pp., illus. $40.00

A discussion of the "best" English guns; round action, over-and-under, boxlocks, hammer guns, bolt action and double rifles as well as accessories.

More Complete Cannoneer, The, by M.C. Switlik, Museum & Collectors Specialties Co., Monroe, MI, 1990. 199 pp., illus. $19.95

Compiled agreeably to the regulations for the U.S. War Department, 1861, and containing current observations on the use of antique cannons.

MP-40 Machine Gun, The, Desert Publications, El Dorado, AZ, 1995. 32 pp., illus. Paper covers. $11.95

A reprint of the hard-to-find operating and maintenance manual for one of the most famous machine guns of World War II.

Naval Percussion Locks and Primers, by Lt. J. A. Dahlgren, Museum Restoration Service, Bloomfield, Canada, 1996. 140 pp., illus. $35.00

First published as an Ordnance Memoranda in 1853, this is the finest existing study of percussion locks and primers origin and development.

Official Soviet AKM Manual, The, translated by Maj. James F. Gebhardt (Ret.), Paladin Press, Boulder, CO, 1999. 120 pp., illustrated. Paper covers. $18.00

This official military manual, available in English for the first time, was originally published by the Soviet Ministry of Defence. Covers the history, function, maintenance, assembly and disassembly, etc. of the 7.62mm AKM assault rifle.

One-Round War: U.S.M.C. Scout-Snipers in Vietnam, The, by Peter Senich, Paladin Press, Boulder, CO, 1996. 384 pp., illus. Paper covers $59.95

Sniping in Vietnam focusing specifically on the Marine Corps program.

Parker Brothers: Knight of the Trigger, by Ed Muderlak. A Fact-Based Historical Novel Describing the Life and Times of Captain Arthur William du Bray, 1848-1928. Davis, IL: Old Reliable Publishing, 2002. 223 pages. $25.00

Knight of the Trigger tells the story of the Old West when Parker's most famous gun saleman traveled the country by rail, competing in the pigeon ring, hunting with the rich and famous, and selling the "Old Reliable" Parker shotgun. The life and times of Captain Arthur William du Bray, Parker Brothers' on-the-road sales agent from 1884 to 1926, is described in a novelized version of his interesting life.

Powder Horns and Their Architecture and Decoration as Used by the Soldier, Indian, Sailor and Traders of the Era, by Madison Grant. York, PA: Privately Printed, 1987. 165 pages, profusely illustrated. Hardcover. $45.00

Covers homemade pieces from the late eighteenth and early nineteenth centuries.

Practically Speaking: An Illustrated Guide — The Game, Guns and Gear of the International Defensive Pistol Association, by Walt Rauch. Lafayette Hills, PA: Privately Printed, 2002. 1st edition. Softcover. $24.95

The game, guns and gear of the International Defensive Pistol Association with real-world applications. 79 pages, illustated with drawings and color photos.

Present Sabers: A Popular History of the U.S. Horse Cavalry, by Allan T. Heninger, Tucson, AZ: Excalibur Publications, 2002. 1st edition. 160 pages, with 148 photographs, 45 illustrations and 4 charts. Softcover. $24.95

An illustrated history of America's involvement with the horse cavalry, from its earliest beginnings during the Revolutionary War through it's demise in World War 2. The book also contains several appendices, as well as depictions of the regular insignia of all the U.S. Cavalry units.

Principles of Personal Defense, by Jeff Cooper, Paladin Press, Boulder, CO, 1999. 56 pp., illustrated. Paper covers. $14.00

This revised edition of Jeff Cooper's classic on personal defense offers great new illustrations and a new preface while retaining the timeliness theory of individual defense behavior presented in the original book.

Quotable Hunter, The, edited by Jay Cassell and Peter Fiduccia, The Lyons Press, N.Y., 1999. 224 pp., illustrated. $20.00

This collection of more than three hundred memorable quotes from hunters through the ages captures the essence of the sport, with all its joys idiosyncrasies, and challenges.

Rifleman Went to War, A, by H. W. McBride, Lancer Militaria, Mt. Ida, AR, 1987. 398 pp., illus. $29.95

The classic account of practical marksmanship on the battlefields of World War I.

Sharpshooting for Sport and War, by W.W. Greener, Wolfe Publishing Co., Prescott, AZ, 1995. 192 pp., illus. $30.00

This classic reprint explores the *first* expanding bullet; service rifles; shooting positions; trajectories; recoil; external ballistics; and other valuable information.

Shooter's Bible 2003, The, No. 94, edited by William S. Jarrett, Stoeger Publishing Co., Wayne, NJ, 2002. 576 pp., illustrated. Paper covers. $23.95

Over 3,000 firearms currently offered by major American and foreign gunmakers. Represented are handguns, rifles, shotguns and black powder arms with complete specifications and retail prices.

Shooting to Live, by Capt. W. E. Fairbairn & Capt. E. A. Sykes, Paladin Press, Boulder, CO, 1997, 4 1/2 x 7, soft cover, illus., 112 pp. $14.00

Shooting to Live is the product of Fairbairn's and Sykes' practical experience with the handgun. Hundreds of incidents provided the basis for the first true book on life-or-death shootouts with the pistol. Shooting to Live teaches all concepts, considerations and applications of combat pistol craft.

Shooting Buffalo Rifles of the Old West, by Mike Venturino, MLV Enterprises, Livingston, MT, 2002. 278 pages, illustrated with black and white photos. Softcover. $30.00

This tome will take you through the history, the usage, the many models, and the actual shooting (and how to's) of the many guns that saw service on the Frontier and are lovingly called "Buffalo Rifles" today. If you love to shoot your Sharps, Ballards, Remingtons, or Springfield "Trapdoors" for hunting or competition, or simply love Old West history, your library WILL NOT be complete without this latest book from Mike Venturino!

Shooting Colt Single Actions, by Mike Venturino, MLV Enterprises, Livingston, MT 1997. 205 pp., illus. Black and white photos throughout. Softcover. $25.00

A complete examination of the Colt Single Action including styles, calibers and generations.

Shooting Lever Guns Of The Old West, by Mike Venturino, MLV Enterprises, Livingston, MT, 1999. 300 pp., illustrated. Softcover. $27.95

Shooting the lever action type repeating rifles of our American West.

Shooting Sixguns of the Old West, by Mike Venturino, MLV Enterprises, Livingston, MT, 1997. 221 pp., illus. Paper covers. $26.50

A comprehensive look at the guns of the early West: Colts, Smith & Wesson and Remingtons, plus blackpowder and reloading specs.

Sniper Training, FM 23-10, Reprint of the U.S. Army field manual of August, 1994, Paladin Press, Boulder, CO, 1995. 352pp., illus. Paper covers. $30.00

The most up-to-date U.S. military sniping information and doctrine.

Sniping in France, by Major H. Hesketh-Prichard, Lancer Militaria, Mt. Ida, AR, 1993. 224 pp., illus. $24.95

The author was a well-known British adventurer and big game hunter. He was called upon in the early days of "The Great War" to develop a program to offset an initial German advantage in sniping. How the British forces came to overcome this advantage.

Special Warfare: Special Weapons, by Kevin Dockery, Emperor's Press, Chicago, IL, 1997. 192 pp., illus. $29.95

The arms and equipment of the UDT and SEALS from 1943 to the present.

Sporting Collectibles, by Dr. Stephen R. Irwin, Stoeger Publishing Co., Wayne, NJ, 1997. 256 pp., illus. Paper covers. $19.95

A must book for serious collectors and admirers of sporting collectibles.

Sporting Craftsmen: A Complete Guide to Contemporary Makers of Custom-Built Sporting Equipment, The, by Art Carter, Countrysport Press, Traverse City, MI, 1994. 240 pp., illus. $35.00

Profiles leading makers of centerfire rifles; muzzleloading rifles; bamboo fly rods; fly reels; flies; waterfowl calls; decoys; handmade knives; and traditional longbows and recurves.

Street Smart Gun Book, The, by John Farnam, Police Bookshelf, Concord, NH, 1986. 45 pp., illus. Paper covers. $11.95

Weapon selection, defensive shooting techniques, and gunfight-winning tactics from one of the world's leading authorities.

Stress Fire, Vol. 1: Stress Fighting for Police, by Massad Ayoob, Police Bookshelf, Concord, NH, 1984. 149 pp., illus. Paper covers. $11.95

Gunfighting for police, advanced tactics and techniques.

Survival Guns, by Mel Tappan, Desert Publications, El Dorado, AZ, 1993. 456 pp., illus. Paper covers. $25.00

Discusses in a frank and forthright manner which handguns, rifles and shotguns to buy for personal defense and securing food, and the ones to avoid.

Tactical Advantage, The, by Gabriel Suarez, Paladin Press, Boulder, CO, 1998. 216 pp., illustrated. Paper covers. $22.00

Learn combat tactics that have been tested in the world's toughest schools.

Tactical Marksman, by Dave M. Lauch, Paladin Press, Boulder, CO, 1996. 165 pp., illus. Paper covers. $35.00

A complete training manual for police and practical shooters.

Thompson Guns 1921-1945, Anubis Press, Houston, TX, 1980. 215 pp., illus. Paper covers. $15.95

Facsimile reprinting of five complete manuals on the Thompson submachine gun.

To Ride, Shoot Straight, and Speak the Truth, by Jeff Cooper, Paladin Press, Boulder, CO, 1997, 5 1/2 x 8 1/2, soft-cover, illus., 384 pp. $32.00

Combat mind-set, proper sighting, tactical residential architecture, nuclear war - these are some of the many subjects explored by Jeff Cooper in this illustrated anthology. The author discusses various arms, fighting skills and the importance of knowing how to defend oneself, and one's honor, in our rapidly changing world.

Trailriders Guide to Cowboy Action Shooting, by James W. Barnard, Pioneer Press, Union City, TN, 1998. 134 pp., plus 91 photos, drawings and charts. Paper covers. $24.95

Covers the complete spectrum of this shooting discipline, from how to dress to authentic leather goods, which guns are legal, calibers, loads and ballistics.

Ultimate Sniper, The, by Major John L. Plaster, Paladin Press, Boulder, CO, 1994. 464 pp., illus. Paper covers. $49.95

An advanced training manual for military and police snipers.

Uniforms and Equipment of the Imperial Japanese Army in World War 2, by Mike Hewitt. Atglen, PA: Schiffer Publications, 2002. 176 pages, with over 520 color and b/w photos. Hardcover. $59.95

Unrepentant Sinner, by Col. Charles Askins, Paladin Press, Boulder, CO, 2000. 322 pp., illustrated. $29.95

The autobiography of Colonel Charles Askins.

U.S. Marine Corp Rifle and Pistol Marksmanship, 1935, reprinting of a government publication, Lancer Militaria, Mt. Ida, AR, 1991. 99 pp., illus. Paper covers. $11.95

The old corps method of precision shooting.

U.S. Marine Corps Scout/Sniper Training Manual, Lancer Militaria, Mt. Ida, AR, 1989. Soft covers. $27.95

Reprint of the original sniper training manual used by the Marksmanship Training Unit of the Marine Corps Development and Education Command in Quantico, Virginia.

U.S. Marine Corps Scout-Sniper, World War II and Korea, by Peter R. Senich, Paladin Press, Boulder, CO, 1994. 236 pp., illus. $44.95

The most thorough and accurate account ever printed on the training, equipment and combat experiences of the U.S. Marine Corps Scout-Snipers.

U.S. Marine Corps Sniping, Lancer Militaria, Mt. Ida, AR, 1989. Irregular pagination. Soft covers. $18.95

A reprint of the official Marine Corps FMFM1-3B.

U.S. Marine Uniforms—1912-1940, by Jim Moran. Williamstown, NJ: Phillips Publications, 2001. 174 pages, illustrated with black and white photographs. Hardcover. $49.95

Weapons of the Waffen-SS, by Bruce Quarrie, Sterling Publishing Co., Inc., 1991. 168 pp., illus. $24.95.

An in-depth look at the weapons that made Hitler's Waffen-SS the fearsome fighting machine it was.

Winchester Era, The, by David Madis, Art & Reference House, Brownsville, TX, 1984. 100 pp., illus. $19.95

Story of the Winchester company, management, employees, etc.

With British Snipers to the Reich, by Capt. C. Shore, Lander Militaria, Mt. Ida, AR, 1988. 420 pp., illus. $29.95

One of the greatest books ever written on the art of combat sniping.

World's Machine Pistols and Submachine Guns - Vol. 2a 1964 to 1980, The, by Nelson & Musgrave, Ironside International, Alexandria, VA, 2000. 673 pages, illustrated. $59.95

Containing data, history and photographs of over 200 weapons. With a special section covering shoulder stocked automatic pistols, 100 additional photos.

World's Sniping Rifles, The, by Ian V. Hogg, Paladin Press, Boulder, CO, 1998. 144 pp., illustrated. $22.95

A detailed manual with descriptions and illustrations of more than 50 high-precision rifles from 14 countries and a complete analysis of sights and systems.

GUNSMITHING

Accurizing the Factory Rifle, by M.L. McPhereson, Precision Shooting, Inc., Manchester, CT, 1999. 335 pp., illustrated. Paper covers. $44.95

A long-awaiting book, which bridges the gap between the rudimentary (mounting sling swivels, scope blocks and that general level of accomplishment) and the advanced (precision chambering, barrel fluting, and that general level of accomplishment) books that are currently available today.

Art of Engraving, The, by James B. Meek, F. Brownell & Son, Montezuma, IA, 1973. 196 pp., illus. $38.95

A complete, authoritative, imaginative and detailed study in training for gun engraving. The first book of its kind—and a great one.

Artistry in Arms, The R. W. Norton Gallery, Shreveport, LA, 1970. 42 pp., illus. Paper covers. $9.95.

The art of gunsmithing and engraving.

Checkering and Carving of Gun Stocks, by Monte Kennedy, Stackpole Books, Harrisburg, PA, 1962. 175 pp., illus. $39.95

Revised, enlarged cloth-bound edition of a much sought-after, dependable work.

Firearms Assembly/Disassembly, Part I: Automatic Pistols, 2nd Revised Edition, The Gun Digest Book of, by J.B. Wood, DBI Books, a division of Krause Publications, Iola, WI, 1999. 480 pp., illus. Paper covers. $24.95

Covers 58 popular autoloading pistols plus nearly 200 variants of those models integrated into the text and completely cross-referenced in the index.

Firearms Assembly/Disassembly Part II: Revolvers, Revised Edition, The Gun Digest Book of, by J.B. Wood, DBI Books, a division of Krause Publications, Iola, WI, 1990. 480 pp., illus. Paper covers. $19.95

Covers 49 popular revolvers plus 130 variants. The most comprehensive and professional presentation available to either hobbyist or gunsmith.

Firearms Assembly/Disassembly Part III: Rimfire Rifles, Revised Edition, The Gun Digest Book of, by J. B. Wood, DBI Books, a division of Krause Publications, Iola, WI., 1994. 480 pp., illus. Paper covers. $19.95

Greatly expanded edition covering 65 popular rimfire rifles plus over 100 variants all completely cross-referenced in the index.

Firearms Assembly/Disassembly Part IV: Centerfire Rifles, Revised Edition, The Gun Digest Book of, by J.B. Wood, DBI Books, a division of Krause Publications, Iola, WI, 1991. 480 pp., illus. Paper covers. $19.95

Covers 54 popular centerfire rifles plus 300 variants. The most comprehensive and professional presentation available to either hobbyist or gunsmith.

Firearms Assembly/Disassembly, Part V: Shotguns, Revised Edition, The Gun Digest Book of, by J.B. Wood, DBI Books, a division of Krause Publications, Iola, WI, 1992. 480 pp., illus. Paper covers. $19.95

Covers 46 popular shotguns plus over 250 variants with step-by-step instructions on how to dismantle and reassemble each. The most comprehensive and professional presentation available to either hobbyist or gunsmith.

Firearms Assembly/Disassembly Part VI: Law Enforcement Weapons, The Gun Digest Book of, by J.B. Wood, DBI Books, a division of Krause Publications, Iola, WI, 1981. 288 pp., illus. Paper covers. $16.95

Step-by-step instructions on how to completely dismantle and reassemble the most commonly used firearms found in law enforcement arsenals.

Firearms Assembly 3: The NRA Guide to Rifle and Shotguns, NRA Books, Wash., DC, 1980. 264 pp., illus. Paper covers. $13.95

Text and illustrations explaining the takedown of 125 rifles and shotguns, domestic and foreign.

Firearms Assembly 4: The NRA Guide to Pistols and Revolvers, NRA Books, Wash., DC, 1980. 253 pp., illus. Paper covers. $13.95

Text and illustrations explaining the takedown of 124 pistol and revolver models, domestic and foreign.

Firearms Bluing and Browning, By R.H. Angier, Stackpole Books, Harrisburg, PA. 151 pp., illus. $19.95

A world master gunsmith reveals his secrets of building, repairing and renewing a gun, quite literally, lock, stock and barrel. A useful, concise text on chemical coloring methods for the gunsmith and mechanic.

Firearms Disassembly—With Exploded Views, by John A. Karns & John E. Traister, Stoeger Publishing Co., S. Hackensack, NJ, 1995. 320 pp., illus. Paper covers. $19.95

Provides the do's and don'ts of firearms disassembly. Enables owners and gunsmiths to disassemble firearms in a professional manner.

Guns and Gunmaking Tools of Southern Appalachia, by John Rice Irwin, Schiffer Publishing Ltd., 1983. 118 pp., illus. Paper covers. $9.95

The story of the Kentucky rifle.

Gunsmith Of Grenville County: Building The American Longrifle, The, by Peter Alexander, Texarkana, TX: Scurlock Publishing Co., 2002. Stiff paper covers. $45.00

The most extensive how to book on building longrifles ever published. Takes you through every step of building your own longrifle, from shop set up and tools to engraving, carving and finishing. 400 pages, with hundreds of illustrations, and six color photos of original rifles. Wire O Bind spine will lay flat on the workbench.

Gunsmithing: Pistols & Revolvers, by Patrick Sweeney, DBI Books, a division of Krause Publications, Iola, WI, 1998. 352 pp., illus. Paper covers. $24.95

Do-it-Yourself projects, diagnosis and repair for pistols and revolvers.

Gunsmithing: Rifles, by Patrick Sweeney, Krause Publications, Iola, WI, 1999. 352 pp., illustrated. Paper covers. $24.95

Tips for lever-action rifles. Building a custom Ruger 10/22. Building a better hunting rifle.

THE ARMS LIBRARY

Gunsmith Kinks, by F.R. (Bob) Brownell, F. Brownell & Son, Montezuma, IA, 1st ed., 1969. 496 pp., well illus. $22.98

A widely useful accumulation of shop kinks, short cuts, techniques and pertinent comments by practicing gunsmiths from all over the world.

Gunsmith Kinks 2, by Bob Brownell, F. Brownell & Son, Publishers, Montezuma, IA, 1983. 496 pp., illus. $22.95

A collection of gunsmithing knowledge, shop kinks, new and old techniques, shortcuts and general know-how straight from those who do them best—the gunsmiths.

Gunsmith Kinks 3, edited by Frank Brownell, Brownells Inc., Montezuma, IA, 1993. 504 pp., illus. $24.95

Tricks, knacks and "kinks" by professional gunsmiths and gun tinkerers. Hundreds of valuable ideas are given in this volume.

Gunsmith Kinks 4, edited by Frank Brownell, Brownells Inc., Montezuma, IA, 2001. 564 pp., illus. $27.75

332 detailed illustrations. 560+ pages with 706 separate subject headings and over 5000 cross-indexed entries. An incredible gold mine of information.

Gunsmithing, by Roy F. Dunlap, Stackpole Books, Harrisburg, PA, 1990. 742 pp., illus. $34.95

A manual of firearm design, construction, alteration and remodeling. For amateur and professional gunsmiths and users of modern firearms.

Gunsmithing at Home: Lock, Stock and Barrel, by John Traister, Stoeger Publishing Co., Wayne, NJ, 1997. 320 pp., illus. Paper covers. $19.95

A complete step-by-step fully illustrated guide to the art of gunsmithing.

Gunsmith's Manual, The, by J.P. Stelle and Wm. B. Harrison, The Gun Room Press, Highland Park, NJ, 1982. 376 pp., illus. $19.95

For the gunsmith in all branches of the trade.

Home Gunsmithing the Colt Single Action Revolvers, by Loren W. Smith, Ray Riling Arms Books, Co., Phila., PA, 2001. 119 pp., illus. $29.95

Affords the Colt Single Action owner detailed, pertinent information on the operating and servicing of this famous and historic handgun.

Mauser M98 & M96, by R.A. Walsh, Wolfe Publishing Co., Prescott, AR, 1998. 123 pp., illustrated. Paper covers. $32.50

How to build your own favorite custom Mauser rifle from two of the best bolt action rifle designs ever produced—the military Mauser Model 1898 and Model 1896 bolt rifles.

Mr. Single Shot's Gunsmithing-Idea-Book, by Frank de Haas, Mark de Haas, Orange City, IA, 1996. 168 pp., illus. Paper covers. $21.50

Offers easy to follow, step-by-step instructions for a wide variety of gunsmithing procedures all reinforced by plenty of photos.

Pistolsmithing, by George C. Nonte, Jr., Stackpole Books, Harrisburg, PA, 1974. 560 pp., illus. $34.95

A single source reference to handgun maintenance, repair, and modification at home, unequaled in value.

Practical Gunsmithing, by the editors of American Gunsmith, DBI Books, a division of Krause Publications, Iola, WI, 1996. 256 pp., illus. Paper covers. $19.95

A book intended primarily for home gunsmithing, but one that will be extremely helpful to professionals as well.

Professional Stockmaking, by D. Wesbrook, Wolfe Publishing Co., Prescott AZ, 1995. 308 pp., illus. $54.00

A step-by-step how-to with complete photographic support for every detail of the art of working wood into riflestocks.

Recreating the American Longrifle, by William Buchele, et al, George Shumway Publisher, York, Pa, 5th edition, 1999. 175 pp., illustrated. $40.00

Includes full size plans for building a Kentucky rifle.

Story of Pope's Barrels, The, by Ray M. Smith, R&R Books, Livonia, NY, 1993. 203 pp., illus. $39.00

A reissue of a 1960 book whose author knew Pope personally. It will be of special interest to Schuetzen rifle fans, since Pope's greatest days were at the height of the Schuetzen-era before WWI.

Survival Gunsmithing, by J.B. Wood, Desert Publications, Cornville, AZ, 1986. 92 pp., illus. Paper covers. $11.95

A guide to repair and maintenance of the most popular rifles, shotguns and handguns.

Tactical 1911, The, by Dave Lauck, Paladin Press, Boulder, CO, 1998. 137 pp., illus. Paper covers. $20.00

Here is the only book you will ever need to teach you how to select, modify, employ and maintain your Colt.

HANDGUNS

Advanced Master Handgunning, by Charles Stephens, Paladin Press, Boulder, CO., 1994. 72 pp., illus. Paper covers. $14.00

Secrets and surefire techniques for winning handgun competitions.

Advanced Tactical Marksman More High Performance Techniques for Police, Military, and Practical Shooters, by Lauck, Dave M. Paladin Press, Boulder, CO 2002. 1st edition. 232 pages, photos, illus. Softcover. $35.00

Lauck, one of the most respected names in high-performance shooting and gunsmithing, refines and updates his 1st book . Dispensing with overcomplicated mil-dot formulas and minute-of-angle calculations, Lauck shows you how to achieve superior accuracy and figure out angle shots, streamline the zero process, hit targets at 2,000 yards, deal with dawn and dusk shoots, train for real-world scenarios, choose optics and accessories and create a mobile shooting platform. He also demonstrates the advantages of his custom reticle design and describes important advancements in the MR-30PG shooting system.

American Beauty: The Prewar Colt National Match Government Model Pistol, by Timothy Mullin, Collector Grade Publications, Canada, 1999. 72 pp., 69 illus. $34.95

69 illustrations, 20 in full color photos of factory engraved guns and other authenticated upgrades, including rare 'double-carved' ivory grips.

Ayoob Files: The Book, The, by Massad Ayoob, Police Bookshelf, Concord, NH, 1995. 223 pp., illus. Paper covers. $14.95

The best of Massad Ayoob's acclaimed series in American Handgunner magazine.

Belgian Browning Pistols 1889-1949, The, by Vanderlinden, Anthony. Wet Dog Publications, Geensboro, NC 2001. Limited edition of 2000 copies, signed by the author. 243 pages, plus index. Illustrated with black and white photos. Hardcover. $65.00

Includes the 1899 compact, 1899 Large, 1900,01903, Grand Browning, 1910, 1922 Grand Rendement and high power pistols. Also includes a chapter on holsters.

Big Bore Handguns, by Taffin, John, Krause Publishing, Iola, WI: 2002. 1st edition. 352 Pages, 320 b&w photos with a 16-page color section. Hardcover. $39.95

Gives honest reviews and an inside look at shooting, hunting, and competing with the biggest handguns around. Covers handguns from major gunmakers, as well as handgun customizing, accessories, reloading, and cowboy activities. Significant coverage is also given to handgun customizing, accessories, reloading, and popular shooting hobbies including hunting and cowboy activities. Accessories consist of stocks, handgun holster rigs, and much more. Firearms include single-shot pistols, revolvers, and semi-automatics.

Big Bore Sixguns, by John Taffin, Krause Publications, Iola, WI, 1997. 336 pp., illus. $39.95

The author takes aim on the entire range of big bores from .357 Magnums to .500 Maximums, single actions and cap-and-ball sixguns to custom touches for big bores.

Browning High Power Automatic Pistol (Expanded Edition), The, by Blake R. Stevens, Collector Grade Publications, Canada, 1996. 310 pages, with 313 illus. $49.95

An in-depth chronicle of seventy years of High Power history, from John M Browning's original 16-shot prototypes to the present. Profusely illustrated with rare original photos and drawings from the FN Archive to describe virtually every sporting and military version of the High Power. The numerous modifications made to the basic design over the years are, for the first time, accurately arranged in chronological order, thus permitting the dating of any High Power to within a few years of its production. Full details on the WWII Canadian-made Inglis Browning High Power pistol. The Expanded Edition contains 30 new pages on the interesting Argentine full-auto High Power, the latest FN 'MK3' and BDA9 pistols, plus FN's revolutionary P90 5.7x28mm Personal Defence Weapon, and more!

Browning Hi-Power Pistols, Desert Publications, Cornville, AZ, 1982. 20 pp., illus. Paper covers. $11.95

Covers all facets of the various military and civilian models of the Browning Hi-Power pistol.

Canadian Military Handguns 1855-1985, by Clive M. Law, Museum Restoration Service, Bloomfield, Ont. Canada, 1994. 130pp., illus. $40.00

A long-awaited and important history for arms historians and pistol collectors.

Collecting U.S. Pistols & Revolvers, 1909-1945, by J. C. Harrison. The Arms Chest, Okla. City, OK. 1999. 2nd edition (revised). 185 pages, illus. with pictures and drawings. Spiral bound. $35.00

Valuable and detailed reference book for the collector of U.S. Pistols & Revolvers. Identifies standard issue original military models of the M1911, M1911A1 and M1917Cal .45 Pistols and Revolvers as produced by all manufacturers from 1911 through 1945. Plus .22 ACE Models, National Match Models, and similar foreign military models produced by Colt or manufactured under Colt license. Plus Arsenal repair, refinish and Lend-Lease Models.

Colt .45 Auto Pistol, The, compiled from U.S. War Dept. Technical Manuals, and reprinted by Desert Publications, Cornville, AZ, 1978. 80 pp., illus. Paper covers. $11.95

Covers every facet of this famous pistol from mechanical training, manual of arms, disassembly, repair and replacement of parts.

Colt Automatic Pistols, by Donald B. Bady, Pioneer Press, Union City, TN, 1999. 368 pp., illustrated. Softcover. $19.95

A revised and enlarged edition of a key work on a fascinating subject. Complete information on every Colt automatic pistol.

Combat Handgunnery, 5th Edition, by Chuck Taylor, Krause Publications, Iola, WI, 2002. 256 pp., illus. Paper covers. $21.95

This all-new edition looks at real world combat handgunnery from three different perspectives—military, police and civilian.

Combat Revolvers, by Duncan Long, Paladin Press, Boulder, CO, 1999, 8 1/2 x 11, soft cover, 115 photos, 152 pp. $21.95

This is an uncompromising look at modern combat revolvers. All the major foreign and domestic guns are covered: the Colt Python, S&W Model 29, Ruger GP 100 and hundreds more. Know the gun that you may one day stake your life on.

Complete Guide to Compact Handguns, by Gene Gangarosa, Jr., Stoeger Publishing Co., Wayne, NJ, 1997. 228 pp., illus. Paper covers. $22.95

Includes hundreds of compact firearms, along with text results conducted by the author.

Complete Guide to Service Handguns, by Gene Gangarosa, Jr., Stoeger Publishing Co., Wayne, NJ, 1998. 320 pp., illus. Paper covers. $22.95

The author explores the revolvers and pistols that are used around the globe by military, law enforcement and civilians.

Concealable Pocket Pistols: How to Choose and Use Small-Caliber Handguns, McLeod, Terence. Paladin Press, 2001. 1st edition. 80 pages. Softcover. $14.00

Small-caliber handguns are often maligned as too puny for serious self-defense, but millions of Americans own and carry these guns and have used them successfully to stop violent assaults. This is the first book ever devoted to eliminating the many misconceptions about the usefulness of these popular guns. "Pocket pistols" are small, easily concealed, inexpensive semiautomatic handguns in .22, .25, .32 and .380 calibers. Their small size and hammerless design enable them to be easily concealed and carried so they are immediately accessible in an emergency. Their purpose is not to knock an assailant off his feet with fire-breathing power (which no handgun is capable of doing) but simply to deter or stop his assault by putting firepower in your hands when you need it most. Concealable Pocket Pistols addresses every aspect of owning, carrying and shooting small-caliber handguns in a realistic manner. It cuts right to the chase and recommends a handful of the best pistols on the market today as well as the best ammunition for them. It then gets into the real-world issues of how to carry a concealed pocket pistol, how to shoot it under stress and how to deal with malfunctions quickly and efficiently. In an emergency, a small-caliber pistol in the pocket is better than the .357 Magnum left at home. Find out what millions of Americans already know about these practical self-defense tools.

Custom Government Model Pistol, The, by Layne Simpson, Wolfe Publishing Co., Prescott, AZ, 1994. 639 pp., illus. Paper covers. $26.95

The book about one of the world's greatest firearms and the things pistolsmiths do to make it even greater.

THE ARMS LIBRARY

CZ-75 Family: The Ultimate Combat Handgun, The, by J.M. Ramos, Paladin Press, Boulder, CO, 1990. 100 pp., illus. Soft covers. $25.00
An in-depth discussion of the early-and-late model CZ-75s, as well as the many newest additions to the Czech pistol family.

Encyclopedia of Pistols & Revolvers, by A.E. Hartnik, Knickerbocker Press, New York, NY, 1997. 272 pp., illus. $19.95
A comprehensive encyclopedia specially written for collectors and owners of pistols and revolvers.

Engraved Handguns of .22 Calibre, by John S. Laidacker, Atglen, PA: Schiffer Publications, 2003. 1st edition. 192 pages, with over 400 color and b/w photos. $69.95

Experiments of a Handgunner, by Walter Roper, Wolfe Publishing Co., Prescott, AZ, 1989. 202 pp., illus. $37.00
A limited edition reprint. A listing of experiments with functioning parts of handguns, with targets, stocks, rests, handloading, etc.

Farnam Method of Defensive Handgunning, The, by John S. Farnam, Police Bookshelf, 1999. 191 pp., illus. Paper covers. $24.00
A book intended to not only educate the new shooter, but also to serve as a guide and textbook for his and his instructor's training courses.

Fast and Fancy Revolver Shooting, by Ed. McGivern, Anniversary Edition, Winchester Press, Piscataway, NJ, 1984. 484 pp., illus. $19.95
A fascinating volume, packed with handgun lore and solid information by the acknowledged dean of revolver shooters.

German Handguns: The Complete Book of the Pistols and Revolvers of Germany, 1869 To The Present, by Ian Hogg. Greenhill Publishing, 2001. 320 pages, 270 illustrations. Hardcover. $49.95
Ian Hogg examines the full range of handguns produced in Germany from such classics as the Luger M1908, Mauser HsC and Walther PPK, to more unusual types such as the Reichsrevolver M1879 and the Dreyse 9mm. He presents the key data (length, weight, muzzle velocity, and range) for each weapon discussed and also gives its date of introduction and service record, evaluates and discusses peculiarities, and examines in detail particular strengths and weaknesses.

Glock: The New Wave in Combat Handguns, by Peter Alan Kasler, Paladin Press, Boulder, CO, 1993. 304 pp., illus. $27.00
Kasler debunks the myths that surround what is the most innovative handgun to be introduced in some time.

Glock's Handguns, by Duncan Long, Desert Publications, El Dorado, AR, 1996. 180 pp., illus. Paper covers. $19.95
An outstanding volume on one of the world's newest and most successful firearms of the century.

Gun Digest Book of the 1911, The, by Patrick Sweeney. Krause Publications, Iola, WI, 2002. 336 pages, with 700 b&w photos. Softcover. $27.95
Compete guide of all models and variations of the Model 1911. The author also includes repair tips and information on buying a used 1911.

Hand Cannons: The World's Most Powerful Handguns, by Duncan Long, Paladin Press, Boulder, CO, 1995. 208 pp., illus. Paper covers. $22.00
Long describes and evaluates each powerful gun according to their features.

Handgun, The, by Geoffrey Boothroyd, Safari Press, Inc., Huntington Beach, CA, 1999. 566 pp., illustrated. $50.00
A very detailed history of the handgun. Now revised and a completely new chapter written to take account of developments since the 1970 edition.

Handguns 2003, 14th Edition, edited by Ken Ramage, DBI Books a division of Krause Publications, Iola, WI, 2002. 352 pp., illustrated. Paper covers. $22.95
Top writers in the handgun industry give you a complete report on new handgun developments, testfire reports on the newest introductions and previews on what's ahead.

Handgun Stopping Power "The Definitive Study", by Evan P. Marshall & Edwin J. Sanow, Paladin Press, Boulder, CO, 1997, soft cover, photos, 240 pp. $45.00
Dramatic first-hand accounts of the results of handgun rounds fired into criminals by cops, storeowners, cabbies and others are the heart and soul of this long-awaited book. This is the definitive methodology for predicting the stopping power of handgun loads, the first to take into account what really happens when a bullet meets a man.

Heckler & Koch's Handguns, by Duncan Long, Desert Publications, El Dorado, AR, 1996. 142 pp., illus. Paper covers. $19.95.
Traces the history and the evolution of H&K's pistols from the company's beginning at the end of WWII to the present.

Hidden in Plain Sight, by Trey Bloodworth & Mike Raley, Professional Press, Chapel Hill, NC, 1995. Paper covers. $19.95.
A practical guide to concealed handgun carry.

High Standard: A Collectors Guide to the Hamden & Hartford Target Pistols, Dance, Tom. Andrew Mowbray, Inc., Lincoln, RI: 1999. 192 pp., Heavily illustrated with black & white photographs and technical drawings. $24.00
From Citation to Supermatic, all of the production models and specials made from 1951 to 1984 are covered according to model number or series, making it easy to understand the evolution to this favorite of shooters and collectors.

High Standard Automatic Pistols 1932-1950, by Charles E. Petty, The Gunroom Press, Highland Park, NJ, 1989. 124 pp., illus. $14.95
A definitive source of information for the collector of High Standard arms.

Hi-Standard Pistols and Revolvers, 1951-1984, by James Spacek, James Spacek, Chesire, CT, 1998. 128 pp., illustrated. Paper covers. $12.50
Technical details, marketing features and instruction/parts manual of every model High Standard pistol and revolver made between 1951 and 1984. Most accurate serial number information available.

Hi-Standard Pistol Guide, The, by Burr Leyson, Duckett's Sporting Books, Tempe AZ, 1995. 128 pp., illus. Paper covers. $26.00
Complete information on selection, care and repair, ammunition, parts, and accessories.

How to Become a Master Handgunner: The Mechanics of X-Count Shooting, by Charles Stephens, Paladin Press, Boulder, CO, 1993. 64 pp., illus. Paper covers. $14.00
Offers a simple formula for success to the handgunner who strives to master the technique of shooting accurately.

Illustrated Encyclopedia of Handguns, by A.B. Zhuk, Stackpole Books, Mechanicsburg, PA, 2002. 256 pp., illus. Softcover, $24.95
Identifies more than 2,000 military and commercial pistols and revolvers with details of more than 100 popular handgun cartridges.

Inglis Diamond: The Canadian High Power Pistol, The, by Clive M. Law, Collector Grade Publications, Canada, 2001. 312 pp., illustrated. $49.95
This definitive work on Canada's first and indeed only mass produced handgun, in production for a very brief span of time and consequently made in relatively few numbers, the venerable Inglis-made Browning High Power covers the pistol's initial history, the story of Chinese and British adoption, use post-war by Holland, Australia, Greece, Belgium, New Zealand, Peru, Brasil and other countries. All new information on the famous light-weights and the Inglis Diamond variations. Completely researched through official archives in a dozen countries. Many of the bewildering variety of markings have never been satisfactorily explained until now. Also included are many photos of holsters and accessories.

Instinct Combat Shooting, by Chuck Klein, The Goose Creek, IN, 1989. 49 pp., illus. Paper covers. $12.00
Defensive handgunning for police.

Know Your 45 Auto Pistols—Models 1911 & A1, by E.J. Hoffschmidt, Blacksmith Corp., Southport, CT, 1974. 58 pp., illus. Paper covers. $14.95
A concise history of the gun with a wide variety of types and copies.

Know Your Ruger Single Actions: The Second Decade 1963-1973, by John C. Dougan. Blacksmith Corp., North Hampton, OH, 1994. 143 pp., illus. Paper covers. $19.95

Know Your Ruger S/A Revolvers 1953-1963 (Revised Edition), by John C. Dougan. Blacksmith Corp., North Hampton, OH, 2002. 191 pp., illus. Paper covers. $19.95

Know Your Walther P38 Pistols, by E.J. Hoffschmidt, Blacksmith Corp., Southport, CT, 1974. 77 pp., illus. Paper covers. $14.95
Covers the Walther models Armee, M.P., H.P., P.38—history and variations.

Know Your Walther PP & PPK Pistols, by E.J. Hoffschmidt, Blacksmith Corp., Southport, CT, 1975. 87 pp., illus. Paper covers. $14.95
A concise history of the guns with a guide to the variety and types.

La Connaissance du Luger, Tome 1, by Gerard Henrotin, H & L Publishing, Belguim, 1996. 144 pages, illustrated. $45.00
(The Knowledge of Luger, Volume 1, translated.) Black & white and color photos. French text.

Living with Glocks: The Complete Guide to the New Standard in Combat Handguns, by Robert H Boatman, Boulder, CO: Paladin Press, 2002. 1st edition. ISBN: 1581603401. 184 pages, illustrated. Hardcover. $29.95
In this book he explains why in no uncertain terms. In addition to demystifying the enigmatic Glock trigger, Boatman describes and critiques each Glock model in production. Separate chapters on the G36, the enhanced G20 and the full-auto G18 emphasize the job-specific talents of these standout models for those seeking insight on which Glock pistol might best meet their needs. And for those interested in optimizing their Glock's capabilities, this book addresses all the peripherals – holsters, ammo, accessories, silencers, modifications and conversions, training programs and more. Whether your focus is on concealed carry, home protection, hunting, competition, training or law enforcement.

Luger Handbook, The, by Aarron Davis, Krause Publications, Iola, WI, 1997. 112 pp., illus. Paper covers. $9.95
Now you can identify any of the legendary Luger variations using a simple decision tree. Each model and variation includes pricing information, proof marks and detailed attributes in a handy, user-friendly format. Plus, it's fully indexed. Instantly identify that Luger!

Lugers of Ralph Shattuck, by Ralph Shattuck, Peoria, AZ, 2000. 49 pages, illus. Hardcover. $29.95
49 pages, illustrated with maps and full color photos of here to now never before shown photos of some of the rarest lugers ever. Written by one of the world's renowned collectors. A MUST have book for any Luger collector.

Lugers at Random (Revised Format Edition), by Charles Kenyon, Jr., Handgun Press, Glenview, IL, 2000. 420 pp., illus. $59.95
A new printing of this classic, comprehensive reference for all Luger collectors.

Luger Story, The, by John Walter, Stackpole Books, Mechanicsburg, PA, 2001. 256 pp., illus. Paper Covers. $19.95
The standard history of the world's most famous handgun.

Mauser Self-Loading Pistol, The, by Belford & Dunlap, Borden Publ. Co., Alhambra, CA. Over 200 pp., 300 illus., large format. $29.95
The long-awaited book on the "Broom Handles," covering their inception in 1894 to the end of production. Complete and in detail: pocket pistols, Chinese and Spanish copies, etc.

Mental Mechanics of Shooting: How to Stay Calm at the Center, by Vishnu Karmakar and Thomas Whitney. Littleton, CO: Center Vision, Inc., 2001. 144 pages. Softcover. $19.95
Not only will this book help you stay free of trigger jerk, it will help you in all areas of your shooting.

9mm Parabellum; The History & Development of the World's 9mm Pistols & Ammunition, by Klaus-Peter Konig and Martin Hugo, Schiffer Publishing Ltd., Atglen, PA, 1993. 304 pp., illus. $39.95
Detailed history of 9mm weapons from Belguim, Italy, Germany, Israel, France, USA, Czechoslovakia, Hungary, Poland, Brazil, Finland and Spain.

Official 9mm Markarov Pistol Manual, The, translated into English by Major James Gebhardt, U.S. Army (Ret.), Desert Publications, El Dorado, AR, 1996. 84 pp., illus. Paper covers. $12.95
The information found in this book will be of enormous benefit and interest to the owner or a prospective owner of one of these pistols.

Official Soviet 7.62mm Handgun Manual, The, by Translation by Maj. James F. Gebhardt Ret.), Paladin Press, Boulder, CO, 1997, soft cover, illus., 104 pp. $20.00
This Soviet military manual, now available in English for the first time, covers instructions for use and maintenance of two side arms, the Nagant 7.62mm revolver, used by the Russian tsarist armed forces and later the Soviet armed forces, and the Tokarev7.62mm semi-auto pistol, which replaced the Nagant.

P-08 Parabellum Luger Automatic Pistol, The, edited by J. David McFarland, Desert Publications, Cornville, AZ, 1982. 20 pp., illus. Paper covers. $13.95
Covers every facet of the Luger, plus a listing of all known Luger models.

REFERENCE

THE ARMS LIBRARY

P08 Luger Pistol, The, by de Vries & Martens. Alexandria, VA: Ironside International, 2002. 152 pages, illustrated with 200 high quality black & white photos. Hardcover. $34.95

Covers all essential information on history and development, ammunition and accessories, codes and markings, and contains photos of nearly every model and accessory. Includes a unique selection of original German WWII propoganda photos, most never published before.

P-38 Automatic Pistol, by Gene Gangarosa, Jr., Stoeger Publishing Co., S. Hackensack, NJ, 1993. 272 pp., illus. Paper covers. $16.95

This book traces the origins and development of the P-38, including the momentous political forces of the World War II era that caused its near demise and, later, its rebirth.

P-38 Pistol: The Walther Pistols, 1930-1945. Volume 1, The, by Warren Buxton, Ucross Books, Los Alamos, MN 1999. $68.50

A limited run reprint of this scarce and sought-after work on the P-38 Pistol. 328 pp. with 160 illustrations.

P-38 Pistol: The Contract Pistols, 1940-1945. Volume 2, The, by Warren Buxton, Ucross Books, Los Alamos, MN 1999. 256 pp. with 237 illustrations. $68.50

P-38 Pistol: Postwar Distributions, 1945-1990. Volume 3, The, by Warren Buxton, Ucross Books, Los Alamos, MN 1999. $68.50

Plus an addendum to Volumes 1 & 2. 272 pp. with 342 illustrations.

Parabellum - A Technical History of Swiss Lugers, by V. Bobba, Italy.1998. 224pp, profuse color photos, large format. $100.00

The is the most beautifully illustrated and well-documented book on the Swiss Lugers yet produced. This splendidly produced book features magnificent images while giving an incredible amount of detail on the Swiss Luger. In-depth coverage of key issues include: the production process, pistol accessories, charts with serial numbers, production figures, variations, markings, patent drawings, etc. Covers the Swiss Luger story from 1894 when the first Bergmann-Schmeisser models were tested till the commercial model 1965. Shows every imaginable production variation in amazing detail and full color! A must for all Luger collectors. This work has been produced in an extremely attractive package using quality materials throughout and housed in a protective slipcase.

Report of Board on Tests of Revolvers and Automatic Pistols, From the Annual Report of the Chief of Ordnance, 1907. Reprinted by J.C. Tillinghast, Marlow, NH, 1969. 34 pp., 7 plates, paper covers. $9.95

A comparison of handguns, including Luger, Savage, Colt, Webley-Fosbery and other makes.

Ruger "P" Family of Handguns, The, by Duncan Long, Desert Publications, El Dorado, AZ, 1993. 128 pp., illus. Paper covers. $14.95

A full-fledged documentary on a remarkable series of Sturm Ruger handguns.

Ruger .22 Automatic Pistol, Standard/Mark I/Mark II Series, The, by Duncan Long, Paladin Press, Boulder, CO, 1989. 168 pp., illus. Paper covers. $16.00

The definitive book about the pistol that has served more than 1 million owners so well.

Semiautomatic Pistols in Police Service and Self Defense, The, by Massad Ayoob, Police Bookshelf, Concord, NH, 1990. 25 pp., illus. Soft covers. $11.95.

First quantitative, documented look at actual police experience with 9mm and 45 police service automatics.

Shooting Colt Single Actions, by Mike Venturino, Livingston, MT, 1997. 205 pp., illus. Paper covers. $25.00

A definitive work on the famous Colt SAA and the ammunition it shoots.

Sig Handguns, by Duncan Long, Desert Publications, El Dorado, AZ, 1995. 150 pp., illus. Paper covers. $19.95

The history of Sig/Sauer handguns, including Sig, Sig-Hammerli and Sig/Sauer variants.

Sixgun Cartridges and Loads, by Elmer Keith, reprint edition by The Gun Room Press, Highland Park, NJ, 1984. 151 pp., illus. $24.95

A manual covering the selection, use and loading of the most suitable and popular revolver cartridges.

Sixguns, by Elmer Keith, Wolfe Publishing Company, Prescott, AZ, 1992. 336 pp. Paper covers. $29.95. Hardcover $35.00

The history, selection, repair, care, loading, and use of this historic frontiersman's friend—the one-hand firearm.

Smith & Wesson's Automatics, by Larry Combs, Desert Publications, El Dorado, AZ, 1994. 143 pp., illus. Paper covers. $19.95

A must for every S&W auto owner or prospective owner.

Spanish Handguns: The History of Spanish Pistols and Revolvers, by Gene Gangarosa, Jr., Stoeger Publishing Co., Accokeek, MD, 2001. 320 pp., illustrated. B & W photos. Paper covers. $21.95

Standard Catalog of Smith & Wesson; 2nd Edition, by Jim Supica and Richard Nahas.Krause Publications, Iola, WI: 2001. 2nd edition. 272 Pages, 350 b&w photos, with a 16 page color section. Pictorial Hardcover. $34.95

Clearly details 775 Smith & Wesson models, knives, holsters, ammunition and police items with complete pricing information, illustrated glossary and index.

Star Firearms, by Leonardo M. Antaris, Davenport, IA: Firac Publications Co., 2002. 640 pages, with over 1,100 b/w photos, 47 pages in full color. Hardcover. $119.95

The definitive work on Star's many models with a historical context, with a review of their mechanical features, & details their development throughout production plus tables of proof marks & codes, serial numbers, annual summaries, procurements by Spanish Guardia Civil & Spanish Police, exports to Bulgaria, Germany, & Switzerland during WW2; text also covers Star's .22 rifles & submachine guns & includes a comprehensive list of Spanish trade names matched to manufacturer for arms made prior to the Spanish Civil War (1936-1939).

Street Stoppers: The Latest Handgun Stopping Power Street Results, by Evan P. Marshall & Edwin J. Sandow, Paladin Press, Boulder, CO, 1997. 392 pp., illus. Paper covers. $42.95

Compilation of the results of real-life shooting incidents involving every major handgun caliber.

Tactical 1911, The, by Dave Lauck, Paladin Press, Boulder, CO, 1999. 152 pp., illustrated. Paper covers. $22.00

The cop's and SWAT operator's guide to employment and maintenance.

Tactical Pistol, The, by Gabriel Suarez with a foreword by Jeff Cooper, Paladin Press, Boulder, CO, 1996. 216 pp., illus. Paper covers. $25.00

Advanced gunfighting concepts and techniques.

Thompson/Center Contender Pistol, The, by Charles Tephens, Paladin Press, Boulder, CO, 1997. 58 pp., illus. Paper covers. $14.00

How to tune and time, load and shoot accurately with the Contender pistol.

.380 Enfield No. 2 Revolver, The, by Mark Stamps and Ian Skennerton, I.D.S.A. Books, Piqua, OH, 1993. 124 pp., 80 illus. Paper covers. $19.95

Truth About Handguns, The, by Duane Thomas, Paladin Press, Boulder, CO, 1997. 136 pp., illus. Paper covers. $18.00

Exploding the myths, hype, and misinformation about handguns.

Walther Pistols: Models 1 Through P99, Factory Variations and Copies, by Dieter H. Marschall, Ucross Books, Los Alamos, NM. 2000. 140 pages, with 140 b & w illustrations, index. Paper Covers. $19.95

This is the English translation, revised and updated, of the highly successful and widely acclaimed German language edition. This book provides the collector with a reference guide and overview of the entire line of the Walther military, police, and self-defense pistols from the very first to the very latest. Models 1-9, PP, PPK, MP, AP, HP, P.38, P1, P4, P38K, P5, P88, P99 and the Manurhin models. Variations, where issued, serial ranges, calibers, marks, proofs, logos, and design aspects in an astonishing quantity and variety are crammed into this very well researched and highly regarded work.

U.S. Handguns of World War 2, The Secondary Pistols and Revolvers, by Charles W. Pate, Mowbray Publishers, Lincoln, RI, 1997. 368 pp., illus. $39.00

This indispensable new book covers all of the American military handguns of W.W.2 except for the M1911A1.

HUNTING

NORTH AMERICA

Advanced Black Powder Hunting, by Toby Bridges, Stoeger Publishing Co., Wayne, NJ, 1998. 288 pp., illus. Paper covers. $21.95

The first modern day publication to be filled from cover to cover with guns, loads, projectiles, accessories and the techniques to get the most from today's front loading guns.

Advanced Strategies for Trophy Whitetails, by David Morris, Safari Press, Inc., Huntington Beach, CA, 1999. 399 pp., illustrated. $29.95

This book is a must-have for any serious trophy hunter.

After the Hunt with Lovett Williams, by Lovett Williams, Krause Publications, Iola, WI, 1996. 256 pp., illus. Paper covers. $15.95

The author carefully instructs you on how to prepare your trophy turkey for a trip to the taxidermist. Plus help on planning a grand slam hunt.

Aggressive Whitetail Hunting, by Greg Miller, Krause Publications, Iola, WI, 1995. 208 pp., illus. Paper covers. $14.95

Learn how to hunt trophy bucks in public forests, private farmlands and exclusive hunting grounds from one of America's foremost hunters.

Alaskan Yukon Trophies Won and Lost, by Young, G.O. Wolfe Publishing, Prescott, AZ. 2002. 273 pp. with B&W photographs and a five-page epilogue by the publisher. Softcover. $35.00

A classic big game hunting tale.

All About Bears, by Duncan Gilchrist, Stoneydale Press Publishing Co., Stevensville, MT, 1989. 176 pp., illus. $19.95

Covers all kinds of bears—black, grizzly, Alaskan brown, polar and leans on a lifetime of hunting and guiding experiences to explore proper hunting techniques.

American Duck Shooting, by George Bird Grinnell, Stackpole Books, Harrisburg, PA, 1991. 640 pp., illus. Paper covers. $19.95

First published in 1901 at the height of the author's career. Describes 50 species of waterfowl, and discusses hunting methods common at the turn of the century.

American Wild Turkey, Hunting Tactics and Techniques, The, by John McDaniel, The Lyons Press, New York, NY, 2000. 240 pp., illustrated. $29.95

Loaded with turkey hunting anecdotes gleaned from a lifetime of experience.

American Wingshooting: A Twentieth Century Pictorial Saga, by Ben O. Williams, Willow Creek Press, Minocqua, WI, 2000. 160 pp., illustrated with 180 color photographs. $35.00

A beautifully photographed celebration of upland bird hunting now and how as it once existed.

Autumn Passages, Compiled by the editors of Ducks Unlimited Magazine, Willow Creek Press, Minocqua, WI, 1997. 320 pp. $27.50

An exceptional collection of duck hunting stories.

Backtracking, by I.T. Taylor, Safari Press, Inc., Huntington Beach, CA, 1998. 201 pp., illustrated. $24.95

Reminiscences of a hunter's life in rural America.

Bare November Days, by George Bird Evans et al, Down East Books, Camden, MA 2002. 136 pp., illus. $39.50

A new, original anthology, a tribute to ruffed grouse, king of upland birds.

Bear Attacks, by K. Etling, Safari Press, Long Beach, CA, 1998. 574 pp., illus. In 2 volumes. $75.00

Classic tales of dangerous North American bears.

Bear Hunter's Century, The, by Paul Schullery, Stackpole Books, Harrisburg, PA, 1989. 240 pp., illus. $19.95

Thrilling tales of the bygone days of wilderness hunting.

Best of Babcock, The, by Havilah Babcock, selected and with an introduction by Hugh Grey, The Gunnerman Press, Auburn Hills, MI, 1985. 262 pp., illus. $19.95

A treasury of memorable pieces, 21 of which have never before appeared in book form.

Best of Nash Buckingham, The, by Nash Buckingham, selected, edited and annotated by George Bird Evans, Winchester Press, Piscataway, NJ, 1973. 320 pp., illus. $35.00

Thirty pieces that represent the very cream of Nash's output on his whole range of outdoor interests—upland shooting, duck hunting, even fishing.

Better on a Rising Tide, by Tom Kelly, Lyons & Burford Publishers, New York, NY, 1995. 184 pp. $22.95

Tales of wild turkeys, turkey hunting and Southern folk.

THE ARMS LIBRARY

Big Bucks the Benoit Way, by Bryce Towsley, Krause Publications Iola, WI, 1998. 208 pp., illus. $24.95
Secrets from America's first family of whitetail hunting.

Big December Canvasbacks, by Worth Mathewson, Sand Lake Press, Amity, OR, 1997. 171 pp., illus. By David Hagenbaumer. Limited, signed and numbered edition. $29.95
Duck hunting stories.

Big Game Hunting, by Duncan Gilchrist, Outdoor Expeditions, books and videos, Corvallis, MT, 1999. 192 pp., illustrated. $14.95
Designed to be a warehouse of hunting information covering the major North American big game species.

Bird Dog Days, Wingshooting Ways, by Archibald Rutledge, edited by Jim Casada, Wilderness Adventure Press, Gallatin Gateway, MT, 1998. 200 pp., illus. $35.00
One of the most popular and enduring outdoor writers of this century, the poet laureate of South Carolina.

Blacktail Trophy Tactics, by Boyd Iverson, Stoneydale Press, Stevensville, MI, 1992. 166 pp., illus. Paper covers. $14.95
A comprehensive analysis of blacktail deer habits, describing a deer's and man's use of scents, still hunting, tree techniques, etc.

Boone & Crockett Club's 23rd Big Game Awards, 1995-1997, Boone & Crockett Club, Missoula, MT, 1999. 600 pp., illustrated with black & white photographs plus a 16 page color section. $39.95
A complete listing of the 3,511 trophies accepted in the 23rd Awards Entry Period.

Bowhunter's Handbook, Expert Strategies and Techniques, by M.R. James with Fred Asbell, Dave Holt, Dwight Schuh & Dave Samuel, DBI Books, a division of Krause Publications, Iola, WI, 1997. 256 pp., illus. Paper covers. $19.95.
Tips from the top on taking your bowhunting skills to the next level.

Buffalo Harvest, The, by Frank Mayer as told to Charles Roth, Pioneer Press, Union City, TN, 1995. 96 pp., illus. Paper covers. $12.50.
The story of a hide hunter during his buffalo hunting days on the plains.

Call of the Quail: A Tribute to the Gentleman Game Bird, by Michael McIntosh, et al., Countrysport Press, Traverse City, MI, 1990. 175 pp., illus. $35.00
A new anthology on quail hunting.

Calling All Elk, by Jim Zumbo, Cody, WY, 1989. 169 pp., illus. Paper covers. $14.95
The only book on the subject of elk hunting that covers every aspect of elk vocalization.

Complete Book of Grouse Hunting, The, by Frank Woolner, The Lyons Press, New York, NY, 2000. 192 pp., illustrated Paper covers. $24.95
The history, habits, and habitat of one of America's great game birds—and the methods used to hunt it.

Complete Book of Mule Deer Hunting, The, by Walt Prothero, The Lyons Press, New York, NY, 2000. 192 pp., illustrated. Paper covers. $24.95
Field-tested practical advice on how to bag the trophy buck of a lifetime.

Complete Book of Wild Turkey Hunting, The, by John Trout Jr., The Lyons Press, New York, NY, 2000. 192 pp., illustrated. Paper covers. $24.95
An illustrated guide to hunting for one of America's most popular game birds.

Complete Book of Woodcock Hunting, The, by Frank Woolner, The Lyons Press, New York, NY, 2000. 192 pp., illustrated. Paper covers. $24.95
A thorough, practical guide to the American woodcock and to woodcock hunting.

Complete Guide to Hunting Wild Boar In California, The, by Kramer, Gary. Safari Press, 2002. 1st edition. 127pp, 37 photos. Softcover. $15.95
Gary Kramer takes the hunter all over California, from north to south and east to west. He discusses natural history, calibers, bullets, rifles, pistols, shotguns, black powder, and bow and arrows. Other chapters discuss equipment, the six major systems of hunting hogs, the top hog-producing counties, and hunting areas--those with public access as well as private hog-hunting ranches and military bases that allow hunting. Suprisingly, there are quite a few areas in California that afford public access for hog hunters. The book is chock-a-block full with details, addresses, telephone numbers, Web sites, and relevant information that will help you bring the bacon home. Hints on photography, caring for the meat, as well as a good, thorough list of meat processors are also included to help with converting your hog into good memories and delightful dishes. And just when you thought Kramer would have nothing else to add, he divulges delicious recipes to appease your spouse and present her with a decent excuse as to why you went hunting! This is THE hogging best book on how to get your pig.

Complete Venison Cookbook from Field to Table, The, by Jim & Ann Casada, Krause Publications, Iola, WI, 1996. 208 pp., Comb-bound. $12.95
More than 200 kitchen tested recipes make this book the answer to a table full of hungry hunters or guests.

Coveys and Singles: The Handbook of Quail Hunting, by Robert Gooch, A.S. Barnes, San Diego, CA, 1981. 196 pp., illus. $11.95
The story of the quail in North America.

Coyote Hunting, by Phil Simonski, Stoneydale Press, Stevensville, MT, 1994. 126 pp., illus. Paper covers. $12.95
Probably the most thorough "How-to-do-it" book on coyote hunting ever written.

Dabblers & Divers: A Duck Hunter's Book, compiled by the editors of Ducks Unlimited Magazine, Willow Creek Press, Minocqua, WI, 1997. 160 pp., illus. $39.95.
A word-and-photographic portrayal of waterfowl hunter's singular intimacy with, and passion for, watery haunts and wildfowl.

Dancers in the Sunset Sky, by Robert F. Jones, The Lyons Press, New York, NY, 1997. 192 pp., illus. $22.95
The musings of a bird hunter.

Deer & Deer Hunting, by Al Hofacker, Krause Publications, Iola, WI, 1993. 208 pp., illus. $34.95
Coffee-table volume packed full of how-to-information that will guide hunts for years to come.

Deer and Deer Hunting: The Serious Hunter's Guide, by Dr. Robert Wegner, Stackpole Books, Harrisburg, PA, 1984. 384 pp., illus. Paper covers. $18.95
In-depth information from the editor of "Deer & Deer Hunting" magazine. Major bibliography of English language books on deer and deer hunting from 1838-1984.

Deer and Deer Hunting Book 2, by Dr. Robert Wegner, Stackpole Books, Harrisburg, PA, 1987. 400 pp., illus. Paper covers. $18.95
Strategies and tactics for the advanced hunter.

Deer and Deer Hunting, Book 3, by Dr. Robert Wegner, Stackpole Books, Harrisburg, PA, 1990. 368 pp., illus. $18.95
This comprehensive volume covers natural history, deer hunting lore, profiles of deer hunters, and discussion of important issues facing deer hunters today.

Deer Hunters: The Tactics, Lore, Legacy and Allure of American Deer Hunting, The, Edited by Patrick Durkin, Krause Publications, Iola, WI, 1997. 208 pp., illus. $29.95
More than twenty years of research from America's top whitetail hunters, researchers, and photographers have gone in to the making of this book.

Deer Hunting, by R. Smith, Stackpole Books, Harrisburg, PA, 1978. 224 pp., illus. Paper covers. $14.95
A professional guide leads the hunt for North America's most popular big game animal.

Dreaming the Lion, by Thomas McIntyre, Countrysport Press, Traverse City, MI, 1994. 309 pp., illus. $35.00
Reflections on hunting, fishing and a search for the wild. Twenty-three stories by *Sports Afield* editor, Tom McIntyre.

Elk and Elk Hunting, by Hart Wixom, Stackpole Books, Harrisburg, PA, 1986. 288 pp., illus. $34.95
Your practical guide to fundamentals and fine points of elk hunting.

Elk Hunting in the Northern Rockies, by Ed. Wolff, Stoneydale Press, Stevensville, MT, 1984. 162 pp., illus. $18.95
Helpful information about hunting the premier elk country of the northern Rocky Mountain states—Wyoming, Montana and Idaho.

Elk Hunting with the Experts, by Bob Robb, Stoneydale Press, Stevensville, MT, 1992. 176 pp., illus. Paper covers. $15.95
A complete guide to elk hunting in North America by America's top elk hunting expert.

Firelight, by Burton L. Spiller, Gunnerman Press, Auburn Hills, MI, 1990. 196 pp., illus. $19.95
Enjoyable tales of the outdoors and stalwart companions.

Getting a Stand, by Miles Gilbert, Pioneer Press, Union City, TN, 1993. 204 pp., illus. Paper covers. $13.95
An anthology of 18 short personal experiences by buffalo hunters of the late 1800s, specifically from 1870-1882.

Gordon MacQuarrie Trilogy: Stories of the Old Duck Hunters, by Gordon MacQuarrie, Willow Creek Press, Minocqua, WI, 1994. $49.00
A slip-cased three volume set of masterpieces by one of America's finest outdoor writers.

Greatest Elk; The Complete Historical and Illustrated Record of North America's Biggest Elk, by R. Selner, Safari Press, Huntington Beach, CA, 2000. 209 pages, profuse color illus. $39.95
Here is the book all elk hunters have been waiting for! This oversized book holds the stories and statistics of the biggest bulls ever killed in North America. Stunning, full-color photographs highlight over 40 world-class heads, including the old world records!

Grouse and Woodcock, A Gunner's Guide, by Don Johnson, Krause Publications, Iola, WI, 1995. 256 pp., illus. Paper covers. $14.95
Find out what you need in guns, ammo, equipment, dogs and terrain.

Gunning for Sea Ducks, by George Howard Gillelan, Tidewater Publishers, Centreville, MD, 1988. 144 pp., illus. $14.95
A book that introduces you to a practically untouched arena of waterfowling.

Heck with Moose Hunting, The, by Jim Zumbo, Wapiti Valley Publishing Co., Cody, WY, 1996. 199 pp., illus. $17.95
Jim's hunts around the continent including encounters with moose, caribou, sheep, antelope and mountain goats.

High Pressure Elk Hunting, by Mike Lapinski, Stoneydale Press Publishing Co., Stevensville, MT, 1996. 192 pp., illus. $19.95
The secrets of hunting educated elk revealed.

Horns in the High Country, by Andy Russell, Alfred A. Knopf, NY, 1973. 259 pp., illus. Paper covers. $12.95
A many-sided view of wild sheep and their natural world.

How to Hunt, by Dave Bowring, Winchester Press, Piscataway, NJ, 1982. 208 pp., illus. Hardcover $15.00
A basic guide to hunting big game, small game, upland birds, and waterfowl.

Hunt Alaska Now: Self-Guiding for Trophy Moose & Caribou, by Dennis W. Confer, Wily Ventures, Anchorage, AK, 1997. 309 pp., illus. Paper covers. $26.95
How to plan affordable, successfull, safe hunts you can do yourself.

Hunter's Road, A, by Jim Fergus, Henry Holt & Co., NY, 1992. 290 pp. $22.50
A journey with gun and dog across the American uplands.

Hunt High for Rocky Mountain Goats, Bighorn Sheep, Chamois & Tahr, by Duncan Gilchrist, Stoneydale Press, Stevensville, MT, 1992. 192 pp., illus. Paper covers. $19.95
The source book for hunting mountain goats.

Hunting Adventure of Me and Joe, by Walt Prothero, Safari Press, Huntington Beach, CA, 1995. 220 pp., illus. $22.50
A collection of the author's best and favorite stories.

Hunting America's Game Animals and Birds, by Robert Elman and George Peper, Winchester Press, Piscataway, NJ, 1975. 368 pp., illus. $16.95
A how-to, where-to, when-to guide—by 40 top experts—covering the continent's big, small, upland game and waterfowl.

Hunting Mature Bucks, by Larry L. Weishuhn, Krause Publications, Iola, WI, 1995. 256 pp., illus. Paper covers. $14.95
One of North America's top white-tailed deer authorities shares his expertise on hunting those big, smart and elusive bucks.

Hunting Open-Country Mule Deer, by Dwight Schuh, Sage Press, Nampa, ID, 1989. 180 pp., illus. $18.95
A guide taking Western bucks with rifle and bow.

Hunting America's Wild Turkey, by Bridges, Toby, Stoeger Publishing Company, Pocomoke, MD, 2001. 256 pp., illus. $16.95
The techniques and tactics of hunting North America's largest, and most popular, woodland game bird.

THE ARMS LIBRARY

Hunting the Rockies, Home of the Giants, by Kirk Darner, Marceline, MO, 1996. 291 pp., illus. $25.00
Understand how and where to hunt Western game in the Rockies.

Hunting Trips in North America, by F.C. Selous, Wolfe Publishing Co., Prescott, AZ, 1988. 395 pp., illus. $52.00
A limited edition reprint. Coverage of caribou, moose and other big game hunting in virgin wilds.

Hunting Trophy Deer, by John Wootters, The Lyons Press, New York, NY, 1997. 272 pp., illus. $24.95.
A revised edition of the definitive manual for identifying, scouting, and successfully hunting a deer of a lifetime.

Hunting Trophy Whitetails, by David Morris, Stoneydale Press, Stevensville, MT, 1993. 483 pp., illus. $29.95
This is one of the best whitetail books published in the last two decades. The author is the former editor of *North American Whitetail* magazine.

Hunting Western Deer, by Jim and Wes Brown, Stoneydale Press, Stevensville, MT, 1994. 174 pp., illus. Paper covers. $14.95
A pair of expert Oregon hunters provide insight into hunting mule deer and blacktail deer in the western states.

Hunting Wild Turkeys in the West, by John Higley, Stoneydale Press, Stevensville, MT, 1992. 154 pp., illus. Paper covers. $12.95
Covers the basics of calling, locating and hunting turkeys in the western states.

Hunting with the Twenty-two, by Charles Singer Landis, R&R Books, Livonia, NY, 1994. 429 pp., illus. $35.00
A miscellany of articles touching on the hunting and shooting of small game.

I Don't Want to Shoot an Elephant, by Havilah Babcock, The Gunnerman Press, Auburn Hills, MI, 1985. 184 pp., illus. $19.95
Eighteen delightful stories that will enthrall the upland gunner for many pleasureable hours.

In Search of the Buffalo, by Charles G. Anderson, Pioneer Press, Union City, TN, 1996. 144 pp., illus. Paper covers. $13.95
The primary study of the life of J. Wright Mooar, one of the few hunters fortunate enough to kill a white buffalo.

In the Turkey Woods, by Jerome B. Robinson, The Lyons Press, N.Y., 1998. 207 pp., illustrated. $24.95
Practical expert advice on all aspects of turkey hunting—from calls to decoys to guns.

Jaybirds Go to Hell on Friday, by Havilah Babcock, The Gunnerman Press, Auburn Hills, MI, 1985. 149 pp., illus. $19.95
Sixteen jewels that reestablish the lost art of good old-fashioned yarn telling.

Mammoth Monarchs of North America, by Odie Sudbeck, HTW Publications, Seneca, KA, 1995. 288 pp., illus. $35.00.
This book reveals eye-opening big buck secrets.

Measuring and Scoring North American Big Game Trophies, 2nd Edition, by Wm. H. Nesbitt and Philip L. Wright, The Boone & Crockett Club, Missoula, MT, 1999. 150 pp., illustrated. $34.95
The definitive manual for anyone wanting to learn the Club's world-famous big game measuring system.

Montana—Land of Giant Rams, Volume 2, by Duncan Gilchrist, Outdoor Expeditions and Books, Corvallis, MT, 1992. 208 pp., illus. $34.95
The reader will find stories of how many of the top-scoring trophies were taken.

Montana—Land of Giant Rams, Volume 3, by Duncan Gilchrist, Outdoor Expeditions, books and videos, Corvallis, MT, 1999. 224 pp., illus. Paper covers. $19.95
All new sheep information including over 70 photos. Learn about how Montana became the "Land of Giant Rams" and what the prospects of the future as we enter a new millenium.

More Tracks: 78 Years of Mountains, People & Happiness, by Howard Copenhaver, Stoneydale Press, Stevensville, MT, 1992. 150 pp., illus. $18.95
A collection of stories by one of the back country's best storytellers about the people who shared with Howard his great adventure in the high places and wild Montana country.

Mostly Huntin', by Bill Jordan, Everett Publishing Co., Bossier City, LA, 1987. 254 pp., illus. $21.95
Jordan's hunting adventures in North America, Africa, Australia, South America and Mexico.

Mule Deer: Hunting Today's Trophies, by Tom Carpenter and Jim Van Norman, Krause Publications, Iola, WI, 1998. 256 pp., illustrated. Paper covers. $19.95
A tribute to both the deer and the people who hunt them. Includes info on where to look for big deer, prime mule deer habitat and effective weapons for the hunt.

Murry Burnham's Hunting Secrets, by Murry Burnham with Russell Tinsley, Winchester Press, Piscataway, NJ, 1984. 244 pp., illus. $17.95
One of the great hunters of our time gives the reasons for his success in the field.

My Health is Better in November, by Havilah Babcock, University of S. Carolina Press, Columbia, SC, 1985. 284 pp., illus. $24.95
Adventures in the field set in the plantation country and backwater streams of SC.

North American Waterfowler, The, by Paul S. Bernsen, Superior Publ. Co., Seattle, WA, 1972. 206 pp. Paper covers. $9.95
The complete inside and outside story of duck and goose shooting. Big and colorful, illustrations by Les Kouba.

Old Man and the Boy, The, by Robert Ruark, Henry Holt & Co., New York, NY, 303 pp., illus. $24.95.
A timeless classic, telling the story of a remarkable friendship between a young boy and his grandfather as they hunt and fish together.

Old Man's Boy Grows Older, The, by Robert Ruark, Henry Holt & Co., Inc., New York, NY, 1993. 300 pp., illus. $24.95
The heartwarming sequel to the best-selling *The Old Man and the Boy*.

Old Wildfowling Tales, Volume 2, edited by Worth Mathewson, Sand Lake Press, Amity, OR, 1996. 240 pp. $21.95
A collection of duck and geese hunting stories based around accounts from the past.

161 Waterfowling Secrets, edited by Matt Young, Willow Creek Press, Minocqua, WI, 1997. 78 pp., Paper covers. $10.95
Time-honored, field-tested waterfowling tips and advice.

One Man, One Rifle, One Land; Hunting all Species of Big Game in North America, by J.Y. Jones, Safari Press, Huntington Beach, CA, 2000. 400 pp., illustrated. $59.95
Journey with J.Y. Jones as he hunts each of the big-game animals of North America—from the polar bear of the high Artic to the jaguar of the low-lands of Mexico—with just one rifle.

Outdoor Pastimes of an American Hunter, by Theodore Roosevelt, Stackpole Books, Mechanicsburg, PA, 1994. 480 pp., illus. Paper covers. $18.95
Stories of hunting big game in the West and notes about animals pursued and observed.

Outlaw Gunner, The, by Harry M. Walsh, Tidewater Publishers, Cambridge, MD, 1973. 178 pp., illus. $22.95.
A colorful story of market gunning in both its legal and illegal phases.

Pheasant Days, by Chris Dorsey, Voyageur Press, Stillwater, MN, 1992. 233 pp., illus. $24.95
The definitive resource on ringnecks. Includes everything from basic hunting techniques to the life cycle of the bird.

Pheasant Hunter's Harvest, by Steve Grooms, Lyons & Burford Publishers, New York, NY, 1990. 180 pp. $22.95
A celebration of pheasant, pheasant dogs and pheasant hunting. Practical advice from a passionate hunter.

Pheasant Tales, by Gene Hill et al, Countrysport Press, Traverse City, MI, 1996. 202 pp., illus. $39.00
Charley Waterman, Michael McIntosh and Phil Bourjaily join the author to tell some of the stories that illustrate why the pheasant is America's favorite game bird.

Pheasants of the Mind, by Datus Proper, Wilderness Adventures Press, Bozeman, MT, 1994. 154 pp., illus. $25.00
No single title sums up the life of the solitary pheasant hunter like this masterful work.

Portraits of Elk Hunting, by Jim Zumbo, Safari Press, Huntington Beach, CA, 2001. 222 pp. illustrated. $39.95
Zumbo has captured in photos as well as in words the essence, charisma, and wonderful components of elk hunting: back-country wilderness camps, sweaty guides, happy hunters, favorite companions, elk woods, and, of course, the majestic elk. Join Zumbo in the uniqueness of the pursuit of the magnificent and noble elk.

Predator Calling with Gerry Blair, by Gerry Blair, Krause Publications, Iola, WI, 1996. 208 pp., illus. Paper covers. $14.95
Time-tested secrets lure predators closer to your camera or gun.

Proven Whitetail Tactics, by Greg Miller, Krause Publications, Iola, WI, 1997. 224 pp., illus. Paper covers. $19.95
Proven tactics for scouting, calling and still-hunting whitetail.

Quest for Dall Rams, by Duncan Gilchrist, Duncan Gilchrist Outdoor Expeditions and Books, Corvallis, MT, 1997. 224 pp., illus. Limited numbered edition. $34.95
The most complete book of Dall sheep ever written. Covers information on Alaska and provinces with Dall sheep and explains hunting techniques, equipment, etc.

Quest for Giant Bighorns, by Duncan Gilchrist, Outdoor Expeditions and Books, Corvallis, MT, 1994. 224 pp., illus. Paper covers. $19.95
How some of the most successful sheep hunters hunt and how some of the best bighorns were taken.

Radical Elk Hunting Strategies, by Mike Lapinski, Stoneydale Press Publishing Co., Stevensville, MT, 1988. 161 pp., illus. $18.95
Secrets of calling elk in close.

Rattling, Calling & Decoying Whitetails, by Gary Clancy, Edited by Patrick Durkin, Krause Publications, Iola, WI, 2000. 208 pp., illustrated. Paper covers. $19.95
How to consistently coax big bucks into range.

Records of North American Big Game 11th Edition, with hunting chapters by Craig Boddington, Tom McIntyre and Jim Zumbo, The Boone and Crockett Club, Missoula, MT, 1999. 700 pp., featuring a 32 page color section. $49.95
Listing over 17,150, of the top trophy big game animals ever recorded. Over 4,000 new listings are featured in this latest edition.

Records of North American Big Game 1932, by Prentis N. Grey, Boone and Crockett Club, Dumfries, VA, 1988. 178 pp., illus. $79.95
A reprint of the book that started the Club's record keeping for native North American big game.

Records of North American Caribou and Moose, Craig Boddington et al, The Boone & Crockett Club, Missoula, MT, 1997. 250 pp., illus. $24.95
More than 1,800 caribou listings and more than 1,500 moose listings, organized by the state or Canadian province where they were taken.

Records of North American Elk and Mule Deer, 2nd Edition, edited by Jack and Susan Reneau, Boone & Crockett Club, Missoula, MT, 1996. 360 pp., illus. Paper cover, $18.95; hardcover, $24.95
Updated and expanded edition featuring more than 150 trophy, field and historical photos of the finest elk and mule deer trophies ever recorded.

Records of North American Sheep, Rocky Mountain Goats and Pronghorn edited by Jack and Susan Reneau, Boone & Crockett Club, Missoula, MT, 1996. 400 pp., illus. Paper cover, $18.95; hardcover $24.95
The first B&C Club records book featuring all 3941 accepted wild sheep, Rocky Mountain goats and pronghorn trophies.

Return of Royalty; Wild Sheep of North America, by Dr. Dale E. Toweill and Dr. Valerius Geist, Boone and Crockett Club, Missoula, MT, 1999. 224 pp., illustrated. $59.95
A celebration of the return of the wild sheep to many of its historical ranges.

Ringneck; A Tribute to Pheasants and Pheasant Hunting, by Steve Grooms, Russ Sewell and Dave Nomsen, The Lyons Press, New York, NY, 2000. 120 pp., illustrated. $40.00
A glorious full-color coffee-table tribute to the pheasant and those who hunt them.

Ringneck! Pheasants & Pheasant Hunting, by Ted Janes, Crown Publ., NY, 1975. 120 pp., illus. $15.95
A thorough study of one of our more popular game birds.

Rub-Line Secrets, by Greg Miller, edited by Patrick Durkin, Krause Publications, Iola, WI, 1999. 208 pp., illustrated. Paper covers. $19.95
Based on nearly 30 years experience. Proven tactics for finding, analyzing and hunting big bucks' rub-lines.

Ruffed Grouse, edited by Sally Atwater and Judith Schnell, Stackpole Books, Harrisburg, PA, 1989. 370 pp., illus. $59.95
Everything you ever wanted to know about the ruffed grouse. More than 25 wildlife professionals provided in-depth information on every aspect of this popular game bird's life. Lavishly illustrated with over 300 full-color photos.

Russell Annabel Adventure Series, The, by Russell Annabel, Safari Press, Huntington Beach, CA: Vol. 2, Adventure is My Business, 1951-1955. $35.00, Vol. 3, Adventure is in My Blood, 1957-1964. $35.00, Vol. 4, High Road to Adventure, 1964-1970. $35.00, Vol. 5, The Way We Were, 1970-1979. $35.00
A complete collection of previously unpublished magazine articles in book form by this gifted outdoor writer.

Season, The, by Tom Kelly, Lyons & Burford, New York, NY, 1997. 160 pp., illus. $22.95
The delight and challenges of a turkey hunter's Spring season.

Secret Strategies from North America's Top Whitetail Hunters, compiled by Nick Sisley, Krause Publications, Iola, WI, 1995. 256 pp., illus. Paper covers. $14.95
Bow and gun hunters share their success stories.

Secrets of the Turkey Pros, by Glenn Sapir, North American Hunting Club, Minnetonka, MN, 1999. 176 pp., illustrated. $19.95
This work written by a seasoned turkey hunter draws on the collective knowledge and experience on some of the most renowned names in the world of wild turkey.

Sheep Hunting in Alaska—The Dall Sheep Hunter's Guide, by Tony Russ, Outdoor Expeditions and Books, Corvallis, MT, 1994. 160 pp., illus. Paper covers. $19.95
A how-to guide for the Dall sheep hunter.

Shots at Big Game, by Craig Boddington, Stackpole Books, Harrisburg, PA, 1989. 198 pp., illus. Softcover $15.95
How to shoot a rifle accurately under hunting conditions.

Some Bears Kill!: True-Life Tales of Terror, by Larry Kanuit, Safari Press, Huntington Beach, CA, 1997. 313 pp., illus. $24.95
A collection of 38 stories as told by the victims, and in the case of fatality, recounted by the author from institutional records, episodes involve all three species of North American bears.

Southern Deer & Deer Hunting, by Larry Weishuhn and Bill Bynum, Krause Publications, Iola, WI, 1995. 256 pp., illus. Paper covers. $14.95
Mount a trophy southern whitetail on your wall with this firsthand account of stalking big bucks below the Mason-Dixon line.

Spring Gobbler Fever, by Michael Hanback, Krause Publications, Iola, WI, 1996. 256 pp., illus. Paper covers. $15.95
Your complete guide to spring turkey hunting.

Spirit of the Wilderness, Compiled by Theodore J. Holsten, Jr., Susan C. Reneau and Jack Reneau, the Boone & Crockett Club, Missoula, MT, 1997 300 pp., illus. $29.95
Stalking wild sheep, tracking a trophy cougar, hiking the back country of British Columbia, fishing for striped bass and coming face-to-face with a grizzly bear are some of the adventures found in this book.

Stand Hunting for Whitetails, by Richard P. Smith, Krause Publications, Iola, WI, 1996. 256 pp., illus. Paper covers. $14.95
The author explains the tricks and strategies for successful stand hunting.

Sultan of Spring: A Hunter's Odyssey Through the World of the Wild Turkey, The, by Bob Saile, The Lyons Press, New York, NY, 1998. 176 pp., illus. $22.95
A literary salute to the magic and mysticism of spring turkey hunting.

Taking Big Bucks, by Ed Wolff, Stoneydale Press, Stevensville, MT, 1987. 169 pp., illus. $18.95
Solving the whitetail riddle.

Taking More Birds, by Dan Carlisle and Dolph Adams, Lyons & Burford Publishers, New York, NY, 1993. 160 pp., illus. Paper covers. $15.95
A practical handbook for success at Sporting Clays and wing shooting.

Tales of Quails 'n Such, by Havilah Babcock, University of S. Carolina Press, Columbia, SC, 1985. 237 pp. $19.95
A group of hunting stories, told in informal style, on field experiences in the South in quest of small game.

They Left Their Tracks, by Howard Coperhaver, Stoneydale Press Publishing Co., Stevensville, MT, 1990. 190 pp., illus. $18.95
Recollections of 60 years as an outfitter in the Bob Marshall Wilderness.

Timberdoodle, by Frank Woolner, Nick Lyons Books, N. Y., NY, 1987. 168 pp., illus. $18.95
The classic guide to woodcock and woodcock hunting.

Timberdoodle Tales: Adventures of a Minnesota Woodcock Hunter, by T. Waters, Safari Press, Huntington Beach, CA, 1997. 220 pp., illus. $35.00
The life history and hunt of the American woodcock by the author. A fresh appreciation of this captivating bird and the ethics of its hunt.

To Heck with Moose Hunting, by Jim Zumbo, Wapiti Publishing Co., Cody, WY, 1996. 199 pp., illus. $17.95
Jim's hunts around the continent and even an African adventure.

The Trickiest Thing in Feathers, by Corey Ford; compiled and edited by Laurie Morrow and illustrated by Christopher Smith, Wilderness Adventures, Gallatin Gateway, MT, 1998. 208 pp., illus. $29.95
Here is a collection of Corey Ford's best wing-shooting stories, many of them previously unpublished.

Upland Equation: A Modern Bird-Hunter's Code, The, by Charles Fergus, Lyons & Burford Publishers, New York, NY, 1996. 86 pp. $18.00
A book that deserves space in every sportsman's library. Observations based on firsthand experience.

Upland Tales, by Worth Mathewson (Ed.), Sand Lake Press, Amity, OR, 1996. 271 pp., illus. $29.95
A collection of articles on grouse, snipe and quail.

Varmint Hunter's Odyssey, A, by Steve Hanson with a guest chapter by Mike Johnson, Precision Shooting, Inc. Manchester, CT, 1999. 279 pp., illustrated. Paper covers. $39.95
A new classic by a writer who eats, drinks and sleeps varmint hunting and varmint rifles.

Waterfowler's World, by Bill Buckley, Ducks Unlimited, Inc., Memphis, TN, 1999. 192 pp., illustrated in color. $37.50
An unprecedented pictorial book on waterfowl and waterfowlers.

Western Hunting Guide, by Mike Lapinski, Stoneydale Press Publishing Co., Stevensville, MT, 1989. 168 pp., illus. $18.95
A complete where-to-go and how-to-do-it guide to Western hunting.

When the Duck Were Plenty, by Ed Muderlak, Safari Press, Inc., Huntington Beach, CA, 2000. 300 pp., illustrated. $29.95
The golden age of waterfowling and duck hunting from 1840 till 1920. An anthology.

Whispering Wings of Autumn, by Gene Hill and Steve Smith, Wilderness Adventures Press, Bozeman, MT, 1994. 150 pp., illus. $29.00
Hill and Smith, masters of hunting literature, treat the reader to the best stories of grouse and woodcock hunting.

Whitetail: Behavior Through the Seasons, by Charles J. Alsheimer, Krause Publications, Iola, WI, 1996. 208 pp., illus. $34.95
In-depth coverage of whitetail behavior presented through striking portraits of the whitetail in every season.

Whitetail: The Ultimate Challenge, by Charles J. Alsheimer, Krause Publications, Iola, WI, 1995. 228 pp., illus. Paper covers. $14.95
Learn deer hunting's most intriguing secrets—fooling deer using decoys, scents and calls—from America's premier authority.

Whitetails by the Moon, by Charles J. Alsheimer, edited by Patrick Durkin, Krause Publications, Iola, WI, 1999. 208 pp., illustrated. Paper covers. $19.95
Predict peak times to hunt whitetails. Learn what triggers the rut.

Wildfowler's Season, by Chris Dorsey, Lyons & Burford Publishers, New York, NY, 1998. 224 pp., illus. $37.95
Modern methods for a classic sport.

Wildfowling Tales, by William C. Hazelton, Wilderness Adventures Press, Belgrade, MT, 1999. 117 pp., illustrated with etchings by Brett Smith. In a slipcase. $50.00
Tales from the great ducking resorts of the Continent.

Wildfowling Tales 1888-1913, Volume One, edited by Worth Mathewson, Sand Lake Press, Amity, OR, 1998. 186 pp., illustrated by David Hagerbaumer. $22.50
A collection of some of the best accounts from our literary heritage.

Windward Crossings: A Treasury of Original Waterfowling Tales, by Chuck Petrie et al, Willow Creek Press, Minocqua, WI, 1999. 144 pp., 48 color art and etching reproductions. $35.00
An illustrated, modern anthology of previously unpublished waterfowl hunting (fiction and creative non fiction) stories by America's finest outdoor journalists.

Wings of Thunder: New Grouse Hunting Revisited, by Steven Mulak, Countrysport Books, Selma, AL, 1998. 168 pp. illustrated. $30.00
The author examines every aspect of New England grouse hunting as it is today - the bird and its habits, the hunter and his dog, guns and loads, shooting and hunting techniques, practice on clay targets, clothing and equipment.

Wisconsin Hunting, by Brian Lovett, Krause Publications, Iola, WI, 1997. 208 pp., illus. Paper covers. $16.95
A comprehensive guide to Wisconsin's public hunting lands.

Woodchuck Hunter, The, by Paul C. Estey, R&R Books, Livonia, NY, 1994. 135 pp., illus. $25.00
This book contains information on woodchuck equipment, the rifle, telescopic sights and includes interesting stories.

World Record Whitetails, by Gordon Whittington, Safari Press, Inc., Huntington Beach, CA, 1998. 246 pp. with over 100 photos in color and black-and-white. $32.95
The first and only complete chronicle of all the bucks that have ever held the title "World record whitetail."

Working Retrievers, The, Tom Quinn, The Lyons Press, New York, NY, 1998. 257 pp., illus. $40.00
The author covers every aspect of the training of dogs for hunting and field trials - from the beginning to the most advanced levels - for Labradors, Chesapeakes, Goldens and others.

AFRICA/ASIA/ELSEWHERE

Adventurous Life of a Vagabond Hunter, The, by Sten Cedergren, Safari Press, Inc., Huntington Beach, CA, 2000. 300 pp., illustrated. Limited edition, numbered, signed, and slipcased. $70.00
An unusual story in the safari business by a remarkable character.

Africa's Greatest Hunter; The Lost Writings of Frederick C. Selous, edited by Dr. james A. Casada, Safari Press, Huntington Beach, CA, 1999. $35.00
All the stories in this volume relate to the continent that fascinated Selous his entire life. With many previously unpublished photos.

African Adventures, by J.F. Burger, Safari Press, Huntington Beach, CA, 1993. 222 pp. $35.00
The reader shares adventures on the trail of the lion, the elephant and buffalo.

African Adventures: A Return to the Silent Places, The, by Peter Hathaway Capstick, St. Martin's Press, New York, NY, 1992. 220 pp., illus. $22.95
This book brings to life four turn-of-the-century adventurers and the savage frontier they braved. Frederick Selous, Constatine "Iodine" Ionides, Johnny Boyes and Jim Sutherland.

African Camp-fire Nights, by J.E. Burger, Safari Press, Huntington Beach, CA, 1993. 192 pp., illus. $32.50
In this book the author writes of the men who made hunting their life's profession.

African Game Trails, by Theodore Roosevelt, Peter Capstick, Series Editor, St. Martin's Press, New York, NY 1988. 583 pp., illustrated. $24.95
The famed safari of the noted sportsman, conservationist, and President.

African Hunter, by James Mellon, Safari Press, Huntington Beach, CA, 1996. 522 pp., illus. Paper Covers, $75.00
Regarded as the most comprehensive title ever published on African hunting.

African Hunting and Adventure, by William Charles Baldwin, Books of Zimbabwe, Bulawayo, 1981. 451 pp., illus. $75.00
Facsimile reprint of the scarce 1863 London edition. African hunting and adventure from Natal to the Zambezi.

THE ARMS LIBRARY

African Jungle Memories, by J.F. Burger, Safari Press, Huntington Beach, CA, 1993. 192 pp., illus. $32.50
A book of reminiscences in which the reader is taken on many exciting adventures on the trail of the buffalo, lion, elephant and leopard.

African Rifles & Cartridges, by John Taylor, The Gun Room Press, Highland Park, NJ, 1977. 431 pp., illus. $35.00
Experiences and opinions of a professional ivory hunter in Africa describing his knowledge of numerous arms and cartridges for big game. A reprint.

African Safaris, by Major G.H. Anderson, Safari Press, Long Beach, CA, 1997. 173 pp., illus. $35.00
A reprinting of one of the rarest books on African hunting, with a foreword by Tony Sanchez.

African Twilight, by Robert F. Jones, Wilderness Adventure Press, Bozeman, MT, 1994. 208 pp., illus. $36.00
Details the hunt, danger and changing face of Africa over a span of three decades.

An Annotated Bibliography of African Big Game Hunting Books, 1785 to 1950, by Kenneth P. Czech, Land's Edge Press, St. Cloud, MN 2000. $50.00
This bibliography features over 600 big game hunting titles describing the regions the authors hunted, species of game bagged, and physical descriptions of the books (pages, maps, plates, bindings, etc.) It also features a suite of 16 colored plates depicting decorated bindings from some of the books. Limited to 700 numbered, signed copies.

Argali: High-Mountain Hunting, by Ricardo Medem, Safari Press, Huntington Beach, CA, 1995. 304 pp., illus. Limited, signed edition. $150.00
Medem describes hunting seven different countries in the pursuit of sheep and other mountain game.

Baron in Africa; The Remarkable Adventures of Werner von Alvensleben, by Brian Marsh, Safari Press, Huntington Beach, CA, 2001. 288 pp., illus. $35.00
Follow his career as he hunts lion, goes after large kudu, kills a full-grown buffalo with a spear, and hunts for elephant and ivory in some of the densest brush in Africa. The adventure and the experience were what counted to this fascinating character, not the money or fame; indeed, in the end he left Mozambique with barely more than the clothes on his back. This is a must-read adventure story on one of the most interesting characters to have come out of Africa after World War II. Foreword by Ian Player.

Big Five; Hunting Adventures in Today's Africa, The, by Dr. S. Lloyd Newberry, Safari Press, Huntington Beach, CA, 2001. 214 pp., illus. Limited edition, numbered, signed and slipcased. $70.00
Many books have been written about the old Africa and its fabled Big Five, but almost nothing exits in print that describes hunting the Big Five as its exists today.

Big Game and Big Game Rifles, by John "Pondoro" Taylor, Safari Press, Huntington Beach, CA, 1999. 215 pp., illus. $24.95
Covers rifles and calibers for elephant, rhino, hippo, buffalo, and lion.

Big Game Hunting Around the World, by Bert Klineburger and Vernon W. Hurst, Exposition Press, Jericho, NY, 1969. 376 pp., illus. $30.00
The first book that takes you on a safari all over the world.

Big Game Shooting in Cooch Behar, the Duars and Assam, by The Maharajah of Cooch Behar, Wolfe Publishing Co., Prescott, AZ, 1993. 461 pp., illus. $49.50
A reprinting of the book that has become legendary. This is the Maharajah's personal diary of killing 365 tigers.

Buffalo, Elephant, and Bongo, by Dr. Reinald von Meurers, Safari Press, Huntington Beach, CA, 1999. Limited edition signed and in a slipcase. $75.00
Alone in the Savannas and Rain Forests of the Cameroon.

Campfire Lies of a Canadian Guide, by Fred Webb, Safari Press, Inc., Huntington Beach, CA, 2000. 250 pp., illustrated. Limited edition, numbered, signed and slipcased. $50.00
Forty years in the life of a guide in the North Country.

Cottar: The Exception was the Rule, by Pat Cottar, Trophy Room Books, Agoura, CA, 1999. 350 pp., illustrated. Limited, numbered and signed edition. $135.00
The remarkable big game hunting stories of one of Kenya's most remarkable pioneers.

Country Boy in Africa, A, by George Hoffman, Trophy Room Books, Agoura, CA, 1998. 267 pp., illustrated with over 100 photos. Limited, numbered edition signed by the author. $85.00
In addition to the author's long and successful hunting career, he is known for developing a most effective big game cartridge, the .416 Hoffman.

Death and Double Rifles, by Mark Sullivan, Nitro Express Safaris, Phoenix, AZ, 2000. 295 pages, illus. $85.00
Sullivan has captured every thrilling detail of hunting dangerous game in this lavishly illustrated book. Full of color pictures of African hunts & rifles.

Death in a Lonely Land, by Peter Capstick, St. Martin's Press, New York, NY, 1990. 284 pp., illus. $22.95
Twenty-three stories of hunting as only the master can tell them.

Death in the Dark Continent, by Peter Capstick, St. Martin's Press, New York, NY, 1983. 238 pp., illus. $22.95
A book that brings to life the suspense, fear and exhilaration of stalking ferocious killers under primitive, savage conditions, with the ever present threat of death.

Death in the Long Grass, by Peter Hathaway Capstick, St. Martin's Press, New York, NY, 1977. 297 pp., illus. $22.95
A big game hunter's adventures in the African bush.

Death in the Silent Places, by Peter Capstick, St. Martin's Press, New York, NY, 1981. 243 pp., illus. $23.95
The author recalls the extraordinary careers of legendary hunters such as Corbett, Karamojo Bell, Stigand and others.

Duck Hunting in Australia, by Dick Eussen, Australia Outdoor Publishers Pty Ltd., Victoria, Australia, 1994. 106 pp., illus. Paper covers. $17.95
Covers the many aspects of duck hunting from hides to hunting methods.

East Africa and its Big Game, by Captain Sir John C. Willowghby, Wolfe Publishing Co., Prescott, AZ, 1990. 312 pp., illus. $52.00
A deluxe limited edition reprint of the very scarce 1889 edition of a narrative of a sporting trip from Zanzibar to the borders of the Masai.

Elephant Hunting in East Equatorial Africa, by A. Neumann, St. Martin's Press, New York, NY, 1994. 455 pp., illus. $26.95
This is a reprint of one of the rarest elephant hunting titles ever.

Elephants of Africa, by Dr. Anthony Hall-Martin, New Holland Publishers, London, England, 1987. 120 pp., illus. $45.00
A superbly illustrated overview of the African elephant with reproductions of paintings by the internationally acclaimed wildlife artist Paul Bosman.

Encounters with Lions, by Jan Hemsing, Trophy Room books, Agoura, CA, 1995. 302 pp., illus. $75.00
Some stories fierce, fatal, frightening and even humorous of when man and lion meet.

Fourteen Years in the African Bush, by A. Marsh, Safari Press Publication, Huntington Beach, CA, 1998. 312 pp., illus. Limited signed, numbered, slipcased. $70.00
An account of a Kenyan game warden. A graphic and well-written story.

From Sailor to Professional Hunter: The Autobiography of John Northcote, Trophy Room Books, Agoura, CA, 1997. 400 pp., illus. Limited edition, signed and numbered. $125.00
Only a handfull of men can boast of having a fifty-year professional hunting career throughout Africa as John Northcote has had.

Gone are the Days; Jungle Hunting for Tiger and other Game in India and Nepal 1953-1969, by Peter Byrne, Safari Press, Inc., Huntington Beach, CA, 2001. 225 pp., illus. Limited signed, numbered, slipcased. $70.00

Great Hunters: Their Trophy Rooms and Collections, Volume 1, compiled and published by Safari Press, Inc., Huntington Beach, CA, 1997. 172 pp., illustrated in color. $60.00
A rare glimpse into the trophy rooms of top international hunters. A few of these trophy rooms are museums.

Great Hunters: Their Trophy Rooms & Collections, Volume 2, compiled and published by Safari Press, Inc., Huntington Beach, CA, 1998. 224 pp., illustrated with 260 full-color photographs. $60.00
Volume two of the world's finest, best produced series of books on trophy rooms and game collections. 46 sportsmen sharing sights you'll never forget on this guided tour.

Great Hunters: Their Trophy Rooms & Collections, Volume 3, compiled and published by Safari Press, Inc., Huntington Beach, CA, 2000. 204 pp., illustrated with 260 full-color photographs. $60.00
At last, the long-awaited third volume in the best photographic series ever published of trophy room collections is finally available. Unbelievable as it may sound, this book tops all previous volumes. Besides some of the greatest North American trophy rooms ever seen, an extra effort was made to include European collections. Believe it or not, volume 3 includes the Sandringham Castle big-game collection, home of Queen Elizabeth II! Also included is the complete Don Cox African and Asian collection as displayed at his alma mater. This stupendous gallery contains the trophy collections of Prince D' Arenberg, Umberto D'Entreves, George and Edward Keller, Paul Roberts, Joe Bishop, and James Clark to name but a few. Whether it be castles, palaces, mansions, or museums, the finest of the finest in trophy room designs and collection unequaled anywhere will be found in this book. As before, each trophy room is accompanied by an informative text explaining the collection and giving you insights into the hunters who went to such great efforts to create their trophy rooms. All professionally photographed in the highest quality possible.

Heart of an African Hunter, by Peter F. Flack, Safari Press, Inc., Huntington Beach, CA, 1999. Limited, numbered, slipcased edition. $70.00
Stories on the Big Five and Tiny Ten.

Horned Death, by John F. Burger, Safari Press, Huntington Beach, CA, 1992. 343 pp.illus. $35.00
The classic work on hunting the African buffalo.

Horn of the Hunter, by Robert Ruark, Safari Press, Long Beach, CA, 1987. 315 pp., illus. $35.00
Ruark's most sought-after title on African hunting, here in reprint.

Horned Giants, by Capt. John Brandt, Safari Press, Inc., Huntington Beach, CA, 1999. 288 pp., illustrated. Limited edition, numbered, signed and slipcased. $80.00
Hunting Eurasian wild cattle.

Hunter, by J.A. Hunter, Safari Press Publications, Huntington Beach, CA, 1999. 263 pp., illus. $24.95
Hunter's best known book on African big-game hunting. Internationally recognized as being one of the all-time African hunting classics.

Hunter's Africa, A, by Gordon Cundill, Trophy Room Books, Agoura, CA, 1998. 298 pp., over 125 photographic illustrations. Limited numbered edition signed by the author. $125.00
A good look by the author at the African safari experience - elephant, lion, spiral-horned antelope, firearms, people and events, as well as the clients that make it worthwhile.

Hunter's Wanderings in Africa, A, by Frederick Courteney Selous, Wolfe Publishing Co., Prescott, Arizona, 1986. 504 pp., illustrated plus folding map. $29.95
A reprinting of the 1920 London edition. A narrative of nine years spent amongst the game of the far interior of South Africa.

Hunter's Tracks, by J.A. Hunter, Safari Press Publications, Huntington Beach, CA, 1999. 240 pp., illustrated. $24.95
This is the exciting story of John Hunter's efforts to capture the shady headman of a gang of ivory poachers and smugglers. The story is interwoven with the tale of one of East Africa's most grandiose safaris taken with an Indian maharaja.

Hunting Adventures Worldwide, by Jack Atcheson, Jack Atcheson & Sons, Butte, MT, 1995. 256 pp., illus. $29.95
The author chronicles the richest adventures of a lifetime spent in quest of big game across the world – including Africa, North America and Asia.

Hunting in Ethiopia, An Anthology, by Tony Sanchez-Arino, Safari Press, Huntington Beach, CA, 1996. 350 pp., illus. Limited, signed and numbered edition. $135.00
The finest selection of hunting stories ever compiled on hunting in this great game country.

Hunting Instinct, The, by Phillip D. Rowter, Safari Press, Inc., Huntington Beach, CA, 1999. Limited edition signed and numbered and in a slipcase. $50.00
Safari chronicles from the Republic of South Africa and Namibia 1990-1998.

512 • GUN DIGEST

THE ARMS LIBRARY

Hunting in Kenya, by Tony Sanchez-Arino, Safari Press, Inc., Huntington Beach, CA, 2000. 350 pp., illustrated. Limited, signed and numbered edition in a slipcase. $135.00

The finest selection of hunting stories ever compiled on hunting in this great game country make up this anthology.

Hunting in Many Lands, by Theodore Roosevelt and George Bird Grinnel, The Boone and Crockett Club, Dumfries, VA, 1987. 447 pp., illus. $40.00

Limited edition reprint of this 1895 classic work on hunting in Africa, India, Mongolia, etc.

Hunting in the Sudan, An Anthology, compiled by Tony Sanchez-Arino, Safari Press, Huntington Beach, CA, 1992. 350 pp., illus. Limited, signed and numbered edition in a slipcase. $125.00

The finest selection of hunting stories ever compiled on hunting in this great game country.

Hunting, Settling and Remembering, by Philip H. Percival, Trophy Room Books, Agoura, CA, 1997. 230 pp., illus. Limited, numbered and signed edition. $85.00

If Philip Percival is to come alive again, it will be through this, the first edition of his easy, intricate and magical book illustrated with some of the best historical big game hunting photos ever taken.

Hunting the Dangerous Game of Africa, by John Kingsley-Heath, Sycamore Island Books, Boulder, CO, 1998. 477 pp., illustrated. $95.00

Written by one of the most respected, successful, and ethical P.H.'s to trek the sunlit plains of Botswana, Kenya, Uganda, Tanganyika, Somaliland, Eritrea, Ethiopia, and Mozambique. Filled with some of the most gripping and terrifying tales ever to come out of Africa.

In the Salt, by Lou Hallamore, Trophy Room Books, Agoura, CA, 1999. 227 pp., illustrated in black & white and full color. Limited, numbered and signed edition. $125.00

A book about people, animals and the big game hunt, about being outwitted and out maneuvered. It is about knowing that sooner or later your luck will change and your trophy will be "in the salt."

International Hunter 1945-1999, Hunting's Greatest Era, by Bert klineburger, Sportsmen on Film, Kerrville, TX, 1999. 400 pp., illustrated. A limited, numbered and signed edition. $125.00

The most important book of the greatest hunting era by the world's preeminent International hunter.

Jaguar Hunting in the Mato Grosso and Bolivia, by T. Almedia, Safari Press, Long Beach, CA, 1989. 256 pp., illus. $35.00

Not since Sacha Siemel has there been a book on jaguar hunting like this one.

Jim Corbett, Master of the Jungle, by Tim Werling, Safari Press, Huntington Beach, CA, 1998. 215 pp., illus. $30.00

A biography of India's most famous hunter of man-eating tigers and leopards.

King of the Wa-Kikuyu, by John Boyes, St. Martin Press, New York, NY, 1993. 240 pp., illus. $19.95

In the 19th and 20th centuries, Africa drew to it a large number of great hunters, explorers, adventurers and rogues. Many have become legendary, but John Boyes (1874-1951) was the most legendary of them all.

Last Horizons: Hunting, Fishing and Shooting on Five Continents, by Peter Capstick, St. Martin's Press, New York, NY, 1989. 288 pp., illus. $19.95

The first in a two volume collection of hunting, fishing and shooting tales from the selected pages of The American Hunter, Guns & Ammo and Outdoor Life.

Last of the Few: Forty-Two Years of African Hunting, by Tony Sanchez-Arino, Safari Press, Huntington Beach, CA, 1996. 250 pp., illus. $39.95

The story of the author's career with all the highlights that come from pursuing the unusual and dangerous animals that are native to Africa.

Last of the Ivory Hunters, by John Taylor, Safari Press, Long Beach, CA, 1990. 354 pp., illus. $29.95

Reprint of the classic book "Pondoro" by one of the most famous elephant hunters of all time.

Legends of the Field: More Early Hunters in Africa, by W.R. Foran, Trophy Room Press, Agoura, CA, 1997. 319 pp., illus. Limited edition. $100.00

This book contains the biographies of some very famous hunters: William Cotton Oswell, F.C. Selous, Sir Samuel Baker, Arthur Neumann, Jim Sutherland, W.D.M. Bell and others.

Lost Classics, The, by Robert Ruark, Safari Press, Huntington Beach, CA, 1996. 260 pp., illus. $35.00

The magazine stories that Ruark wrote in the 1950s and 1960s finally in print in book form.

Lost Wilderness; True Accounts of Hunters and Animals in East Africa, The, by Mohamed Ismail & Alice Pianfetti, Safari Press, Inc., Huntington Beach, CA, 2000. 216 pp, photos, illustrated. Limited edition signed and numbered and slipcased. $60.00

Magic of Big Games, The, by Terry Wieland, Countrysport Books, Selma, AL, 1998. 200 pp., illus. $39.00

Original essays on hunting big game around the world.

Man Called Lion: The Life and Times of John Howard "Pondoro" Taylor, A, by P.H. Capstick, Safari Press, Huntington Beach, CA, 1994. 240 pp., illus. $24.95

With the help of Brian Marsh, an old Taylor acquaintance, Peter Capstick has accumulated over ten years of research into the life of this mysterious man.

Man-Eaters of Tsavo, The, by Lt. Colonel J.H. Patterson, Peter Capstick, series editor, St. Martin's Press, New York, NY, 1986, 5th printing. 346 pp., illus. $22.95

The classic man-eating story of the lions that halted construction of a railway line and reportedly killed one hundred people, told by the man who risked his life to successfully shoot them.

McElroy Hunts Asia, by C.J. McElroy, Safari Press, Inc., Huntington Beach, CA, 1989. 272 pp., illustrated. $50.00

From the founder of SCI comes a book on hunting the great continent of Asia for big game: tiger, bear, sheep and ibex. Includes the story of the all-time record Altai Argali as well as several markhor hunts in Pakistan.

Memoirs of an African Hunter, by Terry Irwin, Safari Press Publications, Huntington Beach, CA, 1998. 421 pp., illustrated. Limited numbered, signed and slipcased. $125.00

A narrative of a professional hunter's experiences in Africa.

Memoirs of a Sheep Hunter, by Rashid Jamsheed, Safari Press, Inc., Huntington Beach, CA, 1996. 330 pp., illustrated. $70.00

The author reveals his exciting accounts of obtaining world-record heads from his native Iran, and his eventual move to the U.S. where he procured a grand-slam of North American sheep.

Months of the Sun; Forty Years of Elephant Hunting in the Zambezi Valley, by Ian Nyschens, Safari Press, Huntington Beach, CA, 1998. 420 pp., illus. $60.00

The author has shot equally as many elephants as Walter Bell, and under much more difficult circumstances. His book will rank, or surpass, the best elephant-ivory hunting books published this century.

Mundjamba: The Life Story of an African Hunter, by Hugo Seia, Trophy Room Books, Agoura, CA, 1996. 400 pp., illus. Limited, numbered and signed by the author. $125.00

An autobiography of one of the most respected and appreciated professional African hunters.

My Last Kambaku, by Leo Kroger, Safari Press, Huntington Beach, CA, 1997. 272 pp., illus. Limited edition signed and numbered and slipcased. $60.00

One of the most engaging hunting memoirs ever published.

The Nature of the Game, by Ben Hoskyns, Quiller Press, Ltd., London, England, 1994. 160 pp., illus. $37.50

The first complete guide to British, European and North American game.

On Target, by Christian Le Noel, Trophy Room Books, Agoura, CA, 1999. 275 pp., illustrated. Limited, numbered and signed edition. $85.00

History and hunting in Central Africa.

One Long Safari, by Peter Hay, Trophy Room Books, Agoura, CA, 1998. 350 pp., with over 200 photographic illustrations and 7 maps. Limited numbered edition signed by the author. $100.00

Contains hunts for leopards, sitatunga, hippo, rhino, snakes and, of course, the general African big game bag.

Optics for the Hunter, by John Barsness, Safari Press, Inc., Huntington Beach, CA, 1999. 236 pp., illustrated. $24.95

An evaluation of binoculars, scopes, range finders, spotting scopes for use in the field.

Out in the Midday Shade, by William York, Safari Press, Inc., Huntington Beach, CA, 1999. Limited, signed and numbered edition in a slipcase. $70.00

Memoirs of an African Hunter 1949-1968.

Path of a Hunter, The, by Gilles Tre-Hardy, Trophy Room Books, Agoura, CA, 1997. 318 pp., illus. Limited Edition, signed and numbered. $85.00

A most unusual hunting autobiography with much about elephant hunting in Africa.

Perfect Shot; Shot Placement for African Big Game, The, by Kevin "Doctari" Robertson, Safari Press, Inc., Huntington Beach, CA, 1999. 230 pp., illustrated. $65.00

The most comprehensive work ever undertaken to show the anatomical features for all classes of African game. Includes caliber and bullet selection, rifle selection, trophy handling.

Perfect Shot: Mini Edition For Africa, The, Long Beach, CA: Safari Press, 2002. Softcover. $15.95

A concise 126 page, pocket-size guide, which is a mini reference for making that "perfect shot." Here it finally is, the scaled-down version of Robertson's best-seller. As in the big book, the mini edition features animal tracks as well as ghost views of vital areas and point of aim for each animal. A brief essay on natural history, trophy assessment, and subspecies is included. In addition, the tables in the back list the minimum requirements for inclusion in the Rowland Ward and SCI record books. While nothing can replace the "big" book, this is a super handy item to throw in your backpack or place in your pocket for your next safari.

Peter Capstick's Africa: A Return to the Long Grass, by Peter Hathaway Capstick, St. Martin's Press, N. Y., NY, 1987. 213 pp., illus. $35.00

A first-person adventure in which the author returns to the long grass for his own dangerous and very personal excursion.

Pondoro, by John Taylor, Safari Press, Inc., Huntington Beach, CA, 1999. 354 pp., illustrated. $29.95

The author is considered one of the best storytellers in the hunting book world, and Pondoro is highly entertaining. A classic African big-game hunting title.

Quotable Hunter, The, by Jay Cassell and Peter Fiduccia, The Lyons Press, N.Y., 1999. 288 pp., illustrated. $20.00

This collection of more than three hundred quotes from hunters through the ages captures the essence of the sport, with all its joys, idosyncrasies, and challenges.

Recollections of an Elephant Hunter 1864-1875, The, by William Finaughty, Books of Zimbabwe, Bulawayo, Zimbabwe, 1980. 244 pp., illus. $45.00

Reprint of the scarce 1916 privately published edition. The early game hunting exploits of William Finaughty in Matabeleland and Nashonaland.

Return To Toonaklut — The Russell Annabel Story, by Jeff Davis. Long Beach, CA: Safari Press, 2002. 248pp, photos, illus. $34.95

This book traces many of Rusty's paths from his early pioneer days in Alaska to his years as a UPI war correspondent to his disillusionment over the increased population in Alaska and his final move to Mexico, where he died in 1979 near Guadalajara, Mexico. Meet the characters that peopled his world--fanciful and real--like Tex Cobb and Blind Nick. Explore the cabins that sheltered him and the rivers and forests that fed him. Follow along in his journeys through Alaska and Mexico, his first mistress and his second love, and look behind the stories, myths, and legends to find the real Rusty Annabel. His sense of adventure and the courage to walk into the unknown brought him into contact with a harsh, beautiful land and the wild two-legged and four-legged characters that lived there. Those of us who grew up after WW II cannot imagine the Alaskan frontier that Rusty Annabel walked into early in the twentieth century. The hardships, the resourcefulness, the natural beauty, not knowing what lay beyond the next horizon, all were a part of his existence. His extraordinary talent allows us even today to share in the excitement and experiences of Alaska in the first half of the twentieth century. This is the story of the man behind the legend, and it is as fascinating as any of the tales Rusty Annabel ever spun for the sporting magazines.

Rifles and Cartridges for Large Game — From Deer to Bear— Advice on the Choice of a Rifle, by Layne Simpson. Long Beach, CA: Safari Press, 2002. Illustrated with 100 color photos, oversize book. 225pp, color illus. $39.95

Layne Simpson, who has been field editor for *Shooting Times* magazine for 20 years, draws from his hunting experiences on five continents to tell you what rifles, cartridges, bullets, loads, and scopes are best for various applications, and he explains why in plain English. Developer of the popular 7mm STW cartridge, Simpson has taken big game with rifle cartridges ranging in power from the .220

REFERENCE

Swift to the .460 Weatherby Magnum, and he pulls no punches when describing their effectiveness in the field. A sample of the thirty chapters includes: "The Woods Rifle," "The Mountain Rifle," "Medicine For Dangerous Game," "The Custom Rifle," "The Beanfield Rifle," "The Saddle Rifle," "All About Rifle Barrels," "The Bolt-Action Rifle," "Hunting With Modern Single Shots," "The Lever-Action Rifle," "Pumps and Autoloaders," "Choosing An Optical Sight," "All About Scope Mounts," "The Trigger," "Notes On Open Sights," "The .22 Calibers On Deer," ".243 Through .458 Caliber Cartridges," "Wildcat Cartridges," "The Big-Game Bullet," "Handloading For Big Game," "Hunting With Factory Ammo," "Selecting The Big-Game Rifle Battery," and "When Old Rifles Go Afield." If you are interested in the equipment needed to successfully hunt white-tailed deer, pronghorn antelope, elk, mule deer, caribou, black bear, moose, Alaska brown bear, Cape buffalo, African lion, or any other big-game animal, this book is a must.

Rifles for Africa; Practical Advice on Rifles and Ammunition for an African Safari, by Gregor Woods. Long Beach, CA: Safari Press, 2002. 1st edition. 430 pages, illustrated. Photos. $39.95

Invaluable to the person who seeks advice and information on what rifles, calibers, and bullets work on African big game, be they the largest land mammals on earth or an antelope barely weighing in at 20 lbs.!

Robert Ruark's Africa, by Robert Ruark, edited by Michael McIntosh, Countrysport Press, Selma, AL, 1999. 256 pp illustrated with 19 original etchings by Bruce Langton. $32.00

These previously uncollected works of Robert Ruark make this a classic big-game hunting book.

Safari: A Chronicle of Adventure, by Bartle Bull, Viking/Penguin, London, England, 1989. 383 pp., illus. $40.00

The thrilling history of the African safari, highlighting some of Africa's best-known personalities.

Safari: A Dangerous Affair, by Walt Prothero, Safari Press, Huntington Beach, CA, 2000. 275 pp., illustrated. Limited edition, numbered, signed and slipcased. $60.00

True accounts of hunters and animals of Africa.

Safari Rifles: Double, Magazine Rifles and Cartridges for African Hunting, by Craig Boddington, Safari Press, Huntington Beach, CA, 1990. 416 pp., illus. $37.50

A wealth of knowledge on the safari rifle. Historical and present double-rifle makers, ballistics for the large bores, and much, much more.

Safari: The Last Adventure, by Peter Capstick, St. Martin's Press, New York, NY, 1984. 291 pp., illus. $22.95

A modern comprehensive guide to the African Safari.

Sands of Silence, by Peter H. Capstick, Saint Martin's Press, New York, NY, 1991. 224 pp., illus. $35.00

Join the author on safari in Nambia for his latest big-game hunting adventures.

Shoot Straight And Stay Alive: A Lifetime of Hunting Experiences, by Fred Bartlett, Safari Press, Huntington Beach, CA, 2000. 256 pp., illus. $35.00

Bartlett grew up on a remote farm in Kenya where he started hunting at an early age. After serving in WWII, he returned to Kenya to farm. After a few years, he decided to join the Kenya Game Department as a game control officer, which required him to shoot buffalo and elephant at very close range. He had a fine reputation as a buffalo hunter and was considered to be one of the quickest shots with a double rifle.

Solo Safari, by T. Cacek, Safari Press, Huntington Beach, CA, 1995. 270 pp., illus. $30.00

Here is the story of Terry Cacek who hunted elephant, buffalo, leopard and plains game in Zimbabwe and Botswana on his own.

Spiral-Horn Dreams, by Terry Wieland, Trophy Room Books, Agoura, CA, 1996. 362 pp., illus. Limited, numbered and signed by the author. $85.00

Everyone who goes to hunt in Africa is looking for something; this is for those who go to hunt the spiral-horned antelope—the bongo, myala, mountain nyala, greater and lesser kudu, etc.

Sport Hunting on Six Continents, by Ken Wilson, Sportsmen of Film, Kerrville, TX, 1999. 300 pp., illustrated. $69.95

Hunting around the world....from Alaska to Australia...from the Americas, to Africa, Asia, and Europe.

Tales of the African Frontier, by J.A. Hunter, Safari Press Publications, Huntington Beach, CA, 1999. 308 pp., illus. $24.95

The early days of East Africa is the subject of this powerful John Hunter book.

Uganda Safaris, by Brian Herne, Winchester Press, Piscataway, NJ, 1979. 236 pp., illus. $24.95

The chronicle of a professional hunter's adventures in Africa.

Under the African Sun, by Dr. Frank Hibben, Safari Press, Inc., Huntington Beach, CA, 1999. Limited edition signed, numbered and in a slipcase. $85.00

Forty-eight years of hunting the African continent.

Under the Shadow of Man Eaters, by Jerry Jaleel, The Jim Corbett Foundation, Edmonton, Alberta, Canada, 1997. 152 pp., illus. A limited, numbered and signed edition. Paper covers. $35.00

The life and legend of Jim Corbett of Kumaon.

Use Enough Gun, by Robert Ruark, Safari Press, Huntington Beach, CA, 1997. 333 pp., illus. $35.00

Robert Ruark on big game hunting.

Warrior: The Legend of Col. Richard Meinertzhagen, by Peter H. Capstick, St. Martins Press, New York, NY, 1998. 320 pp., illus. $23.95

A stirring and vivid biography of the famous British colonial officer Richard Meinertzhagen, whose exploits earned him fame and notoriety as one of the most daring and ruthless men to serve during the glory days of the British Empire.

Waterfowler's World, The, by Bill Buckley, Willow Creek Press, Minocqua, WI, 1999. 176 pp., 225 color photographs. $37.50

Waterfowl hunting from Canadian prairies, across the U.S. heartland, to the wilds of Mexico, from the Atlantic to the Pacific coasts and the Gulf of Mexico.

Where Lions Roar: Ten More Years of African Hunting, by Craig Boddington, Safari Press, Huntington Beach, CA, 1997. 250 pp $35.00

The story of Boddington's hunts in the Dark Continent during the last ten years.

White Hunter, by J.A. Hunter, Safari Press Publications, Huntington Beach, CA, 1999. 282 pp., illustrated. $24.95

This book is a seldom-seen account of John Hunter's adventures in pre-WW2 Africa.

Wind, Dust and Snow, by Robert M. Anderson, Safari Press, Inc., Huntington Beach, CA, 1997. 240 pp., illustrated. $65.00

A complete chronology of modern exploratory and pioneering Asian sheep-hunting expeditions from 1960 until 1996, with wonderful background history and previously untold stories.

With a Gun in Good Country, by Ian Manning, Trophy Room Books, Agoura, CA, 1996. Limited, numbered and signed by the author. $85.00

A book written about that splendid period before the poaching onslaught which almost closed Zambia and continues to the granting of her independence. It then goes on to recount Manning's experiences in Botswana, Congo, and briefly in South Africa.

RIFLES

Accurate Rifle, The, by Warren Page, Claymore Publishing, Ohio, 1997. 254 pages, illustrated. Revised edition. Paper Covers. $17.95

Provides hunters & shooter alike with detailed practical information on the whole range of subjects affecting rifle accuracy, he explains techniques in ammo, sights & shooting methods. With a 1996 equipment update from Dave Brennan.

Accurate Varmint Rifle, The, by Boyd Mace, Precision Shooting, Inc., Whitehall, NY, 1991. 184 pp., illus. $15.00

A long overdue and long needed work on what factors go into the selection of components for and the subsequent assembly of...the accurate varmint rifle.

AK-47 Assault Rifle, The, Desert Publications, Cornville, AZ, 1981. 150 pp., illus. Paper covers. $15.95

Complete and practical technical information on the only weapon in history to be produced in an estimated 30,000,000 units.

American Hunting Rifles: Their Application in the Field for Practical Shooting, by Craig Boddington, Safari Press, Huntington Beach, CA, 1996. 446 pp., illus. Second printing trade edition. Softcover $24.95

Covers all the hunting rifles and calibers that are needed for North America's diverse game.

American Krag Rifle and Carbine, The, by Joe Poyer. North Cape Publications, Tustin, CA: 2002. 1st edition. 317 pages, illustrated with hundreds of black & white drawings and photos. Softcover. $19.95

Provides the arms collector, historian and target shooter with a part by part analysis of what has been called the rifle with the smoothest bolt action ever designed. All changes to all parts are analyzed in detail and matched to serial number ranges. A monthly serial number chart by production year has been devised that will provide the collector with the year and month in which his gun was manufactured. A new and complete exploded view was produced for this book.

AR-15 Complete Owner's Guide, Volume 1, 2nd Edition, The, by Kuleck, Walt and Scott Duff. Export, PA: Scott A. Duff Publications, 2002. 224 pages, 164 photographs & line drawings. Softcover. $21.95

This book provides the prospective, new or experienced AR-15 owner with the in-depth knowledge he or she needs to select, configure, operate, maintain and troubleshoot his or her rifle. The guide covers history, applications, details of components and subassemblies, operating, cleaning, maintenance, and future of perhaps the most versatile rifle system ever produced. A comprehensive Colt model number table and pre-/post-ban serial number information are included. This is the book I wish had existed prior to buying my first AR-15!

AR-15 Complete Assembly Guide, The, Volume 2. by Kuleck, Walt and Clint McKee. Export, PA: Scott A. Duff Publications, 2002. 1st edition. 155 pages, 164 photographs & line drawings. Softcover. $19.95

This book goes beyond the military manuals in depth and scope, using words and pictures to clearly guide the reader through every operation required to assemble their AR-15-type rifle. You'll learn the best and easiest ways to build your rifle. It won't make you an AR-15 armorer, but it will make you a more knowledgeable owner. You'll be able to do more with (and to) your rifle. You'll also be able to better judge the competence of those whom you choose to work on your rifle, and to discuss your needs more intelligently with them. In short, if you build it, you'll know how to repair it.

AR-15/M16, A Practical Guide, The, by Duncan Long. Paladin Press, Boulder, CO, 1985. 168 pp., illus. Paper covers. $22.00

The definitive book on the rifle that has been the inspiration for so many modern assault rifles.

Art of Shooting with the Rifle, The, by Col. Sir H. St. John Halford, Excalibur Publications, Latham, NY, 1996. 96 pp., illus. Paper covers. $12.95

A facsimile edition of the 1888 book by a respected rifleman providing a wealth of detailed information.

Art of the Rifle, The, by Jeff Cooper, Paladin Press, Boulder, CO, 1997. 104 pp., illus. $29.95

Everything you need to know about the rifle whether you use it for security, meat or target shooting.

Australian Military Rifles & Bayonets, 200 Years of, by Ian Skennerton, I.D.S.A. Books, Piqua, OH, 1988. 124 pp., 198 illus. Paper covers. $19.50

Australian Service Machine Guns, 100 Years of, by Ian Skennerton, I.D.S.A. Books, Piqua, OH, 1989. 122 pp., 150 illus. Paper covers. $19.50

Ballard: The Great American Single Shot Rifle, by Dutcher, John T., Denver, CO: Privately Printed, 2002. 1st edition. 380 pages, illustrated with black & white photos, with 8-page color insert. Hardcover. $79.95

Big Game Rifles and Cartridges, by Elmer Keith, reprint edition by The Gun Room Press, Highland Park, NJ, 1984. 161 pp., illus. $17.95

Reprint of Elmer Keith's first book, a most original and accurate work on big game rifles and cartridges.

Black Magic: The Ultra Accurate AR-15, by John Feamster, Precision Shooting, Manchester, CT, 1998. 300 pp., illustrated. $29.95

The author has compiled his experiences pushing the accuracy envelope of the AR-15 to its maximum potential. A wealth of advice on AR-15 loads, modifications and accessories for everything from NRA Highpower and Service Rifle competitions to benchrest and varmint shooting.

REFERENCE

THE ARMS LIBRARY

Black Rifle, M16 Retrospective, The, R. Blake Stevens and Edward C. Ezell, Collector Grade Publications, Toronto, Canada, 1987. 400 pp., illus. $59.95
The complete story of the M16 rifle and its development.

Bolt Action Rifles, 3rd Edition, by Frank de Haas, DBI Books, a division of Krause Publications, Iola, WI, 1995. 528 pp., illus. Paper covers. $24.95
A revised edition of the most definitive work on all major bolt-action rifle designs.

Book of the Garand, The, by Maj. Gen. J.S. Hatcher, The Gun Room Press, Highland Park, NJ, 1977. 292 pp., illus. $26.95
A new printing of the standard reference work on the U.S. Army M1 rifle.

British .22RF Training Rifles, by Dennis Lewis and Robert Washburn, Excaliber Publications, Latham, NY, 1993. 64 pp., illus. Paper covers. $10.95
The story of Britain's training rifles from the early Aiming Tube models to the post-WWII trainers.

Classic Sporting Rifles, by Christopher Austyn, Safari Press, Huntington Beach, CA, 1997. 128 pp., illus. $50.00
As the head of the gun department at Christie's Auction House the author examines the "best" rifles built over the last 150 years.

Collectable '03, The, by J. C. Harrison. The Arms Chest, Okla. City, OK. 1999. 2nd edition (revised). 234 pages, illus. with drawings. Spiral bound. $35.00
Valuable and detailed reference book for the collector of the Model 1903 Springfield rifle.

Collecting Classic Bolt Action Military Rifles, by Paul S. Scarlata. Andrew Mowbray, Inc. Lincoln, RI. 2001. 280 pages, illustrated. $39.95
Over 400 large photographs detail key features you will need to recognize in order to identify guns for your collection. Learn the original military configurations of these service rifles so that you can tell them apart from altered guns and bad restorations. The historical sections are particularly strong, giving readers a clear understanding of how and why these rifles were developed, and which troops used them. Advanced collectors will be fascinated by the countless historical photographs of these guns in the hands of troops.

Collecting the Garand, by J. C. Harrison. The Arms Chest, Okla. City, OK. 2001. 2nd edition (revised). 198 pages, illus. Spiral bound. $35.00
Valuable and detailed reference book for the collector of the Garand.

Collecting the M1 Carbine, by J. C. Harrison. The Arms Chest, Okla. City, OK. 2000. 2nd edition (revised). 247 pages, illus. with pictures and drawings. Spiral bound. $35.00
Valuable and detailed reference book for the collector of the M1 Carbine. Identifies standard issue original military models of M1 and M1A1 Models of 1942, '43, '44, and '45 Carbines as produced by each manufacturer. Plus arsenal repair, refinish and lend-lease.

Complete AR15/M16 Sourcebook, Revised and Updated Edition, The, by Duncan Long, Paladin Press, Boulder, CO, 2002. 336 pp., illus. Paper covers. $39.95
The latest development of the AR15/M16 and the many spin-offs now available, selective-fire conversion systems for the 1990s, the vast selection of new accessories.

Competitive AR15: The Mouse That Roared, The, by Glenn Zediker, Zediker Publishing, Oxford, MS, 1999. 286 pp., illustrated. Paper covers. $29.95
A thorough and detailed study of the newest precision rifle sensation.

Complete Book of U.S. Sniping, by Peter R. Senich, Paladin Press, Boulder, CO, 1997, 8 1/2 x 11, hardcover, photos, 288 pp. $52.95
Trace American sniping materiel from its infancy to today's sophisticated systems with this volume, compiled from Senich's early books, Limited War Sniping and The Pictorial History of U.S. Sniping. Almost 400 photos, plus information gleaned from official documents and military archives, pack this informative work.

Complete Guide To The M1 Garand and The M1 Carbine, by Bruce Canfield, Andrew Mowbray, Inc., Lincoln, RI, 1999. 296 pp., illustrated. $39.50
Covers all of the manufacturers of components, parts, variations and markings. Learn which parts are proper for which guns. The total story behind these guns, from their invention through WWII, Korea, Vietnam and beyond! 300+ photos show you features, markings, overall views and action shots. Thirty-three tables and charts give instant reference to serial numbers, markings, dates of issue and proper configurations. Special sections on Sniper guns, National Match Rifles, exotic variations, and more!

Complete M1 Garand, The, by Jim Thompson, Paladin Press, Boulder, CO, 1998. 160 pp., illustrated. Paper cover. $25.00
A guide for the shooter and collector, heavily illustrated.

FAL Rifle, The, by R. Blake Stevens and Jean van Rutten, Collector Grade Publications, Cobourg, Canada, 1993. 848 pp., illus. $129.95
Originally published in three volumes, this classic edition covers North American, UK and Commonwealth and the metric FAL's.

Fighting Rifle, The, by Chuck Taylor, Paladin Press, Boulder, CO, 1983. 184 pp., illus. Paper covers. $25.00
The difference between assault and battle rifles and auto and light machine guns.

Firearms Assembly/Disassembly Part III: Rimfire Rifles, Revised Edition, The Gun Digest Book of, by J. B. Wood, DBI Books, a division of Krause Publications, Iola, WI., 1994. 480 pp., illus. Paper covers. $19.95
Covers 65 popular rimfires plus over 100 variants, all cross-referenced in the index.

Firearms Assembly/Disassembly Part IV: Centerfire Rifles, Revised Edition, The Gun Digest Book of, by J.B. Wood, DBI Books, a division of Krause Publications, Iola, WI, 1991. 480 pp., illus. Paper covers. $19.95
Covers 54 popular centerfire rifles plus 300 variants. The most comprehensive and professional presentation available to either hobbyist or gunsmith.

FN-FAL Rifle, et al, The, by Duncan Long, Delta Press, El Dorado, AR, 1998. 148 pp., illustrated. Paper covers. $18.95
A comprehensive study of one of the classic assault weapons of all times. Detailed descriptions of the basic models plus the myriad of variants that evolved as a result of its universal acceptance.

Forty Years with the .45-70, second edition, revised and expanded, by Paul A. Matthews, Wolfe Publishing Co., Prescott, AZ, 1997. 184 pp., illus. Paper covers. $17.95
This book is pure gun lore-lore of the .45-70. It not only contains a history of the cartridge, but also years of the author's personal experiences.

F.N.-F.A.L. Auto Rifles, Desert Publications, Cornville, AZ, 1981. 130 pp., illus. Paper covers. $16.95
A definitive study of one of the free world's finest combat rifles.

German Sniper 1914-1945, by Peter R. Senich, Paladin Press, Boulder, CO, 1997 8 1/2 x 11, hardcover, photos, 468 pp. $69.95
The complete story of Germany's sniping arms development through both World Wars. Presents more than 600 photos of Mauser 98's, Selbstladegewehr 41s and 43s, optical sights by Goerz, Zeiss, etc., plus German snipers in action. An exceptional hardcover collector's edition for serious military historians everywhere.

Hints and Advice on Rifle-Shooting, by Private R. McVittie with new introductory material by W.S. Curtis, W.S. Curtis Publishers, Ltd., Clwyd, England, 1993. 32 pp. Paper covers. $10.00
A reprint of the original 1886 London edition.

Historic Henry Rifle: Oliver Winchester's Famous Civil War Repeater, The, by Wiley Sword. Andrew Mowbray, Inc., Lincoln, RI. 2002. Softcover. $29.95
It was perhaps the most important firearm of its era. Tested and proved in the fiery crucible of the Civil War, the Henry Rifle became the forerunner of the famous line of Winchester Repeating Rifles that "Won the West." Here is the fascinating story from the frustrations of early sales efforts aimed at the government to the inspired purchase of the Henry Rifle by veteran soldiers who wanted the best weapon.

Hitler's Garands: German Self-Loading Rifles of World War II, by Darrin W. Weaver. Collector Grade Publications, Canada, 2001. 392 pages, 590 illustrations. $69.95
Hitler's Wehrmacht began World War II armed with the bolt action K98k, a rifle only cosmetically different from that with which Imperial Germany had fought the Great War a quarter-century earlier. Then in 1940, the Heereswaffenamt (HWaA, the Army Weapons Office) issued a requirement for a new self-loading rifle. The resulting Mauser G41(M) and flap-locked Walther G41(W) were both hampered by gas-takeoff at the muzzle, which resulted in arms which were overlong, clumsy, muzzle-heavy, unreliable, and consequently unpopular with the troops. Taking their lead from the Russians, Walther copied (and patented) the gas system of the Tokarev SVT self-loader, grafting it onto the flap-locked bolt of the G41 to create the G43, which was only produced during the last nineteen desperate months of World War II.

How-To's for the Black Powder Cartridge Rifle Shooter, by Paul A. Matthews, Wolfe Publishing Co., Prescott, AZ, 1996. 136 pp., illus. Paper covers. $22.50
Practices and procedures used in the reloading and shooting of blackpowder cartridges.

The Hunter's Guide To Accurate Shooting, by Van Zwoll, Wayne. Guilford, CT: Lyons Press, 2002. 1st edition. 288 pp. Hardcover. $29.95
Firearms expert Van Zwoll explains exactly how to shoot the big-game rifle accurately. Taking into consideration every pertinent factor, he shows a step-by-step analysis of shooting and hunting with the big-game rifle.

Illustrated Handbook of Rifle Shooting, by A.L. Russell, Museum Restoration Service, Alexandria Bay, NY, 1992. 194 pp., illus. $24.50
A new printing of the 1869 edition by one of the leading military marksman of the day.

Johnson Rifles and Machine Guns The Story of Melvin Maynard Johnson, Jr. and his Guns, by Bruce N. Canfield, Lincoln, RI: Andrew Mowbray, Inc., 2002. 1st edition. 272 pages with over 285 photographs. Hardcover. $49.95
The M1941 Johnson Rifle is the hottest WW2 rifle on the collectors market today, and this new book covers them all! From invention and manufacture through issue to the troops.

Kalashnikov: The Arms and the Man, A Revised and Expanded Edition of the AK47 Story, by Edward C. Ezell. Canada: Collector Grade Publications, 2002. 312 pages, 356 illustrations. Hardcover. $59.95
The original edition of The AK47 Story was published in 1986, and the events of the intervening fifteen years have provided much fresh new material. Beginning with an introduction by Dr. Kalashnikov himself, we present a most comprehensive study of the "life and times" of the AK, starting with the early history of small arms manufacture in Czarist Russia and then the Soviet Union. We follow the development of the AK (originally designed in caliber 7.62x41mm) and all the offshoots and clones which make up the Kalashnikov "family" of small arms, including an important new summary of technical information on the numerous loadings of "intermediate" ammunition, right up to the "AK for the 21st Century" - the AK100 series, now being manufactured by the Joint Stock Company "Kalashnikov" in Izhevsk, Russia in three calibers: 7.62x39mm, 5.45x39mm, and 5.56x45mm NATO.

Know Your M1 Garand, by E. J. Hoffschmidt, Blacksmith Corp., Southport, CT, 1975, 84 pp., illus. Paper covers. $14.95
Facts about America's most famous infantry weapon. Covers test and experimental models, Japanese and Italian copies, National Match models.

Know Your Ruger 10/22 Carbine, by William E. Workman, Blacksmith Corp., Chino Valley, AZ, 1991. 96 pp., illus. Paper covers. $14.95
The story and facts about the most popular 22 autoloader ever made.

Krag Rifle Story, The, by Frank Mallory with Ludwig Olson. Springfield Research Service, Silver Springs Md. 2001. (Updated and expanded 2nd edition) $80.00
356 pages organized into 29 chapters dealing with each model and variation of Krag rifle and carbine, foreign as well as U.S., plus bayonets, accouterments, and ammunition. Twenty appendices provide data of interest to collectors on markings, finishes, production changes, serial numbers, etc.

Lee Enfield No. 1 Rifles, The, by Alan M. Petrillo, Excaliber Publications, Latham, NY, 1992. 64 pp., illus. Paper covers. $10.95
Highlights the SMLE rifles from the Mark 1-VI.

Lee Enfield Number 4 Rifles, The, by Alan M. Petrillo, Excalibur Publications, Latham, NY, 1992. 64 pp., illus. Paper covers. $10.95
A pocket-sized, bare-bones reference devoted entirely to the .303 World War II and Korean War vintage service rifle.

Legendary Sporting Rifles, by Sam Fadala, Stoeger Publishing Co., So. Hackensack, NJ, 1992. 288 pp., illus. Paper covers. $16.95
Covers a vast span of time and technology beginning with the Kentucky Long-rifle.

Li'l M1 .30 Cal. Carbine, The, by Duncan Long, Desert Publications, El Dorado, AZ, 1995. 203 pp., illus. Paper covers. $19.95
Traces the history of this little giant from its original creation.

Make It Accurate: Get the Maximum Performance from Your Hunting Rifle, by Craig Boddington, Safari Press Publications, Huntington Beach, CA, 1999. 224 pp., illustrated. $24.95
Tips on how to select the rifle, cartridge, and scope best suited to your needs. A must-have for any hunter who wants to improve his shot.

THE ARMS LIBRARY

Mauser Smallbore Sporting, Target and Training Rifles, by Jon Speed, Collector Grade Publications, Inc., Cobourg, Ont., Canada, 1998. 372 pp., illustrated. $67.50
The history of all the smallbore sporting, target and training rifles produced by the legendary Mauser-Werke of Obendorf am Neckar.

Mauser: Original-Oberndorf Sporting Rifles, by Jon Speed, Collector Grade Publications, Inc., Cobourg, Ont., Canada, 1997. 508 pp., illustrated. $89.95
The most exhaustive study ever published of the design origins and manufacturing history of the original Oberndorf Mauser Sporter.

M14/M14A1 Rifles and Rifle Markmanship, Desert Publications, El Dorado, AZ, 1995. 236 pp., illus. Paper covers. $24.95
Contains a detailed description of the M14 and M14A1 rifles and their general characteristics, procedures for disassembly and assembly, operating and functioning of the rifles, etc.

M14 Owner's Guide and Match Conditioning Instructions, The, by Scott A. Duff and John M. Miller, Scott A. Duff Publications, Export, PA, 1996. 180 pp., illus. Paper covers. $19.95
Traces the history and development from the T44 through the adoption and production of the M14 rifle.

M-14 Rifle, The, facsimile reprint of FM 23-8, Desert Publications, Cornville, AZ, 50 pp., illus. Paper $11.95
Well illustrated and informative reprint covering the M-14 and M-14E2.

M14-Type Rifle: A Shooter's and Collector's Guide, The, by Joe Poyer, North Cape Publications, Tustin, CA, 1997. 82 pp., illus. Paper covers. $14.95
Covers the history and development, commercial copies, cleaning and maintenance instructions, and targeting and shooting.

M16/AR15 Rifle, The, by Joe Poyer, North Cape Publications, Tustin, CA, 1998. 150 pp., illustrated. Paper covers. $19.95
From its inception as the first American assault battle rifle to the firing lines of the National Matches, the M16/AR15 rifle in all its various models and guises has made a significant impact on the American rifleman.

Military Bolt Action Rifles, 1841-1918, by Donald B. Webster, Museum Restoration Service, Alexander Bay, NY, 1993. 150 pp., illus. $34.50
A photographic survey of the principal rifles and carbines of the European and Asiatic powers of the last half of the 19th century and the first years of the 20th century.

Mini-14, The, by Duncan Long, Paladin Press, Boulder, CO, 1987. 120 pp., illus. Paper covers. $17.00
History of the Mini-14, the factory-produced models, specifications, accessories, suppliers, and much more.

Mr. Single Shot's Book of Rifle Plans, by Frank de Haas, Mark de Haas, Orange City, IA, 1996. 85 pp., illus. Paper covers. $22.50
Contains complete and detailed drawings, plans and instructions on how to build four different and unique breech-loading single shot rifles of the author's own proven design.

M1 Carbine Owner's Manual, M1, M2 & M3 .30 Caliber Carbines, Firepower Publications, Cornville, AZ, 1984. 102 pp., illus. Paper covers. $14.95
The complete book for the owner of an M1 Carbine.

M1 Garand Serial Numbers & Data Sheets, The, by Scott A. Duff, Scott A. Duff, Export, PA, 1995. 101 pp. Paper covers. $11.95
This pocket reference book includes serial number tables and data sheets on the Springfield Armory, Gas Trap Rifles, Gas Port Rifles, Winchester Repeating Arms, International Harvester and H&R Arms Co. and more.

M1 Garand: Post World War, The, by Scott A. Duff, Scott A. Duff, Export, PA, 1990. 139 pp., illus. Soft covers. $21.95
A detailed account of the activities at Springfield Armory through this period. International Harvester, H&R, Korean War production and quantities delivered. Serial numbers.

M1 Garand: World War II, The, by Scott A. Duff, Scott A. Duff, Export, PA, 1993. 210 pp., illus. Paper covers. $34.95
The most comprehensive study available to the collector and historian on the M1 Garand of World War II.

MG34-MG42 German Universal Machineguns, by Folke Myrvang. Collector Grade Publications, Canada. 2002. 496 pages, 646 illustrations. $79.95
This is the first-ever COMPLETE study of the MG34 & MG42. Here the author presents in-depth coverage of the historical development, fielding, tactical use of and modifications made to these remarkable guns and their myriad accessories and ancillaries, plus authoritative tips on troubleshooting.

Modern Sniper Rifles, by Duncan Long, Paladin Press, Boulder, CO, 1997, 8 1/2 x 11, soft cover, photos, illus., 120 pp. $20.00
Noted weapons expert Duncan Long describes the .22 LR, single-shot, bolt-action, semiautomatic and large-caliber rifles that can be used for sniping purposes, including the U.S. M21, Ruger Mini-14, AUG and HK-94SG1. These and other models are evaluated on the basis of their features, accuracy, reliability and handiness in the field. The author also looks at the best scopes, ammunition and accessories.

More Single Shot Rifles and Actions, by Frank de Haas, Mark de Haas, Orange City, IA, 1996. 146 pp., illus. Paper covers. $22.50
Covers 45 different single shot rifles. Includes the history plus photos, drawings and personal comments.

No. 4 (T) Sniper Rifle: An Armourer's Perspective, The, by Peter Laidler with Ian Skennerton, I.D.S.A. Books, Piqua, OH, 1993. 125 pp., 75 illus. Paper covers. $19.95

Notes on Rifle-Shooting, by Henry William Heaton, reprinted with a new introduction by W.S. Curtis, W.S. Curtis Publishers, Ltd., Clwyd, England, 1993. 89 pp. $19.95
A reprint of the 1864 London edition. Captain Heaton was one of the great rifle shots from the earliest days of the Volunteer Movement.

Official SKS Manual, The, Translation by Major James F. Gebhardt (Ret.), Paladin Press, Boulder, CO, 1997. 96 pp., illus. Paper covers. $16.95
This Soviet military manual covering the widely distributed SKS is now available in English.

Police Rifles, by Richard Fairburn, Paladin Press, Boulder, CO, 1994. 248 pp., illus. Paper covers. $35.00
Selecting the right rifle for street patrol and special tactical situations.

Poor Man's Sniper Rifle, The, by D. Boone, Paladin Press, Boulder, CO, 1995. 152 pp., illus. Paper covers. $18.95
Here is a complete plan for converting readily available surplus military rifles to high-performance sniper weapons.

Potpourri of Single Shot Rifles and Actions, A, by Frank de Haas, Mark de Haas, Ridgeway, MO, 1993. 153 pp., illus. Paper covers. $22.50
The author's 6th book on non-bolt-action single shots. Covers more than 40 single-shot rifles in historical and technical detail.

Precision Shooting with the M1 Garand, by Roy Baumgardner, Precision Shooting, Inc., Manchester, CT, 1999. 142 pp., illustrated. Paper covers. $12.95
Starts off with the ever popular ten-article series on accurizing the M1 that originally appeared in Precision Shooting in the 1993-95 era. There follows nine more Baumgardner authored articles on the M1 Garand and finally a 1999 updating chapter.

Remington Autoloading and Pump Action Rifles, by Eugene Myszkowski, Tucson, AZ: Excalibur Publications, 2002. 132 pages, with 162 photographs, 6 illustrations and 18 charts. Softcover. $20.95
An illustrated history of Remington's centerfire Models 760, 740, 742, 7400 and 7600. The book is thoroughly researed and features many previously unpublished photos of the rifles, their accessories and accoutrements. Also covers high grade, unusual and experimental rifles. Contains information on collecting, serial numbers and barrel codes.

Remington 700, The, by John F. Lacy, Taylor Publishing Co., Dallas, TX, 2002. 208 pp., illus. $49.95
Covers the different models, limited editions, chamberings, proofmarks, serial numbers, military models, and much more.

Rifle Guide, by Sam Fadala, Stoeger Publishing Co., S. Hackensack, NJ, 1993. 288 pp., illus. Paper covers. $16.95
This comprehensive, fact-filled book beckons to both the seasoned rifleman as well as the novice shooter.

Rifle: Its Development for Big-Game Hunting, The, by S.R. Truesdell, Safari Press, Huntington Beach, CA, 1992. 274 pp., illus. $35.00
The full story of the development of the big-game rifle from 1834-1946.

Rifles of the World, 2nd Edition, edited by John Walter, DBI Books, a division of Krause Publications, Iola, WI, 1998. 384 pp., illus. $24.95
The definitive guide to the world's centerfire and rimfire rifles.

Ned H. Roberts and the Schuetzen Rifle, edited by Gerald O. Kelver, Brighton, CO, 1982. 99 pp., illus. $13.95
A compilation of the writings of Major Ned H. Roberts which appeared in various gun magazines.

Rock Island Rifle Model 1903, by C.S. Ferris. Export, PA: Scott A. Duff Publications, 2002. 177 pages, illustrated with black and white photographs. Foreword by Scott A. Duff. Softcover. $22.95

Schuetzen Rifles, History and Loading, by Gerald O. Kelver, Gerald O. Kelver, Publisher, Brighton, CO, 1972. Illus. $13.95
Reference work on these rifles, their bullets, loading, telescopic sights, accuracy, etc. A limited, numbered ed.

Shooting the Blackpowder Cartridge Rifle, by Paul A. Matthews, Wolfe Publishing Co., Prescott, AZ, 1994. 129 pp., illus. Paper covers. $22.50
A general discourse on shooting the blackpowder cartridge rifle and the procedure required to make a particular rifle perform.

Shooting Lever Guns of the Old West, by Mike Venturino, MLV Enterprises, Livingston, MT, 1999. 300 pp., illustrated. Paper covers. $27.95
Shooting the lever action type repeating rifles of our American west.

Single Shot Rifles and Actions, by Frank de Haas, Orange City, IA, 1990. 352 pp., illus. Soft covers. $27.00
The definitive book on over 60 single shot rifles and actions.

S.L.R.—Australia's F.N. F.A.L. by Ian Skennerton and David Balmer, I.D.S.A. Books, Piqua, OH, 1989. 124 pp., 100 illus. Paper covers. $19.50

Small Arms Identification Series, No. 2—.303 Rifle, No. 4 Marks I, & I*, Marks 1/2, 1/3 & 2, by Ian Skennerton, I.D.S.A. Books, Piqua, OH, 1994. 48 pp. $10.50

Small Arms Identification Series, No. 3—9mm Austen Mk I & 9mm Owen Mk I Sub-Machine Guns, by Ian Skennerton, I.D.S.A. Books, Piqua, OH, 1994. 48 pp. $10.50

Small Arms Identification Series, No. 4—.303 Rifle, No. 5 Mk I, by Ian Skennerton, I.D.S.A. Books, Piqua, OH, 1994. 48 pp. $10.50

Small Arms Identification Series, No. 5—.303-in. Bren Light Machine Gun, by Ian Skennerton, I.D.S.A. Books, Piqua, OH, 1994. 48 pp. $10.50

Small Arms Identification Series, No. 1—.303 Rifle, No. 1 S.M.L.E. Marks III and III*, by Ian Skennerton, I.D.S.A. Books, Piqua, OH, 1981. 48 pp. $10.50

Springfield M1903, M1903A1, M1903A3, M1903A4, The, Desert Publications, Cornville, AZ, 1982. 100 pp., illus. Paper covers. $14.95
Covers every aspect of disassembly and assembly, inspection, repair and maintenance.

Still More Single Shot Rifles, by James J. Grant, Pioneer Press, Union City, TN, 1995. 211 pp., illus. $29.95
This is Volume Four in a series of Single-Shot Rifles by America's foremost authority. It gives more in-depth information on those single-shot rifles which were presented in the first three books.

Sturm, Ruger 10/22 Rifle and .44 Magnum Carbine, The, by Duncan Long, Paladin Press, Boulder, CO, 1988. 108 pp., illus. Paper covers. $15.00
An in-depth look at both weapons detailing the elegant simplicity of the Ruger design. Offers specifications, troubleshooting procedures and ammunition recommendations.

Tactical Rifle, The, by Gabriel Suarez, Paladin Press, Boulder, CO, 1999. 264 pp., illustrated. Paper covers. $25.00
The precision tool for urban police operations.

Target Rifle in Australia, by J.E. Corcoran, R&R, Livonia, NY, 1996. 160 pp., illus. $40.00
A most interesting study of the evolution of these rifles from 1860 - 1900. British rifles from the percussion period through the early smokeless era are discussed.

THE ARMS LIBRARY

To the Dreams of Youth: The .22 Caliber Single Shot Winchester Rifle, by Herbert Houze, Krause Publications, Iola, WI, 1993. 192 pp., illus. $34.95
A thorougly researched history of the 22-caliber Winchester single shot rifle, including interesting photographs.

Ultimate in Rifle Accuracy, The, by Glenn Newick, Stoeger Publishing Co., Wayne, N.J., 1999. 205 pp., illustrated. Paper covers. $11.95
This handbook contains the information you need to extract the best performance from your rifle.

U.S. Marine Corps AR15/M16 A2 Manual, reprinted by Desert Publications, El Dorado, AZ, 1993. 262 pp., illus. Paper covers. $16.95
A reprint of TM05538C-23&P/2, August, 1987. The A-2 manual for the Colt AR15/M16.

U.S. Marine Corps Rifle Marksmanship, by U.S. Marine Corps. Boulder, CO: Paladin Press, 2002. Photos, illus., 120 pp. Softcover. $20.00
This manual is the very latest Marine doctrine on the art and science of shooting effectively in battle. Its 10 chapters teach the versatility, flexibility and skills needed to deal with a situation at any level of intensity across the entire range of military operations. Topics covered include the proper combat mind-set; cleaning your rifle under all weather conditions; rifle handling and marksmanship the Marine way; engaging targets from behind cover; obtaining a battlefield zero; engaging immediate threat, multiple and moving targets; shooting at night and at unknown distances; and much more.

U.S. Rifle M14—From John Garand to the M21, by R. Blake Stevens, Collector Grade Publications, Inc., Toronto, Canada, revised second edition, 1991. 350 pp., illus. $49.50
A classic, in-depth examination of the development, manufacture and fielding of the last wood-and-metal ("lock, stock, and barrel") battle rifle to be issued to U.S. troops.

War Baby!: The U.S. Caliber 30 Carbine, Volume I, by Larry Ruth, Collector Grade Publications, Toronto, Canada, 1992. 512 pp., illus. $69.95
Volume 1 of the in-depth story of the phenomenally popular U.S. caliber 30 carbine. Concentrates on design and production of the military 30 carbine during World War II.

War Baby Comes Home: The U.S. Caliber 30 Carbine, Volume 2, by Larry Ruth, Collector Grade Publications, Toronto, Canada, 1993. 386 pp., illus. $49.95
The triumphant competion of Larry Ruth's two-volume in-depth series on the most popular U.S. military small arm in history.

Winchester Model 52, Perfection in Design, The, by Herbert G. Houze, Krause Publications, Iola, WI, 1997. 192 pp., illus. $34.95
This book covers the complete story of this technically superior gun.

Winchester Model 94: The First 100 Years, The, by Robert C. Renneberg, Krause Publications, Iola, WI, 1991. 208 pp., illus. $34.95
Covers the design and evolution from the early years up to today.

Winchester Slide-Action Rifles, Volume I: Model 1890 and Model 1906 by Ned Schwing, Krause Publications, Iola, WI. 352 pp., illus. $39.95
Traces the history through word and picture in this chronolgy of the Model 1890 and 1906.

SHOTGUNS

Advanced Combat Shotgun: The Stress Fire Concept, by Massad Ayoob, Police Bookshelf, Concord, NH, 1993. 197 pp., illus. Paper covers. $11.95
Advanced combat shotgun fighting for police.

Best Guns, by Michael McIntosh, Countrysport Press, Selma, AL, 1999, revised edition. 418 pp. $45.00
Combines the best shotguns ever made in America with information on British and Continental makers.

Better Shot, The, by Ken Davies, Quiller Press, London, England, 1992. 136 pp., illus. $39.95
Step-by-step shotgun technique with Holland and Holland.

Big Shots; Edwardian Shooting Parties, The, by Jonathan Ruffer, Quiller Press, London, England, 1997 160pp. B & W illus. $24.95
A book about Edwardian shooting parties, now a former pastime and enjoyed by the selected few, who recall the hunting of pheasants. Foreword by HRH The Prince of Wales.

Boss & Co. Builders of the Best Guns Only, by Donald Dallas, Quiller Press, London, 1995. 262 pp., illustrated. $79.95
Large four colour plates, b/w photos, bibliography. The definitive history authorized by Boss & Co.

Browning Superposed: John M. Browning's Last Legacy, The, by Ned Schwing, Krause Publications, Iola, WI, 1996. 496 pp., illus. $49.95
An exclusive story of the man, the company and the best-selling over-and-under shotgun in North America.

Clay Target Handbook, by Jerry Meyer, Lyons & Buford, Publisher, New York, NY, 1993. 182 pp., illus. $22.95
Contains in-depth, how-to-do-it information on trap, skeet, sporting clays, international trap, international skeet and clay target games played around the country.

Clay Target Shooting, by Paul Bentley, A&C Black, London, England, 1987. 144 pp., illus. $25.00
Practical book on clay target shooting written by a very successful international competitor, providing valuable professional advice and instruction for shooters of all disciplines.

Cogswell & Harrison; Two Centuries of Gunmaking, by G. Cooley & J. Newton, Safari Press, Long Beach, CA, 2000. 128pp, 30 color photos, 100 b&w photos. $39.95
The authors have gathered a wealth of fascinating historical and technical material that will make the book indispensable, not only to many thousands of "Coggie" owners worldwide, but also to anyone interested in the general history of British gunmaking.

Collector's Guide to United States Combat Shotguns, A, by Bruce N. Canfield, Andrew Mowbray Inc., Publishers, Lincoln, RI, 1993. 184 pp., illus. Paper covers. $24.00
Full coverage of the combat shotgun, from the earliest examples to the Gulf War and beyond.

Combat Shotgun and Submachine Gun, "A Special Weapons Analysis" by Chuck Taylor, Paladin Press, Boulder, CO, 1997, soft cover, photos, 176 pp. $25.00
From one of America's top shooting instructors comes an analysis of two controversial, misunderstood and misemployed small arms. Hundreds of photos detail field-testing of both, basic and advanced training drills, tactical rules, gun accessories and modifications. Loading procedures, carrying and fighting positions and malfunction clearance drills are included to promote weapon effectiveness.

Defensive Shotgun, The, by Louis Awerbuck, S.W.A.T. Publications, Cornville, AZ, 1989. 77 pp., illus. Soft covers. $14.95
Cuts through the myths concerning the shotgun and its attendant ballistic effects.

Ducks Unlimited Guide to Shotgunning, The, by Don Zutz, Willow Creek Press, Minocqua, WI, 2000. 166 pg. Illustrated. $24.50
This book covers everything from the grand old guns of yesterday to todays best shotguns and loads, from the basic shotgun fit and function to expert advice on ballistics, chocks, and shooting techniques.

Finding the Extra Target, by Coach John R. Linn & Stephen A. Blumenthal, Shotgun Sports, Inc., Auburn, CA, 1989. 126 pp., illus. Paper covers. $14.95
The ultimate training guide for all the clay target sports.

Fine European Gunmakers: Best Continental European Gunmakers & Engravers, by M. Nobili. Long Beach, CA: Safari Press, 2002. 250 pages, illustrated in color. $69.95
Hundreds of books have been published about the British gun trade, but English speakers and publishers have largely ignored the European trade in fine guns until now! Many experts argue that Continental gunmakers produce guns equally as good or better than British makers. Marco Nobili's new work, Fine European Gunmakers, showcases the skills of the best craftsmen from continental Europe, and the author brings to life in words and pictures their finest sporting guns. The book covers the histories of the individual firms and looks at the guns they currently build, tracing the developments of their most influential models. Depicted with profuse color illustrations, it showcases the best guns ever made in Europe. All the greatest names are here, including Piotti, Beretta, Merkel, Kreighoff, Connecticut Shotgun, Perazzi, Hartmann & Weiss, Peter Hofer, Gamba, Fausti, Fanzoj, Lebeau & Courally, Fabbri and many others.

Fine Gunmaking: Double Shotguns, by Steven Dodd Hughes, Krause Publications Iola, WI, 1998. 167 pp., illustrated. $34.95
An in-depth look at the creation of fine shotguns.

Firearms Assembly/Disassembly, Part V: Shotguns, Revised Edition, The Gun Digest Book of, by J.B. Wood, DBI Books, a division of Krause Publications, Iola, WI, 1992. 480 pp., illus. Paper covers. $19.95
Covers 46 popular shotguns plus over 250 variants. The most comprehensive and professional presentation available to either hobbyist or gunsmith.

Fox "The Finest Gun in the World", A.H., revised and enlarged edition, by Michael McIntosh, Countrysport, Inc., New Albany, OH, 1995. 408 pp., illus. $49.00
The first detailed history of one of America's finest shotguns.

Game Shooting, by Robert Churchill, Countrysport Press, Selma, AL, 1998. 258 pp., illus. $30.00
The basis for every shotgun instructional technique devised and the foundation for all wingshooting and the game of sporting clays.

Greener Story, The, by Graham Greener, Safari Press, Long Beach, CA, 2000. 231pp, color and b&w illustrations. $69.95
The history of the Greener Gunmakers and their guns

Gun Digest Book of Sporting Clays, 2nd Edition, edited by Harold A. Murtz, Krause Publications, Iola, WI, 1999. 256 pp., illus. Paper covers. $21.95
A concise Gun Digest book that covers guns, ammo, chokes, targets and course layouts so you'll stay a step ahead.

Gun Review Book, The, by Michael McIntosh, Countrysport Press, Selman, AL, 1999. Paper covers. $19.95
Compiled here for the first time are McIntosh's popular gun reviews from *Shooting Sportsman; The Magazine of Wingshooting* and *Fine Shotguns.* The author traces the history of gunmakes, then examines, analyzes, and critique the fine shotguns of England, Continental Europe and the United States.

Heyday of the Shotgun, The, by David Baker, Safari Press, Inc., Huntington Beach, CA, 2000. 160 pp., illustrated. $39.95
The art of the gunmaker at the turn of the last century when British craftsmen brought forth the finest guns ever made.

House of Churchill, The, by Don Masters. Safari Press, Long Beach, CA, 2000. A limited edition of 1000 copies. Signed and numbered. In a slipcase. 512 pages, profuse color and b&w illustrations. $95.00
The world-renowned Churchill gunmakers was formed in 1891 and is one of the best known of all English gunmakers. Many guns have been made in London over the centuries, but few carry the cachet of a Churchill gun! Here is the colorful history of a company that has seen success and jubilation as well as drama and defeat. Through it all Churchill guns remain some of the most sought-after in the world. The reader will find in these pages the complete history as well as wonderfully entertaining anecdotes of the Churchill family and its colorful gunmaking members, including Edwin J. Churchill, who established the company, and Robert Churchill, who became known as an international gunmaker and ballistics expert. The history of the company and its guns is also thoroughly analyzed. There is detailed information on the glory years, the famous Churchill XXV gun, which was advocated by Robert Churchill but had its detractors, the difficult pre-WWII years, the Atkin, Grant, & Lang years, and the age of conglomerates. This marvelous work on the house of Churchill contains serial numbers and dates of manufacture of its guns from 1891 forward, price lists from 1895 onward, a complete listing of all craftsmen employed at the company, as well as the prices realized at the famous Dallas auction where the "last" production guns were sold. The treatment of all aspects of this gunmaker is so thorough that it contains details that will defy even the greatest expert! This massive work is well illustrated with hundreds of color and black and white photos, period brochures, and gun labels, and it includes dozens of charts, tables, appendices, and a detailed index. Written by Don Masters, a longtime Churchill employee, who is keeping the flame of Churchill alive.

Italian Gun, The, by Steve Smith & Laurie Morrow, wilderness Adventures, Gallatin Gateway, MT, 1997. 325 pp., illus. $49.95
The first book ever written entirely in English for American enthusiasts who own, aspire to own, or simply admire Italian guns.

Ithaca Featherlight Repeater; The Best Gun Going, The, by Walter C. Snyder, Southern Pines, NC, 1998. 300 pp., illus. $89.95
Describes the complete history of each model of the legendary Ithaca Model 37 and Model 87 Repeaters from their conception in 1930 throught 1997.

Ithaca Gun Company from the Beginning, The, by Walter C. Snyder, Cook & Uline Publishing Co., Southern Pines, NC, 2nd edition, 1999. 384 pp., illustrated in color and black and white. $90.00

The entire family of Ithaca Gun Company products is described along with new historical information and the serial number/date of manufacturing listing has been improved.

Little Trapshooting Book, The, by Frank Little, Shotgun Sports Magazine, Auburn, CA, 1994. 168 pp., illus. Paper covers. $19.95

Packed with know-how from one of the greatest trapshooters of all time.

Lock, Stock, and Barrel, by C. Adams & R. Braden, Safari Press, Huntington Beach, CA, 1996. 254 pp., illus. $24.95

The process of making a best grade English gun from a lump of steel and a walnut tree trunk to the ultimate product plus practical advise on consistent field shooting with a double gun.

Mental Training for the Shotgun Sports, by Michael J. Keyes, Shotgun Sports, Auburn, CA, 1996. 160 pp., illus. Paper covers. $27.95

The most comprehensive book ever published on what it takes to shoot winning scores at trap, Skeet and Sporting Clays.

Model 12, 1912-1964, The, by Dave Riffle, Dave Riffle, Ft. Meyers, FL, 1995. 274 pp., illus. $49.95

The story of the greatest hammerless repeating shotgun ever built.

More Shotguns and Shooting, by Michael McIntosh, Countrysport Books, Selma, AL, 1998. 256 pp., illustrated. $30.00

From specifics of shotguns to shooting your way out of a slump, it's McIntosh at his best.

Mossberg Shotguns, by Duncan Long, Delta Press, El Dorado, AR, 2000. 120 pp., illustrated. $24.95

This book contains a brief history of the company and it's founder, full coverage of the pump and semiautomatic shotguns, rare products and a care and maintenance section.

Mysteries of Shotgun Patterns, The, by George G. Oberfell and Charles E. Thompson, Oklahoma State University Press, Stillwater, OK, 1982. 164 pp., illus. Paper covers. $25.00

Shotgun ballistics for the hunter in non-technical language.

Parker Gun, The, by Larry Baer, Gun Room Press, Highland Park, NJ, 1993. 195 pages, illustrated with B & W and Color photos. $35.00

Covers in detail, production of all models on this classic gun. Many fine specimens from great collections are illustrated.

Parker Gun Identification & Serialization, by S.P. Fjestad, Minneapolis, MN: Blue Book Publications, 2002. 1st edition. Softcover. $34.95

This new 608-page publication is the only book that provides an easy reference for Parker shotguns manufactured between 1866-1942. Included is a comprehensive 46-page section on Parker identification, with over 100 detailed images depicting serialization location and explanation, various Parker grades, extra features, stock configurations, action types, and barrel identification.

Parker Story; Volumes 1 & 2, The, by Bill Mullins, "etal". The Double Gun Journal, East Jordan, MI, 2000. 1,025 pages of text and 1,500 color and monochrome illustrations. Hardbound in a gold-embossed cover. $295.00

The most complete and attractive "last word" on America's preeminent double gun maker. Includes tables showing the number of guns made by gauge, barrel length and special features for each grade.

Positive Shooting, by Michael Yardley, Safari Press, Huntington Beach, CA, 1995. 160 pp., illus. $30.00

This book will provide the shooter with a sound foundation from which to develop an effective, personal technique that can dramatically improve shooting performance.

Purdey Gun and Rifle Makers: The Definitive History, by Donald Dallas, Quiller Press, London 2000. 245 pages, illus. $100.00

245 Colour plates, b/w photos, ills, bibliography. The definitive history. A limited edition of 3,000 copies. Signed and Numbered. With a PURDEY book plate.

Reloading for Shotgunners, 4th Edition, by Kurt D. Fackler and M.L. McPherson, DBI Books, a division of Krause Publications, Iola, WI, 1997. 320 pp., illus. Paper covers. $19.95

Expanded reloading tables with over 11,000 loads. Bushing charts for every major press and component maker. All new presentation on all aspects of shotshell reloading by two of the top experts in the field.

Remington Double Shotguns, by Charles G. Semer, Denver, CO, 1997. 617 pp., illus. $60.00

This book deals with the entire production and all grades of double shotguns made by Remington during the period of their production 1873-1910.

75 Years with the Shotgun, by C.T. (Buck) Buckman, Valley Publ., Fresno, CA, 1974. 141 pp., illus. $10.00

An expert hunter and trapshooter shares experiences of a lifetime.

Shotgun Encyclopedia, The, by John Taylor, Safari Press, Inc., Huntington Beach, CA, 2000. 260 pp., illustrated. $34.95

A comprehensive reference work on all aspects of shotguns and shotgun shooting.

Shotgun — A Shooting Instructor's Handbook, The, by Michael Yardley. Long Beach, CA: Safari Press, 2002. 272pp, b&w photos, line drawings. Hardcover. $29.95

This is one of the very few books intended to be read by shooting instructors and other advanced shots. In setting down a complete (but notably flexible) teaching system, Michael Yardley puts the greatest emphasis on safety, and he discusses the problems inherent in shooting because of individual fallibility. He sets out a "layer principal"--a series of checks and procedures to be used at all times--that provides a positive framework from which to build a solid, secure technique. After considering game- and clay-shooting safety comprehensively, he goes on to consider gun condition and proof (vital subjects for the instructor), and he explores shooting vision in unprecedented depth. In further chapters he analyzes the components and development of shooting technique by pointing out the styles of great instructors such as Percy Stanbury and Robert Churchill as well as the shooting techniques of some of the best-known modern competitors. There is practical advice on gunfit and on gun and cartridge selection.

Shotgun: History and Development, The, by Geoffrey Boothroyd, Safari Press, Huntington Beach, CA, 1995. 240 pp., illus. $35.00

The first volume in a series that traces the development of the British shotgun from the 17th century onward.

Shotgun Handbook, The, by Mike George, The Croswood Press, London, England, 1999. 128 pp., illus. $35.00

For all shotgun enthusiasts, this detailed guide ranges from design and selection of a gun to adjustment, cleaning, and maintenance.

Shotgun Stuff, by Don Zutz, Shotgun Sports, Inc., Auburn, CA, 1991. 172 pp., illus. Paper covers. $19.95

This book gives shotgunners all the "stuff" they need to achieve better performance and get more enjoyment from their favorite smoothbore.

Shotgun Technicana, by McIntosh, Michael and David Trevallion. Camden, ME: Down East Books, 2002. Everything you wanted to know about fine double shotguns by the nations formost experts. 272 pages, with 100 illustrations. Hardcover. $28.00

Shotgunning: The Art and the Science, by Bob Brister, Winchester Press, Piscataway, NJ, 1976. 321 pp., illus. $18.95

Hundreds of specific tips and truly novel techniques to improve the field and target shooting of every shotgunner.

Shotgunning Trends in Transition, by Don Zutz, Wolfe Publishing Co., Prescott, AZ, 1990. 314 pp., illus. $29.50

This book updates American shotgunning from post WWII to present.

Shotguns and Cartridges for Game and Clays, by Gough Thomas, edited by Nigel Brown, A & C Black, Ltd., Cambs, England, 1989. 256 pp., illus. Soft covers. $24.95

Gough Thomas' well-known and respected book for game and clay pigeon shooters in a thoroughly up-dated edition.

Shotguns and Gunsmiths: The Vintage Years, by Geoffrey Boothroyd, Safari Press, Huntington Beach, CA, 1995. 240 pp., illus. $35.00

A fascinating insight into the lives and skilled work of gunsmiths who helped develop the British shotgun during the Victorian and Edwardian eras.

Shotguns and Shooting, by Michael McIntosh, Countrysport Press, New Albany, OH, 1995. 258 pp., illus. $30.00

The art of guns and gunmaking, this book is a celebration no lover of fine doubles should miss.

Shotguns for Wingshooting, by John Barsness, DBI Books, a division of Krause Publications, Inc., Iola, WI, 1999. 208 pp., illustrated. $49.95

Detailed information on all styles of shotgun. How to select the correct ammunition for specific hunting applications.

Spanish Best: The Fine Shotguns of Spain, 2nd Ed, by Terry Wieland, Down East Books, Traverse City, MI, 2001. 364 pp., illus. $48.00

A practical source of information for owners of Spanish shotguns and a guide for those considering buying a used shotgun.

Sporting Clay Handbook, The, by Jerry Meyer, Lyons and Burford Publishers, New York, NY, 1990. 140 pp., illus. Soft covers. $17.95

Introduction to the fastest growing, and most exciting, gun game in America.

Streetsweepers, "The Complete Book of Combat Shotguns", by Duncan Long, Paladin Press, Boulder, CO,1997, soft cover, 63 photos, illus., appendices, 160 pp. $24.95

Streetsweepers is the newest, most comprehensive book out on combat shotguns, covering single- and double-barreled, slide-action, semi-auto and rotary cylinder shotguns, plus a chapter on grenade launchers you can mount on your weapon and info about shotgun models not yet on the market. Noted gun writer Duncan Long also advises on which ammo to use, accessories and combat shotgun tactics.

Tactical Shotgun, The, by Gabriel Suzrez, Paladin Press, Boulder, CO, 1996. 232 pp., illus. Paper covers. $25.00

The best techniques and tactics for employing the shotgun in personal combat.

Trap & Skeet Shooting, 4th Edition, by Chris Christian, DBI Books, a division of Krause Publications, Iola, WI, 1994. 288 pp., illus. Paper covers. $21.95

A detailed look at the contemporary world of Trap, Skeet and Sporting Clays.

Trapshooting is a Game of Opposites, by Dick Bennett, Shotgun Sports, Inc., Auburn, CA, 1996. 129 pp., illus. Paper covers. $19.95

Discover everything you need to know about shooting trap like the pros.

Uncle Dan Lefever, Master Gunmaker: Guns of Lasting Fame, by Robert W. Elliott. Privately Printed, 2002. Profusely illustrated with black and white photos, with 45-page color section. 239 pages. Hardcover. $60.00

Handsomely bound, with gilt titled spine and top cover.

U.S. Shotguns, All Types, reprint of TM9-285, Desert Publications, Cornville, AZ, 1987. 257 pp., illus. Paper covers. $16.95

Covers operation, assembly and disassembly of nine shotguns used by the U.S. armed forces.

U.S. Winchester Trench and Riot Guns and Other U.S. Military Combat Shotguns, by Joe Poyer, North Cape Publications, Tustin, CA, 1992. 124 pp., illus. Paper covers. $15.95

A detailed history of the use of military shotguns, and the acquisition procedures used by the U.S. Army's Ordnance Department in both World Wars.

Winchester Model Twelve, The, by George Madis, David Madis, Dallas, TX, 1984. 176 pp., illus. $26.95

A definitive work on this famous American shotgun.

Winchester Model 42, The, by Ned Schwing, Krause Pub., Iola, WI, 1990. 160 pp., illus. $34.95

Behind-the-scenes story of the model 42's invention and its early development. Production totals and manufacturing dates; reference work.

Winchester Shotguns and Shotshells, by Ron Stadt, Krause Pub., Iola, WI. 288 pp., illus. $34.95

Must-have for Winchester collectors of shotguns manufactured through 1961.

Winchester's Finest, the Model 21, by Ned Schwing, Krause Publications, Iola, WI, 1990. 360 pp., illus. $49.95

The classic beauty and the interesting history of the Model 21 Winchester shotgun.

World's Fighting Shotguns, The, by Thomas F. Swearengen, T.B.N. Enterprises, Alexandria, VA, 1998. 500 pp., illus. $39.95

The complete military and police reference work from the shotgun's inception to date, with up-to-date developments.

ARMS ASSOCIATIONS

UNITED STATES

ALABAMA
Alabama Gun Collectors Assn.
Secretary, P.O. Box 70965, Tuscaloosa, AL 35407

ALASKA
Alaska Gun Collectors Assn., Inc.
C.W. Floyd, Pres., 5240 Little Tree, Anchorage, AK 99507

ARIZONA
Arizona Arms Assn.
Don DeBusk, President, 4837 Bryce Ave., Glendale, AZ 85301

CALIFORNIA
California Cartridge Collectors Assn.
Rick Montgomery, 1729 Christina, Stockton, CA 95204/209-463-7216 evs.
California Waterfowl Assn.
4630 Northgate Blvd., #150, Sacramento, CA 95834
Greater Calif. Arms & Collectors Assn.
Donald L. Bullock, 8291 Carburton St., Long Beach, CA 90808-3302
Los Angeles Gun Ctg. Collectors Assn.
F.H. Ruffra, 20810 Amie Ave., Apt. #9, Torrance, CA 90503
Stock Gun Players Assn.
6038 Appian Way, Long Beach, CA, 90803

COLORADO
Colorado Gun Collectors Assn.
L.E.(Bud) Greenwald, 2553 S. Quitman St., Denver, CO 80219/303-935-3850
Rocky Mountain Cartridge Collectors Assn.
John Roth, P.O. Box 757, Conifer, CO 80433

CONNECTICUT
Ye Connecticut Gun Guild, Inc.
Dick Fraser, P.O. Box 425, Windsor, CT 06095

FLORIDA
Unified Sportsmen of Florida
P.O. Box 6565, Tallahassee, FL 32314

GEORGIA
Georgia Arms Collectors Assn., Inc.
Michael Kindberg, President, P.O. Box 277, Alpharetta, GA 30239-0277

ILLINOIS
Illinois State Rifle Assn.
P.O. Box 637, Chatsworth, IL 60921
Mississippi Valley Gun & Cartridge Coll. Assn.
Bob Filbert, P.O. Box 61, Port Byron, IL 61275/309-523-2593
Sauk Trail Gun Collectors
Gordell M. Matson, P.O. Box 1113, Milan, IL 61264
Wabash Valley Gun Collectors Assn., Inc.
Roger L. Dorsett, 2601 Willow Rd., Urbana, IL 61801/217-384-7302

INDIANA
Indiana State Rifle & Pistol Assn.
Thos. Glancy, P.O. Box 552, Chesterton, IN 46304
Southern Indiana Gun Collectors Assn., Inc.
Sheila McClary, 309 W. Monroe St., Boonville, IN 47601/812-897-3742

IOWA
Beaver Creek Plainsmen Inc.
Steve Murphy, Secy., P.O. Box 298, Bondurant, IA 50035
Central States Gun Collectors Assn.
Dennis Greischar, Box 841, Mason City, IA 50402-0841

KANSAS
Kansas Cartridge Collectors Assn.
Bob Linder, Box 84, Plainville, KS 67663

KENTUCKY
Kentuckiana Arms Collectors Assn.
Charles Billips, President, Box 1776, Louisville, KY 40201
Kentucky Gun Collectors Assn., Inc.
Ruth Johnson, Box 64, Owensboro, KY 42302/502-729-4197

LOUISIANA
Washitaw River Renegades
Sandra Rushing, P.O. Box 256, Main St., Grayson, LA 71435

MARYLAND
Baltimore Antique Arms Assn.
Mr. Cillo, 1034 Main St., Darlington, MD 21304

MASSACHUSETTS
Bay Colony Weapons Collectors, Inc.
John Brandt, Box 111, Hingham, MA 02043
Massachusetts Arms Collectors
Bruce E. Skinner, P.O. Box 31, No. Carver, MA 02355/508-866-5259

MICHIGAN
Association for the Study and Research of .22 Caliber Rimfire Cartridges
George Kass, 4512 Nakoma Dr., Okemos, MI 48864

MINNESOTA
Sioux Empire Cartridge Collectors Assn.
Bob Cameron, 14597 Glendale Ave. SE, Prior Lake, MN 55372

MISSISSIPPI
Mississippi Gun Collectors Assn.
Jack E. Swinney, P.O. Box 16323, Hattiesburg, MS 39402

MISSOURI
Greater St. Louis Cartridge Collectors Assn.
Don MacChesney, 634 Scottsdale Rd., Kirkwood, MO 63122-1109
Mineral Belt Gun Collectors Assn.
D.F. Saunders, 1110 Cleveland Ave., Monett, MO 65708
Missouri Valley Arms Collectors Assn., Inc.
L.P Brammer II, Membership Secy., P.O. Box 33033, Kansas City, MO 64114

MONTANA
Montana Arms Collectors Assn.
Dean E. Yearout, Sr., Exec. Secy., 1516 21st Ave. S., Great Falls, MT 59405
Weapons Collectors Society of Montana
R.G. Schipf, Ex. Secy., 3100 Bancroft St., Missoula, MT 59801/406-728-2995

NEBRASKA
Nebraska Cartridge Collectors Club
Gary Muckel, P.O. Box 84442, Lincoln, NE 68501

NEW HAMPSHIRE
New Hampshire Arms Collectors, Inc.
James Stamatelos, Secy., P.O. Box 5, Cambridge, MA 02139

NEW JERSEY
Englishtown Benchrest Shooters Assn.
Michael Toth, 64 Cooke Ave., Carteret, NJ 07008
Jersey Shore Antique Arms Collectors
Joe Sisia, P.O. Box 100, Bayville, NJ 08721-0100
New Jersey Arms Collectors Club, Inc.
Angus Laidlaw, Vice President, 230 Valley Rd., Montclair, NJ 07042/201-746-0939; e-mail: acclaidlaw@juno.com

NEW YORK
Iroquois Arms Collectors Assn.
Bonnie Robinson, Show Secy., P.O. Box 142, Ransomville, NY 14131/716-791-4096
Mid-State Arms Coll. & Shooters Club
Jack Ackerman, 24 S. Mountain Terr., Binghamton, NY 13903

NORTH CAROLINA
North Carolina Gun Collectors Assn.
Jerry Ledford, 3231-7th St. Dr. NE, Hickory, NC 28601

OHIO
Ohio Gun Collectors Assn.
P.O. Box 9007, Maumee, OH 43537-9007/419-897-0861; Fax:419-897-0860
Shotshell Historical and Collectors Society
Madeline Bruemmer, 3886 Dawley Rd., Ravenna, OH 44266
The Stark Gun Collectors, Inc.
William I. Gann, 5666 Waynesburg Dr., Waynesburg, OH 44688

OREGON
Oregon Arms Collectors Assn., Inc.
Phil Bailey, P.O. Box 13000-A, Portland, OR 97213-0017/503-281-6864; off.:503-281-0918
Oregon Cartridge Collectors Assn.
Boyd Northrup, P.O. Box 285, Rhododendron, OR 97049

PENNSYLVANIA
Presque Isle Gun Collectors Assn.
James Welch, 156 E. 37 St., Erie, PA 16504

SOUTH CAROLINA
Belton Gun Club, Inc.
Attn. Secretary, P.O. Box 126, Belton, SC 29627/864-369-6767
Gun Owners of South Carolina
Membership Div.: William Strozier, Secretary, P.O. Box 70, Johns Island, SC 29457-0070/803-762-3240; Fax:803-795-0711; e-mail:76053.222@compuserve.com

SOUTH DAKOTA
Dakota Territory Gun Coll. Assn., Inc.
Curt Carter, Castlewood, SD 57223

TENNESSEE
Smoky Mountain Gun Coll. Assn., Inc.
Hugh W. Yabro, President, P.O. Box 23225, Knoxville, TN 37933

Tennessee Gun Collectors Assn., Inc.
M.H. Parks, 3556 Pleasant Valley Rd., Nashville, TN 37204-3419

TEXAS
Houston Gun Collectors Assn., Inc.
P.O. Box 741429, Houston, TX 77274-1429
Texas Gun Collectors Assn.
Bob Eder, Pres., P.O. Box 12067, El Paso, TX 79913/915-584-8183
Texas State Rifle Assn.
1131 Rockingham Dr., Suite 101, Richardson, TX 75080-4326

VIRGINIA
Virginia Gun Collectors Assn., Inc.
Addison Hurst, Secy., 38802 Charlestown Height, Waterford, VA 20197/540-882-3543

WASHINGTON
Association of Cartridge Collectors on the Pacific Northwest
Robert Jardin, 14214 Meadowlark Drive KPN, Gig Harbor, WA 98329
Washington Arms Collectors, Inc.
Joyce Boss, P.O. Box 389, Renton, WA, 98057-0389/206-255-8410

WISCONSIN
Great Lakes Arms Collectors Assn., Inc.
Edward C. Warnke, 2913 Woodridge Lane, Waukesha, WI 53188
Wisconsin Gun Collectors Assn., Inc.
Lulita Zellmer, P.O. Box 181, Sussex, WI 53089

WYOMING
Wyoming Weapons Collectors
P.O. Box 284, Laramie, WY 82073/307-745-4652 or 745-9530

NATIONAL ORGANIZATIONS

Amateur Trapshooting Assn.
David D. Bopp, Exec. Director, 601 W. National Rd., Vandalia, OH 45377/937-898-4638; Fax:937-898-5472
American Airgun Field Target Assn.
5911 Cherokee Ave., Tampa, FL 33604
American Coon Hunters Assn.
Opal Johnston, P.O. Cadet, Route 1, Box 492, Old Mines, MO 63630
American Custom Gunmakers Guild
Jan Billeb, Exec. Director, 22 Vista View Drive, Cody, WY 82414-9606 (307) 587-4297 (phone/fax). Email: acgg@acgg.org Website: www.acgg.org
American Defense Preparedness Assn.
Two Colonial Place, 2101 Wilson Blvd., Suite 400, Arlington, VA 22201-3061
American Paintball League
P.O. Box 3561, Johnson City, TN 37602/800-541-9169
American Pistolsmiths Guild
Alex B. Hamilton, Pres., 1449 Blue Crest Lane, San Antonio, TX 78232/210-494-3063
American Police Pistol & Rifle Assn.
3801 Biscayne Blvd., Miami, FL 33137

American Single Shot Rifle Assn.
Charles Kriegel, Secy., 1346C Whispering Woods Drive, West Carrollton OH 45449/937-866-9064. Website: www.assra.com
American Society of Arms Collectors
George E. Weatherly, P.O. Box 2567, Waxahachie, TX 75165
American Tactical Shooting Assn.(A.T.S.A.)
c/o Skip Gochenour, 2600 N. Third St., Harrisburg, PA 17110/717-233-0402; Fax:717-233-5340
Association of Firearm and Tool Mark Examiners
Lannie G. Emanuel, Secy., Southwest Institute of Forensic Sciences, P.O. Box 35728, Dallas, TX 75235/214-920-5979; Fax:214-920-5928; Membership Secy., Ann D. Jones, VA Div. of Forensic Science, P.O. Box 999, Richmond, VA 23208/804-786-4706; Fax:804-371-8328
Boone & Crockett Club
250 Station Dr., Missoula, MT 59801-2753
Browning Collectors Assn.
Secretary:Scherrie L. Brennac, 2749 Keith Dr., Villa Ridge, MO 63089/314-742-0571
The Cast Bullet Assn., Inc.
Ralland J. Fortier, Editor, 4103 Foxcraft Dr., Traverse City, MI 49684
Citizens Committee for the Right to Keep and Bear Arms
Natl. Hq., Liberty Park, 12500 NE Tenth Pl., Bellevue, WA 98005
Colt Collectors Assn.
25000 Highland Way, Los Gatos, CA 95030/408-353-2658
Ducks Unlimited, Inc.
Natl. Headquarters, One Waterfowl Way, Memphis, TN 38120/901-758-3937
Fifty Caliber Shooters Assn.
PO Box 111, Monroe UT 84754-0111/435-527-9245; Fax: 435-527-0948
Firearms Coalition/Neal Knox Associates
Box 6537, Silver Spring, MD 20906/301-871-3006
Firearms Engravers Guild of America
Rex C. Pedersen, Secy., 511 N. Rath Ave., Lundington, MI 49431/616-845-7695(Phone and Fax)
Foundation for North American Wild Sheep
720 Allen Ave., Cody, WY 82414-3402/web site: http://iigi.com/os/non/fnaws/fnaws.htm; e-mail: fnaws@wyoming.com
Freedom Arms Collectors Assn.
P.O. Box 160302, Miami, FL 33116-0302
Garand Collectors Assn.
P.O. Box 181, Richmond, KY 40475
German Gun Collectors Assn. U.S.A.
PO Box 385, Meriden, NH 03770/603-469-3438 Fax: 603-469-3800 Website: www.germanguns.com; email: jaeger@valley.net
Glock Collectors Assn.
PO Box 1063, Maryland Heights, MO 63043/314-878-2061 Website: www.glockcollectors.com

ARMS ASSOCIATIONS

Glock Shooting Sports Foundation
PO Box 309, Smyrna, GA 30081
770-432-1202 Website:
www.gssfonline.com
Golden Eagle Collectors Assn. (G.E.C.A.)
Chris Showler, 11144 Slate Creek Rd., Grass Valley, CA 95945
Gun Owners of America
8001 Forbes Place, Suite 102, Springfield, VA 22151/703-321-8585
Handgun Hunters International
J.D. Jones, Director, P.O. Box 357 MAG, Bloomingdale, OH 43910
Harrington & Richardson Gun Coll. Assn.
George L. Cardet, 330 S.W. 27th Ave., Suite 603, Miami, FL 33135
High Standard Collectors' Assn.
John J. Stimson, Jr., Pres., 540 W. 92nd St., Indianapolis, IN 46260
Website: www.highstandard.org
Hopkins & Allen Arms & Memorabilia Society (HAAMS)
P.O. Box 187, 1309 Pamela Circle, Delphos, OH 45833
International Ammunition Association, Inc.
C.R. Punnett, Secy., 8 Hillock Lane, Chadds Ford, PA 19317/610-358-1285;Fax:610-358-1560
International Benchrest Shooters
Joan Borden, RR1, Box 250BB, Springville, PA 18844/717-965-2366
International Blackpowder Hunting Assn.
P.O. Box 1180, Glenrock, WY 82637/307-436-9817
IHMSA (Intl. Handgun Metallic Silhouette Assn.)
PO Box 368, Burlington, IA 52601
Website: www.ihmsa.org
International Society of Mauser Arms Collectors
Michael Kindberg, Pres., P.O. Box 277, Alpharetta, GA 30239-0277
Jews for the Preservation of Firearms Ownership (JPFO) 501(c)(3)
2872 S. Wentworth Ave., Milwaukee, WI 53207/414-769-0760; Fax:414-483-8435
The Mannlicher Collectors Assn.
Membership Office: P.O. Box 1249, The Dalles, Oregon 97058
Marlin Firearms Collectors Assn., Ltd.
Dick Paterson, Secy., 407 Lincoln Bldg., 44 Main St., Champaign, IL 61820
Merwin Hulbert Association,
2503 Kentwood Ct., High Point, NC 27265
Miniature Arms Collectors/Makers Society, Ltd.
Ralph Koebbeman, Pres., 4910 Kilburn Ave., Rockford, IL 61101/815-964-2569
M1 Carbine Collectors Assn. (M1-CCA)
623 Apaloosa Ln., Gardnerville, NV 89410-7840
National Association of Buckskinners (NAB)
Territorial Dispatch—1800s Historical Publication, 4701 Marion St., Suite 324, Livestock Exchange Bldg., Denver, CO 80216/303-297-9671
The National Association of Derringer Collectors
P.O. Box 20572, San Jose, CA 95160

National Assn. of Federally Licensed Firearms Dealers
Andrew Molchan, 2455 E. Sunrise, Ft. Lauderdale, FL 33304
National Association to Keep and Bear Arms
P.O. Box 78336, Seattle, WA 98178
National Automatic Pistol Collectors Assn.
Tom Knox, P.O. Box 15738, Tower Grove Station, St. Louis, MO 63163
National Bench Rest Shooters Assn., Inc.
Pat Ferrell, 2835 Guilford Lane, Oklahoma City, OK 73120-4404/405-842-9585; Fax: 405-842-9575
National Muzzle Loading Rifle Assn.
Box 67, Friendship, IN 47021 / 812-667-5131. Website: www.nmlra.org and nmlra.org
National Professional Paintball League (NPPL)
540 Main St., Mount Kisco, NY 10549/914-241-7400
National Reloading Manufacturers Assn.
One Centerpointe Dr., Suite 300, Lake Oswego, OR 97035
National Rifle Assn. of America
11250 Waples Mill Rd., Fairfax, VA 22030 / 703-267-1000. Website: www.nra.org
National Shooting Sports Foundation, Inc.
Robert T. Delfay, President, Flintlock Ridge Office Center, 11 Mile Hill Rd., Newtown, CT 06470-2359/203-426-1320; FAX: 203-426-1087
National Skeet Shooting Assn.
Dan Snyuder, Director, 5931 Roft Road, San Antonio, TX 78253-9261/800-877-5338. Website: nssa-nsca.com
National Sporting Clays Association
Ann Myers, Director, 5931 Roft Road, San Antonio, TX 78253-9261/800-877-5338. Website: nssa-nsca.com
National Wild Turkey Federation, Inc.
P.O. Box 530, 770 Augusta Rd., Edgefield, SC 29824
North American Hunting Club
P.O. Box 3401, Minnetonka, MN 55343/612-936-9333; Fax: 612-936-9755
North American Paintball Referees Association (NAPRA)
584 Cestaric Dr., Milpitas, CA 95035
North-South Skirmish Assn., Inc.
Stevan F. Meserve, Exec. Secretary, 507 N. Brighton Court, Sterling, VA 20164-3919
Old West Shooter's Association
712 James Street, Hazel TX 76020 817-444-2049
Remington Society of America
Gordon Fosburg, Secretary, 11900 North Brinton Road, Lake, MI 48623
Rocky Mountain Elk Foundation
P.O. Box 8249, Missoula, MT 59807-8249/406-523-4500;Fax: 406-523-4581
Website: www.rmef.org
Ruger Collector's Assn., Inc.
P.O. Box 240, Greens Farms, CT 06436
Safari Club International
4800 W. Gates Pass Rd., Tucson, AZ 85745/520-620-1220

Sako Collectors Assn., Inc.
Jim Lutes, 202 N. Locust, Whitewater, KS 67154
Second Amendment Foundation
James Madison Building, 12500 NE 10th Pl., Bellevue, WA 98005
Single Action Shooting Society (SASS)
23255-A La Palma Avenue, Yorba Linda, CA 92887/714-694-1800; FAX: 714-694-1815/email: sasseot@aol.com Website: www.sassnet.com
Smith & Wesson Collectors Assn.
Cally Pletl, Admin. Asst.,PO Box 444, Afton, NY 13730
The Society of American Bayonet Collectors
P.O. Box 234, East Islip, NY 11730-0234
Southern California Schuetzen Society
Dean Lillard, 34657 Ave. E., Yucaipa, CA 92399
Sporting Arms and Ammunition Manufacturers' Institute (SAAMI)
Flintlock Ridge Office Center, 11 Mile Hill Rd., Newtown, CT 06470-2359/203-426-4358; FAX: 203-426-1087
Sporting Clays of America (SCA)
Ron L. Blosser, Pres., 9257 Buckeye Rd., Sugar Grove, OH 43155-9632/614-746-8334; Fax: 614-746-8605
Steel Challenge
23234 Via Barra, Valencia CA 91355 Website: www.steelchallenge.com
The Thompson/Center Assn.
Joe Wright, President, Box 792, Northboro, MA 01532/508-845-6960
U.S. Practical Shooting Assn./IPSC
Dave Thomas, P.O. Box 811, Sedro Woolley, WA 98284/360-855-2245 Website: www.uspsa.org
U.S. Revolver Assn.
Brian J. Barer, 40 Larchmont Ave., Taunton, MA 02780/508-824-4836
U.S. A. Shooting
U.S. Olympic Shooting Center, One Olympic Plaza, Colorado Springs, CO 80909/719-578-4670. Website: wwwusashooting.org
The Varmint Hunters Assn., Inc.
Box 759, Pierre, SD 57501/Member Services 800-528-4868
Weatherby Collectors Assn., Inc.
P.O. Box 478, Pacific, MO 63069 Website: www.weatherbycollectors.com Email: WCAsecretary@aol.com
The Wildcatters
P.O. Box 170, Greenville, WI 54942
Winchester Arms Collectors Assn.
P.O. Box 230, Brownsboro, TX 75756/903-852-4027
The Women's Shooting Sports Foundation (WSSF)
4620 Edison Avenue, Ste. C, Colorado Springs, CO 80915/719-638-1299; FAX: 719-638-1271/email: wssf@worldnet.att.net

ARGENTINA

Asociacion Argentina de Coleccionistas de Armes y Municiones
Castilla de Correos No. 28, Succursal I B, 1401 Buenos Aires, Republica Argentina

AUSTRALIA

Antique & Historical Arms Collectors of Australia
P.O. Box 5654, GCMC Queensland 9726, Australia
The Arms Collector's Guild of Queensland
Ian Skennerton, P.O. Box 433, Ashmore City 4214, Queensland, Australia
Australian Cartridge Collectors Assn., Inc.
Bob Bennett, 126 Landscape Dr., E. Doncaster 3109, Victoria, Australia
Sporting Shooters Assn. of Australia, Inc.
P.O. Box 2066, Kent Town, SA 5071, Australia

CANADA

ALBERTA
Canadian Historical Arms Society
P.O. Box 901, Edmonton, Alb., Canada T5J 2L8
National Firearms Assn.
Natl. Hq: P.O. Box 1779, Edmonton, Alb., Canada T5J 2P1

BRITISH COLUMBIA
The Historical Arms Collectors of B.C. (Canada)
Harry Moon, Pres., P.O. Box 50117, South Slope RPO, Burnaby, BC V5J 5G3, Canada/604-438-0950; Fax:604-277-3646

ONTARIO
Association of Canadian Cartridge Collectors
Monica Wright, RR 1, Millgrove, ON, LOR IVO, Canada
Tri-County Antique Arms Fair
P.O. Box 122, RR #1, North Lancaster, Ont., Canada K0C 1Z0

EUROPE

BELGIUM
European Cartridge Research Assn.
Graham Irving, 21 Rue Schaltin, 4900 Spa, Belgium/32.87.77.43.40; Fax:32.87.77.27.51

CZECHOSLOVAKIA
Spolecnost Pro Studium Naboju (Czech Cartridge Research Assn.)
JUDr. Jaroslav Bubak, Pod Homolko 1439, 26601 Beroun 2, Czech Republic

DENMARK
Aquila Dansk Jagtpatron Historic Forening (Danish Historical Cartridge Collectors Club)
Steen Elgaard Møller, Ulriksdalsvej 7, 4840 Nr. Alslev, Denmark 10045-53846218;Fax:00455384 6209

ENGLAND
Arms and Armour Society
Hon. Secretary A. Dove, P.O. Box 10232, London, 5W19 2ZD, England
Dutch Paintball Federation
Aceville Publ., Castle House 97 High Street, Colchester, Essex C01 1TH, England/011-44-206-564840
European Paintball Sports Foundation
c/o Aceville Publ., Castle House 97 High St., Colchester, Essex, C01 1TH, England
Historical Breechloading Smallarms Assn.
D.J. Penn M.A., Secy., P.O. Box

12778, London SE1 6BX, England. Journal and newsletter are $23 a yr., including airmail.
National Rifle Assn.
(Great Britain) Bisley Camp, Brookwood, Woking Surrey GU24 OPB, England/01483.797777; Fax: 014730686275
United Kingdom Cartridge Club
Ian Southgate, 20 Millfield, Elmley Castle, Nr. Pershore, Worcestershire, WR10 3HR, England

FRANCE
STAC-Western Co.
3 Ave. Paul Doumer (N.311); 78360 Montesson, France/01.30.53-43-65; Fax: 01.30.53.19.10

GERMANY
Bund Deutscher Sportschützen e.v. (BDS)
Borsigallee 10, 53125 Bonn 1, Germany
Deutscher Schützenbund
Lahnstrasse 120, 65195 Wiesbaden, Germany

SPAIN
Asociacion Espanola de Colleccionistas de Cartuchos (A.E.C.C.)
Secretary: Apdo. Correos No. 1086, 2880-Alcala de Henares (Madrid), Spain. President: Apdo. Correos No. 682, 50080 Zaragoza, Spain

SWEDEN
Scandinavian Ammunition Research Assn.
c/o Morten Stoen, Annerudstubben 3, N-1383 Asker, Norway

NEW ZEALAND
New Zealand Cartridge Collectors Club
Terry Castle, 70 Tiraumea Dr., Pakuranga, Auckland, New Zealand
New Zealand Deerstalkers Assn.
P.O. Box 6514 TE ARO, Wellington, New Zealand

SOUTH AFRICA
Historical Firearms Soc. of South Africa
P.O. Box 145, 7725 Newlands, Republic of South Africa
Republic of South Africa Cartridge Collectors Assn.
Arno Klee, 20 Eugene St., Malanshof Randburg, Gauteng 2194, Republic of South Africa
S.A.A.C.A. (Southern Africa Arms and Ammunition Assn.)
Gauteng office: P.O. Box 7597, Weltevreden Park, 1715, Republic of South Africa/011-679-1151; Fax: 011-679-1131; e-mail: saaaca@iafrica.com. Kwa-Zulu Natal office: P.O. Box 4065, Northway, Kwazulu-Natal 4065, Republic of South Africa
SAGA (S.A. Gunowners' Assn.)
P.O. Box 35203, Northway, Kwazulu-Natal 4065, Republic of South Africa

2004
GUN DIGEST
DIRECTORY OF THE
ARMS TRADE

The **Product Directory** contains 84 product categories. The **Manufacturer's Directory** alphabetically lists the manufacturers with their addresses, phone numbers, FAX numbers and Internet addresses, if available.

DIRECTORY OF THE ARMS TRADE INDEX

DIRECTORY

AMMUNITION COMPONENTS, SHOTSHELL

A.W. Peterson Gun Shop, Inc.
Ballistic Product, Inc.
Blount, Inc., Sporting Equipment Div.
CCI Ammunition ATK
Cheddite, France S.A.
Claybuster Wads & Harvester Bullets
Garcia National Gun Traders, Inc.
Peterson Gun Shop, Inc., A.W.
Precision Reloading, Inc.
Ravell Ltd.
Tar-Hunt Custom Rifles, Inc.
Vitt/Boos

AMMUNITION COMPONENTS-- BULLETS, POWDER, PRIMERS, CASES

A.W. Peterson Gun Shop, Inc.
Acadian Ballistic Specialties
Accuracy Unlimited
Accurate Arms Co., Inc.
Action Bullets & Alloy Inc.
ADCO Sales, Inc.
Alaska Bullet Works, Inc.
Alliant Techsystems Smokeless Powder Group
Allred Bullet Co.
Alpha LaFranck Enterprises
American Products, Inc.
Arizona Ammunition, Inc.
Armfield Custom Bullets
A-Square Co.
Atlantic Rose, Inc.
Baer's Hollows
Ballard Rifle & Cartridge Co., LLC
Barnes
Barnes Bullets, Inc.
Beartooth Bullets
Bell Reloading, Inc.
Berger Bullets Ltd.
Berry's Mfg., Inc.
Big Bore Bullets of Alaska
Big Bore Express
Bitterroot Bullet Co.
Black Belt Bullets (See Big Bore Express)
Black Hills Shooters Supply
Black Powder Products
Blount, Inc., Sporting Equipment Div.
Blue Mountain Bullets
Brenneke GmbH
Briese Bullet Co., Inc.
Brown Co., E. Arthur
Brown Dog Ent.
BRP, Inc. High Performance Cast Bullets
Buck Stix-SOS Products Co.
Buckeye Custom Bullets
Buckskin Bullet Co.
Buffalo Arms Co.
Buffalo Bullet Co., Inc.
Buffalo Rock Shooters Supply
Bullseye Bullets
Bull-X, Inc.
Butler Enterprises
Cambos Outdoorsman
Canyon Cartridge Corp.
Cascade Bullet Co., Inc.
Cast Performance Bullet Company
Casull Arms Corp.
CCI Ammunition ATK
Champion's Choice, Inc.
Cheddite, France S.A.
CheVron Bullets
Chuck's Gun Shop
Clean Shot Technologies
Competitor Corp., Inc.
Cook Engineering Service

Corbin Mfg. & Supply, Inc.
Cummings Bullets
Curtis Cast Bullets
Curtis Gun Shop (See Curtis Cast Bullets)
Custom Bullets by Hoffman
Dakota Arms, Inc.
Davide Pedersoli and Co.
DKT, Inc.
Dohring Bullets
Eichelberger Bullets, Wm.
Federal Cartridge Co.
Fiocchi of America, Inc.
Forkin, Ben (See Belt MTN Arms)
Forkin Arms
Fowler Bullets
Fowler, Bob (See Black Powder Products)
Foy Custom Bullets
Freedom Arms, Inc.
Garcia National Gun Traders, Inc.
Gehmann, Walter (See Huntington Die Specialties)
GOEX, Inc.
Golden Bear Bullets
Gotz Bullets
Grayback Wildcats
Green Mountain Rifle Barrel Co., Inc.
Grier's Hard Cast Bullets
GTB
Gun City
Harris Enterprises
Harrison Bullets
Hart & Son, Inc.
Hawk Laboratories, Inc. (See Hawk, Inc.)
Hawk, Inc.
Haydon Shooters Supply, Russ
Heidenstrom Bullets
Hercules, Inc. (See Alliant Techsystems, Smokeless)
HI-Performance Ammunition Company
Hirtenberger AG
Hobson Precision Mfg. Co.
Hodgdon Powder Co.
Hornady Mfg. Co.
HT Bullets
Hunters Supply, Inc.
Huntington Die Specialties
Impact Case & Container, Inc.
Imperial Magnum Corp.
IMR Powder Co.
Intercontinental Distributors, Ltd.
J&D Components
J&L Superior Bullets (See Huntington Die Special)
J.R. Williams Bullet Co.
James Calhoon Mfg.
James Calhoon Varmint Bullets
Jamison International
Jensen Bullets
Jensen's Firearms Academy
Jericho Tool & Die Co., Inc.
Jester Bullets
JLK Bullets
JRP Custom Bullets
Ka Pu Kapili
Kaswer Custom, Inc.
Keith's Bullets
Keng's Firearms Specialty, Inc./US Tactical Systems
Ken's Kustom Kartridges
Kent Cartridge Mfg. Co. Ltd.
KLA Enterprises
Knight Rifles
Knight Rifles (See Modern Muzzle Loading, Inc.)
Lapua Ltd.
Lawrence Brand Shot (See Precision Reloading)
Legend Products Corp.
Liberty Shooting Supplies

Lightning Performance Innovations, Inc.
Lindsley Arms Cartridge Co.
Littleton, J. F.
Lomont Precision Bullets
Lyman Products Corp.
Magnus Bullets
Maine Custom Bullets
Maionchi-L.M.I.
Marchmon Bullets
Markesbery Muzzle Loaders, Inc.
MarMik, Inc.
Marshall Fish Mfg. Gunsmith Sptg. Co.
MAST Technology, Inc.
McMurdo, Lynn (See Specialty Gunsmithing)
Meister Bullets (See Gander Mountain)
Men-Metallwerk Elisenhuette GmbH
Merkuria Ltd.
Michael's Antiques
Midway Arms, Inc.
Mitchell Bullets, R.F.
MI-TE Bullets
Montana Precision Swaging
Mountain State Muzzleloading Supplies, Inc.
Mulhern, Rick
Murmur Corp.
Nagel's Custom Bullets
National Bullet Co.
Naval Ordnance Works
North American Shooting Systems
North Devon Firearms Services
Northern Precision Custom Swaged Bullets
Nosler, Inc.
OK Weber, Inc.
Oklahoma Ammunition Co.
Old Wagon Bullets
Oregon Trail Bullet Company
Pacific Cartridge, Inc.
Pacific Rifle Co.
Page Custom Bullets
Pease Accuracy
Penn Bullets
Peterson Gun Shop, Inc., A.W.
Petro-Explo Inc.
Phillippi Custom Bullets, Justin
Pinetree Bullets
PMC/Eldorado Cartridge Corp.
Polywad, Inc.
Pony Express Reloaders
Power Plus Enterprises, Inc.
Precision Delta Corp.
Prescott Projectile Co.
Price Bullets, Patrick W.
PRL Bullets, c/o Blackburn Enterprises
Professional Hunter Supplies (See Star Custom Bullets)
Proofmark Corp.
R.I.S. Co., Inc.
Rainier Ballistics Corp.
Ramon B. Gonzalez Guns
Ravell Ltd.
Redwood Bullet Works
Reloading Specialties, Inc.
Remington Arms Co., Inc.
Rhino
Robinson H.V. Bullets
Rubright Bullets
Russ Haydon's Shooters' Supply
SAECO (See Redding Reloading Equipment)
Scharch Mfg., Inc.-Top Brass
Schneider Bullets
Schroeder Bullets
Schumakers Gun Shop
Scot Powder
Seebeck Assoc., R.E.
Shappy Bullets
Sharps Arms Co., Inc., C.
Shilen, Inc.
Sierra Bullets

SOS Products Co. (See Buck Stix-SOS Products Co.)
Southern Ammunition Co., Inc.
Specialty Gunsmithing
Speer Bullets
Spencer's Rifle Barrels, Inc.
SSK Industries
Stanley Bullets
Star Ammunition, Inc.
Star Custom Bullets
Starke Bullet Company
Starline, Inc.
Stewart's Gunsmithing
Swift Bullet Co.
T.F.C. S.p.A.
Taracorp Industries, Inc.
Tar-Hunt Custom Rifles, Inc.
TCCI
TCSR
The A.W. Peterson Gun Shop, Inc.
The Gun Works
The Ordnance Works
Thompson Bullet Lube Co.
Thompson Precision
TMI Products (See Haselbauer Products, Jerry)
Traditions Performance Firearms
Trico Plastics
True Flight Bullet Co.
Tucson Mold, Inc.
Unmussig Bullets, D. L.
USAC
Vann Custom Bullets
Vihtavuori Oy/Kaltron-Pettibone
Vincent's Shop
Viper Bullet and Brass Works
Walters Wads
Warren Muzzleloading Co., Inc.
Watson Trophy Match Bullets
Weatherby, Inc.
Western Nevada West Coast Bullets
Widener's Reloading & Shooting Supply, Inc.
Winchester Div. Olin Corp.
Winkle Bullets
Woodleigh (See Huntington Die Specialties)
Worthy Products, Inc.
Wyant Bullets
Wyoming Custom Bullets
Zero Ammunition Co., Inc.

AMMUNITION, COMMERCIAL

3-Ten Corp.
A.W. Peterson Gun Shop, Inc.
Ace Custom 45's, Inc.
Ad Hominem
Air Arms
American Ammunition
Arizona Ammunition, Inc.
Arms Corporation of the Philippines
Arundel Arms & Ammunition, Inc., A.
A-Square Co.
Atlantic Rose, Inc.
Badger Shooters Supply, Inc.
Ballistic Product, Inc.
Ben William's Gun Shop
Benjamin/Sheridan Co., Crosman
Big Bear Arms & Sporting Goods, Inc.
Black Hills Ammunition, Inc.
Blammo Ammo
Blount, Inc., Sporting Equipment Div.
Brenneke GmbH
Buffalo Bullet Co., Inc.
Bull-X, Inc.
Cabela's
Cambos Outdoorsman
Casull Arms Corp.
CBC
Champion's Choice, Inc.
Cor-Bon Inc./Glaser LLC
Crosman Airguns

Cubic Shot Shell Co., Inc.
Daisy Outdoor Products
Dead Eye's Sport Center
Delta Arms Ltd.
Delta Frangible Ammunition LLC
Dynamit Nobel-RWS, Inc.
Effebi SNC-Dr. Franco Beretta
Eley Ltd.
Elite Ammunition
Estate Cartridge, Inc.
Federal Cartridge Co.
Fiocchi of America, Inc.
Garcia National Gun Traders, Inc.
Garrett Cartridges, Inc.
Garthwaite Pistolsmith, Inc., Jim
Gibbs Rifle Co., Inc.
Gil Hebard Guns Inc.
Glaser LLC
Glaser Safety Slug, Inc.
GOEX, Inc.
Goodwin's Gun Shop
Gun City
Hansen & Co.
Hart & Son, Inc.
Hi-Performance Ammunition Company
Hirtenberger AG
Hornady Mfg. Co.
Hunters Supply, Inc.
Intercontinental Distributors, Ltd.
Ion Industries, Inc.
Keng's Firearms Specialty, Inc./US Tactical Systems
Kent Cartridge America, Inc.
Kent Cartridge Mfg. Co. Ltd.
Knight Rifles
Lapua Ltd.
Lethal Force Institute (See Police Bookshelf)
Lock's Philadelphia Gun Exchange
Magnum Research, Inc.
MagSafe Ammo Co.
Magtech Ammunition Co. Inc.
Maionchi-L.M.I.
Mandall Shooting Supplies Inc.
Markell,Inc.
Marshall Fish Mfg. Gunsmith Sptg. Co.
McBros Rifle Co.
Men-Metallwerk Elisenhuette GmbH
Mullins Ammunition
New England Ammunition Co.
Oklahoma Ammunition Co.
Omark Industries, Div. of Blount, Inc.
Outdoor Sports Headquarters, Inc.
P.S.M.G. Gun Co.
Pacific Cartridge, Inc.
Paragon Sales & Services, Inc.
Parker & Sons Shooting Supply
Parker Gun Finishes
Peterson Gun Shop, Inc., A.W.
PMC/Eldorado Cartridge Corp.
Police Bookshelf
Polywad, Inc.
Pony Express Reloaders
Precision Delta Corp.
Pro Load Ammunition, Inc.
R.E.I.
Ravell Ltd.
Remington Arms Co., Inc.
Rucker Dist. Inc.
RWS (See US Importer-Dynamit Nobel-RWS, Inc.)
Sellier & Bellot, USA Inc.
Southern Ammunition Co., Inc.
Speer Bullets
TCCI
The A.W. Peterson Gun Shop, Inc.
The BulletMakers Workshop
The Gun Room Press
The Gun Works
Thompson Bullet Lube Co.
USAC
VAM Distribution Co. LLC
Victory USA

PRODUCT & SERVICE DIRECTORY

Vihtavuori Oy/Kaltron-Pettibone
Visible Impact Targets
Voere-KGH GmbH
Weatherby, Inc.
Westley Richards & Co.
Whitestone Lumber Corp.
Widener's Reloading & Shooting
  Supply, Inc.
William E. Phillips Firearms
Winchester Div. Olin Corp.
Zero Ammunition Co., Inc.

AMMUNITION, CUSTOM

3-Ten Corp.
A.W. Peterson Gun Shop, Inc.
Accuracy Unlimited
AFSCO Ammunition
Allred Bullet Co.
American Derringer Corp.
American Products, Inc.
Arizona Ammunition, Inc.
Arms Corporation of the Philippines
Atlantic Rose, Inc.
Ballard Rifle & Cartridge Co., LLC
Bear Arms
Belding's Custom Gun Shop
Berger Bullets Ltd.
Big Bore Bullets of Alaska
Black Hills Ammunition, Inc.
Blue Mountain Bullets
Brynin, Milton
Buckskin Bullet Co.
CBC
CFVentures
Champlin Firearms, Inc.
Cubic Shot Shell Co., Inc.
Custom Tackle and Ammo
Dakota Arms, Inc.
Dead Eye's Sport Center
Delta Frangible Ammunition LLC
DKT, Inc.
Elite Ammunition
Estate Cartridge, Inc.
GDL Enterprises
GOEX, Inc.
Grayback Wildcats
Hirtenberger AG
Hobson Precision Mfg. Co.
Horizons Unlimited
Hornady Mfg. Co.
Hunters Supply, Inc.
James Calhoon Mfg.
James Calhoon Varmint Bullets
Jensen Bullets
Jensen's Custom Ammunition
Jensen's Firearms Academy
Kaswer Custom, Inc.
Kent Cartridge Mfg. Co. Ltd.
L. E. Jurras & Assoc.
L.A.R. Mfg., Inc.
Lethal Force Institute (See Police
  Bookshelf)
Lindsley Arms Cartridge Co.
Linebaugh Custom Sixguns
Loch Leven Industries/Convert-A-Pell
MagSafe Ammo Co.
MAST Technology, Inc.
McBros Rifle Co.
McMurdo, Lynn (See Specialty
  Gunsmithing)
Men-Metallwerk Elisenhuette GmbH
Milstor Corp.
Mullins Ammunition
Oklahoma Ammunition Co.
P.S.M.G. Gun Co.
Peterson Gun Shop, Inc., A.W.
Phillippi Custom Bullets, Justin
Police Bookshelf
Power Plus Enterprises, Inc.
Precision Delta Corp.
Professional Hunter Supplies (See
  Star Custom Bullets)
R.E.I.

Ramon B. Gonzalez Guns
Sandia Die & Cartridge Co.
SOS Products Co. (See Buck Stix-SOS
  Products Co.)
Specialty Gunsmithing
Spencer's Rifle Barrels, Inc.
SSK Industries
Star Custom Bullets
Stewart's Gunsmithing
The A.W. Peterson Gun Shop, Inc.
The BulletMakers Workshop
The Country Armourer
Unmussig Bullets, D. L.
Vitt/Boos
Vulpes Ventures, Inc. Fox Cartridge
  Division
Warren Muzzleloading Co., Inc.
Watson Trophy Match Bullets
Worthy Products, Inc.
Zero Ammunition Co., Inc.

AMMUNITION, FOREIGN

A.W. Peterson Gun Shop, Inc.
Ad Hominem
AFSCO Ammunition
Armscorp USA, Inc.
Atlantic Rose, Inc.
B&P America
Beeman Precision Airguns
Cape Outfitters
CBC
Cheddite, France S.A.
Cubic Shot Shell Co., Inc.
Dead Eye's Sport Center
DKT, Inc.
Dynamit Nobel-RWS, Inc.
E. Arthur Brown Co.
Fiocchi of America, Inc.
First Inc., Jack
Gamebore Division, Polywad Inc.
Gibbs Rifle Co., Inc.
GOEX, Inc.
Goodwin's Gun Shop
Gunsmithing, Inc.
Hansen & Co.
Heidenstrom Bullets
Hirtenberger AG
Hornady Mfg. Co.
I.S.S.
Intrac Arms International
K.B.I. Inc.
MagSafe Ammo Co.
Maionchi-L.M.I.
Mandall Shooting Supplies Inc.
Marksman Products
MAST Technology, Inc.
Merkuria Ltd.
Mullins Ammunition
Navy Arms Company
Oklahoma Ammunition Co.
P.S.M.G. Gun Co.
Paragon Sales & Services, Inc.
Peterson Gun Shop, Inc., A.W.
Petro-Explo Inc.
Precision Delta Corp.
R.E.T. Enterprises
Ramon B. Gonzalez Guns
RWS (See US Importer-Dynamit
  Nobel-RWS, Inc.)
Samco Global Arms, Inc.
Sentinel Arms
Southern Ammunition Co., Inc.
Speer Bullets
Stratco, Inc.
T.F.C. S.p.A.
The A.W. Peterson Gun Shop, Inc.
The BulletMakers Workshop
The Paul Co.
Victory Ammunition
Vihtavuori Oy/Kaltron-Pettibone
Vulpes Ventures, Inc. Fox Cartridge
  Division
Wolf Performance Ammunition

ANTIQUE ARMS DEALER

Ackerman & Co.
Ad Hominem
Antique American Firearms
Antique Arms Co.
Aplan Antiques & Art, James O.
Armoury, Inc., The
Arundel Arms & Ammunition, Inc., A.
Ballard Rifle & Cartridge Co., LLC
Bear Mountain Gun & Tool
Bob's Tactical Indoor Shooting Range
  & Gun Shop
Buffalo Arms Co.
Cape Outfitters
Carlson, Douglas R, Antique American
  Firearms
CBC-BRAZIL
Chadick's Ltd.
Chambers Flintlocks Ltd., Jim
Champlin Firearms, Inc.
Chuck's Gun Shop
Clements' Custom Leathercraft, Chas
Cole's Gun Works
D&D Gunsmiths, Ltd.
David R. Chicoine
Dixie Gun Works
Dixon Muzzleloading Shop, Inc.
Duffy, Charles E (See Guns Antique &
  Modern DBA)
Ed's Gun House
Enguix Import-Export
Fagan & Co.Inc
Flayderman & Co., Inc.
Fulmer's Antique Firearms, Chet
George Madis Winchester Consultants
Getz Barrel Co.
Glass, Herb
Goergen's Gun Shop, Inc.
Golden Age Arms Co.
Goodwin's Gun Shop
Gun Hunter Books (See Gun Hunter
  Trading Co.)
Gun Hunter Trading Co.
Guns Antique & Modern DBA / Charles
  E. Duffy
Hallowell & Co.
Hammans, Charles E.
HandCrafts Unltd (See Clements'
  Custom Leather)
Handgun Press
Hansen & Co.
Hunkeler, A (See Buckskin Machine
  Works
Imperial Miniature Armory
James Wayne Firearms for Collectors
  and Investors
Kelley's
Knight's Mfg. Co.
Ledbetter Airguns, Riley
LeFever Arms Co., Inc.
Lever Arms Service Ltd.
Lock's Philadelphia Gun Exchange
Log Cabin Sport Shop
Logdewood Mfg.
Mandall Shooting Supplies Inc.
Marshall Fish Mfg. Gunsmith Sptg. Co.
Martin's Gun Shop
Michael's Antiques
Mid-America Recreation, Inc.
Montana Outfitters, Lewis E. Yearout
Muzzleloaders Etcetera, Inc.
Navy Arms Company
New England Arms Co.
Olathe Gun Shop
Peter Dyson & Son Ltd.
Pony Express Sport Shop
Powder Horn Ltd.
Ravell Ltd.
Reno, Wayne
Retting, Inc., Martin B
Robert Valade Engraving
Rutgers Book Center
Samco Global Arms, Inc.

Sarco, Inc.
Scott Fine Guns Inc., Thad
Shootin' Shack
Sportsmen's Exchange & Western
  Gun Traders, Inc.
Steves House of Guns
Stott's Creek Armory, Inc.
The Gun Room
The Gun Room Press
The Gun Works
Turnbull Restoration, Doug
Vic's Gun Refinishing
Vintage Arms, Inc.
Wallace, Terry
Westley Richards & Co.
Wild West Guns
William Fagan & Co.
Winchester Sutler, Inc., The
Wood, Frank (See Classic Guns, Inc.)
Yearout, Lewis E. (See Montana
  Outfitters)

APPRAISER - GUNS, ETC.

A.W. Peterson Gun Shop, Inc.
Ackerman & Co.
Antique Arms Co.
Armoury, Inc., The
Arundel Arms & Ammunition, Inc., A.
Barta's Gunsmithing
Beitzinger, George
Blue Book Publications, Inc.
Bob's Tactical Indoor Shooting Range
  & Gun Shop
Bullet N Press
Butterfield's
Cape Outfitters
Chadick's Ltd.
Champlin Firearms, Inc.
Christie's East
Chuilli, Stephen
Clark Firearms Engraving
Clements' Custom Leathercraft, Chas
Cole's Gun Works
Colonial Arms, Inc.
Colonial Repair
Corry, John
Custom Tackle and Ammo
D&D Gunsmiths, Ltd.
David R. Chicoine
DGR Custom Rifles
Dietz Gun Shop & Range, Inc.
Dixie Gun Works
Dixon Muzzleloading Shop, Inc.
Duane's Gun Repair (See DGR Custom
  Rifles)
Ed's Gun House
Eversull Co., Inc.
Fagan & Co.Inc
Ferris Firearms
Flayderman & Co., Inc.
Forty Five Ranch Enterprises
Francotte & Cie S.A. Auguste
Frontier Arms Co.,Inc.
Gene's Custom Guns
George E. Mathews & Son, Inc.
George Madis Winchester Consultants
Gerald Pettinger Books (See Pettinger
  Books)
Getz Barrel Co.
Gillmann, Edwin
Gilmore Sports Concepts
Goergen's Gun Shop, Inc.
Golden Age Arms Co.
Goodwin's Gun Shop
Griffin & Howe, Inc.
Griffin & Howe, Inc.
Griffin & Howe, Inc.
Groenewold, John
Gun City
Gun Hunter Books (See Gun Hunter
  Trading Co.)
Gun Hunter Trading Co.

Guncraft Books (See Guncraft Sports
  Inc.)
Guncraft Sports Inc.
Gunsmithing, Inc.
Hallowell & Co.
Hammans, Charles E.
HandCrafts Unltd (See Clements'
  Custom Leather)
Handgun Press
Hank's Gun Shop
Hansen & Co.
Irwin, Campbell H.
Island Pond Gun Shop
Ithaca Classic Doubles
Jackalope Gun Shop
James Wayne Firearms for Collectors
  and Investors
Jensen's Custom Ammunition
Kelley's
L.L. Bean, Inc.
Lampert, Ron
LaRocca Gun Works
Ledbetter Airguns, Riley
LeFever Arms Co., Inc.
Lock's Philadelphia Gun Exchange
Log Cabin Sport Shop
Logdewood Mfg.
Lomont Precision Bullets
Long, George F.
Mahony, Philip Bruce
Mandall Shooting Supplies Inc.
Marshall Fish Mfg. Gunsmith Sptg. Co.
Martin's Gun Shop
Mathews & Son, Inc., George E.
McCann Industries
McCann's Machine & Gun Shop
Mercer Custom Guns
Montana Outfitters, Lewis E. Yearout
Muzzleloaders Etcetera, Inc.
Navy Arms Company
New England Arms Co.
Nitex Gun Shop
Olathe Gun Shop
P&M Sales & Services, LLC
Pasadena Gun Center
Pentheny de Pentheny
Peterson Gun Shop, Inc., A.W.
Pettinger Books, Gerald
Pony Express Sport Shop
Powder Horn Ltd.
R.A. Wells Custom Gunsmith
R.E.T. Enterprises
Ramon B. Gonzalez Guns
Retting, Inc., Martin B
Robert Valade Engraving
Rutgers Book Center
Scott Fine Guns Inc., Thad
Shootin' Shack
Spencer Reblue Service
Sportsmen's Exchange & Western
  Gun Traders, Inc.
Steven Dodd Hughes
Stott's Creek Armory, Inc.
Stratco, Inc.
Ten-Ring Precision, Inc.
The A.W. Peterson Gun Shop, Inc.
The Gun Room Press
The Gun Shop
The Gun Works
The Orvis Co.
The Swampfire Shop (See Peterson
  Gun Shop, Inc.)
Thurston Sports, Inc.
Vic's Gun Refinishing
Walker Arms Co., Inc.
Wallace, Terry
Wasmundt, Jim
Weber & Markin Custom Gunsmiths
Werth, T. W.
Whildin & Sons Ltd, E.H.
Whitestone Lumber Corp.
Wichita Arms, Inc.
Wild West Guns
William Fagan & Co.

PRODUCT & SERVICE DIRECTORY

Williams Shootin' Iron Service, The Lynx-Line
Winchester Sutler, Inc., The
Wood, Frank (See Classic Guns, Inc.)
Yearout, Lewis E. (See Montana Outfitters)

AUCTIONEER - GUNS, ETC.

"Little John's" Antique Arms
Buck Stix-SOS Products Co.
Butterfield's
Christie's East
Fagan & Co.Inc
Sotheby's

BOOKS & MANUALS (PUBLISHERS & DEALERS)

"Su-Press-On", Inc.
Alpha 1 Drop Zone
American Handgunner Magazine
Armory Publications
Arms & Armour Press
Ballistic Product, Inc.
Ballistic Product, Inc.
Barnes Bullets, Inc.
Bauska Barrels
Beartooth Bullets
Beeman Precision Airguns
Blacksmith Corp.
Blacktail Mountain Books
Blue Book Publications, Inc.
Blue Ridge Machinery & Tools, Inc.
Boone's Custom Ivory Grips, Inc.
Brown Co., E. Arthur
Brownells, Inc.
Bullet N Press
C. Sharps Arms Co. Inc./Montana Armory
Cape Outfitters
Cheyenne Pioneer Products
Colonial Repair
Corbin Mfg. & Supply, Inc.
DBI Books Division of Krause Publications
deHaas Barrels
Dixon Muzzleloading Shop, Inc.
Excalibur Publications
Executive Protection Institute
Galati International
Gerald Pettinger Books (See Pettinger Books)
Golden Age Arms Co.
Gun City
Gun List (See Krause Publications)
Guncraft Books (See Guncraft Sports Inc.)
Guncraft Sports Inc.
Gunnerman Books
GUNS Magazine
Gunsmithing, Inc.
H&P Publishing
Handgun Press
Harris Publications
Hawk Laboratories, Inc. (See Hawk, Inc.)
Hawk, Inc.
Heritage/VSP Gun Books
Hodgdon Powder Co.
Home Shop Machinist, The Village Press Publications
Hornady Mfg. Co.
Huntington Die Specialties
I.D.S.A. Books
Info-Arm
Ironside International Publishers, Inc.
Jantz Supply
Kelley's
King & Co.
Koval Knives

Krause Publications, Inc.
L.B.T.
Lapua Ltd.
Lebeau-Courally
Lethal Force Institute (See Police Bookshelf)
Lyman Products Corp.
Madis Books
Magma Engineering Co.
Mandall Shooting Supplies Inc.
MarMik, Inc.
Montana Armory, Inc .(See C. Sharps Arms Co. Inc.)
Mountain South
Mountain State Muzzleloading Supplies, Inc.
Mulberry House Publishing
Navy Arms Company
Numrich Gun Parts Corporation
OK Weber, Inc.
Outdoor Sports Headquarters, Inc.
Paintball Games International Magazine Aceville
Pejsa Ballistics
Petersen Publishing Co.
Pettinger Books, Gerald
PFRB Co.
Police Bookshelf
Precision Shooting, Inc.
Professional Hunter Supplies (See Star Custom Bullets)
Ravell Ltd.
Ray Riling Arms Books Co.
Remington Double Shotguns
Russ Haydon's Shooters' Supply
Rutgers Book Center
S&S Firearms
Safari Press, Inc.
Saunders Gun & Machine Shop
Scharch Mfg., Inc.-Top Brass
Scharch Mfg., Inc.-Top Brass
Semmer, Charles (See Remington Double Shotguns)
Sharps Arms Co., Inc., C.
Shotgun Sports Magazine, dba Shootin' Accessories Ltd.
Sierra Bullets
Speer Bullets
SPG LLC
Stackpole Books
Star Custom Bullets
Stewart Game Calls, Inc., Johnny
Stoeger Industries
Stoeger Publishing Co. (See Stoeger Industries)
Swift Bullet Co.
The A.W. Peterson Gun Shop, Inc.
The Gun Room Press
The Gun Works
The NgraveR Co.
Thomas, Charles C.
Track of the Wolf, Inc.
Trafalgar Square
Trotman, Ken
Tru-Balance Knife Co.
Vega Tool Co.
Vintage Industries, Inc.
VSP Publishers (See Heritage/VSP Gun Books)
W.E. Brownell Checkering Tools
WAMCO-New Mexico
Wells Creek Knife & Gun Works
Wilderness Sound Products Ltd.
Williams Gun Sight Co.
Wolfe Publishing Co.
Wolf's Western Traders

BULLET CASTING, ACCESSORIES

Ballisti-Cast, Inc.
Buffalo Arms Co.
Bullet Metals
Cast Performance Bullet Company

CFVentures
Cooper-Woodward
Davide Pedersoli and Co.
Ferguson, Bill
Huntington Die Specialties
Lee Precision, Inc.
Lithi Bee Bullet Lube
Lyman Products Corp.
Magma Engineering Co.
Ox-Yoke Originals, Inc.
Rapine Bullet Mould Mfg. Co.
SPG LLC
The A.W. Peterson Gun Shop, Inc.
The Hanned Line
United States Products Co.

BULLET CASTING, FURNACES & POTS

Ballisti-Cast, Inc.
Buffalo Arms Co.
Bullet Metals
Ferguson, Bill
GAR
Lee Precision, Inc.
Lyman Products Corp.
Magma Engineering Co.
Rapine Bullet Mould Mfg. Co.
RCBS/ATK
The A.W. Peterson Gun Shop, Inc.
The Gun Works
Thompson Bullet Lube Co.

BULLET CASTING, LEAD

Action Bullets & Alloy Inc.
Ames Metal Products
Belltown Ltd.
Buckskin Bullet Co.
Buffalo Arms Co.
Bullet Metals
Bullseye Bullets
Hunters Supply, Inc.
Jericho Tool & Die Co., Inc.
Lee Precision, Inc.
Lithi Bee Bullet Lube
Magma Engineering Co.
Montana Precision Swaging
Ox-Yoke Originals, Inc.
Penn Bullets
Proofmark Corp.
SPG LLC
Splitfire Sporting Goods, L.L.C.
The A.W. Peterson Gun Shop, Inc.
The Gun Works
Walters Wads

BULLET PULLERS

Battenfeld Technologies
Davide Pedersoli and Co.
Hollywood Engineering
Huntington Die Specialties
Royal Arms Gunstocks
The A.W. Peterson Gun Shop, Inc.
The Gun Works

BULLET TOOLS

Brynin, Milton
Camdex, Inc.
Corbin Mfg. & Supply, Inc.
Cumberland Arms
Eagan, Donald V.
Holland's Gunsmithing
Hollywood Engineering
Lee Precision, Inc.
Niemi Engineering, W. B.
North Devon Firearms Services
Rorschach Precision Products
Sport Flite Manufacturing Co.
The A.W. Peterson Gun Shop, Inc.

The Hanned Line
WTA Manufacturing

BULLET, CASE & DIE LUBRICANTS

Beartooth Bullets
Bonanza (See Forster Products)
Brown Co., E. Arthur
Buckskin Bullet Co.
Buffalo Arms Co.
Camp-Cap Products
CFVentures
Cooper-Woodward
CVA
E-Z-Way Systems
Ferguson, Bill
Forster Products
GAR
Guardsman Products
Heidenstrom Bullets
Hollywood Engineering
Hornady Mfg. Co.
Imperial (See E-Z-Way Systems)
Knoell, Doug
L.B.T.
Le Clear Industries (See E-Z-Way Systems)
Lee Precision, Inc.
Lithi Bee Bullet Lube
MI-TE Bullets
Paco's (See Small Custom Mould & Bullet Co.)
RCBS Operations/ATK
Reardon Products
Rooster Laboratories
Shay's Gunsmithing
Small Custom Mould & Bullet Co.
Tamarack Products, Inc.
The Hanned Line
Uncle Mike's (See Michaels of Oregon Co.)
Warren Muzzleloading Co., Inc.
Widener's Reloading & Shooting Supply, Inc.
Young Country Arms

CARTRIDGES FOR COLLECTORS

Ackerman & Co.
Ad Hominem
Armory Publications
Cameron's
Campbell, Dick
Cartridge Transfer Group, Pete de Coux
Cherry Creek State Park Shooting Center
Cole's Gun Works
Colonial Repair
Cubic Shot Shell Co., Inc.
de Coux, Pete (See Cartridge Transfer Group)
Duane's Gun Repair (See DGR Custom Rifles)
Ed's Gun House
Ed's Gun House
Enguix Import-Export
Epps, Ellwood/Isabella
First Inc., Jack
Forty Five Ranch Enterprises
George Madis Winchester Consultants
Goergen's Gun Shop, Inc.
Goodwin's Gun Shop
Grayback Wildcats
Gun City
Gun Hunter Books (See Gun Hunter Trading Co.)
Gun Hunter Trading Co.
Jack First, Inc.
Kelley's
Liberty Shooting Supplies

Mandall Shooting Supplies Inc.
MAST Technology, Inc.
Michael's Antiques
Montana Outfitters, Lewis E. Yearout
Numrich Gun Parts Corporation
Pasadena Gun Center
Samco Global Arms, Inc.
SOS Products Co. (See Buck Stix-SOS Products Co.)
Stone Enterprises Ltd.
The Country Armourer
The Gun Room Press
Ward & Van Valkenburg
Yearout, Lewis E. (See Montana Outfitters)

CASE & AMMUNITION PROCESSORS, INSPECTORS, BOXERS

Ammo Load, Inc.
Ben's Machines
Hafner World Wide, Inc.
Scharch Mfg., Inc.-Top Brass
The A.W. Peterson Gun Shop, Inc.

CASE CLEANERS & POLISHING MEDIA

Battenfeld Technologies
Belltown Ltd.
Buffalo Arms Co.
G96 Products Co., Inc.
Huntington Die Specialties
Lee Precision, Inc.
Penn Bullets
The A.W. Peterson Gun Shop, Inc.
The Gun Works
Tru-Square Metal Products Inc.
VibraShine, Inc.

CASE PREPARATION TOOLS

Battenfeld Technologies
CONKKO
High Precision
Hoehn Sales, Inc.
Huntington Die Specialties
J. Dewey Mfg. Co., Inc.
K&M Services
Lee Precision, Inc.
Match Prep-Doyle Gracey
Plum City Ballistic Range
RCBS Operations/ATK
Russ Haydon's Shooters' Supply
Sinclair International, Inc.
Stoney Point Products, Inc.
The A.W. Peterson Gun Shop, Inc.

CASE TRIMMERS, TRIM DIES & ACCESSORIES

Buffalo Arms Co.
Creedmoor Sports, Inc.
Fremont Tool Works
Goodwin's Gun Shop
Hollywood Engineering
K&M Services
Lyman Products Corp.
Match Prep-Doyle Gracey
OK Weber, Inc.
Ozark Gun Works
RCBS/ATK
Redding Reloading Equipment
The A.W. Peterson Gun Shop, Inc.
Time Precision

PRODUCT & SERVICE DIRECTORY

CASE TUMBLERS, VIBRATORS, MEDIA & ACCESSORIES

4-D Custom Die Co.
Battenfeld Technologies
Berry's Mfg., Inc.
Dillon Precision Products, Inc.
Goodwin's Gun Shop
Penn Bullets
Raytech Div. of Lyman Products Corp.
The A.W. Peterson Gun Shop, Inc.
Tru-Square Metal Products Inc.
VibraShine, Inc.

CASES, CABINETS, RACKS & SAFES - GUN

All Rite Products, Inc.
Allen Co., Bob
Allen Co., Inc.
Allen Sportswear, Bob (See Allen Co., Bob)
Alumna Sport by Dee Zee
American Display Co.
American Security Products Co.
Americase
Art Jewel Enterprises Ltd.
Ashby Turkey Calls
Bagmaster Mfg., Inc.
Barramundi Corp.
Berry's Mfg., Inc.
Big Spring Enterprises "Bore Stores"
Bill's Custom Cases
Bison Studios
Black Sheep Brand
Brauer Bros.
Brown, H. R. (See Silhouette Leathers)
Browning Arms Co.
Bushmaster Hunting & Fishing
Cannon Safe, Inc.
Chipmunk (See Oregon Arms, Inc.)
Cobalt Mfg., Inc.
CONKKO
Connecticut Shotgun Mfg. Co.
D&L Industries (See D.J. Marketing)
D.J. Marketing
Dara-Nes, Inc. (See Nesci Enterprises, Inc.)
Deepeeka Exports Pvt. Ltd.
Doskocil Mfg. Co., Inc.
DTM International, Inc.
EMF Co., Inc.
English, Inc., A.G.
Enhanced Presentations, Inc.
Eversull Co., Inc.
Fort Knox Security Products
Freedom Arms, Inc.
Frontier Safe Co.
Galati International
GALCO International Ltd.
Gun-Ho Sports Cases
Hall Plastics, Inc., John
Hastings
Homak
Hoppe's Div. Penguin Industries, Inc.
Hunter Co., Inc.
Hydrosorbent Products
Impact Case & Container, Inc.
Johanssons Vapentillbehor, Bert
Johnston Bros. (See C&T Corp. TA Johnson Brothers)
Kalispel Case Line
Kane Products, Inc.
KK Air International (See Impact Case & Container Co.)
Knock on Wood Antiques
Kolpin Mfg., Inc.
Lakewood Products LLC
Liberty Safe
Mandall Shooting Supplies Inc.
Marsh, Mike
McWelco Products

Morton Booth Co.
MPC
MTM Molded Products Co., Inc.
Nalpak
Necessary Concepts, Inc.
Nesci Enterprises Inc.
Oregon Arms, Inc. (See Rogue Rifle Co., Inc.)
Outa-Site Gun Carriers
Pflumm Mfg. Co.
Poburka, Philip (See Bison Studios)
Powell & Son (Gunmakers) Ltd., William
Protektor Model
Prototech Industries, Inc.
Rogue Rifle Co., Inc.
Schulz Industries
Southern Security
Sportsman's Communicators
Sun Welding Safe Co.
Sweet Home, Inc.
Talmage, William G.
The Outdoor Connection, Inc.
The Surecase Co.
Tinks & Ben Lee Hunting Products (See Wellington)
Trulock Tool
Universal Sports
W. Waller & Son, Inc.
Whitestone Lumber Corp.
Wilson Case, Inc.
Woodstream
Zanotti Armor, Inc.
Ziegel Engineering

CHOKE DEVICES, RECOIL ABSORBERS & RECOIL PADS

3-Ten Corp.
Action Products, Inc.
Allen Co., Bob
Allen Sportswear, Bob (See Allen Co., Bob)
Answer Products Co.
Arms Ingenuity Co.
Baer Custom Inc., Les
Bansner's Ultimate Rifles, LLC
Bartlett Engineering
Battenfeld Technologies
Briley Mfg. Inc.
Brooks Tactical Systems-Agrip
Brownells, Inc.
B-Square Company, Inc.
Buffer Technologies
Bull Mountain Rifle Co.
C&H Research
Cation
Chicasaw Gun Works
Clearview Products
Colonial Arms, Inc.
Connecticut Shotgun Mfg. Co.
CRR, Inc./Marble's Inc.
Danuser Machine Co.
Dina Arms Corporation
Gentry Custom Gunmaker, David
Goodwin's Gun Shop
Graybill's Gun Shop
Gruning Precision Inc.
Harry Lawson Co.
Hastings
Haydel's Game Calls, Inc.
Hogue Grips
Holland's Gunsmithing
I.N.C. Inc (See Kickeez I.N.C., Inc.)
J.P. Enterprises Inc.
Jackalope Gun Shop
Jenkins Recoil Pads, Inc.
KDF, Inc.
Kickeez I.N.C., Inc.
Lawson Co., Harry
London Guns Ltd.
Lyman Products Corp.
Mag-Na-Port International, Inc.

Mandall Shooting Supplies Inc.
Marble Arms (See CRR, Inc./Marble's Inc.)
Menck, Gunsmith Inc., T.W.
Middlebrooks Custom Shop
Morrow, Bud
Nelson/Weather-Rite, Inc.
One Of A Kind
Original Box, Inc.
P.S.M.G. Gun Co.
Palsa Outdoor Products
Parker & Sons Shooting Supply
Pro-Port Ltd.
Que Industries, Inc.
Shotguns Unlimited
Simmons Gun Repair, Inc.
Sound Technology
Stan Baker Sports
Stone Enterprises Ltd.
The A.W. Peterson Gun Shop, Inc.
Truglo, Inc.
Trulock Tool
Uncle Mike's (See Michaels of Oregon Co.)
Universal Sports
Virgin Valley Custom Guns
Vortek Products, Inc.
Williams Gun Sight Co.
Wilsom Combat
Wise Guns, Dale

CHRONOGRAPHS & PRESSURE TOOLS

Air Rifle Specialists
Brown Co., E. Arthur
C.W. Erickson's L.L.C.
Canons Delcour
Clearview Products
Competition Electronics, Inc.
Custom Chronograph, Inc.
D&H Precision Tooling
Hege Jagd-u. Sporthandels GmbH
Hutton Rifle Ranch
Kent Cartridge Mfg. Co. Ltd.
Mac-1 Airgun Distributors
Oehler Research,Inc.
P.A.C.T., Inc.
Romain's Custom Guns, Inc.
Savage Arms, Inc.
Stratco, Inc.
Tepeco

CLEANERS & DEGREASERS

Barnes Bullets, Inc.
Belltown Ltd.
Camp-Cap Products
G96 Products Co., Inc.
Goodwin's Gun Shop
Hafner World Wide, Inc.
Half Moon Rifle Shop
Kleen-Bore,Inc.
LEM Gun Specialties, Inc. The Lewis Lead Remover
Modern Muzzleloading, Inc.
Northern Precision Custom Swaged Bullets
Parker & Sons Shooting Supply
Parker Gun Finishes
Perazone-Gunsmith, Brian
PrOlixr Lubricants
R&S Industries Corp.
Ramon B. Gonzalez Guns
Rusteprufe Laboratories
Sheffield Knifemakers Supply, Inc.
Shooter's Choice Gun Care
Sierra Specialty Prod. Co.
Spencer's Rifle Barrels, Inc.
The A.W. Peterson Gun Shop, Inc.
The Gun Works
United States Products Co.

CLEANING & REFINISHING SUPPLIES

AC Dyna-tite Corp.
Alpha 1 Drop Zone
American Gas & Chemical Co., Ltd
Answer Products Co.
Armite Laboratories
Atlantic Mills, Inc.
Atsko/Sno-Seal, Inc.
Barnes Bullets, Inc.
Battenfeld Technologies
Beeman Precision Airguns
Belltown Ltd.
Bill's Gun Repair
Birchwood Casey
Blount, Inc., Sporting Equipment Div.
Blount/Outers ATK
Blue and Gray Products Inc. (See Ox-Yoke Originals)
Break-Free, Inc.
Bridgers Best
Brown Co., E. Arthur
Brownells, Inc.
C.S. Van Gorden & Son, Inc.
Cambos Outdoorsman
Cambos Outdoorsman
Camp-Cap Products
CONKKO
Connecticut Shotgun Mfg. Co.
Creedmoor Sports, Inc.
CRR, Inc./Marble's Inc.
Custom Products (See Jones Custom Products)
Cylinder & Slide, Inc., William R. Laughridge
Dara-Nes, Inc. (See Nesci Enterprises, Inc.)
Deepeeka Exports Pvt. Ltd.
Desert Mountain Mfg.
Du-Lite Corp.
Dykstra, Doug
E&L Mfg., Inc.
Eezox, Inc.
Ekol Leather Care
Faith Associates
Flitz International Ltd.
Fluoramics, Inc.
Frontier Products Co.
G96 Products Co., Inc.
Golden Age Arms Co.
Guardsman Products
Gunsmithing, Inc.
Hafner World Wide, Inc.
Half Moon Rifle Shop
Heatbath Corp.
Hoppe's Div. Penguin Industries, Inc.
Hornady Mfg. Co.
Hydrosorbent Products
Iosso Products
J. Dewey Mfg. Co., Inc.
Jantz Supply
Jantz Supply
Johnston Bros. (See C&T Corp. TA Johnson Brothers)
Jonad Corp.
K&M Industries, Inc.
Kellogg's Professional Products
Kent Cartridge Mfg. Co. Ltd.
Kesselring Gun Shop
Kleen-Bore,Inc.
Knight Rifles
Laurel Mountain Forge
Lee Supplies, Mark
LEM Gun Specialties, Inc. The Lewis Lead Remover
List Precision Engineering
LPS Laboratories, Inc.
Lyman Products Corp.
Mac-1 Airgun Distributors
Mandall Shooting Supplies Inc.
Marble Arms (See CRR, Inc./Marble's Inc.)
Mark Lee Supplies

Micro Sight Co.
Minute Man High Tech Industries
Mountain State Muzzleloading Supplies, Inc.
MTM Molded Products Co., Inc.
Muscle Products Corp.
Nesci Enterprises Inc.
Northern Precision Custom Swaged Bullets
Now Products, Inc.
October Country Muzzleloading
Old World Oil Products
Omark Industries, Div. of Blount, Inc.
Original Mink Oil, Inc.
Otis Technology, Inc.
Outers Laboratories Div. of ATK
Ox-Yoke Originals, Inc.
Parker & Sons Shooting Supply
Parker Gun Finishes
Pendleton Royal, c/o Swingler Buckland Ltd.
Perazone-Gunsmith, Brian
Pete Rickard, Inc.
Peter Dyson & Son Ltd.
Precision Airgun Sales, Inc.
PrOlixr Lubricants
Pro-Shot Products, Inc.
R&S Industries Corp.
Radiator Specialty Co.
Rooster Laboratories
Russ Haydon's Shooters' Supply
Rusteprufe Laboratories
Rusty Duck Premium Gun Care Products
Saunders Gun & Machine Shop
Schumakers Gun Shop
Sheffield Knifemakers Supply, Inc.
Shooter's Choice Gun Care
Shotgun Sports Magazine, dba Shootin' Accessories Ltd.
Silencio/Safety Direct
Sinclair International, Inc.
Sno-Seal, Inc. (See Atsko/Sno-Seal, Inc.)
Southern Bloomer Mfg. Co.
Splitfire Sporting Goods, L.L.C.
Starr Trading Co., Jedediah
Stoney Point Products, Inc.
Svon Corp.
T.F.C. S.p.A
TDP Industries, Inc.
Tetra Gun Care
Texas Platers Supply Co.
The A.W. Peterson Gun Shop, Inc.
The Dutchman's Firearms, Inc.
The Lewis Lead Remover (See LEM Gun Specialties)
The Paul Co.
Track of the Wolf, Inc.
United States Products Co.
Van Gorden & Son Inc., C. S.
Venco Industries, Inc. (See Shooter's Choice Gun Care)
VibraShine, Inc.
Volquartsen Custom Ltd.
Warren Muzzleloading Co., Inc.
Watson Trophy Match Bullets
WD-40 Co.
Wick, David E.
Willow Bend
Wolf's Western Traders
Young Country Arms

COMPUTER SOFTWARE - BALLISTICS

Action Target, Inc.
AmBr Software Group Ltd.
Arms Software
Arms, Programming Solutions (See Arms Software)
Barnes Bullets, Inc.
Canons Delcour
Corbin Mfg. & Supply, Inc.

PRODUCT & SERVICE DIRECTORY

Data Tech Software Systems
Hodgdon Powder Co.
J.I.T. Ltd.
Jensen Bullets
Kent Cartridge Mfg. Co. Ltd.
Maionchi-L.M.I.
Oehler Research,Inc.
Outdoor Sports Headquarters, Inc.
P.A.C.T., Inc.
Pejsa Ballistics
Powley Computer (See Hutton Rifle Ranch)
RCBS Operations/ATK
Sierra Bullets
The Ballistic Program Co., Inc.
The Country Armourer
The Gun Works
Tioga Engineering Co., Inc.
W. Square Enterprises

CUSTOM GUNSMITH

A&W Repair
A.A. Arms, Inc.
Acadian Ballistic Specialties
Accuracy Unlimited
Ace Custom 45's, Inc.
Acra-Bond Laminates
Adair Custom Shop, Bill
Ahlman Guns
Al Lind Custom Guns
Aldis Gunsmithing & Shooting Supply
Alpha Precision, Inc.
Alpine Indoor Shooting Range
Amrine's Gun Shop
Answer Products Co.
Antique Arms Co.
Armament Gunsmithing Co., Inc.
Arms Craft Gunsmithing
Arms Ingenuity Co.
Armscorp USA, Inc.
Artistry in Wood
Art's Gun & Sport Shop, Inc.
Arundel Arms & Ammunition, Inc., A.
Autauga Arms, Inc.
Badger Creek Studio
Baelder, Harry
Baer Custom Inc., Les
Bain & Davis, Inc.
Bansner's Ultimate Rifles, LLC
Barnes Bullets, Inc.
Baron Technology
Barta's Gunsmithing
Bear Arms
Bear Mountain Gun & Tool
Beaver Lodge (See Fellowes, Ted)
Behlert Precision, Inc.
Beitzinger, George
Belding's Custom Gun Shop
Ben William's Gun Shop
Bengtson Arms Co., L.
Bill Adair Custom Shop
Billings Gunsmiths
BlackStar AccuMax Barrels
BlackStar Barrel Accurizing (See BlackStar AccuMax)
Bob Rogers Gunsmithing
Bond Custom Firearms
Borden Ridges Rimrock Stocks
Borovnik KG, Ludwig
Bowen Classic Arms Corp.
Brace, Larry D.
Briese Bullet Co., Inc.
Briganti, A.J.
Briley Mfg. Inc.
Broad Creek Rifle Works, Ltd.
Brockman's Custom Gunsmithing
Broken Gun Ranch
Brown Precision, Inc.
Brown Products, Inc., Ed
Buchsenmachermeister
Buckhorn Gun Works
Budin, Dave
Bull Mountain Rifle Co.

Bullberry Barrel Works, Ltd.
Burkhart Gunsmithing, Don
Cache La Poudre Rifleworks
Cambos Outdoorsman
Cambos Outdoorsman
Campbell, Dick
Carolina Precision Rifles
Carter's Gun Shop
Caywood, Shane J.
CBC-BRAZIL
Chambers Flintlocks Ltd., Jim
Champlin Firearms, Inc.
Chicasaw Gun Works
Chuck's Gun Shop
Chuilli, Stephen
Clark Custom Guns, Inc.
Clark Firearms Engraving
Classic Arms Company
Classic Arms Corp.
Clearview Products
Cleland's Outdoor World, Inc
Coffin, Charles H.
Cogar's Gunsmithing
Cole's Gun Works
Colonial Arms, Inc.
Colonial Repair
Colorado Gunsmithing Academy
Colorado School of Trades
Colt's Mfg. Co., Inc.
Conrad, C. A.
Corkys Gun Clinic
Cox, Ed. C.
Cullity Restoration
Custom Gun Stocks
Custom Single Shot Rifles
D&D Gunsmiths, Ltd.
Dangler, Homer L.
D'Arcy Echols & Co.
Darlington Gun Works, Inc.
Dave's Gun Shop
David Miller Co.
David R. Chicoine
David W. Schwartz Custom Guns
Davis, Don
Delorge, Ed
Del-Sports, Inc.
DGR Custom Rifles
DGS, Inc., Dale A. Storey
Dietz Gun Shop & Range, Inc.
Dilliott Gunsmithing, Inc.
Donnelly, C. P.
Duane A. Hobbie Gunsmithing
Duane's Gun Repair (See DGR Custom Rifles)
Duffy, Charles E (See Guns Antique & Modern DBA)
Duncan's Gun Works, Inc.
E. Arthur Brown Co.
Eckelman Gunsmithing
Ed Brown Products, Inc.
Eggleston, Jere D.
Entre`prise Arms, Inc.
Erhardt, Dennis
Eversull Co., Inc.
Evolution Gun Works Inc.
F.I., Inc. - High Standard Mfg. Co.
FERLIB
Ferris Firearms
Fisher, Jerry A.
Fisher Custom Firearms
Fleming Firearms
Flynn's Custom Guns
Forkin, Ben (See Belt MTN Arms)
Forkin Arms
Forster, Kathy (See Custom Checkering)
Forster, Larry L.
Forthofer's Gunsmithing & Knifemaking
Francesca, Inc.
Francotte & Cie S.A. Auguste
Fred F. Wells/Wells Sport Store
Frontier Arms Co.,Inc.
Fullmer, Geo. M.

G.G. & G.
Galaxy Imports Ltd., Inc.
Garthwaite Pistolsmith, Inc., Jim
Gary Reeder Custom Guns
Gator Guns & Repair
Genecco Gun Works
Gene's Custom Guns
Gentry Custom Gunmaker, David
George E. Mathews & Son, Inc.
George Hoenig, Inc.
Gillmann, Edwin
Gilman-Mayfield, Inc.
Gilmore Sports Concepts
Giron, Robert E.
Goens, Dale W.
Gonic Arms/North American Arm
Goodling's Gunsmithing
Goodwin's Gun Shop
Grace, Charles E.
Grayback Wildcats
Graybill's Gun Shop
Green, Roger M.
Greg Gunsmithing Repair
Gre-Tan Rifles
Griffin & Howe, Inc.
Griffin & Howe, Inc.
Griffin & Howe, Inc.
Gruning Precision Inc.
Guncraft Books (See Guncraft Sports Inc.)
Guncraft Sports Inc.
Guncraft Sports, Inc.
Guns Antique & Modern DBA / Charles E. Duffy
Gunsite Custom Shop
Gunsite Gunsmithy (See Gunsite Custom Shop)
Gunsite Training Center
Gunsmithing Ltd.
Hamilton, Alex B (See Ten-Ring Precision, Inc)
Hammans, Charles E.
Hammerli Service-Precision Mac
Hammond Custom Guns Ltd.
Hank's Gun Shop
Hanson's Gun Center, Dick
Harris Gunworks
Harry Lawson Co.
Hart & Son, Inc.
Hart Rifle Barrels,Inc.
Hartmann & Weiss GmbH
Harwood, Jack O.
Hawken Shop, The (See Dayton Traister)
Hecht, Hubert J, Waffen-Hecht
Heilmann, Stephen
Heinie Specialty Products
Hensley, Gunmaker, Darwin
High Bridge Arms, Inc
High Performance International
High Precision
Highline Machine Co.
Hill, Loring F.
Hiptmayer, Armurier
Hiptmayer, Klaus
Hoag, James W.
Hodgson, Richard
Hoehn Sales, Inc.
Hofer Jagdwaffen, P.
Holland's Gunsmithing
Huebner, Corey O.
Hunkeler, A (See Buckskin Machine Works
Imperial Magnum Corp.
Irwin, Campbell H.
Island Pond Gun Shop
Israel Arms International, Inc.
Ivanoff, Thomas G. (See Tom's Gun Repair)
J&S Heat Treat
J.J. Roberts / Engraver
Jack Dever Co.
Jackalope Gun Shop
James Calhoon Mfg.

James Calhoon Varmint Bullets
Jamison's Forge Works
Jarrett Rifles, Inc.
Jarvis, Inc.
Jay McCament Custom Gunmaker
Jeffredo Gunsight
Jensen's Custom Ammunition
Jim Norman Custom Gunstocks
Jim's Gun Shop (See Spradlin's)
Jim's Precision, Jim Ketchum
John Norrell Arms
John Rigby & Co.
Jones Custom Products, Neil A.
Juenke, Vern
K. Eversull Co., Inc.
KDF, Inc.
Keith's Custom Gunstocks
Ken Eyster Heritage Gunsmiths, Inc.
Ken Starnes Gunmaker
Ketchum, Jim (See Jim's Precision)
Kilham & Co.
King's Gun Works
KLA Enterprises
Klein Custom Guns, Don
Kleinendorst, K. W.
KOGOT
Korzinek Riflesmith, J.
L. E. Jurras & Assoc.
LaFrance Specialties
Lampert, Ron
LaRocca Gun Works
Larry Lyons Gunworks
Lathrop's, Inc.
Laughridge, William R (See Cylinder & Slide Inc)
Lawson Co., Harry
Lazzeroni Arms Co.
LeFever Arms Co., Inc.
Linebaugh Custom Sixguns
List Precision Engineering
Lock's Philadelphia Gun Exchange
Lone Star Rifle Company
Long, George F.
Mag-Na-Port International, Inc.
Mahony, Philip Bruce
Mahony, Philip Bruce
Mahovsky's Metalife
Makinson, Nicholas
Mandall Shooting Supplies Inc.
Marshall Fish Mfg. Gunsmith Sptg. Co.
Martin's Gun Shop
Martz, John V.
Mathews & Son, Inc., George E.
Mazur Restoration, Pete
McCann's Muzzle-Gun Works
McCluskey Precision Rifles
McGowen Rifle Barrels
McMillan Rifle Barrels
MCS, Inc.
Mercer Custom Guns
Michael's Antiques
Mid-America Recreation, Inc.
Middlebrooks Custom Shop
Miller Arms, Inc.
Miller Custom
Mills Jr., Hugh B.
Moeller, Steve
Monell Custom Guns
Montgomery Community College
Morrison Custom Rifles, J. W.
Morrow, Bud
Mo's Competitor Supplies (See MCS, Inc.)
Mowrey's Guns & Gunsmithing
Mullis Guncraft
Muzzleloaders Etcetera, Inc.
NCP Products, Inc.
Neil A. Jones Custom Products
Nelson's Custom Guns, Inc.
Nettestad Gun Works
New England Arms Co.
New England Custom Gun Service
Newman Gunshop
Nicholson Custom

Nickels, Paul R.
Nicklas, Ted
Nitex Gun Shop
North American Shooting Systems
Nu-Line Guns,Inc.
Old World Gunsmithing
Olson, Vic
Ottmar, Maurice
Ox-Yoke Originals, Inc.
Ozark Gun Works
P&M Sales & Services, LLC
P.S.M.G. Gun Co.
PAC-NOR Barreling
Pagel Gun Works, Inc.
Parker & Sons Shooting Supply
Parker Gun Finishes
Pasadena Gun Center
Paterson Gunsmithing
Paulsen Gunstocks
Peacemaker Specialists
PEM's Mfg. Co.
Pence Precision Barrels
Pennsylvania Gunsmith School
Penrod Precision
Pentheny de Pentheny
Performance Specialists
Pete Mazur Restoration
Peter Dyson & Son Ltd.
Peterson Gun Shop, Inc., A.W.
Piquette's Custom Engraving
Plum City Ballistic Range
Powell & Son (Gunmakers) Ltd., William
Power Custom, Inc.
Professional Hunter Supplies (See Star Custom Bullets)
Quality Custom Firearms
R&J Gun Shop
R.A. Wells Custom Gunsmith
Ramon B. Gonzalez Guns
Ray's Gunsmith Shop
Renfrew Guns & Supplies
Ridgetop Sporting Goods
Ries, Chuck
RMS Custom Gunsmithing
Robert Valade Engraving
Robinson, Don
Rocky Mountain Arms, Inc.
Romain's Custom Guns, Inc.
Ron Frank Custom Classic Arms
Ruger's Custom Guns
Rupert's Gun Shop
Savage Arms, Inc.
Schiffman, Mike
Schumakers Gun Shop
Score High Gunsmithing
Sharp Shooter Supply
Shaw, Inc., E. R. (See Small Arms Mfg. Co.)
Shay's Gunsmithing
Shockley, Harold H.
Shooters Supply
Shootin' Shack
Shooting Specialties (See Titus, Daniel)
Shotguns Unlimited
Silver Ridge Gun Shop (See Goodwin, Fred)
Simmons Gun Repair, Inc.
Singletary, Kent
Siskiyou Gun Works (See Donnelly, C. P.)
Skeoch, Brian R.
Sklany's Machine Shop
Slezak, Jerome F.
Small Arms Mfg. Co.
Small Arms Specialists
Smith, Art
Snapp's Gunshop
Sound Technology
Speiser, Fred D.
Spencer Reblue Service
Spencer's Rifle Barrels, Inc.
Splitfire Sporting Goods, L.L.C.

Sportsmen's Exchange & Western Gun Traders, Inc.
Springfield Armory
Springfield, Inc.
SSK Industries
Star Custom Bullets
Steelman's Gun Shop
Steffens, Ron
Steven Dodd Hughes
Stiles Custom Guns
Stott's Creek Armory, Inc.
Sturgeon Valley Sporters
Sullivan, David S .(See Westwind Rifles Inc.)
Swann, D. J.
Swenson's 45 Shop, A. D.
Swift River Gunworks
Szweda, Robert (See RMS Custom Gunsmithing)
Taconic Firearms Ltd., Perry Lane
Talmage, William G.
Tank's Rifle Shop
Tar-Hunt Custom Rifles, Inc.
Tarnhelm Supply Co., Inc.
Taylor & Robbins
Ten-Ring Precision, Inc.
Terry K. Kopp Professional Gunsmithing
The A.W. Peterson Gun Shop, Inc.
The Competitive Pistol Shop
The Custom Shop
The Gun Shop
The Gun Works
The Orvis Co.
The Robar Co.'s, Inc.
The Swampfire Shop (See Peterson Gun Shop, Inc.)
Theis, Terry
Thompson, Randall (See Highline Machine Co.)
Thurston Sports, Inc.
Time Precision
Tom's Gun Repair, Thomas G. Ivanoff
Tom's Gunshop
Trevallion Gunstocks
Trulock Tool
Tucker, James C.
Turnbull Restoration, Doug
Unmussig Bullets, D. L.
Upper Missouri Trading Co.
Van Horn, Gil
Van Patten, J. W.
Van's Gunsmith Service
Vest, John
Vic's Gun Refinishing
Vintage Arms, Inc.
Virgin Valley Custom Guns
Volquartsen Custom Ltd.
Walker Arms Co., Inc.
Wallace, Terry
Wasmundt, Jim
Wayne E. Schwartz Custom Guns
Weatherby, Inc.
Weber & Markin Custom Gunsmiths
Weems, Cecil
Werth, T. W.
Wessinger Custom Guns & Engraving
Western Design (See Alpha Gunsmith Division)
Westley Richards & Co.
Westwind Rifles, Inc., David S. Sullivan
White Barn Wor
White Rifles, Inc.
Wichita Arms, Inc.
Wiebe, Duane
Wild West Guns
William E. Phillips Firearms
Williams Gun Sight Co.
Williams Shootin' Iron Service, The Lynx-Line
Williamson Precision Gunsmithing
Wilsom Combat
Winter, Robert M.

Wise Guns, Dale
Wiseman and Co., Bill
Wood, Frank (See Classic Guns, Inc.)
Working Guns
Wright's Gunstock Blanks
Yankee Gunsmith "Just Glocks"
Zeeryp, Russ

CUSTOM METALSMITH

A&W Repair
Ackerman & Co.
Ahlman Guns
Alaskan Silversmith, The
Aldis Gunsmithing & Shooting Supply
Alpha Precision, Inc.
Amrine's Gun Shop
Answer Products Co.
Antique Arms Co.
Artistry in Wood
Baer Custom Inc., Les
Baron Technology
Bear Mountain Gun & Tool
Behlert Precision, Inc.
Beitzinger, George
Bengtson Arms Co., L.
Bill Adair Custom Shop
Billings Gunsmiths
Billingsley & Brownell
Bob Rogers Gunsmithing
Bowen Classic Arms Corp.
Brace, Larry D.
Briganti, A.J.
Broad Creek Rifle Works, Ltd.
Brown Precision, Inc.
Buckhorn Gun Works
Bull Mountain Rifle Co.
Bullberry Barrel Works, Ltd.
Carter's Gun Shop
Caywood, Shane J.
Checkmate Refinishing
Cleland's Outdoor World, Inc
Colonial Repair
Colorado Gunsmithing Academy
Craftguard
Crandall Tool & Machine Co.
Cullity Restoration
Custom Single Shot Rifles
D&D Gunsmiths, Ltd.
D&H Precision Tooling
D'Arcy Echols & Co.
Dave's Gun Shop
Delorge, Ed
DGS, Inc., Dale A. Storey
Dietz Gun Shop & Range, Inc.
Dilliott Gunsmithing, Inc.
Duane's Gun Repair (See DGR Custom Rifles)
Duncan's Gun Works, Inc.
Erhardt, Dennis
Eversull Co., Inc.
Ferris Firearms
Fisher, Jerry A.
Forster, Larry L.
Forthofer's Gunsmithing & Knifemaking
Francesca, Inc.
Fred F. Wells/Wells Sport Store
Fullmer, Geo. M.
Genecco Gun Works
Gentry Custom Gunmaker, David
Grace, Charles E.
Grayback Wildcats
Graybill's Gun Shop
Green, Roger M.
Gunsmithing Ltd.
Hamilton, Alex B (See Ten-Ring Precision, Inc)
Harry Lawson Co.
Hartmann & Weiss GmbH
Harwood, Jack O.
Hecht, Hubert J, Waffen-Hecht
Heilmann, Stephen
Highline Machine Co.

Hiptmayer, Armurier
Hiptmayer, Klaus
Hoag, James W.
Holland's Gunsmithing
Island Pond Gun Shop
Ivanoff, Thomas G. (See Tom's Gun Repair)
J J Roberts Firearm Engraver
J&S Heat Treat
J.J. Roberts / Engraver
Jamison's Forge Works
Jay McCament Custom Gunmaker
Jeffredo Gunsight
KDF, Inc.
Ken Eyster Heritage Gunsmiths, Inc.
Ken Starnes Gunmaker
Kilham & Co.
Klein Custom Guns, Don
Kleinendorst, K. W.
Lampert, Ron
LaRocca Gun Works
Larry Lyons Gunworks
Lawson Co., Harry
List Precision Engineering
Mahovsky's Metalife
Makinson, Nicholas
Mandall Shooting Supplies Inc.
Mazur Restoration, Pete
McCann Industries
McCann's Machine & Gun Shop
Mid-America Recreation, Inc.
Miller Arms, Inc.
Montgomery Community College
Morrison Custom Rifles, J. W.
Morrow, Bud
Mullis Guncraft
Nelson's Custom Guns, Inc.
Nettestad Gun Works
New England Custom Gun Service
Nicholson Custom
Nitex Gun Shop
Noreen, Peter H.
Nu-Line Guns,Inc.
Olson, Vic
Ozark Gun Works
P.S.M.G. Gun Co.
Pagel Gun Works, Inc.
Parker & Sons Shooting Supply
Parker Gun Finishes
Pasadena Gun Center
Penrod Precision
Pete Mazur Restoration
Precision Specialties
Quality Custom Firearms
R.A. Wells Custom Gunsmith
Rice, Keith (See White Rock Tool & Die)
Robert Valade Engraving
Rocky Mountain Arms, Inc.
Romain's Custom Guns, Inc.
Ron Frank Custom Classic Arms
Score High Gunsmithing
Simmons Gun Repair, Inc.
Singletary, Kent
Skeoch, Brian R.
Sklany's Machine Shop
Small Arms Specialists
Smith, Art
Smith, Sharmon
Snapp's Gunshop
Spencer Reblue Service
Spencer's Rifle Barrels, Inc.
Sportsmen's Exchange & Western Gun Traders, Inc.
SSK Industries
Steffens, Ron
Stiles Custom Guns
Taylor & Robbins
Ten-Ring Precision, Inc.
The A.W. Peterson Gun Shop, Inc.
The Custom Shop
The Gun Shop
The Robar Co.'s, Inc.

Thompson, Randall (See Highline Machine Co.)
Tom's Gun Repair, Thomas G. Ivanoff
Turnbull Restoration, Doug
Van Horn, Gil
Van Patten, J. W.
Waldron, Herman
Wallace, Terry
Weber & Markin Custom Gunsmiths
Werth, T. W.
Wessinger Custom Guns & Engraving
White Rock Tool & Die
Wiebe, Duane
Wild West Guns
Williams Shootin' Iron Service, The Lynx-Line
Williamson Precision Gunsmithing
Winter, Robert M.
Wise Guns, Dale
Wood, Frank (See Classic Guns, Inc.)
Wright's Gunstock Blanks
Zufall, Joseph F.

DECOYS

Ad Hominem
Baekgaard Ltd.
Belding's Custom Gun Shop
Bill Russ Trading Post
Boyds' Gunstock Industries, Inc.
Carry-Lite, Inc.
Farm Form Decoys, Inc.
Feather, Flex Decoys
Flambeau Products Corp.
G&H Decoys,Inc.
Grand Slam Hunting Products
Herter's Manufacturing Inc.
Hiti-Schuch, Atelier Wilma
Klingler Woodcarving
L.L. Bean, Inc.
Molin Industries, Tru-Nord Division
Murphy, R.R. Co., Inc.
Original Deer Formula Co., The.
Quack Decoy & Sporting Clays
Sports Innovations Inc.
Tanglefree Industries
The A.W. Peterson Gun Shop, Inc.
Woods Wise Products

DIE ACCESSORIES, METALLIC

High Precision
King & Co.
MarMik, Inc.
Rapine Bullet Mould Mfg. Co.
Redding Reloading Equipment
Royal Arms Gunstocks
Sport Flite Manufacturing Co.
The A.W. Peterson Gun Shop, Inc.
Wolf's Western Traders

DIES, METALLIC

4-D Custom Die Co.
Badger Creek Studio
Buffalo Arms Co.
Dakota Arms, Inc.
Dillon Precision Products, Inc.
Dixie Gun Works
Fremont Tool Works
Goodwin's Gun Shop
Gruning Precision Inc.
Jones Custom Products, Neil A.
King & Co.
Lee Precision, Inc.
Montana Precision Swaging
Neil A. Jones Custom Products
Ozark Gun Works
Rapine Bullet Mould Mfg. Co.
RCBS Operations/ATK
RCBS/ATK
Redding Reloading Equipment

Thompson, Randall (See Highline Machine Co.)
Tom's Gun Repair, Thomas G. Ivanoff
Turnbull Restoration, Doug
Van Horn, Gil
Van Patten, J. W.
Waldron, Herman
Wallace, Terry
Weber & Markin Custom Gunsmiths
Werth, T. W.
Wessinger Custom Guns & Engraving
White Rock Tool & Die
Wiebe, Duane
Wild West Guns
Williams Shootin' Iron Service, The Lynx-Line
Williamson Precision Gunsmithing
Winter, Robert M.
Wise Guns, Dale
Wood, Frank (See Classic Guns, Inc.)
Wright's Gunstock Blanks
Zufall, Joseph F.

Romain's Custom Guns, Inc.
Spencer's Rifle Barrels, Inc.
Sport Flite Manufacturing Co.
SSK Industries
The A.W. Peterson Gun Shop, Inc.
Vega Tool Co.
Wolf's Western Traders

DIES, SHOTSHELL

Goodwin's Gun Shop
Lee Precision, Inc.
MEC, Inc.
The A.W. Peterson Gun Shop, Inc.

DIES, SWAGE

4-D Custom Die Co.
Bullet Swaging Supply, Inc.
Goodwin's Gun Shop
Hollywood Engineering
Montana Precision Swaging
Sport Flite Manufacturing Co.
The A.W. Peterson Gun Shop, Inc.

ENGRAVER, ENGRAVING TOOLS

Ackerman & Co.
Adair Custom Shop, Bill
Ahlman Guns
Alaskan Silversmith, The
Alfano, Sam
Allard, Gary/Creek Side Metal & Woodcrafters
Allen Firearm Engraving
Altamont Co.
American Pioneer Video
Baron Technology
Barraclough, John K.
Bates Engraving, Billy
Bill Adair Custom Shop
Billy Bates Engraving
Boessler, Erich
Brooker, Dennis
Buchsenmachermeister
Churchill, Winston G.
Clark Firearms Engraving
Collings, Ronald
Creek Side Metal & Woodcrafters
Cullity Restoration
Cupp, Alana, Custom Engraver
Custom Single Shot Rifles
Dayton Traister
Delorge, Ed
Dolbare, Elizabeth
Drain, Mark
Dremel Mfg. Co.
Dubber, Michael W.
Engraving Artistry
Engraving Only
Evans Engraving, Robert
Eversull Co., Inc.
Firearms Engraver's Guild of America
Flannery Engraving Co., Jeff W
Forty Five Ranch Enterprises
Fountain Products
Francotte & Cie S.A. Auguste
Frank Knives
Fred F. Wells/Wells Sport Store
French, Artistic Engraving, J. R.
Gary Reeder Custom Guns
Gene's Custom Guns
George Madis Winchester Consultants
Glimm's Custom Gun Engraving
Golden Age Arms Co.
Gournet Artistic Engraving
Grant, Howard V.
GRS / Glendo Corp.
Gurney, F. R.
Half Moon Rifle Shop
Harris Gunworks
Harris Hand Engraving, Paul A.

Harwood, Jack O.
Hawken Shop, The (See Dayton Traister)
Hiptmayer, Armurier
Hiptmayer, Heidemarie
Hofer Jagdwaffen, P.
Ingle, Ralph W.
J J Roberts Firearm Engraver
J.J. Roberts / Engraver
Jantz Supply
Jeff W. Flannery Engraving Co.
Jim Blair Engraving
John J. Adams & Son Engravers
Kane, Edward
Kehr, Roger
Kelly, Lance
Ken Eyster Heritage Gunsmiths, Inc.
Kenneth W. Warren Engraver
Klingler Woodcarving
Larry Lyons Gunworks
LeFever Arms Co., Inc.
Leibowitz, Leonard
Lindsay Engraving & Tools
Little Trees Ramble (See Scott Pilkington)
McCombs, Leo
McDonald, Dennis
McKenzie, Lynton
Mele, Frank
Mid-America Recreation, Inc.
Mittermeier, Inc., Frank
Montgomery Community College
Nelson, Gary K.
New Orleans Jewelers Supply Co.
Pedersen, C. R.
Pedersen, Rex C.
Peter Hale/Engraver
Pilgrim Pewter,Inc. (See Bell Originals Inc. Sid)
Pilkington, Scott (See Little Trees Ramble)
Piquette's Custom Engraving
Potts, Wayne E.
Quality Custom Firearms
Rabeno, Martin
Ralph Bone Engraving
Reed, Dave
Reno, Wayne
Riggs, Jim
Robert Evans Engraving
Robert Valade Engraving
Rohner, Hans
Rohner, John
Rosser, Bob
Rundell's Gun Shop
Runge, Robert P.
Sam Welch Gun Engraving
Sampson, Roger
Schiffman, Mike
Sheffield Knifemakers Supply, Inc.
Sherwood, George
Singletary, Kent
Smith, Mark A.
Smith, Ron
Smokey Valley Rifles
SSK Industries
Steve Kamyk Engraver
Swanson, Mark
The Gun Room
The NgraveR Co.
Theis, Terry
Thiewes, George W.
Thirion Gun Engraving, Denise
Viramontez Engraving
Vorhes, David
W.E. Brownell Checkering Tools
Wagoner, Vernon G.
Wallace, Terry
Warenski, Julie
Weber & Markin Custom Gunsmiths
Wells, Rachel
Wessinger Custom Guns & Engraving
Ziegel Engineering

GAME CALLS

Adventure Game Calls
African Import Co.
Ashby Turkey Calls
Bill Russ Trading Post
Bostick Wildlife Calls, Inc.
Cedar Hill Game Calls, Inc.
Crit'R Call (See Rocky Mountain Wildlife Products)
Custom Calls
D-Boone Ent., Inc.
Deepeeka Exports Pvt. Ltd.
Dr. O's Products Ltd.
Duck Call Specialists
Faulhaber Wildlocker
Faulk's Game Call Co., Inc.
Fibron Products, Inc.
Glynn Scobey Duck & Goose Calls
Goodwin's Gun Shop
Grand Slam Hunting Products
Green Head Game Call Co.
Hally Caller
Haydel's Game Calls, Inc.
Herter's Manufacturing Inc.
Hunter's Specialties Inc.
Keowee Game Calls
Kingyon, Paul L. (See Custom Calls)
Knight & Hale Game Calls
Lohman Mfg. Co., Inc.
Mallardtone Game Calls
Moss Double Tone, Inc.
Oakman Turkey Calls
Original Deer Formula Co., The.
Outdoor Sports Headquarters, Inc.
Pete Rickard, Inc.
Philip S. Olt Co.
Primos, Inc.
Protektor Model
Quaker Boy, Inc.
Rocky Mountain Wildlife Products
Sceery Game Calls
Sports Innovations Inc.
Stewart Game Calls, Inc., Johnny
Sure-Shot Game Calls, Inc.
Tanglefree Industries
The A.W. Peterson Gun Shop, Inc.
Tinks & Ben Lee Hunting Products (See Wellington)
Tink's Safariland Hunting Corp.
Wellington Outdoors
Wilderness Sound Products Ltd.
Woods Wise Products
Wyant's Outdoor Products, Inc.

GAUGES, CALIPERS & MICROMETERS

Blue Ridge Machinery & Tools, Inc.
Goodwin's Gun Shop
Gruning Precision Inc.
Huntington Die Specialties
K&M Services
King & Co.
Spencer's Rifle Barrels, Inc.
Starrett Co., L. S.
Stoney Point Products, Inc.

GUN PARTS, U.S. & FOREIGN

"Su-Press-On", Inc.
A.A. Arms, Inc.
Ahlman Guns
Amherst Arms
Antique Arms Co.
Armscorp USA, Inc.
Auto-Ordnance Corp.
B.A.C.
Badger Shooters Supply, Inc.
Ballard Rifle & Cartridge Co., LLC
Bar-Sto Precision Machine
Bear Mountain Gun & Tool

Billings Gunsmiths
Bill's Gun Repair
Bob's Gun Shop
Briese Bullet Co., Inc.
Brown Products, Inc., Ed
Brownells, Inc.
Bryan & Assoc.
Buffer Technologies
Cambos Outdoorsman
Cambos Outdoorsman
Cape Outfitters
Caspian Arms, Ltd.
CBC-BRAZIL
Chicasaw Gun Works
Ciener Inc., Jonathan Arthur
Cole's Gun Works
Colonial Arms, Inc.
Colonial Repair
Colt's Mfg. Co., Inc.
Custom Riflestocks, Inc., Michael M. Kokolus
Cylinder & Slide, Inc., William R. Laughridge
David R. Chicoine
Delta Arms Ltd.
DGR Custom Rifles
Dibble, Derek A.
Dixie Gun Works
Duane's Gun Repair (See DGR Custom Rifles)
Duffy, Charles E (See Guns Antique & Modern DBA)
E.A.A. Corp.
Elliott Inc., G. W.
EMF Co., Inc.
Enguix Import-Export
Entre`prise Arms, Inc.
European American Armory Corp (See E.A.A. Corp)
Evolution Gun Works Inc.
F.I., Inc. - High Standard Mfg. Co.
Faloon Industries, Inc.
Federal Arms Corp. of America
Fleming Firearms
Forrest Inc., Tom
Gentry Custom Gunmaker, David
Glimm's Custom Gun Engraving
Goodwin's Gun Shop
Granite Mountain Arms, Inc.
Greider Precision
Gre-Tan Rifles
Groenewold, John
Gun Hunter Books (See Gun Hunter Trading Co.)
Gun Hunter Trading Co.
Guns Antique & Modern DBA / Charles E. Duffy
Gunsmithing, Inc.
Hastings
Hawken Shop, The (See Dayton Traister)
High Performance International
I.S.S.
Irwin, Campbell H.
Jack First, Inc.
Jamison's Forge Works
Jonathan Arthur Ciener, Inc.
Kimber of America, Inc.
Knight's Mfg. Co.
Krico Deutschland GmbH
LaFrance Specialties
Lampert, Ron
LaPrade
Laughridge, William R (See Cylinder & Slide Inc)
Leapers, Inc.
List Precision Engineering
Lodewick, Walter H.
Logdewood Mfg.
Long, George F.
Mandall Shooting Supplies Inc.
Markell,Inc.
Martin's Gun Shop
McCormick Corp., Chip

MCS, Inc.
Merkuria Ltd.
Mid-America Recreation, Inc.
Morrow, Bud
Mo's Competitor Supplies (See MCS, Inc.)
North Star West
Northwest Arms
Nu-Line Guns,Inc.
Numrich Gun Parts Corporation
Nygord Precision Products, Inc.
Olathe Gun Shop
Olympic Arms Inc.
P.S.M.G. Gun Co.
Pacific Armament Corp
Pennsylvania Gun Parts Inc
Performance Specialists
Peter Dyson & Son Ltd.
Peterson Gun Shop, Inc., A.W.
Ranch Products
Randco UK
Ravell Ltd.
Retting, Inc., Martin B
Romain's Custom Guns, Inc.
Ruger (See Sturm, Ruger & Co., Inc.)
Rutgers Book Center
S&S Firearms
Sabatti SPA
Samco Global Arms, Inc.
Sarco, Inc.
Shockley, Harold H.
Shootin' Shack
Silver Ridge Gun Shop (See Goodwin, Fred)
Simmons Gun Repair, Inc.
Smires, C. L.
Smith & Wesson
Southern Ammunition Co., Inc.
Sportsmen's Exchange & Western Gun Traders, Inc.
Springfield Sporters, Inc.
Springfield, Inc.
Steyr Mannlicher GmbH P Co KG
STI International
Strayer-Voigt, Inc.
Sturm Ruger & Co. Inc.
Sunny Hill Enterprises, Inc.
T&S Industries, Inc.
Tank's Rifle Shop
Tarnhelm Supply Co., Inc.
Terry K. Kopp Professional Gunsmithing
The A.W. Peterson Gun Shop, Inc.
The Gun Room Press
The Gun Shop
The Gun Works
The Southern Armory
The Swampfire Shop (See Peterson Gun Shop, Inc.)
VAM Distribution Co. LLC
Vektor USA
Vintage Arms, Inc.
W. Waller & Son, Inc.
W.C. Wolff Co.
Walker Arms Co., Inc.
Wescombe, Bill (See North Star West)
Whitestone Lumber Corp.
Wild West Guns
Williams Mfg. of Oregon
Winchester Sutler, Inc., The
Wise Guns, Dale
Wisners Inc/Twin Pine Armory

GUNS & GUN PARTS, REPLICA & ANTIQUE

Ackerman & Co.
Ahlman Guns
Armi San Paolo
Auto-Ordnance Corp.
Ballard Rifle & Cartridge Co., LLC
Bear Mountain Gun & Tool
Billings Gunsmiths
Bob's Gun Shop

Buffalo Arms Co.
Cache La Poudre Rifleworks
Campbell, Dick
Cash Mfg. Co., Inc.
CBC-BRAZIL
CCL Security Products
Chambers Flintlocks Ltd., Jim
Chicasaw Gun Works
Cimarron F.A. Co.
Cogar's Gunsmithing
Cole's Gun Works
Colonial Repair
Colt Blackpowder Arms Co.
Colt's Mfg. Co., Inc.
Custom Riflestocks, Inc., Michael M. Kokolus
Custom Single Shot Rifles
David R. Chicoine
Delhi Gun House
Delta Arms Ltd.
Dilliott Gunsmithing, Inc.
Dixie Gun Works
Dixon Muzzleloading Shop, Inc.
Ed's Gun House
Euroarms of America, Inc.
Flintlocks, Etc.
George E. Mathews & Son, Inc.
Getz Barrel Co.
Golden Age Arms Co.
Goodwin's Gun Shop
Groenewold, John
Gun Hunter Books (See Gun Hunter Trading Co.)
Gun Hunter Trading Co.
Hastings
Heidenstrom Bullets
Hunkeler, A (See Buckskin Machine Works
IAR Inc.
Imperial Miniature Armory
Ithaca Classic Doubles
Jack First, Inc.
Ken Starnes Gunmaker
Kokolus, Michael M. (See Custom Riflestocks In)
L&R Lock Co.
Leonard Day
List Precision Engineering
Lock's Philadelphia Gun Exchange
Logdewood Mfg.
Lone Star Rifle Company
Lucas, Edward E
Mandall Shooting Supplies Inc.
Martin's Gun Shop
Mathews & Son, Inc., George E.
Mid-America Recreation, Inc.
Mountain State Muzzleloading Supplies, Inc.
Mowrey Gun Works
Navy Arms Company
Neumann GmbH
North Star West
Numrich Gun Parts Corporation
Olathe Gun Shop
Parker & Sons Shooting Supply
Pasadena Gun Center
Pecatonica River Longrifle
PEM's Mfg. Co.
Peter Dyson & Son Ltd.
Pony Express Sport Shop
R.A. Wells Custom Gunsmith
Randco UK
Ravell Ltd.
Retting, Inc., Martin B
Rutgers Book Center
S&S Firearms
Samco Global Arms, Inc.
Sarco, Inc.
Shootin' Shack
Silver Ridge Gun Shop (See Goodwin, Fred)
Simmons Gun Repair, Inc.
Sklany's Machine Shop
Southern Ammunition Co., Inc.

Starr Trading Co., Jedediah
Stott's Creek Armory, Inc.
Taylor's & Co., Inc.
Tennessee Valley Mfg.
The A.W. Peterson Gun Shop, Inc.
The Gun Room Press
The Gun Works
Tiger-Hunt Gunstocks
Turnbull Restoration, Doug
Upper Missouri Trading Co.
Vintage Industries, Inc.
Vortek Products, Inc.
VTI Gun Parts
Weber & Markin Custom Gunsmiths
Wescombe, Bill (See North Star West)
Whitestone Lumber Corp.
Winchester Sutler, Inc., The

GUNS, AIR

Air Arms
Air Rifle Specialists
Air Venture Airguns
AirForce Airguns
Airrow
Allred Bullet Co.
Arms Corporation of the Philippines
BEC, Inc.
Beeman Precision Airguns
Benjamin/Sheridan Co., Crosman
Brass Eagle, Inc.
Brocock Ltd.
Bryan & Assoc.
BSA Guns Ltd.
Compasseco, Ltd.
Component Concepts, Inc.
Conetrol Scope Mounts
Crosman Airguns
Daisy Outdoor Products
Daystate Ltd.
Domino
Dynamit Nobel-RWS, Inc.
European American Armory Corp (See
E.A.A. Corp)
Feinwerkbau Westinger & Altenburger
Gamo USA, Inc.
Gaucher Armes, S.A.
Great Lakes Airguns
Groenewold, John
Hammerli Service-Precision Mac
I.S.S.
IAR Inc.
J.G. Anschutz GmbH & Co. KG
Labanu, Inc.
Leapers, Inc.
List Precision Engineering
Mac-1 Airgun Distributors
Marksman Products
Maryland Paintball Supply
Merkuria Ltd.
Nationwide Airgun Repair
Nygord Precision Products, Inc.
Olympic Arms Inc.
Pardini Armi Srl
Precision Airgun Sales, Inc.
Precision Sales International, Inc.
Ripley Rifles
Robinson, Don
RWS (See US Importer-Dynamit
Nobel-RWS, Inc.)
S.G.S. Sporting Guns Srl.
Safari Arms/Schuetzen Pistol Works
Savage Arms, Inc.
Smart Parts
Smith & Wesson
Steyr Mannlicher GmbH P Co KG
Stone Enterprises Ltd.
The A.W. Peterson Gun Shop, Inc.
The Gun Room Press
The Park Rifle Co., Ltd.
Tippman Pneumatics, Inc.
Tristar Sporting Arms, Ltd.
Trooper Walsh
UltraSport Arms, Inc.

Visible Impact Targets
Vortek Products, Inc.
Walther GmbH, Carl
Webley and Scott Ltd.
Weihrauch KG, Hermann
Whiscombe (See U.S. Importer-
Pelaire Products)

GUNS, FOREIGN MANUFACTURER U.S. IMPORTER

Accuracy Internationl Precision Rifles
(See U.S.)
Accuracy Int'l. North America, Inc.
Ad Hominem
Air Arms
Armas Garbi, S.A.
Armas Kemen S. A. (See U.S.
Importers)
Armi Perazzi S.p.A.
Armi San Marco (See U.S. Importers-
Taylor's & Co I
Armi Sport (See U.S. Importers-Cape
Outfitters)
Arms Corporation of the Philippines
Armscorp USA, Inc.
Arrieta S.L.
Astra Sport, S.A.
Atamec-Bretton
AYA (See U.S. Importer-New England
Custom Gun Serv
B.A.C.
B.C. Outdoors
BEC, Inc.
Benelli Armi S.p.A.
Benelli USA Corp
Beretta S.p.A., Pietro
Beretta U.S.A. Corp.
Bernardelli S.p.A., Vincenzo
Bersa S.A.
Bertuzzi (See U.S. Importer-New
England Arms Co)
Bill Hanus Birdguns
Blaser Jagdwaffen GmbH
Borovnik KG, Ludwig
Bosis (See U.S. Importer-New England
Arms Co.)
Brenneke GmbH
Browning Arms Co.
Bryan & Assoc.
BSA Guns Ltd.
Cabanas (See U.S. Importer-Mandall
Shooting Supply)
Cabela's
Cape Outfitters
CBC
Chapuis Armes
Churchill (See U.S. Importer-Ellett
Bros.)
Conetrol Scope Mounts
Cosmi Americo & Figlio s.n.c.
Crucelegui, Hermanos (See U.S.
Importer-Mandall)
Cubic Shot Shell Co., Inc.
Daewoo Precision Industries Ltd.
Dakota (See U.S. Importer-EMF Co.,
Inc.)
Dakota Arms, Inc.
Daly, Charles (See U.S. Importer)
Davide Pedersoli and Co.
Domino
Dumoulin, Ernest
Eagle Imports, Inc.
EAW (See U.S. Importer-New England
Custom Gun Serv
Ed's Gun House
Effebi SNC-Dr. Franco Beretta
EMF Co., Inc.
Eversull Co., Inc.
F.A.I.R.
Fabarm S.p.A.
FEG
Feinwerkbau Westinger & Altenburger

Felk Pistols Inc.
FERLIB
Fiocchi Munizioni S.p.A. (See U.S.
Importer-Fiocch
Firearms Co Ltd. / Alpine (See U.S.
Importer-Mandall
Firearms International
Flintlocks, Etc.
Franchi S.p.A.
Galaxy Imports Ltd., Inc.
Gamba S.p.A. Societa Armi Bresciane
Srl
Gamo (See U.S. Importers-Arms
United Corp, Daisy M
Gaucher Armes, S.A.
Gibbs Rifle Co., Inc.
Glock GmbH
Goergen's Gun Shop, Inc.
Griffin & Howe, Inc.
Griffin & Howe, Inc.
Griffin & Howe, Inc.
Grulla Armes
Hammerli Ltd.
Hammerli USA
Hartford (See U.S. Importer-EMF Co.
Inc.)
Hartmann & Weiss GmbH
Heckler & Koch, Inc.
Hege Jagd-u. Sporthandels GmbH
Helwan (See U.S. Importer-Interarms)
Holland & Holland Ltd.
Howa Machinery, Ltd.
I.A.B. (See U.S. Importer-Taylor's &
Co. Inc.)
IAR Inc.
IGA (See U.S. Importer-Stoeger
Industries)
Ignacio Ugartechea S.A.
Imperial Magnum Corp.
Imperial Miniature Armory
Import Sports Inc.
Inter Ordnance of America LP
Intrac Arms International
J.G. Anschutz GmbH & Co. KG
JSL Ltd (See U.S. Importer-Specialty
Shooters)
K. Eversull Co., Inc.
Kimar (See U.S. Importer-IAR,Inc)
Korth Germany GmbH
Krico Deutschland GmbH
Krieghoff Gun Co., H.
Lakefield Arms Ltd. (See Savage
Arms, Inc.)
Lapua Ltd.
Laurona Armas Eibar, S.A.L.
Lebeau-Courally
Lever Arms Service Ltd.
Llama Gabilondo Y Cia
London Guns Ltd.
M. Thys (See U.S. Importer-Champlin
Firearms Inc)
Magtech Ammunition Co. Inc.
Mandall Shooting Supplies Inc.
Marocchi F.lli S.p.A
Mauser Werke Oberndorf
Waffensysteme GmbH
McCann Industries
MEC-Gar S.R.L.
Merkel
Miltex, Inc
Morini (See U.S. Importers-Mandall
Shooting Supply)
New England Custom Gun Service
New SKB Arms Co.
Norica, Avnda Otaola
Norinco
Norma Precision AB (See U.S.
Importers-Dynamit)
Northwest Arms
Nygord Precision Products, Inc.
OK Weber, Inc.
Para-Ordnance Mfg., Inc.
Pardini Armi Srl
Perugini Visini & Co. S.r.l.

Peters Stahl GmbH
Pietta (See U.S. Importers-Navy Arms
Co, Taylor's
Piotti (See U.S. Importer-Moore & Co,
Wm. Larkin)
PMC/Eldorado Cartridge Corp.
Powell & Son (Gunmakers) Ltd.,
William
Prairie Gun Works
Ramon B. Gonzalez Guns
Rizzini F.lli (See U.S. Importers-Moore
& C England)
Rizzini SNC
Robinson Armament Co.
Rossi Firearms
Rottweil Compe
Rutten (See U.S. Importer-Labanu Inc)
RWS (See US Importer-Dynamit
Nobel-RWS, Inc.)
S.A.R.L. G. Granger
S.I.A.C.E. (See U.S. Importer-IAR Inc)
Sabatti SPA
Sako Ltd (See U.S. Importer-Stoeger
Industries)
San Marco (See U.S. Importers-Cape
Outfitters-EMF
Sarsilmaz Shotguns - Turkey (see B.C.
Outdoors)
Sauer (See U.S. Importers-Paul Co.,
The, Sigarms I
Savage Arms (Canada), Inc.
SIG
Sigarms, Inc.
SIG-Sauer (See U.S. Importer-
Sigarms Inc.)
SKB Shotguns
Small Arms Specialists
Societa Armi Bresciane Srl (See U.S.
Importer-Cape
Sphinx Systems Ltd.
Springfield Armory
Springfield, Inc.
Starr Trading Co., Jedediah
Steyr Mannlicher GmbH P Co KG
T.F.C. S.p.A.
Tanfoglio Fratelli S.r.l.
Tanner (See U.S. Importer-Mandall
Shooting Supply)
Tar-Hunt Custom Rifles, Inc.
Taurus International Firearms (See
U.S. Importer)
Taurus S.A. Forjas
Taylor's & Co., Inc.
Techno Arms (See U.S. Importer-
Auto-Ordnance Corp
The A.W. Peterson Gun Shop, Inc.
Tikka (See U.S. Importer-Stoeger
Industries)
TOZ (See U.S. Importer-Nygord
Precision Products)
Ugartechea S. A., Ignacio
Ultralux (See U.S. Importer-Keng's
Firearms)
Unique/M.A.P.F.
Valtro USA, Inc
Verney-Carron
Voere-KGH GmbH
Walther GmbH, Carl
Weatherby, Inc.
Webley and Scott Ltd.
Weihrauch KG, Hermann
Westley Richards & Co.
Whiscombe (See U.S. Importer-
Pelaire Products)
Wolf (See J.R. Distribuing)
Yankee Gunsmith "Just Glocks"
Zabala Hermanos S.A.

GUNS, FOREIGN-IMPORTER

Accuracy International
AcuSport Corporation
Air Rifle Specialists

American Frontier Firearms Mfg., Inc
Auto-Ordnance Corp.
B.A.C.
B.C. Outdoors
Bell's Legendary Country Wear
Benelli USA Corp
Big Bear Arms & Sporting Goods, Inc.
Bill Hanus Birdguns
Bridgeman Products
British Sporting Arms
Browning Arms Co.
Cape Outfitters
Century International Arms, Inc.
Champion Shooters' Supply
Champion's Choice, Inc.
Chapuis USA
Cimarron F.A. Co.
CVA
CZ USA
Dixie Gun Works
Dynamit Nobel-RWS, Inc.
E&L Mfg., Inc.
E.A.A. Corp.
Eagle Imports, Inc.
Ellett Bros.
EMF Co., Inc.
Euroarms of America, Inc.
Eversull Co., Inc.
Fiocchi of America, Inc.
Flintlocks, Etc.
Franzen International,Inc (See U.S.
Importer for)
G.U. Inc (See U.S. Importer for New
SKB Arms Co.)
Galaxy Imports Ltd., Inc.
Gamba, USA
Gamo USA, Inc.
Giacomo Sporting USA
Glock, Inc.
Gremmel Enterprises
GSI, Inc.
Guncraft Books (See Guncraft Sports
Inc.)
Guncraft Sports Inc.
Gunsite Custom Shop
Gunsite Training Center
Hammerli USA
I.S.S.
IAR Inc.
Imperial Magnum Corp.
Imperial Miniature Armory
Import Sports Inc.
Intrac Arms International
K. Eversull Co., Inc.
K.B.I. Inc.
Kemen America
Keng's Firearms Specialty, Inc./US
Tactical Systems
Krieghoff International,Inc.
Labanu, Inc.
Legacy Sports International
Lion Country Supply
London Guns Ltd.
Magnum Research, Inc.
Marx, Harry (See U.S. Importer for
FERLIB)
MCS, Inc.
MEC-Gar U.S.A., Inc.
Navy Arms Company
New England Arms Co.
Nygord Precision Products, Inc.
OK Weber, Inc.
P.S.M.G. Gun Co.
Para-Ordnance, Inc.
Parker Reproductions
Pelaire Products
Perazzi U.S.A. Inc.
Powell Agency, William
Precision Sales International, Inc.
Rocky Mountain Armoury
S.D. Meacham
Safari Arms/Schuetzen Pistol Works
Samco Global Arms, Inc.
Savage Arms, Inc.

PRODUCT & SERVICE DIRECTORY

Scott Fine Guns Inc., Thad
Sigarms, Inc.
SKB Shotguns
Small Arms Specialists
Southern Ammunition Co., Inc.
Specialty Shooters Supply, Inc.
Springfield, Inc.
Stoeger Industries
Stone Enterprises Ltd.
Swarovski Optik North America Ltd.
Tar-Hunt Custom Rifles, Inc.
Taurus Firearms, Inc.
Taylor's & Co., Inc.
The A.W. Peterson Gun Shop, Inc.
The Gun Shop
The Orvis Co.
The Paul Co.
Track of the Wolf, Inc.
Traditions Performance Firearms
Tristar Sporting Arms, Ltd.
Trooper Walsh
U.S. Importer-Wm. Larkin Moore
VAM Distribution Co. LLC
Vektor USA
Vintage Arms, Inc.
VTI Gun Parts
Westley Richards Agency USA (See
   U.S. Importer for
Wingshooting Adventures

GUNS, SURPLUS, PARTS & AMMUNITION

Ahlman Guns
Alpha 1 Drop Zone
Armscorp USA, Inc.
Arundel Arms & Ammunition, Inc., A.
B.A.C.
Bondini Paolo
Cambos Outdoorsman
Century International Arms, Inc.
Cole's Gun Works
Conetrol Scope Mounts
Delta Arms Ltd.
Ed's Gun House
First Inc., Jack
Fleming Firearms
Forrest Inc., Tom
Garcia National Gun Traders, Inc.
Goodwin's Gun Shop
Gun City
Gun Hunter Books (See Gun Hunter
   Trading Co.)
Gun Hunter Trading Co.
Hank's Gun Shop
Hege Jagd-u. Sporthandels GmbH
Jackalope Gun Shop
Ken Starnes Gunmaker
LaRocca Gun Works
Lever Arms Service Ltd.
Log Cabin Sport Shop
Martin's Gun Shop
Navy Arms Company
Nevada Pistol Academy, Inc.
Northwest Arms
Numrich Gun Parts Corporation
Oil Rod and Gun Shop
Olathe Gun Shop
Paragon Sales & Services, Inc.
Pasadena Gun Center
Power Plus Enterprises, Inc.
Ravell Ltd.
Retting, Inc., Martin B
Rutgers Book Center
Samco Global Arms, Inc.
Sarco, Inc.
Shootin' Shack
Silver Ridge Gun Shop (See Goodwin,
   Fred)
Simmons Gun Repair, Inc.
Sportsmen's Exchange & Western
   Gun Traders, Inc.
Springfield Sporters, Inc.
T.F.C. S.p.A.

Tarnhelm Supply Co., Inc.
The A.W. Peterson Gun Shop, Inc.
The Gun Room Press
Thurston Sports, Inc.
Williams Shootin' Iron Service, The
   Lynx-Line

GUNS, U.S. MADE

3-Ten Corp.
A.A. Arms, Inc.
Accu-Tek
Ace Custom 45's, Inc.
Acra-Bond Laminates
Ad Hominem
Airrow
Allred Bullet Co.
American Derringer Corp.
American Frontier Firearms Mfg., Inc
AR-7 Industries, LLC
ArmaLite, Inc.
Armscorp USA, Inc.
A-Square Co.
Austin & Halleck, Inc.
Autauga Arms, Inc.
Auto-Ordnance Corp.
Baer Custom Inc., Les
Ballard Rifle & Cartridge Co., LLC
Barrett Firearms Manufacturer, Inc.
Bar-Sto Precision Machine
Benjamin/Sheridan Co., Crosman
Beretta S.p.A., Pietro
Beretta U.S.A. Corp.
Big Bear Arms & Sporting Goods, Inc.
Bill Russ Trading Post
Bond Arms, Inc.
Borden Ridges Rimrock Stocks
Borden Rifles Inc.
Brockman's Custom Gunsmithing
Brown Co., E. Arthur
Brown Products, Inc., Ed
Browning Arms Co.
Bryan & Assoc.
Bushmaster Firearms
C. Sharps Arms Co. Inc./Montana
   Armory
Cabela's
Calico Light Weapon Systems
Cambos Outdoorsman
Cape Outfitters
Casull Arms Corp.
CCL Security Products
Century Gun Dist. Inc.
Champlin Firearms, Inc.
Charter 2000
Cobra Enterprises, Inc.
Colt's Mfg. Co., Inc.
Competitor Corp., Inc.
Conetrol Scope Mounts
Connecticut Shotgun Mfg. Co.
Connecticut Valley Classics (See CVC,
   BPI)
Cooper Arms
Crosman Airguns
Cumberland Arms
Cumberland Mountain Arms
CVA
Daisy Outdoor Products
Dakota Arms, Inc.
Dan Wesson Firearms
Dayton Traister
Dixie Gun Works
Downsizer Corp.
DS Arms, Inc.
DunLyon R&D Inc.
E&L Mfg., Inc.
E. Arthur Brown Co.
Eagle Arms, Inc. (See ArmaLite, Inc.)
Ed Brown Products, Inc.
Emerging Technologies, Inc. (See
   Laseraim Technologies, Inc.)
Entre`prise Arms, Inc.
Essex Arms
Excel Industries Inc.

F.I., Inc. - High Standard Mfg. Co.
Fletcher-Bidwell, LLC.
FN Manufacturing
Fort Worth Firearms
Freedom Arms, Inc.
Fulton Armory
Galena Industries AMT
Garcia National Gun Traders, Inc.
Gary Reeder Custom Guns
Genecco Gun Works
Gentry Custom Gunmaker, David
George Hoenig, Inc.
George Madis Winchester Consultants
Gibbs Rifle Co., Inc.
Gil Hebard Guns Inc.
Gilbert Equipment Co., Inc.
Goergen's Gun Shop, Inc.
Goodwin's Gun Shop
Granite Mountain Arms, Inc.
Grayback Wildcats
Gunsite Custom Shop
Gunsite Gunsmithy (See Gunsite
   Custom Shop)
H&R 1871.LLC
Hammans, Charles E.
Hammerli USA
Harrington & Richardson (See H&R
   1871, Inc.)
Harris Gunworks
Hart & Son, Inc.
Hatfield Gun
Hawken Shop, The (See Dayton
   Traister)
Heritage Firearms (See Heritage Mfg.,
   Inc.)
Heritage Manufacturing, Inc.
Hesco-Meprolight
High Precision
Hi-Point Firearms/MKS Supply
HJS Arms, Inc.
H-S Precision, Inc.
Hutton Rifle Ranch
IAR Inc.
Imperial Miniature Armory
Israel Arms International, Inc.
Ithaca Classic Doubles
Ithaca Gun Company LLC
J.P. Enterprises Inc.
Jim Norman Custom Gunstocks
John Rigby & Co.
John's Custom Leather
K.B.I. Inc.
Kahr Arms
Kehr, Roger
Kelbly, Inc.
Kel-Tec CNC Industries, Inc.
Kimber of America, Inc.
Knight Rifles
Knight's Mfg. Co.
Kolar
L.A.R. Mfg., Inc.
L.W. Seecamp Co., Inc.
LaFrance Specialties
Lakefield Arms Ltd. (See Savage
   Arms, Inc.)
Laseraim Technologies, Inc.
Lever Arms Service Ltd.
Ljutic Industries, Inc.
Lock's Philadelphia Gun Exchange
Lomont Precision Bullets
Lone Star Rifle Company
Mag-Na-Port International, Inc.
Magnum Research, Inc.
Mandall Shooting Supplies Inc.
Marlin Firearms Co.
Maverick Arms, Inc.
McBros Rifle Co.
McCann Industries
Mid-America Recreation, Inc.
Miller Arms, Inc.
MKS Supply, Inc. (See Hi-Point
   Firearms)
MOA Corporation

Montana Armory, Inc .(See C. Sharps
   Arms Co. Inc.)
MPI Stocks
Navy Arms Company
NCP Products, Inc.
New Ultra Light Arms, LLC
Noreen, Peter H.
North American Arms, Inc.
North Star West
Northwest Arms
Nowlin Mfg. Co.
Olympic Arms Inc.
Oregon Arms, Inc. (See Rogue Rifle
   Co., Inc.)
P&M Sales & Services, LLC
Parker & Sons Shooting Supply
Parker Gun Finishes
Phillips & Rogers, Inc.
Phoenix Arms
Precision Small Arms Inc.
ProWare, Inc.
Ramon B. Gonzalez Guns
Rapine Bullet Mould Mfg. Co.
Remington Arms Co., Inc.
Robinson Armament Co.
Rock River Arms
Rocky Mountain Arms, Inc.
Rogue Rifle Co., Inc.
Rogue River Rifleworks
Rohrbaugh
Romain's Custom Guns, Inc.
RPM
Ruger (See Sturm, Ruger & Co., Inc.)
Safari Arms/Schuetzen Pistol Works
Savage Arms (Canada), Inc.
Searcy Enterprises
Sharps Arms Co., Inc., C.
Shiloh Rifle Mfg.
Sklany's Machine Shop
Small Arms Specialists
Smith & Wesson
Sound Technology
Spencer's Rifle Barrels, Inc.
Springfield Armory
Springfield, Inc.
SSK Industries
STI International
Stoeger Industries
Strayer-Voigt, Inc.
Sturm Ruger & Co. Inc.
Sunny Hill Enterprises, Inc.
T&S Industries, Inc.
Taconic Firearms Ltd., Perry Lane
Tank's Rifle Shop
Tar-Hunt Custom Rifles, Inc.
Taurus Firearms, Inc.
Texas Armory (See Bond Arms, Inc.)
The A.W. Peterson Gun Shop, Inc.
The Gun Room Press
The Gun Works
Thompson/Center Arms
Tristar Sporting Arms, Ltd.
U.S. Fire Arms Mfg. Co., Inc.
U.S. Repeating Arms Co., Inc.
Visible Impact Targets
Volquartsen Custom Ltd.
Wallace, Terry
Weatherby, Inc.
Wescombe, Bill (See North Star West)
Wessinger Custom Guns & Engraving
Whildin & Sons Ltd, E.H.
Whitestone Lumber Corp.
Wichita Arms, Inc.
Wichita Arms, Inc.
Wildey, Inc.
Wilsom Combat
Z-M Weapons

GUNSMITH SCHOOL

American Gunsmithing Institute
Bull Mountain Rifle Co.
Colorado Gunsmithing Academy
Colorado School of Trades

Cylinder & Slide, Inc., William R.
   Laughridge
Lassen Community College,
   Gunsmithing Dept.
Laughridge, William R (See Cylinder &
   Slide Inc)
Log Cabin Sport Shop
Modern Gun Repair School
Montgomery Community College
Murray State College
North American Correspondence
   Schools The Gun Pro
Nowlin Mfg. Co.
NRI Gunsmith School
Pennsylvania Gunsmith School
Piedmont Community College
Pine Technical College
Professional Gunsmiths of America
Smith & Wesson
Southeastern Community College
Spencer's Rifle Barrels, Inc.
Trinidad St. Jr. Col. Gunsmith Dept.
Wright's Gunstock Blanks
Yavapai College

GUNSMITH SUPPLIES, TOOLS & SERVICES

Ace Custom 45's, Inc.
Actions by "T" Teddy Jacobson
Alaskan Silversmith, The
Aldis Gunsmithing & Shooting Supply
Alley Supply Co.
Allred Bullet Co.
Alpec Team, Inc.
American Frontier Firearms Mfg., Inc
American Gunsmithing Institute
Baer Custom Inc., Les
Ballard Rifle & Cartridge Co., LLC
Bar-Sto Precision Machine
Bauska Barrels
Bear Mountain Gun & Tool
Bengtson Arms Co., L.
Bill's Gun Repair
Blue Ridge Machinery & Tools, Inc.
Boyds' Gunstock Industries, Inc.
Break-Free, Inc.
Briley Mfg. Inc.
Brockman's Custom Gunsmithing
Brown Products, Inc., Ed
Brownells, Inc.
Bryan & Assoc.
B-Square Company, Inc.
Buffer Technologies
Bull Mountain Rifle Co.
Bushmaster Firearms
C.S. Van Gorden & Son, Inc.
Carbide Checkering Tools (See J&R
   Engineering)
Carter's Gun Shop
Caywood, Shane J.
CBC-BRAZIL
Chapman Manufacturing Co.
Chicasaw Gun Works
Choate Machine & Tool Co., Inc.
Ciener Inc., Jonathan Arthur
Colonial Arms, Inc.
Colorado School of Trades
Colt's Mfg. Co., Inc.
Conetrol Scope Mounts
Corbin Mfg. & Supply, Inc.
CRR, Inc./Marble's Inc.
Cumberland Arms
Cumberland Mountain Arms
Custom Checkering Service, Kathy
   Forster
D'Arcy Echols & Co.
Dem-Bart Checkering Tools, Inc.
Dixie Gun Works
Dixie Gun Works
Dremel Mfg. Co.
Du-Lite Corp.
Efficient Machinery Co.
Entre`prise Arms, Inc.

PRODUCT & SERVICE DIRECTORY

Erhardt, Dennis
Evolution Gun Works Inc.
Faith Associates
Faloon Industries, Inc.
FERLIB
Fisher, Jerry A.
Forgreens Tool & Mfg., Inc.
Forkin, Ben (See Belt MTN Arms)
Forster, Kathy (See Custom
  Checkering)
Gentry Custom Gunmaker, David
Goodwin's Gun Shop
Grace Metal Products
Gre-Tan Rifles
Gruning Precision Inc.
Gunline Tools
Half Moon Rifle Shop
Hammond Custom Guns Ltd.
Hastings
Henriksen Tool Co., Inc.
High Performance International
High Precision
Holland's Gunsmithing
Ironsighter Co.
Israel Arms International, Inc.
Ivanoff, Thomas G. (See Tom's Gun
  Repair)
J&R Engineering
J&S Heat Treat
J. Dewey Mfg. Co., Inc.
Jantz Supply
Jenkins Recoil Pads, Inc.
JGS Precision Tool Mfg., LLC
Jonathan Arthur Ciener, Inc.
Jones Custom Products, Neil A.
Kailua Custom Guns Inc.
Kasenit Co., Inc.
Kleinendorst, K. W.
Korzinek Riflesmith, J.
LaBounty Precision Reboring, Inc
LaFrance Specialties
Laurel Mountain Forge
Lea Mfg. Co.
Lee Supplies, Mark
List Precision Engineering
Lock's Philadelphia Gun Exchange
London Guns Ltd.
Mahovsky's Metalife
Marble Arms (See CRR, Inc./Marble's
  Inc.)
Mark Lee Supplies
Marsh, Mike
Martin's Gun Shop
McFarland, Stan
Menck, Gunsmith Inc., T.W.
Metalife Industries (See Mahovsky's
  Metalife)
Michael's Antiques
Micro Sight Co.
Midway Arms, Inc.
MMC
Mo's Competitor Supplies (See MCS,
  Inc.)
Mowrey's Guns & Gunsmithing
Neil A. Jones Custom Products
New England Custom Gun Service
Ole Frontier Gunsmith Shop
Olympic Arms Inc.
Parker & Sons Shooting Supply
Parker Gun Finishes
Paulsen Gunstocks
PEM's Mfg. Co.
Perazone-Gunsmith, Brian
Peter Dyson & Son Ltd.
Power Custom, Inc.
Practical Tools, Inc.
Precision Specialties
R.A. Wells Custom Gunsmith
Ranch Products
Ransom International Corp.
Reardon Products
Rice, Keith (See White Rock Tool &
  Die)
Robert Valade Engraving

Rocky Mountain Arms, Inc.
Romain's Custom Guns, Inc.
Royal Arms Gunstocks
Rusteprufe Laboratories
Sharp Shooter Supply
Shooter's Choice Gun Care
Simmons Gun Repair, Inc.
Smith Abrasives, Inc.
Southern Bloomer Mfg. Co.
Spencer Reblue Service
Spencer's Rifle Barrels, Inc.
Spradlin's
Starr Trading Co., Jedediah
Starrett Co., L. S.
Stiles Custom Guns
Stoney Point Products, Inc.
Sullivan, David S .(See Westwind
  Rifles Inc.)
Sunny Hill Enterprises, Inc.
T&S Industries, Inc.
T.W. Menck Gunsmith Inc.
Tank's Rifle Shop
Texas Platers Supply Co.
The A.W. Peterson Gun Shop, Inc.
The Dutchman's Firearms, Inc.
The Gun Works
The NgraveR Co.
The Robar Co.'s, Inc.
Theis, Terry
Tom's Gun Repair, Thomas G. Ivanoff
Track of the Wolf, Inc.
Trinidad St. Jr. Col. Gunsmith Dept.
Trulock Tool
Turnbull Restoration, Doug
United States Products Co.
Van Gorden & Son Inc., C. S.
Venco Industries, Inc. (See Shooter's
  Choice Gun Care)
W.C. Wolff Co.
Warne Manufacturing Co.
Washita Mountain Whetstone Co.
Weigand Combat Handguns, Inc.
Wessinger Custom Guns & Engraving
White Rock Tool & Die
Wilcox All-Pro Tools & Supply
Wild West Guns
Will-Burt Co.
Williams Gun Sight Co.
Williams Shootin' Iron Service, The
  Lynx-Line
Willow Bend
Windish, Jim
Winter, Robert M.
Wise Guns, Dale
Wright's Gunstock Blanks
Yavapai College
Ziegel Engineering

HANDGUN ACCESSORIES

"Su-Press-On", Inc.
A.A. Arms, Inc.
Ace Custom 45's, Inc.
Action Direct, Inc.
ADCO Sales, Inc.
Aimtech Mount Systems
Ajax Custom Grips, Inc.
Alpha 1 Drop Zone
American Derringer Corp.
American Frontier Firearms Mfg., Inc
Arms Corporation of the Philippines
Astra Sport, S.A.
Autauga Arms, Inc.
Badger Creek Studio
Baer Custom Inc., Les
Bagmaster Mfg., Inc.
Bar-Sto Precision Machine
Behlert Precision, Inc.
Berry's Mfg., Inc.
Bill's Custom Cases
Blue and Gray Products Inc. (See Ox-
  Yoke Originals)
Bond Custom Firearms

Bowen Classic Arms Corp.
Bridgeman Products
Broken Gun Ranch
Brooks Tactical Systems-Agrip
Brown Products, Inc., Ed
Bushmaster Hunting & Fishing
Butler Creek Corp.
Cannon Safe, Inc.
Centaur Systems, Inc.
Central Specialties Ltd (See Trigger
  Lock Division
Charter 2000
Cheyenne Pioneer Products
Chicasaw Gun Works
Ciener, Jonathan Arthur
Clark Custom Guns, Inc.
Classic Arms Company
Conetrol Scope Mounts
Crimson Trace Lasers
CRR, Inc./Marble's Inc.
Cylinder & Slide, Inc., William R.
  Laughridge
D&L Industries (See D.J. Marketing)
D.J. Marketing
Dade Screw Machine Products
Delhi Gun House
DeSantis Holster & Leather Goods,
  Inc.
Dixie Gun Works
Doskocil Mfg. Co., Inc.
E&L Mfg., Inc.
E. Arthur Brown Co.
E.A.A. Corp.
Ed Brown Products, Inc.
Essex Arms
European American Armory Corp (See
  E.A.A. Corp)
Evolution Gun Works Inc.
F.I., Inc. - High Standard Mfg. Co.
Faloon Industries, Inc.
Federal Arms Corp. of America
Feinwerkbau Westinger & Altenburger
Fisher Custom Firearms
Fleming Firearms
Freedom Arms, Inc.
G.G. & G.
Galati International
GALCO International Ltd.
Garcia National Gun Traders, Inc.
Garthwaite Pistolsmith, Inc., Jim
Gil Hebard Guns Inc.
Gilmore Sports Concepts
Glock, Inc.
Goodwin's Gun Shop
Gould & Goodrich
Gremmel Enterprises
Gun-Alert
Gun-Ho Sports Cases
H.K.S. Products
Hafner World Wide, Inc.
Hammerli USA
Heinie Specialty Products
Henigson & Associates, Steve
Hill Speed Leather, Ernie
Hi-Point Firearms/MKS Supply
Hobson Precision Mfg. Co.
Hoppe's Div. Penguin Industries, Inc.
H-S Precision, Inc.
Hunter Co., Inc.
Impact Case & Container, Inc.
J.P. Enterprises Inc.
Jarvis, Inc.
JB Custom
Jeffredo Gunsight
Jim Noble Co.
John's Custom Leather
Jonathan Arthur Ciener, Inc.
Kalispel Case Line
KeeCo Impressions, Inc.
King's Gun Works
KK Air International (See Impact Case
  & Container Co.)
L&S Technologies Inc. (See Aimtech
  Mount Systems)

Lakewood Products LLC
LaserMax, Inc.
Loch Leven Industries/Convert-A-Pell
Lock's Philadelphia Gun Exchange
Lohman Mfg. Co., Inc.
Mag-Na-Port International, Inc.
Magnolia Sports,Inc.
Mag-Pack Corp.
Mahony, Philip Bruce
Mandall Shooting Supplies Inc.
Marble Arms (See CRR, Inc./Marble's
  Inc.)
Markell,Inc.
McCormick Corp., Chip
MEC-Gar S.R.L.
Menck, Gunsmith Inc., T.W.
Merkuria Ltd.
Middlebrooks Custom Shop
Millett Sights
Mogul Co./Life Jacket
MTM Molded Products Co., Inc.
No-Sho Mfg. Co.
Numrich Gun Parts Corporation
Omega Sales
Outdoor Sports Headquarters, Inc.
Ox-Yoke Originals, Inc.
Pachmayr Div. Lyman Products
Pager Pal
Palmer Security Products
Parker & Sons Shooting Supply
Pearce Grip, Inc.
Perazone-Gunsmith, Brian
Phoenix Arms
Practical Tools, Inc.
Precision Small Arms Inc.
Protektor Model
Ram-Line ATK
Ranch Products
Ransom International Corp.
Ringler Custom Leather Co.
RPM
Seecamp Co. Inc., L. W.
Simmons Gun Repair, Inc.
Sound Technology
Southern Bloomer Mfg. Co.
Springfield Armory
Springfield, Inc.
SSK Industries
Sturm Ruger & Co. Inc.
T.F.C. S.p.A.
Tactical Defense Institute
Tanfoglio Fratelli S.r.l.
The A.W. Peterson Gun Shop, Inc.
The Concealment Shop, Inc.
The Gun Works
The Keller Co.
The Protector Mfg. Co., Inc.
Thompson/Center Arms
Trigger Lock Division / Central
  Specialties Ltd.
Trijicon, Inc.
Triple-K Mfg. Co., Inc.
Truglo, Inc.
Tyler Manufacturing & Distributing
United States Products Co.
Universal Sports
Volquartsen Custom Ltd.
W. Waller & Son, Inc.
W.C. Wolff Co.
Warne Manufacturing Co.
Weigand Combat Handguns, Inc.
Wessinger Custom Guns & Engraving
Western Design (See Alpha Gunsmith
  Division)
Whitestone Lumber Corp.
Wild West Guns
Williams Gun Sight Co.
Wilsom Combat
Yankee Gunsmith "Just Glocks"
Ziegel Engineering

HANDGUN GRIPS

A.A. Arms, Inc.

African Import Co.
Ahrends, Kim (See Custom Firearms,
  Inc.)
Ajax Custom Grips, Inc.
Altamont Co.
American Derringer Corp.
American Frontier Firearms Mfg., Inc
American Gripcraft
Arms Corporation of the Philippines
Art Jewel Enterprises Ltd.
Baelder, Harry
Baer Custom Inc., Les
Big Bear Arms & Sporting Goods, Inc.
Bob's Gun Shop
Boone Trading Co., Inc.
Boone's Custom Ivory Grips, Inc.
Boyds' Gunstock Industries, Inc.
Brooks Tactical Systems-Agrip
Brown Products, Inc., Ed
Clark Custom Guns, Inc.
Cole-Grip
Colonial Repair
Crimson Trace Lasers
Custom Firearms (See Ahrends, Kim)
Cylinder & Slide, Inc., William R.
  Laughridge
Dixie Gun Works
E.A.A. Corp.
EMF Co., Inc.
Essex Arms
European American Armory Corp (See
  E.A.A. Corp)
F.I., Inc. - High Standard Mfg. Co.
Faloon Industries, Inc.
Feinwerkbau Westinger & Altenburger
Fibron Products, Inc.
Fisher Custom Firearms
Forrest Inc., Tom
Garthwaite Pistolsmith, Inc., Jim
Goodwin's Gun Shop
Herrett's Stocks, Inc.
HIP-GRIP Barami Corp.
Hogue Grips
H-S Precision, Inc.
Huebner, Corey O.
I.S.S.
Israel Arms International, Inc.
John Masen Co. Inc.
KeeCo Impressions, Inc.
Kim Ahrends Custom Firearms, Inc.
Korth Germany GmbH
Lett Custom Grips
Linebaugh Custom Sixguns
Lyman Products Corp.
Mandall Shooting Supplies Inc.
Michaels Of Oregon, Co.
Millett Sights
N.C. Ordnance Co.
Newell, Robert H.
Northern Precision Custom Swaged
  Bullets
Pachmayr Div. Lyman Products
Pardini Armi Srl
Parker & Sons Shooting Supply
Perazone-Gunsmith, Brian
Pilgrim Pewter,Inc. (See Bell Originals
  Inc. Sid)
Precision Small Arms Inc.
Radical Concepts
Rosenberg & Son, Jack A
Roy's Custom Grips
Spegel, Craig
Stoeger Industries
Sturm Ruger & Co. Inc.
Sunny Hill Enterprises, Inc.
Tactical Defense Institute
Taurus Firearms, Inc.
The A.W. Peterson Gun Shop, Inc.
Tirelli
Triple-K Mfg. Co., Inc.
Tyler Manufacturing & Distributing
U.S. Fire Arms Mfg. Co., Inc.
Uncle Mike's (See Michaels of Oregon
  Co.)

PRODUCT & SERVICE DIRECTORY

Vintage Industries, Inc.
Volquartsen Custom Ltd.
Western Mfg. Co.
Whitestone Lumber Corp.
Wright's Gunstock Blanks

HEARING PROTECTORS

Aero Peltor
Ajax Custom Grips, Inc.
Brown Co., E. Arthur
Browning Arms Co.
Creedmoor Sports, Inc.
David Clark Co., Inc.
Dillon Precision Products, Inc.
Dixie Gun Works
E-A-R, Inc.
Electronic Shooters Protection, Inc.
Gentex Corp.
Goodwin's Gun Shop
Gunsmithing, Inc.
Hoppe's Div. Penguin Industries, Inc.
Kesselring Gun Shop
Mandall Shooting Supplies Inc.
North Specialty Products
Parker & Sons Shooting Supply
Paterson Gunsmithing
Peltor, Inc. (See Aero Peltor)
R.E.T. Enterprises
Ridgeline, Inc.
Rucker Dist. Inc.
Silencio/Safety Direct
Sound Technology
Tactical Defense Institute
The A.W. Peterson Gun Shop, Inc.
The Gun Room Press
Triple-K Mfg. Co., Inc.
Watson Trophy Match Bullets
Whitestone Lumber Corp.

HOLSTERS & LEATHER GOODS

A&B Industries,Inc (See Top-Line USA Inc)
A.A. Arms, Inc.
Action Direct, Inc.
Action Products, Inc.
Aker International, Inc.
AKJ Concealco
Alessi Holsters, Inc.
Arratoonian, Andy (See Horseshoe Leather Products)
Autauga Arms, Inc.
Bagmaster Mfg., Inc.
Baker's Leather Goods, Roy
Bandcor Industries, Div. of Man-Sew Corp.
Bang-Bang Boutique (See Holster Shop, The)
Beretta S.p.A., Pietro
Bianchi International, Inc.
Bond Arms, Inc.
Brocock Ltd.
Brooks Tactical Systems-Agrip
Brown, H. R. (See Silhouette Leathers)
Browning Arms Co.
Bull-X, Inc.
Cape Outfitters
Cathey Enterprises, Inc.
Chace Leather Products
Churchill Glove Co., James
Cimarron F.A. Co.
Classic Old West Styles
Clements' Custom Leathercraft, Chas
Cobra Sport S.r.l.
Colonial Repair
Counter Assault
Delhi Gun House
DeSantis Holster & Leather Goods, Inc.
Dillon Precision Products, Inc.
Dixie Gun Works

Ekol Leather Care
El Paso Saddlery Co.
EMF Co., Inc.
Faust Inc., T. G.
Freedom Arms, Inc.
Gage Manufacturing
GALCO International Ltd.
Garcia National Gun Traders, Inc.
Gil Hebard Guns Inc.
Gilmore Sports Concepts
GML Products, Inc.
Goodwin's Gun Shop
Gould & Goodrich
Gun Leather Limited
Gunfitters
Hafner World Wide, Inc.
HandCrafts Unltd (See Clements' Custom Leather)
Hank's Gun Shop
Heinie Specialty Products
Henigson & Associates, Steve
Hill Speed Leather, Ernie
HIP-GRIP Barami Corp.
Hobson Precision Mfg. Co.
Hogue Grips
Horseshoe Leather Products
Hume, Don
Hunter Co., Inc.
Jim Noble Co.
John's Custom Leather
K.L. Null Holsters Ltd.
Kane Products, Inc.
Kirkpatrick Leather Co.
Kolpin Mfg., Inc.
Korth Germany GmbH
Kramer Handgun Leather
L.A.R. Mfg., Inc.
Lawrence Leather Co.
Lock's Philadelphia Gun Exchange
Lone Star Gunleather
Magnolia Sports,Inc.
Mandall Shooting Supplies Inc.
Markell,Inc.
Marksman Products
Michaels Of Oregon, Co.
Minute Man High Tech Industries
Navy Arms Company
No-Sho Mfg. Co.
Null Holsters Ltd. K.L.
October Country Muzzleloading
Ojala Holsters, Arvo
Oklahoma Leather Products,Inc.
Old West Reproductions,Inc. R.M. Bachman
Pager Pal
Parker & Sons Shooting Supply
Pathfinder Sports Leather
Protektor Model
PWL Gunleather
Ramon B. Gonzalez Guns
Renegade
Ringler Custom Leather Co.
Rogue Rifle Co., Inc.
Safariland Ltd., Inc.
Safety Speed Holster, Inc.
Scharch Mfg., Inc.-Top Brass
Schulz Industries
Second Chance Body Armor
Silhouette Leathers
Smith Saddlery, Jesse W.
Sparks, Milt
Stalker, Inc.
Starr Trading Co., Jedediah
Strong Holster Co.
Stuart, V. Pat
Tabler Marketing
Tactical Defense Institute
Ted Blocker Holsters, Inc.
Tex Shoemaker & Sons, Inc.
Thad Rybka Custom Leather Equipment
The A.W. Peterson Gun Shop, Inc.
The Concealment Shop, Inc.
The Gun Works

The Keller Co.
The Outdoor Connection, Inc.
Torel, Inc.
Triple-K Mfg. Co., Inc.
Tristar Sporting Arms, Ltd.
Tyler Manufacturing & Distributing
Uncle Mike's (See Michaels of Oregon Co.)
Venus Industries
Walt's Custom Leather, Walt Whinnery
Watson Trophy Match Bullets
Westley Richards & Co.
Whinnery, Walt (See Walt's Custom Leather)
Wild Bill's Originals
Wilsom Combat

HUNTING & CAMP GEAR, CLOTHING, ETC.

Ace Sportswear, Inc.
Action Direct, Inc.
Action Products, Inc.
Adventure 16, Inc.
Adventure Game Calls
All Rite Products, Inc.
Allen Co., Bob
Allen Sportswear, Bob (See Allen Co., Bob)
Alpha 1 Drop Zone
Armor (See Buck Stop Lure Co., Inc.)
Atlanta Cutlery Corp.
Atsko/Sno-Seal, Inc.
B.B. Walker Co.
Baekgaard Ltd.
Bagmaster Mfg., Inc.
Barbour, Inc.
Bauer, Eddie
Bear Archery
Beaver Park Product, Inc.
Beretta S.p.A., Pietro
Better Concepts Co.
Bill Russ Trading Post
Boonie Packer Products
Boss Manufacturing Co.
Browning Arms Co.
Buck Stop Lure Co., Inc.
Bushmaster Hunting & Fishing
Cambos Outdoorsman
Cambos Outdoorsman
Camp-Cap Products
Carhartt, Inc.
Churchill Glove Co., James
Clarkfield Enterprises, Inc.
Classic Old West Styles
Clements' Custom Leathercraft, Chas
Coghlan's Ltd.
Cold Steel Inc.
Coleman Co., Inc.
Coulston Products, Inc.
Counter Assault
Dakota Corp.
Danner Shoe Mfg. Co.
Deepeeka Exports Pvt. Ltd.
Dr. O's Products Ltd.
Duofold, Inc.
Dynalite Products, Inc.
E-A-R, Inc.
Ekol Leather Care
Forrest Tool Co.
Fox River Mills, Inc.
Frontier
G&H Decoys,Inc.
Gerber Legendary Blades
Glacier Glove
Grand Slam Hunting Products
HandCrafts Unltd (See Clements' Custom Leather)
High North Products, Inc.
Hinman Outfitters, Bob
Hodgman, Inc.
Houtz & Barwick
Hunter's Specialties Inc.
James Churchill Glove Co.

John's Custom Leather
K&M Industries, Inc.
Kamik Outdoor Footwear
Kolpin Mfg., Inc.
L.L. Bean, Inc.
LaCrosse Footwear, Inc.
Leapers, Inc.
MAG Instrument, Inc.
Mag-Na-Port International, Inc.
Marathon Rubber Prods. Co., Inc.
McCann Industries
McCann's Machine & Gun Shop
Molin Industries, Tru-Nord Division
Murphy, R.R. Co., Inc.
Nelson/Weather-Rite, Inc.
North Specialty Products
Northlake Outdoor Footwear
Original Deer Formula Co., The.
Original Mink Oil, Inc.
Palsa Outdoor Products
Partridge Sales Ltd., John
Pointing Dog Journal, Village Press Publications
Powell & Son (Gunmakers) Ltd., William
Pro-Mark Div. of Wells Lamont
Ringler Custom Leather Co.
Robert Valade Engraving
Rocky Shoes & Boots
Scansport, Inc.
Sceery Game Calls
Schaefer Shooting Sports
Servus Footwear Co.
Simmons Outdoor Corp.
Sno-Seal, Inc. (See Atsko/Sno-Seal, Inc.)
Streamlight, Inc.
Swanndri New Zealand
T.H.U. Enterprises, Inc.
TEN-X Products Group
The A.W. Peterson Gun Shop, Inc.
The Orvis Co.
The Outdoor Connection, Inc.
Tink's Safariland Hunting Corp.
Torel, Inc.
Triple-K Mfg. Co., Inc.
United Cutlery Corp.
Venus Industries
Wakina by Pic
Walls Industries, Inc.
Wideview Scope Mount Corp.
Wilderness Sound Products Ltd.
Winchester Sutler, Inc., The
Wolverine Footwear Group
Woolrich, Inc.
Wyoming Knife Corp.
Yellowstone Wilderness Supply

KNIVES & KNIFEMAKER'S SUPPLIES

A.G. Russell Knives, Inc.
Action Direct, Inc.
Adventure 16, Inc.
African Import Co.
Aitor-Cuchilleria Del Norte S.A.
American Target Knives
Art Jewel Enterprises Ltd.
Atlanta Cutlery Corp.
B&D Trading Co., Inc.
Barteaux Machete
Belltown Ltd.
Benchmark Knives (See Gerber Legendary Blades)
Beretta S.p.A., Pietro
Beretta U.S.A. Corp.
Big Bear Arms & Sporting Goods, Inc.
Bill Russ Trading Post
Bill's Custom Cases
Boker USA, Inc.
Boone Trading Co., Inc.
Boone's Custom Ivory Grips, Inc.
Bowen Knife Co., Inc.

Brooks Tactical Systems-Agrip
Browning Arms Co.
Buck Knives, Inc.
Buster's Custom Knives
Camillus Cutlery Co.
Campbell, Dick
Case & Sons Cutlery Co., W R
Chicago Cutlery Co.
Clements' Custom Leathercraft, Chas
Cold Steel Inc.
Coleman Co., Inc.
Compass Industries, Inc.
Crosman Blades (See Coleman Co., Inc.)
CRR, Inc./Marble's Inc.
Cutco Cutlery
damascususa@inteliport.com
Dan's Whetstone Co., Inc.
Deepeeka Exports Pvt. Ltd.
Degen Inc. (See Aristocrat Knives)
Delhi Gun House
DeSantis Holster & Leather Goods, Inc.
Diamond Machining Technology, Inc. (See DMT)
Dixie Gun Works
EdgeCraft Corp., S. Weiner
Empire Cutlery Corp.
Eze-Lap Diamond Prods.
Flitz International Ltd.
Forrest Tool Co.
Forthofer's Gunsmithing & Knifemaking
Fortune Products, Inc.
Frank Knives
Frost Cutlery Co.
Galati International
George Ibberson (Sheffield) Ltd.
Gerber Legendary Blades
Gibbs Rifle Co., Inc.
Glock, Inc.
Golden Age Arms Co.
H&B Forge Co.
Hafner World Wide, Inc.
Hammans, Charles E.
HandCrafts Unltd (See Clements' Custom Leather)
Harris Publications
High North Products, Inc.
Hoppe's Div. Penguin Industries, Inc.
Hunter Co., Inc.
Imperial Schrade Corp.
J.A. Blades, Inc. (See Christopher Firearms Co.)
J.A. Henckels Zwillingswerk Inc.
Jackalope Gun Shop
Jantz Supply
Jenco Sales, Inc.
Jim Blair Engraving
Johnson Wood Products
KA-BAR Knives
Kasenit Co., Inc.
Kershaw Knives
Knifeware, Inc.
Koval Knives
Lamson & Goodnow Mfg. Co.
Lansky Sharpeners
Leapers, Inc.
Leatherman Tool Group, Inc.
Lethal Force Institute (See Police Bookshelf)
Linder Solingen Knives
Mandall Shooting Supplies Inc.
Marble Arms (See CRR, Inc./Marble's Inc.)
Marshall Fish Mfg. Gunsmith Sptg. Co.
Matthews Cutlery
McCann Industries
McCann's Machine & Gun Shop
Molin Industries, Tru-Nord Division
Mountain State Muzzleloading Supplies, Inc.
Normark Corp.
October Country Muzzleloading

PRODUCT & SERVICE DIRECTORY

Outdoor Edge Cutlery Corp.
Pilgrim Pewter,Inc. (See Bell Originals Inc. Sid)
Plaza Cutlery, Inc.
Police Bookshelf
Queen Cutlery Co.
R&C Knives & Such
R. Murphy Co., Inc.
Randall-Made Knives
Ringler Custom Leather Co.
Robert Valade Engraving
Rodgers & Sons Ltd., Joseph (See George Ibberson)
Scansport, Inc.
Schiffman, Mike
Sheffield Knifemakers Supply, Inc.
Smith Saddlery, Jesse W.
Springfield Armory
Spyderco, Inc.
T.F.C. S.p.A.
The A.W. Peterson Gun Shop, Inc.
The Creative Craftsman, Inc.
The Gun Room
The Gun Works
Theis, Terry
Traditions Performance Firearms
Traditions Performance Firearms
Tru-Balance Knife Co.
United Cutlery Corp.
Utica Cutlery Co.
Venus Industries
W.R. Case & Sons Cutlery Co.
Washita Mountain Whetstone Co.
Weber Jr., Rudolf
Wells Creek Knife & Gun Works
Wenger North America/Precise Int'l
Western Cutlery (See Camillus Cutlery Co.)
Whinnery, Walt (See Walt's Custom Leather)
Wideview Scope Mount Corp.
Wostenholm (See Ibberson [Sheffield] Ltd., George)
Wyoming Knife Corp.

LABELS, BOXES & CARTRIDGE HOLDERS

Ballistic Product, Inc.
Berry's Mfg., Inc.
Brocock Ltd.
Brown Co., E. Arthur
Cabinet Mtn. Outfitters Scents & Lures
Cheyenne Pioneer Products
Del Rey Products
DeSantis Holster & Leather Goods, Inc.
Flambeau Products Corp.
Goodwin's Gun Shop
Hafner World Wide, Inc.
J&J Products, Inc.
Kolpin Mfg., Inc.
Liberty Shooting Supplies
Midway Arms, Inc.
MTM Molded Products Co., Inc.
Pendleton Royal, c/o Swingler Buckland Ltd.
Protektor Model
Ziegel Engineering

LEAD WIRES & WIRE CUTTERS

Ames Metal Products
Big Bore Express
Bullet Swaging Supply, Inc.
Goodwin's Gun Shop
Liberty Metals
Lightning Performance Innovations, Inc.
Montana Precision Swaging
Northern Precision Custom Swaged Bullets

Sport Flite Manufacturing Co.
Star Ammunition, Inc.
Unmussig Bullets, D. L.

LOAD TESTING & PRODUCT TESTING

Ballistic Research
Bitterroot Bullet Co.
Bridgeman Products
Briese Bullet Co., Inc.
Buckskin Bullet Co.
Bull Mountain Rifle Co.
CFVentures
Claybuster Wads & Harvester Bullets
Clearview Products
D&H Precision Tooling
Dead Eye's Sport Center
Defense Training International, Inc.
Duane's Gun Repair (See DGR Custom Rifles)
Gruning Precision Inc.
Gun Hunter Books (See Gun Hunter Trading Co.)
Gun Hunter Trading Co.
H.P. White Laboratory, Inc.
Hank's Gun Shop
Henigson & Associates, Steve
Hutton Rifle Ranch
J&J Sales
Jackalope Gun Shop
Jensen Bullets
L. E. Jurras & Assoc.
Liberty Shooting Supplies
Linebaugh Custom Sixguns
Lomont Precision Bullets
Maionchi-L.M.I.
MAST Technology, Inc.
McMurdo, Lynn (See Specialty Gunsmithing)
Middlebrooks Custom Shop
Modern Gun Repair School
Multiplex International
Northwest Arms
Oil Rod and Gun Shop
Plum City Ballistic Range
R.A. Wells Custom Gunsmith
Ramon B. Gonzalez Guns
Rupert's Gun Shop
Small Custom Mould & Bullet Co.
SOS Products Co. (See Buck Stix-SOS Products Co.)
Spencer's Rifle Barrels, Inc.
Tar-Hunt Custom Rifles, Inc.
Trinidad St. Jr. Col. Gunsmith Dept.
Vulpes Ventures, Inc. Fox Cartridge Division
W. Square Enterprises
X-Spand Target Systems

LOADING BLOCKS, METALLIC & SHOTSHELL

Battenfeld Technologies
Buffalo Arms Co.
Huntington Die Specialties
Jericho Tool & Die Co., Inc.
Sinclair International, Inc.
The A.W. Peterson Gun Shop, Inc.

LUBRISIZERS, DIES & ACCESSORIES

Ballisti-Cast, Inc.
Ben's Machines
Buffalo Arms Co.
Cast Performance Bullet Company
Cooper-Woodward
Corbin Mfg. & Supply, Inc.
GAR
Hart & Son, Inc.

Javelina Lube Products
Lee Precision, Inc.
Lithi Bee Bullet Lube
Lyman Products Corp.
Magma Engineering Co.
RCBS Operations/ATK
Redding Reloading Equipment
SPG LLC
The A.W. Peterson Gun Shop, Inc.
Thompson Bullet Lube Co.
United States Products Co.
WTA Manufacturing

MOULDS & MOULD ACCESSORIES

Ad Hominem
American Products, Inc.
Ballisti-Cast, Inc.
Buffalo Arms Co.
Bullet Swaging Supply, Inc.
Cast Performance Bullet Company
Corbin Mfg. & Supply, Inc.
Davide Pedersoli and Co.
GAR
Huntington Die Specialties
Lee Precision, Inc.
Lyman Products Corp.
Magma Engineering Co.
NEI Handtools, Inc.
Old West Bullet Moulds
Penn Bullets
Rapine Bullet Mould Mfg. Co.
RCBS Operations/ATK
Redding Reloading Equipment
S&S Firearms
Small Custom Mould & Bullet Co.
The A.W. Peterson Gun Shop, Inc.
The Gun Works
Wolf's Western Traders

MUZZLE-LOADING GUNS, BARRELS & EQUIPMENT

Accuracy Unlimited
Ackerman & Co.
Adkins, Luther
Allen Mfg.
Armi San Paolo
Armoury, Inc., The
Austin & Halleck, Inc.
Bauska Barrels
Beaver Lodge (See Fellowes, Ted)
Bentley, John
Big Bore Express
Birdsong & Assoc., W. E.
Black Powder Products
Blount/Outers ATK
Blue and Gray Products Inc. (See Ox-Yoke Originals)
Bridgers Best
Buckskin Bullet Co.
Bullberry Barrel Works, Ltd.
Butler Creek Corp.
Cabela's
Cache La Poudre Rifleworks
California Sights (See Fautheree, Andy)
Cash Mfg. Co., Inc.
Caywood Gunmakers
CBC-BRAZIL
Chambers Flintlocks Ltd., Jim
Chicasaw Gun Works
Cimarron F.A. Co.
Claybuster Wads & Harvester Bullets
Cogar's Gunsmithing
Colonial Repair
Colt Blackpowder Arms Co.
Conetrol Scope Mounts
Cousin Bob's Mountain Products
Cumberland Arms
Cumberland Mountain Arms

Curly Maple Stock Blanks (See Tiger-Hunt)
CVA
Dangler, Homer L.
Davide Pedersoli and Co.
Dayton Traister
deHaas Barrels
Delhi Gun House
Dixie Gun Works
Dixie Gun Works
Dixon Muzzleloading Shop, Inc.
EMF Co., Inc.
Euroarms of America, Inc.
Feken, Dennis
Fellowes, Ted
Flintlocks, Etc.
Fort Hill Gunstocks
Fowler, Bob (See Black Powder Products)
Frontier
Getz Barrel Co.
Goergen's Gun Shop, Inc.
Golden Age Arms Co.
Gonic Arms/North American Arm
Goodwin's Gun Shop
Green Mountain Rifle Barrel Co., Inc.
H&R 1871.LLC
Hastings
Hawken Shop, The (See Dayton Traister)
Hege Jagd-u. Sporthandels GmbH
Hodgdon Powder Co.
Hoppe's Div. Penguin Industries, Inc.
Hornady Mfg. Co.
House of Muskets, Inc., The
Hunkeler, A (See Buckskin Machine Works
IAR Inc.
Impact Case & Container, Inc.
Ironsighter Co.
J. Dewey Mfg. Co., Inc.
Jamison's Forge Works
Jones Co., Dale
K&M Industries, Inc.
Kalispel Case Line
Kennedy Firearms
Knight Rifles
Knight Rifles (See Modern Muzzle Loading, Inc.)
Kolar
L&R Lock Co.
L&S Technologies Inc. (See Aimtech Mount Systems)
Lakewood Products LLC
Legend Products Corp.
Lodgewood Mfg.
Log Cabin Sport Shop
Lothar Walther Precision Tool Inc.
Lyman Products Corp.
Markesbery Muzzle Loaders, Inc.
Marlin Firearms Co.
McCann's Muzzle-Gun Works
Michaels Of Oregon, Co.
Millennium Designed Muzzleloaders
Modern Muzzleloading, Inc.
Mountain State Muzzleloading Supplies, Inc.
Mowrey Gun Works
Mt. Alto Outdoor Products
Navy Arms Company
Newman Gunshop
North Star West
October Country Muzzleloading
Oklahoma Leather Products,Inc.
Olson, Myron
Orion Rifle Barrel Co.
Ox-Yoke Originals, Inc.
Pacific Rifle Co.
Parker & Sons Shooting Supply
Parker Gun Finishes
Pecatonica River Longrifle
Peter Dyson & Son Ltd.
Pioneer Arms Co.
Prairie River Arms

Rusty Duck Premium Gun Care Products
S&S Firearms
Selsi Co., Inc.
Simmons Gun Repair, Inc.
Sklany's Machine Shop
Smokey Valley Rifles
South Bend Replicas, Inc.
Southern Bloomer Mfg. Co.
Splitfire Sporting Goods, L.L.C.
Starr Trading Co., Jedediah
Stone Mountain Arms
Sturm Ruger & Co. Inc.
Taylor's & Co., Inc.
Tennessee Valley Mfg.
The A.W. Peterson Gun Shop, Inc.
The Gun Works
The Hawken Shop
Thompson Bullet Lube Co.
Thompson/Center Arms
Tiger-Hunt Gunstocks
Track of the Wolf, Inc.
Traditions Performance Firearms
Truglo, Inc.
Uncle Mike's (See Michaels of Oregon Co.)
Universal Sports
Upper Missouri Trading Co.
Venco Industries, Inc. (See Shooter's Choice Gun Care)
Virgin Valley Custom Guns
Voere-KGH GmbH
W.E. Birdsong & Assoc.
Warne Manufacturing Co.
Warren Muzzleloading Co., Inc.
Wescombe, Bill (See North Star West)
White Rifles, Inc.
William E. Phillips Firearms
Woodworker's Supply
Wright's Gunstock Blanks
Young Country Arms
Ziegel Engineering

PISTOLSMITH

A.W. Peterson Gun Shop, Inc.
Acadian Ballistic Specialties
Accuracy Unlimited
Ace Custom 45's, Inc.
Actions by "T" Teddy Jacobson
Adair Custom Shop, Bill
Ahlman Guns
Ahrends, Kim (See Custom Firearms, Inc)
Aldis Gunsmithing & Shooting Supply
Alpha Precision, Inc.
Alpine Indoor Shooting Range
Armament Gunsmithing Co., Inc.
Arundel Arms & Ammunition, Inc., A.
Badger Creek Studio
Baer Custom Inc., Les
Bain & Davis, Inc.
Banks, Ed
Bar-Sto Precision Machine
Behlert Precision, Inc.
Ben William's Gun Shop
Bengtson Arms Co., L.
Bill Adair Custom Shop
Billings Gunsmiths
Bowen Classic Arms Corp.
Broken Gun Ranch
Caraville Manufacturing
Chicasaw Gun Works
Clark Custom Guns, Inc.
Cleland's Outdoor World, Inc
Colonial Repair
Colorado School of Trades
Colt's Mfg. Co., Inc.
Corkys Gun Clinic
Custom Firearms (See Ahrends, Kim)
Cylinder & Slide, Inc., William R. Laughridge
D&D Gunsmiths, Ltd.
D&L Sports

DIRECTORY

David R. Chicoine
Dayton Traister
Dilliott Gunsmithing, Inc.
Ellicott Arms, Inc. / Woods Pistolsmithing
Evolution Gun Works Inc.
F.I., Inc. - High Standard Mfg. Co.
Ferris Firearms
Fisher Custom Firearms
Forkin, Ben (See Belt MTN Arms)
Forkin Arms
Francesca, Inc.
G.G. & G.
Garthwaite Pistolsmith, Inc., Jim
Gary Reeder Custom Guns
Genecco Gun Works
Gentry Custom Gunmaker, David
George E. Mathews & Son, Inc.
Greider Precision
Guncraft Sports Inc.
Guncraft Sports, Inc.
Gunsite Custom Shop
Gunsite Gunsmithy (See Gunsite Custom Shop)
Gunsite Training Center
Hamilton, Alex B (See Ten-Ring Precision, Inc)
Hammerli Service-Precision Mac
Hammond Custom Guns Ltd.
Hank's Gun Shop
Hanson's Gun Center, Dick
Harris Gunworks
Harwood, Jack O.
Hawken Shop, The (See Dayton Traister)
Heinie Specialty Products
High Bridge Arms, Inc
Highline Machine Co.
Hoag, James W.
Irwin, Campbell H.
Island Pond Gun Shop
Ivanoff, Thomas G. (See Tom's Gun Repair)
J&S Heat Treat
Jarvis, Inc.
Jeffredo Gunsight
Jensen's Custom Ammunition
Jungkind, Reeves C.
Kaswer Custom, Inc.
Ken Starnes Gunmaker
Kilham & Co.
Kim Ahrends Custom Firearms, Inc.
King's Gun Works
La Clinique du .45
LaFrance Specialties
LaRocca Gun Works
Lathrop's, Inc.
Lawson, John G (See Sight Shop, The)
Leckie Professional Gunsmithing
Linebaugh Custom Sixguns
List Precision Engineering
Long, George F.
Mag-Na-Port International, Inc.
Mahony, Philip Bruce
Mahovsky's Metalife
Mandall Shooting Supplies Inc.
Marvel, Alan
Mathews & Son, Inc., George E.
McCann's Machine & Gun Shop
MCS, Inc.
Middlebrooks Custom Shop
Miller Custom
Mitchell's Accuracy Shop
MJK Gunsmithing, Inc.
Modern Gun Repair School
Montgomery Community College
Mo's Competitor Supplies (See MCS, Inc.)
Mowrey's Guns & Gunsmithing
Mullis Guncraft
NCP Products, Inc.
Novak's, Inc.
Nowlin Mfg. Co.
Olathe Gun Shop

Paris, Frank J.
Pasadena Gun Center
Peacemaker Specialists
PEM's Mfg. Co.
Performance Specialists
Peterson Gun Shop, Inc., A.W.
Pierce Pistols
Piquette's Custom Engraving
Power Custom, Inc.
Precision Specialties
Ramon B. Gonzalez Guns
Randco UK
Ries, Chuck
Rim Pac Sports, Inc.
Rocky Mountain Arms, Inc.
RPM
Ruger's Custom Guns
Score High Gunsmithing
Shooters Supply
Shootin' Shack
Singletary, Kent
Springfield, Inc.
SSK Industries
Swenson's 45 Shop, A. D.
Swift River Gunworks
Ten-Ring Precision, Inc.
Terry K. Kopp Professional Gunsmithing
The A.W. Peterson Gun Shop, Inc.
The Gun Works
The Robar Co.'s, Inc.
The Sight Shop
Thompson, Randall (See Highline Machine Co.)
Thurston Sports, Inc.
Tom's Gun Repair, Thomas G. Ivanoff
Turnbull Restoration, Doug
Vic's Gun Refinishing
Volquartsen Custom Ltd.
Walker Arms Co., Inc.
Walters Industries
Wardell Precision Handguns Ltd.
Wessinger Custom Guns & Engraving
White Barn Wor
Wichita Arms, Inc.
Wild West Guns
Williams Gun Sight Co.
Williamson Precision Gunsmithing
Wilsom Combat
Wright's Gunstock Blanks

POWDER MEASURES, SCALES, FUNNELS & ACCESSORIES

4-D Custom Die Co.
Battenfeld Technologies
Buffalo Arms Co.
Dillon Precision Products, Inc.
Fremont Tool Works
Frontier
GAR
High Precision
Hoehn Sales, Inc.
Jones Custom Products, Neil A.
Modern Muzzleloading, Inc.
Neil A. Jones Custom Products
Peter Dyson & Son Ltd.
Precision Reloading, Inc.
Ramon B. Gonzalez Guns
RCBS Operations/ATK
RCBS/ATK
Redding Reloading Equipment
Saunders Gun & Machine Shop
Spencer's Rifle Barrels, Inc.
The A.W. Peterson Gun Shop, Inc.
Vega Tool Co.
VibraShine, Inc.
VTI Gun Parts

PRESS ACCESSORIES, METALLIC

Buffalo Arms Co.
Corbin Mfg. & Supply, Inc.
Efficient Machinery Co.
Hollywood Engineering
Huntington Die Specialties
R.E.I.
Redding Reloading Equipment
The A.W. Peterson Gun Shop, Inc.
Thompson Tool Mount
Vega Tool Co.

PRESS ACCESSORIES, SHOTSHELL

Efficient Machinery Co.
Hollywood Engineering
Lee Precision, Inc.
MEC, Inc.
Precision Reloading, Inc.
R.E.I.
The A.W. Peterson Gun Shop, Inc.

PRESSES, ARBOR

Blue Ridge Machinery & Tools, Inc.
Goodwin's Gun Shop
K&M Services
RCBS Operations/ATK
Spencer's Rifle Barrels, Inc.
The A.W. Peterson Gun Shop, Inc.

PRESSES, METALLIC

4-D Custom Die Co.
Battenfeld Technologies
Dillon Precision Products, Inc.
Fremont Tool Works
Goodwin's Gun Shop
Hornady Mfg. Co.
Huntington Die Specialties
Lee Precision, Inc.
Midway Arms, Inc.
R.E.I.
Ramon B. Gonzalez Guns
RCBS Operations/ATK
RCBS/ATK
Redding Reloading Equipment
Spencer's Rifle Barrels, Inc.
The A.W. Peterson Gun Shop, Inc.

PRESSES, SHOTSHELL

Ballistic Product, Inc.
Dillon Precision Products, Inc.
Goodwin's Gun Shop
Hornady Mfg. Co.
MEC, Inc.
Precision Reloading, Inc.
Spolar Power Load Inc.
The A.W. Peterson Gun Shop, Inc.

PRESSES, SWAGE

Bullet Swaging Supply, Inc.
The A.W. Peterson Gun Shop, Inc.

PRIMING TOOLS & ACCESSORIES

Goodwin's Gun Shop
Hart & Son, Inc.
Huntington Die Specialties
K&M Services
RCBS Operations/ATK
Simmons, Jerry
Sinclair International, Inc.
The A.W. Peterson Gun Shop, Inc.

REBORING & RERIFLING

Ahlman Guns
Bauska Barrels
BlackStar AccuMax Barrels
BlackStar Barrel Accurizing (See BlackStar AccuMax)
Buffalo Arms Co.
Champlin Firearms, Inc.
Ed's Gun House
Fred F. Wells/Wells Sport Store
H&S Liner Service
Ivanoff, Thomas G. (See Tom's Gun Repair)
Jackalope Gun Shop
LaBounty Precision Reboring, Inc
NCP Products, Inc.
Pence Precision Barrels
Redman's Rifling & Reboring
Rice, Keith (See White Rock Tool & Die)
Ridgetop Sporting Goods
Savage Arms, Inc.
Shaw, Inc., E. R. (See Small Arms Mfg. Co.)
Siegrist Gun Shop
Simmons Gun Repair, Inc.
Stratco, Inc.
Terry K. Kopp Professional Gunsmithing
The Gun Works
Time Precision
Tom's Gun Repair, Thomas G. Ivanoff
Turnbull Restoration, Doug
Van Patten, J. W.
White Rock Tool & Die
Zufall, Joseph F.

RELOADING TOOLS AND ACCESSORIES

4-D Custom Die Co.
Advance Car Mover Co., Rowell Div.
American Products, Inc.
Ammo Load, Inc.
Armfield Custom Bullets
Armite Laboratories
Arms Corporation of the Philippines
Atlantic Rose, Inc.
Atsko/Sno-Seal, Inc.
Bald Eagle Precision Machine Co.
Ballistic Product, Inc.
Belltown Ltd.
Ben William's Gun Shop
Ben's Machines
Berger Bullets Ltd.
Berry's Mfg., Inc.
Blount, Inc., Sporting Equipment Div.
Blue Mountain Bullets
Blue Ridge Machinery & Tools, Inc.
Bonanza (See Forster Products)
Break-Free, Inc.
Brown Co., E. Arthur
BRP, Inc. High Performance Cast Bullets
Brynin, Milton
B-Square Company, Inc.
Buck Stix-SOS Products Co.
Buffalo Arms Co.
Bull Mountain Rifle Co.
Bullseye Bullets
C&D Special Products (See Claybuster Wads & Harvester Bullets)
Camdex, Inc.
Camp-Cap Products
Canyon Cartridge Corp.
Case Sorting System
CH Tool & Die Co. (See 4-D Custom Die Co.)
CheVron Bullets
Claybuster Wads & Harvester Bullets
CONKKO
Cook Engineering Service
Crouse's Country Cover

Cumberland Arms
Curtis Cast Bullets
Custom Products (See Jones Custom Products)
CVA
D.C.C. Enterprises
Davide Pedersoli and Co.
Davis, Don
Davis Products, Mike
Denver Instrument Co.
Dillon Precision Products, Inc.
Dropkick
E&L Mfg., Inc.
Eagan, Donald V.
Eezox, Inc.
Eichelberger Bullets, Wm.
Enguix Import-Export
Euroarms of America, Inc.
E-Z-Way Systems
Federated-Fry (See Fry Metals)
Feken, Dennis
Ferguson, Bill
First Inc., Jack
Fisher Custom Firearms
Flambeau Products Corp.
Flitz International Ltd.
Forster Products
Fremont Tool Works
Fry Metals
Gehmann, Walter (See Huntington Die Specialties)
Graf & Sons
Graphics Direct
Graves Co.
Green, Arthur S.
Greenwood Precision
GTB
Gun City
Hanned Precision (See The Hanned Line)
Harrell's Precision
Harris Enterprises
Harrison Bullets
Haydon Shooters Supply, Russ
Heidenstrom Bullets
High Precision
Hirtenberger AG
Hodgdon Powder Co.
Hoehn Sales, Inc.
Holland's Gunsmithing
Hondo Ind.
Hornady Mfg. Co.
Howell Machine
Hunters Supply, Inc.
Hutton Rifle Ranch
Image Ind. Inc.
Imperial Magnum Corp.
INTEC International, Inc.
Iosso Products
J&L Superior Bullets (See Huntington Die Special)
Javelina Lube Products
JGS Precision Tool Mfg., LLC
JLK Bullets
Jonad Corp.
Jones Custom Products, Neil A.
Jones Moulds, Paul
K&M Services
Kapro Mfg. Co. Inc. (See R.E.I.)
Knoell, Doug
Korzinek Riflesmith, J.
L.A.R. Mfg., Inc.
L.E. Wilson, Inc.
Lapua Ltd.
Le Clear Industries (See E-Z-Way Systems)
Lee Precision, Inc.
Legend Products Corp.
Liberty Metals
Liberty Shooting Supplies
Lightning Performance Innovations, Inc.
Lithi Bee Bullet Lube
Littleton, J. F.

Lock's Philadelphia Gun Exchange
Lortone Inc.
Lyman Instant Targets, Inc. (See Lyman Products)
Lyman Products Corp.
MA Systems
Magma Engineering Co.
MarMik, Inc.
Marquart Precision Co.
Match Prep-Doyle Gracey
Mayville Engineering Co. (See MEC, Inc.)
MCS, Inc.
MEC, Inc.
Midway Arms, Inc.
MI-TE Bullets
Montana Armory, Inc .(See C. Sharps Arms Co. Inc.)
Mo's Competitor Supplies (See MCS, Inc.)
Mountain South
Mountain State Muzzleloading Supplies, Inc.
MTM Molded Products Co., Inc.
Multi-Scale Charge Ltd.
MWG Co.
Navy Arms Company
Newman Gunshop
North Devon Firearms Services
Old West Bullet Moulds
Omark Industries, Div. of Blount, Inc.
Original Box, Inc.
Outdoor Sports Headquarters, Inc.
Paco's (See Small Custom Mould & Bullet Co.)
Paragon Sales & Services, Inc.
Pease Accuracy
Pinetree Bullets
Ponsness/Warren
Prairie River Arms
Prime Reloading
Professional Hunter Supplies (See Star Custom Bullets)
Pro-Shot Products, Inc.
R.A. Wells Custom Gunsmith
R.E.I.
R.I.S. Co., Inc.
Rapine Bullet Mould Mfg. Co.
Reloading Specialties, Inc.
Rice, Keith (See White Rock Tool & Die)
Rochester Lead Works
Rooster Laboratories
Rorschach Precision Products
SAECO (See Redding Reloading Equipment)
Sandia Die & Cartridge Co.
Saunders Gun & Machine Shop
Saville Iron Co. (See Greenwood Precision)
Seebeck Assoc., R.E.
Sharp Shooter Supply
Sharps Arms Co., Inc., C.
Shiloh Rifle Mfg.
Sierra Specialty Prod. Co.
Silver Eagle Machining
Skip's Machine
Small Custom Mould & Bullet Co.
Sno-Seal, Inc. (See Atsko/Sno-Seal, Inc.)
SOS Products Co. (See Buck Stix-SOS Products Co.)
Spencer's Rifle Barrels, Inc.
SPG LLC
SSK Industries
Stalwart Corporation
Star Custom Bullets
Starr Trading Co., Jedediah
Stillwell, Robert
Stoney Point Products, Inc.
Stratco, Inc.
Tamarack Products, Inc.
Taracorp Industries, Inc.
TCCI

TCSR
TDP Industries, Inc.
Tetra Gun Care
The Hanned Line
The Protector Mfg. Co., Inc.
Thompson/Center Arms
TMI Products (See Haselbauer Products, Jerry)
Vega Tool Co.
Venco Industries, Inc. (See Shooter's Choice Gun Care)
VibraShine, Inc.
Vibra-Tek Co.
Vihtavuori Oy/Kaltron-Pettibone
Vitt/Boos
W.B. Niemi Engineering
W.J. Riebe Co.
WD-40 Co.
Webster Scale Mfg. Co.
White Rock Tool & Die
Widener's Reloading & Shooting Supply, Inc.
Wise Custom Guns
Woodleigh (See Huntington Die Specialties)
Yesteryear Armory & Supply
Young Country Arms

RESTS BENCH, PORTABLE AND ACCESSORIES

Adventure 16, Inc.
Armor Metal Products
Bald Eagle Precision Machine Co.
Bartlett Engineering
Battenfeld Technologies
Blount/Outers ATK
Browning Arms Co.
B-Square Company, Inc.
Bull Mountain Rifle Co.
Canons Delcour
Clift Mfg., L. R.
Desert Mountain Mfg.
Efficient Machinery Co.
Greenwood Precision
Harris Engineering Inc.
Hidalgo, Tony
Hoehn Sales, Inc.
Hoppe's Div. Penguin Industries, Inc.
J&J Sales
Keng's Firearms Specialty, Inc./US Tactical Systems
Kolpin Mfg., Inc.
Kramer Designs
Midway Arms, Inc.
Millett Sights
Protektor Model
Ransom International Corp.
Russ Haydon's Shooters' Supply
Saville Iron Co. (See Greenwood Precision)
Sinclair International, Inc.
Stoney Point Products, Inc.
T.H.U. Enterprises, Inc.
The A.W. Peterson Gun Shop, Inc.
The Outdoor Connection, Inc.
Thompson Target Technology
Tonoloway Tack Drives
Varmint Masters, LLC
Wichita Arms, Inc.
Zanotti Armor, Inc.
Ziegel Engineering

RIFLE BARREL MAKER

Airrow
American Safe Arms, Inc.
Bauska Barrels
BlackStar AccuMax Barrels
BlackStar Barrel Accurizing (See BlackStar AccuMax)
Border Barrels Ltd.

Brown Co., E. Arthur
Buchsenmachermeister
Bullberry Barrel Works, Ltd.
Bushmaster Firearms
Canons Delcour
Carter's Gun Shop
Christensen Arms
Cincinnati Swaging
deHaas Barrels
Dilliott Gunsmithing, Inc.
DKT, Inc.
Donnelly, C. P.
Douglas Barrels, Inc.
Fred F. Wells/Wells Sport Store
Gaillard Barrels
Gary Schneider Rifle Barrels Inc.
Getz Barrel Co.
Granite Mountain Arms, Inc.
Green Mountain Rifle Barrel Co., Inc.
Gruning Precision Inc.
Half Moon Rifle Shop
Harris Gunworks
Hart Rifle Barrels,Inc.
Hastings
Hofer Jagdwaffen, P.
H-S Precision, Inc.
Jackalope Gun Shop
Krieger Barrels, Inc.
Lilja Precision Rifle Barrels
Lothar Walther Precision Tool Inc.
McGowen Rifle Barrels
McMillan Rifle Barrels
Mid-America Recreation, Inc.
Modern Gun Repair School
Morrison Precision
N.C. Ordnance Co.
Obermeyer Rifled Barrels
Olympic Arms Inc.
Orion Rifle Barrel Co.
PAC-NOR Barreling
Pence Precision Barrels
Rogue Rifle Co., Inc.
Sabatti SPA
Savage Arms, Inc.
Schneider Rifle Barrels, Inc., Gary
Shaw, Inc., E. R. (See Small Arms Mfg. Co.)
Shilen, Inc.
Siskiyou Gun Works (See Donnelly, C. P.)
Small Arms Mfg. Co.
Specialty Shooters Supply, Inc.
Spencer's Rifle Barrels, Inc.
Strutz Rifle Barrels, Inc., W. C.
Swift River Gunworks
Terry K. Kopp Professional Gunsmithing
The Gun Works
The Wilson Arms Co.
Turnbull Restoration, Doug
Unmussig Bullets, D. L.
Verney-Carron
Virgin Valley Custom Guns
Wiseman and Co., Bill

SCOPES, MOUNTS, ACCESSORIES, OPTICAL EQUIPMENT

A.R.M.S., Inc.
Accu-Tek
Ackerman, Bill (See Optical Services Co.)
Action Direct, Inc.
ADCO Sales, Inc.
Aimtech Mount Systems
Air Rifle Specialists
Air Venture Airguns
All Rite Products, Inc.
Alley Supply Co.
Alpec Team, Inc.
Apel GmbH, Ernst
ArmaLite, Inc.
Arundel Arms & Ammunition, Inc., A.

B.A.C.
Badger Creek Studio
Baer Custom, Inc.
Bansner's Ultimate Rifles, LLC
Barrett Firearms Manufacturer, Inc.
Beaver Park Product, Inc.
BEC, Inc.
Beeman Precision Airguns
Ben William's Gun Shop
Benjamin/Sheridan Co., Crosman
Bill Russ Trading Post
BKL Technologies
Blount, Inc., Sporting Equipment Div.
Blount/Outers ATK
Borden Rifles Inc.
Brockman's Custom Gunsmithing
Brocock Ltd.
Brown Co., E. Arthur
Brownells, Inc.
Brunton U.S.A.
BSA Optics
B-Square Company, Inc.
Bull Mountain Rifle Co.
Burris Co., Inc.
Bushmaster Firearms
Bushnell Sports Optics Worldwide
Butler Creek Corp.
Cabela's
Carl Zeiss Inc.
Center Lock Scope Rings
Chuck's Gun Shop
Clark Custom Guns, Inc.
Clearview Mfg. Co., Inc.
Compass Industries, Inc.
Compasseco, Ltd.
Concept Development Corp.
Conetrol Scope Mounts
Creedmoor Sports, Inc.
Crimson Trace Lasers
Crosman Airguns
Custom Quality Products, Inc.
D.C.C. Enterprises
Daisy Outdoor Products
Del-Sports, Inc.
DHB Products
E. Arthur Brown Co.
Eclectic Technologies, Inc.
Edmund Scientific Co.
Ednar, Inc.
Eggleston, Jere D.
Emerging Technologies, Inc. (See Laseraim Technologies, Inc.)
Entre`prise Arms, Inc.
Euro-Imports
Evolution Gun Works Inc.
Excalibur Electro Optics Inc.
Excel Industries Inc.
Faloon Industries, Inc.
Farr Studio, Inc.
Federal Arms Corp. of America
Freedom Arms, Inc.
Fujinon, Inc.
G.G. & G.
Galati International
Gentry Custom Gunmaker, David
Gil Hebard Guns Inc.
Gilmore Sports Concepts
Goodwin's Gun Shop
GSI, Inc.
Gun South, Inc. (See GSI, Inc.)
Guns Div. of D.C. Engineering, Inc.
Gunsmithing, Inc.
Hakko Co. Ltd.
Hammerli USA
Harris Gunworks
Harvey, Frank
Highwood Special Products
Hiptmayer, Armurier
Hiptmayer, Klaus
HiTek International
Holland's Gunsmithing
Impact Case & Container, Inc.
Ironsighter Co.
Jeffredo Gunsight

Jena Eur
Jerry Phillips Optics
Jewell Triggers, Inc.
John Masen Co. Inc.
John's Custom Leather
Kahles A. Swarovski Company
Kalispel Case Line
KDF, Inc.
Keng's Firearms Specialty, Inc./US Tactical Systems
Kesselring Gun Shop
Kimber of America, Inc.
Knight's Mfg. Co.
Kowa Optimed, Inc.
KVH Industries, Inc.
Kwik-Site Co.
L&S Technologies Inc. (See Aimtech Mount Systems)
L.A.R. Mfg., Inc.
Laser Devices, Inc.
Laseraim Technologies, Inc.
LaserMax, Inc.
Leapers, Inc.
Leica USA, Inc.
Leupold & Stevens, Inc.
List Precision Engineering
Lohman Mfg. Co., Inc.
Lomont Precision Bullets
London Guns Ltd.
Mac-1 Airgun Distributors
Mag-Na-Port International, Inc.
Mandall Shooting Supplies Inc.
Marksman Products
Maxi-Mount Inc.
McBros Rifle Co.
McCann's Machine & Gun Shop
McMillan Optical Gunsight Co.
MCS, Inc.
MDS
Merit Corp.
Military Armament Corp.
Millett Sights
Mirador Optical Corp.
Mitchell Optics, Inc.
MMC
Mo's Competitor Supplies (See MCS, Inc.)
MWG Co.
Navy Arms Company
New England Custom Gun Service
Nikon, Inc.
Norincoptics (See BEC, Inc.)
Olympic Optical Co.
Optical Services Co.
Orchard Park Enterprise
Oregon Arms, Inc. (See Rogue Rifle Co., Inc.)
Ozark Gun Works
Parker & Sons Shooting Supply
Parsons Optical Mfg. Co.
PECAR Herbert Schwarz GmbH
PEM's Mfg. Co.
Pentax Corp.
PMC/Eldorado Cartridge Corp.
Precision Sport Optics
Premier Reticles
R.A. Wells Custom Gunsmith
Ram-Line ATK
Ramon B. Gonzalez Guns
Ranch Products
Randolph Engineering Inc.
Rice, Keith (See White Rock Tool & Die)
Robinson Armament Co.
Rogue Rifle Co., Inc.
Romain's Custom Guns, Inc.
S&K Scope Mounts
Saunders Gun & Machine Shop
Schmidt & Bender, Inc.
Schumakers Gun Shop
Scope Control, Inc.
Score High Gunsmithing
Seecamp Co. Inc., L. W.
Segway Industries

DIRECTORY

PRODUCT & SERVICE DIRECTORY

Selsi Co., Inc.
Sharp Shooter Supply
Shepherd Enterprises, Inc.
Sightron, Inc.
Simmons Outdoor Corp.
Six Enterprises
Southern Bloomer Mfg. Co.
Spencer's Rifle Barrels, Inc.
Splitfire Sporting Goods, L.L.C.
Sportsmatch U.K. Ltd.
Springfield Armory
Springfield, Inc.
SSK Industries
Stiles Custom Guns
Stoeger Industries
Stoney Point Products, Inc.
Sturm Ruger & Co. Inc.
Sunny Hill Enterprises, Inc.
Swarovski Optik North America Ltd.
Swift Instruments, Inc.
T.K. Lee Co.
Talley, Dave
Tasco Sales, Inc.
Tele-Optics
The A.W. Peterson Gun Shop, Inc.
The Outdoor Connection, Inc.
Thompson/Center Arms
Traditions Performance Firearms
Trijicon, Inc.
Truglo, Inc.
Ultra Dot Distribution
Uncle Mike's (See Michaels of Oregon Co.)
Unertl Optical Co., Inc.
United Binocular Co.
United States Optics Technologies, Inc.
Virgin Valley Custom Guns
Visible Impact Targets
Voere-KGH GmbH
Warne Manufacturing Co.
Warren Muzzleloading Co., Inc.
Watson Trophy Match Bullets
Weaver Products ATK
Weaver Scope Repair Service
Weigand Combat Handguns, Inc.
Wessinger Custom Guns & Engraving
Westley Richards & Co.
White Rifles, Inc.
White Rock Tool & Die
Whitestone Lumber Corp.
Wideview Scope Mount Corp.
Wilcox Industries Corp.
Wild West Guns
Williams Gun Sight Co.
York M-1 Conversions
Zanotti Armor, Inc.

SHELLHOLDERS

Corbin Mfg. & Supply, Inc.
Fremont Tool Works
Goodwin's Gun Shop
Hart & Son, Inc.
Hollywood Engineering
Huntington Die Specialties
K&M Services
King & Co.
RCBS Operations/ATK
Redding Reloading Equipment
The A.W. Peterson Gun Shop, Inc.
Vega Tool Co.

SHOOTING/TRAINING SCHOOL

Alpine Indoor Shooting Range
American Gunsmithing Institute
American Small Arms Academy
Auto Arms
Beretta U.S.A. Corp.
Bob's Tactical Indoor Shooting Range & Gun Shop

Bridgeman Products
Chapman Academy of Practical Shooting
Chelsea Gun Club of New York City Inc.
Cherry Creek State Park Shooting Center
CQB Training
Defense Training International, Inc.
Executive Protection Institute
Ferris Firearms
Front Sight Firearms Training Institute
G.H. Enterprises Ltd.
Gene's Custom Guns
Griffin & Howe, Inc.
Griffin & Howe, Inc.
Griffin & Howe, Inc.
Guncraft Books (See Guncraft Sports Inc.)
Guncraft Sports Inc.
Guncraft Sports, Inc.
Gunsite Training Center
Henigson & Associates, Steve
Jensen's Custom Ammunition
Jensen's Firearms Academy
Kemen America
L.L. Bean, Inc.
Lethal Force Institute (See Police Bookshelf)
Loch Leven Industries/Convert-A-Pell
Long, George F.
McMurdo, Lynn (See Specialty Gunsmithing)
Mendez, John A.
NCP Products, Inc.
Nevada Pistol Academy, Inc.
North American Shooting Systems
North Mountain Pine Training Center (See Executive
Nowlin Mfg. Co.
Paxton Quigley's Personal Protection Strategies
Pentheny de Pentheny
Performance Specialists
Police Bookshelf
SAFE
Shoot Where You Look
Shooter's World
Shooters, Inc.
Sigarms, Inc.
Smith & Wesson
Specialty Gunsmithing
Starlight Training Center, Inc.
Tactical Defense Institute
The Firearm Training Center
The Midwest Shooting School
The Shooting Gallery
Thunden Ranch
Western Missouri Shooters Alliance
Yankee Gunsmith "Just Glocks"
Yavapai Firearms Academy Ltd.

SHOTSHELL MISCELLANY

American Products, Inc.
Ballistic Product, Inc.
Bridgeman Products
Goodwin's Gun Shop
Lee Precision, Inc.
MEC, Inc.
Precision Reloading, Inc.
R.E.I.
RCBS Operations/ATK
T&S Industries, Inc.
The A.W. Peterson Gun Shop, Inc.
The Gun Works
Vitt/Boos
Ziegel Engineering

SIGHTS, METALLIC

100 Straight Products, Inc.

Accura-Site (See All's, The Jim Tembelis Co., Inc.)
Ad Hominem
Alley Supply Co.
All's, The Jim J. Tembelis Co., Inc.
Alpec Team, Inc.
Andela Tool & Machine, Inc.
AO Sight Systems
ArmaLite, Inc.
Ashley Outdoors, Inc.
Aspen Outfitting Co.
Axtell Rifle Co.
B.A.C.
Baer Custom Inc., Les
Ballard Rifle & Cartridge Co., LLC
BEC, Inc.
Bob's Gun Shop
Bo-Mar Tool & Mfg. Co.
Bond Custom Firearms
Bowen Classic Arms Corp.
Brockman's Custom Gunsmithing
Brooks Tactical Systems-Agrip
Brown Co., E. Arthur
Brown Dog Ent.
Brownells, Inc.
Buffalo Arms Co.
Bushmaster Firearms
C. Sharps Arms Co. Inc./Montana Armory
California Sights (See Fautheree, Andy)
Campbell, Dick
Cape Outfitters
Cape Outfitters
Cash Mfg. Co., Inc.
Center Lock Scope Rings
Champion's Choice, Inc.
C-More Systems
Colonial Repair
CRR, Inc./Marble's Inc.
Davide Pedersoli and Co.
DHB Products
Dixie Gun Works
DPMS (Defense Procurement Manufacturing Services, Inc.)
E. Arthur Brown Co.
Evolution Gun Works Inc.
Faloon Industries, Inc.
Farr Studio, Inc.
G.G. & G.
Garthwaite Pistolsmith, Inc., Jim
Goergen's Gun Shop, Inc.
Goodwin's Gun Shop
Guns Div. of D.C. Engineering, Inc.
Gunsmithing, Inc.
Hank's Gun Shop
Heidenstrom Bullets
Heinie Specialty Products
Hesco-Meprolight
Hiptmayer, Armurier
Hiptmayer, Klaus
I.S.S.
Innovative Weaponry Inc.
J.G. Anschutz GmbH & Co. KG
J.P. Enterprises Inc.
Keng's Firearms Specialty, Inc./US Tactical Systems
Knight Rifles
Knight's Mfg. Co.
L.P.A. Inc.
Leapers, Inc.
List Precision Engineering
London Guns Ltd.
Lyman Instant Targets, Inc. (See Lyman Products)
Mandall Shooting Supplies Inc.
Marble Arms (See CRR, Inc./Marble's Inc.)
MCS, Inc.
MEC-Gar S.R.L.
Meprolight (See Hesco-Meprolight)
Merit Corp.
Mid-America Recreation, Inc.
Middlebrooks Custom Shop

Millett Sights
MMC
Modern Muzzleloading, Inc.
Montana Armory, Inc .(See C. Sharps Arms Co. Inc.)
Montana Vintage Arms
Mo's Competitor Supplies (See MCS, Inc.)
Navy Arms Company
New England Custom Gun Service
Newman Gunshop
Novak's, Inc.
OK Weber, Inc.
One Ragged Hole
Parker & Sons Shooting Supply
PEM's Mfg. Co.
Perazone-Gunsmith, Brian
RPM
Sharps Arms Co., Inc., C.
Slug Site
STI International
T.F.C. S.p.A.
Talley, Dave
Tank's Rifle Shop
The A.W. Peterson Gun Shop, Inc.
The Gun Doctor
Trijicon, Inc.
Truglo, Inc.
United States Optics Technologies, Inc.
Warne Manufacturing Co.
Weigand Combat Handguns, Inc.
Wichita Arms, Inc.
Wild West Guns
Williams Gun Sight Co.
Wilsom Combat
Wilsom Combat

STOCK MAKER

Acra-Bond Laminates
Al Lind Custom Guns
Amrine's Gun Shop
Antique Arms Co.
Artistry in Wood
Aspen Outfitting Co.
Bain & Davis, Inc.
Bansner's Ultimate Rifles, LLC
Baron Technology
Belding's Custom Gun Shop
Billings Gunsmiths
Bob Rogers Gunsmithing
Boltin, John M.
Borden Ridges Rimrock Stocks
Bowerly, Kent
Boyds' Gunstock Industries, Inc.
Brace, Larry D.
Briganti, A.J.
Brown Precision, Inc.
Buchsenmachermeister
Bull Mountain Rifle Co.
Bullberry Barrel Works, Ltd.
Burkhart Gunsmithing, Don
Cambos Outdoorsman
Cambos Outdoorsman
Caywood, Shane J.
Chicasaw Gun Works
Chuck's Gun Shop
Claro Walnut Gunstock Co.
Coffin, Charles H.
Colorado Gunsmithing Academy
Custom Riflestocks, Inc., Michael M. Kokolus
Custom Single Shot Rifles
Custom Stocking
D&D Gunsmiths, Ltd.
Dangler, Homer L.
D'Arcy Echols & Co.
DGR Custom Rifles
DGR Custom Rifles
DGS, Inc., Dale A. Storey
Erhardt, Dennis
Eversull Co., Inc.
Fieldsport Ltd.

Fisher, Jerry A.
Forster, Larry L.
Fred F. Wells/Wells Sport Store
Gary Goudy Classic Stocks
Genecco Gun Works
Gene's Custom Guns
George E. Mathews & Son, Inc.
Gillmann, Edwin
Grace, Charles E.
Great American Gunstock Co.
Gruning Precision Inc.
Gunsmithing Ltd.
Hank's Gun Shop
Harper's Custom Stocks
Harry Lawson Co.
Heilmann, Stephen
Hensley, Gunmaker, Darwin
Heydenberk, Warren R.
High Tech Specialties, Inc.
Hofer Jagdwaffen, P.
Huebner, Corey O.
Island Pond Gun Shop
Jack Dever Co.
Jamison's Forge Works
Jay McCament Custom Gunmaker
Jim Norman Custom Gunstocks
John Rigby & Co.
K. Eversull Co., Inc.
Keith's Custom Gunstocks
Ken Eyster Heritage Gunsmiths, Inc.
Klein Custom Guns, Don
L. E. Jurras & Assoc.
Larry Lyons Gunworks
Marshall Fish Mfg. Gunsmith Sptg. Co.
Mathews & Son, Inc., George E.
McGowen Rifle Barrels
Mercer Custom Guns
Mid-America Recreation, Inc.
Mitchell, Jack
Modern Gun Repair School
Morrow, Bud
Nelson's Custom Guns, Inc.
Nettestad Gun Works
Nickels, Paul R.
Paul and Sharon Dressel
Paul D. Hillmer Custom Gunstocks
Paulsen Gunstocks
Pawling Mountain Club
Pecatonica River Longrifle
Pentheny de Pentheny
Quality Custom Firearms
R&J Gun Shop
R.A. Wells Custom Gunsmith
Ralph Bone Engraving
RMS Custom Gunsmithing
Ron Frank Custom Classic Arms
Royal Arms Gunstocks
Ruger's Custom Guns
Six Enterprises
Skeoch, Brian R.
Smith, Art
Smith, Sharmon
Speiser, Fred D.
Steven Dodd Hughes
Stott's Creek Armory, Inc.
Sturgeon Valley Sporters
Talmage, William G.
Taylor & Robbins
The Custom Shop
Tiger-Hunt Gunstocks
Trico Plastics
Tucker, James C.
Turnbull Restoration, Doug
Vest, John
Walker Arms Co., Inc.
Wayne E. Schwartz Custom Guns
Weber & Markin Custom Gunsmiths
Wenig Custom Gunstocks
Wiebe, Duane
Wild West Guns
Williamson Precision Gunsmithing
Winter, Robert M.
Working Guns

PRODUCT & SERVICE DIRECTORY

STOCKS (COMMERCIAL)

Accuracy Unlimited
Acra-Bond Laminates
Ahlman Guns
Al Lind Custom Guns
Arms Ingenuity Co.
Arundel Arms & Ammunition, Inc., A.
Aspen Outfitting Co.
B.A.C.
Baelder, Harry
Balickie, Joe
Bansner's Ultimate Rifles, LLC
Barnes Bullets, Inc.
Battenfeld Technologies
Beitzinger, George
Belding's Custom Gun Shop
Bell & Carlson, Inc.
Blount, Inc., Sporting Equipment Div.
Blount/Outers ATK
Bob's Gun Shop
Borden Ridges Rimrock Stocks
Borden Rifles Inc.
Bowerly, Kent
Boyds' Gunstock Industries, Inc.
Brockman's Custom Gunsmithing
Brown Co., E. Arthur
Buckhorn Gun Works
Bull Mountain Rifle Co.
Butler Creek Corp.
Cali'co Hardwoods, Inc.
Cape Outfitters
Caywood, Shane J.
Chambers Flintlocks Ltd., Jim
Chicasaw Gun Works
Chuilli, Stephen
Claro Walnut Gunstock Co.
Coffin, Charles H.
Coffin, Jim (See Working Guns)
Colonial Repair
Colorado Gunsmithing Academy
Colorado School of Trades
Conrad, C. A.
Curly Maple Stock Blanks (See Tiger-Hunt)
Custom Checkering Service, Kathy Forster
Custom Riflestocks, Inc., Michael M. Kokolus
D&D Gunsmiths, Ltd.
D&G Precision Duplicators (See Greene Precision)
David W. Schwartz Custom Guns
Davide Pedersoli and Co.
DGR Custom Rifles
Duane's Gun Repair (See DGR Custom Rifles)
Duncan's Gun Works, Inc.
Eggleston, Jere D.
Erhardt, Dennis
Eversull Co., Inc.
Faloon Industries, Inc.
Faloon Industries, Inc.
Fibron Products, Inc.
Fieldsport Ltd.
Fisher, Jerry A.
Folks, Donald E.
Forster, Kathy (See Custom Checkering)
Forthofer's Gunsmithing & Knifemaking
Francotte & Cie S.A. Auguste
Game Haven Gunstocks
George Hoenig, Inc.
Gervais, Mike
Gillmann, Edwin
Giron, Robert E.
Goens, Dale W.
Golden Age Arms Co.
Goodwin's Gun Shop
Great American Gunstock Co.
Green, Roger M.
Greenwood Precision
Guns Div. of D.C. Engineering, Inc.

Gunsmithing Ltd.
Hammerli USA
Hanson's Gun Center, Dick
Harper's Custom Stocks
Harris Gunworks
Harry Lawson Co.
Hart & Son, Inc.
Harwood, Jack O.
Hecht, Hubert J, Waffen-Hecht
Hensley, Gunmaker, Darwin
High Tech Specialties, Inc.
Hiptmayer, Armurier
Hiptmayer, Klaus
Hogue Grips
H-S Precision, Inc.
Huebner, Corey O.
Island Pond Gun Shop
Israel Arms International, Inc.
Ivanoff, Thomas G. (See Tom's Gun Repair)
Jackalope Gun Shop
Jarrett Rifles, Inc.
Jay McCament Custom Gunmaker
Jim Norman Custom Gunstocks
John Masen Co. Inc.
Johnson Wood Products
KDF, Inc.
Keith's Custom Gunstocks
Kelbly, Inc.
Kilham & Co.
Klingler Woodcarving
Kokolus, Michael M. (See Custom Riflestocks In)
Lawson Co., Harry
Mandall Shooting Supplies Inc.
McBros Rifle Co.
McDonald, Dennis
McMillan Fiberglass Stocks, Inc.
Michaels Of Oregon, Co.
Mid-America Recreation, Inc.
Miller Arms, Inc.
Mitchell, Jack
Morrison Custom Rifles, J. W.
MPI Stocks
MWG Co.
NCP Products, Inc.
Nelson's Custom Guns, Inc.
New England Arms Co.
New England Custom Gun Service
Newman Gunshop
Nickels, Paul R.
Oil Rod and Gun Shop
Old World Gunsmithing
One Of A Kind
Ottmar, Maurice
Pagel Gun Works, Inc.
Paragon Sales & Services, Inc.
Parker & Sons Shooting Supply
Paul and Sharon Dressel
Paul D. Hillmer Custom Gunstocks
Paulsen Gunstocks
Pawling Mountain Club
Pecatonica River Longrifle
PEM's Mfg. Co.
Pohl, Henry A. (See Great American Gun Co.
Powell & Son (Gunmakers) Ltd., William
Precision Gun Works
R&J Gun Shop
R.A. Wells Custom Gunsmith
Ram-Line ATK
Ramon B. Gonzalez Guns
Rampart International
Reagent Chemical & Research, Inc.
Reiswig, Wallace E. (See Claro Walnut Gunstock
Richards Micro-Fit Stocks
RMS Custom Gunsmithing
Robinson, Don
Robinson Armament Co.
Robinson Firearms Mfg. Ltd.
Romain's Custom Guns, Inc.
Ron Frank Custom Classic Arms

Royal Arms Gunstocks
Saville Iron Co. (See Greenwood Precision)
Schiffman, Curt
Schiffman, Mike
Score High Gunsmithing
Simmons Gun Repair, Inc.
Six Enterprises
Speiser, Fred D.
Stan De Treville & Co.
Stiles Custom Guns
Swann, D. J.
Swift River Gunworks
Szweda, Robert (See RMS Custom Gunsmithing)
T.F.C. S.p.A.
Talmage, William G.
Tecnolegno S.p.A.
The A.W. Peterson Gun Shop, Inc.
The Gun Shop
The Orvis Co.
Tiger-Hunt Gunstocks
Tirelli
Tom's Gun Repair, Thomas G. Ivanoff
Track of the Wolf, Inc.
Trevallion Gunstocks
Tuttle, Dale
Vic's Gun Refinishing
Vintage Industries, Inc.
Virgin Valley Custom Guns
Volquartsen Custom Ltd.
Walker Arms Co., Inc.
Weber & Markin Custom Gunsmiths
Weems, Cecil
Wenig Custom Gunstocks
Werth, T. W.
Western Mfg. Co.
Wild West Guns
Williams Gun Sight Co.
Windish, Jim
Winter, Robert M.
Working Guns
Wright's Gunstock Blanks
Zeeryp, Russ

STUCK CASE REMOVERS

Goodwin's Gun Shop
Huntington Die Specialties
MarMik, Inc.
The A.W. Peterson Gun Shop, Inc.
Tom's Gun Repair, Thomas G. Ivanoff

TARGETS, BULLET & CLAYBIRD TRAPS

Action Target, Inc.
Air Arms
American Target
Autauga Arms, Inc.
Beeman Precision Airguns
Benjamin/Sheridan Co., Crosman
Beomat of America, Inc.
Birchwood Casey
Blount, Inc., Sporting Equipment Div.
Blount/Outers ATK
Blue and Gray Products Inc. (See Ox-Yoke Originals)
Brown Precision, Inc.
Bull-X, Inc.
Champion Target Co.
Creedmoor Sports, Inc.
Crosman Airguns
D.C.C. Enterprises
Daisy Outdoor Products
Detroit-Armor Corp.
Diamond Mfg. Co.
Federal Champion Target Co.
G.H. Enterprises Ltd.
Hiti-Schuch, Atelier Wilma
H-S Precision, Inc.
Hunterjohn

J.G. Dapkus Co., Inc.
Kennebec Journal
Kleen-Bore,Inc.
Lakefield Arms Ltd. (See Savage Arms, Inc.)
Leapers, Inc.
Littler Sales Co.
Lyman Instant Targets, Inc. (See Lyman Products)
Marksman Products
Mendez, John A.
Mountain Plains Industries
MSR Targets
Muscle Products Corp.
N.B.B., Inc.
National Target Co.
North American Shooting Systems
Outers Laboratories Div. of ATK
Ox-Yoke Originals, Inc.
Palsa Outdoor Products
Passive Bullet Traps, Inc. (See Savage Range Systems, Inc.)
PlumFire Press, Inc.
Precision Airgun Sales, Inc.
Protektor Model
Quack Decoy & Sporting Clays
Remington Arms Co., Inc.
Rockwood Corp.
Rocky Mountain Target Co.
Savage Range Systems, Inc.
Schaefer Shooting Sports
Seligman Shooting Products
Shooters Supply
Shoot-N-C Targets (See Birchwood Casey)
Target Shooting, Inc.
The A.W. Peterson Gun Shop, Inc.
Thompson Target Technology
Trius Traps, Inc.
Universal Sports
Visible Impact Targets
Watson Trophy Match Bullets
Woods Wise Products
World of Targets (See Birchwood Casey)
X-Spand Target Systems

TAXIDERMY

African Import Co.
Bill Russ Trading Post
Kulis Freeze Dry Taxidermy
Montgomery Community College
World Trek, Inc.

TRAP & SKEET SHOOTER'S EQUIPMENT

Allen Co., Bob
Allen Sportswear, Bob (See Allen Co., Bob)
American Products, Inc.
Bagmaster Mfg., Inc.
Ballistic Product, Inc.
Beomat of America, Inc.
Beretta S.p.A., Pietro
Blount/Outers ATK
Bridgeman Products
C&H Research
Cape Outfitters
Claybuster Wads & Harvester Bullets
Fiocchi of America, Inc.
G.H. Enterprises Ltd.
Hoppe's Div. Penguin Industries, Inc.
Hunter Co., Inc.
Jamison's Forge Works
Jenkins Recoil Pads, Inc.
Jim Noble Co.
Kalispel Case Line
Kolar
Lakewood Products LLC
Ljutic Industries, Inc.
Mag-Na-Port International, Inc.

Maionchi-L.M.I.
MEC, Inc.
Moneymaker Guncraft Corp.
MTM Molded Products Co., Inc.
NCP Products, Inc.
Pachmayr Div. Lyman Products
Palsa Outdoor Products
Perazone-Gunsmith, Brian
Pro-Port Ltd.
Protektor Model
Quack Decoy & Sporting Clays
Randolph Engineering Inc.
Remington Arms Co., Inc.
Rhodeside, Inc.
Shooting Specialties (See Titus, Daniel)
Shotgun Sports Magazine, dba Shootin' Accessories Ltd.
Stan Baker Sports
T&S Industries, Inc.
TEN-X Products Group
The Gun Works
Trius Traps, Inc.
Truglo, Inc.
Universal Sports
Warne Manufacturing Co.
Weber & Markin Custom Gunsmiths
X-Spand Target Systems
Ziegel Engineering

TRIGGERS, RELATED EQUIPMENT

Actions by "T" Teddy Jacobson
B&D Trading Co., Inc.
Baer Custom Inc., Les
Behlert Precision, Inc.
Bond Custom Firearms
Boyds' Gunstock Industries, Inc.
Bull Mountain Rifle Co.
Chicasaw Gun Works
Dayton Traister
Electronic Trigger Systems, Inc.
Eversull Co., Inc.
Feinwerkbau Westinger & Altenburger
Gentry Custom Gunmaker, David
Goodwin's Gun Shop
Hart & Son, Inc.
Hawken Shop, The (See Dayton Traister)
Hoehn Sales, Inc.
Holland's Gunsmithing
Impact Case & Container, Inc.
J.P. Enterprises Inc.
Jewell Triggers, Inc.
John Masen Co. Inc.
Jones Custom Products, Neil A.
K. Eversull Co., Inc.
KK Air International (See Impact Case & Container Co.)
Knight's Mfg. Co.
L&R Lock Co.
List Precision Engineering
London Guns Ltd.
M.H. Canjar Co.
Mahony, Philip Bruce
Master Lock Co.
Miller Single Trigger Mfg. Co.
NCP Products, Inc.
Neil A. Jones Custom Products
Nowlin Mfg. Co.
PEM's Mfg. Co.
Penrod Precision
Ramon B. Gonzalez Guns
Robinson Armament Co.
Schumakers Gun Shop
Sharp Shooter Supply
Shilen, Inc.
Simmons Gun Repair, Inc.
Spencer's Rifle Barrels, Inc.
Tank's Rifle Shop
Target Shooting, Inc.
The A.W. Peterson Gun Shop, Inc.
The Gun Works
Watson Trophy Match Bullets

MANUFACTURER'S DIRECTORY

A

A Zone Bullets, 2039 Walter Rd., Billings, MT 59105 / 800-252-3111; FAX: 406-248-1961

A&B Industries,Inc (See Top-Line USA Inc)

A&W Repair, 2930 Schneider Dr., Arnold, MO 63010 / 617-287-3725

A.A. Arms, Inc., 4811 Persimmont Ct., Monroe, NC 28110 / 704-289-5356; or 800-935-1119; FAX: 704-289-5859

A.B.S. III, 9238 St. Morritz Dr., Fern Creek, KY 40291

A.G. Russell Knives, Inc., 1920 North 26th Street, Springdale, AR 72764 / 479-751-7341; FAX: 479-751-4520 ag@agrussell.com agrussell.com

A.R.M.S., Inc., 230 W. Center St., West Bridgewater, MA 02379-1620 / 508-584-7816; FAX: 508-588-8045

A.W. Peterson Gun Shop, Inc., 4255 W. Old U.S. 441, Mt. Dora, FL 32757-3299 / 352-383-4258; FAX: 352-735-1001

AC Dyna-tite Corp., 155 Kelly St., P.O. Box 0984, Elk Grove Village, IL 60007 / 847-593-5566; FAX: 847-593-1304

Acadian Ballistic Specialties, P.O. Box 787, Folsom, LA 70437 / 504-796-0078 gunsmith@neasoft.com

Accuracy International, Foster, PO Box 111, Wilsall, MT 59086 / 406-587-7922; FAX: 406-585-9434

Accuracy Internationl Precision Rifles (See U.S.)

Accuracy Int'l. North America, Inc., PO Box 5267, Oak Ridge, TN 37831 / 423-482-0330; FAX: 423-482-0336

Accuracy Unlimited, 16036 N. 49 Ave., Glendale, AZ 85306 / 602-978-9089; FAX: 602-978-9089 fglenn@cox.net www.glenncustom.com

Accuracy Unlimited, 7479 S. DePew St., Littleton, CO 80123

Accura-Site (See All's, The Jim Tembelis Co., Inc.)

Accurate Arms Co., Inc., 5891 Hwy. 230 West, McEwen, TN 37101 / 931-729-4207; FAX: 931-729-4211 email@accuratecompanies.com www.accuratepowder.com

Accu-Tek, 4510 Carter Ct., Chino, CA 91710

Ace Custom 45's, Inc., 1880 1/2 Upper Turtle Creek Rd., Kerrville, TX 78028 / 830-257-4290; FAX: 830-257-5724 www.acecustom45.com

Ace Sportswear, Inc., 700 Quality Rd., Fayetteville, NC 28306 / 919-323-1223; FAX: 919-323-5392

Ackerman & Co., Box 133 US Highway Rt. 7, Pownal, VT 05261 / 802-823-9874 muskets@togsther.net

Ackerman, Bill (See Optical Services Co.)

Acra-Bond Laminates, 134 Zimmerman Rd., Kalispell, MT 59901 / 406-257-9003; FAX: 406-257-9003 merlins@digisys.net www.acrabondlaminates.com

Action Bullets & Alloy Inc., RR 1, P.O. Box 189, Quinter, KS 67752 / 785-754-3609; FAX: 785-754-3629 bullets@ruraltel.net

Action Direct, Inc., P.O. Box 770400, Miami, FL 33177 / 305-969-0056; FAX: 530-734-3760 www.action-direct.com

Action Products, Inc., 22 N. Mulberry St., Hagerstown, MD 21740 / 301-797-1414; FAX: 301-733-2073

Action Target, Inc., PO Box 636, Provo, UT 84603 / 801-377-8033; FAX: 801-377-8096

Actions by "T" Teddy Jacobson, 16315 Redwood Forest Ct., Sugar Land, TX 77478 / 281-277-4008; FAX: 281-277-9112 tjacobson@houston.rr.com www.actionsbyt.com

AcuSport Corporation, 1 Hunter Place, Bellefontaine, OH 43311-3001 / 513-593-7010; FAX: 513-592-5625

Ad Hominem, 3130 Gun Club Lane, RR #3, Orillia, ON L3V 6H3 CANADA / 705-689-5303; FAX: 705-689-5303

Adair Custom Shop, Bill, 2886 Westridge, Carrollton, TX 75006

ADCO Sales, Inc., 4 Draper St. #A, Woburn, MA 01801 / 781-935-1799; FAX: 781-935-1011

Adkins, Luther, 1292 E. McKay Rd., Shelbyville, IN 46176-8706 / 317-392-3795

Advance Car Mover Co., Rowell Div., P.O. Box 1, 240 N. Depot St., Juneau, WI 53039 / 414-386-4464; FAX: 414-386-4416

Adventure 16, Inc., 4620 Alvarado Canyon Rd., San Diego, CA 92120 / 619-283-6314

Adventure Game Calls, R.D. 1, Leonard Rd., Spencer, NY 14883 / 607-589-4611

Aero Peltor, 90 Mechanic St., Southbridge, MA 01550 / 508-764-5500; FAX: 508-764-0188

African Import Co., 22 Goodwin Rd, Plymouth, MA 02360 / 508-746-8552; FAX: 508-746-0404

AFSCO Ammunition, 731 W. Third St., P.O. Box L, Owen, WI 54460 / 715-229-2516

Ahlman Guns, 9525 W. 230th St., Morristown, MN 55052 / 507-685-4243; FAX: 507-685-4280 www.ahlmans.com

Ahrends, Kim (See Custom Firearms, Inc), Box 203, Clarion, IA 50525 / 515-532-3449; FAX: 515-532-3926

Aimtech Mount Systems, P.O. Box 223, Thomasville, GA 31799 / 229-226-4313; FAX: 229-227-0222 mail@aimtech-mounts.com www.aimtech-mounts.com

Air Arms, Hailsham Industrial Park, Diplocks Way, Hailsham, E. Sussex, BN27 3JF ENGLAND / 011-0323-845853

Air Rifle Specialists, P.O. Box 138, 130 Holden Rd., Pine City, NY 14871-0138 / 607-734-7340; FAX: 607-733-3261 ars@stny.rr.com www.air-rifles.com

Air Venture Airguns, 9752 E. Flower St., Bellflower, CA 90706 / 562-867-6355

AirForce Airguns, P.O. Box 2478, Fort Worth, TX 76113 / 817-451-8966; FAX: 817-451-1613 www.airforceairguns.com

Airrow, 11 Monitor Hill Rd., Newtown, CT 06470 / 203-270-6343

Aitor-Cuchilleria Del Norte S.A., Izelaieta, 17, 48260, Ermua, S SPAIN / 43-17-08-50 info@aitor.com www.ailor.com

Ajax Custom Grips, Inc., 9130 Viscount Row, Dallas, TX 75247 / 214-630-8893; FAX: 214-630-4942

Aker International, Inc., 2248 Main St., Suite 6, Chula Vista, CA 91911 / 619-423-5182; FAX: 619-423-1363 aker@akerleather.com www.akerleather.com

AKJ Concealco, P.O. Box 871596, Vancouver, WA 98687-1596 / 360-891-8222; FAX: 360-891-8221 Concealco@aol.com www.greatholsters.com

Al Lind Custom Guns, P.O. Box 97268, Tacoma, WA 98497 / 253-584-6361; FAX: 253-584-6361

Alana Cupp Custom Engraver, P.O. Box 207, Annabella, UT 84711 / 801-896-4834

Alaska Bullet Works, Inc., 9978 Crazy Horse Drive, Juneau, AK 99801 / 907-789-3834; FAX: 907-789-3433

Alaskan Silversmith, The, 2145 Wagner Hollow Rd., Fort Plain, NY 13339 / 518-993-3983 sidbell@capital.net www.sidbell.cizland.com

Aldis Gunsmithing & Shooting Supply, 502 S. Montezuma St., Prescott, AZ 86303 / 602-445-6723; FAX: 602-445-6763

Alessi Holsters, Inc., 2465 Niagara Falls Blvd., Amherst, NY 14228-3527 / 716-691-5615

Alex, Inc., 3420 Cameron Bridge Rd., Manhattan, MT 59741-8523 / 406-282-7396; FAX: 406-282-7396

Alfano, Sam, 36180 Henry Gaines Rd., Pearl River, LA 70452 / 504-863-3364; FAX: 504-863-7715

All American Lead Shot Corp., P.O. Box 224566, Dallas, TX 75062

All Rite Products, Inc., 9554 Wells Circle, Suite D, West Jordan, UT 84088-6226 / 800-771-8471; FAX: 801-280-8302 www.allriteproducts.com

Allard, Gary/Creek Side Metal & Woodcrafters, Fishers Hill, VA 22626 / 703-465-3903

Allen Co., Bob, 214 SW Jackson, P.O. Box 477, Des Moines, IA 50315 / 515-283-2191; or 800-685-7020; FAX: 515-283-0779

Allen Co., Inc., 525 Burbank St., Broomfield, CO 80020 / 303-469-1857; or 800-876-8600; FAX: 303-466-7437

Allen Firearm Engraving, P.O. Box 155, Camp Verde, AZ 86322 / 928-567-6711; FAX: 928-567-3901 rosebudmcko@aol.com

Allen Mfg., 6449 Hodgson Rd., Circle Pines, MN 55014 / 612-429-8231

Allen Sportswear, Bob (See Allen Co., Bob)

Alley Supply Co., PO Box 848, Gardnerville, NV 89410 / 775-782-3800; FAX: 775-782-3827 jetalley@aol.com www.alleysupplyco.com

Alliant Techsystems Smokeless Powder Group, P.O. Box 6, Rt. 114, Bldg. 229, Radford, VA 24141-0096 www.alliantpowder.com

Allred Bullet Co., 932 Evergreen Drive, Logan, UT 84321 / 435-752-6983; FAX: 435-752-6983

All's, The Jim J. Tembelis Co., Inc., 216 Loper Ct., Neenah, WI 54956 / 920-725-5251; FAX: 920-725-5251

Alpec Team, Inc., 201 Ricken Backer Cir., Livermore, CA 94550 / 510-606-8245; FAX: 510-606-4279

Alpha 1 Drop Zone, 2121 N. Tyler, Wichita, KS 67212 / 316-729-0800; FAX: 316-729-4262 www.alpha1dropzone.com

Alpha LaFranck Enterprises, P.O. Box 81072, Lincoln, NE 68501 / 402-466-3193

Alpha Precision, Inc., 3238 Della Slaton Rd., Comer, GA 30629-2212 / 706-783-2131 jim@alphaprecisioninc.com www.alphaprecisioninc.com

Alpine Indoor Shooting Range, 2401 Government Way, Coeur d'Alene, ID 83814 / 208-676-8824; FAX: 208-676-8824

Altamont Co., 901 N. Church St., P.O. Box 309, Thomasboro, IL 61878 / 217-643-3125; or 800-626-5774; FAX: 217-643-7973

Alumna Sport by Dee Zee, 1572 NE 58th Ave., P.O. Box 3090, Des Moines, IA 50316 / 800-798-9899

Amadeo Rossi S.A., Rua: Amadeo Rossi, 143, Sao Leopoldo, RS 93030-220 BRAZIL / 051-592-5566

AmBr Software Group Ltd., P.O. Box 301, Reistertown, MD 21136-0301 / 800-888-1917; FAX: 410-526-7212

American Ammunition, 3545 NW 71st St., Miami, FL 33147 / 305-835-7400; FAX: 305-694-0037

American Derringer Corp., 127 N. Lacy Dr., Waco, TX 76705 / 800-642-7817 or 254-799-9111; FAX: 254-799-7935

American Display Co., 55 Cromwell St., Providence, RI 02907 / 401-331-2464; FAX: 401-421-1264

American Frontier Firearms Mfg., Inc, PO Box 744, Aguanga, CA 92536 / 909-763-0014; FAX: 909-763-0014

American Gas & Chemical Co., Ltd, 220 Pegasus Ave, Northvale, NJ 07647 / 201-767-7300

American Gripcraft, 3230 S Dodge 2, Tucson, AZ 85713 / 602-790-1222

American Gunsmithing Institute, 1325 Imola Ave #504, Napa, CA 94559 / 707-253-0462; FAX: 707-253-7149

American Handgunner Magazine, 591 Camino de la Reina, Ste. 200, San Diego, CA 92108 / 619-297-5350; FAX: 619-297-5353

American Pioneer Video, PO Box 50049, Bowling Green, KY 42102-2649 / 800-743-4675

American Products, Inc., 14729 Spring Valley Road, Morrison, IL 61270 / 815-772-3336; FAX: 815-772-8046

American Safe Arms, Inc., 1240 Riverview Dr., Garland, UT 84312 / 801-257-7472; FAX: 801-785-8156

American Security Products Co., 11925 Pacific Ave., Fontana, CA 92337 / 909-685-9680; or 800-421-6142; FAX: 909-685-9685

American Small Arms Academy, P.O. Box 12111, Prescott, AZ 86304 / 602-778-5623

American Target, 1328 S. Jason St., Denver, CO 80223 / 303-733-0433; FAX: 303-777-0311

American Target Knives, 1030 Brownwood NW, Grand Rapids, MI 49504 / 616-453-1998

Americase, P.O. Box 271, 1610 E. Main, Waxahachie, TX 75165 / 800-880-3629; FAX: 214-937-8373

Ames Metal Products, 4323 S. Western Blvd., Chicago, IL 60609 / 773-523-3230 or 800-255-6937; FAX: 773-523-3854

Amherst Arms, P.O. Box 1457, Englewood, FL 34295 / 941-475-2020; FAX: 941-473-1212

Ammo Load, Inc., 1560 E. Edinger, Suite G, Santa Ana, CA 92705 / 714-558-8858; FAX: 714-569-0319

Amrine's Gun Shop, 937 La Luna, Ojai, CA 93023 / 805-646-2376

Amsec, 11925 Pacific Ave., Fontana, CA 92337

Analog Devices, Box 9106, Norwood, MA 02062

Andela Tool & Machine, Inc., RD3, Box 246, Richfield Springs, NY 13439

Anderson Manufacturing Co., Inc., 22602 53rd Ave. SE, Bothell, WA 98021 / 206-481-1858; FAX: 206-481-7839

Andres & Dworsky KG, Bergstrasse 18, A-3822 Karlstein, Thaya, AUSTRIA / 0 28 44-285; FAX: 02844 28619 andres.dnorsky@wvnet.as

Angelo & Little Custom Gun Stock Blanks, P.O. Box 240046, Dell, MT 59724-0046

Answer Products Co., 1519 Westbury Drive, Davison, MI 48423 / 810-653-2911

Antique American Firearms, P.O. Box 71035, Dept. GD, Des Moines, IA 50325 / 515-224-6552

Antique Arms Co., 1110 Cleveland Ave., Monett, MO 65708 / 417-235-6501

AO Sight Systems, 2401 Ludelle St., Fort Worth, TX 76105 / 888-744-4880 or 817-536-0136; FAX: 817-536-3517

Apel GmbH, Ernst, Am Kirschberg 3, D-97218, Gerbrunn, GERMANY / 0 (931) 707192 info@eaw.de www.eaw.de

Aplan Antiques & Art, James O., James O., HC 80, Box 793-25, Piedmont, SD 57769 / 605-347-5016

AR-7 Industries, LLC, 998 N. Colony Rd., Meriden, CT 06450 / 203-630-3536; FAX: 203-630-3637

Arizona Ammunition, Inc., 21421 No. 14th Ave., Suite E, Phoenix, AZ 85027 / 623-516-9004; FAX: 623-516-9012 www.azammo.com

ArmaLite, Inc., P.O. Box 299, Geneseo, IL 61254 / 800-336-0184 or 309-944-6939; FAX: 309-944-6949

Armament Gunsmithing Co., Inc., 525 Rt. 22, Hillside, NJ 07205 / 908-686-0960; FAX: 718-738-5019 armamentgunsmithing@worldnet.att.net

Armas Garbi, S.A., 12-14 20.600 Urki, 12, Eibar (Guipuzcoa), / 943203873; FAX: 943203873 armosgarbi@euskalnet.n

Armas Kemen S. A. (See U.S. Importers)

Armfield Custom Bullets, 10584 County Road 100, Carthage, MO 64836 / 417-359-8480; FAX: 417-359-8497

Armi Perazzi S.p.A., Via Fontanelle 1/3, 1-25080, Botticino Mattina, / 030-2692591; FAX: 030 2692594

Armi San Marco (See U.S. Importers-Taylor's & Co I

Armi San Paolo, 172-A, I-25062, via Europa, ITALY / 030-2751725

Armi Sport (See U.S. Importers-Cape Outfitters)

538 • GUN DIGEST

Armite Laboratories, 1560 Superior Ave., Costa Mesa, CA 92627 / 213-587-7768; FAX: 213-587-5075

Armoloy Co. of Ft. Worth, 204 E. Daggett St., Fort Worth, TX 76104 / 817-332-5604; FAX: 817-335-6517

Armor (See Buck Stop Lure Co., Inc.)

Armor Metal Products, P.O. Box 4609, Helena, MT 59604 / 406-442-5560; FAX: 406-442-5650

Armory Publications, 17171 Bothall Way NE, #276, Seattle, WA 98155 / 206-364-7653; FAX: 206-362-9413 armorypub@aol.com www.grocities.com/armorypub

Armoury, Inc., The, Rt. 202, Box 2340, New Preston, CT 06777 / 860-868-0001; FAX: 860-868-2919

Arms & Armour Press, Wellington House, 125 Strand, London, WC2R 0BB ENGLAND / 0171-420-5555; FAX: 0171-240-7265

Arms Corporation of the Philippines, Bo. Parang Marikina, Metro Manila, PHILIPPINES / 632-941-6243 or 632-941-6244; FAX: 632-942-0682

Arms Craft Gunsmithing, 1106 Linda Dr., Arroyo Grande, CA 93420 / 805-481-2830

Arms Ingenuity Co., P.O. Box 1, 51 Canal St., Weatogue, CT 06089 / 203-658-5624

Arms Software, 4851 SW Madrona St., Lake Oswego, OR 97035 / 800-366-5559 or 503-697-0533; FAX: 503-697-3337

Arms, Programming Solutions (See Arms Software)

Armscorp USA, Inc., 4424 John Ave., Baltimore, MD 21227 / 410-247-6200; FAX: 410-247-6205 info@armscorpusa.com www.armscorpusa.com

Arratoonian, Andy (See Horseshoe Leather Products)

Arrieta S.L., Morkaiko 5, 20870, Elgoibar, SPAIN / 34-43-743150; FAX: 34-43-743154

Art Jewel Enterprises Ltd., Eagle Business Ctr., 460 Randy Rd., Carol Stream, IL 60188 / 708-260-0400

Artistry in Wood, 134 Zimmerman Rd., Kalispell, MT 59901 / 406-257-9003; FAX: 406-257-9167 merlins@digisys.net www.acrabondlaminates.com

Art's Gun & Sport Shop, Inc., 6008 Hwy. Y, Hillsboro, MO 63050

Arundel Arms & Ammunition, Inc., A., 24A Defense St., Annapolis, MD 21401 / 410-224-8683

Arvo Ojala Holsters, P.O. Box 98, N. Hollywood, CA 91603 / 818-222-9700; FAX: 818-222-0401

Ashby, David. See: ASHBY TURKEY CALLS

Ashby Turkey Calls, David L. Ashby, P.O. Box 1653, Ozark, MO 65721-1653

Ashley Outdoors, Inc., 2401 Ludelle St., Fort Worth, TX 76105 / 888-744-4880; FAX: 800-734-7939

Aspen Outfitting Co., Jon Hollinger, 9 Dean St., Aspen, CO 81611 / 970-925-3406

A-Square Co., 205 Fairfield Ave., Jeffersonville, IN 47130 / 812-283-0577; FAX: 812-283-0375

Astra Sport, S.A., Apartado 3, 48300 Guernica, Espagne, SPAIN / 34-4-6250100; FAX: 34-4-6255186

Atamec-Bretton, 19 rue Victor Grignard, F-42026, St.-Etienne (Cedex 1, / 77-93-54-69; FAX: 33-77-93-57-98

Atlanta Cutlery Corp., 2143 Gees Mill Rd., Box 839 CIS, Conyers, GA 30207 / 800-883-0300; FAX: 404-388-0246

Atlantic Mills, Inc., 1295 Towbin Ave., Lakewood, NJ 08701-5934 / 800-242-7374

Atlantic Rose, Inc., P.O. Box 10717, Bradenton, FL 34282-0717

Atsko/Sno-Seal, Inc., 2664 Russell St., Orangeburg, SC 29115 / 803-531-1820; FAX: 803-531-2139 info@atsko.com www.atsko.com

Auguste Francotte & Cie S.A., rue du Trois Juin 109, 4400 Herstal-Liege, BELGIUM / 32-4-248-13-18; FAX: 32-4-948-11-79

Austin & Halleck, Inc., 2150 South 950 East, Provo, UT 84606-6285 / 877-543-3256; or 801-374-9990; FAX: 801-374-9998 www.austinhallek.com

Austin Sheridan USA, Inc., P.O. Box 577, 36 Haddam Quarter Rd., Durham, CT 06422 / 860-349-1772; FAX: 860-349-1771 swalzer@palm.net

Autauga Arms, Inc., Pratt Plaza Mall No. 13, Prattville, AL 36067 / 800-262-9563; FAX: 334-361-2961

Auto Arms, 738 Clearview, San Antonio, TX 78228 / 512-545-4450

Auto-Ordnance Corp., PO Box 220, Blauvelt, NY 10913 / 914-353-7770

Autumn Sales, Inc. (Blaser), 1320 Lake St., Fort Worth, TX 76102 / 817-335-1634; FAX: 817-338-0119

Avnda Otaola Norica, 16 Apartado 68, 20600, Eibar, SPAIN

AWC Systems Technology, P.O. Box 41938, Phoenix, AZ 85080-1938 / 602-780-1050; FAX: 602-780-2967

Axtell Rifle Co., 353 Mill Creek Road, Sheridan, MT 59749 / 406-842-5814

AYA (See U.S. Importer-New England Custom Gun Serv

B

B&D Trading Co., Inc., 3935 Fair Hill Rd., Fair Oaks, CA 95628 / 800-334-3790 or 916-967-9366; FAX: 916-967-4873

B&P America, 12321 Brittany Cir., Dallas, TX 75230 / 972-726-9069

B.A.C., 17101 Los Modelos St., Fountain Valley, CA 92708 / 435-586-3286

B.B. Walker Co., PO Box 1167, 414 E Dixie Dr, Asheboro, NC 27204 / 910-625-1380; FAX: 910-625-8125

B.C. Outdoors, Larry McGhee, PO Box 61497, Boulder City, NV 89006 / 702-294-3056; FAX: 702-294-0413 jdalton@pmcammo.com www.pmcammo.com

B.M.F. Activator, Inc., 12145 Mill Creek Run, Plantersville, TX 77363 / 936-894-2397; FAX: 936-894-2397

Badger Creek Studio, 1629 Via Monserate, Fallbrook, CA 92028 / 760-723-9279; or 619-728-2663

Badger Shooters Supply, Inc., P.O. Box 397, Owen, WI 54460 / 800-424-9069; FAX: 715-229-2332

Baekgaard Ltd., 1855 Janke Dr., Northbrook, IL 60062 / 708-498-3040; FAX: 708-493-3106

Baelder, Harry, Alte Goennebeker Strasse 5, 24635, Rickling, GERMANY / 04328-722732; FAX: 04328-722733

Baer Custom Inc., Les, 29601 34th Ave., Hillsdale, IL 61257 / 309-658-2716; FAX: 309-658-2610

Baer's Hollows, P.O. Box 284, Eads, CO 81036 / 719-438-5718

Bagmaster Mfg., Inc., 2731 Sutton Ave., St. Louis, MO 63143 / 314-781-8002; FAX: 314-781-3363

Bain & Davis, Inc., 307 E. Valley Blvd., San Gabriel, CA 91776-3522 / 626-573-4241 baindavis@aol.com

Baker, Stan. See: STAN BAKER SPORTS

Baker's Leather Goods, Roy, PO Box 893, Magnolia, AR 71754 / 870-234-0344 pholsters@ipa.net

Bald Eagle Precision Machine Co., 101-A Allison St., Lock Haven, PA 17745 / 570-748-6772; FAX: 570-748-4443

Balickie, Joe, 408 Trelawney Lane, Apex, NC 27502 / 919-362-5185

Ballard, Donald. See: BALLARD INDUSTRIES

Ballard Industries, Donald Ballard Sr., PO Box 2035, Arnold, CA 95223 / 408-996-0957; FAX: 408-257-6828

Ballard Rifle & Cartridge Co., LLC, 113 W. Yellowstone Ave., Cody, WY 82414 / 307-587-4914; FAX: 307-527-6097 ballard@wyoming.com www.ballardrifles.com

Ballistic Product, Inc., 20015 75th Ave. North, Corcoran, MN 55340-9456 / 763-494-9237; FAX: 763-494-9236 info@ballisticproducts.com www.ballisticproducts.com

Ballistic Research, 1108 W. May Ave., McHenry, IL 60050 / 815-385-0037

Ballisti-Cast, Inc., P.O. Box 1057, Minot, ND 58702-1057 / 701-497-3333; FAX: 701-497-3335

Bandcor Industries, Div. of Man-Sew Corp., 6108 Sherwin Dr., Port Richey, FL 34668 / 813-848-0432

Bang-Bang Boutique (See Holster Shop, The)

Banks, Ed, 2011 Alabama Ave., Savannah, GA 31404-2721 / 912-987-4665

Bansner's Ultimate Rifles, LLC, P.O. Box 839, 261 E. Main St., Adamstown, PA 19501 / 717-484-2370; FAX: 717-484-0523 bansner@aol.com www.bansnersrifle.com

Barbour, Inc., 55 Meadowbrook Dr., Milford, NH 03055 / 603-673-1313; FAX: 603-673-6510

Barnes, 4347 Tweed Dr., Eau Claire, WI 54703-6302

Barnes Bullets, Inc., P.O. Box 215, American Fork, UT 84003 / 801-756-4222 or 800-574-9200; FAX: 801-756-2465 email@barnesbullets.com www.barnesbullets.com

Baron Technology, 62 Spring Hill Rd., Trumbull, CT 06611 / 203-452-0515; FAX: 203-452-0663 dbaron@baronengraving.com www.baronengraving.com

Barraclough, John K., 55 Merit Park Dr., Gardena, CA 90247 / 310-324-2574

Barramundi Corp., P.O. Drawer 4259, Homosassa Springs, FL 32687 / 904-628-0200

Barrett Firearms Manufacturer, Inc., P.O. Box 1077, Murfreesboro, TN 37133 / 615-896-2938; FAX: 615-896-7313

Bar-Sto Precision Machine, 73377 Sullivan Rd., PO Box 1838, Twentynine Palms, CA 92277 / 760-367-2747; FAX: 760-367-2407 barsto@eee.org www.barsto.com

Barta's Gunsmithing, 10231 US Hwy. 10, Cato, WI 54230 / 920-732-4472

Barteaux Machete, 1916 SE 50th Ave., Portland, OR 97215-3238 / 503-233-5880

Bartlett Engineering, 40 South 200 East, Smithfield, UT 84335-1645 / 801-563-5910

Bates Engraving, Billy, 2302 Winthrop Dr. SW, Decatur, AL 35603 / 256-355-3690 bbrn@aol.com

Battenfeld Technologies, 5875 W. Van Horn Tavern Rd., Columbia, MO 65203 / 573-445-9200; FAX: 573-447-4158 battenfeldtechnologies.com

Bauer, Eddie, 15010 NE 36th St., Redmond, WA 98052

Baumgartner Bullets, 3011 S. Alane St., W. Valley City, UT 84120

Bauska Barrels, 105 9th Ave. W., Kalispell, MT 59901 / 406-752-7706

Bear Archery, RR 4, 4600 Southwest 41st Blvd., Gainesville, FL 32601 / 904-376-2327

Bear Arms, 374-A Carson Road, St. Mathews, SC 29135

Bear Mountain Gun & Tool, 120 N. Plymouth, New Plymouth, ID 83655 / 208-278-5221; FAX: 208-278-5221

Beartooth Bullets, PO Box 491, Dept. HLD, Dover, ID 83825-0491 / 208-448-1865 bullets@beartoothbullets.com www.beartoothbullets.com

Beaver Lodge (See Fellowes, Ted)

Beaver Park Product, Inc., 840 J St., Penrose, CO 81240 / 719-372-6744

BEC, Inc., 1227 W. Valley Blvd., Suite 204, Alhambra, CA 91803 / 626-281-5751; FAX: 626-293-7073

Beeks, Mike. See: GRAYBACK WILDCATS

Beeman Precision Airguns, 5454 Argosy Dr., Huntington Beach, CA 92649 / 714-890-4800; FAX: 714-890-4808

Behlert Precision, Inc., P.O. Box 288, 7067 Easton Rd., Pipersville, PA 18947 / 215-766-8681 or 215-766-7301; FAX: 215-766-8681

Beitzinger, George, 116-20 Atlantic Ave., Richmond Hill, NY 11419 / 718-847-7661

Belding's Custom Gun Shop, 10691 Sayers Rd., Munith, MI 49259 / 517-596-2388

Bell & Carlson, Inc., Dodge City Industrial Park, 101 Allen Rd., Dodge City, KS 67801 / 800-634-8586 or 620-225-6688; FAX: 620-225-6688 email@belandcarlson.com www.belandcarlson.com

Bell Reloading, Inc., 1725 Harlin Lane Rd., Villa Rica, GA 30180

Bell's Gun & Sport Shop, 3309-19 Mannheim Rd, Franklin Park, IL 60131

Bell's Legendary Country Wear, 22 Circle Dr., Bellmore, NY 11710 / 516-679-1158

Belltown Ltd., 11 Camps Rd., Kent, CT 06757 / 860-354-5750; FAX: 860-354-6764

Ben William's Gun Shop, 1151 S. Cedar Ridge, Duncanville, TX 75137 / 214-780-1807

Benchmark Knives (See Gerber Legendary Blades)

Benelli Armi S.p.A., Via della Stazione, 61029, Urbino, ITALY / 39-722-307-1; FAX: 39-722-327427

Benelli USA Corp, 17603 Indian Head Hwy, Accokeek, MD 20607 / 301-283-6981; FAX: 301-283-6988 benelliusa.com

Bengtson Arms Co., L., 6345-B E. Akron St., Mesa, AZ 85205 / 602-981-6375

Benjamin/Sheridan Co., Crosman, Rts. 5 and 20, E. Bloomfield, NY 14443 / 716-657-6161; FAX: 716-657-5405 www.crosman.com

Ben's Machines, 1151 S. Cedar Ridge, Duncanville, TX 75137 / 214-780-1807; FAX: 214-780-0316

Bentley, John, 128-D Watson Dr., Turtle Creek, PA 15145

Beomat of America, Inc., 300 Railway Ave., Campbell, CA 95008 / 408-379-4829

Beretta S.p.A., Pietro, Via Beretta, 18, 25063, Gardone Vae Trompia, ITALY / 39-30-8341-1 info@benetta.com www.benetta.com

Beretta U.S.A. Corp., 17601 Beretta Drive, Accokeek, MD 20607 / 301-283-2191; FAX: 301-283-0435

Berger Bullets Ltd., 5443 W. Westwind Dr., Glendale, AZ 85310 / 602-842-4001; FAX: 602-934-9083

Bernardelli, Vincenzo, P.O. Box 460243, Houston, TX 77056-8243 www.bernardelli.com

Bernardelli S.p.A., Vincenzo, 125 Via Matteotti, PO Box 74, Brescia, ITALY / 39-30-8912851-2-3; FAX: 39-30-8910249

Berry's Mfg., Inc., 401 North 3050 East St., St. George, UT 84770 / 435-634-1682; FAX: 435-634-1683 sales@berrysmfg.com www.berrysmfg.com

Bersa S.A., Benso Bonadimani, Magallanes 775 B1704 FLC, Ramos Mejia, ARGENTINA / 011-4656-2377; FAX: 011-4656-2093+ info@bersa-sa.com.dr www.bersa-sa.com.ar

Bert Johanssons Vapentillbehor, S-430 20 Veddige, SWEDEN, Bertuzzi (See U.S. Importer-New England Arms Co)

Better Concepts Co., 663 New Castle Rd., Butler, PA 16001 / 412-285-9000

Beverly, Mary, 3201 Horseshoe Trail, Tallahassee, FL 32312

Bianchi International, Inc., 100 Calle Cortez, Temecula, CA 92590 / 909-676-5621; FAX: 909-676-6777

Big Bear Arms & Sporting Goods, Inc., 1112 Milam Way, Carrollton, TX 75006 / 972-416-8051 or 800-400-BEAR; FAX: 972-416-0771

Big Bore Bullets of Alaska, PO Box 521455, Big Lake, AK 99652 / 907-373-2673; FAX: 907-373-2673 doug@mtaonline.net ww.awloo.com/bbb/index.

Big Bore Express, 16345 Midway Rd., Nampa, ID 83651 / 208-466-9975; FAX: 208-466-6927 bigbore.com

Big Spring Enterprises "Bore Stores", P.O. Box 1115, Big Spring Rd., Yellville, AR 72687 / 870-449-5297; FAX: 870-449-4446

Bilal, Mustafa. See: TURK'S HEAD PRODUCTIONS

Bilinski, Bryan. See: FIELDSPORT LTD.

Bill Adair Custom Shop, 2886 Westridge, Carrollton, TX 75006 / 972-418-0950

Bill Austin's Calls, Box 284, Kaycee, WY 82639 / 307-738-2552

Bill Hanus Birdguns, P.O. Box 533, Newport, OR 97365 / 541-265-7433; FAX: 541-265-7400 www.billhanusbirdguns.com

Bill Russ Trading Post, William A. Russ, 23 William St., Addison, NY 14801-1326 / 607-359-3896

Bill Wiseman and Co., P.O. Box 3427, Bryan, TX 77805 / 409-690-3456; FAX: 409-690-0156

Billeb, Stephn. See: QUALITY CUSTOM FIREARMS

Billings Gunsmiths, 1841 Grand Ave., Billings, MT 59102 / 406-256-8390; FAX: 406-256-6530 blgsgunsmiths@msn.com www.billingsgunsmiths.net

Billingsley & Brownell, P.O. Box 25, Dayton, WY 82836 / 307-655-9344

Bill's Custom Cases, P.O. Box 2, Dunsmuir, CA 96025 / 530-235-0177; FAX: 530-235-4959 billscustomcases@mindspring.com

Bill's Gun Repair, 1007 Burlington St., Mendota, IL 61342 / 815-539-5786

Billy Bates Engraving, 2302 Winthrop Dr. SW, Decatur, AL 35603 / 256-355-3690 bbrn@aol.com

Birchwood Casey, 7900 Fuller Rd., Eden Prairie, MN 55344 / 800-328-6156 or 612-937-7933; FAX: 612-937-7979

Birdsong & Assoc., W. E., 1435 Monterey Rd, Florence, MS 39073-9748 / 601-366-8270

Bismuth Cartridge Co., 3500 Maple Ave., Suite 1650, Dallas, TX 75219 / 214-521-5880; FAX: 214-521-9035

Bison Studios, 1409 South Commerce St., Las Vegas, NV 89102 / 702-388-2891; FAX: 702-383-9967

Bitterroot Bullet Co., P.O. Box 412, 2001 Cedar Ave., Lewiston, ID 83501-0412 / 208-743-5635; FAX: 208-743-5635 brootbil@lewiston.com

BKL Technologies, PO Box 5237, Brownsville, TX 78523

Black Belt Bullets (See Big Bore Express)

Black Hills Ammunition, Inc., P.O. Box 3090, Rapid City, SD 57709-3090 / 605-348-5150; FAX: 605-348-9827

Black Hills Shooters Supply, P.O. Box 4220, Rapid City, SD 57709 / 800-289-2506

Black Powder Products, 67 Township Rd. 1411, Chesapeake, OH 45619 / 614-867-8047

Black Sheep Brand, 3220 W. Gentry Parkway, Tyler, TX 75702 / 903-592-3853; FAX: 903-592-0527

Blacksmith Corp., P.O. Box 280, North Hampton, OH 45349 / 800-531-2665; FAX: 937-969-8399 sales@blacksmith.com www.blacksmithcorp.com

BlackStar AccuMax Barrels, 11501 Brittmoore Park Drive, Houston, TX 77041 / 281-721-6040; FAX: 281-721-6041

BlackStar Barrel Accurizing (See BlackStar AccuMax)

Blacktail Mountain Books, 42 First Ave. W., Kalispell, MT 59901 / 406-257-5573

Blammo Ammo, P.O. Box 1677, Seneca, SC 29679 / 803-882-1768

Blaser Jagdwaffen GmbH, D-88316, Isny Im Allgau, GERMANY

Blount, Inc., Sporting Equipment Div., 2299 Snake River Ave., P.O. Box 856, Lewiston, ID 83501 / 800-627-3640 or 208-746-2351; FAX: 208-799-3904

Blount/Outers ATK, P..O Box 39, Onalaska, WI 54650 / 608-781-5800; FAX: 608-781-0368

Blue and Gray Products Inc. (See Ox-Yoke Originals)

Blue Book Publications, Inc., 8009 34th Ave. S., Ste. 175, Minneapolis, MN 55425 / 800-877-4867 or 612-854-5229; FAX: 612-853-1486 bluebook@bluebookinc.com www.bluebookinc.com

Blue Mountain Bullets, 64146 Quail Ln., Box 231, John Day, OR 97845 / 541-820-4594; FAX: 541-820-4594

Blue Ridge Machinery & Tools, Inc., P.O. Box 536-GD, Hurricane, WV 25526 / 800-872-6500; FAX: 304-562-5311 blueridgemachine@worldnet.att.net www.blueridgemachinery.com

BMC Supply, Inc., 26051 - 179th Ave. S.E., Kent, WA 98042

Bob Allen Co.214 SW Jackson, P.O. Box 477, Des Moines, IA 50315 / 800-685-7020; FAX: 515-283-0779

Bob Rogers Gunsmithing, P.O. Box 305, 344 S. Walnut St., Franklin Grove, IL 61031 / 815-456-2685; FAX: 815-456-2777

Bob's Gun Shop, P.O. Box 200, Royal, AR 71968 / 501-767-1970; FAX: 501-767-1970 gunparts@hsnp.com www.gun-parts.com

Bob's Tactical Indoor Shooting Range & Gun Shop, 90 Lafayette Rd., Salisbury, MA 01952 / 508-465-5561

Boessler, Erich, Am Vogeltal 3, 97702, Munnerstadt, GERMANY

Boker USA, Inc., 1550 Balsam Street, Lakewood, CO 80215 / 303-462-0662; FAX: 303-462-0668 sales@bokerusa.com bokerusa.com

Boltin, John M., P.O. Box 644, Estill, SC 29918 / 803-625-2185

Bo-Mar Tool & Mfg. Co., 6136 State Hwy. 300, Longview, TX 75604 / 903-759-4784; FAX: 903-759-9141 marykor@earthlink.net bo-mar.com

Bonadimani, Benso. See: BERSA S.A.

Bonanza (See Forster Products), 310 E. Lanark Ave., Lanark, IL 61046 / 815-493-6360; FAX: 815-493-2371

Bond Arms, Inc., P.O. Box 1296, Granbury, TX 76048 / 817-573-4445; FAX: 817-573-5636

Bond Custom Firearms, 8954 N. Lewis Ln., Bloomington, IN 47408 / 812-332-4519

Bondini Paolo, Via Sorrento 345, San Carlo di Cesena, ITALY / 0547-663-240; FAX: 0547-663-780

Boone Trading Co., Inc., PO Box 669, Brinnon, WA 98320 / 800-423-1945; or 360-796-4330; FAX: 360-796-4511 sales@boonetrading.com boonetrading.com

Boone's Custom Ivory Grips, Inc., 562 Coyote Rd., Brinnon, WA 98320 / 206-796-4330

Boonie Packer Products, P.O. Box 12517, Salem, OR 97309-0517 / 800-477-3244; or 503-581-3244; FAX: 503-581-3191 booniepacker@aol.com www.booniepacker.com

Borden Ridges Rimrock Stocks, RR 1 Box 250 BC, Springville, PA 18844 / 570-965-2505; FAX: 570-965-2328

Borden Rifles Inc., RD 1, Box 250BC, Springville, PA 18844 / 717-965-2505; FAX: 717-965-2328

Border Barrels Ltd., Riccarton Farm, Newcastleton, SCOTLAND UK

Borovnik KG, Ludwig, 9170 Ferlach, Bahnhofstrasse 7, AUSTRIA / 042 27 24 42; FAX: 042 26 43 49

Bosis (See U.S. Importer-New England Arms Co.)

Boss Manufacturing Co., 221 W. First St., Kewanee, IL 61443 / 309-852-2131; or 800-447-4581; FAX: 309-852-0848

Bostick Wildlife Calls, Inc., P.O. Box 728, Estill, SC 29918 / 803-625-2210; or 803-625-4512

Bowen Classic Arms Corp., PO Box 67, Louisville, TN 37777 / 865-984-3583 www.bowenclassicarms.com

Bowen Knife Co., Inc., P.O. Box 590, Blackshear, GA 31516 / 912-449-4794

Bowerly, Kent, 710 Golden Pheasant Dr., Redmond, OR 97756 / 541-923-3501 jkbowerly@aol.com

Boyds' Gunstock Industries, Inc., 25376 403 Rd. Ave., Mitchell, SD 57301 / 605-996-5011; FAX: 605-996-9878

Brace, Larry D., 771 Blackfoot Ave., Eugene, OR 97404 / 541-688-1278; FAX: 541-607-5833

Brass Eagle, Inc., 7050A Bramalea Rd., Unit 19, Mississauga,, ON L4Z 1C7 CANADA / 416-848-4844

Brauer Bros., 1520 Washington Avenue., St. Louis, MO 63103 / 314-231-2864; FAX: 314-249-4952 www.brauerbros.com

Break-Free, Inc., 1035 S. Linwood Ave., Santa Ana, CA 92705 / 714-953-1900; FAX: 714-953-0402

Brennke GmbH, P.O. Box 1646, 30837 Langenhagen, Langenhagen, GERMANY / +49-511-97262-0; FAX: +49-511-97262-62 info@brenneke.de brenneke.com

Bridgeman Products, Harry Jaffin, 153 B Cross Slope Court, Englishtown, NJ 07726 / 732-536-3604; FAX: 732-972-1004

Bridgers Best, P.O. Box 1410, Berthoud, CO 80513

Briese Bullet Co., Inc., RR1, Box 108, Tappen, ND 58487 / 701-327-4578; FAX: 701-327-4579

Brigade Quartermasters, 1025 Cobb International Blvd., Dept. VH, Kennesaw, GA 30144-4300 / 404-428-1248; or 800-241-3125; FAX: 404-426-7726

Briganti, A.J., 512 Rt. 32, Highland Mills, NY 10930 / 914-928-9573

Briley Mfg. Inc., 1230 Lumpkin, Houston, TX 77043 / 800-331-5718; or 713-932-6995; FAX: 713-932-1043

Brill, R. See: ROYAL ARMS INTERNATIONAL

British Sporting Arms, RR1, Box 130, Millbrook, NY 12545 / 914-677-8303

Broad Creek Rifle Works, Ltd., 120 Horsey Ave., Laurel, DE 19956 / 302-875-5446; FAX: 302-875-1448 bcrw4guns@aol.com

Brockman's Custom Gunsmithing, P.O. Box 357, Gooding, ID 83330 / 208-934-5050

Brocock Ltd., 43 River Street, Digbeth, Birmingham, B5 5SA ENGLAND / 011-021-773-1200; FAX: 011-021-773-1211 sales@brocock.co.un www.brocock.co.uk

Broken Gun Ranch, 10739 126 Rd., Spearville, KS 67876 / 316-385-2587; FAX: 316-385-2597

Brooker, Dennis, Rt. 1, Box 12A, Derby, IA 50068 / 515-533-2103

Brooks Tactical Systems-Agrip, 279-C Shorewood Ct., Fox Island, WA 98333 / 253-549-2866 FAX: 253-549-2703 brooks@brookstactical.com www.brookstactical.com

Brown, H. R. (See Silhouette Leathers)

Brown Co., E. Arthur, 3404 Pawnee Dr., Alexandria, MN 56308 / 320-762-8847

Brown Dog Ent., 2200 Calle Camelia, 1000 Oaks, CA 91360 / 805-497-2318; FAX: 805-497-1618

Brown Precision, Inc., 7786 Molinos Ave., Los Molinos, CA 96055 / 530-384-2506; FAX: 916-384-1638 www.brownprecision.com

Brown Products, Inc., Ed, 43825 Muldrow Trail, Perry, MO 63462 / 573-565-3261; FAX: 573-565-2791 www.edbrown.com

Brownells, Inc., 200 S. Front St., Montezuma, IA 50171 / 641-623-5401; FAX: 641-623-3896 orderdesk@brownells.com www.brownells.com

Browning Arms Co., One Browning Place, Morgan, UT 84050 / 801-876-2711; FAX: 801-876-3331

Browning Arms Co. (Parts & Service), 3005 Arnold Tenbrook Rd., Arnold, MO 63010 / 617-287-6800; FAX: 617-287-9751

BRP, Inc. High Performance Cast Bullets, 1210 Alexander Rd., Colorado Springs, CO 80909 / 719-633-0658

Brunton U.S.A., 620 E. Monroe Ave., Riverton, WY 82501 / 307-856-6559; FAX: 307-856-1840

Bryan & Assoc., R D Sauls, PO Box 5772, Anderson, SC 29623-5772 / 864-261-6810 bryanandac@aol.com www.huntersweb.com/bryanandac

Brynin, Milton, P.O. Box 383, Yonkers, NY 10710 / 914-779-4333

BSA Guns Ltd., Armoury Rd. Small Heath, Birmingham B11 2PP, ENGLAND / 011-021-772-8543; FAX: 011-021-773-0845 sales@bsagun.com www.bsagun.com

BSA Optics, 3911 SW 47th Ave., Ste. 914, Ft. Lauderdale, FL 33314 / 954-581-2144; FAX: 954-581-3165 4info@basaoptics.com www.bsaoptics.com

B-Square Company, Inc., ;, P.O. Box 11281, 2708 St. Louis Ave., Ft. Worth, TX 76110 / 817-923-0964 or 800-433-2909; FAX: 817-926-7012

Buchsenmachermeister, Peter Hofer Jagdwaffen, Buchsenmachermeister, Kirchgasse 24 A-9170, Ferlach, AUSTRIA / 43 4227 3683; FAX: 43 4227 368330 peterhofer@hoferwaffen.com www.hoferwaffen.com

Buck Knives, Inc., 1900 Weld Blvd., P.O. Box 1267, El Cajon, CA 92020 / 619-449-1100; or 800-326-2825; FAX: 619-562-5774 8

Buck Stix-SOS Products Co., Box 3, Neenah, WI 54956

Buck Stop Lure Co., Inc., 3600 Grow Rd. NW, P.O. Box 636, Stanton, MI 48888 / 517-762-5091; FAX: 517-762-5124

Buckeye Custom Bullets, 6490 Stewart Rd., Elida, OH 45807 / 419-641-4463

Buckhorn Gun Works, 8109 Woodland Dr., Black Hawk, SD 57718 / 605-787-6472

Buckskin Bullet Co., P.O. Box 1893, Cedar City, UT 84721 / 435-586-3286

Budin, Dave, Main St., Margaretville, NY 12455 / 914-568-4103; FAX: 914-586-4105

Budin, Dave. See: DEL-SPORTS, INC.

Buenger Enterprises/Goldenrod Dehumidifier, 3600 S. Harbor Blvd., Oxnard, CA 93035 / 800-451-6797; or 805-985-5828; FAX: 805-985-1534

Buffalo Arms Co., 660 Vermeer Ct., Ponderay, ID 83852 / 208-263-6953; FAX: 208-265-2096 www.buffaloarms.com

Buffalo Bullet Co., Inc., 12637 Los Nietos Rd., Unit A, Santa Fe Springs, CA 90670 / 800-423-8069; FAX: 562-944-5054

Buffalo Gun Center, 3385 Harlem Rd., Buffalo, NY 14225 / 716-833-2581; FAX: 716-833-2265 www.buffaloguncenter.com

Buffalo Rock Shooters Supply, R.R. 1, Ottawa, IL 61350 / 815-433-2471

Buffer Technologies, P.O. Box 104930, Jefferson City, MO 65110 / 573-634-8529; FAX: 573-634-8522

Bull Mountain Rifle Co., 6327 Golden West Terrace, Billings, MT 59106 / 406-656-0778

Bullberry Barrel Works, Ltd., 2430 W. Bullberry Ln., Hurricane, UT 84737 / 435-635-9866; FAX: 435-635-0348 fred@bullberry.com www.bullberry.com

Bullet Metals, Bill Ferguson, P.O. Box 1238, Sierra Vista, AZ 85636 / 520-458-5321; FAX: 520-458-1421 info@theantimonyman.com www.bullet-metals.com

Bullet N Press, 1210 Jones St., Gastonia, NC 28052 / 704-853-0265 bnpress@quik.com www.nemaine.com/bnpress

Bullet Swaging Supply, Inc., P.O. Box 1056, 303 McMillan Rd., West Monroe, LA 71291 / 318-387-3266; FAX: 318-387-7779 leblackmon@colla.com

Bullseye Bullets, 1808 Turkey Creek Rd. #9, Plant City, FL 33567 / 800-741-6343 bbullets8100@aol.com

Bull-X, Inc., 411 E. Water St., Farmer City, IL 61842-1556 / 309-928-2574 or 800-248-3845; FAX: 309-928-2130

Burkhart Gunsmithing, Don, P.O. Box 852, Rawlins, WY 82301 / 307-324-6007

Burnham Bros., P.O. Box 1148, Menard, TX 78659 / 915-396-4572; FAX: 915-396-4574

Burris Co., Inc., PO Box 1747, 331 E. 8th St., Greeley, CO 80631 / 970-356-1670; FAX: 970-356-8702

Bushmaster Firearms, 999 Roosevelt Trail, Windham, ME 04062 / 800-998-7928; FAX: 207-892-8068 info@bushmaster.com www.bushmaster.com

Bushmaster Hunting & Fishing, 451 Alliance Ave., Toronto, ON M6N 2J1 CANADA / 416-763-4040; FAX: 416-763-0623

Bushnell Sports Optics Worldwide, 9200 Cody, Overland Park, KS 66214 / 913-752-3400 or 800-423-3537; FAX: 913-752-3550

Buster's Custom Knives, P.O. Box 214, Richfield, UT 84701 / 801-896-5319

Butler Creek Corp., 2100 S. Silverstone Way, Meridian, ID 83642-8151 / 800-423-8327 or 406-388-1356; FAX: 406-388-7204

Butler Enterprises, 834 Oberting Rd., Lawrenceburg, IN 47025 / 812-537-3584

Butterfield's, 220 San Bruno Ave., San Francisco, CA 94103 / 415-861-7500; FAX: 415-861-0183 arms@butterfields.com www.butterfields.com

Buzz Fletcher Custom Stockmaker, 117 Silver Road, P.O. Box 189, Taos, NM 87571 / 505-758-3486

C

C&D Special Products (See Claybuster Wads & Harvester Bullets)

C&H Research, 115 Sunnyside Dr., Box 351, Lewis, KS 67552 / 316-324-5445888-324-5445; FAX: 620-324-5984 info@mercuryrecoil.com www.mercuryrecoil.com

C. Palmer Manufacturing Co., Inc., P.O. Box 220, West Newton, PA 15089 / 412-872-8200; FAX: 412-872-8302

C. Sharps Arms Co. Inc./Montana Armory, 100 Centennial Dr., PO Box 885, Big Timber, MT 59011 / 406-932-4353; FAX: 406-932-4443

C.S. Van Gorden & Son, Inc., 1815 Main St., Bloomer, WI 54724 / 715-568-2612 vangorden@bloomer.net

C.W. Erickson's L.L.C., 530 Garrison Ave. NE, PO Box 522, Buffalo, MN 55313 / 763-682-3665; FAX: 763-682-4328 www.archerhunter.com

Cabanas (See U.S. Importer-Mandall Shooting Supply

Cabela's, One Cabela Drive, Sidney, NE 69160 / 308-254-5505; FAX: 308-254-8420

Cabinet Mtn. Outfitters Scents & Lures, P.O. Box 766, Plains, MT 59859 / 406-826-3970

Cache La Poudre Rifleworks, 140 N. College, Ft. Collins, CO 80524 / 920-482-6913

Cali'co Hardwoods, Inc., 3580 Westwind Blvd., Santa Rosa, CA 95403 / 707-546-4045; FAX: 707-546-4027 calicohardwoods@msn.com

Calico Light Weapon Systems, 1489 Greg St., Sparks, NV 89431

California Sights (See Fautheree, Andy)

Cambos Outdoorsman, 532 E. Idaho Ave., Ontario, OR 97914 / 541-889-3135; FAX: 541-889-2633

Cambos Outdoorsman, Fritz Hallberg, 532 E. Idaho Ave., Ontario, OR 97914 / 541-889-3135; FAX: 541-889-2633

Camdex, Inc., 2330 Alger, Troy, MI 48083 / 810-528-2300; FAX: 810-528-0989

Cameron's, 16690 W. 11th Ave., Golden, CO 80401 / 303-279-7365; FAX: 303-628-5413 ncnoremac@aol.com

Camillus Cutlery Co., 54 Main St., Camillus, NY 13031 / 315-672-8111; FAX: 315-672-8832

Campbell, Dick, 20000 Silver Ranch Rd., Conifer, CO 80433 / 303-697-0150; FAX: 303-697-0150 dicksknives@aol.com

Camp-Cap Products, P.O. Box 3805, Chesterfield, MO 63006 / 314-532-4340; FAX: 314-532-4340

Cannon Safe, Inc., 216 S. 2nd Ave. #BLD-932, San Bernardino, CA 92400 / 310-692-0636; or 800-242-1055; FAX: 310-692-7252

Canons Delcour, Rue J.B. Cools, B-4040, Herstal, BELGIUM / 32.(0)42.40.61.40; FAX: 32(0)42.40.22.88

Canyon Cartridge Corp., P.O. Box 152, Albertson, NY 11507 FAX: 516-294-8946

Cape Outfitters, 599 County Rd. 206, Cape Girardeau, MO 63701 / 573-335-4103; FAX: 573-335-1555

Caraville Manufacturing, P.O. Box 4545, Thousand Oaks, CA 91359 / 805-499-1234

Carbide Checkering Tools (See J&R Engineering)

Carhartt,Inc., P.O. Box 600, 3 Parklane Blvd., Dearborn, MI 48121 / 800-358-3825; or 313-271-8460; FAX: 313-271-3455

Carl Walther GmbH, B.P. 4325, D-89033, Ulm, GERMANY

Carl Zeiss Inc., 13005 N. Kingston Ave., Chester, VA 23836 / 800-441-3005; FAX: 804-530-8481

Carlson, Douglas R, Antique American Firearms, P.O. Box 71035, Dept GD, Des Moines, IA 50325 / 515-224-6552

Carolina Precision Rifles, 1200 Old Jackson Hwy., Jackson, SC 29831 / 803-827-2069

Carrell, William. See: CARRELL'S PRECISION FIREARMS

Carrell's Precision Firearms, William Carrell, 1952 W.Silver Falls Ct., Meridian, ID 83642-3837

Carry-Lite, Inc., P.O. Box 1587, Fort Smith, AR 72902 / 479-782-8971; FAX: 479-783-0234

Carter's Gun Shop, 225 G St., Penrose, CO 81240 / 719-372-6240

Cartridge Transfer Group, Pete de Coux, HC 30 Box 932 G, Prescott, AZ 86305-7447 / 928-776-8285; FAX: 928-776-8276 pdbullets@commspeed.net

Cascade Bullet Co., Inc., 2355 South 6th St., Klamath Falls, OR 97601 / 503-884-9316

Cascade Shooters, 2155 N.W. 12th St., Redwood, OR 97756

Case & Sons Cutlery Co., W R, Owens Way, Bradford, PA 16701 / 814-368-4123; or 800-523-6350; FAX: 814-768-5369

Case Sorting System, 12695 Cobblestone Creek Rd., Poway, CA 92064 / 619-486-9340

Cash Mfg. Co., Inc., P.O. Box 130, 201 S. Klein Dr., Waunakee, WI 53597-0130 / 608-849-5664; FAX: 608-849-5664

Caspian Arms, Ltd., 14 North Main St., Hardwick, VT 05843 / 802-472-6454; FAX: 802-472-6709

Cast Performance Bullet Company, PO Box 153, Riverton, WY 82501 / 307-857-2940; FAX: 307-857-3132 castperform@wyoming.com castperformance.com

Casull Arms Corp., P.O. Box 1629, Afton, WY 83110 / 307-886-0200

Cathey Enterprises, Inc., P.O. Box 2202, Brownwood, TX 76804 / 915-643-2553; FAX: 915-643-3653

Cation, 2341 Alger St., Troy, MI 48083 / 810-689-0658; FAX: 810-689-7558

Caywood, Shane J., P.O. Box 321, Minocqua, WI 54548 / 715-277-3866

Caywood Gunmakers, 18 King's Hill Estates, Berryville, AR 72616 / 870-423-4741 www.caywoodguns.com

CBC, Avenida Humberto de Campos 3220, 09400-000, Ribeirao Pires, SP, BRAZIL / 55-11-742-7500; FAX: 55-11-459-7385

CBC-BRAZIL, 3 Cuckoo Lane, Honley, Yorkshire HD7 2BR, ENGLAND / 44-1484-661062; FAX: 44-1484-663709

CCG Enterprises, 5217 E. Belknap St., Halton City, TX 76117 / 800-819-7464

CCI Ammunition ATK, P.O. Box 856, Lewiston, ID 83501 / 208-746-2351 www.cci_ammunition.com

CCL Security Products, 199 Whiting St, New Britain, CT 06051 / 800-733-8588

Cedar Hill Game Calls, Inc., 238 Vic Allen Rd, Downsville, LA 71234 / 318-982-5632; FAX: 318-368-2245

Centaur Systems, Inc., 1602 Foothill Rd., Kalispell, MT 59901 / 406-755-8609; FAX: 406-755-8609

Center Lock Scope Rings, 9901 France Ct., Lakeville, MN 55044 / 612-461-2114

Central Specialties Ltd (See Trigger Lock Division

Century Gun Dist. Inc., 1467 Jason Rd., Greenfield, IN 46140 / 317-462-4524

Century International Arms, Inc., 1161 Holland Dr, Boca Raton, FL 33487

CFVentures, 509 Harvey Dr., Bloomington, IN 47403-1715 paladinwilltravel@yahoo.com

CH Tool & Die Co. (See 4-D Custom Die Co.), 711 N Sandusky St., P.O. Box 889, Mt. Vernon, OH 43050-0889 / 740-397-7214; FAX: 740-397-6600

Chace Leather Products, 507 Alden St., Fall River, MA 02722 / 508-678-7556; FAX: 508-675-9666

Chadick's Ltd., P.O. Box 100, Terrell, TX 75160 / 214-563-7577

Chambers Flintlocks Ltd., Jim, 116 Sams Branch Rd., Candler, NC 28715 / 828-667-8361; FAX: 828-665-0852 www.flintlocks.com

Champion Shooters' Supply, P.O. Box 303, New Albany, OH 43054 / 614-855-1603; FAX: 614-855-1209

Champion Target Co., 232 Industrial Parkway, Richmond, IN 47374 / 800-441-4971

Champion's Choice, Inc., 201 International Blvd., LaVergne, TN 37086 / 615-793-4066; FAX: 615-793-4070 champ.choice@earthlink.net www.champchoice.com

Champlin Firearms, Inc., P.O. Box 3191, Woodring Airport, Enid, OK 73701 / 580-237-7388; FAX: 580-242-6922 info@champlinarms.com www.champlinarms.com

Chapman Academy of Practical Shooting, 4350 Academy Rd., Hallsville, MO 65255 / 573-696-5544; FAX: 573-696-2266 ha@chapmanacademy.com

Chapman, J Ken. See: OLD WEST BULLET MOULDS

Chapman Manufacturing Co., 471 New Haven Rd., PO Box 250, Durham, CT 06422 / 860-349-9228; FAX: 860-349-0084 sales@chapmanmfg.com www.chapmanmfg.com

Chapuis Armes, 21 La Gravoux, BP15, 42380, St. Bonnet-le-Chatea, FRANCE / (33)77.50.06.96

Chapuis USA, 416 Business Park, Bedford, KY 40006

Charter 2000, 273 Canal St, Shelton, CT 06484 / 203-922-1652

Checkmate Refinishing, 370 Champion Dr., Brooksville, FL 34601 / 352-799-5774; FAX: 352-799-2986 checkmatecustom.com

Cheddite, France S.A., 99 Route de Lyon, F-26501, Bourg-les-Valence, FRANCE / 33-75-56-4545; FAX: 33-75-56-3587 export@cheddite.com

Chelsea Gun Club of New York City Inc., 237 Ovington Ave., Apt. D53, Brooklyn, NY 11209 / 718-836-9422; or 718-833-2704

Cherry Creek State Park Shooting Center, 12500 E. Belleview Ave., Englewood, CO 80111 / 303-693-1765

Chet Fulmer's Antique Firearms, P.O. Box 792, Rt. 2 Buffalo Lake, Detroit Lakes, MN 56501 / 218-847-7712

CheVron Bullets, RR1, Ottawa, IL 61350 / 815-433-2471

Cheyenne Pioneer Products, PO Box 28425, Kansas City, MO 64188 / 816-413-9196; FAX: 816-455-2859 cheyennepp@aol.com www.cartridgeboxes.com

Chicago Cutlery Co., 1536 Beech St., Terre Haute, IN 47804 / 800-457-2665

Chicasaw Gun Works, 4 Mi. Mkr., Pluto Rd., Box 868, Shady Spring, WV 25918-0868 / 304-763-2848; FAX: 304-763-3725

Chipmunk (See Oregon Arms, Inc.)

Choate Machine & Tool Co., Inc., P.O. Box 218, 116 Lovers Ln., Bald Knob, AR 72010 / 501-724-6193; or 800-972-6390; FAX: 501-724-5873

Christensen Arms, 192 East 100 North, Fayette, UT 84630 / 435-528-7999; FAX: 435-528-7494 www.christensenarms.com

Christie's East, 20 Rockefeller Plz., New York, NY 10020-1902 / 212-606-0406 christics.com

Chu Tani Ind., Inc., P.O. Box 2064, Cody, WY 82414-2064

Chuck's Gun Shop, P.O. Box 597, Waldo, FL 32694 / 904-468-2264

Chuilli, Stephen, 8895 N. Military Trl. Ste., Ste. 201E, Palm Beach Gardens, FL 33410

Churchill (See U.S. Importer-Ellett Bros.)

Churchill, Winston G., 2838 20 Mile Stream Rd., Proctorville, VT 05153 / 802-226-7772

Churchill Glove Co., James, PO Box 298, Centralia, WA 98531 / 360-736-2816; FAX: 360-330-0151

CIDCO, 21480 Pacific Blvd., Sterling, VA 22170 / 703-444-5353

Ciener Inc., Jonathan Arthur, 8700 Commerce St., Cape Canaveral, FL 32920 / 321-868-2200; FAX: 321-868-2201

Cimarron F.A. Co., P.O. Box 906, Fredericksburg, TX 78624-0906 / 830-997-9090; FAX: 830-997-0802 cimgraph@koc.com www.cimarron-firearms.com

Cincinnati Swaging, 2605 Marlington Ave., Cincinnati, OH 45208

Clark Custom Guns, Inc., 336 Shootout Lane, Princeton, LA 71067 / 318-949-9884; FAX: 318-949-9829

Clark Firearms Engraving, P.O. Box 80746, San Marino, CA 91118 / 818-287-1652

Clarkfield Enterprises, Inc., 1032 10th Ave., Clarkfield, MN 56223 / 612-669-7140

Claro Walnut Gunstock Co., 1235 Stanley Ave., Chico, CA 95928 / 530-342-5188; FAX: 530-342-5199 wally@clarowalnutgunstock.com www.clarowalnutgunstock.com

Classic Arms Company, Rt 1 Box 120F, Burnet, TX 78611 / 512-756-4001

Classic Arms Corp., P.O. Box 106, Dunsmuir, CA 96025-0106 / 530-235-2000

Classic Old West Styles, 1060 Doniphan Park Circle C, El Paso, TX 79936 / 915-587-0684

Claybuster Wads & Harvester Bullets, 309 Sequoya Dr., Hopkinsville, KY 42240 / 800-922-6287 or 800-284-1746; FAX: 502-885-8088 50

Clean Shot Technologies, 21218 St. Andrews Blvd. Ste 504, Boca Raton, FL 33433 / 888-866-2532

Clearview Mfg. Co., Inc., 413 S. Oakley St., Fordyce, AR 71742 / 501-352-8557; FAX: 501-352-7120

Clearview Products, 3021 N. Portland, Oklahoma City, OK 73107

Cleland's Outdoor World, Inc, 10306 Airport Hwy, Swanton, OH 43558 / 419-865-4713; FAX: 419-865-5865

Clements' Custom Leathercraft, Chas, 1741 Dallas St., Aurora, CO 80010-2018 / 303-364-0403; FAX: 303-739-9824 gryphons@home.com kuntaoslcat.com

Clenzoil Worldwide Corp, Jack Fitzgerald, 25670 1st St., Westlake, OH 44145-1430 / 440-899-0482; FAX: 440-899-0483

Clift Mfg., L. R., 3821 Hammonton Rd., Marysville, CA 95901 / 916-755-3390; FAX: 916-755-3393

Clymer Mfg. Co., 1645 W. Hamlin Rd., Rochester Hills, MI 48309-3312 / 248-853-5555; FAX: 248-853-1530

C-More Systems, P.O. Box 1750, 7553 Gary Rd., Manassas, VA 20108 / 703-361-2663; FAX: 703-361-5881

Cobalt Mfg., Inc., 4020 Mcewen Rd Ste 180, Dallas, TX 75244-5090 / 817-382-8986; FAX: 817-383-4281

Cobra Enterprises, Inc., 1960 S. Milestone Drive, Suite F, Salt Lake City, UT 84104 FAX: 801-908-8301 www.cobrapistols@networld.com

Cobra Sport S.r.l., Via Caduti Nei Lager No. 1, 56020 San Romano, Montopoli v/Arno (Pi, ITALY / 0039-571-450490; FAX: 0039-571-450492

Coffin, Charles H., 3719 Scarlet Ave., Odessa, TX 79762 / 915-366-4729; FAX: 915-366-4729

Coffin, Jim (See Working Guns)

Coffin, Jim. See: WORKING GUNS

Cogar's Gunsmithing, 206 Redwine Dr., Houghton Lake, MI 48629 / 517-422-4591

Coghlan's Ltd., 121 Irene St., Winnipeg, MB R3T 4C7 CANADA / 204-284-9550; FAX: 204-475-4127

Cold Steel Inc., 3036 Seaborg Ave. Ste. A, Ventura, CA 93003 / 800-255-4716; or 800-624-2363; FAX: 805-642-9727

Cole-Grip, 16135 Cohasset St., Van Nuys, CA 91406 / 818-782-4424

Coleman Co., Inc., 250 N. St. Francis, Wichita, KS 67201

Cole's Gun Works, Old Bank Building, Rt. 4 Box 250, Moyock, NC 27958 / 919-435-2345

Collings, Ronald, 1006 Cielta Linda, Vista, CA 92083

Colonial Arms, Inc., P.O. Box 636, Selma, AL 36702-0636 / 334-872-9455; FAX: 334-872-9540 colonialarms@mindspring.com www.colonialarms.com

Colonial Repair, 47 Navarre St., Roslindale, MA 02131-4725 / 617-469-4951

Colorado Gunsmithing Academy, RR 3 Box 79B, El Campo, TX 77437 / 719-336-4099 or 800-754-2046; FAX: 719-336-9642

Colorado School of Trades, 1575 Hoyt St., Lakewood, CO 80215 / 800-234-4594; FAX: 303-233-4723

Colt Blackpowder Arms Co., 110 8th Street, Brooklyn, NY 11215 / 718-499-4678; FAX: 718-768-8056

Colt's Mfg. Co., Inc., PO Box 1868, Hartford, CT 06144-1868 / 800-962-COLT; or 860-236-6311; FAX: 860-244-1449

Compass Industries, Inc., 104 East 25th St., New York, NY 10010 / 212-473-2614 or 800-221-9904; FAX: 212-353-0826

Compasseco, Ltd., 151 Atkinson Hill Ave., Bardtown, KY 40004 / 502-349-0910

Competition Electronics, Inc., 3469 Precision Dr., Rockford, IL 61109 / 815-874-8001; FAX: 815-874-8181

Competitor Corp., Inc., Appleton Business Center, 30 Tricnit Road Unit 16, New Ipswich, NH 03071 / 603-878-3891; FAX: 603-878-3950

Component Concepts, Inc., 530 S Springbrook Road, Newberg, OR 97132 / 503-554-8095; FAX: 503-554-9370 cci@cybcon.com www.phantomonline.com

Concept Development Corp., 16610 E. Laser Drive, Suite 5, Fountain Hills, AZ 85268-6644

Conetrol Scope Mounts, 10225 Hwy. 123 S., Seguin, TX 78155 / 830-379-3030 or 800-CONETROL; FAX: 830-379-3030 email@conetrol.com www.conetrol.com

CONKKO, P.O. Box 40, Broomall, PA 19008 / 215-356-0711

Connecticut Shotgun Mfg. Co., P.O. Box 1692, 35 Woodland St., New Britain, CT 06051 / 860-225-6581; FAX: 860-832-8707

Connecticut Valley Classics (See CVC, BPI)

Conrad, C. A., 3964 Ebert St., Winston-Salem, NC 27127 / 919-788-5469

Cook Engineering Service, 891 Highbury Rd., Vict, 3133 AUSTRALIA

Cooper Arms, P.O. Box 114, Stevensville, MT 59870 / 406-777-0373; FAX: 406-777-5228

Cooper-Woodward, 3800 Pelican Rd., Helena, MT 59602 / 406-458-3800 dolymama@msn.com

Corbin Mfg. & Supply, Inc., 600 Industrial Circle, P.O. Box 2659, White City, OR 97503 / 541-826-5211; FAX: 541-826-8669 sales@corbins.com www.corbins.com

Cor-Bon Inc./Glaser LLC, P.O. Box 173, 1311 Industry Rd., Sturgis, SD 57785 / 605-347-4544 or 800-221-3489; FAX: 605-347-5055 email@corbon.com www.corbon.com

Corkys Gun Clinic, 4401 Hot Springs Dr., Greeley, CO 80634-9226 / 970-330-0516

Corry, John, 861 Princeton Ct., Neshanic Station, NJ 08853 / 908-369-8019

Cosmi Americo & Figlio s.n.c., Via Flaminia 307, Ancona, ITALY / 071-888208; FAX: 39-071-887008

Coulston Products, Inc., P.O. Box 30, 201 Ferry St. Suite 212, Easton, PA 18044-0030 / 215-253-0167; or 800-445-9927; FAX: 215-252-1511

Counter Assault, 120 Industrial Court, Kalispell, MT 59901 / 406-257-4740; FAX: 406-257-6674

Cousin Bob's Mountain Products, 7119 Ohio River Blvd., Ben Avon, PA 15202 / 412-766-5114; FAX: 412-766-5114

Cox, Ed. C., RD 2, Box 192, Prosperity, PA 15329 / 412-228-4984

CP Bullets, 1310 Industrial Hwy #5-6, South Hampton, PA 18966 / 215-953-7264; FAX: 215-953-7275

CQB Training, P.O. Box 1739, Manchester, MO 63011

Craftguard, 3624 Logan Ave., Waterloo, IA 50703 / 319-232-2959; FAX: 319-234-0804

Crandall Tool & Machine Co., 19163 21 Mile Rd., Tustin, MI 49688 / 616-829-4430

Creedmoor Sports, Inc., P.O. Box 1040, Oceanside, CA 92051 / 767-757-5529; FAX: 760-757-5558 shoot@creedmoorsports.com www.creedmoorsports.com

Creek Side Metal & Woodcrafters, Fishers Hill, VA 22626 / 703-465-3903

Creighton Audette, 19 Highland Circle, Springfield, VT 05156 / 802-885-2331

Crimson Trace Lasers, 8090 SW Cirrus Dr., Beverton, OR 97008 / 800-442-2406; FAX: 503-627-0166 www.crimsontrace.com

Crit'R Call (See Rocky Mountain Wildlife Products)

Crosman Airguns, Rts. 5 and 20, E. Bloomfield, NY 14443 / 716-657-6161; FAX: 716-657-5405

Crosman Blades (See Coleman Co., Inc.)

Crouse's Country Cover, P.O. Box 160, Storrs, CT 06268 / 860-423-8736

CRR, Inc./Marble's Inc., 420 Industrial Park, P.O. Box 111, Gladstone, MI 49837 / 906-428-3710; FAX: 906-428-3711

Crucelegui, Hermanos (See U.S. Importer-Mandall)

Cubic Shot Shell Co., Inc., 98 Fatima Dr., Campbell, OH 44405 / 330-755-0349

Cullity Restoration, 209 Old Country Rd., East Sandwich, MA 02537 / 508-888-1147

Cumberland Arms, 514 Shafer Road, Manchester, TN 37355 / 800-797-8414

Cumberland Mountain Arms, P.O. Box 710, Winchester, TN 37398 / 615-967-8414; FAX: 615-967-9199

Cummings Bullets, 1417 Esperanza Way, Escondido, CA 92027

Cupp, Alana, Custom Engraver, PO Box 207, Annabella, UT 84711 / 801-896-4834

Curly Maple Stock Blanks (See Tiger-Hunt)

Curtis Cast Bullets, 527 W. Babcock St., Bozeman, MT 59715 / 406-587-8117; FAX: 406-587-8117

Curtis Gun Shop (See Curtis Cast Bullets)

Custom Bullets by Hoffman, 2604 Peconic Ave., Seaford, NY 11783

Custom Calls, 607 N. 5th St., Burlington, IA 52601 / 319-752-4465

Custom Checkering Service, Kathy Forster, 2124 S.E. Yamhill St., Portland, OR 97214 / 503-236-5874

Custom Chronograph, Inc., 5305 Reese Hill Rd., Sumas, WA 98295 / 360-988-7801

Custom Firearms (See Ahrends, Kim)

Custom Gun Stocks, 3062 Turners Bend Rd, McMinnville, TN 37110 / 615-668-3912

Custom Products (See Jones Custom Products)

Custom Quality Products, Inc., 345 W. Girard Ave., P.O. Box 71129, Madison Heights, MI 48071 / 810-585-1616; FAX: 810-585-0644

Custom Riflestocks, Inc., Michael M. Kokolus, 7005 Herber Rd., New Tripoli, PA 18066 / 610-298-3013; FAX: 610-298-2431 mkokolus@prodigy.net

Custom Single Shot Rifles, 9651 Meadows Lane, Guthrie, OK 73044 / 405-282-3634

Custom Stocking, Mike Yee, 29927 56 Pl. S., Auburn, WA 98001 / 253-839-3991

Custom Tackle and Ammo, P.O. Box 1886, Farmington, NM 87499 / 505-632-3539

Cutco Cutlery, P.O. Box 810, Olean, NY 14760 / 716-372-3111

CVA, 5988 Peachtree Corners East, Norcross, GA 30071 / 770-449-4687; FAX: 770-242-8546 info@cva.com www.cva.com

Cylinder & Slide, Inc., William R. Laughridge, 245 E. 4th St., Fremont, NE 68025 / 402-721-4277; FAX: 402-721-0263 bill@cylinder-slide.com www.clinder-slide.com

CZ USA, PO Box 171073, Kansas City, KS 66117 / 913-321-1811; FAX: 913-321-4901

D

D&D Gunsmiths, Ltd., 363 E. Elmwood, Troy, MI 48083 / 810-583-1512; FAX: 810-583-1524

D&G Precision Duplicators (See Greene Precision)

D&H Precision Tooling, 7522 Barnard Mill Rd., Ringwood, IL 60072 / 815-653-4011

D&L Industries (See D.J. Marketing)

D&L Sports, P.O. Box 651, Gillette, WY 82717 / 307-686-4008

D.C.C. Enterprises, 259 Wynburn Ave., Athens, GA 30601

D.J. Marketing, 10602 Horton Ave., Downey, CA 90241 / 310-806-0891; FAX: 310-806-6231

Dade Screw Machine Products, 2319 NW 7th Ave., Miami, FL 33127 / 305-573-5050

Daewoo Precision Industries Ltd., 34-3 Yeoeuido-Dong, Yeongdeungpo-GU 15th Fl., Seoul, KOREA

Daisy Outdoor Products, P.O. Box 220, Rogers, AR 72757 / 479-636-1200; FAX: 479-636-0573 www.daisy.com

Dakota (See U.S. Importer-EMF Co., Inc.)

Dakota Arms, Inc., 130 Industry Road, Sturgis, SD 57785 / 605-347-4686; FAX: 605-347-4459 info@dakotaarms.com www.dakotaarms.com

Dakota Corp., 77 Wales St., P.O. Box 543, Rutland, VT 05701 / 802-775-6062; or 800-451-4167; FAX: 802-773-3919

Daly, Charles (See U.S. Importer), P.O. Box 6625, Harrisburg, PA 17112 / 717-540-8518 www.charlesdaly.com

Da-Mar Gunsmith's Inc., 102 1st St., Solvay, NY 13209 damascususa@inteliport.com, 149 Deans Farm Rd., Tyner, NC 27980 / 252-221-2010; FAX: 252-221-2010 damascususa@inteliport.com

Dan Wesson Firearms, 119 Kemper Lane, Norwich, NY 13815 / 607-336-1174; FAX: 607-336-2730

Danforth, Mikael. See: VEKTOR USA

Dangler, Homer L., 2870 Lee Marie Dr., Adrian, MI 49220 / 517-266-1997

Danner Shoe Mfg. Co., 12722 NE Airport Way, Portland, OR 97230 / 503-251-1100; or 800-345-0430; FAX: 503-251-1119

Dan's Whetstone Co., Inc., 130 Timbs Place, Hot Springs, AR 71913 / 501-767-1616; FAX: 501-767-9598 questions@danswhetstone.com www.danswhetstone.com

Danuser Machine Co., 550 E. Third St., P.O. Box 368, Fulton, MO 65251 / 573-642-2246; FAX: 573-642-2240 sales@danuser.com www.danuser.com

Dara-Nes, Inc. (See Nesci Enterprises, Inc.)

D'Arcy Echols & Co., PO Box 421, Millville, UT 84326 / 435-755-6842

Darlington Gun Works, Inc., P.O. Box 698, 516 S. 52 Bypass, Darlington, SC 29532 / 803-393-3931

Dart Bell/Brass (See MAST Technology)

Darwin Hensley Gunmaker, PO Box 329, Brightwood, OR 97011 / 503-622-5411

Data Tech Software Systems, 19312 East Eldorado Drive, Aurora, CO 80013

Dave Norin Schrank's Smoke & Gun, 2010 Washington St., Waukegan, IL 60085 / 708-662-4034

Dave's Gun Shop, P.O. Box 2824, Casper, WY 82602-2824 / 307-754-9724

David Clark Co., Inc., PO Box 15054, Worcester, MA 01615-0054 / 508-756-6216; FAX: 508-753-5827 sales@davidclark.com www.davidclark.com

David Condon, Inc., 109 E. Washington St., Middleburg, VA 22117 / 703-687-5642

David Miller Co., 3131 E Greenlee Rd, Tucson, AZ 85716 / 520-326-3117

David R. Chicoine, 1210 Jones Street, Gastonia, NC 28052 / 704-853-0265 bnpress@quik.com

David W. Schwartz Custom Guns, 2505 Waller St., Eau Claire, WI 54703 / 715-832-1735

Davide Pedersoli and Co., Via Artigiani 57, Gardone VT, Brescia 25063, ITALY / 030-8912402; or 030-8915000;

MANUFACTURER'S DIRECTORY

FAX: 030-8911019 info@davidepedersoli.com
www.davide_pedersoli.com
Davis, Don, 1619 Heights, Katy, TX 77493 / 713-391-3090
Davis Industries (See Cobra Enterprises, Inc.)
Davis Products, Mike, 643 Loop Dr., Moses Lake, WA 98837 / 509-765-6178; or 509-766-7281
Daystate Ltd., Birch House Lanee, Cotes Heath Staffs, ST15.022, ENGLAND / 01782-791755; FAX: 01782-791617
Dayton Traister, 4778 N. Monkey Hill Rd., P.O. Box 593, Oak Harbor, WA 98277 / 360-679-4657; FAX: 360-675-1114
DBI Books Division of Krause Publications, 700 E. State St., Iola, WI 54990-0001 / 715-445-2214
D-Boone Ent., Inc., 5900 Colwyn Dr., Harrisburg, PA 17109
de Coux, Pete (See Cartridge Transfer Group)
Dead Eye's Sport Center, 76 Baer Rd., Shickshinny, PA 18655 / 570-256-7432 deadeyeprizz@aol.com
Deepeeka Exports Pvt. Ltd., D-78, Saket, Meerut-250-006, INDIA / 011-91-121-640363 or ; FAX: 011-91-121-640988 deepeeka@poboxes.com www.deepeeka.com
Defense Training International, Inc., 749 S. Lemay, Ste. A3-337, Ft. Collins, CO 80524 / 303-482-2520; FAX: 303-482-0548
Degen Inc. (See Aristocrat Knives)
deHaas Barrels, 20049 W. State Hwy. Z, Ridgeway, MO 64481 / 660-872-6308
Del Rey Products, P.O. Box 5134, Playa Del Rey, CA 90296-5134 / 213-823-0494
Delhi Gun House, 1374 Kashmere Gate, New Delhi 110 006, INDIA / 2940974; or 394-0974; FAX: 2917344 dgh@vsnl.com
Delorge, Ed, 6734 W. Main, Houma, LA 70360 / 985-223-0206
Del-Sports, Inc., Dave Budin, Box 685, 817 Main St., Margaretville, NY 12455 / 845-586-4103; FAX: 845-586-4105
Delta Arms Ltd., P.O. Box 1000, Delta, VT 84624-1000
Delta Enterprises, 284 Hagemann Drive, Livermore, CA 94550
Delta Frangible Ammunition LLC, P.O. Box 2350, Stafford, VA 22555-2350 / 540-720-5778 or 800-339-1933; FAX: 540-720-5667 dfa@dfanet.com www.dfanet.com
Dem-Bart Checkering Tools, Inc., 1825 Bickford Ave., Snohomish, WA 98290 / 360-568-7356 walt@dembartco.com www.dembartco.com
Denver Instrument Co., 6542 Fig St., Arvada, CO 80004 / 800-321-1135; or 303-431-7255; FAX: 303-423-4831
DeSantis Holster & Leather Goods, P.O. Box 2039, 149 Denton Ave., New Hyde Park, NY 11040-0701 / 516-354-8000; FAX: 516-354-7501
Desert Mountain Mfg., P.O. Box 130184, Coram, MT 59913 / 800-477-0762; or 406-387-5361; FAX: 406-387-5361
Detroit-Armor Corp., 720 Industrial Dr. No. 112, Cary, IL 60013 / 708-639-7666; FAX: 708-639-7694
DGR Custom Rifles, 4191 37th Ave. SE, Tappen, ND 58487 / 701-327-8135
DGS, Inc., Dale A. Storey, 1117 E. 12th, Casper, WY 82601 / 307-237-2414; FAX: 307-237-2414 dalest@trib.com www.dgsrifle.com
DHB Products, 336 River View Dr., Verona, VA 24482-2547 / 703-836-2648
Diamond Machining Technology, Inc. (See DMT)
Diamond Mfg. Co., P.O. Box 174, Wyoming, PA 18644 / 800-233-9601
Dibble, Derek A., 555 John Downey Dr., New Britain, CT 06051 / 203-224-2630
Dietz Gun Shop & Range, Inc., 421 Range Rd., New Braunfels, TX 78132 / 210-885-4662
Dilliott Gunsmithing, Inc., 657 Scarlett Rd., Dandridge, TN 37725 / 865-397-9204 gunsmithd@aol.com dilliottgunsmithing.com
Dillon Precision Products, Inc., 8009 East Dillon's Way, Scottsdale, AZ 85260 / 480-948-8009; or 800-762-3845; FAX: 480-998-2786 sales@dillonprecision.com www.dillonprecision.com
Dina Arms Corporation, P.O. Box 46, Royersford, PA 19468 / 610-287-0266; FAX: 610-287-0266
Dixie Gun Works, P.O. Box 130, Union City, TN 38281 / 731-885-0700; FAX: 731-885-0440 info@dixiegunworks.com www.dixiegunworks.com
Dixon Muzzleloading Shop, Inc., 9952 Kunkels Mill Rd., Kempton, PA 19529 / 610-756-6271 dixonmuzzleloading.com
DKT, Inc., 14623 Vera Drive, Union, MI 49130-9744 / 800-741-7083 orders; FAX: 616-641-2015
DLO Mfg., 10807 SE Foster Ave., Arcadia, FL 33821-7304
DMT--Diamond Machining Technology Inc., 85 Hayes Memorial Dr., Marlborough, MA 01752 FAX: 508-485-3924

Dohring Bullets, 100 W. 8 Mile Rd., Ferndale, MI 48220
Dolbare, Elizabeth, P.O. Box 502, Dubois, WY 82513-0502
Domino, PO Box 108, 20019 Settimo Milanese, Milano, ITALY / 1-39-2-33512040; FAX: 1-39-2-33511587
Donnelly, C. P., 405 Kubli Rd., Grants Pass, OR 97527 / 541-846-6604
Doskocil Mfg. Co., Inc., P.O. Box 1246, 4209 Barnett, Arlington, TX 76017 / 817-467-5116; FAX: 817-472-9810
Douglas Barrels, Inc., 5504 Big Tyler Rd., Charleston, WV 25313-1398 / 304-776-1341; FAX: 304-776-8560 www.benchrest.com/douglas
Downsizer Corp., P.O. Box 710316, Santee, CA 92072-0316 / 619-448-5510 www.downsizer.com
DPMS (Defense Procurement Manufacturing Services, Inc.), 13983 Industry Avenue, Becker, MN 55308 / 800-578-DPMS; or 763-261-5600 FAX: 763-261-5599
Dr. O's Products Ltd., P.O. Box 111, Niverville, NY 12130 / 518-784-3333; FAX: 518-784-2800
Drain, Mark, SE 3211 Kamilche Point Rd., Shelton, WA 98584 / 206-426-5452
Dremel Mfg. Co., 4915-21st St., Racine, WI 53406
Dri-Slide, Inc., 411 N. Darling, Fremont, MI 49412 / 616-924-3950
Dropkick, 1460 Washington Blvd., Williamsport, PA 17701 / 717-326-6561; FAX: 717-326-4950
DS Arms, Inc., P.O. Box 370, 27 West 990 Industrial Ave., Barrington, IL 60010 / 847-277-7258; FAX: 847-277-7259 www.dsarms.com
DTM International, Inc., 40 Joslyn Rd., P.O. Box 5, Lake Orion, MI 48362 / 313-693-6670
Duane A. Hobbie Gunsmithing, 2412 Pattie Ave, Wichita, KS 67216 / 316-264-8266
Duane's Gun Repair (See DGR Custom Rifles)
Dubber, Michael W., P.O. Box 312, Evansville, IN 47702 / 812-424-9000; FAX: 812-424-6551
Duck Call Specialists, P.O. Box 124, Jerseyville, IL 62052 / 618-498-9855
Duffy, Charles E (See Guns Antique & Modern DBA), Williams Lane, PO Box 2, West Hurley, NY 12491 / 914-679-2997
Du-Lite Corp., 171 River Rd., Middletown, CT 06457 / 203-347-2505; FAX: 203-347-9404
Dumoulin, Ernest, Rue Florent Boclinville 8-10, 13-4041, Votten, BELGIUM / 41 27 78 92
Duncan's Gun Works, Inc., 1619 Grand Ave., San Marcos, CA 92069 / 760-727-0515
DunLyon R&D Inc., 52151 E. US Hwy. 60, Miami, AZ 85539 / 928-473-9027
Duofold, Inc., RD 3 Rt. 309, Valley Square Mall, Tamaqua, PA 18252 / 717-386-2666; FAX: 717-386-3652
Dybala Gun Shop, P.O. Box 1024, FM 3156, Bay City, TX 77414 / 409-245-0866
Dykstra, Doug, 411 N. Darling, Fremont, MI 49412 / 616-924-3950
Dynalite Products, Inc., 215 S. Washington St., Greenfield, OH 45123 / 513-981-2124
Dynamit Nobel-RWS, Inc., 81 Ruckman Rd., Closter, NJ 07624 / 201-767-7971; FAX: 201-767-1589

E

E&L Mfg., Inc., 4177 Riddle By Pass Rd., Riddle, OR 97469 / 541-874-2137; FAX: 541-874-3107
E. Arthur Brown Co., 3404 Pawnee Dr., Alexandria, MN 56308 / 320-762-8847
E.A.A. Corp., P.O. Box 1299, Sharpes, FL 32959 / 407-639-4842; or 800-536-4442; FAX: 407-639-7006
Eagan, Donald V., P.O. Box 196, Benton, PA 17814 / 717-925-6134
Eagle Arms, Inc. (See ArmaLite, Inc.)
Eagle Grips, Eagle Business Center, 460 Randy Rd., Carol Stream, IL 60188 / 800-323-6144; or 708-260-0400; FAX: 708-260-0486
Eagle Imports, Inc., 1750 Brielle Ave., Unit B1, Wanamassa, NJ 07712 / 908-493-0333
E-A-R, Inc., Div. of Cabot Safety Corp., 5457 W. 79th St., Indianapolis, IN 46268 / 800-327-3431; FAX: 800-488-8007
EAW (See U.S. Importer-New England Custom Gun Serv
Eckelman Gunsmithing, 3125 133rd St. SW, Fort Ripley, MN 56449 / 218-829-3176
Eclectic Technologies, Inc., 45 Grandview Dr., Suite A, Farmington, CT 06034
Ed Brown Products, Inc., P.O. Box 492, Perry, MO 63462 / 573-565-3261; FAX: 573-565-2791 edbrown@edbrown.com www.edbrown.com
Edenpine, Inc. c/o Six Enterprises, Inc., 320 D Turtle Creek Ct., San Jose, CA 95125 / 408-999-0201; FAX: 408-999-0216

EdgeCraft Corp., S. Weiner, 825 Southwood Road, Avondale, PA 19311 / 610-268-0500; or 800-342-3255; FAX: 610-268-3545 www.edgecraft.com
Edmisten Co., P.O. Box 1293, Boone, NC 28607
Edmund Scientific Co., 101 E. Gloucester Pike, Barrington, NJ 08033 / 609-543-6250
Ednar, Inc., 2-4-8 Kayabacho, Nihonbashi Chuo-ku, Tokyo, JAPAN / 81(Japan)-3-3667-1651; FAX: 81-3-3661-8113
Ed's Gun House, Ed Kukowski, P.O. Box 62, Minnesota City, MN 55959 / 507-689-2925
Eezox, Inc., P.O. Box 772, Waterford, CT 06385-0772 / 800-462-3331; FAX: 860-447-3484
Effebi SNC-Dr. Franco Beretta, via Rossa, 4, 25062, ITALY / 030-2751955; FAX: 030-2180414
Efficient Machinery Co., 12878 N.E. 15th Pl., Bellevue, WA 98005 / 425-453-9318 or 800-375-8554; FAX: 425-453-9311 priemc@aol.com www.sturdybench.com
Eggleston, Jere D., 400 Saluda Ave., Columbia, SC 29205 / 803-799-3402
Eichelberger Bullets, Wm., 158 Crossfield Rd., King Of Prussia, PA 19406
Ekol Leather Care, P.O. Box 2652, West Lafayette, IN 47906 / 317-463-2250; FAX: 317-463-7004
El Paso Saddlery Co., P.O. Box 27194, El Paso, TX 79926 / 915-544-2233; FAX: 915-544-2535 epsaddlery.com www.epsaddlery.com
Electro Prismatic Collimators, Inc., 1441 Manatt St., Lincoln, NE 68521
Electronic Shooters Protection, Inc., 15290 Gadsden Ct., Brighton, CO 80603 / 800-797-7791; FAX: 303-659-8668
Electronic Trigger Systems, Inc., PO Box 13, 230 Main St. S., Hector, MN 55342 / 320-848-2760; FAX: 320-848-2760
Eley Ltd., P.O. Box 705, Witton, Birmingham, B6 7UT ENGLAND / 021-356-8899; FAX: 021-331-4173
Elite Ammunition, P.O. Box 3251, Oakbrook, IL 60522 / 708-366-9006
Ellett Bros., 267 Columbia Ave., P.O. Box 128, Chapin, SC 29036 / 803-345-3751; or 800-845-3711; FAX: 803-345-1820
Ellicott Arms, Inc. / Woods Pistolsmithing, 8390 Sunset Dr., Ellicott City, MD 21043 / 410-465-7979
Elliott Inc., G. W., 514 Burnside Ave., East Hartford, CT 06108 / 203-289-5741; FAX: 203-289-3137
EMAP USA, 6420 Wilshire Blvd., Los Angeles, CA 90048 / 213-782-2000; FAX: 213-782-2867
Emerging Technologies, Inc. (See Laseraim Technologies, Inc.)
EMF Co., Inc., 1900 E. Warner Ave., Suite 1-D, Santa Ana, CA 92705 / 949-261-6611; FAX: 949-756-0133
Empire Cutlery Corp., 12 Kruger Ct., Clifton, NJ 07013 / 201-472-5155; FAX: 201-779-0759
English, Inc., A.G., 708 S. 12th St., Broken Arrow, OK 74012 / 918-251-3399 agenglish@wedzone.net www.agenglish.com
Engraving Artistry, 36 Alto Rd., Burlington, CT 06013 / 203-673-6837 bobburt44@hotmail.com
Engraving Only, Box 55 Rabbit Gulch, Hill City, SD 57745 / 605-574-2239
Enguix Import-Export, Alpujarras 58, Alzira, Valencia, SPAIN / (96) 241 43 95; FAX: (96) 241 43 95
Enhanced Presentations, Inc., 5929 Market St., Wilmington, NC 28405 / 910-799-1622; FAX: 910-799-5004
Enlow, Charles, 895 Box, Beaver, OK 73932 / 405-625-4487
Entre`prise Arms, Inc., 15861 Business Center Dr., Irwindale, CA 91706
EPC, 1441 Manatt St., Lincoln, NE 68521 / 402-476-3946
Epps, Ellwood/Isabella, Box 341, Washago, ON L0K 2B0 CANADA / 705-689-5348
Erhardt, Dennis, 4508 N. Montana Ave., Helena, MT 59602 / 406-442-4533
Essex Arms, P.O. Box 363, Island Pond, VT 05846 / 802-723-6203; FAX: 802-723-6203
Estate Cartridge, Inc., 900 Bob Ehlen Dr., Anoka, MN 55303-7502 / 409-856-7277; FAX: 409-856-5486
Euber Bullets, No. Orwell Rd., Orwell, VT 05760 / 802-948-2621
Euroarms of America, Inc., P.O. Box 3277, Winchester, VA 22604 / 540-662-1863; FAX: 540-662-4464 www.euroarms.net
Euro-Imports, 905 W. Main St. E., El Cajon, CA 92020 / 619-442-7005; FAX: 619-442-7005
European American Armory Corp (See E.A.A. Corp)
Evans Engraving, Robert, 332 Vine St, Oregon City, OR 97045 / 503-656-5693 norbob-ore@msn.com
Eversull Co., Inc., 1 Tracemont, Boyce, LA 71409 / 318-793-8728; FAX: 318-793-5483 bestguns@aol.com
Evolution Gun Works Inc., 4050 B-8 Skyron Dr., Doylestown, PA 18901 / 215-348-9892; FAX: 215-348-1056 egw@pil.net www.egw-guns.com

Excalibur Electro Optics Inc., P.O. Box 400, Fogelsville, PA 18051-0400 / 610-391-9105; FAX: 610-391-9220
Excalibur Publications, P.O. Box 35369, Tucson, AZ 85740 / 520-575-9057 militarypubs@earthlink.net
Excel Industries Inc., 4510 Carter Ct., Chino, CA 91710 / 909-627-2404; FAX: 909-627-7817
Executive Protection Institute, P.O. Box 802, Berryville, VA 22611 / 540-554-2540 ruk.@creslink.net www.personalprotecion.com
Eze-Lap Diamond Prods., P.O. Box 2229, 15164 West State St., Westminster, CA 92683 / 714-847-1555; FAX: 714-897-0280
E-Z-Way Systems, PO Box 4310, Newark, OH 43058-4310 / 614-345-6645; or 800-848-2072; FAX: 614-345-6600

F

F.A.I.R., Via Gitti, 41, 25060 Marcheno (Bres, ITALY / 030/861162-8610344; FAX: 030/8610179 info@fair.it www.fair.it
F.I., Inc. - High Standard Mfg. Co., 5200 Mitchelldale St., Ste. E17, Houston, TX 77092-7222 / 713-462-4200; or 800-272-7816; FAX: 713-681-5665 info@highstandard.com www.highstandard.com
Fabarm S.p.A., Via Averolda 31, 25039 Travagliato, Brescia, ITALY / 030-6863629; FAX: 030-6863684 info@fabarm.com www.fabarm.com
Fagan & Co.Inc, 22952 15 Mile Rd., Clinton Township, MI 48035 / 810-465-4637; FAX: 810-792-6996
Faith Associates, PO Box 549, Flat Rock, NC 28731-0549 FAX: 828-697-6827
Faloon Industries, Inc., P.O. Box 1060, Tijeras, NM 87059 / 505-281-3783
Far North Outfitters, Box 1252, Bethel, AK 99559
Farm Form Decoys, Inc., 1602 Biovu, P.O. Box 748, Galveston, TX 77553 / 409-744-0762; or 409-765-6361; FAX: 409-765-8513
Farr Studio, Inc., 183 Hunters Rd., Washington, VA 22747-2001 / 615-638-8825
Farrar Tool Co., Inc., 11855 Cog Hill Dr., Whittier, CA 90601-1902 / 310-863-4367; FAX: 310-863-5123
Faulhaber Wildlocker, Dipl.-Ing. Norbert Wittasek, Seilergasse 2, A-1010 Wien, AUSTRIA / OM-43-1-5137001; FAX: 43-1-5137001 faulhaber1ut@net.at
Faulk's Game Call Co., Inc., 616 18th St., Lake Charles, LA 70601 / 318-436-9726; FAX: 318-494-7205
Faust Inc., T. G., 544 minor St, Reading, PA 19602 / 610-375-8549; FAX: 610-375-4488
Fautheree, Andy, P.O. Box 4607, Pagosa Springs, CO 81157 / 970-731-5003; FAX: 970-731-5009
Feather, Flex Decoys, 4500 Doniphan Dr., Neosho, MO 64850 / 318-746-8596; FAX: 318-742-4815
Federal Arms Corp. of America, 7928 University Ave., Fridley, MN 55432 / 612-780-8780; FAX: 612-780-8780
Federal Cartridge Co., 900 Ehlen Dr., Anoka, MN 55303 / 612-323-2300; FAX: 612-323-2506
Federal Champion Target Co., 232 Industrial Parkway, Richmond, IN 47374 / 800-441-4971; FAX: 317-966-7747
Federated-Fry (See Fry Metals)
FEG, Budapest, Soroksariut 158, H-1095, HUNGARY
Feinwerkbau Westinger & Altenburger, Neckarstrasse 43, 78727, Oberndorf a. N., GERMANY / 07423-814-0; FAX: 07423-814-200 info@feinwerkbau.de www.feinwerkbau.de
Feken, Dennis, Rt. 2, Box 124, Perry, OK 73077 / 405-336-5611
Felk Pistols Inc., 2121 Castlebridge Rd., Midlothian, VA 23113 / 804-794-3744; FAX: 208-988-4834
Fellowes, Ted, Beaver Lodge, 9245 16th Ave. SW, Seattle, WA 98106 / 206-763-1698
Ferguson, Bill, P.O. Box 1238, Sierra Vista, AZ 85636 / 520-458-5321; FAX: 520-458-9125
Ferguson, Bill. See: BULLET METALS
FERLIB, Via Parte 33 Marcheno/BS, Marcheno/BS, ITALY / 00390308610191; FAX: 00390308966882 info@ferlib.com www.ferlib.com
Ferris Firearms, 7110 F.M. 1863, Bulverde, TX 78163 / 210-980-4424
Fibron Products, Inc., P.O. Box 430, Buffalo, NY 14209-0430 / 716-886-2378; FAX: 716-886-2394
Fieldsport Ltd., Bryan Bilinski, 3313 W South Airport Rd., Traverse City, MI 49684 / 616-933-0767
Fiocchi Munizioni S.p.A. (See U.S. Importer-Fiocch
Fiocchi of America, Inc., 5030 Fremont Rd., Ozark, MO 65721 / 417-725-4118 or 800-721-2666; FAX: 417-725-1039
Firearms Co Ltd. / Alpine (See U.S. Importer-Mandall
Firearms Engraver's Guild of America, 332 Vine St., Oregon City, OR 97045 / 503-656-5693

Firearms International, 5709 Hartsdale, Houston, TX 77036 / 713-460-2447
First Inc., Jack, 1201 Turbine Dr., Rapid City, SD 57701 / 605-343-9544; FAX: 605-343-9420
Fisher, Jerry A., 631 Crane Mt. Rd., Big Fork, MT 59911 / 406-837-2722
Fisher Custom Firearms, 2199 S. Kittredge Way, Aurora, CO 80013 / 303-755-3710
Fitzgerald, Jack. See: CLENZOIL WORLDWIDE CORP
Flambeau Products Corp., 15981 Valplast Rd., Middlefield, OH 44062 / 216-632-1631; FAX: 216-632-1581
Flannery Engraving Co., Jeff W, 11034 Riddles Run Rd, Union, KY 41091 / 606-384-3127
Flayderman & Co., Inc., PO Box 2446, Ft Lauderdale, FL 33303 / 954-761-8855
Fleming Firearms, 7720 E 126th St. N, Collinsville, OK 74021-7016 / 918-665-3624
Fletcher-Bidwell, LLC., 305 E. Terhune St., Viroqua, WI 54665-1631 / 866-637-1860 fbguns@netscape.net
Flintlocks, Etc., 160 Rossiter Rd., P.O. Box 181, Richmond, MA 01254 / 413-698-3822; FAX: 413-698-3866 flintetc@berkshire.rr.com
Flitz International Ltd., 821 Mohr Ave., Waterford, WI 53185 / 414-534-5898; FAX: 414-534-2991
Fluoramics, Inc., 18 Industrial Ave., Mahwah, NJ 07430 / 800-922-0075; FAX: 201-825-7035
Flynn's Custom Guns, P.O. Box 7461, Alexandria, LA 71306 / 318-455-7130
FN Manufacturing, PO Box 24257, Columbia, SC 29224 / 803-736-0522
Folks, Donald E., 205 W. Lincoln St., Pontiac, IL 61764 / 815-844-7901
Foothills Video Productions, Inc., P.O. Box 651, Spartanburg, SC 29304 / 803-573-7023; or 800-782-5358
Foredom Electric Co., Rt. 6, 16 Stony Hill Rd., Bethel, CT 06801 / 203-792-8622
Forgett, Valmore. See: NAVY ARMS COMPANY
Forgreens Tool & Mfg., Inc., PO Box 955, Robert Lee, TX 76945 / 915-453-2800; FAX: 915-453-2460
Forkin, Ben (See Belt MTN Arms)
Forkin Arms, 205 10th Avenue S.W., White Sulphur Spring, MT 59645 / 406-547-2344
Forrest Inc., Tom, PO Box 326, Lakeside, CA 92040 / 619-561-5800; FAX: 619-561-0227
Forrest Tool Co., P.O. Box 768, 44380 Gordon Lane, Mendocino, CA 95460 / 707-937-2141; FAX: 717-937-1817
Forster, Kathy (See Custom Checkering)
Forster, Larry L., P.O. Box 212, 216 Highway 13 E., Gwinner, ND 58040-0212 / 701-678-2475
Forster Products, 310 E Lanark Ave, Lanark, IL 61046 / 815-493-6360; FAX: 815-493-2371
Fort Hill Gunstocks, 12807 Fort Hill Rd., Hillsboro, OH 45133 / 513-466-2763
Fort Knox Security Products, 1051 N. Industrial Park Rd., Orem, UT 84057 / 801-224-7233; or 800-821-5216; FAX: 801-226-5493
Fort Worth Firearms, 2006-B, Martin Luther King Fwy., Ft. Worth, TX 76104-6303 / 817-536-0718; FAX: 817-535-0290
Forthofer's Gunsmithing & Knifemaking, 5535 U.S. Hwy 93S, Whitefish, MT 59937-8411 / 406-862-2674
Fortune Products, Inc., 205 Hickory Creek Rd, Marble Falls, TX 78654 / 210-693-6111; FAX: 210-693-6394
Forty Five Ranch Enterprises, Box 1080, Miami, OK 74355-1080 / 918-542-5875
Foster, . See: ACCURACY INTERNATIONAL
Fountain Products, 492 Prospect Ave., West Springfield, MA 01089 / 413-781-4651; FAX: 413-733-8217
4-D Custom Die Co., 711 N. Sandusky St., PO Box 889, Mt. Vernon, OH 43050-0889 / 740-397-7214; FAX: 740-397-6600 info@ch4d.com ch4d.com
Fowler Bullets, 806 Dogwood Dr., Gastonia, NC 28054 / 704-867-3259
Fowler, Bob (See Black Powder Products)
Fox River Mills, Inc., P.O. Box 298, 227 Poplar St., Osage, IA 50461 / 515-732-3798; FAX: 515-732-5128
Foy Custom Bullets, 104 Wells Ave., Daleville, AL 36322
Francesca, Inc., 3115 Old Ranch Rd., San Antonio, TX 78217 / 512-826-2584; FAX: 512-826-8211
Franchi S.p.A., Via del Serpente 12, 25131, Brescia, ITALY / 030-3581833; FAX: 030-3581554
Francotte & Cie S.A. Auguste, rue de Trois Juin 109, 4400 Herstal-Liege, BELGIUM / 32-4-248-13-18; FAX: 32-4-948-11-79
Frank Knives, 13868 NW Keleka Pl., Seal Rock, OR 97376 / 541-563-3041; FAX: 541-563-3041
Frank Mittermeier, Inc., P.O. Box 2G, 3577 E. Tremont Ave., Bronx, NY 10465 / 718-828-3843

Franzen International,Inc (See U.S. Importer for)
Fred F. Wells/Wells Sport Store, 110 N Summit St., Prescott, AZ 86301 / 928-445-3655 www.wellssportstore@aol.com
Freedom Arms, Inc., P.O. Box 150, Freedom, WY 83120 / 307-883-2468; FAX: 307-883-2005
Fremont Tool Works, 1214 Prairie, Ford, KS 67842 / 316-369-2327
French, Artistic Engraving, J. R., 1712 Creek Ridge Ct, Irving, TX 75060 / 214-254-2654
Front Sight Firearms Training Institute, P.O. Box 2619, Aptos, CA 95001 / 800-987-7719; FAX: 408-684-2137
Frontier, 2910 San Bernardo, Laredo, TX 78040 / 956-723-5409; FAX: 956-723-1774
Frontier Arms Co.,Inc., 401 W. Rio Santa Cruz, Green Valley, AZ 85614-3932
Frontier Products Co., 2401 Walker Rd., Roswell, NM 88201-8950 / 614-262-9357
Frontier Safe Co., 3201 S. Clinton St., Fort Wayne, IN 46806 / 219-744-7233; FAX: 219-744-6678
Frost Cutlery Co., P.O. Box 22636, Chattanooga, TN 37422 / 615-894-6079; FAX: 615-894-9576
Fry Metals, 4100 6th Ave., Altoona, PA 16602 / 814-946-1611
Fujinon, Inc., 10 High Point Dr., Wayne, NJ 07470 / 201-633-5600; FAX: 201-633-5216
Fullmer, Geo. M., 2499 Mavis St., Oakland, CA 94601 / 510-533-4193
Fulmer's Antique Firearms, Chet, PO Box 792, Rt 2 Buffalo Lake, Detroit Lakes, MN 56501 / 218-847-7712
Fulton Armory, 8725 Bollman Place No. 1, Savage, MD 20763 / 301-490-9485; FAX: 301-490-9547
Furr Arms, 91 N. 970 W., Orem, UT 84057 / 801-226-3877; FAX: 801-226-3877

G

G C Bullet Co. Inc., 40 Mokelumne River Dr., Lodi, CA 95240
G&H Decoys,Inc., P.O. Box 1208, Hwy. 75 North, Henryetta, OK 74437 / 918-652-3314; FAX: 918-652-3400
G.G. & G., 3602 E. 42nd Stravenue, Tucson, AZ 85713 / 520-748-7167; FAX: 520-748-7583 ggg&3@aol.com www.ggg&3.com
G.H. Enterprises Ltd., Bag 10, Okotoks, AB T0L 1T0 CANADA / 403-938-6070
G.U. Inc (See U.S. Importer for New SKB Arms Co.)
G.W. Elliott, Inc., 514 Burnside Ave., East Hartford, CT 06108 / 203-289-5741; FAX: 203-289-3137
G96 Products Co., Inc., 85 5th Ave, Bldg. #6, Paterson, NJ 07544 / 973-684-4050; FAX: 973-684-3848 g96prod@aol
Gage Manufacturing, 663 W. 7th St., A, San Pedro, CA 90731 / 310-832-3546
Gaillard Barrels, P.O. Box 21, Pathlow, SK S0K 3B0 CANADA / 306-752-3769; FAX: 306-752-5969
Gain Twist Barrel Co. Rifle Works and Armory, 707 12th Street, Cody, WY 82414 / 307-587-4919; FAX: 307-527-6097
Galati International, P.O. Box 10, 616 Burley Ridge Rd., Wesco, MO 65586 / 636-584-0785; FAX: 573-775-4308 support@galatiinternational.com www.galatiinternational.com
Galaxy Imports Ltd., Inc., P.O. Box 3361, Victoria, TX 77903 / 361-573-4867; FAX: 361-576-9622 galaxy@cox_internet.com
GALCO International Ltd., 2019 W. Quail Ave., Phoenix, AZ 85027 / 602-258-8295; or 800-874-2526; FAX: 602-582-6854
Galena Industries AMT, 5463 Diaz St, Irwindale, CA 91706 / 626-856-8883; FAX: 626-856-8878
Gamba S.p.A. Societa Armi Bresciane Srl, Renato, Via Artigiani 93, ITALY / 30-8911640; FAX: 30-8911648
Gamba, USA, P.O. Box 60452, Colorado Springs, CO 80960 / 719-578-1145; FAX: 719-444-0731
Game Haven Gunstocks, 13750 Shire Rd., Wolverine, MI 49799 / 616-525-8257
Gamebore Division, Polywad Inc., P.O. Box 7916, Macon, GA 31209 / 478-477-0669 or 800-998-0669
Gamo (See U.S. Importers-Arms United Corp, Daisy M
Gamo USA, Inc., 3911 SW 47th Ave., Suite 914, Ft. Lauderdale, FL 33314 / 954-581-5822; FAX: 954-581-3165 gamousa@gate.net www.gamo.com
Gander Mountain, Inc., 12400 Fox River Rd., Wilmont, WI 53192 / 414-862-6848
GAR, 590 McBride Avenue, West Paterson, NJ 07424 / 973-754-1114; FAX: 973-754-1114 garreloading@aol.com
Garcia National Gun Traders, Inc., 225 SW 22nd Ave., Miami, FL 33135 / 305-642-2355

Garrett Cartridges, Inc., P.O. Box 178, Chehalis, WA 98532 / 360-736-0702 www.garrettcartridges.com

Garthwaite Pistolsmith, Inc., Jim, 12130 State Route 405, Watsontown, PA 17777 / 570-538-1566; FAX: 570-538-2965 www.garthwaite.com

Gary Goudy Classic Stocks, 1512 S. 5th St., Dayton, WA 99328 / 509-382-2726 goudy@innw.net

Gary Reeder Custom Guns, 2601 7th Avenue East, Flagstaff, AZ 86004 / 928-526-3313; FAX: 928-527-0840 gary@reedercustomguns.com www.reedercustomguns.com

Gary Schneider Rifle Barrels Inc., 12202 N. 62nd Pl., Scottsdale, AZ 85254 / 602-948-2525

Gator Guns & Repair, 7952 Kenai Spur Hwy., Kenai, AK 99611-8311

Gaucher Armes, S.A., 46 rue Desjoyaux, 42000, Saint-Etienne, FRANCE / 04-77-33-38-92; FAX: 04-77-61-95-72

GDL Enterprises, 409 Le Gardeur, Slidell, LA 70460 / 504-649-0693

Gehmann, Walter (See Huntington Die Specialties)

Genco, P.O. Box 5704, Asheville, NC 28803

Genecco Gun Works, 10512 Lower Sacramento Rd., Stockton, CA 95210 / 209-951-0706; FAX: 209-931-3872

Gene's Custom Guns, P.O. Box 10534, White Bear Lake, MN 55110 / 651-429-5105; FAX: 651-429-7365

Gentex Corp., 5 Tinkham Ave., Derry, NH 03038 / 603-434-0311; FAX: 603-434-3002 sales@derry.gentexcorp.com www.derry.gentexcorp.com

Gentner Bullets, 109 Woodlawn Ave., Upper Darby, PA 19082 / 610-352-9396

Gentry Custom Gunmaker, David, 314 N Hoffman, Belgrade, MT 59714 / 406-388-GUNS davidgent@mcn.net www.gentrycustom.com

George & Roy's, PO Box 2125, Sisters, OR 97759-2125 / 503-228-5424; or 800-553-3022; FAX: 503-225-9409

George E. Mathews & Son, Inc., 10224 S. Paramount Blvd., Downey, CA 90241 / 562-862-6719; FAX: 562-862-6719

George Hoenig, 6521 Morton Dr., Boise, ID 83704 / 208-375-1116; FAX: 208-375-1116

George Ibberson (Sheffield) Ltd., 25-31 Allen St., Sheffield, S3 7AW ENGLAND / 0114-2766123; FAX: 0114-2738465 sales@ebbintongroupco.uk www.eggintongroup.co.uk

George Madis Winchester Consultants, George Madis, P.O. Box 545, Brownsboro, TX 75756 / 903-852-6480; FAX: 903-852-3045 gmadis@earthlink.net www.georgemadis.com

Gerald Pettinger Books (See Pettinger Books), 47827 300th Ave., Russell, IA 50238 / 641-535-2239 gpettinger@lisco.com

Gerber Legendary Blades, 14200 SW 72nd Ave., Portland, OR 97223 / 503-639-6161; or 800-950-6161; FAX: 503-684-7008

Gervais, Mike, 3804 S. Cruise Dr., Salt Lake City, UT 84109 / 801-277-7729

Getz Barrel Co., P.O. Box 88, Beavertown, PA 17813 / 717-658-7263

Giacomo Sporting USA, 6234 Stokes Lee Center Rd., Lee Center, NY 13363

Gibbs Rifle Co., Inc., 211 Lawn St., Martinsburg, WV 25401 / 304-262-1651; FAX: 304-262-1658

Gil Hebard Guns Inc., 125 Public Square, Knoxville, IL 61448 / 309-289-2700; FAX: 309-289-2233

Gilbert Equipment Co., Inc., 960 Downtowner Rd., Mobile, AL 36609 / 205-344-3322

Gillmann, Edwin, 33 Valley View Dr., Hanover, PA 17331 / 717-632-1662 gillmaned@super-pa.net

Gilman-Mayfield, Inc., 3279 E. Shields, Fresno, CA 93703 / 209-221-9415; FAX: 209-221-9419

Gilmore Sports Concepts, 5949 S. Garnett, Tulsa, OK 74146 / 918-250-3810; FAX: 918-250-3845 gilmore@webzone.net www.gilmoresports.com

Giron, Robert E., 12671 Cousins Rd.., Peosta, IA 52068 / 412-731-6041

Glacier Glove, 4890 Aircenter Circle, Suite 210, Reno, NV 89502 / 702-825-8225; FAX: 702-825-6544

Glaser LLC, P.O. Box 173, Sturgis, SD 57785 / 605-347-4544 or 800-221-3489; FAX: 605-347-5055 email@corbon.com www.safetyslug.com

Glaser Safety Slug, Inc., PO Box 8223, Foster City, CA 94404 / 800-221-3489; FAX: 510-785-6685 safetyslug.com

Glass, Herb, PO Box 25, Bullville, NY 10915 / 914-361-3021

Glimm, Jerome. See: GLIMM'S CUSTOM GUN ENGRAVING

Glimm's Custom Gun Engraving, Jerome C. Glimm, 19 S. Maryland, Conrad, MT 59425 / 406-278-3574 jandlglimm@mcn.net

Glock GmbH, P.O. Box 50, A-2232, Deutsch Wagram, AUSTRIA

Glock, Inc., PO Box 369, Smyrna, GA 30081 / 770-432-1202; FAX: 770-433-8719

Glynn Scobey Duck & Goose Calls, Rt. 3, Box 37, Newbern, TN 38059 / 731-643-6128

GML Products, Inc., 394 Laredo Dr., Birmingham, AL 35226 / 205-979-4867

Gner's Hard Cast Bullets, 1107 11th St., LaGrande, OR 97850 / 503-963-8796

Goens, Dale W., P.O. Box 224, Cedar Crest, NM 87008 / 505-281-5419

Goergen's Gun Shop, Inc., 17985 538th Ave., Austin, MN 55912 / 507-433-9280; FAX: 507-433-9280

GOEX, Inc., P.O. Box 659, Doyline, LA 71023-0659 / 318-382-9300; FAX: 318-382-9303 mfahringer@goexpowder.com www.goexpowder.com

Golden Age Arms Co., 115 E. High St., Ashley, OH 43003 / 614-747-2488

Golden Bear Bullets, 3065 Fairfax Ave., San Jose, CA 95148 / 408-238-9515

Gonic Arms/North American Arm, 134 Flagg Rd., Gonic, NH 03839 / 603-332-8456 or 603-332-8457

Goodling's Gunsmithing, 1950 Stoverstown Road, Spring Grove, PA 17362 / 717-225-3350

Goodwin, Fred. See: GOODWIN'S GUN SHOP

Goodwin's Gun Shop, Fred Goodwin, Sherman Mills, ME 04776 / 207-365-4451

Gotz Bullets, 11426 Edgemere Ter., Roscoe, IL 61073-8232

Gould & Goodrich, 709 E. McNeil, Lillington, NC 27546 / 910-893-2071; FAX: 910-893-4742

Gournet Artistic Engraving, Geoffroy Gournet, 820 Paxinosa Ave., Easton, PA 18042 / 610-559-0710 www.geoffroygournet.com

Gournet, Geoffroy. See: GOURNET ARTISTIC ENGRAVING

Grace, Charles E., 1006 Western Ave., Trinidad, CO 81082 / 719-846-9435

Grace Metal Products, P.O. Box 67, Elk Rapids, MI 49629 / 616-264-8133

Graf & Sons, 4050 S Clark St., Mexico, MO 65265 / 573-581-2266; FAX: 573-581-2875

Grand Slam Hunting Products, Box 121, 25454 Military Rd., Cascade, MD 21719 / 301-241-4900; FAX: 301-241-4900 rlj6call@aol.com

Granite Mountain Arms, Inc., 3145 W Hidden Acres Trail, Prescott, AZ 86305 / 520-541-9758; FAX: 520-445-6826

Grant, Howard V., Hiawatha 15, Woodruff, WI 54568 / 715-356-7146

Graphics Direct, P.O. Box 372421, Reseda, CA 91337-2421 / 818-344-9002

Graves Co., 1800 Andrews Ave., Pompano Beach, FL 33069 / 800-327-9103; FAX: 305-960-0301

Grayback Wildcats, Mike Beeks, 5306 Bryant Ave., Klamath Falls, OR 97603 / 541-884-1072

Graybill's Gun Shop, 1035 Ironville Pike, Columbia, PA 17512 / 717-684-2739

Great American Gunstock Co., 3420 Industrial Drive, Yuba City, CA 95993 / 800-784-4867; FAX: 530-671-3906 gunstox@oro.net www.gunstocks.com

Great Lakes Airguns, 6175 S. Park Ave, Hamburg, NY 14075 / 716-648-6666; FAX: 716-648-6666 www.greatlakesairguns.com

Green, Arthur S., 485 S. Robertson Blvd., Beverly Hills, CA 90211 / 310-274-1283

Green, Roger M., P.O. Box 984, 435 E. Birch, Glenrock, WY 82637 / 307-436-9804

Green Head Game Call Co., RR 1, Box 33, Lacon, IL 61540 / 309-246-2155

Green Mountain Rifle Barrel Co., Inc., P.O. Box 2670, 153 West Main St., Conway, NH 03818 / 603-447-1095; FAX: 603-447-1099

Greenwood Precision, P.O. Box 407, Rogersville, MO 65742 / 417-725-2330

Greg Gunsmithing Repair, 3732 26th Ave. North, Robbinsdale, MN 55422 / 612-529-8103

Greg's Superior Products, P.O. Box 46219, Seattle, WA 98146

Greider Precision, 431 Santa Marina Ct., Escondido, CA 92029 / 760-480-8892; FAX: 760-480-9800 greider@msn.com

Gremmel Enterprises, 2111 Carriage Drive, Eugene, OR 97408-7537 / 541-302-3000

Gre-Tan Rifles, 29742 W.C.R. 50, Kersey, CO 80644 / 970-353-6176; FAX: 970-356-5940 www.gtrtooling.com

Grier's Hard Cast Bullets, 1107 11th St., LaGrande, OR 97850 / 503-963-8796

Griffin & Howe, Inc., 36 W. 44th St., Suite 1011, New York, NY 10036 / 212-921-0980 info@griffinhowe.com www.griffinhowe.com

Griffin & Howe, Inc., 33 Claremont Rd., Bernardsville, NJ 07924 / 908-766-2287; FAX: 908-766-1068 info@griffinhowe.com www.griffinhowe.com

Griffin & Howe, Inc., 340 W Putnam Avenue, Greenwich, CT 06830 / 203-618-0270 info@griffinhowe.com www.griffinhowe.com

Grifon, Inc., 58 Guinam St., Waltham, MS 02154

Groenewold, John, P.O. Box 830, Mundelein, IL 60060 / 847-566-2365; FAX: 847-566-4065 jgairguns@direcway.com http://jwww.gairguns.aupal.com/augmpubl.

GRS / Glendo Corp., P.O. Box 1153, 900 Overlander St., Emporia, KS 66801 / 620-343-1084; or 800-836-3519; FAX: 620-343-9640 glendo@glendo.com www.glendo.com

Grulla Armes, Apartado 453, Avda Otaloa 12, Eiber, SPAIN

Gruning Precision Inc., 7101 Jurupa Ave., No. 12, Riverside, CA 92504 / 909-289-4371; FAX: 909-689-7791 gruningprecision@earthlink.net www.gruningprecision.com

GSI, Inc., 7661 Commerce Ln., Trussville, AL 35173 / 205-655-8299

GTB, 482 Comerwood Court, San Francisco, CA 94080 / 650-583-1550

Guarasi, Robert. See: WILCOX INDUSTRIES CORP.

Guardsman Products, 411 N. Darling, Fremont, MI 49412 / 616-924-3950

Gun City, 212 W. Main Ave., Bismarck, ND 58501 / 701-223-2304

Gun Hunter Books (See Gun Hunter Trading Co.), 5075 Heisig St., Beaumont, TX 77705 / 409-835-3006; FAX: 409-838-2266 gunhuntertrading@hotmail.com

Gun Hunter Trading Co., 5075 Heisig St., Beaumont, TX 77705 / 409-835-3006; FAX: 409-838-2266 gunhuntertrading@hotmail.com

Gun Leather Limited, 116 Lipscomb, Ft. Worth, TX 76104 / 817-334-0225; FAX: 800-247-0609

Gun List (See Krause Publications), 700 E State St., Iola, WI 54945 / 715-445-2214; FAX: 715-445-4087

Gun South, Inc. (See GSI, Inc.)

Gun Vault, 7339 E Acoma Dr., Ste. 7, Scottsdale, AZ 85260 / 602-951-6855

Gun-Alert, 1010 N. Maclay Ave., San Fernando, CA 91340 / 818-365-0864; FAX: 818-365-1308

Guncraft Books (See Guncraft Sports Inc.), 10737 Dutchtown Rd, Knoxville, TN 37932 / 865-966-4545; FAX: 865-966-4500 findit@guncraft.com www.usit.net/guncraft

Guncraft Sports Inc., 10737 Dutchtown Rd., Knoxville, TN 37932 / 865-966-4545; FAX: 865-966-4500 findit@guncraft.com www.usit.net/guncraft

Guncraft Sports, Inc., Marie C. Wiest, 10737 Dutchtown Rd., Knoxville, TN 37932 / 865-966-4545; FAX: 865-966-4500 www.guncraft.com

Gunfitters, P.O. Box 426, Cambridge, WI 53523-0426 / 608-764-8128 gunfitters@aol.com www.gunfitters.com

Gun-Ho Sports Cases, 110 E. 10th St., St. Paul, MN 55101 / 612-224-9491

Gunline Tools, 2950 Saturn St., "O", Brea, CA 92821 / 714-993-5100; FAX: 714-572-4128

Gunnerman Books, P.O. Box 81697, Rochester Hills, MI 48308 / 989-729-7018

Guns Antique & Modern DBA / Charles E. Duffy, Williams Lane, West Hurley, NY 12491 / 914-679-2997

Guns Div. of D.C. Engineering, Inc., 8633 Southfield Fwy., Detroit, MI 48228 / 313-271-7111 or 800-886-7623; FAX: 313-271-7112 guns@rifletech.com www.rifletech.com

GUNS Magazine, 591 Camino de la Reina, Suite 200, San Diego, CA 92108 / 619-297-5350; FAX: 619-297-5353

Gunsite Custom Shop, P.O. Box 451, Paulden, AZ 86334 / 520-636-4104; FAX: 520-636-1236

Gunsite Gunsmithy (See Gunsite Custom Shop)

Gunsite Training Center, P.O. Box 700, Paulden, AZ 86334 / 520-636-4565; FAX: 520-636-1236

Gunsmithing Ltd., 57 Unquowa Rd., Fairfield, CT 06430 / 203-254-0436; FAX: 203-254-1535

Gunsmithing, Inc., 30 West Buchanan St., Colorado Springs, CO 80907 / 719-632-3795; FAX: 719-632-3493

Gurney, F. R., Box 13, Sooke, BC V0S 1N0 CANADA / 604-642-5282; FAX: 604-642-7859

H

H&B Forge Co., Rt. 2, Geisinger Rd., Shiloh, OH 44878 / 419-895-1856

H&P Publishing, 7174 Hoffman Rd., San Angelo, TX 76905 / 915-655-5953

H&R 1871.LLC, 60 Industrial Rowe, Gardner, MA 01440 / 508-632-9393; FAX: 508-632-2300 hr1871@hr1871.com www.hr1871.com

H&S Liner Service, 515 E. 8th, Odessa, TX 79761 / 915-332-1021

H. Krieghoff Gun Co., Boschstrasse 22, D-89079, Ulm, GERMANY / 731-401820; FAX: 731-4018270

H.K.S. Products, 7841 Founion Dr., Florence, KY 41042 / 606-342-7841; or 800-354-9814; FAX: 606-342-5865

H.P. White Laboratory, Inc., 3114 Scarboro Rd., Street, MD 21154 / 410-838-6550; FAX: 410-838-2802

Hafner World Wide, Inc., PO Box 1987, Lake City, FL 32055 / 904-755-6481; FAX: 904-755-6595 hafner@isgroupe.net

Hakko Co. Ltd., 1-13-12, Narimasu, Itabashiku Tokyo, JAPAN / 03-5997-7870/2; FAX: 81-3-5997-7840

Half Moon Rifle Shop, 490 Halfmoon Rd., Columbia Falls, MT 59912 / 406-892-4409 halfmoonrs@centurytel.net

Hall Manufacturing, 142 CR 406, Clanton, AL 35045 / 205-755-4094

Hall Plastics, Inc., John, P.O. Box 1526, Alvin, TX 77512 / 713-489-8709

Hallberg, Fritz. See: CAMBOS OUTDOORSMAN

Hallowell & Co., P.O. Box 1445, Livingston, MT 59047 / 406-222-4770; FAX: 406-222-4792 morris@hallowellco.com www.hallowellco.com

Hally Caller, 443 Wells Rd., Doylestown, PA 18901 / 215-345-6354; FAX: 215-345-8892 info@hallycaller.com www.hallycaller.com

Hamilton, Alex B (See Ten-Ring Precision, Inc)

Hammans, Charles E., P.O. Box 788, 2022 McCracken, Stuttgart, AR 72160-0788 / 870-673-1388

Hammerli Ltd., Seonerstrasse 37, CH-5600, SWITZERLAND / 064-50 11 44; FAX: 064-51 38 27

Hammerli Service-Precision Mac, Rudolf Marent, 9711 Tiltree St., Houston, TX 77075 / 713-946-7028

Hammerli USA, 19296 Oak Grove Circle, Groveland, CA 95321 FAX: 209-962-5311

Hammond Custom Guns Ltd., 619 S. Pandora, Gilbert, AZ 85234 / 602-892-3437

HandCrafts Unltd (See Clements' Custom Leather), 1741 Dallas St, Aurora, CO 80010-2018 / 303-364-0403; FAX: 303-739-9824 gryphons@home.com kuntaoslcat.com

Handgun Press, P.O. Box 406, Glenview, IL 60025 / 847-657-6500; FAX: 847-724-8831 handgunpress@earth-link.net

Hank's Gun Shop, Box 370, 50 West 100 South, Monroe, UT 84754 / 801-527-4456

Hanned Precision (See The Hanned Line)

Hansen & Co., 244-246 Old Post Rd., Southport, CT 06490 / 203-259-6222; FAX: 203-254-3832

Hanson's Gun Center, Dick, 233 Everett Dr, Colorado Springs, CO 80911

Hanusin, John, 3306 Commercial, Northbrook, IL 60062 / 708-564-2706

Harford (See U.S. Importer-EMF Co. Inc.)

Harper's Custom Stocks, 928 Lombrano St., San Antonio, TX 78207 / 210-732-7174

Harrell's Precision, 5756 Hickory Dr., Salem, VA 24153 / 540-380-2683

Harrington & Richardson (See H&R 1871, Inc.)

Harris Engineering Inc., Dept GD54, Barlow, KY 42024 / 502-334-3633; FAX: 502-334-3000

Harris Enterprises, P.O. Box 105, Bly, OR 97622 / 503-353-2625

Harris Gunworks, 11240 N. Cave Creek Rd., Ste. 104, Phoenix, AZ 85020 / 602-582-9627; FAX: 602-582-5178

Harris Hand Engraving, Paul A., 113 Rusty Ln., Boerne, TX 78006-5746 / 512-391-5121

Harris Publications, 1115 Broadway, New York, NY 10010 / 212-807-7100; FAX: 212-627-4678

Harrison Bullets, 6437 E. Hobart St., Mesa, AZ 85205

Harry Lawson Co., 3328 N. Richey Blvd., Tucson, AZ 85716 / 520-326-1117

Hart & Son, Inc., Robert W., 401 Montgomery St., Nescopeck, PA 18635 / 717-752-3655; FAX: 717-752-1088

Hart Rifle Barrels,Inc., PO Box 182, 1690 Apulia Rd., Lafayette, NY 13084 / 315-677-9841; FAX: 315-677-9610 hartrb@aol.com hartbarrels.com

Hartford (See U.S. Importer-EMF Co. Inc.)

Hartmann & Weiss GmbH, Rahlstedter Bahnhofstr. 47, 22143, Hamburg, GERMANY / (40) 677 55 85; FAX: (40) 677 55 92 hartmannundweisst-online.de

Harvey, Frank, 218 Nightfall, Terrace, NV 89015 / 702-558-6998

Harwood, Jack O., 1191 S. Pendlebury Lane, Blackfoot, ID 83221 / 208-785-5368

Hastings, P.O. Box 224, Clay Center, KS 67432 / 785-632-3169; FAX: 785-632-6554

Hatfield Gun, 224 N. 4th St., St. Joseph, MO 64501

Hawk Laboratories, Inc. (See Hawk, Inc.), 849 Hawks Bridge Rd, Salem, NJ 08079 / 609-299-2700; FAX: 609-299-2800

Hawk, Inc., 849 Hawks Bridge Rd., Salem, NJ 08079 / 609-299-2700; FAX: 609-299-2800

Hawken Shop, The (See Dayton Traister)

Haydel's Game Calls, Inc., 5018 Hazel Jones Rd., Bossier City, LA 71111 / 318-746-3586; FAX: 318-746-3711

Haydon Shooters Supply, Russ, 15018 Goodrich Dr. NW, Gig Harbor, WA 98329-9738 / 253-857-7557; FAX: 253-857-7884

Heatbath Corp., P.O. Box 2978, Springfield, MA 01101 / 413-543-3381

Hecht, Hubert J, Waffen-Hecht, PO Box 2635, Fair Oaks, CA 95628 / 916-966-1020

Heckler & Koch GmbH, PO Box 1329, 78722 Oberndorf, Neckar, GERMANY / 49-7423179-0; FAX: 49-7423179-2406

Heckler & Koch, Inc., 21480 Pacific Blvd., Sterling, VA 20166-8900 / 703-450-1900; FAX: 703-450-8160 www.hecklerkoch-usa.com

Hege Jagd-u. Sporthandels GmbH, P.O. Box 101461, W-7770, Ueberlingen a. Boden, GERMANY

Heidenstrom Bullets, Dalghte 86-3660 Rjukan, 35091818, NORWAY, olau.joh@online.tuo

Heilmann, Stephen, P.O. Box 657, Grass Valley, CA 95945 / 530-272-8758; FAX: 530-274-0285 sheilmann@jps.net www.metalwood.com

Heinie Specialty Products, 301 Oak St., Quincy, IL 62301-2500 / 217-228-9500; FAX: 217-228-9502 rheinie@heinie.com www.heinie.com

Helwan (See U.S. Importer-Interarms)

Henigson & Associates, Steve, PO Box 2726, Culver City, CA 90231 / 310-305-8288; FAX: 310-305-1905

Henriksen Tool Co., Inc., 8515 Wagner Creek Rd., Talent, OR 97540 / 541-535-2309; FAX: 541-535-2309

Henry Repeating Arms Co., 110 8th St., Brooklyn, NY 11215 / 718-499-5600

Hensley, Gunmaker, Darwin, PO Box 329, Brightwood, OR 97011 / 503-622-5411

Heppler, Keith. See: KEITH'S CUSTOM GUNSTOCKS

Hercules, Inc. (See Alliant Techsystems, Smokeless)

Heritage Firearms (See Heritage Mfg., Inc.)

Heritage Manufacturing, Inc., 4600 NW 135th St., Opa Locka, FL 33054 or 305-685-5966; FAX: 305-687-6721 infohmi@heritagemfg.com www.heritagemfg.com

Heritage/VSP Gun Books, P.O. Box 887, McCall, ID 83638 / 208-634-4104; FAX: 208-634-3101

Herrett's Stocks, Inc., P.O. Box 741, Twin Falls, ID 83303 / 208-733-1498

Herter's Manufacturing Inc., 111 E. Burnett St., P.O. Box 518, Beaver Dam, WI 53916-1811 / 414-887-1765; FAX: 414-887-8444

Hesco-Meprolight, 2139 Greenville Rd., LaGrange, GA 30241 / 706-884-7967; FAX: 706-882-4683

Hesse Arms, Robert Hesse, 1126 70th Street E., Inver Grove Heights, MN 55077-2416 / 651-455-5760; FAX: 612-455-5760

Hesse, Robert. See: HESSE ARMS

Heydenberk, Warren R., 1059 W. Sawmill Rd., Quakertown, PA 18951 / 215-538-2682

Hickman, Jaclyn, Box 1900, Glenrock, WY 82637

Hidalgo, Tony, 12701 SW 9th Pl., Davie, FL 33325 / 954-476-7645

High Bridge Arms, Inc, 3185 Mission St., San Francisco, CA 94110 / 415-282-8358

High North Products, Inc., P.O. Box 2, Antigo, WI 54409 / 715-627-2331; FAX: 715-623-5451

High Performance International, 5734 W. Florist Ave., Milwaukee, WI 53218 / 414-466-9040

High Precision, Bud Welsh, 80 New Road, E. Amherst, NY 14051 / 716-688-6344; FAX: 716-688-0425 welsh5168@aol.com www.high-precision.com

High Tech Specialties, Inc., P.O. Box 839, 293 E Main St., Rear, Adamstown, PA 19501 / 717-484-0405; FAX: 717-484-0523 bansner@aol.com www.bansmersrifle.com/hightech

Highline Machine Co., Randall Thompson, 654 Lela Place, Grand Junction, CO 81504 / 970-434-4971

Highwood Special Products, 1531 E. Highwood, Pontiac, MI 48340

Hi-Grade Imports, 8655 Monterey Rd., Gilroy, CA 95021 / 408-842-9301; FAX: 408-842-2374

Hill, Loring F., 304 Cedar Rd., Elkins Park, PA 19027

Hill Speed Leather, Ernie, 4507 N 195th Ave, Litchfield Park, AZ 85340 / 602-853-9222; FAX: 602-853-9235

Hinman Outfitters, Bob, 107 N Sanderson Ave, Bartonville, IL 61607-1839 / 309-691-8132

Hi-Performance Ammunition Company, 484 State Route 366, Apollo, PA 15613 / 412-327-8100

HIP-GRIP Barami Corp., P.O. Box 252224, West Bloomfield, MI 48325-2224 / 248-738-0462; FAX: 248-738-2542 hipgripja@aol.com www.hipgrip.com

Hi-Point Firearms/MKS Supply, 8611-A North Dixie Dr., Dayton, OH 45414 / 877-425-4867; FAX: 937-454-0503 www.hi-pointfirearms.com

Hiptmayer, Armurier, RR 112 750, P.O. Box 136, Eastman, PQ JOE 1P0 CANADA / 514-297-2492

Hiptmayer, Heidemarie, RR 112 750, P.O. Box 136, Eastman, PQ JOE 1P0 CANADA / 514-297-2492

Hiptmayer, Klaus, RR 112 750, P.O. Box 136, Eastman, PQ JOE 1P0 CANADA / 514-297-2492

Hirtenberger AG, Leobersdorferstrasse 31, A-2552, Hirtenberg, / 43(0)2256 81184; FAX: 43(0)2256 81808 www.hirtenberger.ot

HiTek International, 484 El Camino Real, Redwood City, CA 94063 / 415-363-1404; or 800-54-NIGHT; FAX: 415-363-1408

Hiti-Schuch, Atelier Wilma, A-8863 Predlitz, Pirming, Y1 AUSTRIA / 0353418278

HJS Arms, Inc., P.O. Box 3711, Brownsville, TX 78523-3711 / 956-542-2767; FAX: 956-542-2767

Hoag, James W., 8523 Canoga Ave., Suite C, Canoga Park, CA 91304 / 818-998-1510

Hobson Precision Mfg. Co., 210 Big Oak Ln, Brent, AL 35034 / 205-926-4662; FAX: 205-926-3193 cahobbob@dbtech.com

Hodgdon Powder Co., 6231 Robinson, Shawnee Mission, KS 66202 / 913-362-9455; FAX: 913-362-1307

Hodgman, Inc., 1750 Orchard Rd., Montgomery, IL 60538 / 708-897-7555; FAX: 708-897-7558

Hodgson, Richard, 9081 Tahoe Lane, Boulder, CO 80301

Hoehn Sales, Inc., 2045 Kohn Road, Wright City, MO 63390 / 636-745-8144; FAX: 636-745-8144 hoehnsal@usmo.com

Hofer Jagdwaffen, P., Buchsenmachermeister, Kirchgasse 24, A-9170 Ferlach, AUSTRIA / 43 4227 3683; FAX: 43 4227 368330 peterhofer@hoferwaffen.com www.hoferwaffen.com

Hoffman New Ideas, 821 Northmoor Rd., Lake Forest, IL 60045 / 312-234-4075

Hogue Grips, P.O. Box 1138, Paso Robles, CA 93447 / 800-438-4747 or 805-239-1440; FAX: 805-239-2553

Holland & Holland Ltd., 33 Bruton St., London, ENGLAND / 44-171-499-4411; FAX: 44-171-408-7962

Holland's Gunsmithing, P.O. Box 69, Powers, OR 97466 / 541-439-5155; FAX: 541-439-5155

Hollinger, Jon. Sec: ASPEN OUTFITTING CO.

Hollywood Engineering, 10642 Arminta St., Sun Valley, CA 91352 / 818-842-8376; FAX: 818-504-4168

Homak, 5151 W. 73rd St., Chicago, IL 60638-6613 / 312-523-3100; FAX: 312-523-9455

Home Shop Machinist, The Village Press Publications, P.O. Box 1810, Traverse City, MI 49685 / 800-447-7367; FAX: 616-946-3289

Hondo Ind., 510 S. 52nd St., I04, Tempe, AZ 85281

Hoppe's Div. Penguin Industries, Inc., P.O. Box 1690, Oregon City, OR 97045-0690 / 610-384-6000

Horizons Unlimited, P.O. Box 426, Warm Springs, GA 31830 / 706-655-3603; FAX: 706-655-3603

Hornady Mfg. Co., P.O. Box 1848, Grand Island, NE 68802 / 800-338-3220 or 308-382-1390; FAX: 308-382-5761

Horseshoe Leather Products, Andy Arratoonian, The Cottage Sharow, Ripon U.K., ENGLAND U.K. / 44-1765-605858 andy@horseshoe.co.uk www.horseshoe.co.uk

House of Muskets, Inc., The, PO Box 4640, Pagosa Springs, CO 81157 / 970-731-2295

Houtz & Barwick, P.O. Box 435, W. Church St., Elizabeth City, NC 27909 / 800-775-0337; or 919-335-4191; FAX: 919-335-1152

Howa Machinery, Ltd., Sukaguchi, Shinkawa-cho Nishikasugai-gun, Aichi 452-8601, JAPAN / 81-52-408-1231; FAX: 81-52-409-4855 howa@howa.co.jp http://www.howa.cojpl

Howell Machine, 815 1/2 D St., Lewiston, ID 83501 / 208-743-7418

H-S Precision, Inc., 1301 Turbine Dr., Rapid City, SD 57701 / 605-341-3006; FAX: 605-342-8964

HT Bullets, 244 Belleville Rd., New Bedford, MA 02745 / 508-999-3338

Hubert J. Hecht Waffen-Hecht, P.O. Box 2635, Fair Oaks, CA 95628 / 916-966-1020

Huebner, Corey O., PO Box 564, Frenchtown, MT 59834 / 406-721-7168

Huey Gun Cases, 820 Indiana St., Lawrence, KS 66044-2645 / 816-444-1637; FAX: 816-444-1637 hueycases@aol.com www.hueycases.com

Hume, Don, P.O. Box 351, Miami, OK 74355 / 800-331-2686; FAX: 918-542-4340 info@donhume.com www.donhume.com

Hunkeler, A (See Buckskin Machine Works, 3235 S 358th St., Auburn, WA 98001 / 206-927-5412

MANUFACTURER'S DIRECTORY

Hunter Co., Inc., 3300 W. 71st Ave., Westminster, CO 80030 / 303-427-4626; FAX: 303-428-3980

Hunterjohn, PO Box 771457, St. Louis, MO 63177 / 314-531-7250

Hunter's Specialties Inc., 6000 Huntington Ct. NE, Cedar Rapids, IA 52402-1268 / 319-395-0321; FAX: 319-395-0326

Hunters Supply, Inc., P.O. Box 313, Tioga, TX 76271 / 940-437-2458; FAX: 940-437-2228 hunterssupply@hotmail.com www.hunterssupply.net

Huntington Die Specialties, 601 Oro Dam Blvd., Oroville, CA 95965 / 530-534-1210; FAX: 530-534-1212 buy@huntingtons.com www.huntingtons.com

Hutton Rifle Ranch, P.O. Box 170317, Boise, ID 83717 / 208-345-8781 www.martinbrevik@aol.com

Hydrosorbent Products, PO Box 437, Ashley Falls, MA 01222 / 800-448-7903; FAX: 413-229-8743 orders@dehumidify.com www.dehumidify.com

I

I.A.B. (See U.S. Importer-Taylor's & Co. Inc.)

I.D.S.A. Books, 1324 Stratford Drive, Piqua, OH 45356 / 937-773-4203; FAX: 937-778-1922

I.N.C. Inc (See Kickeez I.N.C., Inc.)

I.S.S., P.O. Box 185234, Ft. Worth, TX 76181 / 817-595-2090; FAX: 817-595-2090 iss@concentric.net

I.S.W., 106 E. Cairo Dr., Tempe, AZ 85282

IAR Inc., 33171 Camino Capistrano, San Juan Capistrano, CA 92675 / 949-443-3642; FAX: 949-443-3647 sales@iar-arms.com iar-arms.com

Ide, K. See: STURGEON VALLEY SPORTERS

IGA (See U.S. Importer-Stoeger Industries)

Ignacio Ugartechea S.A., Chonta 26, Eibar, 20600 SPAIN / 43-121257; FAX: 43-121669

Image Ind. Inc., 382 Balm Court, Wood Dale, IL 60191 / 630-766-2402; FAX: 630-766-7373

Impact Case & Container, Inc., P.O. Box 1129, Rathdrum, ID 83858 / 877-687-2452; FAX: 208-687-0632 bradk@icc-case.com www.icc-case.com

Imperial (See E-Z-Way Systems), PO Box 4310, Newark, OH 43058-4310 / 614-345-6645; FAX: 614-345-6600 ezway@infinet.com www.jcunald.com

Imperial Magnum Corp., P.O. Box 249, Oroville, WA 98844 / 604-495-3131; FAX: 604-495-2816

Imperial Miniature Armory, 10547 S. Post Oak Road, Houston, TX 77035-3305 / 713-729-8428; FAX: 713-729-2274 miniguns@aol.com www.1800miniature.com

Imperial Schrade Corp., 7 Schrade Ct., Box 7000, Ellenville, NY 12428 / 914-647-7601; FAX: 914-647-8701 csc@schradeknives.com www.schradeknives.com

Import Sports Inc., 1750 Brielle Ave., Unit B1, Wanamassa, NJ 07712 / 908-493-0302; FAX: 908-493-0301

IMR Powder Co., 1080 Military Turnpike, Suite 2, Plattsburgh, NY 12901 / 518-563-2253; FAX: 518-563-6916

Info-Arm, P.O. Box 1262, Champlain, NY 12919 / 514-955-0355; FAX: 514-955-0357

Ingle, Ralph W., Engraver, 112 Manchester Ct., Centerville, GA 31028 / 478-953-5824 riengraver@aol.com www.fega.com

Innovative Weaponry Inc., 2513 E. Loop 820 N., Fort Worth, TX 76118 / 817-284-0099 or 800-334-3573

INTEC International, Inc., P.O. Box 5708, Scottsdale, AZ 85261 / 602-483-1708

Inter Ordnance of America LP, 3305 Westwood Industrial Dr, Monroe, NC 28110-5204 / 704-821-8337; FAX: 704-821-8523

Intercontinental Distributors, Ltd., PO Box 815, Beulah, ND 58523

Intrac Arms International, 5005 Chapman Hwy., Knoxville, TN 37920

Ion Industries, Inc., 3508 E Allerton Ave., Cudahy, WI 53110 / 414-486-2007; FAX: 414-486-2017

Iosso Products, 1485 Lively Blvd., Elk Grove Village, IL 60007 / 847-437-8400; FAX: 847-437-8478

Iron Bench, 12619 Bailey Rd., Redding, CA 96003 / 916-241-4623

Ironside International Publishers, Inc., 3000 S. Eaos St., Arlington, VA 22202 / 703-684-6111; FAX: 703-683-5486

Ironsighter Co., P.O. Box 85070, Westland, MI 48185 / 734-326-8731; FAX: 734-326-3378 www.ironsighter.com

Irwin, Campbell H., 140 Hartland Blvd., East Hartland, CT 06027 / 203-653-3901

Island Pond Gun Shop, Cross St., Island Pond, VT 05846 / 802-723-4546

Israel Arms International, Inc., 1085 Gessner Rd., Ste. F, Houston, TX 77055 / 713-789-0745; FAX: 713-914-9515 iaipro@wt.net www.israelarms.com

Ithaca Classic Doubles, Stephen Lamboy, No. 5 Railroad St., Victor, NY 14564 / 716-924-2710; FAX: 716-924-2737 ithacadoubles.com

Ithaca Gun Company LLC, 901 Rt. 34 B, King Ferry, NY 13081 / 315-364-7171; FAX: 315-364-5134 info@ithacagun.com

Ivanoff, Thomas G. (See Tom's Gun Repair)

J

J J Roberts Firearm Engraver, 7808 Lake Dr, Manassas, VA 20111 / 703-330-0448; FAX: 703-264-8600 james..roberts@angelfire.com www.angelfire.com/va2/engraver

J&D Components, 75 East 350 North, Orem, UT 84057-4719 / 801-225-7007

J&J Products, Inc., 9240 Whitmore, El Monte, CA 91731 / 818-571-5228; FAX: 800-927-8361

J&J Sales, 1501 21st Ave. S., Great Falls, MT 59405 / 406-727-9789 www.j&jsales.us

J&L Superior Bullets (See Huntington Die Special)

J&R Engineering, P.O. Box 77, 200 Lyons Hill Rd., Athol, MA 01331 / 508-249-9241

J&R Enterprises, 4550 Scotts Valley Rd., Lakeport, CA 95453

J&S Heat Treat, 803 S. 16th St., Blue Springs, MO 64015 / 816-229-2149; FAX: 816-228-1135

J. Dewey Mfg. Co., Inc., P.O. Box 2014, Southbury, CT 06488 / 203-264-3064; FAX: 203-262-6907 deweyrods@worldnet.att.net www.deweyrods.com

J. Korzinek Riflesmith, RD 2, Box 73D, Canton, PA 17724 / 717-673-8512

J.A. Blades, Inc. (See Christopher Firearms Co.)

J.A. Henckels Zwillingswerk Inc., 9 Skyline Dr., Hawthorne, NY 10532 / 914-592-7370

J.G. Anschutz GmbH & Co. KG, Daimlerstr. 12, D-89079 Ulm, Ulm, GERMANY / 49 731 40120; FAX: 49 731 4012700 JGA-info@anschuetz-sport.com www.anschuetz-sport.com

J.G. Dapkus Co., Inc., Commerce Circle, P.O. Box 293, Durham, CT 06422 www.explodingtargets.com

J.I.T. Ltd., P.O. Box 230, Freedom, WY 83120 / 708-494-0937

J.J. Roberts / Engraver, 7808 Lake Dr., Manassas, VA 20111 / 703-330-0448 jjrengraver@aol.com www.angelfire.com/va2/engraver

J.P. Enterprises, Inc., P.O. Box 378, Hugo, MN 55110 / 612-486-9064; FAX: 612-482-0970

J.R. Williams Bullet Co., 2008 Tucker Rd., Perry, GA 31069 / 912-987-0274

J.W. Morrison Custom Rifles, 4015 W. Sharon, Phoenix, AZ 85029 / 602-978-3754

J/B Adventures & Safaris Inc., 2275 E. Arapahoe Rd., Ste. 109, Littleton, CO 80122-1521 / 303-771-0977

Jack A. Rosenberg & Sons, 12229 Cox Ln., Dallas, TX 75234 / 214-241-6302

Jack Dever Co., 8520 NW 90th St., Oklahoma City, OK 73132 / 405-721-6393 jbdever1@home.com

Jack First, Inc., 1201 Turbine Dr., Rapid City, SD 57703 / 605-343-8481; FAX: 605-343-9420

Jack Jonas Appraisals & Taki, 13952 E. Marina Dr., #604, Aurora, CO 80014

Jackalope Gun Shop, 1048 S. 5th St., Douglas, WY 82633 / 307-358-3441

Jaffin, Harry. See: BRIDGEMAN PRODUCTS

Jagdwaffen, Peter. See: BUCHSENMACHERMEISTER

James Calhoon Mfg., Shambo Rte. 304, Havre, MT 59501 / 406-395-4079 www.jamescalhoon.com

James Calhoon Varmint Bullets, Shambo Rt., 304, Havre, MT 59501 / 406-395-4079 www.jamescalhoon.com

James Churchill Glove Co., PO Box 298, Centralia, WA 98531 / 360-736-2816; FAX: 360-330-0151 churchillglove@localaccess.com

James Wayne Firearms for Collectors and Investors, 2608 N. Laurent, Victoria, TX 77901 / 361-578-1258; FAX: 361-578-3559

Jamison International, Marc Jamison, 3551 Mayer Ave., Sturgis, SD 57785 / 605-347-5090; FAX: 605-347-4704 jbell2@masttechnology.com

Jamison, Marc. See: JAMISON INTERNATIONAL

Jamison's Forge Works, 4527 Rd. 6.5 NE, Moses Lake, WA 98837 / 509-762-2659

Jantz Supply, 309 West Main Dept HD, Davis, OK 73030-0584 / 580-369-2316; FAX: 580-369-3082 jantz@brightok.net www.knifemaking.com

Jarrett Rifles, Inc., 383 Brown Rd., Jackson, SC 29831 / 803-471-3616 www.jarrettrifles.com

Jarvis, Inc., 1123 Cherry Orchard Lane, Hamilton, MT 59840 / 406-961-4392

Javelina Lube Products, PO Box 337, San Bernardino, CA 92402 / 714-882-5847; FAX: 714-434-6937

Jay McCament Custom Gunmaker, Jay McCament, 1730-134th St. Ct. S., Tacoma, WA 98444 / 253-531-8832

JB Custom, P.O. Box 6912, Leawood, KS 66206 / 913-381-2329

Jeff W. Flannery Engraving Co., 11034 Riddles Run Rd., Union, KY 41091 / 606-384-3127 engraving@fuse.net http://home.fuse.net/engraving/

Jeffredo Gunsight, P.O. Box 669, San Marcos, CA 92079 / 760-728-2695

Jena Eur, PO Box 319, Dunmore, PA 18512

Jenco Sales, Inc., P.O. Box 1000, Manchaca, TX 78652 / 800-531-5301; FAX: 800-266-2373 jencosales@sbcglobal.net

Jenkins Recoil Pads, Inc., 5438 E. Frontage Ln., Olney, IL 62450 / 618-395-3416

Jensen Bullets, RR 1 Box 187, Arco, ID 83213 / 208-785-5590

Jensen's Custom Ammunition, 5146 E. Pima, Tucson, AZ 85712 / 602-325-3346; FAX: 602-322-5704

Jensen's Firearms Academy, 1280 W. Prince, Tucson, AZ 85705 / 602-293-8516

Jericho Tool & Die Co., Inc., 2917 St. Hwy. 7, Bainbridge, NY 13733 / 607-563-8222; FAX: 607-563-8560 jerichotool.com www.jerichotool.com

Jerry Phillips Optics, P.O. Box L632, Langhorne, PA 19047 / 215-757-5037; FAX: 215-757-7097

Jesse W. Smith Saddlery, 0499 County Road J, Pritchett, CO 81064 / 509-325-0622

Jester Bullets, Rt. 1 Box 27, Orienta, OK 73737

Jewell Triggers, Inc., 3620 Hwy. 123, San Marcos, TX 78666 / 512-353-2999; FAX: 512-392-0543

J-Gar Co., 183 Turnpike Rd., Dept. 3, Petersham, MA 01366-9604

JGS Precision Tool Mfg., LLC, 60819 Selander Rd., Coos Bay, OR 97420 / 541-267-4331; FAX: 541-267-5996 jgstools@harborside.com www.jgstools.com

Jim Blair Engraving, P.O. Box 64, Glenrock, WY 82637 / 307-436-8115 jblairengrav@msn.com

Jim Noble Co., 1305 Columbia St, Vancouver, WA 98660 / 360-695-1309; FAX: 360-695-6835 jnobleco@aol.com

Jim Norman Custom Gunstocks, 14281 Cane Rd., Valley Center, CA 92082 / 619-749-6252

Jim's Gun Shop (See Spradlin's)

Jim's Precision, Jim Ketchum, 1725 Moclips Dr., Petaluma, CA 94952 / 707-762-3014

JLK Bullets, 414 Turner Rd., Dover, AR 72837 / 501-331-4194

Johanssons Vapentillbehor, Bert, S-430 20, Veddige, SWEDEN

John Hall Plastics, Inc., P.O. Box 1526, Alvin, TX 77512 / 713-489-8709

John J. Adams & Son Engravers, 7040 VT Rt 113, Vershire, VT 05079 / 802-685-0019

John Masen Co. Inc., 1305 Jelmak, Grand Prairie, TX 75050 / 817-430-8732; FAX: 817-430-1715

John Norrell Arms, 2608 Grist Mill Rd, Little Rock, AR 72207 / 501-225-7864

John Partridge Sales Ltd., Trent Meadows Rugeley, Staffordshire, WS15 2HS ENGLAND

John Rigby & Co., 500 Linne Rd. Ste. D, Paso Robles, CA 93446 / 805-227-4236; FAX: 805-227-4723 jrigby@calinet www.johnrigbyandco.com

Johnny Stewart Game Calls, Inc., P.O. Box 7954, 5100 Fort Ave., Waco, TX 76714 / 817-772-3261; FAX: 817-772-3670

John's Custom Leather, 523 S. Liberty St., Blairsville, PA 15717 / 724-459-6802; FAX: 724-459-5996

Johnson Wood Products, 34897 Crystal Road, Strawberry Point, IA 52076 / 563-933-6504 johnsonwoodproducts@yahoo.com

Johnston Bros. (See C&T Corp. TA Johnson Brothers)

Jonad Corp., 2091 Lakeland Ave., Lakewood, OH 44107 / 216-226-3161

Jonathan Arthur Ciener, Inc., 8700 Commerce St., Cape Canaveral, FL 32920 / 321-868-2200; FAX: 321-868-2201

Jones Co., Dale, 680 Hoffman Draw, Kila, MT 59920 / 406-755-4684

Jones Custom Products, Neil A., 17217 Brookhouser Rd., Saegertown, PA 16433 / 814-763-2769; FAX: 814-763-4228

Jones, J. See: SSK INDUSTRIES

Jones Moulds, Paul, 4901 Telegraph Rd, Los Angeles, CA 90022 / 213-262-1510

JP Sales, Box 307, Anderson, TX 77830

JRP Custom Bullets, RR2 2233 Carlton Rd., Whitehall, NY 12887 / 518-282-0084 or 802-438-5548

JSL Ltd (See U.S. Importer-Specialty Shooters)

Juenke, Vern, 25 Bitterbush Rd., Reno, NV 89523 / 702-345-0225

DIRECTORY

Jungkind, Reeves C., 509 E. Granite St., Llano, TX 78643-3055 / 512-442-1094

Jurras, L. See: L. E. JURRAS & ASSOC.

Justin Phillippi Custom Bullets, P.O. Box 773, Ligonier, PA 15658 / 412-238-9671

K

K&M Industries, Inc., Box 66, 510 S. Main, Troy, ID 83871 / 208-835-2281; FAX: 208-835-5211

K&M Services, 5430 Salmon Run Rd., Dover, PA 17315 / 717-292-3175; FAX: 717-292-3175

K. Eversull Co., Inc., 1 Tracemont, Boyce, LA 71409 / 318-793-8728; FAX: 318-793-5483 bestguns@aol.com

K.B.I. Inc., P.O. Box 6625, Harrisburg, PA 17112 / 717-540-8518; FAX: 717-540-8567

K.L. Null Holsters Ltd., 161 School St. NW, Hill City Station, Resaca, GA 30735 / 706-625-5643; FAX: 706-625-9392 ken@klnullholsters.com www.klnullholsters.com

Ka Pu Kapili, P.O. Box 745, Honokaa, HI 96727 / 808-776-1644; FAX: 808-776-1731

KA-BAR Knives, 1125 E. State St., Olean, NY 14760 / 800-282-0130; FAX: 716-373-6245 info@ka-bar.com www.ka-bar.com

Kahles A. Swarovski Company, 2 Slater Rd., Cranston, RI 02920 / 401-946-2220; FAX: 401-946-2587

Kahr Arms, PO Box 220, 630 Route 303, Blauvelt, NY 10913 / 845-353-7770; FAX: 845-353-7833 www.kahr.com

Kailua Custom Guns Inc., 51 N. Dean Street, Coquille, OR 97423 / 541-396-5413 kailuacustom@aol.com www.kailuacustom.com

Kalispel Case Line, P.O. Box 267, Cusick, WA 99119 / 509-445-1121

Kamik Outdoor Footwear, 554 Montee de Liesse, Montreal, PQ H4T 1P1 CANADA / 514-341-3950; FAX: 514-341-1861

Kane, Edward, P.O. Box 385, Ukiah, CA 95482 / 707-462-2937

Kane Products, Inc., 5572 Brecksville Rd., Cleveland, OH 44131 / 216-524-9962

Kapro Mfg. Co. Inc. (See R.E.I.)

Kasenit Co., Inc., 13 Park Ave., Highland Mills, NY 10930 / 914-928-9595; FAX: 914-928-7292

Kaswer Custom, Inc., 13 Surrey Drive, Brookfield, CT 06804 / 203-775-0564; FAX: 203-775-6872

KDF, Inc., 2485 Hwy. 46 N., Seguin, TX 78155 / 830-379-8141; FAX: 830-379 5420

KeeCo Impressions, Inc., 346 Wood Ave., North Brunswick, NJ 08902 / 800-468-0546

Kehr, Roger, 2131 Agate Ct. SE, Lacy, WA 98503 / 360-491-0691

Keith's Bullets, 942 Twisted Oak, Algonquin, IL 60102 / 708-658-3520

Keith's Custom Gunstocks, Keith M. Heppler, 540 Banyan Circle, Walnut Creek, CA 94598 / 925-934-3509; FAX: 925-934-3143 kmheppler@hotmail.com

Kelbly, Inc., 7222 Dalton Fox Lake Rd., North Lawrence, OH 44666 / 216-683-4674; FAX: 216-683-7349

Kelley's, P.O. Box 125, Woburn, MA 01801-0125 / 800-879-7273; FAX: 781-272-7077 kels@star.net www.kelsmilitary.com

Kellogg's Professional Products, 325 Pearl St., Sandusky, OH 44870 / 419-625-6551; FAX: 419-625-6167 skwigton@aol.com

Kelly, Lance, 1723 Willow Oak Dr., Edgewater, FL 32132 / 904-423-4933

Kel-Tec CNC Industries, Inc., PO Box 236009, Cocoa, FL 32923 / 407-631-0068; FAX: 407-631-1169

Kemen America, 2550 Hwy. 23, Wrenshall, MN 55797 / 218-384-3670 patrickl@midwestshootingschool.com midwestshootingschool.com

Ken Eyster Heritage Gunsmiths, Inc., 6441 Bishop Rd., Centerburg, OH 43011 / 740-625-6131; FAX: 740-625-7811

Ken Starnes Gunmaker, 15940 SW Holly Hill Rd, Hillsboro, OR 97123-9033 / 503-628-0705; FAX: 503-443-2096 kstarnes@kdsa.com

Keng's Firearms Specialty, Inc./US Tactical Systems, 875 Wharton Dr., P.O. Box 44405, Atlanta, GA 30336-1405 / 404-691-7611; FAX: 404-505-8445

Kennebec Journal, 274 Western Ave., Augusta, ME 04330 / 207-622-6288

Kennedy Firearms, 10 N. Market St., Muncy, PA 17756 / 717-546-6695

Kenneth W. Warren Engraver, P.O. Box 2842, Wenatchee, WA 98807 / 509-663-6123; FAX: 509-665-6123

Ken's Kustom Kartridges, 331 Jacobs Rd., Hubbard, OH 44425 / 216-534-4595

Kent Cartridge America, Inc., PO Box 849, 1000 Zigor Rd., Kearneysville, WV 25430

Kent Cartridge Mfg. Co. Ltd., Unit 16 Branbridges Industrial Esta, Tonbridge, Kent, ENGLAND / 622-872255; FAX: 622-872645

Keowee Game Calls, 608 Hwy. 25 North, Travelers Rest, SC 29690 / 864-834-7204; FAX: 864-834-7831

Kershaw Knives, 25300 SW Parkway Ave., Wilsonville, OR 97070 / 503-682-1966; or 800-325-2891; FAX: 503-682-7168

Kesselring Gun Shop, 4024 Old Hwy. 99N, Burlington, WA 98233 / 360-724-3113; FAX: 360-724-7003 info@kesselrings.com www.kesselrings.com

Ketchum, Jim (See Jim's Precision)

Kickeez I.N.C., Inc., 301 Industrial Dr, Carl Junction, MO 64834-8806 / 419-649-2100; FAX: 417-649-2200 kickey@ipa.net

Kilham & Co., Main St., P.O. Box 37, Lyme, NH 03768 / 603-795-4112

Kim Ahrends Custom Firearms, Inc., Box 203, Clarion, IA 50525 / 515-532-3449; FAX: 515-532-3926

Kimar (See U.S. Importer-IAR,Inc)

Kimber of America, Inc., 1 Lawton St., Yonkers, NY 10705 / 800-880-2418; FAX: 914-964-9340

King & Co., P.O. Box 1242, Bloomington, IL 61702 / 309-473-3964; FAX: 309-473-2161

King's Gun Works, 1837 W. Glenoaks Blvd., Glendale, CA 91201 / 818-956-6010; FAX: 818-548-8606

Kingyon, Paul L. (See Custom Calls)

Kirkpatrick Leather Co., PO Box 677, Laredo, TX 78040 / 956-723-6631; FAX: 956-725-0672 mike@kirkpatrickleather.com www.kirkpatrickleather.com

KK Air International (See Impact Case & Container Co.)

KLA Enterprises, P.O. Box 2028, Eaton Park, FL 33840 / 941-682-2829; FAX: 941-682-2829

Kleen-Bore,Inc., 16 Industrial Pkwy., Easthampton, MA 01027 / 413-527-0300; FAX: 413-527-2522 info@kleen-bore.com www.kleen-bore.com

Klein Custom Guns, Don, 433 Murray Park Dr, Ripon, WI 54971 / 920-748-2931 daklein@charter.net

Kleinendorst, K. W., RR 1, Box 1500, Hop Bottom, PA 18824 / 717-289-4687

Klingler Woodcarving, P.O. Box 141, Thistle Hill, Cabot, VT 05647 / 802-426-3811

Knifeware, Inc., P.O. Box 3, Greenville, WV 24945 / 304-832-6878

Knight & Hale Game Calls, Box 468, Industrial Park, Cadiz, KY 42211 / 502-924-1755; FAX: 502-924-1763

Knight Rifles, 21852 Hwy. J46, P.O. Box 130, Centerville, IA 52544 / 515-856-2626; FAX: 515-856-2628

Knight Rifles (See Modern Muzzle Loading, Inc.)

Knight's Mfg. Co., 7750 Ninth St. SW, Vero Beach, FL 32968 / 561-562-5697; FAX: 561-569-2955 civiliansales@knightarmco.com

Knock on Wood Antiques, 355 Post Rd., Darien, CT 06820 / 203-655-9031

Knoell, Doug, 9737 McCardle Way, Santee, CA 92071 / 619-449-5189

Knopp, Gary. See: SUPER 6 LLC

KOGOT, 410 College, Trinidad, CO 81082 / 719-846-9406; FAX: 719-846-9406

Kokolus, Michael M. (See Custom Riflestocks In)

Kolar, 1925 Roosevelt Ave., Racine, WI 53406 / 414-554-0800; FAX: 414-554-9093

Kolpin Mfg., Inc., P.O. Box 107, 205 Depot St., Fox Lake, WI 53933 / 414-928-3118; FAX: 414-928-3687

Korth Germany GmbH, Robert Bosch Strasse, 11, D-23909, 23909 Ratzeburg, GERMANY / 4541-840363; FAX: 4541-84 05 35

Korth USA, 437R Chandler St., Tewksbury, MA 01876 / 978-851-8656; FAX: 978-851-9462 info@kortusa.com www.kortusa.com

Korzinek Riflesmith, J., RD 2 Box 73D, Canton, PA 17724 / 717-673-8512

Koval Knives, 5819 Zarley St., Suite A, New Albany, OH 43054 / 614-855-0777; FAX: 614-855-0945 koval@kovalknives.com www.kovalknives.com

Kowa Optimed, Inc., 20001 S. Vermont Ave., Torrance, CA 90502 / 310-327-1913; FAX: 310-327-4177

Kramer Designs, P.O. Box 129, Clancy, MT 59634 / 406-933-8658; FAX: 406-933-8658

Kramer Handgun Leather, P.O. Box 112154, Tacoma, WA 98411 / 800-510-2666; FAX: 253-564-1214 www.kramerleather.com

Krause Publications, Inc., 700 E. State St., Iola, WI 54990 / 715-445-2214; FAX: 715-445-4087

Krico Deutschland GmbH, Nurnbergerstrasse 6, D-90602, Pyrbaum, GERMANY / 09180-2780; FAX: 09180-2661

Krieger Barrels, Inc., 2024 Mayfield Rd, Richfield, WI 53076 / 262-628-8558; FAX: 262-628-8748

Krieghoff Gun Co., H., Boschstrasse 22, D-89079 Elm, GERMANY or 731-4018270

Krieghoff International,Inc., 7528 Easton Rd., Ottsville, PA 18942 / 610-847-5173; FAX: 610-847-8691

Kukowski, Ed. See: ED'S GUN HOUSE

Kulis Freeze Dry Taxidermy, 725 Broadway Ave., Bedford, OH 44146 / 216-232-8352; FAX: 216-232-7305 jkulis@kastaway.com kastaway.com

KVH Industries, Inc., 110 Enterprise Center, Middletown, RI 02842 / 401-847-3327; FAX: 401-849-0045

Kwik-Site Co., 5555 Treadwell St., Wayne, MI 48184 / 734-326-1500; FAX: 734-326-4120 kwiksiteco@aol.com

L

L&R Lock Co., 1137 Pocalla Rd., Sumter, SC 29150 / 803-775-6127; FAX: 803-775-5171

L&S Technologies Inc. (See Aimtech Mount Systems)

L. Bengtson Arms Co., 6345-B E. Akron St., Mesa, AZ 85205 / 602-981-6375

L. E. Jurras & Assoc., L. E. Jurras, P.O. Box 680, Washington, IN 47501 / 812-254-6170; FAX: 812-254-6170 jurasgun@rtcc.net

L.A.R. Mfg., Inc., 4133 W. Farm Rd., West Jordan, UT 84088 / 801-280-3505; FAX: 801-280-1972

L.B.T., Judy Smith, HCR 62, Box 145, Moyie Springs, ID 83845 / 208-267-3588

L.E. Wilson, Inc., Box 324, 404 Pioneer Ave., Cashmere, WA 98815 / 509-782-1328; FAX: 509-782-7200

L.L. Bean, Inc., Freeport, ME 04032 / 207-865-4761; FAX: 207-552-2802

L.P.A. Inc., Via Alfieri 26, Gardone V.T., Brescia, ITALY / 30-891-14-81; FAX: 30-891-09-51

L.R. Clift Mfg., 3821 Hammonton Rd., Marysville, CA 95901 / 916-755-3390; FAX: 916-755-3393

L.W. Seecamp Co., Inc., PO Box 255, New Haven, CT 06502 / 203-877-3429; FAX: 203-877-3429 seecamp@optonline.net

La Clinique du .45, 1432 Rougemont, Chambly,, PQ J3L 2L8 CANADA / 514-658-1144

Labanu, Inc., 2201-F Fifth Ave., Ronkonkoma, NY 11779 / 516-467-6197; FAX: 516-981-4112

LaBoone, Pat. See: THE MIDWEST SHOOTING SCHOOL

LaBounty Precision Reboring, Inc, 7968 Silver Lake Rd., PO Box 186, Maple Falls, WA 98266 / 360-599-2047; FAX: 360-599-3018

LaCrosse Footwear, Inc., 18550 NE Riverside Parkway, Portland, OR 97230 / 503-766-1010; or 800-323-2668; FAX: 503-766-1015

LaFrance Specialties, P.O. Box 87933, San Diego, CA 92138 / 619-293-3373; FAX: 619-293-7087 timlafrance@att.net

Lake Center Marina, PO Box 670, St. Charles, MO 63302 / 314-946-7500

Lakefield Arms Ltd. (See Savage Arms, Inc.)

Lakewood Products LLC, 275 June St., Berlin, WI 54923 / 800-872-8458; FAX: 920-361-7719 lakewood@dotnet.com www.lakewoodproducts.com

Lamboy, Stephen. See: ITHACA CLASSIC DOUBLES

Lampert, Ron, Rt. 1, 44857 Schoolcraft Trl., Guthrie, MN 56461 / 218-854-7345

Lamson & Goodnow Mfg. Co., 45 Conway St., Shelburne Falls, MA 03170 / 413-625-6564; or 800-872-6564; FAX: 413-625-9816 www.lamsonsharp.com

Lansky Levine, Arthur. See: LANSKY SHARPENERS

Lansky Sharpeners, Arthur Lansky Levine, PO Box 50830, Las Vegas, NV 89016 / 702-361-7511; FAX: 702-896-9511

LaPrade, PO Box 250, Ewing, VA 24248 / 423-733-2615

Lapua Ltd., P.O. Box 5, Lapua, FINLAND / 6-310111; FAX: 6-4388991

LaRocca Gun Works, 51 Union Place, Worcester, MA 01608 / 508-754-2887; FAX: 508-754-2887 www.laroccagunworks.com

Larry Lyons Gunworks, 110 Hamilton St., Dowagiac, MI 49047 / 616-782-9478

Laser Devices, Inc., 2 Harris Ct. A-4, Monterey, CA 93940 / 831-373-0701; FAX: 831-373-0903 sales@laserdevices.com www.laserdevices.com

Laseraim Technologies, Inc., P.O. Box 3548, Little Rock, AR 72203 / 501-375-2227

Laserlyte, 2201 Amapola Ct., Torrance, CA 90501

LaserMax, Inc., 3495 Winton Place, Bldg. B, Rochester, NY 14623-2807 / 800-527-3703; FAX: 716-272-5427 customerservice@lasermax-inc.com www.lasermax-inc.com

Lassen Community College, Gunsmithing Dept., P.O. Box 3000, Hwy. 139, Susanville, CA 96130 / 916-251-8800; FAX: 916-251-8838

Lathrop's, Inc., Inc., 5146 E. Pima, Tucson, AZ 85712 / 520-881-0266; or 800-875-4867; FAX: 520-322-5704

Laughridge, William R (See Cylinder & Slide Inc)
Laurel Mountain Forge, P.O. Box 52, Crown Point, IN 46308 / 219-548-2950; FAX: 219-548-2950
Laurona Armas Eibar, S.A.L., Avenida de Otaola 25, P.O. Box 260, Eibar 20600, SPAIN / 34-43-700600; FAX: 34-43-700616
Lawrence Brand Shot (See Precision Reloading)
Lawrence Leather Co., P.O. Box 1479, Lillington, NC 27546 / 910-893-2071; FAX: 910-893-4742
Lawson Co., Harry, 3328 N Richey Blvd., Tucson, AZ 85716 / 520-326-1117; FAX: 520-326-1117
Lawson, John. See: THE SIGHT SHOP
Lawson, John G (See Sight Shop, The)
Lazzeroni Arms Co., PO Box 26696, Tucson, AZ 85726 / 888-492-7247; FAX: 520-624-4250
Le Clear Industries (See E-Z-Way Systems), PO Box 4310, Newark, OH 43058-4310 / 614-345-6645; FAX: 614-345-6600
Lea Mfg. Co., 237 E. Aurora St., Waterbury, CT 06720 / 203-753-5116
Leapers, Inc., 7675 Five Mile Rd., Northville, MI 48167 / 248-486-1231; FAX: 248-486-1430
Leatherman Tool Group, Inc., 12106 NE Ainsworth Cir., P.O. Box 20595, Portland, OR 97294 / 503-253-7826; FAX: 503-253-7830
Lebeau-Courally, Rue St. Gilles, 386 4000, Liege, BELGIUM / 042-52-48-43; FAX: 32-4-252-2008 info@lebeau-courally.com www.lebeau-courally.com
Leckie Professional Gunsmithing, 546 Quarry Rd., Ottsville, PA 18942 / 215-847-8594
Ledbetter Airguns, Riley, 1804 E Sprague St, Winston Salem, NC 27107-3521 / 919-784-0676
Lee Precision, Inc., 4275 Hwy. U, Hartford, WI 53027 / 262-673-3075; FAX: 262-673-9273 info@leeprecision.com www.leeprecision.com
Lee Supplies, Mark, 9901 France Ct., Lakeville, MN 55044 / 612-461-2114
LeFever Arms Co., Inc., 6234 Stokes, Lee Center Rd., Lee Center, NY 13363 / 315-337-6722; FAX: 315-337-1543
Legacy Sports International, 206 S. Union St., Alexandria, VA 22314 / 703-548-4837 www.legacysports.com
Legend Products Corp., 21218 Saint Andrews Blvd., Boca Raton, FL 33433-2435
Leibowitz, Leonard, 1205 Murrayhill Ave., Pittsburgh, PA 15217 / 412-361-5455
Leica USA, Inc., 156 Ludlow Ave., Northvale, NJ 07647 / 201-767-7500; FAX: 201-767-8666
LEM Gun Specialties, Inc. The Lewis Lead Remover, P.O. Box 2855, Peachtree City, GA 30269-2024 / 770-487-0556
Leonard Day, 6 Linseed Rd Box 1, West Hatfield, MA 01088-7505 / 413-337-8369
Les Baer Custom,Inc., 29601 34th Ave., Hillsdale, IL 61257 / 309-658-2716; FAX: 309-658-2610
LesMerises, Felix. See: ROCKY MOUNTAIN ARMOURY
Lethal Force Institute (See Police Bookshelf), PO Box 122, Concord, NH 03301 / 603-224-6814; FAX: 603-226-3554
Lett Custom Grips, 672 Currier Rd., Hopkinton, NH 03229-2652 / 800-421-5388; FAX: 603-226-4580 info@lettgrips.com www.lettgrips.com
Leupold & Stevens, Inc., 14400 NW Greenbrier Pky., Beaverton, OR 97006 / 503-646-9171; FAX: 503-526-1455
Lever Arms Service Ltd., 2131 Burrard St., Vancouver, BC V6J 3H7 CANADA / 604-736-2711; FAX: 604-738-3503
Lew Horton Dist. Co., Inc., 15 Walkup Dr., Westboro, MA 01581 / 508-366-7400; FAX: 508-366-5332
Liberty Metals, 2233 East 16th St., Los Angeles, CA 90021 / 213-581-9171; FAX: 213-581-9351 libertymfgsolder@hotmail.com
Liberty Safe, 999 W. Utah Ave., Payson, UT 84651-1744 / 800-247-5625; FAX: 801-489-6409
Liberty Shooting Supplies, P.O. Box 357, Hillsboro, OR 97123 / 503-640-5518; FAX: 503-640-5518 info@libertyshootingsupplies.com www.libertyshootingsupplies.com
Lightning Performance Innovations, Inc., RD1 Box 555, Mohawk, NY 13407 / 315-866-8819; FAX: 315-867-5701
Lilja Precision Rifle Barrels, P.O. Box 372, Plains, MT 59859 / 406-826-3084; FAX: 406-826-3083 lilja@riflebarrels.com www.riflebarrels.com
Lincoln, Dean, Box 1886, Farmington, NM 87401
Linder Solingen Knives, 4401 Sentry Dr., Tucker, GA 30084 / 770-939-6915; FAX: 770-939-6738
Lindsay Engraving & Tools, Steve Lindsay, 3714 W. Cedar Hills, Kearney, NE 68845 / 308-236-7885 steve@lindsayengraving.com www.handgravers.com
Lindsay, Steve. See: LINDSAY ENGRAVING & TOOLS
Lindsley Arms Cartridge Co., P.O. Box 757, 20 College Hill Rd., Henniker, NH 03242 / 603-428-3127

Linebaugh Custom Sixguns, P.O. Box 455, Cody, WY 82414 / 307-645-3332 www.sitgunner.com
Lion Country Supply, P.O. Box 480, Port Matilda, PA 16870
List Precision Engineering, Unit 1 Ingley Works, 13 River Road, Barking, ENGLAND / 011-081-594-1686
Lithi Bee Bullet Lube, 1728 Carr Rd., Muskegon, MI 49442 / 616-788-4479
"Little John's" Antique Arms, 1740 W. Laveta, Orange, CA 92668
Little Trees Ramble (See Scott Pilkington)
Littler Sales Co., 20815 W. Chicago, Detroit, MI 48228 / 313-273-6888; FAX: 313-273-1099 littlerptg@aol.com
Littleton, J. F., 275 Pinedale Ave., Oroville, CA 95966 / 916-533-6084
Ljutic Industries, Inc., 732 N. 16th Ave., Suite 22, Yakima, WA 98902 / 509-248-0476; FAX: 509-576-8233 ljuticgun.net www.ljuticgun.com
Llama Gabilondo Y Cia, Apartado 290, E-01080, Victoria, spain, SPAIN
Loch Leven Industries/Convert-A-Pell, P.O. Box 2751, Santa Rosa, CA 95405 / 707-573-8735; FAX: 707-573-0369
Lock's Philadelphia Gun Exchange, 6700 Rowland Ave., Philadelphia, PA 19149 / 215-332-6225; FAX: 215-332-4800 locks.gunshop@verizon.net
Lodewick, Walter H., 2816 NE Halsey St., Portland, OR 97232 / 503-284-2554
Lodgewood Mfg., P.O. Box 611, Whitewater, WI 53190 / 262-473-5444; FAX: 262-473-6448 lodgewd@idcnet.com lodgewood.com
Log Cabin Sport Shop, 8010 Lafayette Rd., Lodi, OH 44254 / 330-948-1082; FAX: 330-948-4307 logcabin@logcabinshop.com www.logcabinshop.com
Logan, Harry M., Box 745, Honokaa, HI 96727 / 808-776-1644
Logdewood Mfg., P.O. Box 611, Whitewater, WI 53190 / 262-473-5444; FAX: 262-473-6448 lodgewd@idcnet.com www.lodgewood.com
Lohman Mfg. Co., Inc., 4500 Doniphan Dr., P.O. Box 220, Neosho, MO 64850 / 417-451-4438; FAX: 417-451-2576
Lomont Precision Bullets, 278 Sandy Creek Rd, Salmon, ID 83467 / 208-756-6819; FAX: 208-756-6824 www.klomont.com
London Guns Ltd., Box 3750, Santa Barbara, CA 93130 / 805-683-4141; FAX: 805-683-1712
Lone Star Gunleather, 1301 Brushy Bend Dr., Round Rock, TX 78681 / 512-255-1805
Lone Star Rifle Company, 11231 Rose Road, Conroe, TX 77303 / 936-856-3363 dave@lonestar.com
Long, George F., 1500 Rogue River Hwy., Ste. F, Grants Pass, OR 97527 / 541-476-7552
Lortone Inc., 2856 NW Market St., Seattle, WA 98107
Lothar Walther Precision Tool Inc., 3425 Hutchinson Rd., Cumming, GA 30040 / 770-889-9998; FAX: 770-889-4919 lotharwalther@mindspring.com www.lothar-walther.com
LPS Laboratories, Inc., 4647 Hugh Howell Rd., P.O. Box 3050, Tucker, GA 30084 / 404-934-7800
Lucas, Edward E, 32 Garfield Ave., East Brunswick, NJ 08816 / 201-251-5526
Lupton, Keith. See: PAWLING MOUNTAIN CLUB
Lyman Instant Targets, Inc. (See Lyman Products)
Lyman Products Corp., 475 Smith Street, Middletown, CT 06457-1541 / 800-423-9704; FAX: 860-632-1699 lymansales@cshore.com www.lymanproducts.com

M

M. Thys (See U.S. Importer-Champlin Firearms Inc)
M.H. Canjar Co., 6510 Raleigh St., Arvada, CO 80003 / 303-295-2638; FAX: 303-295-2638
MA Systems, P.O. Box 894, Pryor, OK 74362-0894 / 918-479-6378
Mac-1 Airgun Distributors, 13974 Van Ness Ave., Gardena, CA 90249-2900 / 310-327-3581; FAX: 310-327-0238 mac1@maclairgun.com www.mac1airgun.com
Madis Books, 2453 West Five Mile Pkwy., Dallas, TX 75233 / 214-330-7168
Madis, George. See: GEORGE MADIS WINCHESTER CONSULTANTS
MAG Instrument, Inc., 1635 S. Sacramento Ave., Ontario, CA 91761 / 909-947-1006; FAX: 909-947-3116
Magma Engineering Co., P.O. Box 161, 20955 E. Ocotillo Rd., Queen Creek, AZ 85242 / 602-987-9008; FAX: 602-987-0148
Mag-Na-Port International, Inc., 41302 Executive Dr., Harrison Twp., MI 48045-1306 / 586-469-6727; FAX: 586-469-0425 email@magnaport.com www.magnaport.com

Magnolia Sports,Inc., 211 W. Main, Magnolia, AR 71753 / 501-234-8410; or 800-530-7816; FAX: 501-234-8117
Magnum Power Products, Inc., P.O. Box 17768, Fountain Hills, AZ 85268
Magnum Research, Inc., 7110 University Ave. NE, Minneapolis, MN 55432 / 800-772-6168 or 763-574-1868; FAX: 763-574-0109 info@magnumresearch.com
Magnus Bullets, P.O. Box 239, Toney, AL 35773 / 256-420-8359; FAX: 256-420-8360
Mag-Pack Corp., P.O. Box 846, Chesterland, OH 44026 / 440-285-9480 magpack@hotmail.com
MagSafe Ammo Co., 4700 S US Highway 17/92, Casselberry, FL 32707-3814 / 407-834-9966; FAX: 407-834-8185 www.magsafeonline.com
Magtech Ammunition Co. Inc., 837 Boston Rd #12, Madison, CT 06443 / 203-245-8983; FAX: 203-245-2883 rfine@mactechammunition.com www.mactech.com.br
Mahony, Philip Bruce, 67 White Hollow Rd., Lime Rock, CT 06039-2418 / 203-435-9341 filbalony-redbeard@snet.net
Mahovsky's Metalife, R.D. 1, Box 149a Eureka Road, Grand Valley, PA 16420 / 814-436-7747
Maine Custom Bullets, RFD 1, Box 1755, Brooks, ME 04921
Maionchi-L.M.I., Via Di Coselli-Zona, Industriale Di Guamo 55060, Lucca, ITALY / 011 39-583 94291
Makinson, Nicholas, RR 3, Komoka, ON N0L 1R0 CANADA / 519-471-5462
Malcolm Enterprises, 1023 E. Prien Lake Rd., Lake Charles, LA 70601
Mallardtone Game Calls, 10406 96th St., Court West, Taylor Ridge, IL 61284 / 309-798-2481; FAX: 309-798-2501
Mandall Shooting Supplies Inc., 3616 N. Scottsdale Rd., Scottsdale, AZ 85251 / 480-945-2553; FAX: 480-949-0734
Marathon Rubber Prods. Co., Inc., 1009 3rd St, Wausau, WI 54403-4765 / 715-845-6255
Marble Arms (See CRR, Inc./Marble's Inc.)
Marchmon Bullets, 8191 Woodland Shore Dr., Brighton, MI 48116
Marent, Rudolf. See: HAMMERLI SERVICE-PRECISION MAC
Mark Lee Supplies, 9901 France Ct., Lakeville, MN 55044 / 952-461-2114; FAX: 952-461-2194 marklee55044@usfamily.net
Markell,Inc., 422 Larkfield Center 235, Santa Rosa, CA 95403 / 707-573-0792; FAX: 707-573-9867
Markesbery Muzzle Loaders, Inc., 7785 Foundation Dr., Ste. 6, Florence, KY 41042 / 606-342-5553 or 606-342-2380
Marksman Products, 5482 Argosy Dr., Huntington Beach, CA 92649 / 714-898-7535; or 800-822-8005; FAX: 714-891-0782
Marlin Firearms Co., 100 Kenna Dr., North Haven, CT 06473 / 203-239-5621; FAX: 203-234-7991
MarMik, Inc., 2116 S. Woodland Ave., Michigan City, IN 46360 / 219-872-7231; FAX: 219-872-7231
Marocchi F.lli S.p.A, Via Galileo Galilei 8, I-25068 Zanano, ITALY
Marquart Precision Co., P.O. Box 1740, Prescott, AZ 86302 / 520-445-5646
Marsh, Mike, Croft Cottage, Main St., Derbyshire, DE4 2BY ENGLAND / 01629 650 669
Marshall Enterprises, 792 Canyon Rd., Redwood City, CA 94062
Marshall Fish Mfg. Gunsmith Sptg. Co., Rd. Box 2439, Westport, NY 12993 / 518-962-4897; FAX: 518-962-4897
Martin B. Retting Inc., 11029 Washington, Culver City, CA 90232 / 213-837-2412
Martini & Hagn, 1264 Jimsmith Lake Rd, Cranbrook, BC V1C 6V6 CANADA / 250-417-2926; FAX: 250-417-2928
Martin's Gun Shop, 937 S. Sheridan Blvd., Lakewood, CO 80226 / 303-922-2184
Martz, John V., 8060 Lakeview Lane, Lincoln, CA 95648 FAX: 916-645-3815
Marvel, Alan, 3922 Madonna Rd., Jarretsville, MD 21084 / 301-557-6545
Marx, Harry (See U.S. Importer for FERLIB)
Maryland Paintball Supply, 8507 Harford Rd., Parkville, MD 21234 / 410-882-5607
MAST Technology, Inc., 14555 US Hwy. 95 S., P.O. Box 60969, Boulder City, NV 89006 / 702-293-6969; FAX: 702-293-7255 info@masttechnology.com www.bellammo.com
Master Lock Co., 2600 N. 32nd St., Milwaukee, WI 53245 / 414-444-2800
Match Prep-Doyle Gracey, P.O. Box 155, Tehachapi, CA 93581 / 661-822-5383; FAX: 661-823-8680
Mathews & Son, Inc., George E., 10224 S Paramount Blvd, Downey, CA 90241 / 562-862-6719; FAX: 562-862-6719

MANUFACTURER'S DIRECTORY

Matthews Cutlery, 4401 Sentry Dr., Tucker, GA 30084 / 770-939-6915
Mauser Werke Oberndorf Waffensysteme GmbH, Postfach 1349, 78722, Oberndorf/N., GERMANY
Maverick Arms, Inc., 7 Grasso Ave., P.O. Box 497, North Haven, CT 06473 / 203-230-5300; FAX: 203-230-5420
Maxi-Mount Inc., P.O. Box 291, Willoughby Hills, OH 44096-0291 / 440-944-9456; FAX: 440-944-9456 maximount454@yahoo.com
Mayville Engineering Co. (See MEC, Inc.)
Mazur Restoration, Pete, 13083 Drummer Way, Grass Valley, CA 95949 / 530-268-2412
McBros Rifle Co., P.O. Box 86549, Phoenix, AZ 85080 / 602-582-3713; FAX: 602-581-3825
McCament, Jay. See: JAY MCCAMENT CUSTOM GUNMAKER
McCann Industries, P.O. Box 641, Spanaway, WA 98387 / 253-537-6919; FAX: 253-537-6919 mccann.machine@worldnet.att.net www.mccannindustries.com
McCann's Machine & Gun Shop, P.O. Box 641, Spanaway, WA 98387 / 253-537-6919; FAX: 253-537-6993 mccann.machine@worldnet.att.net www.mccannindustries.com
McCann's Muzzle-Gun Works, 14 Walton Dr., New Hope, PA 18938 / 215-862-2728
McCluskey Precision Rifles, 10502 14th Ave. NW, Seattle, WA 98177 / 206-781-2776
McCombs, Leo, 1862 White Cemetery Rd., Patriot, OH 45658 / 740-256-1714
McCormick Corp., Chip, 1715 W. FM 1626 Ste. 105, Manchaca, TX 78652 / 800-328-CHIP; FAX: 512-462-0009
McDonald, Dennis, 8359 Brady St., Peosta, IA 52068 / 319-556-7940
McFarland, Stan, 2221 Idella Ct., Grand Junction, CO 81505 / 970-243-4704
McGhee, Larry. See: B.C. OUTDOORS
McGowen Rifle Barrels, 5961 Spruce Lane, St. Anne, IL 60964 / 815-937-9816; FAX: 815-937-4024
Mchalik, Gary. See: ROSSI FIREARMS
McKenzie, Lynton, 6940 N. Alvernon Way, Tucson, AZ 85718 / 520-299-5090
McMillan Fiberglass Stocks, Inc., 1638 W. Knudsen Dr. #102, Phoenix, AZ 85027 / 602-582-9635; FAX: 602-581-3825
McMillan Optical Gunsight Co., 28638 N. 42nd St., Cave Creek, AZ 85331 / 602-585-7868; FAX: 602-585-7872
McMillan Rifle Barrels, P.O. Box 3427, Bryan, TX 77805 / 409-690-3456; FAX: 409-690-0156
McMurdo, Lynn (See Specialty Gunsmithing), PO Box 404, Afton, WY 83110 / 307-886-5535
MCS, Inc., 166 Pocono Rd., Brookfield, CT 06804-2023 / 203-775-1013; FAX: 203-775-9462
McWelco Products, 6730 Santa Fe Ave., Hesperia, CA 92345 / 619-244-8876; FAX: 619-244-9398 products@mcwelco.com www.mawelco.com
MDS, P.O. Box 1441, Brandon, FL 33509-1441 / 813-653-1180; FAX: 813-684-5953
Measurement Group Inc., Box 27777, Raleigh, NC 27611
Measures, Leon. See: SHOOT WHERE YOU LOOK
MEC, Inc., 715 South St., Mayville, WI 53050 / 414-387-4500; FAX: 414-387-5802 reloaders@mayul.com www.mayvl.com
MEC-Gar S.R.L., Via Madonnina 64, Gardone V.T. Brescia, ITALY / 39-30-8912687; FAX: 39-30-8910065
MEC-Gar U.S.A., Inc., Hurley Farms Industr. Park, 115, Hurley Road 6G, Oxofrd, CT 06478 / 203-262-1525; FAX: 203-262-1719 mecgar@aol.com www.mec-gar.com
Mech-Tech Systems, Inc., 1602 Foothill Rd., Kalispell, MT 59901 / 406-755-8055
Meister Bullets (See Gander Mountain)
Mele, Frank, 201 S. Wellow Ave., Cookeville, TN 38501 / 615-526-4860
Menck, Gunsmith Inc., T.W., 5703 S 77th St, Ralston, NE 68127
Mendez, John A., P.O. Box 620984, Orlando, FL 32862 / 407-344-2791
Men-Metallwerk Elisenhuette GmbH, P.O. Box 1263, Nassau/Lahn, D-56372 GERMANY / 2604-7819
Meprolight (See Hesco-Meprolight)
Mercer Custom Guns, 216 S Whitewater Ave, Jefferson, WI 53549 / 920-674-3839
Merit Corp., PO Box 9044, Schenectady, NY 12309 / 518-346-1420 sales@meritcorporation.com www.meritcorporation.com
Merkel, Schutzenstrasse 26, D-98527 Suhl, Suhl, GERMANY FAX: 011-49-3681-854-203 www.merkel-waffen.de
Merkuria Ltd., Argentinska 38, 17005, Praha 7 CZECH, REPUBLIC / 422-875117; FAX: 422-809152
Metal Merchants, PO Box 186, Walled Lake, MI 48390-0186

Metalife Industries (See Mahovsky's Metalife)
Michael's Antiques, Box 591, Waldoboro, ME 04572
Michaels Of Oregon, Co., P.O. Box 1690, Oregon City, OR 97045 www.michaels-oregon.com
Micro Sight Co., 242 Harbor Blvd., Belmont, CA 94002 / 415-591-0769; FAX: 415-591-7531
Microfusion Alfa S.A., Paseo San Andres N8, P.O. Box 271, Eibar, 20600 SPAIN / 34-43-11-89-16; FAX: 34-43-11-40-38
Mid-America Recreation, Inc., 1328 5th Ave., Moline, IL 61265 / 309-764-5089; FAX: 309-764-5089 fmilcusguns@aol.com www.midamericarecreation.com
Middlebrooks Custom Shop, 7366 Colonial Trail East, Surry, VA 23883 / 757-357-0881; FAX: 757-365-0442
Midway Arms, Inc., 5875 W. Van Horn Tavern Rd., Columbia, MO 65203 / 800-243-3220; or 573-445-6363; FAX: 573-446-1018
Midwest Gun Sport, 1108 Herbert Dr., Zebulon, NC 27597 / 919-269-5570
Midwest Sport Distributors, Box 129, Fayette, MO 65248
Mike Davis Products, 643 Loop Dr., Moses Lake, WA 98837 / 509-765-6178; or 509-766-7281
Military Armament Corp., P.O. Box 120, Mt. Zion Rd., Lingleville, TX 76461 / 817-965-3253
Millennium Designed Muzzleloaders, PO Box 536, Routes 11 & 25, Limington, ME 04049 / 207-637-2316
Miller Arms, Inc., P.O. Box 260 Purl St., St. Onge, SD 57779 / 605-642-5160; FAX: 605-642-5160
Miller Custom, 210 E. Julia, Clinton, IL 61727 / 217-935-9362
Miller Single Trigger Mfg. Co., 6680 Rt. 5-20, P.O. Box 471, Bloomfield, NY 14469 / 585-657-6338
Millett Sights, 7275 Murdy Circle, Adm. Office, Huntington Beach, CA 92647 / 714-842-5575 or 800-645-5388; FAX: 714-843-5707
Mills Jr., Hugh B., 3615 Canterbury Rd., New Bern, NC 28560 / 919-637-4631
Milstor Corp., 80-975 Indio Blvd., Indio, CA 92201 / 760-775-9998; FAX: 760-775-5229 milstor@webtv.net
Miltex, Inc, 700 S Lee St, Alexandria, VA 22314-4332 / 888-642-9123; FAX: 301-645-1430
Minute Man High Tech Industries, 10611 Canyon Rd. E., Suite 151, Puyallup, WA 98373 / 800-233-2734
Mirador Optical Corp., P.O. Box 11614, Marina Del Rey, CA 90295-7614 / 310-821-5587; FAX: 310-305-0386
Mitchell, Jack, c/o Geoff Gaebe, Addieville East Farm, 200 Pheasant Dr, Mapleville, RI 02839 / 401-568-3185
Mitchell Bullets, R.F., 430 Walnut St, Westernport, MD 21562
Mitchell Optics, Inc., 2072 CR 1100 N, Sidney, IL 61877 / 217-688-2219; or 217-621-3018; FAX: 217-688-2505 mitche1@attglobal.net
Mitchell's Accuracy Shop, 68 Greenridge Dr., Stafford, VA 22554 / 703-659-0165
MI-TE Bullets, 1396 Ave. K, Ellsworth, KS 67439 / 785-472-4575; FAX: 785-472-5579
Mittermeier, Inc., Frank, PO Box 2G, 3577 E Tremont Ave, Bronx, NY 10465 / 718-828-3843
Mixson Corp., 7635 W. 28th Ave., Hialeah, FL 33016 / 305-821-5190; or 800-327-0078; FAX: 305-558-9318
MJK Gunsmithing, Inc., 417 N. Huber Ct., E. Wenatchee, WA 98802 / 509-884-7683
MKS Supply, Inc. (See Hi-Point Firearms)
MMC, 5050 E. Belknap St., Haltom City, TX 76117 / 817-831-9557; FAX: 817-834-5508
MOA Corporation, 2451 Old Camden Pike, Eaton, OH 45320 / 937-456-3669 www.moaguns.com
Modern Gun Repair School, PO Box 846, Saint Albans, VT 05478 / 802-524-2223; FAX: 802-524-2053 jfwp@dlilearn.com www.mgsinfoadlifearn.com
Modern Muzzleloading, Inc., P.O. Box 130, Centerville, IA 52544 / 515-856-2626
Moeller, Steve, 1213 4th St., Fulton, IL 61252 / 815-589-2300
Mogul Co./Life Jacket, 500 N. Kimball Rd., Ste. 109, South Lake, TX 76092
Molin Industries, Tru-Nord Division, P.O. Box 365, 204 North 9th St., Brainerd, MN 56401 / 218-829-2870
Monell Custom Guns, 228 Red Mills Rd., Pine Bush, NY 12566 / 914-744-3021
Moneymaker Guncraft Corp., 1420 Military Ave., Omaha, NE 68131 / 402-556-0226
Montana Armory, Inc. (See C. Sharps Arms Co. Inc.), 100 Centennial Dr., P.O. Box 885, Big Timber, MT 59011 / 406-932-4353; FAX: 406-932-4443
Montana Outfitters, Lewis E. Yearout, 308 Riverview Dr. E., Great Falls, MT 59404 / 406-761-0859
Montana Precision Swaging, P.O. Box 4746, Butte, MT 59702 / 406-494-0600; FAX: 406-494-0600
Montana Rifleman, Inc., 2593A Hwy. 2 East, Kalispell, MT 59901 / 406-755-4867

Montana Vintage Arms, 2354 Bear Canyon Rd., Bozeman, MT 59715
Montgomery Community College, PO Box 787-GD, Troy, NC 27371 / 910-576-6222; or 800-839-6222; FAX: 910-576-2176 hammondp@mcc.montgomery.cc.nc.us www.montgomery.cc.nc.us
Morini (See U.S. Importers-Mandall Shooting Supply)
Morrison Custom Rifles, J. W., 4015 W Sharon, Phoenix, AZ 85029 / 602-978-3754
Morrison Precision, 6719 Calle Mango, Hereford, AZ 85615 / 520-378-6207 morprec@c2i2.com
Morrow, Bud, 11 Hillside Lane, Sheridan, WY 82801-9729 / 307-674-8360
Morton Booth Co., P.O. Box 123, Joplin, MO 64802 / 417-673-1962; FAX: 417-673-3642
Mo's Competitor Supplies (See MCS, Inc.)
Moss Double Tone, Inc., P.O. Box 1112, 2101 S. Kentucky, Sedalia, MO 65301 / 816-827-0827
Mountain Plains Industries, 244 Glass Hollow Rd., Alton, VA 22920 / 800-687-3000; FAX: 540-456-8134
Mountain South, P.O. Box 381, Barnwell, SC 29812 / FAX: 803-259-3227
Mountain State Muzzleloading Supplies, Inc., Box 154-1, Rt. 2, Williamstown, WV 26187 / 304-375-7842; FAX: 304-375-3737
Mowrey Gun Works, P.O. Box 246, Waldron, IN 46182 / 317-525-6181; FAX: 317-525-9595
Mowrey's Guns & Gunsmithing, 119 Fredericks St., Canajoharie, NY 13317 / 518-673-3483
MPC, P.O. Box 450, McMinnville, TN 37110-0450 / 615-473-5513; FAX: 615-473-5516 thebox@blomand.net www.mpc-thebox.com
MPI Stocks, PO Box 83266, Portland, OR 97283 / 503-226-1215; FAX: 503-226-2661
MSR Targets, P.O. Box 1042, West Covina, CA 91793 / 818-331-7840
Mt. Alto Outdoor Products, Rt. 735, Howardsville, VA 24562
MTM Molded Products Co., Inc., 3370 Obco Ct., Dayton, OH 45414 / 937-890-7461; FAX: 937-890-1747
Mulberry House Publishing, P.O. Box 2180, Apache Junction, AZ 85217 / 888-738-1567; FAX: 480-671-1015
Mulhern, Rick, Rt. 5, Box 152, Rayville, LA 71269 / 318-728-2688
Mullins Ammunition, Rt. 2 Box 304N, Clintwood, VA 24228 / 540-926-6772; FAX: 540-926-6092 www.extremeshockusa.com
Mullis Guncraft, 3523 Lawyers Road E., Monroe, NC 28110 / 704-283-6683
Multiplex International, 26 S. Main St., Concord, NH 03301 FAX: 603-796-2223
Multipropulseurs, La Bertrandiere, 42580, FRANCE / 77 74 01 30; FAX: 77 93 19 34
Multi-Scale Charge Ltd., 3269 Niagara Falls Blvd., N. Tonawanda, NY 14120 / 905-566-1255; FAX: 905-276-6295
Mundy, Thomas A., 69 Robbins Road, Somerville, NJ 08876 / 201-722-2199
Murmur Corp., 2823 N. Westmoreland Ave., Dallas, TX 75222 / 214-630-5400
Murphy, R.R. Murphy Co., Inc. See: MURPHY, R.R. CO., INC.
Murphy, R.R. Co., Inc., R.R. Murphy Co., Inc. Murphy, P.O. Box 102, Ripley, TN 38063 / 901-635-4003; FAX: 901-635-2320
Murray State College, 1 Murray Campus St., Tishomingo, OK 73460 / 508-371-2371
Muscle Products Corp., 112 Fennell Dr., Butler, PA 16002 / 800-227-7049 or 724-283-0567; FAX: 724-283-8310 mpc@mpc_home.com www.mpc_home.com
Muzzleloaders Etcetera, Inc., 9901 Lyndale Ave. S., Bloomington, MN 55420 / 952-884-1161 www.muzzleloaders-etcetera.com
MWG Co., P.O. Box 971202, Miami, FL 33197 / 800-428-9394 or 305-253-8393; FAX: 305-232-1247

N

N.B.B., Inc., 24 Elliot Rd., Sterling, MA 01564 / 508-422-7538; or 800-942-9444
N.C. Ordnance Co., P.O. Box 3254, Wilson, NC 27895 / 919-237-2440; FAX: 919-243-9845
Nagel's Custom Bullets, 100 Scott St., Baytown, TX 77520-2849
Nalpak, 1937-C Friendship Drive, El Cajon, CA 92020 / 619-258-1200
Nastoff, Steve. See: NASTOFFS 45 SHOP, INC.
Nastoffs 45 Shop, Inc., Steve Nastoff, 1057 Laverne Dr., Youngstown, OH 44511
National Bullet Co., 1585 E. 361 St., Eastlake, OH 44095 / 216-951-1854; FAX: 216-951-7761

National Target Co., 4690 Wyaconda Rd., Rockville, MD 20852 / 800-827-7060 or 301-770-7060; FAX: 301-770-7892

Nationwide Airgun Repair, 2310 Windsor Forest Dr, Louisville, KY 40272 / 502-937-2614; FAX: 812-637-1463 airgunrepair@aol.com

Naval Ordnance Works, Rt. 2, Box 919, Sheperdstown, WV 25443 / 304-876-0998

Navy Arms Co., Inc., 219 Lawn St., Martinsburg, WV 25401 / 304-262-1651; FAX: 304-262-1658

Navy Arms Company, Valmore J. Forgett Jr., 815 22nd Street, Union City, NJ 07087 / 201-863-7100; FAX: 201-863-8770 info@navyarms.com www.navyarms.com

NCP Products, Inc., 3500 12th St. N.W., Canton, OH 44708 / 330-456-5130; FAX: 330-456-5234

Necessary Concepts, Inc., P.O. Box 571, Deer Park, NY 11729 / 516-667-8509; FAX: 516-667-8588

NEI Handtools, Inc., 51583 Columbia River Hwy., Scappoose, OR 97056 / 503-543-6776; FAX: 503-543-7865 nei@columbia-center.com www.neihandtools.com

Neil A. Jones Custom Products, 17217 Brookhouser Road, Saegertown, PA 16433 / 814-763-2769; FAX: 814-763-4228

Nelson, Gary K., 975 Terrace Dr., Oakdale, CA 95361 / 209-847-4590

Nelson, Stephen. See: NELSON'S CUSTOM GUNS, INC.

Nelson/Weather-Rite, Inc., 14760 Santa Fe Trail Dr., Lenexa, KS 66215 / 913-492-3200; FAX: 913-492-8749

Nelson's Custom Guns, Inc., Stephen Nelson, 7430 Valley View Dr. N.W., Corvallis, OR 97330 / 541-745-5232 nelsons-custom@attbi.com

Nesci Enterprises Inc., P.O. Box 119, Summit St., East Hampton, CT 06424 / 203-267-2588

Nesika Bay Precision, 22239 Big Valley Rd., Poulsbo, WA 98370 / 206-697-3830

Nettestad Gun Works, 38962 160th Avenue, Pelican Rapids, MN 56572 / 218-863-4301

Neumann GmbH, Am Galgenberg 6, 90575, GERMANY / 09101/8258; FAX: 09101/6356

Nevada Pistol Academy, Inc., 4610 Blue Diamond Rd., Las Vegas, NV 89139 / 702-897-1100

New England Ammunition Co., 1771 Post Rd. East, Suite 223, Westport, CT 06880 / 203-254-8048

New England Arms Co., Box 278, Lawrence Lane, Kittery Point, ME 03905 / 207-439-0593; FAX: 207-439-0525 info@newenglandarms.com www.newenglandarms.com

New England Custom Gun Service, 438 Willow Brook Rd., Plainfield, NH 03781 / 603-469-3450; FAX: 603-469-3471 bestguns@cyborportal.net www.newenglandcustom.com

New Orleans Jewelers Supply Co., 206 Charters St., New Orleans, LA 70130 / 504-523-3839; FAX: 504-523-3836

New SKB Arms Co., C.P.O. Box 1401, Tokyo, JAPAN / 81-3-3943-9550; FAX: 81-3-3943-0695

New Ultra Light Arms, LLC, 1024 Grafton Rd., Morgantown, WV 26508 / 304-292-0600; FAX: 304-292-9662 newultralightarm@cs.com www.NewUltraLightArm

Newark Electronics, 4801 N. Ravenswood Ave., Chicago, IL 60640

Newell, Robert H., 55 Coyote, Los Alamos, NM 87544 / 505-662-7135

Newman Gunshop, 2035 Chester Ave. #411, Ottumwa, IA 52501-3715 / 515-937-5775

Nicholson Custom, 17285 Thornlay Road, Hughesville, MO 65334 / 816-826-8746

Nickels, Paul R., 4328 Seville St., Las Vegas, NV 89121 / 702-435-5318

Nicklas, Ted, 5504 Hegel Rd., Goodrich, MI 48438 / 810-797-4493

Niemi Engineering, W. B., Box 126 Center Rd., Greensboro, VT 05841 / 802-533-7180; FAX: 802-533-7141

Nikon, Inc., 1300 Walt Whitman Rd., Melville, NY 11747 / 516-547-8623; FAX: 516-547-0309

Nitex Gun Shop, P.O. Box 1706, Uvalde, TX 78801 / 830-278-8843

Noreen, Peter H., 5075 Buena Vista Dr., Belgrade, MT 59714 / 406-586-7383

Norica, Avnda Otaola, 16 Apartado 68, Eibar, SPAIN

Norinco, 7A Yun Tan N, Beijing, CHINA

Norincoptics (See BEC, Inc.)

Norma Precision AB (See U.S. Importers-Dynamit)

Normark Corp., 10395 Yellow Circle Dr., Minnetonka, MN 55343-9101 / 612-933-7060; FAX: 612-933-0046

North American Arms, Inc., 2150 South 950 East, Provo, UT 84606-6285 / 800-821-5783; or 801-374-9990; FAX: 801-374-9998

North American Correspondence Schools The Gun Pro, Oak & Pawney St., Scranton, PA 18515 / 717-342-7701

North American Shooting Systems, P.O. Box 306, Osoyoos, BC V0H 1V0 CANADA / 604-495-3131; FAX: 604-495-2816

North Devon Firearms Services, 3 North St., Braunton, EX33 1AJ ENGLAND / 01271 813624; FAX: 01271 813624

North Mountain Pine Training Center (See Executive

North Specialty Products, 10091 Stageline St., Corona, CA 92883 / 714-524-1665

North Star West, P.O. Box 488, Glencoe, CA 95232 / 209-293-7010 northstarwest.com

Northern Precision Custom Swaged Bullets, 329 S. James St., Carthage, NY 13619 / 315-493-1711

Northlake Outdoor Footwear, P.O. Box 10, Franklin, TN 37065-0010 / 615-794-1556; FAX: 615-790-8005

Northside Gun Shop, 2725 NW 109th, Oklahoma City, OK 73120 / 405-840-2353

Northwest Arms, 26884 Pearl Rd., Parma, ID 83660 / 208-722-6771; FAX: 208-722-1062

No-Sho Mfg. Co., 10727 Glenfield Ct., Houston, TX 77096 / 713-723-5332

Nosler, Inc., P.O. Box 671, Bend, OR 97709 / 800-285-3701 or 541-382-3921; FAX: 541-388-4667

Novak's, Inc., 1206 1/2 30th St., P.O. Box 4045, Parkersburg, WV 26101 / 304-485-9295; FAX: 304-428-6722

Now Products, Inc., P.O. Box 27608, Tempe, AZ 85285 / 800-662-6063; FAX: 480-966-0890

Nowlin Mfg. Co., 20622 S 4092 Rd, Claremore, OK 74017 / 918-342-0689; FAX: 918-342-0624 nowlinguns@msn.com nowlinguns.com

NRI Gunsmith School, P.O. Box 182968, Columbus, OH 43218-2968

Nu-Line Guns,Inc., 1053 Caulks Hill Rd., Harvester, MO 63304 / 314-441-4500; or 314-447-4501; FAX: 314-447-5018

Null Holsters Ltd. K.L., 161 School St NW, Resaca, GA 30735 / 706-625-5643; FAX: 706-625-9392

Numrich Arms Corp., 203 Broadway, W. Hurley, NY 12491

Numrich Gun Parts Corporation, 226 Williams Lane, P.O. Box 299, West Hurley, NY 12491 / 866-686-7424; FAX: 877-GUNPART info@gunpartscorp.com www.@-gunparts.com

Nygord Precision Products, Inc., P.O. Box 12578, Prescott, AZ 86304 / 928-717-2315; FAX: 928-717-2198 nygords@northlink.com www.nygordprecision.com

O

O.F. Mossberg & Sons,Inc., 7 Grasso Ave., North Haven, CT 06473 / 203-230-5300; FAX: 203-230-5420

Oakman Turkey Calls, RD 1, Box 825, Harrisonville, PA 17228 / 717-485-4620

Obermeyer Rifled Barrels, 23122 60th St., Bristol, WI 53104 / 262-843-3537; FAX: 262-843-2129

October Country Muzzleloading, P.O. Box 969, Dept. GD, Hayden, ID 83835 / 208-772-2068; FAX: 208-772-9230 ocinfo@octobercountry.com www.octobercountry.com

Oehler Research,Inc., P.O. Box 9135, Austin, TX 78766 / 512-327-6900 or 800-531-5125; FAX: 512-327-6903 www.oehler-research.com

Oil Rod and Gun Shop, 69 Oak St., East Douglas, MA 01516 / 508-476-3687

Ojala Holsters, Arvo, PO Box 98, N Hollywood, CA 91603 / 503-669-1404

OK Weber, Inc., P.O. Box 7485, Eugene, OR 97401 / 541-747-0458; FAX: 541-747-5927 okweber@pacinfo www.okweber.com

Oker's Engraving, P.O. Box 126, Shawnee, CO 80475 / 303-838-6042

Oklahoma Ammunition Co., 3701A S. Harvard Ave., No. 367, Tulsa, OK 74135-2265 / 918-396-3187; FAX: 918-396-4270

Oklahoma Leather Products,Inc., 500 26th NW, Miami, OK 74354 / 918-542-6651; FAX: 918-542-6653

Olathe Gun Shop, 716-A South Rogers Road, Olathe, KS 66062 / 913-782-6900; FAX: 913-782-6902 info@olathegunshop.com www.olathegunshop.com

Old Wagon Bullets, 32 Old Wagon Rd., Wilton, CT 06897

Old West Bullet Moulds, J Ken Chapman, P.O. Box 519, Flora Vista, NM 87415 / 505-334-6970

Old West Reproductions,Inc. R.M. Bachman, 446 Florence S. Loop, Florence, MT 59833 / 406-273-2615; FAX: 406-273-2615 rick@oldwestreproductions.com www.oldwestreproduction.com

Old World Gunsmithing, 2901 SE 122nd St., Portland, OR 97236 / 503-760-7681

Old World Oil Products, 3827 Queen Ave. N., Minneapolis, MN 55412 / 612-522-5037

Ole Frontier Gunsmith Shop, 2617 Hwy. 29 S., Cantonment, FL 32533 / 904-477-8074

Olson, Myron, 989 W. Kemp, Watertown, SD 57201 / 605-886-9787

Olson, Vic, 5002 Countryside Dr., Imperial, MO 63052 / 314-296-8086

Olympic Arms Inc., 620-626 Old Pacific Hwy. SE, Olympia, WA 98513 / 360-456-3471; FAX: 360-491-3447 info@olyarms.com www.olyarms.com

Olympic Optical Co., P.O. Box 752377, Memphis, TN 38175-2377 / 901-794-3890; or 800-238-7120; FAX: 901-794-0676 80

Omark Industries, Div. of Blount, Inc., 2299 Snake River Ave., P.O. Box 856, Lewiston, ID 83501 / 800-627-3640 or 208-746-2351

Omega Sales, P.O. Box 1066, Mt. Clemens, MI 48043 / 810-469-7323; FAX: 810-469-0425

100 Straight Products, Inc., P.O. Box 6148, Omaha, NE 68106 / 402-556-1055; FAX: 402-556-1055

One Of A Kind, 15610 Purple Sage, San Antonio, TX 78255 / 512-695-3364

One Ragged Hole, P.O. Box 13624, Tallahassee, FL 32317-3624

Op-Tec, P.O. Box L632, Langhorn, PA 19047 / 215-757-5037

Optical Services Co., P.O. Box 1174, Santa Teresa, NM 88008-1174 / 505-589-3833

Orchard Park Enterprise, P.O. Box 563, Orchard Park, NY 14127 / 616-656-0356

Oregon Arms, Inc. (See Rogue Rifle Co., Inc.)

Oregon Trail Bullet Company, PO Box 529, Dept. P, Baker City, OR 97814 / 800-811-0548; FAX: 514-523-1803

Original Box, Inc., 700 Linden Ave., York, PA 17404 / 717-854-2897; FAX: 717-845-4276

Original Deer Formula Co., The., PO Box 1705, Dickson, TN 37056 / 800-874-6965; FAX: 615-446-0646 deerformula1@aol.com

Original Mink Oil, Inc., 10652 NE Holman, Portland, OR 97220 / 503-255-2814; or 800-547-5895; FAX: 503-255-2487

Orion Rifle Barrel Co., RR2, 137 Cobler Village, Kalispell, MT 59901 / 406-257-5649

Otis Technology, Inc., RR 1 Box 84, Boonville, NY 13309 / 315-942-3320

Ottmar, Maurice, Box 657, 113 E. Fir, Coulee City, WA 99115 / 509-632-5717

Outa-Site Gun Carriers, 219 Market St., Laredo, TX 78040 / 210-722-4678; or 800-880-9715; FAX: 210-726-4858

Outdoor Edge Cutlery Corp., 4699 Nautilus Ct. S. Ste. 503, Boulder, CO 80301-5310 / 303-652-8212; FAX: 303-652-8238

Outdoor Enthusiast, 3784 W. Woodland, Springfield, MO 65807 / 417-883-9841

Outdoor Sports Headquarters, Inc., 967 Watertower Ln., West Carrollton, OH 45449 / 513-865-5855; FAX: 513-865-5962

Outers Laboratories Div. of ATK, Route 2, P.O. Box 39, Onalaska, WI 54650 / 608-781-5800; FAX: 608-781-0368

Ox-Yoke Originals, Inc., 34 Main St., Milo, ME 04463 / 800-231-8313; or 207-943-7351; FAX: 207-943-2416

Ozark Gun Works, 11830 Cemetery Rd., Rogers, AR 72756 / 479-631-1024; FAX: 479-631-1024 ogw@hotmail.com www.eocities.com/ocarkgunworks

P

P&M Sales & Services, LLC, 4697 Tote Rd. Bldg. H-B, Comins, MI 48619 / 989-848-8364; FAX: 989-848-8364 info@pmsales-online.com

P.A.C.T., Inc., P.O. Box 531525, Grand Prairie, TX 75053 / 214-641-0049

P.S.M.G. Gun Co., 10 Park Ave., Arlington, MA 02174 / 617-646-8845; FAX: 617-646-2133

Pachmayr Div. Lyman Products, 475 Smith St., Middletown, CT 06457 / 860-632-2020; or 800-225-9626; FAX: 860-632-1699 lymansales@cshore.com www.pachmayr.com

Pacific Armament Corp, 4813 Enterprise Way, Unit K, Modesto, CA 95356 / 209-545-2800 gunsparts@att.net

Pacific Cartridge, Inc., 2425 Salashan Loop Road, Ferndale, WA 98248 / 360-366-4444; FAX: 360-366-4445

Pacific Rifle Co., PO Box 1473, Lake Oswego, OR 97035 / 503-538-7437

PAC-NOR Barreling, 99299 Overlook Rd., P.O. Box 6188, Brookings, OR 97415 / 503-469-7330; FAX: 503-469-7331 info@pac-nor.com www.pac-nor.com

Paco's (See Small Custom Mould & Bullet Co.)

Page Custom Bullets, P.O. Box 25, Port Moresby, NEW GUINEA

Pagel Gun Works, Inc., 1407 4th St. NW, Grand Rapids, MN 55744 / 218-326-3003

Pager Pal, 200 W Pleasantview, Hurst, TX 76054 / 800-561-1603; FAX: 817-285-8769 www.pagerpal.com

Paintball Games International Magazine Aceville, Castle House 97 High St., Essex, ENGLAND / 011-44-206-564840

Palmer Security Products, 2930 N. Campbell Ave., Chicago, IL 60618 / 773-267-0200; FAX: 773-267-8080 info@palmersecurity.com www.palmersecurity.com

Palsa Outdoor Products, P.O. Box 81336, Lincoln, NE 68501 / 402-488-5288; FAX: 402-488-2321

Paragon Sales & Services, Inc., 2501 Theodore St, Crest Hill, IL 60435-1613 / 815-725-9212; FAX: 815-725-8974

Para-Ordnance Mfg., Inc., 980 Tapscott Rd., Scarborough, ON M1X 1E7 CANADA / 416-297-7855; FAX: 416-297-1289

Para-Ordnance, Inc., 1919 NE 45th St., Ste 215, Ft. Lauderdale, FL 33308 info@paraord.com www.paraord.com

Pardini Armi Srl, Via Italica 154, 55043, Lido Di Camaiore Lu, ITALY / 584-90121; FAX: 584-90122

Paris, Frank J., 17417 Pershing St., Livonia, MI 48152-3822

Parker & Sons Shooting Supply, 9337 Smoky Row Road, Strawberry Plains, TN 37871 / 865-933-3286; FAX: 865-932-8586

Parker Gun Finishes, 9337 Smokey Row Rd., Strawberry Plains, TN 37871 / 423-933-3286; FAX: 865-932-8586

Parker Reproductions, 114 Broad St., Flemington, NJ 11232 / 718-499-6220; FAX: 718-499-6143

Parsons Optical Mfg. Co., PO Box 192, Ross, OH 45061 / 513-867-0820; FAX: 513-867-8380 psscopes@concentric.net

Partridge Sales Ltd., John, Trent Meadows, Rugeley, ENGLAND

Pasadena Gun Center, 206 E. Shaw, Pasadena, TX 77506 / 713-472-0417; FAX: 713-472-1322

Passive Bullet Traps, Inc. (See Savage Range Systems, Inc.)

Paterson Gunsmithing, 438 Main St., Paterson, NJ 07502 / 201-345-4100

Pathfinder Sports Leather, 2920 E. Chambers St., Phoenix, AZ 85040 / 602-276-0016

Patrick W. Price Bullets, 16520 Worthley Drive, San Lorenzo, CA 94580 / 510-278-1547

Pattern Control, 114 N. Third St., P.O. Box 462105, Garland, TX 75046 / 214-494-3551; FAX: 214-272-8447

Paul A. Harris Hand Engraving, 113 Rusty Lane, Boerne, TX 78006-5746 / 512-391-5121

Paul and Sharon Dressel, 209 N. 92nd Ave., Yakima, WA 98908 / 509-966-9233; FAX: 509-966-3365 dressels@nwinfo.net www.dressels.com

Paul D. Hillmer Custom Gunstocks, 7251 Hudson Heights, Hudson, IA 50643 / 319-988-3941

Paul Jones Moulds, 4901 Telegraph Rd., Los Angeles, CA 90022 / 213-262-1510

Paulsen Gunstocks, Rt. 71, Box 11, Chinook, MT 59523 / 406-357-3403

Pawling Mountain Club, Keith Lupton, PO Box 573, Pawling, NY 12564 / 914-855-3825

Paxton Quigley's Personal Protection Strategies, 9903 Santa Monica Blvd., 300, Beverly Hills, CA 90212 / 310-281-1762 www.defend-net.com/paxton

Payne Photography, Robert, Robert, P.O. Box 141471, Austin, TX 78714 / 512-272-4554

Peacemaker Specialists, P.O. Box 157, Whitmore, CA 96096 / 530-472-3438 www.peacemakerspecialists.com

Pearce Grip, Inc., PO Box 40367, Fort Worth, TX 76140 / 206-485-5488; FAX: 206-488-9497

Pease Accuracy, Bob, P.O. Box 310787, New Braunfels, TX 78131 / 210-625-1342

PECAR Herbert Schwarz GmbH, Kreuzbergstrasse 6, 10965, Berlin, GERMANY / 004930-785-7383; FAX: 004930-785-1934 michael.schwart@pecar-berlin.de www.pecar-berlin.de

Pecatonica River Longrifle, 5205 Nottingham Dr., Rockford, IL 61111 / 815-968-1995; FAX: 815-968-1996

Pedersen, C. R., 2717 S. Pere Marquette Hwy., Ludington, MI 49431 / 231-843-2061; FAX: 231-845-7695 fega@fega.com

Pedersen, Rex C., 2717 S. Pere Marquette Hwy., Ludington, MI 49431 / 231-843-2061; FAX: 231-845-7695 fega@fega.com

Peifer Rifle Co., P.O. Box 192, Nokomis, IL 62075-0192 / 217-563-7050; FAX: 217-563-7060

Pejsa Ballistics, 1314 Marquette Ave., Apt 807, Minneapolis, MN 55403 / 612-374-3337; FAX: 612-374-5383

Pelaire Products, 5346 Bonky Ct., W. Palm Beach, FL 33415 / 561-439-0691; FAX: 561-967-0052

Peltor, Inc. (See Aero Peltor)

PEM's Mfg. Co., 5063 Waterloo Rd., Atwater, OH 44201 / 216-947-3721

Pence Precision Barrels, 7567 E. 900 S., S. Whitley, IN 46787 / 219-839-4745

Pendleton Royal, c/o Swingler Buckland Ltd., 4/7 Highgate St., Birmingham, ENGLAND / 44 121 440 3060; or 44 121 446 5898; FAX: 44 121 446 4165

Pendleton Woolen Mills, P.O. Box 3030, 220 N.W. Broadway, Portland, OR 97208 / 503-226-4801

Penn Bullets, P.O. Box 756, Indianola, PA 15051

Pennsylvania Gun Parts Inc., P.O. Box 665, 300 Third St, East Berlin, PA 17316-0665 / 717-259-8010; FAX: 717-259-0057

Pennsylvania Gunsmith School, 812 Ohio River Blvd., Avalon, Pittsburgh, PA 15202 / 412-766-1812; FAX: 412-766-0855 pgs@pagunsmith.com www.pagunsmith.com

Penrod Precision, 312 College Ave., PO Box 307, N. Manchester, IN 46962 / 260-982-8385; FAX: 260-982-1819

Pentax Corp., 35 Inverness Dr. E., Englewood, CO 80112 / 303-799-8000; FAX: 303-790-1131

Pentheny de Pentheny, 2352 Baggett Ct., Santa Rosa, CA 95401 / 707-573-1390; FAX: 707-573-1390

Perazone-Gunsmith, Brian, Cold Spring Rd., Roxbury, NY 12474 / 607-326-4088; FAX: 607-326-3140

Perazzi U.S.A. Inc., 1010 West Tenth, Azusa, CA 91702 / 626-334-1234; FAX: 626-334-0344 perazziusa@aol.com

Performance Specialists, 308 Eanes School Rd., Austin, TX 78746 / 512-327-0119

Perugini Visini & Co. S.r.l., Via Camprelle, 126, 25080 Nuvolera, ITALY / 30-6897535; FAX: 30-6897821 peruvisi@virgilia.it

Pete Mazur Restoration, 13083 Drummer Way, Grass Valley, CA 95949 / 530-268-2412; FAX: 530-268-2412

Pete Rickard, Inc., 115 Roy Walsh Rd, Cobleskill, NY 12043 / 518-234-2731: FAX: 518-234-2454 rickard@telenet.net www.peterickard.com

Peter Dyson & Son Ltd., 3 Cuckoo Lane, Honley Huddersfield, Yorkshire, HD7 2BR ENGLAND / 44-1484-661062; FAX: 44-1484-663709 info@peterdyson.co.uk www.peterdyson.com

Peter Hale/Engraver, 800 E. Canyon Rd., Spanish Fork, UT 84660 / 801-798-8215

Peters Stahl GmbH, Stettiner Strasse 42, D-33106, Paderborn, GERMANY / 05251-750025; FAX: 05251-75611

Petersen Publishing Co., 6420 Wilshire Blvd., Los Angeles, CA 90048 / 213-782-2000; FAX: 213-782-2867

Peterson Gun Shop, Inc., A.W., 4255 W. Old U.S. 441, Mt. Dora, FL 32757-3299 / 352-383-4258; FAX: 352-735-1001

Petro-Explo Inc., 7650 U.S. Hwy. 287, Suite 100, Arlington, TX 76017 / 817-478-8888

Pettinger Books, Gerald, 47827 300th Ave., Russell, IA 50238 / 641-535-2239 gpettinger@lisco.com

Pflumm Mfg. Co., 10662 Widmer Rd., Lenexa, KS 66215 / 800-888-4867; FAX: 913-451-7857

PFRB Co., P.O. Box 1242, Bloomington, IL 61702 / 309-473-3964 or 800-914-5464; FAX: 309-473-2161

Philip S. Olt Co., P.O. Box 550, 12662 Fifth St., Pekin, IL 61554 / 309-348-3633; FAX: 309-348-3300

Phillippi Custom Bullets, Justin, P.O. Box 773, Ligonier, PA 15658 / 724-238-2962; FAX: 724-238-9671 jrp@wpa.net http://www.wpa.net~jrphil

Phillips & Rogers, Inc., 100 Hilbig #C, Conroe, TX 77301 / 409-435-0011

Phoenix Arms, 1420 S. Archibald Ave., Ontario, CA 91761 / 909-947-4843; FAX: 909-947-6798

Photronic Systems Engineering Company, 6731 Via De La Reina, Bonsall, CA 92003 / 619-758-8000

Piedmont Community College, P.O. Box 1197, Roxboro, NC 27573 / 336-599-1181; FAX: 336-597-3817 www.piedmont.cc.nc.us

Pierce Pistols, 55 Sorrellwood Lane, Sharpsburg, GA 30277-9523 / 404-253-8192

Pietta (See U.S. Importers-Navy Arms Co, Taylor's

Pilgrim Pewter,Inc. (See Bell Originals Inc. Sid)

Pilkington, Scott (See Little Trees Ramble)

Pine Technical College, 1100 4th St., Pine City, MN 55063 / 800-521-7463; FAX: 612-629-6766

Pinetree Bullets, 133 Skeena St., Kitimat, BC V8C 1Z1 CANADA / 604-632-3768; FAX: 604-632-3768

Pioneer Arms Co., 355 Lawrence Rd., Broomall, PA 19008 / 215-356-5203

Piotti (See U.S. Importer-Moore & Co, Wm. Larkin)

Piquette, Paul. See: PIQUETTE'S CUSTOM ENGRAVING

Piquette's Custom Engraving, Paul R. Piquette, 80 Bradford Dr., Feeding Hills, MA 01030 / 413-789-4582; FAX: 413-786-8118 ppiquette@aol.com www.pistoldynamics.com

Plaza Cutlery, Inc., 3333 Bristol, 161 South Coast Plaza, Costa Mesa, CA 92626 / 714-549-3932

Plum City Ballistic Range, N2162 80th St., Plum City, WI 54761 / 715-647-2539

PlumFire Press, Inc., 30-A Grove Ave., Patchogue, NY 11772-4112 / 800-695-7246; FAX: 516-758-4071

PMC/Eldorado Cartridge Corp., P.O. Box 62508, 12801 U.S. Hwy. 95 S., Boulder City, NV 89005 / 702-294-0025; FAX: 702-294-0121 kbauer@pmcammo.com www.pmcammo.com

Poburka, Philip (See Bison Studios)

Pohl, Henry A. (See Great American Gun Co.

Pointing Dog Journal, Village Press Publications, P.O. Box 968, Dept. PGD, Traverse City, MI 49685 / 800-272-3246; FAX: 616-946-3289

Police Bookshelf, PO Box 122, Concord, NH 03301 / 603-224-6814; FAX: 603-226-3554

Polywad, Inc., P.O. Box 7916, Macon, GA 31209 / 478-477-0669; or 800-998-0669 polywadmpb@aol.com www.polywad.com

Ponsness/Warren, 768 Ohio St., Rathdrum, ID 83858 / 800-732-0706; FAX: 208-687-2233

Pony Express Reloaders, 608 E. Co. Rd. D, Suite 3, St. Paul, MN 55117 / 612-483-9406; FAX: 612-483-9884

Pony Express Sport Shop, 23404 Lyons Ave., PMB 448, Newhall, CA 91321-2511 / 818-895-1231

Potts, Wayne E., 912 Poplar St., Denver, CO 80220 / 303-355-5462

Powder Horn Ltd., PO Box 565, Glenview, IL 60025 / 305-565-6060

Powell & Son (Gunmakers) Ltd., William, 35-37 Carrs Lane, Birmingham, B4 7SX ENGLAND / 121-643-0689; FAX: 121-631-3504

Powell Agency, William, 22 Circle Dr., Bellmore, NY 11710 / 516-679-1158

Power Custom, Inc., 29739 Hwy. J, Gravois Mills, MO 65037 / 573-372-5684; FAX: 573-372-5799 rwpowers@laurie.net www.powercustom.com

Power Plus Enterprises, Inc., PO Box 38, Warm Springs, GA 31830 / 706-655-2132

Powley Computer (See Hutton Rifle Ranch)

Practical Tools, Inc., 7067 Easton Rd., P.O. Box 133, Pipersville, PA 18947 / 215-766-7301; FAX: 215-766-8681

Prairie Gun Works, 1-761 Marion St., Winnipeg, MB R2J 0K6 CANADA / 204-231-2976; FAX: 204-231-8566

Prairie River Arms, 1220 N. Sixth St., Princeton, IL 61356 / 815-875-1616 or 800-445-1541; FAX: 815-875-1402

Pranger, Ed G., 1414 7th St., Anacortes, WA 98221 / 206-293-3488

Precision Airgun Sales, Inc., 5247 Warrensville Ctr Rd., Maple Hts., OH 44137 / 216-587-5005; FAX: 216-587-5005

Precision Cast Bullets, 101 Mud Creek Lane, Ronan, MT 59864 / 406-676-5135

Precision Delta Corp., PO Box 128, Ruleville, MS 38771 / 662-756-2810; FAX: 662-756-2590

Precision Firearm Finishing, 25 N.W. 44th Avenue, Des Moines, IA 50313 / 515-288-8680; FAX: 515-244-3925

Precision Gun Works, 104 Sierra Rd.Dept. GD, Kerrville, TX 78028 / 830-367-4587

Precision Reloading, Inc., PO Box 122, Stafford Springs, CT 06076 / 860-684-7979; FAX: 860-684-6788 info@precisionreloading.com www.precisionreloading.com

Precision Sales International, Inc., PO Box 1776, Westfield, MA 01086 / 413-562-5055; FAX: 413-562-5056 precision-sales.com

Precision Shooting, Inc., 222 McKee St., Manchester, CT 06040 / 860-645-8776; FAX: 860-643-8215 www.precisionshooting.com

Precision Small Arms Inc., 9272 Jeronimo Rd, Ste 121, Irvine, CA 92618 / 800-554-5515; or 949-768-3530; FAX: 949-768-4808 www.tcbebe.com

Precision Specialties, 131 Hendom Dr., Feeding Hills, MA 01030 / 413-786-3365; FAX: 413-786-3365

Precision Sport Optics, 15571 Producer Lane, Unit G, Huntington Beach, CA 92649 / 714-891-1309; FAX: 714-892-6920

Premier Reticles, 920 Breckinridge Lane, Winchester, VA 22601-6707 / 540-722-0601; FAX: 540-722-3522

Prescott Projectile Co., 1808 Meadowbrook Road, Prescott, AZ 86303

Preslik's Gunstocks, 4245 Keith Ln., Chico, CA 95926 / 916-891-8236

Price Bullets, Patrick W., 16520 Worthley Dr., San Lorenzo, CA 94580 / 510-278-1547

Prime Reloading, 30 Chiswick End, Meldreth, ROYSTON UK / 0763-260636

Primos, Inc., P.O. Box 12785, Jackson, MS 39236-2785 / 601-366-1288; FAX: 601-362-3274

PRL Bullets, c/o Blackburn Enterprises, 114 Stuart Rd., Ste. 110, Cleveland, TN 37312 / 423-559-0340

Pro Load Ammunition, Inc., 5180 E. Seltice Way, Post Falls, ID 83854 / 208-773-9444; FAX: 208-773-9441

Professional Gunsmiths of America, Rt 1 Box 224, Lexington, MO 64067 / 660-259-2636

Professional Hunter Supplies (See Star Custom Bullets), PO Box 608, 468 Main St., Ferndale, CA 95536 / 707-786-9140; FAX: 707-786-9117 wmebride@humboldt.com

PrOlixr Lubricants, P.O. Box 1348, Victorville, CA 92393 / 760-243-3129; FAX: 760-241-0148 prolix@accex.net www.prolixlubricant.com

Pro-Mark Div. of Wells Lamont, 6640 W. Touhy, Chicago, IL 60648 / 312-647-8200

Proofmark Corp., P.O. Box 610, Burgess, VA 22432 / 804-453-4337; FAX: 804-453-4337 proofmark@rivnet.net

Pro-Port Ltd., 41302 Executive Dr., Harrison Twp., MI 48045-1306 / 586-469-6727; FAX: 586-469-0425 e-mail@magnaport.com www.magnaport.com

Pro-Shot Products, Inc., P.O. Box 763, Taylorville, IL 62568 / 217-824-9133; FAX: 217-824-8861

Protektor Model, 1-11 Bridge St., Galeton, PA 16922 / 814-435-2442 info@protektormodel.com www.protektormodel.com

Prototech Industries, Inc., 10532 E Road, Delia, KS 66418 / 785-771-3571; prototec@grapevine.net

ProWare, Inc., 15847 NE Hancock St., Portland, OR 97230 / 503-239-0159

PWL Gunleather, P.O. Box 450432, Atlanta, GA 31145 / 800-960-4072; FAX: 770-822-1704 covert@pwlusa.com www.pwlusa.com

Pyramyd Stone Inter. Corp., 2447 Suffolk Lane, Pepper Pike, OH 44124-4540

Q

Quack Decoy & Sporting Clays, 4 Ann & Hope Way, P.O. Box 98, Cumberland, RI 02864 / 401-723-8202; FAX: 401-722-5910

Quaker Boy, Inc., 5455 Webster Rd., Orchard Parks, NY 14127 / 716-662-3979; FAX: 716-662-9426

Quality Arms, Inc., Box 19477, Dept. GD, Houston, TX 77224 / 281-870-8377; FAX: 281-870-8524 arrieta2@excite.com www.gunshop.com

Quality Custom Firearms, Stepehn Billeb, 22 Vista View Drive, Cody, WY 82414 / 307-587-4278; FAX: 307-587-4297 stevebilleb@wyoming.com

Que Industries, Inc., PO Box 2471, Everett, WA 98203 / 425-303-9088; FAX: 206-514-3266 queinfo@queindustries.com

Queen Cutlery Company, PO Box 500, Franklinville, NY 14737 / 800-222-5233; FAX: 800-299-2618

R

R&C Knives & Such, 2136 CANDY CANE WALK, Manteca, CA 95336-9501 / 209-239-3722; FAX: 209-825-6947

R&D Gun Repair, Kenny Howell, RR1 Box 283, Beloit, WI 53511

R&J Gun Shop, 337 S. Humbolt St., Canyon City, OR 97820 / 541-575-2130 rjgunshop@highdestertnet.com

R&S Industries Corp., 8255 Brentwood Industrial Dr., St. Louis, MO 63144 / 314-781-5169 ron@miraclepolishingcloth.com www.miraclepolishingcloth.com

R. Murphy Co., Inc., 13 Groton-Harvard Rd., P.O. Box 376, Ayer, MA 01432 / 617-772-3481

R.A. Wells Custom Gunsmith, 3452 1st Ave., Racine, WI 53402 / 414-639-5223

R.E. Seebeck Assoc., P.O. Box 59752, Dallas, TX 75229

R.E.I., P.O. Box 88, Tallevast, FL 34270 / 813-755-0085

R.E.T. Enterprises, 2608 S. Chestnut, Broken Arrow, OK 74012 / 918-251-GUNS; FAX: 918-251-0587

R.F. Mitchell Rifles, 430 Walnut St., Westernport, MD 21562

R.I.S. Co., Inc., 718 Timberlake Circle, Richardson, TX 75080 / 214-235-0933

R.T. Eastman Products, P.O. Box 1531, Jackson, WY 83001 / 307-733-3217; or 800-624-4311

Rabeno, Martin, 92 Spook Hole Rd., Ellenville, NY 12428 / 845-647-2129; FAX: 845-647-2129 fancygun@aol.com

Radack Photography, Lauren, 21140 Jib Court L-12, Aventura, FL 33180 / 305-931-3110

Radiator Specialty Co., 1900 Wilkinson Blvd., P.O. Box 34689, Charlotte, NC 28234 / 800-438-6947; FAX: 800-421-9525

Radical Concepts, P.O. Box 1473, Lake Grove, OR 97035 / 503-538-7437

Rainier Ballistics Corp., 4500 15th St. East, Tacoma, WA 98424 / 800-638-8722 or 206-922-7589; FAX: 206-922-7854

Ralph Bone Engraving, 718 N. Atlanta St., Owasso, OK 74055 / 918-272-9745

Ram-Line ATK, P.O. Box 39, Onalaska, WI 54650

Ramon B. Gonzalez Guns, P.O. Box 370, Monticello, NY 12701 / 914-794-4515

Rampart International, 2781 W. MacArthur Blvd., B-283, Santa Ana, CA 92704 / 800-976-7240 or 714-557-6405

Ranch Products, P.O. Box 145, Malinta, OH 43535 / 313-277-3118; FAX: 313-565-8536

Randall-Made Knives, P.O. Box 1988, Orlando, FL 32802 / 407-855-8075

Randco UK, 286 Gipsy Rd., Welling, DA16 1JJ ENGLAND / 44 81 303 4118

Randolph Engineering Inc., 26 Thomas Patten Dr., Randolph, MA 02368 / 781-961-6070; FAX: 781-961-0337

Randy Duane Custom Stocks, 7822 Church St., Middletown, VA 22645-9521

Range Brass Products Company, P.O. Box 218, Rockport, TX 78381

Ranger Shooting Glasses, 26 Thomas Patten Dr., Randolph, MA 02368 / 800-541-1405; FAX: 617-986-0337

Ransom International Corp., 1027 Spire Dr, Prescott, AZ 86302 / 520-778-7899; FAX: 520-778-7993 ransom@primenet.com www.ransom-intl.com

Rapine Bullet Mould Mfg. Co., 9503 Landis Lane, East Greenville, PA 18041 / 215-679-5413; FAX: 215-679-9795

Ravell Ltd., 289 Diputacion St., 08009, Barcelona, SPAIN / 34(3) 4874486; FAX: 34(3) 4881394

Ray Riling Arms Books Co., 6844 Gorsten St., Philadelphia, PA 19119 / 215-438-2456; FAX: 215-438-5395 sales@rayrilingarmsbooks.com www.rayrilingarmsbooks.com

Ray's Gunsmith Shop, 3199 Elm Ave., Grand Junction, CO 81504 / 970-434-6162; FAX: 970-434-6162

Raytech Div. of Lyman Products Corp., 475 Smith Street, Middletown, CT 06457-1541 / 860-632-2020 or 800-225-9626; FAX: 860-632-1699 lymansales@cshore.com www.lymanproducts.com

RCBS Operations/ATK, 605 Oro Dam Blvd., Oroville, CA 95965 / 530-533-5191 or 800-533-5000; FAX: 530-533-1647 www.rcbs.com

RCBS/ATK, 605 Oro Dam Blvd., Oroville, CA 95965 / 800-533-5000; FAX: 916-533-1647

Reagent Chemical & Research, Inc., 114 Broad St., Flemington, NJ 11232 / 718-499-6220; FAX: 718-499-6143

Reardon Products, P.O. Box 126, Morrison, IL 61270 / 815-772-3155

Red Diamond Dist. Co., 1304 Snowdon Dr., Knoxville, TN 37912

Redding Reloading Equipment, 1089 Starr Rd., Cortland, NY 13045 / 607-753-3331; FAX: 607-756-8445 techline@redding-reloading.com www.redding-reloading.com

Redfield Media Resource Center, 4607 N.E. Cedar Creek Rd., Woodland, WA 98674 / 360-225-5000; FAX: 360-225-7616

Redman's Rifling & Reboring, 189 Nichols Rd., Omak, WA 98841 / 509-826-5512

Redwood Bullet Works, 3559 Bay Rd., Redwood City, CA 94063 / 415-367-6741

Reed, Dave, Rt. 1, Box 374, Minnesota City, MN 55959 / 507-689-2944

Reimer Johannsen, Inc., 438 Willow Brook Rd., Plainfield, NH 03781 / 603-469-3450; FAX: 603-469-3471

Reiswig, Wallace E. (See Claro Walnut Gunstock

Reloaders Equipment Co., 4680 High St., Ecorse, MI 48229

Reloading Specialties, Inc., Box 1130, Pine Island, MN 55463 / 507-356-8500; FAX: 507-356-8800

Remington Arms Co., Inc., 870 Remington Drive, P.O. Box 700, Madison, NC 27025-0700 / 800-243-9700; FAX: 910-548-8700

Remington Double Shotguns, 7885 Cyd Dr., Denver, CO 80221 / 303-429-6947

Renato Gamba S.p.A.-Societa Armi Bresciane Srl., Via Artigiani 93, 25063 Gardone, Val Trompia (BS), ITALY / 30-8911640; FAX: 30-8911648

Renegade, PO Box 31546, Phoenix, AZ 85046 / 602-482-6777; FAX: 602-482-1952

Renfrew Guns & Supplies, R.R. 4, Renfrew, ON K7V 3Z7 CANADA / 613-432-7080

Reno, Wayne, 2808 Stagestop Road, Jefferson, CO 80456

Republic Arms, Inc. (See Cobra Enterprises, Inc.)

Retting, Inc., Martin B, 11029 Washington, Culver City, CA 90232 / 213-837-2412

RG-G, Inc., PO Box 935, Trinidad, CO 81082 / 719-845-1436

RH Machine & Consulting Inc, PO Box 394, Pacific, MO 63069 / 314-271-8465

Rhino, P.O. Box 787, Locust, NC 28097 / 704-753-2198

Rhodeside, Inc., 1704 Commerce Dr., Piqua, OH 45356 / 513-773-5781

Rice, Keith (See White Rock Tool & Die)

Richards Micro-Fit Stocks, 8331 N. San Fernando Ave., Sun Valley, CA 91352 / 818-767-6097; FAX: 818-767-7121

Ridgeline, Inc., Bruce Sheldon, P.O. Box 930, Dewey, AZ 86327-0930 / 800-632-5900; FAX: 520-632-5900

Ridgetop Sporting Goods, P.O. Box 306, 42907 Hilligoss Ln. East, Eatonville, WA 98328 / 360-832-6422; FAX: 360-832-6422

Ries, Chuck, 415 Ridgecrest Dr., Grants Pass, OR 97527 / 503-476-5623

Riggs, Jim, 206 Azalea, Boerne, TX 78006 / 210-249-8567

Riley Ledbetter Airguns, 1804 E. Sprague St., Winston Salem, NC 27107-3521 / 919-784-0676

Rim Pac Sports, Inc., 1034 N. Soldano Ave., Azusa, CA 91702-2135

Ringler Custom Leather Co., 31 Shining Mtn. Rd., Powell, WY 82435 / 307-645-3255

Ripley Rifles, 42 Fletcher Street, Ripley, Derbyshire, DE5 3LP ENGLAND / 011-0773-748353

Rizzini F.lli (See U.S. Importers-Moore & C England)

Rizzini SNC, Via 2 Giugno, 7/7Bis-25060, Marcheno (Brescia), ITALY

RLCM Enterprises, 110 Hill Crest Drive, Burleson, TX 76028

RMS Custom Gunsmithing, 4120 N. Bitterwell, Prescott Valley, AZ 86314 / 520-772-7626

Robert Evans Engraving, 332 Vine St., Oregon City, OR 97045 / 503-656-5693

Robert Valade Engraving, 931 3rd Ave., Seaside, OR 97138 / 503-738-7672

Robinett, R. G., P.O. Box 72, Madrid, IA 50156 / 515-795-2906

Robinson, Don, Pennsylvania Hse, 36 Fairfax Crescent, W Yorkshire, ENGLAND / 0422-364458

Robinson Armament Co., PO Box 16776, Salt Lake City, UT 84116 / 801-355-0401; FAX: 801-355-0402 zdf@robarm.com www.robarm.com

Robinson Firearms Mfg. Ltd., 1699 Blondeaux Crescent, Kelowna, BC V1Y 4J8 CANADA / 604-868-9596

Robinson H.V. Bullets, 3145 Church St., Zachary, LA 70791 / 504-654-4029

Rochester Lead Works, 76 Anderson Ave., Rochester, NY 14607 / 716-442-8500; FAX: 716-442-4712

Rock River Arms, 101 Noble St., Cleveland, IL 61241

Rockwood Corp., Speedwell Division, 136 Lincoln Blvd., Middlesex, NJ 08846 / 800-243-8274; FAX: 980-560-7475

Rocky Mountain Armoury, Mr. Felix LesMerises, 610 Main Street, P.O. Box 691, Frisco, CO 80443-0691 / 970-668-0136; FAX: 970-668-4484 felix@rockymountainarmoury.com

Rocky Mountain Arms, Inc., 1813 Sunset Pl, Unit D, Longmont, CO 80501 / 800-375-0846; FAX: 303-678-8766

Rocky Mountain Target Co., 3 Aloe Way, Leesburg, FL 34788 / 352-365-9598

Rocky Mountain Wildlife Products, P.O. Box 999, La Porte, CO 80535 / 970-484-2768; FAX: 970-484-0807 critrcall@earthlink.net www.critrcall.com

Rocky Shoes & Boots, 294 Harper St., Nelsonville, OH 45764 / 800-848-9452; or 614-753-1951; FAX: 614-753-4024

Rodgers & Sons Ltd., Joseph (See George Ibberson)

Rogue Rifle Co., Inc., P.O. Box 20, Prospect, OR 97536 / 541-560-4040; FAX: 541-560-4041

Rogue River Rifleworks, 500 Linne Road #D, Paso Robles, CA 93446 / 805-227-4706; FAX: 805-227-4723 rrrifles@calinet.com

Rohner, Hans, 1148 Twin Sisters Ranch Rd., Nederland, CO 80466-9600

Rohner, John, 186 Virginia Ave, Asheville, NC 28806 / 303-444-3841

Rohrbaugh, P.O. Box 785, Bayport, NY 11705 / 631-363-2843; FAX: 631-363-2681 API380@aol.com

Romain's Custom Guns, Inc., RD 1, Whetstone Rd., Brockport, PA 15823 / 814-265-1948 romwhetstone@penn.com

Ron Frank Custom Classic Arms, 7131 Richland Rd., Ft. Worth, TX 76118 / 817-284-9300; FAX: 817-284-9300 rfrank3974@aol.com

Rooster Laboratories, P.O. Box 414605, Kansas City, MO 64141 / 816-474-1622; FAX: 816-474-7622

Rorschach Precision Products, 417 Keats Cir., Irving, TX 75061 / 214-790-3487

Rosenberg & Son, Jack A, 12229 Cox Ln, Dallas, TX 75234 / 214-241-6302

Ross, Don, 12813 West 83 Terrace, Lenexa, KS 66215 / 913-492-6982

Rosser, Bob, 1824 29th Ave. So., Suite 214, Homewood, AL 35209 / 205-870-4422; FAX: 205-870-4421 www.hand-engravers.com

MANUFACTURER'S DIRECTORY

Rossi Firearms, Gary Mchalik, 16175 NW 49th Ave, Miami, FL 33014-6314 / 305-474-0401; FAX: 305-623-7506

Rottweil Compe, 1330 Glassell, Orange, CA 92667

Roy Baker's Leather Goods, PO Box 893, Magnolia, AR 71754 / 870-234-0344

Royal Arms Gunstocks, 919 8th Ave. NW, Great Falls, MT 59404 / 406-453-1149 royalarms@lmt.net www.lmt.net/~royalarms

Royal Arms International, R J Brill, P.O. Box 6083, Woodland Hills, CA 91365 / 818-704-5110; FAX: 818-887-2059 royalarms.com

Roy's Custom Grips, 793 Mt. Olivet Church Rd, Lynchburg, VA 24504 / 434-993-3470

RPM, 15481 N. Twin Lakes Dr., Tucson, AZ 85739 / 520-825-1233; FAX: 520-825-3333

Rubright Bullets, 1008 S. Quince Rd., Walnutport, PA 18088 / 215-767-1339

Rucker Dist. Inc., P.O. Box 479, Terrell, TX 75160 / 214-563-2094

Ruger (See Sturm, Ruger & Co., Inc.)

Ruger, Chris. See: RUGER'S CUSTOM GUNS

Ruger's Custom Guns, Chris Ruger, 1050 Morton Blvd., Kingston, NY 12401 / 845-336-7106; FAX: 845-336-7106 rugerscustom@outdrs.net rugergunsmith.com

Rundell's Gun Shop, 6198 Frances Rd., Clio, MI 48420 / 313-687-0559

Runge, Robert P., 1120 Helderberg Trl. #1, Berne, NY 12023-2909

Rupert's Gun Shop, 2202 Dick Rd., Suite B, Fenwick, MI 48834 / 517-248-3252 17rupert@pathwaynet.com

Russ Haydon's Shooters' Supply, 15018 Goodrich Dr. NW, Gig Harbor, WA 98329 / 253-857-7557; FAX: 253-857-7884 www.shooters-supply.com

Russ, William. See: BILL RUSS TRADING POST

Rusteprufe Laboratories, 1319 Jefferson Ave., Sparta, WI 54656 / 608-269-4144; FAX: 608-366-1972 rusteprufe@centurytel.net www.rusteprufe.com

Rusty Duck Premium Gun Care Products, 7785 Foundation Dr., Suite 6, Florence, KY 41042 / 606-342-5553; FAX: 606-342-5556

Rutgers Book Center, 127 Raritan Ave., Highland Park, NJ 08904 / 732-545-4344; FAX: 732-545-6686 gunbooks@rutgersgunbooks.com www.rutgersgunbooks.com

Rutten (See U.S. Importer-Labanu Inc)

RWS (See US Importer-Dynamit Nobel-RWS, Inc.), 81 Ruckman Rd., Closter, NJ 07624 / 201-767-7971; FAX: 201-767-1589

S

S&K Scope Mounts, RD 2 Box 72E, Sugar Grove, PA 16350 / 814-489-3091; or 800-578-9862; FAX: 814-489-5466 comments@scopemounts.com www.scopemounts.com

S&S Firearms, 74-11 Myrtle Ave., Glendale, NY 11385 / 718-497-1100; FAX: 718-497-1105

S.A.R.L. G. Granger, 66 cours Fauriel, 42100, Saint Etienne, FRANCE / 04 77 25 14 73; FAX: 04 77 38 66 99

S.C.R.C., PO Box 660, Katy, TX 77492-0660 FAX: 713-578-2124

S.D. Meacham, 1070 Angel Ridge, Peck, ID 83545

S.G.S. Sporting Guns Srl., Via Della Resistenza, 37 20090, Buccinasco, ITALY / 2-45702446; FAX: 2-45702464

S.I.A.C.E. (See U.S. Importer-IAR Inc)

Sabatti SPA, Via A Volta 90, 25063 Gandome V.T.(BS), Brescia, ITALY / 030-8912207-831312; FAX: 030-8912059 info@sabatti.it www.sabatti.com

SAECO (See Redding Reloading Equipment)

Safari Arms/Schuetzen Pistol Works, 620-626 Old Pacific Hwy. SE, Olympia, WA 98513 / 360-459-3471; FAX: 360-491-3447 info@yarms.com www.olyarms.com

Safari Press, Inc., 15621 Chemical Lane B, Huntington Beach, CA 92649 / 714-894-9080; FAX: 714-894-4949

Safariland Ltd., Inc., 3120 E. Mission Blvd., P.O. Box 51478, Ontario, CA 91761 / 909-923-7300; FAX: 909-923-7400

SAFE, PO Box 864, Post Falls, ID 83877 / 208-773-3624; FAX: 208-773-6819 staysafe@safe-llc.com www.safe-llc.com

Safety Speed Holster, Inc., 910 S. Vail Ave., Montebello, CA 90640 / 323-723-4140; FAX: 323-726-6973 e-mail@safetyspeedholster.com www.safetyspeedholster.com

Saf-T-Lok Corp., 18245 SE, Tesquesta, FL 33469 / 800-723-8565

Sako Ltd (See U.S. Importer-Stoeger Industries)

Sam Welch Gun Engraving, Sam Welch, HC 64 Box 2110, Moab, UT 84532 / 435-259-8131

Samco Global Arms, Inc., 6995 NW 43rd St., Miami, FL 33166 / 305-593-9782; FAX: 305-593-1014 samco@samcoglobal.com www.samcoglobal.com

---

Sampson, Roger, 2316 Mahogany St., Mora, MN 55051 / 612-679-4868

San Marco (See U.S. Importers-Cape Outfitters-EMF

Sandia Die & Cartridge Co., 37 Atancacio Rd. NE, Auquerque, NM 87123 / 505-298-5729

Sarco, Inc., 323 Union St., Stirling, NJ 07980 / 908-647-3800; FAX: 908-647-9413

Sarsilmaz Shotguns - Turkey (see B.C. Outdoors)

Sauer (See U.S. Importers-Paul Co., The, Sigarms I

Sauls, R. See: BRYAN & ASSOC.

Saunders Gun & Machine Shop, 145 Delhi Rd, Manchester, IA 52057 / 563-927-4026

Savage Arms (Canada), Inc., 248 Water St., P.O. Box 1240, Lakefield, ON K0L 2H0 CANADA / 705-652-8000; FAX: 705-652-8431

Savage Arms, Inc., 100 Springdale Rd., Westfield, MA 01085 / 413-568-7001; FAX: 413-562-7764

Savage Range Systems, Inc., 100 Springdale Rd., Westfield, MA 01085 / 413-568-7001; FAX: 413-562-1152

Saville Iron Co. (See Greenwood Precision)

Savino, Barbara J., P.O. Box 51, West Burke, VT 05871-0051

Scansport, Inc., P.O. Box 700, Enfield, NH 03748 / 603-632-7654

Sceery Game Calls, P.O. Box 6520, Sante Fe, NM 87502 / 505-471-9110; FAX: 505-471-3476

Schaefer Shooting Sports, P.O. Box 1515, Melville, NY 11747-0515 / 516-643-5466; FAX: 516-643-2426 robert@robertschaefer.com www.schaefershooting.com

Scharch Mfg., Inc.-Top Brass, 10325 Co. Rd. 120, Salida, CO 81201 / 719-539-7242; or 800-836-4683; FAX: 719-539-3021 scharch@chaffee.net www.topbraass.tv

Scherer, Liz. See: SCHERER SUPPLIES

Scherer Supplies, Liz Scherer, Box 250, Ewing, VA 24248 FAX: 423-733-2073

Schiffman, Curt, 3017 Kevin Cr., Idaho Falls, ID 83402 / 208-524-4684

Schiffman, Mike, 8233 S. Crystal Springs, McCammon, ID 83250 / 208-254-9114

Schmidt & Bender, Inc., P.O. Box 134, Meriden, NH 03770 / 603-469-3565; FAX: 603-469-3471 scopes@cyberportal.net www.schmidtbender.com

Schmidtke Group, 17050 W. Salentine Dr., New Berlin, WI 53151-7349

Schneider Bullets, 3655 West 214th St., Fairview Park, OH 44126

Schneider Rifle Barrels, Inc., Gary, 12202 N 62nd Pl., Scottsdale, AZ 85254 / 602-948-2525

Schroeder Bullets, 1421 Thermal Ave., San Diego, CA 92154 / 619-423-3523; FAX: 619-423-8124

Schulz Industries, 16247 Minnesota Ave., Paramount, CA 90723 / 213-439-5903

Schumakers Gun Shop, 512 Prouty Corner Lp. A, Colville, WA 99114 / 509-684-4848

Scope Control, Inc., 5775 Co. Rd. 23 SE, Alexandria, MN 56308 / 612-762-7295

Score High Gunsmithing, 9812-A, Cochiti SE, Albuquerque, NM 087123 / 800-326-5632 or 505-292-5532; FAX: 505-292-2592

Scot Powder, Rt.1 Box 167, McEwen, TN 37101 / 800-416-3006; FAX: 615-729-4211

Scott Fine Guns Inc., Thad, PO Box 412, Indianola, MS 38751 / 601-887-5929

Searcy Enterprises, PO Box 584, Boron, CA 93596 / 760-762-6771; FAX: 760-762-0191

Second Chance Body Armor, P.O. Box 578, Central Lake, MI 49622 / 616-544-5721; FAX: 616-544-9824

Seebeck Assoc., R.E., P. O. Box 59752, Dallas, TX 75229

Seecamp Co. Inc., L. W., PO Box 255, New Haven, CT 06502 / 203-877-3429; FAX: 203-877-3429

Segway Industries, P.O. Box 783, Suffern, NY 10901-0783 / 914-357-5510

Seligman Shooting Products, Box 133, Seligman, AZ 86337 / 602-422-3607 shootssp@yahoo.com

Sellier & Bellot, USA Inc., P.O. Box 27006, Shawnee Mission, KS 66225 / 913-685-0916; FAX: 913-685-0917

Selsi Co., Inc., P.O. Box 10, Midland Park, NJ 07432-0010 / 201-935-0388; FAX: 201-935-5851

Semmer, Charles (See Remington Double Shotguns), 7885 Cyd Dr, Denver, CO 80221 / 303-429-6947

Sentinel Arms, P.O. Box 57, Detroit, MI 48231 / 313-331-1951; FAX: 313-331-1456

Servus Footwear Co., 1136 2nd St., Rock Island, IL 61204 / 309-786-7741; FAX: 309-786-9808

Shappy Bullets, 76 Milldale Ave., Plantsville, CT 06479 / 203-621-3704

Sharp Shooter Supply, 4970 Lehman Road, Delphos, OH 45833 / 419-695-3179

Sharps Arms Co., Inc., C., 100 Centennial, Box 885, Big Timber, MT 59011 / 406-932-4353

Shaw, Inc., E. R. (See Small Arms Mfg. Co.)

Shay's Gunsmithing, 931 Marvin Ave., Lebanon, PA 17042

Sheffield Knifemakers Supply, Inc., PO Box 741107, Orange City, FL 32774-1107 / 386-775-6453; FAX: 386-774-5754

Sheldon, Bruce. See: RIDGELINE, INC.

Shepherd Enterprises, Inc., Box 189, Waterloo, NE 68069 / 402-779-2424; FAX: 402-779-4010 sshepherd@shepherdscopes.com www.shepherdscopes.com

Sherwood, George, 46 N. River Dr., Roseburg, OR 97470 / 541-672-3159

Shilen, Inc., 205 Metro Park Blvd., Ennis, TX 75119 / 972-875-5318; FAX: 972-875-5402

Shiloh Rifle Mfg., 201 Centennial Dr., Big Timber, MT 59011 / 406-932-4454; FAX: 406-932-5627 lucinda@shilohrifle.com www.shilohrifle.com

Shockley, Harold H., 204 E. Farmington Rd., Hanna City, IL 61536 / 309-565-4524

Shoot Where You Look, Leon Measures, Dept GD, 408 Fair, Livingston, TX 77351

Shooters Arms Manufacturing Inc., Rivergate Mall, Gen. Maxilom Ave., Cebu City 6000, PHILIPPINES / 6332-254-8478 www.shootersarms.com.ph

Shooter's Choice Gun Care, 15050 Berkshire Ind. Pky., Middlefield, OH 44062 / 440-834-8888; FAX: 440-834-3388 www.shooterschoice.com

Shooter's Edge Inc., 3313 Creekstone Dr., Fort Collins, CO 80525

Shooters Supply, 1120 Tieton Dr., Yakima, WA 98902 / 509-452-1181

Shooter's World, 3828 N. 28th Ave., Phoenix, AZ 85017 / 602-266-0170

Shooters, Inc., 5139 Stanart St., Norfolk, VA 23502 / 757-461-9152; FAX: 757-461-9155 gflocker@aol.com

Shootin' Shack, 357 Cypress Drive, No. 10, Tequesta, FL 33469 / 561-842-0990; FAX: 561-545-4861

Shooting Specialties (See Titus, Daniel)

Shooting Star, 1715 FM 1626 Ste 105, Manchaca, TX 78652 / 512-462-0009

Shoot-N-C Targets (See Birchwood Casey)

Shotgun Sports, P.O. Box 6810, Auburn, CA 95604 / 530-889-2220; FAX: 530-889-9106 custsrv@shotgunsportsmagazine.com shotgunsportsmagazine.com

Shotgun Sports Magazine, dba Shootin' Accessories Ltd., P.O. Box 6810, Auburn, CA 95604 / 916-889-2220 custsrv@shotgunsportsmagazine.com shotgunspotsmagazine.com

Shotguns Unlimited, 2307 Fon Du Lac Rd., Richmond, VA 23229 / 804-752-7115

Siegrist Gun Shop, 8752 Turtle Road, Whittemore, MI 48770 / 989-873-3929

Sierra Bullets, 1400 W. Henry St., Sedalia, MO 65301 / 816-827-6300; FAX: 816-827-6300

Sierra Specialty Prod. Co., 1344 Oakhurst Ave., Los Altos, CA 94024 FAX: 415-965-1536

SIG, CH-8212 Neuhausen, SWITZERLAND

Sigarms, Inc., Corporate Park, Exeter, NH 03833 / 603-772-2302; FAX: 603-772-9082 www.sigarms.com

Sightron, Inc., 1672B Hwy. 96, Franklinton, NC 27525 / 919-528-8783; FAX: 919-528-0995 info@sightron.com www.sightron.com

Signet Metal Corp., 551 Stewart Ave., Brooklyn, NY 11222 / 718-384-5400; FAX: 718-388-7488

SIG-Sauer (See U.S. Importer-Sigarms Inc.)

Silencio/Safety Direct, 56 Coney Island Dr., Sparks, NV 89431 / 800-648-1812 or 702-354-4451; FAX: 702-359-1074

Silent Hunter, 1100 Newton Ave., W. Collingswood, NJ 08107 / 609-854-3276

Silhouette Leathers, P.O. Box 1161, Gunnison, CO 81230 / 303-641-6639 oldshooter@yahoo.com

Silver Eagle Machining, 18007 N. 69th Ave., Glendale, AZ 85308

Silver Ridge Gun Shop (See Goodwin, Fred)

Simmons, Jerry, 715 Middlebury St., Goshen, IN 46528-2717 / 574-533-8546

Simmons Gun Repair, Inc., 700 S. Rogers Rd., Olathe, KS 66062 / 913-782-3131; FAX: 913-782-4189

Simmons Outdoor Corp., 6001 Oak Canyon, Irvine, CA 92618 / 949-451-1450; FAX: 949-451-1460 www.meade.com

Sinclair International, Inc., 2330 Wayne Haven St., Fort Wayne, IN 46803 / 260-493-1858; FAX: 260-493-2530 sales@sinclairintl.com www.sinclairintl.com

Singletary, Kent, 4538 W Carol Ave., Glendale, AZ 85302 / 602-526-6836 kent@kscustom.com www.kscustom.com

Siskiyou Gun Works (See Donnelly, C. P.)

Six Enterprises, 320-D Turtle Creek Ct., San Jose, CA 95125 / 408-999-0201; FAX: 408-999-0216

SKB Shotguns, 4325 S. 120th St., Omaha, NE 68137 / 800-752-2767; FAX: 402-330-8040 skb@skbshotguns.com www.skbshotguns.com

Skeoch, Brian R., PO Box 279, Glenrock, WY 82637 / 307-436-9655 brianskeoch@aol.com

Skip's Machine, 364 29 Road, Grand Junction, CO 81501 / 303-245-5417

Sklany's Machine Shop, 566 Birch Grove Dr., Kalispell, MT 59901 / 406-755-4257

Slezak, Jerome F., 1290 Marlowe, Lakewood (Cleveland), OH 44107 / 216-221-1668

Slug Site, Ozark Wilds, 21300 Hwy. 5, Versailles, MO 65084 / 573-378-6430 john@ebeling.com john.ebeling.com

Small Arms Mfg. Co., 5312 Thoms Run Rd., Bridgeville, PA 15017 / 412-221-4343; FAX: 412-221-4303

Small Arms Specialists, 443 Firchburg Rd, Mason, NH 03048 / 603-878-0427; FAX: 603-878-3905 miniguns@empire.net miniguns.com

Small Custom Mould & Bullet Co., Box 17211, Tucson, AZ 85731

Smart Parts, 1203 Spring St., Latrobe, PA 15650 / 412-539-2660; FAX: 412-539-2298

Smires, C. L., 5222 Windmill Lane, Columbia, MD 21044-1328

Smith & Wesson, 2100 Roosevelt Ave., Springfield, MA 01104 / 413-781-8300; FAX: 413-731-8980

Smith, Art, 230 Main St. S., Hector, MN 55342 / 320-848-2760; FAX: 320-848-2760

Smith, Mark A., P.O. Box 182, Sinclair, WY 82334 / 307-324-7929

Smith, Michael, 2612 Ashmore Ave., Red Bank, TN 37415 / 615-267-8341

Smith, Ron, 5869 Straley, Ft. Worth, TX 76114 / 817-732-6768

Smith, Sharmon, 4545 Speas Rd., Fruitland, ID 83619 / 208-452-6329 sharmon@fmtc.com

Smith Abrasives, Inc., 1700 Sleepy Valley Rd., P.O. Box 5095, Hot Springs, AR 71902-5095 / 501-321-2244; FAX: 501-321-9232

Smith, Judy. See: L.B.T.

Smith Saddlery, Jesse W., 0499 County Road J, Pritchett, CO 81064 / 509-325-0622

Smokey Valley Rifles, E1976 Smokey Valley Rd, Scandinavia, WI 54977 / 715-467-2674

Snapp's Gunshop, 6911 E. Washington Rd., Clare, MI 48617 / 989-386-9226

Sno-Seal, Inc. (See Atsko/Sno-Seal, Inc.)

Societa Armi Bresciane Srl (See U.S. Importer-Cape

SOS Products Co. (See Buck Stix-SOS Products Co.), Box 3, Neenah, WI 54956

Sotheby's, 1334 York Ave. at 72nd St., New York, NY 10021 / 212-606-7260

Sound Technology, Box 391, Pelham, AL 35124 / 205-664-5860; or 907-486-2825 rem700P@sprintmail.com www.soundtechsilencers.com

South Bend Replicas, Inc., 61650 Oak Rd.., South Bend, IN 46614 / 219-289-4500

Southeastern Community College, 1015 S. Gear Ave., West Burlington, IA 52655 / 319-752-2731

Southern Ammunition Co., Inc., 4232 Meadow St., Loris, SC 29569-3124 / 803-756-3262; FAX: 803-756-3583

Southern Bloomer Mfg. Co., P.O. Box 1621, Bristol, TN 37620 / 615-878-6660; FAX: 615-878-8761

Southern Security, 1700 Oak Hills Dr., Kingston, TN 37763 / 423-376-6297; FAX: 800-251-9992

Sparks, Milt, 605 E. 44th St. No. 2, Boise, ID 83714-4800

Spartan-Realtree Products, Inc., 1390 Box Circle, Columbus, GA 31907 / 706-569-9101; FAX: 706-569-0042

Specialty Gunsmithing, Lynn McMurdo, P.O. Box 404, Afton, WY 83110 / 307-886-5535

Specialty Shooters Supply, Inc., 3325 Griffin Rd., Suite 9mm, Fort Lauderdale, FL 33317

Speer Bullets, PO Box 856, Lewiston, ID 83501 / 208-746-2351; www.speer-bullets.com

Spegel, Craig, P.O. Box 387, Nehalem, OR 97131 / 503-368-5653

Speiser, Fred D., 2229 Dearborn, Missoula, MT 59801 / 406-549-8133

Spencer Reblue Service, 1820 Tupelo Trail, Holt, MI 48842 / 517-694-7474

Spencer's Rifle Barrels, Inc., 4107 Jacobs Creek Dr, Scottsville, VA 24590 / 804-293-6836; FAX: 804-293-6836 www.spencerriflebarrels.com

SPG LLC, P.O. Box 1625, Cody, WY 82414 / 307-587-7621; FAX: 307-587-7695 spg@cody.wtp.net www.blackpowderspg.com

Sphinx Systems Ltd., Gesteigtstrasse 12, CH-3800, Matten, BRNE, SWITZERLAND

Splitfire Sporting Goods, L.L.C., P.O. Box 1044, Orem, UT 84059-1044 / 801-932-7950; FAX: 801-932-7959 www.splitfireguns.com

Spolar Power Load Inc., 17376 Filbert, Fontana, CA 92335 / 800-227-9667

Sport Flite Manufacturing Co., PO Box 1082, Bloomfield Hills, MI 48303 / 248-647-3747

Sporting Clays Of America, 9257 Bluckeye Rd, Sugar Grove, OH 43155-9632 / 740-746-8334; FAX: 740-746-8605

Sports Innovations Inc., P.O. Box 5181, 8505 Jacksboro Hwy., Wichita Falls, TX 76307 / 817-723-6015

Sportsman Safe Mfg. Co., 6309-6311 Paramount Blvd., Long Beach, CA 90805 / 800-266-7150; or 310-984-5445

Sportsman's Communicators, 588 Radcliffe Ave., Pacific Palisades, CA 90272 / 800-538-3752

Sportsmatch U.K. Ltd., 16 Summer St. Leighton,, Buzzard Beds, Bedfordshire, LU7 8HT ENGLAND / 01525-381638; FAX: 01525-851236 info@sportsmatch-uk.com www.sportsmatch-uk.com

Sportsmen's Exchange & Western Gun Traders, Inc., 560 S. C St., Oxnard, CA 93030 / 805-483-1917

Spradlin's, 457 Shannon Rd, Texas CreekCotopaxi, CO 81223 / 719-275-7105; FAX: 719-275-3852 spradlins@prodigy.net www.spradlins.net

Springfield Armory, 420 W. Main St, Geneseo, IL 61254 / 309-944-5631; FAX: 309-944-3676 sales@springfield-armory.com www.springfieldarmory.com

Springfield Sporters, Inc., RD 1, Penn Run, PA 15765 / 412-254-2626; FAX: 412-254-9173

Springfield, Inc., 420 W. Main St., Geneseo, IL 61254 / 309-944-5631; FAX: 309-944-3676

Spyderco, Inc., 20011 Golden Gate Canyon Rd., Golden, CO 80403 / 800-525-7770; or 800-525-7770; FAX: 303-278-2229 sales@spyderco.com www.spyderco.com

SSK Industries, J. D. Jones, 590 Woodvue Lane, Wintersville, OH 43953 / 740-264-0176; FAX: 740-264-2257 www.sskindustries.com

Stackpole Books, 5067 Ritter Rd., Mechanicsburg, PA 17055-6921 / 717-796-0411 or 800-732-3669; FAX: 717-796-0412 tmanney@stackpolebooks.com www.stackpolebooks.com

Stalker, Inc., P.O. Box 21, Fishermans Wharf Rd., Malakoff, TX 75148 / 903-489-1010

Stalwart Corporation, PO Box 46, Evanston, WY 82931 / 307-789-7687; FAX: 307-789-7688

Stan Baker Sports, Stan Baker, 10000 Lake City Way, Seattle, WA 98125 / 206-522-4575

Stan De Treville & Co., 4129 Normal St., San Diego, CA 92103 / 619-298-3393

Stanley Bullets, 2085 Heatheridge Ln., Reno, NV 89509

Star Ammunition, Inc., 5520 Rock Hampton Ct., Indianapolis, IN 46268 / 800-221-5927; FAX: 317-872-5847

Star Custom Bullets, PO Box 608, 468 Main St., Ferndale, CA 95536 / 707-786-9140; FAX: 707-786-9117 wmebridge@humboldt.com

Star Machine Works, PO Box 1872, Pioneer, CA 95666 / 209-295-5000

Starke Bullet Company, P.O. Box 400, 605 6th St. NW, Cooperstown, ND 58425 / 888-797-3431

Starkey Labs, 6700 Washington Ave. S., Eden Prairie, MN 55344

Starkey's Gun Shop, 9430 McCombs, El Paso, TX 79924 / 915-751-3030

Starlight Training Center, Inc., Rt. 1, P.O. Box 88, Bronaugh, MO 64728 / 417-843-3555

Starline, Inc., 1300 W. Henry St., Sedalia, MO 65301 / 660-827-6640; FAX: 660-827-6650 info@starlinebrass.com http://www.starlinebrass.com

Starr Trading Co., Jedediah, PO Box 2007, Farmington Hills, MI 48333 / 810-683-4343; FAX: 810-683-3282

Starrett Co., L. S., 121 Crescent St., Athol, MA 01331 / 978-249-3551; FAX: 978-249-8495

Steelman's Gun Shop, 10465 Beers Rd., Swartz Creek, MI 48473 / 810-735-4884

Steffens, Ron, 18396 Mariposa Creek Rd., Willits, CA 95490 / 707-485-0873

Stegall, James B., 26 Forest Rd., Wallkill, NY 12589

Steve Henigson & Associates, P.O. Box 2726, Culver City, CA 90231 / 310-305-8288; FAX: 310-305-1905

Steve Kamyk Engraver, 9 Grandview Dr., Westfield, MA 01085-1810 / 413-568-0457 stevek201@attbi

Steven Dodd Hughes, P.O. Box 545, Livingston, MT 59047 / 406-222-9377; FAX: 406-222-9377

Steves House of Guns, Rt. 1, Minnesota City, MN 55959 / 507-689-2573

Stewart Game Calls, Inc., Johnny, PO Box 7954, 5100 Fort Ave, Waco, TX 76714 / 817-772-3261; FAX: 817-772-3670

Stewart's Gunsmithing, P.O. Box 5854, Pietersburg North 0750, Transvaal, SOUTH AFRICA / 01521-89401

Steyr Mannlicher GmbH P Co KG, Mannlicherstrasse 1, 4400 Steyr, Steyr, AUSTRIA / 0043-7252-896-0; FAX: 0043-7252-78620 office@steyr-mannlicher.com www.steyr-mannlicher.com

STI International, 114 Halmar Cove, Georgetown, TX 78628 / 800-959-8201; FAX: 512-819-0465 www.stiguns.com

Stiles Custom Guns, 76 Cherry Run Rd., Box 1605, Homer City, PA 15748 / 712-479-9945

Stillwell, Robert, 421 Judith Ann Dr., Schertz, TX 78154

Stoeger Industries, 17603 Indian Head Hwy., Suite 200, Accokeek, MD 20607-2501 / 301-283-6300; FAX: 301-283-6986 www.stoegerindustries.com

Stoeger Publishing Co. (See Stoeger Industries)

Stone Enterprises Ltd., 426 Harveys Neck Rd., PO Box 335, Wicomico Church, VA 22579 / 804-580-5114; FAX: 804-580-8421

Stone Mountain Arms, 5988 Peachtree Corners E., Norcross, GA 30071 / 800-251-9412

Stoney Point Products, Inc., P.O. Box 234, 1822 N Minnesota St., New Ulm, MN 56073-0234 / 507-354-3360; FAX: 507-354-7236 stoney@newulmtel.net www.stoneypoint.com

Storm, Gary, P.O. Box 5211, Richardson, TX 75083 / 214-385-0862

Stott's Creek Armory, Inc., 2526 S. 475W, Morgantown, IN 46160 / 317-878-5489; FAX: 317-878-9489 sccalendar@aol.com www.sccalendar.com

Stratco, Inc., P.O. Box 2270, Kalispell, MT 59901 / 406-755-1221; FAX: 406-755-1226

Strayer, Sandy. See: STRAYER-VOIGT, INC.

Strayer-Voigt, Inc., Sandy Strayer, 3435 Ray Orr Blvd, Grand Prairie, TX 75050 / 972-513-0575

Streamlight, Inc., 1030 W. Germantown Pike, Norristown, PA 19403 / 215-631-0600; FAX: 610-631-0712

Strong Holster Co., 39 Grove St., Gloucester, MA 01930 / 508-281-3300; FAX: 508-281-6321

Strutz Rifle Barrels, Inc., W. C., P.O. Box 611, Eagle River, WI 54521 / 715-479-4766

Stuart, V. Pat, Rt.1, Box 447-S, Greenville, VA 24440 / 804-556-3845

Sturgeon Valley Sporters, K. Ide, P.O. Box 283, Vanderbilt, MI 49795 / 517-983-4338

Sturm Ruger & Co. Inc., 200 Ruger Rd., Prescott, AZ 86301 / 928-541-8820; FAX: 520-541-8850 www.ruger.com

Sullivan, David S .(See Westwind Rifles Inc.)

Summit Specialties, Inc., P.O. Box 786, Decatur, AL 35602 / 205-353-0634; FAX: 205-353-9818

Sun Welding Safe Co., 290 Easy St. No.3, Simi Valley, CA 93065 / 805-584-6678; or 800-729-SAFE; FAX: 805-584-6169 sunwelding.com

Sunny Hill Enterprises, Inc., W1790 Cty. HHH, Malone, WI 53049 / 920-795-4722; FAX: 920-795-4822

"Su-Press-On", Inc., P.O. Box 09161, Detroit, MI 48209 / 313-842-4222

Super 6 LLC, Gary Knopp, 3806 W. Lisbon Ave., Milwaukee, WI 53208 / 414-344-3343; FAX: 414-344-0304

Sure-Shot Game Calls, Inc., P.O. Box 816, 6835 Capitol, Groves, TX 77619 / 409-962-1636; FAX: 409-962-5465

Survival Arms, Inc., 273 Canal St., Shelton, CT 06484-3173 / 203-924-6533; FAX: 203-924-2581

Svon Corp., 2107 W. Blue Heron Blvd., Riviera Beach, FL 33404 / 508-881-8852

Swann, D. J., 5 Orsova Close, Eltham North Vic., 3095 AUSTRALIA / 03-431-0323

Swanndri New Zealand, 152 Elm Ave., Burlingame, CA 94010 / 415-347-6158

Swanson, Mark, 975 Heap Avenue, Prescott, AZ 86301 / 928-778-4423

Swarovski Optik North America Ltd., 2 Slater Rd., Cranston, RI 02920 / 401-946-2220; or 800-426-3089; FAX: 401-946-2587

Sweet Home, Inc., P.O. Box 900, Orrville, OH 44667-0900

Swenson's 45 Shop, A. D., 3839 Ladera Vista Rd, Fallbrook, CA 92028-9431

Swift Bullet Co., P.O. Box 27, 201 Main St., Quinter, KS 67752 / 913-754-3959; FAX: 913-754-2359

Swift Instruments, Inc., 952 Dorchester Ave., Boston, MA 02125 / 617-436-2960; FAX: 617-436-3232

Swift River Gunworks, 450 State St., Belchertown, MA 01007 / 413-323-4052

Szweda, Robert (See RMS Custom Gunsmithing)

T

T&S Industries, Inc., 1027 Skyview Dr., W. Carrollton, OH 45449 / 513-859-8414

MANUFACTURER'S DIRECTORY

T.F.C. S.p.A., Via G. Marconi 118, B, Villa Carcina 25069, ITALY / 030-881271; FAX: 030-881826

T.G. Faust, Inc., 544 Minor St., Reading, PA 19602 / 610-375-8549; FAX: 610-375-4488

T.H.U. Enterprises, Inc., P.O. Box 418, Lederach, PA 19450 / 215-256-1665; FAX: 215-256-9718

T.K. Lee Co., 1282 Branchwater Ln., Birmingham, AL 35216 / 205-913-5222 odonmich@aol.com www.scopedot.com

T.W. Menck Gunsmith Inc., 5703 S. 77th St., Ralston, NE 68127 guntools@cox.net http://llwww.members.cox.net/guntools

Tabler Marketing, 2554 Lincoln Blvd., Suite 555, Marina Del Rey, CA 90291 / 818-755-4565; FAX: 818-755-0972

Taconic Firearms Ltd., Perry Lane, PO Box 553, Cambridge, NY 12816 / 518-677-2704; FAX: 518-677-5974

Tactical Defense Institute, 2174 Bethany Ridges, West Union, OH 45693 / 937-544-7228; FAX: 937-544-2887

Talley, Dave, P.O. Box 821, Glenrock, WY 82637 / 307-436-8724; or 307-436-9315

Talmage, William G., 10208 N. County Rd. 425 W., Brazil, IN 47834 / 812-442-0804

Talon Industries Inc. (See Cobra Enterprises, Inc.)

Tamarack Products, Inc., PO Box 625, Wauconda, IL 60084 / 708-526-9333; FAX: 708-526-9353

Tanfoglio Fratelli S.r.l., via Valtrompia 39, 41, Brescia, ITALY / 30-8910361; FAX: 30-8910183

Tanglefree Industries, 1261 Heavenly Dr., Martinez, CA 94553 / 800-982-4868; FAX: 510-825-3874

Tank's Rifle Shop, P.O. Box 474, Fremont, NE 68026-0474 / 402-727-1317 jtank@tanksrifleshop.com www.tanksrifleshop.com

Tanner (See U.S. Importer-Mandall Shooting Supply)

Taracorp Industries, Inc., 1200 Sixteenth St., Granite City, IL 62040 / 618-451-4400

Target Shooting, Inc., PO Box 773, Watertown, SD 57201 / 605-882-6955; FAX: 605-882-8840

Tar-Hunt Custom Rifles, Inc., 101 Dogtown Rd., Bloomsburg, PA 17815 / 570-784-6368; FAX: 570-784-6368 www.tar-hunt.com

Tarnhelm Supply Co., Inc., 431 High St., Boscawen, NH 03303 / 603-796-2551; FAX: 603-796-2918 info@tarnhelm.com www.tarnhelm.com

Tasco Sales, Inc., 2889 Commerce Pky., Miramar, FL 33025

Taurus Firearms, Inc., 16175 NW 49th Ave., Miami, FL 33014 / 305-624-1115; FAX: 305-623-7506

Taurus International Firearms (See U.S. Importer)

Taurus S.A. Forjas, Avenida Do Forte 511, Porto Alegre, RS BRAZIL 91360 / 55-51-347-4050; FAX: 55-51-347-3065

Taylor & Robbins, P.O. Box 164, Rixford, PA 16745 / 814-966-3233

Taylor's & Co., Inc., 304 Lenoir Dr., Winchester, VA 22603 / 540-722-2017; FAX: 540-722-2018

TCCI, P.O. Box 302, Phoenix, AZ 85001 / 602-237-3823; FAX: 602-237-3858

TCSR, 3998 Hoffman Rd., White Bear Lake, MN 55110-4626 / 800-328-5323; FAX: 612-429-0526

TDP Industries, Inc., P.O. Box 249, Ottsville, PA 18942-0249 / 215-345-8687; FAX: 215-345-6057

Techno Arms (See U.S. Importer- Auto-Ordnance Corp

Tecnolegno S.p.A., Via A. Locatelli, 6 10, 24019 Zogno, I ITALY / 0345-55111; FAX: 0345-55155

Ted Blocker Holsters, Inc., 9396 S.W. Tigard St., Tigard, OR 97223 / 800-650-9742; FAX: 503-670-9692 www.tedblocker.com

Tele-Optics, 630 E. Rockland Rd., PO Box 6313, Libertyville, IL 60048 / 847-362-7757; FAX: 847-362-7757

Tennessee Valley Mfg., 14 County Road 521, Corinth, MS 38834 / 601-286-5014

Ten-Ring Precision, Inc., Alex B. Hamilton, 1449 Blue Crest Lane, San Antonio, TX 78232 / 210-494-3063; FAX: 210-494-3066

TEN-X Products Group, 1905 N Main St, Suite 133, Cleburne, TX 76031-1305 / 972-243-4016; or 800-433-2225; FAX: 972-243-4112

Tepeco, P.O. Box 342, Friendswood, TX 77546 / 713-482-2702

Terry K. Kopp Professional Gunsmithing, Rt 1 Box 224, Lexington, MO 64067 / 816-259-2636

Testing Systems, Inc., 220 Pegasus Ave., Northvale, NJ 07647

Tetra Gun Care, 8 Vreeland Rd., Florham Park, NJ 07932 / 973-443-0004; FAX: 973-443-0263

Tex Shoemaker & Sons, Inc., 714 W. Cienega Ave., San Dimas, CA 91773 / 909-592-2071; FAX: 909-592-2378 texshoemaker@texshoemaker.com www.texshoemaker.com

Texas Armory (See Bond Arms, Inc.)

Texas Platers Supply Co., 2453 W. Five Mile Parkway, Dallas, TX 75233 / 214-330-7168

Thad Rybka Custom Leather Equipment, 2050 Canoe Creek Rd., Springvale, AL 35146-6709

Thad Scott Fine Guns, Inc., P.O. Box 412, Indianola, MS 38751 / 601-887-5929

The A.W. Peterson Gun Shop, Inc., 4255 West Old U.S. 441, Mount Dora, FL 32757-3299 / 352-383-4258

The Accuracy Den, 25 Bitterbrush Rd., Reno, NV 89523 / 702-345-0225

The Ballistic Program Co., Inc., 2417 N. Patterson St., Thomasville, GA 31792 / 912-228-5739 or 800-368-0835

The BulletMakers Workshop, RFD 1 Box 1755, Brooks, ME 04921

The Competitive Pistol Shop, 5233 Palmer Dr., Ft. Worth, TX 76117-2433 / 817-834-8479

The Concealment Shop, Inc., 617 W. Kearney St., Ste. 205, Mesquite, TX 75149 / 972-289-8997; or 800-444-7090; FAX: 972-289-4410 concealmentshop@email.msn.com www.theconcealmentshop.com

The Country Armourer, P.O. Box 308, Ashby, MA 01431-0308 / 508-827-6797; FAX: 508-827-4845

The Creative Craftsman, Inc., 95 Highway 29 North, P.O. Box 331, Lawrenceville, GA 30246 / 404-963-2112; FAX: 404-513-9488

The Custom Shop, 890 Cochrane Crescent, Peterborough, ON K9H 5N3 CANADA / 705-742-6693

The Dutchman's Firearms, Inc., 4143 Taylor Blvd., Louisville, KY 40215 / 502-366-0555

The Ensign-Bickford Co., 660 Hopmeadow St., Simsbury, CT 06070

The Firearm Training Center, 9555 Blandville Rd., West Paducah, KY 42086 / 502-554-5886

The Fouling Shot, 6465 Parfet St., Arvada, CO 80004

The Gun Doctor, 435 East Maple, Roselle, IL 60172 / 708-894-0668

The Gun Room, 1121 Burlington, Muncie, IN 47302 / 765-282-9073; FAX: 765-282-5270 bshstleguns@aol.com

The Gun Room Press, 127 Raritan Ave., Highland Park, NJ 08904 / 732-545-4344; FAX: 732-545-6686 gunbooks@rutgersgunbooks.com www.rutgersgunbooks.com

The Gun Shop, 5550 S. 900 East, Salt Lake City, UT 84117 / 801-263-3633

The Gun Shop, 62778 Spring Creek Rd., Montrose, CO 81401

The Gun Works, 247 S. 2nd St., Springfield, OR 97477 / 541-741-4118; FAX: 541-988-1097 gunworks@worldnet.att.net www.thegunworks.com

The Gunsight, 1712 North Placentia Ave., Fullerton, CA 92631

The Gunsmith in Elk River, 14021 Victoria Lane, Elk River, MN 55330 / 612-441-7761

The Hanned Line, P.O. Box 2387, Cupertino, CA 95015-2387 smith@hanned.com www.hanned.com

The Hawken Shop, P.O. Box 593, Oak Harbor, WA 98277 / 206-679-4657; FAX: 206-675-1114

The Keller Co., P.O. Box 4057, Port Angeles, WA 98363-0997 / 214-770-8585

The Lewis Lead Remover (See LEM Gun Specialties)

The Midwest Shooting School, Pat LaBoone, 2550 Hwy. 23, Wrenshall, MN 55797 / 218-384-3670 shootingschool@starband.net

The NgraveR Co., 67 Wawecus Hill Rd., Bozrah, CT 06334 / 860-823-1533

The Ordnance Works, 2969 Pidgeon Point Road, Eureka, CA 95501 / 707-443-3252

The Orvis Co., Rt. 7, Manchester, VT 05254 / 802-362-3622; FAX: 802-362-3525

The Outdoor Connection, Inc., 7901 Panther Way, Waco, TX 76712-6556 / 800-533-6076 or 254-772-5575; FAX: 254-776-3553 floyd@outdoorconnection.com www.outdoorconnection.com

The Park Rifle Co., Ltd., Unit 6a Dartford Trade Park, Power Mill Lane, Dartford DA7 7NX, ENGLAND / 011-0322-222512

The Paul Co., 27385 Pressonville Rd., Wellsville, KS 66092 / 785-883-4444; FAX: 785-883-2525

The Protector Mfg. Co., Inc., 443 Ashwood Place, Boca Raton, FL 33431 / 407-394-6011

The Robar Co.'s, Inc., 21438 N. 7th Ave., Suite B, Phoenix, AZ 85027 / 623-581-2648 www.robarguns.com

The School of Gunsmithing, 6065 Roswell Rd., Atlanta, GA 30328 / 800-223-4542

The Shooting Gallery, 8070 Southern Blvd., Boardman, OH 44512 / 216-726-7788

The Sight Shop, John G. Lawson, 1802 E. Columbia Ave., Tacoma, WA 98404 / 253-474-5465 parahellum9@aol.com www.thesightshop.org

The Southern Armory, 25 Millstone Road, Woodlawn, VA 24381 / 703-238-1343; FAX: 703-238-1453

The Surecase Co., 233 Wilshire Blvd., Ste. 900, Santa Monica, CA 90401 / 800-92ARMLOC

The Swampfire Shop (See Peterson Gun Shop, Inc.)

The Wilson Arms Co., 63 Leetes Island Rd., Branford, CT 06405 / 203-488-7297; FAX: 203-488-0135

Theis, Terry, 21452 FM 2093, Harper, TX 78631 / 830-864-4438

Thiewes, George W., 14329 W. Parada Dr., Sun City West, AZ 85375

Things Unlimited, 235 N. Kimbau, Casper, WY 82601 / 307-234-5277

Thirion Gun Engraving, Denise, PO Box 408, Graton, CA 95444 / 707-829-1876

Thomas, Charles C., 2600 S. First St., Springfield, IL 62794 / 217-789-8980; FAX: 217-789-9130

Thompson Bullet Lube Co., P.O. Box 409, Wills Point, TX 75169 / 866-476-1500; FAX: 866-476-1500 thompsonbulletlube.com www.thompsonbulletlube.com

Thompson Precision, 110 Mary St., P.O. Box 251, Warren, IL 61087 / 815-745-3625

Thompson, Randall. See: HIGHLINE MACHINE CO.

Thompson Target Technology, 4804 Sherman Church Ave. S.W., Canton, OH 44710 / 330-484-6480; FAX: 330-491-1087 www.thompsontarget.com

Thompson Tool Mount, 1550 Solomon Rd., Santa Maria, CA 93455 / 805-934-1281 ttm@pronet.net www.thompsontoolmount.com

Thompson, Randall (See Highline Machine Co.)

Thompson/Center Arms, P.O. Box 5002, Rochester, NH 03866 / 603-332-2394; FAX: 603-332-5133 tech@tcarms.com www.tcarms.com

3-Ten Corp., P.O. Box 269, Feeding Hills, MA 01030 / 413-789-2086; FAX: 413-789-1549

Thunden Ranch, HCR 1, Box 53, Mt. Home, TX 78058 / 830-640-3138

Thurston Sports, Inc., RD 3 Donovan Rd., Auburn, NY 13021 / 315-253-0966

Tiger-Hunt Gunstocks, Box 379, Beaverdale, PA 15921 / 814-472-5161 tigerhunt4@aol.com www.gunstockwood.com

Tikka (See U.S. Importer-Stoeger Industries)

Time Precision, 4 Nicholas Sq., New Milford, CT 06776-3506 / 203-775-8343

Tinks & Ben Lee Hunting Products (See Wellington)

Tink's Safariland Hunting Corp., PO Box 244, 1140 Monticello Rd., Madison, GA 30650 / 706-342-4915; FAX: 706-342-7568

Tioga Engineering Co., Inc., P.O. Box 913, 13 Cone St., Wellsboro, PA 16901 / 570-724-3533; FAX: 570-724-3895 tiogaeng@epix.net

Tippman Pneumatics, Inc., 3518 Adams Center Rd., Fort Wayne, IN 46806 / 219-749-6022; FAX: 219-749-6619

Tirelli, Snc Di Tirelli Primo E.C., Via Matteotti No. 359, Gardone V.T. Brescia, I ITALY / 030-8912819; FAX: 030-832240

TM Stockworks, 6355 Maplecrest Rd., Fort Wayne, IN 46835 / 219-485-5389

TMI Products (See Haselbauer Products, Jerry)

Tom Forrest, Inc., P.O. Box 326, Lakeside, CA 92040 / 619-561-5800; FAX: 619-561-0227

Tombstone Smoke`n' Deals, PO Box 31298, Phoenix, AZ 85046 / 602-905-7013; FAX: 602-443-1998

Tom's Gun Repair, Thomas G. Ivanoff, 76-6 Rt. Southfork Rd., Cody, WY 82414 / 307-587-6949

Tom's Gunshop, 3601 Central Ave., Hot Springs, AR 71913 / 501-624-3856

Tonoloway Tack Drives, HCR 81, Box 100, Needmore, PA 17238

Torel, Inc., 1708 N. South St., P.O. Box 592, Yoakum, TX 77995 / 512-293-2341; FAX: 512-293-3413

TOZ (See U.S. Importer-Nygord Precision Products)

Track of the Wolf, Inc., 18308 Joplin St. NW, Elk River, MN 55330-1773 / 763-633-2500; FAX: 763-633-2550

Traditions Performance Firearms, P.O. Box 776, 1375 Boston Post Rd., Old Saybrook, CT 06475 / 860-388-4656; FAX: 860-388-4657 info@traditionsfirearms.com www.traditionsfirearms.com

Trafalgar Square, P.O. Box 257, N. Pomfret, VT 05053 / 802-457-1911

Trail Visions, 5800 N. Ames Terrace, Glendale, WI 53209 / 414-228-1328

Trax America, Inc., PO Box 898, 1150 Eldridge, Forrest City, AR 72335 / 870-633-0410; or 800-232-2327; FAX: 870-633-4788 trax@ipa.net www.traxamerica.com

Treadlok Gun Safe, Inc., 1764 Granby St. NE, Roanoke, VA 24012 / 800-729-8732; or 703-982-6881; FAX: 703-982-1059

Treemaster, P.O. Box 247, Guntersville, AL 35976 / 205-878-3597

Trevallion Gunstocks, 9 Old Mountain Rd., Cape Neddick, ME 03902 / 207-361-1130

Trico Plastics, 28061 Diaz Rd., Temecula, CA 92590 / 909-676-7714; FAX: 909-676-0267 ustinfo@ustplastics.com www.tricoplastics.com

Trigger Lock Division / Central Specialties Ltd., 220-D Exchange Dr., Crystal Lake, IL 60014 / 847-639-3900; FAX: 847-639-3972

Trijicon, Inc., 49385 Shafer Ave., P.O. Box 930059, Wixom, MI 48393-0059 / 248-960-7700 or 800-338-0563

Trilby Sport Shop, 1623 Hagley Rd., Toledo, OH 43612-2024 / 419-472-6222

Trilux, Inc., P.O. Box 24608, Winston-Salem, NC 27114 / 910-659-9438; FAX: 910-768-7720

Trinidad St. Jr. Col. Gunsmith Dept., 600 Prospect St., Trinidad, CO 81082 / 719-846-5631; FAX: 719-846-5667

Triple-K Mfg. Co., Inc., 2222 Commercial St., San Diego, CA 92113 / 619-232-2066; FAX: 619-232-7675 sales@triplek.com www.triplek.com

Tristar Sporting Arms, Ltd., 1814 Linn St. #16, N. Kansas City, MO 64116-3627 / 816-421-1400; FAX: 816-421-4182 tristar@blity-it.net www.tristarsportingarms

Trius Traps, Inc., P.O. Box 25, 221 S. Miami Ave., Cleves, OH 45002 / 513-941-5682; FAX: 513-941-7970 triustraps@fuse.net www.triustraps.com

Trooper Walsh, 2393 N Edgewood St, Arlington, VA 22207

Trotman, Ken, 135 Ditton Walk, Unit 11, Cambridge, CB5 8PY ENGLAND / 01223-211030; FAX: 01223-212317 www.kentrolman.com

Tru-Balance Knife Co., P.O. Box 140555, Grand Rapids, MI 49514 / 616-647-1215

True Flight Bullet Co., 5581 Roosevelt St., Whitehall, PA 18052 / 610-262-7630; FAX: 610-262-7806

Truglo, Inc., P.O. Box 1612, McKinna, TX 75070 / 972-774-0300; FAX: 972-774-0323 www.truglosights.com

Trulock Tool, PO Box 530, Whigham, GA 31797 / 229-762-4678; FAX: 229-762-4050 trulockchokes@hotmail.com trulockchokes.com

Tru-Square Metal Products Inc., 640 First St. SW, P.O. Box 585, Auburn, WA 98071 / 253-833-2310; or 800-225-1017; FAX: 253-833-2349 t-tumbler@qwest.net

Tucker, James C., P.O. Box 1212, Paso Robles, CA 93447-1212

Tucson Mold, Inc., 930 S. Plumer Ave., Tucson, AZ 85719 / 520-792-1075; FAX: 520-792-1075

Turk's Head Productions, Mustafa Bilal, 908 NW 50th St., Seattle, WA 98107-3634 / 206-782-4164; FAX: 206-783-5677 info@turkshead.com www.turkshead.com

Turnbull Restoration, Doug, 6680 Rt. 5 & 20, P.O. Box 471, Bloomfield, NY 14469 / 585-657-6338; FAX: 585-657-6338 turnbullrest@mindspring.com www.turnbullrestoration.com

Tuttle, Dale, 4046 Russell Rd., Muskegon, MI 49445 / 616-766-2250

Tyler Manufacturing & Distributing, 3804 S. Eastern, Oklahoma City, OK 73129 / 405-677-1487; or 800-654-8415

U

U.S. Fire Arms Mfg. Co., Inc., 55 Van Dyke Ave., Hartford, CT 06106 / 877-227-6901; FAX: 800-644-7265 usfirearms.com

U.S. Importer-Wm. Larkin Moore, 8430 E. Raintree Ste. B-7, Scottsdale, AZ 85260

U.S. Repeating Arms Co., Inc., 275 Winchester Ave., Morgan, UT 84050-9333 / 801-876-3440; FAX: 801-876-3737

U.S. Tactical Systems (See Keng's Firearms Specialty)

Ugartechea S. A., Ignacio, Chonta 26, Eibar, SPAIN / 43-121257; FAX: 43-121669

Ultra Dot Distribution, P.O. Box 362, 6304 Riverside Dr., Yankeetown, FL 34498 / 352-447-2255; FAX: 352-447-2266

Ultralux (See U.S. Importer-Keng's Firearms)

UltraSport Arms, Inc., 1955 Norwood Ct., Racine, WI 53403 / 414-554-3237; FAX: 414-554-9731

Uncle Bud's, HCR 81, Box 100, Needmore, PA 17238 / 717-294-6000; FAX: 717-294-6005

Uncle Mike's (See Michaels of Oregon Co.)

Unertl Optical Co., Inc., 103 Grand Avenue, P.O. Box 895, Mars, PA 16046-0895 / 724-625-3810; FAX: 724-625-3819 unertl@nauticom.net www.unertloptics.net

Unique/M.A.P.F., 10 Les Allees, 64700, Hendaye, FRANCE / 33-59 20 71 93

UniTec, 1250 Bedford SW, Canton, OH 44710 / 216-452-4017

United Binocular Co., 9043 S. Western Ave., Chicago, IL 60620

United Cutlery Corp., 1425 United Blvd., Sevierville, TN 37876 / 865-428-2532; or 800-548-0835; FAX: 865-428-2267

United States Optics Technologies, Inc., 5900 Dale St., Buena Park, CA 90621 / 714-994-4901; FAX: 714-994-4904 www.usoptics.com

United States Products Co., 518 Melwood Ave., Pittsburgh, PA 15213-1136 / 412-621-2130; FAX: 412-621-8740 sales@us-products.com www.us-products.com

Universal Sports, PO Box 532, Vincennes, IN 47591 / 812-882-8680; FAX: 812-882-8680

Unmussig Bullets, D. L., 7862 Brentford Dr., Richmond, VA 23225 / 804-320-1165

Upper Missouri Trading Co., P.O. Box 100, 304 Harold St., Crofton, NE 68730-0100 / 402-388-4844

USAC, 4500-15th St. East, Tacoma, WA 98424 / 206-922-7589

Utica Cutlery Co., 820 Noyes St., Utica, NY 13503 / 315-733-4663; FAX: 315-733-6602

V

V.H. Blackinton & Co., Inc., 221 John L. Dietsch, Attleboro Falls, MA 02763-0300 / 508-699-4436; FAX: 508-695-5349

Valdada Enterprises, P.O. Box 773122, 31733 County Road 35, Steamboat Springs, CO 80477 / 970-879-2983; FAX: 970-879-0851 www.valdada.com

Valtro USA, Inc, 1281 Andersen Dr., San Rafael, CA 94901 / 415-256-2575; FAX: 415-256-2576

VAM Distribution Co. LLC, 1141-B Mechanicsburg Rd., Wooster, OH 44691 www.rex10.com

Van Gorden & Son Inc., C. S., 1815 Main St., Bloomer, WI 54724 / 715-568-2612

Van Horn, Gil, P.O. Box 207, Llano, CA 93544

Van Patten, J. W., P.O. Box 145, Foster Hill, Milford, PA 18337 / 717-296-7069

Vann Custom Bullets, 330 Grandview Ave., Novato, CA 94947

Van's Gunsmith Service, 224 Route 69-A, Parish, NY 13131 / 315-625-7251

Varmint Masters, LLC, Rick Vecqueray, PO Box 6724, Bend, OR 97708 / 541-318-7306; FAX: 541-318-7306 varmintmasters@bendcable.com www.varmintmasters.net

Vecqueray, Rick. See: VARMINT MASTERS, LLC

Vega Tool Co., c/o T.R. Ross, 4865 Tanglewood Ct., Boulder, CO 80301 / 303-530-0174 clanlaird@aol.com www.vegatool.com

Vektor USA, Mikael Danforth, 5139 Stanart St, Norfolk, VA 23502 / 888-740-0837; or 757-455-8895; FAX: 757-461-9155

Venco Industries, Inc. (See Shooter's Choice Gun Care)

Venus Industries, P.O. Box 246, Sialkot-1, PAKISTAN FAX: 92 432 85579

Verney-Carron, BP 72-54 Boulevard Thiers, 42002 St Etienne Cedex 1, St Etienne Cedex 1, FRANCE / 33-477791500; FAX: 33-477790702 email@verney-carron.com www.verney-carron.com

Vest, John, 1923 NE 7th St., Redmond, OR 97756 / 541-923-8898

VibraShine, Inc., PO Box 577, Taylorsville, MS 39168 / 601-785-9854; FAX: 601-785-9874

Vibra-Tek Co., 1844 Arroya Rd., Colorado Springs, CO 80906 / 719-634-8611; FAX: 719-634-6886

Vic's Gun Refinishing, 6 Pineview Dr., Dover, NH 03820-6422 / 603-742-0013

Victory Ammunition, PO Box 1022, Milford, PA 18337 / 717-296-5768; FAX: 717-296-9298

Victory USA, P.O. Box 1021, Pine Bush, NY 12566 / 914-744-2060; FAX: 914-744-5181

Vihtavuori Oy, FIN-41330 Vihtavuori, FINLAND, / 358-41-3779211; FAX: 358-41-3771643

Vihtavuori Oy/Kaltron-Pettibone, 1241 Ellis St., Bensenville, IL 60106 / 708-350-1116; FAX: 708-350-1606

Viking Video Productions, P.O. Box 251, Roseburg, OR 97470

Vincent's Shop, 210 Antoinette, Fairbanks, AK 99701

Vincenzo Bernardelli S.p.A., 125 Via Matteotti, P.O. Box 74, Gardone V.T., Bresci, 25063 ITALY / 39-30-8912851-2-3; FAX: 39-30-8910249

Vintage Arms, Inc., 6003 Saddle Horse, Fairfax, VA 22030 / 703-968-0779; FAX: 703-968-0780

Vintage Industries, Inc., 781 Big Tree Dr., Longwood, FL 32750 / 407-831-8949; FAX: 407-831-5346

Viper Bullet and Brass Works, 11 Brock St., Box 582, Norwich, ON N0J 1P0 CANADA

Viramontez Engraving, Ray Viramontez, 601 Springfield Dr., Albany, GA 31721 / 229-432-9683 sgtvira@aol.com

Viramontez, Ray. See: VIRAMONTEZ ENGRAVING

Virgin Valley Custom Guns, 450 E 800 N #20, Hurricane, UT 84737 / 435-635-8941; FAX: 435-635-8943 vvcguns@infowest.com www.virginvalleyguns.com

Visible Impact Targets, Rts. 5 & 20, E. Bloomfield, NY 14443 / 716-657-6161; FAX: 716-657-5405

Vitt/Boos, 1195 Buck Hill Rd., Townshend, VT 05353 / 802-365-9232

Voere-KGH GmbH, Untere Sparchen 56, A-6330 Kufstein, Tirol, AUSTRIA / 0043-5372-62547; FAX: 0043-5372-65752 voere@aon.com www.voere.com

Volquartsen Custom Ltd., 24276 240th Street, PO Box 397, Carroll, IA 51401 / 712-792-4238; FAX: 712-792-2542 vcl@netins.net www.volquartsen.com

Vorhes, David, 3042 Beecham St., Napa, CA 94558 / 707-226-9116; FAX: 707-253-7334

Vortek Products, Inc., P.O. Box 871181, Canton, MI 48187-6181 / 313-397-5656; FAX: 313-397-5656

VSP Publishers (See Heritage/VSP Gun Books), PO Box 887, McCall, ID 83638 / 208-634-4104; FAX: 208-634-3101

VTI Gun Parts, P.O. Box 509, Lakeville, CT 06039 / 860-435-8068; FAX: 860-435-8146 mail@vtigunparts.com www.vtigunparts.com

Vulpes Ventures, Inc. Fox Cartridge Division, P.O. Box 1363, Bolingbrook, IL 60440-7363 / 630-759-1229

W

W. Square Enterprises, 9826 Sagedale Dr., Houston, TX 77089 / 281-484-0935; FAX: 281-464-9940 lfdw@pdq.net www.loadammo.com

W. Waller & Son, Inc., 2221 Stoney Brook Rd., Grantham, NH 03753-7706 / 603-863-4177 www.wallerandson.com

W.B. Niemi Engineering, Box 126 Center Road, Greensboro, VT 05841 / 802-533-7180 or 802-533-7141

W.C. Wolff Co., PO Box 458, Newtown Square, PA 19073 / 610-359-9600; or 800-545-0077; mail@gunsprings.com www.gunsprings.com

W.E. Birdsong & Assoc., 1435 Monterey Rd., Florence, MS 39073-9748 / 601-366-8270

W.E. Brownell Checkering Tools, 9390 Twin Mountain Cir., San Diego, CA 92126 / 858-695-2479; FAX: 858-695-2479

W.J. Riebe Co., 3434 Tucker Rd., Boise, ID 83703

W.R. Case & Sons Cutlery Co., Owens Way, Bradford, PA 16701 / 814-368-4123; or 800-523-6350; FAX: 814-368-1736 jsullivan@wrcase.com www.wrcase.com

Wagoner, Vernon G., 2325 E. Encanto St., Mesa, AZ 85213-5917 / 480-835-1307

Wakina by Pic, 24813 Alderbrook Dr., Santa Clarita, CA 91321 / 800-295-8194

Waldron, Herman, Box 475, 80 N. 17th St., Pomeroy, WA 99347 / 509-843-1404

Walker Arms Co., Inc., 499 County Rd. 820, Selma, AL 36701 / 334-872-6231; FAX: 334-872-6262

Wallace, Terry, 385 San Marino, Vallejo, CA 94589 / 707-642-7041

Walls Industries, Inc., P.O. Box 98, 1905 N. Main, Cleburne, TX 76033 / 817-645-4366; FAX: 817-645-7946 www.wallsoutdoors.com

Walters Industries, 6226 Park Lane, Dallas, TX 75225 / 214-691-6973

Walters, John. See: WALTERS WADS

Walters Wads, John Walters, 500 N. Avery Dr., Moore, OK 73160 / 405-799-0376; FAX: 405-799-7727 www.tinwadman@cs.com

Walther America, PO Box 22, Springfield, MA 01102 / 413-747-3443 www.walther-usa.com

Walther GmbH, Carl, B.P. 4325, D-89033 Ulm, GERMANY

Walt's Custom Leather, Walt Whinnery, 1947 Meadow Creek Dr., Louisville, KY 40218 / 502-458-4361

WAMCO-New Mexico, P.O. Box 205, Peralta, NM 87042-0205 / 505-869-0826

Ward & Van Valkenburg, 114 32nd Ave. N., Fargo, ND 58102 / 701-232-2351

Ward Machine, 5620 Lexington Rd., Corpus Christi, TX 78412 / 512-992-1221

Wardell Precision Handguns Ltd., 48851 N. Fig Springs Rd., New River, AZ 85027-8513 / 602-465-7995

Warenski, Julie, 590 E. 500 N., Richfield, UT 84701 / 801-896-5319; FAX: 801-896-5319

Warne Manufacturing Co., 9057 SE Jannsen Rd., Clackamas, OR 97015 / 503-657-5590 or 800-683-5590; FAX: 503-657-5695 info@warnescopemounts.com www.warnescopemounts.com

Warren Muzzleloading Co., Inc., Hwy. 21 North, P.O. Box 100, Ozone, AR 72854 / 501-292-3268

Washita Mountain Whetstone Co., P.O. Box 378, Lake Hamilton, AR 71951 / 501-525-3914

Wasmundt, Jim, P.O. Box 511, Fossil, OR 97830

Watson Bros., 39 Redcross Way, SE1 1H6, London, ENGLAND FAX: 44-171-403-336

Watson Trophy Match Bullets, 467 Pine Loop, Frostproof, FL 33843 / 863-635-7948 or 864-244-7948 cbestbullet@aol.com

Wayne E. Schwartz Custom Guns, 970 E. Britton Rd., Morrice, MI 48857 / 517-625-4079

Wayne Firearms For Collectors & Investors

Wayne Specialty Services, 260 Waterford Drive, Florissant, MO 63033 / 413-831-7083

WD-40 Co., 1061 Cudahy Pl., San Diego, CA 92110 / 619-275-1400; FAX: 619-275-5823

Weatherby, Inc., 3100 El Camino Real, Atascadero, CA 93422 / 805-466-1767; FAX: 805-466-2527 www.weatherby.com

Weaver Products ATK, P.O. Box 39, Onalaska, WI 54650 / 800-648-9624 or 608-781-5800; FAX: 608-781-0368

Weaver Scope Repair Service, 1121 Larry Mahan Dr., Suite B, El Paso, TX 79925 / 915-593-1005

Webb, Bill, 6504 North Bellefontaine, Kansas City, MO 64119 / 816-453-7431

Weber & Markin Custom Gunsmiths, 4-1691 Powick Rd., Kelowna, BC V1X 4L1 CANADA / 250-762-7575; FAX: 250-861-3655 www.weberandmarkinguns.com

Weber Jr., Rudolf, P.O. Box 160106, D-5650, GERMANY / 0212-592136

Webley and Scott Ltd., Frankley Industrial Park, Tay Rd., Birmingham, B45 0PA ENGLAND / 011-021-453-1864; FAX: 0121-457-7846 guns@webley.co.uk www.webley.co.uk

Webster Scale Mfg. Co., P.O. Box 188, Sebring, FL 33870 / 813-385-6362

Weems, Cecil, 510 W Hubbard St., Mineral Wells, TX 76067-4847 / 817-325-1462

Weigand Combat Handguns, Inc., 1057 South Main Rd., Mountain Top, PA 18707 / 570-868-8358; FAX: 570-868-5218 sales@jackweigand.com www.scopemount.com

Weihrauch KG, Hermann, Industriestrasse 11, 8744 Mellrichstadt, Mellrichstadt, GERMANY

Welch, Sam. See: SAM WELCH GUN ENGRAVING

Wellington Outdoors, P.O. Box 244, 1140 Monticello Rd., Madison, GA 30650 / 706-342-4915; FAX: 706-342-7568

Wells, Rachel, 110 N. Summit St., Prescott, AZ 86301 / 928-445-3655 wellssportstore@aol.com

Wells Creek Knife & Gun Works, 32956 State Hwy. 38, Scottsburg, OR 97473 / 541-587-4202; FAX: 541-587-4223

Welsh, Bud. See: HIGH PRECISION

Wenger North America/Precise Int'l, 15 Corporate Dr., Orangeburg, NY 10962 / 800-431-2996; FAX: 914-425-4700

Wenig Custom Gunstocks, 103 N. Market St., PO Box 249, Lincoln, MO 65338 / 660-547-3334; FAX: 660-547-2881 gustock@wenig.com www.wenig.com

Werth, T. W., 1203 Woodlawn Rd., Lincoln, IL 62656 / 217-732-1300

Wescombe, Bill (See North Star West)

Wessinger Custom Guns & Engraving, 268 Limestone Rd., Chapin, SC 29036 / 803-345-5677

West, Jack L., 1220 W. Fifth, P.O. Box 427, Arlington, OR 97812

Western Cutlery (See Camillus Cutlery Co.)

Western Design (See Alpha Gunsmith Division)

Western Mfg. Co., 550 Valencia School Rd., Aptos, CA 95003 / 831-688-5884 lotsabears@eathlink.net

Western Missouri Shooters Alliance, PO Box 11144, Kansas City, MO 64119 / 816-597-3950; FAX: 816-229-7350

Western Nevada West Coast Bullets, PO BOX 2270, DAYTON, NV 89403-2270 / 702-246-3941; FAX: 702-246-0836

Westley Richards & Co., 40 Grange Rd., Birmingham, ENGLAND / 010-214722953

Westley Richards Agency USA (See U.S. Importer for

Westwind Rifles, Inc., David S. Sullivan, P.O. Box 261, 640 Briggs St., Erie, CO 80516 / 303-828-3823

Weyer International, 2740 Nebraska Ave., Toledo, OH 43607 / 419-534-2020; FAX: 419-534-2697

Whildin & Sons Ltd, E.H., RR 2 Box 119, Tamaqua, PA 18252 / 717-668-6743; FAX: 717-668-6745

Whinnery, Walt (See Walt's Custom Leather)

Whiscombe (See U.S. Importer-Pelaire Products)

White Barn Wor, 431 County Road, Broadlands, IL 61816

White Pine Photographic Services, Hwy. 60, General Delivery, Wilno, ON K0J 2N0 CANADA / 613-756-3452

White Rifles, Inc., 1464 W. 40 South, Linden, UT 84042 / 801-932-7950 www.whiterifles.com

White Rock Tool & Die, 6400 N. Brighton Ave., Kansas City, MO 64119 / 816-454-0478

Whitestone Lumber Corp., 148-02 14th Ave., Whitestone, NY 11357 / 718-746-4400; FAX: 718-767-1748

Wichita Arms, Inc., 923 E. Gilbert, P.O. Box 11371, Wichita, KS 67211 / 316-265-0661; FAX: 316-265-0760

Wick, David E., 1504 Michigan Ave., Columbus, IN 47201 / 812-376-6960

Widener's Reloading & Shooting Supply, Inc., P.O. Box 3009 CRS, Johnson City, TN 37602 / 615-282-6786; FAX: 615-282-6651

Wideview Scope Mount Corp., 13535 S. Hwy. 16, Rapid City, SD 57701 / 605-341-3220; FAX: 605-341-9142 wvdon@rapidnet.com www.jii.to

Wiebe, Duane, 5300 Merchant Cir. #2, Placerville, CA 95667 / 530-344-1357; FAX: 530-344-1357 wiebe@d-wdb.com

Wiest, Marie. See: GUNCRAFT SPORTS, INC.

Wilcox All-Pro Tools & Supply, 4880 147th St., Montezuma, IA 50171 / 515-623-3138; FAX: 515-623-3104

Wilcox Industries Corp., Robert F Guarasi, 53 Durham St., Portsmouth, NH 03801 / 603-431-1331; FAX: 603-431-1221

Wild Bill's Originals, P.O. Box 13037, Burton, WA 98013 / 206-463-5738; FAX: 206-465-5925 wildbill@haleyon.com

Wild West Guns, 7521 Old Seward Hwy., Unit A, Anchorage, AK 99518 / 800-992-4570 or 907-344-4500; FAX: 907-344-4005 wwguns@ak.net www.wildwestguns.com

Wilderness Sound Products Ltd., 4015 Main St. A, Springfield, OR 97478 / 800-47-0006; FAX: 541-741-0263

Wildey, Inc., 45 Angevine Rd, Warren, CT 06754-1818 / 203-355-9000; FAX: 203-354-7759

Wildlife Research Center, Inc., 1050 McKinley St., Anoka, MN 55303 / 612-427-3350; or 800-USE-LURE; FAX: 612-427-8354

Will-Burt Co., 169 S. Main, Orrville, OH 44667

William Fagan & Co., 22952 15 Mile Rd., Clinton Township, MI 48035 / 810-465-4637; FAX: 810-792-6996

William E. Phillips Firearms, 38 Avondale Rd., Wigston, Leicester, ENGLAND / 0116 2886334; FAX: 0116 2810644 wephillips@aol.com

William Powell & Son (Gunmakers) Ltd., 35-37 Carrs Lane, Birmingham, B4 7SX ENGLAND / 121-643-0689; FAX: 121-631-3504

William Powell Agency, 22 Circle Dr., Bellmore, NY 11710 / 516-679-1158

Williams Gun Sight Co., 7389 Lapeer Rd., Box 329, Davison, MI 48423 / 810-653-2131 or 800-530-9028; FAX: 810-658-2140 williamsgunsight.com

Williams Mfg. of Oregon, 110 East B St., Drain, OR 97435 / 503-836-7461; FAX: 503-836-7245

Williams Shootin' Iron Service, The Lynx-Line, Rt. 2 Box 223A, Mountain Grove, MO 65711 / 417-948-0902; FAX: 417-948-0902

Williamson Precision Gunsmithing, 117 W. Pipeline, Hurst, TX 76053 / 817-285-0064; FAX: 817-280-0044

Willow Bend, P.O. Box 203, Chelmsford, MA 01824 / 978-256-8508; FAX: 978-256-8508

Wilsom Combat, 2234 CR 719, Berryville, AR 72616-4573 / 800-955-4856; FAX: 870-545-3310

Wilson Case, Inc., PO Box 1106, Hastings, NE 68902-1106 / 800-322-5493; FAX: 402-463-5276 sales@wilsoncase.com www.wilsoncase.com

Wilson Combat, 2234 CR 719, Berryville, AR 72616-4573 / 800-955-4856

Winchester Div. Olin Corp., 427 N. Shamrock, E. Alton, IL 62024 / 618-258-3566; FAX: 618-258-3599

Winchester Sutler, Inc., The, 270 Shadow Brook Lane, Winchester, VA 22603 / 540-888-3595; FAX: 540-888-4632

Windish, Jim, 2510 Dawn Dr., Alexandria, VA 22306 / 703-765-1994

Wingshooting Adventures, 0-1845 W. Leonard, Grand Rapids, MI 49544 / 616-677-1980; FAX: 616-677-1986

Winkle Bullets, R.R. 1, Box 316, Heyworth, IL 61745

Winter, Robert M., P.O. Box 484, 42975-287th St., Menno, SD 57045 / 605-387-5322

Wise Custom Guns, 1402 Blanco Rd., San Antonio, TX 78212-2716 / 210-828-3388

Wise Guns, Dale, 1402 Blanco Rd., San Antonio, TX 78212 / 210-734-9999

Wiseman and Co., Bill, PO Box 3427, Bryan, TX 77805 / 409-690-3456; FAX: 409-690-0156

Wisners Inc/Twin Pine Armory, P.O. Box 58, Hwy. 6, Adna, WA 98522 / 360-748-4590; FAX: 360-748-1802

Wolf (See J.R. Distributing)

Wolf Performance Ammunition, 2201 E. Winston Rd. Ste. K, Anaheim, CA 92806-5537 / 702-837-8506; FAX: 702-837-9250

Wolfe Publishing Co., 6471 Airpark Dr., Prescott, AZ 86301 / 520-445-7810 or 800-899-7810; FAX: 520-778-5124

Wolf's Western Traders, 1250 Santa Cora Ave. #613, Chula Vista, CA 91913 / 619-482-1701 patwolf4570book@aol.com

Wolverine Footwear Group, 9341 Courtland Dr. NE, Rockford, MI 49351 / 616-866-5500; FAX: 616-866-5658

Wood, Frank (See Classic Guns, Inc.), 5305 Peachtree Ind. Blvd., Norcross, GA 30092 / 404-242-7944

Woodleigh (See Huntington Die Specialties)

Woods Wise Products, P.O. Box 681552, Franklin, TN 37068 / 800-735-8182; FAX: 615-726-2637

Woodstream, P.O. Box 327, Lititz, PA 17543 / 717-626-2125; FAX: 717-626-1912

Woodworker's Supply, 1108 North Glenn Rd., Casper, WY 82601 / 307-237-5354

Woolrich, Inc., Mill St., Woolrich, PA 17701 / 800-995-1299; FAX: 717-769-6234/6259

Working Guns, Jim Coffin, 1224 NW Fernwood Cir., Corvallis, OR 97330-2909 / 541-928-4391

World of Targets (See Birchwood Casey)

World Trek, Inc., 7170 Turkey Creek Rd., Pueblo, CO 81007-1046 / 719-546-2121; FAX: 719-543-6886

Worthy Products, Inc., RR 1, P.O. Box 213, Martville, NY 13111 / 315-324-5298

Wostenholm (See Ibberson [Sheffield] Ltd., George)

Wright's Gunstock Blanks, 8540 SE Kane Rd., Gresham, OR 97080 / 503-666-1705 doyal@wrightsguns.com www.wrightsguns.com

WTA Manufacturing, P.O. Box 164, Kit Carson, CO 80825 / 800-700-3054; FAX: 719-962-3570 wta@rebeltec.net http://www.members.aol.com/ductman249/wta.html

Wyant Bullets, Gen. Del., Swan Lake, MT 59911

Wyant's Outdoor Products, Inc., PO Box 9, Broadway, VA 22815

Wyoming Custom Bullets, 1626 21st St., Cody, WY 82414

Wyoming Knife Corp., 101 Commerce Dr., Ft. Collins, CO 80524 / 303-224-3454

X

X-Spand Target Systems, 26-10th St. SE, Medicine Hat, AB T1A 1P7 CANADA / 403-526-7997; FAX: 403-528-2362

Y

Yankee Gunsmith "Just Glocks", 2901 Deer Flat Dr., Copperas Cove, TX 76522 / 817-547-8433; FAX: 254-547-8887 ed@justglocks.com www.justglocks.com

Yavapai College, 1100 E. Sheldon St., Prescott, AZ 86301 / 520-776-2353; FAX: 520-776-2355

Yavapai Firearms Academy Ltd., P.O. Box 27290, Prescott Valley, AZ 86312 / 928-772-8262; FAX: 928-772-0062 info@yfainc.corn www.yfainc.com

Yearout, Lewis E. (See Montana Outfitters), 308 Riverview Dr E, Great Falls, MT 59404 / 406-761-0859

Yee, Mike. See: CUSTOM STOCKING

Yellowstone Wilderness Supply, P.O. Box 129, W. Yellowstone, MT 59758 / 406-646-7613

Yesteryear Armory & Supply, P.O. Box 408, Carthage, TN 37030

York M-1 Conversions, 12145 Mill Creek Run, Plantersville, TX 77363 / 936-894-2397; FAX: 936-894-2397

Young Country Arms, William, 1409 Kuehner Dr. #13, Simi Valley, CA 93063-4478

Z

Zabala Hermanos S.A., P.O. Box 97, 20600 Elbar, Elgueta, Guipuzcoa, 20600 SPAIN / 943-768076; FAX: 943-768201

Zander's Sporting Goods, 7525 Hwy 154 West, Baldwin, IL 62217-9706 / 800-851-4373; FAX: 618-785-2320

Zanotti Armor, Inc., 123 W. Lone Tree Rd., Cedar Falls, IA 50613 / 319-232-9650

Zeeryp, Russ, 1601 Foard Dr., Lynn Ross Manor, Morristown, TN 37814 / 615-586-2357

Zero Ammunition Co., Inc., 1601 22nd St. SE, PO Box 1188, Cullman, AL 35056-1188 / 800-545-9376; FAX: 205-739-4683

Ziegel Engineering, 1390 E. Bunnett St. #I, Signal Hill, CA 90755 / 562-596-9481; FAX: 562-598-4734 ziegel@aol.com www.ziegeleng.com

Zim's, Inc., 4370 S. 3rd West, Salt Lake City, UT 84107 / 801-268-2505

Z-M Weapons, 203 South St., Bernardston, MA 01337 / 413-648-9501; FAX: 413-648-0219

Zufall, Joseph F., P.O. Box 304, Golden, CO 80402-0304

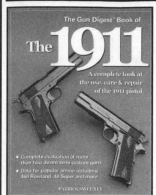
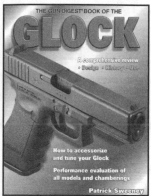

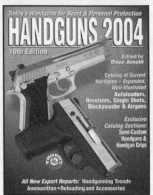
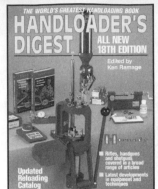

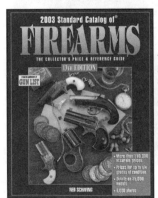